# WRITING

*A LITERARY ANTHOLOGY*

# NEW YORK

# WRITING

## A LITERARY ANTHOLOGY

# NEW YORK

EXPANDED EDITION

A SPECIAL PUBLICATION OF
THE LIBRARY OF AMERICA

PHILLIP LOPATE, EDITOR

*WRITING NEW YORK*
*has been published with support from the*
*SUSAN AND ELIHU ROSE*
*FOUNDATION*

# CONTENTS

[ XI ]

[ XIII ]

# INTRODUCTION

FEW CITIES HAVE INSPIRED AS MUCH GREAT WRITING AS NEW
YORK, OR INDEED AS MUCH WRITING: THE LITERATURE OF THE
city is extraordinary for its variety and sheer volume. Almost every
major American author, if not a New Yorker, at least went through a
New York phase; there were legions of minor authors who specialized in portraying the Empire City; and countless distinguished visitors left a literary record of their sojourns. Yet no one writer can be
said to have encompassed the city as, say, Joyce did Dublin. "New
York is just too big, too complex to be served by any one writer. At
best he can only offer his little tribute to something he loves, but
which is beyond him": so lamented (not without a trace of self-satis-
faction) Robert Moses, that poet of city planning whose own verses
in concrete all New Yorkers still live with.

Let us admit for the sake of argument that Moses was right, and
that New York is too big for any one writer to tell its story (although
Walt Whitman may have come as close as one can). In that case the
only way to undertake a literary portrait of the city would be piece
by piece, through a full-scale anthology of the best New York writing. This volume attempts such a literary record, on the hundredth
anniversary of the city's amalgamation.

We start from the premise that there really is such a thing as
"New York writing," and that it goes beyond the coincidence of many
superb authors having resided and worked in the city. New York writing flows from the rhythm and mode of being that this singular place
imposes on everyone who lives in it or even visits it at length.

New York's essence, literary or otherwise, grows out of the street
experience, the basis for an aesthetic of a ragged, miraculous simultaneity. New York has from the start been an extroverted, not a
covert, place; its man-made geography and network of mass trans-
ports provide the basic cue, the beat from which all else follows.
Writers have again and again described the pedestrian stream, the
crowd (whether perceived as threatening or benign), the street as
emblem of material reality. Henry Miller put it succinctly: "In the

street you learn what human beings really are; otherwise, or afterwards, you invent them. What is not in the open street is false, derived,
that is to say, *literature*." Those preoccupied faces of passersby constitute a scandalous puzzle that invites, yet baffles, decoding. "So a million people are a public secret," wrote the poet Edwin Denby.

There is a characteristic tone as well in New York writing, of
skeptical humor, sardonic wit, disenchanted realism. A famously
*hard* environment, New York inspires both stoic pride and chagrin.
The turn-of-the-century movement of literary realism (William
Dean Howells, Stephen Crane, Theodore Dreiser) often took its lead
from the realities of New York, and the harsh terms the city imposed
on its people. In a very different way, the city prompted the warm,
compensatory sentimentality of an O. Henry or Damon Runyon. The
quintessential New Yorkese blend of hard-nosed disparagement and
down-to-earth sympathy may also be seen as a composite creation of
all those immigrant groups—Jewish, Irish, African-American,
German, Italian, Asian, Hispanic, Caribbean—whose accents and
phrasings thickened the linguistic stock.

To look at the literature chronologically, as we have done here, is
to see how early New York's patterns set in. From the start, the place
was fast, boisterous, crowded, dirty, secular, and on the make. It began
as a cosmopolitan, international port, a walking city with a vital
street life and a housing shortage, and stayed that way. The more the
metropolis grew, the more it attracted writers. Yet no matter how
independent a writer might be, New York has always had a way of
seeming stronger, of bending the individual will to its designs and
obsessions.

Certain themes recur obsessively in the literary record:
+ the city's contradictory faces of glamour and squalor;
+ its man-made quality: the gigantic built environment and the
  relative unimportance of nature;
+ its Mammon-like preoccupation with business and money-
  making, from the days of the Dutch settlement to the present;
+ its concentration of media and information, leading to the
  manufacture of celebrity for the few;
+ its offer of anonymity to the many;

- its uneasy relationship with the rest of America;
- its large, dense population, providing space if not always the warmest of welcomes for the immigrant and the nonconformist;
- its affable, loquacious working-class populace speaking a streetwise vernacular;
- its fabled loneliness and alienation;
- its symbolic importance as the modernist city *par excellence*;
- its addictive, temptress quality, which ensnares newcomers and convinces them—no matter how much they may suffer at its hands—that no place else will do.

Writing about New York reverts again and again to the contrasts of the city, as enunciated by Theodore Dreiser in his collection *The Color of a Great City*: "The thing that interested me then as now about New York—as indeed about any great city, but more definitely New York because it was and is so preponderantly large—was the sharp, and at the same time immense, contrast it showed between the dull and the shrewd, the strong and the weak, the rich and the poor, the wise and the ignorant. This, perhaps, was more by reason of numbers and opportunity than anything else, for of course humanity is much the same everywhere. But the number from which to choose was so great here that the strong, or those who ultimately dominated, were so very strong, and the weak so very, very weak— and so very, very many."

Dreiser chose the impressionistic urban sketch—a highly pliable form, once fashionable in the popular press—to work out many of these ideas. Hatched in the Paris and London of the early nineteenth century, and soon gravitating to the young cities of America, the urban sketch was an attempt to catch on the fly some aspect, high or low, of the burgeoning metropolis. The Argus-eyed commentator satisfied readers' voyeuristic desires to peek around every neglected corner of their city, while taking advantage of the opportunity to sneak in some fancy lyrical passages. "Which one of us, in his moments of ambition, has not dreamed of the miracle of a poetic prose, musical, without rhythm and without rhyme, supple enough to adapt itself to the lyrical impulses of the soul, the undulations of reverie, the jibes of conscience?" wrote Baudelaire, adding tellingly that it was "out of my exploration of huge cities, out of the medley of their innumerable interrelations, that this haunting ideal was born." Many of the writers included in this anthology—Nathaniel P. Willis, Theodore Dreiser, Djuna Barnes, James Huneker, Christopher Morley, Edmund Wilson—responded to the challenge of capturing urban life in quicksilver poetic prose.

Another literary response to New York was the walking-around poem. Once Whitman perfected the catalogue or list, it became a favorite technique among New York poets for conveying sensory saturation. Whitman's impact on later peripatetic city poets (such as Frank O'Hara, Charles Reznikoff, and James Schuyler) was vast, partly because the all-embracing, synthesizing persona he developed offered a solution to the problem of integrating the random stimuli of modern life. The walk poem is a species of travel literature in which the writer puts himself through culture shock in his own city. Precisely because New York is so polyglot and international, it becomes easy for the walker-writer to turn a corner and imagine himself in Prague or Montevideo.

The diaristic impulse is yet another response to the "too-much-ness" of New York daily life. Both O'Hara and Schuyler were masters of the diary-poem, which found some larger resonance in the trivia or detritus of the passing moment. New York has also been exceptionally fortunate in its prose diarists: Philip Hone and George Templeton Strong left a vivid, almost unbroken record of the city for much of the nineteenth century, while Dawn Powell and Ned Rorem have been among the extraordinary diarists of our own era.

Henry James was not alone in deploring what he felt was New York's lack of history, and its eagerness to erase traces of the past. James Merrill ruefully remarked in his poem "An Urban Convalescence":

> *As usual in New York, everything is torn down*
> *Before you have had time to care for it.*

Yet a consistent motif in this anthology is how often New York's writers looked backward, sifting through the city's past, no matter how much others may have been ignoring it. The first significant piece of writing about New York City was Washington Irving's nostalgic history of the Dutch reign. We can further see, from the historical fiction and autobiographical writings of James Fenimore Cooper, Grant Thorburn, Frederick Law Olmsted, Al Smith, Lincoln Steffens, F. Scott Fitzgerald, Edith Wharton, Henry Miller, Langston Hughes, William Carlos Williams, Malcolm Cowley, Alfred Kazin, Lewis Mumford, Mario Puzo, Kate Simon, and so many others, how central to New York writing has been the act of remembering and reflecting on the changing city.

This literary preoccupation with urban archaeology has become even more noticeable in our own period. During the last three decades—let us say, ever since the irreplaceable Pennsylvania Station was torn down in 1962—there has developed, along with a tough Landmark Preservation Law, a poignant veneration for the city's remaining architectural treasures. Meanwhile, some of our best novelists, such as E. L. Doctorow, Toni Morrison, Don DeLillo, and Oscar Hijuelos, have invested considerable energy in stories about the New York of their—or their parents'—youth. The result is a revival of rich historical fiction bordering on memoir—alongside a seeming reluctance to capture the New York City of the present. The power that New York once had to compel tributes of description from even reluctant observers seems to have waned, while young American writers explore the mysteries of small town and suburb. Either the 1990's are not a particularly high point in writing about New York, or we are too close to judge. All the more reason, it would seem, to celebrate the city's past evocations, while we wait to see what its newest literary incarnation will be.

The prospective reader has a right to know the principles that inform the selection process for any anthology, including this one. The goal was to cast as wide a net as possible, with poetry, essays, fiction, memoirs, diaries, letters, and journalism all eligible for inclusion. Preference was given to the literary: this is not intended as a documentary history of New York, nor an anthology of the city's popular culture. It was not enough for a piece of writing to be set in New York, with the city serving as passive backdrop. New York had to be felt as a force, a character—to be engaged as a subject. Rather than attempting thematic divisions, the volume relies on a straight-forward chronological arrangement, in which the placement of each entry has been determined not by the era it describes but by the approximate date of its composition.

The making of anthologies is an activity fated to inspire defensiveness about all that has been left out. It has not been possible, for example, to include excerpts from all the great novels about New York. John Dos Passos's *Manhattan Transfer* is one of my favorites, but its ensemble effects are cumulative, and do not submit well to excerpting. The same can be said for *The House of Mirth, Washington Square, Call It Sleep, The Rise of David Levinsky, A Tree Grows in Brooklyn, Invisible Man, Sister Carrie, The Great Gatsby, You Can't Go Home Again, Seize the Day, Last Exit to Brooklyn, The Bonfire of the Vanities, Jazz, Underworld,* and many other New York-related novels.

I have sought a balance between the familiar and the arcane. It would have been unthinkable to exclude such seminal writings about New York as Herman Melville's "Bartleby, the Scrivener" or Walt Whitman's "Crossing Brooklyn Ferry" simply because they have often been anthologized. But the fun of anthologies is in going off the beaten path and making discoveries, such as George Templeton Strong, Paul Morand, Nathaniel P. Willis, Fanny Kemble, Stephen Graham, Paul Rosenfeld, José Martí. In the end, passion for the subject of New York City has counted more than any presumed hierarchical ranking in the literary pantheon.

It has been my privilege to try to make sense of this great city's literary heritage. I am deeply grateful for the many New York mavens who helped with suggestions and advice, including Thomas Bender, Paul Berman, Dana Brand, John Bryant, Ric Burns, Barbara Cohen, Dan De Simone, Byron Dobell, Eric Foner, Nico Guillen, Bruce Edward Hall, Lawrence Joseph, Justin Kaplan, Neal Karlan, Alfred Kazin, Thomas Kessner, Fran Kiernan, John Lahr, Lawrence Maslon, Ron Padgett, Michel Ridgeway, Steve Rivo, James Sanders, Luc Sante, Richard Sennett, David Shapiro, Richard Snow, Maura Spiegel, Sidney Tillim, Katharine Washburn, and Lee Zimmerman.

PHILLIP LOPATE, 1998

# WASHINGTON IRVING

*Washington Irving (1783–1859), America's first successful man of let-ters, now known primarily for his Hudson Valley tales "Rip Van Winkle" and "The Legend of Sleepy Hollow," made his initial splash at age twenty-six with a comic, mock-learned, rambling volume, whose full title,* A History of New York From the Beginnings of the World to the End of the Dutch Dynasty, *indicates the tongue-in-cheek, mythological manner in which Irving clothed his account of his native city's roots. The book pretended to have been written by an aged, bitter codger of Dutch extraction, Diedrich Knickerbocker—in short, one of history's "losers." Thus began the whole "Knickerbocker" tradition, con-necting that pseudonym with the city's local legends. Though* A History of New York *certainly has passages of farce and satire, Irving (who did considerable research) often followed historical events fairly closely. In any case, this first published history of the city attempted to provide the amnesiac, hustling, nineteenth-century port with a founding myth and a past. Its ironic, disenchanted voice set the tone for much New York literature to come.*

## FROM *A HISTORY OF NEW YORK*

THE ISLAND of Manna-hata, Manhattoes, or as it is vulgarly called Manhattan, having been discovered, as was related in the last chapter; and being unanimously pronounced by the discoverers, the fairest spot in the known world, whereon to build a city, that should surpass all the emporiums of Europe, they immedi-ately returned to Communipaw with the pleasing intelligence. Upon this a considerable colony was forthwith fitted out, who after a pros-perous voyage of half an hour, arrived at Manna hata, and having previously purchased the land of the Indians, (a measure almost un-paralleled in the annals of discovery and colonization) they settled upon the south-west point of the island, and fortified themselves strongly, by throwing up a mud battery, which they named FORT AMSTERDAM. A number of huts soon sprung up in the neighbour-

hood, to protect which, they made an enclosure of strong pallisa-
does. A creek running from the East river, through what at present is
called Whitehall street, and a little inlet from Hudson river to the
bowling green formed the original boundaries; as though nature had
kindly designated the cradle, in which the embryo of this renowned
city was to be nestled. The woods on both sides of the creek were
carefully cleared away, as well as from the space of ground now occupied by the bowling green.—These precautions were taken to
protect the fort from either the open attacks or insidious advances of
its savage neighbours, who wandered in hordes about the forests and
swamps that extended over those tracts of country, at present called
broad way, Wall street, William street and Pearl street.

No sooner was the colony once planted, than like a luxuriant
vine, it took root and throve amazingly; for it would seem, that this
thrice favoured island is like a munificent dung hill, where every
thing finds kindly nourishment, and soon shoots up and expands to
greatness. The thriving state of the settlement, and the astonishing
encrease of houses, gradually awakened the leaders from a profound
lethargy, into which they had fallen, after having built their mud fort.
They began to think it was high time some plan should be devised,
on which the encreasing town should be built; so taking pipe in
mouth, and meeting in close divan, they forthwith fell into a profound deliberation on the subject.

At the very outset of the business, an unexpected difference of
opinion arose, and I mention it with regret, as being the first internal altercation on record among the new settlers. An ingenious plan
was proposed by Mynheer Ten Broek to cut up and intersect the
ground by means of canals; after the manner of the most admired
cities in Holland; but to this Mynheer Hardenbroek was diametri-
cally opposed; suggesting in place thereof, that they should run out
docks and wharves, by means of piles driven into the bottom of the
river, on which the town should be built—By this means said he triumphantly, shall we rescue a considerable space of territory from
these immense rivers, and build a city that shall rival Amsterdam,
Venice, or any amphibious city in Europe. To this proposition, Ten
Broek (or Ten breeches) replied, with a look of as much scorn as he

could possibly assume. He cast the utmost censure upon the plan of his antagonist, as being preposterous, and against the very order of things, as he would leave to every true hollander. "For what," said he, "is a town without canals?—it is like a body without veins and arteries, and must perish for want of a free circulation of the vital fluid"—Tough breeches, on the contrary, retorted with a sarcasm upon his antagonist, who was somewhat of an arid, dry boned habit of body; he remarked that as to the circulation of the blood being necessary to existence, Mynheer Ten breeches was a living contradiction to his own assertion; for every body knew there had not a drop of blood circulated through his wind dried carcass for good ten years, and yet there was not a greater busy body in the whole colony. Personalities have seldom much effect in making converts in argument—nor have I ever seen a man convinced of error, by being convicted of deformity. At least such was not the case at present. Ten Breeches was very acrimonious in reply, and Tough Breeches, who was a sturdy little man, and never gave up the last word, rejoined with encreasing spirit—Ten Breeches had the advantage of the greatest volubility, but Tough Breeches had that invaluable coat of mail in argument called obstinacy—Ten Breeches had, therefore, the most mettle, but Tough Breeches the best bottom—so that though Ten Breeches made a dreadful clattering about his ears, and battered and belaboured him with hard words and sound arguments, yet Tough Breeches hung on most resolutely to the last. They parted therefore, as is usual in all arguments where both parties are in the right, without coming to any conclusion—but they hated each other most heartily forever after, and a similar breach with that between the houses of Capulet and Montague, had well nigh ensued between the families of Ten Breeches and Tough Breeches.

I would not fatigue my reader with these dull matters of fact, but that my duty as a faithful historian, requires that I should be particular—and in truth, as I am now treating of the critical period, when our city, like a young twig, first received the twists and turns, that have since contributed to give it the present picturesque irregularity for which it is celebrated, I cannot be too minute in detailing their first causes.

[ 3 ]

After the unhappy altercation I have just mentioned, I do not find that any thing further was said on the subject, worthy of being recorded. The council, consisting of the largest and oldest heads in the community, met regularly once a week, to ponder on this momentous subject.—But either they were deterred by the war of words they had witnessed, or they were naturally averse to the exercise of the tongue, and the consequent exercise of the brains—certain it is, the most profound silence was maintained—the question as usual lay on the table—the members quietly smoked their pipes, making but few laws, without ever enforcing any, and in the mean time the affairs of the settlement went on—as it pleased God.

As most of the council were but little skilled in the mystery of combining pot hooks and hangers, they determined most judiciously not to puzzle either themselves or posterity, with voluminous records. The secretary however, kept the minutes of each meeting with tolerable precision, in a large vellum folio, fastened with massy brass clasps, with a sight of which I have been politely favoured by my highly respected friends, the Goelets, who have this invaluable relique, at present in their possession. On perusal, however, I do not find much information—The journal of each meeting consists but of two lines, stating in dutch, that, "the council sat this day, and smoked twelve pipes, on the affairs of the colony."—By which it appears that the first settlers did not regulate their time by hours, but pipes, in the same manner as they measure distances in Holland at this very time; an admirably exact measurement, as a pipe in the mouth of a genuine dutchman is never liable to those accidents and irregularities, that are continually putting our clocks out of order.

In this manner did the profound council of NEW AMSTERDAM smoke, and doze, and ponder, from week to week, month to month, and year to year, in what manner they should construct their infant settlement—mean while, the town took care of itself, and like a sturdy brat which is suffered to run about wild, unshackled by clouts and bandages, and other abominations by which your notable nurses and sage old women cripple and disfigure the children of men, encreased so rapidly in strength and magnitude, that before the honest burgomasters had determined upon a plan, it was too late to put it in execution—whereupon they wisely abandoned the subject altogether.

* * * * *

Grievous, and very much to be commiserated, is the task of the feeling historian, who writes the history of his native land. If it falls to his lot to be the sad recorder of calamity or crime, the mournful page is watered with his tears—nor can he recal the most prosperous and blissful eras, without a melancholy sigh at the reflection, that they have passed away forever! I know not whether it be owing to an immoderate love for the simplicity of former times, or to a certain tenderness of heart, natural to a sentimental historian; but I candidly confess, I cannot look back on the halcyon days of the city, which I now describe, without a deep dejection of the spirits. With faultering hand I withdraw the curtain of oblivion, which veils the modest merits of our venerable dutch ancestors, and as their revered figures rise to my mental vision, humble myself before the mighty shades.

Such too are my feelings when I revisit the family mansion of the Knickerbockers and spend a lonely hour in the attic chamber, where hang the portraits of my forefathers, shrouded in dust like the forms they represent. With pious reverence do I gaze on the countenances of those renowned burghers, who have preceded me in the steady march of existence—whose sober and temperate blood now meanders through my veins, flowing slower and slower in its feeble conduits, until its lingering current shall soon be stopped forever!

These, say I to myself, are but frail memorials of the mighty men, who flourished in the days of the patriarchs; but who, alas, have long since mouldered in that tomb, towards which my steps are insensibly and irresistibly hastening! As I pace the darkened chamber and lose myself in melancholy musings, the shadowy images around me, almost seem to steal once more into existence—their countenances appear for an instant to assume the animation of life—their eyes to pursue me in every movement! carried away by the delusion of fancy, I almost imagine myself surrounded by the shades of the departed, and holding sweet converse with the worthies of antiquity!

— Luckless Diedrich! born in a degenerate age—abandoned to the buffettings of fortune—a stranger and a weary pilgrim in thy native land; blest with no weeping wife, nor family of helpless children— but doomed to wander neglected through those crowded streets, and elbowed by foreign upstarts from those fair abodes, where once thine ancestors held sovereign empire. Alas! alas! is then the dutch spirit forever extinct? The days of the patriarchs, have they fled forever? Return—return sweet days of simplicity and ease—dawn once more on the lovely island of Manna hata!—Bear with me my worthy readers, bear with the weakness of my nature—or rather let us sit down together, indulge the full flow of filial piety, and weep over the memories of our great great grand-fathers.

Having thus gratified those feelings irresistibly awakened by the happy scenes I am describing, I return with more composure to my history.

The town of New Amsterdam, being, as I before mentioned, left to its own course and the fostering care of providence, increased as rapidly in importance, as though it had been burthened with a dozen panniers full of those sage laws, which are usually heaped upon the backs of young cities—in order to make them grow. The only measure that remains on record of the worthy council, was to build a chapel within the fort, which they dedicated to the great and good ST. NICHOLAS, who immediately took the infant town of New Amsterdam under his peculiar patronage, and has ever since been, and I devoutly hope will ever be, the tutelar saint of this excellent city. I am moreover told, that there is a little legendary book somewhere extant, written in low dutch, which says that the image of this renowned saint, which whilome graced the bowsprit of the Goede Vrouw, was placed in front of this chapel; and the legend further treats of divers miracles wrought by the mighty pipe which the saint held in his mouth; a whiff of which was a sovereign cure for an indigestion, and consequently of great importance in this colony of huge feeders. But as, notwithstanding the most diligent search, I cannot lay my hands upon this little book, I entertain considerable doubt on the subject.

This much is certain, that from the time of the building of this chapel, the town throve with tenfold prosperity, and soon became the metropolis of numerous settlements, and an extensive territory. The province extended on the north, to Fort Aurania or Orange, now known by the name of Albany, situated about 160 miles up the Mohegan or Hudson River. Indeed the province claimed quite to the river St. Lawrence; but this claim was not much insisted on at the time, as the country beyond Fort Aurania was a perfect wilderness, reported to be inhabited by cannibals, and termed Terra Incognita. Various accounts were given of the people of these unknown parts; by some they are described as being of the race of the *Acephali*, such as Herodotus describes, who have no heads, and carry their eyes in their bellies. Others affirm they were of that race whom father Charlevoix mentions, as having but one leg; adding gravely, that they were exceedingly alert in running. But the most satisfactory account is that given by the reverend Hans Megapolensis, a missionary in these parts, who, in a letter still extant, declares them to be the Mohagues or Mohawks; a nation, according to his description, very loose in their morals, but withal most rare wags. "For," says he, "if theye can get to bedd with another mans wife, theye thinke it a piece of wit."* This excellent old gentleman gives moreover very important additional information, about this country of monsters; for he observes, "theye have plenty of tortoises here, and within land, from two and three to four feet long; some with two heads, very mischievous and addicted to biting."†

1809

---

*Let. of I. Megapol. Hag. S. P.

†Ogilvie, in his excellent account of America, speaking of these parts, makes mention of Lions, which abounded on a high mountain, and likewise observes, "On the borders of Canada there is seen sometimes a kind of beast which hath some resemblance with a horse, having cloven feet, shaggy mayn, one horn just on the forehead, a tail like that of a wild hog, and a deer's neck." He furthermore gives a picture of this strange beast, which resembles exceedingly an unicorn.—It is much to be lamented by philosophers, that this miraculous breed of animals, like that of the horned frog, is totally extinct.

# JAMES KIRKE PAULDING

*In 1807–8 there began to appear in the New York streets a newssheet, called* Salmagundi, *devoted to belletristic wit and whimsy more or less along the lines of Addison and Steele's* Spectator. *It was written by three young men: Washington Irving, his brother William, and their great friend—and future distinguished novelist—from Tarrytown, James Kirke Paulding (1778–1860), who had come down to the city to join them. Though the* Salmagundi *essays (soon collected in book form) were unsigned, scholarly tradition assigns the following piece to Paulding. An early example of the "Walking Down Broadway" genre, it describes a commercial society expanding rapidly, and already bearing its share of tourist landmarks. It also shows how quickly writers began to adopt a hit-and-run approach to inventorying the random plenitude of New York street life.*

## THE STRANGER AT HOME;
## OR, A TOUR IN BROADWAY

BY JEREMY COCKLOFT *the younger.*

. . . . . *Peregre rediit.*

*He is returned home from abroad.*

DICTIONARY.

### PREFACE.

YOUR LEARNED TRAVELLER begins his travels at the commencement of his journey; others begin theirs at the end; and a third class begin any how and any where, which I think is the true way. A late facetious writer begins what he calls, "a Picture of New-York," with a particular description of Glen's Falls, from whence with admirable dexterity he makes a digression to the celebrated Mill Rock, on Long-Island! now this is what I like; and I intend in my present tour to digress as often and as long as I please. If, therefore, I choose to make a hop, skip, and jump to China, or New-Holland, or Terra Incognita, or Communipaw, I can produce a host of examples to justify me even in books that have been praised by the english reviewers, whose *fiat* being all that is necessary to give books a currency in this country, I am determined, as soon as I finish my edition of travels in seventy-five volumes, to transmit it forthwith to them for judgment. If these trans-atlantic censors praise it, I have no fear of its success in this country, where *their* approbation gives, like the tower stamp, a fictitious value, and makes tinsel and wampum pass current for classick gold.

## CHAPTER I.

Battery—flag-staff kept by Louis Kcaffee—Keaffee maintains two spy-glasses by subscriptions—merchants pay two shillings a-year to look through them at the signal poles on Staten-Island—a very pleasant prospect; but not so pleasant as that from the hill of Howth—quere, ever been there?—Young *seniors* go down to the flag-staff to buy peanuts and beer, after the fatigue of their morning studies, and sometimes to play at ball, or some other innocent amusement—digression to the Olympic, and Isthmian games, with a description of the Isthmus of Corinth, and that of Darien: to conclude with a dissertation on the indian custom of offering a whiff of tobacco smoke to their great spirit Areskou.—Return to the battery—delightful place to indulge in the luxury of sentiment.—How various are the mutations of this world! but a few days, a few hours—at least not above two hundred years ago, and this spot was inhabited by a race of aborigines, who dwelt in bark huts, lived upon oysters, and indian corn, danced buffalo dances, and were lords "of the fowl and the brute"—but the spirit of time, and the spirit of brandy, have swept them from their antient inheritance: and as the white wave of the ocean by its ever toiling assiduity, gains on the brown land, so the white man, by slow and sure degrees has gained on the brown savage, and dispossessed him of the land of his forefathers.—Conjectures on the first peopling of America—different opinions on that subject, to the amount of near one hundred—opinion of Augustine Torniel—that they are the descendants of Shem and Japheth, who came by the way of Japan to America—Juffridius Petri, says they came from Friezeland—mem. cold journey.—Mons.

Charron says they are descended from the gauls—bitter enough.—
A Milius from the Celtæ—Kircher from the egyptians—L'Compte
from the phenicians—Lescarbot from the canaanites, alias the an-
thropophagi—Brerewood from the tartars—Grotius from the norwegians—and Linkum Fidelius, has written two folio volumes to
prove that America was first of all peopled either by the antipodeans,
or the cornish miners, who he maintains, might easily have made a
subterraneous passage to this country, particularly the antipodeans,
who, he asserts, can get along under ground, as fast as moles—
quere, which of these is in the right, or are they all wrong?—For my
part, I dont see why America had not as good a right to be peopled
at first, as any little contemptible country of Europe, or Asia; and I
am determined to write a book at my first leisure, to prove that
Noah was born here—and that so far is America from being indebted to any other country for inhabitants, that they were every
one of them peopled by colonies from her!—mem. battery a very
pleasant place to walk on a sunday evening—not quite genteel
though—every body walks there, and a pleasure, however genuine,
is spoiled by general participation—the fashionable ladies of New-
York, turn up their noses if you ask them to walk on the battery on
sunday—quere, have they scruples of conscience, or scruples of delicacy?—neither—they have only scruples of gentility, which are
quite different things.

### CHAPTER II.

Custom-house—origin of duties on merchandize—this place
much frequented by merchants—and why?—different classes of
merchants—importers—a kind of nobility—Wholesale merchants—have the privilege of going to the city assembly!—Retail
traders cannot go to the assembly—Some curious speculations on
the vast distinction betwixt selling tape by the piece or by the
yard.—Wholesale merchants look down upon the retailers, who in
return look down upon the green grocers, who look down upon the
market women, who don't care a straw about any of them.—Origin
of the distinction of ranks—Dr. Johnson once horribly puzzled to
settle the point of precedence between a louse and a flea . . . good

hint enough to humble purse-proud arrogance. . . . Custom house partly used as a lodging house for the pictures belonging to the academy of arts . . . couldn't afford the statues house room, most of them in the cellar of the City hall . . . poor place for the gods and goddesses, . . . after Olympus . . . Pensive reflections on the ups and downs of life . . . Apollo, and the rest of the sett, used to cut a great figure in days of yore.—Mem. . . . every dog has his day . . . sorry for Venus though, poor wench, to be cooped up in a cellar with not a single grace to wait on her! . . . Eulogy on the gentlemen of the academy of arts, for the great spirit with which they began the undertaking, and the perseverance with which they have pursued it . . . It is a pity however, they began at the wrong end . . . maxim . . . If you want a bird and a cage, always buy the cage first . . . hem! . . . a word to the wise!

### CHAPTER III.

Bowling green . . . fine place for pasturing cows . . . a perquisite of the late corporation . . . formerly ornamented with a statue of George the 3d. . . . people pulled it down in the war to make bullets . . . great pity, as it might have been given to the academy . . . it would have become a cellar as well as any other. . . . The pedestal still remains, because, there was no use in pulling *that* down, as it would cost the corporation money, and not sell for any thing . . . mem . . . a penny saved is a penny got. . . . If the pedestal must remain, I would recommend that a statue of somebody, or something be placed on it, for truly it looks quite melancholy and forlorn. . . . Broadway . . . great difference in the gentility of streets . . . a man who resides in Pearl-street, or Chatham-row, derives no kind of dignity from his domicil, but place him in a certain part of Broadway . . . any where between the battery and Wall-street, and he straightway becomes entitled to figure in the beau-monde, and strut as a person of prodigious consequence! . . . Quere, whether there is a degree of purity in the air of that quarter which changes the gross particles of vulgarity, into gems of refinement and polish? . . . A question to be asked but not to be answered. . . . New brick church! . . . what a pity it is the corporation of Trinity church are so poor!

. . . if they could not afford to build a better place of worship, why did they not go about with a subscription? . . . even I would have given them a few shillings rather than our city should have been disgraced by such a pitiful specimen of economy . . . . Wall-street . . . . City-hall, famous place for catch-poles, deputy sheriffs, and young lawyers, which last attended the courts, not because they have business there, but because they have no business any where else. My blood always curdles when I see a catchpole, they being a species of vermin, who feed and fatten on the common wretchedness of mankind, who trade in misery, and in becoming the executioners of the law, by their oppression and villainy, almost counter-balance all the benefits which are derived from its salutary regulations. . . . Story of Quevedo, about a catchpole possessed by a devil, who in being interrogated, declared that he did not come there voluntarily, but by compulsion, and that a decent devil would never of his own free will enter into the body of a catchpole . . . instead therefore of doing him the injustice to say that here was a catchpole be-devilled, they should say it was a devil be-catchpoled . . . that being in reality the truth. . . . Wonder what has become of the old crier of the court, who used to make more noise in preserving silence than the audience did in breaking it. . . . If a man happened to drop his cane, the old hero would sing out silence! in a voice that emulated the "wide-mouthed thunder" . . . . On inquiring, found he had retired from business to enjoy *otium cum dignitate*, as many a great man had done before. . . . Strange that wise men, as they are thought, should toil through a whole existence merely to enjoy a few moments of leisure at last! . . . why don't they begin to be easy at first, and not purchase a moments pleasure with an age of pain? . . . mem . . . posed some of the jockeys . . . eh!

## CHAP. IV.

Barber's Pole—three different orders of *shavers* in New-York—those who shave *pigs*, N. B.—Freshmen and Sophomores—those who cut beards, and those who *shave notes of hand*—the last are the most respectable, because in the course of a year, they make more money and that *honestly*, than the whole corps of other *shavers*, can do in half a century—besides, it would puzzle a common barber to ruin any man, except by cutting his throat; whereas, your higher order of *shavers*, your true blood suckers of the community, seated snugly behind the curtain in watch for prey, live on the vitals of the unfortunate, and grow rich on the ruin of thousands.—Yet this last class of *barbers* are held in high respect in the world—they never offend against the decencies of life, go often to church, look down on honest poverty walking on foot, and call themselves gentlemen—yea, men of honour!—Lottery offices—another set of Capital Shavers! licensed gambling houses good things enough though, as they enable a few *honest industrious gentlemen* to humbug the people—according to law—besides, if the people will be such fools, whose fault is it but their own if they get *bit*?—Messrs. Paff . . . beg pardon for putting them in such bad company, because they are a couple of fine fellows—mem.—to recommend Michael's antique snuff box to all amateurs *in the art*.—Eagle singing Yankey-doodle—N. B.—Buffon, Pennant, and the rest of the naturalists all *naturals*, not to know the eagle was a singing bird—Linkum Fidelius knew better, and gives a long description of a bald eagle that serenaded him once in Canada—digression—particular account of the canadian indians— story about Areskou learning to make fishing nets of a spider—don't believe it though, because, according to Linkum, and many other learned authorities, Areskou is the same as *Mars*, being derived from his greek name of *Ares*, and if so he knew well enough what *a net* was without consulting a spider—story of Arachne being changed into a spider as a reward for having hanged herself—derivation of the word spinster from spider—Colophon, now Altobosco, the birth place of Arachne, remarkable for a famous breed of spiders to this day— mem.—nothing like a little scholarship—make the *ignoramus'* viz. the majority of my readers, stare like wild pigeons—return to New-York by a short cut—meet a dashing belle, in a thick white veil— tried to get a peep at her face . . . saw she squinted a little . . . thought so at first . . . never saw a face covered with a veil that was worth looking at . . . saw some ladies holding a conversation across the street about going to church next Sunday . . . talked so loud they frightened a cartman's horse, who ran away, and overset a basket of

gingerbread with a little boy under it . . . mem. I dont much see the
use of speaking trumpets now-a-days.

CHAP. V.

Bought a pair of gloves—dry-good stores the genuine schools of
politeness—true parisian manners there—got a pair of gloves and a
pistareen's worth of bows for a dollar—dog cheap!—Courtlandt-
street corner—famous place to see the belles go by—quere, ever
been shopping with a lady?—some account of it—ladies go into all
the shops in the city to buy a pair of gloves—good way of spending
time, if they have nothing else to do.—Oswego-Market—looks very
much like a triumphal arch—some account of the manner of erecting them in ancient times—digression to the *arch*-duke Charles, and
some account of the ancient germans.—N. B. quote Tacitus on this
subject.—Particular description of market-baskets, butchers' blocks
and wheelbarrows—mem. queer things run upon one wheel!—Saw
a cartman driving full-tilt through Broadway—run over a child—
good enough for it—what business had it to be in the way?—Hint
concerning the laws against pigs, goats, dogs and cartmen—grand
apostrophe to the sublime science of jurisprudence—comparison
between legislators and tinkers—quere, whether it requires greater
ability to mend a law than to mend a kettle?—inquiry into the utility of making laws that are broken a hundred times in a day with impunity—my lord Coke's opinion on the subject—my lord a very
great man—so was lord Bacon—good story about a criminal named
Hog claiming relationship with him.—Hogg's porter-house—great
haunt of Will Wizard—Will put down there one night by a sea captain, in an argument concerning the area of the Chinese empire,
Whang-po;—Hogg's a capital place for hearing the same stories, the
same jokes and the same songs every night in the year—mem. except Sunday nights—fine school for young politicians too—some of
the longest and thickest heads in the city come there to settle the nation.—Scheme of *Ichabod Fungus* to restore the balance of Europe—
digression—some account of the balance of Europe—comparison
between it, and a pair of scales, with the emperor Alexander in one
and the emperor Napoleon in the other—fine fellows—both of a

weight, can't tell which will kick the beam ... mem. dont care much either ... nothing to me ... *Ichabod* very unhappy about it ... thinks Napoleon has an eye on this country ... capital place to pasture his horses, and provide for the rest of his family .... Dey-street ... ancient dutch name of it, signifying murders'-valley— formerly the site of a great peach orchard ... my grandmother's history of the famous *Peach war* ... arose from an indian stealing peaches out of this orchard ... good cause as need be for a war ... just as good as the balance of power ... Anecdote of a war between two italian states about a bucket ... introduce some capital new *truisms* about the folly of mankind, the ambition of kings, potentates and princes, particularly Alexander, Caesar, Charles the XIIth, Napoleon, little king Pepin and the great Charlemagne .... Conclude with an exhortation to the present race of sovereigns to keep the king's peace, and abstain from all those deadly quarrels which produce battle, murder and sudden death ... Mem. ran my nose against lamp-post ... conclude in great dudgeon.

*SALMAGUNDI,* 1807

# FRANCES TROLLOPE

*Frances Trollope (1780–1863) was the first in a line of English au-
thors who visited America and wrote gossipy, critical accounts of the
new nation. Her amusingly malicious* Domestic Manners of the
Americans *(1832) began the vogue, which touched off a counter-
offensive by patriotic American writers such as James Kirke Paulding.
(Her son, the novelist Anthony Trollope, extended the tradition with his
travel book* North America *in 1862.) Mrs. Trollope's disillusionment
with the United States was understandable, given the circumstances of
her sojourn: having set off at age forty-eight with three of her children to join an Owenite commune in Tennessee, only to find it a sham-
bles, she attempted to open a bazaar in Cincinnati, which failed
dismally. She returned to England broke, and discovered her true
métier as a writer at fifty. Given her devastating remarks about other
sections of the country, her observations of New York seem all the more
enthusiastic.*

## FROM *DOMESTIC MANNERS*
## *OF THE AMERICANS*

I HAVE NEVER SEEN the bay of Naples, I can therefore make no
comparison, but my imagination is incapable of conceiving any
thing of the kind more beautiful than the harbour of New York.
Various and lovely are the objects which meet the eye on every side,
but the naming them would only be to give a list of words, without
conveying the faintest idea of the scene. I doubt if ever the pencil of
Turner could do it justice, bright and glorious as it rose upon us. We
seemed to enter the harbour of New York upon waves of liquid gold,
and as we darted past the green isles which rise from its bosom, like
guardian sentinels of the fair city, the setting sun stretched his horizontal beams farther and farther at each moment, as if to point out
to us some new glory in the landscape.

New York, indeed, appeared to us, even when we saw it by a
soberer light, a lovely and a noble city. To us who had been so long

travelling through half-cleared forests, and sojourning among an "I'm-as-good-as-you" population, it seemed, perhaps, more beauti-ful, more splendid, and more refined than it might have done, had we arrived there directly from London; but making every allowance for this, I must still declare that I think New York one of the finest cities I ever saw, and as much superior to every other in the Union, (Philadelphia not excepted,) as London to Liverpool, or Paris to Rouen. Its advantages of position are, perhaps, unequalled any where. Situated on an island, which I think it will one day cover, it rises, like Venice, from the sea, and like that fairest of cities in the days of her glory, receives into its lap tribute of all the riches of the earth.

The southern point of Manhattan Island divides the waters of the harbour into the north and east rivers; on this point stands the city of New York, extending from river to river, and running northward to the extent of three or four miles. I think it covers nearly as much ground as Paris, but is much less thickly peopled. The extreme point is fortified towards the sea by a battery, and forms an admirable point of defence; but in these piping days of peace, it is converted into a public promenade, and one more beautiful, I should suppose, no city could boast. From hence commences the splendid Broadway, as the fine avenue is called, which runs through the whole city. This noble street may vie with any I ever saw, for its length and breadth, its handsome shops, neat awnings, excellent *trottoir*, and well-dressed pedestrians. It has not the crowded glitter of Bond-street equipages, nor the gorgeous fronted palaces of Regent-street; but it is magnifi-cent in its extent, and ornamented by several handsome buildings, some of them surrounded by grass and trees. The Park, in which stands the noble city-hall, is a very fine area. I never found that the most graphic description of a city could give me any feeling of being there; and even if others have the power, I am very sure I have not, of setting churches and squares, and long drawn streets, before the mind's eye. I will not, therefore, attempt a detailed description of this great metropolis of the new world, but will only say that during the seven weeks we stayed there, we always found something new to see and to admire; and were it not so very far from all the old-world things which cling about the heart of an European, I should say that I never saw a city more desirable as a residence.

The dwelling houses of the higher classes are extremely handsome, and very richly furnished. Silk or satin furniture is as often, or oftener, seen than chintz; the mirrors are as handsome as in London; the cheffoniers, slabs, and marble tables as elegant; and in addition, they have all the pretty tasteful decoration of French porcelaine and or-molu in much greater abundance, because at a much cheaper rate. Every part of their houses is well carpeted, and the exterior finishings, such as steps, railings, and door-frames, are very superior. Almost every house has handsome green blinds on the outside; balconies are not very general, nor do the houses display, externally, so many flowers as those of Paris and London; but I saw many rooms decorated within, exactly like those of an European *petite maîtresse*. Little tables, looking and smelling like flower beds, portfolios, nicknacks, bronzes, busts, cameos, and alabaster vases, illustrated copies of lady-like rhymes bound in silk, and, in short, all the pretty coxcomalities of the drawing-room scattered about with the same profuse and studied negligence as with us.

Hudson Square and its neighbourhood is, I believe, the most fashionable part of the town; the square is beautiful, excellently well planted with a great variety of trees, and only wanting our frequent and careful mowing to make it equal to any square in London. The iron railing which surrounds this enclosure is as high and as handsome as that of the Tuileries, and it will give some idea of the care bestowed on its decoration, to know that the gravel for the walks was conveyed by barges from Boston, not as ballast, but as freight.

The great defect in the houses is their extreme uniformity— when you have seen one you have seen all. Neither do I quite like the arrangement of the rooms. In nearly all the houses the dining and drawing-rooms are on the same floor, with ample folding doors between them; when thrown together they certainly make a very noble apartment; but no doors can be barrier sufficient between dining and drawing-rooms. Mixed dinner parties of ladies and gentlemen, however, are very rare, which is a great defect in the society; not only as depriving them of the most social and hospitable manner of meeting, but as leading to frequent dinner parties of gentlemen without ladies, which certainly does not conduce to refinement.

1832

# FANNY KEMBLE

*Among visitors to New York, few were more passionately embraced than the English actors who performed here and helped to lift the cultural standards of a robustly appreciative but still provincial audience. Fanny Kemble (1809–93) and her trouper-father arrived in the city in 1832, and from there began a barnstorming tour around the country. She kept a delightfully spirited diary of those adventures, rich in theatrical "war stories." Walt Whitman wrote years later, in* Specimen Days, *of the impression she made on him: "Fanny Kemble—name to conjure up great mimic scenes withal—perhaps the greatest. I remember well her rendering of Bianca in 'Fazio,' and Marianna in 'The Wife.' Nothing finer did ever stage exhibit—the veterans of all nations said so, and my boyish heart and head felt it in every minute cell. The lady was just matured, strong, better than merely beautiful, born from the footlights, had had three years' practice in London and through the British towns, and then she came to give America that young maturity and roseate power in all their noon, or rather forenoon, flush. It was my good luck to see her nearly every night she play'd at the old Park—certainly in all her principal characters."*

### FROM THE JOURNAL

*FRIDAY, SEPTEMBER 13TH* Drove all about New York, which more than ever, reminded me of the towns in France. Passed the Bowery Theatre, which is a handsome, finely proportioned building, with a large brazen eagle plastered on the pediment, for all the world like an insurance mark. We passed a pretty house, which Colonel Sibell called an old mansion. Mercy on me and him! Old! I thought of Warwick Castle, of Hatfield, of Chequers, of Hopwood— old! and there it stood, for all the world like one of our own city's yesterday-grown boxes. The woods, waters and hills and skies alone are old here. The works of men are in the very greenness and unmellowed imperfection of youth. But the Americans are not satisfied with glorying in what they are, but are never happy without comparing this, their sapling, to the giant oaks of the old world, and what can one say to that? Is New York like London? No, it is not, but the oak was an acorn once, and New York will surely, if the world holds together long enough, become a lordly city, such as we know of beyond the sea.

*SATURDAY, SEPTEMBER 14TH*  Sat stitching all the blessed day. At five dressed and went to the Hones, where we were to dine. This is one of the first houses here, so I conclude that I am to consider what I see as a tolerable sample of the ways and manners of being and doing of the *best* society in New York. There were about twenty people, the women in a sort of French demi-toilette with bare necks and long sleeves, hair all frizzed out and thread-net handkerchiefs and capes. The whole of which, to my English eye, appeared a strange marrying of incongruities. The younger daughter of our host is beautiful, a young and brilliant likeness of Ellen Tree, but with more refinement. She was much taken up with a youth, to whom, my neighbour at dinner informed me, she was engaged.

The women here, like those of most warm climates, ripen very early and decay proportionally soon. They are, generally speaking, pretty, with good complexions, and an air of freshness, but this I am told is very evanescent. Whereas in England a woman is in the full bloom of health and beauty from twenty to five and thirty, here they scarcely reach the first period without being faded and looking old.

There was a Mr. Dominic Lynch, the magnus Apollo of New York, who is a musical genius. He sings as well as any gentleman need sing, pronounces Italian well, and accompanies himself without any false chords. All of which renders him *the* man round whom the women listen and languish. He sang the "Phantom Bark"—the last time I heard it was from the lips of Moore, with two of the loveliest faces in all the world hanging over him—Mrs. Norton and Mrs. Blackwood, now Lady Dufferin.

The dinner was plenteous and tolerably well dressed, but ill-served. There were not half enough servants, and we had neither water glasses nor finger glasses. Now though I don't eat with my fingers, yet I do hold a finger glass at the conclusion of my dinner, a requisite comfort. After dinner we had coffee, but no tea, whereat my English taste was in high dudgeon. The gentlemen did not sit long, and when they joined us, Mr. Dominic Lynch, as I said before, uttered sweet sounds. I was not a little amused at Mrs. Hone asking me whether I had heard of his singing or their musical soirées, and seeming surprised that I had no revelations of either across the Atlantic. Mercy on me! what fools people are all over the world! The worst is, they are fools of the same sort, and there is no profit whatever in travelling. Mr. Bancroft, who is an Englishman, happened to ask if I knew Captain Whaite, whereupon we immediately struck of a conversation, and talked over English folk and doings, to my entire satisfaction.

I sang to them two or three things, but the piano was pitched too high for my voice. In that large, lofty, fine room, they had a tiny old-fashioned becurtained cabinet piano struck right against the wall, into which the singer's face was turned, and into which his voice was absorbed. We had hardly regained our inn, when in walked Mr. Bancroft to ask if we would not join him and the Cornwalls at supper. He said that besides five being a great deal too early to dine, he had not had half enough dinner. And then began the regular English quizzing of everything and everybody we had left behind. Oh dear! how thoroughly English it was! Of course we did not accept their invitation, but it furnished me a matter of amusement. How we English folk do cling to our own habits, our own views, our own things, our own people.

*MONDAY, SEPTEMBER 16TH* Rose at eight, at twelve went to rehearsal. That washed-out man who failed in London when he acted Romeo with me is to be my Fazio. Let us hope that he will know some of his words tomorrow night, for he is at present innocent of any such knowledge. After rehearsal walked into a shop to buy some gauze. The shopman called me by name, entered into conversation with us, and one of them, after showing me a variety of things I did not want, said that they were anxious to show me every attention, and render my stay in this country aggreable. For my own part, though I had the grace to smile and say "thank you", I longed to add, "but be so good as to measure your ribands and hold your tongue". I have no idea of holding parley with clerks behind a counter, still less of their doing so with me. I should have been better pleased if they had called me "Ma'am", which they did not.

We dined at three. Vincent and Colonel Sibell called after dinner, and at seven we went to the theatre. It was my dear father's first appearance in this new world, and my heart ached with anxiety. The weather was intensely hot, yet the theatre was crowded. When he came on, they gave him what everybody here calls an immense reception, but they should see our London audience get up and wave hats and handkerchiefs, and shout welcome, as they do to us. The tears were in my eyes, and all I could say was—"They might as well get up, I think". My father looked well and acted beyond all praise. I think it is impossible to conceive Hamlet more truly, or execute it more exquisitely than he does. The refinement, the tenderness, the grace, dignity and princely courtesy with which he invests it from beginning to end, are most lovely. His voice was weak from nervousness and the intolerable heat, and he was not well dressed, which was a pity. The play was well got up, and went off very well. The Hones were there, a regiment of them, also Colonel Sibell and Captain Martin.

*TUESDAY, SEPTEMBER 17TH* At eleven went to rehearsal. Mr. Keppel is just as nervous and as imperfect as ever. What on earth will he or I do tonight? Came home and got things out for the theatre. Mr. Hone and his nephew called. The latter asked me if I was at all apprehensive? No, by my troth, I am not. The whole thing is too loathsome to me for either failure or success to affect me in the least.

At half past six went to the theatre. They acted the farce of *Popping the Question* first, in order, I suppose, to get people to their seats before the play began. Poor Mr. Keppel was gasping for breath. I consoled and comforted him all I could, and gave him some of my lemonade to swallow, for he was choking with fright, then sat myself down with my back to the audience, and up went the curtain. Owing to the position in which I was sitting, and my plain dress, the people did not know me, and would not have known me for some time, if that stupid man had done as I kept bidding him, gone on. Instead, he stood stock still, looked at me, and then at the audience, thereupon the latter caught an inkling of the truth, and gave me such a reception as I get at Covent Garden every time I act a new part. The house was very full, all the Hones were there, and Colonel Sibell. Mr. Keppel was frightened to death and in the very second speech was quite out. It was in vain that I prompted him, he was too nervous to take the word and made a complete mess of it. This happened more than once in the first scene, and at the end of the first act, as I left the stage, I said to Dall, "It's all up with me, I can't do anything now!" Having to prompt my Fazio, frightened by his fright, annoyed by his forgetting his crossings and positions, I thought the whole thing must necessarily go to pieces.

However, once rid of my encumbrance, which I am at the end of the second act, I began to move a little more freely, gathered up my strength, and set to work comfortably by myself. Whereupon the people applauded, I warmed, and got through very satisfactorily, or so it seems. After the play, my father introduced me to Mr. Berkley, who was behind the scenes. Came home to bed at half past twelve, weary and half melted away. The ants swarm on the floor, on the tables, in the beds, about one's clothes. The plagues of Egypt were a joke to them.

WEDNESDAY, SEPTEMBER 18TH  After breakfast, went off to rehearsal—*Romeo and Juliet*. Mr. Keppel has been dismissed, poor man! I'm sorry for him. My father is to play Romeo—I'm sorrier still for that. After rehearsal Mr. Berkley called. He is particularly fond of music, and my father asked him to try the piano, and was playing most delightfully when in walked Mr. Hone, followed by Colonel Sibell. At five our dinner party assembled. Our dinner was neither good nor well served, the wine not half iced. At the end of it, my father gave Captain Whaite his claret jug, with which that worthy seemed much satisfied. Then they put me down to the piano, and once or twice I thought I must have screamed. Dear Mr. Bell vibrated at my side, threatening my new gown with a cup of coffee, which he held at an awful angle from the horizontal, singing with everybody who opened their lips, and uttering such dreadfully discordant little squeals and squeaks, that I thought I should have died with suppressed laughter. On the other side, stood the Irishman, who, though warbling a little out of tune, still retained enough of his right senses to discriminate between Mr. Bell's yelps, and singing, properly so-called. They all went away in good time, and we came to bed.

—to bed—to sleep—

*To sleep! perchance to be bitten! Aye, there's the scratch;*
*And in that sleep of ours what bugs may come,*
*Must give us pause.*

*THURSDAY, SEPTEMBER 19TH* After breakfast went to rehearse *Romeo and Juliet.* Poor Mr. Keppel is fairly laid on the shelf— I'm sorry for him. What a funny passion he had, by the way, for going down on his knees. In *Fazio*, at the end of the judgement scene, when I was upon mine, down he went upon his, making the most absurd devout looking vis-à-vis I ever beheld. In the last scene too, when he ought to have been going off to execution, down he went again on his knees, and no power on earth could get him up again for Lord knows how long! Poor fellow, he bothered me a great deal, yet I'm sincerely sorry for him.

Mr. Hone called and asked us to dinner tomorrow to meet Dr. Wainwright, who, poor man, dares neither to go to the play nor to call upon us. So strict are the good people about the behaviour of their pastors and masters. This morning, Essex called to fetch away the Captain's jug. He asked my father for an order, adding, with some hesitation, "It must be for the gallery, if you please, sir, for people of colour are not allowed in the pit, or any other part of the house". I believe I turned black myself, I was so indignant.

At half past six went to the theatre. The house was very full and dreadfully hot. My father acted Romeo beautifully, and I looked very nice and the people applauded my *gown* abundantly. At the end of the play I was half dead with heat and fatigue.

*FRIDAY, SEPTEMBER 20TH* This morning, a letter from Mr. Keppel, soliciting another trial, and urging the harshness of his case, in being condemned upon a part which he had had no time to study. My own opinion of poor Mr. Keppel is that no power on earth or in heaven can make him act decently. However, I don't object to his trying again; he did not swamp me the first night, so I don't suppose he will the fifth. Just before dinner received a most delicious bouquet, which gladdened my heart with its sweet smell and lovely colours. Some of the flowers were strangers to me. After dinner, Colonel Sibell called, and began pulling out heaps of newspapers, and telling us a long story about Mr. Keppel, who, it seems, has been writing to the papers to convince them and the public that he is a good actor.

When he had gone, went to the theatre; the house was very good, the play *The School of Scandal*. I played pretty fairly and looked very nice. The people were stupid to a degree, to be sure—poor things, it was very hot. The few critiques I have seen upon our acting have been, on the whole, laudatory. One was sent to me from a paper called *The Mirror*, which pleased me very much. Not because the praise in it was excessive, and far beyond my deserts, but it was written with great taste and feeling, and was not a product of a common press hack.

*SATURDAY, SEPTEMBER 21ST* After breakfast got into a hackney carriage with Dall, and went to a shop to order a pair of shoes. The shopkeepers with whom I have hitherto had to deal, are either condescendingly familiar, or insolently indifferent in their manner. Your washer-woman sits down before you while you are standing to speak to her; a shop boy bringing things for your inspection, not only sits down, but keeps his hat on in your drawing room. The worthy man to whom I went for my shoes was so amazingly ungracious, that at first I thought I would go out of the shop. But recollecting that I should probably go further and fare worse, I gulped, sat down, and was measured.

Came home, and at five went in to our neighbours. Dr. Wainwright, the Rector of Grace Church, was the only stranger. I like him extremely—a charming and intelligent man. His conversation was clever, with an abundance of goodness and liberal benevolent feeling shining through it. We retired to our drawing room, where Mrs. Bancroft made me laugh extremely with sundry passages of her American experiences. I was particularly amused by her account of their stopping, after a long day's journey, at an inn somewhere, where the hostess, who remained in the room the whole time, addressed her as follows—"D'ye play?", pointing to an open pianoforte. Mrs. Bancroft replied that she did sometimes, whereupon the free and easy landlady ordered candles, and added—"Come, sit down and give us a tune then," to which courteous invitation Mrs. Bancroft replied by taking up her candle and walking out of the room. Dr. Wainwright is perfectly enchanting. They left us about eleven, and I went to bed.

*SUNDAY, SEPTEMBER 22ND* Went to church with Dall. The day was most lovely and my eyes were constantly attracted to the church windows, through which the magnificent willows of the burial ground looked like golden-green fountains rising into the sky. The singing was excellent, and Dr. Wainwright's sermon very good too. After church, Mr. Ogden Hoffman called and sat with us during dinner, telling us stories of the flogging of slaves, as he himself had witnessed it in the south. Rage and indignation forced the colour into my face, tears into my eyes, and strained every muscle in my body. He made me perfectly sick with it.

*MONDAY, SEPTEMBER 23RD* Went to rehearsale—*Venice Preserved*, with Mr. Keppel, who did not appear to know the words even and seemed perfectly bewildered at being asked to do the common business of the piece. "Mercy on me! what will he do tonight!", thought I. After dinner, played and wrote my journal and at six went to the theatre. My gown was horribly ill-plaited and I looked like a blue bag. The house was very full, and they received Mr. Keppel with acclamations and shouts of applause. When I went on, I was all but tumbling down at the sight of my Jaffier, who looked like the apothecary in *Romeo and Juliet,* with the addition of some devilish red slashes along his arms and thighs. The first scene passed well, but oh,

the next, and the next, and the next. Whenever he was not glued to
my side, he stood three yards behind me. He did nothing but seize
my hand and grapple to it so hard, that unless I had knocked him
down (which I felt much inclined to try), I could not disengage myself. In the senate scene, when I was entreating for mercy, and struggling, as Otway has it, for my life, he was prancing around the stage
in every direction, flourishing his dagger in the air. I wish to heaven
I had got up and run away, it would have been natural and served him
right. In the parting scene, instead of going away from me when he
said, "Farewell for ever!", he stuck to my skirts, though in the same
breath that I adjured him in the words of my part not to leave me, I
added aside, "Get away from me, oh do!". When I exclaimed "Not
one kiss at parting", he kept embracing and kissing me like mad, and
when I ought to have been pursuing him, and calling after him,
"Leave thy dagger with me!", he hung himself up against the wing,
and remained dangling there for five minutes. I was half crazy! The
good people sat and swallowed it all. They deserved it, by my troth,
they did. I prompted him constantly, and once, after struggling in
vain to free myself from him, was obliged in the middle of my part,
to exclaim, "You hurt me dreadfully, Mr. Keppel!" He clung to me,
cramped me, crumpled me—dreadful! I never experienced anything
like this before, and made up my mind I never would again. I played
of course like a wretch, finished my part as well as I could, and as
soon as the play was over, went to my father and Mr. Simpson and
declared to them both my determination not to go upon the stage
again with that gentleman for a hero. Come what may, I will not be
subjected to this sort of experiment again.

At the end of the play, the clever New Yorkers actually called for
Mr. Keppel! And this most worthless clapping of hands, most worth-
lessly bestowed upon such a worthless object, is what, by the nature
of my craft, I am bound to care for. I spit at it from the bottom of
my soul! Talking of applause, the man who acted Bedamar tonight
thought fit to be two hours dragging me off the stage, in consequence of which I had to scream, "Jaffier! Jaffier!", till I thought I
should have broken a blood vessel. On my remonstrating with him
about this, he said, "Well, you are rewarded, listen"—the people

were clapping and shouting vehemently. This is the whole history of actors and acting. We came home tired and thoroughly disgusted, and found no supper. The cooks, who do not live in the house, but come and do their work, and depart home whenever it suits their convenience, had not thought to stay and prepare any supper for us. So we had to wait for the readiest things that could be procured out of doors for us. At last appeared a cold boiled fowl, and some monstrous oysters. They were well-flavoured but their size displeased me, and I swallowed but one and went to bed.

1832

# PHILIP HONE

*Philip Hone (1780–1851) rose from humble origins to become a wealthy businessman, mayor of New York, and leader of the patrician set. He also kept a diary of over two million words, from 1828 to his death. Hone was not much given to private confession, but his diary is fascinating as a record of society, politics, and daily life. There remains something very attractive about this public-spirited, gregarious man and the way he brooded over the transformations and growing pains of his beloved city.*

## FROM THE DIARY

*[1832] WEDNESDAY, JULY 4* It is a lovely day, but very different from all the previous anniversaries of independence. The alarm about the cholera has prevented all the usual jollification under the public authority. There are no booths in Broadway, the parade which was ordered here has been countermanded, no corporation dinner, and no ringing of bells. Some troops are marching about the street, "upon their own hook," I suppose. Most of the stores are closed, and there is a pretty smart cannonade of crackers by the boys, but it is not a regular Fourth of July. The Board of Health reports to-day twenty new cases and eleven deaths since noon yesterday. The disease is here in all its violence and will increase. God grant that its ravages may be confined, and its visit short! I wrote to-day for the girls to return from Hyde Park forthwith. They are all going to Rockaway. Catharine is greatly alarmed, and we are to ascertain whether the seashore is a place of safety.

*FRIDAY, JULY 5* Mr. Martin Van Buren arrived last evening in the packet ship *New York* from Liverpool, sailed June 1. His party in this city had made arrangements to receive him on his arrival, and committees waited upon him for the purpose. Processions were to have been formed and speeches made, but with proper delicacy he declined the honor, alleging as a reason the alarm existing in the city on account of the cholera.

*ROCKAWAY, MONDAY, JULY 16* The accounts of the cholera in New York have become dreadfully alarming, and it is spreading rapidly over the whole country. Albany, the towns on the river, different parts of New Jersey and Connecticut, are becoming successively the theater of its ravages. The following reports of the Board of Health for the last three days show a progressive increase: Saturday the 14th, 115 new cases, 66 deaths; Sunday, 133 new cases, 74 deaths; Monday, 163 new cases, 94 deaths.

*MONDAY, JULY 23* I left Rockaway after breakfast this morning and came to the city. Miss Lewis accompanied me. The alarm is very great but the streets are more lively than I expected. I went to Wall Street and transacted some business; there was a considerable number of persons on 'Change, and I saw but few stores closed on my walk. Great alarm has been occasioned by the sudden death of George E. Smith, alderman of the Fourth Ward. He attended the board on Saturday night until eleven o'clock, was taken ill with cholera at three in the morning, and died in seven hours. But I have learned that although he was an active man and a vigilant magistrate, he was habitually addicted to the intemperate use of ardent liquor. I hear many dreadful stories of cholera cases. The last of last week a man was found in the road at Harlem, who had died of cholera. A coroner's inquest was called, and of twenty persons, jury and witnesses, who were present, nine are now dead. John Aspenwall told me this story.

*TUESDAY, JULY 31* I came into town this morning with Mr. Abraham Ogden. The eastern section of the city is nearly deserted, and business of every description appears to be at a stand. Broadway and the lower part of the city is yet tolerably lively, and Wall Street and other parts "where the merchants do congregate" retains much of its usual bustle and animation.

*MONDAY, AUG. 27* My wife, my daughter Margaret, and I came up from Rockaway this morning, and brought Joanna Anthon with us. I presume I have taken my leave of Rockaway for the season. The change in the appearance of the city is very great. The favorable reports of cholera, and the pleasant weather, have brought thousands of the refugees back to their homes. Business has revived, the streets are lively and animated, and everything seems to be resuming its wonted appearance. We are very cautious, however. Beef and mutton are allowed, but vegetables and fruit are strictly interdicted. The peaches and melons in vain throw their fragrance around; we look at them, we sigh for their enjoyment—but we don't touch them. I am well of my diarrhoea, and I find it exceedingly difficult to resist the temptation. It is too much for the frailty of human nature and I am off to the Springs to-morrow to get out of the way.

*[1834] THURSDAY, JULY 10* There has been of late great excitement in consequence of the proceedings of a set of fanatics who are determined to emancipate all the slaves by a *coup de main*, and have held meetings in which black men and women have been introduced. These meetings have been attended with tumult and violence, especially one which was held on Friday evening at the Chatham Street Chapel. Arthur Tappan and his brother Lewis have been conspicuous in these proceedings, and the mob last night, after exhausting their rage at the Bowery Theater, went down in a body to the house of the latter gentleman in Rose Street, broke into the house, destroyed the windows and made a bonfire of the furniture in the street. The police at length interfered, rather tardily, I should think; but the diabolical spirit which prompted this outrage is not quenched, and I apprehend we shall see more of it.

The conduct of the Abolitionists has been very indiscreet, but their number has been too small to give reasonable ground of alarm; and this attack upon one of their leaders will add to their strength by enabling them to raise the cry of persecution.

*[1835] THURSDAY, DEC. 17* How shall I record the events of last night, or how attempt to describe the most awful calamity which has ever visited these United States? The greatest loss by fire that has ever been known, with the exception perhaps of the conflagration of

Moscow, and that was an incidental concomitant of war. I am fatigued in body, disturbed in mind, and my fancy filled with images of horror which my pen is inadequate to describe. Nearly one half of the first ward is in ashes; 500 to 700 stores, which with their contents are valued at $20,000,000 to $40,000,000, are now lying in an indistinguishable mass of ruins. There is not perhaps in the world the same space of ground covered by so great an amount of real and personal property as the scene of this dreadful conflagration. The fire broke out at nine o'clock last evening. I was waiting in the library when the alarm was given and went immediately down. The night was intensely cold, which was one cause of the unprecedented progress of the flames, for the water froze in the hydrants, and the engines and their hose could not be worked without great difficulty. The firemen, too, had been on duty all last night, and were almost incapable of performing their usual services.

The fire originated in the store of Comstock & Adams in Merchant Street, a narrow crooked street, filled with high stores lately erected and occupied by dry goods and hardware merchants, which led from Hanover to Pearl Street. When I arrived at the spot the scene exceeded all description; the progress of the flames, like flashes of lightning, communicated in every direction, and a few minutes sufficed to level the lofty edifices on every side. It had crossed the block to Pearl Street. I perceived that the store of my son John (Brown & Hone) was in danger, and made the best of my way by Front Street around the Old Slip to the spot. We succeeded in getting out the stock of valuable dry goods, but they were put in the square, and in the course of the night our labors were rendered unavailing, for the fire reached and destroyed them, with a great part of all which were saved from the neighboring stores; this part of Pearl Street consisted of dry goods stores, with stocks of immense value of which little or nothing was saved. At this period the flames were unmanageable, and the crowd, including the firemen, appeared to look on with the apathy of despair, and the destruction continued until it reached Coenties Slip, in that direction, and Wall Street down to the river, including all South Street and Water Street; while to the west, Exchange Street, including all Post's stores, Lord's beautiful row, William Street, Beaver and Stone Streets, were destroyed. The splendid edifice erected a few years since by the liberality of the merchants, known as the Merchants' Exchange, and one of the ornaments of the city, took fire in the rear, and is now a heap of ruins. The façade and magnificent marble columns fronting on Wall Street are all that remains of this noble building, and resemble the ruins of an ancient temple rather than the new and beautiful resort of the merchants. When the dome of this edifice fell in, the sight was awfully grand. In its fall it demolished the statue of Hamilton executed by Ball Hughes, which was erected in the rotunda only eight months ago by the public spirit of the merchants. The *Evening Star* has the following paragraphs upon the loss of this fine specimen of art and that of Dr. Mathews' church in Exchange (late Garden) Street:

> Among the ruins, not the least to be lamented was the loss of that splendid statue of Hamilton, which towering brightly amidst the sea of flames, that dashed against its crackling base, cast a mournful glance on the terrific scene, and then fell nobly, perishing under the crush of the edifice of which it had been, as it were, the tutelary genius.
>
> The handsome church of the Rev. Dr. Mathews, Garden Street, a long while resisted the mass of flames in their course toward Broad Street. The bright gold ball and the star above it gleamed brilliantly, and still, while they were both shining with an intensity of splendor which attracted general remark, gave one surge and fell, in all their glory, into the heap of chaos beneath them.

The Exchange and the church, from being considered out of reach of danger, were made the receptacles of an immense amount of valuable dry goods, all of which were consumed.

It would be an idle task to attempt an enumeration of the sufferers; in the number are most of my nearest friends and of my family; my son John, my son-in-law Schermerhorn, and my nephew Isaac S. Hone, and Samuel S. Howland, were all burnt out.

The buildings covered an area a quarter of a mile square, closely built up with fine stores of four and five stories in height, filled with merchandise, all of which lie in a mass of burning, smoking ruins, rendering the streets indistinguishable. . . . A large portion of the valuable estates of the Jones and Schermerhorn families was within these limits, and is not now to be found. The fire has been burning all day in the direction of Coenties Slip, and was not fairly gotten under till towards evening.

A calculation is made in the *Commercial* this afternoon that the number of buildings burnt is 570, and that the whole loss is something over $15,000,000. The insurance offices are all, of course, bankrupt. Their collective capitals amount to $11,750,000; but those downtown have a large proportion of the risks, and will not be able to pay 50 per cent of the losses. The unfortunate stockholders lose all. In this way I suffer directly, and in others indirectly, to a large amount.

The mayor, who has exerted himself greatly in this fearful emergency, called the Common Council together this afternoon for the purpose of establishing private patrols for the protection of the city; for if another fire should break out before the firemen have recovered from the fatigues of the last two nights, and the engines and hose be repaired from the effects of the frost, it would be impossible to arrest its progress. Several companies of uniformed militia and a company of United States marines are under arms, to protect the property scattered over the lower part of the city.

I have been alarmed by some of the signs of the times which this calamity has brought forth: the miserable wretches who prowled about the ruins, and became beastly drunk on the champagne and other wines and liquors with which the streets and wharves were lined, seemed to exult in the misfortune, and such expressions were heard as "Ah! They'll make no more five per cent dividends!" and "This will make the aristocracy haul in their horns!" Poor deluded wretches, little do they know that their own horns "live and move and have their being" in these very horns of the aristocracy, as their instigators teach them to call it. This cant is the very text from which their leaders teach their deluded followers. It forms part of the warfare of the poor against the rich; a warfare which is destined, I fear, to break the hearts of some of the politicians of Tammany Hall, who have used these men to answer a temporary purpose, and find now that the dogs they have taught to bark will bite them as soon as their political opponents.

These remarks are not so much the result of what I have heard of the conduct and conversation of the rabble at the fire as of what I witnessed this afternoon at the Bank for Savings. There was an evident run upon the bank by a gang of low Irishmen, who demanded their money in a peremptory and threatening manner. At this season there is usually a great preponderance of deposits over the drafts, the first of January being the day on which the balances are made up for the semi-annual dividend. All the sums now drawn lose nearly six months interest, which the bank gains. These Irishmen, however, insisted upon having their money, and when they received it were evidently disappointed and would fain have put it back again. This class of men are the most ignorant, and consequently the most obstinate white men in the world, and I have seen enough to satisfy me that, with few exceptions, ignorance and vice go together. These men, rejoicing in the calamity which has ruined so many institutions and individuals, thought it a fine opportunity to use the power which their dirty money gave them, to add to the general distress, and sought to embarrass this excellent institution, which has been established for the sole benefit of the poor. . . . These Irishmen, strangers among us, without a feeling of patriotism or affection in common with American citizens, decide the elections in the city of New York. They make Presidents and Governors, and they send men to represent us in the councils of the nation, and what is worse than all, their importance in these matters is derived from the use which is made of them by political demagogues, who despise the tools they work with. Let them look to it; the time may not be very distant when the same brogue which they have instructed to shout "Hurrah for Jackson!" shall be used to impart additional horror to the cry of "Down with the natives!"

*[1836]* FRIDAY, DEC. 30 I went this evening to a party at Mrs. Charles H. Russell's, given in honor of the bride, Mrs. William H.

Russell. The splendid apartments of this fine house are well adapted to an evening party, and everything was very handsome on this occasion. The home is lighted with gas, and the quantity consumed being greater than common, it gave out suddenly in the midst of a cotillion. "Darkness overspread the land." This accident occasioned great merriment to the company, and some embarrassment to the host and hostess, but a fresh supply of gas was obtained, and in a short time the fair dancers were again "tripping it on the light fantastic toe."

Gas is a handsome light, in a large room like Mr. Russell's, on an occasion of this kind, but liable (I should think) at all times to give the company the slip, and illy calculated for the ordinary uses of a family.

*[1837] TUESDAY, JAN. 3* Mr. Lawrence, the Mayor, kept open house yesterday, according to custom from time immemorable, but the manners as well as the times have sadly changed. Formerly gentlemen visited the mayor, saluted him by an honest shake of the hand, paid him the compliment of the day, and took their leave; one out of twenty perhaps taking a single glass of wine or cherry bounce and a morsel of pound cake or New Year's cookies. But that respectable functionary is now considered the mayor of a party, and the rabble considering him "hail fellow well met," use his house as a Five Points tavern. Mr. Lawrence has been much annoyed on former occasions, but the scene yesterday defies description. At ten o'clock the doors were beset by a crowd of importunate *sovereigns*, some of whom had already laid the foundations of *regal* glory and expected to become *royally* drunk at the hospitable house of His Honor. The rush was tremendous; the tables were taken by storm, the bottles emptied in a moment. Confusion, noise, and quarreling ensued, until the mayor with the assistance of his police cleared the house and locked the doors, which were not reopened until every eatable and drinkable were removed, and a little decency and order restored.

I called soon after this change had taken place. The mayor related the circumstances to me with strong indignation, and I hope the evil will be remedied hereafter. All this comes of Mr. Lawrence being the mayor of a party and not of the city. Every scamp who has bawled out "Huzza for Lawrence" and "Down With the Whigs" considered himself authorized to use him and his house and furniture at his pleasure; to wear his hat in his presence, to smoke and spit upon his carpet, to devour his beef and turkey, and wipe his greasy fingers upon the curtains, to get drunk with his liquor, and discharge the reckoning with riotous shouts of "Huzza for our mayor." *We* put him in and *we* are entitled to the use of him. Mr. Lawrence (party man as he is) is too much of a gentleman to submit to this, and sometimes wishes his constituents and his office all to the devil, if I am not greatly mistaken, and if he rejects (as he has now done) their kind tokens of brotherly affection, they will be for sending him there ere long, and will look out for somebody of their own class less troubled than him with aristocratical notions of decency, order, and sobriety.

*[1838]* FRIDAY, JAN. 26 My wife, daughter Margaret, Jones and I dined with Mr. and Mrs. Olmstead. The dinner was quite *à la française.* The table, covered with confectionery and gew-gaws, looked like one of the shops down Broadway in the Christmas holidays, but not an eatable thing. The dishes were all handed round; in my opinion a most unsatisfactory mode of proceeding in relation to this important part of the business of a man's life. One does not know how to choose, because you are ignorant of what is coming next, or whether anything more is coming. Your conversation is interrupted every minute by greasy dishes thrust between your head and that of your next neighbor, and it is more expensive than the old mode of shewing a handsome dinner to your guests and leaving them free to choose. It will not do. This French influence must be resisted. Give us the nice French dishes, *fricandeau de veau, perdrix au choux,* and *côtelettes à la province,* but let us see what we are to have.

THURSDAY, AUG. 9 I saw in one of the papers the death announced at New Haven of Henry Bedlow, aged 71 years, an old beau who at one time made a great noise in New York. This man, then about 24 years old, was tried for a rape on a Miss Sawyer, stepdaughter of Callahan, a pilot, who lived in Gold Street near my father's. He was acquitted, as I dare say he ought to have been; but her father being well known amongst the seafaring people, and the case, if not a rape, being an aggravated one of seduction, the popular indignation was excited to the highest pitch. A mob collected and pulled down the house to which the libertine had decoyed his victim, a famous brothel kept by a Mother Carey in Beekman Street at the corner of Theater Alley, on the very spot where I built the Clinton Hotel. Well do I remember, although the occurrence took place nearly fifty years ago, sitting in the branches of one of the large buttonwood trees in the burial ground of the Brick Presbyterian Church, opposite the scene of action, and enjoying the dispersion of "Mother Carey's chickens," the destruction of mahogany tables and looking glasses. These excesses did not stop here, for the mob, once excited, continued their riotous proceedings several successive nights, and many houses of ill-fame in other parts of the city were demolished and their miserable inmates driven naked and houseless into the streets.

SATURDAY, DEC. 8 We had to dine with us to-day Mr. Christopher Hughes, American *chargé* at Stockholm, Col. Webb, Mr. William B. Astor, and Dr. Francis. Whilst we were at dinner there was a ring at the street doorbell. The boy Daniel went out and found nobody there; but there was a basket on the sill of the door, which he brought into the dining room, and it was found to contain a lovely infant, apparently about a week old, stowed away nicely in soft cotton. It had on a clean worked muslin frock, lace cap, its underclothes new and perfectly clean, a locket on the neck which opened with a spring and contained a lock of dark hair; the whole covered nicely with a piece of new flannel, and a label pinned on the breast on which was written, in a female hand, Alfred G. Douglas. It was one of the sweetest babies I ever saw; apparently healthy. It did not cry during the time we had it, but lay in a placid, dozing state, and occasionally, on the approach of the light, opened its little, sparkling eyes, and seemed satisfied with the company into which it had been so strangely introduced. Poor little innocent—abandoned by its natural protector, and thrown at its entrance into life upon the sympathy of a selfish world, to be exposed, if it should live, to the sneers and taunts of uncharitable illegitimacy! How often in his future life may the bitter wish swell in his heart and rise to his lips, that those eyes which now opened so mildly upon me whilst I was gazing upon his innocent face had been forever closed. My feelings were strongly interested, and I felt inclined at first to take in and cherish the little stranger; but this was strongly opposed by the company, who urged, very properly, that in that case I would have twenty more such outlets to my benevolence. I reflected, moreover, that if the little urchin should turn out bad, he would prove a troublesome inmate; and if intelligent and good, by the time he became an object of my affection the rightful owners might come and take him away. So John Stotes was summoned, and sent off with the little wanderer to the almshouse.

The group in the kitchen which surrounded the basket, before John took it away, would have furnished a capital subject for a painter. There was the elegant diplomat, the inquisitive doctor, the bluff editor, and the calculating millionaire; my wife and daughters, standing like the daughters of Pharaoh over the infant Moses in the bulrushes—all interested, but differently affected, the maids shoving forward to get a last peep; little Emily, the black cook, ever and anon showing her white teeth; James and Dannie in the background, wondering that so great a fuss should be made about so small a matter; and John, wrapped up in his characteristically neat overcoat, waiting, with all the dignified composure which marks his demeanor, to receive his interesting charge and convey it to its destination.

This affair ended, we returned to the dinner table, the game and oysters cold, but our hearts warm; other topics soon engrossed us, and it was near midnight when we broke up.

*[1839] MONDAY, AUG. 26* I went yesterday morning to St. Thomas's church, where I heard from Dr. Hawks a glorious sermon; in the afternoon to St. Bartholomew's.

We are vagrants now on Sundays, poor old Trinity being nearly razed to the ground, and a new church to be erected on the same spot, which will require two or three years to complete. We shall be compelled during that time to hire a pew in one of the uptown churches or quarter upon our friends.

When the committee of the vestry of Trinity Church began with the edifice, it was intended to repair and remodel the interior only, leaving the venerable exterior and the noble dark-looking spire in their original integrity. But in the progress of the work the building was found to be in such a state of decay as to be rendered irreparable, and the time-honored temple of the Lord, the parish church of New York, the nucleus of Episcopacy, was doomed to destruction. I found on my return to the city a shapeless heap of ruins on the spot where my imperfect devotions have been performed for the last thirty-seven years. It occasions melancholy reflections to see the dark mass of ruins still overlooking the magnificent temples of Mammon in Wall Street, and to think of the changes which have occurred there during the time the venerable spire which is now removed has thrown its shadow over the place "where merchants most do congregate."

May I not also see in this dilapidation a type of my own decay and speedily approaching removal? When I first went to Trinity Church I was young, ardent, and full of hopes, capable and industrious, and I should now be ungrateful not to acknowledge that in most cases my hopes were realized and my industry rewarded; but the storms within the last three years have beaten upon me, the timbers are decayed, the spire no longer "like a tall bully lifts its head," and the vestry has no funds to rebuild me.

[1840] FRIDAY, FEB. 28 The great affair which has occupied the minds of the people of all stations, ranks, and employments, from the fashionable belle who prepared for conquest to the humble *artiste* who made honestly a few welcome dollars in providing the weapons; from the liberal-minded gentleman who could discover no crime in an innocent and refined amusement of this kind to the newspaper reformer striving to sow the seeds of discontentment in an unruly population—this long-anticipated affair came off last evening, and I believe the expectations of all were realized. The mansion of our entertainers, Mr. and Mrs. Brevoort, is better calculated for such a display than any other in the city, and everything which host and hostess could do in preparing and arranging, in receiving their guests and making them feel a full warrant and assurance of welcome, was done to the topmost round of elegant hospitality. Mrs. B. in particular, by her kind and courteous deportment, threw a charm over the splendid pageant which would have been incomplete without it.

My family contributed a large number of actors in the gay scene. I went as Cardinal Wolseley, in a grand robe of new scarlet merino, with an exceedingly well-contrived cap of the same material; a cape of real ermine, which I borrowed from Mrs. Thomas W. Ludlow, gold chain and cross, scarlet stockings, etc.; Mary and Catharine as Day and Night; Margaret, Annot Lyle in "The Legend of Montrose"; John as Washington Irving's royal poet; Schermerhorn as Gessler, the Austrian governor who helped make William Tell immortal; Robert a Highlander, and our sweet neighbor Eliza Russell as Lalla Rookh. We had a great preparatory gathering of friends to see our dresses and those of several others, who took us "in their way up." I am not quite sure whether the pleasantest part of such an affair does not consist in "the note of preparation," the contriving and fixing . . . ; and perhaps, after all is over, the greatest doubt is *si le jeu vaut la chandelle*.

And if ever that question is tested, it must be by this experiment, for never before has New York witnessed a fancy ball so splendidly gotten up, in better taste, or more successfully carried through. We went at ten o'clock, at which time the numerous apartments, brilliantly lighted, were tolerably well filled with characters. The notice on the cards of invitation, *costume à la rigueur*, had virtually closed the door to all others, and with the exception of some eight or ten gentlemen who, in plain dress with a red ribbon at the buttonhole, officiated as managers, every one appeared as some one else; the dresses being generally new, some of them superbly ornamented with gold, silver, and jewelry; others marked by classical elegance, or appropriately designating distinguished characters of ancient and modern history and the drama; and others again most familiarly grotesque and ridiculous. The *coup d'oeil* dazzled the eyes and bewildered the imagination.

Soon after our party arrived the five rooms on the first floor (including the library) were completely filled. I should think there were about 500 ladies and gentlemen. Many a beautiful "point device," which had cost the fair or gallant wearer infinite pains in the selection and adaptation, was doomed to pass unnoticed in the crowd; and many who went there hoping each to be the star of the evening, found themselves eclipsed by some superior luminary, or at best forming a unit in the milky way. Some surprise was expressed at seeing in the crowd a man in the habit of a knight in armor—a Mr. Attree, reporter and one of the editors of an infamous penny paper called the *Herald*. Bennett, the principal editor, called upon Mr. Brevoort to obtain permission for this person to be present to report in his paper an account of the ball. He consented, as I believe I should have done in the same circumstances, as by doing so a sort of obligation was imposed upon him to refrain from abusing the house, the people of the house, and their guests, which would have been done in case of a denial. But this is a hard alternative to submit to. This kind of surveillance is getting to be intolerable, and nothing but the force of public opinion will correct the insolence, which, it is to be feared, will never be applied as long as Mr. Charles A. Davis and other gentlemen make this Mr. Attree "hail fellow well met," as they did on this occasion. Whether the notice which they took of him, and that which they extend to Bennett when he shows his ugly face in Wall Street, may be considered approbatory of the daily slanders and unblushing impudence of the paper they conduct, or is intended to purchase their forbearance toward themselves, the effect is equally mischievous. It affords them countenances and encouragement, and they find that the more personalities they have in their paper the more papers they sell.

MONDAY, NOV. 16 There is a chasm of three days in this journal, and gracious Heaven, how has the time been filled! My strength fails me when I attempt to account for it, and yet I feel that it will afford me a sort of melancholy consolation. My heart sinks within me, whenever my thoughts are concentrated on the greatest grief which has ever oppressed it. May the indulgent Father of Mercies sustain me and my bereaved family in this great hour of my affliction, and teach us with resignation to exclaim, "Father, thy will be done!" My dear, beloved Mary left this world of trouble and affliction, and as I firmly and confidently believe, joined her sister angels in Heaven, on Friday morning at half past six o'clock. Long and severe as her illness has been, and great as her sufferings, at times she has appeared to be so much better that the blessed rays of hope have shone round her, and we have indulged the delusive expectation that the cherished flower would be reanimated and bloom once more in its former loveliness.

Friday was a melancholy day. The body was deposited in its coffin, and placed in the back parlor. After the family had all gone to bed, I obtained the key of the room and taking a lamp went into the chamber of death, seated myself at the side of the cold remains of my darling child, and for half an hour held in imagination delightful converse with the spirit which had of late animated it. The countenance was unchanged, the expression intelligent and lovely as it was wont to be, and that smile, sweet as the smile of a seraph, still hung upon her half-closed lips, and I gazed with fixed eyes upon it, until I almost fancied it moved and spoke to me again. It is strange that I could derive consolation from looking upon the wreck of that which my heart held so dear, and yet it was a half hour of delightful enjoyment. Never shall I desire to have it effaced from my remembrance.

*[1842] TUESDAY, FEB. 15* The agony is over; the Boz ball, the greatest affair in modern times, the tallest compliment ever paid a little man, the fullest libation ever poured upon the altar of the muses, came off last evening in fine style. Everything answered the public expectation, and no untoward circumstance occurred to make anybody sorry he went.

The theater was prepared for the occasion with great splendor and taste. The whole area of the stage and pit was floored over and formed an immense saloon. The decorations and paintings were all "Pickwickian." Shields with scenes painted from the several stories of Dickens, the titles of his works on others surrounded with wreaths, the dome formed of flags, and the side walls in fresco, representing the panels of an ancient oaken hall. A small stage was erected at the extreme end opposite the main entrance, before which a curtain was suspended, exhibiting the portly proportions of the immortal Pickwick, his prince of valets, and his bodyguard of choice cronies. This curtain was raised in the intervals between the cotillions and waltzes to disclose a stage on which were exhibited a series of *tableaux vivants*, forming groups of the characters in the most striking incidents of "Pickwick," "Nicholas Nickleby," "Oliver Twist," "The Old Curiosity Shop," "Barnaby Rudge," etc. The company began to assemble at half past seven o'clock, and at nine, when the committee introduced Mr. and Mrs. Dickens, the crowd was immense; a little upward of two thousand tickets were handed in at the door, and, with the members of committees and their parties who came in by back ways, the assembled multitude numbered about two thousand five hundred. Everybody was there, and every lady was dressed well and in good taste, and decorum and good order were preserved during the whole evening. Refreshments were provided in the saloons on the several floors, and in the green room, which was kept for the members of the committees and their families. This branch of the business was farmed out to Downing, the great man of oysters, who received $2,200. On the arrival of the "observed of all observers," a lane was opened through the crowd, through which he and his lady were marched to the upper end, where the committee of reception were stationed. Here I, as chairman of the committee, received him, and made a short speech, after which they joined in the dancing. Everything went off well except the arrangement for receiving coats, hats, etc., which by the time I came away were all "in pie," as the printers say of their types, and I was fain to make my way home as best I could, without coat or hat. I went this morning and got the former, but the hat is "no more office of mine." The scene in the box office was amusing; there was a pyramid of integuments which had, like mine, been abandoned in despair, large enough to form the stock in trade of a clothing store—hats, cloaks, coats, ladies' shawls, caps, and overshoes, waiting to be claimed by such persons as had not gotten better ones in their stead.

The author of the "Pickwick Papers" is a small, bright-eyed, intelligent-looking young fellow, thirty years of age, somewhat of a dandy in his dress, with "rings and things and fine array," brisk in his manner and of a lively conversation. If he does not get his little head turned by all this, I shall wonder at it. Mrs. Dickens is a little, fat, English-looking woman, of an agreeable countenance, and, I should think, a "nice person."

*[1844] WEDNESDAY, OCT. 9* I went out yesterday to dine at Mr. Blatchford's, at Hell Gate. The party at dinner consisted of old Mr. John Jacob Astor and his train-bearer and prime minister, Mr. Coggeswell; Mr. Jaudon; Ole Bull, the celebrated Norwegian violinist (we used to call it fiddler); and myself. In the evening the party was increased by the addition of Mr. Webster, his brother-in-law Mr. Page, and Mr. and Mrs. Curtis. Ole Bull had his two violins, and astonished and pleased us by his wonderful performance. Every note was sounded, from the roaring of a lion to the whisper of a summer evening's breeze; every instrument of music seemed to send forth its peculiar tones.

After an hour or two passed in the billiard room I retired to bed. When I arose this morning at Mr. Blatchford's I contemplated the delightful scene: the clumps of fine old trees clothed in the gorgeous foliage of autumn, the lawn still bright and green, the mild, refreshing breeze, the rapid waters of Hell Gate covered with sailing vessels and steamboats—all combined to present a picture of consummate beauty. In this place, so rich in the beauties of art and nature, in the enjoyment of pecuniary independence and happy in his family relations, did the former occupant commit suicide! I slept in the room in which Mr. Prime committed the fatal act.

Mr. Astor, one of our dinner companions yesterday, presented a painful example of the insufficiency of wealth to prolong the life of man. This old gentleman with his fifteen millions of dollars would give it all to have my strength and physical ability, and yet with this example and that recorded above, I, with a good conscience and in possession of my bodily faculties, sometimes repine at my lot. He would pay all my debts if I could ensure him one year of my health and strength, but nothing else would extort so much from him. His life has been spent in amassing money, and he loves it as much as ever. He sat at the dinner table with his head down upon his breast, saying very little, and in a voice almost unintelligible; the saliva dropping from his mouth, and a servant behind him to guide the victuals which he was eating, and to watch him as an infant is watched. His mind is good, his observation acute, and he seems to know everything that is going on. But the machinery is all broken up, and there are some people, no doubt, who think he has lived long enough.

*[1846] TUESDAY, OCT. 27* I witnessed this morning, from the steps of Clinton Hall, a scene which is calculated to cause alarm as to future collisions between the citizens of this country,—a trifling incident in the appalling drama which we shall be called to witness, and perhaps bear a part in, during the course of not many years. A negro boy, named George Kirk, a slave from Georgia, secreted himself in a vessel commanded by Captain Buckley, and was brought to New York. Here he was arrested and confined, at the instance of the captain, who is subjected to severe penalties for the abduction of the slave. The claim of the master to have the fugitive sent back to Georgia was tried before Judge Edwards; N. B. Blunt appearing for the captain, and Mr. John Jay and J. L. White for the slave.

The judge's decision set the boy free, for want of evidence to prove his identity; and such a mob, of all colours, from dirty white to shining black, came rushing down Nassau and into Beekman Street as made peaceable people shrink into places of security. Such shouting and jostling, such peals of negro triumph, such uncovering of woolly heads in raising the greasy hats to give effect to the loud huzzas of the sons of Africa, seemed almost to "fright the neighborhood from its propriety." A carriage was brought to convey the hero of the day from his place of concealment, but it went away without him. This is all very pretty; but how will it end? How long will the North and the South remain a united people?

*[1849] MAY 8* Mr. Macready commenced an engagement last evening at the Opera-House, Astor Place, and was to have per-

formed the part of "Macbeth," whilst his rival, Mr. Forrest, appeared in the same part at the Broadway theater. A violent animosity has existed on the part of the latter theatrical hero against his rival, growing out of some differences in England; but with no cause, that I can discover, except that one is a gentleman, and the other is a vulgar, arrogant loafer, with a pack of kindred rowdies at his heels. Of these retainers a regularly organized force was employed to raise a riot at the Opera-House and drive Mr. Macready off the stage, in which, to the disgrace of the city, the ruffians succeeded. On the appearance of the "Thane of Cawdor," he was saluted with a shower of missiles, rotten eggs, and other unsavory objects, with shouts and yells of the most abusive epithets. In the midst of this disgraceful riot the performance was suspended, the respectable part of the audience dispersed, and the vile band of *Forresters* were left in possession of the house. This cannot end here; the respectable part of our citizens will never consent to be put down by a mob raised to serve the purpose of such a fellow as Forrest. Recriminations will be resorted to, and a series of riots will have possession of the theaters of the opposing parties.

MAY 10 The riot at the Opera-House on Monday night was children's play compared with the disgraceful scenes which were enacted in our part of this devoted city this evening, and the melancholy loss of life to which the outrageous proceedings of the mob naturally led.

An appeal to Mr. Macready had been made by many highly respectable citizens, and published in the papers, inviting him to finish his engagement at the Opera-House, with an implied pledge that they would stand by him against the ferocious mob of Mr. Forrest's friends, who had determined that Macready should not be allowed to play, whilst at the same time their oracle was strutting, unmolested, his "hour upon the stage" of the Broadway theater. This announcement served as a firebrand in the mass of combustibles left smoldering from the riot of the former occasion. The *Forresters* perceived that their previous triumph was incomplete, and a new conspiracy was formed to accomplish effectually their nefarious designs.

Inflammatory notices were posted in the upper ward, meetings were regularly organized, and bands of ruffians, gratuitously supplied with tickets by richer rascals, were sent to take possession of the theater. The police, however, were beforehand with them, and a large body of their force was posted in different parts of the house.

When Mr. Macready appeared he was assailed in the same manner as on the former occasion; but he continued on the stage and performed his part with firmness, amidst the yells and hisses of the mob. The strength of the police, and their good conduct, as well as that of the Mayor, Recorder, and other public functionaries, succeeded in preventing any serious injury to the property within doors, and many arrests were made; but the war raged with frightful violence in the adjacent streets. The mob—a dreadful one in numbers and ferocity—assailed the extension of the building, broke in the windows, and demolished some of the doors. I walked up to the corner of Astor Place, but was glad to make my escape. On my way down, opposite the New York Hotel, I met a detachment of troops, consisting of about sixty cavalry and three hundred infantry, fine-looking fellows, well armed, who marched steadily to the field of action. Another detachment went by the way of Lafayette Place. On their arrival they were assailed by the mob, pelted with stones and brickbats, and several were carried off severely wounded.

Under this provocation, with the sanction of the civil authorities, orders were given to fire. Three or four volleys were discharged; about twenty persons were killed and a large number wounded. It is to be lamented that in the number were several innocent persons, as is always the case in such affairs. A large proportion of the mob being lookers-on, who, putting no faith in the declaration of the magistrates that the fatal order was about to be given, refused to retire, and shared the fate of the rioters. What is to be the issue of this unhappy affair cannot be surmised; the end is not yet.

MAY 11    I walked up this morning to the field of battle, in Astor Place. The Opera-House presents a shocking spectacle, and the adjacent buildings were smashed with bullet-holes. Mrs. Langdon's house looks as if it had withstood a siege. Groups of people were standing around, some justifying the interference of the military, but a large proportion were savage as tigers with the smell of blood.

MAY 12  Last night passed off intolerably quietly, owing to the measures taken by the magistrates and police. But it is consolatory to know that law and order have thus far prevailed. The city authorities have acted nobly. The whole military force was under arms all night, and a detachment of United States troops was also held in reserve. All the approaches to the Opera-House were strictly guarded, and no transit permitted. The police force, with the addition of a thousand special constables, were employed in every post of danger; and although the lesson has been dearly bought, it is of great value, inasmuch as the fact has been established that law and order can be maintained under a Republican form of government.

# CHARLES DICKENS

*No foreign visitor to the United States was more ecstatically welcomed than Charles Dickens (see Philip Hone's diary entry for February 15, 1842)—which was why his satiric appraisal of the country in American Notes for General Circulation aroused such wounded feelings in his hosts. His New York chapter starts off jauntily enough but culminates, with its descriptions of the Tombs prison and the notorious Five Points slum, in passionate indignation.*

### FROM *AMERICAN NOTES FOR GENERAL CIRCULATION*

T HE BEAUTIFUL METROPOLIS of America is by no means so clean a city as Boston, but many of its streets have the same characteristics; except that the houses are not quite so fresh-coloured, the sign-boards are not quite so gaudy, the gilded letters not quite so golden, the bricks not quite so red, the stone not quite so white, the blinds and area railings not quite so green, the knobs and plates upon the street doors not quite so bright and twinkling. There are many bye-streets, almost as neutral in clean colours, and positive in dirty ones, as bye-streets in London; and there is one quarter, commonly called the Five Points, which, in respect of filth and wretchedness, may be safely backed against Seven Dials, or any other part of famed St. Giles's.

The great promenade and thoroughfare, as most people know, is Broadway; a wide and bustling street, which, from the Battery Gardens to its opposite termination in a country road, may be four miles long. Shall we sit down in an upper floor of the Carlton House Hotel (situated in the best part of this main artery of New York), and when we are tired of looking down upon the life below, sally forth arm-in-arm, and mingle with the stream?

Warm weather! The sun strikes upon our heads at this open window, as though its rays were concentrated through a burning-glass;

but the day is in its zenith, and the season an unusual one. Was there ever such a sunny street as this Broadway? The pavement stones are polished with the tread of feet until they shine again; the red bricks of the houses might be yet in the dry, hot kilns; and the roofs of those omnibuses look as though, if water were poured on them, they would hiss and smoke, and smell like half-quenched fires. No stint of omnibuses here! Half a dozen have gone by within as many minutes. Plenty of hackney cabs and coaches too; gigs, phaetons, large-wheeled tilburies, and private carriages—rather of a clumsy make, and not very different from the public vehicles, but built for the heavy roads beyond the city pavement. Negro coachmen and white; in straw hats, black hats, white hats, glazed caps, fur caps; in coats of drab, black, brown, green, blue, nankeen, striped jean and linen; and there, in that one instance (look while it passes, or it will be too late), in suits of livery. Some southern republican that, who puts his blacks in uniform, and swells with Sultan pomp and power. Yonder, where that phaeton with the well-clipped pair of greys has stopped—standing at their heads now—is a Yorkshire groom, who has not been very long in these parts, and looks sorrowfully round for a companion pair of top-boots, which he may traverse the city half a year without meeting. Heaven save the ladies, how they dress! We have seen more colours in these ten minutes, than we should have seen elsewhere, in as many days. What various parasols! what rainbow silks and satins! what pinking of thin stockings, and pinching of thin shoes, and fluttering of ribbons and silk tassels, and display of rich cloaks with gaudy hoods and linings! The young gentlemen are fond, you see, of turning down their shirt-collars and cultivating their whiskers, especially under the chin; but they cannot approach the ladies in their dress or bearing, being, to say the truth, humanity of quite another sort. Byrons of the desk and counter, pass on, and let us see what kind of men those are behind ye: those two labourers in holiday clothes, of whom one carries in his hand a crumpled scrap of paper from which he tries to spell out a hard name, while the other looks about for it on all the doors and windows.

Irishmen both! You might know them, if they were masked, by

their long-tailed blue coats and bright buttons, and their drab trousers, which they wear like men well used to working dresses, who are easy in no others. It would be hard to keep your model republics going, without the countrymen and countrywomen of those two labourers. For who else would dig, and delve, and drudge, and do domestic work, and make canals and roads, and execute great lines of Internal Improvement! Irishmen both, and sorely puzzled too, to find out what they seek. Let us go down, and help them, for the love of home, and that spirit of liberty which admits of honest service to honest men, and honest work for honest bread, no matter what it be.

That's well! We have got at the right address at last, though it is written in strange characters truly, and might have been scrawled with the blunt handle of the spade the writer better knows the use of, than a pen. Their way lies yonder, but what business takes them there? They carry savings: to hoard up? No. They are brothers, those men. One crossed the sea alone, and working very hard for one half year, and living harder, saved funds enough to bring the other out. That done, they worked together, side by side, contentedly sharing hard labour and hard living for another term, and then their sisters came, and then another brother, and, lastly, their old mother. And what now? Why, the poor old crone is restless in a strange land, and yearns to lay her bones, she says, among her people in the old graveyard at home: and so they go to pay her passage back: and God help her and them, and every simple heart, and all who turn to the Jerusalem of their younger days, and have an altar-fire upon the cold hearth of their fathers.

This narrow thoroughfare, baking and blistering in the sun, is Wall Street: the Stock Exchange and Lombard Street of New York. Many a rapid fortune has been made in this street, and many a no less rapid ruin. Some of these very merchants whom you see hanging about here now, have locked up Money in their strong-boxes, like the man in the Arabian Nights, and opening them again, have found but withered leaves. Below, here by the water-side, where the bowsprits of ships stretch across the footway, and almost thrust themselves into the windows, lie the noble American vessels which have made their Packet Service the finest in the world. They have brought hither the foreigners who abound in all the streets: not perhaps, that there are more here, than in other commercial cities; but elsewhere, they have particular haunts, and you must find them out; here, they pervade the town.

We must cross Broadway again; gaining some refreshment from the heat, in the sight of the great blocks of clean ice which are being carried into shops and bar-rooms; and the pine-apples and water-melons profusely displayed for sale. Fine streets of spacious houses here, you see!—Wall Street has furnished and dismantled many of them very often—and here a deep green leafy square. Be sure that is a hospitable house with inmates to be affectionately remembered always, where they have the open door and pretty show of plants within, and where the child with laughing eyes is peeping out of window at the little dog below. You wonder what may be the use of this tall flagstaff in the bye-street, with something like Liberty's head-dress on its top: so do I. But there is a passion for tall flagstaffs hereabout, and you may see its twin brother in five minutes, if you have a mind.

Again across Broadway, and so—passing from the many-coloured crowd and glittering shops—into another long main street, the Bowery. A railroad yonder, see, where two stout horses trot along, drawing a score or two of people and a great wooden ark, with ease. The stores are poorer here; the passengers less gay. Clothes ready-made, and meat ready-cooked, are to be bought in these parts; and the lively whirl of carriages is exchanged for the deep rumble of carts and waggons. These signs which are so plentiful, in shape like river buoys, or small balloons, hoisted by cords to poles, and dangling there, announce, as you may see by looking up, "OYSTERS IN EVERY STYLE." They tempt the hungry most at night, for then dull candles glimmering inside, illuminate these dainty words, and make the mouths of idlers water, as they read and linger.

What is this dismal-fronted pile of bastard Egyptian, like an enchanter's palace in a melodrama!—a famous prison, called The Tombs. Shall we go in?

So. A long narrow lofty building, stove-heated as usual, with four galleries, one above the other, going round it, and communicating by stairs. Between the two sides of each gallery, and in its centre, a bridge, for the greater convenience of crossing. On each of these bridges sits a man: dozing or reading, or talking to an idle companion. On each tier, are two opposite rows of small iron doors. They look like furnace-doors, but are cold and black, as though the fires within had all gone out. Some two or three are open, and women, with drooping heads bent down, are talking to the inmates. The whole is lighted by a skylight, but it is fast closed; and from the roof there dangle, limp and drooping, two useless windsails.

A man with keys appears, to show us round. A good-looking fellow, and, in his way, civil and obliging.

"Are those black doors the cells?"

"Yes."

"Are they all full?"

"Well, they're pretty nigh full, and that's a fact, and no two ways about it."

"Those at the bottom are unwholesome, surely?"

"Why, we *do* only put coloured people in 'em. That's the truth."

"When do the prisoners take exercise?"

"Well, they do without it pretty much."

"Do they never walk in the yard?"

"Considerable seldom."

"Sometimes, I suppose?"

"Well, it's rare they do. They keep pretty bright without it."

"But suppose a man were here for a twelvemonth. I know this is only a prison for criminals who are charged with grave offences, while they are awaiting their trial, or are under remand, but the law here, affords criminals many means of delay. What with motions for new trials, and in arrest of judgment, and what not, a prisoner might be here for twelve months, I take it, might he not?"

"Well, I guess he might."

"Do you mean to say that in all that time he would never come out at that little iron door, for exercise?"

"He might walk some, perhaps—not much."

"Will you open one of the doors?"

"All, if you like."

The fastenings jar and rattle, and one of the doors turns slowly on its hinges. Let us look in. A small bare cell, into which the light enters through a high chink in the wall. There is a rude means of washing, a table, and a bedstead. Upon the latter, sits a man of sixty; reading. He looks up for a moment; gives an impatient dogged shake; and fixes his eyes upon his book again. As we withdraw our heads, the door closes on him, and is fastened as before. This man has murdered his wife, and will probably be hanged.

"How long has he been here?"

"A month."

"When will he be tried?"

"Next term."

"When is that?"

"Next month."

"In England, if a man be under sentence of death, even, he has air and exercise at certain periods of the day."

"Possible?"

With what stupendous and untranslatable coolness he says this, and how loungingly he leads on to the women's side: making, as he goes, a kind of iron castanet of the key and the stair-rail!

Each cell door on this side has a square aperture in it. Some of the women peep anxiously through it at the sound of footsteps; others shrink away in shame.—For what offence can that lonely child, of ten or twelve years old, be shut up here? Oh! that boy? He is the son of the prisoner we saw just now; is a witness against his father; and is detained here for safe keeping, until the trial: that's all.

But it is a dreadful place for the child to pass the long days and nights in. This is rather hard treatment for a young witness, is it not?—What says our conductor?

"Well, it an't a very rowdy life, and *that's* a fact!"

Again he clinks his metal castanet, and leads us leisurely away. I have a question to ask him as we go.

"Pray, why do they call this place The Tombs?"

"Well, it's the cant name."

"I know it is. Why?"

"Some suicides happened here, when it was first built. I expect it come about from that."

"I saw just now, that that man's clothes were scattered about the floor of his cell. Don't you oblige the prisoners to be orderly, and put such things away?"

"Where should they put 'em?"

"Not on the ground surely What do you say to hanging them up?"

He stops, and looks round to emphasise his answer:

"Why, I say that's just it. When they had hooks they *would* hang themselves, so they're taken out of every cell, and there's only the marks left where they used to be!"

The prison-yard in which he pauses now, has been the scene of terrible performances. Into this narrow, grave-like place, men are brought out to die. The wretched creature stands beneath the gibbet on the ground; the rope about his neck; and when the sign is given, a weight at its other end comes running down, and swings him up into the air—a corpse.

The law requires that there be present at this dismal spectacle, the judge, the jury, and citizens to the amount of twenty-five. From the community it is hidden. To the dissolute and bad, the thing remains a frightful mystery. Between the criminal and them, the prison-wall is interposed as a thick gloomy veil. It is the curtain to his bed of death, his winding-sheet, and grave. From him it shuts out life, and all the motives to unrepenting hardihood in that last hour, which its mere sight and presence is often all-sufficient to sustain. There are no bold eyes to make him bold; no ruffians to uphold a ruffian's name before. All beyond the pitiless stone wall, is unknown space.

Let us go forth again into the cheerful streets.

Once more in Broadway! Here are the same ladies in bright colours, walking to and fro, in pairs and singly; yonder the very same light blue parasol which passed and repassed the hotel-window twenty times while we were sitting there. We are going to cross here. Take care of the pigs. Two portly sows are trotting up behind this carriage, and a select party of half-a-dozen gentlemen-hogs have just now turned the corner.

Here is a solitary swine, lounging homeward by himself. He has only one ear; having parted with the other to vagrant-dogs in the course of his city rambles. But he gets on very well without it; and leads a roving, gentlemanly, vagabond kind of life, somewhat answering to that of our club-men at home. He leaves his lodgings every morning at a certain hour, throws himself upon the town, gets through his day in some manner quite satisfactory to himself, and regularly appears at the door of his own house again at night, like the mysterious master of Gil Blas. He is a free-and-easy, careless, indifferent kind of pig, having a very large acquaintance among other pigs of the same character, whom he rather knows by sight than conversation, as he seldom troubles himself to stop and exchange civilities, but goes grunting down the kennel, turning up the news and small-talk of the city, in the shape of cabbage-stalks and offal, and bearing no tails but his own: which is a very short one, for his old enemies, the dogs, have been at that too, and have left him hardly enough to swear by. He is in every respect a republican pig, going wherever he pleases, and mingling with the best society, on an equal, if not superior footing, for every one makes way when he appears, and the haughtiest give him the wall, if he prefer it. He is a great philosopher, and seldom moved, unless by the dogs before mentioned. Sometimes, indeed, you may see his small eye twinkling on a slaughtered friend, whose carcase garnishes a butcher's door-post, but he grunts out "Such is life: all flesh is pork!" buries his nose in the mire again, and waddles down the gutter: comforting himself with the reflection that there is one snout the less to anticipate stray cabbage-stalks, at any rate.

They are the city scavengers, these pigs. Ugly brutes they are; having, for the most part, scanty, brown backs, like the lids of old horse-hair trunks: spotted with unwholesome black blotches. They have long, gaunt legs, too, and such peaked snouts, that if one of them could be persuaded to sit for his profile, nobody would recognise it for a pig's likeness. They are never attended upon, or fed, or driven, or caught, but are thrown upon their own resources in early life, and become preternaturally knowing in consequence. Every pig knows where he lives, much better than anybody could tell him. At this hour, just as evening is closing in, you will see them roaming towards bed by scores, eating their way to the last. Occasionally, some youth among them who has over-eaten himself, or has been worried by dogs, trots shrinkingly homeward, like a prodigal son: but this is a rare case: perfect self-possession and self-reliance, and immovable composure, being their foremost attributes.

The streets and shops are lighted now; and as the eye travels down the long thoroughfare, dotted with bright jets of gas, it is reminded of Oxford Street, or Piccadilly. Here and there a flight of broad stone cellar-steps appears, and a painted lamp directs you to the Bowling Saloon, or Ten-Pin alley: Ten-Pins being a game of mingled chance and skill, invented when the legislature passed an act forbidding Nine-Pins. At other downward flights of steps, are other lamps, marking the whereabouts of oyster-cellars—pleasant retreats, say I: not only by reason of their wonderful cookery of oysters, pretty nigh as large as cheese-plates, (or for thy dear sake, heartiest of Greek Professors!) but because of all kinds of eaters of fish, or flesh, or fowl, in these latitudes, the swallowers of oysters alone are not gregarious; but subduing themselves, as it were, to the nature of what they work in, and copying the coyness of the thing they eat, do sit apart in curtained boxes, and consort by twos, not by two hundreds.

But how quiet the streets are! Are there no itinerant bands; no wind or stringed instruments? No, not one. By day, are there no Punches, Fantoccinis, Dancing-dogs, Jugglers, Conjurors, Orchestrinas, or even Barrel-organs? No, not one. Yes, I remember one. One barrel-organ and a dancing-monkey—sportive by nature, but fast fading into a dull, lumpish monkey, of the Utilitarian school. Beyond that, nothing lively; no, not so much as a white mouse in a twirling cage.

Are there no amusements? Yes. There is a lecture-room across the way, from which that glare of light proceeds, and there may be evening service for the ladies thrice a week, or oftener. For the young gentlemen, there is the counting-house, the store, the bar-room: the latter, as you may see through these windows, pretty full. Hark! to the clinking sound of hammers breaking lumps of ice, and to the cool gurgling of the pounded bits, as, in the process of mixing, they are poured from glass to glass! No amusements? What are these suckers of cigars and swallowers of strong drinks, whose hats and legs we see in every possible variety of twist, doing, but amusing themselves? What are the fifty newspapers, which those precocious urchins are bawling down the street, and which are kept filed within, what are they but amusements? Not vapid waterish amusements, but good strong stuff; dealing in round abuse and blackguard names; pulling off the roofs of private houses, as the Halting Devil did in Spain; pimping and pandering for all degrees of vicious taste, and gorging with coined lies the most voracious maw; imputing to every man in public life the coarsest and the vilest motives; scaring away from the stabbed and prostrate body-politic, every Samaritan of clear conscience and good deeds; and setting on, with yell and whistle and the clapping of foul hands, the vilest vermin and worst birds of prey.—No amusements!

Let us go on again; and passing this wilderness of an hotel with stores about its base, like some Continental theatre, or the London Opera House shorn of its colonnade, plunge into the Five Points. But it is needful, first, that we take as our escort these two heads of the police, whom you would know for sharp and well-trained officers if you met them in the Great Desert. So true it is, that certain pursuits, wherever carried on, will stamp men with the same character. These two might have been begotten, born, and bred, in Bow Street.

We have seen no beggars in the streets by night or day; but of other kinds of strollers, plenty. Poverty, wretchedness, and vice, are rife enough where we are going now.

This is the place: these narrow ways, diverging to the right and left, and reeking everywhere with dirt and filth. Such lives as are led here, bear the same fruits here as elsewhere. The coarse and bloated faces at the doors, have counterparts at home, and all the wide world over. Debauchery has made the very houses prematurely old. See how the rotten beams are tumbling down, and how the patched and broken windows seem to scowl dimly, like eyes that have been hurt in drunken frays. Many of those pigs live here. Do they ever wonder why their masters walk upright in lieu of going on all-fours? and why they talk instead of grunting?

So far, nearly every house is a low tavern; and on the bar-room walls, are coloured prints of Washington, and Queen Victoria of England, and the American Eagle. Among the pigeon-holes that hold the bottles, are pieces of plate-glass and coloured paper, for there is, in some sort, a taste for decoration, even here. And as seamen frequent these haunts, there are maritime pictures by the dozen: of partings between sailors and their lady-loves, portraits of William, of the ballad, and his Black-Eyed Susan; of Will Watch, the Bold Smuggler; of Paul Jones the Pirate, and the like: on which the painted eyes of Queen Victoria, and of Washington to boot, rest in as strange companionship, as on most of the scenes that are enacted in their wondering presence.

What place is this, to which the squalid street conducts us? A kind of square of leprous houses, some of which are attainable only by crazy wooden stairs without. What lies beyond this tottering flight of steps, that creak beneath our tread?—a miserable room, lighted by one dim candle, and destitute of all comfort, save that which may be hidden in a wretched bed. Beside it, sits a man: his elbows on his knees: his forehead hidden in his hands. "What ails that man?" asks the foremost officer. "Fever," he sullenly replies, without looking up. Conceive the fancies of a feverish brain, in such a place as this!

Ascend these pitch-dark stairs, heedful of a false footing on the trembling boards, and grope your way with me into this wolfish den, where neither ray of light nor breath of air, appears to come. A negro lad, startled from his sleep by the officer's voice—he knows it well—but comforted by his assurance that he has not come on business, officiously bestirs himself to light a candle. The match flickers for a moment, and shows great mounds of dusty rags upon the ground; then dies away and leaves a denser darkness than before, if there can be degrees in such extremes. He stumbles down the stairs and presently comes back, shading a flaring taper with his hand. Then the mounds of rags are seen to be astir, and rise slowly up, and the floor is covered with heaps of negro women, waking from their sleep: their white teeth chattering, and their bright eyes glistening and winking on all sides with surprise and fear, like the countless repetition of one astonished African face in some strange mirror.

Mount up these other stairs with no less caution (there are traps and pitfalls here, for those who are not so well escorted as ourselves) into the housetop; where the bare beams and rafters meet overhead, and calm night looks down through the crevices in the roof. Open the door of one of these cramped hutches full of sleeping negroes. Pah! They have a charcoal fire within; there is a smell of singeing clothes, or flesh, so close they gather round the brazier; and vapours issue forth that blind and suffocate. From every corner, as you glance about you in these dark retreats, some figure crawls half-awakened, as if the judgment-hour were near at hand, and every obscene grave were giving up its dead. Where dogs would howl to lie, women, and men, and boys slink off to sleep, forcing the dislodged rats to move away in quest of better lodgings.

Here too are lanes and alleys, paved with mud knee-deep: underground chambers, where they dance and game; the walls bedecked with rough designs of ships, and forts, and flags, and American Eagles out of number: ruined houses, open to the street, whence, through wide gaps in the walls, other ruins loom upon the eye, as though the world of vice and misery had nothing else to show: hideous tenements which take their name from robbery and murder: all that is loathsome, drooping, and decayed is here.

Our leader has his hand upon the latch of "Almack's," and calls to us from the bottom of the steps; for the assembly-room of the Five-Point fashionables is approached by a descent. Shall we go in? It is but a moment.

Heyday! the landlady of Almack's thrives! A buxom fat mulatto woman, with sparkling eyes, whose head is daintily ornamented with a handkerchief of many colours. Nor is the landlord much behind her in his finery, being attired in a smart blue jacket, like a ship's steward, with a thick gold ring upon his little finger, and round his neck a gleaming golden watch-guard. How glad he is to see us! What will we please to call for? A dance? It shall be done directly, sir: "a regular break-down."

The corpulent black fiddler, and his friend who plays the tambourine, stamp upon the boarding of the small raised orchestra in which they sit, and play a lively measure. Five or six couples come upon the floor, marshalled by a lively young negro, who is the wit of the assembly, and the greatest dancer known. He never leaves off making queer faces, and is the delight of all the rest, who grin from ear to ear incessantly. Among the dancers are two young mulatto girls, with large, black, drooping eyes, and head-gear after the fashion of the hostess, who are as shy or feign to be, as though they never danced before, and so look down before the visitors, that their partners can see nothing but the long fringed lashes.

But the dance commences. Every gentleman sets as long as he likes to the opposite lady, and the opposite lady to him, and all are so long about it that the sport begins to languish, when suddenly the lively hero dashes in to the rescue. Instantly the fiddler grins, and goes at it tooth and nail; there is new energy in the tambourine; new laughter in the dancers; new smiles in the landlady; new confidence in the landlord; new brightness in the very candles. Single shuffle, double shuffle, cut and cross-cut; snapping his fingers, rolling his eyes, turning in his knees, presenting the backs of his legs in front, spinning about on his toes and heels like nothing but the man's fingers on the tambourine; dancing with two left legs, two right legs, two wooden legs, two wire legs, two spring legs—all sorts of legs and no legs—what is this to him? And in what walk of life, or dance of life, does man ever get such stimulating applause as thunders about him, when, having danced his partner off her feet, and himself too, he finishes by leaping gloriously on the bar-counter, and calling for something to drink, with the chuckle of a million of counterfeit Jim Crows, in one inimitable sound!

The air, even in these distempered parts, is fresh after the stifling atmosphere of the houses; and now, as we emerge into a broader street, it blows upon us with a purer breath, and the stars look bright again. Here are The Tombs once more. The city watch-house is a part of the building. It follows naturally on the sights we have just left. Let us see that, and then to bed.

What! do you thrust your common offenders against the police discipline of the town, into such holes as these? Do men and women, against whom no crime is proved, lie here all night in perfect darkness, surrounded by the noisome vapours which encircle that flagging lamp you light us with, and breathing this filthy and offensive stench! Why, such indecent and disgusting dungeons as these cells, would bring disgrace upon the most despotic empire in the world! Look at them, man—you, who see them every night, and keep the keys. Do you see what they are? Do you know how drains are made below the streets, and wherein these human sewers differ, except in being always stagnant?

Well, he don't know. He has had five-and-twenty young women locked up in this very cell at one time, and you'd hardly realise what handsome faces there were among 'em.

In God's name! shut the door upon the wretched creature who is in it now, and put its screen before a place, quite unsurpassed in all the vice, neglect, and devilry, of the worst old town in Europe.

Are people really left all night, untried, in those black sties?—Every night. The watch is set at seven in the evening. The magistrate opens his court at five in the morning. That is the earliest hour at which the first prisoner can be released; and if an officer appear against him, he is not taken out till nine o'clock or ten.—But if any one among them die in the interval, as one man did, not long ago? Then he is half-eaten by the rats in an hour's time; as that man was; and there an end.

What is this intolerable tolling of great bells, and crashing of wheels, and shouting in the distance? A fire. And what that deep red light in the opposite direction? Another fire. And what these charred and blackened walls we stand before? A dwelling where a fire has been. It was more than hinted, in an official report, not long ago, that some of these conflagrations were not wholly accidental, and that speculation and enterprise found a field of exertion, even in flames: but be this as it may, there was a fire last night, there are two to-night, and you may lay an even wager there will be at least one, to-morrow. So, carrying that with us for our comfort let us say, Good night, and climb upstairs to bed.

1842

# HENRY DAVID THOREAU

*Hard as it may be to imagine the great nature writer and reclusive sage of Walden Pond let loose in New York City, Henry David Thoreau (1817–62) did spend a few months on Staten Island in 1843, as tutor to William Emerson's son, Haven. He communed with as much nature as he could find around Sandy Hook, while also making numerous trips to Manhattan to drum up business for future articles. In this respect, Thoreau exemplified Walter Benjamin's remark that the nineteenth-century writer came to the city market ostensibly to observe, but actually to sell his wares. Thoreau found few takers, and left the city with relief.*

### LETTERS FROM STATEN ISLAND

WE ARRIVED HERE safely at ten o'clock on Sunday morning, having had as good a passage as usual, though we ran aground and were detained a couple of hours in the Thames River, till the tide came to our relief. At length we curtseyed up to a wharf just the other side of their Castle Garden,—very incurious about them and their city. I believe my vacant looks, absolutely inaccessible to questions, did at length satisfy an army of starving cabmen that I did not want a hack, cab, or anything of that sort as yet. It was the only demand the city made on us; as if a wheeled vehicle of some sort were the sum and summit of a reasonable man's wants. "Having tried the water," they seemed to say, "will you not return to the pleasant securities of land carriage? Else why your boat's prow turned toward the shore at last?" They are a sad-looking set of fellows, not permitted to come on board, and I pitied them. They had been expecting me, it would seem, and did really wish that I should take a cab; though they did not seem rich enough to supply me with one.

It was a confused jumble of heads and soiled coats, dangling from flesh-colored faces,—all swaying to and fro, as by a sort of undertow, while each whipstick, true as the needle to the pole, still preserved that level and direction in which its proprietor had dismissed his forlorn interrogatory. They took sight from them,—the lash be-ing wound up thereon, to prevent your attention from wandering, or to make it concentre upon its object by the spiral line. They began at first, perhaps, with the modest, but rather confident inquiry, "Want a cab, sir?" but as their despair increased, it took the affirmative tone, as the disheartened and irresolute are apt to do: "You want a cab, sir," or even, "You want a nice cab, sir, to take you to Fourth Street." The question which one had bravely and hopefully begun to put, another had the tact to take up and conclude with fresh emphasis,—twirling it from his particular whipstick as if it had emanated from his lips— as the sentiment did from his heart. Each one could truly say, "Them's my sentiments." But it was a sad sight.

I am seven and a half miles from New York, and, as it would take half a day at least, have not been there yet. I have already run over no small part of the island, to the highest hill, and some way along the shore. From the hill directly behind the house I can see New York, Brooklyn, Long Island, the Narrows, through which vessels bound to and from all parts of the world chiefly pass,—Sandy Hook and the Highlands of Neversink (part of the coast of New Jersey)—and, by going still farther up the hill, the Kill van Kull, and Newark Bay. From the pinnacle of one Madame Grimes' house the other night at sunset, I could see almost round the island. Far in the horizon there was a fleet of sloops bound up the Hudson, which seemed to be going over the edge of the earth; and in view of these trading ships, commerce seems quite imposing.

But it is rather derogatory that your dwelling-place should be only a neighborhood to a great city,—to live on an inclined plane. I do not like their cities and forts, with their morning and evening guns, and sails flapping in one's eye. I want a whole continent to breathe in, and a good deal of solitude and silence, such as all Wall Street cannot buy,—nor Broadway with its wooden pavement. I must live along the beach, on the southern shore, which looks di-rectly out to sea,—and see what that great parade of water means, that dashes and roars, and has not yet wet me, as long as I have lived.

I must not know anything about my condition and relations here till what is not permanent is worn off. I have not yet subsided. Give me time enough, and I may like it. All my inner man heretofore has been a Concord impression; and here come these Sandy Hook and Coney Island breakers to meet and modify the former; but it will be long before I can make nature look as innocently grand and inspiring as in Concord.

TO MRS. JOHN THOREAU, MAY 11, 1843

I was just going to write to you when I received your letter. I was waiting till I had got away from Concord. I should have sent you something for the Dial before, but I have been sick ever since I came here—rather unaccountably, what with a cold, bronchitis, acclimation &c—still unaccountably. I send you some verses from my journal which will help make a packet. I have not time to correct them—if this goes by Rockwood Hoar. If I can finish an account of a winter's walk in Concord in the midst of a Staten Island summer—not so wise or true I trust—I will send it to you soon.

I have had no "later experiences" yet. You must not count much upon what I can do or learn in New York. I feel a good way off here—and it is not to be visited, but seen and dwelt in. I have been there but once, and have been confined to the house since. Every thing there disappoints me but the crowd—rather I was disappointed with the rest before I came. I have no eyes for their churches and what else they find to brag of. Though I know but little about Boston, yet what attracts me in a quiet way seems much meaner and more pretending than these—Libraries—Pictures—and faces in the street—You don't know where any respectability inhabits.—It is in the crowd in Chatham street. The crowd is something new and to be attended to. It is worth a thousand Trinity Churches and Exchanges while it is looking at them—and will run over them and trample them under foot one day. There are two things I hear, and am aware that I live in the neighborhood of—The roar of the sea—and the hum of the city. I have just come from the beach (to find your letter) and I like it much. Every thing there is on a grand and generous scale—sea-weed, water, and sand; and even the dead fishes, horses and hogs have a rank luxuriant odor. Great shad nets spread to dry, crabs and horse-shoes crawling over the sand—Clumsy boats, only for service, dancing like sea-fowl on the surf, and ships afar off going about their business.

TO RALPH WALDO EMERSON, MAY 23, 1843

I have been to see Henry James, and like him very much. It was a great pleasure to meet him. It makes humanity seem more erect and respectable. I never was more kindly and faithfully catechised. It made me respect myself more to be thought worthy of such wise questions. He is a man, and takes his own way, or stands still in his own place. I know of no one so patient and determined to have the good of you. It is almost friendship, such plain and human dealing. I think that he will not write or speak inspiringly; but he is a refreshing forward-looking and forward-moving man, and he has naturalized and humanized New York for me.

✦ ✦ ✦ ✦ ✦

I don't like the city better, the more I see it, but worse. I am ashamed of my eyes that behold it. It is a thousand times meaner than I could have imagined. It will be something to hate,—that's the advantage it will be to me; and even the best people in it are a part of it and talk coolly about it. The pigs in the street are the most respectable part of the population. When will the world learn that a million men are of no importance compared with *one* man? But I must wait for a shower of shillings, or at least a slight dew or mizzling of sixpences, before I explore New York very far.

The sea-beach is the best thing I have seen. It is very solitary and remote, and you only remember New York occasionally. The distances, too, along the shore, and inland in sight of it, are unaccountably great and startling. The sea seems very near from the hills but it proves a long way over the plain, and yet you may be wet with the spray before you can believe that you are there. The far seems near, and the near far. Many rods from the beach, I step aside for the

Atlantic, and I see men drag up their boats on to the sand, with oxen, stepping about amid the surf, as if it were possible they might draw up Sandy Hook.

TO RALPH WALDO EMERSON, JUNE 8, 1843

I am not in such haste to write home when I remember that I make my readers pay the postage—But I believe I have not taxed you before—I have pretty much explored this island—inland and along the shore—finding my health inclined me to the peripatetic philosophy—I have visited Telegraph Stations—Sailor's Snug Harbors—Seaman's Retreats—Old Elm Trees, where the Hugonots landed —Brittons Mills—and all the villages on the island. Last Sunday I walked over to Lake Island Farm—8 or 9 miles from here—where Moses Prichard lived, and found the present occupant, one Mr Davenport formerly from Mass.—with 3 or four men to help him— raising sweet potatoes and tomatoes by the acre. It seemed a cool and pleasant retreat, but a hungry soil. As I was coming away I took my toll out of the soil in the shape of arrowheads—which may after all be the surest crop—certainly not affected by drought.

I am well enough situated here to observe one aspect of the modern world at least—I mean the migratory—the western movement. Sixteen hundred imigrants arrived at quarantine ground on the fourth of July, and more or less every day since I have been here. I see them occasionally washing their persons and clothes, or men women and children gathered on an isolated quay near the shore, stretching their limbs and taking the air, the children running races and swinging—on their artificial piece of the land of liberty—while the vessels are undergoing purification. They are detained but a day or two, and then go up to the city, for the most part without having *landed* here.

In the city I have seen since I wrote last—W. H. Channing—at whose house in 15th St. I spent a few pleasant hours, discussing the all absorbing question—What to do for the race. (He is sadly in earnest—about going up the river to rusticate for six weeks—and issues a new periodical called The Present in September.)—Also Horace Greeley Editor of the Tribune—who is cheerfully in earnest.—at his office of all work—a hearty New Hampshire boy as one would wish to meet. And says "now be neighborly"—and believes only or mainly, first, in the Sylvania Association somewhere in Pennsylvania—and secondly and most of all, in a new association to go into operation soon in New Jersey, with which he is connected.—Edward Palmer came down to see me Sunday before last. As for Waldo and Tappan we have strangely dodged one another and have not met for some weeks.

I believe I have not told you anything about Lucretia Mott. It was a good while ago that I heard her at the Quaker Church in Hester St. She is a preacher, and it was advertised that she would be present on that day. I liked all the proceedings very well—their plainly greater harmony and sincerity than elsewhere. They do nothing in a hurry. Every one that walks up the aisle in his square coat and expansive hat—has a history, and comes from a house to a house. The women come in one after another in their Quaker bonnets and handkerchiefs, looking all like sisters and so many chic-a-dees—At length, after a long silence, waiting for the spirit, Mrs Mott rose, took off her bonnet, and began to utter very deliberately what the spirit suggested. Her self-possession was something to say, if all else failed—but it did not. Her subject was the abuse of the Bible—and thence she straightway digressed to slavery and the degradation of woman. It was a good speech—transcendentalism in its mildest form. She sat down at length and after a long and decorous silence in which some seemed to be really digesting her words, the elders shook hands and the meeting dispersed. On the whole I liked their ways, and the plainness of their meeting house. It looked as if it was indeed made for service.

TO  HELEN  THOREAU,  JULY  21,  1843

I go moping about the fields and woods here as I did in Concord, and, it seems, am thought to be a surveyor,—an Eastern man inquiring narrowly into the condition and value of land, etc., here, preparatory to an extensive speculation. One neighbor observed to me, in a mysterious and half inquisitive way, that he supposed I must be pretty well acquainted with the state of things; that I kept pretty close; he didn't see any surveying instruments, but perhaps I had them in my pocket.

TO MRS. JOHN THOREAU, AUGUST 6, 1843

Mr Emerson has just given me a short warning that he is about to send to Concord, which I will endeavor to improve—I am a good deal more wakeful than I was, and growing stout in other respects— so that I may yet accomplish something in the literary way— indeed I should have done so before now but for the slowness and poverty of the Reviews themselves. I have tried sundry methods of earning money in the city of late but without success, have rambled into every book-sellers or publisher's house and discussed their affairs with them. Some propose to me to do what an honest man cannot— Among others I conversed with the Harpers—to see if they might not find me useful to them—but they say that they are making fifty thousand dollars annually, and their motto is to let well alone. I find that I talk with these poor men as if I were over head and ears in business and a few thousands were no consideration with me—I almost reproach myself for bothering them thus to no purpose—but it is very valuable experience—and the best introduction I could have.

TO MRS. JOHN THOREAU, AUGUST 29, 1843

Miss Fuller will tell you the news from these parts, so I will only devote these few moments to what she does not know as well. I was absent only one day and night from the Island, the family expecting me back immediately. I was to earn a certain sum before winter, and thought it worth the while to try various experiments. I carried the Agriculturist about the city, and up as far as Manhattanville, and called at the Croton Reservoir, where indeed they did not want any

Agriculturist, but paid well enough in their way. Literature comes to a poor market here, and even the little that I write is more than will sell. I have tried the Democratic Review, the New Mirror, and Brother Jonathan. The last two, as well as the New World, are overwhelmed with contributions which cost nothing, and are worth no more. The Knickerbocker is too poor, and only the Ladies' Companion pays. O'Sullivan is printing the manuscript I sent him some time ago, having objected only to my want of sympathy with the Communities.

TO RALPH WALDO EMERSON, SEPTEMBER 14, 1843

I hold together remarkably well as yet, speaking of my outward linen and woolen man, no holes more than I brought away, and no stitches needed yet. It is marvellous. I think the Fates must be on my side, for there is less than a plank between me and—Time, to say the least. As for Eldorado that is far off yet. My bait will not tempt the rats; they are too well fed. The Democratic Review is poor, and can only afford half or quarter pay—which it *will* do—and they say there is a Ldy's Companion that pays—but I could not write anything companionable. However, speculate as we will, it is quite gratuitous, for life never the less, and never the more, goes steadily on, well or ill fed and clothed, somehow, and "honor bright" withal. It is very gratifying to live in the prospect of great successes always, and for that purpose, we must leave a sufficient foreground to see them through. All the painters prefer distant prospects for the greater breadth of view, and delicacy of tint.—But this is no news, and describes no new conditions. Meanwhile I am somnambulic at least— stirring in my sleep—indeed, quite awake. I read a good deal and am pretty well known in the libraries of New York. Am in with the Librarian, one Dr Forbes, of the Society Library—who has lately been to Cambridge to learn liberality, and has come back to let me take out some untake-out-able-books, which I was threatening to read on the spot. And Mr Mackean, of the Mercantile Library, is a true gentleman—a former tutor of mine—and offers me every privilege there. I have from him a perpetual stranger's ticket, and a citizen's rights besides—all which privileges I pay handsomely for by improving.

A canoe-race "came off" on the Hudson the other day, between Chippeways and New Yorkers, which must have been as moving a sight as the buffalo hunt which I witnessed. But canoes and buffaloes are all lost, as is everything here, in the mob. It is only the people have come to see one another. Let them advertise that there will be a gathering at Hoboken—having bargained with the ferry boats, and there will be, and they need not throw in the buffaloes.

I have crossed the bay 20 or 30 times and have seen a great many immigrants going up to the city for the first time—Norwegians who carry their old fashioned farming tools to the west with them, and will buy nothing here for fear of being cheated.—English operatives, known by their pale faces and stained hands, who will recover their birth-rights in a little cheap sun and wind,—English travellers on their way to the Astor House, to whom I have done the honors of the city.—Whole families of imigrants cooking their dinner upon the pavements, all sun-burnt—so that you are in doubt where the foreigner's face of flesh begins—their tidy clothes laid on, and then tied to their swathed bodies which move about like a bandaged finger—caps set on the head, as if woven of the hair, which is still growing at the roots—each and all busily cooking, stooping from time to time over the pot, and having something to drop into it, that so they may be entitled to take something out, forsooth. They look like respectable but straightened people, who may turn out to be counts when they get to Wisconsin—and will have their experience to relate to their children.

Seeing so many people from day to day one comes to have less respect for flesh and bones, and thinks they must be more loosely joined of less firm fibre, than the few he had known. It must have a very bad influence on children to see so many human beings at once—mere herds of men.

TO MRS. JOHN THOREAU, OCTOBER 1, 1843

# NATHANIEL PARKER WILLIS

*Nathaniel Parker Willis (1806–67), barely remembered today, was a fix-
ture of the nineteenth-century New York literary scene. Poet, essayist, and
newspaper editor, he collected his magazine pieces into popular volumes
such as* Pencillings by the Way, Dashes at Life with a Free Pencil,
*and* People I Have Met, *which built on the polished "sketchbook"
manner introduced by Washington Irving. Handsome and something of a
dandy, Willis was an accomplished flaneur, or connoisseur of the sidewalk, whom James Russell Lowell described as "the topmost bright
bubble on the wave of the Town." Granted, he had "no profundity—no
genius," as his friend Poe cruelly put it, but it is remarkable with what
urbanity he assumed the then-novel role of the "New Yorker."*

## FROM *OPEN-AIR MUSINGS IN THE CITY*

ROM THE WINDOW at which I sit, I look directly on the most
frequented portion in Broadway—the *sidewalk in front of
St. Paul's.* You walk over it every day. Familiarity with most
things alters their aspect, however. Let me, after long acquaintance
with this bit of sidewalk, sketch how it looks to me at the various
hours of the day. I may jot down, also, one or two trifles I have observed while looking into the street in the intervals of writing.

*Eight in the morning.*—The sidewalk is comparatively deserted.
The early clerks have gone by, and the bookkeepers and younger
partners not being abroad, the current sets no particular way. A vigorous female exerciser or two may be seen returning from a smart
walk to the Battery, and the orange-women are getting their tables
ready at the corners. There is to be a funeral in the course of the day
in St. Paul's church-yard, and one or two boys are on the coping of
the iron fence, watching the grave-digger. Seamstresses and
schoolmistresses, with veils down, in impenetrable incognito, hurry
by with a step which says unmistakeably, "Don't look at me in this
dress!" The return omnibuses come from Wall street empty, on a
walk.

*Nine and after.*—A rapid throng of well-dressed men, all walking smartly, and all bound Mammon-ward. Glanced at vaguely, the side-walk seems like a floor with a swarm of black beetles running races across it. The single pedestrians who are struggling up stream, keep close to the curbstone or get rudely jostled. The omnibuses all stop opposite St. Paul's at this hour, letting out passengers, who invariably start on a trot down Ann street or Fulton. The Museum people are on the top of the building drawing their flags across Broadway and Ann, by pulleys fastened to trees and chimneys. Burgess and Stringer hanging out their literary placards, with a listless deliberation, as if nobody was abroad yet who had leisure to read them.

*Twelve and after.*—Discount-seekers crowding into the Chemical Bank with hats over their eyes. Flower-merchants setting their pots of roses and geraniums along the iron fence. The blind beggar arrived, and set with his back against the church gate by an old woman. And now the streaks, drawn across my side vision by the passers under, glide at a more leisurely pace, and are of gayer hues. The street full of sunshine. Omnibuses going slowly, both ways. Female exclusives gliding to and fro in studiously plain dresses, and with very occupied air—(never in Broadway without "the carriage," *of course*, except to shop.) Strangers sprinkled in couples, exhausting their strength and spirits by promenading before the show hour. The grave dug in St. Paul's, and the grave-digger gone home to dinner. Woman run over at the Fulton crossing. Boys out of school. Tombs' bell ringing fire in the third district.

*One and after.*—The ornamentals are abroad. A crowd on St. Paul's sidewalk, watching the accomplished canary-bird, whose cage hangs on the fence. He draws his seed and water up an inclined plane in a rail-car, and does his complicated feeding to the great approbation of his audience. The price is high—his value being in proportion (aristocracy-wise) to his wants! It is the smoothest and broadest sidewalk in Broadway—the frontage of St. Paul's—and the ladies and dandies walk most at their ease just here, loitering a little, per-haps, to glance at the flowers for sale. My window, commanding this *pavé*, is a particularly good place, therefore, to study street habits, and I have noted a trifle or so, that, if not new, may be newly put down. I observe that a very well-dressed woman is noticed by none so much as by the women themselves. This is the week for the first spring dresses, and, to-day, there is a specimen or two of Miss Lawson's April *avatar*, taking its first sun on the promenade. A lady passed, just now, with a charming straw hat and primrose shawl— not a *very* pretty woman, but, dress and all, a fresh and sweet object to look at—like a new-blown cowslip, that stops you in your walk, though it is not a violet. Not a *male* eye observed her, from curb-stone in Vesey to curb-stone in Fulton, but *every woman* turned to look after her! *Query*, is this the notice of envy or admiration; and, if the former, is it desirable or worth the pains and money of toilet? *Query*, again—the men's notice being admiration (not envy) what *will* attract it, and is *that* (whatever it is) worth while? I query what I should, myself, like to know.

*Half past three.*—The sidewalk is in shade. The orange-man sits on a lemon-box, with his legs and arms all crossed together in his lap, listening to the band who have just commenced playing in the Museum balcony. The principal listeners, who have stopped for nothing but to listen, are three negro boys, (one sitting on the Croton hydrant, and the other two leaning on his back,) and to them this gratuitous music seems a charming dispensation. (Tune, "Ole Dan Tucker.") The omnibus horses prick up their ears in going under the trumpets, but evidently feel that to show fright would be a luxury beyond their means. Saddle-horse, tied at the bank, breaks bridle and runs away. Three is universal dinner time for *bosses*—(what other word expresses the head men of all trades and professions?)— and probably not a single portly man will pass under my window in this hour.

*Four to five.*—Sidewalk more crowded. Hotel boarders lounging along with toothpicks. Stout men going down toward Wall street with coats unbuttoned. Hearse stopped at St. Paul's, and the Museum band playing, "Take your time, Miss Lucy," while the mourners are getting out. A gentleman, separated from two ladies by the passing of the coffin across the sidewalk, rejoins them, apparently with some funny remark. Bell tolls. No one in the crowd is interested to inquire the age or sex of the person breaking the current of Broadway to pass to the grave. Hearse drives off on a trot.

*Five and after.*——Broadway one gay procession. Few ladies accompanied by gentlemen——fewer than in the promenades of any other country. Men in couples and women in couples. Dandies strolling and stealing an occasional look at their loose *demi-saison* pantaloons and gaiter-shoes, newly sported with the sudden advent of warm weather. No private carriage passing, except those bound to the ferries for a drive into the country. The crowd is unlike the morning crowd. There is as much or more beauty, but the fashionable ladies are not out. You would be puzzled to discover who these lovely women are. Their toilets are unexceptionable, their style is a *very* near approach to *comme il faut*. They look perfectly satisfied with their position and with themselves, and they do——(what fashionable women do *not*)——meet the eye of the promenader with a coquettish confidence he will misinterpret——if he be green or a puppy. Among these ladies are accidents of feature, form, and manner——charms of which the possessor is unconscious——that, if transplanted into a high-bred sphere of society abroad, would be bowed to as the stamp of lovely aristocracy. Possibly——probably, indeed——the very woman who is a marked instance of this, is not called pretty by her friends. She is only spoken to by those whose taste is commonplace and unrefined. She walks Broadway, and has a vague suspicion that the men of fashion look at her more admiringly than could be accounted for by any credit she has for beauty at home. Yet she is not likely to be enlightened as to the secret of it. When tired of her promenade, she disappears by some side-street leading away from the great thoroughfares, and there is no clue to her unless by inquiries that would be properly resented as impertinence. I see at least twenty pass daily under my window, who would be ornaments of any society, yet who, I know, (by the men I see occasionally with them,) are unacknowledgable by the aristocrats up town. What a field for a Columbus! How charming to go on a voyage of discovery and search for these unprized pearls among the unconscious pebbles! How delightful to see these rare plants without hedges about them——exquisite women without fashionable affectations, fashionable hindrances, penalties, exactions, pretensions, and all the wearying nonsenses that embarrass and stupefy the society of most of our female pretenders to exclusiveness!

*Half-past six and after.*—The flower-seller loading up his pots into a fragrant wagon-load. Twilight's rosy mist falling into the street. Gas-lamps alight, here and there. The Museum band increased by two instruments, to play more noisily for the night-custom. The magic wheel lit up, and ground rather capriciously by the tired boy inside. The gaudy transparencies one by one illuminated. Great difference now in the paces at which people walk. Business-men bound home, apprentices and shop-boys carrying parcels, ladies belated—are among the hurrying ones. Gentlemen strolling for amusement take it very leisurely, and with a careless gait that is more graceful and becoming than their mien of circumspect daylight. And now thicken the flaunting dresses of the unfortunate outlaws of charity and pity. Some among them (not many) have a remainder of lady-likeness in their gait, as if, but for the need there is to attract attention, they could seem modest—but the most of them are promoted to fine dress from sculleries and low life, and show their shameless vulgarity through silk and feathers. They are not all to be pitied. The gentleman cit passes them by like the rails in St. Paul's fence—wholly unnoticed. If he is vicious, it is not those in the street who could attract him. The "loafers" return their bold looks, and the boys pull their dresses as they go along, and now and then a greenish youth, well-dressed, shows signs of being attracted. Sailors, rowdies, country-people, and strangers who have dined freely, are those whose steps are arrested by them. It is dark now. The omnibuses, that were heavily laden through the twilight, now go more noisily, because lighter. Carriages make their way toward the Park theatre. My window shows but the two lines of lamps and the glittering shops, and all else vaguely.

I have repeatedly taken five minutes, at a time, to pick out a well-dressed man, and see if he would walk from Fulton street to Vesey without getting a look at his boots. You might safely bet against it. If he is an idle man, and out only for a walk, two to one he would glance downward to his feet three or four times in that distance. Men betray their subterfuges of toilet—women never. Once in the street, women are armed at all points against undesirable observation—men have an ostrich's obtusity, being wholly unconscious even of that battery of critics, a passing omnibus! How many substitutes and secrets of dress a woman carries about her, the angels know!— but she *looks* defiance to suspicion on that subject. Sit in my window, on the contrary, and you can pick out every false shirt-bosom that passes, and every pair of false wristbands, and the dandy's economical half-boots, gaiter-cut trowsers notwithstanding.

Indeed, while it is always difficult, sometimes impossible, to distinguish *female* genuine from the imitation, nothing is easier than to know at sight the "glossed (*male*) worsted from the patrician sarsnet." The "fashion" of women, above a certain guide, can seldom be guessed at in the street, except by the men who are with them.

You should sit in a window like mine, to know how few men *walk* with even passable grace. Nothing so corrupts the gait as business— (a fact that would be offensive to mention in a purely business country, if it were not that the "unmannerly haste" of parcel-bearing and money-seeking, *may be* laid aside with low-heeled boots and sample cards.) The bent-kneed celerity, learned in dodging clerks and jumping over boxes on sidewalks, betrays its trick in the gait, as the face shows the pucker of calculation and the suavity of sale. I observe that the man used to hurry, relies principally on his heel, and keeps his foot at right angles. The ornamental man drops his toe slightly downward in taking a step, and uses, for elasticity, the spring of his instep. Nature has provided muscles of grace which are only incorporated into the gait by habitually walking with leisure. All women walk with comparative grace who are not cramped with tight shoes, but there are many degrees of gracefulness in women, and oh, what a charm is the highest degree of it! How pleasurable even to see from my window a woman walking like a queen!

The February rehearsal of spring is over—the popular play of April having been well represented by the reigning stars and that pleasant company of players, the Breezes. The drop-curtain has fallen, representing a winter-scene, principally clouds and snow, and the beauties of the dress-circle have retired (from Broadway) discontented only with the beauty of the piece. By-the-way, the acting was so true to Nature, that several trees in Broadway were affected to— budding!

> "Ah, friends, methinks it were a pleasant sphere
> If, like the trees, *we* budded every year!
> If locks grew thick again, and rosy dyes
> Returned in cheeks, a raciness in eyes,
> And all around us vital to their tips,
> The human orchard laughed with rosy lips."

So says Leigh Hunt.

February should be called the *month of hope*, for it is invariably more enjoyable than the first nominal fruition—more spring-like than the first month of Spring. This is a morning that makes the hand open and the fingers spread—a morning that should be consecrated to sacred idleness. I should like to exchange work with any out-of-doors man—even with a driver of an omnibus—specially with the farmer tinkering his fences. Cities are convenient places of refuge from winter and bad weather, but one longs to get out into the country, like a sheep from a shed, with the first warm gleam of sunshine.

March made an expiring effort to give us a spring-day yesterday. The morning dawned mild and bright, and there was a voluptuous contralto in the cries of the milkmen and the sweeps, which satisfied me, before I was out of bed, that there was an arrival of a south wind. The Chinese proverb says, "when thou hast a day to be idle, be idle for a day;" but for that very elusive "time when," I irresistibly substitute the day the wind sweetens, after a sour northeaster. Oh, the luxury (or *curse*, as the case may be) of breakfasting leisurely with an idle day before one!

I strolled up Broadway between nine and ten, and encountered the *morning tide down*; and if you never have studied the physiognomy of this great thoroughfare in its various fluxes and refluxes, the differences would amuse you. The clerks and workies have passed down an hour before the nine o'clock tide, and the sidewalk is filled at this time with bankers, brokers, and speculators, bound to Wall Street; old merchants and junior partners, bound to Pearl and Water; and lawyers, young and old, bound for Nassau and Pine. Ah, the faces of care! The day's operations are working out in their eyes; their hats are pitched forward at the angle of a stage-coach, with all the load on the driver's seat; their shoulders are raised with the shrug of anxiety, their steps are hurried and short, and mortal face and gait could scarcely express a heavier burden of solicitude than every man seems to bear. They nod to you without a smile, and with a kind of unconscious recognition; and, if you are unaccustomed to walk out at that hour, you might fancy that, if there were not some great public calamity, your friends at least had done smiling on you. Walk as far as Niblo's, stop at the greenhouse there, and breathe an hour in the delicious atmosphere of flowering plants, and then return. There is no longer any particular current in Broadway. Foreigners coming out from the *cafés*, after their late breakfast, and idling up and down, for fresh air; country-people shopping early; ladies going to their dress-makers in close veils and demi-toilets; errand-boys, news-boys, duns, and doctors, make up the throng. Toward twelve o'clock there is a sprinkling of mechanics going to dinner—a merry, short-jack-eted, independent-looking troop, glancing gayly at the women as they pass, and disappearing around corners and up alleys, and an hour later Broadway begins to brighten. The omnibuses go along empty, and at a slow pace, for people would rather walk than ride. The side-streets are tributaries of silks and velvets, flowers and feathers, to the great thoroughfare; and ladies, whose proper mates (judging by the dress alone) should be lords and princes, and dandies, shoppers, and loungers of every description, take crowded possession of the *pavé*. At nine o'clock you look into the troubled faces of men going to their business, and ask yourself "to what end is all this burden of care?" and, at two, you gaze on the universal prodigality of exterior, and wonder what fills the multitude of pockets that pay for it! The faces are beautiful, the shops are thronged, the sidewalks crowded for an hour, and then the full tide turns and sets upward. The most of those who are out at three are bound to the upper part

of the city to dine; and the merchants and lawyers, excited by colli-
sion and contest above the depression of care, join, smiling, in the
throng. The physiognomy of the crowd is at its brightest. Dinner is
the smile of the day to most people, and the hour approaches.
Whatever has happened in stocks or politics, whoever is dead, whoever ruined, since morning, Broadway is thronged with cheerful
faces and good appetites at three! The world will probably dine with
pleasure up to the last day—perhaps breakfast with worldly care for
the future on doomsday morning! And here I must break off my
Daguerreotype of yesterday's idling, for the wind came round east-
erly and raw at three o'clock, and I was driven in-doors to try industry as an opiate.

The first day of freedom from medical embargo is equivalent, in
most men's memories, to a new first impression of existence. Dame
Nature, like a provident housewife, seems to take the opportunity of
a sick man's absence to whitewash and freshen the world he occupies. Certainly, I never saw the bay of New York look so beautiful as
on Sunday noon; and you may attribute as much as you please of this
impression to the "Claude Lorraine spectacles" of convalescence, and
as much more as pleases you to the fact that it was an intoxicating
and dissolving day of Spring.

The Battery on Sunday is the Champs Elysées of foreigners. I
heard nothing spoken around me but French and German. Wrapped
in my cloak, and seated on a bench, I watched the children and the
poodle-dogs at their gambols, and it seemed to me as if I were in
some public resort over the water. They bring such happiness to a
day of idleness—these foreigners—laughing, talking nonsense, totally unconscious of observation, and delighted as much with the
passing of a rowboat, or a steamer, as an American with the arrival
of his own "argosy" from sea. They are not the better class of foreigners who frequent the Battery on Sunday. They are the newly
arrived, the artisans, the German toymakers and the French boot-
makers—people who still wear the spacious-hipped trowsers and
scant coats, the gold rings in the ears, and the ruffled shirts of the
lands of undandyfied poverty. They are there by hundreds. They hang

over the railing and look off upon the sea. They sit and smoke on the long benches. They run hither and thither with their children, and behave as they would in their own garden, using and enjoying it just as if it were their own. And an enviable power they have of it!

There had been a heavy fog on the water all the morning, and quite a fleet of the river-craft had drifted with the tide close on to the Battery. The soft south wind was lifting the mist in undulating sweeps, and covering and disclosing the spars and sails with a phantom effect quite melo-dramatic. By two o'clock the breeze was steady and the bay clear, and the horizon was completely concealed with the spread of canvass. The grass in the Battery plots seemed to be growing visibly meantime, and to this animated sea-picture gave a foreground of tender and sparkling green; the trees looked feathery with the opening buds; the children rolled on the grass, and the summer seemed come. Much as Nature loves the country, she opens her green lap first in the cities. The valleys are asleep under the snow, and will be, for weeks.

I am inclined to think it is not peculiar to myself to have a Sabbath taste for the water-side. There is an affinity, felt I think by man and boy, between the stillness of the day and the audible hush of boundaries to water. Premising that it was at first with the turned-up nose of conscious travestie, I have to confess the finding of a Sabbath solitude, to my mind, along the river-side in New-York— the first mile toward Albany on the bank of the Hudson. Indeed, if quiet be the object, the nearer the water the less jostled the walk on Sunday. You would think, to cross the city anywhere from river to river, that there was a general hydrophobia—the entire population crowding to the high ridge of Broadway, and hardly a soul to be seen on either the East River or the Hudson. But, with a little thoughtful frequenting, those deserted river-sides become contemplative and pleasant rambling-places; and, if some whim of fashion do not make the bank of the Hudson like the Marina of Smyrna, a fashionable resort, I have my Sunday afternoons provided for, during the pigritude of city durance.

Yesterday (Sunday) it blew one of those unfolding west winds,

chartered expressly to pull the kinks out of the belated leaves—a
breeze it was delightful to set the face to—strong, genial, and inspir-
iting, and smelling (in New-York) of the snubbed twigs of Hoboken.
The Battery looked very delightful, with the grass laying its cheek to
the ground, and the trees all astir and trinkling; but on Sunday this
lovely resort is full of smokers of bad cigars—unpleasant gentlemen to take the wind of. I turned the corner with a look through the
fence, and was in comparative solitude the next moment.

The monarch of our deep water-streams, the gigantic "Massachusetts," lay at her wharf, washed by the waving hands of the
waters taking leave of the Hudson. The river ends under the prow—
or, as we might say with a poetic license, joins on, at this point, to
Stonington—so easy is the transit from wharf to wharf in that magnificent conveyance. From this point up, extends a line of ships, rubbing against the pier the fearless noses that have nudged the poles
and the tropics, and been breathed on by spice-islands and ice-
bergs—an array of nobly-built merchantmen, that, with the association of their triumphant and richly-freighted comings and goings,
grows upon my eye with a certain majesty. It is a broad street here,
of made land, and the sidewalks in front of the new stores are lum-
bered with pitch and molasses, flour and red ochre, bales, bags, and
barrels, in unsightly confusion—but the wharf-side, with its long
line of carved figure-heads, and bowsprits projecting over the street,
is an unobstructed walk—on Sundays at least—and more suggestive
than many a gallery of marble statues. The vessels that trade to the
North Sea harbor here, unloading their hemp and iron; and the superb French packet-ships, with their gilded prows; and, leaning over
the gangways and taffrails, the Swedish and Norwegian sailors jabber
away their Sunday's idle time; and the negro-cooks lie and look into
the puddles; and, altogether, it is a strangely-mixed picture—Power
reposing, and Fret and Business gone from the six-days' whip and
chain. I sat down on a short hawser-post, and conjured the spirits of
ships around me. They were as communicative as would naturally be
expected in a *tête-à-tête* when quite at leisure. Things they had seen
and got wind of in the Indian seas, strange fishes that had tried the
metal of their copper bottoms, porpoises they had run over asleep,

wrecks and skeletons they had thrown a shadow across when under prosperous headway—these and particulars of the fortunes they had brought home, and the passengers coming to look through one more country to find happiness, and the terrors and dangers, heart-aches and dreams, that had come and gone with each bill of lading—the talkative old bowsprits told me all. I sat and watched the sun setting between two outlandish-looking vessels, and, at twilight, turned to go home, leaving the spars and lines drawn in clear tracery, on a sky as rosy and fading as a poet's prospects at seventeen.

We know nothing of a more restless tendency than a fine, old-fashioned June day—one that begins with a morning damp with a fresh south wind, and gradually clears away in a thin white mist, till the sun shines through at last, genial and luxurious, but not sultry, and everything looks clear and bright in the transparent atmosphere. We know nothing which so seduces the very eye and spirit of a man, and stirs in him that gipsy longing, which, spite of warning and punishment, made him a truant in his boyhood. There is an expansive rarity in the air of such a day—a something that lifts up the lungs, and plays in the nostrils with a delicious sensation of freshness and elasticity. The close room grows sadly dull under it. The half-open blind, with its tempting glimpse of the sky, and branch of idle leaves flickering in the sun, has a strange witchery. The poor pursuits of this drossy world grow passing insignificant; and the scrawled and blotted manuscripts of an editor's table—pleasant anodyne as they are when the wind is in the east—are, at these seasons, but the "Diary of an Ennuyée"—the notched calendar of confinement and unrest. The commendatory sentence stands half-completed; the fate of the author under review, with his two volumes, is altogether of less importance than five minutes of the life of that tame pigeon that sits on the eaves washing his white breast in the spout; and the public good-will, and the cause of literature, and our own precarious livelihood, all fade into dim shadow, and leave us listening dreamily to the creeping of the sweet south upon the vine, or the far-off rattle of the hourly, with its freight of happy bowlers and gentlemen of suburban idleness.

What is it to us when the sun is shining, and the winds bland and balmy, and the moist roads with their fresh smell of earth tempting us away to the hills—what is it, then, to us, whether a poor-devil-author has a flaw in his style, or our own leading article a "local habitation and a name?" Are we to thrust down our heart like a reptile into its cage, and close our shutter to the cheerful light, and our ear to all sounds of out-door happiness? Are we to smother our uneasy impulses, and chain ourselves down to a poor, dry thought, that has neither light, nor music, nor any spell in it, save the poor necessity of occupation? Shall we forget the turn in the green lane where we are wont to loiter in our drive, and the cool claret of our friend at the Hermitage, and the glorious golden summer sunset in which we bowl away to the city—musing and refreshed? Alas—yes! the heart *must* be closed, and the green lane and the friend that is happier than we (for he is idle) *must* be forgotten, and the dry thought *must* be dragged up like a willful steer and yoked to its fellow, and the magnificent sunset, with all its glorious dreams and forgetful happiness, *must* be seen in the pauses of articles, and the "bleared een" of painful attention—and all this in June—prodigal June—when the very worm is all day out in the sun, and the birds scarce stop their singing from the gray light to the dewfall!

What an insufferable state of the thermometer! We knock under to Heraclitus, that fire is the first principle of all things. Fahrenheit at one hundred degrees in the shade! Our curtain in the attic unstirred! Our japonica drooping its great white flowers lower and lower. It is a fair scene, indeed! not a ripple from the pier to the castle, and the surface of the water as Shelley says, "like a plane of glass spread out between two heavens"—and there is a solitary sloop, with the light and shade flickering on its loose sail, positively hung in the air—and a gull, it is refreshing to see him, keeping down with his white wings close to the water, as if to meet his own snowy and perfect shadow. Was ever such intense, unmitigated sunshine? There is nothing on the hard, opaque sky, but a mere rag of a cloud, like a handkerchief on a tablet of blue marble, and the edge of the shadow of that tall chimney is as definite as a hair; and the young elm that leans over the fence is copied in perfect and motionless leaves, like a very painting on the broad sidewalk. How delightful the night will be after such a deluge of light! How beautiful the modest rays of the starlight, and the cool dark blue of the heavens will seem after the dazzling clearness of this sultry noon! It reminds one of that exquisite passage in Thalaba, where the spirit-bird comes, when his eyes are blinded with the intense brightness of the snow, and spreads her green wings before him!

There is no struggling against it—*we have a need* to pass the summer in some place that God made. We have argued the instinct down—every morning since May-day—while shaving. It is as cool in the city as in the country, we believe. We see as many trees, from our window, (living opposite St. Paul's church-yard,) and as much grass, as we could take in at a glance. The air we breathe, outside the embrasures of Castle Garden, every afternoon, and on board the Hoboken and Jersey boats, every warm evening, are entire recompenses to the lungs for the day's dust and stony heat. And then God intends that *somebody* shall live in the city in summer-time, and why not we? By the time this argument is over, our chin and our rebellious spirit are both smoothed down. Breakfast is ready—as cool fruit, as delicious butter under the ice, and as beloved a *vis-à-vis* over the white cloth and coffee-tray as we should have in the country. We go to work after breakfast with passable content. The city cries, and the city wheels, the clang of the charcoal cart and the importunities of printer's imp—all blend in the passages of our outer ear as unconsciously and fitly as brook-noises and breeze-doings. We are well enough till two. An hour to dinner—somewhat a weary hour, we must say, with a subdued longing for some earth to walk upon. Dinner—pretty well! Discontent and sorrow dwell in a man's throat, and go abroad while it is watered and swept. The hour after dinner has its little resignation also—coffee, music, and the "angel-visit" from the nursery. Five o'clock comes round, and with it Nature's demand for a pair of horses. (Alas! why are we not centaurs, to have a pair of horses when we marry?) We get into an omnibus, and as we get toward the porcelain end of the city, our porcclain friends pass us in their carriages, bound out where the earth breathes and the grass grows. An irresistible discontent overwhelms us! The paved hand of the city spreads out beneath us, holding down the grass and shutting off the salutary earth-pores, and we pine for balm and moisture! The over-worked mind offers no asylum of thought. It is the out-door time of day. Nature calls us to her bared bosom, and there is a floor of impenetrable stone between us and her! At the end of the omnibus-line we turn and go back, and resume our paved and walled-up existence; and all the logic of philosophy, aided by ice-creams and bands of music, would fail to convince us, that night, that we are not victims and wretches. For Heaven's sake, some kind old man, give us an acre off the pavement, and money enough to go and lie on the outside of it, of summer afternoons!

We had a June May, and a May June, and the brick world of Manhattan has not, as yet, become too hot to hold us. This is to be our first experiment at passing the entire summer in the city, and we had laid up a few alleviations which have as yet kept the shelf, with our white hat, uncalled for by any great rise in the thermometer. There is no knowing, however, when we shall hear from Texas and the warm "girdle round the earth," (the equator—no reference to English dominion,) and our advice to the stayers in town may be called for by a south wind before it is fairly printed. First—*our substitute for a private yacht*. Not having twenty thousand dollars to defray our aquatic tendencies—having, on the contrary, an occasional spare shilling—we take our moonlight trip on the river—dividing the cool breezes, 'twixt shore and shore—*in the Jersey ferry-boat*. Smile those who have private yachts! We know no pleasanter trip, after the dusk of the evening, than to stroll down to the ferry, haul a bench to the bow of the ferry-boat, and "open up" the evening breeze for two miles and back, for a shilling! After eight o'clock, there are, on an average, ten people in the boat, and you have the cool shoulder under the railing, as nearly as possible, to yourself. The long line of lamps on either shore makes a gold flounce to the "starry skirt of heaven"—the air is as pure as the rich man has it in his grounds, and all the money in the world could not mend the outside of your head, as far as the horizon. (And the horizon, at such a place and hour, becomes a substitute for the small hoop you have stepped out of.) No man is richer than we, or could be better off—till we reach the Jersey shore—and we are as rich going back. Try this of a hot evening, all who prefer coolness and have a mind that is good company.

Then, there is our *substitute for an airing.* There is a succession of coaches, lined with red velvet, that, in the slope of the afternoon, ply, nearly empty, the whole length of Broadway—two or three miles, at an easy pace, for sixpence. We have had vehicles, or friends who had vehicles, in most times and places that we remember, and we *crave* our ride after dinner. We need to get away from walls and ceiling stuck over with cares and brain-work, and to be amused without effort—particularly without the effort of walking or talking. So—

"Taking our hat in our hand, *that* remarkably requisite practice"—

we step out from our side-street to the brink of Broadway, and *presto*, like magic, up drives an empty coach with two horses, red velvet lining, and windows open; and, by an adroit slackening of the tendons of his left leg, the driver opens the door to us. With the leisurely pace suited to the hour and its *besoin*, our carriage rolls up Broadway, giving us a sliding panorama of such charms as are peculiar to the afternoon of the great thoroughfare, (quite the best part of the day, for a spectator merely.) Every bonnet we see wipes off a care from our mental slate, and every nudge to our curiosity shoves up our spirits a peg. Easily and uncrowded, we are set down for our sixpence at "Fourteenth street," and turning our face once more toward Texas, we take the next velvet-lined vehicle bound down. The main difference betwixt us and the rich man, for that hour, is, that he rides in a green lane, and we in Broadway—he sees green leaves, and we pretty women—he pays much and we pay little. The question of *envy*, therefore, depends upon which of these categories you honestly prefer. While Providence furnishes the spare shilling, *we*, at any rate, will not complain. Such of our friends as are prepared to condole with us for our summer among the bricks, will please credit us with the two foregoing alleviations.

1843–45

# EDGAR ALLAN POE

*Edgar Allan Poe (1809–49) made a good part of his living as a prolific literary critic and newspaper essayist. In* Doings of Gotham, *the pungent and alert series of articles he wrote about New York for a Columbia, Pennsylvania, newspaper, Poe exhibited his critic's capacity for fastidious underpraise and acerbic judgments, as well as his meandering curiosity. Poe's ties to New York City were actually much closer than his somewhat cavalier pose in these pieces might indicate; he resided twice in the city, edited the* Broadway Journal, *and occupied a cottage in Fordham which is now a museum. Incidentally, Poe himself was responsible for the "balloon hoax" to which he alludes with feigned bafflement.*

## FROM *DOINGS OF GOTHAM*

IT WILL GIVE ME much pleasure, gentlemen, to comply with your suggestions and, by dint of a weekly epistle, keep you *au fait* to a certain portion of the doings of Gotham. And here if, in the beginning, for "certain" you read "*uncertain,*" you will the more readily arrive at my design. For, in fact, I must deal chiefly in gossip—in gossip, whose empire is unlimited, whose influence is universal, whose devotees are legion;—in gossip which is the true safety-valve of society—engrossing at least seven-eights of the whole waking existence of mankind. It has been never better defined than by Basil, who calls it "talk for talk's sake," nor more thoroughly comprehended than by Lady Wortley Montague, who made it a profession and a purpose. Although coextensive with the world, it is well known, however, to have neither beginning, middle, nor end. Thus, of the gossiper it was not acutely said that "he commences his discourse by jumping *in medias res.*" Herein it was Jeremy Taylor who deceived himself. For, clearly, your gossiper begins not at all. He is begun. He is already begun. He is always begun. In the matter of end he is indeterminate, and by these things shall you know him to be of the Caesars—*porphyrogenitus*—born in the purple—a gossiper of the "right vein"—of the true blood—of the blue blood—of the *sangre azula*. As for law, he is cognizant of but one, and that negative—the invariable absence of all. And, for his road, were it as straight as the Appia, and as broad as "that which leadeth to destruction," nevertheless would he be malcontent without a frequent hop-skip-and-jump over the hedges, into the tempting pastures of digression beyond. Thus, although my avowed purpose be Gotham, I shall not be expected to give up the privilege of touching, when it suits me, *de omnibus rebus et quibusdam aliis*—upon everything and something besides.

✦  ✦  ✦  ✦  ✦

I have been roaming far and wide over this island of Mannahatta. Some portions of its interior have a certain air of rocky sterility which may impress some imaginations as simply *dreary*—to me it conveys the sublime. Trees are few; but some of the shrubbery is exceedingly picturesque. Not less so are the prevalent shanties of the Irish squatters. I have one of these *tabernacles* (I use the term primitively) at present in the eye of my mind. It is, perhaps, nine feet by six, with a pigsty applied externally, by way both of portico and support. The whole fabric (which is of mud) has been erected in somewhat too obvious an imitation of the Tower of Pisa. A dozen rough planks, "pitched" together, form the roof. The door is a barrel on end. There is a garden, too; and this is encircled by a ditch at one point, a large stone at another, a bramble at a third. A dog and a cat are inevitable in these habitations; and, apparently, there are no dogs and no cats more entirely happy.

On the eastern or "Sound" face of Mannahatta (*why* do we persist in *de-euphonizing* the true names?) are some of the most picturesque sites for villas to be found within the limits of Christendom. These localities, however, are neglected—unimproved. The old mansions upon them (principally wooden) are suffered to remain unrepaired, and present a melancholy spectacle of decrepitude. In fact, these magnificent places are doomed. The spirit of Improvement has withered them with its acrid breath. Streets are already "mapped" through them, and they are no longer suburban residences, but "town-lots." In some thirty years every noble cliff will be a pier, and the whole island will be densely desecrated by buildings of brick, with portentous *facades* of brown-stone, or brown-*stonn*, as the Gothamites have it.

The fountain in the Park is in so much good, as it fulfils its design. That at the Bowling-Green is an absurdity—and is it for this reason that it has been pronounced sublime? The idea, you know,—the original conception was rusticity—Nature, in short. The water was designed to fall and flow naturally, over natural rocks. And how has this design been carried into execution? By piling some hundred nearly rectangular cubes of stone, into *one* nearly rectangular cube. The whole has much the air of a small country jail in a hard thunder shower.

MAY 14, 1844

In the way of mere news there is nothing—nothing, at least, which I could reconcile it to my conscience to make matter of record.

The city is thronged with strangers, and everything wears an aspect of intense life. Business has experienced a thorough revival, and "all goes merry as a marriage bell." Notwithstanding the Croton water, or "the Crot'n," as the Gothamites have it, the streets are, with rare exception, insufferably dirty. The exceptions are to be found in Bond Street, Waverly Place, and some others of the upper, more retired, and more fashionable quarters. These surpass in purity the cleanest districts of Philadelphia; but, in general, there is no comparison between the two cities. I believe that New York is "scavengered," to use an English verb, by contract, at an annual expense of $50,000. If this is really the case, there must be either great stupidity, or ignorance, somewhere—or at all events some partisan chicanery. Contractors might pay roundly *for the privilege* of cleaning the streets, receiving the sweepings for their perquisite, and find themselves great gainers by the arrangement. In any large city, a company of market gardeners would be induced to accept a contract of this character.

Mr. Harper has commenced his reign with vigor, and will, no doubt, make an efficient Mayor. Of course, there has been, and will be, the usual proscription, notwithstanding the usual promises. The anticipation, or rather the certainty of removal from office, has given rise to some high-handed, and at the same time ludicrous instances of the *sauve qui peut* principle. Entire districts, for example, are left, for weeks, in outer darkness, at night; the lamp-lighting function-aries flatly refusing to light up; preferring to appropriate the oil to their own private and personal emolument, and thus have a penny in pocket, with which to console themselves for that dismissal which is inevitable. Three-quarters of a mile on the Third Avenue, one of the most important and most thronged thoroughfares, have been thus left in darkness visible for the last fortnight or more. When the question is asked—"cannot these scoundrels be made to suffer for their high-handed peculations?"—the reply is invariably—"oh, no—to be sure not—the thing is expected, and will only be laughed at as an excellent practical joke. The comers-in to office will be in too high glee to be severe, and as for the turned-out, it is no longer any business of theirs."

I presume you have seen, by the papers, that some person has been so good as to publish what he calls "The Life and Writings of James Gordon Bennett." Mr. Bennett, calling the book "an infamous and atrocious libel," charges Mr. Moses Y. Beach of the "Sun" with its perpetration, and announces his intention to sue. Mr. Beach denies the parentage, and Mr. T. L. Nichols avows it. Mr. N. was, for a year, associated with Mr. Bennett in the conduct of the "Herald," and is a man of much talent. He declares that the *brochure* in question is chiefly a *rifacimento* of Mr. Bennett's own articles extracted from the "Herald" itself. I have not seen the production, nor shall I see it. It is said to be *very* severe.

The arrival of the Brittannia at Boston, on Saturday, just as the western train was leaving the city, rendered nugatory the various "express" arrangements in contemplation, and thus put an end to di-verse excellent quarrels in prospectu. One, especially, of ominous aspect, had been gradually gathering itself into shape, between

Beach, on the one hand, and Messieurs Bennett and Greeley, in co-partnership, on the other.

Talking of "expresses"—the "Balloon-Hoax" made a far more intense sensation than anything of that character since the "Moon-Story" of Locke. On the morning (Saturday) of its announcement, the whole square surrounding the "Sun" building was literally besieged, blocked up—ingress and egress being alike impossible, from a period soon after sunrise until about two o'clock P. M. In Saturday's regular issue, it was stated that the news had been just received, and that an "Extra" was then in preparation, which would be ready at ten. It was not delivered, however, until nearly noon. In the meantime I never witnessed more intense excitement to get possession of a newspaper. As soon as the few first copies made their way into the streets, they were bought up, at almost any price, from the news-boys, who made a profitable speculation beyond doubt. I saw a half-dollar given, in one instance, for a single paper, and a shilling was a frequent price. I tried, in vain, during the whole day, to get possession of a copy. It was excessively amusing, however, to hear the comments of those who had read the "Extra." Of course there was great discrepancy of opinion as regards the authenticity of the story; but I observed that the more intelligent believed, while the rabble, for the most part, rejected the whole with disdain. Twenty years ago credulity was the characteristic trait of the mob, incredulity the distinctive feature of the philosophic; now the case is exactly conversed. The wise are disinclined to *disbelief*—and justly so. The only grounds, in this instance, for doubt, with those who knew anything of Natural Philosophy, were the publication of the marvel in the suspected "Sun" (the organ of the Moon-Hoax) and the great difficulty of running an Express from Charleston, in advance of the mail. As for internal evidence of falsehood, there is, positively, *none*—while the more generally accredited fable of Locke would not bear even momentary examination by the scientific. There is nothing put forth in the Balloon-Story which is not in full keeping with the known facts of aeronautic experience—which might not really have occurred. An expedition of the kind has been long contemplated, and this *jeu d'esprit* will, beyond doubt give the intention a new impulse. For my own part, I shall not be in the least surprised to learn, in the course of next month, or the next, that a balloon has made the actual voyage so elaborately described by the hoaxer. The trip might be made in even less time than seventy-five hours—which give only about forty miles to the hour.

The publishing world is very busy here, just now, and it has become a truism that "everything *sells*." The "Mirror" still thrives, and will, in the end, be a fortune to its very worthy proprietors. The popularity of General Morris is, perhaps, a little on the wane; but that of Mr. Willis is gradually increasing. He is well constituted for dazzling the masses—with brilliant, agreeable talents—no profundity—no *genius*. A more estimable man, in his private relations, never existed.

The Magazines for June are already out. "Graham," I see, has a portrait of Judge Conrad, the author of "Aylmere," which is no portrait at all—altogether too baby-ish—character-less. The biography (by a friend of yours) does no more than justice.

MAY 21, 1844

The city is brimful of all kinds of *legitimate* liveliness—the life of money-making, and the life of pleasure;—but political excitement seems, for the moment, to pause—I presume by way of getting breath, and new vigor, for the approaching Presidential contest; while all apprehension of danger from the mob-disorder which so lately beset Philadelphia, is fairly at an end. A crisis, however, was very nearly at hand, and was averted principally, I think, by the firmness and prudence of the new authorities.

You may remember the futile attempt made a short time since, in the city of Brotherly Love, to close the Rum Palaces, and Rum Hovels, on the Sabbath. The point has been carried here by Mr. Harper—at least so far as a point of this character *can* be carried at all. As to the direct benefits accruing to the community at large, by the closing of these hot-houses of iniquity on Sunday—or at all times, indeed—as to this, I say, no one can entertain a doubt. But it appears to me that municipal, or any other regulations for the purpose, are in palpable violation of the Constitution. To declare a thing immoral, and therefore inexpedient, at *all* times, is one thing—to declare it immoral on Sunday, and therefore to forbid it on that particular day, is quite another. Why not equally forbid it on Saturday, which is the Sabbath of the Jew? In particularizing Sunday, we legislate for the protection and convenience of a sect; and although this sect are the majority, this fact can by no means justify the violation of a great principle—the perfect freedom of conscience—the entire separation of Church and State. Were every individual in America known to be in favor of any "Sunday" enactment, even Congress would have no authority to enact it, and it might be violated with impunity. Nothing short of a change in the Constitution could effect what even the *whole people*, in the case I have supposed, should desire.

When you visit Gotham, you should ride out the Fifth Avenue, as far as the distributing reservoir, near Forty-third Street, I believe. The prospect from the walk around the reservoir is particularly beautiful. You can see, from this elevation, the north reservoir at Yorkville; the whole city to the Battery; with a large portion of the harbor, and long reaches of the Hudson and East rivers. Perhaps even a finer view, however, is to be obtained from the summit of the white, light-house-looking shot-tower which stands on the East river, at Fifty-fifth Street, or thereabouts.

A day or two since I procured a light skiff, and with the aid of a pair of *sculls* (as they here term short oars, or paddles) made my way around Blackwell's Island, on a voyage of discovery and exploration. The chief interest of the adventure lay in the scenery of the Manhattan shore, which is here particularly picturesque. The houses are, without exception, *frame*, and antique. Nothing very modern has been attempted—a necessary result of the subdivision of the whole island into streets and town-lots. I could not look on the magnificent cliffs, and stately trees, which at every moment met my view, without a sigh for their inevitable doom—inevitable and swift. In twenty years, or thirty at farthest, we shall see here nothing more romantic than shipping, warehouses, and wharves.

Trinity Church is making rapid strides to completion. When finished, it will be unequalled in America, for richness, elegance, and general beauty. I suppose you know that the property of this Church is some fifteen millions, but that, at present, its income is narrow (about seventy thousand dollars, I believe) on account of the long leases at which most of its estates are held. They are now, however, generally expiring.

*    *    *    *    *

The Gothamites, not yet having made sufficient fools of themselves in their fete-ing and festival-ing of Dickens, are already on the *qui vive* to receive Bulwer in a similar manner. If I mistake not, however, the author of "The Last Days of Pompeii" will not be willing "to play Punch and Judy" for the amusement of an American rabble. His character, apart from his book-reputation, is little understood in this country, where he is regarded very much in the light of a mere dandy, a *roue*, and a misanthrope. He has many high qualities— among which generosity and indomitable energy are conspicuous. It is much in his favor that, although born to independence, he has not suffered his talents to be buried in indolence, or pleasure. *He* never went to any public school;—this is not generally known. He graduated at Cambridge; but owes his education chiefly to himself. He once made the tour of England and Scotland, on foot, and of France on horseback; these things smack little of the dandy. His first publication was a poem, at three and twenty.

When I spoke of Bulwer's probably refusing to do, what Dickens made no scruple of doing, I by no means intended a disparagement of the latter. Dickens is a man of *far higher genius* than Bulwer. Bulwer is thoughtful, analytic, industrious, artistical; and therefore will write the better book upon the whole; but Dickens, at times, rises to an unpremeditated elevation altogether beyond the flight—beyond the ability—perhaps even beyond the appreciation, of his contemporary. Dickens, with care and education, might have written "The Last of the Barons"; but nothing short of a miracle could have galvanized Bulwer into the conception of the concluding portion of the "Curiosity Shop."

MAY 27, 1844

The foot-race, yesterday, at the Beacon Course, attracted a wonderful share of the public attention.—Eleven thousand persons are said to have been present, and several of our morning papers issued Extras, to satisfy the general curiosity, at a late hour in the afternoon. You have already heard that Stannard was the winner, and that he did *not* accomplish the ten miles within the hour; being one hour, four minutes, and thirty seconds, on the road. He *walked* the last two or three hundred yards, however; his sole antagonist (towards the end of the race) having fallen, shortly after completing his ninth mile. There can be no doubt that Stannard could have run the ten miles within the time stipulated (as he did, easily, in 1835), and thus have secured five hundred, in place of three hundred dollars. He was, no doubt, influenced, in holding back, by the hope of a future bet. I myself did not see the contest; feeling little interest in feats of merely physical strength, or agility, when performed by rational beings. The speed of a horse is sublime—that of a man absurd. I always find myself fancying how very readily he could be beaten by an ass. In the same way, when Herr Kline curvets upon a rope, I say to myself "how any ordinary baboon would turn up its nose at his antics!" Touching the actual feat now in question—ten miles within the hour—I have not only accomplished it myself, but firmly believe that there are at least one thousand men, in our western districts, who could perform, with proper training, *twelve*, with all ease. The true reason why "ten miles within the hour" is considered a marvel, is to be found in the fact (not generally understood) that the most active men—those in the highest physical condition—are seldom to be met with among "the lower classes" of society—among those who alone ever contend, in public, for the honors of the *athletae*.

One of the truest curiosities of Gotham is the great raree-show of Messieurs Tiffany, Young, and Ellis, Broadway, at the corner of Warren. They are very tasteful and industrious importers of the various fancy manufactures of France, England, Germany, and China. Their warehouses are, beyond doubt, the most richly filled of any in America; forming one immense *knicknackatory* of *virtu*. The perfumery department is especially rare. I notice, also, particularly, a beautiful assortment of Swiss osier-work; chess-men—some sets costing five hundred dollars; paintings on rice-paper, in books and sheets; tile for fencing ornamental grounds; fine old bronzes and curiosities from the ancient temples; fillogram articles, in great variety; a vast display of bizarre fans; ranging, in price, from sixpence to seventy-five dollars; solid carved ebony and "landscape-marble" chairs, tables, sofas, &c.; apparatus for stamping initials on paper; Berlin iron and "*artistique*" candle-sticks, taper-stands, perfume-burners, *et cetera, et cetera.*

There is little political excitement; or else it lies "too deep for tears"—too profound for ordinary observation. "Polk Houses," "Polk Oyster Cellars," and "Polk hats, gloves, and walking-canes," are already contending with their rivals of Clay. One poor hotel-keeper had half-painted the sign of a "Wright Restaurant"; but the next mail convinced him that Wright was wrong, and so he plastered it over with "Dallas."

Mr. Harper has failed, I am truly happy to say, in an attempt to stop the running of the Harlaem rail-road cars upon Sunday. There are loud complaints, on the part of the "original Natives," that the new authorities have made nearly all the appointments from the ranks of the Whigs. There can be no doubt that patriotism (well paid) is a capital thing.

JUNE 4, 1844

Brooklyn has been increasing with great rapidity of late years. This is owing, partly, to the salubrity of its situation; but chiefly to its vicinity to the business portion of the city; the low price of ferriage (two cents); the facility of access, which can be obtained at all hours, except two in the morning; and, especially, to the high rents of New York. Brooklyn, you know, is much admired by the Gothamites; and, in fact, much has been done by Nature for the place. But this much the New Yorkers have contrived very thoroughly to spoil. I know few towns which inspire me with so great disgust and contempt. It puts me often in mind of a city of silvered-gingerbread; no doubt you have seen this article of confectionery in some of the Dutch boroughs of Pennsylvania. Brooklyn, on the immediate shore of the

Sound, has, it is true, some tolerable residences; but the majority, throughout, are several steps beyond the preposterous. What can be more sillily and pitiably absurd than palaces of painted white pine, fifteen feet by twenty?—and of such is this boasted "city of villas." You see nowhere a cottage—everywhere a temple which "might have been Grecian had it not been Dutch"—which might have been tasteful had it not been Gothamite—a square box, with Doric or Corinthian pillars, supporting a frieze of unseasoned timber, roughly planed, and daubed with, at best, a couple of coats of whitey-brown paint. This "pavilion" has, usually, a flat roof, covered with red zinc, and surrounded by a balustrade; if not surmounted by something nondescript, intended for a cupola, but wavering in character, between a pigeon-house, a sentry-box, and a pig-sty. The steps, at the front-door, are many, and bright yellow, and from their foot a straight alley of tan-bark, arranged between box-hedges, conducts the tenant, in glory, to the front-gate—which, with the wall of the whole, is of tall white pine boards, painted sky-blue. If we add to this a fountain, giving out a pint of real water per hour, through the mouth of a leaden cat-fish standing upon the tip-end of his tail, and surrounded by a circle of admiring "conchs" (as they here call the strombuses), we have a quite perfect picture of a Brooklynite "villa." In point of downright iniquity—of absolute atrocity—such sin, I mean, as would consign a man, inevitably, to the regions of Pluto— I really can see little difference between the putting up such a house as this, and blowing up a House of Parliament, or cutting the throat of one's grandfather.

The street-cries, and other nuisances to the same effect, are particularly disagreeable here. Immense charcoal-waggons infest the most frequented thorough-fares, and give forth a din which I can liken to nothing earthly (unless, perhaps, a gong), from some metallic, triangular contrivance within the bowels of the "infernal machine." This is a free country, I have heard, and wish to believe if I can; but I cannot perceive how it would materially interfere with our freedom to put an end to these *tintamarres*. A man may do what he pleases with his own (and the principle applies as well to a man's waggon, as to a man's snuff-box, or wife), provided, in so doing, he incommode not his neighbor; this is one of the commonest precepts of common law. But the amount of general annoyances wrought by street-noises is incalculable; and this matter is worthy our very serious attention. It would be difficult to say, for example, how much of *time*, more valuable than money, is lost, in a large city, to no purpose, for the convenience of the fishwomen, the charcoal-men, and the monkey-exhibitors. How often does it happen that where two individuals are transacting business of vital importance, where fate hangs upon every syllable and upon every moment—how frequently does it occur that all conversation is delayed, for five or even ten minutes at a time, until these devil's-triangles have got out of hearing, or until the leathern throats of the clam-and-cat-fish venders have been hallooed, and shrieked, and yelled, into a temporary hoarseness and silence!

The din of the vehicles, however, is even more thoroughly, and more intolerably a nuisance. Are we never to have done with these unmeaning round stones?—than which a more ingenious contrivance for driving men mad through sheer noise, was undoubtedly never invented. It is difficult to foresee what mode of street-pavement will come, finally, into vogue; but we should have *some* change, and that forthwith, or we must have new and more plentiful remedies for headache. The twelve-inch cubes of stone (square, with the upper surface roughened) make, perhaps, the most durable, and, in many respects, the best road; they are, however, expensive, and the noise they emit is objectionable, although in a much less degree than the round stones. Of the stereatomic wooden pavement, we hear nothing, now, at all. The people seem to have given it up altogether—but nothing better could be invented. We inserted the blocks, without preparation, and they failed. Therefore, we abandoned the experiment. Had they been Kyanized, the result would have been very different, and the wooden causeways would have been in extensive use throughout the country. In England, where wood is costly, it might not be preferred to stone, but here it must and, finally, will. The Kyanizing, or mineralizing, is a simple process, and cheap. Put a pound of corrosive sublimate (bi-chloride of Mercury) into sixteen gallons of water, and in this mixture immerse a piece of sound wood (either green or seasoned) for forty-eight hours (more or less as the wood is thicker or thinner). At the end of this time the wood *cannot be rotted*. It has assumed a metallic hardness and texture, is much increased in weight, and will last as long as granite. In the pavement with ordinary wood, although the road be arched, the soft, rotting material yields to heavy pressure, the whole arch sinks, and the fabric is soon destroyed—to say nothing of the speedy decay of the upper surface. The Kyanized wood would not yield an inch, and therefore would never be displaced; and, never rotting, would last for ages as good as in the beginning. The present retail cost of the bi-chloride of Mercury is, I believe, about ninety cents per pound; but if an extensive demand for the article should arise (as would be the case were we to adopt the Kyanized road) the quick-silver mines of South America, now abandoned, would be again put into operation, and we might get the mineral for thirty or forty cents, if not for less. In point of cheapness, freedom from noise, ease of cleaning, pleasantness to the hoof, and, finally, in point of durability, there is *no* causeway equal to that of the Kyanized wood. But it will take us, as usual, fully ten years to make this discovery. In the meantime, the present experiments with the un-prepared wood will answer very well for the profit of the street-menders, and for the amusement of common-councils—who will, perhaps, in the next instance, experiment with soft-soap, or sauer-kraut.

Some person, falling from the roof of a house, and receiving se-vere injury, has been wrapped up, by somebody else, in a wet sheet, and not immediately dying in consequence, but getting well in spite of the sheets, somebody else, again, has written a letter to the "Tribune," extolling the "Hydropathy," or water-cure, of that monarch of the charlatans, Priessnitz. Whereupon, all the medical world of Gotham are by the ears. They will remain so, I hope, until you hear from me again.

J U N E   1 2 ,   1 8 4 4

In point of *natural* beauty, as well as of convenience, the harbor of New York has scarcely its equal in the northern hemisphere; but, as

in the case of Brooklyn, the Gothamites have most grievously disfigured it by displays of landscape and architectural *taste*. More atrocious *pagodas*, or what not—for it is indeed difficult to find a name
for them—were certainly never imagined than the greater portion
of those which affront the eye, in every nook and corner of the bay,
and, more particularly, in the vicinity of New Brighton. If these
monstrosities appertain to taste, then it is to taste in its dying
agonies.

Speaking of harbors; I have been much surprised at observing an
attempt, on the part of a Philadelphian paper, to compare Boston, as
a port, with New York; and in instituting the comparison, the journal in question is so bold as to assert that the largest class of ships
cannot pass the bar of this harbor at low water. I believe this to be
quite a mistake:——is it not?

Foreigners are apt to speak of the great length of Broadway. It is
no doubt a long street; but we have many much longer in
Philadelphia. If I do not greatly err, Front street offers an unbroken
line of houses for *four miles*, and is, unquestionably, the longest street
in America, if not in the world. Grant, the gossiping and twaddling
author of "Random Recollections of the House of Lords," "The Great
Metropolis," &c., &c., in mentioning some London thoroughfare of
two miles and three-quarters, calls it, with an absolute air, "the most
extensive in the world." The dogmatic bow-wow of this man is the
most amusing thing imaginable. I do believe that out of every ten
matters which he gives to the public as fact, eight, at least, are downright lies, while the other two may be classed either as "doubtful" or
"rigmarole."

The trial of Polly Bodine will take place at Richmond, on
Monday next, and will, no doubt, excite much interest. This woman
may, possibly, escape;—for they manage these matters wretchedly in
New York. It is difficult to conceive anything more preposterous than
the whole conduct, for example, of the Mary Rogers affair. The police seemed blown about, in all directions, by every varying puff of
the most unconsidered newspaper opinion. The *truth*, as an end, appeared to be lost sight of altogether. The magistracy suffered the
murderer to escape, while they amused themselves with playing

court, and chopping the technicalities of jurisprudence. Not the least usual error, in such investigations, is the limiting of inquiry to the immediate, with total disregard of the collateral, or circumstantial events. It is malpractice to confine evidence and discussion too vigorously within the limits of the seemingly relevant. Experience has shown, and Philosophy will always show, that a vast portion, perhaps the larger portion of truth, arises from the apparently *ir*relevant. It is through the spirit of this principle that modern science has resolved to *calculate upon the unforseen*. The history of human knowledge has so uniformly shown that to collateral, or incidental, or accidental events, we are indebted for the most numerous and most valuable discoveries, that it has, at length, become necessary, in any prospective view of improvements to make not only large, but the largest allowances for inventions that shall arise by chance—out of the range of expectation. It is, thus, no longer philosophical to base upon what *has been*, a vision of what *is to be*. Accident is admitted as a portion of the substructure. We make chance a matter of absolute certainty. We subject the unlooked-for and unimagined to the mathematical *formulae* of the schools. But what I wish now to observe is, that the small magistracies are too prone to ape the airs and echo the rectangular precepts of the courts. And, moreover, *very* much of what is rejected as evidence by a court, is the best of evidence to the intellect. For the court, guiding itself by the general principles of evidence—the recognized and *booked* principles—is adverse from swerving at particular instances. And this steadfast adherence to principle, with systematic disregard of the conflicting exception, is a sure mode of attaining the *maximum* of attainable truth, in any long sequence of time. The practice, *in mass*, is, therefore, philosophical; but it is none the less certain that it engenders, in many extraordinary instances, a vast amount of individual error. I have good reason to believe that it will do public mischief in the coming trial of Polly Bodine.

The literary world of Gotham is not particularly busy. Mr. Willis, I see, has issued a very handsome edition of his poems—the only complete edition—with a portrait. Few men have received more abuse, deserving it less, than the author of "Melanie." I never read a paper from his pen, in the "New-Mirror," without regretting his abandonment of Glen-Mary, and the tranquility and leisure he might there have found. In its retirement he might have accomplished much, both for himself and for posterity; but, chained to the oar of a mere weekly paper, professedly addressing the frivolous and the fashionable, what can he now hope for but a gradual sinking into the slough of the Public Disregard? For his *sake*, I do sincerely wish the "New-Mirror" would go the way of all flesh. Did you see his Biography in "Graham's Magazine"? The style was a little stilted, but the matter was *true*. Mr. W. deserves nearly all, if not quite all, the commendation there bestowed. Some of the newspapers, in the habit of seeing through mill-stones, attributed the article to Longfellow, whose manner it about as much resembled as a virgin of Massaccio does a virgin of Raphael. The real author (Mr. Landor), although a man of high talent, has a certain set of phrases which cannot easily be mistaken, and is as much a uni-stylist as Cardinal Chigi, who boasted that he wrote with the same pen for fifty years.

JUNE 18, 1844

# JAMES FENIMORE COOPER

*James Fenimore Cooper (1789–1851), America's first great novelist, may be best known for Natty Bumppo stalking through the wilderness; but he lived for some years in New York City, where he shared the literary laurels with Washington Irving. Growing conservative and bitterly litigious as his career advanced, Cooper came to despise New York, seeing it as a symbol of the mass values corrupting American democracy—and in his novel* Home as Found *he even put it to the torch. Here, however, in this excerpt from* Satanstoe *(1845), a novel set in the mid-eighteenth century, he wrote memorably about the black community's Pinkster holiday, in the early and, to Cooper, still innocent days of the city's youth.*

## FROM *SATANSTOE*

WE PROCEEDED along the wharves in a body, admiring the different vessels that lined them. About nine o'clock, all three of us passed up Wall-Street, on the stoops of which no small portion of its tenants were already seated, enjoying the sight of the negroes, as, with happy, "shining," faces they left the different dwellings, to hasten to the Pinkster field. Our passage through the street attracted a good deal of attention, for, being all three strangers it was not to be supposed we could be thus seen in a body, without exciting a remark. Such a thing could hardly have been expected in London itself.

After showing Jason the City Hall, Trinity Church, and the City Tavern, we went out of town, taking the direction of a large common that the King's officers had long used for a parade ground, and which has since been called the Park, though it would be difficult to say why, since it is barely a paddock in size, and certainly has never been used to keep any animals wilder than the boys of the town. A park I suppose it will one day become, though it has little at present that comports with my ideas of such a thing. On this common there was the Pinkster ground, which was now quite full of people, as well as of animation.

There was nothing new in a Pinkster frolic either to Dirck, or to myself, though Jason gazed at the whole procedure with wonder. He was born within seventy miles of that very spot, but had not the smallest notion, before, of such a holiday as Pinkster. There are few blacks in Connecticut, I believe, and those that are there, are so ground down in the Puritan mill, that they are neither fish, flesh, nor red herring, as we say of a non-descript. No man ever heard of a festival in New-England that had not some immediate connection with the saints, or with politics.

Jason was at first confounded with the noises, dances, music, and games that were going on. By this time, nine-tenths of the blacks of the city, and of the whole country within thirty, or forty miles, indeed, were collected in thousands in those fields, beating banjoes, singing African songs, drinking, and most of all laughing, in a way that seemed to set their very hearts rattling within their ribs. Every thing wore the aspect of good humour, though it was good humour in its broadest and coarsest forms. Every sort of common game was in requisition while drinking was far from being neglected. Still, not a soul was drunk. A drunken negro, indeed, is by no means a common thing. The features that distinguish a Pinkster frolic from the usual scenes at fairs, and other merry makings, however, were of African origin. It is true, there are not now, nor were there then, many blacks among us of African birth; but the traditions and usages of their original country were so far preserved as to produce a marked difference between this festival, and one of European origin. Among other things, some were making music, by beating on skins drawn over the ends of hollow logs, while others were dancing to it, in a manner to show that they felt infinite delight. This, in particular, was said to be a usage of their African progenitors.

Hundreds of whites were walking through the fields, amused spectators. Among these last, were a great many children of the better class, who had come to look at the enjoyment of those who attended them in their own ordinary amusements. Many a sable nurse did I see that day, chaperoning her young master, or young mistress, or both together, through the various groups, demanding of all, and

receiving from all the respect that one of these classes was accustomed to pay to the other.

A great many young ladies between the ages of fifteen and twenty
were also in the fields, either escorted by male companions, or, what
was equally as certain of producing deference, under the care of old
female nurses, who belonged to the race that kept the festival.

✦ ✦ ✦ ✦ ✦

As has been said, most of the blacks had been born in the colony, but
there were some native Africans among them. New York never had
slaves on the system of the southern planters, or in gangs of hundreds, to labour in the fields under overseers, and who lived apart in
cabins of their own; but, our system of slavery was strictly domestic,
the negro almost invariably living under the same roof with the master, or, if his habitation was detached, as certainly sometimes happened, it was still near at hand, leaving both races as parts of a
common family. In the country, the negro men toiled in the fields,
but it was as ordinary husbandmen; and, in the cases of those who
laboured on their own property, or as tenants of some extensive
landlord, the black did his work at his master's side. Then all, or
nearly all, our household servants were, and still are, blacks, leaving
that department of domestic economy almost exclusively in their
hands, with the exception of those cases in which the white females
busied themselves also in such occupations, united to the usual su-
pervision of the mistresses. Among the Dutch, in particular, the
treatment of the negro was of the kindest character, a trusty field
slave often having quite as much to say on the subject of the tillage
and the crops, as the man who owned both the land he worked, and
himself.

A party of native Africans kept us for half an hour. The scene
seemed to have revived their early associations, and they were carried away with their own representation of semi-savage sports. The
American-born blacks gazed at this group with intense interest also,
regarding them as so many ambassadors from the land of their ancestors, to enlighten them in usages, and superstitious lore, that

were more peculiarly suited to their race. The last even endeavoured to imitate the acts of the first, and, though the attempt was often ludicrous, it never failed on the score of intention and gravity. Nothing was done in the way of caricature, but much in the way of respect and affection.

Lest the habits of this generation should pass away and be forgotten, of which I see some evidence, I will mention a usage that was quite common among the Dutch, and which has passed in some measure, into the English families that have formed connections with the children of Holland. Two of these intermarriages had so far brought the Littlepages within the pale, that the usage to which I allude, was practised in my own case. The custom was this: when a child of the family reached the age of six, or eight, a young slave of the same age and sex, was given to him, or her, with some little formality, and from that moment the fortunes of the two were considered to be, within the limits of their respective pursuits and positions, as those of man and wife. It is true, divorces do occur, but it is only in cases of gross misconduct, and quite as often the misconduct is on the side of the master, as on that of the slave. A drunkard may get in debt, and be compelled to part with his blacks; this one among the rest; but this particular negro remains with him as long as any thing remains. Slaves that seriously misbehave, are usually sent to the islands, where the toil on the sugar plantations proves a very sufficient punishment.

1845

# MARGARET FULLER

When Margaret Fuller (1810–50) accepted Horace Greeley's offer to contribute articles to his New-York Tribune, she was already known as the author of Woman in the Nineteenth Century, editor of the Transcendentalist journal The Dial, and organizer of a famous series of seminars, the Boston "Conversations." In moving from Boston to New York and writing for the penny press, she saw more than an opportunity to expand her readership. As the writer Hans Bergmann has commented, "She thought of working for the newspapers as an erasure of the self, a conscious decision to use her talent for the benefit of others, and seemed to struggle to imagine a kind of writing that was selfless and yet serious." Greeley invited her to describe the city's public charity institutions—then, oddly enough, part of the standard visitor's tour. Fuller's pieces avoided the patronizingly "colorful," emphasizing instead issues of client dignity, privacy, and rehabilitation. Her twenty-month encounter with New York City, she wrote, had offered "a richer and more varied exercise for thought than twenty years could in any other part of these United States."

OUR CITY CHARITIES
VISIT TO BELLEVUE ALMS HOUSE, TO THE
FARM SCHOOL, THE ASYLUM FOR THE INSANE,
AND PENITENTIARY ON BLACKWELL'S ISLAND.

THE ASPECT of Nature was sad; what is worse, it was dull and dubious, when we set forth on these visits. The sky was leaden and lowering, the air unkind and piercing, the little birds sat mute and astonished at the departure of the beautiful days which had lured them to premature song. It was a suitable day for such visits. The pauper establishments that belong to a great city take the place of the skeleton at the banquets of old. They admonish us of stern realities, which must bear the same explanation as the frequent blight of Nature's bloom. They should be looked at by all, if only for their own sakes, that they may not sink listlessly into selfish ease, in a world so full of disease. They should be looked at by all who wish to enlighten themselves as to the means of aiding their fellow-creatures in any way, public or private. For nothing can really be done till the right principles are discovered, and it would seem they still need to be discovered or elucidated, so little is done, with a great deal of desire in the heart of the community to do what is right. Such visits are not yet calculated to encourage and exhilarate, as does the story of the Prodigal Son; they wear a grave aspect and suit the grave mood of a *cold* Spring day.

At the Alms House there is every appearance of kindness in the guardians of the poor, and there was a greater degree of cleanliness and comfort than we had expected. But the want of suitable and sufficient employment is a great evil. The persons who find here either a permanent or temporary refuge have scarcely any occupation provided except to raise vegetables for the establishment, and prepare clothing for themselves. The men especially have the most vagrant, degraded air, and so much indolence must tend to confirm them in every bad habit. We were told that, as they are under no strict discipline, their labor at the various trades could not be made profitable; yet surely the means of such should be provided, even at some expense. Employments of various kinds must be absolutely needed, if only to counteract the bad effects of such a position. Every establishment in aid of the poor should be planned with a view to their education. There should be instruction, both practical and in the use of books, openings to a better intercourse than they can obtain from their miserable homes, correct notions, as to cleanliness, diet, and fresh air. A great deal of pains would be lost in their case, as with all other arrangements for the good of the many, but here and there the seed would fall into the right places, and some members of the downtrodden million, rising a little from the mud, would raise the whole body with them.

As we saw old women enjoying their dish of gossip and their dish of tea, and mothers able for a while to take care in peace of their poor little children, we longed and hoped for that genius, who shall teach how to make, of these establishments, places of rest and instruction, not of degradation.

The causes which make the acceptance of public charity so much more injurious to the receiver than that of private are obvious, but surely not such that the human mind which has just invented the magnetic telegraph and Anastatic printing, may not obviate them. A deeper religion at the heart of Society would devise such means. Why should it be that the poor may still feel themselves men; paupers not? The poor man does not feel himself injured but benefitted by the charity of the doctor who gives him back the bill he is unable to pay, because the doctor is acting from intelligent sympathy—from love. Let Society do the same. She might raise the man, who is accepting her bounty, instead of degrading him.

Indeed, it requires great nobleness and faith in human nature, and God's will concerning it, for the officials not to take the tone toward these under their care, which their vices and bad habits prompt, but which must confirm them in the same. Men treated with respect are reminded of self-respect, and if there is a sound spot left in the character, the healthy influence spreads.

We were sorry to see mothers with their new-born infants exposed to the careless scrutiny of male visitors. In the hospital, those who had children scarce a day old were not secure from the gaze of the stranger. This cannot be pleasant to them, and, if they have not refinement to dislike it, those who have should teach it to them. But we suppose there is no woman who has so entirely lost sight of the feelings of girlhood as not to dislike the scrutiny of strangers at a time which is sacred, if any in life is. Women they may like to see, even strangers, if they can approach them with delicacy.

In the yard of the hospital, we saw a little Dutch girl, a dwarf, who would have suggested a thousand poetical images and fictions to the mind of Victor Hugo or Sir Walter Scott. She had been brought here to New-York, as we understood, by some showman and then deserted, so that this place was her only refuge. No one could communicate with her or know her feelings, but she showed what they were, by running to the gate whenever it was opened, though treated with familiar kindness and seeming pleased by it. She had a large head, ragged dark hair, a glowering wizard eye, an uncouth yet pleasant smile, like an old child;—she wore a gold ring, and her complexion was as yellow as gold, if not as bright; altogether she looked like a gnome, more than any attempt we have ever known to embody in Art that fabled inhabitant of the mines and secret caves of earth.

From the Alms House we passed in an open boat to the Farm School. We were unprepared to find this, as we did, only a school upon a small farm, instead of one in which study is associated with labor. The children are simply taken care of and taught the common English branches till they are twelve years old, when they are bound out to various kinds of work. We think this plan very injudicious. It is bad enough for the children of rich parents, not likely in after life to bear a hard burden, and who are, at any rate, supplied with those various excitements required to develope the character in the earliest years; it is bad enough, we say, for these to have no kind of useful labor mingled with their plays and studies. Even these children would expand more, and be more variously called forth, and better prepared for common life, if another course were pursued. But, in schools like this at the farm, where the children, on leaving it, will be at once called on for adroitness and readiness of mind and body, and where the absence of natural ties and the various excitements that rise from them inevitably give to life a mechanical routine calculated to cramp and chill the character, it would be peculiarly desirable to provide various occupations, and such as are calculated to prepare for common life. As to economy of time, there is never time lost, by mingling other pursuits with the studies of children; they have vital energy enough for many things at once, and learn more from books when their attention is quickened by other kinds of culture.

Some of these children were pretty, and they were healthy and well-grown, considering the general poverty or vice of the class from which they were taken. That terrible scourge, opthalmia, disfigured many among them. This disease, from some cause not yet detected, has been prevalent here for many years. We trust it may yield to the change of location next summer. There is not water enough here to give the children decent advantages as to bathing. This, too, will be remedied by the change. The Principal, who has been almost all his life connected with this establishment and that at Bellevue, seemed to feel a lively interest in his charge. He has arranged the dormitories with excellent judgment, both as to ventilation and neatness. This, alone, is a great advantage these children have over those of poor families living at home. They may pass the night in healthy sleep, and have thereby a chance for innocent and active days.

We saw with pleasure the little children engaged in the kind of drill they so much enjoy, of gesticulation regulated by singing. It was also pretty to see the babies sitting in a circle and the nurses in the midst feeding them, alternately, with a spoon. It seemed like a nest full of little birds, each opening its bill as the parent returns from her flight.

Hence we passed to the Asylum for the Insane. Only a part of this building is completed, and it is well known that the space is insufficient. Twice as many are inmates here as can be properly accommodated. A tolerable degree, however, of order and cleanliness is preserved. We could not but observe the vast difference between the appearance of the insane here and at Bloomingdale, or other Institutions where the number of attendants and nature of the arrangements permit them to be the objects of individual treatment; that is, where the wants and difficulties of each patient can be distinctly and carefully attended to. At Bloomingdale, the shades of character and feeling were nicely kept up, decorum of manners preserved, and the insane showed in every way that they felt no violent separation betwixt them and the rest of the world, and might easily return to it. The eye, though bewildered, seemed lively, and the tongue prompt. But *here*, insanity appeared in its more stupid, wild, or despairing forms. They crouched in corners; they had no eye for the stranger, no heart for hope, no habitual expectation of light. Just as at the Farm School, where the children show by their unformed features and mechanical movements that they are treated by wholesale, so do these poor sufferers. It is an evil incident to public establishments, and which only a more intelligent public attention can obviate.

One figure we saw, here also, of high poetical interest. It was a woman seated on the floor, in the corner of her cell, with a shawl wrapped gracefully around her head and chest, like a Nun's veil. Her hair was grey, her face attenuated and very pallid, her eyes large, open, fixed and bright with a still fire. She never moved them nor ceased chanting the service of the Church. She was a Catholic, who became insane while preparing to be a Nun. She is surely a Nun now in her heart; and a figure from which a painter might study for some of the most consecrated subjects.

Passing to the Penitentiary, we entered on one of the gloomiest scenes that deforms this great metropolis. Here are the twelve hundred, who receive the punishment due to the vices of so large a portion of the rest. And under what circumstances! Never was punishment treated more simply as a social convenience, without regard to pure right, or a hope of reformation.

Public attention is now so far awake to the state of the Penitentiary that it cannot be long, we trust, before proper means of classification are devised, a temporary asylum provided for those who leave this purgatory, even now, unwilling to return to the inferno from which it has for a time kept them, and means presented likely to lead some, at least, among the many, who seem hardened, to better views and hopes. It must be that the more righteous feeling which has shown itself in regard to the prisons at Sing Sing and elsewhere, must take some effect as to the Penitentiary also. The present Superintendent enters into the necessity of such improvements, and, should he remain there, will do what he can to carry them into effect.

The want of proper matrons, or any matrons, to take the care so necessary for the bodily or mental improvement or even decent condition of the seven hundred women assembled here, is an offence that cries aloud. It is impossible to take the most cursory survey of this assembly of women; especially it is impossible to see them in the Hospital, where the circumstances are a little more favorable, without seeing how many there are in whom the feelings of innocent childhood are not dead, who need only good influences and steady aid to raise them from the pit of infamy and wo into which they have fallen. And, if there was not one that could be helped, at least Society owes them the insurance of a decent condition while here. We trust that interest on this subject will not slumber.

The recognized principles of all such institutions which have any higher object than the punishment of fault, (and we believe few among us are so ignorant as to avow that as the only object, though they may, from want of thought, act as if it were,) are—Classification as the first step, that the bad may not impede those who wish to do well; 2d. Instruction, practical, oral, and by furnishing books which may open entirely new hopes and thoughts to minds oftener darkened than corrupted; 3d. A good Sanitary system, which promotes self-respect, and, through health and purity of body, the same in mind.

In visiting the Tombs the other day, we found the air in the upper galleries unendurable, and felt great regret that those confined there should be constantly subjected to it. Give the free breath of Heaven to all who are still permitted to breathe.—We cannot, however, wonder at finding this barbarity in a prison, having been subjected to it at the most fashionable places of public resort. Dr. Griscom has sent us his excellent lecture on the health of New-York, which we recommend to all who take a vital interest in the city where they live, and have intellect to discern that a cancer on the body must in time affect the head and heart also. We thought, while reading, that it was not surprising typhus fever and opthalmia should be bred in the cellars, while the families of those who live in palaces breathe such infected air at public places, and receive their visitors on New Year's day by candle-light. (That was a sad omen for the New Year— did they mean to class themselves among those who love darkness rather than light?)

We hope to see the two thousand poor people, and the poor children, better situated in their new abode, when we visit them again. The Insane Asylum will gain at once by enlargement of accommodations; but more attendance is also necessary, and, for that purpose, the best persons should be selected. We saw, with pleasure, tame pigeons walking about among the most violent of the insane, but we also saw two attendants with faces brutal and stolid. Such a charge is too delicate to be intrusted to any but excellent persons. Of the

Penitentiary we shall write again. All criticism, however imperfect, should be welcome. There is no reason why New-York should not become a model for other States in these things. There is wealth enough, intelligence, and good desire enough, and *surely, need enough.* If she be not the best cared for city in the world, she threatens to surpass in corruption London and Paris. Such bane as is constantly poured into her veins demands powerful antidotes.

But nothing effectual can be achieved while both measures and men are made the sport of political changes. It is a most crying and shameful evil, which does not belong to our institutions, but is a careless distortion of them, that the men and measures are changed in these institutions with changes from Whig to Democrat, from Democrat to Whig. Churches, Schools, Colleges, the care of the Insane, and suffering Poor, should be preserved from the uneasy tossings of this delirium. The Country, the State, should look to it that only those fit for such officers should be chosen for such, apart from all considerations of political party. Let this be thought of; for without an absolute change in this respect no permanent good whatever can be effected; and farther, let not economy but utility be the rule of expenditure, for, here, parsimony is the worst prodigality.

*NEW-YORK TRIBUNE, 1845*

# GEORGE G. FOSTER

*Like Margaret Fuller, George G. Foster (1814–56) wrote urban sketches for the* Tribune, *where he served as "City Items" editor in the mid-1840's. He was also something of a scoundrel, and was eventually jailed for passing bad checks to his tailor. Foster's books, such as* Fifteen Minutes Around New York, New York In Slices, *and* New York By Gaslight, *capitalized on the city's growing self-consciousness as a metropolis with a set of definable "characters" and habits. The promised rapidity of the takes says something about the perceived pace of New York. (In an addendum to the piece below, he attributes the success of New York's business district to its "fast food" establishments.) While claiming to be writing urban sociology like London's Henry Mayhew, Foster was really a literary entertainer, not above sensationalism (one of his books is called* New York Naked), *and with a talent for framing local color into delectable "slices."*

## THE EATING-HOUSES

"Beefsteakandtatersvegetábesnumbertwenty—Injinhardand sparrowgrassnumbérsixteen!" "Waiter! Waiter! WA-Y-TER!" "Comingsir"—while the rascal's *going* as fast as he can! "*Is* that beef killed for my porterhouse steak I ordered last week?" "Readynminitsir, comingsir, drcklysir—twonsixpence, biledamand cabbage shillin, ricepudn sixpnce, eighteenpence—at the barf you please—lobstaucensammingnumberfour—yes sir!" Imagine a continuous stream of such sounds as these, about the size of the Croton river, flowing through the banks of clattering plates and clashing knives and forks, perfumed with the steam from a mammoth kitchen, roasting, boiling, baking, frying, beneath the floor—crowds of animals with a pair of jaws apiece, wagging in emulation of the one wielded with such terrific effect by SAMSON—and the thermometer which has become ashamed of itself and hides away behind a mountain of hats in the corner, melting up *by degrees* to boiling heat—and you will have some notion of a New York eating-house.

We once undertook to count these establishments in the lower part of the City, but got surfeited on the smell of fried grease before we got half through the first street, and were obliged to go home in a cab. We believe, however, that there can't be less than a hundred of them within half a mile of the Exchange. They are too important a "slice" of New York to be overlooked, and strangers who stop curiosity-hunting after they have climbed the big clock-case at the head of Wall-street, haven't seen half the sights.

A New York eating-house at high tide is a scene which would well repay the labors of an antiquarian or a panoramist, if its spirit and details could be but half preserved. Every thing is done differently in New York from anywhere else—but in eating the difference is more striking than in any other branch of human economy. A thorough-bred diner-down-town will look at a bill of fare, order his dinner, bolt it and himself, and be engaged in putting off a lot of goods upon a greenhorn, while you are getting your napkin fixed over your nankeens (we think the cotton article preferable) and deciding whether you will take ox-tail or mock-turtle. A regular down-towner surveys the kitchen with his nose as he comes up-stairs—selects his dish by intuition, and swallows it by steam and the electro-galvanic battery. As to digesting it, that is none of his business. He has paid all liabilities to his stomach, and that is all he knows or cares about the matter. The stomach must manage its own affairs—he is not in that "line."

Not less than thirty thousand persons engaged in mercantile or financial affairs, dine at eating-houses every day. The work commences punctually at twelve; and from that hour until three or four the havoc is immense and incessant. Taylor at Buena Vista was nothing to it. They sweep every thing—not a fragment is left. The fare is generally bad enough—not nearly equal to that which the cook at the Home above Bleecker saves for the beggars, (generally her own thirteen cousins, "just come over.") It is really wonderful how men of refined tastes and pampered habits, who at home are as fastidious as luxury and a delicate appetite can make them, find it in their hearts—or stomachs either—to gorge such disgusting masses of stringy meat and tepid vegetables, and to go about their business again under the fond delusion that they have dined. But "custom," they say, does wonders; and it seems that the fear of losing it makes our merchant-princes willing to put up with and put down warm swill in lieu of soup, perspiring joints for delicate *entrées*, and corn meal and molasses instead of *meringues à la crême à la rose*.

There are three distinct classes of eating-houses, and each has its model or type. Linnæus would probably classify them as Sweenyorum, Browniverous, and Delmonican. The Sweenyorum is but an extension downward of the Browniverous, which we have already described. The chief difference to be noted between the two is, that while at Brown's the waiters *actually do* pass by you within hail now and then, at Sweeney's no such phenomenon ever by any possibility occurs. The room is laid out like the floor of a church, with tables and benches for four, in place of pews. Along the aisles (of Greece, if you judge by the smell) are ranged at "stated" intervals, the attentive waiters, who receive the dishes, small plate sixpnce, large plate shillin, as they are cut off by the man at the helm, and distribute them on either side, with surprising dexterity and precision. Sometimes a nice bit of rosegoose, tender, may be seen flying down the aisle, without its original wings, followed closely in playful sport by a small plate bilebeef, vegetables, until both arrive at their destination; when goose leaps lightly in front of a poet of the Sunday press, who ordered it probably through a commendable preference for a brother of the quill; while the fat and lazy beef dumps itself down with perfect resignation before the "monstrous jaws" of one of the b'hoys, who has just come from a fire in 49th-street, and is hungry, *some!*

At Brown's we get a bill of fare, with the "extras" all honestly marked off and priced at the margin. But at Sweeney's we save our sixpence and dispense with superfluities. The bill of fare is delivered by a man at the door, regularly engaged for that purpose, and is as follows:

> Biledlamancapersors.
> Rosebeefrosegoorosemuttonantaters—
> Biledamancabbage, vegetables—
> Walkinsirtakaseatsir.

This is certainly clear and distinct as General Taylor's political opinions, and does away with a great deal of lying in print, to which bills of fare as well as newspapers are too much addicted. The Sweeney, or sixpenny cut, is frequented by a more diversified set of customers than either of the others. It is not impossible to see, here, Professor Bush dining cheek-by-jowl with a hod-man off duty, nor to find a blackleg from Park-row seated opposite the police-officer whose manifest destiny it will be one of these days to take him to quod—unless he should happen to have money enough about him to pay for being let go. The editor, the author, the young lawyer, the publisher, the ice-cream man round the corner, the poor physician on his way to patients who don't pay, the young student of divinity learning humility at six shillings a week; the journeyman printer on a batter, and afraid to go home to his wife before he gets sober; in short, all classes who go to make up the great middle stripe of population, concentrate and commingle at Sweeney's. Yet all these varied elements never effervesce into any thing in the slightest degree resembling a disturbance; for eating is a serious business—especially when you have but sixpence and no idea whether the next one has been coined.

It is true that Sweeney's "is emphatically a sixpenny eating-house"—but you must take care what you are about, or you may as well have dined at the Astor.—Unless you know how it is done, you will be nicely done yourself. If you indulge in a second piece of bread, a pickle, a bit of cheese, &c., &c., your bill will be summed up to you something after this fashion:—"Clamsoup sixpnce, rosebeef large, shilln, roastchikn eighteen, extra bread three, butter sixpnce, pickle sixpnce, pudn sixpnce, cheese three, claret (logwood and water alumized) two shilln—seven shilln." If you wish to dine cheaply, be contented with a cheap dinner. Call simply for a small plate of roast beef mixed, (this means mashed turnips and potatoes in equal quantities.) After you have eaten this frugal dish,—and it is as much as any one really *needs* for dinner,—you may send for "bread, hard," drink a tumbler of cool Croton, pay one shilling for the whole, and go about your business like a refreshed and sensible man.

There is still another class of eating-houses, which deserve honorable mention—the cake and coffee shops, of which "Butter-cake Dick's" is a favorable sample.—The chief merit of these establishments is that they are kept open all night, and that hungry Editors or belated idlers can get a plate of biscuits with a lump of butter in the belly for three cents, and a cup of coffee for as much more—or he can regale himself on pumpkin pie at four cents the quarter-section, with a cup of Croton, fresh from the hydrant, gratis. The principal supporters of these luxurious establishments, however, are the firemen and the upper circles of the newsboys, who have made a good business during the day, or have succeeded in pummeling some smaller boy and taking his pennies from him. Here, ranged on wooden benches, the butter-cakes and coffee spread ostentatiously before them, and their intelligent faces supported in the crotch of their joined hands, these autocrats of the press, and the b'hoys, discuss the grave questions as to whether Fourteen *was* at the fire in Front-street first, or whether it is all gas. Here also are decided in advance the relative merits and speed of the boats entered for the next regatta, and points of great pith and moment in the science of the Ring are definitively settled. As midnight comes and passes, the firemen, those children of the dark, gather from unimaginable places, and soon a panorama of red shirts and brown faces lines the walls and fills the whole area of the little cellar. They are generally far more moderate than politicians and less noisy than gentlemen. At the first tingle of the fire-bell they leap like crouching greyhounds, and are in an instant darting through the street towards their respective engine-houses—whence they emerge dragging their ponderous machines behind them, ready to work like Titans all night and all day, exposing themselves to every peril of life and limb, and performing incredible feats of daring strength, to save the property of people who know nothing about them, care nothing for them, and perhaps will scarcely take the trouble to thank them.

But of all this by itself. The type of eating-house of which we have not spoken is the expensive and aristocratic *restaurant* of which Delmonico's is the only complete specimen in the United States— and this, we have it on the authority of travelled epicures, is equal in every respect, in its appointments and attendance as well as the quality and execution of its dishes, to any similar establishment in Paris itself. We have not left ourselves room in this number to speak in detail of this famous *restaurant*, nor of its *habitués*. It well deserves, however, a separate notice; and a look through its well-filled yet not crowded saloons, and into its admirable *cuisine* will enable us to pass an hour very profitably—besides obtaining a dinner which, as a work of art, ranks with a picture by Huntingdon, a poem by Willis, or a statue by Powers—a dinner which is not merely a quantity of food deposited in the stomach, but is in every sense and to all the senses a great work of art.

Some persons who eat—and they form a pretty large portion of the community—may have experienced a shudder of horror at the freedom with which we sliced up the Eating-Houses. As if we were not at liberty to make free with an old friend! Why, we have lived, man and boy, something over a quarter of a century at the downtown Eating-Houses—being in the habit of breakfasting at Lovejoy's, dining at Brown's, and taking our tea and biscuit at Sweeney's. But a picture is a picture; and in order to give the reader or spectator a correct idea of the subject under treatment, it is necessary to dash in the light and shade with a free hand. Exact portraiture is as common-place as—as—the National Academy; while an artistic representation relieves the mind of the material lumber which oppresses it, and presents nothing but the abstract picture to the eye. Whether we possess the faculty of painting such a picture or not, does not depend on the Eating-Houses—they are as economical and as indispensable as ever.

And now, since we are at the confessional, we are willing to admit that the Eating-Houses are immensely valuable. New York could no more exist without her Eating-Houses, than you, reader, could get along without your stomach. In the Winter, when the days are as short as pie-crust, and one has scarcely time to get to his counting-house before it is time to shut up, what business could be transacted, if the fifty thousand people who do business down-town were obliged to go home for their dinners? The progress of trade and population has driven the dwelling-houses all so far uptown, that if it were not for the Eating-Houses, one meal a day would be all that a business man would have any right to expect. Now, he carries on till a favorable lull occurs—an eddy in the vast *counter*-current that is bearing him on to fortune—and slipping quietly out to Brown's or the Alderman's, refreshes the inward man, and is back again in ten minutes, ready to serve a customer, or make out a bill. Consider that this is done by at least fifty thousand every day in New York, and you will be able to begin to calculate the immense amount of time saved to the mercantile and business community by the Eating-Houses.

If the Eating-Houses are so useful in Winter, they become absolutely indispensable in Summer. The thrifty merchant or tradesman sends his wife and children to board in some cool and sequestered place in the vicinity of the city, (and surely nothing can compare with the facilities of New York in this respect,) and where he can join them every evening after the business of the day is over. But all through the hot and glaring day, he must be in town working, working, working. What would he do without the Eating-Houses? Why, literally, he must starve! And then, what would become of his wife and children? Horrible thought!

Indeed, upon taking a cool and calm view of the matter, we are inclined to believe that, notwithstanding their steaming-rooms and thin soups, it is to the Eating-Houses that New York is in a great measure indebted for that continuous rush of commercial activity around her great business centres, which so strikingly distinguishes her from all other cities. Her geographical position doubtless contributes also to this; but without the Eating-Houses, situated right in the heart of trade, and providing abundant and wholesome meals at a cost absolutely nothing to a business man, compared with the value of ten minutes' time in the middle of the day, neither the mere geographical position, nor the immense pressure of trade, would produce that inexhaustible glow of excitement, that ceaseless whirl of activity, which keeps the wine of life continually effervescing and sending off sparks and scintillations which imbue the very atmosphere with a vital and intoxicating essence—the pungent perfume of gold.

In such extensive establishments as the New York Eating-Houses, conducted with such incredible celerity, and dining hungry men by the regiment, some "noise and confusion" are absolutely indispensable. Just think of it—two or three thousand people going up and down the same stairs, and dining at the same tables, within three hours! Such a scene cannot be imagined by any but a New Yorker. Nowhere else, either in Europe or America, does any thing like it exist. It is the culmination, the consummation, the concentration of Americanism; with all its activity, perseverance, energy, and practicality in their highest state of development. In this view the Eating-Houses of New York rise to the dignity of a national institution, and are well worth the most observant analysis.

NEW YORK IN SLICES, 1848

# GRANT THORBURN

In his autobiography, the tradesman-writer Grant Thorburn (1773–1863) left a detailed account of life in post-colonial New York. A native Scotsman, he landed in the city in 1794. After his grocery was forced out of business by the opening of a larger store nearby (retail competition, ever the New York story—see Malamud's "The Cost of Living," page 712), he stumbled into selling plants, although at first he knew nothing about gardening. Eventually, he built the first thriving seed catalogue business in the United States. Success enabled him to indulge his taste for writing and for mingling in cultured society (the actress Fanny Kemble, who became friendly with Thorburn, described him as "the little man, whose appearance is that of a dwarf in some fairy tale"). Credulous yet tough, pious but happy to befriend the deist Tom Paine, he appears before us the literary version of a Copley portrait.

## FROM *LIFE AND WRITINGS OF GRANT THORBURN*

I NOW kept a grocery, and had a good run of customers: I still resided at No. 22 Nassau street.

On the east corner of Nassau and Liberty streets there lived the venerable old gentleman, Mr. Isaac Van Hook, so well known as the sexton of the New Dutch church opposite his house, for nearly fifty years. James Laing and William Smith, both cabinet-makers, and carrying on a respectable business, having in their employment ten or twelve journeymen and apprentices; these men took a mad resolution, gave up the business, sold their stock, hired the corner house over the head of poor old Van Hook,* turned him and his tobacco-

---

*This Mr. Van Hook was so great a smoker, that the pipe was not out of his mouth perhaps one hour in the twenty-four: he used the longest kind of Liverpool pipes. In the house, in the street, in the church, and in his bed, have I seen him with the pipe in his mouth. One day, a wag sent a countryman to ask if he sold any *smoked tongues?* The old man took the hint, said he had none to sell, but directed him across the street to old Mr. Watkey's, another noted smoker; between them they *smoked* the man, and, after drinking some good old Hollands, parted good friends.

pipes out of doors, and commenced the grocery business. Theirs being a corner, took away the most of my customers; insomuch that I was obliged to look round for some other mode to support my family. This, you may be sure, I considered a great misfortune; but, in the sequel, you will see that Providence was thus preparing the way to put me into a more agreeable and profitable business; and what we may often think is a great misfortune at the time, is only making the way for a greater blessing.

About this time the ladies in New York were beginning to show their taste for flowers; and it was customary to sell the empty flower-pots in the grocery stores; these articles also comprised part of my stock.

In the fall of the year, when the plants wanted shifting, preparatory to their being placed in the parlor, I was often asked for pots of a handsomer quality, or better make. As I stated above, I was looking round for some other means to support my family. All at once it came into my mind to take and paint some of my common flower-pots with green varnish paint, thinking it would better suit the taste of the ladies than the common brick-bat colored ones. I painted two pair, and exposed them in front of my window. I remember, just as I had placed the two pair of pots in front of my window on the outside, I was standing on the sidewalk, admiring their appearance, a carriage came along, having the glasses let down, and one lady only in the carriage. As the carriage passed my shop, her eye lit on the pots; she put her head out at the window, and looked back, as far as she could see, on the pots. Thinks I, this will take; and it did take—for these two pots were the links of a chain by means of which Providence was leading me into my extensive seed establishment. They soon drew attention, and were sold. I painted six pair; they soon went the same way. Being thus encouraged, I continued painting and selling to good advantage: this was in the fall of 1802.

One day, in the month of April following, I observed a man, for the first time, selling flower-plants in the Fly Market, which then stood at the foot of Maiden Lane. As I carelessly passed along, I took a leaf, and rubbing it between my fingers and thumb, asked him what was the name of it. He answered, a rose-geranium. This, as far as I can recollect, was the first time that I ever heard that there was a geranium in the world; as, before this, I had no taste for, nor paid any attention to, plants. I looked a few minutes at the plant, thought it had a pleasant smell, and thought it would look well if removed into one of my green flower-pots, to stand on my counter to draw attention. I remember, after smelling the first leaf of the rose-geranium, and also when I received additions to my stock, how I was struck with wonder and amazement, at the power, wisdom, and goodness of God, in imparting to the *green leaf* of one plant the fragrance of another, such as the balm, musk, pennyroyal, &c. How condescending to our senses, how indulgent, as it were, even to our childish and playful fancies! It was thus my mind was struck when I smelt the first leaf. Thought I, it is strange that a *green leaf* plucked from a plant no way similar, should possess all the flavor of the *flower* plucked from another.

Observe, I did not purchase this plant with the intention of selling it again, but merely to draw attention to my green pots, and let the people see how well the pots looked when the plant was in them. Next day, some one fancied and purchased plant and pot. Next day I went when the market was nearly over, judging the man would sell cheaper, rather than have the trouble of carrying them over the river, as he lived at Brooklyn,—and in those days there was neither steam nor horse-boats. Accordingly I purchased two plants; and having sold them, I began to think that something might be done this way; and so I continued to go at the close of the market, and always bargained for the unsold plants. And the man finding me a useful customer, would assist me to carry them home, and show me how to shift the plants out of his pots and put them into green pots, if my customers wished it. So I soon found by his tongue that he was a Scotchman, and being countrymen, we wrought to one another's hands: thus, from having one plant, in a short time I had fifty. The thing being a novelty, began to draw attention; people carrying their country friends to see the curiosities of the city, would step in to see my plants. In some of these visits the strangers would express a wish to have some of these plants, but having so far to go, could not carry them. Then they would ask if I had no seed of such plants; then, again, others would ask for cabbage, turnip, or radish seed, &c.

These frequent inquiries at length set me to thinking, that if I could get seeds I would be able to sell them; but here lay the difficulty, as no one sold seed in New York, no one of the farmers or gardeners saved more than what they wanted for their own use; there being no market for an overplus. In this dilemma I told my situation to George Inglis, the man from whom I had always bought the plants in the Fly Market. He said he was now raising seeds, with the intention of selling them next spring, along with his plants, in the market; but if I would take his seeds he would quit the market, and stay at home and raise plants and seeds for me to sell. A bargain was immediately struck; I purchased his stock of seeds, amounting to *fifteen dollars*; and thus commenced a business on the 17th of September, 1805, that became the most extensive of the sort in the United States.

It is worth while to look back on the steps by which Providence led me into this business, without my ever planning or intending to become a seedsman.

1. By the introduction of cut-nail machines cutting me off from making a living by my own trade of nail-making.

2. By shutting me up, so that I could not make a living by keeping grocery.

3. By directing my mind to the painting of green pots, which induced me to purchase the first plant that ever drew my attention; and this merely with a view of ornamenting my store, and not for the purpose of sale.

4. In being led, by the sale of this plant, to keep a quantity of them for the same purpose, which induced people to ask for the seed of the plants, and also for vegetable seeds, long before I ever thought of selling seeds.

I now advertised in the papers of the day garden-seeds. In a short time my small stock was all sold out; I knew not where to replace them. In this difficulty a friend stepped into the store, and introduced me to his friend, Mr. Morgan, just arrived from London, having a small invoice of garden-seeds, which he was willing to sell at a small advance. A bargain was soon struck, for the invoice contained the very articles I was daily asked for, and knew not where to obtain. Next day, on opening the casks, I found a catalogue of seeds for sale by William Malcolm & Co., London; this was at that time a prize to me, for never before this had I seen a seed-catalogue. This catalogue had noted on the margin the time of sowing—a thing I was totally ignorant of. Having now a plan, I published a catalogue of my own, and, with the assistance of my friend the gardener, at Brooklyn, adapted the time to suit our own climate; so that now, when my customers asked when such and such seeds ought to be sown, I was able to give the necessary information. Next fall, I sent a small remittance with an order to Mr. M. The seeds arrived in good season, and, with the seeds raised by my friend at Brooklyn, composed a good assortment to commence business in the spring. The seeds I had imported and got raised here, proving very good, my sales increased beyond what my friend could supply; and some of the market-gardeners, supposing they might be able to sell me seeds, had this year raised seeds for that purpose. Having no other resource, I was fain to purchase such as were offered; and, being a mechanic by profession, and alike ignorant of seeds and gardening, I had long to struggle with the impositions of unprincipled seed-raisers, they often selling me spurious seeds, and asserting they were of the most genuine quality.

Having at length brought the business to a pretty respectable footing, it narrowly escaped total destruction in 1808, by a great fire, which commenced in a soap and candle manufactory adjoining the store. This fire broke out at midnight, the 25th of August, and was so rapid that five of the inmates of the house where it commenced, perished in the flames. Several circumstances occurred in connection with this fire in which I could discern the kind hand of Providence, and are in themselves so remarkable that they deserve never to be forgotten. It was impressed on my mind, long before it took place, that the factory would be burned. For many months previous, when the fire company belonging to engine No. 16 came to the pump, corner of Liberty and Nassau streets, on the first Monday in every month (according to law), to wash and clean the engine, I used to tell them, in a jocose manner, how I wished them to act

when the candle-box (as I termed the building) should take fire. I got
my property insured a short time before the fire took place; it was
in time of the long embargo. I had on hand a large stock of early York
cabbage and other seeds, which I was obliged to import, but which
could not then be imported, on account of the restrictions existing.
At dinner, the day previous to the fire, I told my wife I was going to
pack my most valuable seeds, and head them up in flour barrels, that
they might be safely removed when the fire broke out next door. I
came from my store between nine and ten o'clock that evening. My
wife was much fatigued with nursing our youngest child, who was
sick at the time; I told her to lie down, and I would nurse till she got
some sleep. She arose about five minutes before twelve. As I laid my
head on the pillow, the clock in the corner of my room struck
twelve. I must have dropped to sleep immediately; for the next day
I found my clock in the New Dutch Church, with the hands stopped
at fifteen minutes past twelve; it having been seized and carried into
the church at that minute, to save it from the fire. I was awoke by a
loud scream from my wife, who was then rocking the cradle; I
sprung on the floor before my eyes were opened, and asked what
was the matter. She said we were all on fire. I opened the back window, and was saluted by a column of smoke and fire, issuing from the
back of the soap-works. Having for many months previous resolved
in my mind how I would act when the thing took place, I was in no-
wise alarmed; she being dressed, I told her to take herself and child
to a place of safety, and I would wake up and take care of the other
children and servants. I afterwards dressed, and put on a pair of dou-
ble-soled boots, fearing that in the confusion I should tread on a
rusty nail in some of the boards that might be pulled down. I then
went in my store, which was by this time on fire, and secured my
valuable papers and money, by pinning them in my jacket-pocket; I
wet my night-cap and put it on, to preserve my hair from being
singed. As the engines came up, I directed them to the place where
their services would be most useful, and then ran from place to
place, saving and preserving such property as I could.

The buildings where the fire originated stood on the south side of
my premises, my back store, a wooden building two stories high. The

wind blew fresh from the south, which covered this building with flame; but, notwithstanding, there was so little damage done this building, that ten dollars put it in as good repair as it was before the fire began. There was only an inch-board between the factory and my back building. The day previous, I had been painting pots with green varnish. The shelf on which the painted pots stood was next to the factory; one pot contained about four pounds of verdigris, mixed with spirits of turpentine and varnish; a pitcher also contained half a gallon of rosin, varnish, &c., with a jug containing half a gallon of spirits of turpentine. The fire burned through the boards directly opposite where these inflammable articles stood; the end of the shelf burned through, and dropping about twelve inches, rested on the floor, and then was extinguished; but by what means no one could tell, as no engine, person, or water, could reach that spot during the fire. The heat melted the paint that was on the outside of the pots and jug, running down the sides; when the fire subsided, they were found glued fast to the board. The jug with spirits of turpentine was corked; the pots containing paint and varnish were without covering, but completely filled up with black coals, which must have fallen in while burning. Yet for all this, these inflammable articles did not take fire; had they taken fire, my whole premises must have been consumed.

Next day, when the carpenter and his men came to repair what little damage was done, they were the first to observe this circumstance; and being struck with surprise, not only called me, but several of the neighbors, besides others, to see it, before they removed the articles. One of the neighbors observed, it was impossible that they could have stood there during the fire without being burned; when one of the carpenters told them to lift up the pots and jugs. They found them glued fast to the board, and were then convinced that, however strange, it was true. For my own part, I saw in it the power of Him whose hand is in every thing, whether it is the fall of an empire or a sparrow. In short, the small damage that was done to my premises surprised many; and many came from a distance to view the buildings for months after. Eight or nine houses were burned on the rear and on the windward side of the factory where the fire commenced; while my store, which was joined by nails and boards, had scarcely the smell of fire on its roof.

In 1808, when all intercourse between America and Britain was suspended, and we were therefore prevented from importing such seeds as were necessary in our business, I was advised by my friends to attempt the raising of them myself. I was drawn into this business much against my own inclination and better judgment, as you will see in the sequel.

A few years previous, a gardener from England, by the name of Thornly, purchased about seven acres of land near Newark Bridge, which he improved as a kitchen-garden, and for raising a few seeds; but failing of success, and getting in debt, he absconded. He owed me a hundred dollars at the time; so, when he got to Philadelphia he executed a deed, whereby he constituted me owner of the soil, the first intimation of which was my receiving said deed per mail. As there was a considerable crop of seeds on the ground at the time, I resolved to gather the seeds as part payment; and as there was a mortgage for two hundred dollars on the premises, to let the land go to whomsoever had the best claim. The seeds were gathered, and the crop hardly paid the men's wages; but still I was persuaded to pay the mortgage and keep the place, as my well-intending friends all said it would do wonders under the management of an active man. It did wonders with a witness; for, after striving and toiling by sunlight and moonlight, in wet weather and dry weather, I found, at the end of five years, I had spent the whole earnings of my life, and was several thousands worse than nothing. I now gave up my all to my creditors; and, that I might be enabled to commence business anew, I applied, with an empty pocket and a clear conscience, for the benefit of the insolvent act. For this end it was necessary, as a first step, that I should either go to jail or the limits. I preferred the former, as I could board for half the expense. So, in December, 1813, I left my wife with one dollar and sixty-two cents, and four young children to support, without any certainty where the next dollar was to come from, in a solitary house, the nearest neighbor being one-fourth of a mile distant, and on a stormy day. You may suppose my feelings at this moment were not of the most pleasant kind.

The following circumstance took place, which struck me forcibly at the time, and on which I often reflect with wonder and gratitude. As I was walking down the main street in Newark, on my way to jail, the sheriff's officer politely going some distance either before or behind me, it matters not which, I was accosted by a man whom I had not seen for two years previous. Says he, "Mr. Thorburn, I have owed you fifteen dollars for a long time, but it never was in my power to pay you till now; just step in this store and I will pay you," pointing to one close by. I received the money with as much wonder and thankfulness as if I had seen it drop from the clouds in my path. I had not seen this man for so long a time, that I never expected the money. This circumstance inspired me with so much confidence in a superintending Providence, that I went into jail with a light heart, and *slept*—yes, my mind was so composed, after witnessing this signal proof of the goodness of God as a *Provider*, that all my anxieties on account of my family fled, and I *slept*. I knew that He who hangs creation on his arm, and feeds her at his board, would not suffer my children to starve. This man told me, some months after, that at the time he paid me that money he knew nothing of my difficulties. Well, having stayed the time appointed in jail, and gone through the forms by law prescribed, I came out whitewashed from all claims as far as the *law* could go; but I thought I was as much bound in *justice* as ever I was to pay my honest debts, should Providence put it in my power, by prospering my future exertions. He did prosper my future exertions, and I can now show receipts for thousands of dollars which were by law cancelled.

In the course of my life I have experienced at times the depths of sorrow and the heights of delight; but just enough of the former to give a relish to the latter. When I failed, and gave up my property to my creditors, as usual, it was sold by the sheriff. At the public sale of my furniture, a cradle, in which lay one of my children asleep, then about two months old, was sold among the rest. This was more than my philosophy could stand. A gentleman among the company had it knocked down to him; he observed, with a smile, he supposed the child now was his property, as well as the cradle. Being answered in the affirmative, he called the mother of the child, and made her a present of both. Such seasonable acts of kindness, in times of trouble, give a double relish to the deed. While I was filled with gratitude to the instrument, I was also thankful to Him who has the hearts of all in his hands, believing that all men are to me what he makes them to be. He who gave Joseph favor in the eyes of his fellow-men is the same yesterday, to-day, and forever.

In 1815 I returned to New York with my family, and only about twelve dollars in my pocket. Being out of employment, I hired myself as porter to the store of Mr. D. Durham. He always treated me with kindness, though the other servants about his office complained of him as being a hard master. In January, 1816, a friend advanced me five hundred dollars, with which I commenced business in the cellar of a house corner of Nassau street and Liberty. For seven years previous, in spite of all my exertions, every thing went backwards,—now every thing seemed to thrive of itself.

Previous to my removal to New Jersey, my seed establishment was kept at No. 20 Nassau street. After my failure it was occupied by Mr. Grundy as a seed shop; and he, being in possession of the original stand, nearly engrossed all my former custom. He, however, neglected his business, took to habits of dissipation, was sold out by the sheriff in turn, when I purchased part of the stock and all the fixtures, and continued the business in my old stand.

On the day of my discharge under the insolvent act, Mr. Grundy was the only person who brought forward any opposition. It was not founded on the plea of fraud, but in trying to make out some sort of a flaw in the papers, as not having got the full two-thirds of my creditors to sign off, or something to that purpose: and had it not been that the recorder saw through the motive, and withal being a man proverbial for leaning to the side of mercy, he would have frustrated my discharge at that time.

When Mr. Grundy arrived in America he lodged first in my house, and continued under my roof several years, where he was always treated with kind attention; yet, when I was surrounded with difficulties and trouble, he proved my most determined enemy.

Again I had an opportunity of returning good for evil. When he got low I gave him employment: the last shilling he received in the world was from my hand. The streets were glazed with ice: I urged him to go home before night; he stopped on the way with a friend; it was very dark; he fell backwards, and was dead before morning.

Finding my business again in a prosperous state, I left New York the 8th of July, on a visit to my friends in Scotland.

1852

# WALT WHITMAN

*Walt Whitman (1819–92) saw in the jostle and tumult of the New York crowd the embodiment of democracy as a spiritual force. The crowd was also a continually tantalizing, pullulating field of erotic potential. ("Are you the New Person Drawn toward Me?" he asks in one poem.) He employed long poetic lines, like a walker following out the gridded avenues. He was also fascinated with the spectacle of early mass transit, the Broadway omnibuses and the ferries. "Living in Brooklyn or New York city from this time forward, my life, then, and still more the following years, was curiously identified with the Fulton ferry . . . Almost daily, later ('50 to '60), I cross'd on the boats, often up in the pilot-houses, where I could get a full sweep, absorbing shows, accompaniments, surroundings. What oceanic currents, eddies, underneath—the great tides of humanity also, with ever-shifting movements. Indeed, I have always had a passion for ferries; to me they afford inimitable, streaming, never-failing, living poems," he wrote in* Specimen Days. *That same eye for the theater and poetry of urban daily life informs his reminiscences of the Old Bowery playhouse.*

CROSSING BROOKLYN FERRY

I

Flood-tide below me! I see you face to face!
  Clouds of the west—sun there half an hour high—I see you
    also face to face.
Crowds of men and women attired in the usual costumes, how
    curious you are to me!
On the ferry-boats the hundreds and hundreds that cross, returning
    home, are more curious to me than you suppose,
And you that shall cross from shore to shore years hence are more to
    me, and more in my meditations, than you might suppose.

2

The impalpable sustenance of me from all things at all hours of the
day,
The simple, compact, well-join'd scheme, myself disintegrated,
every one disintegrated yet part of the scheme,
The similitudes of the past and those of the future,
The glories strung like beads on my smallest sights and hearings, on
the walk in the street and the passage over the river,
The current rushing so swiftly and swimming with me far away,
The others that are to follow me, the ties between me and them,
The certainty of others, the life, love, sight, hearing of others.

Others will enter the gates of the ferry and cross from shore to
shore,
Others will watch the run of the flood-tide,
Others will see the shipping of Manhattan north and west, and the
heights of Brooklyn to the south and east,
Others will see the islands large and small;
Fifty years hence, others will see them as they cross, the sun half an
hour high,
A hundred years hence, or ever so many hundred years hence,
others will see them,
Will enjoy the sunset, the pouring-in of the flood-tide, the falling-
back to the sea of the ebb-tide.

3

It avails not, time nor place—distance avails not,
I am with you, you men and women of a generation, or ever so many
generations hence,
Just as you feel when you look on the river and sky, so I felt,
Just as any of you is one of a living crowd, I was one of a crowd,
Just as you are refresh'd by the gladness of the river and the bright
flow, I was refresh'd,
Just as you stand and lean on the rail, yet hurry with the swift
current, I stood yet was hurried,

Just as you look on the numberless masts of ships and the thick-
    stemm'd pipes of steamboats, I look'd.

I too many and many a time cross'd the river of old,
Watched the Twelfth-month sea-gulls, saw them high in the air
    floating with motionless wings, oscillating their bodies,
Saw how the glistening yellow lit up parts of their bodies and left the
    rest in strong shadow,
Saw the slow-wheeling circles and the gradual edging toward the
    south,
Saw the reflection of the summer sky in the water,
Had my eyes dazzled by the shimmering track of beams,
Look'd at the fine centrifugal spokes of light round the shape of my
    head in the sunlit water,
Look'd on the haze on the hills southward and southwestward,
Look'd on the vapor as it flew in fleeces tinged with violet,
Look'd toward the lower bay to notice the vessels arriving,
Saw their approach, saw aboard those that were near me,
Saw the white sails of schooners and sloops, saw the ships at
    anchor,
The sailors at work in the rigging or out astride the spars,
The round masts, the swinging motion of the hulls, the slender
    serpentine pennants,
The large and small steamers in motion, the pilots in their pilot-
    houses,
The white wake left by the passage, the quick tremulous whirl of the
    wheels,
The flags of all nations, the falling of them at sunset,
The scallop-edged waves in the twilight, the ladled cups, the
    frolicsome crests and glistening,
The stretch afar growing dimmer and dimmer, the gray walls of the
    granite storehouses by the docks,
On the river the shadowy group, the big steam-tug closely flank'd on
    each side by the barges, the hay-boat, the belated lighter,
On the neighboring shore the fires from the foundry chimneys
    burning high and glaringly into the night,

Casting their flicker of black contrasted with wild red and yellow
    light over the tops of houses, and down into the clefts of
    streets.

4

These and all else were to me the same as they are to you,
I loved well those cities, loved well the stately and rapid river,
The men and women I saw were all near to me,
Others the same—others who look back on me because I look'd
    forward to them,
(The time will come, though I stop here to-day and to-night.)

5

What is it then between us?
What is the count of the scores or hundreds of years between us?

Whatever it is, it avails not—distance avails not, and place avails
    not,
I too lived, Brooklyn of ample hills was mine,
I too walk'd the streets of Manhattan island, and bathed in the waters
    around it,
I too felt the curious abrupt questionings stir within me,
In the day among crowds of people sometimes they came upon me,
In my walks home late at night or as I lay in my bed they came upon
    me,
I too had been struck from the float forever held in solution,
I too had receiv'd identity by my body,
That I was I knew was of my body, and what I should be I knew I
    should be of my body.

6

It is not upon you alone the dark patches fall,
The dark threw its patches down upon me also,
The best I had done seem'd to me blank and suspicious,
My great thoughts as I supposed them, were they not in reality
    meagre?

Nor is it you alone who know what it is to be evil,
I am he who knew what it was to be evil,
I too knotted the old knot of contrariety,
Blabb'd, blush'd, resented, lied, stole, grudg'd,
Had guile, anger, lust, hot wishes I dared not speak,
Was wayward, vain, greedy, shallow, sly, cowardly, malignant,
The wolf, the snake, the hog, not wanting in me,
The cheating look, the frivolous word, the adulterous wish, not
    wanting,
Refusals, hates, postponements, meanness, laziness, none of these
    wanting,
Was one with the rest, the days and haps of the rest,
Was call'd by my nighest name by clear loud voices of young men as
    they saw me approaching or passing,
Felt their arms on my neck as I stood, or the negligent leaning of
    their flesh against me as I sat,
Saw many I loved in the street or ferry-boat or public assembly, yet
    never told them a word,
Lived the same life with the rest, the same old laughing, gnawing,
    sleeping,
Play'd the part that still looks back on the actor or actress,
The same old role, the role that is what we make it, as great as we
    like,
Or as small as we like, or both great and small.

## 7

Closer yet I approach you,
What thought you have of me now, I had as much of you—I laid in
    my stores in advance,
I consider'd long and seriously of you before you were born.

Who was to know what should come home to me?
Who knows but I am enjoying this?
Who knows, for all the distance, but I am as good as looking at you
    now, for all you cannot see me?

8

Ah, what can ever be more stately and admirable to me than mast-
    hemm'd Manhattan?
River and sunset and scallop-edg'd waves of flood-tide?
The sea-gulls oscillating their bodies, the hay-boat in the twilight,
    and the belated lighter?
What gods can exceed these that clasp me by the hand, and with
    voices I love call me promptly and loudly by my nighest name
    as I approach?
What is more subtle than this which ties me to the woman or man
    that looks in my face?
Which fuses me into you now, and pours my meaning into you?

We understand then do we not?
What I promis'd without mentioning it, have you not accepted?
What the study could not teach—what the preaching could not
    accomplish is accomplish'd, is it not?

9

Flow on, river! flow with the flood-tide, and ebb with the ebb-tide!
Frolic on, crested and scallop-edg'd waves!
Gorgeous clouds of the sunset! drench with your splendor me, or
    the men and women generations after me!
Cross from shore to shore, countless crowds of passengers!
Stand up, tall masts of Mannahatta! stand up, beautiful hills of
    Brooklyn!
Throb, baffled and curious brain! throw out questions and answers!
Suspend here and everywhere, eternal float of solution!
Gaze, loving and thirsting eyes, in the house or street or public
    assembly!
Sound out, voices of young men! loudly and musically call me by my
    nighest name!
Live, old life! play the part that looks back on the actor or actress!
Play the old role, the role that is great or small according as one
    makes it!

Consider, you who peruse me, whether I may not in unknown ways
    be looking upon you;
Be firm, rail over the river, to support those who lean idly, yet haste
    with the hasting current;
Fly on, sea-birds! fly sideways, or wheel in large circles high in the
    air;
Receive the summer sky, you water, and faithfully hold it till all
    downcast eyes have time to take it from you!
Diverge, fine spokes of light, from the shape of my head, or any
    one's head, in the sunlit water!
Come on, ships from the lower bay! pass up or down, white-sail'd
    schooners, sloops, lighters!
Flaunt away, flags of all nations! be duly lower'd at sunset!
Burn high your fires, foundry chimneys! cast black shadows at
    nightfall! cast red and yellow light over the tops of the houses!
Appearances, now or henceforth, indicate what you are,
You necessary film, continue to envelop the soul,
About my body for me, and your body for you, be hung out divinest
    aromas,
Thrive, cities—bring your freight, bring your shows, ample and
    sufficient rivers,
Expand, being than which none else is perhaps more spiritual,
Keep your places, objects than which none else is more lasting.

You have waited, you always wait, you dumb, beautiful ministers,
We receive you with free sense at last, and are insatiate
    henceforward,
Not you any more shall be able to foil us, or withhold yourselves
    from us,
We use you, and do not cast you aside—we plant you permanently
    within us,
We fathom you not—we love you—there is perfection in you also,
You furnish your parts toward eternity,
Great or small, you furnish your parts toward the soul.

1856, REVISED 1892

# THE OLD BOWERY

## A REMINISCENCE OF NEW YORK PLAYS
## AND ACTING FIFTY YEARS AGO

I
N AN ARTICLE not long since, "Mrs. Siddons as Lady Macbeth," in "The Nineteenth Century," after describing the bitter regretfulness to mankind from the loss of those first-class poems, temples, pictures, gone and vanish'd from any record of men, the writer (Fleeming Jenkin) continues:

> If this be our feeling as to the more durable works of art, what shall we say of those triumphs which, by their very nature, last no longer than the action which creates them—the triumphs of the orator, the singer or the actor? There is an anodyne in the words, "must be so," "inevitable," and there is even some absurdity in longing for the impossible. This anodyne and our sense of humor temper the unhappiness we feel when, after hearing some great performance, we leave the theatre and think, "Well, this great thing has been, and all that is now left of it is the feeble print upon my brain, the little thrill which memory will send along my nerves, mine and my neighbors, as we live longer the print and thrill must be feebler, and when we pass away the impress of the great artist will vanish from the world." The regret that a great art should in its nature be transitory, explains the lively interest which many feel in reading anecdotes or descriptions of a great actor.

All this is emphatically my own feeling and reminiscence about the best dramatic and lyric artists I have seen in bygone days—for instance, Marietta Alboni, the elder Booth, Forrest, the tenor Bettini, the baritone Badiali, "old man Clarke"—(I could write a whole paper on the latter's peerless rendering of the Ghost in "Hamlet" at the Park, when I was a young fellow)—an actor named Ranger, who appear'd in America forty years ago in *genre* characters; Henry Placide, and many others. But I will make a few memoranda at least of the best one I knew.

For the elderly New Yorker of to-day, perhaps, nothing were more likely to start up memories of his early manhood than the mention of the Bowery and the elder Booth. At the date given, the more stylish and select theatre (prices, 50 cents pit, $1 boxes) was "The Park," a large and well-appointed house on Park Row, opposite the present Post-office. English opera and the old comedies were often given in capital style; the principal foreign stars appear'd here, with Italian opera at wide intervals. The Park held a large part in my boyhood's and young manhood's life. Here I heard the English actor, Anderson, in "Charles de Moor," and in the fine part of "Gisippus." Here I heard Fanny Kemble, Charlotte Cushman, the Seguins, Daddy Rice, Hackett as Falstaff, Nimrod Wildfire, Rip Van Winkle, and in his Yankee characters. (See *Specimen Days.*) It was here (some years later than the date in the headline) I also heard Mario many times, and at his best. In such parts as Gennaro, in "Lucrezia Borgia," he was inimitable—the sweetest of voices, a pure tenor, of considerable compass and respectable power. His wife, Grisi, was with him, no longer first-class or young—a fine Norma, though, to the last.

Perhaps my dearest amusement reminiscences are those musical ones. I doubt if ever the senses and emotions of the future will be thrill'd as were the auditors of a generation ago by the deep passion of Alboni's contralto (at the Broadway Theatre, south side, near Pearl street)—or by the trumpet notes of Badiali's baritone, or Bettini's pensive and incomparable tenor in Fernando in "Favorita," or Marini's bass in "Faliero," among the Havana troupe, Castle Garden.

But getting back more specifically to the date and theme I started from—the heavy tragedy business prevail'd more decidedly at the Bowery Theatre, where Booth and Forrest were frequently to be heard. Though Booth *pere*, then in his prime, ranging in age from 40 to 44 years (he was born in 1796,) was the loyal child and continuer of the traditions of orthodox English play-acting, he stood out "himself alone" in many respects beyond any of his kind on record, and with effects and ways that broke through all rules and all traditions. He has been well describ'd as an actor "whose instant and tremendous concentration of passion in his delineations overwhelm'd his audience, and wrought into it such enthusiasm that it partook of the fever of inspiration surging through his own veins." He seems to have been of beautiful private character, very honorable, affectionate, good-natured, no arrogance, glad to give the other actors the best chances. He knew all stage points thoroughly, and curiously ignored the mere dignities. I once talk'd with a man who had seen him do the Second Actor in the mock play to Charles Kean's Hamlet in Baltimore. He was a marvellous linguist. He play'd Shylock once in London, giving the dialogue in Hebrew, and in New Orleans Oreste (Racine's "Andromaque") in French. One trait of his habits, I have heard, was strict vegetarianism. He was exceptionally kind to the brute creation. Every once in a while he would make a break for solitude or wild freedom, sometimes for a few hours, sometimes for days. (He illustrated Plato's rule that to the forming an artist of the very highest rank a dash of insanity or what the world calls insanity is indispensable.) He was a small-sized man—yet sharp observers noticed that however crowded the stage might be in certain scenes, Booth never seem'd overtopt or hidden. He was singularly spontaneous and fluctuating; in the same part each rendering differ'd from any and all others. He had no stereotyped positions and made no arbitrary requirements on his fellow-performers.

As is well known to old play-goers, Booth's most effective part was Richard III. Either that, or Iago, or Shylock, or Pescara in "The Apostate," was sure to draw a crowded house. (Remember heavy pieces were much more in demand those days than now.) He was also unapproachably grand in Sir Giles Overreach, in "A New Way to Pay Old Debts," and the principal character in "The Iron Chest."

In any portraiture of Booth, those years, the Bowery Theatre, with its leading lights, and the lessee and manager, Thomas Hamblin, cannot be left out. It was at the Bowery I first saw Edwin Forrest (the play was John Howard Payne's "Brutus, or the Fall of Tarquin," and it affected me for weeks; or rather I might say permanently filter'd into my whole nature,) then in the zenith of his fame and ability. Sometimes (perhaps a veteran's benefit night,) the Bowery would group together five or six of the first-class actors of those days—

Booth, Forrest, Cooper, Hamblin, and John R. Scott, for instance. At that time and here George Jones ("Count Joannes") was a young, handsome actor, and quite a favorite. I remember seeing him in the title role in "Julius Cæsar," and a capital performance it was.

To return specially to the manager. Thomas Hamblin made a first-rate foil to Booth, and was frequently cast with him. He had a large, shapely, imposing presence, and dark and flashing eyes. I remember well his rendering of the main role in Maturin's "Bertram, or the Castle of St. Aldobrand." But I thought Tom Hamblin's best acting was in the comparatively minor part of Faulconbridge in "King John"—he himself evidently revell'd in the part, and took away the house's applause from young Kean (the King) and Ellen Tree (Constance,) and everybody else on the stage—some time afterward at the Park. Some of the Bowery actresses were remarkably good. I remember Mrs. Pritchard in "Tour de Nesle," and Mrs. McClure in "Fatal Curiosity," and as Millwood in "George Barnwell." (I wonder what old fellow reading these lines will recall the fine comedietta of "The Youth That Never Saw a Woman," and the jolly acting in it of Mrs. Herring and old Gates.)

The Bowery, now and then, was the place, too, for spectacular pieces, such as "The Last Days of Pompeii," "The Lion-Doom'd" and the yet undying "Mazeppa." At one time "Jonathan Bradford, or the Murder at the Roadside Inn," had a long and crowded run; John Sefton and his brother William acted in it. I remember well the Frenchwoman Celeste, a splendid pantomimist, and her emotional "Wept of the Wish-ton-Wish." But certainly the main "reason for being" of the Bowery Theatre those years was to furnish the public with Forrest's and Booth's performances—the latter having a popularity and circles of enthusiastic admirers and critics fully equal to the former—though people were divided as always. For some reason or other, neither Forrest nor Booth would accept engagements at the more fashionable theatre, the Park. And it is a curious reminiscence, but a true one, that both these great actors and their performances were taboo'd by "polite society" in New York and Boston at the time—probably as being too robustuous. But no such scruples affected the Bowery.

Recalling from that period the occasion of either Forrest or Booth, any good night at the old Bowery, pack'd from ceiling to pit with its audience mainly of alert, well dress'd, full-blooded young and middle-aged men, the best average of American-born mechanics—the emotional nature of the whole mass arous'd by the power and magnetism of as mighty mimes as ever trod the stage—the whole crowded auditorium, and what seeth'd in it, and flush'd from its faces and eyes, to me as much a part of the show as any—bursting forth in one of those long-kept-up tempests of hand-clapping peculiar to the Bowery—no dainty kid-glove business, but electric force and muscle from perhaps 2000 full-sinew'd men—(the inimitable and chromatic tempest of one of those ovations to Edwin Forrest, welcoming him back after an absence, comes up to me this moment)—Such sounds and scenes as here resumed will surely afford to many old New Yorkers some fruitful recollections.

I can yet remember (for I always scann'd an audience as rigidly as a play) the faces of the leading authors, poets, editors, of those times—Fenimore Cooper, Bryant, Paulding, Irving, Charles King, Watson Webb, N. P. Willis, Hoffman, Halleck, Mumford, Morris, Leggett, L. G. Clarke, R. A. Locke and others, occasionally peering from the first tier boxes; and even the great National Eminences, Presidents Adams, Jackson, Van Buren and Tyler, all made short visits there on their Eastern tours.

Awhile after 1840 the character of the Bowery as hitherto described completely changed. Cheap prices and vulgar programmes came in. People who of after years saw the pandemonium of the pit and the doings on the boards must not gauge by them the times and characters I am describing. Not but what there was more or less rankness in the crowd even then. For types of sectional New York those days—the streets East of the Bowery, that intersect Division, Grand, and up to Third Avenue—types that never found their Dickens, or Hogarth, or Balzac, and have pass'd away unportraitured—the young ship-builders, cartmen, butchers, firemen (the old-time "soap-lock" or exaggerated "Mose" or "Sikesey," of Chanfrau's plays,) they, too, were always to be seen in these audiences, racy of the East River and the Dry Dock. Slang, wit, occasional shirt sleeves, and a picturesque freedom of looks and manners, with a rude good-nature and restless movement, were generally noticeable. Yet there never were audiences that paid a good actor or an interesting play the compliment of more sustain'd attention or quicker rapport. Then at times came the exceptionally decorous and intellectual congregations I have hinted at; for the Bowery really furnish'd plays and players you could get nowhere else. Notably, Booth always drew the best hearers; and to a specimen of his acting I will now attend in some detail.

I happen'd to see what has been reckon'd by experts one of the most marvelous pieces of histrionism ever known. It must have been about 1834 or '35. A favorite comedian and actress at the Bowery, Thomas Flynn and his wife, were to have a joint benefit, and, securing Booth for Richard, advertised the fact many days before-hand. The house fill'd early from top to bottom. There was some uneasiness behind the scenes, for the afternoon arrived, and Booth had not come from down in Maryland, where he lived. However, a few minutes before ringing-up time he made his appearance in lively condition.

After a one-act farce over, as contrast and prelude, the curtain rising for the tragedy, I can, from my good seat in the pit, pretty well front, see again Booth's quiet entrance from the side, as, with head bent, he slowly and in silence, (amid the tempest of boisterous hand-clapping,) walks down the stage to the footlights with that peculiar and abstracted gesture, musingly kicking his sword, which he holds off from him by its sash. Though fifty years have pass'd since then, I can hear the clank, and feel the perfect following hush of perhaps three thousand people waiting. (I never saw an actor who could make more of the said hush or wait, and hold the audience in an indescribable, half-delicious, half-irritating suspense.) And so throughout the entire play, all parts, voice, atmosphere, magnetism, from

"Now is the winter of our discontent,"

to the closing death fight with Richmond, were of the finest and grandest. The latter character was play'd by a stalwart young fellow named Ingersoll. Indeed, all the renderings were wonderfully good. But the great spell cast upon the mass of hearers came from Booth. Especially was the dream scene very impressive. A shudder went through every nervous system in the audience; it certainly did through mine.

Without question Booth was royal heir and legitimate representative of the Garrick-Kemble-Siddons dramatic traditions; but he vitalized and gave an unnamable *race* to those traditions with his own electric personal idiosyncrasy. (As in all art-utterance it was the subtle and powerful something *special to the individual* that really conquer'd.)

To me, too, Booth stands for much else besides theatricals. I consider that my seeing the man those years glimps'd for me, beyond all else, that inner spirit and form—the unquestionable charm and vivacity, but intrinsic sophistication and artificiality—crystallizing rapidly upon the English stage and literature at and after Shakspere's time, and coming on accumulatively through the seventeenth and eighteenth centuries to the beginning, fifty or forty years ago, of those disintegrating, decomposing processes now authoritatively going on. Yes; although Booth must be class'd in that antique, almost extinct school, inflated, stagy, rendering Shakspere (perhaps inevitably, appropriately) from the growth of arbitrary and often cockney conventions, his genius was to me one of the grandest revelations of my life, a lesson of artistic expression. The words fire, energy, *abandon*, found in him unprecedented meanings. I never heard a speaker or actor who could give such a sting to hauteur or the taunt. I never heard from any other the charm of unswervingly perfect vocalization without trenching at all on mere melody, the province of music.

So much for a Thespian temple of New York fifty years since, where "sceptred tragedy went trailing by" under the gaze of the Dry Dock youth, and both players and auditors were of a character and like we shall never see again. And so much for the grandest historian of modern times, as near as I can deliberately judge (and the phrenologists put my "caution" at 7)—grander, I believe, than Kean in the expression of electric passion, the prime eligibility of the tragic artist. For though those brilliant years had many fine and even magnificent actors, undoubtedly at Booth's death (in 1852) went the last and by far the noblest Roman of them all.

*NEW-YORK TRIBUNE*, 1885

# HERMAN MELVILLE

*Herman Melville (1819–91) was born in the city; spent close to twenty-five years working as a customs inspector at the port; set the beginning of* Moby-Dick *in "the insular city of the Manhattoes," and much of* Pierre *as well; and wrote what is arguably the greatest New York story of all, "Bartleby, the Scrivener." Many opposing interpretations of "Bartleby" have been offered, as befits a work that refuses to resolve the inexplicable. Whatever symbolic interpretations may be made of Melville's supremely enigmatic story, it powerfully evokes the realities of 1850's New York: the emergence of Wall Street and a lawyer-managed economy; the office world with its opportunities and alienations; the new army of copy-clerks whose hidden inner lives piqued the imaginations of those more privileged. Recent scholarship has revealed that a whole sub-genre of stories about New York lawyers and their scriveners flourished around the time that Melville wrote "Bartleby." His was simply the best.*

## BARTLEBY, THE SCRIVENER
### A STORY OF WALL-STREET

I AM a rather elderly man. The nature of my avocations for the last thirty years has brought me into more than ordinary contact with what would seem an interesting and somewhat singular set of men, of whom as yet nothing that I know of has ever been written:—I mean the law-copyists or scriveners. I have known very many of them, professionally and privately, and if I pleased, could relate divers histories, at which good-natured gentlemen might smile, and sentimental souls might weep. But I waive the biographies of all other scriveners for a few passages in the life of Bartleby, who was a scrivener the strangest I ever saw or heard of. While of other law-copyists I might write the complete life, of Bartleby nothing of that sort can be done. I believe that no materials exist for a full and satisfactory biography of this man. It is an irreparable loss to literature. Bartleby was one of those beings of whom nothing is ascertainable, except from the original sources, and in his case those are very small. What my own astonished eyes saw of Bartleby, *that* is all I know of him, except, indeed, one vague report which will appear in the sequel.

Ere introducing the scrivener, as he first appeared to me, it is fit I make some mention of myself, my *employés*, my business, my chambers, and general surroundings; because some such description is indispensable to an adequate understanding of the chief character about to be presented.

Imprimis: I am a man who, from his youth upwards, has been filled with a profound conviction that the easiest way of life is the best. Hence, though I belong to a profession proverbially energetic and nervous, even to turbulence, at times, yet nothing of that sort have I ever suffered to invade my peace. I am one of those unambitious lawyers who never addresses a jury, or in any way draws down public applause; but in the cool tranquillity of a snug retreat, do a snug business among rich men's bonds and mortgages and title-deeds. All who know me, consider me an eminently *safe* man. The late John Jacob Astor, a personage little given to poetic enthusiasm, had no hesitation in pronouncing my first grand point to be prudence; my next, method. I do not speak it in vanity, but simply record the fact, that I was not unemployed in my profession by the late John Jacob Astor; a name which, I admit, I love to repeat, for it hath a rounded and orbicular sound to it, and rings like unto bullion. I will freely add, that I was not insensible to the late John Jacob Astor's good opinion.

Some time prior to the period at which this little history begins, my avocations had been largely increased. The good old office, now extinct in the State of New-York, of a Master in Chancery, had been conferred upon me. It was not a very arduous office, but very pleasantly remunerative. I seldom lose my temper; much more seldom indulge in dangerous indignation at wrongs and outrages; but I must be permitted to be rash here and declare, that I consider the sudden and violent abrogation of the office of Master in Chancery, by the new Constitution, as a ——— premature act; inasmuch as I had counted upon a life-lease of the profits, whereas I only received those of a few short years. But this is by the way.

My chambers were up stairs at No. — Wall-street. At one end they looked upon the white wall of the interior of a spacious sky-light shaft, penetrating the building from top to bottom. This view might have been considered rather tame than otherwise, deficient in what landscape painters call "life." But if so, the view from the other end of my chambers offered, at least, a contrast, if nothing more. In that direction my windows commanded an unobstructed view of a lofty brick wall, black by age and everlasting shade; which wall required no spy-glass to bring out its lurking beauties, but for the benefit of all near-sighted spectators, was pushed up to within ten feet of my window panes. Owing to the great height of the surrounding buildings, and my chambers being on the second floor, the interval between this wall and mine not a little resembled a huge square cistern.

At the period just preceding the advent of Bartleby, I had two persons as copyists in my employment, and a promising lad as an office-boy. First, Turkey; second, Nippers; third, Ginger Nut. These may seem names, the like of which are not usually found in the Directory. In truth they were nicknames, mutually conferred upon each other by my three clerks, and were deemed expressive of their respective persons or characters. Turkey was a short, pursy Englishman of about my own age, that is, somewhere not far from sixty. In the morning, one might say, his face was of a fine florid hue, but after twelve o'clock, meridian—his dinner hour—it blazed like a grate full of Christmas coals; and continued blazing—but, as it were, with a gradual wane—till 6 o'clock, P.M. or thereabouts, after which I saw no more of the proprietor of the face, which gaining its meridian with the sun, seemed to set with it, to rise, culminate, and decline the following day, with the like regularity and undiminished glory. There are many singular coincidences I have known in the course of my life, not the least among which was the fact, that exactly when Turkey displayed his fullest beams from his red and radiant countenance, just then, too, at that critical moment, began the daily period when I considered his business capacities as seriously disturbed for the remainder of the twenty-four hours. Not that he was absolutely idle, or averse to business then; far from it. The difficulty was, he was apt to be altogether too energetic. There was a strange, inflamed, flurried, flighty recklessness of activity about him. He would be incautious in dipping his pen into his inkstand. All his blots upon my documents, were dropped there after twelve o'clock, meridian. Indeed, not only would he be reckless and sadly given to making blots in the afternoon, but some days he went further, and was rather noisy. At such times, too, his face flamed with augmented blazonry, as if cannel coal had been heaped on anthracite. He made an unpleasant racket with his chair; spilled his sand-box; in mending his pens, impatiently split them all to pieces, and threw them on the floor in a sudden passion; stood up and leaned over his table, boxing his papers about in a most indecorous manner, very sad to behold in an elderly man like him. Nevertheless, as he was in many ways a most valuable person to me, and all the time before twelve o'clock, meridian, was the quickest, steadiest creature too, accomplishing a great deal of work in a style not easy to be matched—for these reasons, I was willing to overlook his eccentricities, though indeed, occasionally, I remonstrated with him. I did this very gently, however, because, though the civilest, nay, the blandest and most reverential of men in the morning, yet in the afternoon he was disposed, upon provocation, to be slightly rash with his tongue, in fact, insolent. Now, valuing his morning services as I did, and resolved not to lose them; yet, at the same time made uncomfortable by his inflamed ways after twelve o'clock; and being a man of peace, unwilling by my admonitions to call forth unseemly retorts from him; I took upon me, one Saturday noon (he was always worse on Saturdays), to hint to him, very kindly, that perhaps now that he was growing old, it might be well to abridge his labors; in short, he need not come to my chambers after twelve o'clock, but, dinner over, had best go home to his lodgings and rest himself till tea-time. But no; he insisted upon his afternoon devotions. His countenance became intolerably fervid, as he oratorically assured me—gesticulating with a long ruler at the other end of the room—that if his services in the morning were useful, how indispensable, then, in the afternoon?

"With submission, sir," said Turkey on this occasion, "I consider myself your right-hand man. In the morning I but marshal and deploy my columns; but in the afternoon I put myself at their head, and gallantly charge the foe, thus!"—and he made a violent thrust with the ruler.

"But the blots, Turkey," intimated I.

"True,—but, with submission, sir, behold these hairs! I am getting old. Surely, sir, a blot or two of a warm afternoon is not to be severely urged against gray hairs. Old age—even if it blot the page—is honorable. With submission, sir, we *both* are getting old."

This appeal to my fellow-feeling was hardly to be resisted. At all events, I saw that go he would not. So I made up my mind to let him stay, resolving, nevertheless, to see to it, that during the afternoon he had to do with my less important papers.

Nippers, the second on my list, was a whiskered, sallow, and, upon the whole, rather piratical-looking young man of about five and twenty. I always deemed him the victim of two evil powers—ambition and indigestion. The ambition was evinced by a certain impatience of the duties of a mere copyist, an unwarrantable usurpation of strictly professional affairs, such as the original drawing up of legal documents. The indigestion seemed betokened in an occasional nervous testiness and grinning irritability, causing the teeth to audibly grind together over mistakes committed in copying; unnecessary maledictions, hissed, rather than spoken, in the heat of business; and especially by a continual discontent with the height of the table where he worked. Though of a very ingenious mechanical turn, Nippers could never get this table to suit him. He put chips under it, blocks of various sorts, bits of pasteboard, and at last went so far as to attempt an exquisite adjustment by final pieces of folded blotting-paper. But no invention would answer. If, for the sake of easing his back, he brought the table lid at a sharp angle well up towards his chin, and wrote there like a man using the steep roof of a Dutch house for his desk:—then he declared that it stopped the circulation in his arms. If now he lowered the table to his waistbands, and stooped over it in writing, then there was a sore aching in his back. In short, the truth of the matter was, Nippers knew not what he wanted. Or, if he wanted any thing, it was to be rid of a scrivener's table altogether. Among the manifestations of his diseased ambition was a fondness he had for receiving visits from certain ambiguous-looking fellows in seedy coats, whom he called his clients. Indeed I was aware that not only was he, at times, considerable of a ward-politician, but he occasionally did a little business at the Justices' courts, and was not unknown on the steps of the Tombs. I have good reason to believe, however, that one individual who called upon him at my chambers, and who, with a grand air, he insisted was his client, was no other than a dun, and the alleged title-deed, a bill. But with all his failings, and the annoyances he caused me, Nippers, like his compatriot Turkey, was a very useful man to me; wrote a neat, swift hand; and, when he chose, was not deficient in a gentlemanly sort of deportment. Added to this, he always dressed in a gentlemanly sort of way; and so, incidentally, reflected credit upon my chambers. Whereas with respect to Turkey, I had much ado to keep him from being a reproach to me. His clothes were apt to look oily and smell of eating-houses. He wore his pantaloons very loose and baggy in summer. His coats were execrable; his hat not to be handled. But while the hat was a thing of indifference to me, inasmuch as his natural civility and deference, as a dependent Englishman, always led him to doff it the moment he entered the room, yet his coat was another matter. Concerning his coats, I reasoned with him; but with no effect. The truth was, I suppose, that a man with so small an income, could not afford to sport such a lustrous face and a lustrous coat at one and the same time. As Nippers once observed, Turkey's money went chiefly for red ink. One winter day I presented Turkey with a highly-respectable looking coat of my own, a padded gray coat, of a most comfortable warmth, and which buttoned straight up from the knee to the neck. I thought Turkey would appreciate the favor, and abate his rashness and obstreperousness of afternoons. But no. I verily believe that buttoning himself up in so downy and blanket-like a coat had a pernicious effect upon him; upon the same principle that too much oats are bad for horses. In fact, precisely as a rash, restive horse is said to feel his oats, so Turkey felt his coat. It made him insolent. He was a man whom prosperity harmed.

Though concerning the self-indulgent habits of Turkey I had my own private surmises, yet touching Nippers I was well persuaded that whatever might be his faults in other respects, he was, at least, a temperate young man. But indeed, nature herself seemed to have been his vintner, and at his birth charged him so thoroughly with an irritable, brandy-like disposition, that all subsequent potations were needless. When I consider how, amid the stillness of my chambers, Nippers would sometimes impatiently rise from his seat, and stooping over his table, spread his arms wide apart, seize the whole desk, and move it, and jerk it, with a grim, grinding motion on the floor, as if the table were a perverse voluntary agent, intent on thwarting and vexing him; I plainly perceive that for Nippers, brandy and water were altogether superfluous.

It was fortunate for me that, owing to its peculiar cause—indigestion—the irritability and consequent nervousness of Nippers, were mainly observable in the morning, while in the afternoon he was comparatively mild. So that Turkey's paroxysms only coming on about twelve o'clock, I never had to do with their eccentricities at one time. Their fits relieved each other like guards. When Nippers' was on, Turkey's was off; and *vice versa*. This was a good natural arrangement under the circumstances.

Ginger Nut, the third on my list, was a lad some twelve years old. His father was a carman, ambitious of seeing his son on the bench instead of a cart, before he died. So he sent him to my office as student at law, errand boy, and cleaner and sweeper, at the rate of one dollar a week. He had a little desk to himself, but he did not use it much. Upon inspection, the drawer exhibited a great array of the shells of various sorts of nuts. Indeed, to this quick-witted youth the whole noble science of the law was contained in a nut-shell. Not the least among the employments of Ginger Nut, as well as one which he discharged with the most alacrity, was his duty as cake and apple purveyor for Turkey and Nippers. Copying law papers being proverbially a dry, husky sort of business, my two scriveners were fain to moisten their mouths very often with Spitzenbergs to be had at the

numerous stalls nigh the Custom House and Post Office. Also, they
sent Ginger Nut very frequently for that peculiar cake—small, flat,
round, and very spicy—after which he had been named by them. Of
a cold morning when business was but dull, Turkey would gobble up
scores of these cakes, as if they were mere wafers—indeed they sell
them at the rate of six or eight for a penny—the scrape of his pen
blending with the crunching of the crisp particles in his mouth. Of
all the fiery afternoon blunders and flurried rashnesses of Turkey, was
his once moistening a ginger-cake between his lips, and clapping it
on to a mortgage for a seal. I came within an ace of dismissing him
then. But he mollified me by making an oriental bow, and saying—
"With submission, sir, it was generous of me to find you in stationery
on my own account."

Now my original business—that of a conveyancer and title
hunter, and drawer-up of recondite documents of all sorts—was
considerably increased by receiving the master's office. There was
now great work for scriveners. Not only must I push the clerks already with me, but I must have additional help. In answer to my advertisement, a motionless young man one morning, stood upon my
office threshold, the door being open, for it was summer. I can see
that figure now—pallidly neat, pitiably respectable, incurably forlorn! It was Bartleby.

After a few words touching his qualifications, I engaged him, glad
to have among my corps of copyists a man of so singularly sedate an
aspect, which I thought might operate beneficially upon the flighty
temper of Turkey, and the fiery one of Nippers.

I should have stated before that ground glass folding-doors divided my premises into two parts, one of which was occupied by my
scriveners, the other by myself. According to my humor I threw
open these doors, or closed them. I resolved to assign Bartleby a
corner by the folding-doors, but on my side of them, so as to have
this quiet man within easy call, in case any trifling thing was to be
done. I placed his desk close up to a small side-window in that part
of the room, a window which originally had afforded a lateral view
of certain grimy back-yards and bricks, but which, owing to subsequent erections, commanded at present no view at all, though it gave

some light. Within three feet of the panes was a wall, and the light came down from far above, between two lofty buildings, as from a very small opening in a dome. Still further to a satisfactory arrangement, I procured a high green folding screen, which might entirely isolate Bartleby from my sight, though not remove him from my voice. And thus, in a manner, privacy and society were conjoined.

At first Bartleby did an extraordinary quantity of writing. As if long famishing for something to copy, he seemed to gorge himself on my documents. There was no pause for digestion. He ran a day and night line, copying by sun-light and by candle-light. I should have been quite delighted with his application, had he been cheerfully industrious. But he wrote on silently, palely, mechanically.

It is, of course, an indispensable part of a scrivener's business to verify the accuracy of his copy, word by word. Where there are two or more scriveners in an office, they assist each other in this examination, one reading from the copy, the other holding the original. It is a very dull, wearisome, and lethargic affair. I can readily imagine that to some sanguine temperaments it would be altogether intolerable. For example, I cannot credit that the mettlesome poet Byron would have contentedly sat down with Bartleby to examine a law document of, say five hundred pages, closely written in a crimpy hand.

Now and then, in the haste of business, it had been my habit to assist in comparing some brief document myself, calling Turkey or Nippers for this purpose. One object I had in placing Bartleby so handy to me behind the screen, was to avail myself of his services on such trivial occasions. It was on the third day, I think, of his being with me, and before any necessity had arisen for having his own writing examined, that, being much hurried to complete a small affair I had in hand, I abruptly called to Bartleby. In my haste and natural expectancy of instant compliance, I sat with my head bent over the original on my desk, and my right hand sideways, and somewhat nervously extended with the copy, so that immediately upon emerging from his retreat, Bartleby might snatch it and proceed to business without the least delay.

In this very attitude did I sit when I called to him, rapidly stating what it was I wanted him to do—namely, to examine a small paper with me. Imagine my surprise, nay, my consternation, when without moving from his privacy, Bartleby in a singularly mild, firm voice, replied, "I would prefer not to."

I sat awhile in perfect silence, rallying my stunned faculties. Immediately it occurred to me that my ears had deceived me, or Bartleby had entirely misunderstood my meaning. I repeated my request in the clearest tone I could assume. But in quite as clear a one came the previous reply, "I would prefer not to."

"Prefer not to," echoed I, rising in high excitement, and crossing the room with a stride. "What do you mean? Are you moon-struck? I want you to help me compare this sheet here—take it," and I thrust it towards him.

"I would prefer not to," said he.

I looked at him steadfastly. His face was leanly composed; his gray eye dimly calm. Not a wrinkle of agitation rippled him. Had there been the least uneasiness, anger, impatience or impertinence in his manner; in other words, had there been any thing ordinarily human about him, doubtless I should have violently dismissed him from the premises. But as it was, I should have as soon thought of turning my pale plaster-of-paris bust of Cicero out of doors. I stood gazing at him awhile, as he went on with his own writing, and then reseated myself at my desk. This is very strange, thought I. What had one best do? But my business hurried me. I concluded to forget the matter for the present, reserving it for my future leisure. So calling Nippers from the other room, the paper was speedily examined.

A few days after this, Bartleby concluded four lengthy documents, being quadruplicates of a week's testimony taken before me in my High Court of Chancery. It became necessary to examine them. It was an important suit, and great accuracy was imperative. Having all things arranged I called Turkey, Nippers and Ginger Nut from the next room, meaning to place the four copies in the hands of my four clerks, while I should read from the original. Accordingly Turkey, Nippers and Ginger Nut had taken their seats in a row, each with his document in hand, when I called to Bartleby to join this interesting group.

"Bartleby! quick, I am waiting."

I heard a slow scrape of his chair legs on the uncarpeted floor, and soon he appeared standing at the entrance of his hermitage.

"What is wanted?" said he mildly.

"The copies, the copies," said I hurriedly. "We are going to examine them. There"—and I held towards him the fourth quadruplicate.

"I would prefer not to," he said, and gently disappeared behind the screen.

For a few moments I was turned into a pillar of salt, standing at the head of my seated column of clerks. Recovering myself, I advanced towards the screen, and demanded the reason for such extraordinary conduct.

"*Why* do you refuse?"

"I would prefer not to."

With any other man I should have flown outright into a dreadful passion, scorned all further words, and thrust him ignominiously from my presence. But there was something about Bartleby that not only strangely disarmed me, but in a wonderful manner touched and disconcerted me. I began to reason with him.

"These are your own copies we are about to examine. It is labor saving to you, because one examination will answer for your four papers. It is common usage. Every copyist is bound to help examine his copy. Is it not so? Will you not speak? Answer!"

"I prefer not to," he replied in a flute-like tone. It seemed to me that while I had been addressing him, he carefully revolved every statement that I made; fully comprehended the meaning; could not gainsay the irresistible conclusion; but, at the same time, some paramount consideration prevailed with him to reply as he did.

"You are decided, then, not to comply with my request—a request made according to common usage and common sense?"

He briefly gave me to understand that on that point my judgment was sound. Yes: his decision was irreversible.

It is not seldom the case that when a man is browbeaten in some unprecedented and violently unreasonable way, he begins to stagger in his own plainest faith. He begins, as it were, vaguely to surmise that, wonderful as it may be, all the justice and all the reason is on the other side. Accordingly, if any disinterested persons are present, he turns to them for some reinforcement for his own faltering mind.

"Turkey," said I, "what do you think of this? Am I not right?"

"With submission, sir," said Turkey, with his blandest tone, "I think that you are."

"Nippers," said I, "what do *you* think of it?"

"I think I should kick him out of the office."

(The reader of nice perceptions will here perceive that, it being morning, Turkey's answer is couched in polite and tranquil terms, but Nippers replies in ill-tempered ones. Or, to repeat a previous sentence, Nippers's ugly mood was on duty, and Turkey's off.)

"Ginger Nut," said I, willing to enlist the smallest suffrage in my behalf, "what do *you* think of it?"

"I think, sir, he's a little *luny*," replied Ginger Nut, with a grin.

"You hear what they say," said I, turning towards the screen, "come forth and do your duty."

But he vouchsafed no reply. I pondered a moment in sore perplexity. But once more business hurried me. I determined again to postpone the consideration of this dilemma to my future leisure. With a little trouble we made out to examine the papers without Bartleby, though at every page or two, Turkey deferentially dropped his opinion that this proceeding was quite out of the common; while Nippers, twitching in his chair with a dyspeptic nervousness, ground out between his set teeth occasional hissing maledictions against the stubborn oaf behind the screen. And for his (Nippers's) part, this was the first and the last time he would do another man's business without pay.

Meanwhile Bartleby sat in his hermitage, oblivious to every thing but his own peculiar business there.

Some days passed, the scrivener being employed upon another lengthy work. His late remarkable conduct led me to regard his ways narrowly. I observed that he never went to dinner; indeed that he never went any where. As yet I had never of my personal knowledge known him to be outside of my office. He was a perpetual sentry in the corner. At about eleven o'clock though, in the morning, I noticed that Ginger Nut would advance toward the opening in

Bartleby's screen, as if silently beckoned thither by a gesture invisible to me where I sat. The boy would then leave the office jingling a few pence, and reappear with a handful of ginger-nuts which he delivered in the hermitage, receiving two of the cakes for his trouble.

He lives, then, on ginger-nuts, thought I; never eats a dinner, properly speaking; he must be a vegetarian then; but no; he never eats even vegetables, he eats nothing but ginger-nuts. My mind then ran on in reveries concerning the probable effects upon the human constitution of living entirely on ginger-nuts. Ginger-nuts are so called because they contain ginger as one of their peculiar constituents, and the final flavoring one. Now what was ginger? A hot, spicy thing. Was Bartleby hot and spicy? Not at all. Ginger, then, had no effect upon Bartleby. Probably he preferred it should have none.

Nothing so aggravates an earnest person as a passive resistance. If the individual so resisted be of a not inhumane temper, and the resisting one perfectly harmless in his passivity; then, in the better moods of the former, he will endeavor charitably to construe to his imagination what proves impossible to be solved by his judgment. Even so, for the most part, I regarded Bartleby and his ways. Poor fellow! thought I, he means no mischief; it is plain he intends no insolence; his aspect sufficiently evinces that his eccentricities are involuntary. He is useful to me. I can get along with him. If I turn him away, the chances are he will fall in with some less indulgent employer, and then he will be rudely treated, and perhaps driven forth miserably to starve. Yes. Here I can cheaply purchase a delicious self-approval. To befriend Bartleby; to humor him in his strange wilfulness, will cost me little or nothing, while I lay up in my soul what will eventually prove a sweet morsel for my conscience. But this mood was not invariable with me. The passiveness of Bartleby sometimes irritated me. I felt strangely goaded on to encounter him in new opposition, to elicit some angry spark from him answerable to my own. But indeed I might as well have essayed to strike fire with my knuckles against a bit of Windsor soap. But one afternoon the evil impulse in me mastered me, and the following little scene ensued:

"Bartleby," said I, "when those papers are all copied, I will compare them with you."

"I would prefer not to."

"How? Surely you do not mean to persist in that mulish vagary?"

No answer.

I threw open the folding-doors near by, and turning upon Turkey and Nippers, exclaimed:

"Bartleby a second time says, he won't examine his papers. What do you think of it, Turkey?"

It was afternoon, be it remembered. Turkey sat glowing like a brass boiler, his bald head steaming, his hands reeling among his blotted papers.

"Think of it?" roared Turkey; "I think I'll just step behind his screen, and black his eyes for him!"

So saying, Turkey rose to his feet and threw his arms into a pugilistic position. He was hurrying away to make good his promise, when I detained him, alarmed at the effect of incautiously rousing Turkey's combativeness after dinner.

"Sit down, Turkey," said I, "and hear what Nippers has to say. What do you think of it, Nippers? Would I not be justified in immediately dismissing Bartleby?"

"Excuse me, that is for you to decide, sir. I think his conduct quite unusual, and indeed unjust, as regards Turkey and myself. But it may only be a passing whim."

"Ah," exclaimed I, "you have strangely changed your mind then—you speak very gently of him now."

"All beer," cried Turkey; "gentleness is effects of beer—Nippers and I dined together to-day. You see how gentle *I* am, sir. Shall I go and black his eyes?"

"You refer to Bartleby, I suppose. No, not to-day, Turkey," I replied; "pray, put up your fists."

I closed the doors, and again advanced towards Bartleby. I felt additional incentives tempting me to my fate. I burned to be rebelled against again. I remembered that Bartleby never left the office.

"Bartleby," said I, "Ginger Nut is away; just step round to the Post Office, won't you? (it was but a three minutes walk,) and see if there is any thing for me."

"I would prefer not to."

"You *will* not?"

"I *prefer* not."

I staggered to my desk, and sat there in a deep study. My blind inveteracy returned. Was there any other thing in which I could procure myself to be ignominiously repulsed by this lean, penniless wight?—my hired clerk? What added thing is there, perfectly reasonable, that he will be sure to refuse to do?

"Bartleby!"

No answer.

"Bartleby," in a louder tone.

No answer.

"Bartleby," I roared.

Like a very ghost, agreeably to the laws of magical invocation, at the third summons, he appeared at the entrance of his hermitage.

"Go to the next room, and tell Nippers to come to me."

"I prefer not to," he respectfully and slowly said, and mildly disappeared.

"Very good, Bartleby," said I, in a quiet sort of serenely severe self-possessed tone, intimating the unalterable purpose of some terrible retribution very close at hand. At the moment I half intended something of the kind. But upon the whole, as it was drawing towards my dinner-hour, I thought it best to put on my hat and walk home for the day, suffering much from perplexity and distress of mind.

Shall I acknowledge it? The conclusion of this whole business was, that it soon became a fixed fact of my chambers, that a pale young scrivener, by the name of Bartleby, had a desk there; that he copied for me at the usual rate of four cents a folio (one hundred words); but he was permanently exempt from examining the work done by him, that duty being transferred to Turkey and Nippers, out of compliment doubtless to their superior acuteness; moreover, said Bartleby was never on any account to be dispatched on the most trivial errand of any sort; and that even if entreated to take upon him such a matter, it was generally understood that he would prefer not to—in other words, that he would refuse point-blank.

As days passed on, I became considerably reconciled to Bartleby.

His steadiness, his freedom from all dissipation, his incessant industry (except when he chose to throw himself into a standing revery
behind his screen), his great stillness, his unalterableness of demeanor under all circumstances, made him a valuable acquisition.
One prime thing was this,—*he was always there*;—first in the morning, continually through the day, and the last at night. I had a singular confidence in his honesty. I felt my most precious papers
perfectly safe in his hands. Sometimes to be sure I could not, for the
very soul of me, avoid falling into sudden spasmodic passions with
him. For it was exceeding difficult to bear in mind all the time those
strange peculiarities, privileges, and unheard of exemptions, forming the tacit stipulations on Bartleby's part under which he remained
in my office. Now and then, in the eagerness of dispatching pressing
business, I would inadvertently summon Bartleby, in a short, rapid
tone, to put his finger, say, on the incipient tie of a bit of red tape
with which I was about compressing some papers. Of course, from
behind the screen the usual answer, "I prefer not to," was sure to
come; and then, how could a human creature with the common in-
firmities of our nature, refrain from bitterly exclaiming upon such
perverseness—such unreasonableness. However, every added re-
pulse of this sort which I received only tended to lessen the probability of my repeating the inadvertence.

Here it must be said, that according to the custom of most legal
gentlemen occupying chambers in densely-populated law buildings,
there were several keys to my door. One was kept by a woman re-
siding in the attic, which person weekly scrubbed and daily swept
and dusted my apartments. Another was kept by Turkey for convenience sake. The third I sometimes carried in my own pocket. The
fourth I knew not who had.

Now, one Sunday morning I happened to go to Trinity Church, to
hear a celebrated preacher, and finding myself rather early on the
ground, I thought I would walk round to my chambers for a while.
Luckily I had my key with me; but upon applying it to the lock, I
found it resisted by something inserted from the inside. Quite surprised, I called out; when to my consternation a key was turned
from within; and thrusting his lean visage at me, and holding the

door ajar, the apparition of Bartleby appeared, in his shirt sleeves, and otherwise in a strangely tattered dishabille, saying quietly that he was sorry, but he was deeply engaged just then, and—preferred not admitting me at present. In a brief word or two, he moreover added, that perhaps I had better walk round the block two or three times, and by that time he would probably have concluded his affairs.

Now, the utterly unsurmised appearance of Bartleby, tenanting my law-chambers of a Sunday morning, with his cadaverously gentlemanly *nonchalance*, yet withal firm and self-possessed, had such a strange effect upon me, that incontinently I slunk away from my own door, and did as desired. But not without sundry twinges of impotent rebellion against the mild effrontery of this unaccountable scrivener. Indeed, it was his wonderful mildness chiefly, which not only disarmed me, but unmanned me, as it were. For I consider that one, for the time, is a sort of unmanned when he tranquilly permits his hired clerk to dictate to him, and order him away from his own premises. Furthermore, I was full of uneasiness as to what Bartleby could possibly be doing in my office in his shirt sleeves, and in an otherwise dismantled condition of a Sunday morning. Was any thing amiss going on? Nay, that was out of the question. It was not to be thought of for a moment that Bartleby was an immoral person. But what could he be doing there?—copying? Nay again, whatever might be his eccentricities, Bartleby was an eminently decorous person. He would be the last man to sit down to his desk in any state approaching to nudity. Besides, it was Sunday; and there was something about Bartleby that forbade the supposition that he would by any secular occupation violate the proprieties of the day.

Nevertheless, my mind was not pacified; and full of a restless curiosity, at last I returned to the door. Without hindrance I inserted my key, opened it, and entered. Bartleby was not to be seen. I looked round anxiously, peeped behind his screen; but it was very plain that he was gone. Upon more closely examining the place, I surmised that for an indefinite period Bartleby must have ate, dressed, and slept in my office, and that too without plate, mirror, or bed. The cushioned seat of a ricketty old sofa in one corner bore the faint impress of a lean, reclining form. Rolled away under his desk, I found a blanket; under the empty grate, a blacking box and brush; on a chair, a tin basin, with soap and a ragged towel; in a newspaper a few crumbs of ginger-nuts and a morsel of cheese. Yes, thought I, it is evident enough that Bartleby has been making his home here, keeping bachelor's hall all by himself. Immediately then the thought came sweeping across me, What miserable friendlessness and loneliness are here revealed! His poverty is great; but his solitude, how horrible! Think of it. Of a Sunday, Wall-street is deserted as Petra; and every night of every day it is an emptiness. This building too, which of week-days hums with industry and life, at nightfall echoes with sheer vacancy, and all through Sunday is forlorn. And here Bartleby makes his home; sole spectator of a solitude which he has seen all populous—a sort of innocent and transformed Marius brooding among the ruins of Carthage!

For the first time in my life a feeling of overpowering stinging melancholy seized me. Before, I had never experienced aught but a not-unpleasing sadness. The bond of a common humanity now drew me irresistibly to gloom. A fraternal melancholy! For both I and Bartleby were sons of Adam. I remembered the bright silks and sparkling faces I had seen that day, in gala trim, swan-like sailing down the Mississippi of Broadway; and I contrasted them with the pallid copyist, and thought to myself, Ah, happiness courts the light, so we deem the world is gay; but misery hides aloof, so we deem that misery there is none. These sad fancyings—chimeras, doubtless, of a sick and silly brain—led on to other and more special thoughts, concerning the eccentricities of Bartleby. Presentiments of strange discoveries hovered round me. The scrivener's pale form appeared to me laid out, among uncaring strangers, in its shivering winding sheet.

Suddenly I was attracted by Bartleby's closed desk, the key in open sight left in the lock.

I mean no mischief, seek the gratification of no heartless curiosity, thought I; besides, the desk is mine, and its contents too, so I will make bold to look within. Every thing was methodically arranged, the papers smoothly placed. The pigeon holes were deep, and removing the files of documents, I groped into their recesses. Presently

I felt something there, and dragged it out. It was an old bandanna handkerchief, heavy and knotted. I opened it, and saw it was a savings' bank.

I now recalled all the quiet mysteries which I had noted in the man. I remembered that he never spoke but to answer; that though at intervals he had considerable time to himself, yet I had never seen him reading—no, not even a newspaper; that for long periods he would stand looking out, at his pale window behind the screen, upon the dead brick wall; I was quite sure he never visited any refectory or eating house; while his pale face clearly indicated that he never drank beer like Turkey, or tea and coffee even, like other men; that he never went any where in particular that I could learn; never went out for a walk, unless indeed that was the case at present; that he had declined telling who he was, or whence he came, or whether he had any relatives in the world; that though so thin and pale, he never complained of ill health. And more than all, I remembered a certain unconscious air of pallid—how shall I call it?—of pallid haughtiness, say, or rather an austere reserve about him, which had positively awed me into my tame compliance with his eccentricities, when I had feared to ask him to do the slightest incidental thing for me, even though I might know, from his long-continued motionlessness, that behind his screen he must be standing in one of those dead-wall reveries of his.

Revolving all these things, and coupling them with the recently discovered fact that he made my office his constant abiding place and home, and not forgetful of his morbid moodiness; revolving all these things, a prudential feeling began to steal over me. My first emotions had been those of pure melancholy and sincerest pity; but just in proportion as the forlornness of Bartleby grew and grew to my imagination, did that same melancholy merge into fear, that pity into repulsion. So true it is, and so terrible too, that up to a certain point the thought or sight of misery enlists our best affections; but, in certain special cases, beyond that point it does not. They err who would assert that invariably this is owing to the inherent selfishness of the human heart. It rather proceeds from a certain hopelessness of remedying excessive and organic ill. To a sensitive being, pity is not seldom pain. And when at last it is perceived that such pity cannot lead to effectual succor, common sense bids the soul be rid of it. What I saw that morning persuaded me that the scrivener was the victim of innate and incurable disorder. I might give alms to his body; but his body did not pain him; it was his soul that suffered, and his soul I could not reach.

I did not accomplish the purpose of going to Trinity Church that morning. Somehow, the things I had seen disqualified me for the time from church-going. I walked homeward, thinking what I would do with Bartleby. Finally, I resolved upon this;—I would put certain calm questions to him the next morning, touching his history, &c., and if he declined to answer them openly and unreservedly (and I supposed he would prefer not), then to give him a twenty dollar bill over and above whatever I might owe him, and tell him his services were no longer required; but that if in any other way I could assist him, I would be happy to do so, especially if he desired to return to his native place, wherever that might be, I would willingly help to defray the expenses. Moreover, if, after reaching home, he found himself at any time in want of aid, a letter from him would be sure of a reply.

The next morning came.

"Bartleby," said I, gently calling to him behind his screen.

No reply.

"Bartleby," said I, in a still gentler tone, "come here; I am not going to ask you to do any thing you would prefer not to do—I simply wish to speak to you."

Upon this he noiselessly slid into view.

"Will you tell me, Bartleby, where you were born?"

"I would prefer not to."

"Will you tell me *any thing* about yourself?"

"I would prefer not to."

"But what reasonable objection can you have to speak to me? I feel friendly towards you."

He did not look at me while I spoke, but kept his glance fixed upon my bust of Cicero, which as I then sat, was directly behind me, some six inches above my head.

"What is your answer, Bartleby?" said I, after waiting a considerable time for a reply, during which his countenance remained immovable, only there was the faintest conceivable tremor of the white attenuated mouth.

"At present I prefer to give no answer," he said, and retired into his hermitage.

It was rather weak in me I confess, but his manner on this occasion nettled me. Not only did there seem to lurk in it a certain calm disdain, but his perverseness seemed ungrateful, considering the undeniable good usage and indulgence he had received from me.

Again I sat ruminating what I should do. Mortified as I was at his behavior, and resolved as I had been to dismiss him when I entered my office, nevertheless I strangely felt something superstitious knocking at my heart, and forbidding me to carry out my purpose, and denouncing me for a villain if I dared to breathe one bitter word against this forlornest of mankind. At last, familiarly drawing my chair behind his screen, I sat down and said: "Bartleby, never mind then about revealing your history; but let me entreat you, as a friend, to comply as far as may be with the usages of this office. Say now you will help to examine papers to-morrow or next day: in short, say now that in a day or two you will begin to be a little reasonable:—say so, Bartleby."

"At present I would prefer not to be a little reasonable," was his mildly cadaverous reply.

Just then the folding-doors opened, and Nippers approached. He seemed suffering from an unusually bad night's rest, induced by severer indigestion than common. He overheard those final words of Bartleby.

"*Prefer not*, eh?" gritted Nippers—"I'd *prefer* him, if I were you, sir," addressing me—"I'd *prefer* him; I'd give him preferences, the stubborn mule! What is it, sir, pray, that he *prefers* not to do now?"

Bartleby moved not a limb.

"Mr. Nippers," said I, "I'd prefer that you would withdraw for the present."

Somehow, of late I had got into the way of involuntarily using this word "prefer" upon all sorts of not exactly suitable occasions. And I trembled to think that my contact with the scrivener had already and seriously affected me in a mental way. And what further and deeper aberration might it not yet produce? This apprehension had not been without efficacy in determining me to summary measures.

As Nippers, looking very sour and sulky, was departing, Turkey blandly and deferentially approached.

"With submission, sir," said he, "yesterday I was thinking about Bartleby here, and I think that if he would but prefer to take a quart of good ale every day, it would do much towards mending him, and enabling him to assist in examining his papers."

"So you have got the word too," said I, slightly excited.

"With submission, what word, sir," asked Turkey, respectfully crowding himself into the contracted space behind the screen, and by so doing, making me jostle the scrivener. "What word, sir?"

"I would prefer to be left alone here," said Bartleby, as if offended at being mobbed in his privacy.

"*That's* the word, Turkey," said I—"*that's* it."

"Oh, *prefer*? oh yes—queer word. I never use it myself. But, sir, as I was saying, if he would but prefer—"

"Turkey," interrupted I, "you will please withdraw."

"Oh certainly, sir, if you prefer that I should."

As he opened the folding-door to retire, Nippers at his desk caught a glimpse of me, and asked whether I would prefer to have a certain paper copied on blue paper or white. He did not in the least roguishly accent the word prefer. It was plain that it involuntarily rolled from his tongue. I thought to myself, surely I must get rid of a demented man, who already has in some degree turned the tongues, if not the heads of myself and clerks. But I thought it prudent not to break the dismission at once.

The next day I noticed that Bartleby did nothing but stand at his window in his dead-wall revery. Upon asking him why he did not write, he said that he had decided upon doing no more writing.

"Why, how now? what next?" exclaimed I, "do no more writing?"

"No more."

"And what is the reason?"

"Do you not see the reason for yourself," he indifferently replied.

I looked steadfastly at him, and perceived that his eyes looked dull and glazed. Instantly it occurred to me, that his unexampled diligence in copying by his dim window for the first few weeks of his stay with me might have temporarily impaired his vision.

I was touched. I said something in condolence with him. I hinted that of course he did wisely in abstaining from writing for a while; and urged him to embrace that opportunity of taking wholesome exercise in the open air. This, however, he did not do. A few days after this, my other clerks being absent, and being in a great hurry to dispatch certain letters by the mail, I thought that, having nothing else earthly to do, Bartleby would surely be less inflexible than usual, and carry these letters to the post-office. But he blankly declined. So, much to my inconvenience, I went myself.

Still added days went by. Whether Bartleby's eyes improved or not, I could not say. To all appearance, I thought they did. But when I asked him if they did, he vouchsafed no answer. At all events, he would do no copying. At last, in reply to my urgings, he informed me that he had permanently given up copying.

"What!" exclaimed I; "suppose your eyes should get entirely well—better than ever before—would you not copy then?"

"I have given up copying," he answered, and slid aside.

He remained as ever, a fixture in my chamber. Nay—if that were possible—he became still more of a fixture than before. What was to be done? He would do nothing in the office: why should he stay there? In plain fact, he had now become a millstone to me, not only useless as a necklace, but afflictive to bear. Yet I was sorry for him. I speak less than truth when I say that, on his own account, he occasioned me uneasiness. If he would but have named a single relative or friend, I would instantly have written, and urged their taking the poor fellow away to some convenient retreat. But he seemed alone, absolutely alone in the universe. A bit of wreck in the mid Atlantic. At length, necessities connected with my business tyrannized over all other considerations. Decently as I could, I told Bartleby that in six days' time he must unconditionally leave the office. I warned him to take measures, in the interval, for procuring some other abode. I offered to assist him in this endeavor, if he himself would but take the first step towards a removal. "And when you finally quit me, Bartleby," added I, "I shall see that you go not away entirely unprovided. Six days from this hour, remember."

At the expiration of that period, I peeped behind the screen, and lo! Bartleby was there.

I buttoned up my coat, balanced myself; advanced slowly towards him, touched his shoulder, and said, "The time has come; you must quit this place; I am sorry for you; here is money; but you must go."

"I would prefer not," he replied, with his back still towards me.

"You *must*."

He remained silent.

Now I had an unbounded confidence in this man's common honesty. He had frequently restored to me sixpences and shillings carelessly dropped upon the floor, for I am apt to be very reckless in such shirt-button affairs. The proceeding then which followed will not be deemed extraordinary.

"Bartleby," said I, "I owe you twelve dollars on account; here are thirty-two; the odd twenty are yours.—Will you take it?" and I handed the bills towards him.

But he made no motion.

"I will leave them here then," putting them under a weight on the table. Then taking my hat and cane and going to the door I tranquilly turned and added— "After you have removed your things from these offices, Bartleby, you will of course lock the door—since every one is now gone for the day but you—and if you please, slip your key underneath the mat, so that I may have it in the morning. I shall not see you again; so good-bye to you. If hereafter in your new place of abode I can be of any service to you, do not fail to advise me by letter. Good-bye, Bartleby, and fare you well."

But he answered not a word; like the last column of some ruined temple, he remained standing mute and solitary in the middle of the otherwise deserted room.

As I walked home in a pensive mood, my vanity got the better of my pity. I could not but highly plume myself on my masterly management in getting rid of Bartleby. Masterly I call it, and such it must appear to any dispassionate thinker. The beauty of my procedure

seemed to consist in its perfect quietness. There was no vulgar bully-
ing, no bravado of any sort, no choleric hectoring, and striding to
and fro across the apartment, jerking out vehement commands for
Bartleby to bundle himself off with his beggarly traps. Nothing of the
kind. Without loudly bidding Bartleby depart—as an inferior genius
might have done—I *assumed* the ground that depart he must; and
upon that assumption built all I had to say. The more I thought over
my procedure, the more I was charmed with it. Nevertheless, next
morning, upon awakening, I had my doubts,—I had somehow slept
off the fumes of vanity. One of the coolest and wisest hours a man
has, is just after he awakes in the morning. My procedure seemed as
sagacious as ever,—but only in theory. How it would prove in practice—there was the rub. It was truly a beautiful thought to have assumed Bartleby's departure; but, after all, that assumption was
simply my own, and none of Bartleby's. The great point was, not
whether I had assumed that he would quit me, but whether he would
prefer so to do. He was more a man of preferences than assumptions.

After breakfast, I walked down town, arguing the probabilities
*pro* and *con*. One moment I thought it would prove a miserable failure, and Bartleby would be found all alive at my office as usual; the
next moment it seemed certain that I should find his chair empty.
And so I kept veering about. At the corner of Broadway and Canal-
street, I saw quite an excited group of people standing in earnest
conversation.

"I'll take odds he doesn't," said a voice as I passed.

"Doesn't go?—done!" said I, "put up your money."

I was instinctively putting my hand in my pocket to produce my
own, when I remembered that this was an election day. The words I
had overheard bore no reference to Bartleby, but to the success or
non-success of some candidate for the mayoralty. In my intent frame
of mind, I had, as it were, imagined that all Broadway shared in my
excitement, and were debating the same question with me. I passed
on, very thankful that the uproar of the street screened my momentary absent-mindedness.

As I had intended, I was earlier than usual at my office door. I
stood listening for a moment. All was still. He must be gone. I tried

the knob. The door was locked. Yes, my procedure had worked to a charm; he indeed must be vanished. Yet a certain melancholy mixed with this: I was almost sorry for my brilliant success. I was fumbling under the door mat for the key, which Bartleby was to have left there for me, when accidentally my knee knocked against a panel, producing a summoning sound, and in response a voice came to me from within—"Not yet; I am occupied."

It was Bartleby.

I was thunderstruck. For an instant I stood like the man who, pipe in mouth, was killed one cloudless afternoon long ago in Virginia, by summer lightning; at his own warm open window he was killed, and remained leaning out there upon the dreamy afternoon, till some one touched him, when he fell.

"Not gone!" I murmured at last. But again obeying that wondrous ascendancy which the inscrutable scrivener had over me, and from which ascendency, for all my chafing, I could not completely escape, I slowly went down stairs and out into the street, and while walking round the block, considered what I should next do in this unheard-of perplexity. Turn the man out by an actual thrusting I could not; to drive him away by calling him hard names would not do; calling in the police was an unpleasant idea; and yet, permit him to enjoy his cadaverous triumph over me,—this too I could not think of. What was to be done? or, if nothing could be done, was there any thing further that I could *assume* in the matter? Yes, as before I had prospectively assumed that Bartleby would depart, so now I might retrospectively assume that departed he was. In the legitimate carrying out of this assumption, I might enter my office in a great hurry, and pretending not to see Bartleby at all, walk straight against him as if he were air. Such a proceeding would in a singular degree have the appearance of a home-thrust. It was hardly possible that Bartleby could withstand such an application of the doctrine of assumptions. But upon second thoughts the success of the plan seemed rather dubious. I resolved to argue the matter over with him again.

"Bartleby," said I, entering the office, with a quietly severe expression, "I am seriously displeased. I am pained, Bartleby. I had thought better of you. I had imagined you of such a gentlemanly or-

ganization, that in any delicate dilemma a slight hint would suffice—
in short, an assumption. But it appears I am deceived. Why," I added,
unaffectedly starting, "you have not even touched that money yet,"
pointing to it, just where I had left it the evening previous.

He answered nothing.

"Will you, or will you not, quit me?" I now demanded in a sudden passion, advancing close to him.

"I would prefer *not* to quit you," he replied, gently emphasizing
the *not*.

"What earthly right have you to stay here? Do you pay any rent?
Do you pay my taxes? Or is this property yours?"

He answered nothing.

"Are you ready to go on and write now? Are your eyes recovered? Could you copy a small paper for me this morning? or help examine a few lines? or step round to the post-office? In a word, will
you do any thing at all, to give a coloring to your refusal to depart
the premises?"

He silently retired into his hermitage.

I was now in such a state of nervous resentment that I thought it
but prudent to check myself at present from further demonstrations.
Bartleby and I were alone. I remembered the tragedy of the unfortunate Adams and the still more unfortunate Colt in the solitary office of the latter; and how poor Colt, being dreadfully incensed by
Adams, and imprudently permitting himself to get wildly excited,
was at unawares hurried into his fatal act—an act which certainly no
man could possibly deplore more than the actor himself. Often it
had occurred to me in my ponderings upon the subject, that had that
altercation taken place in the public street, or at a private residence,
it would not have terminated as it did. It was the circumstance of
being alone in a solitary office, up stairs, of a building entirely un-
hallowed by humanizing domestic associations—an uncarpeted office, doubtless, of a dusty, haggard sort of appearance;—this it must
have been, which greatly helped to enhance the irritable desperation
of the hapless Colt.

But when this old Adam of resentment rose in me and tempted
me concerning Bartleby, I grappled him and threw him. How? Why,

simply by recalling the divine injunction: "A new commandment give I unto you, that ye love one another." Yes, this it was that saved me. Aside from higher considerations, charity often operates as a vastly wise and prudent principle—a great safeguard to its possessor. Men have committed murder for jealousy's sake, and anger's sake, and hatred's sake, and selfishness' sake, and spiritual pride's sake; but no man that ever I heard of, ever committed a diabolical murder for sweet charity's sake. Mere self-interest, then, if no better motive can be enlisted, should, especially with high-tempered men, prompt all beings to charity and philanthropy. At any rate, upon the occasion in question, I strove to drown my exasperated feelings towards the scrivener by benevolently construing his conduct. Poor fellow, poor fellow! thought I, he don't mean any thing; and besides, he has seen hard times, and ought to be indulged.

I endeavored also immediately to occupy myself, and at the same time to comfort my despondency. I tried to fancy that in the course of the morning, at such time as might prove agreeable to him, Bartleby, of his own free accord, would emerge from his hermitage, and take up some decided line of march in the direction of the door. But no. Half-past twelve o'clock came; Turkey began to glow in the face, overturn his inkstand, and become generally obstreperous; Nippers abated down into quietude and courtesy; Ginger Nut munched his noon apple; and Bartleby remained standing at his window in one of his profoundest dead-wall reveries. Will it be credited? Ought I to acknowledge it? That afternoon I left the office without saying one further word to him.

Some days now passed, during which, at leisure intervals I looked a little into "Edwards on the Will," and "Priestley on Necessity." Under the circumstances, those books induced a salutary feeling. Gradually I slid into the persuasion that these troubles of mine touching the scrivener, had been all predestinated from eternity, and Bartleby was billeted upon me for some mysterious purpose of an all-wise Providence, which it was not for a mere mortal like me to fathom. Yes, Bartleby, stay there behind your screen, thought I; I shall persecute you no more; you are harmless and noiseless as any of these old chairs; in short, I never feel so private as when I know you

are here. At last I see it, I feel it; I penetrate to the predestinated purpose of my life. I am content. Others may have loftier parts to enact;
but my mission in this world, Bartleby, is to furnish you with office-
room for such period as you may see fit to remain.

I believe that this wise and blessed frame of mind would have
continued with me, had it not been for the unsolicited and uncharitable remarks obtruded upon me by my professional friends who visited the rooms. But this it often is, that the constant friction of
illiberal minds wears out at last the best resolves of the more generous. Though to be sure, when I reflected upon it, it was not strange
that people entering my office should be struck by the peculiar aspect of the unaccountable Bartleby, and so be tempted to throw out
some sinister observations concerning him. Sometimes an attorney
having business with me, and calling at my office, and finding no one
but the scrivener there, would undertake to obtain some sort of precise information from him touching my whereabouts; but without
heeding his idle talk, Bartleby would remain standing immovable in
the middle of the room. So after contemplating him in that position
for a time, the attorney would depart, no wiser than he came.

Also, when a Reference was going on, and the room full of
lawyers and witnesses and business was driving fast; some deeply occupied legal gentleman present, seeing Bartleby wholly unemployed,
would request him to run round to his (the legal gentleman's) office
and fetch some papers for him. Thereupon, Bartleby would tranquilly decline, and yet remain idle as before. Then the lawyer would
give a great stare, and turn to me. And what could I say? At last I was
made aware that all through the circle of my professional acquaintance, a whisper of wonder was running round, having reference to
the strange creature I kept at my office. This worried me very much.
And as the idea came upon me of his possibly turning out a long-
lived man, and keep occupying my chambers, and denying my authority; and perplexing my visitors; and scandalizing my professional
reputation; and casting a general gloom over the premises; keeping
soul and body together to the last upon his savings (for doubtless he
spent but half a dime a day), and in the end perhaps outlive me, and
claim possession of my office by right of his perpetual occupancy: as

all these dark anticipations crowded upon me more and more, and my friends continually intruded their relentless remarks upon the apparition in my room; a great change was wrought in me. I resolved to gather all my faculties together, and for ever rid me of this intolerable incubus.

Ere revolving any complicated project, however, adapted to this end, I first simply suggested to Bartleby the propriety of his permanent departure. In a calm and serious tone, I commended the idea to his careful and mature consideration. But having taken three days to meditate upon it, he apprised me that his original determination remained the same; in short, that he still preferred to abide with me.

What shall I do? I now said to myself, buttoning up my coat to the last button. What shall I do? what ought I to do? what does conscience say I *should* do with this man, or rather ghost? Rid myself of him, I must; go, he shall. But how? You will not thrust him, the poor, pale, passive mortal,—you will not thrust such a helpless creature out of your door? you will not dishonor yourself by such cruelty? No, I will not, I cannot do that. Rather would I let him live and die here, and then mason up his remains in the wall. What then will you do? For all your coaxing, he will not budge. Bribes he leaves under your own paper-weight on your table; in short, it is quite plain that he prefers to cling to you.

Then something severe, something unusual must be done. What! surely you will not have him collared by a constable, and commit his innocent pallor to the common jail? And upon what ground could you procure such a thing to be done?—a vagrant, is he? What! he a vagrant, a wanderer, who refuses to budge? It is because he will *not* be a vagrant, then, that you seek to count him *as* a vagrant. That is too absurd. No visible means of support: there I have him. Wrong again: for indubitably he *does* support himself, and that is the only unanswerable proof that any man can show of his possessing the means so to do. No more then. Since he will not quit me, I must quit him. I will change my offices; I will move elsewhere; and give him fair notice, that if I find him on my new premises I will then proceed against him as a common trespasser.

Acting accordingly, next day I thus addressed him: "I find these chambers too far from the City Hall; the air is unwholesome. In a word, I propose to remove my offices next week, and shall no longer require your services. I tell you this now, in order that you may seek another place."

He made no reply, and nothing more was said.

On the appointed day I engaged carts and men, proceeded to my chambers, and having but little furniture, every thing was removed in a few hours. Throughout, the scrivener remained standing behind the screen, which I directed to be removed the last thing. It was withdrawn; and being folded up like a huge folio, left him the motionless occupant of a naked room. I stood in the entry watching him a moment, while something from within me upbraided me.

I re-entered, with my hand in my pocket—and—and my heart in my mouth.

"Good-bye, Bartleby; I am going—good-bye, and God some way bless you; and take that," slipping something in his hand. But it dropped upon the floor, and then,—strange to say—I tore myself from him whom I had so longed to be rid of.

Established in my new quarters, for a day or two I kept the door locked, and started at every footfall in the passages. When I returned to my rooms after any little absence, I would pause at the threshold for an instant, and attentively listen, ere applying my key. But these fears were needless. Bartleby never came nigh me.

I thought all was going well, when a perturbed looking stranger visited me, inquiring whether I was the person who had recently occupied rooms at No. — Wall-street.

Full of forebodings, I replied that I was.

"Then sir," said the stranger, who proved a lawyer, "you are responsible for the man you left there. He refuses to do any copying; he refuses to do any thing; he says he prefers not to; and he refuses to quit the premises."

"I am very sorry, sir," said I, with assumed tranquillity, but an inward tremor, "but, really, the man you allude to is nothing to me— he is no relation or apprentice of mine, that you should hold me responsible for him."

"In mercy's name, who is he?"

"I certainly cannot inform you. I know nothing about him. Formerly I employed him as a copyist; but he has done nothing for me now for some time past."

"I shall settle him then,—good morning, sir."

Several days passed, and I heard nothing more; and though I often felt a charitable prompting to call at the place and see poor Bartleby, yet a certain squeamishness of I know not what withheld me.

All is over with him, by this time, thought I at last, when through another week no further intelligence reached me. But coming to my room the day after, I found several persons waiting at my door in a high state of nervous excitement.

"That's the man—here he comes," cried the foremost one, whom I recognized as the lawyer who had previously called upon me alone.

"You must take him away, sir, at once," cried a portly person among them, advancing upon me, and whom I knew to be the landlord of No. — Wall-street. "These gentlemen, my tenants, cannot stand it any longer; Mr. B——" pointing to the lawyer, "has turned him out of his room, and he now persists in haunting the building generally, sitting upon the banisters of the stairs by day, and sleeping in the entry by night. Every body is concerned; clients are leaving the offices; some fears are entertained of a mob; something you must do, and that without delay."

Aghast at this torrent, I fell back before it, and would fain have locked myself in my new quarters. In vain I persisted that Bartleby was nothing to me—no more than to any one else. In vain:—I was the last person known to have any thing to do with him, and they held me to the terrible account. Fearful then of being exposed in the papers (as one person present obscurely threatened) I considered the matter, and at length said, that if the lawyer would give me a confidential interview with the scrivener, in his (the lawyer's) own room, I would that afternoon strive my best to rid them of the nuisance they complained of.

Going up stairs to my old haunt, there was Bartleby silently sitting upon the banister at the landing.

"What are you doing here, Bartleby?" said I.

"Sitting upon the banister," he mildly replied.

I motioned him into the lawyer's room, who then left us.

"Bartleby," said I, "are you aware that you are the cause of great tribulation to me, by persisting in occupying the entry after being dismissed from the office?"

No answer.

"Now one of two things must take place. Either you must do something, or something must be done to you. Now what sort of business would you like to engage in? Would you like to re-engage in copying for some one?"

"No; I would prefer not to make any change."

"Would you like a clerkship in a dry-goods store?"

"There is too much confinement about that. No, I would not like a clerkship; but I am not particular."

"Too much confinement," I cried, "why you keep yourself confined all the time!"

"I would prefer not to take a clerkship," he rejoined, as if to settle that little item at once.

"How would a bar-tender's business suit you? There is no trying of the eyesight in that."

"I would not like it at all; though, as I said before, I am not particular."

His unwonted wordiness inspirited me. I returned to the charge.

"Well then, would you like to travel through the country collecting bills for the merchants? That would improve your health."

"No, I would prefer to be doing something else."

"How then would going as a companion to Europe, to entertain some young gentleman with your conversation,—how would that suit you?"

"Not at all. It does not strike me that there is any thing definite about that. I like to be stationary. But I am not particular."

"Stationary you shall be then," I cried, now losing all patience, and for the first time in all my exasperating connection with him fairly flying into a passion. "If you do not go away from these premises before night, I shall feel bound—indeed I *am* bound—to—to—to quit the premises myself!" I rather absurdly concluded, knowing not with what possible threat to try to frighten his immobility into compliance. Despairing of all further efforts, I was precipitately leaving him, when a final thought occurred to me—one which had not been wholly unindulged before.

"Bartleby," said I, in the kindest tone I could assume under such exciting circumstances, "will you go home with me now—not to my office, but my dwelling—and remain there till we can conclude upon some convenient arrangement for you at our leisure? Come, let us start now, right away."

"No: at present I would prefer not to make any change at all."

I answered nothing; but effectually dodging every one by the suddenness and rapidity of my flight, rushed from the building, ran up Wall-street towards Broadway, and jumping into the first omnibus was soon removed from pursuit. As soon as tranquillity returned I distinctly perceived that I had now done all that I possibly could, both in respect to the demands of the landlord and his tenants, and with regard to my own desire and sense of duty, to benefit Bartleby, and shield him from rude persecution. I now strove to be entirely care-free and quiescent; and my conscience justified me in the attempt; though indeed it was not so successful as I could have wished. So fearful was I of being again hunted out by the incensed landlord and his exasperated tenants, that, surrendering my business to Nippers, for a few days I drove about the upper part of the town and through the suburbs, in my rockaway; crossed over to Jersey City and Hoboken, and paid fugitive visits to Manhattanville and Astoria. In fact I almost lived in my rockaway for the time.

When again I entered my office, lo, a note from the landlord lay upon the desk. I opened it with trembling hands. It informed me that the writer had sent to the police, and had Bartleby removed to the Tombs as a vagrant. Moreover, since I knew more about him than any one else, he wished me to appear at that place, and make a suitable statement of the facts. These tidings had a conflicting effect upon me. At first I was indignant; but at last almost approved. The landlord's energetic, summary disposition, had led him to adopt a procedure which I do not think I would have decided upon myself; and yet as a last resort, under such peculiar circumstances, it seemed the only plan.

As I afterwards learned, the poor scrivener, when told that he must be conducted to the Tombs, offered not the slightest obstacle, but in his pale unmoving way, silently acquiesced.

Some of the compassionate and curious bystanders joined the party; and headed by one of the constables arm in arm with Bartleby, the silent procession filed its way through all the noise, and heat, and joy of the roaring thoroughfares at noon.

The same day I received the note I went to the Tombs, or to speak more properly, the Halls of Justice. Seeking the right officer, I stated the purpose of my call, and was informed that the individual I described was indeed within. I then assured the functionary that Bartleby was a perfectly honest man, and greatly to be compassionated, however unaccountably eccentric. I narrated all I knew, and closed by suggesting the idea of letting him remain in as indulgent confinement as possible till something less harsh might be done— though indeed I hardly knew what. At all events, if nothing else could be decided upon, the alms-house must receive him. I then begged to have an interview.

Being under no disgraceful charge, and quite serene and harmless in all his ways, they had permitted him freely to wander about the prison, and especially in the inclosed grass-platted yards thereof. And so I found him there, standing all alone in the quietest of the yards, his face towards a high wall, while all around, from the narrow slits of the jail windows, I thought I saw peering out upon him the eyes of murderers and thieves.

"Bartleby!"

"I know you," he said, without looking round,—"and I want nothing to say to you."

"It was not I that brought you here, Bartleby," said I, keenly pained at his implied suspicion. "And to you, this should not be so vile a place. Nothing reproachful attaches to you by being here. And see, it is not so sad a place as one might think. Look, there is the sky, and here is the grass."

"I know where I am," he replied, but would say nothing more, and so I left him.

As I entered the corridor again, a broad meat-like man, in an apron, accosted me, and jerking his thumb over his shoulder said— "Is that your friend?"

"Yes."

"Does he want to starve? If he does, let him live on the prison fare, that's all."

"Who are you?" asked I, not knowing what to make of such an unofficially speaking person in such a place.

"I am the grub-man. Such gentlemen as have friends here, hire me to provide them with something good to eat."

"Is this so?" said I, turning to the turnkey.

He said it was.

"Well then," said I, slipping some silver into the grub-man's hands (for so they called him). "I want you to give particular attention to my friend there; let him have the best dinner you can get. And you must be as polite to him as possible."

"Introduce me, will you?" said the grub-man, looking at me with an expression which seemed to say he was all impatience for an op- portunity to give a specimen of his breeding.

Thinking it would prove of benefit to the scrivener, I acquiesced; and asking the grub-man his name, went up with him to Bartleby.

"Bartleby, this is Mr. Cutlets; you will find him very useful to you."

"Your sarvant, sir, your sarvant," said the grub-man, making a low salutation behind his apron. "Hope you find it pleasant here, sir; nice grounds—cool apartments, sir—hope you'll stay with us some time—try to make it agreeable. May Mrs. Cutlets and I have the pleasure of your company to dinner, sir, in Mrs. Cutlets' private room?"

"I prefer not to dine to-day," said Bartleby, turning away. "It would disagree with me; I am unused to dinners." So saying he slowly moved to the other side of the inclosure, and took up a posi- tion fronting the dead-wall.

"How's this?" said the grub-man, addressing me with a stare of as- tonishment. "He's odd, aint he?"

"I think he is a little deranged," said I, sadly.

"Deranged? deranged is it? Well now, upon my word, I thought that friend of yourn was a gentleman forger; they are always pale and genteel-like, them forgers. I can't help pity 'em—can't help it, sir. Did you know Monroe Edwards?" he added touchingly, and paused. Then, laying his hand pityingly on my shoulder, sighed, "he died of consumption at Sing-Sing. So you weren't acquainted with Monroe?"

"No, I was never socially acquainted with any forgers. But I cannot stop longer. Look to my friend yonder. You will not lose by it. I will see you again."

Some few days after this, I again obtained admission to the Tombs, and went through the corridors in quest of Bartleby; but without finding him.

"I saw him coming from his cell not long ago," said a turnkey, "may be he's gone to loiter in the yards."

So I went in that direction.

"Are you looking for the silent man?" said another turnkey passing me. "Yonder he lies—sleeping in the yard there. 'Tis not twenty minutes since I saw him lie down."

The yard was entirely quiet. It was not accessible to the common prisoners. The surrounding walls, of amazing thickness, kept off all sounds behind them. The Egyptian character of the masonry weighed upon me with its gloom. But a soft imprisoned turf grew under foot. The heart of the eternal pyramids, it seemed, wherein, by some strange magic, through the clefts, grass-seed, dropped by birds, had sprung.

Strangely huddled at the base of the wall, his knees drawn up, and lying on his side, his head touching the cold stones, I saw the wasted Bartleby. But nothing stirred. I paused; then went close up to him; stooped over, and saw that his dim eyes were open; otherwise he seemed profoundly sleeping. Something prompted me to touch him. I felt his hand, when a tingling shiver ran up my arm and down my spine to my feet.

The round face of the grub-man peered upon me now. "His dinner is ready. Won't he dine to-day, either? Or does he live without dining?"

"Lives without dining," said I, and closed the eyes.

"Eh!—He's asleep, aint he?"

"With kings and counsellors," murmured I.

\*

There would seem little need for proceeding further in this history. Imagination will readily supply the meagre recital of poor Bartleby's interment. But ere parting with the reader, let me say, that if this little narrative has sufficiently interested him, to awaken curiosity as to who Bartleby was, and what manner of life he led prior to the present narrator's making his acquaintance, I can only reply, that in such curiosity I fully share, but am wholly unable to gratify it. Yet here I hardly know whether I should divulge one little item of rumor, which came to my ear a few months after the scrivener's decease. Upon what basis it rested, I could never ascertain; and hence, how true it is I cannot now tell. But inasmuch as this vague report has not been without a certain strange suggestive interest to me, however sad, it may prove the same with some others; and so I will briefly mention it. The report was this: that Bartleby had been a subordinate clerk in the Dead Letter Office at Washington, from which he had been suddenly removed by a change in the administration. When I think over this rumor, hardly can I express the emotions which seize me. Dead letters! does it not sound like dead men? Conceive a man by nature and misfortune prone to a pallid hopelessness, can any business seem more fitted to heighten it than that of continually handling these dead letters, and assorting them for the flames? For by the cart-load they are annually burned. Sometimes from out the folded paper the pale clerk takes a ring:— the finger it was meant for, perhaps, moulders in the grave; a banknote sent in swiftest charity:—he whom it would relieve, nor eats nor hungers any more; pardon for those who died despairing; hope for those who died unhoping; good tidings for those who died stifled by unrelieved calamities. On errands of life, these letters speed to death.

Ah Bartleby! Ah humanity!

1856

# GEORGE TEMPLETON STRONG

*The greatest American diary in the nineteenth century was kept by a Wall Street lawyer named George Templeton Strong (1820–75). It is remarkable not only for its length—some four million words—but for the flavorsome precision of the writing. Though it came to light only after his death, it is obvious that, as historian Allan Nevins put it, "Strong was an artist who was consciously trying to render his own city, his own time, his own personality in such form that later generations could comprehend them." Strong emerges as an intensely human confidant: we see his enthusiasms (classical music, chasing fires), his strong sense of civic duty (as a trustee of Columbia College and Trinity Church), his failures of sympathy (with regard to the Irish, Jews, socialists). While Strong shared many of the prejudices of his aristocratic, nativist class, his humanity and penetrating intelligence are equally in evidence. The Civil War brought out his best qualities: he served on the Sanitary Commission, which sought to alleviate wounds and sickness in the field, and enlisted his friend Frederick Law Olmsted to head it, and he came to revere Lincoln, about whom he was initially lukewarm. His horrified description of the draft riots of 1863 remains the most vivid account of that low point in New York City's history.*

## FROM THE DIARIES

*[1850] OCTOBER 27, SUNDAY* How this city marches northward! The progress of 1835 and 1836 was nothing to the luxuriant, rank growth of this year. Streets are springing up, whole strata of sandstone have transferred themselves from their ancient resting-places to look down on bustling thoroughfares for long years to come. Wealth is rushing in upon us like a freshet.

*NOVEMBER 13, WEDNESDAY* Busy times; last new botheration a sharp transaction of the Griswolds, for which they are in trouble, and I'm fagging at an answer to help them. . . . I'm beginning to feel a desire to make money, and I avow and asseverate that it's a new feeling with me. In this city the feeling is necessary to enable one to sympathize with the rest of mankind and be sure of his common humanity with the people about him.

*[1851] JANUARY 16, THURSDAY* Bad accident in this street between Fifth and Sixth Avenues yesterday. The houses Tom Emmet and Ferris Pell (or rather his widow) were putting up and on which the Bank has a rather large loan, tumbled down spontaneously, killing or mangling and mutilating some two dozen people. Cause, the criminal economy of the contractor. Saw some of the *mortar*, a greasy, pulverulent earth or clay, apparently far less tenacious than an average specimen of Broadway mud. The contractor, who certified to the sufficiency of his work three hours before the crash, has discreetly run away.

*JULY 29, TUESDAY* Heard one act of *Sonnambula* at Castle Garden tonight, and the first chorus of the second. Immense crowd. The opera has created quite a furor. Everybody goes, and nob and snob, Fifth Avenue and Chatham Street, sit side by side fraternally on the hard benches. Perhaps there is hardly so attractive a summer theatre in the world as Castle Garden when so good a company is performing as we have there now. Ample room; cool sea breeze on the balcony, where one can sit and smoke and listen and look out on the bay studded with the lights of anchored vessels, and white sails gleaming. . . . I don't wonder that the people are *Sonnambula*-mad. The plot of the opera is pretty for an opera plot; the music is pretty and shallow and taking and is sung by Bosio and Salvi. It's not very reasonable, to be sure, to prefer "Ah, non giunge" to "Vedrai, Carino," but that delusion is less debasing than the superstitious belief in Donizetti and Verdi that prevails so lamentably.

*SEPTEMBER 26* Money market desperately tight. Two or three New Jersey banks have collapsed, and people are talking ominously today about possible explosions among our own, and prophesying a panic and a run. Don't believe it will happen. If it does happen, it is a consolatory reflection that my own bank account is particularly small. I'm sadly vulgarized and degraded of late by the itching for money that has come over me. Oh, for $100,000—well invested! A skilful operation resulting in an enormous profit with no risk has all the charm for me now of poetry or romance.

*NOVEMBER 23, SUNDAY AFTERNOON* Fearful calamity at a public school in Ninth Ward Thursday afternoon, a false alarm of fire, a panic, a stampede downstairs of 1,800 children, and near fifty killed on the spot and many more wounded—a massacre of the innocents. The stair banisters gave way, and the children fell into the square well round which the stairs wound, where the heap of killed and wounded lay for hours before help could reach them. The doors opened inwards. The bodies were piled up to the top of the doors; they did not dare to burst them open and had to cut them slowly away with knives.

*[1852] MARCH 8* N. P. Willis is stricken with deadly disease, epilepsy and consumption together. The idea of death and of the man who writes editorials for the *Home Journal* are an unnatural combination. Death seems too solemn a matter for him to have any business with it.

*MAY 5, WEDNESDAY NIGHT* Quite indefatigable in the affairs of St. Luke's Hospital. I'm getting to be an Aminadab Sleek. Astor, by the by, has (unsolicited) raised his $3,000 to $13,000. This is very creditable. If he and Whitney and the other twenty or thirty millionaires of the city would do such things a little oftener, they would never feel the difference, and in ten years could control the course of things in New York by the public confidence and gratitude they would gain. Property is the ruling element in our society. Wealthy men are meant to have supreme influence in the long run; they do not possess it because they will not use the power wealth gives them.

*JULY 2, FRIDAY NIGHT* We shall have to get up a volunteer force in this city before long, a sort of Holy Vehm or Vigilance Committee, if rowdyism continues to grow on us at its present rate. The Common Council is notoriously profligate and corrupt; the police force partly awed by the blackguards of the brothel and grog-gery, partly intimate with them. And if some drunken ruffian is ar-rested, he's sure to be discharged by some justice or alderman, who feels that it won't do to lose the support of the particular gang to which he belongs. An organized amateur society of supporters of law would be wholesome, an association that should employ agents to prosecute violence and corruption vigorously, and to follow up with the penalties of the law those of its ministers who are too timid or dishonest to enforce it. It might not effect a cure, though, unless it went further and took the law into its own hands.

*JULY 5, MONDAY EVENING* Have been at home all day writing. Tonight went on the roof awhile. It's a beautiful sight the city pre-sents. In every direction one incessant sparkle of fire balls, rockets, roman candles, and stars of all colors shooting thick into the air and disappearing for miles around, with now and then a glare of colored light coming out in some neighborhood where fireworks on a large scale are going off. A foreigner would put it in his book of travels as one of the marvels of New York, and compare it to a swarm of trop-ical fireflies gleaming in and out through a Brazilian forest.

*[1853] MARCH 11* Stocks down. Wonder whether I'd better invest some loose savings in another Erie bond at present prices, or wait for a farther depression? Alas, alas, alas, for all the dreams of former times, the dreams to which this journal bears witness! Is it the doom of all men in this nineteenth century to be weighed down with the incumbrance of a desire to make money and save money, all their days? I suppose if my career is prosperous, it will be spent in the thoughtful, diligent accumulation of dollars, till I suddenly wake up to the sense that the career is ended and the dollars dross. So are we gradually carried into the social currents that belong to our time, whether it be the tenth century, or this cold-blooded, interest-calculating age of our own.

*DECEMBER 5* Meeting of the Trustees of Columbia College this afternoon, at which I was elected to one of the three vacancies in the

Board, Dr. Wainwright and a certain Presbyterian or Dutch Reformed Dr. Beadle being put into the other two. So I was certified by Ruggles and Ogden Hoffman as I walked uptown this afternoon, and by Professor Anderson tonight at a St. Luke's Hospital meeting. On many accounts much gratified by the result.

DECEMBER 10  Great fire today. Saw the smoke swelling out in great masses against the clear sky at two o'clock, and put for the scene. The "devouring element" was occupied with Harpers' premises (Cliff Street through to Pearl) and the Walton House (I believe) on the opposite side of Pearl. Very fierce and obstinate, and more than commonly dramatic and splendid was the conflagration. From the corner of Peck Slip and Pearl Street you looked up a little ascent to Franklin Square, crowded and busy, with three or four great double-banked engines rising above the crowd and working slowly. Fire on both sides, sometimes arching the street, more generally kept down by the columns of water that *stood*, like bars, penetrating the smoke and ruin. Walls thundering down at intervals, each fall followed by a rush upwards of tawny, ropy, blinding smoke and a rain of powdered mortar. Across Pearl Street there stood in beautiful contrast with the lurid masses of flame and smoke, an arch of rainbow, brightening and fading as the northwest wind fell, formed on the spray of the engines. The Walton House saved; I think only the roof destroyed. The loss to the Harpers must be immense and they are probably able to bear it.

DECEMBER 15  Prospect of a No-Popery riot here. Very numerous and bitter indignation meeting in the Park yesterday, growing out of the arrest of a loafer who undertook to preach Native Americanism and anti-priestcraft in the streets last Sunday and was taken in custody to prevent a riot. He sets up for a Protestant martyr on the strength of his detention, and swears that he will preach in the same place next Sunday; in which case there will be a mob originating with the Irish and German Papishes if he's not arrested, and with the Order of United Americans and the godly butcher boys of the Hook and the First Avenue if he is.

If Roman Catholicism as transplanted here shall retain all its aggressive and exclusive features, in other words, its identity, I don't see but that a great religious war is a probable event in the history of the next hundred years; notwithstanding all our national indifference to religious forms.

*[1854] JANUARY 14* Have been turning over *Hot Corn Stories*, a book that has sold more abundantly than any since *Uncle Tom's Cabin*. Not meritorious as a work of art; melodramatic, and I think appealing to depraved curiosity in its details about assignation houses and kept women. But (at least as to the former fault) it must be remembered that the book seems honestly meant to promote a certain end, for the sake of which artistic errors, violations of artistic truth, may well be pardoned. If perfectly correct in form and taste, it would have made less impression on an unaesthetic community.

The cleverest thing about it is its choice of a title. *Hot Corn* suggests so many reminiscences of sultry nights in August or early September, when one has walked through close, unfragrant air and flooding moonlight and crowds, in Broadway or the Bowery, and heard the cry rising at every corner, or has been lulled to sleep by its mournful cadence in the distance as he lay under only a sheet and wondered if tomorrow would be cooler. Alas for some far-off times when I remember so to have heard it!

*JUNE 20* After the everlasting rains of the spring, we are entering on a period of drowth. The sun sets, a well-defined, coppery disk like a red-hot penny in a dark room, and all the western sky is curtained with dull, coppery haze. Cholera is in town, and pretty active—fifty-odd deaths last week. But many of these cases were doubtless aggravated diarrhœa and cholera morbus, and all are thus far confined to the lowest and filthiest classes, whose existence from one day to another in their atmosphere of morphic influences is a triumph of vital organization and illustrates the vigorous tenacity of life (under the deadliest conditions) bestowed on the human species. But we may well be destined to undergo an epidemic this summer. Coleridge's

Cologne was not more fetid or mephitic than this metropolis. The stinks of Centre Street lift up their voices. Malarious aromata rampage invisible through every street, and in the second-rate regions of the city, such as Cherry Street, poor old Greenwich Street, and so on, atmospheric poison and pungent foetor and gaseous filth cry aloud and spare not, and the wayfaring man inhales at every breath a pair of lungs full of vaporized decomposing gutter mud and rottenness. Alas for our civic rulers, whose office it is to see that this be not so.

*[1855] JANUARY 21* In this city financial pressure continues. The unemployed workmen, chiefly Germans, are assembling daily in the Park and listening to inflammatory speeches by demagogues who should be "clapt up" for preaching sedition and marching in procession through the streets. The large majority of the distressed multitude is decently clad and looks well fed and comfortable. People anticipate riot and disturbance; there have been two or three rumors of it in various quarters. Friday night it was rumored that a Socialist mob was sacking the Schiff mansion in the Fifth Avenue, where was a great ball and mass meeting of the aristocracy. Certainly the destitute are a thankless set and deserve little sympathy in their complaints. The efforts to provide employment and relief, the activity of individuals and of benevolent organizations, the readiness with which money is contributed do credit to the city. More could be done and ought to be done, of course, but what is done is beyond precedent here, and more than our "unemployed" friends had a right to count on.

There has been vast improvement during the last three or four years in the dealings of our "upper class" with the poor; not merely in the comparative abundance of their bounty, but in the fact that it has become fashionable and creditable and not unusual for people to busy themselves in personal labors for the very poor and in personal intercourse with them. It is a very significant thing and would have been held a marvel ten years ago that women like Mrs. Eleanor Curtis, Mrs. Lewis Jones, Miss Field, Mrs. Peters, Miss Gibbs, and others should be working hard in "ragged schools" and the like.

Perhaps it may be but a short-lived fashion, but it is an indication most encouraging of progress toward social health.

✦   ✦   ✦   ✦   ✦

Thursday night at Mrs. Robert Gracie's third and (happily) last *reception*. Such transactions are sheer lunacy. The house is small, and the rooms were hot and crowded, so that one moved about like a fly in a glue pot through a stifling, viscid, glutinous medium of perspiring humanity and dilute carbonic acid gas. In the plentitude of their folly, people actually cleared away a narrow space in the middle room, where half a dozen idiotic couples polkaed and waltzed to a faintly audible piano-jingle, increasing thereby the pressure on the house to one hundred atmospheres. The crowd must have nearly burst out the walls.

*FEBRUARY 14*  Mayor Wood continues our Civic Hero—inquiring, reforming, redressing, laboring hard with ample result of good. If he goes on this way to the end of his term, he will be a public benefactor, recognized as such and honored with statues. His predecessors, reported of average honesty, did little or nothing to diminish the systematic profligacy of our city government. He is the first mayor, for thirty years at least, who has set himself seriously to the work of giving the civic administration a decent appearance of common honesty. He is a very strange phenomenon. It is not a citizen of high repute for integrity, entitled to the respect of all classes, known to be a good and true man, not even one of whom little or nothing was known and who might very well be an undeveloped hero till he found himself in his proper sphere of action, that is doing all this good work. It is a man whose former career shews him a scoundrel of special magnitude.

*MARCH 31, SATURDAY*  Chief among the civic notabilia is the Mayor's foray or razzia among the unhappy fallen women who perambulate Broadway, the noctivagous strumpetocracy. Its legality is much debated, and Morris decided against it today on habeas corpus, rightly I think. What the Mayor seeks to abolish or abate is not the terrible evil of prostitution (for the great, notorious "ladies' boarding houses" of Leonard and Mercer Streets are left in peace), but simply the scandal and offence of the *peripatetic* whorearchy. He is right in assailing it and in trying to keep vice from proclaiming its allurements in the market place; for its conspicuousness and publicity are disgraceful and mischievous and inexpressibly bad. But are his *means* and *policy* legal and right, or lawless and wrong? Most people applaud him, naturally enough, for our civic affairs have sunk into such corruption that a public officer seeking to promote a good end is upheld though he overstep his authority. He becomes the more popular for his courage in taking the responsibility of action unsupported by precedent and statute. So rise dictators in degenerate commonwealths. I think his policy dangerous and bad. It enables any scoundrel of a policeman to lay hands on any woman whom he finds unattended in the street after dark, against whose husband or brother he may have a grudge, who may be hurrying home from church or from a day's work, or may have been separated by some accident from her escort, and to consign her for a night to a station house. Till morning no interference can liberate her; and if the policeman did make a mistake, the morning would find her disgraced for life, maddened perhaps by shame and mortification. The possibility of such remediless mischief and abuse cannot be authorized by law.

*APRIL 17, TUESDAY* Trinity Chapel duly consecrated this morning. I didn't get into Wall Street till three o'clock. The services were well conducted and impressive; church packed full, of course. I was there at nine and found people assembling. Fussed about with Livingston and others for an hour and three-quarters between the chapel and the two houses opposite, where the clergy and others assembled——making arrangements and keenly sensible of my own importance. The entering procession was imposing; sextons of the church and chapels with very big staves gilded and colored in the early decorated style; the "parochial" church-wardens with lesser staves (like the pointers used by lecturers to indicate and demonstrate on their diagrams), which the committee had licensed them to "bear" on their solemn written request. I wanted to give them letters-patent authorizing cocked hats, also. Lots of clergy in surplices. Happily, it was a fine day and the distance walked by the procession very small, so they did not have to wear their hats and present the appearance of a holiday turnout of cartmen in clean frocks. The university cap or some ecclesiastical headpiece is wanted on such occasions. The string of fifty or sixty priests and deacons, and as many divinity students, passed into the chapel under my nose as "we" received them on the chapel porch, and I must say I was not favorably impressed by my review of their physiognomies. They don't contrast so very advantageously with the Roman Catholic clergy against whose outward appearance so much is said, except in point of cleanliness. If one must judge of their physiognomy, they are below the average trader, physician, attorney even, in expression, moral and intellectual. There were sensual pig-faces, white vacant sheep-faces, silly green gosling-faces, solemn donkey-faces; but the prevailing type was that of the commonplace fourth-rate snob, without any particular expression but mediocrity and grim professional Pharisaism. Here and there was a nice, manly, earnest face, now and then, among the elder clergy, one that shewed energy and cleanness. But they were mostly a sad set. Why does that profession attract so few men of mark, moral vigor, and commanding talent?

SEPTEMBER 14 Ate nothing till my five o'clock dinner with Anthon at the new Chambers Street Delmonico's, where we fared rather sumptuously. Walked up and stopped at Greene Street synagogue. Israel does not make a joyful noise. The monotonous solo ululations of the reader, or rabbi, are sufficiently dismal, but the people vociferate their responses in discord unspeakable, like eager bidders at a sale of stocks. It is strange that the sentiment and expression of their worship should be so utterly unlike that of any Christian culture I ever witnessed.

OCTOBER 8 Have done an unusual amount of walking today, which I chronicle as a cheering sign of improvement. Started with Eloise after breakfast, as with a newly transported country cousin, marched her out to Fortieth Street on the Fifth Avenue, and thence downtown, and took a melancholy look at poor old shabby 108 Greenwich Street, and left her at the corner of Broadway and Rector Street to find her way back again. Had some locomotion to do in and about Wall Street. Walked uptown, and down again to a vestry meeting, and on my return, perceiving a promising fire somewhere to the northwest, I left the railroad car and went in pursuit on a dog-trot. My pyrotechnic tour was fruitless, the fire began to fade in the sky, and finding myself in an unknown region on the outskirts of the city, somewhere among the thirties or forties, where it was dark and vacant lots abounded, and there was a sparse and Celtic population, I turned about and walked back again.

*NOVEMBER 23, FRIDAY* I must ascertain whether the mighty bug-destroyer Lyons has no modification of his cockroach powder that will exterminate organ-grinders. We suffer peculiarly here, for the street is very quiet, and they play all round the square before they leave it and are more or less audible at each successive station. I have been undergoing the performances of one of the tribe for an hour and a half and have heard "Casta Diva," "Ah, Non Giunge," the first chorus of *Ernani*, and some platitude from the *Trovatore* languidly ground out six times each. It makes me feel homicidal. If Abel had gone about with hand organs, I shouldn't censure Cain so very harshly. There goes "Casta Diva" for the seventh time!

*NOVEMBER 26* Professor Hare's lecture last Friday night somewhat talked of. As reported it seemed sad stuff. . . . What would I have said six years ago to anybody who predicted that before the enlightened nineteenth century was ended hundreds of thousands of people in this country would believe themselves able to communicate daily with the ghosts of their grandfathers?—that ex-judges of the Supreme Court, senators, clergymen, professors of physical sciences, should be lecturing and writing books on the new treasures of all this, and that others among the steadiest and most conservative of my acquaintance should acknowledge that they look on the subject with distrust and dread, as a visible manifestation of diabolic agency?

I am surprised that some of my friends regard the prevalence of this delusion with so much indifference. It is surely one of the most startling events that have occurred for centuries and one of the most significant. A new Revelation, hostile to that of the Church and the Bible, finding acceptance on the authority of knocking ghosts and oscillating tables, is a momentous fact in history as throwing light on the intellectual calibre and moral tone of the age in which multitudes adopt it.

*[1857] FEBRUARY 1, SUNDAY* An epidemic of crime this winter. "Garotting" stories abound, some true, some no doubt fictitious, devised to explain the absence of one's watch and pocketbook after a secret visit to some disreputable place, or to put a good face on some tipsy street fracas. But a tradesman was attacked the other afternoon in broad daylight at his own shop door in the Third Avenue near Thirteenth Street by a couple of men, one of whom was caught, and will probably get his deserts in the State Prison, for life—the doom of two of the fraternity already tried and sentenced. Most of my friends are investing in revolvers and carry them about at night, and if I expected to have to do a great deal of late street-walking off Broadway, I think I should make the like provision; though it's a very bad practice carrying concealed weapons. Moreover, there was an uncommonly shocking murder in Bond Street (No. 31) Friday night; one Burdell, a dentist, strangled and riddled with stabs in his own room by some person unknown who must have been concealed in the room. Motive unknown, evidently not plunder.

*FEBRUARY 4, WEDNESDAY NIGHT* The chief subject of discourse, excluding all others nearly, is the Burdell murder, Mrs. Cunningham and Miss Cunningham, Eckel and Snodgrass, and the extravaganzas and indecencies of that ignorant blackguard the Coroner, Connery, who is conducting from day to day a broad farce called an inquest as afterpiece to the tragedy. When that is ended, I guess the audience will be dismissed. Probably no one will even be indicted. At present strong suspicion rests on Mrs. Cunningham and Eckel, but no item of legal evidence is yet disclosed against them.

The prevalent theory is that Mrs. Cunningham and the doctor had certain love-passages (she sued him for seduction and breach of promise, and the suits were compromised); that Eckel and the lady also carried their mutual friendship to fanaticism; that they laid their heads together to get the doctor's property; that they called on a certain Dutch Reformed Rev. Marvin, Eckel personating the doctor, and a marriage was performed, the certificate whereof the lady holds, but which she says the doctor preferred not to have disclosed till June; that the two thereupon murdered the man, intending to use the cord alone and to throw the body into the street, so that it might be taken for granted the case belonged to the prevailing epidemic "garotting"—whereupon Mrs. Cunningham would come into a very desirable slice of her victim's property; that their plans were deranged by his proving a tougher subject than they expected; and that they were obliged to use a knife and to cover the carpet and furniture with marks that made it impossible to conceal the fact that the crime had been committed on the premises. This theory is consistent with the facts, and there are considerable probabilities in its favor. But this investigation has been so bungled that there is now little chance of the truth being reached and sustained by proofs that will call for action even by the Grand Jury.

The excitement about the matter exceeds that produced by any crime of violence committed here in my time, even the Colt and Helen Jewett cases. Through all this miserable weather a crowd of several hundred people of all classes is in permanent position in front of the house. Well-dressed women occupy the doorsteps of houses on the opposite side of Bond Street, and stare steadily at No. 31, and seem to derive relief from protracted contemplation of its front door.

I had quite forgotten Burdell. He was frequently in the office a year or fifteen months ago, and used to pay my father interest on a mortgage held by the Lloyd estate, some transaction about which some shifting of securities took place at that time.

*OCTOBER 10* People's faces in Wall Street look fearfully gaunt and desperate. There are two or three millionaire friends of mine whose expression is enough to knock off three per cent a month extra from the market value of their paper. I know of at least two "great houses" that are trembling to their foundations. No merchant or banker, no man who has an obligation outstanding, can feel safe unless he has the needful gold in his own custody. He may be worth any amount in stocks or bonds or land, and yet be unable to raise five thousand dollars a week hence.

The Bowery Bank stopped yesterday. So did the little "East River Bank," I believe. This afternoon as I came uptown there was a crowd besieging the Bowery Savings Bank. I don't know how strong it may be, but if it fall, there will be a run on the other savings banks.

Henry A. Coit suspended today!!! He has accepted drafts against his usual consignments of sugar, and finds himself afraid to trust purchasers or to sell for each, and unable to raise money on his securities. There are other most significant failures, among them old Corlies. . . .

The remedy for this crisis must be psychological rather than financial. It is an epidemic of fear and distrust that every one admits to be without real ground *except* the very sufficient ground that everyone else is known to share them. I share the panic simply because I know the whole community feels it and because I know that a frightened community will not buy property at its true value or give business men the credit to which they are entitled.

OCTOBER 14, WEDNESDAY   We have *burst*. All the banks declined paying specie this morning, with the ridiculous exception of the Chemical, which is a little private shaving-shop of the Joneses with no depositors but its own stockholders.

Wall Street has been palpitating uneasily all day, but the first effect of the suspension is, of course, to make men breathe more freely. A special session is confidently expected, and the meeting of merchants at the Exchange at 3:30 P.M. appointed a committee that has gone to Albany to lay the case before Governor King. He ought to decline interference, but were I in his place I dare say my virtue would give way.

My great anxiety has been for the savings banks. Saw the officers of the two in which I feel a special interest (the Bleecker Street and Seamen's). Both were suicidally paying specie and thus inviting depositors to come forward to get the gold they could get nowhere else and could sell at a premium. The latter changes from specie to bills tomorrow; the former did so this afternoon. All the savings banks are to do so tomorrow. The run has been very formidable; some say not so severe as it was yesterday, but bad enough. I think they will get through.

*OCTOBER 22* We are a very sick people just now. The outward and visible signs of disease, the cutaneous symptoms, are many. Walking down Broadway you pass great $200,000 buildings begun last spring or summer that have gone up two stories, and stopped, and may stand unfinished and desolate for years, or on which six Celts are working instead of sixty. Almost every shop has its placards (*written*, not *printed*) announcing a great sacrifice, vast reduction of prices, sales at less than cost. Many of them protrude their stock of goods into unusual positions outside the door, after the manner of Chatham Street, with tickets conspicuously announcing the price of each lot and interjection marks. Great dry-goods houses like Bowen & McNamee's condescend to implore mankind to come in and buy at retail and notify the universe that "this store will be kept open till 9 P.M." Traders who have notes out must sell or perish. In Wall Street every man carries Pressure, Anxiety, Loss, written on his forehead. This is far the worst period of public calamity and distress I've ever seen, and I fear it is but the beginning.

*NOVEMBER 10* This financial crisis has thrown thousands of the working class out of employment and made it a difficult matter enough to maintain peace and order in the city through the winter. But that arch-demagogue Wood, the appropriate punishment of property holders and respectable people generally for their years of fainéance, inertia, and neglect of the city government, has lately put forth an incendiary message recommending the Common Council to apply a few hundred thousand dollars in buying provisions for the poor and inviting attention to the difference between "the rich who produce nothing and have everything and the poor who produce everything and have nothing." Probably he has also used his talents for tortuous, subterranean operations to get up some movement among the "dangerous classes." His object has been either to gain votes among the unwashed by assuming to act as their patron, or to stimulate them to an outbreak on the eve of election, and to suppress it with a high hand, and gain votes among men of peace by showing himself able to maintain order, and so forth. However this may be, his policy has produced sundry rather alarming demonstrations by the *canaille* of the city. They have been marching in procession—holding meetings in Wall Street—listening to seditious speeches—passing resolutions that they were entitled to work and the wages of work, and that if they were not provided with work they would take the means of subsistence *vi et armis.*

This morning the Hall was in a state of siege; all its front portico and a large space in the park occupied by a mob; some three hundred policemen on duty and ready for action inside. About one hundred and fifty United States soldiers from Governor's Island and marines were posted in the Custom-House and the adjoining Assay Office. General Scott was under orders from Washington to see that the treasure of the Federal Government be not violated. The mob in the park was mostly made up of blackguard boys under twenty-one, with some natural proclivity to a muss, Celts of the lower grade, loving whiskey rather than work, "yawping" about, too stolid to understand their own alleged grievances, and a few Germans. These last, the really dangerous class, were not fully represented. The Tompkins Square crowd did not come downtown. The orators were mostly fluent Hibernians. They spoke with ease and with some command of forcible and accurate language, and with great intensity of feeling, but I saw no sign of any deep earnest sentiment among the mob. They hurrahed and yelled, but I think the great majority of the vagabonds considered themselves merely on a lark. It seemed to me that there was no reason to apprehend serious disturbance, *at present.* The precautions that have been taken seem superfluous, but they can do no harm.

Wood is frightened. He has raised a spirit he can't control, a

spirit that threatens to turn and rend him. The orators of this morning denounced him as a humbug, promising aid but unable to afford
it. He will probably lose more votes than he gains by this dodge.

*NOVEMBER 17* If the stock market be a reliable index of our condition, we're reacting toward prosperous times. There are other
signs, too, of returning confidence and ease. But this will be an anxious winter at best.

*NOVEMBER 21* Nothing very new downtown, except that the
large intelligent and spontaneous assemblage of my fellow citizens in
front of the Merchants' Exchange yesterday gave the best evidence of
their sagacity by putting *me* on their "Executive Committee." *A bas*
Fernando! *Vive* Tiemann! I shall commence a series of philippics.
"Strong's First Oration against Wood." "Second ditto." "How long, O
Fernando Wood, wilt thou abuse our patience?" Walked down with
Jack Ehninger and George Anthon. Didn't do much in Wall Street.
Walked up again; went with Ellie to the Philharmonic concert.
Crowd. Clack. At last an excited individual, Teutonic, rose up in the
midst of a dreary adagio on the violoncello by one of these inevitable
Mollenhauers, and exclaimed with much emphasis, as if in continu-
ation of some fruitless private remonstrance: "Well, I can talk, too.
So that everybody can hear me! Is it not possible for us to have some
place where we can *hear?*" and then subsided with like abruptness.
People were still as mice in that neighborhood for some time. This
self-sacrificing champion of silence should receive some testimonial.
At these concerts especially, the music is drowned, or at least one's
capacity for enjoying it is paralyzed with vexation, by incessant, ill-
bred, and obstreperous gabblings.

*DECEMBER 28* *Tonight is a great anniversary.* Ten years ago this
minute I was in Mrs. John A. Stevens' house, in Bleecker Street, at a
big party, in the crowded supper-room, where poor Johnny Parish
had lodged himself in a very strong position at the supper table, and
Walter Cutting was vainly trying to do likewise and telling me that
he thought the true way was for men to "fire and fall back," and

Frank Griffin (I can see him now) was urging me to go to Europe and descanting on his emotions when he entered Rome. And I was thinking about the young lady in blue silk (or blue something) I'd been talking with so pleasantly and sympathetically before supper. God bless her; she's now my dear wife and the mother of my little boys upstairs. I remember just where she stood, at the end of a dance, when I plucked up a sheepish courage (doubting much whether she'd recognize me), and accosted the young lady and the precise topography of the sofa in the back parlor where we discoursed somewhat at length. Just at this hour, about one A.M., I was no doubt walking fast down Broadway with Johnny Parish and the biggest of cigars. I remember his facetious enquiry whether I had fallen in love with Miss Ellen Ruggles. Next time I saw her was New Year's Day, 1848, ten years ago this coming January 1st. I'd been in the house once before, at a "Bee" the preceding spring, of which I remember little but that I thought the young lady wonderful and delightful to behold, and that I contrived to knock over a glass that stood on the little table just by the front parlor door (only a wine glass) with a rose bud or two in it, and to reduce the same to small fragments. Like most shy and awkward people, I was inexpressibly humiliated and crushed, and the graceful simple way in which Miss Ellen passed over the accident only made my anguish more poignant. I expatiated on it, I remember, to George Anthon, who tried to console me. The party of which tonight is the decenniversary was my first interview after that distressing contretemps.

*[1858] APRIL 10* I could not refuse the invitation of today's sunshine. I strolled out with George Anthon on some frivolous pretext or other, walked farther than I intended, and roamed far away, at last, among the remote regions of Southern Brooklyn, near Gowanus and the place where was of old the Penny Bridge. The growth of that region is marvelous. A great city has been built there within my memory. The compact miles of monotonous, ephemeral houses which one overlooks from the Greenwood Cemetery ridge impress me as does some great reef half bare at low tide and dense with barnacles. Each is a *home*, each is throwing out its prehensile cilii into

the great sea, with better fortune or worse, good investments or bad, credit or disrepute, progress up or down. Each has (or had) its children, its young girls, its boys hopeful or otherwise, its own domestic history and prospects, its memories of joy and sorrow, each is an epitome of human life within each shabby domicile.

*APRIL 27* Walked to 109th Street Sunday afternoon with George Anthon. The cutting on Fourth Avenue at Fiftieth Street through the old Potters Field is a disgrace and scandal. It exposes a fossiliferous stratum some three feet thick of close-packed coffins or shells, and debris of dead paupers. Ribs, clavicles, and vertebra abound all along the railroad tracks, and one might easily construct a perfect skeleton from these stray fragments without resorting to the remains *in situ*, were not many of the specimens imperfect, having been gnawed and crunched by the gaunt swine that are co-tenants with Hibernian humanity of the adjoining shanties. This is within a hundred yards of a dense population.

*[1860] JANUARY 1, SUNDAY* New Year's Day. God prosper the New Year to those I love. Church with Ellie and Johnny; an effective sermon by Higby. Thereafter we took a cold "constitutional" up the Fifth Avenue to Forty-second Street, a rather vigorous winter day, still and sharp. Tonight is overcast, with promise of snow tomorrow.

*JANUARY 5* With Ellie to the Artists' "Reception" in Dodworth's Rooms; a vast crowd. Discovered Mrs. D. C. Murray and Mrs. John Weeks, General Dix, Wenzler, Stone, Rossiter, Mrs. Field (commonly distinguished as "the murderess," being mixed up a little with the Duc de Praslin affair), the Rev. Mr. Frothingham, Lewis Rutherfurd, and others. Many bad pictures on the walls, and some few good ones. Eastman Johnson and Charles Dix are making progress. Wenzler has a lovely portrait of one of Dr. Potts's daughters. Stone's portrait of my two little men was there, and people praised it—to *me*.

Monday the second was kept for New Year's Day. It was a fine specimen of crisp frosty weather, with a serene sky and a cutting wind from the northwest. I set forth at eleven o'clock in my own particular hack, *en grand seigneur*, and effected more than twenty calls, beginning with Mrs. Samuel Whitlock in 37th Street. My lowest south latitude was Dr. Berrian's and the Lydigs'. There were no incidents. Bishop Potter's drawing-room was perhaps the dullest place I visited. The Bishop is always kindly and cordial, but nature has given him no organ for the secretion of the small talk appropriate to a five minutes' call. He feels the deficiency and is nervous and uncomfortable. Very nice at Mrs. George F. Jones's, and at Mrs. William Schermerhorn's. At Mrs. Peter A. Schermerhorn's, in University Place, I discovered the mamma and Miss Ellen, both very gracious. At Mrs. William Astor's, Miss Ward (the granddaughter of the house; Sam Ward's daughter by his first wife) talked of her friend Miss Annie Leavenworth. . . . Mrs. Edgar was charming in her little bit of a house, the "Petit Trianon." Poor Mrs. Douglas Cruger seems growing old, is less vivacious and less garrulous. At Mrs. Serena Fearing's I was honored with a revelation of the baby that was produced last summer. Pleasant visit to Mrs. Christine Griffin, née Kean—where little Miss Mary was looking her loveliest. That little creature will make havoc in society a year or two hence, when she "comes out." She is very beautiful and seems full of life and intelligence. Mrs. Isaac Wright in Waverley Place, with her brood of four noble children rampaging about her, was good to see. . . .

Home at six, tired after a pleasant day's work. We had a comfortable session at dinner with Dr. Peters and Mrs. Georgey Peters, Miss Annie Leavenworth, Miss Josephine Strong, Walter Cutting, Richard Hunt, Murray Hoffman, George C. Anthon, Jem Ruggles, and Jack Ehninger. Dinner was successful.

*FEBRUARY 3* Last night's Elm Street fire was a sad business. Some eighteen or twenty people perished. There was another fire in Lexington Avenue (dwelling houses) due to these pestilent furnaces. Two factories have just been blown to bits in Brooklyn by defective or neglected steam-boilers, with great destruction of life. We are still a semi-barbarous race. But the civilizing element also revealed itself this morning at the Tombs, when Mr. Stephens was hanged for poi-

soning his wife. If a few owners or builders of factories and tenement houses could be hanged tomorrow, life would become less insecure.

*MARCH 2, FRIDAY*  Stopped at Barnum's on my way downtown to
see the much advertised nondescript, the "What-is-it." Some say it's
an advanced chimpanzee, others that it's a cross between nigger and
baboon. But it seems to me clearly an idiotic negro dwarf, raised,
perhaps, in Alabama or Virginia. The showman's story of its capture
(with three other specimens that died) by a party in pursuit of the
gorilla on the western coast of Africa is probably bosh. The creature's
look and action when playing with his keeper are those of a nigger
boy. But his anatomical details are fearfully simian, and he's a great
fact for Darwin.

*MARCH 3*  George Anthon called in Wall Street, and before going
uptown, we stopped at Barnum's. The "What-is-it?" is palpably a little nigger and not a good-looking one. There are other animals in the
establishment much more interesting; for example, a grand grizzly
bear from California, a big sea lion, a very intelligent and attractive
marbled or mottled seal (*phoca vitulina?*), a pair of sociable kanga-
roos, and (in the happy family cage) an armadillo, a curious spotted
rodent said to be Australian, two fine owls, and so forth.

*MAY 19*  Thy Nose, O W. H. Seward, is out of joint! The Chicago
Convention nominates Lincoln and Hamlin. They will be beat, unless
the South perpetrate some special act of idiocy, arrogance, or brutality before next fall.
  Lincoln will be strong in the Western states. He is unknown here.
The *Tribune* and other papers commend him to popular favor as having had but six months' schooling in his whole life; and because he
cut a great many rails, and worked on a flatboat in early youth; all
which is somehow presumptive evidence of his statesmanship. The
watchword of the campaign is already indicated. It is to be "Honest
Abe" (our candidate being a namesake of the Father of the Faithful).
Mass-meetings and conventions and committees are to become

enthusiastic and vociferous whenever an orator says Abe. But that monosyllable does not seem to me likely to prove a word of power. "Honest Abe" sounds less efficient than "Frémont and Jessie," and that failed four years ago.

*MAY 28, MONDAY* The park below the reservoir begins to look intelligible. Unfinished still, and in process of manufacture, but shewing the outline now of what it is to be. Many points are already beautiful. What will they be when their trees are grown and I'm dead and forgotten?

One thinks sometimes that one would like re-juvenescence, or a new birth. One would prefer, if he could, to annihilate his past and commence life, say in this A.D. 1860, and so enjoy longer acquaintance with this era of special development and material progress, watch the splendid march of science on earth, share the benefits of the steam engine and the electric telegraph, and grow up with this park—which is to be so great a fact for the young men and maidens of New York in 1880, if all goes well and we do not decompose into anarchy meanwhile. The boy of that year is likely to have larger privileges and a better time than were conceded to the boy of 1830. Central Park and Astor Library and a developed Columbia University promise to make the city twenty years hence a real center of culture and civilization, furnishing privileges to youth far beyond what it gave me in my boyhood.

*MAY 30, WEDNESDAY* Invited to be a vice-president of a great Republican ratification meeting tomorrow night. Declined on the plea of "engagements," but the truth is I do not know whether I am a Republican at all.

*JUNE 1, FRIDAY* Pleasant beginning of another summer. Light showers at noon, and the afternoon a little too cool and breezy. But Ellie enjoyed her drive in the new park and her stroll through the "Ramble." We were an ample carriage-load—poor Miss Annie Leavenworth, Mr. Ruggles, Ellie, I, Babbins, and Johnny on the box. Mr. Ruggles dined here. . . .

Poor Ike Fowler said to be at Havana. Old associations make me share most fully the general sympathy for him in his fall and exile, but it does seem strange that nobody speaks of him as criminal; that one hears no denunciation of his crime, in stealing $158,000 of somebody's money. Everybody says "poor Fowler," "what a pity," "I'm very sorry for Fowler," and the like, just as if this catastrophe were a case of misfortune, the failure of a trader or speculator. Can a community maintain itself long without revolution, being so utterly wanting in perception of the difference between night and morning?

*AUGUST 16* Made my debut in the New York Club this afternoon. Dined there with Charles Strong better and more cheaply than at Delmonico's. One enjoys, moreover, a sensation of being nobby and exclusive when one dines there, which ought to promote digestion, but it has failed to do so this time, for I'm dyspeptic tonight with cephalalgic tendencies. Saw but a few men there, including Bill Pennington, who was a little tight and exuberantly cordial. My respect for the Club has greatly increased since Baron Rothschild's friends had to withdraw his name, because the Baron, though illustrious and a millionaire, was immoderately given to lewd talk and nude photographs. I did not give the Council credit for moral courage enough to deny him admission.

*OCTOBER 2* Diligent day. Having been put on the reception committee for the Prince of Wales's ball, I attended a meeting thereof. There were Hamilton Fish, Luther Bradish, Perit, Maunsell Field, Minturn, Cisco, and myself. There was severe prosing on "nice sharp quillets" of etiquette. Bradish and Field were uncommonly solemn and impressive. With what manner of reception shall we receive General Scott? "Can he be separated from his military family?" There's the rub. Shall we ten reception committeemen dress alike? Shall it be white vests and black cravats or vice versa? Are silk vests considered provincial in Paris? What manner of gloves prevailed at the Tuileries when Governor Fish was there last, and what light is thrown on the whole subject by Bradish's little souvenirs of court society at the several capitals of Europe? Cisco and I are a subcommittee on the carriages that are to convey His Royal Highness and suite from the Fifth Avenue Hotel to the Opera House. O happy carriages, and horses too much blessed! I am a Committee of One to provide drinks for the special consolation of His Royal Highness in a small withdrawing room to be consecrated to that use. The Prince is said to be partial to sherry and seltzer water.

*OCTOBER 5, FRIDAY* Much occupied with divers matters growing out of the expected advent of our "sweet young Prince." "Long may he wave," but I wish he were at home again with his royal mamma, and I hope the community won't utterly disgrace itself before he goes away. The amount of tuft-hunting and Prince-worshiping threatens to be fearful; and, I don't know how it happens, but I fear my share in the demonstration is to be much larger than I expected or desired. The Reception Committee met today and passed on divers weighty matters. It is proposed that we "wait on the Prince" the evening before the ball, which seems to me a very superfluous work of supererogation. All we can say or do is to express the hope that His Royal Highness finds himself pretty well, considering, and I think His Royal Highness will be inclined to take it for granted that we hope so, whether we call or not.

*OCTOBER 11* I begin to be weary of this "sweet young Prince." The Hope of England threatens to become a bore. In fact, he is a bore of the first order. Everybody has talked of nothing but His Royal Highness for the last week. Reaction is inevitable. It has set in, and by Monday next, the remotest allusion to His Royal Highness will act like ipecac. It has been a mild, bland, half-cloudy day. By ten o'clock, people were stationing themselves along the curbstones of Broadway and securing a good place to see the Prince. What a spectacle-loving people we are! Shops were closed and business paralyzed; Wall Street deserted. I spent the morning mostly at the Trinity vestry office, signing tickets, and so forth. We had to pass on a bushel of applications for admission next Sunday. Lots of Fifth Avenueites sent in letters, tendering a private carriage for the conveyance of His Royal Highness to church, with a postscript asking for a "few" tickets. Corporators of Trinity Church bluster about their rights and insist on reserved pews. I fear we are a city of snobs.

I lounged uptown at two o'clock, feeling my way through the crowd that filled Broadway. Omnibusses and carriages were turned into the side streets and all Broadway was one long dense mass of impatient humanity. All the windows on either side were filled. Temporary platforms crowded, at five dollars a seat. It was beyond the Japanese demonstration, though Mr. Superintendent Kennedy assured me the other day that the Prince of Wales would be less popular than Tommy.

At three, I went into the New York Club and took a seat with Charley, Seton, Pinckney, Stewart, Jem Strong, Bankhead, and others, at a convenient window. We watched and waited, and united in denunciation of F. Wood, Mayor, whom we assumed to have got the Prince in his grasp and to be detaining him with a speech at the City Hall. It was six o'clock and quite dark before the head of the procession reached us. We saw a six-horse barouche pass. We hurrahed. Ladies in the opposite windows waved their handkerchiefs. Little boys in the street hay-hayed. Elder loafers yelled, and the Prince was gone. Keen-sighted and self-confident men insisted that they had actually seen someone in scarlet uniform bowing his acknowledgments, but their assertions inspired no confidence. It was too dark to distinguish colors.

I fought my way home through the crowd. We dined at seven. Ellie and Johnny had "seen" the royal procession at Mrs. Cutting's in Fifth Avenue, and Babbins at Union Square.

OCTOBER 13, SATURDAY  At eight to the Academy of Music. The doors were not yet opened to the common herd, but my exalted official position on the committee admitted me by the royal entrance on Fourteenth Street. The house looked brilliant, blazing with lights and decorated with great masses of flowers. My post was with Charles King, Ben Silliman, and Cyrus Field in the room appointed for the reception of invited guests generally. Certain other committees had interfered with our arrangements in an unwarrantable and unconstitutional manner. The consequence of this outrage was (as we had distinctly foreseen and predicted) that the great majority of the invited guests found their way to "the floor" for themselves without being conducted thither by any legitimate organ. Our duties were therefore light. We "received" a few South American and Portuguese diplomats and General Paez and Major Delafield and Captain Cullum and sundry army and navy people and a score of city militia, colonels in most elaborate uniforms, and Mayor Wood (I had a very intimate talk with that limb of Satan); and at ten we adjourned to the special reception room and joined Hamilton Fish and old Pelatiah Perit (who looked like a duke in his dress coat and white cravat), and Peter Cooper, who looked like one of Gulliver's Yahoos caught and cleaned and dressed up.

In came the royal party at last, with the Reception Committeemen, who had been assigned the pleasing duty of escorting them. We were presented to His Royal Highness *seriatim*. I had supposed that shaking hands with a Prince of Wales was indecorous, and that a bow was the proper acknowledgment of introduction to so august a personage; but when the Prince puts out his hand, or extends and proffers his fingers like anybody else, it seems ungracious to decline the honor and say, "Sir, I am so well bred as to know my place, and I am unworthy to shake hands with a descendant of James I and George III and a probable King of England hereafter." I think of having my right-hand glove framed and glazed, with an appropriate inscription.

Fish had assigned to each of the committee the duty of conducting one of the Prince's suite into the ballroom, and I was charged with Lord Hinchinbrooke. I had implored Fish to bear in mind that most of our committee (myself included) were unable to distinguish dukes from mere honorables and asked him to be sure to introduce each notable to his committeeman godfather (*vide* programmes of autos-da-fè). But he forgot to do so, and we marched into the ballroom in a very promiscuous way—Fish escorting Monseigneur, Peter Cooper tagging after them, and the rest like a flock of sheep—and took our place at the head of the room; that is, the east end. Orchestra plays "God Save the Queen," followed by "Hail Columbia!" Aspect of the house and the crowd brilliant and satisfactory. I fall into talk with a pleasant-looking Englisher, and introduce myself. He proves to be Englehart, the Duke of Newcastle's private secretary, and an amiable, agreeable man.

A space in our front was kept clean by the Floor Committee, and through this the crowd began to defile, Fish presenting them as they passed and people making "murgeons and jenny-fluxions" to H.R.H. George Anthon passed with Ellie. . . . I was pointing out notabilities to Englehart and the Honorable Mr. Somebody, and just indicating John Van Buren as the son of one of our ex-kings, when there was a dull, ugly, jarring report, quickly followed by another of the same sort. Everybody started and peered in vain over the heads of the densely packed crowd, and wondered what it was. But there was no panic and no rush. Presently we learned that the temporary flooring had given way in two places; over the stage a couple of beams broke, causing the reports we had heard. Ellie went down into one of the pits and was frightened, but did not lose her footing, nor her self-possession.

Of course, people crowded away from this dangerous region in all directions. The promenade became impracticable, and the Prince and his suite and most of the committee retreated to the reception and supper-rooms. A large space was presently roped off, including the two chasms in the floor, and revealing the scandalous, criminal negligence with which the work of constructing the supports had been done. A score of carpenters and policemen and the illustrious Brown were energetically repairing the damage within fifteen minutes after the accident. But there was a general sense of failure and calamity. Everything looked bilious. Everyone said the whole floor was unsafe. There could be no dancing; the ball was a disgraceful fiasco. I explained to many persons that the Reception Committee had nothing to do with the arrangements of the house. Meantime, the carpenters were working for their lives. Brown peering down into the oblong hole looked as if engaged in his ordinary sextonical duties at an interment. . . .

By midnight damages had been repaired and dancing set in. People streamed over every part of the floor the moment the Prince appeared on it. Danger was forgotten. His Royal Highness's partners, Mrs. Goold Hoyt, Miss Lily Mason, Mrs. John Kernochan, and others, were among our prettiest women. Mrs. Governor Morgan, with whom the Prince opened the ball officially, is elderly and stout, but presentable enough. It is said that she had been taking dancing lessons for the last fortnight, rubbing up her old steps, and that when the quadrille commenced, she timidly inquired, "Your Royal Highness, isn't it time for us to *balancer?*" Miss Helen Russell was overpowered when the Prince was presented. Her voice failed her for fear, and she astonished H.R.H. with a series of contortions and muscular twitchings before she succeeded in articulating an audible word. So they say; I saw little of the dancing. The way people crowded round was snobbish and rude and indecent, and I kept on the outskirts, where I loafed and lounged dejectedly. . . .

While the Prince was waiting for Mrs. Camilla Hoyt, his partner, Walker, the Presbyterian bookbinder, bustled up with a young woman under his arm, introduced himself, and proceeded, "The lady with whom Your Highness was to dance doesn't seem to be ready; allow me to introduce my daughter." The Prince said, "Yes, the crowd is very dense," or some such thing, and evaded this ambitious plebeian rather gracefully for so young a person. Ellie heard this *propriis auribus*. She was presented to the Illustrious Stranger and discoursed with him and danced in the same "Lancers." I had a very pleasant talk with Mrs. Colonel Scott, and was introduced to Millard Fillmore, who is well-bred and cordial, but I spent most of the evening, or night rather, dawdling about and wishing it were over.

Got home at daylight, weary and worn after nearly nine hours spent in a new pair of patent leathers. Very tired. If H.R.H. appreciate my exertions, he will send me the Victoria Cross or make me a duke *in partibus*, at least.

This evening at Mr. Ruggles's awhile and saw part of the Firemen's procession pass up the Fourth Avenue. It was very brilliant, with torches, colored lights, and so forth. On Madison Square, where they no doubt displayed all their resources of Roman candles and portable fireworks, it must have been a really attractive spectacle.

*OCTOBER 14* So that matter is over. My judgment of the future King of England, from the little I've seen of him, is that he is not re-

markably bright or forward for his years, and that he has been carefully trained to remember the duty of courtesy to all classes.
Everyone has some little instance to tell of his good-breeding, under
difficulties at the ball, when he must have been sorely tried by the
well-meant gaucheries of a few and the unpardonable flunkeyism of
others. Today, when he got out of his carriage and bade Cisco good-
bye, he added a request to bid Mr. Strong goodbye and thank him
for his attention in accompanying me, or some such thing. Many
young Americans of eighteen would have forgotten this little civil
formality. . . .

His visit has occasioned a week of excitement beyond that of any
event in my time, and pervading all classes. Its permanent effect, if
any, will be good here and in England. The unanimity of the feeling
is wonderful, when one thinks of twenty years ago. The protest of
certain militia companies of Irishmen against parading to do honor
to a Saxon and an oppressor of Ireland is the single exception. I've
not heard a single growl or sneer about the fuss we have been making over this young man, who is no better than anybody else, after
all, or anything tending that way even remotely.

NOVEMBER 2    Think I will vote the Republican ticket next
Tuesday. One vote is insignificant, but I want to be able to remember that I voted right at this grave crisis. The North must assert its
rights, now, and take the consequences.

Think of James J. Roosevelt, United States District Attorney,
bringing up certain persons under indictment for piracy as slave-
traders to be arraigned the other day, and talking to the Court about
the plea the defendants should put in, and saying that "there had been
a great change in public sentiment about the slave trade," and that "of
course the President would pardon the defendants if they were capi-
tally convicted." !!! Is Judge Roosevelt more deficient in common
sense or in moral sense? If we accede to Southern exactions, we must
re-open the slave trade with all its horrors, establish a Slave Code for
the territories, and acquiesce in a decision of the United States
Supreme Court in the Lemmon case that will entitle every
Southerner to bring his slaves into New York and Massachusetts and

keep them there. We must confess that our federal government exists chiefly for the sake of nigger-owners. *I can't do that.* Rather let South Carolina and Georgia secede. We will coerce and punish the traitorous seceders if we can; but if we can't, we are well rid of them.

*NOVEMBER 6, TUESDAY* A memorable day. We do not know yet for what. Perhaps for the disintegration of the country, perhaps for another proof that the North is timid and mercenary, perhaps for demonstration that Southern bluster is worthless. We cannot tell yet what historical lesson the event of November 6, 1860, will teach, but the lesson cannot fail to be weighty.

Clear and cool. Vote very large, probably far beyond that of 1856. Tried to vote this morning and found people in a queue extending a whole block from the polls. Abandoned the effort and went downtown. Life and Trust Company meeting. The magnates of that board showed no sign of fluster and seemed to expect no financial crisis. Uptown again at two, and got in my vote after only an hour's detention. I voted for Lincoln.

After dinner to the Trinity School Board at 762 Broadway. Thence downtown, looking for election returns. Great crowd about the newspapers of Fulton and Nassau Streets and Park Row. It was cold, and I was alone and tired and came home sooner than I intended. City returns are all one way, but they will hardly foot up a Fusion majority of much above 25,000. Brooklyn said to be Fusion by 14,000. An anti-Lincoln majority of 40,000 in New York and Kings, well backed by the river counties, may possibly outweigh the Republican majorities in the western counties, but that is unlikely. The Republicans have gained in the city since 1856, and have no doubt gained still more in the interior.

*[1861] APRIL 15* Events multiply. The President is out with a proclamation calling for 75,000 volunteers and an extra session of Congress July 4. It is said 200,000 more will be called within a few days. Every man of them will be wanted before this game is lost and won. Change in public feeling marked, and a thing to thank God for. We begin to look like a United North. Willy Duncan (!) says it may

be necessary to hang Lincoln and Seward and Greeley hereafter, but our present duty is to sustain Government and Law, and give the South a lesson. The New York *Herald* is *in equilibrio* today, just at the turning point. Tomorrow it will denounce Jefferson Davis as it denounced Lincoln a week ago. The *Express* is half traitorous and half in favor of energetic action against traitors. The *Journal of Commerce* and the little *Day-Book* show no signs of reformation yet, but though they are contemptible and without material influence for evil, the growing excitement against their treasonable talk will soon make them more cautious in its utterance. The *Herald* office has already been threatened with an attack.

Mayor Wood out with a "proclamation." He must still be talking. It is brief and commonplace, but winds up with a recommendation to everybody to obey the laws of the land. This is significant. The cunning scoundrel sees which way the cat is jumping and puts himself right on the record in a vague general way, giving the least possible offence to his allies of the Southern Democracy.

*APRIL 16* A fine storm of wind and rain all day. The conversion of the New York *Herald* is complete. It rejoices that rebellion is to be put down and is delighted with Civil War, because it will so stimulate the business of New York, and all this is what "we" (the *Herald*, to wit) have been vainly preaching for months. This impudence of old J. G. Bennett's is too vast to be appreciated at once. You must look at it and meditate over it for some time (as at Niagara and St. Peter's) before you can take in its immensity. His capitulation is a set-off against the loss of Sumter. He's a discreditable ally for the North, but when you see a rat leaving the enemy's ship for your own, you overlook the offensiveness of the vermin for the sake of what its movement indicates. This brazen old scoundrel was hooted up Fulton Street yesterday afternoon by a mob, and the police interfered to prevent it from sacking his printing office. Though converted, one can hardly call him penitent. St. Paul did not call himself the Chief of the Apostles and brag of having been a Christian from the first.

✦  ✦  ✦  ✦  ✦

Subscribed to a fund for equipment of the Twelfth Regiment and put down my name for a projected Rifle Corps, but I fear my near-sightedness is a grave objection to my adopting that arm.

✦ ✦ ✦ ✦ ✦

GOD SAVE THE UNION, AND CONFOUND ITS ENEMIES. AMEN.

*APRIL 17* Dull weather, but it has cleared up tonight. No material change in the complexion of affairs, except that a crisis is drawing very near in Virginia and Kentucky. I count on the loyalty of no Border State, except Maryland. We are on the eve of a civil war that will be bitter and bloody, and probably indecisive.

There was a slight outbreak here today. I was sitting in my office at three o'clock when I heard unwonted sounds in Wall Street, and looking out, saw a straggling column of men running toward the East River. My first notion was that they were chasing a runaway horse, but they soon became too numerous to be engaged in that. They halted in front of the *Journal of Commerce* office and filled the street densely for about a block. There were outcries, which I could not distinctly hear for a minute, and then the American flag was hung out from a window, and the crowd sent up a cheer that stirred one's blood a little, and the surface of the black mass was suddenly all in motion with waving hats. Then a line of policemen came down the street on a dog-trot, and the crowd thereupon moved promptly up Wall Street again, cheering lustily.

They were mostly decently-dressed people, but with a sprinkling of laboring men. I understand they paid a like domiciliary visit to the *Express*, the *Day-Book*, and the *Daily News*, requiring each to put up the flag. They intended to call on the New York Hotel, it is said, but Cranston was forewarned and the American flag was flying from its roof as I came uptown.

*APRIL 18* Fine day; drizzly evening. Journalizing is a serious job just now. We are living a month of common life every day. One general proposition to begin with. My habit is to despond and find fault, but the attitude of New York and the whole North at this time is magnificent. Perfect unanimity, earnestness, and readiness to make every sacrifice for the support of law and national life. Especially impressive after our long forbearance and vain efforts to conciliate, our readiness to humble ourselves for the sake of peace.

✦  ✦  ✦  ✦  ✦

The national flag flying everywhere; every cart horse decorated. It occurred to me that it would be a good thing to hoist it on the tower of Trinity—an unprecedented demonstration, but these are unprecedented times; not only good in itself, as a symbol of the sympathy of the Church Catholic with all movements to suppress privy conspiracy and sedition, but a politic move for Trinity Church at this memorable hour of excitement. Somewhat to my surprise, General Dix, Cisco, Skidmore, Swift, and Gouverneur Ogden cordially concurred with me and signed a note to Dr. Berrian, asking his permission to hoist it.

Posted up to the Rector's in Varick Street, but he was out. Again at four, but he was not very well and could not see me. So I left the note and announced that I should call tomorrow morning for an answer. I expected a negative answer, supported by platitudes of fogyism, easily to be imagined. But while I was at dinner came a note from the Rector, who "very cheerfully" complies with our request. Hurrah for Dr. Berrian! His consent to this is the strongest indication yet of the intensity of our national feeling just now. May we dare to hope it will last?

*APRIL 19* Busy this morning in pursuit of a flag for Trinity Church steeple. Hunted through the city with Vinton in vain; went off on my own account and secured one at last (20 by 40) from Robert B. Minturn, who was most kind and obliging. He went to one of his ships with me and insisted on sending up riggers to help Secor's people hoist it. At half-past two, it went up; the chimes saluting it with "Hail Columbia," "Yankee Doodle," and "Old Hundred," and a crowd in Wall Street and Broadway cheering. Higby, Vinton, and Ogilby led the cheers. The flinging out of the flag, the clang of the bells, and the enthusiastic cheering, gave me a new sensation. I am amazed by the strong feeling of gratification strengthened by surprise that this little flourish called out. The solution is, probably, that the ideas of Church and State, Religion and Politics, have been practically separated so long that people are specially delighted with any manifestation of the Church's sympathy with the State and recognition of our national life on any fitting occasion. This flag was a symbol of the truth that the Church is no esoteric organization, no private soul-saving society; that it has a position to take in every great public national crisis, and that its position is important. Some sense of this truth must have been at the bottom of the many emphatic expressions I heard this afternoon (from strangers) of approval of the flag-raising on Trinity spire; for example, "Are they really going to hoist the flag on the steeple, Sir?—Well, now, *I* tell *you*, that's the *biggest thing* that's been done in New York in my time!"

APRIL 23  Everyone's future has changed in these six months last past. This is to be a terrible, ruinous war, and a war in which the nation cannot succeed. It can never subjugate these savage millions of the South. It must make peace at last with the barbarous communities off its Southern frontier. I was prosperous and well off last November. I believe my assets to be reduced fifty per cent, at least. But I hope I can still provide wholesome training for my three boys. With that patrimony they can fight out the battle of life for themselves. Their mother is plucky and can stand self-denial. I clearly see that this is a most severe personal calamity to me, but I welcome it cordially, for it has shown that I belong to a community that is brave and generous, and that the City of New York is not sordid and selfish.

APRIL 25  Our "New York Rifles" met at 7:30 at rooms hired for the evening, a loft at 814 Broadway. It was crowded, so two squads adjourned to the old club house at the corner of Astor Place, where we were drilled more than two hours. Everybody awkward, but earnest and diligent. Then we marched back. I was solemnly elected president of the association till our military commandant shall be chosen, and got through my duties decently well, I believe, keeping the mob of men in tolerable order, though all were on their feet, having nothing but the floor to sit down on.

MAY 6 Walked uptown with Agnew, stopped awhile at the New York Hospital, and then at Colonel Bliss's, where we learned that the *Daniel Webster* had been telegraphed below. Omnibussed at once to Whitehall and found she was lying off Castle Garden. I took a boat. Made a hurried inspection. She came away yesterday morning with 187 sick, of whom four have died. Two more are moribund, if appearances be reliable. Some thirty or forty are convalescent. They are on deck enjoying the tonic northwest wind and bright sunshine and doubtless appreciating the visible signs of home and civilization all around them. In the wards below we found excellent ventilation, no smells, attentive and vigilant officers, comfort and order. But with all this, the bunks of the forward cabin were tragic. Gaunt, wan, wild faces, restless tossing forms, arms that were ready to strike hard for the country against the country's enemy strapped relentlessly to the fevered body. Great big eyes looking at us without intelligence. One poor fellow had just died, and lay with unclosed eyes glaring upwards, as if appealing to the God of Justice for vengeance on those who have brought this murderous war upon us.

I was much gratified by the talk of the soldiers. "Nothing at all to complain of, sir." "Have you been treated as well as you were in your shore hospitals?" "Oh, there ain't no comparison, sir. We've been treated like gentlemen *here*, but in them holes there wasn't nobody to look after us." This is satisfactory; a tangible result that justifies our appeal to the public for aid and support, and the time we have spent in work for the Sanitary Commission.

*[1863]* APRIL 23 A Broadway Railroad seems inflicted on us at last. A corrupt bill to establish it was just passing our disgraceful, profligate legislature, under the pilotage of George Law, when the Common Council intervened, seeing that they could make no money out of this Albany job, and authorized the Harlem Railroad Company to lay a track down Broadway. A large force of Celts is

tearing up the pavement and laying down sleepers this afternoon at the corner of Broadway and Fourteenth Street. I fear our old familiar Broadway, with its packed omnibusses and difficult travel, is gone. The new regime with its railroad cars may prove more convenient, but I distrust it.

*JULY 13, MONDAY* A notable day. Stopped at the Sanitary Commission office on my way downtown to endorse a lot of checks that had accumulated during my absence, and heard there of rioting in the upper part of the city. As Charley is at Newport and Bidwell in Berkshire County, I went to Wall Street nevertheless; but the rumors grew more and more unpleasant, so I left it at once and took a Third Avenue car for uptown. At the Park were groups and small crowds in more or less excitement (which found relief afterwards, I hear, in hunting down and maltreating sundry unoffending niggers), but there was nothing to indicate serious trouble. The crowded car went slowly on its way, with its perspiring passengers, for the weather was still of this deadly muggy sort with a muddy sky and lifeless air. At Thirteenth Street the track was blocked by a long line of stationary cars that stretched indefinitely up the Avenue, and I took to the sidewalk. Above Twentieth Street all shops were closed, and many people standing and staring or strolling uptown, not riotously disposed but eager and curious. Here and there a rough could be heard damning the draft. No policemen to be seen anywhere. Reached the seat of war at last, Forty-sixth Street and Third Avenue. Three houses on the Avenue and two or three on the street were burned down: engines playing on the ruins—more energetically, I'm told, than they did when their efforts would have been useful.

The crowd seemed just what one commonly sees at any fire, but its nucleus of riot was concealed by an outside layer of ordinary peaceable lookers-on. Was told they had beat off a squad of police and another of "regulars" (probably the Twelfth Militia). At last, it opened and out streamed a posse of perhaps five hundred, certainly less than one thousand, of the lowest Irish day laborers. The rabble was perfectly homogeneous. Every brute in the drove was pure

Celtic—hod-carrier or loafer. They were unarmed. A few carried pieces of fence-paling and the like. They turned off west into Forty-fifth Street and gradually collected in front of two three-story dwelling houses on Lexington Avenue, just below that street, that stand alone together on a nearly vacant block. Nobody could tell why these houses were singled out. Some said a drafting officer lived in one of them, others that a damaged policeman had taken refuge there. The mob was in no hurry; they had no need to be; there was no one to molest them or make them afraid. The beastly ruffians were masters of the situation and of the city. After a while sporadic paving-stones began to fly at the windows, ladies and children emerged from the rear and had a rather hard scramble over a high board fence, and then scudded off across the open, Heaven knows whither. Then men and small boys appeared at rear windows and began smashing the sashes and the blinds and shied out light articles, such as books and crockery, and dropped chairs and mirrors into the back yard; the rear fence was demolished and loafers were seen marching off with portable articles of furniture. And at last a light smoke began to float out of the windows and I came away. I could endure the disgraceful, sickening sight no longer, and what could I *do*?

The fury of the low Irish women in that region was noteworthy. Stalwart young vixens and withered old hags were swarming everywhere, all cursing the "bloody draft" and egging on their men to mischief.

Omnibussed down to No. 823, where is news that the Colored Half Orphan Asylum on Fifth Avenue, just above the reservoir, is burned. "*Tribune* office to be burned tonight." Railroad rails torn up, telegraph wires cut, and so on. If a quarter one hears be true, this is an organized insurrection in the interest of the rebellion and Jefferson Davis rules New York today.

Attended to business. Then with Wolcott Gibbs to dinner at Maison Dorée. During our symposium, there was an alarm of a coming mob, and we went to the window to see. The "mob" was moving down Fourteenth Street and consisted of just thirty-four lousy, blackguardly Irishmen with a tail of small boys. Whither they went, I cannot say, nor can I guess what mischief the handful of *canaille* chose to do. A dozen policemen would have been more than a match for the whole crew, but there were no policemen in sight.

Walked uptown with Wolcott Gibbs. Large fire on Broadway and Twenty-eighth Street. Signs of another to the east, said to be on Second Avenue. Stopped awhile at Gibbs's in Twenty-ninth Street, where was madame, frightened nearly to death, and then to St. Nicholas Hotel to see the mayor and General Wool. We found a lot of people with them. There were John Jay and George W. Blunt and Colonel Howe and John Austin Stevens, Jr., all urging strong measures. But the substantial and weighty and influential men were not represented; out of town, I suppose. Their absence emboldened Gibbs and myself to make pressure for instant action, but it was vain. We begged that martial law might be declared. Opdyke said that was Wool's business, and Wool said it was Opdyke's, and neither would act. "Then, Mr. Mayor, issue a proclamation calling on all loyal and law-abiding citizens to enroll themselves as a volunteer force for defense of life and property." "Why," quoth Opdyke, "that is *civil war* at once." Long talk with Colonel Cram, Wool's chief of staff, who professes to believe that everything is as it should be and sufficient force on the ground to prevent further mischief. Don't believe it. Neither Opdyke nor General Wool is nearly equal to this crisis. Came off disgusted. Went to Union League Club awhile. No comfort there. Much talk, but no one ready to do anything whatever, not even to telegraph to Washington.

We telegraphed, two or three of us, from General Wool's rooms, to the President, begging that troops be sent on and stringent measures taken. The great misfortune is that nearly all our militia regiments have been despatched to Pennsylvania. All the military force I have seen or heard of today were in Fifth Avenue at about seven P.M. There were two or three feeble companies of infantry, a couple of howitzers, and a squadron or two of unhappy-looking "dragoons."

These wretched rioters have been plundering freely, I hear. Their outbreak will either destroy the city or damage the Copperhead cause fatally. Could we but catch the scoundrels who have stirred them up, what a blessing it would be! God knows what tonight or tomorrow may bring forth. We may be thankful that it is now (quarter past twelve) raining briskly. Mobs have no taste for the effusion of cold water. I'm thankful, moreover, that Ellie and the children are out of town. I sent Johnny off to Cornwall this afternoon in charge of John the waiter.

*j u l y   14*  Eleven P.M. Fire bells clanking, as they have clanked at intervals through the evening. Plenty of rumors throughout the day and evening, but nothing very precise or authentic. There have been sundry collisions between the rabble and the authorities, civil and military. Mob fired upon. It generally runs, but on one occasion appears to have rallied, charged the police and militia, and forced them back in disorder. The people are waking up, and by tomorrow there will be adequate organization to protect property and life. Many details come in of yesterday's brutal, cowardly ruffianism and plunder. Shops were cleaned out and a black man hanged in Carmine Street, for no offence but that of Nigritude. Opdyke's house again attacked this morning by a roaming handful of Irish blackguards. Two or three gentlemen who chanced to be passing saved it from sack by a vigorous charge and dispersed the popular uprising (as the *Herald*, *World*, and *News* call it), with their walking sticks and their fists.

Walked uptown perforce, for no cars and few omnibi were running. They are suppressed by threats of burning railroad and omnibus stables, the drivers being wanted to reinforce the mob. Tiffany's shop, Ball & Black's, and a few other Broadway establishments are closed. (Here I am interrupted by report of a fire near at hand, and a great glare on the houses across the Park. Sally forth, and find the Eighteenth Ward station house, Twenty-second Street, near First Avenue, in full blaze. A splendid blaze it made, but I did not venture below Second Avenue, finding myself in a crowd of Celtic spectators disgorged by the circumjacent tenement houses. They were exulting over the damage to "them bloody police," and so on. I thought discretion the better part of curiosity. Distance lent enchantment to that view.)

At 823 with Bellows four to six; then home. At eight to Union League Club. Rumor it's to be attacked tonight. Some say there is to be great mischief tonight and that the rabble is getting the upper hand. Home at ten and sent for by Dudley Field, Jr., to confer about an expected attack on his house and his father's, which adjoin each other in this street just below Lexington Avenue. He has a party there with muskets and talks of fearful trouble before morning, but he is always a blower and a very poor devil. Fire bells again at twelve-fifteen. No light of conflagration is visible.

Bellows's report from Gettysburg and from Meade's headquarters very interesting. Thinks highly of Meade. Thinks the battle around Williamsport will be tolerably evenly matched, Lee having been decidedly beaten a week ago, but not at all demoralized. But there's a despatch at the Union League Club tonight that Lee has moved his whole army safely across, except his rear guard, which we captured.

A good deal of yelling to the eastward just now. The Fields and their near neighbour, Colonel Frank Howe, are as likely to be attacked by this traitor-guided mob as any people I know. If they *are*, we shall see trouble in this quarter, and Gramercy Park will acquire historical associations. O, how tired I am! But I feel reluctant to go to bed. I believe I dozed off a minute or two. There came something like two reports of artillery, perhaps only falling walls. There go two jolly Celts along the street, singing a genuine Celtic howl, something about "Tim O'Laggerty," with a refrain of pure Erse. Long live the sovereigns of New York, Brian Boroo *redivivus* and multiplied. Paddy has left his Egypt—Connaught—and reigns in this promised land of milk and honey and perfect freedom. Hurrah, there goes a strong squad of police marching eastward down this street, followed by a company of infantry with gleaming bayonets. One A.M. Fire bells again, southeastward, "Swinging slow with sullen roar." Now they are silent, and I shall go to bed, at least for a season.

*J U L Y   1 5* Wednesday begins with heavy showers, and now (ten A.M.) cloudy, hot, and steaming. Morning papers report nothing specially grave as occurring since midnight. But there will be much trouble today. Rabbledom is not yet dethroned any more than its ally and instigator, Rebeldom.

News from the South is consolatory. Port Hudson surrendered. Sherman said to have beaten Joseph Johnston somewhere near Vicksburg. Operations commencing against Charleston. Bragg seems to be abandoning Chattanooga and retiring on Atlanta. *Per contra*, Lee has got safely off. I thought he would. . . . Lots of talk and rumors about attacks on the New York Custom-house (*ci-devant* Merchants' Exchange) and the Treasury (late Custom-house). Went to see Cisco and found his establishment in military occupation—sentinels pacing, windows barricaded, and so on. He was as serene and bland as the loveliest May morning ("so cool, so calm, so bright") and showed me the live shell ready to throw out of the window and the "battery" to project Assay Office oil-of-vitriol and the like. He's all right. Then called on Collector Barney and had another long talk with him. Find him well prepared with shells, grenades, muskets, and men, but a little timid and anxious, "wanting counsel," doubtful about his right to fire on the mob, and generally flaccid and tremulous—poor devil!

Walked uptown with Charley Strong and Hoppin, and after my cup of coffee, went to Union League Club. A delegation returned from police headquarters, having vainly asked for a squad of men to garrison the clubhouse. *None can be spared*. What is worse, we were badly repulsed in an attack on the mob in First Avenue, near Nineteenth Street, at about six P.M. Fired upon from houses, and had to leave sixteen wounded men and a Lieutenant Colonel Jardine in the hands of these brutes and devils. This is very bad indeed. But tonight is quieter than the last, though there seems to be a large fire downtown, and we hear occasional gun-shots.

At the club was George Biggs, full of the loudest and most emphatic jawing. "General Frémont's house and Craven's to be attacked tonight, Croton mains to be cut, and gas works destroyed," and so on. By way of precaution, I had had the bathtubs filled, and also all the pots, kettles, and pails in the house. . . . Twelve-thirty: Light as of a large fire to the south.

*JULY 16* Rather quiet downtown. No trustworthy accounts of riot on any large scale during the day. General talk downtown is that the trouble is over. We shall see. It will be as it pleases the scoundrels who are privily engineering the outbreak—agents of Jefferson Davis, permitted to work here in New York.

Omnibusses and railroad cars in full career again. Coming uptown tonight I find Gramercy Park in military occupation. Strong parties drawn up across Twentieth Street and Twenty-first Streets at the east end of the Square, by the G House, each with a flanking squad, forming an L. Occasional shots fired at them from the region of Second or First Avenue, which were replied to by volleys that seem to have done little execution. An unlucky cart-horse was knocked over, I hear. This force was relieved at seven by a company of regulars and a party of the Seventh with a couple of howitzers, and there has been but a stray shot or two since dark. The regulars do not look like steady men. I have just gone over to the hotel with John Robertson and ordered a pail of strong coffee to put a little life into them.

Never knew exasperation so intense, unqualified, and general as that which prevails against these rioters and the politic knaves who are supposed to have set them going, Governor Seymour not excepted. Men who voted for him mention the fact with contrition and self-abasement, and the Democratic Party is at a discount with all the people I meet. (Apropos of discount, gold fell to one hundred and twenty-six today, with the city in insurrection, a gunboat at the foot of Wall Street, the Custom-house and Treasury full of soldiers and live shells, and two howitzers in position to rake Nassau Street from Wall to Fulton!!!!)

Every impression that's made on our people passes away so soon, almost as if stamped on the sand of the sea-beach. Were our moods a little less fleeting, I should have great hope of permanent good from the general wrath these outrages have provoked, and should put some faith in people's prophesyings that Fernando Wood and McCunn, and the New York *Herald*, and the Brookses and others, are doomed henceforth to obscurity and contempt. But we shall forget all about it before next November. Perhaps the lesson of the last four days is to be taught us still more emphatically, and we have got to be worse before we are better. It is not clear that the resources of the conspiracy are yet exhausted. The rioters of yesterday were better armed and organized than those of Monday, and their inaction today may possibly be meant to throw us off our guard, or their time may be employed perfecting plans for a campaign of plundering and brutality in yet greater force. They are in full possession of the western and the eastern sides of the city, from Tenth Street upward, and of a good many districts beside. I could not walk four blocks eastward from this house this minute without peril. The outbreak is spreading by concerted action in many quarters. Albany, Troy, Yonkers, Hartford, Boston, and other cities have each their Irish anti-conscription Nigger-murdering mob, of the same type with ours. It is a grave business, a *jacquerie* that must be put down by heroic doses of lead and steel.

Dr. Peters and Charley Strong called at eleven P.M. They have been exploring and report things quiet except on First Avenue from Nineteenth to Thirtieth Street, where there is said to be trouble. A detachment of the Seventh Regiment, five hundred or six hundred strong, marched to that quarter from their armory an hour ago.

*JULY 17* The Army of Gramercy Park has advanced its headquarters to Third Avenue, leaving only a picket guard in sight. Rain will keep the rabble quiet tonight. We are said to have fifteen thousand men under arms, and I incline to hope that this movement in aid of the rebellion is played out.

*JULY 19, SUNDAY* Have been out seeking information and getting none that is to be trusted. Colonel Frank Howe talks darkly and predicts an outbreak on the east side of the town tonight, but that's his way. I think this Celtic beast with many heads is driven back to his hole for the present. When government begins enforcing the draft, we shall have more trouble, but not till then.

Not half the history of this memorable week has been written. I could put down pages of incidents that the newspapers have omitted, any one of which would in ordinary times be the town's talk. Men and ladies attacked and plundered by daylight in the streets; private houses suddenly invaded by gangs of a dozen ruffians and sacked, while the women and children run off for their lives. Then there is the unspeakable infamy of the nigger persecution. They are the most peaceable, sober, and inoffensive of our poor, and the outrages they have suffered during this last week are less excusable—are founded on worse pretext and less provocation—than St. Bartholomew's or the Jew-hunting of the Middle Ages. This is a nice town to call itself a centre of civilization! Life and personal property less safe than in Tipperary, and the "people" (as the *Herald* calls them) burning orphan asylums and conducting a massacre. How this infernal slavery system has corrupted our blood, North as well as South! There should be terrible vengeance for these atrocities, but McCunn, Barnard & Co. are our judges and the disgrace will rest upon us without atonement.

I am sorry to find that England is right about the lower class of Irish. They are brutal, base, cruel, cowards, and as insolent as base. Choate (at the Union League Club) tells me he heard this proposition put forth by one of their political philosophers in conversation with a knot of his brethren last Monday: "Sure and if them dam Dutch would jine us we'd drive the dam Yankees out of New York entirely!" These caitiffs have a trick, I hear, of posting themselves at the window of a tenement house with a musket, while a woman with a baby in her arms squats at their feet. Paddy fires on the police and instantly squats to reload, while Mrs. Paddy rises and looks out. Of course, one can't fire at a window where there is a woman with a child!! But how is one to deal with women who assemble around the lamp-post to which a Negro had been hanged and cut off certain parts of his body to keep as souvenirs? Have they any womanly privilege, immunity, or sanctity?

No wonder St. Patrick drove all the venomous vermin out of Ireland! Its biped mammalia supply that island its full average share of creatures that crawl and eat dirt and poison every community they infest. Vipers were superfluous. But my own theory is that St. Patrick's campaign against the snakes is a Popish delusion. They perished of biting the Irish people.

*[1865] MARCH 18*   Very energetic in Wall Street. Walked off with George Anthon at two, crossed at Wall Street ferry, and explored

sundry new districts of Brooklyn. Visited "Fort Greene," a noble public square with fine views in every direction. I hereby prophesy that
in 1900 A.D. Brooklyn will be the city and New York will be the suburb. It is inevitable if both go on growing as they have grown for the
last forty years. Brooklyn has room to spread and New York has not.
The New Yorker of Thirty-fifth Street already finds it a tedious and
annoying job to make his way downtown to business and home
again. How will the New Yorker of One-hundredth Street get about
forty years hence? Brooklyn must out number this city before very
many years, and then places of amusement and fashionable residences will begin to emigrate across the East River. New York will
become "the city" in the London sense of that word. Its Belgravia will
be transferred from the Fifth Avenue to King's County. A like change
is within my own memory. When I was a boy, the aristocracy lived
around the Battery, on the Bowling Green, and in the western streets
below Chambers; in Wall Street, Cedar Street, and Beekman Street,
on the east of the town. Greenwich Street, now a hissing and a desolation, a place of lager beer saloons, emigrant boarding houses,
and the vilest dens, was what Madison Avenue is now. There were the
Griswolds in Chambers Street, Philip Hone in Broadway below Park
Place, Mrs. Cruger at No. 55, and so on. Between 1828 and 1832,
emigration to the regions of Fourth Street, Bond Street, and
Lafayette Place set in, and the centres of fashion were moved again,
for we are a nomadic people, and our finest brownstone houses are
merely tents of new pattern and material. Brooklyn has advantages,
too, that will speed the change. The situations on the Heights overlooking the bay can hardly be matched in any great city of Christendom. How often have I wished I could exchange this house for one
of them, and that I could see from my library windows that noble
prospect and that wide open expanse of sky, and the going down of
the sun every evening!

MARCH 21   Fifth Avenue from Forty-ninth Street down was absolutely thronged with costly new equipages on their way to Central
Park this bright, bland afternoon. It was a broad torrent of vehicular
gentility, wherein profits of shoddy and of petroleum were largely

represented. Not a few of the ladies who were driving in the most sumptuous turn-outs, with liveried servants, looked as if they might have been cooks or chambermaids a very few years ago.

*APRIL 3* Walking down Wall Street, I saw something on the *Commercial Advertiser* bulletin board at the corner of Pine and William Streets and turned off to investigate. I read the announcement "Petersburg is taken" and went into the office in quest of particulars. The man behind the counter was slowly painting in large letters on a large sheet of brown paper another annunciation for the board outside: "Richmond is"—"What's that about Richmond?" said I. "Anything more?" He was too busy for speech, but he went on with a capital C, and a capital A, and so on, till I read the word *CAPTURED*!!! Finding that this was official, I posted up to Trinity Church to tell the sexton to suggest to Vinton to ask the Rector's permission to set the chimes going (which was duly done). When I came back, all William Street in front of the *Advertiser* office was impenetrably crowded, and people were rushing together in front of the Custom House (the *ci-devant* Merchants' Exchange), where Prosper M. Wetmore and Simeon Draper were getting up a meeting on the spur of the moment.

✦  ✦  ✦  ✦  ✦

I walked about on the outskirts of the crowd, shaking hands with everybody, congratulating and being congratulated by scores of men I hardly know even by sight. Men embraced and hugged each other, *kissed* each other, retreated into doorways to dry their eyes and came out again to flourish their hats and hurrah. There will be many sore throats in New York tomorrow. My only experience of a people stirred up to like intensity of feeling was at the great Union meeting at Union Square in April, 1861. But the feeling of today's crowd was not at all identical with that of the memorable mass-meeting four years ago. It was no less earnest and serious, but it was founded on memories of years of failure, all but hopeless, and on the consciousness that national victory was at last secured, through much tribulation.

*APRIL 15, SATURDAY* Nine o'clock in the morning. *LINCOLN AND SEWARD ASSASSINATED LAST NIGHT!!!!*

The South has nearly filled up the measure of her iniquities at last! Lincoln's death not yet certainly announced, but the one o'clock despatch states that he was then dying. Seward's side room was entered by the same or another assassin, and his throat cut. It is unlikely he will survive, for he was suffering from a broken arm and other injuries, the consequence of a fall, and is advanced in life. Ellie brought this news two hours ago, but I can hardly *take it in* even yet. *Eheu* A. Lincoln!

I have been expecting this. I predicted an attempt would be made on Lincoln's life when he went into Richmond; but just now, after his generous dealings with Lee, I should have said the danger was past. But the ferocious malignity of Southerners is infinite and inexhaustible. I am stunned, as by a fearful personal calamity, though I can see that this thing, occurring just at this time, may be overruled to our great good. Poor Ellie is heartbroken, though never an admirer of Lincoln's. We shall appreciate him at last.

*Up with the Black Flag now!*

Ten P.M. What a day it has been! Excitement and suspension of business even more general than on the 3rd instant. Tone of feeling very like that of four years ago when the news came of Sumter. This atrocity has invigorated national feeling in the same way, almost in the same degree. People who pitied our misguided brethren yesterday, and thought they had been punished enough already, and hoped there would be a general amnesty, including J. Davis himself, talk approvingly today of vindictive justice and favor the introduction of judges, juries, gaolers, and hangmen among the dramatis personae. Above all, there is a profound, awe-stricken feeling that we are, as it were, in immediate presence of a fearful, gigantic crime, such as has not been committed in our day and can hardly be matched in history.

Faulkner, one of our Kenzua directors, called for me by appointment at half-past nine, and we drove to the foot of Jane Street to inspect apparatus for the reduction of gold ore by amalgamation, which he considers a great improvement on the machinery generally used for that purpose. Returned uptown and saw Bellows to advise about adjournment of our Sanitary Commission meeting next week. Thence to Wall Street. Immense crowd. Bulletins and extras following each other in quick, contradictory succession. Seward and his Fred had died and had not. Booth (one of the assassins, a Marylander, brother of Edwin Booth) had been taken and had not. So it has gone on all day. Tonight the case stands thus:

*Abraham Lincoln died at twenty-two minutes after seven this morning.* He never regained consciousness after the pistol ball fired at him from behind, over his wife's shoulder, entered his brain. Seward is living and may recover. The gentleman assigned to the duty of murdering him did his butchery badly. The throat is severely lacerated by his knife, but it's believed that no arteries are injured. Fred Seward's situation is less hopeful, his skull being fractured by a bludgeon or sling shot used by the same gentleman. The attendant who was stabbed, is dead. (Is not.)

The temper of the great meeting I found assembled in front of the Custom House (the old Exchange) was grim. A Southerner would compare it with that of the first session of the Jacobins after Marat's death. I thought it healthy and virile. It was the first great patriotic meeting since the war began at which there was no talk of concession and conciliation. It would have endured no such talk. Its sentiment seemed like this: "Now it is plain at last to everybody that there can be no terms with the woman-flogging aristocracy. Grant's generous dealing with Lee was a blunder. The *Tribune*'s talk for the last fortnight was folly. Let us henceforth deal with rebels as they deserve. The rose-water treatment does not meet their case." I have heard it said fifty times today: "These madmen have murdered the two best friends they had in the world!" I heard of three or four men in Wall Street and near the Post Office who spoke lightly of the tragedy, and were instantly set upon by the bystanders and pummelled. One of them narrowly escaped death. It was Charles E. Anderson, brother of our friend Professor Henry James Anderson, father of pretty Miss Louisa. Moses H. Grinnell and the police had hard work to save him. I never supposed him a secessionist.

*APRIL 17* All over the city, people have been at work all day, draping street fronts, so that hardly a building on Wall Street, Broadway, Chambers Street, Bowery, Fourth Avenue is without its symbol of the profound public sorrow. What a place this man, whom his friends have been patronizing for four years as a well-meaning, sagacious, kind-hearted, ignorant, old codger, had won for himself in the hearts of the people! What a place he will fill in history! I foresaw most clearly that he would be ranked high as the Great Emancipator twenty years hence, but I did not suppose his death would instantly reveal—even to Copperhead newspaper editors— the nobleness and the glory of his part in this great contest. It reminds one of the last line of Blanco White's great sonnet, "If Light can thus deceive, wherefore not Life?" *Death* has suddenly opened the eyes of the people (and I think of the world) to the fact that a hero has been holding high place among them for four years, closely watched and studied, but despised and rejected by a third of this community, and only tolerated by the other two-thirds.

*MAY 29* PEACE.

*Peace* herself at last, for Smith and Magruder have surrendered, if General Canby's dispatch to the War Department be truthful. So here I hope and believe ends, by God's great and undeserved mercy, the chapter of this journal I opened with the heading of *War* on the night of April 13, 1861. We have lived a century of common life since then. Only within the last two months have I dared to hope that this fearful struggle would be settled so soon. . . .

What a time it has been, say from December 21, 1860, when we heard that the process of national decomposition had set in with the secession of cantankerous little South Carolina, on through disaster and depression for four years and nearly six months, till today, with its tidings that the last army Rebeldom has organized out of the many hundred thousand men it has seduced or coerced into fighting for its felonious flag, exists no longer. As I look back now to Bull Run, Fort Donelson, the Seven Days, Antietam, Gettysburg, Chancellorsville, and other battles, I wonder my thoughts have not been even more engrossed by the developments of the great tragedy, that I have been able to pay any attention to my common routine and to be interested in anything outside the tremendous chapter that history has been taking down in shorthand.

# FREDERICK LAW OLMSTED

*The creation of Central Park was a defining moment in the city's history. Frederick Law Olmsted (1822–1903), who designed the park (with Calvert Vaux) and superintended its execution, had already gained some literary distinction for his travel accounts of the slaveholding South and his agricultural writings when, at age thirty-five, he was persuaded to oversee this massive task. That problems of financing public works or dealing with political corruption and construction-crew ineptitude are not new to New York City is evident from Olmsted's memoir fragment below.*

## PASSAGES IN THE LIFE OF
## AN UNPRACTICAL MAN

THE AGITATION for a public park in New York began with an article published by Mr. Downing in 1848 in which he eloquently urged his strong conviction that properly planned and managed public recreation grounds would have a most civilizing and refining influence on the people of our great cities. This was followed from time to time by other papers having the same object until his lamentable death four years afterwards.

Mr. Downing's writings on the subject were much copied and favorably noticed by the leading newspapers and shortly before he died the Common Council of New York, at the instigation of Mayor A. C. Kingsland, took action which led to an act of the state legislature providing for a park on a tract of 150 acres of land situated on the East River. The following year a small politician, jealous of the advantages which another might gain by the success of this scheme, undertook to "head it off" by an alternate project. The idea striking him that a plausible argument could be made for a larger park more centrally situated, in a moment he adopted for his purpose the site afterwards accepted as that of the Central Park, neither knowing nor caring whether the ground was at all suitable in other respects than its geographical centrality.

The land was not fully acquired until 1856 and, the legislature having as yet made no provision for its government, in the latter part of that year Fernando Wood, the Mayor, near the end of his second term, obtained an act of the Common Council under which he with his Street Commissioner Joseph S. Taylor took charge of it. They appointed a chief Engineer and a large corps of assistants, and expenditures were made and liabilities incurred on account of the park, as was alleged by their opponents, to the amount of $60,000, as the result of which all that could afterwards be found of value to the city was an inaccurate topographical map of the ground.

There is a power which ordinarily lies ineffective back of all the political vices of our cities. At times it is stirred with shame, disgust and indignation; organizes itself and makes a loud demand for reform. The politicians out of office take advantage of the opportunity not only to secure the removal of those who have been in office but to make them as they go forth serve the purpose of scape goats. A few changes of form and method are made and the citizens are reconciled to a system under which the old vices are cherished only more warmly than before.

One of these storms of reform was rising at the period of which I have spoken and Fernando Wood was to be the chief scape goat by whose outgoing the indignation and wrath of the people was to be appeased.

Wood being a Democrat, the Republicans, who held the majority of the state legislature, took advantage of the momentary popular disgust with him and his associates to take the regulation of certain parts of the city business from the elected government of the city and to give it to a series of professedly non partisan Commissions. One of these, composed of nine members, part Republicans, part Wood Democrats, part "reform" Democrats, part non-descript, was appointed to supersede Wood and Taylor in the special government of the Central Park. It had to go to the Common Council of the city for its supplies, and a majority of the members of the Common Council siding with the Mayor were disposed not to honor its requisitions. Eventually they would be obliged to do so unless indeed a decision of the court could be obtained, as they professed to expect, declaring the Act of the legislature unconstitutional. But supplies could be delayed, and when yielded given in driblets, and various difficulties and obstructions could be put in the way of the Commission.

Two considerable influences were working in favor of the Commission: first, a desire with many that some progress should be made in turning to use the property in the land appropriated to the park which had cost the city five million dollars; second, the desire of the laboring population to obtain the employment which the construction of the Park was expected to give. This latter influence was strongest in those parts of the city where Wood and his supporters in the Common Council had hitherto obtained the most votes and on their popularity in which they depended for reelection.

To counteract it, the act of the Legislature was denounced as a tyrannical usurpation of power by which the Black Republicans and Abolitionists were to put themselves in office and plunder the city against the will of the local majority.

But these denunciations had to be uttered in the face of the fact that the Commissioners were to receive no pay; that they had elected a Democrat as their President, another Democrat as the Treasurer, and had reappointed Wood's whole Engineer corps. They had gone so far in this respect that a clamor was beginning to rise from the Republican side that the Commission was wholly given over to the Democrats.

At this period in its history one of the Commissioners came to spend a Sunday at a sea side inn near New Haven where I had been finishing the manuscript of my Journey in the Back Country. Sitting next to him at the tea table, he told me what I have just recited of the history of the Commission and added that they were now taking on a force of laborers. Having no money as yet at their command, each of the men employed was required to sign an agreement releasing the Commissioners from personal liability on account of the wages he might earn, and in lieu of wages, due bills against the city were to be issued which would be payable when the Common Council should make the appropriation, in favor of which an additional element of popular interest would thus be established. He added that at their next meeting they intended to elect a Superintendent and it was thought necessary that he should be a Republican. There were several candidates, but no Republican had offered with whom he was much pleased, and he asked if I knew of a suitable man. I inquired what would be the duties of the Superintendent?

He would be the Executive Officer of the Chief Engineer with respect to the labor force and would have charge of the police and see that proper regulations were enforced in regard to public use of the Park.

Must he be a politician?

No, a Republican but not a politician; much better he should not have been a practical politician. The Republicans could do little without the cooperation of the reform Democrats and were ready to compromise, on the understanding that the park shall be managed independently of politics.

"I am delighted to hear it," I said; "There's no limit to the good influence a park rightly managed would have in New York and that seems to be the first necessity of good management."

"I wish we had you on the Commission, but as we have not, why not take the Superintendency yourself? Come now."

Till he asked the question, the possibility of my doing so had never occurred to me, though he probably suspected I was thinking of it. I at once answered, however, smiling:

"I take it? I'm not sure that I would not if it were offered me. Nothing interested me in London like the parks and yet I thought a great deal more might be made of them."

"Well, it will not be offered you; that's not the way we do business. But if you'll go to work I believe you may get it. I wish that you would!"

"You are serious?"

"Yes; but there's no time to lose."

"What is to be done?"

"Go to New York and file an application; see the Commissioners and get your friends to back you."

"I'll take the boat tonight and think it out as I go. If no serious objection occurs to me before morning, I'll do it."

Accordingly, the next day I was looking for my friends in New York. At that season they were much scattered, but one I found who took up the matter warmly and my application was in a few days fortified by a number of weighty signatures. I shall presently refer to the fact that there among them was that of Washington Irving.

The President of the Commission being out of town on my arrival in New York, I first called on the Vice President, bearing a letter to him from my friend in New Haven.

The Vice President, who was a Republican, repeated that it was desirable that the Superintendent should not be a Democrat, yet that he should be as little objectionable as possible to the Democrats. He seemed to think that my prospects in this respect were good. He offered to introduce me to one of the Democratic Commissioners who was a very practical man, and also to the Engineer who again he described as a very practical man; if their judgment should be favorable, I might count on his support.

The practical Democratic Commissioner having ascertained that I had had no experience in practical politics, even no personal acquaintance with the Republican leaders in the city, that my backing would be from unpractical men, and that I responded warmly to virtuous sentiments with regard to corruption in both parties, after a long conversation gave me to understand that I might hope that if the Republicans brought me forward he should be less inclined to oppose me than a possible Republican who had been deep in the mire of city politics and who disapproved of the practice of virtue in politics.

The Engineer I found at a house on the Park about which was a crowd of laboring men, each bearing a letter addressed to him. On the ground that my letter was from a Commissioner, I was allowed to precede those who had stood waiting outside the door before me. The room in which the Engineer sat at a desk was crowded with applicants for employment whose letters were collected in batches by men wearing a golden star on the breast of a very dirty and seedy jacket and handed to the Engineer. These letters were chiefly from members of the Common Council. As each was opened and its writer's name recognized, the bearer was either abruptly told that there was no work for him at present or his name was taken and looked for on a list furnished by the writer of his letter in which it appeared that a limited number had been named whom he wished to have preferred among all those to whom he gave letters. If found there, the applicant was without further examination given a ticket and told to call again on a given day.

At the first opportunity I presented my letter and card. Reading a few lines, the Engineer glanced at me, dropped the letter and went on with his canvass of the laborers. I stood among them half an hour and then pointing to my card asked if I might hope to find him less engaged later in the day. As he seemed to assent, I walked out a little way looking at the ground for the park. I returned and withdrew again three times before I found the enlisting business ended. As I came in the last time, the engineer was about leaving. I walked with him & took a seat by his side in the street car running to the city.

I then had an opportunity to state on what grounds I had ventured to think that he would find me useful as an assistant in his work. He replied that he would rather have a practical man. I did not learn why I could not be regarded as a possibly practical man, but it was only too evident that the gate of hope was closed to me in that direction.

Calling by appointment on the Vice President the next day, I was not surprised to find that doubts had been growing over night in his mind, as to whether the office of Superintendent should not be filled by a practical man.

Some time after my election, which occurred at the first subsequent meeting of the Park Board, another of the Commissioners told me that this objection would have defeated me had it not been for the autograph of Washington Irving on my papers. That turned the balance.

But one member in a full board of nine stood out in the final vote; it was Mr. Thomas C. Fields, the best partisan I ever knew, and he never forgave me for it.

It is hardly necessary to say that even after my election I did not quite feel myself out of the woods. Had it been concluded that it was after all just as well not to have a practical man? Or had they been convinced that after all I was a practical man?

These gentlemen, most of whom had themselves made large fortunes in business, would hardly defer to Washington Irving on such a point. No, I owed my election to something else than their estimate of my value as a practical man—and to what I did not understand.

When I next came to the office on the park, my first experience was repeated until I said to the Engineer; "I was instructed to report to you for orders, Sir;" Upon this he called to one of the starred men: "Tell Hawkin to come here." Then to me: "I have given my orders to Mr. Hawkin. He is what I call a practical man and I will tell him to show you what you have to do."

Mr. Hawkin, a cautious, close-mouthed, sensible looking gentleman, wearing no coat and with trousers tucked in the legs of a heavy and dirty pair of boots, here opened the door and said, "Want me?"

"Yes; this is Mr. Olmsted, the new Superintendent. Take him round the park and show him what work is going on and tell the foremen they will take their orders from him after this."

"Now?"

The Engineer looked at me.

"I am quite ready, Sir."

"Yes, now."

In truth, as I had intended this to be rather a call of ceremony or preliminary report to my superior officer, I was not quite as well prepared as I could have wished to be for what followed.

Striking across the hill into what is now the Ramble, we came first upon a number of men with bill hooks and forks collecting and burning brush wood. Under a tree near by a man sat smoking. He rose as we approached:

"Smith, this is Mr. Olmsted, your new Superintendent. You'll take your orders from him after this."

All the men within hearing dropped their tools and looked at me. Smith said, "Oh! that's the man is it? Expect we shall be pushed up, now." He laughed and the men grinned.

"What is Mr. Smith doing?" I asked.

"He's grubbing round here and burning up what he can get together," and Mr. Hawkin moved on.

"See you again, I suppose," said Smith still laughing.

"Yes Sir; good day for the present."

And this process was repeated with little variation as we passed from gang to gang to the number of perhaps fifteen, there being at this time about 500 men at work. As they were nearly all Democrats and all appointed by a Democrat, and a Democrat who had himself been appointed first by Wood, and as they were mostly introduced to him by Democratic members of the Common Council, the presumption that the Commission was to be managed exclusively in the interests of the Republicans and as a means of defeating Wood was considerably weakened.

As I stood in the office, I had not been able to observe that the slightest consideration was given to the apparent strength or activity of the laborers. Each man undoubtedly supposed that he owed the fact of his preference over others, often much abler than himself to do a good day's work, to the fact that a member of the Common Council had asked his appointment. He also knew that the request of his patron was made not because of his supposed special fitness to serve the city or the park, but because of service that he was expected to render at primary meetings and otherwise with a view to the approaching municipal election. He knew too that he was for an indefinite period to receive no pay for his work, but only a promise to pay which he must turn to account by selling it at a discount.

Under all the circumstances it was plain enough that when Foreman Smith pleasantly remarked that he supposed that they would be pushed up now and the men laughed with him at the suggestion, it was because the idea that I might expect a day's work from them for each day's due-bill was thought a good joke.

Neither Foreman Smith nor any other that day said anything aloud to me about my not being a practical man, but I saw it in their eyes and their smile and I felt it deeply. In fact, for other reasons, I could have wished long before our round was finished that I had worn a pair of high legged boots and left my coat behind me, for it was a sultry afternoon in the height of the dog days and my conductor exhibited his practical ability by leading me through the midst of a number of vile sloughs in the black and unctuous slime of which I sometimes sank nearly half leg deep.

He said but one word to me during the afternoon beyond what his commission strictly required. As I stopped for an instant to kick the mire off my legs against a stump as we came out of the last bog, he turned and remarked:

"Suppose you are used to this sort of business."

I believe that he was some years my junior and it is probable that I had been through fifty miles of swamp for his one. There was not an operation in progress on the park in which I had not considerable personal experience, and he spoke with apparent gravity. Nevertheless, I felt very deeply that he was laughing in his sleeve, and that I was still a very young man. So I avoided a direct reply by saying that I had not been aware that the park was such a very nasty place. In fact the low grounds were steeped in overflow and mush of pig sties, slaughter houses and bone boiling works, and the stench was sickening.

For several days there continued to be something that stimulated good humor in my appearance and in the inquiries and suggestions which I made as I walked from gang to gang feeling my way to an intelligent command of the business. It was as if we were all engaged in playing a practical joke. The most striking illustration of this good fellowship that I remember occurred, I think on the third day, when a foreman who was reading a newspaper as I came suddenly upon him, exclaimed "Hallo Fred—get round pretty often, don't you?"

Having no power to discharge or secure the discharge of a man, I found it was better to give every offender the benefit of the largest possible assumption of ignorance, forgetfulness and accident and urge him to give more attention to his duties and use more care.

1857

# ERNEST DUVERGIER
# DE HAURANNE

*In the midst of the Civil War, Ernest Duvergier de Hauranne (1843–76), a twenty-one-year-old Frenchman from a liberal, well-off family, undertook to travel across America. Sympathetic to the Union cause, and much influenced by Tocqueville's* Democracy in America *(1835), he wanted to observe the war's impact on American liberty. His letters to his father were published in the influential* Revue des Deux Mondes; *their style was praised by the critic Sainte-Beuve, who wrote that "the whole panorama unrolls before our eyes, one scene after another, with a swiftness that is very exciting." All in all, Duvergier de Hauranne was not much taken with New York, which he found dirty and overrun with immigrants, though he did compare the new Central Park to the Bois de Boulogne. The scene below captures the bombast and ballyhoo of nineteenth-century American political life.*

FROM *EIGHT MONTHS IN AMERICA*

New York
September 27, 1864

I HAVE just returned from a large Unionist meeting held at the Cooper Institute; the resulting tumult still keeps the city awake. The electoral campaign is getting lively in New York. Last week there was a giant Democratic meeting in Union Square attended by an immense crowd from the suburbs and the surrounding areas. The Republicans wanted to turn the tables and make a big noise of their own. Guided by the light of the usual fireworks, I arrived at a large triangular open space where in the midst of a milling throng there stood a dozen lighted stands filled with volunteer speakers who began to harangue the crowd. From each platform Roman candles and fiery serpents were set off; many people in the crowd were throwing firecrackers which exploded with a loud noise. From each platform, a speech was being made to a group of listeners, or a song was being sung, only to be swallowed up in the general uproar.

These exhibitions of oratorical prowess in the public streets were only the overflow of the official meeting in the hall of Cooper Union which I did not even try to enter. Mr. Blair, Mr. Noyes and other important men made speeches that were published by the newspapers the next day. But this was the "outside meeting," the truly popular assembly, whose details were of more interest to me than all the speeches; it was here that all the most extravagant inspirations of street-corner orators and barroom statesmen were freely produced. There is truly nothing less worthy of respect than the people of New York when aroused by political emotion.

Many people heckled the speakers, only a few listened to them: most gave themselves the intelligent pleasure of cheering loudly and continually. The orators themselves, gesticulating on their platforms surrounded by lanterns, torches, Bengal flares, pinwheels and rockets—a noisy accompaniment kept up by their supporters—could have been medicine men stomping on their trestles. As I listened to them exchanging shouts and insults from one platform to another, it seemed to me more like a civil war than a harmonious assembly of men of the same party.

But what were they saying? Let us lend an ear. Here a German is haranguing a group of compatriots in his native tongue. Over there is a Pole wearing a tragic expression who stammers out with much stamping of feet and pounding of fists this remarkable bit of eloquence: "If you want to save your families, your children and your country, vote for Lincoln." The idea was thin and the grammar bad, but the intention was good, everything was well-seasoned with blasphemy, and there is nothing this public—hardly a gathering of ancient Athenians—wouldn't swallow with a sauce of two or three spicy oaths.

Nearby there was a sort of giant who, in a voice as loud as a trumpet-call, tossed off a Miltonian apostrophe to McClellan, the prince of Hades; this is the everyday metaphor of American rhetoric, and I have hardly heard one speech in which the devil was not put to work. Elsewhere a Texas refugee recounted his lengthy sufferings for the good cause and the no doubt very real cruelties by means of which he made his tale a melodrama worthy of inclusion in a criminal anthology. Another one calls President Lincoln "the immortal," the man "raised up by Providence," "the new Washington." Still another puts the crowd in good humor by giving them Europeans to eat alive, a good of which they are very fond. A Hungarian eloquently delivers in his outlandish language an imprecation against Austria. An Irishman seizes the occasion to accuse the English monarchy of Asiatic despotism. All the races of the globe misuse the language of their new homeland to their hearts' content. It was a confusion of tongues, and one wondered where in this cosmopolitan Babel were the authentic Americans. Are there any in the triumphal processions that wind through the streets, following the drummers and the brass band? I saw uniforms, braid, flags, cannons, wagons full of orators like our carnival floats; but, alas! they are men who are hired to wear the colors of the ward and carry its banner through the city. They were present the other day in Union Square among the Democrats; they have come here this evening with the same enthusiasm to swell the ranks of the Republicans.

Meanwhile a few small Democratic meetings were being organized along Broadway; stones were thrown at the marchers as they passed by. Tempers became heated. Suddenly a movement occurred in the crowd; the noise of firecrackers redoubled and the sound of drums and brasses increased. The ward delegates appeared on the scene, marching with a military step in long columns, led by their chiefs and followed by their cannons and their illuminated wagons filled with orators. These speakers began to hurl abuse; insults to McClellan echoed through the streets. Some "peace-men" protested, interrupting with loud shouts of "Down with the Negroes!" "You damned scoundrels!" "It's a damned nigger war!" During all this the cannons boomed, the crowd roared and the band played fortissimo: the bellowing orators, foaming with fury and fatigue, still tried to make themselves heard above the tumult. Orators in antiquity were recalled to measure and harmony by a flute player; what is one to think of this American eloquence that takes its pitch from a salvo of field artillery?

It is said that the great meeting of last week was much more significant and solemn. Not only did the whole city come, but also the McClellanites, the "Little Mackerels" (as certain ill-mannered papers call them) from the whole region, including representatives from the country districts. Union Square could hardly hold the densely packed throng. The excitement was such that when a cannon unfortunately burst, mowing swathes through the crowd, the wounded were carried off with no sign of distress, without interrupting even for a moment the cheers and shouts of joy. The Republican demonstration was in worse taste and showed their weakness; but it made me realize what New York politics is like.

In this motley, cosmopolitan city, a broth enriched by two worlds, true citizens are hard to find. The rabble, the plebeian mass, dominates. I have seen meetings where the deep emotion of the audience imposed a character of gravity on the ritual clowning that accompanied it. But here the reality is in accord with the appearance. Politics is an occasion for disorder, the meeting is a spectacle; the arrangements are flamboyant, like trivial plays whose only merit is in the sets. In vain does one look for any thought in this mob, gathered solely for excitement and noise. It is like a rally arranged in advance by some political Barnum or Godillot.

Moreover, New York, located in the very heart of the Northern States, is the place where the President meets with the most violent opposition. Among its one million five hundred thousand inhabitants, there are at least six hundred thousand foreigners who are neither Europeans nor Americans. This multitude of adventurers without a country is a great source of trouble. They have received with the title of citizen an unofficial baptism as supporters of republican ideals, but they have not yet learned to practice the rights and duties of a free people. They have neither political principles nor clear goals, but only a blind, turbulent and venal disposition which certain unscrupulous demagogues exploit. Though but newly arrived, they take it oddly for granted that they have been freed from all public responsibilities, but are entitled to lay down the law to the country that has adopted them. Every party finds mercenaries among them; nowhere has the Republic bought more soldiers than in New York; but they prefer in general to follow the Democrats rather than the Republicans. The latter ask for men, money and sacrifices; the former promise tax exemptions and offer rebellion and looting as entertainment. The Democratic leaders win municipal office by threatening the timid, honest people with riots. In this country, where liberty wages such uncompromising warfare against ignorance and class hatreds, the people of New York are still at a level of primitive tribalism that expresses itself in looting and street-fighting. The Americans are right in not wanting to have as their capital a city that hardly even belongs to their country.

# FANNY FERN

*Fanny Fern (real name Sara Payson Willis, 1811–72) was the first woman newspaper columnist in the United States. Her popularity encouraged her to take on controversial social issues such as women's rights, prostitution, and prison reform. She had a clear, biting style; as Nathaniel Hawthorne admiringly put it, "The woman writes as if the devil was in her." The sister of author-editor Nathaniel Parker Willis, she portrayed him satirically in her novel* Ruth Hall *(1855) in retaliation for his lack of support for her earlier writing efforts, when she was scraping by as a seamstress. Here she shows sympathy for working women, while illuminating an overlooked corner of New York's mercantile Ladies' Mile culture.*

## TYRANTS OF THE SHOP

THERE ARE PERSONS who can regard oppression and injustice without any acceleration of the pulse. There are others who never witness it, how frequent soever, without a desperate struggle against non-interference, though prudence and policy may both whisper "it's none of your business." I believe, as a general thing, that the shopkeepers of New York who employ girls and women to tend in their stores, treat them courteously; but now and then I have been witness to such brutal language to them, in the presence of customers, for that which seemed to me no offence, or at least a very trifling one, that I have longed for a man's strong right arm, summarily to settle matters with the oppressor. And when one has been the innocent cause of it, merely by entering the store to make a purchase, the obligation to see the victim safe through, seems almost imperative. The bad policy of such an exhibition of unmanliness on the part of a shopkeeper would be, one would think, sufficient to stifle the "damn you" to the blushing, tearful girl, who is powerless to escape, or to clear herself from the charge of misbehavior. When ladies "go shopping," in New York, they generally expect to enjoy themselves; though Heaven knows, they must be hard up for resources to fancy this mode of spending their time, when it can be avoided. But, be that as it may, the most vapid can scarcely fancy this sort of scene.

The most disgusting part of such an exhibition is, when the gentlemanly employer, having got through "damning" his embarrassed victim, turns, with a sweet smile and dulcet voice, to yourself, and inquires, "what else he can have the pleasure of showing you?" You are tempted to reply, "Sir, I would like you to show me that you can respect womanhood, although it may not be hedged about with fine raiment, or be able to buy civil words with a full purse." But you bite your tongue to keep it quiet, and you linger till this Nero has strolled off, and then you say to the girl, "I am sorry to have been the innocent cause of this!" and you ask, "Does he often speak this way to you?" and she says, quietly, as she rolls up the ribbons or replaces the boxes on the shelves, "Never in any other!" It is useless to ask her why she stays, because you know something about women's wages and women's work in the crowded city; and you know that, till she is sure of another place, it is folly for her to think of leaving this. And you think many other things as you say Good-morning to her as kindly as you know how; and you turn over this whole "woman-question" as you run the risk of being knocked down and run over in the crowded thoroughfare through which you pass; and the jostle, and hurry, and rush about you, seem to make it more hopeless as each eager face passes you, intent on its own plans, busy with its own hopes and fears—staggering perhaps under a load either of the soul or body, or both, as heavy as the poor shop-girl's, and you gasp as if the air about had suddenly become too thick to breathe. And then you reach your own door-step, and like a guilty creature, face your dressmaker, having forgotten to "match that trimming;" and you wonder if you were to sit down and write about this evil, if it would deter even one employer from such brutality to the shop-girls in his employ; not because of the brutality, perhaps, but because by such a short-sighted policy, he might often drive away from his store, ladies who would otherwise be profitable and steady customers.

*NEW YORK LEDGER*, 1867

# MARK TWAIN

*Mark Twain (real name Samuel Clemens, 1835–1910) first came to New York as a teenager, working as a printer's apprentice. Returning some twenty years later a respected author, he wrote a series of curmudgeonly dispatches on the city which were published in the San Francisco news-paper* Alta California. *Twain, as always the unimpressed tourist, com-plains that New York was "a splendid desert—a domed and steepled solitude, where the stranger is lonely in the midst of a million of his race." In the article below he pokes fun at the vogue for "personals" ads. At the time a novel convenience for New Yorkers, isolated in the crowd and unsure how to find companionship, the personals also offered a peek into the lives and dramas of others.*

## PERSONALS

YOU MAY SIT in a New York restaurant in the morning for a few hours, and you will observe that the very first thing each man does, before ordering his breakfast, is to call for the *Herald*—and the next thing he does is to look at the top of the first column and read the "Personals." Such is the fascination mystery has for the human race! Your man has not the least idea in the world that there is ever going to be a Personal in the paper that will be of private individual interest to himself, and he knows very well that he cannot make head or tail of those he finds there, and that as a vehicle for fun they do not amount to much—yet, as I have said, he is bound to read those "Personals" the very first thing. There is such a toothsome flavor of mystery about them! It is the whole secret. The advertising public appre-ciate the value of a word under that "Personal" head, and many are the dodges they invent to get an airing for their wares there. But it don't succeed. The ingeniously-worded squibs are ruthlessly set aside and buried in the midst of solid cases of advertisements in the desert wastes of the paper, where a man might hunt them with a blood-hound and not find them. True, I have seen three of these dodges win, lately, but they never hinted at a single attraction in the matters they were meant to advertise—mentioned places of business—that was all—nothing but the barest mention. For instance:

"CAROLINE—Be in the same place, at Worrell Sisters' performance, to-night. White rose, left temple. Do not fail, dearest.

ROBERT."

And again:

"IF the gentlemanly manager of the New York Theatre, who was smiled upon by a lady in the dress circle last night, and who was generously befriended by him in Philadelphia two years ago, will approach the footlights again to night, he will recognize her by the lily in the parting of her hair."

And get smiled on again, likely, poor devil. Here is the third:

"THE LADY who left a pair of gloves at Mrs. Mills' Mammarial Balm and Bust Elevator establishment, Washington place, can have them returned by calling or sending address."

I will bet a million dollars, seller ten, no deposit, that that advertisement read "*Celebrated* Mammarial," etc., etc., etc., originally, and the *Herald* people scratched it out. That worried Mrs. Mills, no doubt. It must have made the old bust elevator feel a little humiliated. [Which reminds me that I have not been through the mammarial bust establishments yet. I must make a note of that. I might as well go there and get busted as anywhere else.]

The "sick" kind of personals are very frequent. For instance, this:

"BLACK EYES—Oh, dear, how anxious I am to hear from you!

W. DE ANGELO."

And this.

"HENRY—Don't kill me. Remember, Fourth avenue car runs all night.                                                             SWEET KATE."

That is suggestive, to say the least. She don't want to be killed, but if he is determined to do it, why, he knows where she puts up, and the Fourth avenue car offers every facility for murder.

And how is this?

"H.—Have recovered from accident. Will see you at the old

place in Thirteenth street, between Sixth and Seventh avenues, on Friday, at half-past four, rain or shine.      EMMA FRANCIS W."

She calls it an accident. Well, accidents will happen, even in the best regulated families.

But this is the usual style, and altogether the most nauseating:

"SIX P. M., Bleecker street car, up from Fulton Ferry. Will the lady who was embarrassed in making change and was kindly assisted by a gentleman, whom she smiled upon and who smiled upon her and bowed when she got out, please address Harold, *Herald* office, stating where an interview may be had?"

There seems to be a pack of wooden-headed louts about this town, who fall in love with every old strumpet who smiles a flabby smile at them in a street car, and forthwith they pop a personal into the *Herald*, beseeching an "interview"—a favor they could have had with infinitely less circumlocution if they were half as full of gab as they are of self-complacency. And behold, if a respectable woman dares to look at one of these by accident, or to see if he has got hind legs and a brass collar on, up comes the inevitable personal, with a lot of stuff in it about "the lady who kindly took notice of a gentle-man," and so forth and so on, and the equally inevitable supplication for an "interview." Perdition catch these whelps! But how is this one?

"MR. WM. F. LAWLER, late landsman, U.S. Navy, will call at 271 Broadway, to receive some money.      CHIPMAN, HOSMER & CO."

That has got a very comfortable ring about it, after all that gruel and nonsense. Only a landsman in the Navy, yet they call him "Mr." Lawler? That appears to me to suggest that Lawler is to receive something more than a month's back wages. These Broadway firms do not call a plebeian Mr. without due and sufficient cause.

And here is a sad one; it tells its own story:

"MARY—Come back home, and all will be forgiven. My old heart is breaking.      YOUR MOTHER."

Many a New Yorker is proof against the seductions of the Cable's despatches, but none of them can resist the *Herald's* "Personals."

*ALTA CALIFORNIA*, MAY 19, 1867

# JAMES D. McCABE

*In the nineteenth century a fad arose for "sunshine and shadow" guidebooks that purported to unravel the mysteries of New York, florid tomes (some written by ministers) that warned about fallen women and dangerous neighborhoods, and often titillated under the guise of moralizing. Some works in this genre, such as those by James D. McCabe (1842–83), were better written and more journalistically scrupulous. McCabe dug deep into the criminal world in his book* Lights and Shadows of New York Life *(1872). His section on "Impostors" emphasized an emblematic New York problem: in a young city composed largely of immigrants and strangers knowing nothing of one another's backgrounds, it was all too easy for a newcomer to adopt a manufactured identity, often for fraudulent ends.*

## IMPOSTORS

THERE IS no city in the Union in which impostors of all kinds flourish so well as in New York. The immense size of the city, the heterogeneous character of its population, and the great variety of the interests and pursuits of the people, are all so many advantages to the cheat and swindler. It would require a volume to detail the tricks of these people, and some of their adventures would equal anything to be found in the annals of romance. All manner of tricks are practised upon the unsuspecting, and generally the perpetrator escapes without punishment. They come here from all parts of the country, and indeed from all parts of the world, in the hope of reaping a rich harvest, and the majority end by eking out a miserable existence in a manner which even the police who watch them so closely are sometimes unable to understand.

They find their way into all classes. One cannot mingle much in society here without meeting some bewhiskered, mysterious individual, who claims to be of noble birth. Sometimes he palms himself off as a political exile, sometimes he is travelling, and is so charmed with New York that he makes it his headquarters, and sometimes he lets a few friends into the secret of his rank, and begs that they will not reveal his true title, as a little unpleasant affair, a mere social scandal in his own country, made it necessary for him to absent himself for a while. He hopes the matter will blow over in a few months, and then he will go home. The fashionable New-Yorker, male or female, is powerless against the charms of aristocracy. The "foreign nobleman" is welcomed everywhere, fêted, petted, and allowed almost any privilege he chooses to claim—and he is far from being very modest in this respect; and by and by he is found out to be an impostor, probably the valet of some gentleman of rank in Europe. Then society holds up its hands in holy horror, and vows it always did suspect him. The men in society are weak enough in this respect; but the women are most frequently the victims.

Not long since, a handsome, well got up Englishman came to New York on a brief visit. He called himself Lord Richard X——. Society received him with open arms. Invitations were showered upon him. Brown's hands were always full of cards for his Lordship. The women went wild over him, especially since it was whispered that the young man was heir to a property worth ever so many millions of pounds. In short, his Lordship found himself so popular, and hints of his departure were received with such disfavor by his new found friends, that he concluded to extend his stay in New York indefinitely. He made a fine show, and his toilettes, turnouts, and presents were magnificent. The men did not fancy him. He was too haughty and uncivil, but the ladies found him intensely agreeable. It was whispered by his male acquaintances that he was a good hand at borrowing, and that he was remarkably lucky at cards and at the races. One or two of the large faro banks of the city were certainly the losers by his visits. The ladies, however, were indignant at such stories. His Lordship was divine. All the women were crazy after him, and any of them would have taken him at the first offer.

By and by the newspapers began to take notice of the young man, and boldly asserted that there was no such name as Lord Richard X—— in the British peerage. Society laughed at this, and declared that everybody but ignorant newspaper men was aware that the published lists of titled personages in England were notoriously incomplete.

Meanwhile, his Lordship played his cards well, and it was soon announced that he was "to be married shortly to a well-known belle of Fifth avenue." The women were green with jealousy, and the men, I think, were not a little relieved to find that the lion did not intend devouring all the Fifth avenue belles. The marriage came off in due season; the wedding-presents fairly poured in, and were magnificent. The new Lady X—— was at the summit of her felicity, and was the envied of all who knew her. The happy pair departed on their honeymoon, but his Lordship made no effort to return home to England.

During their absence, it leaked out that Lord X—— was an impostor. Creditors began to pour in upon his father-in-law with anxious inquiries after his Lordship, against whom they held heavy accounts. Proofs of the imposture were numerous and indisputable, and the newspapers declared that Lord X—— would not dare to show his face again in New York. Everybody was laughing at the result of the affair.

What passed between the father-in-law and the young couple is not known; but the bride decided to cling to her husband in spite of the imposture. Father-in-law was a prudent and a sensitive man, and very rich. For his daughter's sake, he accepted the situation. He paid Lord X——'s debts, laughed at the charge of imposture, and spoke warmly to every one he met of the great happiness of his "dear children, Lord and Lady X——." On their return to the city, he received them with a grand party, at which all Fifth avenue was present, and, though he could not silence the comments of society, he succeeded in retaining for his children their places in the world of fashion. He was a nabob, and he knew the power of his wealth. He shook his purse in the face of society, and commanded it to continue to recognize the impostor as Lord X——, and society meekly obeyed him.

Impostures of this kind do not always terminate so fortunately for the parties concerned. New York gossip has many a well-authenticated story of foreign counts and lords, who have set society in a flutter, and have married some foolish, trusting woman, only to be detected when it was too late to prevent the trouble. Some of these scoundrels have been proved to be married men already, and the consequences of their falsehood have, of course, been more serious to the bride. Others again do not enter the matrimonial market at all, but use their arts to secure loans from their new acquaintances. Not long since a foreigner, calling himself a Russian Count, and claiming to be sent here on a mission connected with the Russian navy, succeeded in borrowing from some credulous acquaintances, who were dazzled by his pretended rank, sums ranging from $500 to $2,000, and amounting in the aggregate to $30,000. When the time of payment arrived, the Count had disappeared, and it was ascertained that he had escaped to Europe.

Impostors of other kinds are numerous. Men and women are always to be found in the city, seeking aid for some charitable institution, with which they claim to be connected. They carry memorandum books and pencils, in the former of which the donor is requested to inscribe his name and the amount of his gift, in order that it may be acknowledged in due form by the proper officers of the institution. Small favors are thankfully received, and they depart, assuring you in the most humble and sanctimonious manner that "the Lord loveth a cheerful giver." If you cannot give to-day, they are willing to call to-morrow—next week—any time that may suit your convenience. You cannot insult them by a sharp refusal, or in any way, for like Uriah Heep they are always "so 'umble." You find it hard to suspect them, but, in truth, they are the most genuine impostors to be met with in the city. They are soliciting money for themselves alone, and have no connection with any charitable institution whatever.

One-armed, or one-legged beggars, whose missing member, sound as your own, is strapped to their bodies so as to be safely out of sight, women wishing to bury their husbands or children, women with hired babies, and sundry other objects calculated to excite your pity, meet you at every step. They are vagabonds. God knows there is misery enough in this great city, but how to tell it from barefaced imposture, is perplexing and harassing to a charitably disposed person. Nine out of ten street beggars in New York are unworthy objects, and to give to them is simply to encourage vagrancy; and yet to know how to discriminate. That would be valuable knowledge to many people in the great city.

In the fall of 1870, a middle aged woman committed suicide in New York. For some months she had pursued a singular career in the great city, and had literally lived by her wits. While her main object was to live comfortably at other people's expense, she also devoted herself to an attempt to acquire property without paying for it. She arrived in New York in the spring of 1868, and took lodgings at an up-town hotel. She brought no baggage, but assured the clerk that her trunks had been unjustly detained by a boarding house keeper in Boston with whom she had had a difficulty. She succeeded in winning the confidence of the clerk, and told him that she had just come into possession of a fortune of one million dollars, left her by a rich relative, and that she had come to New York to purchase a home. She completely deceived the clerk, who vouched for her respectability and responsibility, and thus satisfied the proprietor of the hotel. She made the acquaintance of nearly all the resident guests of the house, and so won their sympathy and confidence that she was able to borrow from them considerable sums of money. In this way she lived from house to house, making payments on account only when obliged to do so, and when she could no longer remain at the hotels, she took up her quarters at a private boarding house, passing thence to another, and so on. She spent two years in this way, borrowing money continually, and paying very little for her board.

In pursuance of her plan to acquire real estate without paying for it, she made her appearance in the market as a purchaser. In the summer of 1870, she obtained permits of one of the leading real estate agents of the city to examine property in his hands for sale, and finally selected a house on Madison avenue. The price asked was $100,000, but she coolly declared her readiness to pay the full amount in cash as soon as the necessary deeds could be prepared. The real estate dealer was completely deceived by her seeming frankness, and assured her that he would give his personal attention to the details of the transaction, so that her interests would not suffer, and a day was agreed upon for the completion of the purchase.

The woman then assumed a confidential tone, and told the gentleman of her immense fortune. She was absolutely alone in the city, she said, without relatives or friends to whom she could apply for advice in the management of her property, and she urged him to become her trustee and manage the estate for her, offering him a liberal compensation for his services. Her object was to make him her trustee, induce him to act for her in the purchase of the house, and involve him so far as to secure the success of her scheme for getting possession of the property. The dealer, however, thanked her for her preference, but assured her that it was impossible for him to accept her proposition, as he had made it a rule never to act as trustee for any one. He did not in the least suspect her real design, and but for this previous and fixed determination would have acceded to her request. Finding that she could not shake his resolution, the lady took her departure, promising to return on the day appointed for the payment of the purchase money.

At the time designated, the deeds were ready, and the real estate agent and the owner of the Madison avenue mansion awaited the coming of the lady; but she did not appear, and, after a lapse of several days, the two gentlemen concluded they had been victimized, and then the true character of the trusteeship he had been asked to assume broke upon the real estate agent. The audacity and skill of the scheme fairly staggered him.

After the failure of this scheme, the woman tried several others of a similar character, with the same success. In October, 1870, a city newspaper, having obtained information respecting her transactions from some of her victims, published an account of her career. The next day she committed suicide, and was found dead in her bed.

Not long since a city lawyer, whom we shall call Smith, and who is much given to the procuring of patent divorces for dissatisfied husbands and wives, was visited by a richly dressed lady, who informed him that she was Mrs. P——, the wife of Mr. P——, of Fifth avenue, and that she wished to retain his services in procuring a divorce from her husband, on the ground of ill treatment. Mr. P—— was personally a stranger to the lawyer, who knew him, however, as a man of great wealth. Visions of a heavy fee flashed before him, and he encouraged the lady to make a full statement of her grievances, promising to do his best to secure the desired divorce in the shortest possible time. He made full notes of her statement, and assured her that he felt confident that he would be able to obtain not only the divorce, but a very large sum as alimony. In reply to her question as to his charge for his services, he replied:

"Well, I ought to charge you $1000, but out of consideration for your sufferings, I will only take a retainer of $100, and when we have gained our suit, you will pay me $500 additional."

"That is very reasonable," said the lady, "and I accept the terms. Unfortunately, I have nothing with me but a check for $200, given me by my husband this morning to use in shopping. I shall only need half of it, and if you could get it cashed for me—but, no matter, I'll call to-morrow, and make the payment."

Smith, who had seen the millionaire's heavy signature at the bottom of the check, thought he had better make sure of his retainer, and offered to accept the check on the spot. He had just $100 in his pocket, and this he gave to the lady who handed him the check, with the urgent entreaty that he would not betray her to her husband.

"He shall know nothing of the matter until it is too late for him to harm you," said the lawyer, gallantly, as he bowed his fair client out of the office.

It was after three o'clock, and Smith was forced to wait until the next morning before presenting his check at the bank on which it was drawn. Then, to his astonishment, the teller informed him that the signature of Mr. P—— was a forgery. Thoroughly incensed, Smith hastened to the office of the millionaire, and, laying the check before him, informed him that his wife had been guilty of forging his name, and that he must make the check good, or the lady would be exposed and punished. The millionaire listened blandly, stroking his whiskers musingly, and when the lawyer paused, overcome with excitement, quietly informed him that he was sorry for him, but that he, Mr. P——, had the misfortune to be without a wife. He had been a widower for five years.

How Smith found his way into the street again, he could never tell, but he went back to his work a sadder and a wiser man, musing upon the trickiness of mankind in general, and of women in particular.

*LIGHTS AND SHADOWS OF NEW YORK LIFE*, 1872

# WONG CHIN FOO

*In the Chinese immigrant community, not given to drawing attention to itself, the journalist Wong Chin Foo cut a conspicuous figure. Educated at American universities, Wong became a lecturer on Chinese culture and religion, attempting to correct popular misconceptions about his people. He twitted Christian missionaries with a mock-serious article called "Why I Am a Heathen," campaigned for the repeal of the Chinese exclusion laws, fell briefly under the theosophical spell of Madame Blavatsky, and later supported Sun Yat-Sen's New China movement. His efforts to start a Chinese-American newspaper failed, as he recounts in this piece for the humor magazine* Puck.

## EXPERIENCE OF A CHINESE JOURNALIST

IT IS not necessary for me to remark that I was born in the Middle Empire, and that I am now an American citizen; for ever since my advent in this land of the free I have been systematically styled a "pig-tailed renegade," a "moon-eyed leper," a "demon of the Orient," a "gangrened laundryman," a "rat-eating Mongol," etc.

I started life as a lecturer, and, through my connection with a Literary Bureau, was very successful in purveying to the intellectual pleasures of Western Sunday-schools and Southern clubs. That they seldom asked me to come back and lecture again does not invalidate my statement; neither is it inconsistent with popularity when an enthusiastic audience welcomes a speaker with revolvers and shotguns, and otherwise induces him to depart via a second-story window rather than the stairs. These are incidents in the life of every lecturer.

In an unguarded moment I listened to the voice of the tempter, and fell from my high estate. Persuaded that I was the coming journalist of the Occident and Orient alike, I came to New York City and started the *Chinese American*. I knew nothing of journalism save in a vague way, and went to work accordingly. I took an American partner and a Chinese one, engaged a city editor, a staff, and an artist.

The first issue, after many sleepless nights, appeared. I shall never forget it. It circulated fifty thousand copies, and brought in one thousand five hundred dollars.

That is, it brought in three hundred dollars cash, and one thousand two hundred dollars in notes, bills receivable, and promises. I have a hundred of the latter assorted, which I will sell at one cent on the dollar. I was proud of the issue until I had read the criticisms upon it in my E. C.s. The American E. C.s were contradictory in substance, but unanimous in their drift. The English articles were badly written, poorly thought and wretchedly printed; they were also splendidly written and composed, but displaying signs of some trained journalist, who was posing in my name. The editor, they said, was a Chinese gentleman with more money than brains. He was also a myth and a joke. He was also a Jesuit, a Buddhist missionary, and an Imperial emissary in disguise. Then came the Chinese E. C.s. My native tongue, as I wrote it, was uncouth, illiterate, unintelligent, vapid, hollow, fantastic, bombastic and idiotic. I was a wretch who was endeavoring to ruin the Flowery Kingdom in the eyes of Christendom; I was a renegade, an apostle, and the victim of American gold.

I had written a moral screed against gambling and opium-smoking. The gamblers and joint-keepers invaded my office a week after, and proceeded to flog the associate editor, cashier, and city reporter. The trio did not wait for the end of the performance, but departed for the Empire the same day.

I heard from them at—Panama. They were intact; but the nine hundred and fifty dollars, my entire assets they had carried with them, were not.

I did not come out altogether unscathed. I was "knocked out" twice, arrested four times for criminal libel, once for civil libel, under twenty-five thousand dollars bail, locked up in Ludlow Street jail, and twice poisoned.

I think the paper would have succeeded, if I had had more experience—say a hundred years. But my artist, Jung Fan Tai, became a Bohemian and used too much beer in his designs. Chinese art does not present many differences to the civilized eye; but it does to the Mongolian connaisseur.

Jung's second sacred dragon contained a superfluous cocktail, and was denounced in Chinatown as blasphemy. The luckless draughtsman was thereupon put under the ban of ostracism, and in a fortnight had shaken the dust of Gotham from off his feet. My second cashier was a reporter in bad luck. I do not think he was dishonest; but when you miss your treasurer and treasury, and find the first paralyzed in a neighboring bar-room the next day, and don't find the second at all, it's high time for a head editor to kick. I kicked; but the reporter, with an indescribable oath, swore that no "almond-eyed double blank" could kick him with impunity, and in less time than it takes to tell it had converted me into a ghastly ruin.

My journalistic career culminated recently in the Supreme Court. I had, with the best intentions in the world, allowed an article to appear in my sheet which "showed up" a certain individual in a moderately sensational way.

The style was patented after that employed in many E. C.s, and contained such pleasing epithets as "assassins, cut-throats, viper, scorpion, thief, embezzler, robber, liar, and a member of the Young Men's Christian Association." In short, it was a thoroughly American article. Yet, an imbecile jury gave a verdict for the fellow against me in one thousand dollars. At present there is an order of arrest out for me, and a deputy-sheriff is watching my regular haunts.

It's the old story. I had the capital; now I haven't; but I have the experience. Any paper wishing the services of an experienced editor, who can write in every vein and on every subject, and create libel-suits, can obtain a gem by applying to

WONG CHIN FOO,
*CARE OF* PUCK.

1885

# JOSÉ MARTÍ

*The man-made environment of New York often seems impervious to na-
ture, until an event like the blizzard of 1888 paralyzes the city. José
Martí (1853–95), the Cuban poet and revolutionary who lived for several years in New York and wrote a series of impressionistic pieces about
the United States for* La Nación *(Buenos Aires), describes this snowstorm in a visually haunting reverie which, along the way, acknowledges
New Yorkers' collective capacity for rising to the catastrophic occasion.*

## NEW YORK UNDER THE SNOW

THE FIRST ORIOLE had already been spied hanging its nest
from a cedar in Central Park; the bare poplars were putting
forth their plush of spring; and the leaves of the chestnut were
burgeoning, like chattering women poking their heads out of their
hoods after a storm. Notified by the cheeping of the birds, the
brooks were coming out from under their icy covering to see the
sun's return, and winter, defeated by the flowers, had fled away, covering its retreat with the month of winds. The first straw hats had
made their appearance, and the streets of New York were gay with
Easter attire, when, on opening its eyes after the hurricane had spent
its force, the city found itself silent, deserted, shrouded, buried
under the snow. Doughty Italians, braving the icy winds, load their
street-cleaning carts with fine, glittering snow, which they empty
into the river to the accompaniment of neighs, songs, jokes, and
oaths. The elevated train, stranded in a two-day death vigil beside the
body of the engineer who set out to defy the blizzard, is running
again, creaking and shivering, over the clogged rails that glitter and
flash. Sleigh bells jingle; the newsvendors cry their papers; snow-
plows, drawn by stout percherons, throw up banks of snow on both
sides of the street as they clear the horsecar's path; through the
breast-high snow, the city makes its way back to the trains, paralyzed
on the white plains; to the rivers, become bridges; to the silent
wharfs.

The clash of the combatants echoes through the vault-like streets of the city. For two days the snow has had New York in its power, encircled, terrified, like a prize fighter driven to the canvas by a sneak punch. But the moment the attack of the enemy slackened, as soon as the blizzard had spent its first fury, New York, like the victim of an outrage, goes about freeing itself of its shroud. Through the white hummocks move leagues of men. The snow already runs in dirty rivers in the busiest streets under the onslaught of its assailants. With spades, with shovels, with their own chests and those of the horses, they push back the snow, which retreats to the rivers.

Man's defeat was great, but so was his triumph. The city is still white; the Sound remains white and frozen. There have been deaths, cruelties, kindness, fatigue, and bravery. Man has given a good account of himself in this disaster.

At no time in this century has New York experienced a storm like that of March 13. It had rained the preceding Sunday, and the writer working into the dawn, the newspaper vendor at the railroad station, the milkman on his round of the sleeping houses, could hear the whiplash of the wind that had descended on the city against the chimneys, against walls and roofs, as it vented its fury on slate and mortar, shattered windows, demolished porches, clutched and uprooted trees, and howled, as though ambushed, as it fled down the narrow streets. Electric wires, snapping under its impact, sputtered and died. Telegraph lines, which had withstood so many storms, were wrenched from their posts. And when the sun should have appeared, it could not be seen, for like a shrieking, panic-stricken army, with its broken squadrons, gun carriages and infantry, the snow whirled past the darkened windows, without interruption, day and night. Man refused to be vanquished. He came out to defy the storm.

But by this time the overpowered streetcar lay horseless beneath the storm; the elevated train, which paid in blood for its first attempt to brave the elements, let the steam escape from its helpless engine; the suburban train, halted en route by the tempest or stalled by the drifting snow, higher than the engines, struggled in vain to reach its destination. The streetcars attempted one trip, and the horses plunged and reared, defending themselves with their hoofs from the suffocating storm. The elevated train took on a load of passengers, and ground to a halt half-way through the trip, paralyzed by the snow; after six hours of waiting, the men and women climbed down by ladder from their wind-tossed prison. The wealthy, or those faced with an emergency, paid twenty-five or fifty dollars for carriages drawn by stout horses to carry them a short distance, step by step. The angry wind, heavy with snow, buffeted them, pounded them, hurled them to the ground.

It was impossible to see the sidewalks. Intersections could no longer be distinguished, and one street looked like the next. On Twenty-third Street, one of the busiest thoroughfares, a thoughtful merchant put a sign on a corner-post: "This is 23rd Street." The snow was knee deep, and the drifts, waist-high. The angry wind nipped at the hands of pedestrians, knifed through their clothing, froze their noses and ears, blinded them, hurled them backward into the slippery snow, its fury making it impossible for them to get to their feet, flung them hatless and groping for support against the walls, or left them to sleep, to sleep forever, under the snow. A shopkeeper, a man in the prime of life, was found buried today, with only a hand sticking from the snow to show where he lay. A messenger boy, as blue as his uniform, was dug out of a white, cool tomb, a fit resting place for his innocent soul, and lifted up in the compassionate arms of his comrades. Another, buried to the neck, sleeps with two red patches on his white cheeks, his eyes a filmy blue.

The old, the young, women, children inch along Broadway and the avenues on their way to work. Some fall, and struggle to their feet. Some, exhausted, sink into a doorway, their only desire to struggle no more; others, generous souls, take them by the arm, encouraging them, shouting and singing. An old woman, who had made herself a kind of mask of her handkerchief with two slits for the eyes, leans against a wall and bursts into tears; the president of a neighboring bank, making his way on foot, carries her in his arms to a nearby pharmacy, which can be made out through the driving snow by its yellow and green lights. "I'm not going any further," said one. "I don't care if I lose my job." "I'm going on," says another. "I need my day's pay." The clerk takes the working girl by the arm; she helps her weary friend with an arm around his waist. At the entrance to the Brooklyn Bridge, a new bank clerk pleads with the policeman to let him pass, although at that moment only death can cross the bridge. "I will lose the job it has taken me three years to find," he supplicates. He starts across, and the wind reaches a terrible height, throws him to the ground with one gust, lifts him up again, snatches off his hat, rips open his coat, knocks him down at every step; he falls back, clutches at the railing, drags himself along. Notified by telegraph from Brooklyn, the police on the New York side of the bridge pick him up, utterly spent.

But why all this effort, when hardly a store is open, when the whole city has surrendered, huddled like a mole in its burrow, when if they reach the factory or office they will find the iron doors locked? Only a fellow man's pity, or the power of money, or the happy accident of living beside the only train which is running in one section of the city, valiantly inching along from hour to hour, can give comfort to so many faithful employes, so many courageous old men, so many heroic factory girls on this terrible day. From corner to corner they make their way, sheltering themselves in doorways until one opens to the feeble knocking of their numbed hands, like sparrows tapping against the window panes. Suddenly the fury of the wind mounts; it hurls the group fleeing for shelter against the wall; the poor working women cling to one another in the middle of the street until the snarling, screeching wind puts them to flight again. Men and women fight their way uptown, struggling against the gale, clearing the snow from their eyes, shielding them with their hands to find their way through the storm. Hotels? The chairs have been rented out for beds, and the baths for rooms. Drinks? Not even the men can find anything to drink; the saloons have exhausted their stock; and the women, dragging their numb feet homeward, have only their tears to drink.

After the first surprise of the dawn, people find ways to adjust their clothing so the fury of the tempest will not do them so much harm. There is an overturned wagon at every step; a shade, hanging from its spring, flaps against the wall like the wing of a dying bird;

an awning is torn to ribbons; a cornice dangles from its wall; an eave lies in the street. Walls, hallways, windows are all banked with snow. And the blizzard blows without respite, piling up drifts, scattering destruction, whistling and howling. And men and women keep walking with the snow to their armpits.

One has made a mask of silk from his umbrella, with two holes for the eyes, and another for the mouth, and thus, with his hands behind his back, he cuts his way through the wind. Others have tied stockings over their shoes, or bags of salt, or wrapping paper, or strips of rubber, fastened with twine. Others protect themselves with leggings, with fur caps; another, half dead, is being carried, wrapped in his buffalo-hide overcoat. "Sir," pleads the voice of a child, who cannot be seen for the snow, "help me out of here, I am dying." It is a messenger boy whom some heartless employer has sent out in this storm. There are many on horseback; one, who came out in a sled, is carried away with it at the first gust, and nearly loses his life. A determined old lady, who set out to buy a wreath of orange blossoms for her daughter's marriage, loses the wreath to the wind. Night fell over the arctic waste of New York, and terror took over. The postman on his round fell face down, blinded and benumbed, protecting his leather bag with his body. Families trapped in the roofless houses sought madly and in vain to find a way out through the snow-banked doors. When water hydrants lay buried under five feet of snow, a raging fire broke out, lighting up the snowy landscape like the Northern Lights, and swiftly burned three apartment houses to the ground. The fire wagons arrived! The firemen dug with their hands, and found the hydrant. The walls and the snowy street were scarlet, and the sky was blue velvet. Although the water they played against the flames was hurled back in their faces in stinging pellets by the fury of the wind, although the tongues of crimson flame leaped higher than the cross on the church steeple, although the wind-tossed columns of smoke bearing golden sparks singed their beards, there, without giving an inch, the firemen fought the fire with the snow at their breasts, brought it under control, and vanquished it. And then, with their arms, they opened a path for the engine through the snow.

Without milk, without coal, without mail, without newspapers, without streetcars, without telephone, without telegraph, the city arose today. What eagerness on the part of those living uptown to read the newspapers, which thanks to the intrepidity of the poor newsboys, finally came up from the downtown presses! There were four theatres open last night, but all the stores and offices are closed, and the elevated struggles in vain to carry the unwitting crowds that gather at its station to their places of work.

The trains and their human cargoes stand snowbound on the tracks. The city is cut off from the rest of the country and no news goes in or out. The rivers are ice, and the courageous cross them on foot; suddenly the ice gives way, and cakes of it float aimlessly with men aboard them; a tug goes out to rescue them, skirting the ice cake, nosing it toward the bank, edging it to a nearby dock. They are saved. What a cheer goes up from both sides of the river! There are also cheers as the fireman passes, the policeman, and the brave post-man. What can have happened to the trains that never arrive? The railroad companies, with admirable despatch, send out food and coal, hauled by their most powerful engines. What of those at sea? How many bodies lie buried under the snow?

Like a routed army that unexpectedly turns on its vanquisher, the snow had come in the night and covered the proud city with death.

These unpredictable onslaughts show utilitarian countries to advantage more than any others, for as was amply proven yesterday, in the hour of stress, the virtues that work heightens completely overshadowed those which selfishness withers. How brave the children, how loyal the workers, how uncomplaining and noble the women, how generous the men! The whole city spoke in loud voices today, as though it were afraid of finding itself alone. Those who unfeelingly push and jostle one another all the rest of the year, smile on each other today, tell of the dangers they escaped, exchange addresses, and walk along with new friends. The squares are mountains of snow, over which the icy lacework clinging like filigree to the branches of the trees glitters in the morning sun.

Houses of snow crown the rooftops, where the merry sparrows dig fragile nests. It is amazing and frightening, as though a shroud should suddenly flower in blood, to see the red roofs of the houses reappear in this city of snow. The telegraph poles ruefully contemplate the destruction, their tangled, fallen wires like unkempt heads. The city digs out, buries its dead, and with men, horses, and machines all working together, clears away the snow with streams of boiling water, with shovels, plows, and bonfires. But one is touched by a sense of great humility and a sudden rush of kindness, as though the dread hand had touched the shoulders of all men.

*LA NACIÓN*, 1888

# WILLIAM DEAN HOWELLS

*Since colonial times, the geographical limits of Manhattan Island have resulted in a chronic housing shortage, and real estate has played a major part in New York City's daily life. A Hazard of New Fortunes, by the great champion of literary realism William Dean Howells (1837–1920), depicts unforgettably the familiar process of accommodation by which the newcomer adjusts his residential standards to the available rental stock.*

## FROM *A HAZARD OF NEW FORTUNES*

THEY WENT to a quiet hotel far down town, and took a small apartment which they thought they could easily afford for the day or two they need spend in looking up a furnished flat. They were used to staying at this hotel when they came on for a little outing in New York, after some rigid winter in Boston, at the time of the spring exhibitions. They were remembered there from year to year; the colored call-boys, who never seemed to get any older, smiled upon them, and the clerk called March by name even before he registered. He asked if Mrs. March were with him, and said then he supposed they would want their usual quarters; and in a moment they were domesticated in a far interior that seemed to have been waiting for them in a clean, quiet, patient disoccupation ever since they left it two years before. The little parlor, with its gilt paper and ebonized furniture, was the lightest of the rooms, but it was not very light at noonday without the gas, which the bell-boy now flared up for them. The uproar of the city came to it in a soothing murmur, and they took possession of its peace and comfort with open celebration. After all, they agreed, there *was* no place in the world so delightful as a hotel apartment like that; the boasted charms of home were nothing to it; and then the magic of its being always there, ready for any one, every one, just as if it were for some one alone: it was like the experience of an Arabian Nights hero come true for all the race.

"Oh, *why* can't we always stay here, just we two!" Mrs. March sighed to her husband, as he came out of his room rubbing his face red with the towel, while she studied a new arrangement of her bonnet and hand-bag on the mantel.

"And ignore the past? I'm willing. I've no doubt that the children could get on perfectly well without us, and could find some lot in the scheme of Providence that would really be just as well for them."

"Yes; or could contrive somehow never to have existed. I should insist upon that. If they *are*, don't you see that we couldn't wish them *not to be?*"

"Oh yes; I see your point; it's simply incontrovertible."

She laughed, and said: "Well, at any rate, if we can't find a flat to suit us, we can all crowd into these three rooms somehow, for the winter, and then browse about for meals. By the week we could get them much cheaper; and we could save on the eating, as they do in Europe. Or on something else."

"Something else, probably," said March. "But we won't take this apartment till the ideal furnished flat winks out altogether. We shall not have any trouble. We can easily find some one who is going South for the winter, and will be glad to give up their flat 'to the right party' at a nominal rent. That's my notion. That's what the Evanses did one winter when they came on here in February. All but the nominality of the rent."

"Yes, and we could pay a very good rent and still save something on letting our house. You can settle yourselves in a hundred different ways in New York; that *is* one merit of the place. But if everything else fails, we can come back to this. I want you to take the refusal of it, Basil. And we'll commence looking this very evening as soon as we've had dinner. I cut a lot of things out of the *Herald* as we came on. See here!"

She took a long strip of paper out of her hand-bag with minute advertisements pinned transversely upon it, and forming the effect of some glittering nondescript vertebrate.

"Looks something like the sea-serpent," said March, drying his hands on the towel, while he glanced up and down the list. "But we sha'n't have any trouble. I've no doubt there are half a dozen things there that will do. You haven't gone uptown? Because we must be near the *Every Other Week* office."

"No; but I *wish* Mr. Fulkerson hadn't called it that! It always makes one think of 'jam yesterday and jam to-morrow, but never jam to-day,' in *Through the Looking-glass*. They're all in this region."

They were still at their table, beside a low window, where some sort of never-blooming shrub symmetrically balanced itself in a large pot, with a leaf to the right and a leaf to the left and a spear up the middle, when Fulkerson came stepping square-footedly over the thick dining-room carpet. He wagged in the air a gay hand of saluta-tion at sight of them, and of repression when they offered to rise to meet him; then, with an apparent simultaneity of action, he gave a hand to each, pulled up a chair from the next table, put his hat and stick on the floor beside it, and seated himself.

"Well, you've burnt your ships behind you, sure enough," he said, beaming his satisfaction upon them from eyes and teeth.

"The ships are burnt," said March, "though I'm not sure we did it alone. But here we are, looking for shelter, and a little anxious about the disposition of the natives."

"Oh, they're an awful peaceable lot," said Fulkerson. "I've been round amongst the caciques a little, and I think I've got two or three places that will just suit you, Mrs. March. How did you leave the children?"

"Oh, how kind of you! Very well, and very proud to be left in charge of the smoking wrecks."

Fulkerson naturally paid no attention to what she said, being but secondarily interested in the children at the best. "Here are some things right in this neighborhood, within gunshot of the office, and if you want you can go and look at them to-night; the agents gave me houses where the people would be in."

"We will go and look at them instantly," said Isabel. "Or, as soon as you've had coffee with us."

"Never do," Fulkerson replied. He gathered up his hat and stick. "Just rushed in to say Hello, and got to run right away again. I tell you, March, things are humming. I'm after those fellows with a sharp stick all the while to keep them from loafing on my house, and at the same time I'm just bubbling over with ideas about *The Lone Hand*—wish we *could* call it that!—that I want to talk up with you."

"Well, come to breakfast," said Isabel, cordially.

"No; the ideas will keep till you've secured your lodge in this vast wilderness. Good-by."

"You're as nice as you can be, Mr. Fulkerson," she said, "to keep us in mind when you have so much to occupy you."

"I wouldn't have *any*thing to occupy me if I *hadn't* kept you in mind, Mrs. March," said Fulkerson, going off upon as good a speech as he could apparently hope to make.

"Why, Basil," said Mrs. March, when he was gone, "he's charming! But now we mustn't lose an instant. Let's see where the places are." She ran over the half-dozen agents' permits. "Capital—first-rate—the very thing—every one. Well, I consider ourselves settled! We can go back to the children to-morrow if we like, though I rather think I should like to stay over another day and get a little rested for the final pulling up that's got to come. But this simplifies everything enormously, and Mr. Fulkerson is as thoughtful and as sweet as he can be. I know you will get on well with him. He has such a good heart. And his attitude toward you, Basil, is beautiful always—so respectful; or not that so much as appreciative. Yes, appreciative—that's the word; I must always keep that in mind."

"It's quite important to do so," said March.

"Yes," she assented, seriously; "and we must not forget just what kind of flat we are going to look for. The *sine qua nons* are an elevator and steam heat, not above the third floor, to begin with. Then we must each have a room, and you must have your study and I must have my parlor; and the two girls must each have a room. With the kitchen and dining-room, how many does that make?"

"Ten."

"I thought eight. Well, no matter. You can work in the parlor, and run into your bedroom when anybody comes; and I can sit in mine, and the girls must put up with one, if it's large and sunny, though I've always given them two at home. And the kitchen must be sunny, so they can sit in it. And the rooms must *all* have outside light. And the rent must not be over eight hundred for the winter. We only get a thousand for our whole house, and we *must* save something out of that, so as to cover the expenses of moving. Now, do you think you can remember all that?"

"Not the half of it," said March. "But *you* can; or if you forget a third of it, I can come in with my partial half, and more than make it up."

She had brought her bonnet and sack down-stairs with her, and was transferring them from the hat-rack to her person while she talked. The friendly door-boy let them into the street, and the clear October evening air inspirited her so that as she tucked her hand under her husband's arm and began to pull him along, she said, "If we find something right away—and we're just as likely to get the right flat soon as late; it's all a lottery—we'll go to the theatre somewhere."

She had a moment's panic about having left the agents' permits on the table, and after remembering that she had put them into her little shopping bag, where she kept her money (each note crushed into a round wad), and had left that on the hat-rack, where it would certainly be stolen, she found it on her wrist. She did not think that very funny, but after a first impulse to inculpate her husband, she let him laugh, while they stopped under a lamp, and she held the permits half a yard away to read the numbers on them.

"Where are your glasses, Isabel?"

"On the mantel in our room, of course."

"Then you ought to have brought a pair of tongs."

"I wouldn't get off second-hand jokes, Basil," she said; and "Why, here!" she cried, whirling round to the door before which they had halted, "this is the very number! Well, I do believe it's a sign!"

One of those colored men who soften the trade of janitor in many of the smaller apartment-houses in New York by the sweetness of their race, let the Marches in, or, rather, welcomed them to the possession of the premises by the bow with which he acknowledged their permit. It was a large old mansion cut up into five or six dwellings; but it had kept some traits of its former dignity, which pleased people of their sympathetic tastes. The dark mahogany trim, of sufficiently ugly design, gave a rich gloom to the hallway, which was wide, and paved with marble; the carpeted stairs curved aloft through a generous space.

"There is no elevator?" Mrs. March asked of the janitor.

He answered, "No, ma'am; only two flights up," so winningly that she said,

"Oh!" in courteous apology, and whispered her husband as she followed lightly up, "We'll take it, Basil, if it's like the rest."

"If it's like him, you mean."

"I don't wonder they wanted to own them," she hurriedly philosophized. "If I had such a creature, nothing but death should part us, and I should no more think of giving him his *freedom*——"

"No; we couldn't afford it," returned her husband.

The apartment the janitor unlocked for them, and lit up from those chandeliers and brackets of gilt brass in the form of vine bunches, leaves, and tendrils in which the early gas-fitter realized most of his conceptions of beauty, had rather more of the ugliness than the dignity of the hall. But the rooms were large, and they grouped themselves in a reminiscence of the time when they were part of a dwelling, that had its charm, its pathos, its impressiveness. Where they were cut up into smaller spaces, it had been done with the frankness with which a proud old family of fallen fortunes practises its economies. The rough pine floors showed a black border of tack heads where carpets had been lifted and put down for generations; the white paint was yellow with age; the apartment had light at the front and at the back, and two or three rooms had glimpses of the day through small windows let into their corners; another one seemed lifting an appealing eye to heaven through a glass circle in its ceiling; the rest must darkle in perpetual twilight. Yet something pleased in it all, and Mrs. March had gone far to adapt the different rooms to the members of her family, when she suddenly thought (and for her to think was to say), "Why, but there's no steam heat!"

"No, ma'am," the janitor admitted; "but dere's grates in most o' de rooms, and dere's furnace heat in de halls."

"That's true," she admitted, and having placed her family in the apartments, it was hard to get them out again. "Could we manage?" she referred to her husband.

"Why, *I* shouldn't care for the steam heat if— What is the rent?" he broke off to ask the janitor.

"Nine hundred, sir."

March concluded to his wife, "If it were furnished."

"Why, of course! What could I have been thinking of? We're look-ing for a furnished flat," she explained to the janitor, "and this was so pleasant and home-like that I never thought whether it was furnished or not."

She smiled upon the janitor, and he entered into the joke and chuckled so amiably at her flattering oversight on the way down-stairs that she said, as she pinched her husband's arm, "Now, if you don't give him a quarter, I'll never speak to you again, Basil!"

"I would have given half a dollar willingly to get you beyond his glamour," said March, when they were safely on the pavement out-side. "If it hadn't been for my strength of character, you'd have taken an unfurnished flat without heat and with no elevator, at nine hun-dred a year, when you had just sworn me to steam heat, an elevator, furniture, and eight hundred."

"Yes! How could I have lost my head so completely?" she said, with a lenient amusement in her aberration which she was not al-ways able to feel in her husband's.

"The next time a colored janitor opens the door to us, I'll tell him the apartment doesn't suit at the threshold. It's the only way to manage you, Isabel."

"It's true. I *am* in love with the whole race. I never saw one of them that didn't have perfectly angelic manners. I think we shall all be black in heaven—that is, black-souled."

"That isn't the usual theory," said March.

"Well, perhaps not," she assented. "Where are we going now? Oh yes, to the Xenophon!"

She pulled him gayly along again, and after they had walked a block down and half a block over, they stood before the apartment-house of that name, which was cut on the gas lamps on either side of

the heavily spiked, aesthetic-hinged black door. The titter of an electric bell brought a large fat Buttons, with a stage effect of being
dressed to look small, who said he would call the janitor, and they
waited in the dimly splendid, copper-colored interior, admiring the
whorls and waves into which the wall paint was combed, till the janitor came in his gold-banded cap, like a continental *portier*. When
they said they would like to see Mrs. Grosvenor Green's apartment
he owned his inability to cope with the affair, and said he must send
for the superintendent; he was either in the Herodotus or the
Thucydides, and would be there in a minute. The Buttons brought
him—a Yankee of browbeating presence in plain clothes—almost before they had time to exchange a frightened whisper in recognition
of the fact that there could be no doubt of the steam heat and elevator in this case. Half stifled in the one, they mounted in the other
eight stories, while they tried to keep their self-respect under the
gaze of the superintendent, which they felt was classing and assess-
ing them with unfriendly accuracy. They could not, and they faltered
abashed at the threshold of Mrs. Grosvenor Green's apartment,
while the superintendent lit the gas in the gangway that he called a
private hall, and in the drawing-room and the succession of chambers stretching rearward to the kitchen. Everything had been done
by the architect to save space, and everything to waste it by Mrs.
Grosvenor Green. She had conformed to a law for the necessity of
turning round in each room, and had folding-beds in the chambers;
but there her subordination had ended, and wherever you might
have turned round she had put a gimcrack so that you would knock
it over if you did turn. The place was rather pretty and even imposing at first glance, and it took several joint ballots for March and his
wife to make sure that with the kitchen there were only six rooms.
At every door hung a portière from large rings on a brass rod; every
shelf and dressing-case and mantle was littered with gimcracks, and
the corners of the tiny rooms were curtained off, and behind these
portières swarmed more gimcracks. The front of the upright piano
had what March called a short-skirted portière on it, and the top
was covered with vases, with dragon candlesticks, and with Jap fans,
which also expanded themselves bat-wise on the walls between the

etchings and the water-colors. The floors were covered with filling, and then rugs, and then skins; the easy-chairs all had tidies, Armenian and Turkish and Persian; the lounges and sofas had embroidered cushions hidden under tidies. The radiator was concealed by a Jap screen, and over the top of this some Arab scarfs were flung. There was a superabundance of clocks. China pugs guarded the hearth; a brass sunflower smiled from the top of either andiron, and a brass peacock spread its tail before them inside a high filigree fender; on one side was a coal-hod in repoussé brass, and on the other a wrought-iron wood-basket. Some red Japanese bird-kites were stuck about in the necks of spelter vases, a crimson Jap umbrella hung opened beneath the chandelier, and each globe had a shade of yellow silk.

March, when he had recovered his self-command a little in the presence of the agglomeration, comforted himself by calling the bric-à-brac Jamescracks, as if this was their full name.

The disrespect he was able to show the whole apartment by means of this joke strengthened him to say boldly to the superintendent that it was altogether too small; then he asked carelessly what the rent was.

"Two hundred and fifty."

The Marches gave a start, and looked at each other.

"Don't you think we could make it do?" she asked him, and he could see that she had mentally saved five hundred dollars as the difference between the rent of their house and that of this flat. "It has some very pretty features, and we could manage to squeeze in, couldn't we?"

"You won't find another furnished flat like it for no two fifty a month in the whole city," the superintendent put in.

They exchanged glances again, and March said, carelessly, "It's too small."

"There's a vacant flat in the Herodotus for eighteen hundred a year, and one in the Thucydides for fifteen," the superintendent suggested, clicking his keys together as they sank down in the elevator; "seven rooms and a bath."

"Thank you," said March; "we're looking for a furnished flat."

They felt that the superintendent parted from them with repressed sarcasm.

"Oh, Basil, do you think we *really* made him think it was the smallness and not the dearness?"

"No; but we saved our self-respect in the attempt; and that's a great deal."

"Of course I *wouldn't* have taken it, anyway, with only six rooms, and so high up. But what prices! Now we must be very circumspect about the next place."

It was a janitress, large, fat, with her arms wound up in her apron, who received them there. Mrs. March gave her a succinct but perfect statement of their needs. She failed to grasp the nature of them, or feigned to do so. She shook her head, and said that her son would show them the flat. There was a radiator visible in the narrow hall, and Isabel tacitly compromised on steam heat without an elevator, as the flat was only one flight up. When the son appeared from below with a small kerosene hand-lamp, it appeared that the flat was unfurnished, but there was no stopping him till he had shown it in all its impossibility. When they got safely away from it and into the street, March said, "Well, have you had enough for to-night, Isabel? Shall we go to the theatre now?"

"Not on any account. I want to see the whole list of flats that Mr. Fulkerson thought would be the very thing for us." She laughed, but with a certain bitterness.

"You'll be calling him my Mr. Fulkerson next, Isabel."

"Oh no!"

The fourth address was a furnished flat without a kitchen, in a house with a general restaurant. The fifth was a furnished house. At the sixth a pathetic widow and her pretty daughter wanted to take a family to board, and would give them a private table at a rate which the Marches would have thought low in Boston.

Mrs. March came away tingling with compassion for their evident anxiety, and this pity naturally soured into a sense of injury. "Well, I must say I have completely lost confidence in Mr. Fulkerson's judgment. Anything more utterly different from what I told him we wanted I couldn't imagine. If he doesn't manage any better about his business than he has done about this, it will be a perfect failure."

"Well, well, let's hope he'll be more circumspect about that," her husband returned, with ironical propitiation. "But I don't think it's Fulkerson's fault altogether. Perhaps it's the house agents'. They're a very illusory generation. There seems to be something in the human habitation that corrupts the natures of those who deal in it, to buy or sell it, to hire or let it. You go to an agent and tell him what kind of a house you want. He has no such house, and he sends you to look at something altogether different, upon the well-ascertained principle that if you can't get what you want, you will take what you can get. You don't suppose the 'party' that took our house in Boston was looking for any such house? He was looking for a totally different kind of house in another part of the town."

"I don't believe that!" his wife broke in.

"Well, no matter. But see what a scandalous rent you asked for it!"

"We didn't get much more than half; and, besides, the agent told me to ask fourteen hundred."

"Oh, I'm not blaming you, Isabel. I'm only analyzing the house agent, and exonerating Fulkerson."

"Well, I don't believe he told them just what we wanted; and, at any rate, I'm done with agents. To-morrow, I'm going entirely by advertisements."

✦ ✦ ✦ ✦ ✦

In their search they were obliged, as March complained, to the acquisition of useless information in a degree unequalled in their experience. They came to excel in the sad knowledge of the line at which respectability distinguishes itself from shabbiness. Flattering advertisements took them to numbers of huge apartment-houses chiefly distinguishable from tenement-houses by the absence of fire-escapes on their façades, till Mrs. March refused to stop at any door where there were more than six bell-ratchets and speaking-tubes on either hand. Before the middle of the afternoon she decided against

ratchets altogether, and confined herself to knobs neatly set in the
door-trim. Her husband was still sunk in the superstition that you
can live anywhere you like in New York, and he would have paused
at some places where her quicker eye caught the fatal sign of
"Modes" in the ground-floor windows. She found that there was an
east and west line beyond which they could not go if they wished to
keep their self-respect, and that within the region to which they had
restricted themselves there was a choice of streets. At first all the
New York streets looked to them ill paved, dirty, and repulsive; the
general infamy imparted itself in their casual impression to streets in
no wise guilty. But they began to notice that some streets were quiet
and clean, and though never so quiet and clean as Boston streets, that
they wore an air of encouraging reform, and suggested a future of
greater and greater domesticity. Whole blocks of these down-town
cross streets seemed to have been redeemed from decay, and even in
the midst of squalor a dwelling here and there had been seized,
painted a dull red as to its brick-work, and a glossy black as to its
wood-work, and with a bright brass bell-pull and door-knob and a
large brass plate for its key-hole escutcheon, had been endowed with
an effect of purity and pride which removed its shabby neighborhood
far from it.

Some of these houses were quite small, and imaginably within
their means; but, as March said, somebody seemed always to be
living there himself, and the fact that none of them were to rent
kept Mrs. March true to her ideal of a flat. Nothing prevented its
realization so much as its difference from the New York ideal of a
flat, which was inflexibly seven rooms and a bath. One or two
rooms might be at the front, the rest crooked and cornered backward through increasing and then decreasing darkness till they
reached a light bedroom or kitchen at the rear. It might be the
one or the other, but it was always the seventh room with the
bath; or if, as sometimes happened, it was the eighth, it was so
after having counted the bath as one. In this case the janitor
said you always counted the bath as one. If the flats were advertised as having "all light rooms," he explained that any room with

a window giving into the open air of a court or shaft was counted a light room.

The Marches tried to make out why it was that these flats were so much more repulsive than the apartments which every one lived in abroad; but they could do so only upon the supposition that in their European days they were too young, too happy, too full of the future, to notice whether rooms were inside or outside, light or dark, big or little, high or low. "Now we're imprisoned in the present," he said, "and we have to make the worst of it."

In their despair he had an inspiration, which she declared worthy of him: it was to take two small flats, of four or five rooms and a bath, and live in both. They tried this in a great many places; but they never could get two flats of the kind on the same floor where there were steam heat and an elevator. At one place they almost did it. They had resigned themselves to the humility of the neighborhood, to the prevalence of modistes and livery-stablemen (they seem to consort much in New York), to the garbage in the gutters and the litter of paper in the streets, to the faltering slats in the surrounding window-shutters and the crumbled brown-stone steps and sills, when it turned out that one of the apartments had been taken between two visits they made. Then the only combination left open to them was of a ground-floor flat to the right and a third-floor flat to the left.

Still they kept this inspiration in reserve for use at the first opportunity. In the mean time there were several flats which they thought they could almost make do: notably one where they could get an extra servant's room in the basement four flights down, and another where they could get it in the roof five flights up. At the first the janitor was respectful and enthusiastic; at the second he had an effect of ironical pessimism. When they trembled on the verge of taking his apartment, he pointed out a spot in the kalsomining of the parlor ceiling, and gratuitously said, Now such a thing as that he should not agree to put in shape unless they took the apartment for a term of years. The apartment was unfurnished, and they recurred to the fact that they wanted a furnished apartment, and made their escape. This saved them in several other extremities; but short of extremity they could not keep their different requirements in mind, and were always about to decide without regard to some one of them.

They went to several places twice without intending: once to that old-fashioned house with the pleasant colored janitor, and wandered all over the apartment again with a haunting sense of familiarity, and then recognized the janitor and laughed; and to that house with the pathetic widow and the pretty daughter who wished to take them to board. They staid to excuse their blunder, and easily came by the fact that the mother had taken the house that the girl might have a home while she was in New York studying art, and they hoped to pay their way by taking boarders. Her daughter was at her class now, the mother concluded; and they encouraged her to believe that it could only be a few days till the rest of her scheme was realized.

"I dare say we could be perfectly comfortable there," March suggested when they had got away. "Now if we were truly humane, we would modify our desires to meet their needs, and end this sickening search, wouldn't we?"

"Yes; but we're *not* truly humane," his wife answered, "or at least not in that sense. You know you hate boarding; and if we went there I should have them on my sympathies the whole time."

"I see. And then you would take it out of me."

"Then I should take it out of you. And if you are going to be so weak, Basil, and let every little thing work upon you in that way, you'd better not come to New York. You'll see enough misery here."

"Well, don't take that superior tone with me, as if I were a child that had its mind set on an undesirable toy, Isabel."

"Ah, don't you suppose it's because you *are* such a child in some respects that I like you, dear?" she demanded, without relenting.

"But I don't find so much misery in New York. I don't suppose there's any more suffering here to the population than there is in the country. And they're so gay about it all. I think the outward aspect of the place and the hilarity of the sky and air must get into the people's blood. The weather is simply unapproachable; and I don't care if it is the ugliest place in the world, as you say. I suppose it is. It shrieks and yells with ugliness here and there; but it never loses its spirits. That widow is from the country. When she's been a year in New York she'll be as gay—as gay as an L road." He celebrated a satisfaction they both had in the L roads. "They kill the streets and avenues; but at least they partially hide them, and that is some comfort; and they do triumph over their prostrate forms with a savage exultation that is intoxicating. Those bends in the L that you get at the corner of Washington Square, and just below the Cooper Institute—they're the gayest things in the world. Perfectly atrocious, of course, but incomparably picturesque! And the whole city is so," said March, "or else the L would never have got built here. New York may be splendidly gay or squalidly gay, but, prince or pauper, it's gay always."

"Yes, gay is the word," she admitted, with a sigh. "But frantic. I can't get used to it. They forget death, Basil: they forget death in New York."

"Well, I don't know that I've ever found much advantage in remembering it."

"Don't say such a thing, dearest."

He could see that she had got to the end of her nervous strength for the present, and he proposed that they should take the elevated road as far as it would carry them into the country, and shake off their nightmare of flat-hunting for an hour or two; but her conscience would not let her. She convicted him of levity equal to that of the New-Yorkers in proposing such a thing; and they dragged through the day. She was too tired to care for dinner, and in the night she had a dream from which she woke herself with a cry that roused him too. It was something about the children at first, whom they had talked of wistfully before falling asleep, and then it was of a hideous thing with two square eyes and a series of sections growing darker and then lighter, till the tail of the monstrous articulate was quite luminous again. She shuddered at the vague description she was able to give; but he asked, "Did it offer to bite you?"

"No. That was the most frightful thing about it: it had no mouth."

March laughed. "Why, my dear, it was nothing but a harmless New York flat—seven rooms and a bath."

"I really believe it was," she consented, recognizing an architectural resemblance, and she fell asleep again, and woke renewed for the work before them.

1 8 9 0

# JACOB RIIS

*Jacob Riis (1849–1914) was a Danish immigrant who had experienced homelessness and poverty on arriving in New York. His study of the city's slums,* How the Other Half Lives, *was informed by his own intimate knowledge of those scenes of misery, and animated by a desire for real change; it led to a new tenement construction law which guaranteed better light and ventilation to tenants. (For a glimpse of Riis's career as a police reporter, see Lincoln Steffens'"Roosevelt and Reform,"page 528.)*

## THE DOWN TOWN BACK-ALLEYS

DOWN BELOW Chatham Square, in the old Fourth Ward, where the cradle of the tenement stood, we shall find New York's Other Half at home, receiving such as care to call and are not afraid. Not all of it, to be sure, there is not room for that; but a fairly representative gathering, representative of its earliest and worst traditions. There is nothing to be afraid of. In this metropolis, let it be understood, there is no public street where the stranger may not go safely by day and by night, provided he knows how to mind his own business and is sober. His coming and going will excite little interest, unless he is suspected of being a truant officer, in which case he will be impressed with the truth of the observation that the American stock is dying out for want of children. If he escapes this suspicion and the risk of trampling upon, or being himself run down by the bewildering swarms of youngsters that are everywhere or nowhere as the exigency and their quick scent of danger direct, he will see no reason for dissenting from that observation. Glimpses caught of the parents watching the youngsters play from windows or open doorways will soon convince him that the native stock is in no way involved.

Leaving the Elevated Railroad where it dives under the Brooklyn Bridge at Franklin Square, scarce a dozen steps will take us where we wish to go. With its rush and roar echoing yet in our ears, we have turned the corner from prosperity to poverty. We stand upon the domain of the tenement. In the shadow of the great stone abutments the old Knickerbocker houses linger like ghosts of a departed day. Down the winding slope of Cherry Street—proud and fashionable Cherry Hill that was—their broad steps, sloping roofs, and dormer windows are easily made out; all the more easily for the contrast with the ugly barracks that elbow them right and left. These never had other design than to shelter, at as little outlay as possible, the greatest crowds out of which rent could be wrung. They were the bad after-thought of a heedless day. The years have brought to the old houses unhonored age, a querulous second childhood that is out of tune with the time, their tenants, the neighbors, and cries out against them and against you in fretful protest in every step on their rotten floors or squeaky stairs. Good cause have they for their fretting. This one, with its shabby front and poorly patched roof, what glowing firesides, what happy children may it once have owned? Heavy feet, too often with unsteady step, for the pot-house is next door—where is it not next door in these slums?—have worn away the brown-stone steps since; the broken columns at the door have rotted away at the base. Of the handsome cornice barely a trace is left. Dirt and desolation reign in the wide hallway, and danger lurks on the stairs. Rough pine boards fence off the roomy fire-places— where coal is bought by the pail at the rate of twelve dollars a ton these have no place. The arched gateway leads no longer to a shady bower on the banks of the rushing stream, inviting to day-dreams with its gentle repose, but to a dark and nameless alley, shut in by high brick walls, cheerless as the lives of those they shelter. The wolf knocks loudly at the gate in the troubled dreams that come to this alley, echoes of the day's cares. A horde of dirty children play about the dripping hydrant, the only thing in the alley that thinks enough of its chance to make the most of it: it is the best it can do. These are the children of the tenements, the growing generation of the slums; this their home. From the great highway overhead, along which throbs the life-tide of two great cities, one might drop a pebble into half a dozen such alleys.

One yawns just across the street; not very broadly, but it is not to blame. The builder of the old gateway had no thought of its ever becoming a public thoroughfare. Once inside it widens, but only to make room for a big box-like building with the worn and greasy look of the slum tenement that is stamped alike on the houses and their tenants down here, even on the homeless cur that romps with the children in yonder building lot, with an air of expectant interest plainly betraying the forlorn hope that at some stage of the game a meat-bone may show up in the role of "It." Vain hope, truly! Nothing more appetizing than a bare-legged ragamuffin appears. Meat-bones, not long since picked clean, are as scarce in Blind Man's Alley as elbow-room in any Fourth Ward back-yard. The shouts of the children come hushed over the house-tops, as if apologizing for the intrusion. Few glad noises make this old alley ring. Morning and evening it echoes with the gentle, groping tap of the blind man's staff as he feels his way to the street. Blind Man's Alley bears its name for a reason. Until little more than a year ago its dark burrows harbored a colony of blind beggars, tenants of a blind landlord, old Daniel Murphy, whom every child in the ward knows, if he never heard of the President of the United States. "Old Dan" made a big fortune— he told me once four hundred thousand dollars—out of his alley and the surrounding tenements, only to grow blind himself in extreme old age, sharing in the end the chief hardship of the wretched beings whose lot he had stubbornly refused to better that he might increase his wealth. Even when the Board of Health at last compelled him to repair and clean up the worst of the old buildings, under threat of driving out the tenants and locking the doors behind them, the work was accomplished against the old man's angry protests. He appeared in person before the Board to argue his case, and his argument was characteristic.

"I have made my will," he said. "My monument stands waiting for me in Calvary. I stand on the very brink of the grave, blind and helpless, and now (here the pathos of the appeal was swept under in a burst of angry indignation) do you want me to build and get skinned, skinned? These people are not fit to live in a nice house. Let them go where they can, and let my house stand."

In spite of the genuine anguish of the appeal, it was downright amusing to find that his anger was provoked less by the anticipated waste of luxury on his tenants than by distrust of his own kind, the builder. He knew intuitively what to expect. The result showed that Mr. Murphy had gauged his tenants correctly. The cleaning up process apparently destroyed the home-feeling of the alley; many of the blind people moved away and did not return. Some remained, however, and the name has clung to the place.

Some idea of what is meant by a sanitary "cleaning up" in these slums may be gained from the account of a mishap I met with once, in taking a flash-light picture of a group of blind beggars in one of the tenements down here. With unpractised hands I managed to set fire to the house. When the blinding effect of the flash had passed away and I could see once more, I discovered that a lot of paper and rags that hung on the wall were ablaze. There were six of us, five blind men and women who knew nothing of their danger, and my-self, in an attic room with a dozen crooked, rickety stairs between us and the street, and as many households as helpless as the one whose guest I was all about us. The thought: how were they ever to be got out? made my blood run cold as I saw the flames creeping up the wall, and my first impulse was to bolt for the street and shout for help. The next was to smother the fire myself, and I did, with a vast deal of trouble. Afterward, when I came down to the street I told a friendly policeman of my trouble. For some reason he thought it rather a good joke, and laughed immoderately at my concern lest even then sparks should be burrowing in the rotten wall that might yet break out in flame and destroy the house with all that were in it. He told me why, when he found time to draw breath. "Why, don't you know," he said, "that house is the Dirty Spoon? It caught fire six times last winter, but it wouldn't burn. The dirt was so thick on the walls, it smothered the fire!" Which, if true, shows that water and dirt, not usually held to be harmonious elements, work together for the good of those who insure houses.

Sunless and joyless though it be, Blind Man's Alley has that which its compeers of the slums vainly yearn for. It has a pay-day. Once a year sunlight shines into the lives of its forlorn crew, past and present. In June, when the Superintendent of Out-door Poor distributes the twenty thousand dollars annually allowed the poor blind by the city, in half-hearted recognition of its failure to otherwise provide for them, Blindman's Alley takes a day off and goes to "see" Mr. Blake. That night it is noisy with unwonted merriment. There is scraping of squeaky fiddles in the dark rooms, and cracked old voices sing long-forgotten songs. Even the blind landlord rejoices, for much of the money goes into his coffers.

From their perch up among the rafters Mrs. Gallagher's blind boarders might hear, did they listen, the tramp of the policeman always on duty in Gotham Court, half a stone's throw away. His beat, though it takes in but a small portion of a single block, is quite as lively as most larger patrol rounds. A double row of five-story tenements, back to back under a common roof, extending back from the street two hundred and thirty-four feet, with barred openings in the dividing wall, so that the tenants may see but cannot get at each other from the stairs, makes the "court." Alleys—one wider by a couple of feet than the other, whence the distinction Single and Double Alley—skirt the barracks on either side. Such, briefly, is the tenement that has challenged public attention more than any other in the whole city and tested the power of sanitary law and rule for forty years. The name of the pile is not down in the City Directory, but in the public records it holds an unenviable place. It was here the mortality rose during the last great cholera epidemic to the unprecedented rate of 195 in 1,000 inhabitants. In its worst days a full thousand could not be packed into the court, though the number did probably not fall far short of it. Even now, under the management of men of conscience, and an agent, a King's Daughter, whose practical energy, kindliness and good sense have done much to redeem its foul reputation, the swarms it shelters would make more than one fair-sized country village. The mixed character of the population, by this time about equally divided between the Celtic and the Italian stock, accounts for the iron bars and the policeman. It was an eminently Irish suggestion that the latter was to be credited to the presence of two German families in the court, who "made trouble all the time." A Chinaman whom I questioned as he hurried past the iron gate of the alley, put the matter in a different light. "Lem Ilish velly bad," he said. Gotham Court has been the entering wedge for the Italian hordes, which until recently had not attained a foothold in the Fourth Ward, but are now trailing across Chatham Street from their stronghold in "the Bend" in ever increasing numbers, seeking, according to their wont, the lowest level.

It is curious to find that this notorious block, whose name was so long synonymous with all that was desperately bad, was originally built (in 1851) by a benevolent Quaker for the express purpose of rescuing the poor people from the dreadful rookeries they were then living in. How long it continued a model tenement is not on record. It could not have been very long, for already in 1862, ten years after it was finished, a sanitary official counted 146 cases of sickness in the court, including "all kinds of infectious disease," from small-pox down, and reported that of 138 children born in it in less than three years 61 had died, mostly before they were one year old. Seven years later the inspector of the district reported to the Board of Health that "nearly ten per cent. of the population is sent to the public hospitals each year." When the alley was finally taken in hand by the authorities, and, as a first step toward its reclamation, the entire population was driven out by the police, experience dictated, as one of the first improvements to be made, the putting in of a kind of sewer-grating, so constructed, as the official report patiently puts it, "as to prevent the ingress of persons disposed to make a hiding-place" of the sewer and the cellars into which they opened. The fact was that the big vaulted sewers had long been a runway for thieves—the Swamp Angels—who through them easily escaped when chased by the police, as well as a storehouse for their plunder. The sewers are there to-day; in fact the two alleys are nothing but the roofs of these enormous tunnels in which a man may walk upright the full distance of the block and into the Cherry Street sewer—if he likes the fun and is not afraid of rats. Could their grimy walls speak, the big canals might tell many a startling tale. But they are silent enough, and so are most of those whose secrets they might betray. The flood-gates connecting with the Cherry Street main are closed now, except when the water is drained off. Then there were no gates, and it is on record that the sewers were chosen as a short cut habitually by residents of the court whose business lay on the line of them, near a manhole, perhaps, in Cherry Street, or at the river mouth of the big pipe when it was clear at low tide. "Me Jimmy," said one wrinkled old dame, who looked in while we were nosing about under Double Alley, "he used to go to his work along down Cherry Street that way every morning and come back at night." The associations must have been congenial. Probably "Jimmy" himself fitted into the landscape.

Half-way back from the street in this latter alley is a tenement, facing the main building, on the west side of the way, that was not originally part of the court proper. It stands there a curious monument to a Quaker's revenge, a living illustration of the power of hate to perpetuate its bitter fruit beyond the grave. The lot upon which it is built was the property of John Wood, brother of Silas, the builder of Gotham Court. He sold the Cherry Street front to a man who built upon it a tenement with entrance only from the street. Mr. Wood afterward quarrelled about the partition line with his neighbor, Alderman Mullins, who had put up a long tenement barrack on his lot after the style of the Court, and the Alderman knocked him down. Tradition records that the Quaker picked himself up with the quiet remark, "I will pay thee for that, friend Alderman," and went his way. His manner of paying was to put up the big building in the rear of 34 Cherry Street with an immense blank wall right in front of the windows of Alderman Mullins's tenements, shutting out effectually light and air from them. But as he had no access to the street from his building for many years it could not be let or used for anything, and remained vacant until it passed under the management of the Gotham Court property. Mullins's Court is there yet, and so is the Quaker's vengeful wall that has cursed the lives of thousands of innocent people since. At its farther end the alley between the two that begins inside the Cherry Street tenement, six or seven feet wide, narrows down to less than two feet. It is barely possible to squeeze through; but few care to do it, for the rift leads to the jail of the Oak Street police station, and therefore is not popular with the growing youth of the district.

There is crape on the door of the Alderman's court as we pass out, and upstairs in one of the tenements preparations are making for a wake. A man lies dead in the hospital who was cut to pieces in a "can racket" in the alley on Sunday. The sway of the excise law is not extended to these back alleys. It would matter little if it were. There are secret by-ways, and some it is not held worth while to keep secret, along which the "growler" wanders at all hours and all seasons unmolested. It climbed the stairs so long and so often that day that murder resulted. It is nothing unusual on Cherry Street, nothing to "make a fuss" about. Not a week before, two or three blocks up the street, the police felt called upon to interfere in one of these can rackets at two o'clock in the morning, to secure peace for the neighborhood. The interference took the form of a general fusillade, during which one of the disturbers fell off the roof and was killed. There was the usual wake and nothing more was heard of it. What, indeed, was there to say?

The "Rock of Ages" is the name over the door of a low saloon that blocks the entrance to another alley, if possible more forlorn and dreary than the rest, as we pass out of the Alderman's court. It sounds like a jeer from the days, happily past, when the "wickedest man in New York" lived around the corner a little way and boasted of his title. One cannot take many steps in Cherry Street without encountering some relic of past or present prominence in the ways of crime, scarce one that does not turn up specimen bricks of the coming thief. The Cherry Street tough is all-pervading. Ask Superintendent Murray, who, as captain of the Oak Street squad, in seven months secured convictions for theft, robbery, and murder aggregating no less than five hundred and thirty years of penal servitude, and he will tell you his opinion that the Fourth Ward, even in the last twenty years, has turned out more criminals than all the rest of the city together.

But though the "Swamp Angels" have gone to their reward, their successors carry on business at the old stand as successfully, if not as boldly. There goes one who was once a shining light in thiefdom. He has reformed since, they say. The policeman on the corner, who is addicted to a professional unbelief in reform of any kind, will tell you that while on the Island once he sailed away on a shutter, paddling along until he was picked up in Hell Gate by a schooner's crew, whom he persuaded that he was a fanatic performing some sort of religious penance by his singular expedition. Over yonder, Tweed, the arch-thief, worked in a brush-shop and earned an honest living before he took to politics. As we stroll from one narrow street to another the odd contrast between the low, old-looking houses in front and the towering tenements in the back yards grows even more striking, perhaps because we expect and are looking for it. Nobody who was not would suspect the presence of the rear houses, though they have been there long enough. Here is one seven stories high behind one with only three floors. Take a look into this Roosevelt Street alley; just about one step wide, with a five-story house on one side that gets its light and air—God help us for pitiful mockery!—from this slit between brick walls. There are no windows in the wall on the other side; it is perfectly blank. The fire-escapes of the long tenement fairly touch it; but the rays of the sun, rising, setting, or at high noon, never do. It never shone into the alley from the day the devil planned and man built it. There was once an English doctor who experimented with the sunlight in the soldiers' barracks, and found that on the side that was shut off altogether from the sun the mortality was one hundred per cent. greater than on the light side, where its rays had free access. But then soldiers are of some account, have a fixed value, if not a very high one. The people who live here have not. The horse that pulls the dirt-cart one of these laborers loads and unloads is of ever so much more account to the employer of his labor than he and all that belongs to him. Ask the owner; he will not attempt to deny it, if the horse is worth anything. The man too knows it. It is the one thought that occasionally troubles the owner of the horse in the enjoyment of his prosperity, built of and upon the successful assertion of the truth that all men are created equal.

With what a shock did the story of yonder Madison Street alley come home to New Yorkers one morning, eight or ten years ago, when a fire that broke out after the men had gone to their work swept up those narrow stairs and burned up women and children to the number of a full half score. There were fire-escapes, yes! but so placed that they could not be reached. The firemen had to look twice

before they could find the opening that passes for a thoroughfare; a
stout man would never venture in. Some wonderfully heroic rescues
were made at that fire by people living in the adjoining tenements.
Danger and trouble—of the imminent kind, not the everyday sort
that excites neither interest nor commiseration—run even this common clay into heroic moulds on occasion; occasions that help us to
remember that the gap that separates the man with the patched coat
from his wealthy neighbor is, after all, perhaps but a tenement. Yet,
what a gap! and of whose making? Here, as we stroll along Madison
Street, workmen are busy putting the finishing touches to the
brown-stone front of a tall new tenement. This one will probably be
called an apartment house. They are carving satyrs' heads in the
stone, with a crowd of gaping youngsters looking on in admiring
wonder. Next door are two other tenements, likewise with brown-
stone fronts, fair to look at. The youngest of the children in the
group is not too young to remember how their army of tenants was
turned out by the health officers because the houses had been condemned as unfit for human beings to live in. The owner was a
wealthy builder who "stood high in the community." Is it only in our
fancy that the sardonic leer on the stone faces seems to list that way?
Or is it an introspective grin? We will not ask if the new house belongs to the same builder. He too may have reformed.

We have crossed the boundary of the Seventh Ward. Penitentiary
Row, suggestive name for a block of Cherry Street tenements, is
behind us. Within recent days it has become peopled wholly with
Hebrews, the overflow from Jewtown adjoining, pedlars and tailors,
all of them. It is odd to read this legend from other days over the
door: "No pedlars allowed in this house." These thrifty people are not
only crowding into the tenements of this once exclusive district—
they are buying them. The Jew runs to real estate as soon as he can
save up enough for a deposit to clinch the bargain. As fast as the old
houses are torn down, towering structures go up in their place, and
Hebrews are found to be the builders. Here is a whole alley nicknamed after the intruder, Jews' Alley. But abuse and ridicule are not
weapons to fight the Israelite with. He pockets them quietly with the
rent and bides his time. He knows from experience, both sweet and

bitter, that all things come to those who wait, including the houses and lands of their persecutors.

Here comes a pleasure party, as gay as any on the avenue, though the carry-all is an ash-cart. The father is the driver and he has taken his brown-legged boy for a ride. How proud and happy they both look up there on their perch! The queer old building they have halted in front of is "The Ship," famous for fifty years as a ramshackle tenement filled with the oddest crowd. No one knows why it is called "The Ship," though there is a tradition that once the river came clear up here to Hamilton Street, and boats were moored along-side it. More likely it is because it is as bewildering inside as a crazy old ship, with its ups and downs of ladders parading as stairs, and its unexpected pitfalls. But Hamilton Street, like Water Street, is not what it was. The missions drove from the latter the worst of its dives. A sailors' mission has lately made its appearance in Hamilton Street, but there are no dives there, nothing worse than the ubiquitous saloon and tough tenements.

Enough of them everywhere. Suppose we look into one? No. — Cherry Street. Be a little careful, please! The hall is dark and you might stumble over the children pitching pennies back there. Not that it would hurt them; kicks and cuffs are their daily diet. They have little else. Here where the hall turns and dives into utter darkness is a step, and another, another. A flight of stairs. You can feel your way, if you cannot see it. Close? Yes! What would you have? All the fresh air that ever enters these stairs comes from the hall-door that is forever slamming, and from the windows of dark bedrooms that in turn receive from the stairs their sole supply of the elements God meant to be free, but man deals out with such niggardly hand. That was a woman filling her pail by the hydrant you just bumped against. The sinks are in the hallway, that all the tenants may have access—and all be poisoned alike by their summer stenches. Hear the pump squeak! It is the lullaby of tenement-house babes. In summer, when a thousand thirsty throats pant for a cooling drink in this block, it is worked in vain. But the saloon, whose open door you passed in the hall, is always there. The smell of it has followed you up. Here is a door. Listen! That short hacking cough, that tiny, helpless wail—what do they mean? They mean that the soiled bow of white you saw on the door downstairs will have another story to tell—Oh! a sadly familiar story—before the day is at an end. The child is dying with measles. With half a chance it might have lived; but it had none. That dark bedroom killed it.

"It was took all of a suddint," says the mother, smoothing the throbbing little body with trembling hands. There is no unkindness in the rough voice of the man in the jumper, who sits by the window grimly smoking a clay pipe, with the little life ebbing out in his sight, bitter as his words sound: "Hush, Mary! If we cannot keep the baby, need we complain—such as we?"

Such as we! What if the words ring in your ears as we grope our way up the stairs and down from floor to floor, listening to the sounds behind the closed doors—some of quarrelling, some of coarse songs, more of profanity. They are true. When the summer heats come with their suffering they have meaning more terrible than words can tell. Come over here. Step carefully over this baby— it is a baby, spite of its rags and dirt—under these iron bridges called fire-escapes, but loaded down, despite the incessant watchfulness of the firemen, with broken household goods, with wash-tubs and bar-rels, over which no man could climb from a fire. This gap between dingy brick-walls is the yard. That strip of smoke-colored sky up there is the heaven of these people. Do you wonder the name does not attract them to the churches? That baby's parents live in the rear tenement here. She is at least as clean as the steps we are now climb-ing. There are plenty of houses with half a hundred such in. The ten-ement is much like the one in front we just left, only fouler, closer, darker—we will not say more cheerless. The word is a mockery. A hundred thousand people lived in rear tenements in New York last year. Here is a room neater than the rest. The woman, a stout ma-tron with hard lines of care in her face, is at the wash-tub. "I try to keep the childer clean," she says, apologetically, but with a hopeless glance around. The spice of hot soap-suds is added to the air already tainted with the smell of boiling cabbage, of rags and uncleanliness all about. It makes an overpowering compound. It is Thursday, but patched linen is hung upon the pulley-line from the window. There is no Monday cleaning in the tenements. It is wash-day all the week round, for a change of clothing is scarce among the poor. They are poverty's honest badge, these perennial lines of rags hung out to dry, those that are not the washerwoman's professional shingle. The true line to be drawn between pauperism and honest poverty is the clothes-line. With it begins the effort to be clean that is the first and the best evidence of a desire to be honest.

What sort of an answer, think you, would come from these tenements to the question "Is life worth living?" were they heard at all in the discussion? It may be that this, cut from the last report but one of the Association for the Improvement of the Condition of the Poor, a long name for a weary task, has a suggestion of it: "In the depth of winter the attention of the Association was called to a Protestant family living in a garret in a miserable tenement in Cherry Street. The family's condition was most deplorable. The man, his wife, and three small children shivering in one room through the roof of which the pitiless winds of winter whistled. The room was almost barren of furniture; the parents slept on the floor, the elder children in boxes, and the baby was swung in an old shawl attached to the rafters by cords by way of a hammock. The father, a seaman, had been obliged to give up that calling because he was in consumption, and was unable to provide either bread or fire for his little ones."

Perhaps this may be put down as an exceptional case, but one that came to my notice some months ago in a Seventh Ward tenement was typical enough to escape that reproach. There were nine in the family: husband, wife, an aged grandmother, and six children; honest, hard-working Germans, scrupulously neat, but poor. All nine lived in two rooms, one about ten feet square that served as parlor, bedroom, and eating-room, the other a small hall-room made into a kitchen. The rent was seven dollars and a half a month, more than a week's wages for the husband and father, who was the only bread-winner in the family. That day the mother had thrown herself out of the window, and was carried up from the street dead. She was "discouraged," said some of the other women from the tenement, who had come in to look after the children while a messenger carried the news to the father at the shop. They went stolidly about their task, although they were evidently not without feeling for the dead woman. No doubt she was wrong in not taking life philosophically, as did the four families a city missionary found housekeeping in the four corners of one room. They got along well enough together until one of the families took a boarder and made trouble. Philosophy, according to my optimistic friend, naturally inhabits the tenements. The people who live there come to look upon death in a different way from the rest of us—do not take it as hard. He has never found time to explain how the fact fits into his general theory that life is not unbearable in the tenements. Unhappily for the philosophy of the slums, it is too apt to be of the kind that readily recognizes the saloon, always handy, as the refuge from every trouble, and shapes its practice according to the discovery.

*HOW THE OTHER HALF LIVES*, 1890

# STEPHEN CRANE

*Stephen Crane (1871–1900) was a pioneering realist who uncovered the low life of New York, in stories about the destitute ("An Experiment in Misery") or those driven to prostitution (Maggie: A Girl of the Streets). Building on Jacob Riis's investigative reporting about the slums and William Dean Howells' realistic fiction, Crane achieved a new level of harsh verisimilitude and artistic rigor. In his exemplary journalistic sketches about New York, as well as in his fiction, Crane pares down his prose, stripping it of Victorian moralisms, quaint locutions, and unnecessary adjectives, arriving at the prototype of the modern American sentence.*

## OPIUM'S VARIED DREAMS

OPIUM SMOKING in this country is believed to be more particularly a pastime of the Chinese, but in truth the greater number of the smokers are white men and white women. Chinatown furnishes the pipe, lamp and yen-hock, but let a man once possess a "layout" and a common American drug store furnishes him with the opium, and afterward China is discernible only in the traditions that cling to the habit.

There are 25,000 opium-smokers in the city of New York alone. At one time there were two great colonies, one in the Tenderloin, one of course in Chinatown. This was before the hammer of reform struck them. Now the two colonies are splintered into something less than 25,000 fragments. The smokers are disorganized, but they still exist.

The Tenderloin district of New York fell an early victim to opium. That part of the population which is known as the sporting class adopted the habit quickly. Cheap actors, race track touts, gamblers and the different kinds of confidence men took to it generally. Opium raised its yellow banner over the Tenderloin, attaining the dignity of a common vice.

Splendid "joints" were not uncommon then in New York. There

was one on Forty-second street which would have been palatial if it were not for the bad taste of the decorations. An occasional man from Fifth avenue or Madison avenue would there have his private "layout," an elegant equipment of silver, ivory, gold. The bunks which lined all sides of the two rooms were nightly crowded and some of the people owned names which are not altogether unknown to the public. This place was raided because of sensational stories in the newspapers and the little wicket no longer opens to allow the anxious "fiend" to enter.

Upon the appearance of reform, opium retired to private flats. Here it now reigns and it will undoubtedly be an extremely long century before the police can root it from these little strongholds. Once, Billie Rostetter got drunk on whisky and emptied three scuttles of coal down the dumb-waiter shaft. This made a noise and Billie naturally was arrested. But opium is silent. These smokers do not rave. They lay and dream, or talk in low tones. The opium vice does not betray itself by heaving coal down dumb-waiter shafts.

People who declare themselves able to pick out opium-smokers on the street are usually deluded. An opium-smoker may look like a deacon or a deacon may look like an opium-smoker. One case is as probable as the other. The "fiends" can easily conceal their vice. They get up from the "layout," adjust their cravats, straighten their coat-tails and march off like ordinary people, and the best kind of an expert would not be willing to bet that they were or were not addicted to the habit.

It would be very hard to say just exactly what constitutes a "habit." With the fiends it is an elastic word. Ask a smoker if he has a habit and he will deny it. Ask him if some one who smokes the same amount has a habit and he will gracefully admit it. Perhaps the ordinary smoker consumes 25 cents worth of opium each day. There are others who smoke $1 worth. This is rather extraordinary and in this case at least it is safe to say that it is a "habit." The $1 smokers usually indulge in "high hats," which is the term for a large pill. The ordinary smoker is satisfied with "pin-heads." "Pin-heads" are about the size of a French pea.

"Habit-smokers" have a contempt for the "sensation-smoker." This

latter is a person who has been won by the false glamour which surrounds the vice and who goes about really pretending that he has a
ravenous hunger for the pipe. There are more "sensation-smokers"
than one would imagine.

It is said to take one year of devotion to the pipe before one can
contract a habit. As far as the writer's observation goes, he should
say that it does not take any such long time. Sometimes an individual who has only smoked a few months will speak of nothing but
pipe and when they "talk pipe" persistently it is a pretty sure sign that
the drug has fastened its grip upon them so that at any rate they are
not able to easily stop its use.

When a man arises from his first trial of the pipe, the nausea that
clutches him is something that can give cards and spades and big
casino to seasickness. If he had swallowed a live chimney-sweep he
could not feel more like dying. The room and everything in it whirls
like the inside of an electric light plant. There appears a thirst, a
great thirst, and this thirst is so sinister and so misleading that if the
novice drank spirits to satisfy it he would presently be much worse.
The one thing that will make him feel again that life may be a joy is
a cup of strong black coffee.

If there is a sentiment in the pipe for him he returns to it after
this first unpleasant trial. Gradually, the power of the drug sinks into
his heart. It absorbs his thought. He begins to lie with more and
more grace to cover the shortcomings and little failures of his life.
And then finally he may become a full-fledged "pipe fiend," a man
with a "yen-yen."

A "yen-yen," be it known, is the hunger, the craving. It comes to
a "fiend" when he separates himself from his pipe and takes him by
the heart strings. If indeed he will not buck through a brick wall to
get to the pipe, he at least will become the most disagreeable, sour-
tempered person on earth until he finds a way to satisfy his craving.

When the victim arrives at the point where his soul calls for the
drug, he usually learns to cook. The operation of rolling the pill and
cooking it over the little lamp is a delicate task and it takes time to
learn it. When a man can cook for himself and buys his own "layout,"
he is gone, probably. He has placed upon his shoulders an elephant

which he may carry to the edge of forever. The Chinese have a preparation which they call a cure, but the first difficulty is to get the hop-
fiend to take the preparation, and the second difficulty is to cure
anything with this cure.

A "hop-fiend" will defend opium with eloquence and energy. He
very seldom drinks spirits and so he gains an opportunity to make
the most ferocious parallels between the effects of rum and the effects of opium. Ask him to free his mind and he will probably say:
"Opium does not deprive you of your senses. It does not make a
madman of you. But drink does! See? Who ever heard of a man committing murder when full of hop? Get him full of whisky and he
might kill his father. I don't see why people kick so about opium
smoking. If they knew anything about it they wouldn't talk that way.
Let anybody drink rum who cares to, but as for me I would rather
be what I am."

As before mentioned, there were at one time gorgeous opium
dens in New York, but at the present time there is probably not one
with any pretense to splendid decoration. The Chinamen will smoke
in a cellar, bare, squalid, occupied by an odor that will float wooden
chips. The police took the adornments from the vice and left nothing but the pipe itself. Yet the pipe is sufficient for its slant-eyed
lover.

When prepared for smoking purposes, opium is a heavy liquid
much like molasses. Ordinarily it is sold in hollow li-shi nuts or in
little round tins resembling the old percussion cap-boxes. The pipe is
a curious affair, particularly notable for the way in which it does not
resemble the drawings of it that appear in print. The stem is of thick
bamboo, the mouthpiece usually of ivory. The bowl crops out suddenly about four inches from the end of the stem. It is a heavy affair
of clay or stone. The cavity is a mere hole, of the diameter of a lead
pencil, drilled through the centre. The "yen-hock" is a sort of sharpened darning-needle. With it the cook takes the opium from the
box. He twirls it dexterously with his thumb and forefinger until
enough of the gummy substance adheres to the sharp point. Then he
holds it over the tiny flame of the lamp which burns only peanut oil
or sweet oil. The pill now exactly resembles boiling molasses. The

clever fingers of the cook twirl it above the flame. Lying on his side comfortably, he takes the pipe in his left hand and transfers the cooked pill from the yen-hock to the bowl of the pipe where he again molds it with the yen-hock until it is a little button-like thing with a hole in the centre fitting squarely over the hole in the bowl. Dropping the yen-hock, the cook now uses two hands for the pipe. He extends the mouthpiece toward the one whose turn it is to smoke and as this latter leans forward in readiness, the cook draws the bowl toward the flame until the heat sets the pill to boiling. Whereupon, the smoker takes a long, deep draw at the pipe, the pill splutters and fries and a moment later the smoker sinks back tranquilly. An odor, heavy, aromatic, agreeable and yet disagreeable, hangs in the air and makes its way with peculiar powers of penetration. The group about the layout talk in low voices and watch the cook deftly molding another pill. The little flame casts a strong yellow light on their faces as they cuddle about the layout. As the pipe passes and passes around the circle, the voices drop to a mere indolent cooing, and the eyes that so lazily watch the cook at his work glisten and glisten from the influence of the drug until they resemble flashing bits of silver.

There is a similarity in coloring and composition in a group of men about a midnight camp-fire in a forest and a group of smokers about the layout tray with its tiny light. Everything, of course, is on a smaller scale with the smoking. The flame is only an inch and a half perhaps in height and the smokers huddle closely in order that every person may smoke undisturbed. But there is something in the abandon of the poses, the wealth of light on the faces and the strong mystery of shadow at the backs of the people that bring the two scenes into some kind of artistic brotherhood. And just as the lazy eyes about a camp-fire fasten themselves dreamfully upon the blaze of logs so do the lazy eyes about an opium layout fasten themselves upon the little yellow flame.

There is but one pipe, one lamp and one cook to each smoking layout. Pictures of nine or ten persons sitting in arm-chairs and smoking various kinds of curiously carved tobacco pipes probably serve well enough, but when they are named "Interior of an Opium

Den" and that sort of thing, it is absurd. Opium could not be smoked like tobacco. A pill is good for one long draw. After that the cook molds another. A smoker would just as soon choose a gallows as an arm-chair for smoking purposes. He likes to curl down on a mattress placed on the floor in the quietest corner of a Tenderloin flat, and smoke there with no light but the tiny yellow spear from the layout lamp.

It is a curious fact that it is rather the custom to purchase for a layout tray one of those innocent black tin affairs which are supposed to be placed before baby as he takes his high chair for dinner.

If a beginner expects to have dreams of an earth dotted with white porcelain towers and a sky of green silk, he will, from all accounts, be much mistaken. "The Opium Smoker's Dream" seems to be mostly a mistake. The influence of "dope" is evidently a fine languor, a complete mental rest. The problems of life no longer appear. Existence is peace. The virtues of a man's friends, for instance, loom beautifully against his own sudden perfection. The universe is readjusted. Wrong departs, injustice vanishes; there is nothing but a quiet, a soothing harmony of all things—until the next morning.

And who should invade this momentary land of rest, this dream country, if not the people of the Tenderloin, they who are at once supersensitive and hopeless, the people who think more upon death and the mysteries of life, the chances of the hereafter, than any other class, educated or uneducated. Opium holds out to them its lie, and they embrace it eagerly, expecting to find a definition of peace, but they awake to find the formidable labors of life grown more formidable. And if the pipe should happen to ruin their lives they cling the more closely to it because then it stands between them and thought.

*N E W   Y O R K   S U N ,   1 8 9 6*

## A D V E N T U R E S   O F   A   N O V E L I S T

T HIS IS a plain tale of two chorus girls, a woman of the streets and a reluctant laggard witness. The tale properly begins in a resort on Broadway, where the two chorus girls and the reluctant witness sat the entire evening. They were on the verge of departing their several ways when a young woman approached one of the chorus girls, with outstretched hand.

"Why, how do you do?" she said. "I haven't seen you for a long time."

The chorus girl recognized some acquaintance of the past, and the young woman then took a seat and joined the party. Finally they left the table in this resort, and the quartet walked down Broadway together. At the corner of Thirty-first street one of the chorus girls said that she wished to take a car immediately for home, and so the reluctant witness left one of the chorus girls and the young woman on the corner of Thirty-first street while he placed the other chorus girl aboard an uptown cable car. The two girls who waited on the corner were deep in conversation.

The reluctant witness was returning leisurely to them. In the semi-conscious manner in which people note details which do not appear at the time important, he saw two men passing along Broadway. They passed swiftly, like men who are going home. They paid attention to none, and none at the corner of Thirty-first street and Broadway paid attention to them.

The two girls were still deep in conversation. They were standing at the curb facing the street. The two men passed unseen—in all human probability—by the two girls. The reluctant witness continued his leisurely way. He was within four feet of these two girls when suddenly and silently a man appeared from nowhere in particular and grabbed them both.

The astonishment of the reluctant witness was so great for the ensuing seconds that he was hardly aware of what transpired during that time, save that both girls screamed. Then he heard this man, who was now evidently an officer, say to them: "Come to the station house. You are under arrest for soliciting two men."

With one voice the unknown woman, the chorus girl and the reluctant witness cried out: "What two men?"

The officer said: "Those two men who have just passed."

And here began the wildest and most hysterical sobbing of the two girls, accompanied by spasmodic attempts to pull their arms away from the grip of the policeman. The chorus girl seemed nearly insane with fright and fury. Finally she screamed:

"Well, he's my husband." And with her finger she indicated the reluctant witness. The witness at once replied to the swift, questioning glance of the officer, "Yes; I am."

If it was necessary to avow a marriage to save a girl who is not a prostitute from being arrested as a prostitute, it must be done, though the man suffer eternally. And then the officer forgot immediately—without a second's hesitation, he forgot that a moment previously he had arrested this girl for soliciting, and so, dropping her arm, released her.

"But," said he, "I have got this other one." He was as picturesque as a wolf.

"Why arrest her, either?" said the reluctant witness.

"For soliciting those two men."

"But she didn't solicit those two men."

"Say," said the officer, turning, "do you know this woman?"

The chorus girl had it in mind to lie then for the purpose of saving this woman easily and simply from the palpable wrong she seemed to be about to experience. "Yes; I know her"—"I have seen her two or three times"—"Yes; I have met her before——" But the reluctant witness said at once that he knew nothing whatever of the girl.

"Well," said the officer, "she's a common prostitute."

There was a short silence then, but the reluctant witness presently said: "Are you arresting her as a common prostitute? She has been perfectly respectable since she has been with us. She hasn't done anything wrong since she has been in our company."

"I am arresting her for soliciting those two men," answered the officer, "and if you people don't want to get pinched, too, you had better not be seen with her."

Then began a parade to the station house—the officer and his prisoner ahead and two simpletons following.

At the station house the officer said to the sergeant behind the desk that he had seen the woman come from the resort on Broadway alone, and on the way to the corner of Thirty-first street solicit two men, and that immediately afterward she had met a man and a woman—meaning the chorus girl and the reluctant witness—on the said corner, and was in conversation with them when he arrested her. He did not mention to the sergeant at this time the arrest and release of the chorus girl.

At the conclusion of the officer's story the sergeant said, shortly: "Take her back." This did not mean to take the woman back to the corner of Thirty-first street and Broadway. It meant to take her back to the cells, and she was accordingly led away.

The chorus girl had undoubtedly intended to be an intrepid champion; she had avowedly come to the station house for that purpose, but her entire time had been devoted to sobbing in the wildest form of hysteria. The reluctant witness was obliged to devote his entire time to an attempt to keep her from making an uproar of some kind. This paroxysm of terror, of indignation, and the extreme mental anguish caused by her unconventional and strange situation, was so violent that the reluctant witness could not take time from her to give any testimony to the sergeant.

After the woman was sent to the cell the reluctant witness reflected a moment in silence; then he said:

"Well, we might as well go."

On the way out of Thirtieth street the chorus girl continued to sob. "If you don't go to court and speak for that girl you are no man!" she cried. The arrested woman had, by the way, screamed out a request to appear in her behalf before the Magistrate.

"By George! I cannot," said the reluctant witness. "I can't afford to do that sort of thing. I—I——"

After he had left this girl safely, he continued to reflect: "Now this arrest I firmly believe to be wrong. This girl may be a courtesan, for anything that I know at all to the contrary. The sergeant at the station house seemed to know her as well as he knew the Madison square tower. She is then, in all probability, a courtesan. She is arrested, however, for soliciting those two men. If I have ever had a conviction in my life, I am convinced that she did not solicit those two men. Now, if these affairs occur from time to time, they must be witnessed occasionally by men of character. Do these reputable citizens interfere? No, they go home and thank God that they can still attend piously to their own affairs. Suppose I were a clerk and I interfered in this sort of a case. When it became known to my employers they would say to me: 'We are sorry, but we cannot have men in our employ who stay out until 2:30 in the morning in the company of chorus girls.'

"Suppose, for instance, I had a wife and seven children in Harlem. As soon as my wife read the papers she would say: 'Ha! You told me you had a business engagement! Half-past two in the morning with questionable company!'

"Suppose, for instance, I were engaged to the beautiful Countess of Kalamazoo. If she were to hear it, she would write: 'All is over between us. My future husband cannot rescue prostitutes at 2:30 in the morning.'

"These, then, must be three small general illustrations of why men of character say nothing if they happen to witness some possible affair of this sort, and perhaps these illustrations could be multiplied to infinity. I possess nothing so tangible as a clerkship, as a wife and seven children in Harlem, as an engagement to the beautiful Countess of Kalamazoo; but all that I value may be chanced in this affair. Shall I take this risk for the benefit of a girl of the streets?

"But this girl, be she prostitute or whatever, was at this time manifestly in my escort, and—Heaven save the blasphemous philosophy—a wrong done to a prostitute must be as purely a wrong as a wrong done to a queen," said the reluctant witness—this blockhead.

"Moreover, I believe that this officer has dishonored his obligation as a public servant. Have I a duty as a citizen, or do citizens have duty, as a citizen, or do citizens have no duties? Is it a mere myth that there was at one time a man who possessed a consciousness of civic responsibility, or has it become a distinction of our municipal civilization that men of this character shall be licensed to deprecate in such a manner upon those who are completely at their mercy?"

He returned to the sergeant at the police station, and, after asking if he could send anything to the girl to make her more comfortable for the night, he told the sergeant the story of the arrest, as he knew it.

"Well," said the sergeant, "that may be all true. I don't defend the officer. I do not say that he was right, or that he was wrong, but it seems to me that I have seen you somewhere before and know you vaguely as a man of good repute; so why interfere in this thing? As for this girl, I know her to be a common prostitute. That's why I sent her back."

"But she was not arrested as a common prostitute. She was arrested for soliciting two men, and I know that she didn't solicit the two men."

"Well," said the sergeant, "that, too, may all be true, but I give you the plain advice of a man who has been behind this desk for years, and knows how these things go, and I advise you simply to stay home. If you monkey with this case, you are pretty sure to come out with mud all over you."

"I suppose so," said the reluctant witness. "I haven't a doubt of it. But I don't see how I can, in honesty, stay away from court in the morning."

"Well, do it anyhow," said the sergeant.

"But I don't see how I can do it."

The sergeant was bored. "Oh, I tell you, the girl is nothing but a common prostitute," he said, wearily.

The reluctant witness on reaching his room set the alarm clock for the proper hour.

In the court at 8:30 he met a reporter acquaintance. "Go home," said the reporter, when he had heard the story. "Go home; your own participation in the affair doesn't look very respectable. Go home."

"But it is a wrong," said the reluctant witness.

"Oh, it is only a temporary wrong," said the reporter. The definition of a temporary wrong did not appear at that time to the reluctant witness, but the reporter was too much in earnest to consider terms. "Go home," said he.

Thus—if the girl was wronged—it is to be seen that all circumstances, all forces, all opinions, all men were combined to militate against her. Apparently the united wisdom of the world declared that no man should do anything but throw his sense of justice to the winds in an affair of this description. "Let a man have a conscience for the daytime," said wisdom. "Let him have a conscience for the daytime, but it is idiocy for a man to have a conscience at 2:30 in the morning, in the case of an arrested prostitute."

The officer who had made the arrest told a story of the occurrence. The girl at the bar told a story of the occurrence. And the girl's story as to this affair was, to the reluctant witness, perfectly true. Nevertheless, her word could not be accounted of any value. It was impossible that any one in the courtroom could suppose that she was telling the truth, save the reluctant witness and the reporter to whom he had told the tale.

The reluctant witness recited what he believed to be a true accounting, and the Magistrate discharged the prisoner.

The reluctant witness has told this story merely because it is a story which the public of New York should know for once.

*N E W   Y O R K   J O U R N A L* , 1896

# ABRAHAM CAHAN

*Abraham Cahan (1860–1951) was at the intellectual center of the large Jewish immigrant community that took shape in New York City at the turn of the century. Born in Russia, he came to New York in 1882 and supported himself as a laborer, union organizer, teacher of English, author, and editor. He co-founded the* Jewish Daily Forward, *a successful Yiddish socialist newspaper, and, at William Dean Howells' urging, wrote fiction. In his novels (especially* The Rise of David Levinsky, *his masterpiece) and his journalism, he offered pioneering accounts of the painful adjustments by which "greenhorns" became Americanized, sometimes losing touch with their roots and their moral compass.*

## DROWNED THEIR SINS

Two of Roosevelt's Rough Riders, accompanied by an admiring civilian, were crossing the Brooklyn Bridge yesterday afternoon when their attention and progress were suddenly arrested by the sight of a knot of old women nodding and murmuring over the rail. Some of them wore heavy wigs on their heads, others had their hair carefully concealed under white silk kerchiefs, but they were all bent upon open books over which they were swaying to and fro as they whispered and sighed to the gleaming water below.

"What in —— is that?" asked the Rough Riders in duet. The question was addressed to the civilian, who was apparently their guide about town, but instead of an answer he stood gaping at the old women himself.

"You've got me this time," he muttered, as his eyes ran from one woman to the other. "Look, there are others and over there some more. They are Jew women, that's all I can tell you."

A bridge policeman who had been watching the movements of the cavalrymen with lazy interest noticed their perplexity and with an affected yawn dropped the explanation that it was "the Jewish New Year and them Jew women come to chuck their sins into the river."

The Rough Riders did not quite understand what he meant, and they stood gazing at the growing crowd of worshippers and expressing their astonishment in their own way, when they saw some of the women shake their skirts over the water.

"See that?" said the policeman. "That's the way they shake their sins off into the river."

"Gee!" exclaimed the Rough Riders.

The women went on shaking their skirts, murmuring and swaying more fervently than ever. Their number grew. Men, old and young, with shaggy beards and without, came along, and opening their books, joined the women, who, however, remained an overwhelming majority.

By 5 o'clock the bridge was swarming with these people. In one place a cluster of women were sighing and sobbing or nodding their heads dolefully, while they were repeating the words of prayer recited from a book by one of their number.

"They cannot read it themselves," an intelligent Jew explained, "and the one who can is their *sogerke* [reader]. The original prayer they are saying now is in Hebrew, of which they don't understand a word, but the *sogerke* reads a Yiddish translation. Still they will shed tears, even when they don't understand what they say. Tears are simply in the air in a 'Day of Awe' like this. It is the day of judgment, when one's account with God is settled and when one's fate for the coming year is determined."

"Today Thou sittest upon Thy throne of judgment," reads a passage of the prayer over which the good pious women were sighing and weeping, "to judge the whole world, the great and the lowly, the rich and the poor—to award them happiness or misery, life or death—each according to his or her deeds and deserts. We know that we are filled with wickedness. We have not fulfilled what Thou didst write in Thy holy laws. We have sinned against Thee and against one another. Therefore we are awed on this day of judgment, and we tremble for fear lest Thou judgest us according to our evil deeds. Therefore do we come to the edge of the water to shed tears like water and to pray for Thy mercy which flows in its abundance like this river. We pray Thee, Lord of the Universe, to erase all our sins from Thy book. Heartbroken we pray Thee to grant us a year of health, peace, and happiness; not to take away a father or a mother from their children, nor a child from its parents. Hear our sighs today and let there be no sighs and no tears during the new year. We know we have sinned but now our hearts are pure even as this water is pure. Help us, O God, that we may serve Thee, guard us against hunger and distress, against illness and grief. Amen."

Another part of the rail was occupied by a crowd of men and women, who recited their prayer aloud and shook their skirts more violently than the others. Conspicuous among these was an elderly man in a high hat and short sack coat. He was neatly dressed, his beard was well kept and he wore no sidelocks. He looked more prosperous and intelligent than the others, yet he read from his prayerbook louder and gesticulated more vehemently than the rest. Gentiles passing by stopped to look at him and to pry into his book, but he heeded nobody and nothing, and went on singing and jerking himself as fervently as ever.

"What is that you want?" he suddenly faced about to say to a bystander angrily. "I have finished, and now I can satisfy your curiosity. No, I am not angry at all. I am glad to explain it to you. Well, we call it *tashlich*, which means 'casting'——the casting of the sins upon the waters, as it stands in Micah, verse 19, Chapter VII, 'He will again have mercy on us; he will suppress our iniquities; yea, thou wilt cast all their sins into the sea.'

"Now, I don't want you to run away with the idea that we are fools enough to think that you can get rid of your sins by shaking them off your coat or skirt, as if they were a lot of fleas clinging to you. It's only some of these foolish old women who take the verse in its literal sense and come here to shake themselves clear of all sins. The Jew who understands his holy books takes it as a beautiful figure of speech," he went on, the vigorous, angry look on his face somewhat relaxing as he spoke. "Yet it is an old custom and a pretty custom, and why should I not pray here over the waters, rather than in my suffocating rooms in the tenement house?" he shouted again, taking on a wrathful look. "Here is God's flowing river, His pure, flowing, peaceful water. Here I feel nearer to Him, and my prayer seems more ardent to me. That's why I come to the river. But all talk about throwing your sins to the fish is stuff and nonsense. You don't see many men here, do you? It's all women, silly creatures who take everything literally."

The docks were also crowded with people going to *tashlich*, and the lakes at Central Park, especially near the 110th Street end, in which neighborhood the new uptown ghetto lies, were surrounded with Jewish men, women and children nodding and murmuring over their prayerbooks as did the people on the bridge. But the true women of piety preferred to walk many blocks to throw their sins into the river.

"You want flowing water, my son," said a little woman of seventy. "The stagnant water of a pond or a lake is not fresh enough, nor pure, nor does it move like a living creature. It's only in a country of sinners like this that people will put up with a lake for *tashlich*," she concluded with a sigh.

At the Pike Street dock the worshippers had a good deal of trouble with some "Gentile rowdies," as they characterized them, who pelted the devout old women with stones. One Christian boy stole up to an old Jewess as she stood weeping over the waters as if her heart would break and tore off her wig. The commotion which ensued bade fair to develop into a riot, for the older Christians present, including some laborers or watchmen of the dock, relished the practical jokes of the boys and encouraged them. The police were rather slow in making their appearance, and so at one time stones and other missiles flew thick and fast. The news spread through the Jewish district like wildfire, and the devout people, armed with their prayerbooks, carried their sins to other docks. Some of these people seemed to take it all as a matter of course, as if it was the most natural thing in the world that "Irish *shegotzim*" (Gentile boys) should molest Jews with prayerbooks on the street.

"Still throwing stones?" asked one man of another on Pike Street, with the air of one who asks whether the rain is still falling.

Police Headquarters was notified, and the disturbance was soon stopped by the appearance of several bluecoats. Then the crowd at the Pike Street dock began to grow rapidly. Toward the evening it was literally thronged with *tashlich* worshippers.

When dusk was gathering on the dock it was so crowded that many belated had to go back. Presently strains of song and music rang out near the praying multitude. It was Gentile music, and as it was first heard many of the worshippers turned about with a pained air. It was a detachment of Salvation Army workers. A knot of sailors and dock hands surrounded them. The Jews after a little resumed their prayer. The hum and buzz of *tashlich* mingled with the song and prayer of the Gentiles, the caps of the latter gleaming red amid a sea of white kerchiefs and wigs.

*NEW YORK COMMERCIAL ADVERTISER*, 1898

## SUMMER COMPLAINT: THE ANNUAL STRIKE

THE SHIRTWAIST MAKERS' STRIKE has accentuated the disappearance of the annual tailor strike. It was during the months of July and August that the cloakmakers, cutters or tailors, etc., used to break out, like a sort of summer complaint. It came every year, regular as the heat, unavoidable as malaria in swampy districts, and specialists came from as far away as Europe to study it. The phenomenon has disappeared. There was something like a children's jacket strike last year. The pantsmakers and the knee-pants makers had a fight with their sweaters some few weeks after. But these were all small, one-horse affairs. The big annual tailor strike, *the* strike of the East Side, where hundreds of sweatshops were deserted, the streets of the ghetto were swarming with gesticulating, chattering, groaning men and women, and the newspapers were full of pictures of long-bearded patriarchs, has been gone now three years.

Where has it gone? What has become of the great annual tailor strike? The question has been asked by the curious, superficial observer, and it has been asked by the student of economics, but when it was put to the East Side labor leaders most of them only smiled and shrugged their shoulders, as if it were an idle query not worth racking one's brains over. Still, there are East Side labor leaders and East Side labor leaders. Some of them are said to have gone into the movement as philosophers, students of sociology, observers of human nature, workers for the cause of humanity, and what-not, and several of these took the question rather seriously. They had thought of it before, they said, and discussed it in Yiddish editorials and from the ghetto platform.

These labor philosophers did not quite agree as to some particular phases of the question, but they all seemed to endorse the opinion uttered by one of them, George Pine, that the contract system in the tailoring industries makes the old-time strikes futile, and that the experience of former victories has taught the tailors to attach no weight to such triumphs. They all failed in the long run.

A better mode of warfare has evolved from all these successes which have proven worse than failures, and organizations are in process of formation whose object will be to "open an era of rational and fruitful conflicts" between capital and labor. The seeming disappearance of the annual tailor strike is only the calm which precedes the storm, said one of the philosophers. A big fight is near at hand, and its great aim will be the abolition of the "un-American" sweating system.

Getting down to the gist of the subject, Mr. Pine pointed out that in all former strikes the "hands" did not come in direct contact with the clothing firms, their real employers, but dealt with the contractors or sweaters, a poor, irresponsible lot, who were willing to sign any contract and yield to any demand of the union simply because they knew their contracts were not worth the paper they were written on.

"During the busy season these 'cockroach capitalists,' as we call them, would give in to all our demands and sign any scale of wages we submitted. And we, inexperienced fools that we were, would celebrate our victory and go back to work with a flourish of trumpets. The busy season over, the sweaters would discharge all the good union men, leaving only such hands as were willing to work for less than the price which was paid before the strike broke out. This usually had a demoralizing effect on the organization, for there are always plenty of weaklings who, when jobs are scarce, will work for $4 a week rather than stick to the union and uphold the scale of wages.

"Thus a year would pass. By July or August, when the busy season set in in the many branches of our industry, these weaklings would recover part of their dignity and ask for more wages. This would bring them back to our fold (the union), the general demand for better pay would infuse fresh life into our unions and find expression in a general big conflict between sweaters and their employees. The new strike met with the same sort of success as its predecessors; that is to say, we had an easy victory, but we soon found that we had conquered a lot of dead flies.

"Thus it was that what you call 'the annual tailor strike' used to make its appearance. It came and went regularly every summer, year in and year out. The first big strike of this kind broke out in 1883. Fifteen years elapsed. Fifteen 'great victories' had been recorded in the history of the East Side labor movement. The people began to ask themselves what they had to show for their trouble. Hours were as long as ever. Filth, misery of every kind—especially of that kind which is peculiar to the sweating system and is absolutely unknown to the American citizen outside the ghetto—every curse that goes hand in hand with the blessings of modern civilization reigned supreme in the pestiferous tenement houses of the tailoring district. We have opened our eyes. We have lost faith in victories over impecunious, irresponsible sweaters. Our next big fight will be directed against the clothing magnates of the Broadway warehouses. Let them sign the contracts, if they want their work done. And by and by the middleman must go altogether. Why can't we work in large, well-ventilated factories instead of in tenement house pestholes? Do away with the sweating system and all the filth of the East Side, physical and moral, will disappear, like the perennial strike."

*N E W   Y O R K   C O M M E R C I A L   A D V E R T I S E R* , 1 9 0 0

# THEODORE DREISER

---

*When Indiana-born Theodore Dreiser (1871–1945) arrived in New York in 1894, he found "the city of my dreams" and explored it avidly, fascinated by its sharp contrasts. In his first masterpiece,* Sister Carrie *(1900), and his later Frank Cowperwood trilogy, he portrayed New York as a Social Darwinist winnowing machine, elevating some to the top while pushing others under. Dreiser's remarkable sketches of New York at the turn of the century, collected in* The Color of a Great City *(1923), deserve to be much more widely known.*

## WHENCE THE SONG

ALONG BROADWAY in the height of the theatrical season, but more particularly in that laggard time from June to September, when the great city is given over to those who may not travel, and to actors seeking engagements, there is ever to be seen a certain representative figure, now one individual and now another, of a world so singular that it might well engage the pen of a Balzac or that of a Cervantes. I have in mind an individual whose high hat and smooth Prince Albert coat are still a delicious presence. In his coat lapel is a ruddy boutonnière, in his hand a novel walking-stick. His vest is of a gorgeous and affluent pattern, his shoes shiny-new and topped with pearl-gray spats. With dignity he carries his body and his chin. He is the cynosure of many eyes, the envy of all men, and he knows it. He is the successful author of the latest popular song.

Along Broadway, from Union to Greeley Squares, any fair day during the period of his artistic elevation, he is to be seen. Past the rich shops and splendid theaters he betakes himself with leisurely grace. In Thirtieth Street he may turn for a few moments, but it is only to say good-morning to his publishers. In Twenty-eighth Street, where range the host of those who rival his successful house, he stops to talk with lounging actors and ballad singers. Well-known variety stars nod to him familiarly. Women whose sole claim to distinction lies in their knack of singing a song, smile in greeting as he passes. Occasionally there comes a figure of a needy ballad-monger, trudging from publisher to publisher with an unavailable manuscript, who turns upon him, in passing, the glint of an envious glance. To these he is an important figure, satisfied as much with their envy as with their praise, for is not this also his due, the reward of all who have triumphed?

I have in mind another figure, equally singular: a rouged and powdered little maiden, rich in feathers and ornaments of the latest vogue; gloved in blue and shod in yellow; pretty, self-assured, daring, and even bold. There has gone here all the traditional maidenly reserve you would expect to find in one so young and pleasing, and yet she is not evil. The daughter of a Chicago butcher, you knew her when she first came to the city—a shabby, wondering little thing, clerk to a music publisher transferring his business east, and all eyes for the marvels of city life.

Gradually the scenes and superlatives of elegance, those showy men and women coming daily to secure or sell songs, have aroused her longings and ambitions. Why may not she sing, why not she be a theatrical celebrity? She will. The world shall not keep her down. That elusive and almost imaginary company known as *they*, whose hands are ever against the young, shall not hold her back.

Behold, for a time, then, she has gone; and now, elegant, jingling with silver ornaments, hale and merry from good living, she has returned. To-day she is playing at one of the foremost vaudeville houses. To-morrow she leaves for Pittsburgh. Her one object is still a salary of five hundred or a thousand a week and a three-sheet litho of herself in every window and upon every billboard.

"I'm all right now," she will tell you gleefully. "I'm way ahead of the knockers. They can't keep me down. You ought to have seen the reception I got in Pittsburgh. Say, it was the biggest yet."

Blessed be Pittsburgh, which has honored one who has struggled so hard, and you say so.

"Are you here for long?"

"Only this week. Come up and see my turn. Hey, cabbie!"

A passing cabman turns in close to the walk with considerable alacrity.

"Take me to Keith's. So long. Come up and see my turn to-night."

This is the woman singer, the complement of the male of the same art, the couple who make for the acceptance and spread of the popular song as well as the fame of its author. They sing them in every part of the country, and here in New York, returned from a long season on the road, they form a very important portion of this song-writing, song-singing world. They and the authors and the successful publishers—but we may simplify by yet another picture.

In Twenty-seventh or Twenty-eighth Street, or anywhere along Broadway from Madison to Greeley Squares, are the parlors of a score of publishers, gentlemen who coördinate this divided world for song publishing purposes. There is an office and a reception-room; a music-chamber, where songs are tried, and a stock room. Perhaps, in the case of the larger publishers, the music-rooms are two or three, but the air of each is much the same. Rugs, divans, imitation palms make this publishing house more bower than office. Three or four pianos give to each chamber a parlor-like appearance. The walls are hung with the photos of celebrities, neatly framed, celebrities of the kind described. In the private music-rooms, rocking-chairs. A boy or two waits to bring *professional copies* at a word. A salaried pianist or two wait to run over pieces which the singer may desire to hear. Arrangers wait to make orchestrations or take down newly schemed out melodies which the popular composer himself cannot play. He has evolved the melody by a process of whistling and must have its fleeting beauty registered before it escapes him forever. Hence the salaried arranger.

Into these parlors then, come the mixed company of this distinctive world: authors who have or have not succeeded, variety artists who have some word from touring fellows or know the firm, masters of small bands throughout the city or the country, of which the name is legion, orchestra-leaders of Bowery theaters and uptown variety halls, and singers.

"You haven't got a song that will do for a tenor, have you?"

The inquirer is a little, stout, ruddy-faced Irish boy from the gas-house district. His common clothes are not out of the ordinary here, but they mark him as possibly a non-professional seeking free copies.

"Sure, let me see. For what do you want it?"

"Well, I'm from the Arcadia Pleasure Club. We're going to give a little entertainment next Wednesday and we want some songs."

"I think I've got just the thing you want. Wait till I call the boy. Harry! Bring me some professional copies of ballads."

The youth is probably a representative of one of the many Tammany pleasure organizations, the members of which are known for their propensity to gather about east and west side corners at night and sing. One or two famous songs are known to have secured their start by the airing given them in this fashion on the street corners of the great city.

Upon his heels treads a lady whose ruffled sedateness marks her as one unfamiliar with this half-musical, half-theatrical atmosphere.

"I have a song I would like to have you try over, if you care to."

The attending publisher hesitates before even extending a form of reception.

"What sort of a song is it?"

"Well, I don't exactly know. I guess you'd call it a sentimental ballad. If you'd hear it I think you might——"

"We are so over-stocked with songs now, Madam, that I don't believe there's much use in our hearing it. Could you come in next Friday? We'll have more leisure then and can give you more attention."

The lady looks the failure she has scored, but retreats, leaving the ground clear for the chance arrival of the real author, the individual whose position is attested by one hit or mayhap many. His due is that deference which all publishers, if not the public, feel called upon to render, even if at the time he may have no reigning success.

"Hello, Frank, how are you? What's new?"

The author, cane in hand, may know of nothing in particular.

"Sit down. How are things with you, anyhow?"

"Oh, so-so."

"That new song of yours will be out Friday. We have a rush order on it."

"Is that so?"

"Yes, and I've got good news for you. Windom is going to sing it next year with the minstrels. He was in here the other day and thought it was great."

"Well, that's good."

"That song's going to go, all right. You haven't got any others, have you?"

"No, but I've got a tune. Would you mind having one of the boys take it down for me?"

"Surest thing you know. Here, Harry! Call Hatcher."

Now comes the pianist and arranger, and a hearing and jotting down of the new melody in a private room. The favored author may have piano and pianist for an indefinite period any time. Lunch with the publishers awaits him if he remains until noon. His song, when ready, is heard with attention. The details which make for its publication are rushed. His royalties are paid with that rare smile which accompanies the payment of anything to one who earns money for another. He is to be petted, conciliated, handled with gloves.

At his heels, perhaps, another author, equally successful, maybe, but almost intolerable because of certain marked eccentricities of life and clothing. He is a negro, small, slangy, strong in his cups, but able to write a good song, occasionally a truly pathetic ballad.

"Say, where's that gem o' mine?"

"What?"

"That effusion."

"What are you talking about?"

"That audience-killer—that there thing that's goin' to sweep the country like wildfire—that there song."

Much laughter and apology.

"It will be here Friday, Gussie."

"Thought it was to be here last Monday?"

"So it was, but the printers didn't get it done. You know how those things are, Gussie."

"I know. Gimme twenty-five dollars."

"Sure. But what are you going to do with it?"

"Never you mind. Gimme twenty-five bones. To-morrow's rent day up my way."

Twenty-five is given as if it were all a splendid joke. Gussie is a bad negro, one day radiant in bombastic clothing, the next wretched from dissipation and neglect. He has no royalty coming to him, really. That is, he never accepts royalty. All his songs are sold out-right. But these have earned the house so much that if he were to de-mand royalties the sum to be paid would beggar anything he has ever troubled to ask for.

"I wouldn't take no royalty," he announces at one time, with a bombastic and yet mellow negro emphasis, which is always amusing. "Doan want it. Too much trouble. All I want is money when I needs it and wants it."

Seeing that nearly every song that he writes is successful, this is a most equitable arrangement. He could have several thousand instead of a few hundred, but being shiftless he does not care. Ready money is the thing with him, twenty-five or fifty when he needs it.

And then those "peerless singers of popular ballads," as their pro-grams announce them, men and women whose pictures you will see upon every song-sheet, their physiognomy underscored with their own "Yours Sincerely" in their own handwriting. Every day they are here, arriving and departing, carrying the latest songs to all parts of the land. These are the individuals who in their own estimation "make" the songs the successes they are. In all justice, they have some claim to the distinction. One such, raising his or her voice nightly in a melodic interpretation of a new ballad, may, if the mu-sic be sufficiently catchy, bring it so thoroughly to the public ear as to cause it to begin to sell. These individuals are not unaware of their services in the matter, nor slow to voice their claims. In flocks and droves they come, whenever good fortune brings "the company" to New York or the end of the season causes them to return, to tell of their success and pick new songs for the ensuing season. Also to col-lect certain pre-arranged bonuses. Also to gather news and dispense it. Then, indeed, is the day of the publisher's volubility and grace. These gentlemen and ladies must be attended to with that deference which is the right of the successful. The ladies must be praised and cajoled.

"Did you hear about the hit I made with 'Sweet Kitty Leary' in Kansas City? I knocked 'em cold. Say, it was the biggest thing on the bill."

The publisher may not have heard of it. The song, for all the uproarious success depicted, may not have sold an extra copy, and yet this is not for him to say. Has the lady a good voice? Is she with a good company? He may so ingratiate himself that she will yet sing one of his newer and as yet unheard of compositions into popularity.

"Was it? Well, I'm glad to hear it. You have the voice for that sort of a song, you know, Marie. I've got something new, though, that will just suit you—oh, a dandy. It's by Harry Welch."

For all this flood of geniality the singer may only smile indifferently. Secretly her hand is against all publishers. They are out for themselves. Successful singers must mind their P's and Q's. Payment is the word, some arrangement by which she shall receive a stated sum per week for singing a song. The honeyed phrases are well enough for beginners, but we who have succeeded need something more.

"Let me show you something new. I've got a song here that is fine. Come right into the music-room. Charlie, get a copy of 'She May Have Seen Better Days.' I want you to play it over for Miss Yaeger."

The boy departs and returns. In the exclusive music-room sits the singer, critically listening while the song is played.

"Isn't that a pretty chorus?"

"Well, yes, I rather like that."

"That will suit your voice exactly. Don't ever doubt it. I think that's one of the best songs we have published in years."

"Have you the orchestration?"

"Sure; I'll get you that."

Somehow, however, the effect has not been satisfactory. The singer has not enthused. He must try other songs and give her the orchestrations of many. Perhaps, out of all, she will sing one. That is the chance of the work.

[ 333 ]

As for her point of view, she may object to the quality of anything except for that which she is paid. It is for the publisher to see whether she is worth subsidizing or not. If not, perhaps another house will see her merits in a different light. Yet she takes the songs and orchestrations along. And the publisher turning, as she goes, announces, "Gee, there's a cold proposition for you. Get her to sing anything for you for nothing?—Nix. Not her. Cash or no song." And he thumbs his fingers after the fashion of one who pays out money.

Your male singer is often a bird of the same fine feather. If you wish to see the ideal of dressiness as exemplified by the gentlemen of the road, see these individuals arrive at the offices of the publishers. The radiance of half-hose and neckties is not outdone by the sprightliness of the suit pattern or the glint of the stone in the shirt-front. Fresh from Chicago or Buffalo they arrive, rich in self-opinion fostered by rural praise, perhaps possessed of a new droll story, always loaded with the details of the hit they made.

"Well, well! You should have seen how that song went in Baltimore. I never saw anything like it. Why, it's the hit of the season!"

New songs are forthcoming, a new batch delivered for his service next year.

Is he absolutely sure of the estimation in which the house holds his services? You will hear a sequel to this, not this day perhaps but a week or a month later, during his idle summer in New York.

"You haven't twenty-five handy you could let me have, have you, Pat? I'm a little short to-day."

Into the publisher's eye steals the light of wisdom and decision. Is this individual worth it? Will he do the songs of the house twenty-five dollars' worth of good next season? Blessed be fate if there is a partner to consult. He will have time to reflect.

"Well, George, I haven't it right here in the drawer, but I can get it for you. I always like to consult my partner about these things, you know. Can you wait until this afternoon?"

Of course the applicant can wait, and between whiles are conferences and decisions. All things considered, it may be advisable to do it.

"We will get twenty-five out of him, any way. He's got a fine tenor voice. You never can tell what he might do."

So a pleasant smile and the money may be waiting when he returns. Or, he may be put off, with excuses and apologies. It all depends.

There are cases, however, where not even so much delay can be risked, where a hearty "sure" *must* be given. This is to that lord of the stage whose fame as a singer is announced by every minstrel billboard as "the renowned baritone, Mr. Calvin Johnson," or some such. For him the glad hand and the ready check, and he is to be petted, flattered, taken to lunch, dinner, a box theater party—anything—everything, really. And then, there is that less important one who has over-measured his importance. For him the solemn countenance and the suave excuse, at an hour when his need is greatest. Lastly, there is the sub-strata applicant in tawdry, make-believe clothes, whose want peeps out of every seam and pocket. His day has never been as yet, or mayhap was, and is over. He has a pinched face, a livid hunger, a forlorn appearance. Shall he be given anything? Never. He is not worth it. He is a "dead one." Is it not enough if the publisher looks after those of whose ability he is absolutely sure. Certainly. Therefore this one must slop the streets in old shoes and thin clothing, waiting. And he may never obtain a dime from any publisher.

Out of such grim situations, however, occasionally springs a success. These "down and out" individuals do not always understand why fate should be against them, why they should be down, and are not willing to cease trying.

"I'll write a song yet, you bet," is the dogged, grim decision. "I'll get up, you bet."

Once in a while the threat is made good, some mood allowing. Strolling along the by-streets, ignored and self-commiserating, the mood seizes them. Words bubble up and a melody, some crude commentary on the contrasts, the losses or the hopes of life, rhyming, swinging as they come, straight from the heart. Now it is for pencil and paper, quick. Any old scrap will do—the edge of a newspaper, the back of an envelope, the edge of a cuff. Written so, the words are safe and the melody can be whistled until some one will take it down. And so, occasionally, is born—has been often—the great success, the land-sweeping melody, selling by the hundreds of thousands and netting the author a thousand a month for a year or more.

Then, for him, the glory of the one who is at last successful. Was he commonplace, hungry, envious, wretchedly clothed before? Well, now, see! And do not talk to him of other authors who once struck it, had their little day and went down again, never to rise. He is not of them—not like them. For him, now, the sunlight and the bright places. No clothing too showy or too expensive, no jewelry too rare. Broadway is the place for him, the fine cafés and rich hotel lobbies. What about those other people who looked down on him once? Ha! they scorned him, did they? They sneered, eh? Would not give him a cent, eh? Let them come and look now! Let them stare in envy. Let them make way. He is a great man at last and the whole world knows it. The whole country is making acclaim over that which he has done.

For the time being, then, this little center of song-writing and publishing is for him the all-inclusive of life's importance. From the street organs at every corner is being ground the *one* melody, so expressive of his personality, into the ears of all men. In the vaudeville houses and cheaper concert halls men and women are singing it nightly to uproarious applause. Parodies are made and catch-phrases coined, all speaking of his work. Newsboys whistle and older men pipe its peculiar notes. Out of open windows falls the distinguished melody, accompanied by voices both new and strange. All men seem to recognize that which he has done, and for the time being compliment his presence and his personality.

Then the wane.

Of all the tragedies, this is perhaps the bitterest, because of the long-drawn memory of the thing. Organs continue to play it, but the sale ceases. Quarter after quarter, the royalties are less, until at last a few dollars per month will measure them completely. Meanwhile his publishers ask for other songs. One he writes, and then another, and yet another, vainly endeavoring to duplicate that original note which made for his splendid success the year before. But it will not come. And, in the meanwhile, other song-writers displace him for the time being in the public eye. His publishers have a new hit, but it is not his. A new author is being bowed to and taken out to dinner. But he is not that author. A new tile-crowned celebrity is strolling up his favorite Broadway path. At last, after a dozen attempts and failures, there is no hurry to publish his songs. If the period of failure is too long extended he may even be neglected. More and more, celebrities crowd in between him and that delightful period when he was greatest. At last, chagrined by the contrast of things, he changes his publishers, changes his haunts and, bitterest of all, his style of living. Soon it is the old grind again, and then, if thoughtless spending has been his failing, shabby clothing and want. You may see the doubles of these in any publisher's sanctum at any time, the sarcastically referred-to *has been.*

Here, also, the disengaged ballad singer, "peerless tenor" of some last year's company, suffering a period of misfortune. He is down on his luck in everything but appearances, last year's gorgeousness still surviving in a modified and sedate form. He is a singer of songs, now, for the publishers, by toleration. His one lounging-place in all New York where he is welcome and not looked at askance is the chair they may allow him. Once a day he makes the rounds of the theatrical agencies; once, or if fortune favors, twice a day he visits some cheap eating-house. At night, after a lone stroll through that fairyland of theaters and gaudy palaces to which, as he sees it, he properly belongs—Broadway, he returns to his bed, the carpeted floor of a room in some tolerant publisher's office, where he sleeps by permission, perhaps, and not even there, too often.

Oh, the glory of success in this little world in his eye at this time—how now, in want, it looms large and essential! Outside, as he stretches himself, may even now be heard the murmur of that shiny, joyous rout of which he was so recently a part. The lights, the laughter; the songs, the mirth—all are for others. Only he, only he must linger in shadows, alone.

To-morrow it will come out in words, if you talk with him. It is in the publisher's office, perhaps, where gaudy ladies are trying songs, or on the street, where others, passing, notice him not but go their way in elegance.

"I had it once, all right," he will tell you. "I had my handful. You bet I'll get it next year."

Is it of money he is thinking?

An automobile swings past and some fine lady, looking out, wakes to bitterness his sense of need.

"New York's tough without the coin, isn't it? You never get a glance when you're out of the game. I spend too easy, that's what's the matter with me. But I'll get back, you bet. Next time I'll know enough to save. I'll get up again, and next time I'll stay up, see?"

Next year his hopes may be realized again, his dreams come true. If so, be present and witness the glories of radiance after shadow.

"Ah, me boy, back again, you see!"

"So I see. Quite a change since last season."

"Well, I should smile. I was down on my luck then. That won't happen any more. They won't catch me. I've learned a lesson. Say, we had a great season."

Rings and pins attest it. A cravat of marvelous radiance speaks for itself in no uncertain tones. Striped clothes, yellow shoes, a new hat and cane. Ah, the glory, the glory! He is not to be caught any more, "you bet," and yet here is half of his subsistence blooming upon his merry body.

*They* will catch him, though, him and all in the length of time. One by one they come, old, angular misfortune grabbing them all by the coat-tails. The rich, the proud, the great among them sinking, sinking, staggering backward until they are where he was and deeper, far deeper. I wish I could quote those little notices so common in all our metropolitan dailies, those little perfunctory records which appear from time to time in theatrical and sporting and "song" papers, telling volumes in a line. One day one such singer's voice is failing; another day he has been snatched by disease; one day one radiant author arrives at that white beneficence which is the hospital bed and stretches himself to a final period of suffering; one day a black boat steaming northward along the East River to a barren island and a field of weeds carries the last of all that was so gay, so unthinking, so, after all, childlike of him who was greatest in his world. Weeds and a headboard, salt winds and the cry of seagulls, lone blowings and moanings, and all that light and mirth is buried here.

Here and there in the world are those who are still singing melodies created by those who have gone this unfortunate way, singers of "Two Little Girls in Blue" and "White Wings," "Little Annie Rooney" and "The Picture and the Ring," the authors of "In the Baggage Coach Ahead" and "Trinity Chimes," of "Sweet Marie" and "Eileen"—all are here. There might be recited the successes of a score of years, quaint, pleasing melodies which were sung the land over, which even to-day find an occasional voice and a responsive chord, but of the authors not one but could be found in some field for the outcasts, forgotten. Somehow the world forgets, the peculiar world in which they moved, and the larger one which knew them only by their songs.

It seems strange, really, that so many of them should have come to this. And yet it is true—authors, singers, publishers, even—and yet not more strange is it than that their little feeling, worked into a melody and a set of words, should reach far out over land and water, touching the hearts of the nation. In mansion and hovel, by some blazing furnace of a steel mill, or through the open window of a farmland cottage, is trolled the simple story, written in halting phraseology, tuned as only a popular melody is tuned. All have seen the theater uproarious with those noisy recalls which bring back the sunny singer, harping his one indifferent lay. All have heard the street bands and the organs, the street boys and the street loungers, all expressing a brief melody, snatched from the unknown by some process of the heart. Yes, here it is, wandering the land over like a sweet breath of summer, making for matings and partings, for happiness and pain. That it may not endure is also meet, going back into the soil, as it does, with those who hear it and those who create.

Yet only those who venture here in merry Broadway shall witness the contrast, however. Only they who meet these radiant presences in the flesh will ever know the marvel of the common song.

*HARPER'S WEEKLY*, 1900

## A VANISHED SEASIDE RESORT

AT BROADWAY and Twenty-third Street, where later, on this and some other ground, the once famed Flatiron Building was placed, there stood at one time a smaller building, not more than six stories high, the northward looking blank wall of which was completely covered with a huge electric sign which read:

SWEPT BY OCEAN BREEZES

THE GREAT HOTELS

PAIN'S FIREWORKS

SOUSA'S BAND

SEIDL'S GREAT ORCHESTRA

THE RACES

NOW——MANHATTAN BEACH——NOW

Each line was done in a different color of lights, light green for the ocean breezes, white for Manhattan Beach and the great hotels, red for Pain's fireworks and the races, blue and yellow for the orchestra and band. As one line was illuminated the others were made dark, until all had been flashed separately, when they would again be flashed simultaneously and held thus for a time. Walking up or down Broadway of a hot summer night, this sign was an inspiration and an invitation. It made one long to go to Manhattan Beach. I had heard as much or more about Atlantic City and Coney Island, but this blazing sign lifted Manhattan Beach into rivalry with fairyland.

"Where is Manhattan Beach?" I asked of my brother once on my first coming to New York. "Is it very far from here?"

"Not more than fifteen miles," he replied. "That's the place you ought to see. I'll take you there on Sunday if you will stay that long."

Since I had been in the city only a day or two, and Sunday was close at hand, I agreed. When Sunday came we made our way, via horse-cars first to the East Thirty-fourth Street ferry and then by ferry and train, eventually reaching the beach about noon.

Never before, except possibly at the World's Fair in Chicago, had I ever seen anything to equal this seaward-moving throng. The day was hot and bright, and all New York seemed anxious to get away.

The crowded streets and ferries and trains! Indeed, Thirty-fourth Street near the ferry was packed with people carrying bags and parasols and all but fighting each other to gain access to the dozen or more ticket windows. The boat on which we crossed was packed to suffocation, and all such ferries as led to Manhattan Beach of summer week-ends for years afterward, or until the automobile arrived, were similarly crowded. The clerk and his prettiest girl, the actress and her admirer, the actor and his playmate, brokers, small and exclusive tradesmen, men of obvious political or commercial position, their wives, daughters, relatives and friends, all were outbound toward this much above the average resort.

It was some such place, I found, as Atlantic City and Asbury Park are to-day, yet considerably more restricted. There was but one way to get there, unless one could travel by yacht or sail-boat, and that was via train service across Long Island. As for carriage roads to this wonderful place there were none, the intervening distance being in part occupied by marsh grass and water. The long, hot, red trains leaving Long Island City threaded a devious way past many pretty Long Island villages, until at last, leaving possible home sites behind, the road took to the great meadows on trestles, and traversing miles of bending marsh grass astir in the wind, and crossing a half hundred winding and mucky lagoons where lay water as agate in green frames and where were white cranes, their long legs looking like reeds, standing in the water or the grass, and the occasional boat of a fisherman hugging some mucky bank, it arrived finally at the white sands of the sea and this great scene. White sails of small yachts, the property of those who used some of these lagoons as a safe harbor, might be seen over the distant grass, their sails full spread, as one sped outward on these trains. It was romance, poetry, fairyland.

And the beach, with its great hotels, held and contained all summer long all that was best and most leisurely and pleasure-loving in New York's great middle class of that day. There were, as I knew all the time, other and more exclusive or worse beaches, such as those at Newport and Coney Island, but this was one which served a world which was plainly between the two, a world of politicians and merchants, and dramatic and commercial life generally. I never saw so many prosperous-looking people in one place, more with better and smarter clothes, even though they were a little showy. The straw hat with its blue or striped ribbon, the flannel suit with its accompanying white shoes, light cane, the pearl-gray derby, the check suit, the diamond and pearl pin in necktie, the silk shirt. What a cool, summery, airy-fairy realm!

And the women! I was young and not very experienced at the time, hence the effect, in part. But as I stepped out of the train at the beach that day and walked along the boardwalks which paralleled the sea, looking now at the blue waters and their distant white sails, now at the great sward of green before the hotels with its formal beds of flowers and its fountains, and now at the enormous hotels themselves, the Manhattan and the Oriental, each with its wide veranda packed with a great company seated at tables or in rockers, eating, drinking, smoking and looking outward over gardens to the blue sea beyond, I could scarcely believe my eyes—the airy, colorful, summery costumes of the women who made it, the gay, ribbony, flowery hats, the brilliant parasols, the beach swings and chairs and shades and the floating diving platforms. And the costumes of the women bathing. I had never seen a seaside bathing scene before. It seemed to me that the fabled days of the Greeks had returned. These were nymphs, nereids, sirens in truth. Old Triton might well have raised his head above the blue waves and sounded his spiral horn.

And now my brother explained to me that here in these two enormous hotels were crowded thousands who came here and lived the summer through. The wealth, as I saw it then, which permitted this! Some few Western senators and millionaires brought their yachts and private cars. Senator Platt, the State boss, along with one or more of the important politicians of the State, made the Oriental, the larger and more exclusive of the two hotels, his home for the summer. Along the verandas of these two hotels might be seen of a Saturday afternoon or of a Sunday almost the entire company of Brooklyn and New York politicians and bosses, basking in the shade and enjoying the beautiful view and the breezes. It was no trouble for any one acquainted with the city to point out nearly all of those most famous on Broadway and in the commercial and political worlds. They swarmed here. They lolled and greeted and chatted. The bows and the recognitions were innumerable. By dusk it seemed as though nearly all had nodded or spoken to each other.

And the interesting and to me different character of the amusements offered here! Out over the sea, at one end of the huge Manhattan Hotel, had been built a circular pavilion of great size, in which by turns were housed Seidl's great symphony orchestra and Sousa's band. Even now I can hear the music carried by the wind of the sea. As we strolled along the beach wall or sat upon one or the other of the great verandas we could hear the strains of either the orchestra or the band. Beyond the hotels, in a great field surrounded by a board fence, began at dusk, at which time the distant lighthouses over the bay were beginning to blink, a brilliant display of fireworks, almost as visible to the public as to those who paid a dollar to enter the grounds. Earlier in the afternoon I saw many whose only desire appeared to be to reach the race track in time for the afternoon races. There were hundreds and even thousands of others to whom the enclosed beach appeared to be all. The hundreds of dining-tables along the veranda of the Manhattan facing the sea seemed to call to still other hundreds. And yet again the walks among the parked flowers, the wide walk along the sea, and the more exclusive verandas of the Oriental, which provided no restaurant but plenty of rocking-chairs, seemed to draw still other hundreds, possibly thousands.

But the beauty of it all, the wonder, the airy, insubstantial, almost transparent quality of it all! Never before had I seen the sea, and here it was before me, a great, blue, rocking floor, its distant horizon dotted with white sails and the smoke of but faintly visible steamers dissolving in the clear air above them. Wide-winged gulls were flying by. Hardy rowers in red and yellow and green canoes paddled an uncertain course beyond the breaker line. Flowers most artfully arranged decorated the parapet of the porch, and about us rose a babel of laughing and joking voices, while from somewhere came the strains of a great orchestra, this time within one of the hotels, mingling betimes with the smash of the waves beyond the seawall. And as dusk came on, the lights of the lighthouses, and later the glimmer of the stars above the water, added an impressive and to me melancholy quality to it all. It was so insubstantial and yet so beautiful. I was so wrought up by it that I could scarcely eat. Beauty, beauty, beauty—that was the message and the import of it all, beauty that changes and fades and will not stay. And the eternal search for beauty. By the hard processes of trade, profit and loss, and the driving forces of ambition and necessity and the love of and search for pleasure, this very wonderful thing had been accomplished. Unimportant to me then, how hard some of these people looked, how selfish or vain or indifferent! By that which they sought and bought and paid for had this thing been achieved, and it was beautiful. How sweet the sea here, how beautiful the flowers and the music and these parading men and women. I saw women and girls for the favor of any one of whom, in the first flush of youthful ebullience and ignorance, I imagined I would have done anything. And at the very same time I was being seized with a tremendous depression and dissatisfaction with myself. Who was I? What did I amount to? What must one do to be worthy of all this? How little of all this had I known or would ever know! How little of true beauty or fortune or love! It mattered not that life for me was only then beginning, that I was seeing much and might yet see much more; my heart was miserable. I could have invested and beleaguered the world with my unimportant desires and my capacity. How dare life, with its brutal non-perception of values, withhold so much from one so worthy as myself and give so much to others? Why had not the dice of fortune been loaded in my favor instead of theirs? Why, why, why? I made a very doleful companion for my very good brother, I am sure.

And yet, at that very time I was asking myself who was I that I should complain so, and why was I not content to wait? Those about me, as I told myself, were better swimmers, that was all. There was nothing to be done about it. Life cared no whit for anything save strength and beauty. Let one complain as one would, only beauty or strength or both would save one. And all about, in sky and sea and sun, was that relentless force, illimitable oceans of it, which seemed not to know man, yet one tiny measure of which would make him of the elect of the earth. In the dark, over the whispering and muttering waters, and under the bright stars and in eyeshot of the lamps of the sea, I hung brooding, listening, thinking; only, after a time, to return to the hot city and the small room that was mine to meditate on what life could do for one if it would. The flowers it could strew in one's path! The beauty it could offer one—without price, as I then imagined—the pleasures with which it could beset one's path.

With what fever and fury it is that the heart seeks in youth. How intensely the little flame of life burns! And yet where is its true haven? What is it that will truly satisfy it? Has any one ever found it? In subsequent years I came by some of the things which my soul at that time so eagerly craved, the possession of which I then imagined would satisfy me, but was mine or any other heart ever really satisfied? No. And again no.

Each day the sun rises, and with it how few with whom a sense of contentment dwells! For each how many old dreams unfulfilled, old and new needs unsatisfied. Onward, onward is the lure; what life may still do, not what it has done, is the all-important. And to ask of any one that he count his blessings is but an ungrateful bit of meddling at best. He will none of it. At twenty, at thirty, at sixty, at eighty, the lure is still there, however feeble. More and ever more. Only the wearing of the body, the snapping of the string, the weakening of the inherent urge, ends the search. And with it comes the sad by-thought that what is not realized here may never again be anywhere. For if not here, where is that which could satisfy it as it is here? Of all pathetic dreams that which pictures a spiritual salvation elsewhere for one who has failed in his dreams here is the thinnest and palest, a beggar's dole indeed. But that youthful day by the sea!

Twenty-five years later I chanced to visit a home on the very site of one of these hotels, a home which was a part of a new real-estate division. But of that old, sweet, fair, summery life not a trace. Gone were the great hotels, the wall, the flowers, the parklike nature of the scene. In twenty-five years the beautiful circular pavilion had fallen into the sea and a part of the grounds of the great Manhattan Hotel had been eaten away by winter storms. The Jersey Coast, Connecticut, Atlantic City, aided by the automobile, had superseded and effaced all this. Even the great Oriental, hanging on for a few years and struggling to accommodate itself to new conditions, had at last been torn down. Only the beach remained, and even that was changed to meet new conditions. The land about and beyond the hotels had been filled in, planted to trees, divided by streets and sold to those who craved the freshness of this seaside isle.

But of this older place not one of those with whom I visited knew aught. They had never seen it, had but dimly heard of it. So clouds gather in the sky, are perchance illuminated by the sun, dissolve, and are gone. And youth, viewing old realms of grandeur or terror, views the world as new, untainted, virgin, a realm to be newly and freshly exploited—as, in truth, it ever is.

But we who were——!

*THE COLOR OF A GREAT CITY*, 1923

# GEORGE W. PLUNKITT
# &
# WILLIAM L. RIORDAN

*George Washington Plunkitt (1842–1924) was a successful politician of Tammany Hall, the Democratic party machine that ran New York, off and on, for a hundred years. Tammany's power was largely based on dispensing jobs and other favors for the immigrants and poor in return for their votes. Plunkitt explained the intricate workings of Tammany in a series of charmingly frank monologues that were taken down (and shaped) by his interviewer, the newspaperman William L. Riordan (1861–1909), and published as* Plunkitt of Tammany Hall: A Series of Very Plain Talks on Very Practical Politics *(1905).*

## HONEST GRAFT AND DISHONEST GRAFT

"EVERYBODY is talkin' these days about Tammany men growin' rich on graft, but nobody thinks of drawin' the distinction between honest graft and dishonest graft. There's all the difference in the world between the two. Yes, many of our men have grown rich in politics. I have myself. I've made a big fortune out of the game, and I'm gettin' richer every day, but I've not gone in for dishonest graft—blackmailin' gamblers, saloon-keepers, disorderly people, etc.—and neither has any of the men who have made big fortunes in politics.

"There's an honest graft, and I'm an example of how it works. I might sum up the whole thing by sayin': 'I seen my opportunities and I took 'em.'

"Just let me explain by examples. My party's in power in the city, and it's goin' to undertake a lot of public improvements. Well, I'm tipped off, say, that they're going to lay out a new park at a certain place.

"I see my opportunity and I take it. I go to that place and I buy up all the land I can in the neighborhood. Then the board of this or that makes its plan public, and there is a rush to get my land, which nobody cared particular for before.

"Ain't it perfectly honest to charge a good price and make a profit on my investment and foresight? Of course, it is. Well, that's honest graft.

"Or, supposin' it's a new bridge they're goin' to build. I get tipped off and I buy as much property as I can that has to be taken for approaches. I sell at my own price later on and drop some more money in the bank.

"Wouldn't you? It's just like lookin' ahead in Wall Street or in the coffee or cotton market. It's honest graft, and I'm lookin' for it every day in the year. I will tell you frankly that I've got a good lot of it, too.

"I'll tell you of one case. They were goin' to fix up a big park, no matter where. I got on to it, and went lookin' about for land in that neighborhood.

"I could get nothin' at a bargain but a big piece of swamp, but I took it fast enough and held on to it. What turned out was just what I counted on. They couldn't make the park complete without Plunkitt's swamp, and they had to pay a good price for it. Anything dishonest in that?

"Up in the watershed I made some money, too. I bought up several bits of land there some years ago and made a pretty good guess that they would be bought up for water purposes later by the city.

"Somehow, I always guessed about right, and shouldn't I enjoy the profit of my foresight? It was rather amusin' when the condemnation commissioners came along and found piece after piece of the land in the name of George Plunkitt of the Fifteenth Assembly District, New York City. They wondered how I knew just what to buy. The answer is—I seen my opportunity and I took it. I haven't confined myself to land; anything that pays is in my line.

"For instance, the city is repavin' a street and has several hundred thousand old granite blocks to sell. I am on hand to buy, and I know just what they are worth.

"How? Never mind that. I had a sort of monopoly of this business for a while, but once a newspaper tried to do me. It got some outside men to come over from Brooklyn and New Jersey to bid against me.

"Was I done? Not much. I went to each of the men and said: 'How many of these 250,000 stones do you want?' One said 20,000, and another wanted 15,000, and other wanted 10,000. I said: 'All right, let me bid for the lot, and I'll give each of you all you want for nothin'.'

"They agreed, of course. Then the auctioneer yelled: 'How much am I bid for these 250,000 fine pavin' stones?'

"'Two dollars and fifty cents,' says I.

"'Two dollars and fifty cents!' screamed the auctioneer. 'Oh, that's a joke! Give me a real bid.'

"He found the bid was real enough. My rivals stood silent. I got the lot for $2.50 and gave them their share. That's how the attempt to do Plunkitt ended, and that's how all such attempts end.

"I've told you how I got rich by honest graft. Now, let me tell you that most politicians who are accused of robbin' the city get rich the same way.

"They didn't steal a dollar from the city treasury. They just seen their opportunities and took them. That is why, when a reform administration comes in and spends a half million dollars in tryin' to find the public robberies they talked about in the campaign, they don't find them.

"The books are always all right. The money in the city treasury is all right. Everything is all right. All they can show is that the Tammany heads of departments looked after their friends, within the law, and gave them what opportunities they could to make honest graft. Now, let me tell you that's never goin' to hurt Tammany with the people. Every good man looks after his friends, and any man who doesn't isn't likely to be popular. If I have a good thing to hand out in private life, I give it to a friend. Why shouldn't I do the same in public life?

"Another kind of honest graft. Tammany has raised a good many salaries. There was an awful howl by the reformers, but don't you know that Tammany gains ten votes for every one it lost by salary raisin'?

"The Wall Street banker thinks it shameful to raise a department clerk's salary from $1500 to $1800 a year, but every man who draws a salary himself says: 'That's all right. I wish it was me.' And he feels very much like votin' the Tammany ticket on election day, just out of sympathy.

"Tammany was beat in 1901 because the people were deceived into believin' that it worked dishonest graft. They didn't draw a distinction between dishonest and honest graft, but they saw that some Tammany men grew rich, and supposed they had been robbin' the city treasury or levyin' blackmail on disorderly houses, or workin' in with the gamblers and lawbreakers.

"As a matter of policy, if nothing else, why should the Tammany leaders go into such dirty business, when there is so much honest graft lyin' around when they are in power? Did you ever consider that?

"Now, in conclusion, I want to say that I don't own a dishonest dollar. If my worst enemy was given the job of writin' my epitaph when I'm gone, he couldn't do more than write:

"'George W. Plunkitt. He Seen His Opportunities, and He Took 'Em.'"

## THE CURSE OF CIVIL SERVICE REFORM

"THIS CIVIL SERVICE LAW is the biggest fraud of the age. It is the curse of the nation. There can't be no real patriotism while it lasts. How are you goin' to interest our young men in their country if you have no offices to give them when they work for their party? Just look at things in this city to-day. There are ten thousand good offices, but we can't get at more than a few hundred of them. How are we goin' to provide for the thousands of men who worked for the Tammany ticket? It can't be done. These men were full of patriotism a short time ago. They expected to be servin' their city, but when we tell them that we can't place them, do you think their patriotism is goin' to last? Not much. They say: 'What's the use of workin' for your country anyhow? There's nothin' in the game.' And what can they do? I don't know, but I'll tell you what I do know.

I know more than one young man in past years who worked for the ticket and was just overflowin' with patriotism, but when he was knocked out by the civil service humbug he got to hate his country and became an Anarchist.

"This ain't no exaggeration. I have good reason for sayin' that most of the Anarchists in this city to-day are men who ran up against civil service examinations. Isn't it enough to make a man sour on his country when he wants to serve it and won't be allowed unless he answers a lot of fool questions about the number of cubic inches of water in the Atlantic and the quality of sand in the Sahara desert? There was once a bright young man in my district who tackled one of these examinations. The next I heard of him he had settled down in Herr Most's saloon smokin' and drinkin' beer and talkin' socialism all day. Before that time he had never drank anything but whisky. I knew what was comin' when a young Irishman drops whisky and takes to beer and long pipes in a German saloon. That young man is to-day one of the wildest Anarchists in town. And just to think! He might be a patriot but for that cussed civil service.

"Say, did you hear about that Civil Service Reform Association kickin' because the tax commissioners want to put their fifty-five deputies on the exempt list, and fire the outfit left to them by Low? That's civil service for you. Just think! Fifty-five Republicans and mugwumps holdin' $3000 and $4000 and $5000 jobs in the tax department when 1555 good Tammany men are ready and willin' to take their places! It's an outrage! What did the people mean when they voted for Tammany? What is representative government, anyhow? Is it all a fake that this is a government of the people, by the people and for the people? If it isn't a fake, then why isn't the people's voice obeyed and Tammany men put in all the offices?

"When the people elected Tammany, they knew just what they were doin'. We didn't put up any false pretenses. We didn't go in for humbug civil service and all that rot. We stood as we have always stood, for rewardin' the men that won the victory. They call that the spoils system. All right; Tammany is for the spoils system, and when we go in we fire every anti-Tammany man from office that can be fired under the law. It's an elastic sort of law and you can bet it will be stretched to the limit. Of course the Republican State Civil Service Board will stand in the way of our local Civil Service Commission all it can; but say!—suppose we carry the State some time, won't we fire the up-State Board all right? Or we'll make it work in harmony with the local board, and that means that Tammany will get everything in sight. I know that the civil service humbug is stuck into the constitution, too, but, as Tim Campbell said: 'What's the constitution among friends?'

"Say, the people's voice is smothered by the cursed civil service law; it is the root of all evil in our government. You hear of this thing or that thing goin' wrong in the nation, the State or the city. Look down beneath the surface and you can trace everything wrong to civil service. I have studied the subject and I know. The civil service humbug is underminin' our institutions and if a halt ain't called soon this great republic will tumble down like a Park-avenue house when they were buildin' the subway, and on its ruins will rise another Russian government.

"This is an awful serious proposition. Free silver and the tariff and imperialism and the Panama Canal are triflin' issues when compared to it. We could worry along without any of these things, but civil service is sappin' the foundation of the whole shootin' match. Let me argue it out for you. I ain't up on sillygisms, but I can give you some arguments that nobody can answer.

"First, this great and glorious country was built up by political parties; second, parties can't hold together if their workers don't get the offices when they win; third, if the parties go to pieces, the government they built up must go to pieces, too; fourth, then there'll be h—— to pay.

"Could anything be clearer than that? Say, honest now; can you answer that argument? Of course you won't deny that the government was built up by the great parties. That's history, and you can't go back of the returns. As to my second proposition, you can't deny that either. When parties can't get offices, they'll bust. They ain't far from the bustin' point now, with all this civil service business keepin' most of the good things from them. How are you goin' to keep up patriotism if this thing goes on? You can't do it. Let me tell you that patriotism has been dying out fast for the last twenty years. Before then when a party won, its workers got everything in sight. That was somethin' to make a man patriotic. Now, when a party wins and its men come forward and ask for their reward, the reply is, 'Nothin' doin', unless you can answer a list of questions about Egyptian mummies and how many years it will take for a bird to wear out a mass of iron as big as the earth by steppin' on it once in a century?'

"I have studied politics and men for forty-five years, and I see how things are driftin'. Sad indeed is the change that has come over the young men, even in my district, where I try to keep up the fire of patriotism by gettin' a lot of jobs for my constituents, whether Tammany is in or out. The boys and men don't get excited any more when they see a United States flag or hear 'The Star-Spangled Banner.' They don't care no more for fire-crackers on the Fourth of July. And why should they? What is there in it for them? They know that no matter how hard they work for their country in a campaign, the jobs will go to fellows who can tell about the mummies and the bird steppin' on the iron. Are you surprised then that the young men of the country are beginnin' to look coldly on the flag and don't care to put up a nickel for fire-crackers?

"Say, let me tell of one case. After the battle of San Juan Hill, the Americans found a dead man with a light complexion, red hair and blue eyes. They could see he wasn't a Spaniard, although he had on a Spanish uniform. Several officers looked him over, and then a private of the Seventy-first Regiment saw him and yelled, 'Good Lord, that's Flaherty.' That man grew up in my district, and he was once the most patriotic American boy on the West Side. He couldn't see a flag without yellin' himself hoarse.

"Now, how did he come to be lying dead with a Spanish uniform on? I found out all about it, and I'll vouch for the story. Well, in the municipal campaign of 1897, that young man, chockful of patriotism, worked day and night for the Tammany ticket. Tammany won, and the young man determined to devote his life to the service of the city. He picked out a place that would suit him, and sent in his application to the head of department. He got a reply that he must take a civil service examination to get the place. He didn't know what these examinations were, so he went, all light-hearted, to the Civil Service Board. He read the questions about the mummies, the bird on the iron, and all the other fool questions—and he left that office an enemy of the country that he had loved so well. The mummies and the bird blasted his patriotism. He went to Cuba, enlisted in the Spanish army at the breakin' out of the war, and died fightin' his country.

"That is but one victim of the infamous civil service. If that young man had not run up against the civil examination, but had been allowed to serve his country as he wished, he would be in a good office to-day, drawin' a good salary. Ah, how many young men have had their patriotism blasted in the same way!

"Now, what is goin' to happen when civil service crushes out patriotism? Only one thing can happen—the republic will go to pieces. Then a czar or a sultan will turn up, which brings me to the fourthly of my argument: that is, there will be h—— to pay. And that ain't no lie."

*PLUNKITT OF TAMMANY HALL*, 1905

# MAXIM GORKY

Maxim Gorky (real name Alexi Maximovich Peshkov, 1868–1936), the Russian novelist and playwright (Mother, The Lower Depths), was one of many Marxist authors who visited New York City and found it, predictably, the capital of Mammon. What distinguishes Gorky's account from most of these disapproving polemics is the passionate descriptive energy and near-surrealism he brings to his depiction of Coney Island. This new pleasure park for the masses is seen by him as basically another aspect of worker exploitation, sinister yet inadvertently compelling.

## BOREDOM

WITH THE ADVENT of night a fantastic city all of fire suddenly rises from the ocean into the sky. Thousands of ruddy sparks glimmer in the darkness, limning in fine, sensitive outline on the black background of the sky, shapely towers of miraculous castles, palaces and temples. Golden gossamer threads tremble in the air. They intertwine in transparent, flaming patterns, which flutter and melt away in love with their own beauty mirrored in the waters. Fabulous and beyond conceiving, ineffably beautiful, is this fiery scintillation. It burns but does not consume. Its palpitations are scarce visible. In the wilderness of sky and ocean rises the magic picture of a flaming city. Over it quiver the reddened heavens, and below the water reflects its contours, blending them into a whimsical blotch of molten gold.

Strange thoughts fill the mind at the sight of this play of fire. In the halls of the palaces, in the radiant gleam of flaming mirth, methinks, strains of music float, soft and proud, such as mortal ear has never heard. On the melodious current of their sounds the best thoughts of the world are carried along like sailing stars. The stars meet in a sacred dance, they throw out dazzling sparks, and as they clasp in a momentary embrace, they give birth to new flames, new thoughts.

I see a huge cradle, marvelously wrought of golden tissue, flowers and stars rocking yonder in the soft darkness, upon the trembling bosom of the ocean.

There at night rests the sun.

But the sun of the day brings man nearer to the truth of life. Then the fiery magic castles are tall white buildings.

The blue mist of the ocean vapors mingles with the drab smoke of the metropolis across the harbor. Its flimsy white structures are enveloped in a transparent sheet, in which they quiver like a mirage. They seem to beckon alluringly, and offer quiet and beauty.

The city hums with its constant, insatiate, hungry roar. The strained sound, agitating the air and the soul, the ceaseless bellow of iron, the melancholy wail of life driven by the power of gold, the cold, cynical whistle of the Yellow Devil scare the people away from the turmoil of the earth burdened and besmirched by the ill-smelling body of the city. And the people go forth to the shore of the sea, where the beautiful white buildings stand and promise respite and tranquillity.

The buildings huddle close together on a long, sandy strip of land, which, like a sharp knife, plunges deep into the dark water. The sand glitters in the sun with a warm, yellow gleam, and the transparent buildings stand out on its velvety expanse like thin white silk embroidery. The effect is as of rich garments thrown carelessly on the bosom of the island by some bather before plunging into the waters.

I turn my gaze wistfully upon this island. I long to nestle in its downy texture. I would recline on its luxurious folds, and from there look out into the wide spaces, where white birds dart swiftly and noiselessly, where ocean and sky lie drowsing in the scorching gleam of the sun.

This is Coney Island.

On Monday the metropolitan newspapers triumphantly announce:

"Three Hundred Thousand People in Coney Island Yesterday. Twenty-three Children Lost."

"There's something doing there," the reader thinks.

First a long ride by trolley thru Brooklyn and Long Island amid the dust and noise of the streets. Then the gaze is met by the sight of dazzling, magnificent Coney Island. From the very first moment of arrival at this city of fire, the eye is blinded. It is assailed by thousands of cold, white sparks, and for a long time can distinguish nothing in the scintillating dust round about. Everything whirls and dazzles, and blends into a tempestuous ferment of fiery foam. The visitor is stunned; his consciousness is withered by the intense gleam; his thoughts are routed from his mind; he becomes a particle in the crowd. People wander about in the flashing, blinding fire intoxicated and devoid of will. A dull-white mist penetrates their brains, greedy expectation envelopes their souls. Dazed by the brilliancy the throngs wind about like dark bands in the surging sea of light, pressed upon all sides by the black bournes of night.

Everywhere electric bulbs shed their cold, garish gleam. They shine on posts and walls, on window casings and cornices; they stretch in an even line along the high tubes of the power-house; they burn on all the roofs, and prick the eye with the sharp needles of their dead, indifferent sparkle. The people screw up their eyes, and smiling disconcertedly crawl along the ground like the heavy line of a tangled chain.

A man must make a great effort not to lose himself in the crowd, not to be overwhelmed by his amazement—an amazement in which there is neither transport nor joy. But if he succeeds in individualizing himself, he finds that these millions of fires produce a dismal, all-revealing light. Tho they hint at the possibility of beauty, they everywhere discover a dull, gloomy ugliness. The city, magic and fantastic from afar, now appears an absurd jumble of straight lines of wood, a cheap, hastily constructed toy-house for the amusement of children. Dozens of white buildings, monstrously diverse, not one with even the suggestion of beauty. They are built of wood, and smeared over with peeling white paint, which gives them the appearance of suffering with the same skin disease. The high turrets and low colonnades extend in two dead-even lines insipidly pressing upon each other. Everything is stripped naked by the dispassionate glare. The glare is everywhere, and nowhere a shadow. Each building stands there like a dumbfounded fool with wide-open mouth, and sends forth the glare of brass trumpets and the whining rumble of orchestrions. Inside is a cloud of smoke and the dark figures of the people. The people eat, drink and smoke.

But no human voice is heard. The monotonous hissing of the arc lights fills the air, the sounds of music, the cheap notes of the orchestrions, and the thin, continuous sputtering of the sausage-frying counters. All these sounds mingle in an importunate hum, as of some thick, taut chord. And if the human voice breaks into this ceaseless resonance, it is like a frightened whisper. Everything 'round about glitters insolently and reveals its own dismal ugliness.

The soul is seized with a desire for a living, beautiful fire, a sublime fire, which should free the people from the slavery of a varied boredom. For this boredom deafens their ears and blinds their eyes. The soul would burn away all this allurement, all this mad frenzy, this dead magnificence and spiritual penury. It would have a merry dancing and shouting and singing; it would see a passionate play of the motley tongues of fire; it would have joyousness and life.

The people huddled together in this city actually number hundreds of thousands. They swarm into the cages like black flies. Children walk about, silent, with gaping mouths and dazzled eyes. They look around with such intensity, such seriousness, that the sight of them feeding their little souls upon this hideousness, which they mistake for beauty, inspires a pained sense of pity. The men's faces, shaven even to the mustache, all strangely like one another, are grave and immobile. The majority bring their wives and children along, and feel that they are benefactors of their families, because they provide not only bread, but also magnificent shows. They enjoy the tinsel, but, too serious to betray their pleasure, they keep their thin lips pressed together, and look from the corners of their screwed-up eyes, like people whom nothing can astonish. Yet, under the mask of indifference simulated by the man of mature experience, a strained desire can be detected to take in all the delights of the city. The men with the serious faces, smiling indifferently and concealing the satisfied gleam of their sparkling eyes, seat themselves on the backs of the wooden horses and elephants of the merry-go-round and, dangling their feet, wait with nervous impatience for the keen pleasure of flying along the rails. With a whoop they dart up to the top, with a whistle they descend again. After this stirring journey they draw their skin tight on their faces again and go to taste of new pleasures.

The amusements are without number. There on the summit of an iron tower two long white wings rock slowly up and down. At the end of each wing hang cages, and in these cages are people. When one of the wings rises heavily toward the sky the faces of the occupants of the cages grow sadly serious. They all look in round-eyed silence at the ground receding from them. In the cages of the other wing, then carefully descending, the faces of the people are radiant with smiles. Joyous screams are heard, which strangely remind one of the merry yelp of a puppy let to the floor after he has been held up in the air by the scruff of his neck.

Boats fly in the air around the top of another tower, a third keeps turning about and impels some sort of iron balloon, a fourth, a fifth—they all move and blaze and call with the mute shouts of cold fire. Everything rocks and roars and bellows and turns the heads of the people. They are filled with contented *ennui*, their nerves are racked by an intricate maze of motion and dazzling fire. Bright eyes grow still brighter, as if the brain paled and lost blood in the strange turmoil of the white, glittering wood. The *ennui*, which issues from under the pressure of self-disgust, seems to turn and turn in a slow circle of agony. It drags tens of thousands of uniformly dark people into its somber dance, and sweeps them into a will-less heap, as the wind sweeps the rubbish of the street. Then it scatters them apart and sweeps them together again.

Inside the buildings the people are also seeking pleasure, and here, too, all look serious. The amusement offered is educational. The people are shown hell, with all the terrors and punishments that await those who have transgressed the sacred laws created for them.

Hell is constructed of papier maché, and painted dark red. Everything in it is on fire—paper fire—and it is filled with the thick, dirty odor of grease. Hell is very badly done. It would arouse disgust in a man of even modest demands. It is represented by a cave with stones thrown together in chaotic masses. The cave is penetrated by a reddish darkness. On one of the stones sits Satan, clothed in red. Grimaces distort his lean, brown face. He rubs his hands contentedly, as a man who is doing a good business. He must be very uncomfortable on his perch, a paper stone, which cracks and rocks. But he pretends not to notice his discomfort, and looks down at the evil demons busying themselves with the sinners.

A girl is there who has just bought a new hat. She is trying it on before a mirror, happy and contented. But a pair of little fiends, apparently very greedy, steal up behind her and seize her under the armpits. She screams, but it is too late. The demons put her into a long, smooth trough, which descends tightly into a pit in the middle of the cave. From the pit issue a gray vapor and tongues of fire made of red paper. The girl, with her mirror and her new hat, goes down into the pit, lying on her back in the trough.

A young man has drunk a glass of whisky. Instantly the devils clutch him, and down he goes thru that same hole in the floor of the platform.

The atmosphere in hell is stifling. The demons are insignificant looking and feeble. Apparently they are greatly exhausted by their work and irritated by its sameness and evident futility. When they fling the sinners unceremoniously into the trough like logs of wood, you feel like crying out:

"Enough, enough nonsense, boys!"

A girl extracts some coins from her companion's purse. Forthwith the spies, the demons, attack her, to the great satisfaction of Satan, who sits there snickering and dangling his crooked legs joyfully. The demons frown angrily up at the idle fellow, and spitefully hurl into the jaws of the burning pit everybody who enters hell by chance, on business or out of curiosity.

The audience looks on these horrors in silence with serious faces. The hall is dark. Some sturdy fellow with curly hair holds forth in a lugubrious voice while he points to the stage.

He says that if the people do not want to be the victims of Satan with the red garments and the crooked legs, they should not kiss girls to whom they are not married, because then the girls might become bad women. Women outcasts ought not to steal money from the pockets of their companions, and people should not drink whisky or beer or other liquors that arouse the passions; they should not visit saloons, but the churches, for churches are not only more beneficial to the soul, but they are also cheaper.

He talks monotonously, wearily. He himself does not seem to believe in what he was told to preach.

You involuntarily apostrophize the owners of this corrective amusement for sinners:

"Gentlemen, if you wish morality to work on men's souls with the force of castor oil, you ought to pay your preachers more."

At the conclusion of the terrible story a nauseatingly beautiful angel appears from a corner of the cavern. He hangs on a wire, and moves across the entire cave, holding a wooden trumpet, pasted over with gilt paper, between his teeth. On catching sight of him, Satan dives like a fish into the pit after the sinners. A crash is heard, the paper stones are hurled down, and the devils run off cheerfully to rest from their labor. The curtain drops. The public rises and leaves. Some venture to laugh. The majority, however, seem absorbed in reflection. Perhaps they think:

"If hell is so nasty, it isn't worth sinning."

They proceed further. In the next place they are shown "The World Beyond the Grave." It is large, and also made of papier maché. Here the souls of the dead, hideously garbed, wander in confusion. You may wink at them, but you may not touch them. This is a fact. They must feel greatly bored in the dusk of the subterranean labyrinth, shut up within rugged walls, in a cold, damp atmosphere. Some souls cough disagreeably, other silently chew tobacco, spitting yellow saliva on the ground. One soul, leaning in a corner against the wall, smokes a cigar.

When you pass by them they look into your face with colorless eyes. They compress their lips tightly, and shiver with cold as they thrust their hands into the gray folds of their rags of the other world. They are hungry, these poor souls, and many of them evidently suffer from rheumatism. The public looks at them silently. It breathes in the moist air, and feels its soul with dismal *ennui*, which extinguishes thought, as a wet, dirty cloth extinguishes the fire of a smoldering coal.

In another place again "The Flood" is displayed. The flood, you know, was brought on to punish the inhabitants of the earth for their sins.

And all the spectacles in this city have one purpose: to show the people how they will be punished after death for their sins, to teach them to live upon earth humbly, and to obey the laws.

Everywhere the one commandment is repeated:

"Don't!"

For it helps to crush the spirit of the majority of the public—the working people.

But it is necessary to make money, and in the commodious corners of the bright city, as everywhere in the world, depravity laughs disdainfully at hypocrisy and falsehood. Of course the depravity is hidden, and, of course, it's a wearying, tiresome depravity, but it also is "for the people." It is organized as a paying business, as a means to extract their earnings from the pockets of the people. Fed by the passion for gold it appears in a form vile and despicable indeed in this marsh of glittering boredom.

The people feed on it.

The people are always constrained. As yet they have never acted as free men. So they permit the enslavement of their bodies and their souls; for this alone are they to blame.

They pour in thick streams between two lines of dazzlingly illuminated houses, and the houses snap them up with their hungry jaws. On the right they are intimidated by the terrors of eternal torture.

"Do not sin!" they are warned. "Sin is dangerous!"

On the left, in the spacious dancing hall, women slowly waltz about, and here everything cries out to them:

"Sin! For sin is pleasant!"

Blinded by the gleam of the light, lured by the cheap, but glittering sumptuousness, intoxicated by the noise, they turn about in a slow dance of weary boredom. To the left they go willingly and blindly to Sin, to the right to hear exhortations to Holy Living.

This aimless straying stupefies the people. But for that very reason it is profitable both to the traders in morality and the venders of depravity.

Life is made for the people to work six days in the week, sin on the seventh, and pay for their sins, confess their sins, and pay for the confession.

The fires hiss like thousands of excited serpents, dark swarms of insects buzz feebly and dismally, and the people slowly wind about in the dazzling cobwebs of the amusement halls. Without haste, without a laugh or a smile on their smoothly shaven faces, they lazily crowd thru all the doors, stand long before the animal cages and chew tobacco and spit.

In one huge cage a man chases Bengal tigers with shots from a revolver and the merciless blows of a thin whip. The handsome beasts maddened by terror, blinded by the lights, deafened by the music and revolver shots, fling themselves about between the iron bars, and snort and roar. Their green eyes flash, their lips tremble; they gnash their teeth in fury, and menacingly raise now one forepaw now the other. But the man keeps shooting straight into their eyes, and the loud report of the blank cartridges and the smart blows of the whip, drive one powerful, supple creature into a corner of the cage. All in a tremble of revolt, seized with the impotent anguish of the powerful, choking with the sharp pang of humiliation, the imprisoned beast sinks down, for a moment, and looks on with dazed eyes, his serpentine tail writhing nervously.

The elastic body rolls itself into a firm ball, and twitches, ready to leap into the air, to bury its claws in the flesh of the man with the whip, rend him, annihilate him.

The hind legs of the animal quiver like a spring, his neck stretches, the green irises flash blood-red sparks. The watchful, waiting eyes that blaze in the vindictive countenance confront beyond the bars the dim, coppery blotch of a thousand colorless eyes, set in uniform, yellow faces, coldly expectant.

The face of the crowd, terrible in its dead immobility, waits. The crowd, too, hankers for blood and it waits, not out of revengefulness, but from curiosity, like a satiated, long-subdued beast.

The tiger draws his head in his shoulders and looks out sadly with his wide-open eyes. His whole body sinks back softly, and his skin wrinkles up, as if an icy rain had fallen on a surface heated by the passion for vengeance.

The man runs about the cage, shoots his pistol and cracks his whip, and shouts like a madman. His shouts are intended to hide his painful dread of the animals. The crowd regards the capers of the man, and waits in suspense for the fatal attack. They wait; unconsciously the primitive instinct is awakened in them. They crave fight, they want to feel the delicious shiver produced by the sight of two bodies intertwining, the splutter of blood and pieces of torn, steaming human flesh flying thru the cage and falling on the floor. They want to hear the roar, the cries, the shrieks of agony.

But the brain of the throng is already infected by the poison of various prohibitions and intimidations. Desiring blood, the crowd is afraid. It wishes, yet does not wish. In this struggle within itself it experiences a sharp gratification—it lives.

The man has frightened all the animals. The tigers softly withdraw into a corner of the cage, and the man, all in a sweat, satisfied that he has remained alive that day, bows to the coppery face of the crowd, as to an idol. He endeavors to conceal the tremor on his pale lips with a smile.

The crowd shouts and claps its hands and sighs—is it relief or is it regret?

Then the crowd breaks into dark pieces, and disperses over the slimy marsh of boredom.

Having delighted their eyes with the picture of man's rivalry with beasts, the human animals go in search of other amusements. There is a circus. In the center of the arena a man tosses two children into the air with his long legs. The children dart over them like two white doves with broken wings. Sometimes they fall to the ground. Then they cautiously look into the blood-suffused face of their father or master, and again ascend into the air. The crowd have disposed themselves about the arena, and look on. When the children slip from the performer's legs, a thrill of animation passes over all the countenances, as a wind sends a light ripple over the slumbering waters of a stagnant pool.

You long to see a drunken man with a jovial face, who would push and sing and bawl, happy because he is drunk, and sincerely wishing all good people the same.

The music rends the air. The orchestra is poor, the musicians worn out. The sounds of the brass instruments stray about as if they limped, as if no even course were possible for them. Even the circus horses, who are used to everything, turn cautiously aside, and nervously twitch their sharp ears, as if they wanted to shake off the rasping tin sounds. This music of the poor for the amusement of slaves puts strange notions into your head. You would like to tear the very largest brass trumpet from the musician's hand, and blow into it with all the power of your lungs, long and loud, so terribly that all the people would run from this prison, driven by the fury of the mad sounds.

Not far from the orchestra is a cage with bears. One of them, a stout brown bear with little, shrewd eyes, stands in the middle of the cage, and shakes his head deliberately. Apparently he thinks:

"All this is sensible only if it's contrived to blind, deafen and mutilate the people. Then, of course, the end justifies the means. But if people come here to be amused, I have no faith in their sanity."

Two other bears sit opposite each other, as if playing chess. Another is busy raking up straw in a corner of the cage. He knocks his claws against the bars. His snout is disappointedly calm. He seems to expect nothing from this life, and has made up his mind to go to bed.

The animals arouse the keenest interest. The waiting eyes of the spectators follow them steadily and minutely. The people appear to be searching for something long forgotten in the free and powerful movements of the beautiful bodies of the lion and panther. They thrust sticks thru the gratings, and silently experimenting prod the animals' stomachs and sides and tickle their paws, and look to see what will happen.

[ 365 ]

The animals that have not yet become familiarized with the character of human beings are angry. They thrust their paws against the bars, and roar. This pleases the spectators. Protected from the beast by the iron grill, and assured of their safety, the people look calmly into the blood-shot eyes and smile contentedly. But the majority of the animals pay no heed to the people. When they receive a blow with a stick, or are spat upon, they slowly rise, and without looking at the insulter retire into a distant corner of the cage. There the lions, tigers, panthers and leopards couch their beautiful, powerful bodies. In the darkness their round irises burn with the green fire of scorn for mankind. And the people glancing at them once again walk away, saying:

"Uninteresting!"

A brass band plays desperately at a semi-circular entrance, a kind of dark, wide-gaping jaw, within which the backs of chairs stare like a row of teeth. In front of the musicians is a post to which a pair of monkeys are tied by a thin chain. It is a mother and her child. The child presses closely against the mother's breast, and its long, thin hands, with their little fingers cross over the mother's back. The mother encircles the baby in a firm embrace with one arm. The other is cautiously extended forward, its fingers nervously crooked, ready to seize, to scratch, to strike. The mother's strained, wide-open gaze clearly bespeaks impotent despair, the anguished expectation of unavoidable insult and injury, melancholy rage. The child has nestled its cheek against its mother's breast and looks slantwise at the people with cold terror, motionless, hopeless. Apparently it has been filled with dread from the first day of its life, and the dread has frozen and congealed in it for all days to come. Displaying her white teeth the mother, without for a second removing the hand that clasps the child of her flesh, continually rebuffs the canes, the umbrellas, the hands of the onlookers, her tormentors.

The spectators are many. They are all white-skinned savages, men and women in straw hats and hats with feathers. It is fearfully amusing for all of them to see how skillfully the monkey mother shields her child from the blows they aim at its little body.

The mother quickly turns on a smooth space the size of a plate. She risks falling any second under the feet of the crowd, but she tirelessly repels everything that threatens to come in contact with her child. Sometimes she does not succeed in warding off a blow, and then she shrieks out pitifully. Her arm quickly cuts the air like a lash, but the onlookers are so many, and every one desires so much to pinch, to strike, to pull the monkey by the tail or by the chain around its neck, that sometimes she misses. Her eyes blink thoughtlessly, and radiate wrinkles of injury and distress appear around her mouth.

The child's hands squeeze her bosom. It clasps her so firmly that its hands are almost hidden in her thin hair. It has sunk down motionless, and its eyes stare fixedly at the coppery blotch of the faces all around.

Sometimes one of the musicians turns the stupid, brass bellow of his instrument upon the monkey and overwhelms the animal with a deafening noise. The little baby timidly clasps the mother's body still harder, shows its teeth and looks at the musician sharply.

The people laugh and nod their heads approvingly to the musician. He is satisfied and a minute later repeats the feat.

Among the spectators are women, some apparently mothers. But no one utters a word of protest against this cruel fun. All are satisfied.

Man is nurtured on terror, so he endeavors to inspire others with terror of himself. But he arouses only disgust, the poor, unfortunate wretch!

This torture continues thru the whole long night and part of the morning.

Alongside the orchestra is the cage of an elephant. He is an elderly gentleman, with a worn, glossy skin. He thrusts his trunk thru the grating and swings it with serious mien. He looks at the public, and, good wise animal that he is, he thinks:

"Of course, these scoundrels, swept together by the dirty broom of tedium, are capable of making sport even of their prophets. So I've heard old elephants tell. But I'm sorry for the monkey, any way. I've heard also that human beings, like jackals and hyenas, sometimes tear one another to pieces. But that's no consolation to the monkey."

You look at the pair of eyes in which is depicted the grief of a mother powerless to protect her child, and at the eyes of the baby, in which the deep, cold, dread of man has congealed into immobile rigidity. You look at the people capable of deriving amusement from the torture of a living creature, and turning to the monkey, you say:

"Little beast, forgive them! They know not what they do. They will become better in time."

Thus, when night comes, a fantastic magic city, all of fire, suddenly blazes up from the ocean. Without consuming, it burns long against the dark background of the sky, its beauty mirrored in the broad, gleaming bosom of the sea.

In the glittering gossamer of its fantastic buildings, tens of thousands of gray people, like patches on the ragged clothes of a beggar, creep along with weary faces and colorless eyes.

Mean panderers to debased tastes unfold the disgusting nakedness of their falsehood, the *naïveté* of their shrewdness, the hypocrisy and insatiable force of their greed. The cold gleam of the dead fire bares the stupidity of it all. Its pompous glitter rests upon everything 'round about the people.

But the precaution has been taken to blind the people, and they drink in the vile poison with silent rapture. The poison contaminates their souls. Boredom whirls about in an idle dance, expiring in the agony of its inanition.

One thing alone is good in the garish city: You can drink in hatred to your soul's content, hatred sufficient to last thruout life, hatred of the power of stupidity!

*THE INDEPENDENT*, 1907

# HENRY JAMES

*Henry James (1843–1916) brought a double focus to New York; he was on the one hand a native son, who grew up in the genteel district immortalized by his novella* Washington Square, *and on the other an expatriate who spent most of his adult life in Europe. In* The American Scene, *an account of his visit to America in 1904 after decades of absence, James balks at signs of bustle and vulgarity and registers his "sense of dispossession" in the face of immigrant influx; at the same time he is exhilarated by the scope and power of the city.* The American Scene *is above all a masterpiece of impressionistic prose, in which the tentacular complexity of James's late style reaches its highest point of evolution.*

## FROM *THE AMERICAN SCENE*

THE SINGLE IMPRESSION or particular vision most answering to the greatness of the subject would have been, I think, a certain hour of large circumnavigation that I found prescribed, in the fulness of the spring, as the almost immediate crown of a return from the Far West. I had arrived at one of the transpontine stations of the Pennsylvania Railroad; the question was of proceeding to Boston, for the occasion, without pushing through the terrible town—why "terrible," to my sense, in many ways, I shall presently explain—and the easy and agreeable attainment of this great advantage was to embark on one of the mightiest (as appeared to me) of train-bearing barges and, descending the western waters, pass round the bottom of the city and remount the other current to Harlem; all without "losing touch" of the Pullman that had brought me from Washington. This absence of the need of losing touch, this breadth of effect, as to the whole process, involved in the prompt floating of the huge concatenated cars not only without arrest or confusion, but as for positive prodigal beguilement of the artless traveller, had doubtless much to say to the ensuing state of mind, the happily-excited and amused view of the great face of New York. The extent, the ease, the energy, the quantity and number, all notes scattered about as if, in the whole business and in the splendid light, nature and science were joyously romping together, might have been taking on again, for their symbol, some collective presence of great circling and plunging, hovering and perching sea-birds, white-winged images of the spirit, of the restless freedom of the Bay. The Bay had always, on other opportunities, seemed to blow its immense character straight into one's face—coming "at" you, so to speak, bearing down on you, with the full force of a thousand prows of steamers seen exactly on the line of their longitudinal axis; but I had never before been so conscious of its boundless cool assurance or seemed to see its genius so grandly at play. This was presumably indeed because I had never before enjoyed the remarkable adventure of taking in so much of the vast bristling promontory from the water, of ascending the East River, in especial, to its upper diminishing expanses.

Something of the air of the occasion and of the mood of the moment caused the whole picture to speak with its largest suggestion; which suggestion is irresistible when once it is sounded clear. It is all, absolutely, an expression of things lately and currently *done*, done on a large impersonal stage and on the basis of inordinate gain—it is not an expression of any other matters whatever; and yet the sense of the scene (which had at several previous junctures, as well, put forth to my imagination its power) was commanding and thrilling, was in certain lights almost charming. So it befell, exactly, that an element of mystery and wonder entered into the impression—the interest of trying to make out, in the absence of features of the sort usually supposed indispensable, the reason of the beauty and the joy. It is indubitably a "great" bay, a great harbour, but no one item of the romantic, or even of the picturesque, as commonly understood, contributes to its effect. The shores are low and for the most part depressingly furnished and prosaically peopled; the islands, though numerous, have not a grace to exhibit, and one thinks of the other, the real flowers of geography in this order, of Naples, of Capetown, of Sydney, of Seattle, of San Francisco, of Rio, asking how if *they* justify a reputation, New York should seem to justify one. Then, after all, we remember that there are reputations and reputations; we remember above all that the imaginative response to the conditions here presented may just happen to proceed from the intellectual extravagance of the given observer. When this personage is open to corruption by almost any large view of an intensity of life, his vibrations tend to become a matter difficult even for *him* to explain. He may have to confess that the group of evident facts fails to account by itself for the complacency of his appreciation. Therefore it is that I find myself rather backward with a perceived sanction, of an at all proportionate kind, for the fine exhilaration with which, in this free wayfaring relation to them, the wide waters of New York inspire me. There is the beauty of light and air, the great scale of space, and, seen far away to the west, the open gates of the Hudson, majestic in their degree, even at a distance, and announcing still nobler things. But the real appeal, unmistakably, is in that note of vehemence in the local life of which I have spoken, for it is the appeal of a particular type of dauntless power.

The aspect the power wears then is indescribable; it is the power of the most extravagant of cities, rejoicing, as with the voice of the morning, in its might, its fortune, its unsurpassable conditions, and imparting to every object and element, to the motion and expression of every floating, hurrying, panting thing, to the throb of ferries and tugs, to the plash of waves and the play of winds and the glint of lights and the shrill of whistles and the quality and authority of breeze-borne cries—all, practically, a diffused, wasted clamour of *detonations*—something of its sharp free accent and, above all, of its sovereign sense of being "backed" and able to back. The universal *applied* passion struck me as shining unprecedentedly out of the composition; in the bigness and bravery and insolence, especially, of everything that rushed and shrieked; in the air as of a great intricate frenzied dance, half merry, half desperate, or at least half defiant, performed on the huge watery floor. This appearance of the bold lacing-together, across the waters, of the scattered members of the monstrous organism—lacing as by the ceaseless play of an enormous system of steam-shuttles or electric bobbins (I scarce know what to call them), commensurate in form with their infinite work—does perhaps more than anything else to give the pitch of the vision of

energy. One has the sense that the monster grows and grows, flinging abroad its loose limbs even as some unmannered young giant at
his "larks," and that the binding stitches must for ever fly further and
faster and draw harder; the future complexity of the web, all under
the sky and over the sea, becoming thus that of some colossal set of
clockworks, some steel-souled machine-room of brandished arms
and hammering fists and opening and closing jaws. The immeasur-
able bridges are but as the horizontal sheaths of pistons working at
high pressure, day and night, and subject, one apprehends with perhaps inconsistent gloom, to certain, to fantastic, to merciless multi-
plication. In the light of this apprehension indeed the breezy
brightness of the Bay puts on the semblance of the vast white page
that awaits beyond any other perhaps the black overscoring of
science.

Let me hasten to add that its present whiteness is precisely its
charming note, the frankest of the signs you recognize and remember it by. That is the distinction I was just feeling my way to name as
the main ground of its doing so well, for effect, without technical
scenery. There are great imposing ports—Glasgow and Liverpool
and London—that have already their page blackened almost beyond
redemption from any such light of the picturesque as can hope to
irradiate fog and grime, and there are others, Marseilles and
Constantinople say, or, for all I know to the contrary, New Orleans,
that contrive to abound before everything else in colour, and so to
make a rich and instant and obvious show. But memory and the actual impression keep investing New York with the tone, predominantly, of summer dawns and winter frosts, of sea-foam, of bleached
sails and stretched awnings, of blanched hulls, of scoured decks, of
new ropes, of polished brasses, of streamers clear in the blue air; and
it is by this harmony, doubtless, that the projection of the individual
character of the place, of the candour of its avidity and the freshness
of its audacity, is most conveyed. The "tall buildings," which have so
promptly usurped a glory that affects you as rather surprised, as yet,
at itself, the multitudinous sky-scrapers standing up to the view,
from the water, like extravagant pins in a cushion already over-
planted, and stuck in as in the dark, anywhere and anyhow, have at

least the felicity of carrying out the fairness of tone, of taking the sun and the shade in the manner of towers of marble. They are not all of marble, I believe, by any means, even if some may be, but they are impudently new and still more impudently "novel"—this in common with so many other terrible things in America—and they are triumphant payers of dividends; all of which uncontested and unabashed pride, with flash of innumerable windows and flicker of subordinate gilt attributions, is like the flare, up and down their long, narrow faces, of the lamps of some general permanent "celebration."

You see the pin-cushion in profile, so to speak, on passing between Jersey City and Twenty-third Street, but you get it broadside on, this loose nosegay of architectural flowers, if you skirt the Battery, well out, and embrace the whole plantation. Then the "American beauty," the rose of interminable stem, becomes the token of the cluster at large—to that degree that, positively, this is all that is wanted for emphasis of your final impression. Such growths, you feel, have confessedly arisen but to be "picked," in time, with a shears; nipped short off, by waiting fate, as soon as "science," applied to gain, has put upon the table, from far up its sleeve, some more winning card. Crowned not only with no history, but with no credible possibility of time for history, and consecrated by no uses save the commercial at any cost, they are simply the most piercing notes in that concert of the expensively provisional into which your supreme sense of New York resolves itself. They never begin to speak to you, in the manner of the builded majesties of the world as we have heretofore known such—towers or temples or fortresses or palaces—with the authority of things of permanence or even of things of long duration. One story is good only till another is told, and sky-scrapers are the last word of economic ingenuity only till another word be written. This shall be possibly a word of still uglier meaning, but the vocabulary of thrift at any price shows boundless resources, and the consciousness of that truth, the consciousness of the finite, the menaced, the essentially *invented* state, twinkles ever, to my perception, in the thousand glassy eyes of these giants of the mere market. Such a structure as the comparatively windowless bell-tower of Giotto, in Florence, looks supremely serene in its beauty. You don't feel it to have risen by the breath of an interested passion that, restless beyond all passions, is for ever seeking more pliable forms. Beauty has been the object of its creator's idea, and, having found beauty, it has found the form in which it splendidly rests.

Beauty indeed was the aim of the creator of the spire of Trinity Church, so cruelly overtopped and so barely distinguishable, from your train-bearing barge, as you stand off, in its abject helpless humility; and it may of course be asked how much of this superstition finds voice in the actual shrunken presence of that laudable effort. Where, for the eye, is the felicity of simplified Gothic, of noble preeminence, that once made of this highly-pleasing edifice the pride of the town and the feature of Broadway? The answer is, as obviously, that these charming elements are still there, just where they ever were, but that they have been mercilessly deprived of their visibility. It aches and throbs, this smothered visibility, we easily feel, in its caged and dishonoured condition, supported only by the consciousness that the dishonour is no fault of its own. We commune with it, in tenderness and pity, through the encumbered air; our eyes, made, however unwillingly, at home in strange vertiginous upper atmospheres, look down on it as on a poor ineffectual thing, an architectural object addressed, even in its prime aspiration, to the patient pedestrian sense and permitting thereby a relation of intimacy. It was to speak to me audibly enough on two or three other occasions—even through the thick of that frenzy of Broadway just where Broadway receives from Wall Street the fiercest application of the maddening lash; it was to put its tragic case there with irresistible lucidity. "Yes, the wretched figure I am making is as little as you see my fault—it is the fault of the buildings whose very first care is to deprive churches of their visibility. There are but two or three—two or three outward and visible churches—left in New York 'anyway,' as you must have noticed, and even they are hideously threatened: a fact at which no one, indeed, appears to be shocked, from which no one draws the least of the inferences that stick straight out of it, which every one seems in short to take for granted either with remarkable stupidity or with remarkable cynicism." So, at any rate, they may still effectively communicate, ruddy-brown (where not browny-black) old Trinity and any pausing, any attending survivor of the clearer age—and there is yet more of the bitterness of history to be tasted in such a tacit passage, as I shall presently show.

Was it not the bitterness of history, meanwhile, that on that day of circumnavigation, that day of highest intensity of impression, of which I began by speaking, the ancient rotunda of Castle Garden, viewed from just opposite, should have lurked there as a vague nonentity? One had known it from far, far back and with the indelibility of the childish vision—from the time when it was the commodious concert-hall of New York, the firmament of long-extinguished stars; in spite of which extinction there outlives for me the image of the infant phenomenon Adelina Patti, whom (another large-eyed infant) I had been benevolently taken to hear: Adelina Patti, in a fan-like little white frock and "pantalettes" and a hussar-like red jacket, mounted on an armchair, its back supporting her, wheeled to the front of the stage and warbling like a tiny thrush even in the nest. Shabby, shrunken, barely discernible to-day, the ancient rotunda, adjusted to other uses, had afterwards, for many decades, carried on a conspicuous life—and it was the present remoteness, the repudiated barbarism of all this, foreshortened by one's own experience, that dropped the acid into the cup. The sky-scrapers and the league-long bridges, present and to come, marked the point where the age—the age for which Castle Garden could have been, in its day, a "value"—had come out. That in itself was nothing—ages do come out, as a matter of course, so far from where they have gone in. But it had done so, the latter half of the nineteenth century, in one's own more or less immediate presence; the difference, from pole to pole, was so vivid and concrete that no single shade of any one of its aspects was lost. This impact of the whole condensed past at once produced a horrible, hateful sense of personal antiquity.

Yet was it after all that those monsters of the mere market, as I have called them, had more to say, on the question of "effect," than I had at first allowed? since they are the element that looms largest for me through a particular impression, with remembered parts and pieces melting together rather richly now, of "down-town" seen and felt from the inside. "Felt"—I use that word, I dare say, all presumptuously, for a relation to matters of magnitude and mystery that I could begin neither to measure nor to penetrate, hovering about them only in magnanimous wonder, staring at them as at a world of immovably-closed doors behind which immense "material" lurked, material for the artist, the painter of life, as we say, who shouldn't have begun so early and so fatally to fall away from possible initiations. This sense of a baffled curiosity, an intellectual adventure forever renounced, was surely enough a state of feeling, and indeed in presence of the different half-hours, as memory presents them, at which I gave myself up both to the thrill of Wall Street (by which I mean that of the whole wide edge of the whirlpool), and the too accepted, too irredeemable ignorance, I am at a loss to see what intensity of response was wanting. The imagination might have responded more if there had been a slightly less settled inability to understand what every one, what any one, was really doing; but the picture, as it comes back to me, is, for all this foolish subjective poverty, so crowded with its features that I rejoice, I confess, in not having more of them to handle. No open apprehension, even if it be as open as a public vehicle plying for hire, can carry more than a certain amount of life, of a kind; and there was nothing at play in the outer air, at least, of the scene, during these glimpses, that didn't scramble for admission into mine very much as I had seen the mob seeking entrance to an up-town or a down-town electric car fight for life at one of the apertures. If it had been the final function of the Bay to make one feel one's age, so, assuredly, the mouth of Wall Street proclaimed it, for one's private ear, distinctly enough; the breath of existence being taken, wherever one turned, as that of youth on the run and with the prize of the race in sight, and the new landmarks crushing the old quite as violent children stamp on snails and caterpillars.

The hour I first recall was a morning of winter drizzle and mist, of dense fog in the Bay, one of the strangest sights of which I was on my way to enjoy; and I had stopped in the heart of the business quarter to pick up a friend who was to be my companion. The weather,

such as it was, worked wonders for the upper reaches of the buildings, round which it drifted and hung very much as about the flanks
and summits of emergent mountain-masses—for, to be just all
round, there *was* some evidence of their having a message for the
eyes. Let me parenthesize, once for all, that there are other glimpses
of this message, up and down the city, frequently to be caught; lights
and shades of winter and summer air, of the literally "finishing" afternoon in particular, when refinement of modelling descends from
the skies and lends the white towers, all new and crude and commercial and over-windowed as they are, a fleeting distinction. The
morning I speak of offered me my first chance of seeing one of them
from the inside—which was an opportunity I sought again, repeatedly, in respect to others; and I became conscious of the force with
which this vision of their prodigious working, and of the multitudinous life, as if each were a swarming city in itself, that they are capable of housing, may beget, on the part of the free observer, in
other words of the restless analyst, the impulse to describe and present the facts and express the sense of them. Each of these huge
constructed and compressed communities, throbbing, through its
myriad arteries and pores, with a single passion, even as a complicated watch throbs with the one purpose of telling you the hour and
the minute, testified overwhelmingly to the *character* of New York—
and the passion of the restless analyst, on his side, is for the extraction of character. But there would be too much to say, just here,
were this incurable eccentric to let himself go; the impression in
question, fed by however brief an experience, kept overflowing the
cup and spreading in a wide waste of speculation. I must dip into
these depths, if it prove possible, later on; let me content myself for
the moment with remembering how from the first, on all such
ground, my thought went straight to poor great wonder-working
Émile Zola and *his* love of the human aggregation, the artificial microcosm, which had to spend itself on great shops, great businesses,
great "apartment-houses," of inferior, of mere Parisian scale. His image, it seemed to me, really asked for compassion—in the presence
of this material that his energy of evocation, his alone, would have
been of a stature to meddle with. What if *Le Ventre de Paris*, what if *Au*

*Bonheur des Dames*, what if *Pot-Bouille* and *L'Argent*, could but have come into being under the New York inspiration?

The answer to that, however, for the hour, was that, in all probability, New York was not going (as it turns such remarks) to produce both the maximum of "business" spectacle and the maximum of ironic reflection of it. Zola's huge reflector got itself formed, after all, in a far other air; it had hung there, in essence, awaiting the scene that was to play over it, long before the scene really approached it in scale. The reflecting surfaces, of the ironic, of the epic order, suspended in the New York atmosphere, have yet to show symptoms of shining out, and the monstrous phenomena themselves, meanwhile, strike me as having, with their immense momentum, got the start, got ahead of, in proper parlance, any possibility of poetic, of dramatic capture. That conviction came to me most perhaps while I gazed across at the special sky-scraper that overhangs poor old Trinity to the north—a south face as high and wide as the mountain-wall that drops the Alpine avalanche, from time to time, upon the village, and the village spire, at its foot; the interest of this case being above all, as I learned, to my stupefaction, in the fact that the very creators of the extinguisher are the church-wardens themselves, or at least the trustees of the church property. What was the case but magnificent for pitiless ferocity?—that inexorable law of the growing invisibility of churches, their everywhere reduced or abolished *presence*, which is nine-tenths of their virtue, receiving thus, at such hands, its supreme consecration. This consecration was positively the greater that just then, as I have said, the vast money-making structure quite horribly, quite romantically justified itself, looming through the weather with an insolent cliff-like sublimity. The weather, for all that experience, mixes intimately with the fulness of my impression; speaking not least, for instance, of the way "the state of the streets" and the assault of the turbid air seemed all one with the look, the tramp, the whole quality and *allure*, the consummate monotonous commonness, of the pushing male crowd, moving in its dense mass—with the confusion carried to chaos for any intelligence, any perception; a welter of objects and sounds in which relief, detachment, dignity, meaning, perished utterly and lost all rights. It appeared, the muddy medium, all one with every other element and note as well, all the signs of the heaped industrial battle-field, all the sounds and silences, grim, pushing, trudging silences too, of the universal will to move—to move, move, move, as an end in itself, an appetite at any price.

In the Bay, the rest of the morning, the dense raw fog that delayed the big boat, allowing sight but of the immediate ice-masses through which it thumped its way, was not less of the essence. Anything blander, as a medium, would have seemed a mockery of the facts of the terrible little Ellis Island, the first harbour of refuge and stage of patience for the million or so of immigrants annually knocking at our official door. Before this door, which opens to them there only with a hundred forms and ceremonies, grindings and grumblings of the key, they stand appealing and waiting, marshalled, herded, divided, subdivided, sorted, sifted, searched, fumigated, for longer or shorter periods—the effect of all which prodigious process, an intendedly "scientific" feeding of the mill, is again to give the earnest observer a thousand more things to think of than he can pretend to retail. The impression of Ellis Island, in fine, would be— as I was to find throughout that so many of my impressions would be—a chapter by itself; and with a particular page for recognition of the degree in which the liberal hospitality of the eminent Commissioner of this wonderful service, to whom I had been introduced, helped to make the interest of the whole watched drama poignant and unforgettable. It is a drama that goes on, without a pause, day by day and year by year, this visible act of ingurgitation on the part of our body politic and social, and constituting really an appeal to amazement beyond that of any sword-swallowing or fire-swallowing of the circus. The wonder that one couldn't keep down was the thought that these two or three hours of one's own chance vision of the business were but as a tick or two of the mighty clock, the clock that never, never stops—least of all when it strikes, for a sign of so much winding-up, some louder hour of our national fate than usual. I think indeed that the simplest account of the action of Ellis Island on the spirit of any sensitive citizen who may have happened to "look in" is that he comes back from his visit not at all the same person that he went. He has eaten of the tree of knowledge, and the taste will be for ever in his mouth. He had thought he knew before, thought he had the sense of the degree in which it is his American fate to share the sanctity of his American consciousness, the intimacy of his American patriotism, with the inconceivable alien; but the truth had never come home to him with any such force. In the lurid light projected upon it by those courts of dismay it shakes him—or I like at least to imagine it shakes him—to the depths of his being; I like to think of him, I positively *have* to think of him, as going about ever afterwards with a new look, for those who can see it, in his face, the outward sign of the new chill in his heart. So is stamped, for detection, the questionably privileged person who has had an apparition, seen a ghost in his supposedly safe old house. Let not the unwary, therefore, visit Ellis Island.

The after-sense of that acute experience, however, I myself found, was by no means to be brushed away; I felt it grow and grow, on the contrary, wherever I turned: other impressions might come and go, but this affirmed claim of the alien, however immeasurably alien, to share in one's supreme relation was everywhere the fixed element, the reminder not to be dodged. One's supreme relation, as one had always put it, was one's relation to one's country—a conception made up so largely of one's countrymen and one's country-women. Thus it was as if, all the while, with such a fond tradition of what these products predominantly were, the idea of the country itself underwent something of that profane overhauling through which it appears to suffer the indignity of change. Is not our instinct in this matter, in general, essentially the safe one—that of keeping the idea simple and strong and continuous, so that it shall be perfectly sound? To touch it overmuch, to pull it about, is to put it in peril of weakening; yet on this free assault upon it, this readjustment of it in *their* monstrous, presumptuous interest, the aliens, in New York, seemed perpetually to insist. The combination there of their quantity and their quality—that loud primary stage of alienism which New York most offers to sight—operates, for the native, as their note of settled possession, something they have nobody to thank for; so that *un*-settled possession is what we, on our side, seem reduced to—the implication of which, in its turn, is that, to recover confidence and regain lost ground, we, not they, must make the surrender and accept the orientation. We must go, in other words, *more* than half-way to meet them; which is all the difference, for us, between possession and dispossession. This sense of dispossession, to be brief about it, haunted me so, I was to feel, in the New York streets and in the packed trajectiles to which one clingingly appeals from the streets, just as one tumbles back into the streets in appalled reaction from *them*, that the art of beguiling or duping it became an art to be cultivated—though the fond alternative vision was never long to be obscured, the imagination, exasperated to envy, of the ideal, in the order in question; of the luxury of some such close and sweet and *whole* national consciousness as that of the Switzer and the Scot.

1907

# O. HENRY

*When O. Henry (real name William Sydney Porter, 1862–1910) came to New York in 1902, he was a convicted embezzler who had begun writing fiction in prison. He sought anonymity and a fresh start in a city which was to furnish him with material for more than 125 stories. O. Henry was interested not in the upper-crust "four hundred" but in "the four million" after whom his first collection was named, the ordinary people who battled the city for survival and often found its will stronger than their own. "The Duel" presents this struggle in stark terms, with a signature O. Henry switch: New York, for all its flaws, turns out to be curiously addictive, a toxin that enters the blood.*

### THE DUEL

THE GODS, lying beside their nectar on 'Lympus and peeping over the edge of the cliff, perceive a difference in cities. Although it would seem that to their vision towns must appear as large or small ant-hills without special characteristics, yet it is not so. Studying the habits of ants from so great a height should be but a mild diversion when coupled with the soft drink that mythology tells us is their only solace. But doubtless they have amused themselves by the comparison of villages and towns; and it will be no news to them (nor, perhaps, to many mortals), that in one particularity New York stands unique among the cities of the world. This shall be the theme of a little story addressed to the man who sits smoking with his Sabbath-slippered feet on another chair, and to the woman who snatches the paper for a moment while boiling greens or a narcotized baby leaves her free. With these I love to sit upon the ground and tell sad stories of the death of Kings.

New York City is inhabited by 4,000,000 mysterious strangers; thus beating Bird Centre by three millions and half a dozen nine's. They came here in various ways and for many reasons—Hendrik Hudson, the art schools, green goods, the stork, the annual dressmakers' convention, the Pennsylvania Railroad, love of money, the stage, cheap excursion rates, brains, personal column ads., heavy walking shoes, ambition, freight trains—all these have had a hand in making up the population.

But every man Jack when he first sets foot on the stones of Manhattan has got to fight. He has got to fight at once until either he or his adversary wins. There is no resting between rounds, for there are no rounds. It is slugging from the first. It is a fight to a finish.

Your opponent is the City. You must do battle with it from the time the ferry-boat lands you on the island until either it is yours or it has conquered you. It is the same whether you have a million in your pocket or only the price of a week's lodging.

The battle is to decide whether you shall become a New Yorker or turn the rankest outlander and Philistine. You must be one or the other. You cannot remain neutral. You must be for or against—lover or enemy—bosom friend or outcast. And, oh, the city is a general in the ring. Not only by blows does it seek to subdue you. It woos you to its heart with the subtlety of a siren. It is a combination of Delilah, green Chartreuse, Beethoven, chloral and John L. in his best days.

In other cities you may wander and abide as a stranger man as long as you please. You may live in Chicago until your hair whitens, and be a citizen and still prate of beans if Boston mothered you, and without rebuke. You may become a civic pillar in any other town but Knickerbocker's, and all the time publicly sneering at its buildings, comparing them with the architecture of Colonel Telfair's residence in Jackson, Miss., whence you hail, and you will not be set upon. But in New York you must be either a New Yorker or an invader of a modern Troy, concealed in the wooden horse of your conceited provincialism. And this dreary preamble is only to introduce to you the unimportant figures of William and Jack.

They came out of the West together, where they had been friends. They came to dig their fortunes out of the big city.

Father Knickerbocker met them at the ferry, giving one a right-hander on the nose and the other an uppercut with his left, just to let them know that the fight was on.

William was for business; Jack was for Art. Both were young and ambitious; so they countered and clinched. I think they were from

Nebraska or possibly Missouri or Minnesota. Anyhow, they were out for success and scraps and scads, and they tackled the city like two Lockinvars with brass knucks and a pull at the City Hall.

Four years afterward William and Jack met at luncheon. The business man blew in like a March wind, hurled his silk hat at a waiter, dropped into the chair that was pushed under him, seized the bill of fare, and had ordered as far as cheese before the artist had time to do more than nod. After the nod a humorous smile came into his eyes.

"Billy," he said, "you're done for. The city has gobbled you up. It has taken you and cut you to its pattern and stamped you with its brand. You are so nearly like ten thousand men I have seen to-day that you couldn't be picked out from them if it weren't for your laundry marks."

"Camembert," finished William. "What's that? Oh, you've still got your hammer out for New York, have you? Well, little old Noisyville-on-the-Subway is good enough for me. It's giving me mine. And, say, I used to think the West was the whole round world—only slightly flattened at the poles whenever Bryan ran. I used to yell myself hoarse about the free expanse, and hang my hat on the horizon, and say cutting things in the grocery to little soap drummers from the East. But I'd never seen New York, then, Jack. Me for it from the rathskellers up. Sixth Avenue is the West to me now. Have you heard this fellow Crusoe sing? The desert isle for him, I say, but my wife made me go. Give me May Irwin or E. S. Willard any time."

"Poor Billy," said the artist, delicately fingering a cigarette. "You remember, when we were on our way to the East, how we talked about this great, wonderful city, and how we meant to conquer it and never let it get the best of us? We were going to be just the same fellows we had always been, and never let it master us. It has downed you, old man. You have changed from a maverick into a butterick."

"Don't see exactly what you are driving at," said William. "I don't wear an alpaca coat with blue trousers and a seersucker vest on dress occasions, like I used to do at home. You talk about being cut to a pattern—well, ain't the pattern all right? When you're in Rome you've got to do as the Dagoes do. This town seems to me to have other alleged metropolises skinned to flag stations. According to the

railroad schedule I've got in my mind, Chicago and Saint Jo and
Paris, France, are asterisk stops—which means you wave a red flag
and get on every other Tuesday. I like this little suburb of Tarrytown-
on-the Hudson. There's something or somebody doing all the time.
I'm clearing $8,000 a year selling automatic pumps, and I'm living
like kings-up. Why, yesterday, I was introduced to John W. Gates. I
took an auto ride with a wine agent's sister. I saw two men run over
by a street car, and I seen Edna May play in the evening. Talk about
the West, why, the other night I woke everybody up in the hotel hollering. I dreamed I was walking on a board sidewalk in Oshkosh.
What have you got against this town, Jack? There's only one thing in
it that I don't care for, and that's a ferry-boat."

The artist gazed dreamily at the cartridge paper on the wall.
"This town," said he, "is a leech. It drains the blood of the country.
Whoever comes to it accepts a challenge to a duel. Abandoning the
figure of the leech, it is a juggernaut, a Moloch, a monster to which
the innocence, the genius, and the beauty of the land must pay tribute. Hand to hand every newcomer must struggle with the leviathan.
You've lost, Billy. It shall never conquer me. I hate it as one hates sin
or pestilence or—the color work in a ten-cent magazine. I despise
its very vastness and power. It has the poorest millionaires, the lit-
tlest great men, the haughtiest beggars, the plainest beauties, the
lowest skyscrapers, the dolefulest pleasures of any town I ever saw.
It has caught you, old man, but I will never run beside its chariot
wheels. It glosses itself as the Chinaman glosses his collars. Give me
the domestic finish. I could stand a town ruled by wealth or one
ruled by an aristocracy; but this is one controlled by its lowest in-
gredients. Claiming culture, it is the crudest; asseverating its preeminence, it is the basest; denying all outside values and virtue, it is
the narrowest. Give me the pure air and the open heart of the West
country. I would go back there to-morrow if I could."

"Don't you like this *filet mignon?*" said William. "Shucks, now,
what's the use to knock the town! It's the greatest ever. I couldn't
sell one automatic pump between Harrisburg and Tommy O'Keefe's
saloon, in Sacramento, where I sell twenty here. And have you seen
Sara Bernhardt in 'Andrew Mack' yet?"

"The town's got you, Billy," said Jack.

"All right," said William. "I'm going to buy a cottage on Lake Ronkonkoma next summer."

At midnight Jack raised his window and sat close to it. He caught his breath at what he saw, though he had seen and felt it a hundred times.

Far below and around lay the city like a ragged purple dream. The irregular houses were like the broken exteriors of cliffs lining deep gulches and winding streams. Some were mountainous; some lay in long, monotonous rows like the basalt precipices hanging over desert cañons. Such was the background of the wonderful, cruel, enchanting, bewildering, fatal, great city. But into this background were cut myriads of brilliant parallelograms and circles and squares through which glowed many colored lights. And out of the violet and purple depths ascended like the city's soul sounds and odors and thrills that make up the civic body. There arose the breath of gaiety unrestrained, of love, of hate, of all the passions that man can know. There below him lay all things, good or bad, that can be brought from the four corners of the earth to instruct, please, thrill, enrich, despoil, elevate, cast down, nurture or kill. Thus the flavor of it came up to him and went into his blood.

There was a knock on his door. A telegram had come for him. It came from the West, and these were its words:

"Come back home and the answer will be yes.

"DOLLY."

He kept the boy waiting ten minutes, and then wrote the reply: "Impossible to leave here at present." Then he sat at the window again and let the city put its cup of mandragora to his lips again.

After all it isn't a story; but I wanted to know which one of the heroes won the battle against the city. So I went to a very learned friend and laid the case before him. What he said was: "Please don't bother me; I have Christmas presents to buy."

So there it rests; and you will have to decide for yourself.

1 9 1 0

# JAMES WELDON JOHNSON

James Weldon Johnson (1871–1938) was a poet (God's Trombones), songwriter ("Under the Bamboo Tree"), diplomatic consul (to Venezuela and Nicaragua), sociologist and historian (Black Manhattan), and civil rights activist for the NAACP. In his 1912 novel The Autobiography of an Ex-Colored Man, he wrote a classic scene of arrival in New York City. The novelty of metropolitan life to a newcomer is here exemplified by ragtime, the new music beginning to shape the new century.

## FROM *THE AUTOBIOGRAPHY OF AN EX-COLORED MAN*

WE STEAMED up into New York harbor late one afternoon in spring. The last efforts of the sun were being put forth in turning the waters of the bay to glistening gold; the green islands on either side, in spite of their warlike mountings, looked calm and peaceful; the buildings of the town shone out in a reflected light which gave the city an air of enchantment; and, truly, it is an enchanted spot. New York City is the most fatally fascinating thing in America. She sits like a great witch at the gate of the country, showing her alluring white face, and hiding her crooked hands and feet under the folds of her wide garments,—constantly enticing thousands from far within, and tempting those who come from across the seas to go no farther. And all these become the victims of her caprice. Some she at once crushes beneath her cruel feet; others she condemns to a fate like that of galley slaves; a few she favors and fondles, riding them high on the bubbles of fortune; then with a sudden breath she blows the bubbles out and laughs mockingly as she watches them fall.

Twice I had passed through it; but this was really my first visit to New York; and as I walked about that evening I began to feel the dread power of the city; the crowds, the lights, the excitement, the gayety and all its subtler stimulating influences began to take effect upon me. My blood ran quicker, and I felt that I was just beginning to live. To some natures this stimulant of life in a great city becomes a thing as binding and necessary as opium is to one addicted to the habit. It becomes their breath of life; they cannot exist outside of it; rather than be deprived of it they are content to suffer hunger, want, pain and misery; they would not exchange even a ragged and wretched condition among the great crowd for any degree of comfort away from it.

As soon as we landed, four of us went directly to a lodging-house in 27th Street, just west of Sixth Avenue. The house was run by a short, stout mulatto man, who was exceedingly talkative and inquisitive. In fifteen minutes he not only knew the history of the past life of each one of us, but had a clearer idea of what we intended to do in the future than we ourselves. He sought this information so much with an air of being very particular as to whom he admitted into his house that we tremblingly answered every question that he asked. When we had become located we went out and got supper; then walked around until about ten o'clock. At that hour we met a couple of young fellows who lived in New York and were known to one of the members of our party. It was suggested we go to a certain place which was known by the proprietor's name. We turned into one of the cross streets and mounted the stoop of a house in about the middle of a block between Sixth and Seventh Avenues. One of the young men whom we had met rang a bell, and a man on the inside cracked the door a couple of inches; then opened it and let us in. We found ourselves in the hallway of what had once been a residence. The front parlor had been converted into a bar, and a half dozen or so of well dressed men were in the room. We went in, and after a general introduction had several rounds of beer. In the back parlor a crowd was sitting and standing around the walls of the room watching an exciting and noisy game of pool. I walked back and joined this crowd to watch the game, and principally to get away from the drinking party. The game was really interesting, the players being quite expert, and the excitement was heightened by the bets which were being made on the result. At times the antics and remarks of both players and spectators were amusing. When, at a critical point, a player missed a shot he was deluged by those financially interested in his making it with a flood of epithets synonymous to "chump"; while from the others he would be jeered by such remarks as "Nigger, dat cue ain't no hoe-handle." I noticed that among this class of colored men the word "nigger" was freely used in about the same sense as the word "fellow," and sometimes as a term of almost endearment; but I soon learned that its use was positively and absolutely prohibited to white men.

I stood watching this pool game until I was called by my friends, who were still in the bar-room, to go upstairs. On the second floor there were two large rooms. From the hall I looked into the one on the front. There was a large, round table in the center, at which five or six men were seated playing poker. The air and conduct here were greatly in contrast to what I had just seen in the pool-room; these men were evidently the aristocrats of the place; they were well, perhaps a bit flashily, dressed and spoke in low modulated voices, frequently using the word "gentlemen"; in fact, they seemed to be practicing a sort of Chesterfieldian politeness towards each other. I was watching these men with a great deal of interest and some degree of admiration, when I was again called by the members of our party, and I followed them on to the back room. There was a doorkeeper at this room, and we were admitted only after inspection. When we got inside I saw a crowd of men of all ages and kinds grouped about an old billiard table, regarding some of whom, in supposing them to be white, I made no mistake. At first I did not know what these men were doing; they were using terms that were strange to me. I could hear only a confusion of voices exclaiming, "Shoot the two!" "Shoot the four!" "Fate me!" "Fate me!" "I've got you fated!" "Twenty-five cents he don't turn!" This was the ancient and terribly fascinating game of dice, popularly known as "craps." I, myself, had played pool in Jacksonville; it is a favorite game among cigar-makers, and I had seen others play cards; but here was something new. I edged my way in to the table and stood between one of my new-found New York friends and a tall, slender, black fellow, who was making side bets while the dice were at the other end of the table. My companion explained to me the principles of the game;

and they are so simple that they hardly need to be explained twice. The dice came around the table until they reached the man on the other side of the tall, black fellow. He lost, and the latter said, "Gimme the bones." He threw a dollar on the table and said, "Shoot the dollar." His style of play was so strenuous that he had to be allowed plenty of room. He shook the dice high above his head, and each time he threw them on the table he emitted a grunt such as men give when they are putting forth physical exertion with a rhythmic regularity. He frequently whirled completely around on his heels, throwing the dice the entire length of the table, and talking to them as though they were trained animals. He appealed to them in short singsong phrases. "Come dice," he would say. "Little Phoebe," "Little Joe," "Way down yonder in the cornfield." Whether these mystic incantations were efficacious or not I could not say, but, at any rate, his luck was great, and he had what gamblers term "nerve." "Shoot the dollar!" "Shoot the two!" "Shoot the four!" "Shoot the eight!" came from his lips as quickly as the dice turned to his advantage. My companion asked me if I had ever played. I told him no. He said that I ought to try my luck; that everybody won at first. The tall man at my side was waving his arms in the air exclaiming "Shoot the sixteen!" "Shoot the sixteen!" "Fate me!" Whether it was my companion's suggestion or some latent dare-devil strain in my blood which suddenly sprang into activity I do not know; but with a thrill of excitement which went through my whole body I threw a twenty dollar bill on the table and said in a trembling voice, "I fate you."

I could feel that I had gained the attention and respect of everybody in the room, every eye was fixed on me, and the widespread question, "Who is he?" went around. This was gratifying to a certain sense of vanity of which I have never been able to rid myself, and I felt that it was worth the money even if I lost. The tall man with a whirl on his heels and a double grunt threw the dice; four was the number which turned up. This is considered as a hard "point" to make. He redoubled his contortions and his grunts and his pleadings to the dice; but on his third or fourth throw the fateful seven turned up, and I had won. My companion and all my friends shouted to me to follow up my luck. The fever was on me. I seized the dice. My hands were so hot that the bits of bone felt like pieces of ice. I shouted as loudly as I could, "Shoot it all!" but the blood was tingling so about my ears that I could not hear my own voice. I was soon "fated." I threw the dice—seven—I had won. "Shoot it all!" I cried again. There was a pause; the stake was more than one man cared to or could cover. I was finally "fated" by several men taking "a part" of it. I then threw the dice again. Seven. I had won. "Shoot it all!" I shouted excitedly. After a short delay I was "fated." Again I rolled the dice. Eleven. Again I had won. My friends now surrounded me and, much against my inclination, forced me to take down all of the money except five dollars. I tried my luck once more, and threw some small "Point" which I failed to make, and the dice passed on to the next man.

In less than three minutes I had won more than two hundred dollars, a sum which afterwards cost me dearly. I was the hero of the moment, and was soon surrounded by a group of men who expressed admiration for my "nerve" and predicted for me a brilliant future as a gambler. Although at the time I had no thought of becoming a gambler I felt proud of my success. I felt a bit ashamed, too, that I had allowed my friends to persuade me to take down my money so soon. Another set of men also got around me, and begged me for twenty-five or fifty cents to put them back into the game. I gave each of them something. I saw that several of them had on linen dusters, and as I looked about I noticed that there were perhaps a dozen men in the room similarly clad. I asked the fellow who had been my prompter at the dice table why they dressed in such a manner. He told me that men who had lost all the money and jewelry they possessed, frequently, in an effort to recoup their losses, would gamble away all their outer clothing and even their shoes; and that the proprietor kept on hand a supply of linen dusters for all who were so unfortunate. My informant went on to say that sometimes a fellow would become almost completely dressed and then, by a turn of the dice, would be thrown back into a state of semi-nakedness. Some of them were virtually prisoners and unable to get into the streets for days at a time. They ate at the lunch counter, where their credit was good so long as they were fair gamblers and did not attempt to jump their debts, and they slept around in chairs. They importuned friends and winners to put them back in the game, and kept at it until fortune again smiled on them. I laughed heartily at this, not thinking the day was coming which would find me in the same ludicrous predicament.

On passing downstairs I was told that the third and top floor of the house was occupied by the proprietor. When we passed through the bar I treated everybody in the room,—and that was no small number, for eight or ten had followed us down. Then our party went out. It was now about half-past twelve, but my nerves were at such a tension that I could not endure the mere thought of going to bed. I asked if there was no other place to which we could go; our guides said yes, and suggested that we go to the "Club." We went to Sixth Avenue, walked two blocks, and turned to the west into another street. We stopped in front of a house with three stories and a basement. In the basement was a Chinese Chop-suey restaurant. There was a red lantern at the iron gate to the areaway, inside of which the Chinaman's name was printed. We went up the steps of the stoop, rang the bell, and were admitted without any delay. From the outside the house bore a rather gloomy aspect, the windows being absolutely dark, but within it was a veritable house of mirth. When we had passed through a small vestibule and reached the hallway we heard mingled sounds of music and laughter, the clink of glasses and the pop of bottles. We went into the main room, and I was little prepared for what I saw. The brilliancy of the place, the display of diamond rings, scarf-pins, ear-rings and breast-pins, the big rolls of money that were brought into evidence when drinks were paid for, and the air of gayety that pervaded, all completely dazzled and dazed me. I felt positively giddy, and it was several minutes before I was able to make any clear and definite observations.

We at length secured places at a table in a corner of the room, and as soon as we could attract the attention of one of the busy waiters ordered a round of drinks. When I had somewhat collected my senses I realized that in a large back room into which the main room opened, there was a young fellow singing a song, accompanied on the piano by a short, thick-set, dark man. Between each verse he did some dance steps, which brought forth great applause and a shower of small coins at his feet. After the singer had responded to a rousing encore, the stout man at the piano began to run his fingers up and down the keyboard. This he did in a manner which indicated that he was master of a good deal of technic. Then he began to play; and such playing! I stopped talking to listen. It was music of a kind I had never heard before. It was music that demanded physical response, patting of the feet, drumming of the fingers, or nodding of the head in time with the beat. The barbaric harmonies, the audacious resolutions often consisting of an abrupt jump from one key to another, the intricate rhythms in which the accents fell in the most unexpected places, but in which the beat was never lost, produced a most curious effect. And, too, the player,—the dexterity of his left hand in making rapid octave runs and jumps was little short of marvelous; and, with his right hand, he frequently swept half the keyboard with clean cut chromatics which he fitted in so nicely as never to fail to arouse in his listeners a sort of pleasant surprise at the accomplishment of the feat.

This was ragtime music, then a novelty in New York, and just growing to be a rage which has not yet subsided. It was originated in the questionable resorts about Memphis and St. Louis by Negro piano players, who knew no more of the theory of music than they did of the theory of the universe, but were guided by natural musical instinct and talent. It made its way to Chicago, where it was popular some time before it reached New York. These players often improvised crude and, at times, vulgar words to fit the melodies. This was the beginning of the ragtime song. Several of these improvisations were taken down by white men, the words slightly altered, and published under the names of the arrangers. They sprang into immediate popularity and earned small fortunes, of which the Negro originators got only a few dollars. But I have learned that since that time a number of colored men, of not only musical talent, but training, are writing out their own melodies and words and reaping the reward of their work. I have learned also that they have a large number of white imitators and adulterators.

American musicians, instead of investigating ragtime, attempt to ignore it or dismiss it with a contemptuous word. But that has always been the course of scholasticism in every branch of art. Whatever new thing the *people* like is pooh-poohed; whatever is *popular* is spoken of as not worth the while. The fact is, nothing great or enduring, especially in music, has ever sprung full-fledged and unprecedented from the brain of any master; the best that he gives to the world he gathers from the hearts of the people, and runs it through the alembic of his genius. In spite of the bans which musicians and music teachers have placed upon it, the people still demand and enjoy ragtime. One thing cannot be denied; it is music which possesses at least one strong element of greatness; it appeals universally; not only the American, but the English, the French, and even the German people, find delight in it. In fact, there is not a corner of the civilized world in which it is not known, and this proves its originality; for if it were an imitation, the people of Europe, anyhow, would not have found it a novelty. Anyone who doubts that there is a peculiar heel-tickling, smile-provoking, joy-awakening charm in ragtime needs only to hear a skillful performer play the genuine article to be convinced. I believe that it has its place as well as the music which draws from us sighs and tears.

I became so interested in both the music and the player that I left the table where I was sitting, and made my way through the hall into the back room, where I could see as well as hear. I talked to the piano player between the musical numbers, and found out that he was just a natural musician, never having taken a lesson in his life. Not only could he play almost anything he heard, but could accompany singers in songs he had never heard. He had by ear alone, composed some pieces, several of which he played over for me; each of them was properly proportioned and balanced. I began to wonder what this man with such a lavish natural endowment would have done had he been trained. Perhaps he wouldn't have done anything at all; he might have become, at best, a mediocre imitator of the great masters in what they have already done to a finish, or one of the modern innovators who strive after originality by seeing how cleverly they can dodge about through the rules of harmony, and at the same time avoid melody. It is certain that he would not have been so delightful as he was in ragtime.

I sat by watching and listening to this man until I was dragged away by my friends. The place was now almost deserted; only a few stragglers hung on, and they were all the worse for drink. My friends were well up in this class. We passed into the street; the lamps were pale against the sky; day was just breaking. We went home and got into bed. I fell into a fitful sort of sleep with ragtime music ringing continually in my ears.

1912

# JAMES HUNEKER

*James Gibbons Huneker (1860–1921) was a critic and novelist who discoursed with equal gusto on music, drama, art, and literature. It was as a music critic that he made his greatest mark. He developed a mellifluous, musical prose style, casual, quickly responsive, and personably judgmental. (H. L. Mencken acknowledged he had been much influenced by Huneker.) In this section from his book about the great cities of the modern world,* New Cosmopolis *(1915), we get a quick panoramic tour of the city's parks, showing among other things how early the automobile had begun to change the texture of New York life.*

## THE LUNGS

### I

A BROAD CHEST usually means healthy lungs. Now, Manhattan Island is notoriously narrow-chested. Her scanty space across is not redeemed by greater length. Crowded with humans and their houses, there is consequently little space for the expansion of her normal breathing powers. Her lungs, *i. e.*, her parks, are contracted and not enough of them; there never will be. But more than some people think.

New Yorkers, even the most convinced cockneys, know little of their city, or of its lungs. Not only provincial, but parochial, they are only acquainted with the square or little park that adorns—it's a poor park that doesn't bring a sense of adornment—their native ward. Imagine my amazement when I learned after nearly thirty years' residence here that there were one hundred and eighty-two parks in the five boroughs. I read it in a newspaper and couldn't understand why I hadn't discovered the fact, for I've always been a rambler and my happy hunting-ground usually has been the East Side.

However, seeing is believing, and last summer, with my eyes made innocent by several years' residence in Germany, Austria,

Holland, Belgium, France, and England, I determined to verify certain vague suspicions that had been assailing my consciousness: that perhaps New York was not inferior in attractiveness to London, Paris, Vienna, Berlin, or Brussels. Perhaps many who go down to the sea in steamers, their pockets filled with letters of credit, might be equally shocked when confronted by the sights and sounds of Manhattan. Perhaps—but let us start on a little tour into intimate New York, without a megaphone or a ready-made enthusiasm; above all, let us be meek and avoid boastful rhetoric; also dodge statistics. Go to the guide-books, thou sluggard, for the latter!

When a writer tackles such a big theme as New York he as a rule fetches a deep breath in the lower bay, steams as far as Staten Island, and then lets loose the flood-gate of adjectives. How the city looks as you enter it is the conventional point of attack. I am sorry to say that whenever I have returned from Europe, the first peep of lower Manhattan, with its craggy battlements, its spires splintering the very firmament, and the horrid Statue of Liberty, all these do so work on my spirit that I feel like repining. Not because I am home again—not, my friend, because the spectacle is an uplifting one, but, shame that I must confess the truth, because my return means back to toil, back to the newspaper forge, there to resume my old job of wordsmith. Why, the very symbol of liberty, that stupid giant female, with her illuminating torch, becomes a monster of hated mien, her torch a club that ominously threatens us: Get to work! Get to work!

Therefore I'll begin at Battery Park, leaving the waterways, the arteries and veins of the city, for a future disquisition.

The image stamped on my memory is the reverse of the immobile. A plastic picture. The elevated roads debouching here are ugly, but characteristic. I'm afraid I can't see in our city anything downright ugly—it is never an absolute for me; as Dostoievsky said, there are no ugly women. The elevated road structure is hideous if æsthetically considered, and that is precisely the way it should not be considered. It rolls thousands daily to this end of the town; they usually take the ferries or subways, a few stroll under the scanty trees, or visit the Aquarium, so we must be critically charitable, too.

Oh, how tired I am of being told that Jenny Lind made her début in this same Castle Garden, "presented" by the late Phineas T. Barnum! Wasn't it a historical fort before it became a hall of immigrants and the abode of the fishes? This much may be said for the latter—it is a real aquarium, and, excepting the absence of an octopus or two, the collection rivals those at Brighton, England (where there are octopi); Naples, Hamburg, and elsewhere. More exciting than the fish, the seal, or the porpoises are the people. Thousands elbow through the rather narrow aisles and stare as solemnly at the finny inhabitants as they are stared at in return. The sightseeing coaches give their passengers a quarter of an hour's grace to "do" the show, while ragged boys dance about them, obsequiously pilot them, mock them, quite after the manner of the ragged boy on the Marina at Naples.

A veritable boon is this open Battery Park when the gang of wage-earners have fled the lower reaches of the city, when the dishes have been washed, when the janitors and caretakers of the tall buildings bring their wives and children to catch the breeze from the bay. On moonlit nights there are few situations more romantic. Here is freedom for the eye, for the lungs. There are not enough benches, but the walking is good, and to stand on the edge of the "wharf" and watch the bright eyes of ferries, the blazing eyes of the Jersey and Brooklyn shores, and the eyes of Staten Island as the unstable floor of the water mirrors (a cracked mirror) the moonlight and distorts the tiny flames about it, is to enjoy a spectacle fit for men and women who are not afraid to love their birthplace. I like it better when the weather has a nipping freshness and the day is grey-coloured and full of the noises of broken waters, and the cry of birds.

The seamy side of Battery Park is the poor castaway who has sought its coolness after a hot day of panhandling. But—given a certain amount of leeway—he is harmless. When a woman, the case assumes the pathetic. Begging is semisecretly indulged in. You drop your nickel and escape. If it be daytime you make for South Street to pay that long-deferred visit to Coenties Slip and Jeannette Park.

Perhaps you have seen C. F. W. Mielatz's coloured etching of the slip; if you have, the optical repercussion will be all the stronger when looking at the place itself. The fine old musty flavour of the slip, the canal-boats near the little Jeannette Park—a backwater with its stranded humanity stolidly waiting for something to turn up—and the lofty, lowering warehouses bring memories of London docks; docks where slunk Rogue Riderhood in search of rum after he had landed his dead cargo; docks from which sailed, still sail, wooden ships with real wooden masts, canvas sails, and sailors of flesh and blood, bound on some secret errand to southern seas where under the large few stars they may mutiny and cut the captain's throat; or else return to live immortally in fascinating legends of Joseph Conrad. I almost became sentimental over Coenties Slip, probably because Mielatz had etched it, and also because I had been reading Conrad. Art always reacts on nature, and the reactions may be perfectly sincere.

However, I thought it time to ask a policeman the direction of Corlears Park. He didn't know. No one knew, until an old chap who smelt of fish and whisky said: "It's Cor-*lears*, you want?" I had misplaced the accent, and the ear of the average longshoreman in South Street for quantity would please a college professor of Greek.

I went my winding way, finally enlightened. I like the London bobby, for he is obliging and instructive, but I also like our policeman. He is gruffer than his English contemporary—a shy sort of gruffness. I found myself at Canal Street and the Bowery—I don't know why—and was told to continue eastward. If I had taken a Grand Street car to the ferry my journey would have been simplified, but then I should have missed East Broadway and a lot of sights, of which more anon.

I dived into the east. It was a noisy, narrow lane rather than a street, and the inhabitants, mostly babies, were sprawling over the sidewalks. Often I followed the line of the gutter. Then I reached an open space and was disappointed. It was Corlears Park, and the absence of shade was painful. This lack of trees is a fault to be found in the majority of municipal parks and playgrounds. Night, if you don't feel too scared or lonely, is the proper time to enjoy the Hook. The view of the East River is unimpeded. The water is crowded with craft. A breeze always fans one. Women and children, principally Italians and Jews, sit or walk. Cats are friendly. So is the small boy who knocks off your straw tile with his stick. A venerable steamboat, rotting and dismal, the relic of a once proud excursion career, is warped to the wharf. It has flowers on its upper deck, and pale, sick people sit on the lower. You are informed by the inevitable busybody who traipses after strangers that the old boat is now for tuberculosis patients, living or dying, in the neighbourhood. What an ending for man and machine! Hecker's huge structure dominates the upper end of the park, as does Hoe's building over in Grand Street. The chief thing is the cleanliness and spaciousness. The same may be found at Rutgers Park, but without a water-front, always an added attraction.

Tompkins Square stirred memories. It lies between Seventh and Tenth Streets and Avenues A and B. When I first remember it, it was also called the Weisse-Garten, and no foreign nationality but German lived on its arid fringes.

The anarchists of those days gathered at Justus Schwab's, whose saloon was on First Street. There I first became acquainted with Johann Most, an intelligent and stubborn man, if ever there was one, and other "reds," the majority of them now dead. I remember, in 1887, the funeral parade in commemoration of the anarchists executed in Chicago because of the Haymarket affair. A sombre procession of proletarians with muffled drums, black flags, and dense masses of humans. I didn't go home that night. To my surprise I found the old-fashioned bird store—where they once sold folding bird-cages (collapsible)—in the same place, on Avenue A, near Seventh Street. The park is mightily improved. There are more trees, and also playgrounds for boys and girls, a band-stand, and refreshment pavilions.

I entered. On the benches I found "lobbies" of old men, Germans, Israelites for the most part. They were very old, very active, contented, and loquacious. They settled at a "sitzung" the affairs of the nation, keeping all the while a sharp lookout on the antics of their grandchildren, curly-haired, bright-eyed kiddies who rolled on the grass. The boys and girls literally made the welkin ring with their games, in the enclosures. They seemed healthy and happy. There are vice and poverty on the East Side—and the West—but there are also youth and decency and pride. I should say that optimism was the rule. Naturally, in summer, even poverty wears its rue with a difference. I saw little save cheerfulness, and heard much music-making by talented children.

The Tenth Street side of Tompkins Square reminds me of upper Stuyvesant Square. It is positively well-to-do, many doctors and dentists hanging out their shingles on the quaint, pleasant-looking brick houses. A very old German Lutheran meeting-house is at the corner of Ninth Street and Avenue B, and one block lower is St. Bridget's Church. Not afar is a synagogue or "Shool," as they call it, and you may catch a glimpse of the stately Church of the Holy Redeemer on Third Street near Avenue A, with its cartridge-shaped spire (easily seen from Brooklyn Bridge), that suggests shooting the soul to heaven if you are willing.

Time was when the Felsenkeller, at the foot of Fifty-seventh Street, East River, was an agreeable spot of summer nights. It was an open-air café, and while sipping your beverage you could watch the wheels of passing steamboats. It exists no longer. You must go up to East River Park, at Eighty-sixth Street and the river, or to Jefferson Park, opposite Ward's Island, to enjoy the water. There are little grassy hills, with rocks, at the former park that give you the illusion of nature.

I can't say much in favor of Union Square—now hopelessly encumbered with débris—or of Gramercy Park, locked to the public (you are permitted the barren enjoyment of gazing at the bleak enclosure), or of Madison Square, with its wonderful surroundings. These be places familiar. Nor do I care to drag you over to Hudson Park, on the West Side, to Abingdon Square, to Chelsea, De Witt Clinton, Seward, to other parks of another kind duplicated everywhere, even to the scarcity of foliage and benches. Mount Morris Park, at One Hundred and Twenty-fourth Street and Madison Avenue, was, a few decades ago, not so crowded as it is to-day. The hegira up-town has made it as populous as Tompkins Square. And not so pleasant. A little café, with a back garden on the west side of the square, was once a favourite resort years ago. Schmierkäse and pumpernickel, and—Tempus fugit!

II

I positively refuse to sing the praises of Central Park—which was laid out in 1857 (avaunt, statistics!)—simply because that once haughty and always artificial dame is fast becoming an old lady in plain decadence. Who has not sung her praises! Hardly a park, rather a cluster of graceful arboreal arabesques, which surprise and charm, Central Park is, nevertheless, moribund, and all the king's horses and all the king's men can never set her up again in her former estate. The city itself has assassinated her, not by official neglect, but by the proximity of stone, steel, and brick, which is slowly robbing her of her sustenance of earth, air, and moisture.

In the first flush of spring or a few early summer days she wears her old smile of brightness. How welcome the leafy arch of the Mall, how impressive, how "European" the vista of the Bethesda fountain, the terrace, and the lake; how pleasing it is to sit under the arbour of the Casino piazza and watch the golden girls and slim gilt lads arrive in motor-cars!

Then the Ramble, or the numerous bypaths that lead to the reservoir, or that give on the bridle-paths, wherein joyous youth with grooms flit by, or prosperous cits showing lean, crooked shanks painfully bump on horses too wide for them. Ah, yes! Central Park will continue for years to furnish amusement (if that wretched Zoo were only banished to the Bronx!) and deep breathing for the lucky rider who lives on its borders. Also furnish fun for May parties, June walks, and July depredations. It is a miracle of landscape-gardening, notwithstanding its absence of monotony—it abounds in too many twists and turns; it is seldom reposeful, because broad meadows are absent. You can't do much in decoration without flat surfaces. But what mortal could accomplish what Frederick Law Olmsted and Calvert Vaux accomplished; the impending ruin is the result of pitiless natural causes.

I once said that one can't be a flâneur in a city without trees. New York is almost treeless, and Central Park soon will be. When not so

long ago I saluted the Obelisk on the Thames embankment, that antique and morose stylite sent its regards to its brother in our Park.
Some day when the last Yankee (the breed is rapidly running out)
will look at the plans of what was once Central Park, hanging in the
Metropolitan Museum, his eye will caress the Obelisk across the
way. That strange shaft will endure when New York is become an
abomination and a desolation.

Arthur Brisbane's notion that the nasty little lakes and water
pools be drained and refilled with salt water for bathing purposes is
a capital one. Gone at a swoop malaria and evil odours; gone, too,
the mosquitoes which make life miserable for nigh dwellers. But the
park is doomed; let us enjoy its ancient bravery while we may.

I never skated at Van Cortlandt Park, because I can't skate; but I
love the spot, love the old mansion and its relics, love the open feeling about it. Atop of the highest part of the island is Isham Park. To
reach it get off at the Two Hundred and Seventh Street Subway station and walk westwardly up the hill, or through Isham Street. On
the brow is the little park, looking up and down the Hudson and
across Spuyten Duyvil. A rare spot to watch aeroplane races. Not far
away is the Billings castle, and across the Fort Washington Road the
studio and Gothic cloisters of the sculptor George Grey Barnard.

Often have I enjoyed the Zoological Garden in the Bronx, the
Botanical Garden, and the Bronx Park. Our Zoo is easily the largest
and most complete in the world. I've visited all the European Zoos,
from Amsterdam and Hamburg to Vienna and Budapest. As for the
Botanical Garden, I have the famous botanist Hugo de Vries of
Amsterdam as a witness, who told me he would be happy to live
near it always. The Bronx River is an "intimate" creek and malodor-
ous, but do you remember what cunning little French restaurants
were in vogue up there two or three decades ago? F. Hopkinson
Smith celebrated one of them in a short story. To-day they charge
you more for wine and cookery that are inferior to the old-time
establishments. Or has Time intervened with its soft pedal on the
gustatory sense? I don't believe it. The enjoyment of the table is
the longest surviving of the sociable peccadillos, and nothing can
prove to me that either my Burgundy or my Bordeaux palate has

deteriorated. But if I get on the subject of food we shall never see Pelham Parkway.

I didn't drive the devil wagon, else I should never have seen what I did—at least not in such brief time and in such a pleasant way. For ten hours my friend wheeled me up Tremont Avenue, the Southern Boulevard—and such boulevards!—to Pelham Parkway, with the park of one thousand seven hundred acres and more (I read this in a guide-book) up from the Harlem River, through magnificent shore and country, the Sound in sight, and a general sense of being in a primeval forest that had been cultivated by super-apes. On grey days the mist along the sedge grass of the water evokes delightful melancholy. We whizzed through towns I had heard of but never visited. Oh, shame! Think of Mount Vernon, Yonkers, Irvington, and Tarrytown! All new to this desperate cockney.

However, it was Pelham Bay that set me shouting. There's a park for you! The entire cityful could go out there, hold a cyclopean picnic, and have plenty of room to turn around in. It is not Fairmount Park, for that is the largest in the East, but it's the nearest thing to it. It is the combination of water and woods that is attractive. The Philadelphia park has the same, but on a vaster scale. Of European parks I can recall none that approaches Pelham—the Boboli Gardens and Cascine at Florence, Hyde, Regent, St. James's, and other London Parks, the Bois, Tuileries, and the Jardin d'Acclimatation, Paris, the Prater, Vienna (a lovely spot), Charlottenburg Chaussée, Berlin—none of these matches Pelham Parkway. The automobiles seem to eat space on the smooth road-beds. When the projected Bronx Parkway is an accomplished fact, the motorists ought to be forever satisfied.

We crossed from the Sound over to the Hudson on excellent roads. I began to wonder why any one could abide living in Gotham when such a delectable land of milk and honey is so near. I have noticed that when I ride in another man's motor-car I feel optimistic and inclined to see the "slaves of toil" in a rosy mood. And this mood was not banished by our arrival at the Sleepy Hollow Club. From its terraced lawns the Hudson may be viewed in all its majesty. This former home of Elliott F. Shepard is a palace, and, forgetting the joys and woes of Corlears Hook and Tompkins Square, I trained my eyes on the prospect. There is justice in the boast that nowhere may be seen such an extraordinary collocation of the grandiose and the familiar in landscape and waterscape. The Rhine is domestic, colloquial by comparison. Down the Danube at the Iron Gates there is some hint of the dazzling perspectives of Palisades and Hudson, but there again the barbaric note sounds too loud in the symphony of rugged rocks and vegetation. And great Highland Park, Bear's Nose, the new State Park, gift of Mrs. Harriman—what a wealth of natural park lands! When the wicked blasters blast no more, restrained from sinful destruction by the law courts (when?), and there are better travelling facilities, the Palisades side of the river will entertain thousands where to-day it hardly counts its hundreds.

We flew along the riverside. I had renounced all hope of seeing Jerome Park, St. Mary's, Claremont, and Crotona Parks, or even the little Poe Park at Fordham—we had passed High Bridge, Fort Washington, and Macomb's Dam Parks earlier—and farther down I had often visited Morris Heights and Audubon Park, but I was consoled by the sharp contrasts of the shifting landscape. Of course, there was a "panne" on upper Broadway, a burst tire, and the ensuing boredom, but nothing lasts, even impatience, and soon we were through Yonkers, and then across the city line past Palisades Park, with its lights, and, finally, on Riverside Drive, surely vantage-ground from which the ravishing spectacle of down-river may be enjoyed.

It would be unjust to pass City Hall and its park, not because it allures—it does not—but because City Hall is the priceless gem in our architectural tiara. Buried as it is by the patronising bulk and height of its neighbours, it more than holds its own in dignity, simplicity, and pure linear beauty—qualities conspicuous by their absence in the adjacent parvenu structures.

Nor must I miss Prospect Park, Brooklyn, near enough to reach in a half-hour, and from the grassy knolls of which the turrets and pinnacles of Manhattan may be seen. It is far more captivating than Central Park, and the Flatbush Avenue entrance reminds one of some vast plaza in a European capital, upper Brussels, for example.

It is imposing with its MacMonnies monument, its spaciousness, and general decorative effect—an effect enhanced by the Italianate water-tower and the Museum farther down, whose vast galleries house so little original art, with the exception of the Sargent water-colours and former Chapman pictures. It is only fair to add that Prospect Park began with natural advantages superior to Central Park, advantages made the most of. This park really makes Brooklyn habitable and not merely an interlude of bricks and mortar before achieving the seashore.

Well, we are not far from Battery Park, whence we started. It is only a swallow's flight this—for I could have dwelt on the special characteristics of each park, on the elevated playgrounds at Williamsburg Bridge, on the various recreation piers—but celerity was my aim, the impression as we skimmed; all the rest is guide-book literature—as Paul Verlaine did not say. I didn't start out to prove anything, yet I think I have suggested that, despite its con-tracted chest and waist, the lungs of Manhattan are both vigorous and varied.

*NEW COSMOPOLIS*, 1915

# SARA TEASDALE

Sara Teasdale (1884–1933) was a popular poet in her day, who in delicate and musically polished verse often expressed a disturbingly raw anguish. Her poems set in New York locations—Riverside Park, Union Square, 42nd Street—accentuate the gap between public insouciance and private grief. The sickly and increasingly reclusive Teasdale, who lived to see her type of verse declared outmoded, committed suicide in Greenwich Village.

## GRAMERCY PARK
### FOR W. P.

The little park was filled with peace,
    The walks were carpeted with snow,
But every iron gate was locked,
    Lest if we entered, peace would go.

We circled it a dozen times,
    The wind was blowing from the sea,
I only felt your restless eyes
    Whose love was like a cloak for me.

Oh heavy gates that fate has locked
    To bar the joy we may not win,
Peace would go out forevermore
    If we should dare to enter in.

## IN THE METROPOLITAN MUSEUM

Within the tiny Pantheon
    We stood together silently,
Leaving the restless crowd awhile
    As ships find shelter from the sea.

The ancient centuries came back
    To cover us a moment's space,
And thro' the dome the light was glad
    Because it shone upon your face.

Ah, not from Rome but farther still,
    Beyond sun-smitten Salamis,
The moment took us, till you stooped
    To find the present with a kiss.


CONEY ISLAND

Why did you bring me here?
The sand is white with snow,
Over the wooden domes
The winter sea-winds blow—
There is no shelter near,
    Come, let us go.

With foam of icy lace
The sea creeps up the sand,
The wind is like a hand
That strikes us in the face.
Doors that June set a-swing
Are bolted long ago;
We try them uselessly—
Alas, there cannot be
For us a second spring;
    Come, let us go.


UNION SQUARE

With the man I love who loves me not,
    I walked in the street-lamps' flare;
We watched the world go home that night
    In a flood through Union Square.

I leaned to catch the words he said
   That were light as a snowflake falling;
Ah well that he never leaned to hear
   The words my heart was calling.

And on we walked and on we walked
   Past the fiery lights of the picture shows—
Where the girls with thirsty eyes go by
   On the errand each man knows.

And on we walked and on we walked,
   At the door at last we said good-bye;
I knew by his smile he had not heard
   My heart's unuttered cry.

With the man I love who loves me not
   I walked in the street-lamps' flare—
But oh, the girls who can ask for love
   In the lights of Union Square.

                                 1911

## BROADWAY

This is the quiet hour; the theaters
   Have gathered in their crowds, and steadily
   The million lights blaze on for few to see,
Robbing the sky of stars that should be hers.
A woman waits with bag and shabby furs,
   A somber man drifts by, and only we
   Pass up the street unwearied, warm and free,
For over us the olden magic stirs.
Beneath the liquid splendor of the lights
   We live a little ere the charm is spent;
This night is ours, of all the golden nights,
    The pavement an enchanted palace floor,
   And Youth the player on the viol, who sent
    A strain of music thru an open door.

                                 1913

# DJUNA BARNES

―――――――――

*Before she wrote the experimental novel* Nightwood *(1936), Djuna Barnes (1892–1982) sharpened her prose on some extraordinary urban sketches for the popular press. Hers was a city of spectacle: dance halls, boxing matches, World War I soldiers on a pass, feminist protests, and bohemian flamboyance in her own beloved Greenwich Village. Here she turns to the craze for roof gardens, which provided both a means to enjoy the newly romantic vistas of skyscraper New York and a palliative, in the days before air-conditioning, to the city's hot weather.*

## "COME INTO THE ROOF GARDEN, MAUD"

FIRST OF ALL, enter the atmosphere.

And this, the atmosphere of a roof garden, is 10 per cent. soft June air and 10 per cent. gold June twilight, and a goodly per cent. of high-hung lanterns and the music of hidden mechanical birds, swinging under the tangle of paper wistaria, fifty feet above, where, between guarding panes of glass, shine the electric signs, plus a few stars, of Broadway.

A good deal of the grace of God is there, too. It is a majestic something that keeps a distance east of the champagne bucket, and goes out upon the dancing space not at all.

The thing that is really lacking is a sense of humor. There are not ten people with a really good laugh in their systems in a whole evening on a roof garden. A sense of humor, of course, is never well fed. Here people scan the menu too often and too long to allow the humor to get upon its basic legs. A woman is a terribly good sport and wants to enjoy herself; her escort is growing old in the attempt to make it an evening of evenings.

"That," she says, in the very first appeal of the thing, "is the most hideous gown I ever saw; all sliced up where she should be careful and all bunched around where she should be coming out; no arm at all, no arm."

"What's wrong?"

"Everything!" she said with high held glasses. "Everything. Why don't women get a sense of the decorative when they dress?"

"But, you know," he soothes, "they are really fearfully and terribly magnetic; they make an appeal."

And therefore he has gone into history as a blind innocent, with no sense of order, or the law that stands next to the things that are right.

And yet he is right. They make an appeal. Everything on, in and about a roof garden, from the little white and green match-stands to the wide spanning arches of red light, is an appeal. Sometimes it is an appeal for silence; sometimes it is an appeal for laughter; often it is an appeal for help.

Terribly appealing is the soft melange of the French sisters, wound about in their yard or so of silk, their wide, comprehending eyes, their wider, less comprehending mouths, with a generous space for rouge. Appealing the little foot that waits the tango; appealing, too, the dumb, rigid silences of the chaperon, who feels that there is nothing here for her but to maintain her sense of right.

A typical roof garden is the Jardin de Danse. It is at least the best in the sense of its fullness of spectacular dancing, both the dancing of the professionals and those who go up to do likewise—if they can.

The fifty-mile look is here, too. Let me explain.

People from out of town can't hide it. Even people no further away from home than The Bronx hide it very badly. The born-in-the blood persons, those who seem a part of the place, are those who live in the hotel opposite, or in the apartment just around the corner, or at most, no more than five blocks away.

This doesn't include Judy O'Grady, who dances up stairs upon the roof of the garden of children's and husbands' clothing, swinging in the breeze off a back alley. It is those places about Broadway where the sound of a taxi is personal.

And now the band begins to play.

The conductor, a great, towering figure in white flannels, stands knee-deep in green foliage, which may or may not be false, but which looks extremely like asparagus gone to seed, fine and green and feathery—a soft accompaniment to a fearsome pair of legs.

Up and down and sideways goes the little conducting stick; and up and down and sideways go the head and the bow of the violinist, and up and out goes the laboring chest of the cornetist; and the Chalmerses and the De Vans from Yonkers drift out upon the floor, while the esthetic Four Hundred (who are aware only of that part of their body where rests money in stock and bond value—the breast-bone where hangs the string of pearls, the waist girded tight with priceless stones, the buckled shoe and the fingers holding the brittle champagne glass with Tiffany-encircled fingers); wait a second before they arise, for to be late is to be fashionable, to be hesitant is to be haughty.

"Some day I shall put in such a floor. I don't think the floors along the avenue have received their proper share of attention. Why not have a dancing space like this in the Blue Room?"

"What's the matter?" some one says at a table adjoining, and a voice comes back over your shoulder, high and feminine:

"I am suffering; I am unhappy."

"And why so?"

"Ah," the voice goes on, dramatically broken, clinging softly to its feminine cadences, "I left the pudding in the oven and the canary hasn't been fed." Then the snip snip of pistachio nuts being cracked at the table to the left and the dancers are coming back.

"I felt like a perfect fool," giggles the youngest Miss Van Allen, "when the music stopped and they just threw about a sort of noise like rice in a sieve and that silly negro with a grin on his face kept batting that poor old drum."

"I always feel like a nut, anyway," returns the young man with the hair thrust back as though he has just been reverently handled by an archdeacon.

"Oh, well, we're having an awfully good time, aren't we?" they say in chorus, and decide that they are.

Taken from an artistic point of view, the best moment to catch the atmosphere of a roof garden is when every one is just about to sit down, the colors rise and fall and scintillate and surge, crouch, scream and cry and grope and cough and are bold and are clever and are witty and are wise; and every tone is so very apparent in his or her temperament and taste is so good and so foolish and all taste is worth its modicum of moments.

Around comes the white-coated attendant thrusting a dog with a musical inside at you.

"I just love those little joyous animals," gush the Van Allens, and the white attendant passes on, the basket of furry folk held out in front of him.

Some one says something about the types of women that find their way into the atmosphere. Each hour has its particular type— those who come in the beginning and care so much, those who come behind and care less, and those who come in almost too late to have made it seem worth while. There is the couple that comes in at 8.30 sharp, intent upon getting all that's to be got; like a boy at a circus; those who come at 10.30 and dawdle with a glass of something; those who come in from 11 to 12, not even deceptive in their care-less ease.

The real element knows its garden so well that if blindness found them suddenly they could walk with their hands behind them up to a particular table; could, still with their hands behind them, pick out a particular chair, and in the end could find the floor. These men may range from banker to mere journalist, but the woman who comes with them is languid, impressive, wears long, lassitudinous side curls, and strings the contour of her face to the sharp-pitched key of a large expanse of white forehead and a sudden downward wave of well ordered hair. She is essentially crepe; she moves in long, pa-thetic lines; she is boldly conscious of large hands and ample feet— she has even made them fashionable by endlessly displaying them with a studied simplicity.

A lot of anything can become fashionable if one gets used to it— even the Rosetti neck.

She is called the "dangerous woman." She likes the name, and she has made the most of it. The pillar of fame is her background; the best possibilities in an ordinary future are hers to do with as the small woman may not. One expects to see Juno pluck grapes——

She doesn't make a good talker, but he does not wish to talk. She makes few attempts, because she knows that what looked good in Shakespeare's eyes as a quality to be desired in woman is still good.

"You mustn't take any more of that curry," she tells him, her chin in her palm; "it's too late at night." Thus she has even his dreams in mind.

"It won't hurt me."

She shrugs and, chin still in hand, turns away. He shouldn't feel rebuked, but he does. He knows that the things that may be in an ordinary mind about the effects of curry are doubly full of import in the mind of the dangerous woman. He takes the fork out and lays it across the plate from rim to rim. He has not given up. He's given in.

He could find it in his heart to love her if she would yearn, but she won't. He could become eloquent if she were roguish, but she isn't.

We have all seen her trimphant, sitting high over the tide of lesser beings, a passage to the deeper sea, brooding over the moonlight, queen in her nautical learning, smiling still.

The Miss Van Allens have spotted her long since; they have taken in the shape of her head, the way she does her hair, the exact whole, separately and collectively, they turn to each other and feign horror, and in their mental notes they don't forget.

Women are supreme when it comes to getting back to—shall we say?—supper. If she does nothing else well, this at least she does magnificently. She will leave, thereby making it necessary for the man in the case to leave also, the most picturesque little order of a salad, even if it is lobster in its most excruciating intimacy; she will arise and walk slowly away from the most ravishing pasties and the most vitally tempting glasses of something; she will abandon the best of a bird delayed in its flight; leave it all languidly to go through the mazes of some new step, and finally come back to it coldly, as though she had never known that it existed, or, rather, as if it did not matter whether it existed or not.

And yet of a certainty she is the hungriest thing in the whole of creation!

And then, too, she is as illogical as usual.

"Where is the roof?" she says, stepping out of the elevator and casting her eyes up toward the perfectly substantial roof of lights and twining flowers.

"We're on it now," he assures her, leading her by the elbow to a seat near the red ropes leading from the Dollys' dressing room; she can see the inimitable Sebastian rush on with the whole of a girl in his arms and dance like a Spaniard of old, with the burden material of his love.

"But I don't see the sky," she insists, puffing her three rows of silk girdle about her hips and breaking the paper around the tip of her fan. "I don't see a single piece of sky."

"The sky hasn't come out yet," he returns, beckoning the waiter, who has already insinuated them into place around the symmetry of one of the thousand little green tables.

"You see, this is a place where people come to enjoy themselves."

"Well?"

"Well, you can't, if the sky and mosquitoes get in."

"Yes, but this is a roof garden."

"Well, a roof garden can have a roof, can't it?"

Subsiding, she looks at him as though it were all his fault, which it is partly; for, ten to one, if only women visited roof gardens there would be no roof to the garden. Even if it rained buckets they would prefer to sit under individual umbrellas and soak themselves in the truth of the thing to the very letter.

Therefore, having talked about the dresses, which never seem to please two people alike, and having remarked on some hat and upon some coiffure, and having left the champagne bucket unnoticed upon the floor, and having taken their fair share of the dances, she accepts it, in its good and its bad points, and is humanly sweet about it to him who has disappointed her. She is loyal ever after, as a fact, and brings huddles of other women to see it and explains nonchalantly all the things she could not understand, and is one more of those who can come in without looking interested—the very essence of refinement.

But there's some one who has got them all beaten, for love of life—little, dark-faced, handsome-eyed, lithe Don Carlos Sebastian with palpitating Dolly in his arms. Breaking through the roses of the flowering arch, stampeding onto the floor, round and round he whirls, laughing, exuberant, bursting with life, throwing all of a passionate race's feeling into a passionate dance, and the morsel of French in the morsel of silk clings to him and springs away and laughs, too, and grows reckless in his recklessness, and is thrown from foot to foot and balance to balance in a wild movement-loving whirl.

And there they sit, by Jove, the onlookers, and are commonplacedly interested and say they wonder what the man is saying who gets up to announce the prize winners; and finally the woman glides off in front, coaxing a tired man into just one more step.

Oh, well, it's an awfully jolly thing to be able to dance and to watch others dance; and the roof could come off if you wanted it to, and you loyally don't.

*NEW YORK PRESS,* 1914

# EDNA ST. VINCENT MILLAY

*Edna St. Vincent Millay (1892–1950) was a legend during the 1920's, a poetic magnet of Greenwich Village. Her "Recuerdo" became the anthem for aspiring bohemians, and her line "My candle burns at both ends" their motto. She was a tough, resilient formalist, about whom her admirer Edmund Wilson wrote: "What was impressive and rather unsettling when she read such poems aloud was her power of imposing herself on others through a medium that unburdened the emotions of solitude."*

If I should learn, in some quite casual way,
    That you were gone, not to return again—
Read from the back-page of a paper, say,
    Held by a neighbor in a subway train,
How at the corner of this avenue
    And such a street (so are the papers filled)
A hurrying man—who happened to be you—
    At noon to-day had happened to be killed,
I should not cry aloud—I could not cry
    Aloud, or wring my hands in such a place—
I should but watch the station lights rush by
    With a more careful interest on my face,
Or raise my eyes and read with greater care
Where to store furs and how to treat the hair.

1916

## RECUERDO

We were very tired, we were very merry—
We had gone back and forth all night on the ferry.
It was bare and bright, and smelled like a stable—
But we looked into a fire, we leaned across a table,
We lay on the hill-top underneath the moon;
And the whistles kept blowing, and the dawn came soon.

We were very tired, we were very merry—
We had gone back and forth all night on the ferry;
And you ate an apple, and I ate a pear,
From a dozen of each we had bought somewhere;
And the sky went wan, and the wind came cold,
And the sun rose dripping, a bucketful of gold.

We were very tired, we were very merry,
We had gone back and forth all night on the ferry.
We hailed, "Good morrow, mother!" to a shawl-covered head,
And bought a morning paper, which neither of us read;
And she wept, "God bless you!" for the apples and the pears,
And we gave her all our money but our subway fares.

1919

# WILLA CATHER

*Willa Cather (1873–1947) wrote her greatest novels of the prairie and the Southwest in a small house on Bank Street in Greenwich Village. She rarely portrayed the city around her, though there are passages in* My Mortal Enemy *and the shorter fiction that touch on her adopted home. Her most "New York" piece is the marvelous "Coming, Aphrodite!" This long story has some of the spacious unhurriedness of her prairie novels, along with a keen feeling for the density of contiguous lives in a Greenwich Village walkup. On the other side of the wall might be an infuriatingly noisy neighbor, or the girl of one's dreams.*

## COMING, APHRODITE!

### I

DON HEDGER had lived for four years on the top floor of an old house on the south side of Washington Square, and nobody had ever disturbed him. He occupied one big room with no outside exposure except on the north, where he had built in a many-paned studio window that looked upon a court and upon the roofs and walls of other buildings. His room was very cheerless, since he never got a ray of direct sunlight; the south corners were always in shadow. In one of the corners was a clothes closet, built against the partition, in another a wide divan, serving as a seat by day and a bed by night. In the front corner, the one farther from the window, was a sink, and a table with two gas burners where he sometimes cooked his food. There, too, in the perpetual dusk, was the dog's bed, and often a bone or two for his comfort.

The dog was a Boston bull terrier, and Hedger explained his surly disposition by the fact that he had been bred to the point where it told on his nerves. His name was Caesar III, and he had taken prizes at very exclusive dog shows. When he and his master went out to prowl about University Place or to promenade along West Street, Caesar III was invariably fresh and shining. His pink skin showed through his mottled coat, which glistened as if it had just been rubbed with olive oil, and he wore a brass-studded collar, bought at the smartest saddler's. Hedger, as often as not, was hunched up in an old striped blanket coat, with a shapeless felt hat pulled over his bushy hair, wearing black shoes that had become grey, or brown ones that had become black, and he never put on gloves unless the day was biting cold.

Early in May, Hedger learned that he was to have a new neighbour in the rear apartment—two rooms, one large and one small, that faced the west. His studio was shut off from the larger of these rooms by double doors, which, though they were fairly tight, left him a good deal at the mercy of the occupant. The rooms had been leased, long before he came there, by a trained nurse who considered herself knowing in old furniture. She went to auction sales and bought up mahogany and dirty brass and stored it away here, where she meant to live when she retired from nursing. Meanwhile, she sub-let her rooms, with their precious furniture, to young people who came to New York to "write" or to "paint"—who proposed to live by the sweat of the brow rather than of the hand, and who desired artistic surroundings. When Hedger first moved in, these rooms were occupied by a young man who tried to write plays,— and who kept on trying until a week ago, when the nurse had put him out for unpaid rent.

A few days after the playwright left, Hedger heard an ominous murmur of voices through the bolted double doors: the lady-like intonation of the nurse—doubtless exhibiting her treasures—and another voice, also a woman's, but very different; young, fresh, unguarded, confident. All the same, it would be very annoying to have a woman in there. The only bath-room on the floor was at the top of the stairs in the front hall, and he would always be running into her as he came or went from his bath. He would have to be more careful to see that Caesar didn't leave bones about the hall, too; and she might object when he cooked steak and onions on his gas burner.

As soon as the talking ceased and the women left, he forgot them. He was absorbed in a study of paradise fish at the Aquarium, staring out at people through the glass and green water of their tank. It was a highly gratifying idea; the incommunicability of one stratum of animal life with another,—though Hedger pretended it was only an experiment in unusual lighting. When he heard trunks knocking against the sides of the narrow hall, then he realized that she was moving in at once. Toward noon, groans and deep gasps and the creaking of ropes, made him aware that a piano was arriving. After the tramp of the movers died away down the stairs, somebody touched off a few scales and chords on the instrument, and then there was peace. Presently he heard her lock her door and go down the hall humming something; going out to lunch, probably. He stuck his brushes in a can of turpentine and put on his hat, not stopping to wash his hands. Caesar was smelling along the crack under the bolted doors; his bony tail stuck out hard as a hickory withe, and the hair was standing up about his elegant collar.

Hedger encouraged him. "Come along, Caesar. You'll soon get used to a new smell."

In the hall stood an enormous trunk, behind the ladder that led to the roof, just opposite Hedger's door. The dog flew at it with a growl of hurt amazement. They went down three flights of stairs and out into the brilliant May afternoon.

Behind the Square, Hedger and his dog descended into a basement oyster house where there were no tablecloths on the tables and no handles on the coffee cups, and the floor was covered with sawdust, and Caesar was always welcome,—not that he needed any such precautionary flooring. All the carpets of Persia would have been safe for him. Hedger ordered steak and onions absentmindedly, not realizing why he had an apprehension that this dish might be less readily at hand hereafter. While he ate, Caesar sat beside his chair, gravely disturbing the sawdust with his tail.

After lunch Hedger strolled about the Square for the dog's health and watched the stages pull out;—that was almost the very last summer of the old horse stages on Fifth Avenue. The fountain had but lately begun operations for the season and was throwing up a mist of rainbow water which now and then blew south and sprayed a bunch of Italian babies that were being supported on the outer rim by older, very little older, brothers and sisters. Plump robins were hopping about on the soil; the grass was newly cut and blindly green. Looking up the Avenue through the Arch, one could see the young poplars with their bright, sticky leaves, and the Brevoort glistening in its spring coat of paint, and shining horses and carriages,—occasionally an automobile, mis-shapen and sullen, like an ugly threat in a stream of things that were bright and beautiful and alive.

While Caesar and his master were standing by the fountain, a girl approached them, crossing the Square. Hedger noticed her because she wore a lavender cloth suit and carried in her arms a big bunch of fresh lilacs. He saw that she was young and handsome,—beautiful, in fact, with a splendid figure and good action. She, too, paused by the fountain and looked back through the Arch up the Avenue. She smiled rather patronizingly as she looked, and at the same time seemed delighted. Her slowly curving upper lip and half-closed eyes seemed to say: "You're gay, you're exciting, you are quite the right sort of thing; but you're none too fine for me!"

In the moment she tarried, Caesar stealthily approached her and sniffed at the hem of her lavender skirt, then, when she went south like an arrow, he ran back to his master and lifted a face full of emotion and alarm, his lower lip twitching under his sharp white teeth and his hazel eyes pointed with a very definite discovery. He stood thus, motionless, while Hedger watched the lavender girl go up the steps and through the door of the house in which he lived.

"You're right, my boy, it's she! She might be worse looking, you know."

When they mounted to the studio, the new lodger's door, at the back of the hall, was a little ajar, and Hedger caught the warm perfume of lilacs just brought in out of the sun. He was used to the musty smell of the old hall carpet. (The nurse-lessee had once knocked at his studio door and complained that Caesar must be somewhat responsible for the particular flavour of that mustiness, and Hedger had never spoken to her since.) He was used to the old smell, and he preferred it to that of the lilacs, and so did his companion, whose nose was so much more discriminating. Hedger shut his door vehemently, and fell to work.

Most young men who dwell in obscure studios in New York have had a beginning, come out of something, have somewhere a home town, a family, a paternal roof. But Don Hedger had no such background. He was a foundling, and had grown up in a school for homeless boys, where book-learning was a negligible part of the curriculum. When he was sixteen, a Catholic priest took him to Greensburg, Pennsylvania, to keep house for him. The priest did something to fill in the large gaps in the boy's education,—taught him to like "Don Quixote" and "The Golden Legend," and encouraged him to mess with paints and crayons in his room up under the slope of the mansard. When Don wanted to go to New York to study at the Art League, the priest got him a night job as packer in one of the big department stores. Since then, Hedger had taken care of himself; that was his only responsibility. He was singularly unencumbered; had no family duties, no social ties, no obligations toward any one but his landlord. Since he travelled light, he had travelled rather far. He had got over a good deal of the earth's surface, in spite of the fact that he never in his life had more than three hundred dollars ahead at any one time, and he had already outlived a succession of convictions and revelations about his art.

Though he was now but twenty-six years old, he had twice been on the verge of becoming a marketable product; once through some studies of New York streets he did for a magazine, and once through a collection of pastels he brought home from New Mexico, which Remington, then at the height of his popularity, happened to see, and generously tried to push. But on both occasions Hedger decided that this was something he didn't wish to carry further,—simply the old thing over again and got nowhere,—so he took enquiring dealers experiments in a "later manner," that made them put him out of the shop. When he ran short of money, he could always get any amount of commercial work; he was an expert draughtsman and worked with lightning speed. The rest of his time he spent in groping his way from one kind of painting into another, or travelling about without luggage, like a tramp, and he was chiefly occupied with getting rid of ideas he had once thought very fine.

Hedger's circumstances, since he had moved to Washington

Square, were affluent compared to anything he had ever known before. He was now able to pay advance rent and turn the key on his studio when he went away for four months at a stretch. It didn't occur to him to wish to be richer than this. To be sure, he did without a great many things other people think necessary, but he didn't miss them, because he had never had them. He belonged to no clubs, visited no houses, had no studio friends, and he ate his dinner alone in some decent little restaurant, even on Christmas and New Year's. For days together he talked to nobody but his dog and the janitress and the lame oysterman.

After he shut the door and settled down to his paradise fish on that first Tuesday in May, Hedger forgot all about his new neighbour. When the light failed, he took Caesar out for a walk. On the way home he did his marketing on West Houston Street, with a one-eyed Italian woman who always cheated him. After he had cooked his beans and scallopini, and drunk half a bottle of Chianti, he put his dishes in the sink and went up on the roof to smoke. He was the only person in the house who ever went to the roof, and he had a secret understanding with the janitress about it. He was to have "the privilege of the roof," as she said, if he opened the heavy trapdoor on sunny days to air out the upper hall, and was watchful to close it when rain threatened. Mrs. Foley was fat and dirty and hated to climb stairs,— besides, the roof was reached by a perpendicular iron ladder, definitely inaccessible to a woman of her bulk, and the iron door at the top of it was too heavy for any but Hedger's strong arm to lift. Hedger was not above medium height, but he practised with weights and dumb-bells, and in the shoulders he was as strong as a gorilla.

So Hedger had the roof to himself. He and Caesar often slept up there on hot nights, rolled in blankets he had brought home from Arizona. He mounted with Caesar under his left arm. The dog had never learned to climb a perpendicular ladder, and never did he feel so much his master's greatness and his own dependence upon him, as when he crept under his arm for this perilous ascent. Up there was even gravel to scratch in, and a dog could do whatever he liked, so long as he did not bark. It was a kind of Heaven, which no one was strong enough to reach but his great, paint-smelling master.

On this blue May night there was a slender, girlish looking young moon in the west, playing with a whole company of silver stars. Now and then one of them darted away from the group and shot off into the gauzy blue with a soft little trail of light, like laughter. Hedger and his dog were delighted when a star did this. They were quite lost in watching the glittering game, when they were suddenly diverted by a sound,—not from the stars, though it was music. It was not the Prologue to Pagliacci, which rose ever and anon on hot evenings from an Italian tenement on Thompson Street, with the gasps of the corpulent baritone who got behind it; nor was it the hurdy-gurdy man, who often played at the corner in the balmy twilight. No, this was a woman's voice, singing the tempestuous, over-lapping phrases of Signor Puccini, then comparatively new in the world, but already so popular that even Hedger recognized his unmistakable gusts of breath. He looked about over the roofs; all was blue and still, with the well-built chimneys that were never used now standing up dark and mournful. He moved softly toward the yellow quadrangle where the gas from the hall shone up through the half-lifted trapdoor. Oh yes! It came up through the hole like a strong draught, a big, beautiful voice, and it sounded rather like a professional's. A piano had arrived in the morning, Hedger remembered. This might be a very great nuisance. It would be pleasant enough to listen to, if you could turn it on and off as you wished; but you couldn't. Caesar, with the gas light shining on his collar and his ugly but sensitive face, panted and looked up for information. Hedger put down a reassuring hand.

"I don't know. We can't tell yet. It may not be so bad."

He stayed on the roof until all was still below, and finally descended, with quite a new feeling about his neighbour. Her voice, like her figure, inspired respect,—if one did not choose to call it admiration. Her door was shut, the transom was dark; nothing remained of her but the obtrusive trunk, unrightfully taking up room in the narrow hall.

II

For two days Hedger didn't see her. He was painting eight hours a day just then, and only went out to hunt for food. He noticed that she practised scales and exercises for about an hour in the morning; then she locked her door, went humming down the hall, and left him in peace. He heard her getting her coffee ready at about the same time he got his. Earlier still, she passed his room on her way to her bath. In the evening she sometimes sang, but on the whole she didn't bother him. When he was working well he did not notice anything much. The morning paper lay before his door until he reached out for his milk bottle, then he kicked the sheet inside and it lay on the floor until evening. Sometimes he read it and sometimes he did not. He forgot there was anything of importance going on in the world outside of his third floor studio. Nobody had ever taught him that he ought to be interested in other people; in the Pittsburgh steel strike, in the Fresh Air Fund, in the scandal about the Babies' Hospital. A grey wolf, living in a Wyoming canyon, would hardly have been less concerned about these things than was Don Hedger.

One morning he was coming out of the bathroom at the front end of the hall, having just given Caesar his bath and rubbed him into a glow with a heavy towel. Before the door, lying in wait for him, as it were, stood a tall figure in a flowing blue silk dressing gown that fell away from her marble arms. In her hands she carried various accessories of the bath.

"I wish," she said distinctly, standing in his way, "I wish you wouldn't wash your dog in the tub. I never heard of such a thing! I've found his hair in the tub, and I've smelled a doggy smell, and now I've caught you at it. It's an outrage!"

Hedger was badly frightened. She was so tall and positive, and was fairly blazing with beauty and anger. He stood blinking, holding on to his sponge and dog-soap, feeling that he ought to bow very low to her. But what he actually said was:

"Nobody has ever objected before. I always wash the tub,—and, anyhow, he's cleaner than most people."

"Cleaner than me?" her eyebrows went up, her white arms and neck and her fragrant person seemed to scream at him like a band of outraged nymphs. Something flashed through his mind about a man who was turned into a dog, or was pursued by dogs, because he unwittingly intruded upon the bath of beauty.

"No, I didn't mean that," he muttered, turning scarlet under the bluish stubble of his muscular jaws. "But I know he's cleaner than I am."

"That I don't doubt!" Her voice sounded like a soft shivering of crystal, and with a smile of pity she drew the folds of her voluminous blue robe close about her and allowed the wretched man to pass. Even Caesar was frightened; he darted like a streak down the hall, through the door and to his own bed in the corner among the bones.

Hedger stood still in the doorway, listening to indignant sniffs and coughs and a great swishing of water about the sides of the tub. He had washed it; but as he had washed it with Caesar's sponge, it was quite possible that a few bristles remained; the dog was shedding now. The playwright had never objected, nor had the jovial illustrator who occupied the front apartment,—but he, as he admitted, "was usually pye-eyed, when he wasn't in Buffalo." He went home to Buffalo sometimes to rest his nerves.

It had never occurred to Hedger that any one would mind using the tub after Caesar;—but then, he had never seen a beautiful girl caparisoned for the bath before. As soon as he beheld her standing there, he realized the unfitness of it. For that matter, she ought not to step into a tub that any other mortal had bathed in; the illustrator was sloppy and left cigarette ends on the moulding.

All morning as he worked he was gnawed by a spiteful desire to get back at her. It rankled that he had been so vanquished by her disdain. When he heard her locking her door to go out for lunch, he stepped quickly into the hall in his messy painting coat, and addressed her.

"I don't wish to be exigent, Miss,"—he had certain grand words that he used upon occasion—"but if this is your trunk, it's rather in the way here."

"Oh, very well!" she exclaimed carelessly, dropping her keys into her handbag. "I'll have it moved when I can get a man to do it," and she went down the hall with her free, roving stride.

Her name, Hedger discovered from her letters, which the post-man left on the table in the lower hall, was Eden Bower.

### III

In the closet that was built against the partition separating his room from Miss Bower's, Hedger kept all his wearing apparel, some of it on hooks and hangers, some of it on the floor. When he opened his closet door now-a-days, little dust-coloured insects flew out on downy wing, and he suspected that a brood of moths were hatching in his winter overcoat. Mrs. Foley, the janitress, told him to bring down all his heavy clothes and she would give them a beating and hang them in the court. The closet was in such disorder that he shunned the encounter, but one hot afternoon he set himself to the task. First he threw out a pile of forgotten laundry and tied it up in a sheet. The bundle stood as high as his middle when he had knotted the corners. Then he got his shoes and overshoes together. When he took his overcoat from its place against the partition, a long ray of yellow light shot across the dark enclosure,—a knot hole, evidently, in the high wainscoting of the west room. He had never noticed it before, and without realizing what he was doing, he stooped and squinted through it.

Yonder, in a pool of sunlight, stood his new neighbour, wholly unclad, doing exercises of some sort before a long gilt mirror. Hedger did not happen to think how unpardonable it was of him to watch her. Nudity was not improper to any one who had worked so much from the figure, and he continued to look, simply because he had never seen a woman's body so beautiful as this one,—positively glorious in action. As she swung her arms and changed from one pivot of motion to another, muscular energy seemed to flow through her from her toes to her finger-tips. The soft flush of exercise and the gold of afternoon sun played over her flesh together, enveloped her in a luminous mist which, as she turned and twisted, made now an arm, now a shoulder, now a thigh, dissolve in pure light and instantly recover its outline with the next gesture. Hedger's fingers curved as if he were holding a crayon; mentally he was doing the whole figure in a single running line, and the charcoal seemed to explode in his hand at the point where the energy of each gesture was discharged into the whirling disc of light, from a foot or shoulder, from the up-thrust chin or the lifted breasts.

He could not have told whether he watched her for six minutes or sixteen. When her gymnastics were over, she paused to catch up a lock of hair that had come down, and examined with solicitude a little reddish mole that grew under her left arm-pit. Then, with her hand on her hip, she walked unconcernedly across the room and disappeared through the door into her bedchamber.

Disappeared—Don Hedger was crouching on his knees, staring at the golden shower which poured in through the west windows, at the lake of gold sleeping on the faded Turkish carpet. The spot was enchanted; a vision out of Alexandria, out of the remote pagan past, had bathed itself there in Helianthine fire.

When he crawled out of his closet, he stood blinking at the grey sheet stuffed with laundry, not knowing what had happened to him. He felt a little sick as he contemplated the bundle. Everything here was different; he hated the disorder of the place, the grey prison light, his old shoes and himself and all his slovenly habits. The black calico curtains that ran on wires over his big window were white with dust. There were three greasy frying pans in the sink, and the sink itself— He felt desperate. He couldn't stand this another minute. He took up an armful of winter clothes and ran down four flights into the basement.

"Mrs. Foley," he began, "I want my room cleaned this afternoon, thoroughly cleaned. Can you get a woman for me right away?"

"Is it company you're having?" the fat, dirty janitress enquired. Mrs. Foley was the widow of a useful Tammany man, and she owned real estate in Flatbush. She was huge and soft as a feather bed. Her face and arms were permanently coated with dust, grained like wood where the sweat had trickled.

"Yes, company. That's it."

"Well, this is a queer time of the day to be asking for a cleaning woman. It's likely I can get you old Lizzie, if she's not drunk. I'll send Willy round to see."

Willy, the son of fourteen, roused from the stupor and stain of his fifth box of cigarettes by the gleam of a quarter, went out. In five minutes he returned with old Lizzie,—she smelling strong of spirits and wearing several jackets which she had put on one over the other, and a number of skirts, long and short, which made her resemble an animated dish-clout. She had, of course, to borrow her equipment from Mrs. Foley, and toiled up the long flights, dragging mop and pail and broom. She told Hedger to be of good cheer, for he had got the right woman for the job, and showed him a great leather strap she wore about her wrist to prevent dislocation of tendons. She swished about the place, scattering dust and splashing soapsuds, while he watched her in nervous despair. He stood over Lizzie and made her scour the sink, directing her roughly, then paid her and got rid of her. Shutting the door on his failure, he hurried off with his dog to lose himself among the stevedores and dock labourers on West Street.

A strange chapter began for Don Hedger. Day after day, at that hour in the afternoon, the hour before his neighbour dressed for dinner, he crouched down in his closet to watch her go through her mysterious exercises. It did not occur to him that his conduct was detestable; there was nothing shy or retreating about this unclad girl,—a bold body, studying itself quite coolly and evidently well pleased with itself, doing all this for a purpose. Hedger scarcely regarded his action as conduct at all; it was something that had happened to him. More than once he went out and tried to stay away for the whole afternoon, but at about five o'clock he was sure to find himself among his old shoes in the dark. The pull of that aperture was stronger than his will,—and he had always considered his will the strongest thing about him. When she threw herself upon the divan and lay resting, he still stared, holding his breath. His nerves were so on edge that a sudden noise made him start and brought out the sweat on his forehead. The dog would come and tug at his sleeve, knowing that something was wrong with his master. If he attempted a mournful whine, those strong hands closed about his throat.

When Hedger came slinking out of his closet, he sat down on the edge of the couch, sat for hours without moving. He was not painting at all now. This thing, whatever it was, drank him up as ideas had sometimes done, and he sank into a stupor of idleness as deep and dark as the stupor of work. He could not understand it; he was no boy, he had worked from models for years, and a woman's body was no mystery to him. Yet now he did nothing but sit and think about one. He slept very little, and with the first light of morning he awoke as completely possessed by this woman as if he had been with her all the night before. The unconscious operations of life went on in him only to perpetuate this excitement. His brain held but one image now—vibrated, burned with it. It was a heathenish feeling; without friendliness, almost without tenderness.

Women had come and gone in Hedger's life. Not having had a mother to begin with, his relations with them, whether amorous or friendly, had been casual. He got on well with janitresses and wash-women, with Indians and with the peasant women of foreign countries. He had friends among the silk-skirt factory girls who came to eat their lunch in Washington Square, and he sometimes took a model for a day in the country. He felt an unreasoning antipathy toward the well-dressed women he saw coming out of big shops, or driving in the Park. If, on his way to the Art Museum, he noticed a pretty girl standing on the steps of one of the houses on upper Fifth Avenue, he frowned at her and went by with his shoulders hunched up as if he were cold. He had never known such girls, or heard them talk, or seen the inside of the houses in which they lived; but he believed them all to be artificial and, in an aesthetic sense, perverted. He saw them enslaved by desire of merchandise and manufactured articles, effective only in making life complicated and insincere and in embroidering it with ugly and meaningless trivialities. They were enough, he thought, to make one almost forget woman as she existed in art, in thought, and in the universe.

He had no desire to know the woman who had, for the time at least, so broken up his life,—no curiosity about her every-day personality. He shunned any revelation of it, and he listened for Miss Bower's coming and going, not to encounter, but to avoid her. He wished that the girl who wore shirt-waists and got letters from Chicago would keep out of his way, that she did not exist. With her he had naught to make. But in a room full of sun, before an old mirror, on a little enchanted rug of sleeping colours, he had seen a woman who emerged naked through a door, and disappeared naked. He thought of that body as never having been clad, or as having worn the stuffs and dyes of all the centuries but his own. And for him she had no geographical associations; unless with Crete, or Alexandria, or Veronese's Venice. She was the immortal conception, the perennial theme.

The first break in Hedger's lethargy occurred one afternoon when two young men came to take Eden Bower out to dine. They went into her music room, laughed and talked for a few minutes, and then took her away with them. They were gone a long while, but he did not go out for food himself; he waited for them to come back. At last he heard them coming down the hall, gayer and more talkative than when they left. One of them sat down at the piano, and they all began to sing. This Hedger found absolutely unendurable. He snatched up his hat and went running down the stairs. Caesar leaped beside him, hoping that old times were coming back. They had supper in the oysterman's basement and then sat down in front of their own doorway. The moon stood full over the Square, a thing of regal glory; but Hedger did not see the moon; he was looking, murderously, for men. Presently two, wearing straw hats and white trousers and carrying canes, came down the steps from his house. He rose and dogged them across the Square. They were laughing and seemed very much elated about something. As one stopped to light a cigarette, Hedger caught from the other:

"Don't you think she has a beautiful talent?"

His companion threw away his match. "She has a beautiful figure." They both ran to catch the stage.

Hedger went back to his studio. The light was shining from her transom. For the first time he violated her privacy at night, and peered through that fatal aperture. She was sitting, fully dressed, in the window, smoking a cigarette and looking out over the housetops. He watched her until she rose, looked about her with a disdainful, crafty smile, and turned out the light.

The next morning, when Miss Bower went out, Hedger followed her. Her white skirt gleamed ahead of him as she sauntered about the

Square. She sat down behind the Garibaldi statue and opened a music book she carried. She turned the leaves carelessly, and several times glanced in his direction. He was on the point of going over to her, when she rose quickly and looked up at the sky. A flock of pigeons had risen from somewhere in the crowded Italian quarter to the south, and were wheeling rapidly up through the morning air, soaring and dropping, scattering and coming together, now grey, now white as silver, as they caught or intercepted the sunlight. She put up her hand to shade her eyes and followed them with a kind of defiant delight in her face.

Hedger came and stood beside her. "You've surely seen them before?"

"Oh, yes," she replied, still looking up. "I see them every day from my windows. They always come home about five o'clock. Where do they live?"

"I don't know. Probably some Italian raises them for the market. They were here long before I came, and I've been here four years."

"In that same gloomy room? Why didn't you take mine when it was vacant?"

"It isn't gloomy. That's the best light for painting."

"Oh, is it? I don't know anything about painting. I'd like to see your pictures sometime. You have such a lot in there. Don't they get dusty, piled up against the wall like that?"

"Not very. I'd be glad to show them to you. Is your name really Eden Bower? I've seen your letters on the table."

"Well, it's the name I'm going to sing under. My father's name is Bowers, but my friend Mr. Jones, a Chicago newspaper man who writes about music, told me to drop the 's.' He's crazy about my voice."

Miss Bower didn't usually tell the whole story,—about anything. Her first name, when she lived in Huntington, Illinois, was Edna, but Mr. Jones had persuaded her to change it to one which he felt would be worthy of her future. She was quick to take suggestions, though she told him she "didn't see what was the matter with 'Edna.'"

She explained to Hedger that she was going to Paris to study. She was waiting in New York for Chicago friends who were to take her over, but who had been detained. "Did you study in Paris?" she asked.

"No, I've never been in Paris. But I was in the south of France all last summer, studying with C———. He's the biggest man among the moderns,—at least I think so."

Miss Bower sat down and made room for him on the bench. "Do tell me about it. I expected to be there by this time, and I can't wait to find out what it's like."

Hedger began to relate how he had seen some of this Frenchman's work in an exhibition, and deciding at once that this was the man for him, he had taken a boat for Marseilles the next week, going over steerage. He proceeded at once to the little town on the coast where his painter lived, and presented himself. The man never took pupils, but because Hedger had come so far, he let him stay. Hedger lived at the master's house and every day they went out together to paint, sometimes on the blazing rocks down by the sea. They wrapped themselves in light woollen blankets and didn't feel the heat. Being there and working with C——— was being in Paradise, Hedger concluded; he learned more in three months than in all his life before.

Eden Bower laughed. "You're a funny fellow. Didn't you do anything but work? Are the women very beautiful? Did you have awfully good things to eat and drink?"

Hedger said some of the women were fine looking, especially one girl who went about selling fish and lobsters. About the food there was nothing remarkable,—except the ripe figs, he liked those. They drank sour wine, and used goat-butter, which was strong and full of hair, as it was churned in a goat skin.

"But don't they have parties or banquets? Aren't there any fine hotels down there?"

"Yes, but they are all closed in summer, and the country people are poor. It's a beautiful country, though."

"How, beautiful?" she persisted.

"If you want to go in, I'll show you some sketches, and you'll see."

Miss Bower rose. "All right. I won't go to my fencing lesson this morning. Do you fence? Here comes your dog. You can't move but he's after you. He always makes a face at me when I meet him in the hall, and shows his nasty little teeth as if he wanted to bite me."

In the studio Hedger got out his sketches, but to Miss Bower, whose favourite pictures were Christ Before Pilate and a redhaired Magdalen of Henner, these landscapes were not at all beautiful, and they gave her no idea of any country whatsoever. She was careful not to commit herself, however. Her vocal teacher had already convinced her that she had a great deal to learn about many things.

"Why don't we go out to lunch somewhere?" Hedger asked, and began to dust his fingers with a handkerchief—which he got out of sight as swiftly as possible.

"All right, the Brevoort," she said carelessly. "I think that's a good place, and they have good wine. I don't care for cocktails."

Hedger felt his chin uneasily. "I'm afraid I haven't shaved this morning. If you could wait for me in the Square? It won't take me ten minutes."

Left alone, he found a clean collar and handkerchief, brushed his coat and blacked his shoes, and last of all dug up ten dollars from the bottom of an old copper kettle he had brought from Spain. His winter hat was of such a complexion that the Brevoort hall boy winked at the porter as he took it and placed it on the rack in a row of fresh straw ones.

IV

That afternoon Eden Bower was lying on the couch in her music room, her face turned to the window, watching the pigeons. Reclining thus she could see none of the neighbouring roofs, only the sky itself and the birds that crossed and recrossed her field of vision, white as scraps of paper blowing in the wind. She was thinking that she was young and handsome and had had a good lunch, that a very easy-going, light-hearted city lay in the streets below her; and she was wondering why she found this queer painter chap, with his lean, bluish cheeks and heavy black eyebrows, more interesting than the smart young men she met at her teacher's studio.

Eden Bower was, at twenty, very much the same person that we all know her to be at forty, except that she knew a great deal less.

But one thing she knew: that she was to be Eden Bower. She was like some one standing before a great show window full of beautiful and costly things, deciding which she will order. She understands that they will not all be delivered immediately, but one by one they will arrive at her door. She already knew some of the many things that were to happen to her; for instance, that the Chicago millionaire who was going to take her abroad with his sister as chaperone, would eventually press his claim in quite another manner. He was the most circumspect of bachelors, afraid of everything obvious, even of women who were too flagrantly handsome. He was a nervous collector of pictures and furniture, a nervous patron of music, and a nervous host; very cautious about his health, and about any course of conduct that might make him ridiculous. But she knew that he would at last throw all his precautions to the winds.

People like Eden Bower are inexplicable. Her father sold farming machinery in Huntington, Illinois, and she had grown up with no acquaintances or experiences outside of that prairie town. Yet from her earliest childhood she had not one conviction or opinion in common with the people about her,—the only people she knew. Before she was out of short dresses she had made up her mind that she was going to be an actress, that she would live far away in great cities, that she would be much admired by men and would have everything she wanted. When she was thirteen, and was already singing and reciting for church entertainments, she read in some illustrated magazine a long article about the late Czar of Russia, then just come to the throne or about to come to it. After that, lying in the hammock on the front porch on summer evenings, or sitting through a long sermon in the family pew, she amused herself by trying to make up her mind whether she would or would not be the Czar's mistress when she played in his Capital. Now Edna had met this fascinating word only in the novels of Ouida,—her hard-worked little mother kept a long row of them in the upstairs storeroom, behind the linen chest. In Huntington, women who bore that relation to men were called by a very different name, and their lot was not an enviable one; of all the shabby and poor, they were the shabbiest. But then, Edna had never lived in Huntington, not even before she began to find books like "Sapho" and "Mademoiselle de Maupin," secretly sold in paper covers throughout Illinois. It was as if she had come into Huntington, into the Bowers family, on one of the trains that puffed over the marshes behind their back fence all day long, and was waiting for another train to take her out.

As she grew older and handsomer, she had many beaux, but these small-town boys didn't interest her. If a lad kissed her when he brought her home from a dance, she was indulgent and she rather liked it. But if he pressed her further, she slipped away from him, laughing. After she began to sing in Chicago, she was consistently discreet. She stayed as a guest in rich people's houses, and she knew that she was being watched like a rabbit in a laboratory. Covered up in bed, with the lights out, she thought her own thoughts, and laughed.

This summer in New York was her first taste of freedom. The Chicago capitalist, after all his arrangements were made for sailing, had been compelled to go to Mexico to look after oil interests. His sister knew an excellent singing master in New York. Why should not a discreet, well-balanced girl like Miss Bower spend the summer there, studying quietly? The capitalist suggested that his sister might enjoy a summer on Long Island; he would rent the Griffiths' place for her, with all the servants, and Eden could stay there. But his sister met this proposal with a cold stare. So it fell out, that between selfishness and greed, Eden got a summer all her own,—which really did a great deal toward making her an artist and whatever else she was afterward to become. She had time to look about, to watch without being watched; to select diamonds in one window and furs in another, to select shoulders and moustaches in the big hotels where she went to lunch. She had the easy freedom of obscurity and the consciousness of power. She enjoyed both. She was in no hurry.

While Eden Bower watched the pigeons, Don Hedger sat on the other side of the bolted doors, looking into a pool of dark turpentine, at his idle brushes, wondering why a woman could do this to him. He, too, was sure of his future and knew that he was a chosen man. He could not know, of course, that he was merely the first to fall under a fascination which was to be disastrous to a few men and pleasantly stimulating to many thousands. Each of these two young people sensed the future, but not completely. Don Hedger knew that nothing much would ever happen to him. Eden Bower understood that to her a great deal would happen. But she did not guess that her neighbour would have more tempestuous adventures sitting in his dark studio than she would find in all the capitals of Europe, or in all the latitude of conduct she was prepared to permit herself.

V

One Sunday morning Eden was crossing the Square with a spruce young man in a white flannel suit and a panama hat. They had been breakfasting at the Brevoort and he was coaxing her to let him come up to her rooms and sing for an hour.

"No, I've got to write letters. You must run along now. I see a friend of mine over there, and I want to ask him about something before I go up."

"That fellow with the dog? Where did you pick him up?" the young man glanced toward the seat under a sycamore where Hedger was reading the morning paper.

"Oh, he's an old friend from the West," said Eden easily. "I won't introduce you, because he doesn't like people. He's a recluse. Good-bye. I can't be sure about Tuesday. I'll go with you if I have time after my lesson." She nodded, left him, and went over to the seat littered with newspapers. The young man went up the Avenue without looking back.

"Well, what are you going to do today? Shampoo this animal all morning?" Eden enquired teasingly.

Hedger made room for her on the seat. "No, at twelve o'clock I'm going out to Coney Island. One of my models is going up in a balloon this afternoon. I've often promised to go and see her, and now I'm going."

Eden asked if models usually did such stunts. No, Hedger told her, but Molly Welch added to her earnings in that way. "I believe," he added, "she likes the excitement of it. She's got a good deal of spirit. That's why I like to paint her. So many models have flaccid bodies."

"And she hasn't, eh? Is she the one who comes to see you? I can't help hearing her, she talks so loud."

"Yes, she has a rough voice, but she's a fine girl. I don't suppose you'd be interested in going?"

"I don't know." Eden sat tracing patterns on the asphalt with the end of her parasol. "Is it any fun? I got up feeling I'd like to do something different today. It's the first Sunday I've not had to sing in church. I had that engagement for breakfast at the Brevoort, but it wasn't very exciting. That chap can't talk about anything but himself."

Hedger warmed a little. "If you've never been to Coney Island, you ought to go. It's nice to see all the people; tailors and bartenders and prize-fighters with their best girls, and all sorts of folks taking a holiday."

Eden looked sidewise at him. So one ought to be interested in people of that kind, ought one? He was certainly a funny fellow. Yet he was never, somehow, tiresome. She had seen a good deal of him lately, but she kept wanting to know him better, to find out what made him different from men like the one she had just left— whether he really was as different as he seemed. "I'll go with you," she said at last, "if you'll leave that at home." She pointed to Caesar's flickering ears with her sunshade.

"But he's half the fun. You'd like to hear him bark at the waves when they come in."

"No, I wouldn't. He's jealous and disagreeable if he sees you talking to any one else. Look at him now."

"Of course, if you make a face at him. He knows what that means, and he makes a worse face. He likes Molly Welch, and she'll be disappointed if I don't bring him."

Eden said decidedly that he couldn't take both of them. So at twelve o'clock when she and Hedger got on the boat at Desbrosses street, Caesar was lying on his pallet, with a bone.

Eden enjoyed the boat-ride. It was the first time she had been on the water, and she felt as if she were embarking for France. The light warm breeze and the plunge of the waves made her very wide awake, and she liked crowds of any kind. They went to the balcony of a big, noisy restaurant and had a shore dinner, with tall steins of beer. Hedger had got a big advance from his advertising firm since he first lunched with Miss Bower ten days ago, and he was ready for anything.

After dinner they went to the tent behind the bathing beach, where the tops of two balloons bulged out over the canvas. A red-faced man in a linen suit stood in front of the tent, shouting in a hoarse voice and telling the people that if the crowd was good for five dollars more, a beautiful young woman would risk her life for their entertainment. Four little boys in dirty red uniforms ran about taking contributions in their pill-box hats. One of the balloons was bobbing up and down in its tether and people were shoving forward to get nearer the tent.

"Is it dangerous, as he pretends?" Eden asked.

"Molly says it's simple enough if nothing goes wrong with the balloon. Then it would be all over, I suppose."

"Wouldn't you like to go up with her?"

"I? Of course not. I'm not fond of taking foolish risks."

Eden sniffed. "I shouldn't think sensible risks would be very much fun."

Hedger did not answer, for just then every one began to shove the other way and shout, "Look out. There she goes!" and a band of six pieces commenced playing furiously.

As the balloon rose from its tent enclosure, they saw a girl in green tights standing in the basket, holding carelessly to one of the ropes with one hand and with the other waving to the spectators. A long rope trailed behind to keep the balloon from blowing out to sea.

As it soared, the figure in green tights in the basket diminished to a mere spot, and the balloon itself, in the brilliant light, looked like a big silver-grey bat, with its wings folded. When it began to sink, the girl stepped through the hole in the basket to a trapeze that hung below, and gracefully descended through the air, holding to the rod with both hands, keeping her body taut and her feet close together. The crowd, which had grown very large by this time, cheered vociferously. The men took off their hats and waved, little boys shouted, and fat old women, shining with the heat and a beer lunch, murmured admiring comments upon the balloonist's figure. "Beautiful legs, she has!"

"That's so," Hedger whispered. "Not many girls would look well in that position." Then, for some reason, he blushed a slow, dark, painful crimson.

The balloon descended slowly, a little way from the tent, and the red-faced man in the linen suit caught Molly Welch before her feet touched the ground, and pulled her to one side. The band struck up "Blue Bell" by way of welcome, and one of the sweaty pages ran forward and presented the balloonist with a large bouquet of artificial flowers. She smiled and thanked him, and ran back across the sand to the tent.

"Can't we go inside and see her?" Eden asked. "You can explain to the door man. I want to meet her." Edging forward, she herself addressed the man in the linen suit and slipped something from her purse into his hand.

They found Molly seated before a trunk that had a mirror in the lid and a "make-up" outfit spread upon the tray. She was wiping the cold cream and powder from her neck with a discarded chemise.

"Hello, Don," she said cordially. "Brought a friend?"

Eden liked her. She had an easy, friendly manner, and there was something boyish and devil-may-care about her.

"Yes, it's fun. I'm mad about it," she said in reply to Eden's questions. "I always want to let go, when I come down on the bar. You don't feel your weight at all, as you would on a stationary trapeze."

The big drum boomed outside, and the publicity man began shouting to newly arrived boatloads. Miss Welch took a last pull at her cigarette. "Now you'll have to get out, Don. I change for the next act. This time I go up in a black evening dress, and lose the skirt in the basket before I start down."

"Yes, go along," said Eden. "Wait for me outside the door. I'll stay and help her dress."

Hedger waited and waited, while women of every build bumped into him and begged his pardon, and the red pages ran about holding out their caps for coins, and the people ate and perspired and shifted parasols against the sun. When the band began to play a two-step, all the bathers ran up out of the surf to watch the ascent. The second balloon bumped and rose, and the crowd began shouting to the girl in a black evening dress who stood leaning against the ropes and smiling. "It's a new girl," they called. "It ain't the Countess this time. You're a peach, girlie!"

The balloonist acknowledged these compliments, bowing and looking down over the sea of upturned faces,—but Hedger was determined she should not see him, and he darted behind the tent-fly. He was suddenly dripping with cold sweat, his mouth was full of the bitter taste of anger and his tongue felt stiff behind his teeth. Molly Welch, in a shirt-waist and a white tam-o'-shanter cap, slipped out from the tent under his arm and laughed up in his face. "She's a crazy one you brought along. She'll get what she wants!"

"Oh, I'll settle with you, all right!" Hedger brought out with difficulty.

"It's not my fault, Donnie. I couldn't do anything with her. She bought me off. What's the matter with you? Are you soft on her? She's safe enough. It's as easy as rolling off a log, if you keep cool." Molly Welch was rather excited herself, and she was chewing gum at a high speed as she stood beside him, looking up at the floating silver cone. "Now watch," she exclaimed suddenly. "She's coming down on the bar. I advised her to cut that out, but you see she does it first-rate. And she got rid of the skirt, too. Those black tights show off her legs very well. She keeps her feet together like I told her, and makes a good line along the back. See the light on those silver slippers,— that was a good idea I had. Come along to meet her. Don't be a grouch; she's done it fine!"

Molly tweaked his elbow, and then left him standing like a stump, while she ran down the beach with the crowd.

Though Hedger was sulking, his eye could not help seeing the low blue welter of the sea, the arrested bathers, standing in the surf, their arms and legs stained red by the dropping sun, all shading their eyes and gazing upward at the slowly falling silver star.

Molly Welch and the manager caught Eden under the arms and lifted her aside, a red page dashed up with a bouquet, and the band struck up "Blue Bell." Eden laughed and bowed, took Molly's arm, and ran up the sand in her black tights and silver slippers, dodging the friendly old women, and the gallant sports who wanted to offer their homage on the spot.

When she emerged from the tent, dressed in her own clothes, that part of the beach was almost deserted. She stepped to her companion's side and said carelessly: "Hadn't we better try to catch this boat? I hope you're not sore at me. Really, it was lots of fun."

Hedger looked at his watch. "Yes, we have fifteen minutes to get to the boat," he said politely.

As they walked toward the pier, one of the pages ran up panting. "Lady, you're carrying off the bouquet," he said, aggrievedly.

Eden stopped and looked at the bunch of spotty cotton roses in her hand. "Of course. I want them for a souvenir. You gave them to me yourself."

"I give 'em to you for looks, but you can't take 'em away. They belong to the show."

"Oh, you always use the same bunch?"

"Sure we do. There ain't too much money in this business."

She laughed and tossed them back to him. "Why are you angry?" she asked Hedger. "I wouldn't have done it if I'd been with some fellows, but I thought you were the sort who wouldn't mind. Molly didn't for a minute think you would."

"What possessed you to do such a fool thing?" he asked roughly.

"I don't know. When I saw her coming down, I wanted to try it. It looked exciting. Didn't I hold myself as well as she did?"

Hedger shrugged his shoulders, but in his heart he forgave her.

The return boat was not crowded, though the boats that passed them, going out, were packed to the rails. The sun was setting. Boys and girls sat on the long benches with their arms about each other, singing. Eden felt a strong wish to propitiate her companion, to be alone with him. She had been curiously wrought up by her balloon trip; it was a lark, but not very satisfying unless one came back to something after the flight. She wanted to be admired and adored. Though Eden said nothing, and sat with her arms limp on the rail in front of her, looking languidly at the rising silhouette of the city and the bright path of the sun, Hedger felt a strange drawing near to her. If he but brushed her white skirt with his knee, there was an instant communication between them, such as there had never been before. They did not talk at all, but when they went over the gang-plank she took his arm and kept her shoulder close to his. He felt as if they were enveloped in a highly charged atmosphere, an invisible network of subtle, almost painful sensibility. They had somehow taken hold of each other.

An hour later, they were dining in the back garden of a little French hotel on Ninth Street, long since passed away. It was cool and leafy there, and the mosquitoes were not very numerous. A party of South Americans at another table were drinking champagne, and Eden murmured that she thought she would like some, if it were not too expensive. "Perhaps it will make me think I am in the balloon again. That was a very nice feeling. You've forgiven me, haven't you?"

Hedger gave her a quick straight look from under his black eyebrows, and something went over her that was like a chill, except that it was warm and feathery. She drank most of the wine; her companion was indifferent to it. He was talking more to her tonight than he had ever done before. She asked him about a new picture she had seen in his room; a queer thing full of stiff, supplicating female figures. "It's Indian, isn't it?"

"Yes. I call it Rain Spirits, or maybe, Indian Rain. In the Southwest, where I've been a good deal, the Indian traditions make women have to do with the rain-fall. They were supposed to control it, somehow, and to be able to find springs, and make moisture come out of the earth. You see I'm trying to learn to paint what people think and feel; to get away from all that photographic stuff. When I look at you, I don't see what a camera would see, do I?"

"How can I tell?"

"Well, if I should paint you, I could make you understand what I see." For the second time that day Hedger crimsoned unexpectedly, and his eyes fell and steadily contemplated a dish of little radishes. "That particular picture I got from a story a Mexican priest told me; he said he found it in an old manuscript book in a monastery down there, written by some Spanish Missionary, who got his stories from the Aztecs. This one he called 'The Forty Lovers of the Queen,' and it was more or less about rain-making."

"Aren't you going to tell it to me?" Eden asked.

Hedger fumbled among the radishes. "I don't know if it's the proper kind of story to tell a girl."

She smiled; "Oh, forget about that! I've been balloon riding to-day. I like to hear you talk."

Her low voice was flattering. She had seemed like clay in his hands ever since they got on the boat to come home. He leaned back in his chair, forgot his food, and, looking at her intently, began to tell his story, the theme of which he somehow felt was dangerous tonight.

The tale began, he said, somewhere in Ancient Mexico, and con-cerned the daughter of a king. The birth of this Princess was pre-ceded by unusual portents. Three times her mother dreamed that she was delivered of serpents, which betokened that the child she car-ried would have power with the rain gods. The serpent was the sym-bol of water. The Princess grew up dedicated to the gods, and wise men taught her the rain-making mysteries. She was with difficulty restrained from men and was guarded at all times, for it was the law of the Thunder that she be maiden until her marriage. In the years of her adolescence, rain was abundant with her people. The oldest man could not remember such fertility. When the Princess had counted eighteen summers, her father went to drive out a war party that har-ried his borders on the north and troubled his prosperity. The King destroyed the invaders and brought home many prisoners. Among the prisoners was a young chief, taller than any of his captors, of such strength and ferocity that the King's people came a day's jour-ney to look at him. When the Princess beheld his great stature, and saw that his arms and breast were covered with the figures of wild animals, bitten into the skin and coloured, she begged his life from her father. She desired that he should practise his art upon her, and prick upon her skin the signs of Rain and Lightning and Thunder, and stain the wounds with herb-juices, as they were upon his own body. For many days, upon the roof of the King's house, the Princess submitted herself to the bone needle, and the women with her marvelled at her fortitude. But the Princess was without shame before the Captive, and it came about that he threw from him his needles and his stains, and fell upon the Princess to violate her honour; and her women ran down from the roof screaming, to call the guard which stood at the gateway of the King's house, and none stayed to protect their mistress. When the guard came, the Captive was thrown into bonds, and he was gelded, and his tongue was torn out, and he was given for a slave to the Rain Princess.

The country of the Aztecs to the east was tormented by thirst, and their king, hearing much of the rain-making arts of the Princess, sent an embassy to her father, with presents and an offer of marriage. So the Princess went from her father to be the Queen of the Aztecs, and she took with her the Captive, who served her in everything with entire fidelity and slept upon a mat before her door.

The King gave his bride a fortress on the outskirts of the city, whither she retired to entreat the rain gods. This fortress was called the Queen's House, and on the night of the new moon the Queen came to it from the palace. But when the moon waxed and grew toward the round, because the god of Thunder had had his will of her, then the Queen returned to the King. Drouth abated in the country and rain fell abundantly by reason of the Queen's power with the stars.

When the Queen went to her own house she took with her no servant but the Captive, and he slept outside her door and brought her food after she had fasted. The Queen had a jewel of great value, a turquoise that had fallen from the sun, and had the image of the sun upon it. And when she desired a young man whom she had seen in the army or among the slaves, she sent the Captive to him with the jewel, for a sign that he should come to her secretly at the Queen's House upon business concerning the welfare of all. And some, after she had talked with them, she sent away with rewards; and some she took into her chamber and kept them by her for one night or two. Afterward she called the Captive and bade him conduct the youth by the secret way he had come, underneath the chambers of the fortress. But for the going away of the Queen's lovers the Captive took out the bar that was beneath a stone in the floor of the passage, and put in its stead a rush-reed, and the youth stepped upon it and fell through into a cavern that was the bed of an underground river, and whatever was thrown into it was not seen again. In this service nor in any other did the Captive fail the Queen.

But when the Queen sent for the Captain of the Archers, she detained him four days in her chamber, calling often for food and wine, and was greatly content with him. On the fourth day she went to the Captive outside her door and said: "Tomorrow take this man up by the sure way, by which the King comes, and let him live."

In the Queen's door were arrows, purple and white. When she desired the King to come to her publicly, with his guard, she sent him a white arrow; but when she sent the purple, he came secretly, and covered himself with his mantle to be hidden from the stone gods at the gate. On the fifth night that the Queen was with her lover, the Captive took a purple arrow to the King, and the King came secretly and found them together. He killed the Captain with his own hand, but the Queen he brought to public trial. The Captive, when he was put to the question, told on his fingers forty men that he had let through the underground passage into the river. The Captive and the Queen were put to death by fire, both on the same day, and afterward there was scarcity of rain.

Eden Bower sat shivering a little as she listened. Hedger was not trying to please her, she thought, but to antagonize and frighten her by his brutal story. She had often told herself that his lean, big-boned lower jaw was like his bull-dog's, but tonight his face made Caesar's most savage and determined expression seem an affectation. Now she was looking at the man he really was. Nobody's eyes had ever defied her like this. They were searching her and seeing everything; all she had concealed from Livingston, and from the millionaire and his friends, and from the newspaper man. He was testing her, trying her out, and she was more ill at ease than she wished to show.

"That's quite a thrilling story," she said at last, rising and winding her scarf about her throat. "It must be getting late. Almost every one has gone."

They walked down the Avenue like people who have quarrelled, or who wish to get rid of each other. Hedger did not take her arm at the street crossings, and they did not linger in the Square. At her door he tried none of the old devices of the Livingston boys. He stood like a post, having forgotten to take off his hat, gave her a harsh, threatening glance, muttered "goodnight," and shut his own door noisily.

There was no question of sleep for Eden Bower. Her brain was working like a machine that would never stop. After she undressed, she tried to calm her nerves by smoking a cigarette, lying on the divan by the open window. But she grew wider and wider awake, combating the challenge that had flamed all evening in Hedger's eyes. The balloon had been one kind of excitement, the wine another; but the thing that had roused her, as a blow rouses a proud man, was the doubt, the contempt, the sneering hostility with which the painter had looked at her when he told his savage story. Crowds and balloons were all very well, she reflected, but woman's chief adventure is man. With a mind over active and a sense of life over strong, she wanted to walk across the roofs in the starlight, to sail over the sea and face at once a world of which she had never been afraid.

Hedger must be asleep; his dog had stopped sniffing under the double doors. Eden put on her wrapper and slippers and stole softly down the hall over the old carpet; one loose board creaked just as she reached the ladder. The trapdoor was open, as always on hot nights. When she stepped out on the roof she drew a long breath and walked across it, looking up at the sky. Her foot touched something soft; she heard a low growl, and on the instant Caesar's sharp little teeth caught her ankle and waited. His breath was like steam on her leg. Nobody had ever intruded upon his roof before, and he panted for the movement or the word that would let him spring his jaw. Instead, Hedger's hand seized his throat.

"Wait a minute. I'll settle with him," he said grimly. He dragged the dog toward the manhole and disappeared. When he came back, he found Eden standing over by the dark chimney, looking away in an offended attitude.

"I caned him unmercifully," he panted. "Of course you didn't hear anything; he never whines when I beat him. He didn't nip you, did he?"

"I don't know whether he broke the skin or not," she answered aggrievedly, still looking off into the west.

"If I were one of your friends in white pants, I'd strike a match to find whether you were hurt, though I know you are not, and then I'd see your ankle, wouldn't I?"

"I suppose so."

He shook his head and stood with his hands in the pockets of his old painting jacket. "I'm not up to such boy-tricks. If you want the place to yourself, I'll clear out. There are plenty of places where I can spend the night, what's left of it. But if you stay here and I stay here——" He shrugged his shoulders.

Eden did not stir, and she made no reply. Her head drooped slightly, as if she were considering. But the moment he put his arms about her they began to talk, both at once, as people do in an opera. The instant avowal brought out a flood of trivial admissions. Hedger confessed his crime, was reproached and forgiven, and now Eden knew what it was in his look that she had found so disturbing of late.

Standing against the black chimney, with the sky behind and blue shadows before, they looked like one of Hedger's own paintings of that period; two figures, one white and one dark, and nothing whatever distinguishable about them but that they were male and female. The faces were lost, the contours blurred in shadow, but the figures were a man and a woman, and that was their whole concern and their mysterious beauty,——it was the rhythm in which they moved, at last, along the roof and down into the dark hole; he first, drawing her gently after him. She came down very slowly. The excitement and bravado and uncertainty of that long day and night seemed all at once to tell upon her. When his feet were on the carpet and he reached up to lift her down, she twined her arms about his neck as after a long separation, and turned her face to him, and her lips, with their perfume of youth and passion.

One Saturday afternoon Hedger was sitting in the window of Eden's music room. They had been watching the pigeons come wheeling over the roofs from their unknown feeding grounds.

"Why," said Eden suddenly, "don't we fix those big doors into your studio so they will open? Then, if I want you, I won't have to go through the hall. That illustrator is loafing about a good deal of late."

"I'll open them, if you wish. The bolt is on your side."

"Isn't there one on yours, too?"

"No. I believe a man lived there for years before I came in, and the nurse used to have these rooms herself. Naturally, the lock was on the lady's side."

Eden laughed and began to examine the bolt. "It's all stuck up with paint." Looking about, her eye lighted upon a bronze Buddha which was one of the nurse's treasures. Taking him by his head, she struck the bolt a blow with his squatting posteriors. The two doors creaked, sagged, and swung weakly inward a little way, as if they were too old for such escapades. Eden tossed the heavy idol into a stuffed chair. "That's better," she exclaimed exultantly. "So the bolts are always on the lady's side? What a lot society takes for granted!"

Hedger laughed, sprang up and caught her arms roughly. "Whoever takes you for granted— Did anybody, ever?"

"Everybody does. That's why I'm here. You are the only one who knows anything about me. Now I'll have to dress if we're going out for dinner."

He lingered, keeping his hold on her. "But I won't always be the only one, Eden Bower. I won't be the last."

"No, I suppose not," she said carelessly. "But what does that matter? You are the first."

As a long, despairing whine broke in the warm stillness, they drew apart. Caesar, lying on his bed in the dark corner, had lifted his head at this invasion of sunlight, and realized that the side of his room was broken open, and his whole world shattered by change. There stood his master and this woman, laughing at him! The woman was pulling the long black hair of this mightiest of men, who bowed his head and permitted it.

VI

In time they quarrelled, of course, and about an abstraction,—as young people often do, as mature people almost never do. Eden came in late one afternoon. She had been with some of her musical friends to lunch at Burton Ives' studio, and she began telling Hedger about its splendours. He listened a moment and then threw down his brushes. "I know exactly what it's like," he said impatiently. "A very good department-store conception of a studio. It's one of the show places."

"Well, it's gorgeous, and he said I could bring you to see him. The boys tell me he's awfully kind about giving people a lift, and you might get something out of it."

Hedger started up and pushed his canvas out of the way. "What could I possibly get from Burton Ives? He's almost the worst painter in the world; the stupidest, I mean."

Eden was annoyed. Burton Ives had been very nice to her and had begged her to sit for him. "You must admit that he's a very successful one," she said coldly.

"Of course he is! Anybody can be successful who will do that sort of thing. I wouldn't paint his pictures for all the money in New York."

"Well, I saw a lot of them, and I think they are beautiful."

Hedger bowed stiffly.

"What's the use of being a great painter if nobody knows about you?" Eden went on persuasively. "Why don't you paint the kind of pictures people can understand, and then, after you're successful, do whatever you like?"

"As I look at it," said Hedger brusquely, "I am successful."

Eden glanced about. "Well, I don't see any evidences of it," she said, biting her lip. "He has a Japanese servant and a wine cellar, and keeps a riding horse."

Hedger melted a little. "My dear, I have the most expensive luxury in the world, and I am much more extravagant than Burton Ives, for I work to please nobody but myself."

"You mean you could make money and don't? That you don't try to get a public?"

"Exactly. A public only wants what has been done over and over. I'm painting for painters,—who haven't been born."

"What would you do if I brought Mr. Ives down here to see your things?"

"Well, for God's sake, don't! Before he left I'd probably tell him what I thought of him."

Eden rose. "I give you up. You know very well there's only one kind of success that's real."

"Yes, but it's not the kind you mean. So you've been thinking me a scrub painter, who needs a helping hand from some fashionable studio man? What the devil have you had anything to do with me for, then?"

"There's no use talking to you," said Eden walking slowly toward the door. "I've been trying to pull wires for you all afternoon, and this is what it comes to." She had expected that the tidings of a prospective call from the great man would be received very differently, and had been thinking as she came home in the stage how, as with a magic wand, she might gild Hedger's future, float him out of his dark hole on a tide of prosperity, see his name in the papers and his pictures in the windows on Fifth Avenue.

Hedger mechanically snapped the midsummer leash on Caesar's collar and they ran downstairs and hurried through Sullivan Street off toward the river. He wanted to be among rough, honest people, to get down where the big drays bumped over stone paving blocks and the men wore corduroy trowsers and kept their shirts open at the neck. He stopped for a drink in one of the sagging bar-rooms on the water front. He had never in his life been so deeply wounded; he did not know he could be so hurt. He had told this girl all his secrets. On the roof, in these warm, heavy summer nights, with her hands locked in his, he had been able to explain all his misty ideas about an unborn art the world was waiting for; had been able to explain them better than he had ever done to himself. And she had looked away to the chattels of this uptown studio and coveted them for him! To her he was only an unsuccessful Burton Ives.

Then why, as he had put it to her, did she take up with him? Young, beautiful, talented as she was, why had she wasted herself on a scrub? Pity? Hardly; she wasn't sentimental. There was no explaining her. But in this passion that had seemed so fearless and so fated to be, his own position now looked to him ridiculous; a poor dauber without money or fame,—it was her caprice to load him with favours. Hedger ground his teeth so loud that his dog, trotting beside him, heard him and looked up.

While they were having supper at the oysterman's, he planned his escape. Whenever he saw her again, everything he had told her, that he should never have told any one, would come back to him; ideas he had never whispered even to the painter whom he worshipped and had gone all the way to France to see. To her they must seem his apology for not having horses and a valet, or merely the puerile boastfulness of a weak man. Yet if she slipped the bolt tonight and came through the doors and said, "Oh, weak man, I belong to you!" what could he do? That was the danger. He would catch the train out to Long Beach tonight, and tomorrow he would go on to the north end of Long Island, where an old friend of his had a summer studio among the sand dunes. He would stay until things came right in his mind. And she could find a smart painter, or take her punishment.

When he went home, Eden's room was dark; she was dining out somewhere. He threw his things into a hold-all he had carried about the world with him, strapped up some colours and canvases, and ran downstairs.

VII

Five days later Hedger was a restless passenger on a dirty, crowded Sunday train, coming back to town. Of course he saw now how unreasonable he had been in expecting a Huntington girl to know anything about pictures; here was a whole continent full of people who knew nothing about pictures and he didn't hold it against them. What had such things to do with him and Eden Bower? When he lay out on the dunes, watching the moon come up out of the sea, it had seemed to him that there was no wonder in the world like the wonder of Eden Bower. He was going back to her because she was older than art, because she was the most overwhelming thing that had ever come into his life.

He had written her yesterday, begging her to be at home this evening, telling her that he was contrite, and wretched enough.

Now that he was on his way to her, his stronger feeling unaccountably changed to a mood that was playful and tender. He wanted to share everything with her, even the most trivial things. He wanted to tell her about the people on the train, coming back tired from their holiday with bunches of wilted flowers and dirty daisies; to tell her that the fish-man, to whom she had often sent him for lobsters, was among the passengers, disguised in a silk shirt and a spotted tie, and how his wife looked exactly like a fish, even to her eyes, on which cataracts were forming. He could tell her, too, that he hadn't as much as unstrapped his canvases,—that ought to convince her.

In those days passengers from Long Island came into New York by ferry. Hedger had to be quick about getting his dog out of the express car in order to catch the first boat. The East River, and the bridges, and the city to the west, were burning in the conflagration of the sunset; there was that great home-coming reach of evening in the air.

The car changes from Thirty-fourth Street were too many and too perplexing; for the first time in his life Hedger took a hansom cab for Washington Square. Caesar sat bolt upright on the worn leather cushion beside him, and they jogged off, looking down on the rest of the world.

It was twilight when they drove down lower Fifth Avenue into the Square, and through the Arch behind them were the two long rows of pale violet lights that used to bloom so beautifully against the grey stone and asphalt. Here and yonder about the Square hung globes that shed a radiance not unlike the blue mists of evening, emerging softly when daylight died, as the stars emerged in the thin blue sky. Under them the sharp shadows of the trees fell on the cracked pavement and the sleeping grass. The first stars and the first lights were growing silver against the gradual darkening, when Hedger paid his driver and went into the house,—which, thank God, was still there! On the hall table lay his letter of yesterday, unopened.

He went upstairs with every sort of fear and every sort of hope clutching at his heart; it was as if tigers were tearing him. Why was there no gas burning in the top hall? He found matches and the gas bracket. He knocked, but got no answer; nobody was there. Before his own door were exactly five bottles of milk, standing in a row. The milk-boy had taken spiteful pleasure in thus reminding him that he forgot to stop his order.

Hedger went down to the basement; it, too, was dark. The janitress was taking her evening airing on the basement steps. She sat waving a palm-leaf fan majestically, her dirty calico dress open at the neck. She told him at once that there had been "changes." Miss Bower's room was to let again, and the piano would go tomorrow. Yes, she left yesterday, she sailed for Europe with friends from Chicago. They arrived on Friday, heralded by many telegrams. Very rich people they were said to be, though the man had refused to pay the nurse a month's rent in lieu of notice,—which would have been only right, as the young lady had agreed to take the rooms until October. Mrs. Foley had observed, too, that he didn't overpay her or Willy for their trouble, and a great deal of trouble they had been put to, certainly. Yes, the young lady was very pleasant, but the nurse said there were rings on the mahogany table where she had put tumblers and wine glasses. It was just as well she was gone. The Chicago man was uppish in his ways, but not much to look at. She supposed he had poor health, for there was nothing to him inside his clothes.

Hedger went slowly up the stairs—never had they seemed so long, or his legs so heavy. The upper floor was emptiness and silence. He unlocked his room, lit the gas, and opened the windows. When he went to put his coat in the closet, he found, hanging among his clothes, a pale, flesh-tinted dressing gown he had liked to see her wear, with a perfume—oh, a perfume that was still Eden Bower! He shut the door behind him and there, in the dark, for a moment he lost his manliness. It was when he held this garment to him that he found a letter in the pocket.

The note was written with a lead pencil, in haste: She was sorry that he was angry, but she still didn't know just what she had done. She had thought Mr. Ives would be useful to him; she guessed he was too proud. She wanted awfully to see him again, but Fate came knocking at her door after he had left her. She believed in Fate. She would never forget him, and she knew he would become the greatest painter in the world. Now she must pack. She hoped he wouldn't mind her leaving the dressing gown; somehow, she could never wear it again.

After Hedger read this, standing under the gas, he went back into the closet and knelt down before the wall; the knot hole had been plugged up with a ball of wet paper,—the same blue note-paper on which her letter was written.

He was hard hit. Tonight he had to bear the loneliness of a whole lifetime. Knowing himself so well, he could hardly believe that such a thing had ever happened to him, that such a woman had lain happy and contented in his arms. And now it was over. He turned out the light and sat down on his painter's stool before the big window. Caesar, on the floor beside him, rested his head on his master's knee. We must leave Hedger thus, sitting in his tank with his dog, looking up at the stars.

COMING, APHRODITE! This legend, in electric lights over the Lexington Opera House, had long announced the return of Eden Bower to New York after years of spectacular success in Paris. She came at last, under the management of an American Opera Company, but bringing her own *chef d'orchestre*.

One bright December afternoon Eden Bower was going down Fifth Avenue in her car, on the way to her broker, in Williams Street. Her thoughts were entirely upon stocks,—Cerro de Pasco, and how much she should buy of it,—when she suddenly looked up and realized that she was skirting Washington Square. She had not seen the place since she rolled out of it in an old-fashioned four-wheeler to seek her fortune, eighteen years ago.

"*Arrêtez, Alphonse. Attendez moi*," she called, and opened the door before he could reach it. The children who were streaking over the asphalt on roller skates saw a lady in a long fur coat, and short, high-heeled shoes, alight from a French car and pace slowly about the Square, holding her muff to her chin. This spot, at least, had changed very little, she reflected; the same trees, the same fountain, the white arch, and over yonder, Garibaldi, drawing the sword for freedom. There, just opposite her, was the old red brick house.

"Yes, that is the place," she was thinking. "I can smell the carpets now, and the dog,—what was his name? That grubby bathroom at the end of the hall, and that dreadful Hedger—still, there was something about him, you know—" She glanced up and blinked against the sun. From somewhere in the crowded quarter south of the Square a flock of pigeons rose, wheeling quickly upward into the brilliant blue sky. She threw back her head, pressed her muff closer to her chin, and watched them with a smile of amazement and delight. So they still rose, out of all that dirt and noise and squalor, fleet and silvery, just as they used to rise that summer when she was twenty and went up in a balloon on Coney Island!

Alphonse opened the door and tucked her robes about her. All the way down town her mind wandered from Cerro de Pasco, and she kept smiling and looking up at the sky.

When she had finished her business with the broker, she asked him to look in the telephone book for the address of M. Gaston Jules, the picture dealer, and slipped the paper on which he wrote it into her glove. It was five o'clock when she reached the French Galleries, as they were called. On entering she gave the attendant her card, asking him to take it to M. Jules. The dealer appeared very promptly and begged her to come into his private office, where he pushed a great chair toward his desk for her and signalled his secretary to leave the room.

"How good your lighting is in here," she observed, glancing about. "I met you at Simon's studio, didn't I? Oh, no! I never forget anybody who interests me." She threw her muff on his writing table and sank into the deep chair. "I have come to you for some information that's not in my line. Do you know anything about an American painter named Hedger?"

He took the seat opposite her. "Don Hedger? But, certainly! There are some very interesting things of his in an exhibition at V——'s. If you would care to—"

She held up her hand. "No, no. I've no time to go to exhibitions. Is he a man of any importance?"

"Certainly. He is one of the first men among the moderns. That is to say, among the very moderns. He is always coming up with something different. He often exhibits in Paris, you must have seen—"

"No, I tell you I don't go to exhibitions. Has he had great success? That is what I want to know."

M. Jules pulled at his short grey moustache. "But, Madame, there are many kinds of success," he began cautiously.

Madame gave a dry laugh. "Yes, so he used to say. We once quarrelled on that issue. And how would you define his particular kind?"

M. Jules grew thoughtful. "He is a great name with all the young men, and he is decidedly an influence in art. But one can't definitely place a man who is original, erratic, and who is changing all the time."

She cut him short. "Is he much talked about at home? In Paris, I mean? Thanks. That's all I want to know." She rose and began buttoning her coat. "One doesn't like to have been an utter fool, even at twenty."

*"Mais, non!"* M. Jules handed her her muff with a quick, sympathetic glance. He followed her out through the carpeted show-room, now closed to the public and draped in cheesecloth, and put her into her car with words appreciative of the honour she had done him in calling.

Leaning back in the cushions, Eden Bower closed her eyes, and her face, as the street lamps flashed their ugly orange light upon it, became hard and settled, like a plaster cast; so a sail, that has been filled by a strong breeze, behaves when the wind suddenly dies. Tomorrow night the wind would blow again, and this mask would be the golden face of Aphrodite. But a "big" career takes its toll, even with the best of luck.

1 9 2 0

# CLAUDE McKAY

Claude McKay (1890–1948) grew up in Jamaica, and his poems often express nostalgia for an easier, more sensual Caribbean life. After leaving Jamaica in 1912, he led a peripatetic existence, studying at the Tuskegee Institute and Kansas State University before arriving in New York in 1914, where he established himself as a poet and radical spokesman (he was associate editor of The Liberator for a time). Subsequently he was to spend time in England, Russia, Germany, France, and North Africa, and ultimately settled in Chicago. He is best remembered, however, for the poems collected in Harlem Shadows and the novel Home to Harlem.

## THE TROPICS IN NEW YORK

Bananas ripe and green, and ginger-root,
   Cocoa in pods and alligator pears,
And tangerines and mangoes and grape fruit,
   Fit for the highest prize at parish fairs,

Set in the window, bringing memories
   Of fruit-trees laden by low-singing rills,
And dewy dawns, and mystical blue skies
   In benediction over nun-like hills.

My eyes grew dim, and I could no more gaze;
   A wave of longing through my body swept,
And, hungry for the old, familiar ways,
   I turned aside and bowed my head and wept.

1920

## THE HARLEM DANCER

Applauding youths laughed with young prostitutes
And watched her perfect, half-clothed body sway;
Her voice was like the sound of blended flutes
Blown by black players upon a picnic day.
She sang and danced on gracefully and calm,
The light gauze hanging loose about her form;
To me she seemed a proudly-swaying palm
Grown lovelier for passing through a storm.
Upon her swarthy neck black shiny curls
Luxuriant fell; and tossing coins in praise,
The wine-flushed, bold-eyed boys, and even the girls,
Devoured her shape with eager, passionate gaze;
But looking at her falsely-smiling face,
I knew her self was not in that strange place.

1922

# MARIANNE MOORE

Marianne Moore (1887–1972) was one of America's leading modernist poets. Many of her poems operate essayistically, circling a subject and taking notes, until some difficult insight is pried loose. She drew on a fantastically wide range of materials and associations. In "New York" she appropriates a remark of Isabella, Duchess of Gonzaga, as quoted in Frank Alvah Parsons' The Psychology of Dress, a descriptive passage from an article in Forest and Stream, and a phrase ("accessibility to experience") of Henry James; and by way of historical background to the poem observes in a note that "in 1921 New York succeeded St. Louis as the center of the wholesale fur trade." Of the city itself, she wrote in later years: "I like Santa Barbara, Vancouver, British Columbia; have an incurable fondness for London. But of any cities I have seen, I like New York best."

## NEW YORK

the savage's romance,
accreted where we need the space for commerce—
the center of the wholesale fur trade,
starred with tepees of ermine and peopled with foxes,
the long guard-hairs waving two inches beyond the body of the pelt;
the ground dotted with deer-skins—white with white spots,
"as satin needlework in a single color may carry a varied pattern,"
and wilting eagle's-down compacted by the wind;
and picardels of beaver-skin; white ones alert with snow.
It is a far cry from the "queen full of jewels"
and the beau with the muff,
from the gilt coach shaped like a perfume-bottle,
to the conjunction of the Monongahela and the Allegheny,
and the scholastic philosophy of the wilderness.
It is not the dime-novel exterior,
Niagara Falls, the calico horses and the war-canoe;
it is not that "if the fur is not finer than such as one sees others wear,

one would rather be without it"——
that estimated in raw meat and berries, we could feed the universe;
it is not the atmosphere of ingenuity,
the otter, the beaver, the puma skins
without shooting-irons or dogs;
it is not the plunder,
but "accessibility to experience."

1921, 1952

# PAUL ROSENFELD

Paul Rosenfeld (1890–1946) was a generous, influential interpeter of American modernism in the 1920's, whose particular inspiration was the creative efflorescence centering on photographer Alfred Stieglitz's "291" group. His highly wrought style attempted to lift critical writing to a level of artistry comparable to that of his heroes Stieglitz, William Carlos Williams, Marsden Hartley, John Marin, Georgia O'Keeffe, and Roger Sessions. In Port of New York, a collection of analytical essays about these artists, he concludes with a lyrical epilogue that celebrates the moment when New York artists realized that the center of cultural gravity had shifted from Europe to their own city.

## FROM *PORT OF NEW YORK*

THE LINERS emerge from the lower bay. Up through the Narrows they heave their sharp prows. In sleety, in blue, in sullen weather, throughout the lighted hours, mouse-colored shapes are stretched off Quarantine. Between cheesebox fort and fume of nondescript South Brooklyn waterfront, metal abdomens which were not seated there yesterday are submitted to rising concrete sides, masts, red iron, ferryslips. In New York harbor, always, new-come bodies foreign to it; issued from Southampton and Bergen, Gibraltar and Bremen, Naples and Antwerp; now engirdled by sullen shorelines and lapped by tired crisscrossed wavelets.

The lean voyagers steer under the tower-jumbled point of Manhattan. Flanks are lashed to the town; holds thrown open to the cobbled street. Decks are annexes of the littoral, portion of New York no less than the leagues of "L" sweeping past dismal brick over caverned thoroughfares. And through periods of many days, for weeks, even, the liners lie roped to their piersides, rows of captives handcuffed to policemen. The plated sides list obediently toward bald sheds. Only feeble brownish wisps of smoke adrift from silent smokestacks betray the incorporation incomplete. Then, one day, a pierside is found stripped. Next day, another; two. The vigilantes stand stupid. In the open quadrangle between docks, merely a dingy freighter, and small lighter-fry. By sea-coated piles, the muckerish North River water shrugs its shoulders. The liners have evaded; fled again through the straits. Beyond where eye can reach iron rumps dwindle down the ocean.

And has it really faded from the port, the painful glamour? Has it really gone off them, the fiction that was always on the movements of the liners in and out the upper bay? Or has it merely retreated for a while behind the bluffs of the Jersey shore, to return on us again to-morrow and draw the breast away once more into the distance beneath Staten Island hill? It was on a day just like this one, year before last or last year even—and outside the window the sun fell much as it does now across asphalt grimy with a little last snow, and people came about the corner house and walked past brick walls, and motors ticked and drays banged—that the harbor of New York was somehow the inexplicable scene of a mysterious cruel translation. And nothing in the traffic of the port and in the city streets has changed. Below Battery point, the liners stand off Quarantine all through the lighted hours; and here inside the town the solid gazing houses and shadowed walls have not gone. Steel hooves ring brilliant in the lightening air. Coal roars as it slides down iron into the neighbors' cellars. The truckmen stand like Pharaohs behind their horses and yell at the chickens. From a block away the elevated train comes up like a thunderstorm. These and the bells and the fire-escapes are where they were last year and the year before. How is it that the strange dream light should have gone off the port, and left us in another New York City?

It seemed the liners did not come across the Atlantic on a single plane. Somewhere, in the course of their voyage from the European coasts, they left one plane and descended to another. True, they were steam-packets plying in a huge oceanic ferryboat business, moving in well-known lanes through fog with smell of boilers and pounding of machines. Nevertheless, a mysterious translation took place before they reached their American terminus. If indeed they did plow over the regular surface of the globe, they also came out of delicious unknown qualities of light, and out of wafts of air lighter and fierier than any aplay this side the water. In coming, they had descended as one descends from a heaven-near plateau under blue skylands into a dank and shadowy vale. Going to Europe, coming from Europe, might abolish the illusion; at a touch of the new world earth it was upon one again, not to be rationalized and not to be expelled. But a few hours before their entrance into Ambrose channel, the mighty voyagers now ringed about with smoky land and the sullen objects of the rawly furnished shores had experienced, it seemed, not alone the fishy white Atlantic, but the clear, free, ineffable space which does not know the port. Against steel plates and salt-soaked yellow, white, and pitch-black paint; about funnels and masts erect against the stars, there had lain the otherwhere than New York, the hidden side of the city moon; the unknown aspect of the flower of the moment. Rock lighter than sea-water, the visitor had swum in the space relieved of all the depressure of new world objects; the space that the gas-tuns, chimney pennons of coal-fume, smoky length of Staten Island hill would not let be seen, and stood upon like gravestones upon graves. About it with the sky and salt and ocean was the place that labors in man's behalf, and calls forth and lets bloom in beauty the stuff the new world sites repress and force back and will not let grow. Warming suns and long mild days had poured on it.

But here, in the workman bay, the mysterious water-world it seemed was wrenched from the liners, wrenched as eelskins are drawn. A bad change had been worked. Upon the very sides which had known the free untrammeled space and moved through rich elastic stuff, another vulgarer world had imposed itself. Brightness was no longer about the ship. The city horizon was the one horizon. And when once more the cables were thrown off, the departed liners seemed marine expresses less than they had ever seemed. They were exiled princes gone to regain their thrones. They had shaken from them the situation of frustrating objects and mediocre unsatisfying forms quite as they had shaken from the tired choppy waters and rims of murky brown. Experienced once again was the spirit morning. The liners had left New York.

There was a sun overhead here in New York, blazing cruelly enough in the Yankee summer. But the sun which makes life fragrant and rich did not stand overhead. That sun shone far away across the Atlantic, upon the coasts of Europe. High up, one saw the European coast-line gleaming a fertile yellow and green, shining with a soft gold like Alp pinnacles saluted by the first liquor of daylight. But the sun which shone direct upon the eastern margent of the ocean struck the western slantingly and faint. New York lay in blue twilight as in a valley which the sun never comes to bake with heat. One lived, here in New York, upon ultimate edge of life, a kind of hyperborean edge midmost the temperate zone; the border of a perpetual shadow. For behind us, to the west, a continent lay submerged in chaotic pre-creation darkness. Movement, noise, rise and fall of perpetually displaced matter, all these seeming products of sun-power, were unsubstantial quite, dusty mirages of all the senses. For the very heat was not here. Or merely faintly enough to let us know what it was we wanted. Nothing moved indeed. Nothing came into relation.

The seed inside did not take root. It was a curious thing to know that one had been born here; to know that in precisely this dull red house on the avenue corner, with the precise number, say of 1186, one had undergone the experience which the Englishman underwent in his little island, or the Frenchman in his pleasant land of France, or the German in deep Germany. For, when the European was born, did he not begin the process of coming into relationship with the people and the things which stood about him? Did not something in him, the free-moving particle, cleave to the sites, the walls, the trees, the waters amid which he found himself, so that forever after the sight and memory of these objects had power to bring him nourishment comparable to the nourishment the tree draws from out its rock and loam? But here one did not come into blood relation. Oh, yes, here it was very formally inscribed in the records that on a certain day in a certain month of a certain year, a child had been born a certain citizen and his wife, with the sex male; which meant that one could, legally, become President; and, failing that, vote, sit on a jury, and have consular protection when traveling. But they only said one belonged to these things here, and they to one. In truth, a red spired village seen from railway windows over German cornfields; a prim

Holland garden descending from a glass-enclosed verandah; the vision of an avenue with iron balconies in Paris; these foreign things were more life-giving, more feeding and familiar to one for all their strangeness, than the corner of New York rounded regularly each morning and evening. For in the city, things were very definitely outside you, apart from you; you were very definitely over here, they very definitely over there. You were alien to them, it seemed, and for your part you could not move closer to them, no more than to the people who moved amongst them; even to those of the people you were supposed to know the best of all and with whom you had spent years. It was as useless trying to feel yourself through the crowding towers of the lower town, and feel a whole, as it was trying to feel yourself through the forbidding people in the streets. The towers were not a whit less hard, less mutually exclusive, less eager to crowd each other out, than the people who had made them. They snatched the light from each other; rough-shouldered each other; were loud, anarchical, showy, . . . unfriendly; flaunting money; calling for money. Edges stood, knife against knife. Nothing ever came with the warmth of heaven to do the work of the sun and melt the many antagonistic particles. The breast entire strained toward the place of fruitful suns. With sad wonder, one was aware of the movements of liners. For these were things which through the power of motion threw off like an old coat the hyperborean state which held them awhile, and regained climates fertilized by spirit pours.

Nevertheless, one could not break with New York. If one floated aimlessly about inside its walls, within them one nevertheless remained. The suction which drew the psyche out of New York harbor was exerted upon one only in the city. The voyage to Europe once actually undertaken, the pumping force relaxed and dwindled down under the horizon. Two weeks of the green and gold of the Parisian boulevards; and a counter-magnet began exerting its attractive rays. The free, low-arching skies and Louvre flanks and chestnut avenues, what had their beauty really to do with us? This beauty was in its way as remote from us as the awful meaninglessness of the ways and granites of New York. It had its roots in a past which was not ours, and which we might never adopt. To feel it was to squander the best stuff of the bosom not on the true wife, but on the indifferent courtesan. It was beauty in America one wanted, not in France or Switzerland. It was the towers of Manhattan one wanted to see suddenly garlanded with loveliness. One wanted life for them and for oneself together. Somewhere in one always there had been the will to take root in New York; to come into relation with the things and the people, not in the insane self-abnegation of current patriotism and nationalism, but in the form of one's utmost self; in the form of realizing all the possibilities for life shut inside one, and simultaneously finding oneself one with the people. Somewhere within, perhaps in obedience to some outer voice trusted in childhood, there was a voice which promised one day the consummation. One day a miracle should happen over the magnificent harbor, and set life thrilling and rhythming through the place of New York. How it was to happen, one did not know. And sometimes, one supposed that where the immigrant ships had come in, a supernatural and winged visitor would have to appear, fall into the port as a meteorite might fall from the sky, before the new state which had not been reached when the immigrant feet had touched earth at Castle Garden would declare itself. But it was to happen, that one knew; and within, slumbrous power patiently awaited the divine event. And in Europe, one heard, distinct again, the promise. One knew the secret allegiance to the unfriendly new world; and if it did not take the form of a red, white, and blue rosette in the buttonhole, nevertheless something like a precious promissory letter was carried underneath the heart through all the monuments and treasure houses.

So one went back over the sea, eyes peeled for the moment when the arms of the port would open up and receive one, and the sense of home be written large over every crevice and electric sign. But the welcome proved cold, and the day after landing the buildings recommenced their languid snubbing. The restlessness came back. The water world beyond Sandy Hook began to draw again. There was scarcely a place, two or three at the very utmost, which did anything for you, and urged you out into life and adventure and experiment. The city would not give and stood defiant. There were moments: the river at sundown, West Street with its purple blotches on walls, one pile against another. But one became sore so easily. One could accomplish only a little at a time; one became sore and shrank away, and found it impossible to press further. It was impossible as ever to sit before a table and work for long. One gave a little; here was a little trickle of beauty, a moment of absorption. Then something gave out, and one wanted to run off, to hide, to forget, to go out of doors, anything rather than sit before the table and press further. And, in dreams; in the dreams of many, in the dreams of a whole city and country perhaps, steamers departed for Europe, steamers silently discharged from New York harbor, great iron liners headed and predestined for the opposite coasts of the North Atlantic.

It may be that it was yesteryear they still went forth. It was not long ago. And yet, this year, it is certain they have ceased to move. The line has passed away. If any dream-voyagers stir in dreams, their bows are presented to us. The steamers, small, dogged, shoulderful, come headed America-ward. Merely a fistful of months may separate us from the time they still moved out; and sometimes it seems the time cannot indeed be gone. But it is gone. The enormous spaces that divide world from world separate us from it. The impossible thing has indeed come to pass on us. What seemed a miracle alone could accomplish has taken place. There is no one not aware something has happened in New York. What, it is possible, may not be clearly seen. But that an event has taken place is universally sure. No supernatural and winged flyer has descended into the bay. No enchanter has touched the buildings and made them change their forms. The town still stands the same; no littoral has rearranged itself about the bay. Morning upon morning mouse-colored newcome shapes are stretched off Quarantine; and in the North River tugboats drag the departers into midstream. Nevertheless, we could go from the world to-day and still feel that life had been wonderfully good.

The steamers no longer descend from one plane onto another when they come into New York harbor. The port is not the inferior situation, depressive to every spiritual excellence and every impulse to life, which once it was. Glamour lies upon it still; but not the painful dreamlight of yesteryear. A kind of strong, hearty daylight has come upon the port. Once, thought of it filled us with nostalgia and wander-dreams. To-day, it brings a wash of strength and power over us. Sudden, at the foot of a street, the vague wandering eye perceives with a joyous shock a loading steamer carrying high its mast as a child carries a cross in an all-saints procession. The port-nights loom blue and enormous over the leagues of massy masonries. Out of the purpling evening above office piles there comes a breeze, and in that breath there are, like two delicious positive words in an evasive letter, the fishy hoarse Atlantic. The tall street lamps in brownstone gulches on winter nights press back a soft fog that has in it the gray rims and biting wind and tramps of all nations steering. Or, some afternoon, from a bridge train, the salt tide unrolls before our eyes; the sun casts a little orange onto the tide off Battery, and illuminates Bayonne beyond with the cadences of daylight; and the clay giants of the lower city fuse into a bluish mass. Then it is almost beauty that comes to dress the slipshod harbor of New York.

For what we once could feel only by quitting New York: the fundamental oneness we have with the place and the people in it, that is sensible to us to-day in the very jostling, abstracted streets of the city. We know it here, our relationship with this place in which we live. The buildings cannot deprive us of it. For they and we have suddenly commenced growing together. A state of relation has timidly commenced—between the objects, and between the objects and ourselves. The form is still very vague. One is still alone; among people who are alone, scattered like seed or pebbles thrown. And perhaps the form is still most like the faint scum-like build first taken by the embryo in the womb. It seems a misty architectural shape taking up into itself like individual building stones the skyscrapers, tenements, thoroughfares, and people; and with the mass of them erecting a tower higher than any of them, even the highest, toward the sky. But if it is faint, still, it is none the less evident. Day after day in gray and desperate weather even, one can see its mystic aspiration above the skyscrapers of New York. Over our melancholy it rises high. It seems that we have taken root. The place has gotten a grav-

ity that holds us. The suction outward has abated. No longer do we
yearn to quit New York. We are not drawn away. We are content to
remain in New York. In the very middle of the city, we can feel the
fluid of life to be present. We know the space beyond Staten Island
hill is no more filled with the elixir than the air about the buildings.
Other places may have it no whit less than New York; but New York
has it no whit less than they; the stuff of the breast can make its way
into the world here too. Something outside works with it. The city is
a center like every other point upon the circumference of the globe.
The circle of the globe commences here, too. The port of New York
lies on a single plane with all the world to-day. A single plane unites
it with every other port and seacoast and point of the whole world.
Out of the American hinterland, out of the depths of the inarticulate
American unconsciousness, a spring has come, a push and a re-
silience; and here where Europe meets America we have come to sit
at the focal point where two upspringing forces balance. The sun is
rising overhead, the sun which once shone brightly on Europe alone
and threw slanting rays merely upon New York. The sun has moved
across the Atlantic. The far coasts of Europe still shine with his light.
But they shine mildly, softly, like eastern coasts in late summer afternoon when the sun commences to slope toward the western sea.
And behind us, over the American hinterland, morning rays slant
where deep, impenetrable murkiness lay, and begin to unveil the face
of a continent. But over New York the dayspring commences to flood
his fruity warmth.

It is that the values have come to stand among us. It is they that
outtop the heaven-storming piles, and make the sun to float aloft and
the steam to shoot like flags. It was their absence that made the
buildings stand like tombstones, and life to lie inert. We never knew
them here. They may have stood before, in earlier American days.
But in our time they were gone. What bore their name and aped
their style were the conventions of middleclass trading society giving
themselves out for the worths of civilization. We had the smug safe
bourgeois values of the "humanists," the pontifical allies of the anar-
chistic business men. But the principles which lift men out of them
selves and lead them to human growth and human beauty were gone

from the scene; and unrelation of all things and all people filled the land with black. For values and religion and relation rise together. So it stood until the second decade of the new century when the new orientation began. What gave it to a dozen or more of artists to find the values again here on the soil, to restate ideas of work and growth and love, and run the flag of mature developed life once more to the masthead, we do not know. It may be that conditions were favorable to the new erection. Life has perhaps commenced to stabilize itself on the new continent, and men begun to cease excluding one another. Perhaps the new world of new expression of life which should have been reached when the feet first stepped from off the boats on American soil has faintly begun. Perhaps the tradition of life imported over the Atlantic has commenced expressing itself in terms of the new environment, giving the Port of New York a sense at last, and the entire land the sense of the Port of New York. It seems possible the European war helped the values to the masthead. We had been sponging on Europe for direction instead of developing our own, and Europe had been handing out nice little packages of spiritual direction to us. But then Europe fell into disorder and lost her way, and we were thrown back on ourselves to find inside ourselves sustaining faith. Yet, whether there was indeed a general movement anterior to the work of the worth-givers or whether the movement which we feel to-day merely flows from the songs they sang and the cries they uttered, we cannot know for sure. We saw it only after they had spoken. But what we do know, whatever the cause, is that we have to thank them for a wondrous gift. For, if to-day, the values stand aloft; if to-day the commencement of a religious sense is here; if to-day men on American land are commencing to come into relationship with one another and with the places in which they dwell, it is through the labor of some dozens of artist hands. Through words, lights, colors, the new world has been reached at last. We have to thank a few people—for the gift that is likest the gift of life.

1 9 2 4

# EDMUND WILSON

*The critic Edmund Wilson (1895–1972) delighted in reporting on nightclubs, Broadway shows, circuses, chorus girls backstage at the Ziegfeld Follies, and other facets of popular culture for* The New Republic *during the 1920's and 30's. Even as Wilson was evolving the magisterial style of his literary criticism and historical studies, he experimented with a more mercurial, notational approach in his New York reportage, one that would mirror the city's jazzy clamor.*

## THE FINALE AT THE FOLLIES

### DRESS REHEARSAL

IN THE DUSK of the darkened house, the Tiller girls link in a swinging line, practicing their steps and humming their refrain: alone in the dark, without orchestra, their voices sound girlish and soft. *Finale!* They troop to the back. The little waitresses in lavender come off—the pale green and lavender set folds away with large leisure and ease. An incisive New York voice—Florenz Ziegfeld, who is standing at the front of the house: *You've got to get those stockings right!* Their garters are out of alignment. *There's nothing to the costume but the stockings!* A rustle of laughter. *Darn right!* A Spanish mission has been unfolded—behind it, a backdrop of bright orange sandstone and bright purple cactus. A tall girl with a flopping sombrero mounts a pedestal and begins to pose. *All right: let's go!* The Tenor takes the stage: *Although I stand here singing, A rope I should be swinging, But I've really got to get it off my chest!* The show girls—white, green, white, white, black, orange; purple, green, orange, black, white, green. *You've got two white ones together! Put somebody between them. You go over on the end, Gladys. Now, begin again!* The girl who is doing the Circassian slave in the number *The Pearl of the East*, soft-molded in a fawn-colored robe under which she is almost nude, pale hair smoothed close to her calm little head to accommodate the flooding yellow wig, moves softly down the house toward a friend.

The show girls come in again: one is missing. *Who died?* She appears. *Now do that over.* In the wide space behind the backdrop, a great long-legged loose-legged girl is throwing herself about like a colt; a man holds up his gray hat for her; smiling, amiable, superb, she kicks it; then he sets out to sketch her. *Now, what's the matter with the light? Keep the light off the scenery!* The electrical lighting apparatus with military urgency is rushed to the wings. *Look out!* the smart nasal voice of the liveliest girl in a small town, *You'll get killed like that some day! I suppose you've come to make some more sketches. Yes? Well, you can't sketch them when they're leaping around like that!——I want to look before they leap.* She is gone. *I don't think she got that.——Say, do they ever get anything?* The lighting uncomfortably wavers from a warm orange to a cold pink. *Say: the girls are all right. It's the lights!——I know it: I'm explaining to the girls about the lights!*

The ponies are trooping downstairs with the pink legs and arms of the South Seas. *Come on, dumbbell!*——one reaches back for the hand of the girl behind her. A toe dancer sits rubbing her feet, strapping on her silk shoes. Another stands on one white leg, lifting the other straight up before her—hugging it, she leans against the scenery; with young intent eyes she watches the show. *You'll find it rough but gentle, Romantic, sentimental, Though I'm not a butter and egg man from the West! I would LIKE to corRAL*—The Tiller girls burst in, in a line—orange leggings and orange sombreros. *No: they don't come in yet.* The music of the orchestra stops: their voices sound girlish and foolish. *You don't come in on the beginning of the refrain: you come in on the second half of the refrain.* He sings the verse and half the refrain. *You come in on the second half of the refrain. Now do it over!* The girl on the pedestal, bored, breaks her pose and performs a shimmy step. The toe dancer drops her upright leg and lifts the other leg up, nursing it as she watches. *No brains! no beauty! no personality! Can't sing—can't dance—can't act!—stand 'em on their heads and they're all alike—you know!—Who's fucking her?—I don't know—but she's got a built-in radio in her apartment—so she says.—You still here? Still sketching, eh? Say: the doorman has orders not to let in any more synthetic men—what I call synthetic men. I've got to go on again! So long!* Will Rogers mounts the block, about which the Tiller girls are wheeling. *Say: he's going to whirl the lasso around the whole thing. Yeah: he's clever!* They crowd the wings. Behind them waits the Negro wardrobe woman, patient with a shade of sullenness—knowing herself handsome in another kind, she bides there, blinking at all that white beauty, those open-eyed confident white girls in their paradise of bright dresses: turquoise skirts and canary cloaks, pink bodies hung with dark green leaves, tall white flowerlike stalks that burst into purple and orange—all of them excited by the costumes and the music, proud to have been picked by Ziegfeld, happy to look like the covers of popular magazines— brown-eyed, clear-skinned, straight-browed, straight-backed.—A touch of the hand in passing: *Tomorrow at 11 o'clock?* The thin girl comic, a little strained: *How long has this been going on?* The curtains close. *No: listen here! The second time you close in—the second time! The curtains close: you're turning. They open: you're still turning. They close again: you close in and you stop! Now, go through it again from the beginning!*

The Tenor takes the stage: *Although I stand here singing, A rope I should be swinging, But I've really got to get it off my chest!* The towering shapes of the show girls, blooming in their enormous sombreros: black, white, green, white, orange, white; purple, green, orange, black, white, green. *You'll find it rough but gentle, Romantic, sentimental, Though I'm not a butter and egg man from the West!* The show girls droop away. *I would LIKE to corRAL, A very merry necessary little gal!* At the signal, the Tiller girls enter: white with orange leggings and sombreros, white with purple leggings and sombreros. They make a swinging line: all together, with the strong urgent beats of their kicking they send home the strong beats of the music. *I would LIKE to corRAL!* They crack their whips all together. Will Rogers mounts the pedestal: the tall girl drops to a sitting pose, hugging one knee, hanging the other. The Tiller girls circle about the pedestal, two rings, one inside the other and turning in opposite directions. He drops his lariat down about them, making it whirl in the opposite direction to the outer circle of girls. *I would LIKE to corRAL!* The beat has mastered everything; it pounds fast in a crash of orange. For two minutes, in wheeling speed, focused in the green-gilt proscenium frame, they concentrate the pulse of the city. The bronze gilded curtains close on the girls and the turning lariat. They open: the rings are still turning. They close, as the circles draw in and halt.

*THE NEW REPUBLIC*, 1925

## THOUGHTS ON LEAVING NEW YORK FOR NEW ORLEANS

A T THE AQUARIUM, a tropical booby bird, imprisoned in a small tank, is shivering with the cold.

Horses are slipping in downtown streets and cutting their knees on the ice.

The boys in the office of the *Daily Graphic* are hot on the trail of Earl Carroll's orgy; the boys in the office of the *Herald Tribune* are hot on the trail of the Countess Cathcart.

Young lawyers in the District Attorney's office are forswearing the use of alcohol in order that they may act as *agents provocateurs* in fashionable bootlegging night clubs. Young lawyers in private firms are protecting the interests of the Consolidated Gas Company.

Young men in bond-selling houses are worrying for fear they may not have enough self-confidence to put over the sale of their bonds.

Typists are looking forward to the moment when they can go to the water-cooler.

Gray snow, which matches the sky, is falling.

The students at New York University are making a loyal effort to pretend that Washington Square is their campus.

At a dance in Webster Hall, the waiters are picking the pockets of a fat Greenwich Village bookdealer who has come in a pirate costume.

Young poets, who cannot afford night clubs, are writing poems on the hollowness of modern life.

The Brevoort and the Lafayette are being unattractively renovated in the style of the lavatory of the Pennsylvania Station.

The gray snow, as soon as it has fallen, begins rising in exhalations, and many people come down with bronchitis, tonsilitis, pneumonia, pleurisy, influenza and tuberculosis.

Clothing stores on Fourteenth Street are selling out their entire stock.

In the textile district, the textile workers are pumped in early in the morning, in and out at the lunch hour and out at the end of the day.

Furniture imprisoned in the fortress of the Manhattan Storage Company is running up enormous bills.

In drug-stores, miscellaneous women, as they wait to use the telephone booths, are buying banana-nut sundaes and listening to phonograph records of Ukulele Ike.

At the Grand Central Palace there is a big Bathroom Fixture Exhibition.

At the Algonquin, when a popular dramatic critic says, "I'm going to South America," an eminent humorist will flash, "Going in for the big Honduras contest?"

At the Opera, they are working on the revival of a long-forgotten opera by Meyerbeer.

Highbrow theaters are straining every nerve to discover another Michael Arlen.

People are waiting in line in the cold to see the new Gloria Swanson picture.

Popular actors in the West Fifties are endeavoring to seduce young actresses by showing them oil portraits of themselves; the young actresses are extorting contracts before they consent to yield.

The hostesses and hosts of night clubs are working on quaint accents and wisecracks which will make it seem worthwhile to their clientele to pay their exorbitant cover charges.

Antique stores on Madison Avenue are selling pairs of faked china dogs for sixty-five dollars apiece.

On Park Avenue, above the Grand Central, many people—at a very high cost—believe they are living in style.

People on Lexington Avenue are wishing that they lived in a more cheerful street.

At the concerts of modern music, the ladies wear auburn sideboards and corpse-white toques.

At the concerts of the Philadelphia orchestra, Mr. Stokowski wears a handsome dress suit.

Big theatrical men with their mistresses, both shaped like well-stuffed ottomans, are eating sandwiches at sandwich palaces.

Detectives and tarts in collusion are framing victims in the upper Forties.

Smart book-stores on the side streets in the Forties are disposing of first editions of Joseph Hergesheimer for seven dollars apiece.

The art galleries are lined with carpets, like Campbell's Funeral Church.

Bishop Manning has made public statements on the importance of Christian faith.

People suffering from exhaustion, despondency and acute self-dissatisfaction are being treated by expensive specialists for dental trouble, mastoiditis, astigmatism, inflammatory rheumatism, ophthalmic goiter and fallen arches, then finally turned over to analysts.

People coming home late at night in the upper East Eighties and Nineties are compelled to struggle with three Yale locks in order to get into apartments which they will subsequently find have been robbed.

Corner drug-stores will supply bad gin to people who are well enough known to them.

Students at Columbia University are electing courses in Collective Bargaining, The History of Modern Thought and Problems of Abnormal Psychology.

In Harlem, the whites come to visit the Negroes in the hope of enjoying among them a little color and warmth; and the Negroes are making an effort to live as much as possible like the whites.

*THE NEW REPUBLIC*, 1926

# VLADIMIR MAYAKOVSKY

*The Russian poet Vladimir Mayakovsky (1893–1930) wrote this poem on the Brooklyn Bridge during a three-month stay in the United States in 1925. Mayakovsky, who promoted the legend of himself as a larger-than-life Bolshevik dynamo, salutes the bridge as one outsized force to another.*

### BROOKLYN BRIDGE

Give, Coolidge,
a shout of joy!
I too will spare no words
                          about good things.
Blush
      at my praise,
                   go red as our flag,
however
          united-states
                  -of
-america you may be.
As a crazed believer
                enters
                    a church,
retreats
      into a monastery cell,
                      austere and plain;
so I,
    in graying evening
              haze,
humbly set foot
          on Brooklyn Bridge.
As a conqueror presses
             into a city
                  all shattered,

on cannon with muzzles
                    craning high as a giraffe—
so, drunk with glory,
                    eager to live,
I clamber,
        in pride,
                    upon Brooklyn Bridge.
As a foolish painter
                    plunges his eye,
sharp and loving,
                    into a museum madonna,
so I
    from the near skies
                    bestrewn with stars,
gaze
    at New York
                    through the Brooklyn Bridge.
New York,
        heavy and stifling
                    till night,
has forgotten
            its hardships
                    and height;
and only
        the household ghosts
ascend
        in the lucid glow of its windows.
Here
    the elevateds
                    drone softly.
And only
        their gentle
                    droning
tell us:
        here trains
                    are crawling and rattling

like dishes
        being cleared into a cupboard.
While
      a shopkeeper fetched sugar
from a mill
        that seemed to project
                out of the water—
the masts
      passing under the bridge
looked
      no larger than pins.
I am proud
      of just this
         mile of steel;
upon it,
      my visions come to life, erect—
here's a fight
      for construction
          instead of style,
an austere disposition
        of bolts
          and steel.
If
  the end of the world
        befall—
and chaos
      smash our planet
        to bits,
and what remains
      will be
        this
bridge, rearing above the dust of destruction;
then,
    as huge ancient lizards
        are rebuilt

from bones
               finer than needles,
                              to tower in museums,
so,
    from this bridge,
                   a geologist of the centuries
will succeed
             in recreating
                       our contemporary world.
He will say:
           —Yonder paw
                 of steel
once joined
           the seas and the prairies;
from this spot,
            Europe
                 rushed to the West,
scattering
         to the wind
                Indian feathers.
This rib
       reminds us
             of a machine—
just imagine,
           would there be hands enough,
after planting
           a steel foot
               in Manhattan,
to yank
       Brooklyn to oneself
                   by the lip?
By the cables
         of electric strands,
I recognize
         the era succeeding
                the steam age—

here
    men
        had ranted
             on radio.
Here
    men
        had ascended
             in planes.
For some,
      life
         here
            had no worries;
for others,
       it was a prolonged
             and hungry howl.
From this spot,
         jobless men
leapt
    headlong
         into the Hudson.
Now
    my canvas
        is unobstructed
as it stretches on cables of string
               to the feet of the stars.
I see:
    here
        stood Mayakovsky,
stood,
      composing verse, syllable by syllable.
I stare
      as an Eskimo gapes at a train,
I seize on it
        as a tick fastens to an ear.

Brooklyn Bridge—
yes . . .
   That's quite a thing!

1925

# HART CRANE

Hart Crane (1899–1932) came to New York from Cleveland, and developed an ecstatic, highly rhetorical verse to encapsulate the rhythms and imagery of the modern city. His long poem "The Bridge," of which this is the prelude, sought to combine the epic modernism of Eliot's "The Waste Land" with the affirmation of Whitman, taking the Brooklyn Bridge as its symbol of exaltation. The poem evolved out of Crane's experience of living in a Brooklyn Heights apartment adjacent to the bridge, a location he described in a 1924 letter to his family: "Every time one looks at the harbor and the NY skyline across the river it is quite different, and the range of atmospheric effects is endless. . . . Look far to your left toward Staten Island and there is the statue of Liberty, with that remarkable lamp of hers that makes her seen for miles. And up at the right Brooklyn Bridge, the most superb piece of construction in the modern world, I'm sure, with strings of light crossing it like glowing worms as the Ls and surface cars pass each other coming and going. It is particularly fine to feel the greatest city in the world from enough distance, as I do here, to see its larger proportions."

## TO BROOKLYN BRIDGE

How many dawns, chill from his rippling rest
The seagull's wings shall dip and pivot him,
Shedding white rings of tumult, building high
Over the chained bay waters Liberty—

Then, with inviolate curve, forsake our eyes
As apparitional as sails that cross
Some page of figures to be filed away;
—Till elevators drop us from our day . . .

I think of cinemas, panoramic sleights
With multitudes bent toward some flashing scene
Never disclosed, but hastened to again,
Foretold to other eyes on the same screen;

And Thee, across the harbor, silver-paced
As though the sun took step of thee, yet left
Some motion ever unspent in thy stride,—
Implicitly thy freedom staying thee!

Out of some subway scuttle, cell or loft
A bedlamite speeds to thy parapets,
Tilting there momently, shrill shirt ballooning,
A jest falls from the speechless caravan.

Down Wall, from girder into street noon leaks,
A rip-tooth of the sky's acetylene;
All afternoon the cloud-flown derricks turn . . .
Thy cables breathe the North Atlantic still.

And obscure as that heaven of the Jews,
Thy guerdon . . . Accolade thou dost bestow
Of anonymity time cannot raise:
Vibrant reprieve and pardon thou dost show.

O harp and altar, of the fury fused,
(How could mere toil align thy choiring strings!)
Terrific threshold of the prophet's pledge,
Prayer of pariah, and the lover's cry,—

Again the traffic lights that skim thy swift
Unfractioned idiom, immaculate sigh of stars,
Beading thy path—condense eternity:
And we have seen night lifted in thine arms.

Under thy shadow by the piers I waited;
Only in darkness is thy shadow clear.
The City's fiery parcels all undone,
Already snow submerges an iron year . . .

O Sleepless as the river under thee,
Vaulting the sea, the prairies' dreaming sod,
Unto us lowliest sometime sweep, descend
And of the curveship lend a myth to God.

1927, 1930

[ 486 ]

# STEPHEN GRAHAM

*The English travel writer Stephen Graham (1884–1975) was best known for his long series of books on Russia and the Middle East; he also wrote biographies of Ivan the Terrible, Peter the Great, and Stalin.* New York Nights, *from which this description of his nocturnal perambulations through Manhattan is taken, remains one of the best, most sure-footed books by a visitor to the city.*

## EXTERIOR STREET

I STARTED OFF from South Ferry one night upon a zigzag walk. Sleepless tramps were huddled in the seats in Battery Park; others were lying on the grass, flat and dazed as if they had fallen from balloons. There were hoots and howls from across the river, red lights and green lights, the hum-grum of machinery, and the strange electric-light cascade of moving elevated trains. 'Twas one by the clock. Syria slept. Greece slept.

I walked by Front Street to Moore Street, to Water Street, to Broad, to Pearl, to Coenties Slip, to Stone, to Mill Lane, to South William Street, to Broad again, past a blank empty lighted telegraph office, to Exchange Place, to New Street, to Wall Street. Thus I arrived at the financial anvil of the world. But all was still, no hammering, no bellows blowing, no flying sparks. Yellow stars looked down on the deserted Exchange. But I saw what appeared to be some Pagan temple, a stark altar of human sacrifice, and it proved to be a famous Christian Church, none other than Holy Trinity on Broadway, and as I stood by the strange little graveyard the church clock struck half past one. The little white headstones looked like the dead popping up from the tomb. There was heard the resounding hoot of a steamer on the river—yea, the last trump. Fast cars scooted along wet empty Broadway as if fleeing the wrath to come—and all were going up town.

Then I went on by Little Thames Street, and felt for a moment as if I were in part of the City of London. It also is deserted in the regions of Capel Court at that hour of the night. There are no night-shifts in stockbroking. You do not see a relief of stenographers being marched up Wall Street by a Managing Clerk; the stenographer's relief is prancing in the White Friars and Tangoland.

I was in Cedar Street and Greenwich Street, walking under the "El" like a rat, and came to Liberty Street—O Liberty, most empty was thy street—and to Washington above that sleeping Syria and sleeping Greece, and so, going by Cortland Street, I came to West Street and its great market. It was two o'clock, and New York here was very much alive.

There were horse waggons and motor waggons, cases and baskets of vegetables and fruit, and porters innumerable hurrying hither and thither with gleaming white-wood boxes on their shoulders. I emerged from the dead city where never a blade of grass twinkles before square toes and came into a fairyland of cucumbers and corn, cabbages and melons and Malaga grapes. Refreshing fruit odours invaded the nostrils.

Heaps of small black grapes looked in the dim light like exaggerated caviare. I kicked a peach as I walked along. What largesse in the night, peaches are like stones in the roadway! They tumbled from wooden troughs and buckets uncovered and overfilled. There were South Mountain oranges and California lemons. There were crates of greens stacked higher than men. There were cabinets of blackberries and raspberries. The nose whispered to the heart "Raspberries, raspberries" as it tasted the air. Coloured porters with perspiring gleaming faces shouldered boxes of green varnish-surfaced peppers along narrow alley ways between piles of other boxes. Carrots peeped out of their ventilated crates like brown ribbons. Side streets were blocked with potatoes and yams. Activity, activity, activity—and quietude. The workers do not help themselves along with foul expletives and abuse as in London. They seem to be conserving their energy, or imitating the electric lamps which do their job and say nothing about it. But it is a big market, bigger than Covent Garden in London, and I reflected that New Yorkers eat more fruit and vegetables than we do. There is more for them to eat. Their reserves are greater.

The quayside beyond the market is long and spacious and empty. The freer air seems to be minus something—is it the mental ozone of New York? West Street is a long backyard. It has no mechanical turnings on the left. If you wish to take a turning on the left, the way of the heart, you must take a ship. There are ships in the wharves still as birds dozing head on wing in a covert at night. Not a rustle nor a whisper comes from the giant Cunarder. West Street is the landing stage of the Atlantic ferry. You stand on West Street and you think Southampton. You stand in West Street and you think Havana, San Juan, Cristobal, Panama, Valparaiso. You stand on West Street and think Cherbourg, Naples, the Piræus. But now no one is thinking anything. The gangways may be down, but no one is on them. Eastward New York's luminosity lies in layers like masonry of light and darkness built from the rocks to the night-sky. Westward lies the beautiful river flowing away to the calm ocean. And on the wide roadway of the quay laden lorries rush and crash bearing produce to the market or away.

I sought a turning on the left and did not find one till Fourteenth Street. It was a lonely walk. A drunken man sitting on a bit of paving addressed me vaguely. He was looking at the heavens with lacklustre eye.

"There's only one star left. How far's that from here?" he queried.

I passed an empty "Goulash Kitchen," passed standing freight cars, passed the embarkation for Tampa and Mobile, passed the Boston and Providence pier, passed the R.M.S.P., passed the Hoboken Ferry and entered the Gansevoort market stirring feebly. A black and white cat was squatting in the roadway fastidiously eating melon.

My turning to the left proved to be the virtual one of Eleventh Avenue where it starts North near West Fourteenth Street, and there, like a derelict trolley car left stranded on the ooze after the subsidence of a flood, was a windowed shed with the explicit word LUNCH printed on it. This was kept by a lonely Greek.

"Where do you come from?" I asked, perched on my revolving stool at the counter and munching pie.

"Island," he answered.

"What? From Ireland? You don't look it."

"No. Island. Crete. Greek, yes."

"Fine country."

"No. Some nations go up. Some nations go down. The great Alexander thousand year ago take whole world. Then Venetians come. Before Jesus. Romans. Yes, the French. Napoleon. Germans. Now English, I guess."

"Not Americans?"

"No, English now. But in two hundred year maybe England go down. Other nation rise up."

"How d'ye like New York?"

"Not like it. Bad place here. Kill you for a dime. Want woman; cost ten dollars. Take her hotel two more. Drinks bad poison. Good drink cost big money. Not like New York."

A friend from the island of Rhodes rolled in for his morning coffee on his way to work at the National Biscuit Factory. "Rhodes no good. Italians there. They turn out Greeks. New York fine. Plenty money. Rodos bad."

I said Good Morning and Good-bye, and walked out on to Fourteenth Street, turned into Tenth Avenue and then into West Fifteenth Street where the "fleet" of the Biscuit Company was waiting in the dark like a string of camels before dawn on the outskirts of Baghdad.

Biscuits are not made all night. They are evidently partly compounded of daylight. But here was where my friend from Rhodes belonged, or in local parlance here the islander "held down his jahb."

Ninth Avenue was drear. Orion up above the roofs was striding hastily across Sixteenth Street. On Eighth Avenue a big fruiterer's stood wide open, very still and empty. What zest for trade!

West Seventeenth Street, Seventh Avenue, West Eighteenth, Sixth Avenue, West Nineteenth, passed as one. I was thinking of London and did not notice them. At Fifth Avenue I paused, for the speedway had had its nightly wash and was all aswill with water like a bath-house floor.

I zigzagged across to Lexington and saw an iceman dragging blocks of ice into a large clean-swept and ready but empty cafeteria.

On Twenty-third Street I stopped at a shop window which was stacked with dollar shirts. A tall notice said "FORCED TO SELL." The shop was closed but it was flooded with electric light. I saw many offices and barber shops where the lights had been left on all night. And on Twenty-ninth Street I paused in front of a locked undertaker's where a white-lined baby's coffin was exposed, charmingly illuminated.

On Avenue A, the ashpan of the other avenues, there were notices which struck an Englishman as strange. The words TRANSIENTS met my eye. We advertise "Short Garage" but New Yorkers talk of "Transients." What poetry there is in the word! In some streets all other lighted signs have been put out and the one word remains brilliantly enshrined, now here, now there, "Transients!" "Transients!"

After all, every one in the great caravanserai of New York is a transient. Every one in the caravanserai of the world is a transient. The world itself is a transient. Look up among the stars; you will see it as a celestial sky sign. There it is pricked out all over the dark deep of space—TRANSIENTS.

I am a transient in the city of New York at night. I am gyrating across the fitfully sleeping city from the Hudson to the East River. No other great city can be got across so quickly. One could run across it in less than half an hour. I was soon out at the water edge on the other side of the island, listening to the ceaseless Edison works. Oh, what is Edison contriving there, are they engines of death or of life? The wonder name of Edison stirs the imagination as if he were an arch wizard, the Michael Scott of the New World. The river of Time flows by and the great works climb upward on its banks.

It is five a.m. Something of the burden of the city has been lifted. The air is light. The heart seems freed. I feel happy to be walking. I love the space and the quietness. I have got rid of the idea of going to bed, got rid of the routine of daily life. New York and its millions, its wealth, its mysteries, are mine. There is a sense of conquest. The bustle has died down and I am still walking. The majority of people are asleep—but I am not the least sleepy. It seems as if life has just begun. I am dancing on a springed floor. The stones of the side-walks help me to leap along First Avenue, grim, empty, gloomy Avenue

One, which has no turning to the right except little bottle-neck lanes which go down to the edge of the water of the East River.

I spent many nights in this way wandering about the city and returning at dawn, resuming next night at the point where I had left off the night before.

Whoever would know the poetry of New York must walk it in the after-midnight hours, see the red light come out on the Metropolitan tower preliminary to the striking of the hour; one is too pre-occupied and diverted to observe it in the livelier hours; enter the Central station at four a.m. and see it anew, deserted, silent, beautiful as on the morning of Opening Day; see the City Hall at dawn hanging down from on high like the sky's apron.

Queensboro Bridge, seen from the foot of East Fifty-third Street late at night, is a marvellous spectacle. There is light in the sky above and wandering light on the river below. There is all the grandeur which circumambient shade can give. "What have I come to?" you ask, astonished after the sordidness of the Avenue, with its many garbage cans. Suddenly you see a mirage. It is called Queensboro Bridge. It takes the mind to the finest parts of the Seine and the Thames. You feel you must be at the centre of a great city, near its Parliament, its palaces, its pontifical grandeurs. But this is Rome without a Pope—a mere bridge, beautiful and awe-inspiring by accident, a convenience whose formal magnificence goes unheeded in the daytime, when business absorbs all the interest and takes the first and only place in men's eyes.

Still as I walk on I find the influence of the bridge expressed in men's habitations. As I approach the great viaduct of the bridge the poor district smartens up dramatically. The massive piles of the viaduct and the lofty exaggerated attendant factory chimneys, the vague Colossus of a gas works, all suggest more spacious living, and Sutton Place is the reply.

But I descend rapidly a long straight empty street nameless here for evermore, and it becomes Avenue A—the old ashpan once again. People of no social prominence are herded in grim unremarkable blocks. Fire ladders disfigure the houses, or do they merely hide them, like black veils the ravaged faces of elderly ladies. Perhaps the houses look worse than a similar variety in London. But imagine Bow and Whitechapel all festooned with rusty fire ladders! There is something queer about these ladders. They look like the old black ladders of tramp steamers let down to the wharves. The immigrant never gets away from the debarkation gangway. All New York is a quay. I see all the vessels that have arrived there—then the population swarming on the streets are all people who have come off ships.

But it is the most extraordinary shore in the world. It is well to have arrived there sometime or other on life's voyage.

Solitary walking along the empty streets seems to attune the mind to the city. True thoughts flow like music from the mind. I came to another outside street happily named Exterior Street. It has a Venetian view of river, lights, ferries, and small boats. Away beyond the river the sparse lights of Welfare Island diamond the dark. On the right is the grandeur of the bridge. But Exterior Street is below New York. It is bounded by the great grey cliff of the original Manhattan Island. Somewhere up above there are houses and gardens. Children perhaps come and drop pebbles down into Exterior Street or on to the shaggy tufts of old grass. It is like a bit of mountain road. There are hunks of uncontrolled rock. The shoulder of the world juts out. The silence is only accented by the rustling of the wind. No, there is another sound which is part of the silence, it is the undying whirr of rotary machines. I am walking towards a huge factory and from its little doors strange dwarfs with darkened faces come out, look round, and go in again—the workers, they don't belong. I sit on the grass under the cliff and look over the water. It is Exterior Street: I am outside New York.

To understand any experience you must get outside of it.

King Canute went to Exterior Street and bade the waves keep away from his toes. The gentry from Park Avenue and Upper Fifth might well make a pilgrimage to Exterior Street at four in the morning and sit there in the grass, outside the scene of their wealth and their power.

I left this curious street by smart residential East Seventy-ninth, thence by East End Avenue to East Eightieth. I had been *outside*; soon I was very much *inside*. I came to a steaming curtained window, lighted and murmurous. The one word STUBE was explanatory. I went inside and asked for cider. This seemed to amuse the bar-tender who, however, poured out two mugs of it at once and set them before me. There was a big notice on one of the walls, NO GAMBLING, and under it a vociferous throng were throwing scarlet dice.

"Splitz!" "Splitz!"—every one at the bar was asking for "Splitz."

I was invited to join the "Wilhelm Union." No one spoke a word of English. Mine host kept saying something about *zwei kasen Scotch verkauft*. I had a glass of whisky with a red-faced and puffing, very drunken man who showed me an iron cross and very paradoxically wanted to kiss me. I pointed to the only girl in the establishment, sitting sulkily in a corner. He took me over to a poster depicting the American Unknown Soldier which was inscribed—"Work for the Living," and he nodded his head sententiously. A fig for unknown soldiers; all German soldiers were unknown. At least, so I surmised.

In this tavern ended another night and when next I resumed I quickly reached luxuriant, spacious, Southern-looking Fifth Avenue, *the* Avenue, as it is affectionately called. Curious fact about the avenues—the word avenue means approach; in England avenues are usually bordered with trees; in order to make a road into an avenue you plant trees. An avenue's trees are its guard of honour leading to the portals of country house, castle, or palace. But the avenues of New York do not lead anywhere. They are paved rivers which go on and on through various districts to lose themselves eventually in wildernesses, to be dried up in social deserts. But Fifth Avenue for one hundred and ten streets does preserve its character of grandeur, and it is one of the most exhilarating ways to walk in any city.

With Central Park on one side and fine houses on the other, I walked twenty blocks, the Harlem moon standing over the street and raising gleaming reflections all the way. Moonlight also glinted from the highly polished varnish of fast moving automobiles. No one was walking except myself, and many men and women passed in cars and taxis, mostly lovers indulgently petting one another in course of transit from one night-club to another, or from a dance to their homes.

I turned with the park railings along Hundred-and-Tenth Street and came to the gay base of Lenox Avenue, then went in a circle through the Morningside district back to Fifth Avenue. I came to Harlem all aflare with the lure of pleasure—cabarets, night-clubs, dance-halls, chop-suey restaurants, parlours. At three in the morning I watched a bevy of coloured girls operating a barber shop, cutting the fuzzy hair of Harlem dandies in a brilliantly lighted hairdressing saloon. I strayed into Capitol Club and saw white women dreamily trotting with Negroes in slow jazz, strange women who defy the custom of night to enjoy the sensual thrill of the black man's dance.

By the cross-streets I passed through Africa. Street after street was entirely black, housing swarms of families, all black. Banjoes still throbbed in some; the ukuleles gurgled dance music, but most houses were silent. They were sleeping and snoring. They were bathed in the deep physical ardour of Negro sleep—only in doorways here and there petting couples lingered awake, oblivious of the clock.

I left Harlem by Edgecombe Avenue and St. Nicholas Avenue, the road dug up and dotted with red lanterns, and came to a substantial quiet and English-looking neighbourhood, Hamilton Terrace, 144th Street and Convent Avenue, very respectable.

But respectability only held a strip, and having crossed it I was in Amsterdam Avenue. Then I came to Broadway still very much Broadway and, making a sharp descent by 147th Street, came once more to the end of New York—the grandest backway of all—Riverside Drive. The view was very beautiful. I could imagine that the Hudson River was the Danube and that I was in Bratislava again. The esplanade was high, serene, and wind-blown, fresh with raindrops flickering across the eyes. Little boats, like sleeping ducks, lay upon the surface of the water. The automobiles which whirled along the drive seemed unreal; the river is the great reality. It is on view here. It knows it was before all the rest and will survive it, with thousands of years both before and after.

A ferry boat crosses the river like a tram on the sea—transients once more, transients. Three shooting stars follow and pass over New Jersey—transients, transients. All is transient. New York is a setting for a drama that is being played, a spectacle which is being rehearsed. At four in the morning I am walking along like the

Wandering Jew, but my taste is shared by two lovers in a solemn closed car drawn up overlooking the river. Through the misty glass I see them in one another's arms, in close embrace.

Through silver-tinted clouds the moon seems to beat her way, keeping coming out, keeping going in, and as I climb Washington Heights I seem to be making another exit from the city, upward to the stars. All the way from South Ferry to the sky—I have skated the stairways of the city. I have gone from outside to inside, by Exterior Street to the heart. The mystic closes his eyes that he may see better. The curtain which comes down gives leisure to the mind to consider the hidden springs of drama. Night reveals the day.

*NEW YORK NIGHTS*, 1927

# AL SMITH

*Al Smith (1873–1944), the child of immigrants, was reared in a ghetto on the Lower East Side, went to work early to support his family, and eventually entered politics. Though initially rising through the Tammany machine, he showed increasing independence, and became a progressive governor of New York and a leading reformer of the Democratic Party. He was the first Roman Catholic candidate for the presidency, in 1928. In Smith's charming autobiography* Up to Now, *he describes what it was like to be a poor but resourceful youth growing up on the streets of New York in the 1880's (incidentally noting the same snowstorm José Martí describes in his entry, page 271).*

### FROM *UP TO NOW*

IN 1888, on March twelfth, New York witnessed a phenomenal snowstorm referred to ever since as "the blizzard." On the Sunday night before the blizzard, carrying out my part of the work of management of our little store, I put up the shutters, at the suggestion of my mother, at ten o'clock. It was then misting rain. No high wind was apparent and no warning of the impending storm. When we awoke on the morning of March twelfth the candy store was buried under snow, and there being no way of reaching it from the inside, we lost all track of it until midday on the following Tuesday. I distinctly remember that I was not very much concerned with the inconvenience of our customers or the fear for the perishable quality of the merchandise, but I was very deeply concerned about the welfare of a Scotch terrier dog with four puppies to which I wanted to get food. The terrier dog was down in the back room of the store.

On Tuesday, the thirteenth of March, the day after the blizzard, for the first time within the knowledge of anybody alive at that period, the East River froze over. Some very busy fellows, with an eye to private profit, erected a ladder at Pier 28 on the East River, charging five cents to go down the ladder so that you could walk across to Brooklyn. In company with a number of small boys, I beat the ladder game, slid down the side of the pier, got down on the ice and walked over to Martin's Stores, just opposite in Brooklyn, and back. There is always one individual around who wants to outdo everybody else. He wants to be able to say that he did something nobody else did. Together with the same crowd, I saw a harnessed horse swung onto the ice, and a man ride across on horseback.

Toward three o'clock that afternoon, a large piece of ice broke away and went down the river with the tide with some twenty or thirty people on it. The tow-boats on the river went alongside the cake of ice and picked the people off safely. The cake broke up before it reached Governor's Island.

The schools were closed and there was not much for the school boys and girls to do, so I became a volunteer member of No. 32 Engine Company located on John Street. The engine company had borrowed four sleighs from a leather concern, manned them with firemen and hose, and used the horses of the Fire Department to make their way as best they could through lower New York.

I can distinctly remember the predictions made by experienced fire fighters that had a fire of any consequence broken out on the lower end of Manhattan Island on the Monday morning of the blizzard, nothing could have stopped it from sweeping Manhattan right off the earth.

Volunteer work of that nature was agreeable to me because I had always had a strong desire to be a fireman and performed my probationary duties under what was then called the Buffaloes. The Buffaloes was an order of young boys interested in fire fighting and in the glamour and excitement of the engine house who were willing to give volunteer service. In my after-school hours, for recreation, I practically lived in the engine house of Engine Company No. 32 on John Street. I rode on the hose cart and performed the various duties around the engine house required of the boys belonging to the Buffalo corps.

✦  ✦  ✦  ✦  ✦

In the summer of '88, when I was not quite fifteen years old, the pressure upon the family treasury was so great that it was necessary for me to branch out and find greater earning capacity. I left school before graduation and engaged in the trucking business with a man by the name of William J. Redmond. I held the position known in those days as truck chaser. There were no telephones or other means of easy communication and the truck chaser was a young man or boy who could run along the water front, pick up the trucks of his employer and deliver orders to them before they came back to the base of operation.

As a truck chaser, I earned three dollars a week. In an effort to better myself I went to work as an assistant shipping clerk and general all-round handy boy in the oil establishment known as Clarkson & Ford, in Front Street near Peck Slip, for eight dollars a week. I took advantage of opportunities in the nighttime to earn a little more for the promotion of the welfare of the family.

I remember one night's work very distinctly. Gifted with a good loud voice, I was paid to read off the ticker tape on the night of the Sullivan-Corbett fight. Like most of the young fellows of my time, I was a strong rooter for John L. Sullivan. A few months ago I told this story to James J. Corbett, the victor on that occasion, who has since that time become a warm personal friend.

In 1892 the pressure of necessity again made itself apparent, and as the ordinary clerical position of that day did not pay sufficient for the needs that I was compelled to meet, I found employment, at what at that time was regarded as a very good salary, in the Fulton Fish Market. I received twelve dollars a week. Salaries were large because the work was very hard. I reported for duty at four o'clock in the morning and worked until four o'clock in the afternoon, five days of the week, and reported at three o'clock in the morning on Friday.

I was employed by the wholesale commission house of John Feeney & Co. My position had the lofty title of assistant bookkeeper, and consisted of doing about everything there was to be done around the market. In addition to the salary, all employees were permitted to take home for their own use and the use of their families as much fish as they wanted. I think I may well say that for a long time we had such a complete fish diet that the entire family developed a fear of them. A live one might at some time or other wreak his vengeance for the devoured members of his finny family.

The great science about the wholesale fish business in my time was a knowledge ahead of time of the catch. Fish had to be sold when caught, as the only known means of preservation was packing in loose ice. Economy suggested that the market be cleaned every day, and the shrewd commission merchant was the man who had a knowledge in advance of either a glut or a scarcity. Part of my job was the use of a pair of strong marine glasses from the roof of the fish market in order to pick out the fishing smacks of the fleet operated by my employers as they turned out of Buttermilk Channel into the lower East River. A low draft was a big catch. Riding high on the crest of the wave meant a failure, and as it was known to the owners of the business where each particular smack was operating, so also was the cargo known. In September, the smack that was operating off Seabright, New Jersey, was in quest of bluefish. The well-laden smack, turning out of the Channel, indicated a plentiful supply of blue, and that regulated the price. Cold-storage warehouses had not been invented to circumvent the economic law of supply and demand.

From the fish market I naturally sought promotion and went to work in Brooklyn as shipping clerk for the Davison Steam Pump Works. It was while I was in their employ, in January, 1895, that I received my first political appointment as a clerk in the office of the commissioner of jurors.

During my governorship I have been interested in the setting-up of playgrounds and places of recreation for the children of New York. Naturally, my mind drifts back to the lack of playground facilities and of ordered and properly directed recreation when I was a small boy. But somehow or other, everybody is cared for and we were not without means of amusement and opportunities for exercise and recreation, even though they may have been very crude. No gymnasium that was ever built, no athletic club in the country, could offer to anybody the opportunities given to the small boy along the water front, using the bowsprit and the rigging of ships as a gymnasium. When the ship came to port laden to the water line, trapezes, parallel bars, everything that would take the place of the modern gymnasium was available. As the ship was unloaded over a period of weeks—all by man and horse power—she rose with the tide, and when one bowsprit was no longer available, there was a new arrival every day; so that, while the gymnasium might move a block or a block and a half, there was always one at hand well stocked and ready for use.

The East River was the place for swimming, and as early as April and as late as October the refreshing waters of the East River, free entirely at that time from pollution, offered the small boy all the joys that now come to the winter or summer bather on the shores of the Atlantic Ocean. The dressing rooms were under the dock. Bathing suits were not heard of. In fact, it would have been dangerous to suggest them, for fear you might be accused of setting a fashion that everybody else could not follow.

The popular swimming place was the dock at the foot of Pike Street, built well out into the river, and there was a rather good-natured caretaker who paid no attention to small boys seeking the pleasure and recreation of swimming in the East River.

In the warm summer days it was great fun sliding under the dock while the men were unloading the boat-loads of bananas from Central America. An occasional overripe banana would drop from the green bunch being handed from one dock laborer to another, and the short space between the dock and the boat contained room enough for at least a dozen of us to dive after the banana.

Beginners learned to swim in the fish cars. These were directly back of the fish market. The water in them was about three feet deep and the cars were six feet wide and about twelve feet long. They were used for preserving fish caught alive, and particularly for green turtles. When empty, the covers were lifted from them and they provided a kind of swimming pool for the amateur who was not quite ready to trust himself in the East River.

Roller skating in City Hall Park was something of a luxury, and a trip to Central Park, with a ride in the goat wagon, was something that came to you on your birthday if you were lucky. Our favorite way of reaching Central Park was on the open cars of the Second

Avenue horse-car line in the summertime. They started from Fulton Ferry and gathered in all the downtown children lucky enough to get a trip to Central Park.

Coney Island was entirely out of the world. The favorite way of reaching it was by boat from Jewell's Wharf, which lay alongside the foot of Fulton Street, Brooklyn. We went by boat from the wharf to the foot of Sixty-Fifth Street, South Brooklyn, there transferring to the old Sea Beach route through which the subway trains are now running. We transferred to cars pulled by a steam locomotive and landed at Vanderveer's Hotel at the extreme westerly end of the busy section of Coney Island as we know it today.

Less than a mile of the Atlantic Ocean water front was then Coney Island. The largely built-up residential section now known as Sea Gate was then called Norton's Point, because it was the property of a man named Norton, and was entirely undeveloped, there being no way of getting to it. In 1889, Norton offered the property to Richard Croker and Phil Dwyer as a possible site for a race track. Croker and Dwyer conferred with Austin Corbin, of the Long Island Railroad, in an effort to have a railroad station established there. Failing to secure this, they were obliged to decline Norton's offer. Norton had offered them the entire property for $80,000, and in 1922, when I spent the summer in Sea Gate with my family, a single house with three lots attached thereto was appraised at $75,000.

The playthings for boys in my neighborhood were the animals brought to the port of New York from the West Indian islands and Central and South America. Goats, parrots and monkeys were the favorites. They were brought to port by sailors as pets, and when a sailor was short of funds and ready to ship again, it was easy to drive a sharp bargain with him for his pet monkey.

For a time I had a West Indian goat, four dogs, a parrot and a monkey, all living in peace and harmony in the garret of the South Street house. Sailors' boarding houses located on the streets adjacent to the water front were small menageries, and many of the stories about talking parrots were invented in sailors' boarding houses.

There were no dog catchers. Dogs of all kinds and varieties were allowed the absolute freedom of the city, and one of the hobbies of the small boy was collecting dogs. At one time, in company with half a dozen companions, I had gathered together as many as seven dogs. Being unable to take them home at night, we left them in the shed of a warehouse in Front Street near Dover, and each member of the firm was charged with bringing his share of food from home to take care of the dogs. My familiarity, in later years, with various breeds of dogs makes me realize that this early collection in which I had an interest was probably just dogs.

My early relations with animals and my recollections of them probably account in at least some degree for the private zoological garden at the Albany Executive Mansion that has since been so frequently commented upon.

The New York tower of the Brooklyn Bridge was completed the year that I was born, and I often heard my mother say—she having knowledge of what was going on, because we lived directly under that tower—that if the people of New York City had had any idea of the number of human lives sacrificed in the sinking of the caissons for the towers of the Brooklyn Bridge in all probability they would have halted its progress.

The Brooklyn Bridge was built by hand. Pneumatic tools and compressed air were unknown. All the riveting of the steel in the structure of that great bridge was done by hand, and it was the pride of New York and Brooklyn when, on Queen Victoria's birthday, on the twenty-fourth of May, 1883, it was opened to the public. Newspapers of the time contained a great many stories about the character of its construction, its strength, the load it could carry, and the other details of its construction. Militia crossing it in step or too many elephants crossing it at one time, because they are known to keep in step, were mentioned as dangerous because of the rhythmic vibration they would cause.

It must have been these newspaper stories stirring in the minds of some of the pedestrians on Decoration Day, 1883, six days after the opening of the bridge, which caused the cry that the bridge was falling. Regiments of the national guard, in celebration of the opening of the bridge as well as in celebration of Decoration Day, were crossing it. The cry of alarm started a stampede for the New York end and twelve people were killed and thirty-five injured in the mad scramble to get to the masonry work and away from the suspended steel.

I was a boy of ten, and with other boys was standing under the bridge in South Street. We were unable to discover what was the matter when we saw hats, coats, parasols, umbrellas and pocket-books dropping from the bridge into the street, until we later found that there was an emergency call to all the hospitals of the city to send ambulances to the New York end of the bridge. We learned then that it was due to what was called the "crush," in the effort of the people to get to what they considered to be a place of safety.

In its early days the bridge served as more than a utility for transportation between the two cities. It soon became a place of recreation and of pleasure. So much so that it was referred to in songs and popularized on the variety stage. I can still sing "Danny by my side."

> The Brooklyn Bridge on Sunday is known as lover's lane,
> I stroll there with my sweetheart, oh, time and time again;
> Oh, how I love to ramble, oh, yes, it is my pride,
> Dressed in my best, each day of rest, with Danny by my side.
>
> CHORUS:
> Then, oh my, do try, on the bridge on a Sunday,
> Laughing, chaffing, happy the lovers go by;
> Moonlight, starlight, watching the silvery tide,
> Dressed in my best, each day of rest, with Danny by my side.

1929

# HELEN KELLER

---

*Helen Keller (1880–1968) felt a deep connection to New York, a city whose relentless energy matched her own. Deaf and blind since early childhood, Keller was an active Socialist, suffragist, and Swedenborgian, who lectured with her teacher Anne Sullivan on the Chautauqua circuit and before vaudeville audiences. She also wrote fourteen books, including* Midstream: My Later Life, *from which this excerpt is taken.*

## I GO ADVENTURING

C UT OFF as I am, it is inevitable that I should sometimes feel like a shadow walking in a shadowy world. When this happens I ask to be taken to New York City. Always I return home weary but I have the comforting certainty that mankind is real flesh and I myself am not a dream.

In order to get to New York from my home it is necessary to cross one of the great bridges that separate Manhattan from Long Island. The oldest and most interesting of them is the Brooklyn Bridge, built by my friend, Colonel Roebling, but the one I cross oftenest is the Queensborough Bridge at 59th Street. How often I have had Manhattan described to me from these bridges! They tell me the view is loveliest in the morning and at sunset when one sees the skyscrapers rising like fairy palaces, their million windows gleaming in the rosy-tinted atmosphere.

I like to feel that all poetry is not between the covers of poetry books, that much of it is written in great enterprises of engineering and flying, that into mighty utility man has poured and is pouring his dreams, his emotions, his philosophy. This materializing of his genius is sometimes inchoate and monstrous, but even then sublime in its extravagance and courage. Who can deny that the Queensborough Bridge is the work of a creative artist? It never fails to give me a poignant desire to capture the noble cadence of its music. To my friends I say·

Behold its liberal loveliness of length—
A flowing span from shore to shore,
A brimming reach of beauty matched with strength,
It shines and climbs like some miraculous dream,
Like some vision multitudinous and agleam,
A passion of desire held captive in the clasp of vast utility.

New York has a special interest for me when it is wrapped in fog. Then it behaves very much like a blind person. I once crossed from Jersey City to Manhattan in a dense fog. The ferry-boat felt its way cautiously through the river traffic. More timid than a blind man, its horn brayed incessantly. Fog-bound, surrounded by menacing, unseen craft and dangers, it halted every now and then as a blind man halts at a crowded thoroughfare crossing, tapping his cane, tense and anxious.

One of my never-to-be-forgotten experiences was circumnavigating New York in a boat. The trip took all day. I had with me four people who could use the hand alphabet—my teacher, my sister, my niece, and Mr. Holmes. One who has not seen New York in this way would be amazed at the number of people who live on the water. Someone has called them "harbour gypsies." Their homes are on boats—whole fleets of them, decorated with flower boxes and bright-coloured awnings. It is amusing to note how many of these stumbling, awkward harbour gypsies have pretty feminine names— *Bella, Floradora, Rosalind, Pearl of the Deep, Minnehaha, Sister Nell.* The occupants can be seen going about their household tasks—cooking, washing, sewing, gossiping from one barge to another, and there is a flood of smells which gives eyes to the mind. The children and dogs play on the tiny deck, and chase each other into the water, where they are perfectly at home. These water-babies are familiar with all manner of craft, they know what countries they come from, and what cargoes they carry. There are brick barges from Holland and fruitboats coming in from Havana, and craft loaded with meat, cobblestones, and sand push their way up bays and canals. There are old ships which have been stripped of their majesty and doomed to follow tow ropes up and down the harbour. These ships make me think of old blind people led up and down the city streets. There are aristocratic craft from Albany, Nyack, Newburg. There are also boats from New London and Boston, from the Potomac and Baltimore and Virginia, from Portland, Maine, bringing terra cotta to Manhattan. Here comes the fishing fleet from Gloucester hurrying past the barge houses, and crawling, coal-laden tramps. Tracking the turmoil in every direction are the saucy ferry boats, bellowing rudely to everyone to get out of the way.

It is a sail of vivid contrast—up the Hudson between green hills, past the stately mansions of Riverside Drive, through the narrow straits that separate Manhattan from the mainland, into Harlem and the East River, past Welfare Island, where a great modern city shelters its human derelicts, on to the welter of downtown docks, where longshoremen heave the barge cargoes ashore, and the crash of traffic is deafening, and back to your pier in the moonlight when the harbour gypsies sleep and the sense of peace is balm to the tired nerves.

As I walk up Broadway, the people that brush past me seem always hastening toward a destination they never reach. Their motions are eager, as if they said, "We are on our way, we shall arrive in a moment." They keep up the pace—they almost run. Each on his quest intent, in endless procession they pass, tragic, grotesque, gay, they all sweep onward like rain falling upon leaves. I wonder where they are going. I puzzle my brain; but the mystery is never solved. Will they at last come somewhere? Will anybody be waiting for them? The march never ceases. Their feet have worn the pavements unevenly. I wish I knew where they are going. Some are nonchalant, some walk with their eyes on the ground, others step lightly, as if they might fly if their wings were not bound by the multitude. A pale little woman is guiding the steps of a blind man. His great hand drags on her arm. Awkwardly he shortens his stride to her gait. He trips when the curb is uneven; his grip tightens on the arm of the woman. Where are they going?

Like figures in a meaningless pageant, they pass. There are young girls laughing, loitering. They have beauty, youth, lovers. They look in the shop windows, they look at the huge winking signs; they jostle the crowds, their feet keep time to the music of their hearts. They must be going to a pleasant place. I think I should like to go where they are going.

Tremulously I stand in the subways, absorbed into the terrible reverberations of exploding energy. Fearful, I touch the forest of steel girders loud with the thunder of oncoming trains that shoot past me like projectiles. Inert I stand, riveted in my place. My limbs, paralyzed, refuse to obey the will insistent on haste to board the train while the lightning steed is leashed and its reeling speed checked for a moment. Before my mind flashes in clairvoyant vision what all this speed portends—the lightning crashing into life, the accidents, railroad wrecks, steam bursting free like geysers from bands of steel, thousands of racing motors and children caught at play, flying heroes diving into the sea, dying for speed—all this because of strange, unsatisfied ambitions. Another train bursts into the station like a volcano, the people crowd me on, on into the chasm—into the dark depths of awful forces and fates. In a few minutes, still trembling, I am spilled into the streets.

*MIDSTREAM: MY LATER LIFE*, 1929

# PAUL MORAND

―――――

*Of all the visitors who came to New York in the 1920's, none opened himself to the city more enthusiastically than the French poet, novelist, and diplomat Paul Morand (1888–1976). His* New York *is a giddy fusion of guidebook, lyrical ode, and philosophical meditation on a city "supercharged with electricity," in which he concludes: "If life in towns is madness, New York is at least a madness that is worthwhile."*

## FROM *NEW YORK*

THE NEW YORK STOCK EXCHANGE is not a majestic, state-owned building; it occupies merely the lower floors of an ordinary building, the rest of which is rented to private offices. In the elevator I crowd in amongst people whose arms and pockets are laden with stocks and shares, and I stop on the twenty-second floor, at the offices of the only French brokerage firm on the Stock Exchange. Up in the skies, A. de S. P.―― is waiting for me in his room; Atlantic and Hudson form a beautiful background for the energetic features of this youthful man of business; in a neighboring room I catch a glimpse of people sitting in armchairs watching a sort of blackboard like that on which the position of Basque pelota teams are shown; on this one the ebb and flow of values are figured in white and red. We climb up two stories higher, and I am right in an army central exchange during a battle. A panting, sweating, shirt-sleeved personnel is plunged in its task, helmeted men connected with the ceiling by wires that enter their ears, and clamped to the floor by curving tubes that enter their mouths, one hand on the telegraph, the other entering 0's and staff and serpent dollar signs in huge ledgers.

"You see," says S. P.――, "orders are flowing in from Berlin and Paris. There's still some money in old Europe!"

One hundred United Steel . . .

One thousand Coty . . .

Ten thousand Canadian Pacific . . .

The European Bourses have not known in recent years the steady powerful advance that the New York Exchange has known. So European capital, once free to stir out, has come seeking gold where gold is.

"Within six minutes we receive an order from Paris, or even from the French provinces, and the stock is bought in New York. We do not recommend any; we aren't bankers, but simply the rapid messengers of the public, purely a broking house."

In another room transfers are being put through. All Stock Exchange shares are in the holder's name, and the great increase in speculation has therefore made this work formidable; building cannot keep pace with it, and the rents of premises have doubled in no time; there are now Sunday-shifts and night-shifts. The downtown section, which before the War was plunged in darkness after seven in the evening, is now lighted all night long.

We fall back twenty floors into the corridors, meeting a flood of excited secretaries, a storm of messengers, a cyclone of page-boys, a hurricane of middle-men dashing bareheaded, in black coats and striped trousers, as in London. Among them I recognize, from so often seeing their caricatures, a few specimens of the old white-spatted business men with carnations in their buttonholes. . . . (To wear a *boutonnière* when you're too young lowers you in Wall Street's esteem. . . .) Every one is whispering "tips."

"They'll touch one hundred and eighty within a week . . ."

"If I'd only guessed . . !"

Famous names are mentioned to me. Do these men really hold my fortune in their keeping? Just when I am about to question them they take the lead, and ask me:

"Well, what do you think of the market?"

Lord Rothermere has compared Wall Street to a huge suction pump swallowing up the world's capital, draining Europe dry. I am coming down to see the machinery working.

Here I am leaning on the balcony of the first story, whence I can now distinguish an ant-heap at work; this is the sanctuary of the temple, the railway-station of money, the terminus of fortune. Nine stockbrokers used to meet under a tree at the end of the eighteenth century and formed the first kernel of the Stock Exchange; they now number eleven hundred. The great statesmen whose genius contrived to center the American money market here were Hamilton and Jay; with the Bank of New York, in 1784, the town's fortune was made. I can hear the dull, disturbing noise of all those silver dollars rolling, heaping hugely up, like sacred wafers, and slipping from one pocket into another, in an instant. On the walls the announcement blackboards, attached to electric wires, flick open their little shutters, each disclosing a number, which is that of a broker. Paul Adam, in his notes on America, grew lyrical over "these figures which gleam for an instant on the heights of the walls, just as the *Mene 'Tekel Upharsin* must have gleamed at Babylon to the terror of the prophet." These figures are not in the least alarming in themselves as they are only a summons signal. As soon as an order to buy reaches a bank, it is transmitted to the bank's Stock Exchange representative, who occupies a box just here on the aisles, and is not permitted to leave the telephone post allotted him. The representative can only inform a broker by calling him, as we have seen, by his number; and he then passes on the order to him. Instantly the broker stations himself at the spot where the stock in question is for sale; consulting the list, he announces its price; the seller answers, "Take it," and in this way, with no further procedure, with no exchange of paper, without there being any mistake, notwithstanding the shouts and confusion of orders being given, fabulous sums change hands. The ground is strewn with colored slips of paper, like a race-course. This litter of discarded orders is augmented by the unrolled strips from the "tickers," which register the quotations. Millionaires on their yachts or special trains, tourists on board liners, ordinary people in all the forty-eight states of the Union, ladies in the great uptown hotels between their luncheon courses, and the big gamblers settled in their deep club armchairs—all, at this moment, are intent on forwarding their orders. (A California purchase is effected in New York in less than a minute.) The gray-uniformed attendants seem to be the only calm creatures there.

For several years back the man-in-the-street has been won by the lure of easy money, the glamor of the "inside tip." He had to pay somehow for all the useless and expensive things he has been made to buy on the installment plan; and every one began to speculate, on credit of course, with far less capital than he would do in France; for although money is dearer, the advances asked for are smaller; and so the typist has her own broker and the policeman makes his own fortnightly settlements.* This began in 1916, when the munitions companies were showing unheard-of profits, and continued after the armistice with the increased values in national stocks; since then the New Yorker has never stopped gambling; information and "inside" rumors run through the town in a few hours, and it is no longer uncommon for six million shares to change hands in one day's trading.† The Federal Reserve Bank is alarmed, and periodically tightens credits. The great Stock Exchange kings of former days are no more— the Goulds, Fisks, Carnegies, Harrimans. . . . Nowadays things are in the hands of the nameless immensity of small investors. So often have they been told that their banking account is the best friend, that they believe it. They have seen Radio rise from forty to four hundred; they have taken a taste for this game in which, until recently, there were no losers. The crisis at the end of 1929 had no deep economic causes; it was merely an immense collective panic of Wall Street.

The fatal landslide continues to be audible, while charges fluctuate for the ever-tempting call-money, always ready to hand against security, at six, eight, and recently even twelve and twenty per cent. And in this way the daily battle goes forward, from ten o'clock till three, between those who are pushing prices down and those who are pushing them up, the war of bulls and bears.

The closing gong booms out. The turmoil settles. The great generals instantly leave the battlefield, leap into the still empty subway, in the trains of which, a couple of hours later, the man-in-the-street will be avidly reading the price-columns. . . . This underground line provides for express trains which pass most of the stations without stopping, and only make two or three halts before reaching the

*M. Morand is speaking, of course, of the dear, dead days before the crash in the autumn of 1929.

†Still uncommon, but not unprecedented.

suburbs; there motor-cars and mahogany launches are waiting, ready to take the exhausted financiers away into the country. . . . Evening falls. The skyscrapers, these great presses of humanity, disgorge their exhausted contents. The vertical arrangement of individuals will now give way to the new, horizontal arrangement for night-time. At the foot of the buildings the revolving doors are whirling like crazy wheels, each fan blowing out human beings on to the sidewalk. In Europe there are no crowds. One must go to Asia or come here to get the feel of that air-current, that unsubstantial monster, impersonal and cowardly and tender, calling for the death of a black boxer, writhing for love before the coffin of Valentino, mourning a father before the bier of Lincoln, welcoming a bridegroom in Lindbergh. The flood streams up Broadway, washes over Brooklyn Bridge, invades the "L"—as the Elevated Railroad is called—and swamps the subway stations. Then an individual order follows this momentary chaos; some stop before the newspaper display windows where the fleeting news-strips announce that Trotsky is going to settle at Monte Carlo, or congregate round the special editions which pile up at the street-crossings, or make for suburban repose, for the cottage or bungalow with its aerial on the roof and its artificial flowers, or for supper at the Y.M.C.A., while others seek their aspirations in the great luminous halo of the cinemas and theaters of Times Square and the Forties. . . .

✦   ✦   ✦   ✦   ✦

Open a book or newspaper of a few years ago and you will seek the term "speakeasy" in vain. It was born of Prohibition, but later than Prohibition. The speakeasy (the name suggests a whispered password) is a clandestine refreshment-bar selling spirits or wine. They must be visited to understand present-day New York. One must see a speakeasy, if only to avoid the places for the future—I know nothing so depressing.* There are a few in the downtown streets, but they are mainly set up between Fortieth Street and Sixtieth Street; they are usually situated downstairs, and are identifiable by the large

*M. Morand was, perhaps, merely unfortunate in his choice of speakeasies.

number of empty cars standing at their doors. The door is closed, and is only opened after you have been scrutinized through a door-catch or a barred opening. At night an electric torch suddenly gleams through a pink silk curtain. There is a truly New York atmosphere of humbug in the whole thing. The interior is that of a criminal house; shutters are closed in full daylight, and one is caught in the smell of a cremation furnace, for the ventilation is defective and grills are prepared under the mantelpiece of the fireplace. Italians with a too familiar manner, or plump, blue pseudo-bullfighters, carrying bunches of monastic keys, guide you through the deserted rooms of the abandoned house. Facetious inscriptions grimace from the walls. There are a few very flushed diners. At one table some habitués are asleep, their heads sunk on their arms; behind a screen somebody is trying to restore a young woman who has had an attack of hysteria, while an old gentleman with spectacles is dancing all by himself. The food is almost always poor, the service deplorable; the staff regard you with the eyes of confederates and care not two pins about you. The Sauterne is a sort of glycerine; it has to go with a partridge brought from the refrigerator of a French vessel; the champagne would not be touched at a Vincennes wedding-party.

Yet the speakeasy pervades Manhattan with a fascinating atmosphere of mystery. If only one could drink water there! Some speakeasies are disguised behind florists' shops, or behind undertakers' coffins. I know one, right in Broadway, which is entered through an imitation telephone-box; it has excellent beer; appetizing sausages and Welsh rabbits are sizzling in chafing-dishes and are given to customers without extra charge; drunks are expelled through a side-door which seems to open out into the nether world, as in *Chicago Nights*. In the poorer quarters many former saloons for the ordinary people have secretly reopened. All these secret shrines are readily accessible, for there are, it is said, 20,000 speakeasies in New York,* and it is unlikely that the police do not know them; I think myself that they are only forced to close down when they refuse to make themselves pleasant to persons in authority, or when they sell too

*Grover Whalen's estimate was 32,000. The guess was made while he was Police Commissioner.

much poison. Spirits have their market-quotations in New York, as fluctuating as those of the Stock Exchange; champagne averages forty dollars, cognac and gin twelve dollars, the bottle.* The speakeasy is very popular in all classes of society; women go there gladly, even a few young girls, who at least provide a diversion for the Frenchman, who is not accustomed to American habits of drinking.

✦  ✦  ✦  ✦  ✦

To-day, on a winter evening, I arrive in Times Square about six o'clock. It is Broadway's finest hour. Here, until midnight, New York takes its bath of light.

Light that is not only white, but yellow, red, green, mauve, blue; lights that are not only fixed, but moving, tumbling, running, turning, zigzagging, rolling, vertical, perpendicular, dancing, epileptic; frames are whirling, letters flash out from the night. That yellow, blue and green Chevrolet sign did not exist last year; nor did those flaming telegrams which now run round the buildings, circling them with luminous happenings. The crowds raise their faces to spell out the news: "C-O-O-L-I-D-G-E  L-E-A-V-E-S  F-O-R  M-I-A-M-I."

Dark and empty after seven o'clock, when offices close, the skyscrapers hereabouts now flame on their outer surface, right up to where they merge with the fog.

In Forty-second Street it is a glowing summer afternoon all night: one might almost wear white trousers and straw hat. Theaters, night-clubs, movie palaces, restaurants, are all lighted up at every port-hole. Undiscovered prisms; rainbows squared. In rain, or when there are mists floating round, it is still more beautiful; the rain becomes golden water; the skyscrapers vanish half-way up, and nothing more can be seen but the haloes of their cupolas suspended in a colored mist, like Lenin's tomb on the Red Square before the Kremlin on certain evenings. And when those formidable blizzards, which

---

*Gin has never been this high since Prohibition—it is even more evident that M. Morand got into the wrong speakeasy. Current quotations are: Cognac, $8; Gin [bathtub, or Gout Americaine] $2; imported (?), $3.50 to $4. The champagne also seems to be quoted at night-club, not speakeasy, prices.

sweep down on New York in a few seconds, shower down their fine dry snow, a fine blinding dust like handfuls of salt, freezing instantly on the ground, the passers-by are covered with red snow and green snow, the varnished cars sparkle, the flakes fall on to ermines.

The "Great White Way"—the "Roaring Forties"—all America dreams of having a Broadway. The craving for amusement breaks out like a revolution. Broadway is the port towards which America tacks; compared with this the streets of Shanghai and Hamburg are dark lanes. The festival offers all the false promises of city festival, but, like all its kind, false only on the morrow. There is but one truth— the truth of to-night! "Stimulating," "spectacular"—the newspapers keep on shouting; this is life at its most spectacular. Twenty thousand electric signs on this open space; twenty-five million candle-power. When the fronts of the buildings are overcrowded, reflectors push forward, hanging from steel poles over the pavements. What were the first words of the admiral who has just bombarded Nicaragua, uttered immediately after the battle? Here they are, in letters of fire:

"—— CIGARETTES DO NOT HURT THE THROAT"

Forty-second Street is like a thousand Places Pigalle, on Christmas night, placed end to end. History is forgotten. Nature, gods, the sea, are replaced by new words that must be mastered. In Paris there is but one which the skies spasmodically teach us—Citroën. In New York there are Lasky, Ziegfeld, Goldwyn, Mayer . . . Beauty, renown, talent, are brought to their climax in an instant. The fashion of the Boulevards, they used to say in France, was quick to burn its favorites—yet sixty years later they are still with us. On Broadway the career of genius is as brief as a pugilist's; he picks up a million in a couple of months, and then gets a blow on the chin; he is carried off, and then it's somebody else's turn.

Sellers of caramel nuts, roasted peanuts, sables—where have we seen them before? Further down, in Orchard Street in the ghetto. Once again *The End of St. Petersburg*, but here the class war has no longer any meaning. This is victory! The electric lamp is no longer a lighting device, it is a machine for fascinating, a machine for obliterating. Electricity bedizens this weary throng, determined not to go home, determined to spend its money, determined to blind itself with false daylight.

In Forty-second Street there are no more windows in the build-ings—nothing but letters. It is a kindled alphabet, a conspiracy of commerce against night; in the sky, an advertising airplane.

A whistle! Motor-cars shooting forward at crazy speed, breathing hot in your face; at half-past eight pass those which are taking their passengers to non-musical plays, at twenty minutes to nine, those on their way to musical shows—so orders the new police regulation. And the others? Broadway contains nothing but people going to the theater ... CANDY in blue ... SODAS in green ... One no longer knows what one ought to think or say or see or believe or chew or drink or smoke. It is neither hot nor cold nor damp, there is only one latitude left, the latitude of pleasure.

Searchlights are sweeping up the remains of the sky.

1930

# LINCOLN STEFFENS

*Lincoln Steffens (1866–1936) made his name as a muckraking jour-nalist exposing municipal corruption (*The Shame of the Cities) *and championing reform candidates. By the time he wrote his* Autobiog-raphy *(1931), he had developed a more ironic perspective toward the zeal of reformers (including his younger self), and sought deeper causes of urban malaise than the cupidity of this or that official. He also frankly admitted the paradox that the corrupt political machine may at times have responded better to the needs of the working poor than high-minded reformers who spoke for the business class.*

## THE POLICE

EVERY NEWSPAPER that I know anything about suffers from politics, "newspaper politics." The men on it decide on some question of policy or control or places, and everybody be-comes more or less involved. Joseph Pulitzer, the founder, owner, and editor of the New York *World*, cultivated warring factions. Whether his theory was that disloyalty to one another made his heads of departments loyal to him or that rivalry developed the ad-vantages of competition, he had a business manager who did not speak to some editors, who did not all speak to one another. Charles A. Dana had the most united staff; his competition was between his morning and evening papers, but we used to hear of quarrels and contempts even on the morning edition which was the *Sun*. Godkin may never have heard of parties on the *Evening Post*; the division was not sharp and open, but Henry J. Wright, and the publisher, J. S. Seymour, were, however quietly, against Linn, the managing editor, who represented instinctively the taste and policy of the editor-in-chief. He was for keeping all police and sensational news out of the paper, and in the main he had his way. Wright and Seymour, who wanted to build up circulation and business by printing all the news, had one great victory, and it was most profitable for me.

One afternoon when I was back on my general reporting the city editor called me up to his desk and asked me if I would like to cover police headquarters. A startling suggestion. The *Post* had never had a man in Mulberry Street, where the heads of the police and detective service had their offices. It was the source of crime news—and Mr. Wright said, quick, that I was to pay no attention to crime; I was to cover the activities of Dr. Parkhurst, whom I had already interviewed several times for the paper.

The Rev. Dr. Charles H. Parkhurst was discovering the corruption of the police and denouncing the force from his pulpit. He sounded like a prophet of old in his sermons, but personally he was a calm, smiling, earnest, but not unhumorous gentleman who frankly enjoyed his notoriety and his exposures. He knew some of the doings of the police; they were dangerous facts to allege; libelous. He had to be careful, and he was cautious, but he was persistent, methodically, thoroughly. He organized in and out of his congregation a society to investigate the police, procure evidence, and put him in a position to describe New York police methods and their relations with Tammany Hall, the liquor interests, and criminals. The *Post* was interested, of course, in anybody that came out openly against Tammany; there was some suspicion of a clergyman who "profaned his pulpit with police filth," even as against Tammany; and my first assignments to see Parkhurst were reluctant. Dr. Parkhurst talked moderately, sensibly, briefly, and, as I reported him, in tone with the paper. Following up a police news lead, as I always did, I called on him every few days; we became rather friendly, and I was soon able to warn my chief of news to come; which came—at police headquarters. Mr. Wright had seen, I think, that Dr. Parkhurst offered him a good excuse for assigning a reporter to police headquarters: to report the police side of an opening controversy; and since the clergyman and I seemed to get along well together I was the man to go.

"Not to report crimes and that sort of thing," said Wright, in effect. "You will keep in touch with Dr. Parkhurst, know what he is doing, and work in with him for the purpose of reporting his findings with the police department for a background." But I got from him somehow the idea that, if I could find a way, not a sensational, conventional, but, say, a political, a literary, way to write about robberies, murders, etc., I might try putting some crime into the *Post*.

No urging was needed to make me accept the assignment. I was eager for it. "The police" meant to me a dark, mysterious layer of the life of a great city into which I had not yet penetrated. My experience in Wall Street, especially my mocking relations with James B. Dill, had driven it into my consciousness that it was possible to think that I knew all about something and yet be an innocent ignoramus. Dill had taught me that back of my bankers and brokers and their news of Wall Street there was a world which I had not even glimpsed and which the Wall Street men themselves did not really picture as it was. Few of them ever saw it. My reports of "the American X & Y Company receivership," columns long, were not "the" story, as Dill told it afterward. I had never got and printed the truth back of the financial news. It was probably so with the police news; there was probably a still greater truth back of the petty, monstrous abuses Dr. Parkhurst was disclosing. And then there were the murders, fires, robberies, and politics. I might not write, but I could learn all about such events. I went to police headquarters as I had gone to Wall Street, as I had gone to Europe, and as I had come home to America, with the suppressed ardor of a young student and with the same throbbing anxiety that an orator feels just before he rises to speak.

But, first, I called on Dr. Parkhurst to tell him of my assignment and make with him the kind of agreement I had had with my Wall Street bankers: to work together with him and exchange news and confidences. He was interested, of course; it meant support for him by the *Evening Post*, and he spent several forenoons describing his plans, methods, and best of all, the police chiefs and their system of corruption, as he knew and could not yet prove. As it turned out, Dr. Parkhurst knew well what he knew, but he did not know the system as it was exposed later by the Lexow Committee; nobody had pictured that; and that, even that, was not all. However, after a few talks with Dr. Parkhurst I felt that I knew both the chief police officers and their worst crimes, and so, with no little dread and a solid foundation of certainty, I went one morning early to police headquarters with my card to present to the Superintendent of Police, Thomas F. Byrnes.

It was his hour for receiving citizens with complaints, his inspectors, captains, heads of departments with reports, and "the press." His small outer office was crowded with people, uniformed and in plain clothes. I was embarrassed, but I handed my card to the chief's favorite sergeant, Mangin, and as he bade me wait my turn, a tall, handsome inspector of police, whom I, of course, did not know, spoke out loud into the silence.

"A reporter from the *Evening Post*," he said, clear and distinct like a pistol shot. "The *Post* has always despised police news, true police news, but now when we are under fire they are to have a man up here to expose and clean us all out, us rascals."

I felt as if his shots had hit me, and I sank wounded into a chair; the man was not through. Sneering and pointing at my red-hot face, he said, "We'll see how long he stays here."

The challenge braced me. I asked Sergeant Mangin, "Who is that man?"

Mangin hesitated, glanced at my foe, and then said, softly but audibly, "Inspector Williams."

I knew that name. Dr. Parkhurst had told me of the audacity and force and badness of the "clubbing inspector," so I rallied to him.

"Oh," I said, "Clubber Williams. I know about him," and to him I made my bluff. "I shall stay here till you are driven out."

There was a sense of quick excitement. Mangin darted through the swinging doors into Superintendent Byrnes' inner office, an officer came out, and I was bidden to enter—out of my turn. Mangin undoubtedly had told Byrnes what had happened. The Superintendent rose to meet and greet me, reading my name from the card in his hand, and adding, "The *Evening Post*." Indicating a chair beside his desk, he said in his most formal fashion that I was welcome at police headquarters. The force was irritated, naturally, being subjected just then to criticism from places where "the finest" might expect support.

"When you stop to think that it is we, the police, who protect your lives and property, guarding you not only from thieves and robbers, but from strikers and mobs, you can see, no doubt, that it hurts us to be denounced as Dr. Parkhurst, for example, is denouncing us—from the pulpit and in the newspapers. I hope and trust that the *Evening Post*, a Wall Street paper, an organ of good business and all decent property interests, will give us aid and comfort—"

I wanted to protest; I probably gave some sign of a wish to correct him, as I did, early; he saw that and changed his note a little.

"Yes, yes, I know," he said, "the *Evening Post* will not take sides. A fair paper, it will be just and true to the facts. Right; I know that. None better. You will seek the truth, and the truth you will report, as you find it. Right. But, my dear Mr.—Mr."—he couldn't find the card—"you cannot get the truth from Dr. Parkhurst nor from any other enemy of the police."

Again he saw me shy.

"Yes, yes, you must see Dr. Parkhurst, listen to him, but you will listen to us, too, to me. You will want the news. Well, sir, I control the news from the police department, and I can—I can give and I can withhold the news. No, no, keep your seat. I am only endeavoring to say to you that I am going to put you on the same basis here as the old reporters who have been with us for years, most of them, and in return I ask you, in all fairness, not to print the stuff you get from the enemies of the police without submitting it to me for correction or—at any rate—comment."

It was worse, it was plainer, than I had expected it to be. I could see through this doughty chief of police; he was not the awe-inspiring figure I had imagined. For Tom Byrnes was a famous police chief; few people ever saw him; he was only a name, but there were stories told about him, of his cunning, as a detective, as a master of men, as a manhandler of criminals, and as a retriever of stolen properties— stories that filled the upper world with respect and the lower with terror. He struck me as simple, no complications at all—a man who would buy you or beat you, as you might choose, but get you he would.

Not me. So I thought, and I think he felt as I meant him to: that I was going to be a free lance at police headquarters. His eyes narrowed into two slits as he read me. To meet his covert threat to keep news from me I said that I had no use for his ordinary police news; I was sent there only to see what I might see, hear what might be said, and print what I could prove—of politics. That was all. I was willing to tell him in advance whatever of importance I meant to report—if he would always see me promptly: I could not allow any delays in news, of course.

Byrnes looked at me, listening and drumming with his fingers on the desk. When I had finished he rose, walked to his window, and drummed on the glass with his nails till, turning suddenly, he dismissed me.

"All right," he said, and he pressed a button which summoned Mangin, who came darting in as I went out through the swinging doors into and through the silent, staring crowd in the outer office into the hall. A reporter followed me, an elderly man, who turned out to be the day man of a morning newspaper.

"You have made a bad start," he said as he joined me. "You have made an enemy of the first inspector. I hope you made a friend of the chief. You'll need him, with Williams against you."

I believed this; I was depressed, but I am sure I did not show it.

"What do I need friends for?" I said. "They would only embarrass me in what I am here to do."

He did not ask me what it was that I meant to do. Like Williams, he, everybody, seemed to know what I was there for; maybe Williams had told the crowd while I was with Byrnes. But how did Williams know? I was awed by their detective sagacity; it was frightening. I did not learn till much later that the police are professional guessers, and not good ones, except in obvious cases.

"I know your city editor, Harry Wright," the reporter was saying, "and I know that he will expect you to get some news. And I can help you, if you will work with me for a while and take my advice till you know the ropes yourself."

This did not attract, it repelled me, this proposition, and I wanted to get away from this friend. He was talking about how to find an office. The best place for a police reporter was in the buildings across the street; there one could watch police headquarters, see who came and went, and run across in a moment for any news that might turn up. But all the rooms were taken; I would better have a desk in his office and pay him for half the telephone, heat, and light rates. I hardly heard. My attention was caught by a shaggy-looking fellow coming down the street and yelling, "M-m-ma-a-x. M-m-a-x."

"Who is that?" I asked.

"Oh, that! That's Jake Riis, the *Evening Sun* man."

So! That was Jacob A. Riis, the author of *How the Other Half Lives*, and not only a famous police reporter, but a well-known character in one half of the life of New York. I liked his looks.

"But what's he bawling for?" I asked.

"For his boy, Max, who gets his news for him. There he is."

And there was Max Fischel, a little old round, happy Jewish boy, coming out of the basement door of headquarters, his hand full of pieces of paper: notes. He ran across the street to Riis, who was just coming to work, and the two—geniuses—that's what they were, both of them—went into the building opposite, where on the first floor Riis reappeared to throw up his window, through which you could see him and Max settle down to work. Every morning for two or three years I saw this scene, and it came to have a meaning to me; I was soon imitating it as nearly as I could.

Jake Riis was a Danish American who "covered" police headquarters, the Health Department, which was then in the same building, and "the East Side," which was a short name for the poor and the foreign quarters of the city. And he not only got the news; he cared about the news. He hated passionately all tyrannies, abuses, miseries, and he fought them. He was a "terror" to the officials and landlords responsible, as he saw it, for the desperate condition of the tenements where the poor lived. He had "exposed" them in articles, books, and public speeches, and with results. All the philanthropists in town knew and backed Riis, who was able then, as a reformer and a reporter, too, to force the appointment of a Tenement House Commission that he gently led and fiercely drove to an investigation and a report which—followed up by this terrible reporter—resulted in the wiping out of whole blocks of rookeries, the making of small parks, and the regulation of the tenements. He had discovered these evils as a reporter, reporting, say, a suicide, a fire, or a murder. These were the news, which all the reporters got; only Riis wrote them as stories, with heart, humor, and understanding. And having "seen" the human side of the crime or the disaster, he had taken note also of the house or the block or the street where it happened. He went back and he described that, too; he called on the officers and landlords who permitted the conditions, and "blackmailed" them into reforms.

This had been going on for years when I came to police head-quarters. Riis was growing old, but he had found and trained his boy, Max, to see and to understand as Riis did; and Max could see. It seemed to me that Max was born and not made. He did the early morning work, which was the key to the day. The police, stationed all over the city, reported all happenings in their precincts to head-quarters—fires, accidents, crimes, and arrests—which were posted briefly in the basement telegraph office, where the reporters could see them. The morning newspaper men watched these bulletins, weighed them, and went out to investigate those that seemed likely to have a story back of them. They stayed up till their papers went to press, at two or three o'clock in the morning. When Riis first came to police headquarters as a young man, the evening newspaper men appeared at about eight or nine o'clock and began their work by conning the accumulation of bulletins dated from three o'clock on down to eight. These they divided up among themselves, each re-porter going out on one. When they returned with their several sto-ries, they exchanged the news, wrote each one all the stories, and then could settle down for the day to a poker game, which only big news could interrupt. Riis did not play poker; he joined in no "com-bine"; he worked alone, sometimes giving but never asking help. He began to beat the combine, which had to quit poker and work all day, still together, to keep up with and, if possible, beat Riis. They, all veterans, had the advantage of knowing the town and the police, who did not like Riis, but he carried the war into their camp by coming to work at seven o'clock, which gave him time to take two or three of the early morning bulletins, cover and write them all, and since most of the sensational incidents of a city are reported in those late night hours, the *Evening Sun* had such a lead on police news as the *Post* had had on Wall Street. And when the beaten editors drove their police reporters to work at seven o'clock, Riis, the scab, began to come at six, then five, then four. Nobody else started that early: no editor could demand it, and Riis himself could not stand it long. But each reporter had a copy boy, a messenger, to carry his stories downtown. Riis hit upon the idea of a boy who, besides carrying copy, could "cover" the city from three till seven, eight, nine, when Riis turned up to write the news. Max, who began with the facts, soon learned to see and form and deliver to Riis the stories of the night for which the *Evening Sun* was noted. Beautiful stories they were, too, sometimes, for Riis could write.

This, then, was what I was seeing, my first morning at police headquarters: Max furnishing Riis the night's stories, all ready made. I must know Riis. Waiting out in the street till he was through writing—when I saw Max take the copy and set off for his office downtown, I crossed over and called on Riis. In a loud, cheerful, hearty voice, he greeted me.

"Glad you've come," he said. "The *Post* can help a lot up here, and you've begun well."

"Begun well!" I exclaimed. "I haven't begun yet."

Riis roared his great laugh. "Oh, yes, you have. Max says you banged Alec Williams one and disappointed the old man himself."

He meant that I had failed with Superintendent Byrnes! I was about to protest, but Riis was shouting through that open window.

"That's the way to handle them! Knock 'em down, then you can pick them up and be the good Samaritan. It's their own way with us reporters. They put the fear of God into us, then they are kind to us—if we'll let them. Not to me. They are afraid of me, not I of them, and so with you. You have started off on top. Stay there."

He bade me keep out of the combine. "Play alone," he said. "The combine will beat you for a while; so will I, of course. The whole police force will help beat you. Sure. But you'll soon learn the game and hold your own."

He said, still embarrassingly aloud, that he had seen me talking with the other reporter.

"I know what he wanted," he laughed. "He proposed that you share his office, pay him—not his office, him—half the rent costs, be his Max, and—"

"How did you know that?"

"I didn't," Riis shouted, as the reporter we were talking about walked across the street and up the stairs to headquarters. "But ——— tries to get every new reporter to fag for him; and most of them do. No. Don't you do it. I can't show you around much; too busy; but Max will," and he called "M-a-a-x" out of the window; then remembered: "Oh, yes, Max is gone downtown. Come on. I'll show you around."

He broke into all the offices, police and health, walked right in upon everybody he thought I should know, laughed, made them all laugh, and introduced me, not by name, but as the new *Evening Post* man. When we were coming back out of the building, at the front end of the hall, we saw two policemen half forcing, half carrying, a poor, broken, bandaged East Side Jew into the office opposite that of the Superintendent of Police. There were officers and citizens all about us, but Riis grasped my arm, and pointing to the prisoner as he stumbled in through the open door, he shouted—not, I think, for me alone to hear: "There you have a daily scene in Inspector Williams' office! That's a prisoner. Maybe he's done something wrong, that miserable Russian Jew; anyway he's done something the police don't like. But they haven't only arrested him, as you see; they have beaten him up. And look—"

The door opened, showed a row of bandaged Jews sitting against the wall in the inspector's office, and at his desk, Clubber Williams.

"See the others. There's a strike on the East Side, and there are always clubbed strikers here in this office. I'll tell you what to do while you are learning our ways up here; you hang around this office every morning, watch the broken heads brought in, and as the prisoners are discharged, ask them for their stories. No paper will print them, but you yourself might as well see and hear how strikes are broken by the police."

Inspector Williams had heard. He rose from his desk, pointed at the door, shouted something, and the doorman closed the door with a bang. And Jake Riis laughed. But there was no merriment in that loud laugh of Jake Riis; there was bold rage in his face, as he left me, banging out of the building. I stayed, as he suggested, and watched the scene. Many a morning when I had nothing else to do I stood and saw the police bring in and kick out their bandaged, bloody prisoners, not only strikers and foreigners, but thieves, too, and others of the miserable, friendless, troublesome poor.

## ROOSEVELT AND REFORM

THE MAN the reformers united upon for mayor was William L. Strong. He was a merchant; he knew nothing of politics, and the politicians knew nothing of him. He was an ideal candidate, therefore. He was the good business man who would throw out the rascally politicians and give us a good business administration. For him were the "honest Republicans," the fine old aristocratic Democrats, the reformers called goo-goos after their Good Government Clubs, the "decent" newspapers, and the good people generally. Richard Croker, who managed the fight against us, had his own machine, parts of the Republican machine, the saloons, gambling-houses, all vice interests, sportsmen generally, and to my curious surprise many business men—the ablest, biggest, richest business men in local business: gas, transportation, banks, and the great financiers.

"Sure," said Croker one night to me, "your reformer friends talk about business, but the business men who have business with the city government and so know about the Tammany administration—they are with us."

That was during the campaign. Croker had plenty of money from his rich backers and assurance from himself. "You won't get a look-in," he declared. He talked, he looked, he behaved in a way that convinced me, for one, that our ticket would be defeated and Tammany and the crooked police vindicated. I did not report the reform side of the fight; the political reporters covered that and indeed the whole campaign, but I used to go out of personal curiosity to reform headquarters, and the managers there tried to, but could not, radiate confidence as Croker did. They could say that we were sure to win, but they looked anxious and spoke dubiously; their willing lies did not ring true. The first time I was persuaded that we would win was after the polls closed on Election Day, when, as the counting of the ballots began, Croker received us, as his habit was on Election Day, and calmly told us, not only that Tammany was beaten, but by how large a majority.

I was so astonished, so disappointed in Croker, whom I had believed, that I hung back as the other reporters ran off—not to quote the boss; it was understood that Croker's figures were not for publication, but—to whisper the "truth" to their chiefs. Croker saw me, came over, and laid his hand on my shoulder.

"You look flabbergasted," he said. "Why? You knew all along that it was a reform wave, didn't you?"

"How should I know that?" I protested.

"A political reporter, like a politician, has to know politics," he smiled. "The betting showed; the gamblers have our figures. But one trip of inquiry into any Tammany ward would have told you that Tammany voters were going to vote against us this year, and one ward is all wards in a city. Our people could not stand the rotten police corruption. They'll be back at the next election; they can't stand reform either. But this year they—as you see—" and, giving me a gentle shove, he added, smiling kindly, "as you ought to have known, boy."

The other reporters did, they said. "What do you do, read the papers or work for them?" one of them asked me, when I had sounded him.

Police headquarters was the proper background for my humiliation the day after the election. Everybody there was humble, too, and I sympathized with them. But they did not sympathize with me. Byrnes had nothing to say; Clubber Williams, hate in his eyes, stood with some papers in his hand to watch me come into the hall.

"Well, are you satisfied now?" he sneered at me.

"Not yet," I answered boldly, but I did not feel bold. I felt ashamed. Would I never see through the appearance of things to the facts? Never get past the lie to the truth? Victory was defeat for me.

Dr. Parkhurst was calmly pleased. His attention, however, was fixed on the next step, the appointments to the police board. The fight was not over, he said; Mayor Strong was making "deals." Everybody was pulling and hauling upon him to do this or not do that, to name this man and not to name the other; the police board he had to appoint was the bone of contention among the groups who thought and said that they had "made him mayor." A business man, he did not know the ethics or the ways of politics. He gave promises that could not be kept because they were contradictory. I saw enough of it to realize that reform politics was still politics, only worse; reformers were not so smooth as the professional politicians, and it seemed to me they were not so honest—which was a very confusing theory to me. I remember having a talk with Jake Riis about it. His mind was single and simple. He declared that God was running it.

"Theodore Roosevelt is the man for president of the police board, and God will attend to his appointment. That's all I want to know. I don't care who the other commissioners are. T.R. is enough."

My academic interest in the difference between reformers and politicians did not interest him; my suggestion that maybe the ethics of politics and the ethics of business were different and that, therefore, a man like Croker was better in politics than a merchant like Strong, whereas a business man in business would be better than Croker—that bored Riis. He let me express my thoughts, but after all, I could think aloud more clearly with my mother-in-law than with Riis and other reporters. She was neither religious nor cynical. But Riis was right, in a way.

Roosevelt was appointed police commissioner. We got the news from our offices one day; Riis came shouting it out in the street, and within an hour up walked T.R. and three other gentlemen: Frederick Dent Grant, the son of General Grant; Avery D. Andrews, an ex-army officer, and Andrew D. Parker. I said that they walked. I mean that they came on foot; and three of them did walk, but T.R. ran. He came ahead down the street; he yelled, "Hello, Jake," to Riis, and running up the stairs to the front door of police headquarters, he waved us reporters to follow. We did. With the police officials standing around watching, the new board went up to the second story, where the old commissioners were waiting in their offices. T.R. seized Riis, who introduced me, and still running, he asked questions: "Where are our offices? Where is the board room? What do we do first?" Out of the half-heard answers he gathered the way to the board room, where the old commissioners waited, like three of the new commissioners, stiff, formal, and dignified. Not T.R. He introduced himself, his colleagues, with hand-shakes and then called a meeting of the new board; had himself elected president—this had been prearranged—and then adjourned to pull Riis and me with him into his office.

"Now, then, what'll we do?"

It was all breathless and sudden, but Riis and I were soon describing the situation to him, telling him which higher officers to consult, which to ignore and punish; what the forms were, the customs, rules, methods. It was just as if we three were the police board, T.R., Riis, and I, and as we got T.R. calmed down we made him promise to go a bit slow, to consult with his colleagues also. Then we went out into the hall, and there stood the three other commissioners together, waiting for us to go so that they could see T.R.

They did not like it a bit, as Parker told me afterward. "Thinks he's the whole board," he said; and the subsequent split of the commission was started right then and there. We warned T.R., and he tried to make it up to his colleagues. He consulted them when he thought of it, but Grant and Andrews did not know anything about the police, and Parker, a New Yorker, familiar with the conditions, had it in for T.R., who, he said, was stepping up on the police job as a ladder to something higher.

"Of course," Riis answered, when I told him Parker's opinion. "Teddy is bound for the presidency."

My theory of T.R. was that he merely forgot the courtesies due the board. He had been asked to take the police job, he had been urged to clean out the department, and considering it with his friends, had been thinking of it as his job, his alone, forgetting that it was a board; and so, when the others were appointed, he kept forgetting them. He was so intent upon the task that he did not think of his associates or anything else.

"Except the presidency," Riis would roar, and he was so happy in his certainty that God and T.R. were working toward that end that I challenged him one day.

"Let's ask him," I said.

Riis sprang up, and with a "come on" to me, dashed across the street up to T.R.'s office. And bursting in, Riis did ask him to settle our dispute. Was he working toward the presidency? The effect was frightening.

T.R. leaped to his feet, ran around his desk, and fists clenched, teeth bared, he seemed about to strike or throttle Riis, who cowered away, amazed.

"Don't you dare ask me that," T.R. yelled at Riis. "Don't you put such ideas into my head. No friend of mine would ever say a thing like that, you—you—"

Riis's shocked face or T.R.'s recollection that he had few friends as devoted as Jake Riis halted him. He backed away, came up again to Riis, and put his arm over his shoulder. Then he beckoned me close and in an awed tone of voice explained.

"Never, never, you must never either of you ever remind a man at work on a political job that he may be president. It almost always kills him politically. He loses his nerve; he can't do his work; he gives up the very traits that are making him a possibility. I, for instance, I am going to do great things here, hard things that require all the courage, ability, work that I am capable of, and I can do them if I think of them alone. But if I get to thinking of what it might lead to—"

He stopped, held us off, and looked into our faces with his face screwed up into a knot, as with lowered voice he said slowly: "I must be wanting to be president. Every young man does. But I won't let myself think of it; I must not, because if I do, I will begin to work for it, I'll be careful, calculating, cautious in word and act, and so— I'll beat myself. See?"

Again he looked at us as if we were enemies; then he threw us away from him and went back to his desk.

"Go on away, now," he said, "and don't you ever mention the— don't you ever mention that to me again."

As Riis and I were going, crestfallen, thoughtful, down the stairs, I said, "Well, you win, Riis."

"I do not," he answered, hot; so loyal was Jake Riis; but he was honest, too. He hurried on ahead, and we never mentioned the matter again even to each other.

The first thing the new police board did was to order the police to enforce the law, and when they did not obey, the second step was taken: the removal of the bad police officers. Byrnes had retired voluntarily, unprompted, and the day of his going is memorable to me. There were rumors of his retirement, and many business men and politicians called quietly, saw him, and as quietly slipped away. "What will happen to us now I dread to think," said a banker, who really looked frightened. I believe there were people who felt that all that stood between them and crime was this mysterious master of the police force. But thieves came too, and they were more frightened than the honest men. They did not call on Byrnes; they simply walked along the streets around police headquarters, and one man sat on the steps going up to the high stoop of the building. He sat with his head in his hands, his elbows on his knees, and seemed to heed nothing. I asked Tom the doorman who he was.

"Oh, just an old dip that the old man was good to sometimes. Thinks the world is coming to an end."

The crooks and the business men, and for that matter many of the police and police reporters (including myself), did not understand that it was not Byrnes but a well-nigh universal system that they were living and working under, a system of compromise and privilege for crooks and detectives that "the inspector" inherited and left intact. When Superintendent Byrnes retired that day and walked without good-by to any of us out of his office forever, men stopped and stood to watch him go, silent, respectful, sad, and the next day the world went on as usual.

Roosevelt had to decide whether to let the other higher officers retire on a pension or be tried. Some of the commissioners and public opinion were for punishment. "Discipline," they said; "revenge," they meant. Riis and I were against trials. With Riis, the veteran police reporter, it was sentiment, I think. He was fond even of some of the worst men. My attitude was instinctive: against punishment; but it was not clear and straight. There were exceptions. I wanted satisfaction from the clubber, Williams, and I told T.R. I wanted to be present when he fired him, and why. My argument, however, was that trials were long, the law technical and unsure, and T.R., who was swift, stood in the main for retirement. And he was strengthened by his experience. As he began to send for officers and tell them they must go; either reluctantly resign, retire, or be put on trial, "pull" interfered, and not political pull alone.

"Hey, there," he yelled to me from his window one day, "come up here." I ran upstairs to his outer office, which was filled with all sorts of respectable people, evidently business men, lawyers, doctors, women, and two priests. Waving his hand around the circle of them, he squeezed through his teeth aloud: "I just want you to see the kind of people that are coming here to intercede for proven crooks. Come on, come into my office and listen to the reasons they give for letting bribers, clubbers, and crime-protectors stay on the police force and go on grafting on the public."

Of course he spoiled the sport for that day and that crowd. I sat with him awhile, but the callers who had heard what he said could not make their pleas very well. They were too embarrassed. But on other days when I saw a "string of pulls" calling on him, I went up and listened. They were amusing; they did not know what they were talking about. Most of them merely liked personally some officer who had asked them to intercede to keep him on the force. What I got out of it was that so-called "political influence" is really a common, human plea which politicians use best. The average good citizen tried to tell T.R. that the man he was pulling for was a good officer lied about. Since the officers T.R. was firing were all men fully exposed by the Lexow Committee—the worst of them—the good citizens' appeals only angered him. But when a politician came breezing in and said: "Sure, Mr. President, Captain Bill's a crook; most of 'em are crooks; most of all of us is so crooked we get cramps in our beds at night, but, hell, why pick on Bill? He knows you're straight, and if you ask him to go straight he will. Sure he will. I know Bill since he was a kid. All I ask you is to call him up, look into his face, and tell him what to do. You'll see: he'll do it."

That sort of song and dance would tempt us; and I mean us.

"What'll we do?" T.R. would say after a plea like that from some regular Tammany leader, and I could not help laughing. I knew just how the commissioner felt. I wanted to see Captain Bill and ask him to stay and help reform, as T.R. did; and sometimes we did send for Bill, and, well, sometimes T.R. kept a proved crook for a crooked politician. The reporters observed and reported it, too.

Looking back at it now, I can see it better than I could then. I can see that the police assumed that T.R., being a reformer, might respond to a clergyman's appeal or "a word" from a business man or any other "good man" and be affronted by the plea of a politician, especially a Tammany opponent of reform. They did not know what false and offensive reasonings good people make. It was long before they learned that—for some reason, which they never did discover—the reform commission was, like the old board, subject to political pull. When they did learn it the character of the callers at police headquarters changed. Politicians came after that, prominent leaders of all parties—and failed often; they gave political reasons for mercy. The police never learned what it was that "got" T.R.

"What gets me," said an old police sergeant (the wisest rank on the police force), "what I can't unpuzzle is why he'll listen to Tim Sullivan and throw down the reform Mayor himself and laugh a Platt Republican leader out of his office; and then turn right around and tell Charlie Murphy [a Tammany leader] to go sing his song to the high marines in the harbor, and do a favor for Lem Quigg [a Platt machine leader] up the river."

Nor could I solve the riddle, any more than T.R. could. He thought he was carrying out the reform policy of "throwing out" the crooks and enforcing the law. He was having a hard time of it. He could not make the policemen on their beats close up the saloons at the closing hour. He told them to. He issued formal orders, he made personal appeals, and nothing happened. Talking it over, we guessed that the rank and file would not obey the board because the higher officers, like Inspector Williams, who gave T.R.'s instructions to their men, did so with a wink. By way of experiment I suggested that he force Williams out and then see what happened in his district. He agreed. He knew what had been disclosed of Williams's share in the blackmail fund; everybody remembered the rich inspector's "lots in Japan." I told about my experiences with this man and his brutal clubbings of East Side strikers.

"I said I'd be here at police headquarters till he was fired," I concluded.

"Did you?" T.R. asked. "Well, you will. You'll be right here in this room."

A few days later T.R. threw up his second-story window, leaned out, and yelled his famous cowboy call, "Hi yi yi." He often summoned Riis and me thus. When we poked our heads out of my window across the street this time, he called me alone.

"Not you, Jake. Steffens, come up here."

I hurried over up to his office, and there in the hall stood Williams, who glared as usual at me with eyes that looked like clubs. I passed on in to T.R., who bade me sit down on a certain chair at the back of the room. Then he summoned Williams and fired him; that is to say, he forced him to retire. It was done almost without words. Williams had been warned; the papers were all ready. He "signed there," rose, turned and looked at me, and disappeared.

He did, this one clubber; he went, but not the clubs. Skulls are still cracked—literally—in New York. My triumph was personal, mean, and incomplete.

T.R.'s was a little better. With Williams out and an acting inspector in command of that district, a young, inexperienced patrolman "took a chance," as he said. One night this young cop walked into Pat Callighan's saloon, laid his hand on Pat, and told him he was under arrest. Now Pat was a man of strength as well as power, and his gang was all there. He fought, the gang fought, there was a boozy, bloody battle, but the young cop with his night stick laid out enough men to hold off the rest. He arrested Pat Callighan. I saw this in the morning papers, and when T.R. arrived at his office I showed him his chance.

"Promote that cop," I said, "and you will show all the young policemen that you mean business. Pat Callighan is a sacred person in the underworld, a symbol. The key to his saloon was thrown in the river when he opened, and his door has never been locked since. If a patrolman dare arrest Pat and can get away with it, then all saloons can be closed."

T.R. did it. This young policeman was too newly appointed to be eligible for promotion, and there was strong opposition in the name of the law, but T.R. had announced that he would make a roundsman of this, the first policeman to believe him, and the board consented.

And sure enough, other policemen of all ranks began to obey the orders of the board. Some saloons and some gamblers were raided—not many; not all laws were enforced. T.R. went about at night with Riis as his guide to see the police at work. He had some bizarre experiences. He caught men off post, talking together; he caught them in all sorts of misconduct and had funny, picturesque adventures, which Riis described to all of us (so fair was he as a reporter) and which we all wrote to the amusement of newspaper readers. But what T.R. was really doing—the idea of Riis in proposing it—was to talk personally with the individual policemen and ask them to believe in him, in the law, which they were to enforce. T.R. knew, he said, the power they were up against, the tremendous, enduring power of organized evil, but he promised he would take care of them.

"It worked—a little," he used to say. "I told them that we would back up and not only defend but promote those that served on our side, and I threatened we would pursue and punish those that served on the other side."

This he said, and while he was saying it, he was planning to "fire" Schmittberger, the captain, the key to the old system.

*THE AUTOBIOGRAPHY OF LINCOLN STEFFENS*, 1931

# DAWN POWELL

During her lifetime, novelist and playwright Dawn Powell (1897–1965) won the respect of fellow writers, but had little commercial success. Hers was the characteristic fate of the "midlist" writer. While the seven novels that make up what Gore Vidal has called her "New York cycle" are satirically tinged, her diaries are more poignant, sometimes devastating, in tone. Powell anatomizes, from her privileged position of failure, the shallowness and competitiveness that New York at its worst inspires; the hard choice is often between the claustrophobia of loneliness and the casual cruelty and self-absorption encountered at cocktail parties.

## FROM THE DIARIES

*[1931] JUNE 19*   I am in as serene a state now as I can ever expect to be. I think it's because I'm more or less a flop, I suppose. This means I'm not invited to any smart houses where I am furious at not having clothes, carfare and so on. Since I'm not asked, I don't mind a bit. Even seeing shops doesn't fill me with frustrations and envy; they're out of my life. This may mean that poverty—and we certainly are poor now—is my proper state and I'll always see things out of focus when (or rather if) we have funds.

*JULY 8*   An evening up on the Empire State roof—the strangest experience. The huge tomb in steel and glass, the ride to the 84th floor and there, under the clouds, a Hawaiian string quartet, lounge, concessions and, a thousand feet below, New York—a garden of golden lights winking on and off, automobiles, trucks winding in and out, and not a sound. All as silent as a dead city—it looks *adagio* down there.

*JULY 15*   Dreadful evening with Coby and Joe. Not doing a thing in town but bite my nails and wait, so best go to country where at least I sleep well. All most people do is complicate my responsibilities and force me to worry about them and make up their deficiencies. Selfish, ungracious thing to say—I don't know what's gotten into me, but I've certainly turned into a bitter, ill-tempered, acid, selfish, frustrated old maid.

*J U L Y  2 0*   When writing was a hobby I wrote five to seven hours a day regularly. Now that it is a profession, I find it almost impossible. Is it because I am tired, in bad condition, worried by finances or, as I suspect, because my life is so complicated it takes all my energy weaving in and out of it?

Nostalgia for the old days at *Snappy Stories*—a salary every week, nice clothes, independence, routined life. Finding myself driven more and more into the position of helpless neurotic wife who has dropped her dear little hobby for the time being. That is what I dread—being unarmed, even against one's friends and husband, so that one has no rights but the little privileges permitted a capricious little wife. I want the dignity of my own work, my own earnings and control of my own life. The only way to accomplish this is by constant production. One can't just run from the idle futility of town (not even dissipation is possible there now) to the lazy sleep-and-eat of the country forever, without accomplishing something somewhere. It's up to me.

It seems to me that ever since I finished *Dance Night* I have been marking time, waiting for something that doesn't happen. I can't buckle down seriously to big job but just do little odd pieces—marking time, really, in my mind, waiting for *Dance Night* to come out with great *éclat*. As if it had never come out—a rocket that only sizzled because it was rained on. Still wait for the blaze in the sky. It did a very funny thing to me, that dead rocket.

*J U L Y  2 2*   Even out here, I cannot escape the tension of false expectations. In New York it is unbearable—$10,000 in movie money always about to happen but never quite closing, phones ring but never bring business.

*J U L Y  2 9*   Went Sunday to Mastic to the Lawsons and yachted around till we broke the propeller. Did some work on novel—up to page 52. When Stanley [Rinehart] and John [Farrar] asked me, hopefully, if my new book was about New York, I explained a little of the plot—enough to make their faces fall in obvious consternation.

*OCTOBER 12* Moved to 9 East 10th Street and love it passionately. So quiet—calm, spacious, one's soul breathes deep breaths in it and feels at rest. I am almost neurotic about it: I want it all alone—with Joe and family, of course—but outside of Port Jefferson, this is first material thing I've loved. It comes over one suddenly—like love—that this is home.

*NOVEMBER 21* Party with Vincent Sheean, Coby and Mr. Baby. I asked where was Mrs. Baby (I'd forgotten their names, only remembered they called each other Baby) and he gravely said "bust up." That's what happens to these babies.

Tighter than I've been in years.

*[1932] FEBRUARY 8* Lunch with John Farrar who disturbed me by saying no hurry on novel—not coming out till August. Since I was getting along fine by being in a hurry, what to do?

*JUNE 17* Harassing day fixing everything up with Group. Then Jack sold his play to the Group, too and we went to Sam's and drank with E. E. Cummings till five in the morning—a simply heavenly spree. Cummings' conversation (in its drunken fantastic aspects) permits no interchange—it is a dazzling, glittering spectacle, a parade of wonders and fantastic nonsense. His sarcasm is savage but I note that art and humor both vanish when pretty young girls ask him the meaning of his work—his explanations are as pompous and flattened as any Floyd Dells.

*JULY 5* Dinner at the Brewery, later to Horace Liveright's penthouse. He's a man in a book all right—a semi-glamorous, cheap, New York novel.

*SEPTEMBER 15* To dinner at Sam's with Jack and later to Empire State Building. It was divinely beautiful and strange up there. Clouds, as white as if the sky were baby blue, swam beneath us and stars were below us. They glittered through the clouds and the town lay spread out in its spangles like Christmas presents waiting to be opened, its clangor sifted through space into a whispering silence. It held a secret and when suddenly letters flamed together in the sky you felt—ah, so that's it. "Sunshine Biscuits," the message of the city.

*[1933] JANUARY 25* [. . .] I am in my usual winter state of amazed loneliness though by this time I should be adjusted to a life free of Andrews, Chambers, Lawsons, Dos Passos, etc. [. . .]

Dos has been so sweet and kind during this whole play mess—he is the only person aside from Joe and Coby who hasn't made things worse by manner or speech. Most people are furious at me for not lying down and screaming so they can forgive me and have a friendly pleasure in seeing the punishment sink in—the Olympian privilege of providing big-hearted consolation. Failing in this—I persist in regarding the whole thing as near a success as I've ever had—they decide to take digs.

I wish I could get this novel swinging along. Since I have no other immediate plans I don't see why I shouldn't be up to page 50 at least by the end of February—90 by March 30—140 by April 30—190 by May 30—235 by June 30—290 by July 30, finish—330—by August 30—publish December 15.

In the Brevoort at lunch a fat, petulant, pretty woman implored a sleek, foxy Jewish man of 50. "Let me be yours again for the next few years—I'll be nice—I'll change—I know you think I'm frumpy but I'm going to change. I'm going to branch out. I'm going to get a blue cape and a hat to match—you'll be sorry if you don't take me back." The Brevoort manager stood at all the tables saying "how-do-you-do?" and "how's-the-steak?" She was just saying "I'm going to change and look wonderful—I'm going to get thin—be like I used to when you liked me so much" and sailing into a huge steak when he stood there. "And how is the steak, Madame?" "Oh, fine," she said.

*JUNE 6* Today I posed eating a pineapple at my typewriter for the J. Walter Thompson Agency—the funniest thing I ever heard of, so funny I couldn't help doing it even though Coby Gilman thought it was a hideous lowering of myself. People came and went all day— Edgar, Adolph Dehn, Al Saxe the little Agit-Prop boy, etc.—and I wondered how I ever did any work when my days in New York are so cluttered with people.

*JULY 14*  To Katherine Brush's party for Stan Rinehart. Her house is so fabulous it does not inspire either envy or pleasure but knocks one on the head and leaves one unconscious. It is hard to imagine what it must be like to live in such a world, since it is neither society nor bohemia, but as bare, bottomless, roofless as Hollywood. It has to be warmed by one's meager body and that isn't enough.

Dwight's book, dedicated to me, is receiving tremendous acclaim. He has set his traps so well, managed himself like a shrewd business-man managing an artist—not a bit of his own value does he miss or underestimate. All this means work and he deserves his success. Of the 25 stories, I did a large part of 13, so it seems bitterly ironic that the reviewers (like Stark Young) who were so savage about my play should rave so about lines (usually mine) from this book. Book re-viewers who have ignored my hard-fought novels find whole columns to rave over this work by Dwight in which I helped so considerably.

I cannot envy his success, for he worked far too hard, maneu-vered, fought, and it is not as a writer but as a personality that he seeks a unique recognition. I do despise the reviewers so easily bought, as Dwight sardonically knows, by a mere smell from Society, so cringing before Money and Social Register when they should di-vert that reverence to a Wells or Balzac or even an O'Neill. I have al-most equal contempt for myself for trying to attain any celebrity by sheer hard work and a sincere desire to tell a story that the country annals need for social history. I hope I have learned enough by this time to waste no time on attempts at absolute perfection. Life is too short and appreciation can only come if the work is sufficiently cheap to make the reviewer feel superior or socially set up.

*JULY 18*  This is the last month of my money from Farrar and Rinehart or from anywhere—from now on, nothing—and the morbidity has set in that invariably has its base in finance. I am appalled at this secret, iron determination to make money—to win the artistic esteem its possession automatically confers. What I want is only possible after the world has seen and envied. It is the lesson I learned from Dwight—he set out for years to win something he personally despised but had a worldly significance. Now—having his smart world licked, his serious reviewers off guard—he can give them a symphony and they will listen. A sincere symphony from a serious composer is nothing—but one from a celebrity is something else again. From now on, by God, I am determined to distort every thought into the tawdry easy lines the world can applaud.

By this time next year I will have a fortune, have cut the throats of my best friends, have kicked my inferiors in the pants, have refused to be connected with any strangers except properly identified ones, and be loved and respected by all. And, if I can show enough automobiles and the proper manner, perhaps I will be considered a real artist, a positive dreamer, a genius.

*NOVEMBER 24* Endless weeks of never more than a dollar at best and usually two or three nickels instead, three year old clothes, morbid fat, make me increasingly tired and depressed. Nothing ahead but dreary, unrewarded and limping work. Sustained hate and bitter envy of everyone—very unlike me but so tired and discouraged that almost everyone seems more blessed.

*[1934] FEBRUARY 10* Evening at Pietro Montana's—an Italian sculptor with a house on W. 70th, a beautiful, simple Italian with a Swedish, huge-busted wife and two floors of great plaster saints, harrowed pilgrims. I was surprised at the devotion to *respectability* these midtown foreign artists had—less of the vaunted artistic flare than in any Cleveland candy salesman. Pleasant, sincere good people but I derive no comfort or stimulus from these; I prefer discontents.

*FEBRUARY 12* I want this new novel to be delicate and cutting—nothing will cut New York but a diamond. Probably should do a night job on it as on *Tenth Moon*—it should not be a daylight book but intense and brilliant and fine like night thoughts. No wandering but each detail should point to the one far-off star and be keyed by Lila's own waiting excitement and preserved youth. It should be crystal in quality, sharp as the skyline and relentlessly true. No external details beyond the swift eager glance over the shoulder.

*[1935] AUGUST 14* Weight 137 and ¼—lost 3 and ½ lbs. in less than three weeks due to exercise again, light breakfast—much grapefruit juice.

*NOVEMBER 2* Finished novel late at night.

*NOVEMBER 18* No word from Farrar and Rinehart and have curious sickness as result, something I seem to get when my work is affected, as if work was a gland secretion and when circumstance blocks it, the physique reacts as to any disease—slight fever, aches, weakness, definite mental vagueness.

*NOVEMBER 20* Sickish but no longer tense, due to fine rage at F & R, so wrote firm, angry letter to Carol about them on backbone engendered by Bergdorf clothes, no doubt. Going up today to get evening dress. In that place models wander in and out of dressing rooms. Perfume girl comes in with trace of Matchabelli to squirt at you.

*NOVEMBER 21* Figures on books.

|              |             |      |
| ------------ | ----------- | ---- |
| *Dance Night* | reg edition | 4972 |
|              | reprint     | 7500 |
| *Tenth Moon* | reg         | 1932 |
|              |             | 1089 |
| *Country Boy* | reg        | 1842 |
| "Jig-Saw"    |             | 281  |

*NOVEMBER 22* In *Turn, Magic Wheel*, I believe firmly that I have the perfect New York story, one woman's tragedy viewed through the chinks of a writer's book about her, newspaper clippings, cafe con-

versations, restaurant brawls, New York night life, so that the story is tangled in the fritter of New York—it could not happen anyplace else. The front she keeps up is the front peculiar to the New York broken heart; peoples' deeds and reactions are peculiarly New York. "What? Our friend committed suicide—that's terrible . . . that's the kind of suit I'm going to get, there in Altman's . . . She jumped out of the window? No!—are you getting out here, why don't you get a gold belt . . . ?"

Publisher and critic (but not public which—once it can be reached—is always more sane and sound than critical interpreters) would say these women, discussing the deaths of their friends, must be hard, bitter. The truth is that in New York, a city of perpetual distraction—where superficial senses are perpetually forced to react to superficial impressions—the inner tragedies, no matter how intense, are viewed through the tawdry lace of New York life.

DECEMBER 2  Lunch with John Farrar. He told me how fine my book was; it probably wouldn't sell, etc. Lunch with him is taxing for he is such a complete self-dramatizer. Even his face takes on a cartoon quality, a cartoon of whatever he's talking about—guinea pig—senator—burlesque queen. The flaccid features become these people.

[1936] JANUARY 2  "What'd you think of the show?" asked Odets, firmly fixing me with blue eye. "You saw 'Paradise,' didn't you?"

"Well," I said uneasily, "I can't say just what I thought. I was only sure it wasn't bad."

Group actors and directors took a step forward, like Gods of the Mountain closing in about me. I stammered more inadequacies.

"The reason I ask," said Clifford, "is that about ten of the leading playwrights are testifying for it in an ad, and I'd like to get you in on it. Some of the biggest people in the theater."

Later he talked of the Odets Plays, the audience joy over Odets Plays, as if Odets, the genius, was quite apart from Odets, the "modest" citizen.

*FEBRUARY 10* The book is looking up. Robert Nathan, Rex Stout, Inez Haynes Irwin all read it and are enthusiastic. Mary Ross has too and reviewed it favorably.

At Studin's yesterday the place was filled with charming sensitive, *passé* women, the saddest sight in all the world, except for the elderly men at parties. One once-beautiful woman of about 55, pounced eagerly on people, me particularly, and chattered lightly, vivaciously, of a million things, never pausing, alarming you now and then by a phrase like "of course my son is a raving maniac, has been in a State Institution for 20 years" and "don't mistake me for *Ethel Watts* Mumford, my husband's first wife and ruined his life, really, spent all his money, was indiscriminate to put it mildly . . ."

There was no graceful way to escape the incessant bombardment of her chatter, and just as I was leaving she said, ". . . of course it took all my own fortune and my husband's. I had to sell my diamonds, then my little boy insane. We tried to normalize him—in three months he went stark mad—only 14 years old. But you're such a dear child; why should I put this on you? Please don't look so serious—yes, 20 years he's been there and when I say 'what are those welts on his arm?' the warden says remember he is a Butterfield and a Butterfield can always upset 2000 people. Right, I said. Of course he can upset the other inmates, he's a Butterfield. They're remarkable people; his grandfather built the Pennsylvania Railroad. But the thousands I spent to begin with—as long as we had it—private institutions where he cut his throat and his wrists— a *private* institution, mind you—just a little boy, a fine, beautiful child, everyone adored him but no, they said, he could be normalized, so there he was, uprooted from his tutors, his house—he went to the boy's school, little Eton jackets, whippings every day—in three months he was mad—and me there alone to cope with it for four months. But don't let me burden you—why do you look that way?"

"You're not burdening me," I said. "My own little boy is 14 and we have been worried . . ."

"Oh, my God," she said. "It mustn't happen. You can stop it. I could have stopped Dan. Sit down."

It was a cocktail party for Margaret Widdemer and people were very gay. It was odd for two women in the middle of this confusion, sandwiches and martinis politely being passed, introductions to new-comers offered, to find that strange bond in common—a 14-year old only son—one 20 years ago and the other now—quivering on the brink of a nightmare future. I understood then her incessant gay chatter—for 20 years she had sparkled and chattered to drown the roar of her own tragedy, a little boy raving mad.

"Where do you come from?" Mrs. Dana Butterfield Mumford asked, examining me penetratingly.

"My people come from Ohio," I said.

"Nonsense, child, of course they did, everyone's people spent a few generations in the Middlewest but where were they *from?* Virginia?"

Later I went to lunch at the Women's City Club, where she is chair-man. "The old Butler home," she explained, whisking people in and out of the reception rooms downstairs, waving her program, acci-dentally spilling butter over her new dress while arranging the place-cards at the Chairman's Table. There was an odd air of Alumnae Day about the place, the women had the frozen, wizened masks of their young, athletic faces, the way women have now instead of the serene, relaxed middle-aged faces of their mothers at that age. Not made up but an inner seeking restless look that preserves but shriv-els youth far into the forties.

In the dining room they gathered to hear speeches. "There is Portia Willis, a militant suffragette," said the woman beside me, pointing to a blooming Brünnhilde in red. "She used to be put on a white horse at the front of the suffrage parades. And there is Elizabeth Freeman, another militant, who was chained to the House of Commons one time . . . Of course we're not all militants. We're interested in Civics. Non-partisan. We even have one Communist— a friend of several of us, of course, or we might have hesitated. But in a way it's helpful having all angles. By the way, I wanted to ask about your book. My son died two months ago—and I don't like to read any books that might bring it up."

The women sat around, looking the way they used to look, then the sun shone in and the wrinkles popped into view, hinting the way they would look twenty years from now. Beside me the women listened eagerly to the speakers talk of glamorous worlds. They laid a place in their mental luncheon table for every great name that was mentioned; they drank in H. G. Wells, Pauline Lord, Ellen Terry, Bernard Shaw, David Belasco, Ruth Draper. They were on the same jolly pal basis with these great names as was the speaker. Here was their life, their outside world. From here, they returned to their more modest worlds, their sad worlds, too, with valentines from dead lovers, dead sons, dead husbands.

MARCH 10   The gal, Lilla Worthington, who died at the Brandt's cocktail party. The rainy day. The elevator strike so that streets were crowded with strikers, picketers, rain, cold, blowing off hats and umbrellas inside-out, taxis stuck for hours on sidestreets. By 5:45 only six people in the baronial Brandt living room to meet the Minnesota author, Margaret Culkin Banning, and those six ladies of little importance. "No one is coming to this party," complained Carol, looking with curious dislike on those who had been so common as to come.

In the adjoining dining room three colored waiters (one to every two guests) hovered over a table laden with seltzer, whiskey, sherry and martini mixes. They patiently and constantly passed the trays of little toasted sausages, the stuffed olives in bacon on the pretty colored toothpicks. People talked vivaciously to each other trying to be a crowd and eyes lit up when the bell rang and the row of too handsome young men from the motion picture offices came in. Carol looked pained with the bare bones of her ten percent party too obviously revealed—office employees and movie buyers, usually decently lost in groups of social and literary figures.

The pretty, sweet-faced Miss Worthington and I tried to remember where we met. I had never seen her at the Brandt parties as they rather dislike having their underlings in the home socially. A few minutes later she was standing talking to other people—a commotion, a slight exclamation, she was on the floor. Window raised, wet

cloth brought, suddenly Carl picked her up and carried her into another room, her curly head dangling over his arm, strange animal
gurgling noises coming from her, someone running along beside her
with an inadequate little folded wet handkerchief. People looked at
each other with expressions of mingled polite concern and natural
distaste for the bad manners of the thing. The polite thing obviously
was to continue to chat, forgive the rather vulgar interruption, and
so groups closed in again. The several motion picture people argued
about the value of Vincent Price's profile to pictures; those for him
insisted that the photographer taking his tests declared "I don't know
who this Price is but I will say this—he is without doubt the most
gorgeous boy I've ever photographed."

Miss Banning moved about bravely, guest of honor to the end;
someone occasionally asked about the girl inside; the three butlers
passed their canapés furiously to get rid of these too plentiful
supplies and then the Old Guard began to arrive—the three name
old-time writers, gray, immense, evening-cloaked and furred majestic wives, old Cosmopolitan plots wrapped around their necks,
ready for formal dinner and *Tristan* later at the Met, the Samuel
Hopkins Adams, etc. Just then someone came out from the
bedroom in the midst of this new cheer from outside and said we
were all to leave, the girl was very sick. We left—but she couldn't be
dead! But she was, and her last moments had been full of sweet little Southern banalities and she dropped off as if her name had suddenly thundered through the world—"Lilla Worthington—paging
Lilla Worthington"—the first time in all her modest, kind little life
she'd been vulgarly conspicuous, the first time she'd ever made a
scene.

Later someone said her husband and relatives came—the great
apartment with the three colored butlers, the untouched cocktails,
the cold sausages and congealed toasted cheese—deserted, untouched and uncleaned. The hostess, still in her new hostess gown
with trailing train, carefully matched slippers, rushed over to a hotel
with mink coat over her arm. It was the dead woman's party, it was
a home she'd never dreamed of having, a place she had often wanted
to show her husband though he was never asked there. Now he could

see the lovely rugs, the Sheraton cupboard and the gold Venetian bed she had often described to him; now he could see it for she was dead upon it. Taking her two little boys to school in the morning she had fainted, she had fainted other days, too, but she was afraid of the doctor. She couldn't be very sick; a doctor would scare her, would try to make something serious out of it.

*[1937] MAY 26* Marie came in very happy today, knuckles scraped. Just beat up a man on the subway, she explained; boy, did she feel fine! Old man about 50 sitting opposite her exposing himself. She called a colored man over and he said lady, there's nothing I can do. Oh no? she said, well I can. So she sailed in socking the old boy, let her bundles and purse fly, everyone tried to stop her—men came up. "Let me handle this," she told them and socko, while passengers gathered round and said "Look at the little lady giving it to him. That old boy's getting the beating of his life. Let her be!" Conductor expostulated—she said "The law's on my side." A lady said "Something might happen." "Never mind that," cried Marie happily. "I can always offend myself!"

*JULY 8* How wretched human beings are! Last night I heard a woman's voice late at night and I looked out the window. All windows were dark so it seemed a bedtime quarrel and not a drunken one. "Get out of here, you dirty bum," she cried. "Get out, you low-life, I'll tell your mother. What do you think this is, a whore-house? Get out, you filthy bum, playing with yourself all night long in front of me, stop it, what do you think your mother will say when I tell her—!"

The voice was hopeless, wretched, uneducated in epithet, and the sinister misery of the black, hot city night left me frozen with horror. She went on wearily, a tone of such unhappiness in her voice that it was almost a sob, as if she was trapped and knew it, perhaps by real love that she could not turn to the scorn she would like, bewilderment and confusion over the monstrous sex exhibition, unable to cope with it, understand it. A dreadful night voice praying to a leering city night god.

Three taximen in front of a store on 8th Street. "You wouldn't know the girl now," said one.

"She sure has changed," said the next. "She used to be a nice girl, too."

"She's all right," said the third. "She is a nice girl. I don't believe you fellows."

"Listen, you can tell it by lookin' at her," said the second. "She *walks* guilty."

*SEPTEMBER 13* In the bus (Riverside) the heavy bilious man finally recognized the two fat women. What was he doing now? Playing bridge all afternoon. That's all he did. He played at the best place, the Union Club, 74th Street. What a business, what a business! Fifty couples every afternoon, a hundred and fifty in the evening! Did the ladies play now as much as before? Yes, she did, she played every night. Where did she play? Home, she said. Home?—he asked as if he had never heard of such a place. Yes, home. He was rather reserved after that, as if she had said she played polo at home. Both ladies became voluble in their excuses. "She don't like to play them clubs," one said. "Too much smoke, too much excitement! She likes better to play home!" "Yeah?" he politely said, unconcerned, and then shook hands with them and got off. A play could be written about a bridge club—a melodrama: crooks running it, contrast of boresome bridge-playing innocents with an underworld background.

Riverside Drive is still the loveliest, most glamorous place in New York by night, particularly now with the drive opposite.

*[1938] SEPTEMBER 18* Felipe Alfau called, now a Francoite, as ostracized as a Conscientious Objector in the war. He originally was thrown on the rebel side by simple animalistic reasons—his brother, a mayor in a Spanish town, was assassinated by the Loyalists. Another brother intensified Felipe's vengeance necessity by accepting a Loyalist salary to live on, in spite of the family honor. All very Spanish. From then on he was pushed into more drastic Fascistic positions than before—anti-Jewish talks when all of his friends had

been Jewish. He is a Latin and naturally intellectual, so gravitated automatically to the Jews. They are the ones who start war, who start persecution, is his point. His life is worth nothing, he says, why not go fight if Europe is in war? He would join the Nazi army of Hitler's.

*[1939] MAY 1*  Bobby Lewis said Saroyan's egotism came from his grandmother. An Armenian, she settled in Fresno, California and remained thoroughly Armenian all her days. Commenting on her next-door neighbor she said, "She is so stupid. Think of it. She has lived next door to me for 28 years and still can't speak a word of Armenian."

He wrote a play about two people which he hoped the Group would produce. Saroyan, his hero, is in bed onstage with a woman, in darkness. On screen behind them are pictures of waves breaking.

"You're the best lay I ever had," said the prostitute.

"Not only that," he answers, "but I'm the best writer you ever had."

After a silence, one enormous wave sweeps all the others and the screen blacks out. Lights go on as woman gets up naked and crosses stage to bathroom. "The greatest play ever written," says Saroyan.

*MAY 4*  Frederick Kiesler—a penthouse at 14th and 7th, overlooking the river and New York. 60 guests coming and going, Russians, Tunisians. French, Germans. Buckminster Fuller, neat, gray architect-engineer of 60, carries official Naval Ordinance book around, book on ballistics, pointing out that the first two pages are in verse—The Elongation of the Pressure and the Velocity—etc. Gorky's grandson, tall, mournful, black mustached, essayed a Russian dance. Later, in a small room, in darkness I saw him earnestly talking to the tall, exotic, stagey Russian from Hollywood, with daisies for earrings and a handsome red spangled shawl. "Permeet me to say," he was saying, "permeet me to say that you are like so many dead feesh."

"No! You deed not say it, Arshile! You deed not?"

"I said it," he repeated stiffly. "I said—permeet me to say that to me, I said, you are like so many dead feesh!"

I left and went inside where the Frenchman, the Viennese doctor who had been beaten up by the Nazis, Noguchi the Japanese sculptor and a French Tunisian were all in an open-eyed dither over the blondeness of Peter Jack's wife. The Tunisian was particularly blunt. "How do you do?" he said. "You have a beautiful bosom, do you speak French?" Later he saw her again and reached out his hand. "How do you do, will you come on the terrace?" he said. Peter was jealous, not only of her but more because *he* was the one who should be flirting. He is a strong masculinist.

*[1940] MAY 24* Lunch with Max Perkins. War everywhere.

*SEPTEMBER 15* George Davis—ruddy, clear-eyed, frankly homo but untroubled by it, honest royalist, honest snob, but his clarity about it removes it from sophistication.

*SEPTEMBER 18* In spite of pleasure over Max Perkins' editorial work on me, now that the book is to come out the usual deadly hopelessness and weariness comes in. The lack of any ad or announcement, the silence from publishing end, the all-too-familiar signals of another blank shot, and once again the weary packing up and readying another book—never understanding why I am unable to follow the arrogance of my writing with an arrogance of personality or why the luck should so unfailingly fall elsewhere.

*[1942] DECEMBER 21* At 5 A.M., after usual curious night of not quite being asleep and not quite being awake, woke up and had feeling of tremendous exhilaration—the kind that usually ends in tears but I willed it not so, with my old-time power to will. But nothing beyond a marvelously constructive idea to quit this incredibly silly and kindergarten job at *Mademoiselle*, which I did because of George Davis, whom I like. Then lunch and this usual but new business of people *I* know but am sure don't recognize me waving to someone behind me and bowing and finally coming over and saying "Well, well, *Dawn!*" I am still so amazed at the brazenness of people—completely New York people—who only remember you when you've gone into your fourth printing.

# LOUIS-FERDINAND CÉLINE

---

*The French physician and novelist Louis-Ferdinand Céline (real name Louis-Ferdinand Destouches, 1894–1961) employed splenetic argot, ferocious gallows humor, and torrential narrative drive in chronicling the misadventures of his fictional alter ego Ferdinand. In this scene from his first novel,* Journey to the End of Night, *Ferdinand, newly arrived in New York, becomes one of the movie-going zombies drawn to the lurid "dream palaces" of Times Square.*

FROM *JOURNEY TO THE END OF NIGHT*

As if I knew where I was going, I put on an air of choosing and changed my direction, taking a different street on my right, one that was better lit. "Broadway" it was called. I read the name on a sign. High up, far above the uppermost stories, there was still a bit of daylight, with sea gulls and patches of sky. We moved in the lower light, a sick sort of jungle light, so gray that the street seemed to be full of grimy cotton waste.

That street was like a dismal gash, endless, with us at the bottom of it filling it from side to side, advancing from sorrow to sorrow, toward an end that is never in sight, the end of all the streets in the world.

There were no cars or carriages, only people and more people.

This was the priceless district, I was told later, the gold district: Manhattan. You can enter it only on foot, like a church. It's the banking heart and center of the present-day world. Yet some of those people spit on the sidewalk as they pass. You've got to have your nerve with you.

It's a district filled with gold, a miracle, and through the doors you can actually hear the miracle, the sound of dollars being crumpled, for the Dollar is always too light, a genuine Holy Ghost, more precious than blood.

I found time to go and see them, I even went in and spoke to the employees who guard the cash. They're sad and underpaid.

When the faithful enter their bank, don't go thinking they can help themselves as they please. Far from it. In speaking to Dollar, they mumble words through a little grill; that's their confessional. Not much sound, dim light, a tiny wicket between high arches, that's all. They don't swallow the Host, they put it on their hearts. I couldn't stay there long admiring them. I had to follow the crowd in the street, between those walls of smooth shadow.

Suddenly our street widened, like a crevasse opening out into a bright clearing. Up ahead of us we saw a great pool of sea-green light, wedged between hordes of monstrous buildings. And in the middle of the clearing stood a rather countrified-looking house, surrounded by woebegone lawns.

I asked several people in the crowd what this edifice was, but most of them pretended not to hear me. They couldn't spare the time. But one young fellow right next to me was kind enough to tell me it was City Hall, adding that it was an ancient monument dating back to colonial times, ever so historical . . . so they'd left it there . . . The fringes of this oasis formed a kind of park with benches, where you could sit comfortably enough and look at the building. When I got there, there was hardly anything else to see.

I waited more than an hour in the same place, and then toward noon, from the half-light, from the shuffling, discontinuous, dismal crowd, there erupted a sudden avalanche of absolutely and undeniably beautiful women.

What a discovery! What an America! What ecstasy! I thought of Lola . . . Her promises had not deceived me! It was true.

I had come to the heart of my pilgrimage. And if my appetite hadn't kept calling itself to my attention, that would have struck me as one of those moments of supernatural aesthetic revelation. If I'd been a little more comfortable and confident, the incessant beauties I was discovering might have ravished me from my base human condition. In short, all I needed was a sandwich to make me believe in miracles. But how I needed that sandwich!

And yet, what supple grace! What incredible delicacy of form and feature! What inspired harmonies! What perilous nuances! Triumphant where the danger is greatest! Every conceivable promise of face and figure fulfilled! Those blondes! Those brunettes! Those Titian redheads! And more and more kept coming! Maybe, I thought, this is Greece starting all over again. Looks like I got here just in time.

What made those apparitions all the more divine in my eyes was that they seemed totally unaware of my existence as I sat on a bench close by, slap-happy, drooling with erotico-mystical admiration and quinine, but also, I have to admit, with hunger. If it were possible for a man to jump out of his skin, I'd have done it then, once and for all. There was nothing to hold me back.

Those unlikely midinettes could have wafted me away, sublimated me; a gesture, a word would have sufficed, and in that moment I'd have been transported, all of me, into the world of dreams. But I suppose they had other fish to fry.

I sat there for an hour, two hours, in that state of stupefaction. I had nothing more in the world to hope for.

You know about innards? The trick they play on tramps in the country? They stuff an old wallet with putrid chicken innards. Well, take it from me, a man is just like that, except that he's fatter and hungrier and can move around, and inside there's a dream.

I had to look at the practical side of things and not dip into my small supply of money right away. I didn't have much. I was even afraid to count it. I couldn't have anyway, because I was seeing double. I could only feel those thin, bashful banknotes through the material of my pocket, side by side with my phony statistics.

Men were passing, too, mostly young ones with faces that seemed to be made of pink wood, with a dry, monotonous expression, and jowls so wide and coarse they were hard to get used to . . . Well, maybe that was the kind of jowls their womenfolk wanted. The sexes seemed to stay on different sides of the street. The women looked only at the shopwindows, their whole attention was taken by the handbags, scarves, and little silk doodads, displayed very little at a time, but with precision and authority. You didn't see many old people in that crowd. Not many couples either. Nobody seemed to find it strange that I should sit on that bench for hours all by myself, watching the people pass. But all at once the policeman standing like an inkwell in the middle of the street seemed to suspect me of sinister intentions. I could tell.

Wherever you may be, the moment you draw the attention of the authorities, the best thing you can do is disappear in a hurry. Don't try to explain. Sink into the earth! I said to myself.

It so happened that just to one side of my bench there was a big hole in the sidewalk, something like the Métro at home. That hole seemed propitious, so vast, with a stairway all of pink marble inside it. I'd seen quite a few people from the street disappear into it and come out again. It was in that underground vault that they answered the call of nature. I caught on right away. The hall where the business was done was likewise of marble. A kind of swimming pool, but drained of all its water, a fetid swimming pool, filled only with filtered, moribund light, which fell on the forms of unbuttoned men surrounded by their smells, red in the face from the effect of expelling their stinking feces with barbarous noises in front of everybody.

Men among men, all free and easy, they laughed and joked and cheered one another on, it made me think of a football game. The first thing you did when you got there was to take off your jacket, as if in preparation for strenuous exercise. This was a rite and shirtsleeves were the uniform.

In that state of undress, belching and worse, gesticulating like lunatics, they settled down in the fecal grotto. The new arrivals were assailed with a thousand revolting jokes while descending the stairs from the street, but they all seemed delighted.

The morose aloofness of the men on the street above was equaled only by the air of liberation and rejoicing that came over them at the prospect of emptying their bowels in tumultuous company.

The splotched and spotted doors to the cabins hung loose, wrenched from their hinges. Some customers went from one cell to another for a little chat, those waiting for an empty seat smoked heavy cigars and slapped the backs of the obstinately toiling occupants, who sat there straining with their heads between their hands. Some groaned like wounded men or women in labor. The constipated were threatened with ingenious tortures.

When a gush of water announced a vacancy, the clamor around the free compartment redoubled, and as often as not a coin would be tossed for its possession. No sooner read, newspapers, though as thick as pillows, were dismembered by the horde of rectal toilers. The smoke made it hard to distinguish faces, and the smells deterred me from going too close.

To a foreigner the contrast was disconcerting. Such free-and-easy intimacy, such extraordinary intestinal familiarity, and up on the street such perfect restraint. It left me stunned.

I returned to the light of day by the same stairway and went back to the same bench to rest. Sudden outburst of digestive vulgarity. Discovery of a joyous shitting communism. I ignored both these disconcerting aspects of the same adventure. I hadn't the strength for analysis or synthesis. My pressing desire was to sleep. O rare, delicious frenzy!

So I joined the line of pedestrians entering one of the neighboring streets. We progressed by fits and starts because of the shop-windows, which fragmented the crowd. At one point, the door of a hotel created a great eddy. People poured out on to the sidewalk through a big revolving door. I was caught up and poured the other way, into the big lobby inside.

Instant amazement . . . You had to divine, to imagine the majesty of the edifice, the generous proportions, because the lights were so veiled that it took you some time to know what you were looking at.

Lots of young women in the half-light, plunged in deep arm-chairs as in jewel cases. Around them attentive men, moving silently, with timid curiosity, to and fro, just offshore from the row of crossed legs and magnificent silk-encased thighs. Those miraculous beings seemed to be waiting for grave and costly events. Obviously they weren't giving me a thought. So, ever so furtively, I in my turn passed that long and palpable temptation.

Since at least a hundred of those divine leg owners were sitting in a single row of chairs, I reached the reception desk in so dreamy a condition, having absorbed a ration of beauty so much too strong for my constitution that I was reeling.

At the desk, a pomaded clerk violently offered me a room. I asked for the smallest in the hotel. I can't have had more than fifty dollars at the time. Also, I was pretty well out of ideas and self-assurance.

I hoped the room the clerk was giving me was really the smallest, because his hotel, the Laugh Calvin, was advertised as the most luxurious and sumptuously furnished on the whole North American continent!

Over my head, what an infinity of furnished rooms! And all around me, in those chairs, what inducements to multiple rape! What abysses! What perils! Is the poor man's aesthetic torment to have no end? Is it to be even more long-lasting than his hunger? But there was no time to succumb; before I knew it, the clerk had thrust a heavy key into my hand. I was afraid to move.

A sharp youngster, dressed like a juvenile brigadier general, stepped, imperious and commanding, out of the gloom. The smooth reception clerk rang his metallic bell three times, and the little boy started whistling. That was my send-off. Time to go. And away we went.

As black and resolute as a subway train, we raced down a corridor. The youngster in the lead. A twist, a turn, another. We didn't dawdle. We veered a bit to the left. Here we go. The elevator. Stitch in my side. Is this it? No. Another corridor. Even darker. Ebony paneling, it looks like, all along the walls. No time to examine it. The kid's whistling. He's carrying my frail valise. I don't dare ask him questions. My job was to keep walking, that was clear to me. In the darkness here and there, as we passed, a red-and-green light flashed a command. Long lines of gold marked the doors. We had passed the 1800s long ago and then the 3000s, and still we were on our way, drawn by our invincible destiny. As though driven by instinct, the little bellhop in his braid and stripes pursued the Nameless in the darkness. Nothing in this cavern seemed to take him unawares. His whistling modulated plaintively when we passed a black man and a black chambermaid. And that was all.

Struggling to walk faster in those corridors, I lost what little self-assurance I had left when I escaped from quarantine. I was falling apart, just as I had seen my shack fall apart in the African wind and the floods of warm water. Here I was attacked by a torrent of unfamiliar sensations. There's a moment between two brands of humanity when you find yourself thrashing around in a vacuum.

Suddenly, without warning, the youngster pivoted. We had arrived. I bumped into a chair, it was my room, a big box with ebony walls. The only light was a faint ring surrounding the bashful greenish lamp on the table. The manager of the Laugh Calvin Hotel begged the visitor to look upon him as a friend and assured him that he, the manager, would make a special point of keeping him, the visitor, cheerful throughout his stay in New York. Reading this notice, which was displayed where no one could possibly miss it, added if possible to my depression.

Once I was left alone, it deepened. All America had followed me to my room, and was asking me enormous questions, reviving awful forebodings.

Reclining anxiously on the bed, I tried to adjust to the darkness of my cubbyhole. At regular intervals the walls on the window side trembled. An Elevated Railway train was passing. It bounded between two streets like a cannonball filled with quivering flesh, jolting from section to section of this lunatic city. You could see it far away, its carcass trembling as it passed over a torrent of steel girders, which went on echoing from rampart to rampart long after the train had roared by at seventy miles an hour. Dinnertime passed as I lay thus prostrate, and bedtime as well.

What had horrified me most of all was that Elevated Railway. On the other side of the court, which was more like a well shaft, the wall began to light up, first one, then two rooms, then dozens. I could see what was going on in some of them. Couples going to bed. These Americans seemed as worn out as our own people after their vertical hours. The women had very full, very pale thighs, at least the ones I was able to get a good look at. Before going to bed, most of the men shaved without taking the cigars out of their mouths.

In bed they first took off their glasses, then put their false teeth in a glass of water, which they left in evidence. Same as in the street, the sexes didn't seem to talk to each other. They impressed me as fat, docile animals, used to being bored. In all, I only saw two couples engaging, with the light on, in the kind of thing I'd expected, and not at all violently. The other women ate chocolates in bed, while waiting for their husbands to finish shaving. And then they all put their lights out.

There's something sad about people going to bed. You can see they don't give a damn whether they're getting what they want out of life or not, you can see they don't even try to understand what we're here for. They just don't care. Americans or not, they sleep no matter what, they're bloated mollusks, no sensibility, no trouble with their conscience.

I'd seen too many puzzling things to be easy in my mind. I knew too much and not enough. I'd better go out, I said to myself, I'd better go out again. Maybe I'll meet Robinson. Naturally that was an idiotic idea, but I dreamed it up as an excuse for going out again, because no matter how much I tossed and turned on my narrow bed, I couldn't snatch the tiniest scrap of sleep. Even masturbation, at times like that, provides neither comfort nor entertainment. Then you're really in despair.

The worst part is wondering how you'll find the strength tomorrow to go on doing what you did today and have been doing for much too long, where you'll find the strength for all that stupid running around, those projects that come to nothing, those attempts to escape from crushing necessity, which always founder and serve only to convince you one more time that destiny is implacable, that every night will find you down and out, crushed by the dread of more and more sordid and insecure tomorrows.

And maybe it's treacherous old age coming on, threatening the worst. Not much music left inside us for life to dance to. Our youth has gone to the ends of the earth to die in the silence of the truth. And where, I ask you, can a man escape to, when he hasn't enough madness left inside him? The truth is an endless death agony. The truth is death. You have to choose: death or lies. I've never been able to kill myself.

I'd better go out into the street, a partial suicide. Everyone has his little knacks, his ways of getting sleep and food. I'd need to sleep if I wanted to recover the strength I'd need to go to work next day. Get back the zip it would take to find a job in the morning, and in the meantime force my way into the unknown realm of sleep. Don't go thinking it's easy to fall asleep when you've started doubting everything, mostly because of the awful fears people have given you.

I dressed and somehow found my way to the elevator, but feeling kind of foggy. I still had to cross the lobby, to pass more rows of ravishing enigmas with legs so tempting, faces so delicate and severe. Goddesses, in short, hustling goddesses. We might have tried to make an arrangement. But I was afraid of being arrested. Complications. Nearly all a poor bastard's desires are punishable by jail. So there I was on the street again. It wasn't the same crowd as before. This one billowed over the sidewalks and showed a little more life, as if it had landed in a country less arid, the land of entertainment, of night life.

The people surged in the direction of lights suspended far off in the darkness, writhing multicolored snakes. They flowed in from all the neighboring streets. A crowd like that, I said to myself, adds up to a lot of dollars in handkerchiefs alone or silk stockings! Or just in cigarettes for that matter! And to think that you can go out among all that money, and nobody'll give you a single penny, not even to go and eat with! It's heartbreaking to think how people shut themselves off from one another, like houses.

I, too, dragged myself toward the lights, a movie house, and then another right next to it, and another, all along the street. We lost big chunks of crowd to each of them. I picked a movie house with posters of women in slips, and what legs! Boyohboy! Heavy! Ample! Shapely! And pretty faces on top, as though drawn for the contrast, no need of retouching, not a blemish, not a flaw, perfect I tell you, delicate but firm and concise. Life can engender no greater peril than these incautious beauties, these indiscreet variations on perfect divine harmony.

It was warm and cozy in the movie house. An enormous organ, as mellow as in a cathedral, a heated cathedral I mean, organ pipes like thighs. They don't waste a moment. Before you know it, you're bathing in an all-forgiving warmth. Just let yourself go and you'll begin to think the world has been converted to loving-kindness. I almost was myself.

Dreams rise in the darkness and catch fire from the mirage of moving light. What happens on the screen isn't quite real; it leaves open a vague cloudy space for the poor, for dreams and the dead. Hurry hurry, cram yourself full of dreams to carry you through the life that's waiting for you outside, when you leave here, to help you last a few days more in that nightmare of things and people. Among the dreams, choose the ones most likely to warm your soul. I have to confess that I picked the sexy ones. No point in being proud; when it comes to miracles, take the ones that will stay with you. A blonde with unforgettable tits and shoulders saw fit to break the silence of the screen with a song about her loneliness. I'd have been glad to cry about it with her.

There's nothing like it! What a lift it gives you! After that, I knew I'd have courage enough in my guts to last me at least two days. I didn't even wait for the lights to go on. Once I'd absorbed a small dose of that admirable ecstasy, I knew I'd sleep, my mind was made up.

When I got back to the Laugh Calvin, the night clerk, despite my greeting, neglected to say good evening the way they do at home. But his contempt didn't mean a thing to me anymore. An intense inner life suffices to itself, it can melt an icepack that has been building up for twenty years. That's a fact.

In my room I'd barely closed my eyes when the blonde from the movie house came along and sang her whole song of sorrow just for me. I helped her put me to sleep, so to speak, and succeeded pretty well . . . I wasn't entirely alone . . . It's not possible to sleep alone . . .

1932

# CHRISTOPHER MORLEY

*Christopher Morley (1890–1957) wrote fifty volumes, in just about every genre—including fiction realistic (Kitty Foyle) and fantastic (Thunder on the Left), memoir (John Mistletoe), light verse (The Rocking Horse)—and served for thirty years as a judge for the Book-of-the-Month Club. In a succession of essays written during the 1920's and 30's, he caught the city at ground level: here, for example, he celebrates the unglamorous but solidly middle-class West End Avenue.*

### WEST END AVENUE

YOU HEAR LITTLE about West End Avenue. It is too genteel to have much taste for publicity. But like all very decorous personalities it has its secret ligatures with grim fact. It begins at 106th Street, spliced into the western bend of Broadway, with a memory of the *Titanic* disaster (the Straus Memorial Fountain). It ends at 59th Street in Dead Storage and Loans on Cars, and in the gigantic Interborough Power House. Below that, though its uniformed hall-boys do not like to admit it, it becomes Eleventh Avenue. 59th Street was the latitude where all those baseborn avenues of the old Tenderloin decided to go respectable by changing their names. Eighth became Central Park West, Ninth became Columbus, Tenth became Amsterdam, and Eleventh (or Death Avenue) became West End. But reform is as difficult for streets as for persons. Broadway, careering diagonally across (trollops follow the Trade), drew ever upward its witch-fires and its sulphurous glow. Good old strongholds of middle-class manners were swamped. Apartments once gravid with refinement were given over to the dentist and the private detective (who cries *Confidentially Yours* in the window). When the MacFadden Publications burst into that part of town, reticences tottered. Even as far up as the 70's the West Side struggles to disengage from sombre origins or too gaudy companionship. Then a Childs restaurant—unquestionable banner of fair repute—stems the tide on Broadway. Childs is too shrewd to step in on Doubtful Street. The church also comes to the rescue: a place of worship is combined with an apartment house. "The Cross on top of this building," says a notice, "Guarantees Safety, Security, and Enjoyment."

Of all this shifting struggle—so characteristic of New York and repeated in scores of regions all over town—West End Avenue is perfect symbol. The Interborough Power House, I dare say, gives it vitality to struggle successfully with the New York Central freight yards. It is humble enough here: it eats in Gibbs Diner and smokes its cob pipe in the switchman's little house. It sees lines of milk cans on the sidings and is aware of the solid realities of provender and communication on which citizens depend. (Much of West End Avenue's milk comes from Grand Gorge, N.Y., which is an encouraging name to find printed on the cardboard bottle-top when you rummage the ice-box late at night.) Then the Dodge and other automobile warehouses put ambition into it. It rises to a belt of garages and groceries. At 70th Street it makes as sudden a transformation as any street ever did—except perhaps that social abyss where Tudor City looks over the parapet onto First Avenue. "Here in A.D. 1877," says the tablet in difficult Tudor script, as hen-track as Shakespeare's, "was Paddy Corcoran's Roost." Who was Paddy? They have him in stone with an inverted Irish pipe. One day I walked through Tudor City with W. S. H., a heraldic expert, pursuivant of the various shields, emblems, armorial bearings and stained glaziery of that architect's heyday. Cockle-shells, pelicans, griffons, lymphiads, bars and bends most sinister, nearly made an imbecile of my poor friend. Rouge Dragon himself could never unscramble that débris of the College of Arms. "They intended a boar, but it turned to a talbot," cried W. S. H., examining one fierce escutcheon.

But West End Avenue, when it goes residential at 70th Street, does so in solid fashion, without freak or fantasy. For thirty-five blocks it has probably the most uniform skyline of any avenue in New York. It indulges little in terraces or penthouses; just even bulks of masonry. What other street can show me a run of thirty-five blocks without a shop-window? Few of its apartments have individual names. The Esplanade and the Windermere are two rare exceptions, as also the grand old Apthorp, the Gibraltar of our up-town conservatism. Inside its awful courtyard I have never dared to tread. We leave to the crosstown streets the need to hyperbolize their apartments with pretentious names.

West End is incomparably the most agreeable and convenient of large residential streets, second only to Riverside Drive—whose decline in prestige is mysterious. For that famous old glue-pot stench that used to come drifting across from Jersey has vanished altogether. West End is well churched and doctored. The abandoned hospital at the 72nd Street corner is something of a shock, but the Avenue hurries on uptown, consoling itself with Mr. Schwab's château, its proudest architectural surprise. I wander past Mr. Schwab's railings at night, noting the caretaker's light in the attic and regretting that Charley seems to get so little use of his braw mansion. I like to see the homes of our great barons gay with lights and wassail: I have a thoroughly feudal view of society and believe that we small gentry acquiesce gladly in our restricted orbit provided the nabobs are kicking up a dust at the top of the scale. Sometimes I fear that our rich men have been intimidated by modern doctrines and do not like to be seen at frolic. Nonsense! They owe it to us. When a man builds a French château he should live in it like a French seigneur. For the gayety of West End Avenue I desire to see more lights in that castle, and hear the organ shaking the tall panes.

Certainly with so many doctors (their names provide the only sociological data West End Avenue offers to the student) the street must be healthy. In older days many expectant couples used to come in from the country to West End Avenue to patronize its private maternity hospitals. I knew one fortunate pair to whom the avenue always meant just that. Years later they revisited it, merely to hibernate, and the wife looked round the comfortable sitting-room of the apartment. "I feel as if I ought to be having a baby," she said.

Exceptionally discreet and undemonstrative, West End Avenue offers little drama to the eye. It makes no cajolery to the various arts and Bohemianisms: the modest signs of a Harp Teacher and Hungarian Table Board in one of its few remaining rows of old pri-

vate domiciles come with a pleasant surprise. It is mainly the battle-
ground of the great apartment brokers, Slawson & Hobbs *versus* Bing
& Bing, or Sharp & Nassoit *versus* Wood Dolson. Occasionally appears the mysterious ensign of the Rebus Corporation. Bing, Bing, as
Penrod used to say, and another monthly payment bit the dust. SUPT
ON PREMISES is the motto of West End Avenue. If your necessity is an
apartment with 12 rooms and 3 or 4 baths I think you will have no
difficulty in finding one At certain times of day you will see ladies
urging their small dogs for an airing. It is a highway of both leases
and leashes.

Behind those regular parallels of stone is plenty of tumultuous
life. There are not only doctors and churches but schools also. The
avenue is at its prettiest when the children come pouring out of
Number 9 at lunch time. In apartment windows you can see the
bright eyes of mothers looking down to see that the youngsters are
safely on the way. In the afternoons games are chalked on pavements
and the youthful bicyclist undulates among pedestrians. Riverside
Park and the keen Hudson breeze are only a block away. It is the
same breeze and the same river that Edgar Allan Poe knew when he
was writing *The Raven* at Broadway and 84th Street. It seems unlikely,
and yet perhaps somewhere in those honeycombed cubes of building
is a forehead as full of heat and music as his. They cannot spend all
their lives with Amos 'n' Andy or Mickey Mouse? When something
thrilling comes along good Mr. Levy, the bookseller near Poe's corner, will be quick to welcome it.

It would come from one of the side streets perhaps, rather than
from West End Avenue itself. The side streets are more frank with
life. There the little notice *Vacancies* is frequent. Not that West End
does not have its moments of relaxation. Above 90th Street there are
still a few genial old brownstones with curved bays and alluring circular windows in the attics. At 87th a kindergarten pastes on the
windowpanes facsimile autumn leaves, cut from paper and crayon-
colored, to remind its small prisoners what November is really like.
At 95th and 96th are the open tennis courts that have been there
many years, and against the western end of the settlement called
Pomander Walk old ladies come out, when the sun is warm, and sit

in chairs on the pavement. High overhead on clear days you will observe sea-gulls swinging and soaring in the sky.

But in the main West End Avenue must remain an enigma. I have often walked it at night, scanning the rectangles of lighted panes and wondering. Between the dark stream on one side, the bright slices of Broadway on the other, what does it think about? It is too wise to be fashionable, yet it has a certain unostentatious dignity of its own, the more impressive because it has not thought much about it. Those massive portals of glass and iron have doormen with starched neck-cloths and white gloves and braided trousers: I see them off duty sometimes at Bickford's sitting to a cup of coffee. I know they are human, and perhaps profoundly bored; but speculation, a tender plant, abashes before such splendor. Alas, can it be that West End Avenue, like so many other things, has only the meanings we ourselves bring to it? It remains one of my favorite mysteries, and one of the few citadels (in this random city) of the most powerful order in the world: the not easily shakable Medium Class. It has its feet on a Power House.

1932

# F. SCOTT FITZGERALD

F. Scott Fitzgerald (1896–1940) named and epitomized the Jazz Age, yet lived to see the end of that era and the decline of his own reputation. "My Lost City," with its seductive rhythms, inaugurated a tradition of elegiac farewells to New York (see Cheever, page 820, and Didion, page 904). Astonishingly, this classic essay did not appear during Fitzgerald's lifetime. Cosmopolitan magazine, which bought the piece as part of a series of articles about the city, ultimately decided, in the words of Fitzgerald's agent, "that the readers might get a little tired of them so stopped publication." The essay only came to light when Edmund Wilson included it in his posthumous gathering of Fitzgerald's uncollected writings, The Crack-Up.

## MY LOST CITY

THERE WAS FIRST the ferry boat moving softly from the Jersey shore at dawn—the moment crystalized into my first symbol of New York. Five years later when I was fifteen I went into the city from school to see Ina Claire in *The Quaker Girl* and Gertrude Bryan in *Little Boy Blue*. Confused by my hopeless and melancholy love for them both, I was unable to choose between them—so they blurred into one lovely entity, the girl. She was my second symbol of New York. The ferry boat stood for triumph, the girl for romance. In time I was to achieve some of both, but there was a third symbol that I have lost somewhere, and lost forever.

I found it on a dark April afternoon after five more years.

"Oh, Bunny," I yelled. *"Bunny!"*

He did not hear me—my taxi lost him, picked him up again half a block down the street. There were black spots of rain on the sidewalk and I saw him walking briskly through the crowd wearing a tan raincoat over his inevitable brown get-up; I noted with a shock that he was carrying a light cane.

"Bunny!" I called again, and stopped. I was still an undergraduate at Princeton while he had become a New Yorker. This was his afternoon walk, this hurry along with his stick through the gathering rain, and as I was not to meet him for an hour it seemed an intrusion to happen upon him engrossed in his private life. But the taxi kept pace with him and as I continued to watch I was impressed: he was no longer the shy little scholar of Holder Court—he walked with confidence, wrapped in his thoughts and looking straight ahead, and it was obvious that his new background was entirely sufficient to him. I knew that he had an apartment where he lived with three other men, released now from all undergraduate taboos, but there was something else that was nourishing him and I got my first impression of that new thing—the Metropolitan spirit.

Up to this time I had seen only the New York that offered itself for inspection—I was Dick Whittington up from the country gaping at the trained bears, or a youth of the Midi dazzled by the boulevards of Paris. I had come only to stare at the show, though the designers of the Woolworth Building and the Chariot Race Sign, the producers of musical comedies and problem plays, could ask for no more appreciative spectator, for I took the style and glitter of New York even above its own valuation. But I had never accepted any of the practically anonymous invitations to debutante balls that turned up in an undergraduate's mail, perhaps because I felt that no actuality could live up to my conception of New York's splendor. Moreover, she to whom I fatuously referred as "my girl" was a Middle Westerner, a fact which kept the warm center of the world out there, so I thought of New York as essentially cynical and heartless—save for one night when she made luminous the Ritz Roof on a brief passage through.

Lately, however, I had definitely lost her and I wanted a man's world, and this sight of Bunny made me see New York as just that. A week before, Monsignor Fay had taken me to the Lafayette where there was spread before us a brilliant flag of food, called an *hors d'oeuvre*, and with it we drank claret that was as brave as Bunny's confident cane—but after all it was a restaurant and afterwards we would drive back over a bridge into the hinterland. The New York of undergraduate dissipation, of Bustanoby's, Shanley's, Jack's, had become a horror and though I returned to it, alas, through many an alcoholic mist, I felt each time a betrayal of a persistent idealism. My participance was prurient rather than licentious and scarcely one pleasant memory of it remains from those days; as Ernest Hemingway once remarked, the sole purpose of the cabaret is for unattached men to find complaisant women. All the rest is a wasting of time in bad air.

But that night, in Bunny's apartment, life was mellow and safe, a finer distillation of all that I had come to love at Princeton. The gentle playing of an oboe mingled with city noises from the street outside, which penetrated into the room with difficulty through great barricades of books; only the crisp tearing open of invitations by one man was a discordant note. I had found a third symbol of New York and I began wondering about the rent of such apartments and casting about for the appropriate friends to share one with me.

Fat chance—for the next two years I had as much control over my own destiny as a convict over the cut of his clothes. When I got back to New York in 1919 I was so entangled in life that a period of mellow monasticism in Washington Square was not to be dreamed of. The thing was to make enough money in the advertising business to rent a stuffy apartment for two in the Bronx. The girl concerned had never seen New York but she was wise enough to be rather reluctant. And in a haze of anxiety and unhappiness I passed the four most impressionable months of my life.

New York had all the iridescence of the beginning of the world. The returning troops marched up Fifth Avenue and girls were instinctively drawn East and North toward them—this was the greatest nation and there was gala in the air. As I hovered ghost-like in the Plaza Red Room of a Saturday afternoon, or went to lush and liquid garden parties in the East Sixties or tippled with Princetonians in the Biltmore Bar I was haunted always by my other life—my drab room in the Bronx, my square foot of the subway, my fixation upon the day's letter from Alabama—would it come and what would it say?— my shabby suits, my poverty, and love. While my friends were launching decently into life I had muscled my inadequate bark into midstream. The gilded youth circling around young Constance Bennett in the Club de Vingt, the classmates in the Yale-Princeton Club whooping up our first after-the-war reunion, the atmosphere of the millionaires' houses that I sometimes frequented—these things were empty for me, though I recognized them as impressive scenery and regretted that I was committed to other romance. The most hilarious luncheon table or the most moony cabaret—it was all the same; from them I returned eagerly to my home on Claremont Avenue—home because there might be a letter waiting outside the door. One by one my great dreams of New York became tainted. The remembered charm of Bunny's apartment faded with the rest when I interviewed a blowsy landlady in Greenwich Village. She told me I could bring girls to the room, and the idea filled me with dismay— why should I want to bring girls to my room?—I had a girl. I wandered through the town of 127th Street, resenting its vibrant life; or else I bought cheap theatre seats at Gray's drugstore and tried to lose myself for a few hours in my old passion for Broadway. I was a failure—mediocre at advertising work and unable to get started as a writer. Hating the city, I got roaring, weeping drunk on my last penny and went home. . . .

. . . Incalculable city. What ensued was only one of a thousand success stories of those gaudy days, but it plays a part in my own movie of New York. When I returned six months later the offices of editors and publishers were open to me, impresarios begged plays, the movies panted for screen material. To my bewilderment, I was adopted, not as a Middle Westerner, not even as a detached observer, but as the arch type of what New York wanted. This statement requires some account of the metropolis in 1920.

There was already the tall white city of today, already the feverish activity of the boom, but there was a general inarticulateness. As much as anyone the columnist F. P. A. guessed the pulse of the individual and the crowd, but shyly, as one watching from a window. Society and the native arts had not mingled—Ellen Mackay was not yet married to Irving Berlin. Many of Peter Arno's people would have been meaningless to the citizen of 1920, and save for F. P. A.'s column there was no forum for metropolitan urbanity.

Then, for just a moment, the "younger generation" idea became a fusion of many elements in New York life. People of fifty might pretend there was still a four hundred or Maxwell Bodenheim might

pretend there was a Bohemia worth its paint and pencils—but the
blending of the bright, gay, vigorous elements began then and for the
first time there appeared a society a little livelier than the solid mahogany dinner parties of Emily Price Post. If this society produced
the cocktail party, it also evolved Park Avenue wit and for the first
time an educated European could envisage a trip to New York as
something more amusing than a gold-trek into a formalized Australian Bush.

For just a moment, before it was demonstrated that I was unable
to play the role, I, who knew less of New York than any reporter of
six months standing and less of its society than any hall-room boy in
a Ritz stag line, was pushed into the position not only of spokesman
for the time but of the typical product of that same moment. I, or
rather it was "we" now, did not know exactly what New York expected of us and found it rather confusing. Within a few months after our embarkation on the Metropolitan venture we scarcely knew
any more who we were and we hadn't a notion what we were. A dive
into a civic fountain, a casual brush with the law, was enough to get
us into the gossip columns, and we were quoted on a variety of subjects we knew nothing about. Actually our "contacts" included half a
dozen unmarried college friends and a few new literary acquaintances—I remember a lonesome Christmas when we had not one
friend in the city, nor one house we could go to. Finding no nucleus
to which we could cling, we became a small nucleus ourselves and
gradually we fitted our disruptive personalities into the contemporary scene of New York. Or rather New York forgot us and let us
stay.

This is not an account of the city's changes but of the changes in
this writer's feeling for the city. From the confusion of the year 1920
I remember riding on top of a taxi-cab along deserted Fifth Avenue
on a hot Sunday night, and a luncheon in the cool Japanese gardens
at the Ritz with the wistful Kay Laurel and George Jean Nathan, and
writing all night again and again, and paying too much for minute
apartments, and buying magnificent but broken-down cars. The first
speakeasies had arrived, the toddle was *passé*, the Montmartre was
the smart place to dance and Lillian Tashman's fair hair weaved

around the floor among the enliquored college boys. The plays were *Declassée* and *Sacred and Profane Love*, and at the Midnight Frolic you danced elbow to elbow with Marion Davies and perhaps picked out the vivacious Mary Hay in the pony chorus. We thought we were apart from all that; perhaps everyone thinks they are apart from their milieu. We felt like small children in a great bright unexplored barn. Summoned out to Griffith's studio on Long Island, we trembled in the presence of the familiar faces of the *Birth of a Nation*; later I realized that behind much of the entertainment that the city poured forth into the nation there were only a lot of rather lost and lonely people. The world of the picture actors was like our own in that it was in New York and not of it. It had little sense of itself and no center: when I first met Dorothy Gish I had the feeling that we were both standing on the North Pole and it was snowing. Since then they have found a home but it was not destined to be New York.

When bored we took our city with a Huysmans-like perversity. An afternoon alone in our "apartment" eating olive sandwiches and drinking a quart of Bushmill's whiskey presented by Zoë Atkins, then out into the freshly bewitched city, through strange doors into strange apartments with intermittent swings along in taxis through the soft nights. At last we were one with New York, pulling it after us through every portal. Even now I go into many flats with the sense that I have been there before or in the one above or below—was it the night I tried to disrobe in the *Scandals*, or the night when (as I read with astonishment in the paper next morning) "Fitzgerald Knocks Officer This Side of Paradise"? Successful scrapping not being among my accomplishments, I tried in vain to reconstruct the sequence of events which led up to this dénouement in Webster Hall. And lastly from that period I remember riding in a taxi one afternoon between very tall buildings under a mauve and rosy sky; I began to bawl because I had everything I wanted and knew I would never be so happy again.

It was typical of our precarious position in New York that when our child was to be born we played safe and went home to St. Paul—it seemed inappropriate to bring a baby into all that glamor and loneliness. But in a year we were back and we began doing the same things over again and not liking them so much. We had run through a lot, though we had retained an almost theatrical innocence by preferring the role of the observed to that of the observer. But innocence is no end in itself and as our minds unwillingly matured we began to see New York whole and try to save some of it for the selves we would inevitably become.

It was too late—or too soon. For us the city was inevitably linked up with Bacchic diversions, mild or fantastic. We could organize ourselves only on our return to Long Island and not always there. We had no incentive to meet the city half way. My first symbol was now a memory, for I knew that triumph is in oneself; my second one had grown commonplace—two of the actresses whom I had worshipped from afar in 1913 had dined in our house. But it filled me with a certain fear that even the third symbol had grown dim—the tranquillity of Bunny's apartment was not to be found in the ever-quickening city. Bunny himself was married, and about to become a father, other friends had gone to Europe, and the bachelors had become cadets of houses larger and more social than ours. By this time we "knew everybody"—which is to say most of those whom Ralph Barton would draw as in the orchestra on an opening night.

But we were no longer important. The flapper, upon whose activities the popularity of my first books was based, had become *passé* by 1923—anyhow in the East. I decided to crash Broadway with a play, but Broadway sent its scouts to Atlantic City and quashed the idea in advance, so I felt that, for the moment, the city and I had little to offer each other. I would take the Long Island atmosphere that I had familiarly breathed and materialize it beneath unfamiliar skies.

It was three years before we saw New York again. As the ship glided up the river, the city burst thunderously upon us in the early dusk—the white glacier of lower New York swooping down like a strand of a bridge to rise into uptown New York, a miracle of foamy light suspended by the stars. A band started to play on deck, but the majesty of the city made the march trivial and tinkling. From that moment I knew that New York, however often I might leave it, was home.

The tempo of the city had changed sharply. The uncertainties of

1920 were drowned in a steady golden roar and many of our friends had grown wealthy. But the restlessness of New York in 1927 approached hysteria. The parties were bigger—those of Condé Nast, for example, rivaled in their way the fabled balls of the nineties; the pace was faster—the catering to dissipation set an example to Paris; the shows were broader, the buildings were higher, the morals were looser and the liquor was cheaper; but all these benefits did not really minister to much delight. Young people wore out early—they were hard and languid at twenty-one and save for Peter Arno none of them contributed anything new; perhaps Peter Arno and his collaborators said everything there was to say about the boom days in New York that couldn't be said by a jazz band. Many people who were not alcoholics were lit up four days out of seven, and frayed nerves were strewn everywhere; groups were held together by a generic nervousness and the hangover became a part of the day as well allowed-for as the Spanish siesta. Most of my friends drank too much—the more they were in tune to the times the more they drank. And as effort *per se* had no dignity against the mere bounty of those days in New York, a depreciatory word was found for it: a successful programme became a racket—I was in the literary racket.

We settled a few hours from New York and I found that every time I came to the city I was caught up into a complication of events that deposited me a few days later in a somewhat exhausted state on the train for Delaware. Whole sections of the city had grown rather poisonous, but invariably I found a moment of utter peace in riding south through Central Park at dark toward where the façade of 59th Street thrusts its lights through the trees. There again was my lost city, wrapped cool in its mystery and promise. But that detachment never lasted long—as the toiler must live in the city's belly, so I was compelled to live in its disordered mind.

Instead there were the speakeasies—the moving from luxurious bars, which advertised in the campus publications of Yale and Princeton, to the beer gardens where the snarling face of the underworld peered through the German good nature of the entertainment, then on to strange and even more sinister localities where one was eyed by granite-faced boys and there was nothing left of joviality but only a brutishness that corrupted the new day into which one presently went out. Back in 1920 I shocked a rising young business man by suggesting a cocktail before lunch. In 1929 there was liquor in half the downtown offices, and a speakeasy in half the large buildings.

One was increasingly conscious of the speakeasy and of Park Avenue. In the past decade Greenwich Village, Washington Square, Murray Hill, the châteaux of Fifth Avenue had somehow disappeared, or become unexpressive of anything. The city was bloated, glutted, stupid with cake and circuses, and a new expression "Oh yeah?" summed up all the enthusiasm evoked by the announcement of the last super-skyscrapers. My barber retired on a half million bet in the market and I was conscious that the head waiters who bowed me, or failed to bow me, to my table were far, far wealthier than I. This was no fun—once again I had enough of New York and it was good to be safe on shipboard where the ceaseless revelry remained in the bar in transport to the fleecing rooms of France.

"What news from New York?"

"Stocks go up. A baby murdered a gangster."

"Nothing more?"

"Nothing. Radios blare in the street."

I once thought that there were no second acts in American lives, but there was certainly to be a second act to New York's boom days. We were somewhere in North Africa when we heard a dull distant crash which echoed to the farthest wastes of the desert.

"What was that?"

"Did you hear it?"

"It was nothing."

"Do you think we ought to go home and see?"

"No—it was nothing."

In the dark autumn of two years later we saw New York again. We passed through curiously polite customs agents, and then with bowed head and hat in hand I walked reverently through the echoing tomb. Among the ruins a few childish wraiths still played to keep up the pretense that they were alive, betraying by their feverish voices and hectic cheeks the thinness of the masquerade. Cocktail parties, a last hollow survival from the days of carnival, echoed to the plaints of the wounded: "Shoot me, for the love of God, someone shoot me!", and the groans and wails of the dying: "Did you see that United States Steel is down three more points?" My barber was back at work in his shop; again the head waiters bowed people to their tables, if there were people to be bowed. From the ruins, lonely and inexplicable as the sphinx, rose the Empire State Building and, just as it had been a tradition of mine to climb to the Plaza Roof to take leave of the beautiful city, extending as far as eyes could reach, so now I went to the roof of the last and most magnificent of towers. Then I understood—everything was explained: I had discovered the crowning error of the city, its Pandora's box. Full of vaunting pride the New Yorker had climbed here and seen with dismay what he had never suspected, that the city was not the endless succession of canyons that he had supposed but that *it had limits*—from the tallest structure he saw for the first time that it faded out into the country on all sides, into an expanse of green and blue that alone was limitless. And with the awful realization that New York was a city after all and not a universe, the whole shining edifice that he had reared in his imagination came crashing to the ground. That was the rash gift of Alfred E. Smith to the citizens of New York.

Thus I take leave of my lost city. Seen from the ferry boat in the early morning, it no longer whispers of fantastic success and eternal youth. The whoopee mamas who prance before its empty parquets do not suggest to me the ineffable beauty of my dream girls of 1914. And Bunny, swinging along confidently with his cane toward his cloister in a carnival, has gone over to Communism and frets about the wrongs of southern mill workers and western farmers whose voices, fifteen years ago, would not have penetrated his study walls.

All is lost save memory, yet sometimes I imagine myself reading, with curious interest, a *Daily News* of the issue of 1945:

MAN OF FIFTY RUNS AMUCK IN NEW YORK
Fizgerald Feathered Many Love Nests Cutie Avers
Bumped Off By Outraged Gunman

So perhaps I am destined to return some day and find in the city new experiences that so far I have only read about. For the moment I can only cry out that I have lost my splendid mirage. Come back, come back, O glittering and white!

1932

# EDITH WHARTON

Edith Wharton (1862–1937) set some of her most important novels (The House of Mirth, The Age of Innocence) in the placid yet constricting world of aristocratic New York in which she grew up. While her heroines often flailed against the oppressive codes of that society, Wharton herself, in this first chapter of A Backward Glance, describes it with fondness and balanced appreciation. Perhaps this was because Old New York had vanished by the time she wrote this memoir, and so could be cherished in retrospect.

## THE BACKGROUND

Gute Gesellschaft hab ich gesehen; man nennt sie die gute
Wenn sie zum kleinsten Gedicht nicht die Gelegenheit giebt.
GOETHE: *Venezianische Epigrammen*

## 1

IT WAS ON a bright day of midwinter, in New York. The little girl who eventually became me, but as yet was neither me nor anybody else in particular, but merely a soft anonymous morsel of humanity—this little girl, who bore my name, was going for a walk with her father. The episode is literally the first thing I can remember about her, and therefore I date the birth of her identity from that day.

She had been put into her warmest coat, and into a new and very pretty bonnet, which she had surveyed in the glass with considerable satisfaction. The bonnet (I can see it today) was of white satin, patterned with a pink and green plaid in raised velvet. It was all drawn into close gathers, with a *bavolet* in the neck to keep out the cold, and thick ruffles of silky *blonde* lace under the brim in front. As the air was very cold a gossamer veil of the finest white Shetland wool was drawn about the bonnet and hung down over the wearer's round red cheeks like the white paper filigree over a Valentine; and her hands were encased in white woollen mittens.

One of them lay in the large safe hollow of her father's bare hand; her tall handsome father, who was so warm-blooded that in the coldest weather he always went out without gloves, and whose head, with its ruddy complexion and intensely blue eyes, was so far aloft that when she walked beside him she was too near to see his face. It was always an event in the little girl's life to take a walk with her father, and more particularly so today, because she had on her new winter bonnet, which was so beautiful (and so becoming) that for the first time she woke to the importance of dress, and of herself as a subject for adornment—so that I may date from that hour the birth of the conscious and feminine *me* in the little girl's vague soul.

The little girl and her father walked up Fifth Avenue: the old Fifth Avenue with its double line of low brown-stone houses, of a desperate uniformity of style, broken only—and surprisingly—by two equally unexpected features: the fenced-in plot of ground where the old Miss Kennedys' cows were pastured, and the truncated Egyptian pyramid which so strangely served as a reservoir for New York's water supply. The Fifth Avenue of that day was a placid and uneventful thoroughfare, along which genteel landaus, broughams and victorias, and more countrified vehicles of the "carry-all" and "surrey" type, moved up and down at decent intervals and a decorous pace. On Sundays after church the fashionable of various denominations paraded there on foot, in gathered satin bonnets and tall hats; but at other times it presented long stretches of empty pavement, so that the little girl, advancing at her father's side was able to see at a considerable distance the approach of another pair of legs, not as long but considerably stockier than her father's. The little girl was so very little that she never got much higher than the knees in her survey of grown-up people, and would not have known, if her father had not told her, that the approaching legs belonged to his cousin Henry. The news was very interesting, because in attendance on Cousin Henry was a small person, no bigger than herself, who must obviously be Cousin Henry's little boy Daniel, and therefore somehow belong to the little girl. So when the tall legs and the stocky ones halted for a talk, which took place somewhere high up in the air, and the small Daniel and Edith found themselves face to face close to the pavement, the little girl peered with interest at the little boy through the white woollen mist over her face. The little boy, who was very round and rosy, looked back with equal interest; and suddenly he put out a chubby hand, lifted the little girl's veil, and boldly planted a kiss on her cheek. It was the first time—and the little girl found it very pleasant.

This is my earliest definite memory of anything happening to me; and it will be seen that I was wakened to conscious life by the two tremendous forces of love and vanity.

It may have been just after this memorable day—at any rate it was nearly at the same time—that a snowy-headed old gentleman with a red face and a spun-sugar moustache and imperial gave me a white Spitz puppy which looked as if its coat had been woven out of the donor's luxuriant locks. The old gentleman, in whose veins ran the purest blood of Dutch Colonial New York, was called Mr. Lydig Suydam, and I should like his name to survive till this page has crumbled, for with his gift a new life began for me. The owning of my first dog made me into a conscious sentient person, fiercely possessive, anxiously watchful, and woke in me that long ache of pity for animals, and for all inarticulate beings, which nothing has ever stilled. How I loved that first "Foxy" of mine, how I cherished and yearned over and understood him! And how quickly he relegated all dolls and other inanimate toys to the region of my everlasting indifference!

I never cared much in my little-childhood for fairy tales, or any appeals to my fancy through the fabulous or legendary. My imagination lay there, coiled and sleeping, a mute hibernating creature, and at the least touch of common things—flowers, animals, words, especially the sound of words, apart from their meaning—it already stirred in its sleep, and then sank back into its own rich dream, which needed so little feeding from the outside that it instinctively rejected whatever another imagination had already adorned and completed. There was, however, one fairy tale at which I always thrilled—the story of the boy who could talk with the birds and hear what the grasses said. Very early, earlier than my conscious memory can reach, I must have felt myself to be of kin to that happy child. I cannot remember when the grasses first spoke to me, though I think it was when, a few years later, one of my uncles took me, with some little cousins, to spend a long spring day in some marshy woods near Mamaroneck, where the earth was starred with pink trailing arbutus, where pouch-like white and rosy flowers grew in a swamp, and leafless branches against the sky were netted with buds of mother-of-pearl; but on the day when Foxy was given to me I learned what the animals say to each other, and to us. . . .

2

The readers (and I should doubtless have been among them) who twenty years ago would have smiled at the idea that time could transform a group of *bourgeois* colonials and their republican descendants into a sort of social aristocracy, are now better able to measure the formative value of nearly three hundred years of social observance: the concerted living up to long-established standards of honour and conduct, of education and manners. The value of duration is slowly asserting itself against the welter of change, and sociologists without a drop of American blood in them have been the first to recognize what the traditions of three centuries have contributed to the moral wealth of our country. Even negatively, these traditions have acquired, with the passing of time, an unsuspected value. When I was young it used to seem to me that the group in which I grew up was like an empty vessel into which no new wine would ever again be poured. Now I see that one of its uses lay in preserving a few drops of an old vintage too rare to be savoured by a youthful palate; and I should like to atone for my unappreciativeness by trying to revive that faint fragrance.

If any one had suggested to me, before 1914, to write my reminiscences, I should have answered that my life had been too uneventful to be worth recording. Indeed, I had never even thought of recording it for my own amusement, and the fact that until 1918 I never kept even the briefest of diaries has greatly hampered this tardy reconstruction. Not until the successive upheavals which culminated in the catastrophe of 1914 had "cut all likeness from the name" of my old New York, did I begin to see its pathetic picturesqueness. The first change came in the 'eighties, with the earliest detachment of big money-makers from the West, soon to be followed by the lords of Pittsburgh. But their infiltration did not greatly affect old manners and customs, since the dearest ambition of the newcomers was to assimilate existing traditions. Social life, with us as in the rest of the world, went on with hardly perceptible changes till the war abruptly tore down the old frame-work, and what had seemed unalterable rules of conduct became of a sudden observances as quaintly arbitrary as the domestic rites of the Pharaohs. Between the point of view of my Huguenot great-great-grandfather, who came from the French Palatinate to participate in the founding of New Rochelle, and my own father, who died in 1882, there were fewer differences than between my father and the post-war generation of Americans. That I was born into a world in which telephones, motors, electric light, central heating (except by hot-air furnaces), X-rays, cinemas, radium, aeroplanes and wireless telegraphy were not only unknown but still mostly unforeseen, may seem the most striking difference between then and now; but the really vital change is that, in my youth, the Americans of the original States, who in moments of crisis still shaped the national point of view, were the heirs of an old tradition of European culture which the country has now totally rejected. This rejection (which Mr. Walter Lippmann regards as the chief cause of the country's present moral impoverishment) has opened a gulf between those days and these. The compact world of my youth has receded into a past from which it can only be dug up in bits by the assiduous relic-hunter; and its smallest fragments begin to be worth collecting and putting together before the last of those who knew the live structure are swept away with it.

3

My little-girl life, safe, guarded, monotonous, was cradled in the only world about which, according to Goethe, it is impossible to write poetry. The small society into which I was born was "good" in the most prosaic sense of the term, and its only interest, for the generality of readers, lies in the fact of its sudden and total extinction, and for the imaginative few in the recognition of the moral treasures that went with it. Let me try to call it back. . . .

Once, when I was about fifteen, my parents took me to Annapolis for the graduating ceremonies of the Naval Academy. In my infancy I had travelled extensively on the farther side of the globe, and it was thought high time that I should begin to see something of my own half.

I recall with delight the charming old Academic buildings grouped about turf and trees, and the smartness of the cadets (among whom were some of my young friends) in their dress uniforms; and thrilling memories of speeches, marchings, military music and strawberry ice, flutter pleasingly about the scene. On the way back we stopped in Baltimore and Washington; but neither city offered much to youthful eyes formed by the spectacle of Rome and Paris. Washington, in the days before Charles McKim had seen its possibilities, and resolved to develop them on Major L'Enfant's lines, was in truth a doleful desert; and it was a weary and bored little girl who trailed after her parents through the echoing emptiness of the Capitol, and at last into the famous Rotunda with its paintings of Revolutionary victories. Trumbull was little thought of as a painter in those days (Munkacsky would doubtless have been preferred to him), and when one great panel after another was pointed out to me, and I was led up first to the "Surrender of Burgoyne" and then to the "Surrender of Cornwallis", and told: "There's your great-grandfather," the tall thin young man in the sober uniform of a general of artillery, leaning against a cannon in the foreground of one picture, in the other galloping across the battlefield, impressed me much less than the beautiful youths to whom I had just said good-bye at Annapolis. If anything, I was vaguely sorry to have any one belonging to me represented in those stiff old-fashioned pictures, so visibly inferior to the battle-scenes of Horace Vernet and Detaille. I remember feeling no curiosity about my great-grandfather, and my parents said nothing to rouse my interest in him. The New Yorker of that day was singularly, inexplicably indifferent to his descent, and my father and mother were no exception to the rule.

It was many years later that I began to suspect that Trumbull was very nearly a great painter, and my great-grandfather Stevens very nearly a great man; but by that time all who had known him, and could have spoken of him familiarly, had long been dead, and he was no more than a museum-piece to me. It is a pity, for he must have been worth knowing, even at second hand.

On both sides our colonial ancestry goes back for nearly three hundred years, and on both sides the colonists in question seem to have been identified since early days with New York, though my earliest Stevens forbears went first to Massachusetts. Some of the first Stevens's grandsons, however, probably not being of the stripe of religious fanatic or political reformer to breathe easily in that passionate province, transferred their activities to the easier-going New York, where people seem from the outset to have been more interested in making money and acquiring property than in Predestination and witch-burning. I have always wondered if those old New Yorkers did not owe their greater suavity and tolerance to the fact that the Church of England (so little changed under its later name of Episcopal Church of America) provided from the first their prevalent form of worship. May not the matchless beauty of an ancient rite have protected our ancestors from what Huxley called the "fissiparous tendency of the Protestant sects", sparing them sanguinary wrangles over uncomprehended points of doctrine, and all those extravagances of self-constituted prophets and evangelists which rent and harrowed New England? Milder manners, a greater love of ease, and a franker interest in money-making and good food, certainly distinguished the colonial New Yorkers from the conscience-searching children of the "Mayflower". Apart from some of the old Dutch colonial families, who continued to follow the "Dutch Reformed" rite, the New York of my youth was distinctively Episcopalian; and to this happy chance I owe my early saturation with the noble cadences of the Book of Common Prayer, and my reverence for an ordered ritual in which the officiant's personality is strictly subordinated to the rite he performs.

Colonial New York was mostly composed of merchants and bankers; my own ancestors were mainly merchant shipowners, and my great-grandmother Stevens's wedding-dress, a gauzy Directoire web of embroidered "India mull", was made for her in India and brought to New York on one of her father's merchant-men. My mother, who had a hearty contempt for the tardy discovery of aristocratic genealogies, always said that old New York was composed of Dutch and British middle-class families, and that only four or five could show a pedigree leading back to the aristocracy of their ancestral country. These, if I remember rightly, were the Duers, the Livingstons, the Rutherfurds, the de Grasses and the Van Rensselaers (descendants, these latter, of the original Dutch "Patroon"). I name here only families settled in colonial New York; others, from the southern states, but well known in New York—such as the Fairfaxes, Carys, Calverts and Whartons—should be added if the list included the other colonies.

My own ancestry, as far as I know, was purely middle-class; though my family belonged to the same group as this little aristocratic nucleus I do not think there was any blood-relationship with it. The Schermerhorns, Joneses, Pendletons, on my father's side, the Stevenses, Ledyards, Rhinelanders on my mother's, the Gallatins on both, seem all to have belonged to the same prosperous class of merchants, bankers and lawyers. It was a society from which all dealers in retail business were excluded as a matter of course. The man who "kept a shop" was more rigorously shut out of polite society in the original Thirteen States than in post-revolutionary France—witness the surprise (and amusement) of the Paris solicitor, Moreau de St Méry, who, fleeing from the Terror, earned his living by keeping a bookshop in Philadelphia, and for this reason, though his shop was the meeting-place of the most blue-blooded of his fellow *émigrés*, and Talleyrand and the Marquis de la Tour du Pin were among his intimates, yet could not be invited to the ball given for Washington's inauguration. So little did the Revolution revolutionize a society at once middle-class and provincial that no retail dealer, no matter how palatial his shop-front or how tempting his millions, was received in New York society until long after I was grown up.

My great-grandfather, the Major-General Ebenezer Stevens of the Rotunda, seems to have been the only marked figure among my forbears. He was born in Boston in 1751 and, having a pronounced tendency to mechanical pursuits, was naturally drafted into the artillery at the Revolution. He served in Lieutenant Adino Paddock's artillery company, and took part in the "Boston tea-party", where, as he told one of his sons, "none of the party was painted as Indians, nor, that I know of, disguised; though," (he adds a trifle casuistically) "some of them stopped at a paint-shop on the way and daubed their faces with paint." Thereafter he is heard of as a house-builder and contractor in Rhode Island; but at the news of the battle of Lexington he abandoned his business and began the raising and organizing of artillery companies. He was a first lieutenant in the Rhode Island artillery, then in that of Massachusetts, and in 1776 was transferred as captain to the regiment besieging Quebec. At Ticonderoga, Stillwater and Saratoga he commanded a division of artillery, and it was he who directed the operations leading to General Burgoyne's surrender. For these feats he was specially commended by Generals Knox, Gates and Schuyler, and in 1778 he was in command of the entire artillery service of the northern department. Under Lafayette he took part in the expedition which ended in the defeat of Lord Cornwallis; his skilful manoeuvres are said to have broken the English blockade at Annapolis, and when the English evacuated New York he was among the first to enter the city.

The war over, he declined further military advancement and returned to civil life. His services, however, were still frequently required, and in 1812 he was put in command of the New York Brigade of artillery. One of the forts built at this time for the defence of New York harbour was called Fort Stevens, in his honour, and after the laying of the foundation stone he "gave the party a dinner at his country seat, 'Mount Buonaparte'", which he had named after the hero who restored order in France.

My great-grandfather next became an East-India merchant, and carried on a large and successful trade with foreign ports. The United States War Department still entrusted him with important private missions; he was a confidential agent of both the French and English governments, and at the same time took a leading part in the municipal business of New York, and served on numerous commissions dealing with public affairs. He divided his year between his New York house in Warren Street, and Mount Buonaparte, the country place on Long Island created by the fortune he had made as a

merchant; but when his hero dropped the *u* from his name and became Emperor, my scandalized great-grandfather, irrevocably committed to the Republican idea, indignantly re-named his place "The
Mount". It stood, as its name suggests, on a terraced height in what
is now the dreary waste of Astoria, and my mother could remember
the stately colonnaded orangery, and the big orange-trees in tubs that
were set out every summer on the upper terrace. But in her day the
classical mantelpieces imported from Italy, with designs in white
marble relieved against red or green, had already been torn out and
replaced by black marble arches and ugly grates, and she recalled
seeing the old mantelpieces stacked away in the stables. In his
Bonapartist days General Stevens must have imported a good deal of
Empire furniture from Paris, and one relic, a pair of fine gilt
andirons crowned with Napoleonic eagles, has descended to his
distant great-grand-daughter; but much was doubtless discarded
when the mantelpieces went, and the stuffy day of Regency uphol-
stery set in.

If I have dwelt too long on the career of this model citizen it is
because of a secret partiality for him—for his stern high-nosed good
looks, his gallantry in war, his love of luxury, his tireless commercial
activities. I like above all the abounding energy, the swift adaptability
and the *joie de vivre* which hurried him from one adventure to another, with war, commerce and domesticity (he had two wives and
fourteen children) all carried on to the same heroic tune. But perhaps I feel nearest to him when I look at my eagle andirons, and
think of the exquisite polychrome mantels that he found the time to
bring all the way from Italy, to keep company with the orange-trees
on his terrace.

In his delightful book on Walter Scott Mr. John Buchan, excusing
Scott's inability to create a lifelike woman of his own class, says that,
after all, to the men of his generation, gentlewomen were "a toast"
and little else. Nothing could be truer. Child-bearing was their task,
fine needlework their recreation, being respected their privilege.
Only in aristocratic society, and in the most sophisticated capitals of
Europe, had they added to this repertory a good many private dis-
tractions. In the upper middle class "the ladies, God bless 'em", sums

it up. And so it happens that I know less than nothing of the particular virtues, gifts and modest accomplishments of the young women with pearls in their looped hair or cambric ruffs round their slim necks, who prepared the way for my generation. A few shreds of anecdote, no more than the faded flowers between the leaves of a great-grandmother's Bible, are all that remain to me.

Of my lovely great-grandmother Rhinelander (Mary Robart) I know only that she was of French descent, as her spirited profile declares, and properly jealous of her rights; for if she chanced to drive to New York in her yellow coach with its fringed hammer-cloth at the same hour when her daughter-in-law, from lower down the East River, was following the same road, the latter's carriage had to take the old lady's dust all the way, even though her horses were faster and her errand might be more urgent. I may add that once, several years after my marriage, a new coachman, who did not know my mother's carriage by sight, accidentally drove me past it on the fashionable Ocean Drive at Newport, and that I had to hasten the next morning to apologize to my mother, whose only comment was, when I explained that the coachman could not have known the offence he was committing: "You might have told him".

One of my great-grandmothers, Lucretia Ledyard (the second wife of General Stevens), lost her "handsome sable cloak" one day when she was driving out General Washington in her sleigh, while on another occasion, when she was walking on the Battery in 1812, the gentleman who was with her, glancing seaward, suddenly exclaimed: "My God, madam, there are the British!"

Meagre relics of the past; and when it comes to the next generation, that of my own grandparents, I am little better informed. My maternal grandfather Rhinelander, son of the proud dame of the yellow coach, married Mary Stevens, daughter of the General and his dusky handsome Ledyard wife. The young pair had four children, and then my grandfather died, when he was little more than thirty. He too was handsome, with frank blue eyes and a wide intelligent brow. My mother said he "loved reading", and that particular drop of his blood must have descended to my veins, for I know of no other bookworm in the family. His young widow and her children continued to live at the country place at Hell Gate, lived there, in fact, from motives of economy, in winter as well as summer while the children were young; for my grandmother, whose property was left to the management of her husband's eldest brother, remained poor though her brother-in-law grew rich. The children, however, were carefully educated by English governesses and tutors; and to one of the latter is owing the charming study of the view across Hell Gate to Long Island, taken from my grandmother's lawn, which is here reproduced.

The little girls were taught needle-work, music, drawing and "the languages" (their Italian teacher was Professor Foresti, a distinguished fugitive from the Austrian political prisons). In winter their "best dresses" were low-necked and short-sleeved frocks, of pea-green merino, with gray beaver hats trimmed with tartan ribbons, white cotton stockings and heelless prunella slippers. When they walked in the snow hand-knitted woollen stockings were drawn over this frail footgear, and woollen shawls wrapped about their poor bare shoulders. They suffered, like all young ladies of their day, from chilblains and excruciating sick-headaches, yet all lived to a vigorous old age. When the eldest (my mother) "came out", she wore a home-made gown of white tarlatan, looped up with red and white camellias from the greenhouse, and her mother's old white satin slippers; and her feet being of a different shape from grandmamma's, she suffered martyrdom, and never ceased to resent the indignity inflicted on her, and the impediment to her dancing, the more so as her younger sisters, who were prettier and probably more indulged, were given new slippers when their turn came. The girls appear to have had their horses (in that almost roadless day Americans still went everywhere in the saddle), and my mother, whose memory for the details of dress was inexhaustible, told me that she wore a beaver hat with a drooping ostrich plume, and a green veil to protect her complexion, and that from motives of modesty riding-habits were cut to trail on the ground, so that it was almost impossible to mount unassisted.

A little lower down the Sound (on the actual site of East Eighty-first Street) stood my grandfather Jones's pretty country house with classic pilasters and balustraded roof. A print in my possession shows a low-studded log-cabin adjoining it under the elms, described as the aboriginal Jones habitation; but it was more probably the slaves' quarter. In this pleasant house lived a young man of twenty, handsome, simple and kind, who was madly in love with Lucretia, the eldest of the "poor Rhinelander" girls. George Frederic's parents thought him too young to marry; perhaps they had other ambitions for him; they bade him break off his attentions to Miss Rhinelander of Hell Gate. But George Frederic was the owner of a rowing-boat. His stern papa, perhaps on account of the proximity of the beloved, refused to give him a sailing-craft, though every youth of the day had his "cat-boat", and the smiling expanse of the Sound was flecked with the coming and going of white wings. But George was not to be thwarted. He contrived to turn an oar into a mast; he stole down before dawn, his bed-quilt under his arm, rigged it to the oar in guise of a sail, and flying over the waters of the Sound hurried to his lady's feet across the lawn depicted in the tutor's painting. His devotion at last overcame the paternal opposition, and George and "Lou" were married when they were respectively twenty-one and nineteen. My grandfather was rich, and must have made his sons a generous allowance; for the young couple, after an adventurous honeymoon in Cuba (of which my father kept a conscientious record, full of drives in *volantes* and visits to fashionable plantations) set up a house of their own in Gramercy Park, then just within the built-on limits of New York, and Mrs. George Frederic took her place among the most elegant young married women of her day. At last the home-made tarlatans and the inherited satin shoes were avenged, and there began a long career of hospitality at home and travels abroad. My father, as a boy, had been to Europe with his father on one of the last of the great sailing passenger-ships; and he often told me of the delights of that crossing, on a yacht-like vessel with few passengers and spacious airy cabins, as compared with subsequent voyages on the cramped foul-smelling steamers that superseded the sailing ships. A year or so after the birth of my eldest brother my parents went abroad on a long tour. The new railways were beginning to transform continental travel, and after driving by *diligence* from Calais to Amiens my family journeyed thence by rail to Paris. Later they took train from Paris to Brussels, a day or two after the inauguration of this line; and my father notes in his diary: "We were told to be at the station at one o'clock, *and by four we were actually off.*" By various means of conveyance the young couple with their infant son pursued their way through France, Belgium, Germany and Italy. They met other young New Yorkers of fashion, also on their travels, and would have had a merry time of it had not little Freddy's youthful ailments so frequently altered their plans—sometimes to a degree so disturbing that the patient young father (of twenty-three) confides to his diary how "awful a thing it is to travel in Europe with an infant of twenty months".

In spite of Freddy they saw many cities and countries, and on February 24, 1848, toward the hour of noon, incidentally witnessed, from the balcony of their hotel in the rue de Rivoli, the flight of Louis Philippe and Queen Marie Amélie across the Tuileries gardens. Though my mother often described this scene to me, I suspect that the study of the Paris fashions made a more vivid impression on her than the fall of monarchies. The humiliation of the pea-green merino and the maternal slippers led to a good many extravagances; among them there is the white satin bonnet trimmed with white marabout and crystal drops in which the bride made her wedding visits, and a "capeline" of *gorge de pigeon* taffetas with a wreath of flowers in shiny brown kid, which was one of the triumphs of her Paris shopping. She had a beautiful carriage, and her sloping shoulders and slim waist were becomingly set off by the wonderful gowns brought home from that first visit to the capital of fashion. All this happened years before I was born; but the tradition of elegance was never abandoned, and when we finally returned to live in New York (in 1872) I shared the excitement caused by the annual arrival of the "trunk from Paris", and the enchantment of seeing one resplendent dress after another shaken out of its tissue-paper. Once, when I was a small child, my mother's younger sister, my beautiful and serious-minded Aunt Mary Newbold, asked me, with edifying interest: "What would you like to be when you grow up?" and on my replying in all good faith, and with a dutiful air: "The best-dressed woman

in New York," she uttered the horrified cry: "Oh, don't say that, darling!" to which I could only rejoin in wonder: "But, Auntie, you
know Mamma *is*."

When my grandfather died my father came into an independent
fortune; but even before that my father and uncles seem to have had
allowances permitting them to lead a life of leisure and amiable hospitality. The customs of the day were simple, and in my father's set
the chief diversions were sea-fishing, boat-racing and wild-fowl
shooting. There were no clubs as yet in New York, and my mother,
whose view of life was incurably prosaic, always said that this accounted for the early marriages, as the young men of that day "had
nowhere else to go". The young married couples, Langdons, Hones,
Newbolds, Edgars, Joneses, Gallatins, etc., entertained each other a
good deal, and my mother's sloping shoulders were often displayed
above the elegant fringed and ruffled "berthas" of her Parisian dinner
gowns. The amusing diary of Mr. Philip Hone gives a good idea of
the simple but incessant exchange of hospitality between the young
people who ruled New York society before the Civil War.

My readers, by this time, may be wondering what were the particular merits, private or civic, of these amiable persons. Their lives,
as one looks back, certainly seem lacking in relief; but I believe their
value lay in upholding two standards of importance in any community, that of education and good manners, and of scrupulous probity
in business and private affairs. New York has always been a commercial community, and in my infancy the merits and defects of its citizens were those of a mercantile middle class. The first duty of such a
class was to maintain a strict standard of uprightness in affairs; and
the gentlemen of my father's day did maintain it, whether in the law,
in banking, shipping or wholesale commercial enterprises. I well remember the horror excited by any irregularity in affairs, and the relentless social ostracism inflicted on the families of those who lapsed
from professional or business integrity. In one case, where two or
three men of high social standing were involved in a discreditable
bank failure, their families were made to suffer to a degree that
would seem merciless to our modern judgment. But perhaps the
New Yorkers of that day were unconsciously trying to atone for their

culpable neglect of state and national politics, from which they had long disdainfully held aloof, by upholding the sternest principles of business probity, and inflicting the severest social penalties on whoever lapsed from them. At any rate I should say that the qualities justifying the existence of our old society were social amenity and financial incorruptibility; and we have travelled far enough from both to begin to estimate their value.

The weakness of the social structure of my parents' day was a blind dread of innovation, an instinctive shrinking from responsibility. In 1824 (or thereabouts) a group of New York gentlemen who were appointed to examine various plans for the proposed laying-out of the city, and whose private sympathies were notoriously anti-Jeffersonian and undemocratic, decided against reproducing the beautiful system of squares, circles and radiating avenues which Major L'Enfant, the brilliant French engineer, had designed for Washington, because it was thought "undemocratic" for citizens of the new republic to own building-plots which were not all of exactly the same shape, size—and *value*! This naïf document, shown to me by Robert Minturn, a descendant of a member of the original committee, and doubtless often since published, typified the prudent attitude of a society of prosperous business men who have no desire to row against the current.

A little world so well-ordered and well-to-do does not often produce either eagles or fanatics, and both seem to have been conspicuously absent from the circle in which my forbears moved. In old-established and powerful societies originality of character is smiled at, and even encouraged to assert itself; but conformity is the bane of middle-class communities, and as far as I can recall, only two of my relations stepped out of the strait path of the usual. One was a mild and inoffensive old bachelor cousin, very small and frail, and reputed of immense wealth and morbid miserliness, who built himself a fine house in his youth, and lived in it for fifty or sixty years, in a state of negativeness and insignificance which made him proverbial even in our conforming class—and then, in his last years (so we children were told) *sat on a marble shelf, and thought he was a bust of Napoleon.*

Cousin Edmund's final illusion was not without pathos, but as a source of inspiration to my childish fancy he was a poor thing compared with George Alfred. George Alfred was another cousin, but one whom I had never seen, and could never hope to see, because years before he had—vanished. Vanished, that is, out of society, out of respectability, out of the safe daylight world of "nice people" and reputable doings. Before naming George Alfred my mother altered her expression and lowered her voice. Thank heaven *she* was not responsible for him—he belonged to my father's side of the family! But they too had long since washed their hands of George Alfred— had ceased even to be aware of his existence. If my mother pronounced his name it was solely, I believe, out of malice, out of the child's naughty desire to evoke some nursery hobgoblin by muttering a dark incantation like *Eena Meena Mina Mo*, and then darting away with affrighted backward looks to see if there is anything there.

My mother always darted away from George Alfred's name after pronouncing it, and it was not until I was grown up, and had acquired greater courage and persistency, that one day I drove her to the wall by suddenly asking: "But, Mamma, *what did he do?*" "Some woman"—my mother muttered; and no one accustomed to the innocuous word as now used can imagine the shades of disapproval, scorn and yet excited curiosity, that "some" could then connote on the lips of virtue.

George Alfred—and some woman! Who was she? From what heights had she fallen with him, to what depths dragged him down? For in those simple days it was always a case of "the woman tempted me". To her respectable sisters her culpability was as certain in advance as Predestination to the Calvinist. But I was not fated to know more—thank heaven I was not! For our shadowy Paolo and Francesca, circling together on the "accursèd air", somewhere outside the safe boundaries of our old New York, gave me, I verily believe, my earliest glimpse of the poetry that Goethe missed in the respectable world of the Hirschgraben, and that my ancestors assuredly failed to find, or to create, between the Battery and Union Square. The vision of poor featureless unknown Alfred and his siren, lurking in some cranny of my imagination, hinted at regions perilous, dark and yet lit with mysterious fires, just outside the world of copy-book axioms, and the old obediences that were in my blood; and the hint was useful—for a novelist.

*A BACKWARD GLANCE*, 1934

# THOMAS WOLFE

When Thomas Wolfe (1900–38) first settled in Brooklyn in 1931, he described it to a friend as "a fine town—a nice, big country town, a long way from New York. . . . You couldn't find a better place to work." Within a few months, however, his impression of the borough grew darker: he now saw it as "a vast sprawl upon the face of the earth, which no man alive or dead has yet seen in its foul, dismal entirety." This more somber vision finds expression in his most famous story, told in a brilliant adaptation of Brooklynese demotic.

## ONLY THE DEAD KNOW BROOKLYN

DERE'S NO GUY livin' dat knows Brooklyn t'roo an' t'roo, because it'd take a guy a lifetime just to find his way aroun' duh f—— town.

So like I say, I'm waitin' for my train t' come when I sees dis big guy standin' deh—dis is duh foist I eveh see of him. Well, he's lookin' wild, y'know, an' I can see dat he's had plenty, but still he's holdin' it; he talks good an' is walkin' straight enough. So den, dis big guy steps up to a little guy dat's standin' deh, an' says, "How d'yuh get t' Eighteent' Avenoo an' Sixty-sevent' Street?" he says.

"Jesus! Yuh got me, chief," duh little guy says to him. "I ain't been heah long myself. Where is duh place?" he says. "Out in duh Flatbush section somewhere?"

"Nah," duh big guy says. "It's out in Bensonhoist. But I was neveh deh befoeh. How d'yuh get deh?"

"Jesus," duh little guy says, scratchin' his head, y'know—yuh could see duh little guy didn't know his way about—"yuh got me, chief. I neveh hoid of it. Do any of youse guys know where it is?" he says to me.

"Sure," I says. "It's out in Bensonhoist. Yuh take duh Fourt' Avenoo express, get off at Fifty-nint' Street, change to a Sea Beach local deh, get off at Eighteent' Avenoo an' Sixty-toid, an' den walk down foeh blocks. Dat's all yuh got to do," I says.

"G'wan!" some wise guy dat I neveh seen befoeh pipes up. "Whatcha talkin' about?" he says—oh, he was wise, y'know. "Duh guy is crazy! I tell yuh what yuh do," he says to duh big guy. "Yuh change to duh West End line at Toity-sixt'," he tells him. "Get off at Noo Utrecht an' Sixteent' Avenoo," he says. "Walk two blocks oveh, foeh blocks up," he says, "an' you'll be right deh." Oh, a *wise* guy, y'know.

"Oh, yeah?" I says. "Who told *you* so much?" He got me sore because he was so wise about it. "How long you been livin' heah?" I says.

"All my life," he says. "I was bawn in Williamsboig," he says. "An' I can tell you t'ings about dis town you neveh hoid of," he says.

"Yeah?" I says.

"Yeah," he says.

"Well, den, you can tell me t'ings about dis town dat nobody else has eveh hoid of, either. Maybe you make it all up yoehself at night," I says, "befoeh you go to sleep –like cuttin' out papeh dolls, or somp'n."

"Oh, yeah?" he says. "You're pretty wise, ain't yuh?"

"Oh, I don't know," I says. "Duh boids ain't usin' my head for Lincoln's statue yet," I says. "But I'm wise enough to know a phony when I see one."

"Yeah?" he says. "A wise guy, huh? Well, you're so wise dat some one's goin' t'bust yuh one right on duh snoot some day," he says. "Dat's how wise *you* are."

Well, my train was comin', or I'da smacked him den and dere, but when I seen duh train was comin', all I said was, "All right, mugg! I'm sorry I can't stay to take keh of you, but I'll be seein' yuh sometime, I hope, out in duh cemetery." So den I says to duh big guy, who'd been standin' deh all duh time, "You come wit me," I says. So when we gets onto duh train I says to him, "Where yuh goin' out in Bensonhoist?" I says. "What numbeh are yuh lookin' for?" I says. *You* know—I t'ought if he told me duh address I might be able to help him out.

"Oh," he says, "I'm not lookin' for no one. I don't know no one out deh."

"Then whatcha goin' out deh for?" I says.

"Oh," duh guy says, "I'm just goin' out to see duh place," he says. "I like duh sound of duh name—Bensonhoist, y'know—so I t'ought I'd go out an' have a look at it."

"Whatcha tryin' t'hand me?" I says. "Whatcha tryin' t'do—kid me?" *You* know, I t'ought duh guy was bein' wise wit me.

"No," he says, "I'm tellin' yuh duh troot. I like to go out an' take a look at places wit nice names like dat. I like to go out an' look at all kinds of places," he says.

"How'd yuh know deh was such a place," I says, "if yuh neveh been deh befoeh?"

"Oh," he says, "I got a map."

"A *map?*" I says.

"Sure," he says, "I got a map dat tells me about all dese places. I take it wit me every time I come out heah," he says.

And Jesus! Wit dat, he pulls it out of his pocket, an' so help me, but he's *got* it—he's tellin' duh troot—a big map of duh whole f—— place with all duh different pahts mahked out. You know—Canarsie an' East Noo Yawk an' Flatbush, Bensonhoist, Sout' Brooklyn, duh Heights, Bay Ridge, Greenpernt—duh whole goddam layout, he's got it right deh on duh map.

"You been to any of dose places?" I says.

"Sure," he says, "I been to most of 'em. I was down in Red Hook just last night," he says.

"Jesus! Red Hook!" I says. "Whatcha do down deh?"

"Oh," he says, "nuttin' much. I just walked aroun'. I went into a coupla places an' had a drink," he says, "but most of the time I just walked aroun'."

"Just walked aroun'?" I says.

"Sure," he says, "just lookin' at t'ings, y'know."

"Where'd yuh go?" I asts him.

"Oh," he says, "I don't know duh name of duh place, but I could find it on my map," he says. "One time I was walkin' across some big fields where deh ain't no houses," he says, "but I could see ships oveh deh all lighted up. Dey was loadin'. So I walks across duh fields," he says, "to where duh ships are."

"Sure," I says, "I know where you was. You was down to duh Erie Basin."

"Yeah," he says, "I guess dat was it. Dey had some of dose big elevators an' cranes an' dey was loadin' ships, an' I could see some ships in drydock all lighted up, so I walks across duh fields to where dey are," he says.

"Den what did yuh do?" I says.

"Oh," he says, "nuttin' much. I came on back across duh fields after a while an' went into a coupla places an' had a drink."

"Didn't nuttin' happen while yuh was in dere?" I says.

"No," he says. "Nuttin' much. A coupla guys was drunk in one of duh places an' started a fight, but dey bounced 'em out," he says, "an' den one of duh guys stahted to come back again, but duh bartender gets his baseball bat out from under duh counteh, so duh guy goes on."

"Jesus!" I said. "Red Hook!"

"Sure," he says. "Dat's where it was, all right."

"Well, you keep outa deh," I says. "You stay away from deh."

"Why?" he says. "What's wrong wit it?"

"Oh," I says, "it's a good place to stay away from, dat's all. It's a good place to keep out of."

"Why?" he says. "Why is it?"

Jesus! Whatcha gonna do wit a guy as dumb as dat? I saw it wasn't no use to try to tell him nuttin', he wouldn't know what I was talkin' about, so I just says to him, "Oh, nuttin'. Yuh might get lost down deh, dat's all."

"Lost?" he says. "No, I wouldn't get lost, I got a map," he says.

A map! Red Hook! Jesus!

So den duh guy begins to ast me all kinds of nutty questions: how big was Brooklyn an' could I find my way aroun' in it, an' how long would it take a guy to know duh place.

"Listen!" I says. "You get dat idea outa yoeh head right now," I says. "You ain't neveh gonna get to know Brooklyn," I says. "Not in a hunderd yeahs. I been livin' heah all my life," I says, "an' I don't even know all deh is to know about it, so how do you expect to know duh town," I says, "when you don't even live heah?"

"Yes," he says, "but I got a map to help me find my way about."

"Map or no map," I says, "yuh ain't gonna get to know Brooklyn wit no map," I says.

"Can you swim?" he says, just like dat. Jesus! By dat time, y'know, I begun to see dat duh guy was some kind of nut. He'd had plenty to drink, of course, but he had dat crazy look in his eye I didn't like. "Can you swim?" he says.

"Sure," I says. "Can't you?"

"No," he says. "Not more'n a stroke or two. I neveh loined good."

"Well, it's easy," I says. "All yuh need is a little confidence. Duh way I loined, me older bruddeh pitched me off duh dock one day when I was eight yeahs old, cloes an' all. 'You'll swim,' he says. 'You'll swim all right—or drown.' An', believe me, I *swam*! When yuh know yuh got to, you'll do it. Duh only t'ing yuh need is confidence. An' once you've loined," I says, "you've got nuttin' else to worry about. You'll neveh forget it. It's somp'n dat stays wit yuh as long as yuh live."

"Can yuh swim good?" he says.

"Like a fish," I tells him. "I'm a regulah fish in duh wateh," I says. "I loined to swim right off duh docks wit all duh oddeh kids," I says.

"What would you do if yuh saw a man drownin'?" duh guy says.

"Do? Why, i'd jump in an' pull him out," I says. "Dat's what I'd do."

"Did yuh eveh see a man drown?" he says.

"Sure," I says. "I see two guys—bot' times at Coney Island. Dey got out too far, an' neider one could swim. Dey drowned befoeh any one could get to 'em."

"What becomes of people after dey've drowned out heah?" he says.

"Drowned out where?" I says.

"Out heah in Brooklyn."

"I don't know whatcha mean," I says. "Neveh hoid of no one drownin' heah in Brooklyn, unless you mean a swimmin' pool. Yuh can't drown in Brooklyn," I says. "Yuh gotta drown somewhere else—in duh ocean, where dere's wateh."

"Drownin'," duh guy says, lookin' at his map. "Drownin'." Jesus!

I could see by den he was some kind of nut, he had dat crazy expression in his eyes when he looked at you, an' I didn't know what
he might do. So we was comin' to a station, an' it wasn't my stop,
but I got off anyway, an' waited for duh next train.

"Well, so long, chief," I says. "Take it easy, now."

"Drownin'," duh guy says, lookin' at his map. "Drownin'."

Jesus! I've t'ought about dat guy a t'ousand times since den an'
wondered what eveh happened to 'm goin' out to look at
Bensonhoist because he liked duh name! Walkin' aroun' t'roo Red
Hook by himself at night an' lookin' at his map! How many people
did I see get drowned out hcah in Brooklyn! How long would it take
a guy wit a good map to know all deh was to know about Brooklyn!

Jesus! What a nut *he* was! I wondeh what eveh happened to 'im,
anyway! I wondeh if some one knocked him on duh head, or if he's
still wanderin' aroun' in duh subway in duh middle of duh night wit
his little map! Duh poor guy! Say, I've got to laugh, at dat, when I
t'ink about him! Maybe he's found out by now dat he'll neveh live
long enough to know duh whole of Brooklyn! It'd take a guy a lifetime to know Brooklyn t'roo an' t'roo. An' even den, yuh wouldn't
know it all.

1 9 3 5

# DAMON RUNYON

*A successful sportswriter and crime reporter, Damon Runyon (1884–1946) became famous for his short stories about a corner of Broadway he made as much his own territory as Faulkner's Yokna-patawpha County. Extrapolating from genuine New York types, he created a set of characters—gangsters, chorus girls, bookies, the "guys and dolls" who hung out in Mindy's restaurant—who spoke a combina-tion of New York slang, invented argot, and pseudo-educated euphemisms sometimes known as "Runyonese." These shady types often behave with implausible, almost Arthurian chivalry, but occasionally revert (as be-low) to a more realistic ruthlessness.*

### SENSE OF HUMOR

ONE NIGHT I am standing in front of Mindy's restaurant on Broadway, thinking of practically nothing whatever, when all of a sudden I feel a very terrible pain in my left foot.

In fact, this pain is so very terrible that it causes me to leap up and down like a bullfrog, and to let out loud cries of agony, and to speak some very profane language, which is by no means my custom, although of course I recognize the pain as coming from a hot foot, because I often experience this pain before.

Furthermore, I know Joe the Joker must be in the neighborhood, as Joe the Joker has the most wonderful sense of humor of anybody in this town, and is always around giving people the hot foot, and gives it to me more times than I can remember. In fact, I hear Joe the Joker invents the hot foot, and it finally becomes a very popular idea all over the country.

The way you give a hot foot is to sneak up behind some guy who is standing around thinking of not much, and stick a paper match in his shoe between the sole and the upper along about where his little toe ought to be, and then light the match. By and by the guy will feel a terrible pain in his foot, and will start stamp-ing around, and hollering, and carrying on generally, and it is always a most comical sight and a wonderful laugh to one and all to see him suffer.

No one in the world can give a hot foot as good as Joe the Joker, because it takes a guy who can sneak up very quiet on the guy who is to get the hot foot, and Joe can sneak up so quiet many guys on Broadway are willing to lay you odds that he can give a mouse a hot foot if you can find a mouse that wears shoes. Furthermore, Joe the Joker can take plenty of care of himself in case the guy who gets the hot foot feels like taking the matter up, which sometimes happens, especially with guys who get their shoes made to order at forty bobs per copy and do not care to have holes burned in these shoes.

But Joe does not care what kind of shoes the guys are wearing when he feels like giving out hot foots, and furthermore, he does not care who the guys are, although many citizens think he makes a mistake the time he gives a hot foot to Frankie Ferocious. In fact, many citizens are greatly horrified by this action, and go around saying no good will come of it.

This Frankie Ferocious comes from over in Brooklyn, where he is considered a rising citizen in many respects, and by no means a guy to give hot foots to, especially as Frankie Ferocious has no sense of humor whatever. In fact, he is always very solemn, and nobody ever sees him laugh, and he certainly does not laugh when Joe the Joker gives him a hot foot one day on Broadway when Frankie Ferocious is standing talking over a business matter with some guys from the Bronx.

He only scowls at Joe, and says something in Italian, and while I do not understand Italian, it sounds so unpleasant that I guarantee I will leave town inside of the next two hours if he says it to me.

Of course Frankie Ferocious' name is not really Ferocious, but something in Italian like Feroccio, and I hear he originally comes from Sicily, although he lives in Brooklyn for quite some years, and from a modest beginning he builds himself up until he is a very large operator in merchandise of one kind and another, especially alcohol. He is a big guy of maybe thirty-odd, and he has hair blacker than a yard up a chimney, and black eyes, and black eyebrows, and a slow way of looking at people.

Nobody knows a whole lot about Frankie Ferocious, because he never has much to say, and he takes his time saying it, but everybody gives him plenty of room when he comes around, as there are rumors that Frankie never likes to be crowded. As far as I am concerned, I do not care for any part of Frankie Ferocious, because his slow way of looking at people always makes me nervous, and I am always sorry Joe the Joker gives him a hot foot, because I figure Frankie Ferocious is bound to consider it a most disrespectful action, and hold it against everybody that lives on the Island of Manhattan.

But Joe the Joker only laughs when anybody tells him he is out of line in giving Frankie the hot foot, and says it is not his fault if Frankie has no sense of humor. Furthermore, Joe says he will not only give Frankie another hot foot if he gets a chance, but that he will give hot foots to the Prince of Wales or Mussolini, if he catches them in the right spot, although Regret, the horse player, states that Joe can have twenty to one any time that he will not give Mussolini any hot foots and get away with it.

Anyway, just as I suspect, there is Joe the Joker watching me when I feel the hot foot, and he is laughing very heartily, and furthermore, a large number of other citizens are also laughing heartily, because Joe the Joker never sees any fun in giving people the hot foot unless others are present to enjoy the joke.

Well, naturally when I see who it is gives me the hot foot I join in the laughter, and go over and shake hands with Joe, and when I shake hands with him there is more laughter, because it seems Joe has a hunk of Limburger cheese in his duke, and what I shake hands with is this Limburger. Furthermore, it is some of Mindy's Limburger cheese, and everybody knows Mindy's Limburger is very squashy, and also very loud.

Of course I laugh at this, too, although to tell the truth I will laugh much more heartily if Joe the Joker drops dead in front of me, because I do not like to be made the subject of laughter on Broadway. But my laugh is really quite hearty when Joe takes the rest of the cheese that is not on my fingers and smears it on the steering wheels of some automobiles parked in front of Mindy's, because I get to thinking of what the drivers will say when they start steering their cars.

Then I get to talking to Joe the Joker, and I ask him how things are up in Harlem, where Joe and his younger brother, Freddy, and several other guys have a small organization operating in beer, and Joe says things are as good as can be expected considering business conditions. Then I ask him how Rosa is getting along, this Rosa being Joe the Joker's ever-loving wife, and a personal friend of mine, as I know her when she is Rosa Midnight and is singing in the old Hot Box before Joe hauls off and marries her.

Well, at this question Joe the Joker starts laughing, and I can see that something appeals to his sense of humor, and finally he speaks as follows:

"Why," he says, "do you not hear the news about Rosa? She takes the wind on me a couple of months ago for my friend Frankie Ferocious, and is living in an apartment over in Brooklyn, right near his house, although," Joe says, "of course you understand I am telling you this only to answer your question, and not to holler copper on Rosa."

Then he lets out another large ha-ha, and in fact Joe the Joker keeps laughing until I am afraid he will injure himself internally. Personally, I do not see anything comical in a guy's ever-loving wife taking the wind on him for a guy like Frankie Ferocious, so when Joe the Joker quiets down a bit I ask him what is funny about the proposition.

"Why," Joe says, "I have to laugh every time I think of how the big greaseball is going to feel when he finds out how expensive Rosa is. I do not know how many things Frankie Ferocious has running for him in Brooklyn," Joe says, "but he better try to move himself in on the mint if he wishes to keep Rosa going."

Then he laughs again, and I consider it wonderful the way Joe is able to keep his sense of humor even in such a situation as this, although up to this time I always think Joe is very daffy indeed about Rosa, who is a little doll, weighing maybe ninety pounds with her hat on and quite cute.

Now I judge from what Joe the Joker tells me that Frankie

Ferocious knows Rosa before Joe marries her and is always pitching to her when she is singing in the Hot Box, and even after she is Joe's ever-loving wife, Frankie occasionally calls her up, especially when he commences to be a rising citizen of Brooklyn, although of course Joe does not learn about these calls until later. And about the time Frankie Ferocious commences to be a rising citizen of Brooklyn, things begin breaking a little tough for Joe the Joker, what with the depression and all, and he has to economize on Rosa in spots, and if there is one thing Rosa cannot stand it is being economized on.

Along about now, Joe the Joker gives Frankie Ferocious the hot foot, and just as many citizens state at the time, it is a mistake, for Frankie starts calling Rosa up more than somewhat, and speaking of what a nice place Brooklyn is to live in—which it is, at that—and between these boosts for Brooklyn and Joe the Joker's economy, Rosa hauls off and takes the subway to Borough Hall, leaving Joe a note telling him that if he does not like it he knows what he can do.

"Well, Joe," I say, after listening to his story, "I always hate to hear of these little domestic difficulties among my friends, but maybe this is all for the best. Still, I feel sorry for you, if it will do you any good," I say.

"Do not feel sorry for me," Joe says. "If you wish to feel sorry for anybody, feel sorry for Frankie Ferocious, and," he says, "if you can spare a little more sorrow, give it to Rosa."

And Joe the Joker laughs very hearty again and starts telling me about a little scatter that he has up in Harlem where he keeps a chair fixed up with electric wires so he can give anybody that sits down in it a nice jolt, which sounds very humorous to me, at that, especially when Joe tells me how they turn on too much juice one night and almost kill Commodore Jake.

Finally Joe says he has to get back to Harlem, but first he goes to the telephone in the corner cigar store and calls up Mindy's and imitates a doll's voice, and tells Mindy he is Peggy Joyce, or somebody, and orders fifty dozen sandwiches sent up at once to an apartment in West Seventy-second Street for a birthday party, although of course there is no such number as he gives, and nobody there will wish fifty dozen sandwiches if there is such a number.

Then Joe gets in his car and starts off, and while he is waiting for the traffic lights at Fiftieth Street, I see citizens on the sidewalks making sudden leaps, and looking around very fierce, and I know Joe the Joker is plugging them with pellets made out of tin foil, which he fires from a rubber band hooked between his thumb and forefinger.

Joe the Joker is very expert with this proposition, and it is very funny to see the citizens jump, although once or twice in his life Joe makes a miscue and knocks out somebody's eye. But it is all in fun, and shows you what a wonderful sense of humor Joe has.

Well, a few days later I see by the papers where a couple of Harlem guys Joe the Joker is mobbed up with are found done up in sacks over in Brooklyn, very dead indeed, and the coppers say it is because they are trying to move in on certain business enterprises that belong to nobody but Frankie Ferocious. But of course the coppers do not say Frankie Ferocious puts these guys in the sacks, because in the first place Frankie will report them to Headquarters if the coppers say such a thing about him, and in the second place putting guys in sacks is strictly a St. Louis idea and to have a guy put in a sack properly you have to send to St. Louis for experts in this matter.

Now, putting a guy in a sack is not as easy as it sounds, and in fact it takes quite a lot of practice and experience. To put a guy in a sack properly, you first have to put him to sleep, because naturally no guy is going to walk into a sack wide awake unless he is a plumb sucker. Some people claim the best way to put a guy to sleep is to give him a sleeping powder of some kind in a drink, but the real experts just tap the guy on the noggin with a blackjack, which saves the expense of buying the drink.

Anyway, after the guy is asleep, you double him up like a pocketknife, and tie a cord or a wire around his neck and under his knees. Then you put him in a gunny sack, and leave him some place, and by and by when the guy wakes up and finds himself in the sack, naturally he wants to get out and the first thing he does is to try to straighten out his knees. This pulls the cord around his neck up so tight that after a while the guy is all out of breath.

So then when somebody comes along and opens the sack they find the guy dead, and nobody is responsible for this unfortunate situation, because after all the guy really commits suicide, because if he does not try to straighten out his knees he may live to a ripe old age, if he recovers from the tap on the noggin.

Well, a couple of days later I see by the papers where three Brooklyn citizens are scragged as they are walking peaceably along Clinton Street, the scragging being done by some parties in an automobile who seem to have a machine gun, and the papers state that the citizens are friends of Frankie Ferocious, and that it is rumored the parties with the machine gun are from Harlem.

I judge by this that there is some trouble in Brooklyn, especially as about a week after the citizens are scragged in Clinton Street, another Harlem guy is found done up in a sack like a Virginia ham near Prospect Park, and now who is it but Joe the Joker's brother, Freddy, and I know Joe is going to be greatly displeased by this.

By and by it gets so nobody in Brooklyn will open as much as a sack of potatoes without first calling in the gendarmes, for fear a pair of No. 8 shoes will jump out at them.

Now one night I see Joe the Joker, and this time he is all alone, and I wish to say I am willing to leave him all alone, because something tells me he is hotter than a stove. But he grabs me as I am going past, so naturally I stop to talk to him, and the first thing I say is how sorry I am about his brother.

"Well," Joe the Joker says, "Freddy is always a kind of a sap. Rosa calls him up and asks him to come over to Brooklyn to see her. She wishes to talk to Freddy about getting me to give her a divorce," Joe says, "so she can marry Frankie Ferocious, I suppose. Anyway," he says, "Freddy tells Commodore Jake why he is going to see her. Freddy always likes Rosa, and thinks maybe he can patch it up between us. So," Joe says, "he winds up in a sack. They get him after he leaves her apartment. I do not claim Rosa will ask him to come over if she has any idea he will be sacked," Joe says, "but," he says, "she is responsible. She is a bad-luck doll."

Then he starts to laugh, and at first I am greatly horrified, thinking it is because something about Freddy being sacked strikes his sense of humor, when he says to me like this:

"Say," he says, "I am going to play a wonderful joke on Frankie Ferocious."

"Well, Joe," I say, "you are not asking me for advice, but I am going to give you some free gratis, and for nothing. Do not play any jokes on Frankie Ferocious, as I hear he has no more sense of humor than a nanny goat. I hear Frankie Ferocious will not laugh if you have Al Jolson, Eddie Cantor, Ed Wynn and Joe Cook telling him jokes all at once. In fact," I say, "I hear he is a tough audience."

"Oh," Joe the Joker says, "he must have some sense of humor somewhere to stand for Rosa. I hear he is daffy about her. In fact, I understand she is the only person in the world he really likes, and trusts. But I must play a joke on him. I am going to have myself delivered to Frankie Ferocious in a sack."

Well, of course I have to laugh at this myself, and Joe the Joker laughs with me. Personally, I am laughing just at the idea of anybody having themselves delivered to Frankie Ferocious in a sack, and especially Joe the Joker, but of course I have no idea Joe really means what he says.

"Listen," Joe says, finally. "A guy from St. Louis who is a friend of mine is doing most of the sacking for Frankie Ferocious. His name is Ropes McGonnigle. In fact," Joe says, "he is a very dear old pal of mine, and he has a wonderful sense of humor like me. Ropes McGonnigle has nothing whatever to do with sacking Freddy," Joe says, "and he is very indignant about it since he finds out Freddy is my brother, so he is anxious to help me play a joke on Frankie.

"Only last night," Joe says, "Frankie Ferocious sends for Ropes and tells him he will appreciate it as a special favor if Ropes will bring me to him in a sack. I suppose," Joe says, "that Frankie Ferocious hears from Rosa what Freddy is bound to tell her about my ideas on divorce. I have very strict ideas on divorce," Joe says, "especially where Rosa is concerned. I will see her in what's-this before I ever do her and Frankie Ferocious such a favor as giving her a divorce.

"Anyway," Joe the Joker says, "Ropes tells me about Frankie

Ferocious propositioning him, so I send Ropes back to Frankie Ferocious to tell him he knows I am to be in Brooklyn to-morrow night, and furthermore, Ropes tells Frankie that he will have me in a sack in no time. And so he will," Joe says.

"Well," I say, "personally, I see no percentage in being delivered to Frankie Ferocious in a sack, because as near as I can make out from what I read in the papers, there is no future for a guy in a sack that goes to Frankie Ferocious. What I cannot figure out," I say, "is where the joke on Frankie comes in."

"Why," Joe the Joker says, "the joke is, I will not be asleep in the sack, and my hands will not be tied, and in each of my hands I will have a John Roscoe, so when the sack is delivered to Frankie Ferocious and I pop out blasting away, can you not imagine his astonishment?"

Well, I can imagine this, all right. In fact, when I get to thinking of the look of surprise that is bound to come to Frankie Ferocious' face when Joe the Joker comes out of the sack I have to laugh, and Joe the Joker laughs right along with me.

"Of course," Joe says, "Ropes McGonnigle will be there to start blasting with me, in case Frankie Ferocious happens to have any company."

Then Joe the Joker goes on up the street, leaving me still laughing from thinking of how amazed Frankie Ferocious will be when Joe bounces out of the sack and starts throwing slugs around and about. I do not hear of Joe from that time to this, but I hear the rest of the story from very reliable parties.

It seems that Ropes McGonnigle does not deliver the sack himself, after all, but sends it by an expressman to Frankie Ferocious' home. Frankie Ferocious receives many sacks such as this in his time, because it seems that it is a sort of passion with him to personally view the contents of the sacks and check up on them before they are distributed about the city, and of course Ropes McGonnigle knows about this passion from doing so much sacking for Frankie.

When the expressman takes the sack into Frankie's house, Frankie personally lugs it down into his basement, and there he outs with a big John Roscoe and fires six shots into the sack, because it seems Ropes McGonnigle tips him off to Joe the Joker's plan to pop out of the sack and start blasting.

I hear Frankie Ferocious has a very strange expression on his pan and is laughing the only laugh anybody ever hears from him when the gendarmes break in and put the arm on him for murder, because it seems that when Ropes McGonnigle tells Frankie of Joe the Joker's plan, Frankie tells Ropes what he is going to do with his own hands before opening the sack. Naturally, Ropes speaks to Joe the Joker of Frankie's idea about filling the sack full of slugs, and Joe's sense of humor comes right out again.

So, bound and gagged, but otherwise as right as rain in the sack that is delivered to Frankie Ferocious, is by no means Joe the Joker, but Rosa.

1935

# HENRY MILLER

Henry Miller (1891–1980) achieved his literary breakthrough in *Paris*, but made no secret of where his real inspiration lay: in the Brooklyn that he celebrated and excoriated in Tropic of Capricorn and Black Spring *(and whose distinct accent he retained into his* Big Sur *retirement). Miller's imagination was never more fertile than when he was re-creating the texture of life in the Fourteenth Ward.*

### FROM *BLACK SPRING*

I AM A PATRIOT——of the 14th Ward Brooklyn, where I was raised. The rest of the United States doesn't exist for me, except as idea, or history, or literature. At ten years of age I was uprooted from my native soil and removed to a cemetery, a *Lutheran* cemetery, where the tomb-stones were always in order and the wreaths never faded.

But I was born in the street and raised in the street. "The post-mechanical open street where the most beautiful and hallucinating iron vegetation," etc . . . Born under the sign of Aries which gives a fiery, active, energetic and somewhat restless body. *With Mars in the ninth house!*

To be born in the street means to wander all your life, to be free. It means accident and incident, drama, movement. It means above all dream. A harmony of irrelevant facts which gives to your wandering a metaphysical certitude. In the street you learn what human beings really are; otherwise, or afterwards, you invent them. What is not in the open street is false, derived, that is to say, *literature*. Nothing of what is called "adventure" ever approaches the flavor of the street. It doesn't matter whether you fly to the Pole, whether you sit on the floor of the ocean with a pad in your hand, whether you pull up nine cities one after the other, or whether, like Kurtz, you sail up the river and go mad. No matter how exciting, how intolerable the situation, there are always exits, always ameliorations, comforts, compensations, newspapers, religions. But once there was none of this. Once you were free, wild, murderous . . .

The boys you worshipped when you first came down into the street remain with you all your life. They are the only real heroes. Napoleon, Lenin, Capone—all fiction. Napoleon is nothing to me in comparison with Eddie Carney, who gave me my first black eye. No man I have ever met seems as princely, as regal, as noble, as Lester Reardon who, by the mere act of walking down the street, inspired fear and admiration. Jules Verne never led me to the places that Stanley Borowski had up his sleeve when it came dark. Robinson Crusoe lacked imagination in comparison with Johnny Paul. All these boys of the 14th Ward have a flavor about them still. They were not invented or imagined: they were real. Their names ring out like gold coins—Tom Fowler, Jim Buckley, Matt Owen, Rob Ramsay, Harry Martin, Johnny Dunne, to say nothing of Eddie Carney or the great Lester Reardon. Why, even now when I say Johnny Paul the names of the saints leave a bad taste in my mouth. Johnny Paul was the living Odyssey of the 14th Ward; that he later became a truck driver is an irrelevant fact.

Before the great change no one seemed to notice that the streets were ugly or dirty. If the sewer mains were opened you held your nose. If you blew your nose you found snot in your handkerchief and not your nose. There was more of inward peace and contentment. There was the saloon, the racetrack, bicycles, fast women and trot horses. Life was still moving along leisurely. In the 14th Ward, at least Sunday mornings no one was dressed. If Mrs. Gorman came down in her wrapper with dirt in her eyes to bow to the priest— "Good morning, Father!" "Good morning, Mrs. Gorman!"—the street was purged of all sin. Pat McCarren carried his handkerchief in the tail-flap of his frock coat; it was nice and handy there, like the shamrock in his buttonhole. The foam was on the lager and people stopped to chat with one another.

In my dreams I come back to the 14th Ward as a paranoiac returns to his obsessions. When I think of those steel-gray battleships in the Navy Yard I see them lying there in some astrologic dimension in which I am the gunnersmith, the chemist, the dealer in high explosives, the undertaker, the coroner, the cuckold, the sadist, the lawyer and contender, the scholar, the restless one, the jolt-head and the brazen-faced.

Where others remember of their youth a beautiful garden, a fond mother, a sojourn at the seashore, I remember, with a vividness as if it were etched in acid, the grim, soot-covered walls and chimneys of the tin factory opposite us and the bright, circular pieces of tin that were strewn in the street, some bright and gleaming, others rusted, dull, copperish, leaving a stain on the fingers; I remember the iron-works where the red furnace glowed and men walked toward the glowing pit with huge shovels in their hands, while outside were the shallow wooden forms like coffins with rods through them on which you scraped your shins or broke your neck. I remember the black hands of the iron-moulders, the grit that had sunk so deep into the skin that nothing could remove it, not soap, nor elbow grease, nor money, nor love, nor death. Like a black mark on them! Walking into the furnace like devils with black hands—and later, with flowers over them, cool and rigid in their Sunday suits, not even the rain can wash away the grit. All these beautiful gorillas going up to God with swollen muscles and lumbago and black hands . . .

For me the whole world was embraced in the confines of the 14th Ward. If anything happened outside it either didn't happen or it was unimportant. If my father went outside that world to fish it was of no interest to me. I remember only his boozy breath when he came home in the evening and opening the big green basket spilled the squirming, goggle-eyed monsters on the floor. If a man went off to the war I remember only that he came back of a Sunday afternoon and standing in front of the minister's house puked up his guts and then wiped it up with his vest. Such was Rob Ramsay, the minister's son. I remember that everybody liked Rob Ramsay—he was the black sheep of the family. They liked him because he was a good-for-nothing and he made no bones about it. Sundays or Wednesdays made no difference to him: you could see him coming down the street under the drooping awnings with his coat over his arm and the sweat rolling down his face; his legs wobbly, with that long, steady roll of a sailor coming ashore after a long cruise; the tobacco juice dribbling from his lips, together with warm, silent curses and some loud and foul ones too. The utter indolence, the insouciance of the man, the obscenities, the sacrilege. Not a man of God, like his father. No, a man who inspired love! His frailties were human frailties and he wore them jauntily, tauntingly, flauntingly, like banderillas. He would come down the warm open street with the gas mains bursting and the air full of sun and shit and oaths and maybe his fly would be open and his suspenders undone, or maybe his vest bright with vomit. Sometimes he came charging down the street, like a bull skidding on all fours, and then the street cleared magically, as if the manholes had opened up and swallowed their offal. Crazy Willie Maine would be standing on the shed over the paint shop, with his pants down, jerking away for dear life. There they stood in the dry electrical crackle of the open street with the gas mains bursting. A tandem that broke the minister's heart.

That was how he was then, Rob Ramsay. A man on a perpetual spree. He came back from the war with medals, and with fire in his guts. He puked up in front of his own door and he wiped up his puke with his own vest. He could clear the street quicker than a machine gun. *Faugh a balla!* That was his way. And a little later, in his warm-heartedness, in that fine, careless way he had, he walked off the end of a pier and drowned himself.

I remember him so well and the house he lived in. Because it was on the door-step of Rob Ramsay's house that we used to congregate in the warm summer evenings and watch the goings-on over the saloon across the street. A coming and going all night long and nobody bothered to pull down the shades. Just a stone's throw away from the little burlesque house called "The Bum." All around "The Bum" were the saloons, and Saturday nights there was a long line outside, milling and pushing and squirming to get at the ticket window. Saturday nights, when the Girl in Blue was in her glory, some wild tar from the Navy Yard would be sure to jump out of his seat and grab off one of Millie de Leon's garters. And a little later that night they'd be sure to come strolling down the street and turn in at the family entrance. And soon they'd be standing in the bed-room over the saloon, pulling off their tight pants and the women yanking off their corsets and scratching themselves like monkeys, while down below they were scuttling the suds and biting each other's ears off, and such a wild, shrill laughter all bottled up inside there, like dynamite evaporating. All this from Rob Ramsay's door-step, the old man upstairs saying his prayers over a kerosene lamp, praying like an obscene nanny goat for an end to come, or when he got tired of praying coming down in his nightshirt, like an old leprechaun, and belaying us with a broomstick.

From Saturday afternoon on until Monday morning it was a period without end, one thing melting into another. Saturday morning already—how it happened God only knows—you could *feel* the war vessels lying at anchor in the big basin. Saturday mornings my heart was in my mouth. I could see the decks being scrubbed down and the guns polished and the weight of those big sea-monsters resting on the dirty glass lake of the basin was a luxurious weight on me. I was already dreaming of running away, of going to far places. But I got only as far as the other side of the river, about as far north as Second Avenue and 28th Street, via the Belt Line. There I played the Orange Blossom Waltz and in the entr'actes I washed my eyes at the iron sink. The piano stood in the rear of the saloon. The keys were very yellow and my feet wouldn't reach to the pedals. I wore a velvet suit because velvet was the order of the day.

Everything that passed on the other side of the river was sheer lunacy: the sanded floor, the Argand lamps, the mica pictures in which the snow never melted, the crazy Dutchmen with steins in their hands, the iron sink that had grown such a mossy coat of slime, the woman from Hamburg whose ass always hung over the back of the chair, the court-yard choked with sauerkraut . . . Everything in three-quarter time that goes on forever. I walk between my parents, with one hand in my mother's muff and the other in my father's sleeve. My eyes are shut tight, tight as clams which draw back their lids only to weep.

All the changing tides and weather that passed over the river are in my blood. I can still feel the slipperiness of the big handrail which I leaned against in fog and rain, which sent through my cool forehead the shrill blasts of the ferry-boat as she slid out of the slip. I can still see the mossy planks of the ferry slip buckling as the big round prow grazed her sides and the green, juicy water sloshed through the heaving, groaning planks of the slip. And overhead the sea-gulls wheeling and diving, making a dirty noise with their dirty beaks, a hoarse, preying sound of inhuman feasting, of mouths fastened down on refuse, of scabby legs skimming the green-churned water.

One passes imperceptibly from one scene, one age, one life to another. Suddenly, walking down a street, be it real or be it a dream, one realizes for the first time that the years have flown, that all this has passed forever and will live on only in memory; and then the memory turns inward with a strange, clutching brilliance and one goes over these scenes and incidents perpetually, in dream and reverie, while walking a street, while lying with a woman, while reading a book, while talking to a stranger . . . suddenly, but always with terrific insistence and always with terrific accuracy, these memories intrude, rise up like ghosts and permeate every fibre of one's being. Henceforward everything moves on shifting levels—our thoughts, our dreams, our actions, our whole life. A parallelogram in which we drop from one platform of our scaffold to another. Henceforward we walk split into myriad fragments, like an insect with a hundred feet, a centipede with soft-stirring feet that drinks in the atmosphere; we walk with sensitive filaments that drink avidly of past and future, and all things melt into music and sorrow; we walk against a united world, asserting our dividedness. All things, as we walk, splitting with us into a myriad iridescent fragments. The great fragmentation of maturity. The great change. In youth we were whole and the terror and pain of the world penetrated us through and through. There was no sharp separation between joy and sorrow: they fused into one, as our waking life fuses with dream and sleep. We rose one being in the morning and at night we went down into an ocean, drowned out completely, clutching the stars and the fever of the day.

And then comes a time when suddenly all seems to be reversed. We live in the mind, in ideas, in fragments. We no longer drink in the wild outer music of the streets—we *remember* only. Like a monomaniac we relive the drama of youth.

1936

# CHARLES REZNIKOFF

*Charles Reznikoff (1894–1976) was a great walker who would start from his Upper West Side home each morning and put in twenty miles a day. The streets were his chief source of inspiration; returning home, he would focus on just those isolated incidents or images that moved him. Many of his poems record encounters with strangers or overheard conversations and function like short stories in verse. In spare language, he wrote with sympathy and affectionate amusement about ordinary people—poor, suffering, resilient.*

## MILLINERY DISTRICT

The clouds, piled in rows like merchandise,
become dark; lights are lit in the lofts;
the milliners, tacking bright flowers on straw shapes,
say, glancing out of the windows,
It is going to snow;
and soon they hear the snow scratching the panes. By night
it is high on the sills.
The snow fills up the footprints
in the streets, the ruts of wagons and of motor trucks.
Except for the whir of the car
brushing the tracks clear of snow,
the streets are hushed.
At closing time, the girls breathe deeply
the clean air of the streets
sweet after the smell of merchandise.

1936

The elevator man, working long hours
for little—whose work is dull and trivial—
must also greet each passenger
pleasantly:
to be so heroic
he wears a uniform.

1941

When I came for my laundry, I found a shirt missing.
The laundryman—a Jew—considered the situation:
"There are four ways of losing a shirt," he said thoughtfully;
"in the first place, it may never have been delivered by the steam
        laundry;
in the second place, it may be lying around here, unpacked;
in the third place, it may have been delivered and packed in someone
        else's bundle;
and in the fourth place it may be really lost.
Come in again at the end of the week and I'll know what has
        happened."
And his wife, recognizing a fellow Jew,
smiled and spoke up in Yiddish,
"We won't have to go to the rabbi about it, will we?"

———

The new janitor is a Puerto Rican;
still a young man and he has four small children.
He has been hired because he is cheap—
not because he is the handy man
a good janitor is supposed to be.
I doubt if he ever saw any plumbing

before he came to this country,
to say nothing of a boiler and radiators.
Anyway, he was soon overwhelmed by requests from the tenants
to do this and fix that.
He does his best and spends hours at simple jobs,
and seldom does them well—or can do them at all.
He was in my flat once
to do something or other and, when he was through,
asked me if he might sit down.

"Of course," I said and offered him a drink,
but he would not take it.
"It is so quiet here," he explained.
And then he began to talk about a man who lived in the house and
    taught Spanish.
"He talks to me in Spanish," the janitor said,
"but I do not understand.
You see, I am not an educated man."
His eye caught the print of a water-color by Winslow Homer
which I have hanging: a palm tree in the Bahamas.
"That is my country," he said,
and kept looking at the print
as one might look at a photograph of one's mother
long dead.

———

The Chinese girl in the waiting-room of the busy railway station
writing on a pad
in columns
as if she were adding figures
instead of words—
words in blue ink
that look like small flowers
stylized into squares:
she is planting a small private garden.

———

The dark subway-station was almost empty at a little after ten
that summer morning. The man who sold tokens for the turnstiles
was going back to his booth with a broad smile on his face.
I supposed he had been engaged in an amusing conversation
with the Negro alone on the platform.
The black man's face was wrinkled. As he stood there,
stooped over a stick, he kept on talking:
"I cuss my mother in her grave," he was saying in a loud angry voice,
"because she borned me!"
What a line for a "Mammy" song, I thought.
By this time there were two or three other passengers on the
        platform
and we stood at a distance from the Negro and watched him,
though we pretended not to. He turned to us and said,
"I wonder how it feels to be white."

Just then the train came in and we went inside
hoping that the Negro with his disturbance
would not enter the brightly-lit car.

———

Two men were seated near me in a bus:
well-dressed, well-fed; in the forties;
obviously respected members of their community;
talking together calmly,
the way men of good breeding and education talk,
and the speech may have been Greek or Italian.
I could not hear enough of it to decide.
Suddenly a woman seated directly behind them
began in a loud voice:
"Why don't you talk American?
You live here, don't you?
You make your living here!
Talk American!"

One of the men turned to glance at her
and then the two went on talking in Greek or Italian,

[ 623 ]

calmly, quietly
although every now and then the woman cried out,
"Talk American, why don't you?"

If these men were Jews, I thought,
how uneasy they would have become,
and their faces would show it.
One of them might even say to the woman—
if he knew enough English,
"This is a free country, isn't it?"
And there would be a noisy argument.
Or they might become silent.
The two men, however, continued to talk
as they had been doing
and neither turned to glance at the woman
or show by gesture or grimace
that they heard her.
Finally, she jumped up and sat down beside me.
"What do you think of these men?" she asked.
"Why don't they talk American?
They live here, don't they?
They make their money here!"

"You must not be so impatient," I said.
"English is not an easy language to learn.
Besides, if they don't learn it, their children will:
we have good schools, you know."
She looked at me suspiciously
and, when the bus stopped, hurried off—
fleeing our contamination.
One of the men then turned to me and said quietly
in the best of American with not a trace of a foreign accent:
"She's a little cracked, isn't she?"

———

I was walking along Forty-Second Street as night was falling.
On the other side of the street was Bryant Park.
Walking behind me were two men
and I could hear some of their conversation:
"What you must do," one of them was saying to his companion,
"is to decide on what you want to do
and then stick to it. Stick to it!
And you are sure to succeed finally."

I turned to look at the speaker giving such good advice
and was not surprised to see that he was old.
But his companion
to whom the advice was given so earnestly,
was just as old;
and just then the great clock on top of a building across the park
began to shine.

———

In the street, nine stories below, the horn of an automobile out of
        order
began sounding its loudest
steadily—without having to stop for breath.
We tried to keep on talking
in spite of that unceasing scream;
raised our voices somewhat, no longer calm and serene.
Our civilization was somewhat out of order, it seemed.

But, just as we began to knit our brows,
tighten our jaws, twist our lips,
the noise stopped;
and we dipped our heads,
like ducks on a stream, into the cool silence,
and talked again quietly, smiling at each other.

1969

# A. J. LIEBLING

*It has been suggested that the cultural innovator who makes waves in New York usually hails from elsewhere, while the homegrown New Yorker tends to be skeptical and traditionalist about the incessant claims of new fashions. Certainly the latter tendency predominates in A. J. Liebling's "Apology for Breathing," the introductory essay from his collection of New York pieces,* Back Where I Came From. *Liebling (1904–63), a connoisseur of boxing, food, Paris, and good prose, was among the writers at* The New Yorker *who helped define the city's modern ethos, with much more of a native's self-mocking growl than either Joseph Mitchell or E. B. White.*

### APOLOGY FOR BREATHING

**P**EOPLE I know in New York are incessantly on the point of going back where they came from to write a book, or of staying on and writing a book about back where they came from. Back where they came from, I gather, is the American scene (New York, of course, just isn't America). It is all pretty hard on me because I have no place to go back to. I was born in an apartment house at Ninety-third Street and Lexington Avenue, about three miles from where I now live. Friends often tell me of their excitement when the train on which they are riding passes from Indiana into Illinois, or back again. I am ashamed to admit that when the Jerome Avenue express rolls into Eighty-sixth Street station I have absolutely no reaction.

I always think of back where my friends came from as one place, possessing a homogeneous quality of not being New York. The thought has been well expressed by my literary adviser, Whitey Bimstein, who also trains prize-fighters. I once asked him how he liked the country. He said, "It is a nice spot." I have been to the country myself. I went to a college in New Hampshire. But I seldom mention this, because I would like to be considered quaint and regional, like Jesse Stuart or Kenneth Roberts.

[ 626 ]

The finest thing about New York City, I think, is that it is like one of those complicated Renaissance clocks where on one level an allegorical marionette pops out to mark the day of the week, on another a skeleton death bangs the quarter hour with his scythe, and on a third the Twelve Apostles do a cakewalk. The variety of the sideshows distracts one's attention from the advance of the hour hand. I know people who say that, as in the clock, all the exhibits depend upon the same movement. This they insist is economic. But they are the sort of people who look at a fine woman and remind you that the human body is composed of one dollar and sixty-two cents worth of chemicals.*

I like to think of all the city microcosms so nicely synchronized though unaware of one another: the worlds of the weight-lifters, yodelers, tugboat captains and sideshow barkers, of the book-dutchers, sparring partners, song pluggers, sporting girls and religious painters, of the dealers in rhesus monkeys and the bishops of churches that they establish themselves under the religious corporations law. It strengthens my hold on reality to know when I awake with a brandy headache in my house which is nine blocks due south of the Chrysler Building and four blocks due east of the Empire State, that Eddie Arcaro, the jockey, is galloping a horse around the track at Belmont while Ollie Thomas, a colored clocker of my acquaintance, is holding a watch on him. I can be sure that Kit Coates, at the Aquarium, is worrying over the liverish deportment of a new tropical fish, that presently Whitey will be laying out the gloves and headguards for the fighters he trains at Stillman's gymnasium, while Miss Ira, the Harlem modiste, will be trying to talk a dark-complexioned girl out of buying herself an orange turban and Hymie the Tummler ruminates a plan for opening a new night club. It would be easier to predicate the existence of God on such recurrences than on the cracking of ice in ponds, the peeping of spring peepers in their peeperies and the shy green sprigs of poison ivy so well advertised by writers like Thoreau.

There are New Yorkers so completely submerged in one

*The author has not checked on this figure.—The Editor

environment, like the Garment Centre or Jack and Charlie's, that they live and die oblivious of the other worlds around them. Others are instinctively aware of the wonders of New York natural history, but think them hardly worthy of mention. My father was a New Yorker of the latter sort. In separate phases of his business life, he had occasion to retain Monk Eastman, a leading pre-war gangster, and the Rev. Charles Parkhurst, a notorious crusader against vice. This seemed to him no more paradoxical than going to Coward's for his shoes while he bought his hats of Knox. When Father was President of an association of furriers during a strike he hired Eastman to break up a strikers' mass meeting. His employment of Dr. Parkhurst was more subtle. In about 1910 Father bought some real estate in West Twenty-sixth Street on which he purposed to put several loft buildings. He believed that the fur industry was going to move up in that direction from below Twenty-third. But Twenty-sixth Street between Sixth and Seventh Avenues was full of brothels, and there was no hope of getting tenants for the new buildings until the block was made respectable. First Father dispossessed the hock shops from the houses which he had acquired with his building lots. But the watchmen rented the empty rooms to the drabs for fifty cents a night. Then Father made a substantial gift to Dr. Parkhurst's society, enclosing with his check a letter that called attention to the sinful conditions on West Twenty-sixth Street. Dr. Parkhurst raised Hell with the police, who made the girls move on to another block, and then Father put up his buildings. Father always said Monk and Dr. Parkhurst gave him his money's worth, but he never liked either of them. He became labor conscious after he retired from business, and toward the end of his life often said that unions were a fine thing, but that they had doubtless changed a lot since the time he hired Eastman. He died a staunch Roosevelt man.

Even though he made his home during the second part of his life among middle-class enterprisers with horizons slimmer than a gnat's waist, Father lived in other milieus in restrospect. He liked to talk of the lower East Side in the eighties, when the carters left their wagons in the streets of nights and the small boys would roll the wains away and burn them on election day, and of how he, a workingman at ten, boxed with the other furriers' apprentices using beaver muffs for mitts. He would even tell of the gay life of London and Paris and Leipzig in the late nineties when he was a bachelor buyer, although, he always protested, he had finished with that sort of thing when he got married. And he early introduced me to those worlds into which one may escape temporarily for the payment of a fee, the race course and the baseball park. These have their own conflicts that do not follow scenarios pre-determined in Hollywood.

Since this is a regional book about people I met back where I came from, I should like to say something here about the local language. This is a regional tongue imported from the British Isles, as is the dialect spoken by the retarded inhabitants of the Great Smoky Mountains back where *they* come from. Being spoken by several million people, it has not been considered of any philological importance. Basically, New Yorkese is the common speech of early nineteenth century Cork, transplanted during the mass immigration of the South Irish a hundred years ago. Of this Cork dialect Thomas Crofton Croker in 1839 wrote: "The vernacular of this region may be regarded as the ancient cockneyism of the mixed race who held the old city—Danes, English and Irish. It is a jargon, whose principal characteristic appears in the pronunciation of *th*, as exemplified in *dis, dat, den, dey*—this, that, then, they; and in the dovetailing of words as, 'kum our rish' for 'come of this.'" New York example, "gerradahere" for "get out of here." The neo-Corkonian proved particularly suited to the later immigrants who came here from continental Europe—the *th* sound is equally impossible for French, Germans and Italians. Moreover, it was impressed upon the latecomers because it was the talk of the police and the elementary school teachers, the only Americans who would talk to them at all. Father, who was born in Austria but came here when he was seven years old, spoke New Yorkese perfectly.

It is true that since the diaspora the modern dialects of Cork and New York have diverged slightly like Italian and Provencal, both of which stem from vulgar Latin. Yet Sean O'Faolain's modern story of Cork, "A Born Genius," contains dialogue that might have come out of Eleventh Avenue: "He's after painting two swans on deh kitchen windes. Wan is facin' wan way and d'oder is facin' d'oder way.——So dat so help me God dis day you'd tink deh swans was floatin' in a garden! And deh garden was floatin' in trough deh winda! And dere was no winda!"

There are interesting things about New York besides the language. It is one of the oldest places in the United States, but doesn't live in retrospect like the professionally picturesque provinces. Any city may have one period of magnificence, like Boston or New Orleans or San Francisco, but it takes a real one to keep renewing itself until the past is perennially forgotten. There were plenty of clipper ships out of New York in the old days and privateers before them, but there are better ships out of here today. The Revolution was fought all over town, from Harlem to Red Hook and back again, but that isn't the revolution you will hear New Yorkers discussing now.

Native New Yorkers are the best mannered people in America; they never speak out of turn in saloons, because they have experience in group etiquette. Whenever you hear a drinker let a blat out of him you can be sure he is a recent immigrant from the south or middle west. New Yorkers are modest. It is a distinction for a child in New York to be the brightest on one block; he acquires no exaggerated idea of his own relative intelligence. Prairie geniuses are raced in cheap company when young. They are intoxicated by the feel of being boy wonders in Amarillo, and when they bounce off New York's skin as adults they resent it.

New York women are the most beautiful in the world. They have their teeth straightened in early youth. They get their notions of chic from S. Klein's windows instead of the movies. Really loud and funny New Yorkers, like Bruce Barton, are invariably carpetbaggers. The climate is extremely healthy. The death rate is lower in Queens and the Bronx than in any other large city in the United States, and the average life expectancy is so high that one of our morning newspapers specializes in interviewing people a hundred years old and upward. The average is slightly lowered, however, by the inlanders who come here and insist on eating in Little Southern Tea Roomes on side streets.

The natives put up with a lot back here where I came from. If the inhabitants of Kentucky are distrustful of strangers, that is duly noted as an entertaining local trait. But if a New Yorker says that he doesn't like Kentuckians he is marked a cold churl. It is perennially difficult for the New Yorker who subscribes to a circulating library to understand how the city survived destruction during the Civil War. When he reads about those regional demigods haunted by ancestral daemons and festooned in magnolia blossoms and ghosts who composed practically the whole Confederate Army, he wonders what happened to them en route. I asked Whitey Bimstein what he thought of that one. He said: "Our guys must have slapped their ears down." Whitey does not know that we have been paying a war indemnity ever since in the form of royalties.

*B A C K   W H E R E   I   C A M E   F R O M* , 1 9 3 8

# LANGSTON HUGHES

*Poet, playwright, and novelist Langston Hughes (1902–67) was at the center of what has since been called the Harlem Renaissance. He was also critical about some of its implications, writing in 1926 that "the present vogue in things Negro . . . may do as much harm as good for the budding colored artist." In this chapter from his autobiography,* The Big Sea, *perhaps the most succinct, judicious summary of that era, Hughes looks back wryly at Harlem's fashionable phase, when the curious flocked uptown—and celebrates the heyday of Harlem's rent parties, beyond the reaches of the tourists.*

## WHEN THE NEGRO WAS IN VOGUE

THE 1920's were the years of Manhattan's black Renaissance. It began with *Shuffle Along*, *Running Wild*, and the Charleston. Perhaps some people would say even with *The Emperor Jones*, Charles Gilpin, and the tom-toms at the Provincetown. But certainly it was the musical revue, *Shuffle Along*, that gave a scintillating send-off to that Negro vogue in Manhattan, which reached its peak just before the crash of 1929, the crash that sent Negroes, white folks, and all rolling down the hill toward the Works Progress Administration.

*Shuffle Along* was a honey of a show. Swift, bright, funny, rollicking, and gay, with a dozen danceable, singable tunes. Besides, look who were in it: The now famous choir director, Hall Johnson, and the composer, William Grant Still, were a part of the orchestra. Eubie Blake and Noble Sissle wrote the music and played and acted in the show. Miller and Lyles were the comics. Florence Mills skyrocketed to fame in the second act. Trixie Smith sang "He May Be Your Man But He Comes to See Me Sometimes." And Caterina Jarboro, now a European prima donna, and the internationally celebrated Josephine Baker were merely in the chorus. Everybody was in the audience—including me. People came back to see it innumerable times. It was always packed.

To see *Shuffle Along* was the main reason I wanted to go to Columbia. When I saw it, I was thrilled and delighted. From then on I was in the gallery of the Cort Theatre every time I got a chance. That year, too, I saw Katharine Cornell in *A Bill of Divorcement*, Margaret Wycherly in *The Verge*, Maugham's *The Circle* with Mrs. Leslie Carter, and the Theatre Guild production of Kaiser's *From Morn Till Midnight*. But I remember *Shuffle Along* best of all. It gave just the proper push—a pre-Charleston kick—to that Negro vogue of the 20's, that spread to books, African sculpture, music, and dancing.

Put down the 1920's for the rise of Roland Hayes, who packed Carnegie Hall, the rise of Paul Robeson in New York and London, of Florence Mills over two continents, of Rose McClendon in Broadway parts that never measured up to her, the booming voice of Bessie Smith and the low moan of Clara on thousands of records, and the rise of that grand comedienne of song, Ethel Waters, singing: "Charlie's elected now! He's in right for sure!" Put down the 1920's for Louis Armstrong and Gladys Bentley and Josephine Baker.

White people began to come to Harlem in droves. For several years they packed the expensive Cotton Club on Lenox Avenue. But I was never there, because the Cotton Club was a Jim Crow club for gangsters and monied whites. They were not cordial to Negro patronage, unless you were a celebrity like Bojangles. So Harlem Negroes did not like the Cotton Club and never appreciated its Jim Crow policy in the very heart of their dark community. Nor did ordinary Negroes like the growing influx of whites toward Harlem after sundown, flooding the little cabarets and bars where formerly only colored people laughed and sang, and where now the strangers were given the best ringside tables to sit and stare at the Negro customers—like amusing animals in a zoo.

The Negroes said: "We can't go downtown and sit and stare at you in your clubs. You won't even let us in your clubs." But they didn't say it out loud—for Negroes are practically never rude to white people. So thousands of whites came to Harlem night after night, thinking the Negroes loved to have them there, and firmly believing that all Harlemites left their houses at sundown to sing and dance in cabarets, because most of the whites saw nothing but the cabarets, not the houses.

Some of the owners of Harlem clubs, delighted at the flood of white patronage, made the grievous error of barring their own race, after the manner of the famous Cotton Club. But most of these quickly lost business and folded up, because they failed to realize that a large part of the Harlem attraction for downtown New Yorkers lay in simply watching the colored customers amuse themselves. And the smaller clubs, of course, had no big floor shows or a name band like the Cotton Club, where Duke Ellington usually held forth, so, without black patronage, they were not amusing at all.

Some of the small clubs, however, had people like Gladys Bentley, who was something worth discovering in those days, before she got famous, acquired an accompanist, specially written material, and conscious vulgarity. But for two or three amazing years, Miss Bentley sat, and played a big piano all night long, literally all night, without stopping—singing songs like "The St. James Infirmary," from ten in the evening until dawn, with scarcely a break between the notes, sliding from one song to another, with a powerful and continuous underbeat of jungle rhythm. Miss Bentley was an amazing exhibition of musical energy—a large, dark, masculine lady, whose feet pounded the floor while her fingers pounded the keyboard—a perfect piece of African sculpture, animated by her own rhythm.

But when the place where she played became too well known, she began to sing with an accompanist, became a star, moved to a larger place, then downtown, and is now in Hollywood. The old magic of the woman and the piano and the night and the rhythm being one is gone. But everything goes, one way or another. The '20's are gone and lots of fine things in Harlem night life have disappeared like snow in the sun—since it became utterly commercial, planned for the downtown tourist trade, and therefore dull.

The lindy-hoppers at the Savoy even began to practise acrobatic routines, and to do absurd things for the entertainment of the whites, that probably never would have entered their heads to attempt merely for their own effortless amusement. Some of the

lindy-hoppers had cards printed with their names on them and became dance professors teaching the tourists. Then Harlem nights became show nights for the Nordics.

Some critics say that that is what happened to certain Negro
writers, too—that they ceased to write to amuse themselves and began to write to amuse and entertain white people, and in so doing
distorted and over-colored their material, and left out a great many
things they thought would offend their American brothers of a
lighter complexion. Maybe—since Negroes have writer-racketeers,
as has any other race. But I have known almost all of them, and most
of the good ones have tried to be honest, write honestly, and express
their world as they saw it.

All of us know that the gay and sparkling life of the so-called
Negro Renaissance of the '20's was not so gay and sparkling beneath
the surface as it looked. Carl Van Vechten, in the character of Byron
in *Nigger Heaven*, captured some of the bitterness and frustration of
literary Harlem that Wallace Thurman later so effectively poured
into his *Infants of the Spring*—the only novel by a Negro about that
fantastic period when Harlem was in vogue.

It was a period when, at almost every Harlem upper-crust dance
or party, one would be introduced to various distinguished white
celebrities there as guests. It was a period when almost any Harlem
Negro of any social importance at all would be likely to say casually:
"As I was remarking the other day to Heywood—," meaning
Heywood Broun. Or: "As I said to George—," referring to George
Gershwin. It was a period when local and visiting royalty were not
at all uncommon in Harlem. And when the parties of A'Lelia Walker,
the Negro heiress, were filled with guests whose names would turn
any Nordic social climber green with envy. It was a period when
Harold Jackman, a handsome young Harlem school teacher of modest means, calmly announced one day that he was sailing for the
Riviera for a fortnight, to attend Princess Murat's yachting party. It
was a period when Charleston preachers opened up shouting
churches as sideshows for white tourists. It was a period when at
least one charming colored chorus girl, amber enough to pass for a
Latin American, was living in a pent house, with all her bills paid by

a gentleman whose name was banker's magic on Wall Street. It was a period when every season there was at least one hit play on Broadway acted by a Negro cast. And when books by Negro authors were being published with much greater frequency and much more publicity than ever before or since in history. It was a period when white writers wrote about Negroes more successfully (commercially speaking) than Negroes did about themselves. It was the period (God help us!) when Ethel Barrymore appeared in blackface in *Scarlet Sister Mary*! It was the period when the Negro was in vogue.

I was there. I had a swell time while it lasted. But I thought it wouldn't last long. (I remember the vogue for things Russian, the season the Chauve-Souris first came to town.) For how could a large and enthusiastic number of people be crazy about Negroes forever? But some Harlemites thought the millennium had come. They thought the race problem had at last been solved through Art plus Gladys Bentley. They were sure the New Negro would lead a new life from then on in green pastures of tolerance created by Countee Cullen, Ethel Waters, Claude McKay, Duke Ellington, Bojangles, and Alain Locke.

I don't know what made any Negroes think that—except that they were mostly intellectuals doing the thinking. The ordinary Negroes hadn't heard of the Negro Renaissance. And if they had, it hadn't raised their wages any. As for all those white folks in the speakeasies and night clubs of Harlem—well, maybe a colored man could find *some* place to have a drink that the tourists hadn't yet discovered.

Then it was that house-rent parties began to flourish—and not always to raise the rent either. But, as often as not, to have a get-to-gether of one's own, where you could do the black-bottom with no stranger behind you trying to do it, too. Non-theatrical, non-intellectual Harlem was an unwilling victim of its own vogue. It didn't like to be stared at by white folks. But perhaps the downtowners never knew this—for the cabaret owners, the entertainers, and the speakeasy proprietors treated them fine—as long as they paid.

The Saturday night rent parties that I attended were often more

amusing than any night club, in small apartments where God knows
who lived—because the guests seldom did—but where the piano
would often be augmented by a guitar, or an odd cornet, or somebody with a pair of drums walking in off the street. And where awful bootleg whiskey and good fried fish or steaming chitterling were
sold at very low prices. And the dancing and singing and impromptu
entertaining went on until dawn came in at the windows.

These parties, often termed whist parties or dances, were usually
announced by brightly colored cards stuck in the grille of apartment
house elevators. Some of the cards were highly entertaining in
themselves:

We got yellow girls, we've got black and tan
Will you have a good time? - YEAH MAN !

## A Social Whist Party
—GIVEN BY—
**MARY WINSTON**

147 West 145th Street                                    Apt. 5

**SATURDAY EVE., MARCH 19th, 1932**

GOOD MUSIC                                    REFRESHMENTS

# H U R R A Y
COME AND SEE WHAT IS IN STORE FOR YOU AT THE

# TEA CUP PARTY
GIVEN BY MRS. VANDERBILT SMITH

## at 409 EDGECOMBE AVENUE
## NEW YORK CITY
Apartment 10-A

### on Thursday evening, January 23rd, 1930
at 8:30 P. M.

ORIENTAL - GYPSY - SOUTHERN MAMMY -
STARLIGHT
and other readers will be present

Music and Talent            —        —        Refreshments Served

Ribbons-Maws and Trotters A Specialty

Fall in line, and watch your step, For there'll be Lots of Browns with plenty of Pep At

## A Social Whist Party

Given by

## Lucille & Minnie

149 West 117th Street, N. Y. Gr. floor, W,

## Saturday Evening, Nov. 2nd 1929

Refreshments Just It          Music Won't Quit

---

If Sweet Mamma is running wild, and you are looking for a Do-right child, just come around and linger awhile at a

## SOCIAL WHIST PARTY

GIVEN BY

### PINKNEY & EPPS

260 West 129th Street                    Apartment 10

## SATURDAY EVENING, JUNE 9, 1928

GOOD MUSIC                              REFRESHMENTS

---

## Railroad Men's Ball

AT CANDY'S PLACE

*FRIDAY, SATURDAY & SUNDAY,*

## April 29-30, May 1, 1927

Black Wax, says change your mind and say they do and he will give you a hearing, while MEAT HOUSE SLIM, laying in the bin killing all good men.

L. A. VAUGH, *President*

OH BOY                                      OH JOY

## The Eleven Brown Skins
of the
## Evening Shadow Social Club
are giving their

### Second Annual St. Valentine Dance
Saturday evening, Feb. 18th, 1928

At 129 West 136th Street, New York City

Good Music                                 Refreshments Served

**Subscription**                                 **25 Cents**

---

*Some wear pajamas, some wear pants, what does it matter just so you can dance, at*

## A Social Whist Party
GIVEN BY

Mr. & Mrs. Brown

AT 258 w. 115th street, apt. 9

### SATURDAY EVE., SEPT. 14, 1929

*The music is sweet and everything good to eat!*

---

Almost every Saturday night when I was in Harlem I went to a house-rent party. I wrote lots of poems about house-rent parties, and ate thereat many a fried fish and pig's foot—with liquid refreshments on the side. I met ladies' maids and truck drivers, laundry workers and shoe shine boys, seamstresses and porters. I can still hear their laughter in my ears, hear the soft slow music, and feel the floor shaking as the dancers danced.

*THE BIG SEA, 1940*

# ELIZABETH BISHOP

Elizabeth Bishop (1911–79) spent much of her adult life as a traveler, with long residences in New York, Key West, Brazil, and Boston. Her poetry, celebrated for its clarity, formality, and understated emotion, often expressed an ambivalent blend of wanderlust and longing for home. In her poem "Questions of Travel," she asks: "Should we have stayed at home, / Wherever that may be?" Despite deep familiarity with New York, she would continue to view the city with an outsider's detachment. That mix of ease and dreamlike uncertainty comes across in this poem.


LETTER TO N.Y.

In your next letter I wish you'd say
where you are going and what you are doing;
how are the plays, and after the plays
what other pleasures you're pursuing:

taking cabs in the middle of the night,
driving as if to save your soul
where the road goes round and round the park
and the meter glares like a moral owl,

and the trees look so queer and green
standing alone in big black caves
and suddenly you're in a different place
where everything seems to happen in waves,

and most of the jokes you just can't catch,
like dirty words rubbed off a slate,
and the songs are loud but somehow dim
and it gets so terribly late,

and coming out of the brownstone house
to the gray sidewalk, the watered street,
one side of the buildings rises with the sun
like a glistening field of wheat.

—Wheat, not oats, dear. I'm afraid
if its wheat its none of your sowing,
nevertheless I'd like to know
what you are doing and where you are going.

1 9 4 0

# JOHN McNULTY

*No one came closer to catching the common parlance of New York in all its uncommonness than John McNulty (1895–1956), a newspaperman who regularly contributed carefully crafted, sometimes heartbreaking human-interest stories to* The New Yorker. *A habitué of racetracks and Third Avenue barrooms, McNulty had a phenomenal ear and a rare gift for drawing people out.*

## ATHEIST HIT BY TRUCK

THIS DRUNK came down the "L" stairs, and at the bottom he made a wrong turn. This led him into the gutter instead of onto the sidewalk, and a truck hit him and knocked him down.

It is a busy corner there at Forty-second Street and Second Avenue, in front of the Shanty, and there's a hack line there. Naturally, a little crowd and a cop gathered around the drunk and some hackies were in the crowd.

The cop was fairly young. After he hauled the guy up and sat him on the bottom step of the "L" stairs, he saw there wasn't much wrong with him. His pants were torn and maybe his knee was twisted slightly—maybe cut.

The cop got out his notebook and began asking questions and writing the answers down. Between questions he had to prop the man up. Fellow gave his name—Wilson, Martin, some noncommittal name—and his address. Everybody around was interested in these facts.

The blind man in the newspaper hut under the stairs felt a little put out because nobody was telling him what was going on, and he could hear beguiling fragments of it. "What happen? What happen?" the blind man kept asking, but the event wasn't deemed sensational enough for anybody to run and tell him, at least until afterward.

"What religion are yuh?" the policeman asked the man, who propped himself up this time and blurted out, "Atheist! I'm an atheist!"

For some reason, a lot of people laughed.

"Jeez, he's an atheist!" one of the hackies said. He shouted to a comrade who was still sitting behind the wheel of a parked cab at the corner, "Feller says he's an atheist!"

"Wuddaya laughing at?" the cop asked, addressing himself to the crowd generally. "Says he's an atheist, so he's an atheist. Wuddaya laughing at?" He wrote something in the book.

Another policeman, from over by Whelan's drugstore, where there was a picket line, strolled up. He was an older cop, more lines in his face, bigger belly, less humps around his hips, because the equipment—twisters, mace, and all that stuff—fitted on him better after all these years. "Wuzzamadder with 'im?" he asked his colleague.

"This here truck hit him. He isn't hurt bad. Says he's an atheist."

"I *am* an atheist!" the man yelled.

The crowd laughed again.

"Did you put that down—atheist?" the older cop asked.

"Yuh, I put it in where it says, 'religion.'"

"Rubbid out. Rubbid out. Put in Cat'lic. He looks like a Cat'lic to me. He got an Irish name? Anyway, rubbid out. When he sobers up, he'll be sorry he said that atheist business. Put in Cat'lic. We gotta send him to Bellevue just for safety's sake." The young cop started for the drugstore to put in a call.

"Never mind safety's sake. I'm an atheist, I'm telling you," the drunk said, loud as he could.

"Cuddid out, cuddid out," the older cop said. Then he leaned over like a lecturer or somebody. "An' another thing—if you wouldn't go round sayin' you're an atheist, maybe you wouldn't be gettin' hit by trucks."

The crowd sensed a great moral lesson and didn't laugh.

"Jeez! The guy says he's an atheist," the hackie said again.

A little later the Bellevue ambulance came.

"I yam a natheist," the man kept muttering as they put him into the ambulance.

*THE NEW YORKER*, 1941

## THE TELEVISION HELPS,
### BUT NOT VERY MUCH

WHEN I got into the cab to go down from Seventy-second and Second to Forty-fourth and Fifth, it seemed stuffy, so I gave the handle a twist and let the window down a little.

"That's all right," the driver said. "I'll take and close this here one up, if it's all right with you."

"Oh, sure," I said.

"If they're both open, it makes a draft on the back of my neck," he explained, nicely. "I ought to be home, I got a cold."

"That's about all you can do for these colds," I said.

"Go to bed is the best thing," he said. "Only with me, maybe I'm better off milling around in the hack. Too lonesome home. I lost my wife."

"Oh," I said. "Was it recently it happened? I mean when did she die?"

"Pretty near a year ago at that," he said.

We were moving along Seventy-second, getting near Fifth. Traffic was slow even before we hit Fifth.

Some of them are gabby, the hack drivers. This one wasn't, even though it turned out we talked all the way. It didn't seem to be gab. It seemed natural talk, almost as if we had known each other a long while.

"I got myself a television," he said. "For company like. The television helps, but not very much, at that."

"No kids or anything?" I asked.

"No, we didn't," he said. "We didn't have any children at all. No in-laws, even. See, we come from another city here. More than twenty years here. We made out all right. It ain't the best job in the world, but we battle along all right together, twenty years. Long time."

"Yes," I said.

"Like I say about the television, I can get interested, all right, like a fight or even sometimes those cowboy movies they put on. Just the same, sooner or later the television got to wind up, don't it? I mean, it comes to the end of whatever the show is or wrassling or whatever it is."

"I know what you mean. The thing goes off," I said.

"Yeah, the thing winds up and there I am again," he said. "I'm alone again and I maybe go to the icebox and get a beer, but it's lonesome. Do you think it wouldn't be so bad if I had kids somewheres? Even if they were grown up somewheres?"

"I don't know," I said. "I don't have any children."

"They say it's different if you have kids," he said. "Even if you lose your wife. That's what they say."

"Some people say that," I said. "I don't know. Did she die suddenly?"

"She was sick about two weeks, that's all," he said. "But the more I think about it, she must have been sick a long while. The doctor said she must have been. She didn't like to have doctors. Matter of fact, it was me got him finally. And I had to go to him and say to him, look, I said to him, she's going to be sore at you coming in. I said, she's against you before she even lays an eye on you, I says, so please don't mind if she acts sore. Later on, after it's all over, he tells me it was too late, the thing that was the matter with her it was too late to do anything."

"That was tough," I said.

"Thing is I keep worrying," he said. "Was it my fault maybe I wasn't more bossy and make her get a doctor? What do you think? I worry about it all the time. Like that's why I didn't stay home with this damn cold. I'd be around the house thinking maybe we'd be together just the same as always, me coming home and having supper and help with the dishes and we both sit down and have a couple beers, listen to the radio, if I made her get a doctor and never mind how much beefing, squawking she do about it. What do you think?"

"Oh, I don't know," I said. "That's a tough one to answer." It wasn't that I wanted to give the driver a short answer, but there I was, thrown into the middle of a man's life, and I didn't know the man.

"You're telling me it's a tough one!" he said. "Just the same, I got the notion you're kind of sensible, and after all, what harm is there?

Like I tell you, I got no in-laws, no kids, I had an idea I'd talk it over with somebody. Them guys around the garage, what the hell, they're dumber than me, even. What do they know? Know what I mean?"

"Yes," I said.

"Like, the truth of the matter, I could get married again right away," he said. "Those guys all said don't be a sucker—don't be a sucker, they said."

"About what?" I asked.

"Well, might as well out with it," he said. "There's this girl I could get married with. Do you think I look forty-eight?"

"I don't know," I said. "I hardly looked at you much. Just got in the cab, hardly looked at anything except that it was a cab."

"I guess I look forty-eight all right," he said. "Well, this girl is thirty-one. She has a little baby. I met her at a guy's house, he had me there eating Christmas. Didn't want me eating in a coffeepot first Christmas I had no wife, he said."

"She divorced or what, the girl with the baby?" I asked.

"No," he said. "Thing is she was a Wac—you know, in the war they had women they called them Wacs. She was in Chicago and she married this fellow, and it's only three months after and he dies on her. So in a little while she had the baby, and that's the way it is. She's a very nice woman, only seventeen years younger. I mean seventeen years younger than me. I told you I'm forty-eight, didn't I? Well, this girl, or maybe I should say woman, she's thirty-one and got the baby and thirty-one from forty-eight, that's seventeen, see what I mean?"

"Yes," I said.

"The guys at the garage say that's too much difference, and with the kid and all," he said. "What they don't understand is I like the kid, see what I mean? I bought the kid a couple toys, and you should see how this girl appreciated it I bought toys for the kid. Don't think for a minute this is any kind of a fly-around dame. She's nice. She lives with her mother now, and she works when she can get work."

"I bet she's all right," I said.

"You can say that again," he said. "Just between ourselves, she proposed to me, you might say. Know what I mean? Honest to God, it ain't this sex stuff, that ain't the main thing at all, no matter what the guys in the garage say; they're always harping about that angle. What I mean is—well, I would like to have her around, kid and all. I like the kid. He ain't very big yet, but he could look at the television, too. Like I say, it helps keep me from getting so goddam lonesome but it don't take care of things altogether, know what I mean? Will you tell me one thing? I mean, I want you give me your opinion—it's pretty near Forty-fourth Street after we get this light."

"O.K., what is it?" I said.

"Never mind the guys in the garage—do *you* think it'd be all right if we got married? You think it would work out?"

"You're coming at me rather suddenly with this," I said, sparring for time.

"I know," he said. "I don't say I'll do what you tell me, but just the same, you got an idea now how things are, don't you?"

"Well, I think I understand," I said.

"O.K., then, what do you think?"

"All right, you asked me," I said, and drew a deep breath. "I say go ahead and get married. That's what I say, sight unseen."

"Right!" he said, speaking almost loud for the first time in our rolling acquaintance. "That settles it. I guess I only needed somebody, anybody, say go ahead. Like give me a little shove, you might say. I'm going to do it. It's too goddam lonesome. And I like the kid, no fooling. This is Forty-fourth. Do you want this corner or the downtown side?"

"This corner's all right," I said, and got out and hollered back, "Good luck!"

"O.K., doc," he said. He was smiling, and now I guess he'll go ahead and get married. Probably never see him again. I didn't even look at his name beside the picture in the frame, but I hope they make out all right.

*THE NEW YORKER*, 1951

# IRWIN SHAW

*For five decades Irwin Shaw (1913–84) wrote memorable stories about New York, including such classics as "Girls in Their Summer Dresses," "Sailor Off the Bremen," and "Welcome to the City," which dramatizes the town's seedy, anonymous hotel life and its compensations. Shaw's later bestselling novels have obscured his high achievements in the shorter form, and he is due for a reevaluation.*

## WELCOME TO THE CITY

AS HE DREW NEARER to it, Enders looked up at his hotel through the black drizzle of the city that filled the streets with rain and soot and despair. A small red neon sign bloomed over the hotel entrance, spelling out CIRCUS HOTEL, REASONABLE, turning the drizzle falling profoundly around it into blood.

Enders sighed, shivered inside his raincoat, and walked slowly up the five steps to the entrance and went in. His nostrils curled, as they did each time he opened the door of the hotel, and his nose was hit by the ancient odor of ammonia and lysol and old linoleum and old beds and people who must depend on two bathrooms to the floor, and over the other odors the odor of age and sin, all at reasonable rates.

Wysocki was at the desk, in his gray suit with the markings of all the cafeteria soup in the city on it, and the pale face shaven down to a point where at any moment you half-expected to see the bone exposed, gleaming and green. Wysocki stood against the desk with the thirty-watt bulb shining down on his thinning hair and his navy-blue shirt and the solid orange tie, bright as hope in the dark hotel lobby, gravely reading the next morning's *Mirror*, his pale, hairy hands spread importantly, with delicate possessiveness, on the desk in front of him.

Josephine was sitting in one of the three lobby chairs, facing Wysocki. She wore a purple tailored suit with a ruffled waist, and open-toed red shoes, even though the streets outside were as damp and penetratingly cold as any marsh, and Enders could see the high red polish under her stockings, on her toenails. She sat there, not reading, not talking, her face carved out of powder and rouge under the blonde hair whose last surge of life had been strangled from it a dozen years before by peroxide and small-town hairdressers and curling irons that could have been used to primp the hair of General Sherman's granite horse.

"The English," Wysocki was saying, without looking up from his paper. "I wouldn't let them conduct a war for me for one million dollars in gilt-edged securities. Debaters and herring-fishermen," he said. "That's what they are."

"I thought Jews ate herring," Josephine said. Her voice scraped in the lobby, as though the Circus Hotel itself had suddenly broken into speech in its own voice, lysol and ammonia and rotting ancient wood finally put into sound.

"Jews eat herring," Wysocki said. "And the English eat herring."

Enders sighed again and walked up to the desk. In the chair near the stairway, he noticed, a girl was sitting, a pretty girl in a handsome green coat trimmed with lynx. He watched her obliquely as he talked to Wysocki, noticed that her legs were good and the expression cool, dignified, somehow hauntingly familiar.

"Hello, Wysocki," Enders said.

"Mr. Enders," Wysocki looked up pleasantly from the newspaper. "So you decided to come in out of the rain to your cozy little nest."

"Yes," said Enders, watching the girl.

"Did you know," Josephine asked, "that the English eat herring?"

"Yes," Enders said, digging into his mind for the face the girl reminded him of.

"That's what Wysocki said." Josephine shrugged. "I was living in happy ignorance."

Enders leaned over so that he could whisper into Wysocki's ear. "Who is she?" Enders asked.

Wysocki peered at the girl in the green coat, his eyes sly and guilty, as a thief might peer at a window at Tiffany's through which he intended to heave a brick later in the evening. "Zelinka," Wysocki whispered. "Her name's Bertha Zelinka. She checked in this after-noon. You could do worse, couldn't you?" He chuckled soundlessly, his bone-shaven face creasing without mirth, green and gleaming under the thirty-watt bulb.

"I've seen her some place," Enders whispered, looking at the girl over his shoulder. She sat remote, cold, her legs crossed beautifully under the green coat, looking under heavy lids at the scarred and battered clock over Wysocki's head. "I know that face," Enders said. "But from where?"

"She looks like Greta Garbo," Wysocki said. "That's where you know her from."

Enders stared at the girl in the green coat. She did look like Greta Garbo, the long pale face, the long eyes, the wide, firm mouth, the whole thing a mirror of passion and pain and deep Northern melancholy and bony, stubborn beauty. Suddenly Enders realized that he was a stranger in a strange city, a thousand miles from home, that it was raining out, that he had no girl, and that no one in this huge and wrangling seven-million town had ever said anything more tender to him than, "Pass the mustard." And here, be-fore him, solid as his hand, in a green coat with a lynx collar, sat a tall, melancholy girl who looked enough like Greta Garbo, pain and passion and beauty and understanding all mixed on the bony, pale face, to be her twin sister. His voice charged at his throat, leaping to say the first tender word in this rat-eaten, roach-claimed hotel lobby.

"Enders!" His name was spoken gaily, warmly. He turned from looking at Bertha Zelinka, wrenching his soul. "Mr. Enders, I was waiting for your appearance." It was Bishop, the owner of the hotel, a little fat gray-faced man with wet mustaches. He was rubbing his hands jovially now. "You were just the person I wanted to see tonight," he said.

"Thanks," said Enders.

"Wait!" Bishop's voice trilled. "Don't move an inch from the spot! I have a treat in store for you."

He darted back of the desk through the door into his office.

Enders turned and looked at Bertha Zelinka, sitting there as calmly, as remotely, as Garbo herself.

"Observe!" Bishop darted out again from his office. "Look!" He held his hand high above his head. From it dangled a dead, wet chicken. "See what I've saved for you. I am willing to give you this chicken for sixty cents, Mr. Enders."

Enders looked politely at the chicken, hanging sadly in death from Bishop's proud hand.

"Thanks, Mr. Bishop," Enders said. "But I have no place to cook a chicken."

"Take it to your home," Bishop whirled the chicken lovingly, giving it a spruce and electric appearance of life, the wings spreading, the feathers ruffling. "Your mother would be delighted with this bird."

"My mother's in Davenport, Iowa," Enders said.

"You must have some relatives in the city." Bishop pushed it lovingly under his nose, spreading the limp wings for inspection. "They'll receive you with open arms with this chicken. This is a guaranteed Plymouth Rock chicken. Birds like this are exhibited in poultry shows from coast to coast. Sixty cents, Mr. Enders," Bishop said winningly. "Can you go wrong for sixty cents?"

Enders shook his head. "I have no relatives in the city," he said. "Thanks a lot, but I can't use it."

Bishop looked at him coldly. He shrugged. "I could've sold this chicken five times already," he said, "but I was saving it for you because you looked so pale. You gained my sympathy." He shrugged again, and holding the Plymouth Rock by the neck, he went into his office.

"Well," said Enders loudly, looking squarely at Bertha Zelinka. "I guess I'll turn in for the night."

"Want some company, Baby?" Josephine asked, in her voice the first note of hope she had allowed to sound there all evening.

"No, thank you," Enders said, embarrassedly, glad that Miss Zelinka wasn't looking at him at the moment.

"You certainly are a great ladies' man," Josephine said, her voice rasping through the lobby. "Don't you know you'll go crazy, you go so long without a woman? You been here two weeks, you haven't had a woman all that time. They face that problem in Sing Sing, the convicts climb on the walls."

Enders looked uneasily at Miss Zelinka. He didn't want a girl who looked like Greta Garbo to hear him mixed up in that kind of a conversation. "Good night," he said, and walked past Miss Zelinka, down the hallway to his own room, which was on the ground floor, at the bottom of an airwell, three dollars a week. He looked back regretfully. Miss Zelinka's legs were visible, jutting out, like a promise of poetry and flowers, past the grime and gloom of the hallway. Sadly he opened the door and went into his room, took off his hat and coat and fell on the bed. He could hear Josephine talking, as though the walls, the vermin, the old and wailing plumbing, the very rats hurrying on their gloomy errands between the floors, had at last found a voice.

"The papers are full of boys like him," Josephine was saying. "Turning the gas on and stuffing their heads into the oven. What a night! What a stinking whore of a night! They'll find plenty of bodies in the river tomorrow morning."

"Josephine," Wysocki's voice floated down the hallway. "You ought to learn to talk with more cheerfulness. You're ruining your business, Josephine. The wholesale butchers from Tenth Avenue, the slaughterhouse workers, your whole regular clientele, they're all avoiding you. Should I tell you why?"

"Tell me why," Josephine said.

"Because you're gloomy!" Wysocki said. "Because you depress them with your talk. People like a woman to be cheerful. You can't expect to succeed in your line if you walk around like the last day of the world is beginning in two and three-quarter hours, Bulova watch time."

"The butchers from Tenth Avenue!" Josephine snarled. "Who wants them? I give them to you as a gift."

Enders lay on the bed, regretting that a proud and beautiful woman like Bertha Zelinka had to sit in one of the three chairs of the lobby of the Circus Hotel on a rainy night and listen to a conversation like that. He put on the light and picked up the book he was reading.

I was neither at the hot gates
Nor fought in the warm rain
Nor knee deep in the salt marsh, heaving a cutlass,
Bitten by flies, fought . . .

"What a night!" Josephine's voice scraped down the hallway. "The river will be stuffed with bodies in the morning."

Enders put down T. S. Eliot. It was hard to read T. S. Eliot in the Circus Hotel without a deep feeling of irony. Enders got up and looked around the doorpost, down the hall. The proud, poetic legs were still there, lean, muscular, beautifully shaped, aristocratic, stemming down into slim ankles and narrow feet. Enders leaned dreamily against the doorpost, regarding Miss Zelinka's legs. Music played from a well-known orchestra in a night club lit by orange lamps, where no dish cost less than a dollar seventy-five, even tomato juice, and he danced with Bertha Zelinka, both of them dressed beautifully, shiningly, and he made those deep, long eyes, charged with Northern melancholy, crinkle with laughter, and later grow sober and reflective as he talked swiftly of culture, of art, of poetry. " 'Nor fought in the warm rain,' in the phrase of T. S. Eliot, a favorite of mine, 'nor knee deep in the salt marsh . . .' "

He walked quickly down the hallway, looking neither to right nor left until he stopped at the desk. "Have there been any telephone calls for me today?" he asked Wysocki, carefully avoiding looking at Miss Zelinka.

"No," said Wysocki. "Not a thing."

Enders turned and stared full at Miss Zelinka, trying, with the deep intensity of his glance, to get her to look at him, smile at him . . .

"Heads like yours, my friend," Josephine said, "they find in ovens."

Miss Zelinka sat passionless, expressionless, heedless, looking at a point twenty-five feet over Wysocki's shoulder, patiently, but coolly, in the attitude of a woman who is expecting a Lincoln to drive up at any moment and a uniformed chauffeur to spring from it and lead her fastidiously to the heavy, upholstered door, rich with heavy hardware.

Enders walked slowly back to his room. He tried to read some more. "April is the cruellest month . . ." He thumbed through the book. "Here, said she, is your card, the drowned Phoenician Sailor . . ." Enders put the book down. He couldn't read tonight. He went to the door and looked out. The legs, silk and skin and firm muscle, were still there. Enders took a deep breath and walked back toward the desk.

"Look," said Josephine, "the shuttle's back."

"I forgot to ask." He looked straight at Wysocki. "Is there any mail for me?"

"No mail," said Wysocki.

"I'll tell you frankly, friend," Josephine said. "You should've stayed in Davenport, Iowa. That's my honest opinion. New York City will break you like a peanut shell."

"Nobody asked for your opinion," Wysocki said, noticing Enders peering uneasily at Miss Zelinka to see what impression Josephine's advice had made on her. "He's a nice boy, he's educated, he's going to go a long way. Leave him alone."

"I'm only giving him my honest opinion," Josephine said. "I've been in New York a dozen years. I see them begin and I see them wind up in the river."

"Will you, for Christ's sake, stop talking about the river?" Wysocki slammed his hand on the desk.

Gratefully, Enders noticed that Miss Zelinka was listening to the conversation, that her head tilted just a little, a shade went across her disdainful, beautiful eyes.

"I come from Fall River," Josephine said. "I should've stayed there. At least when you're dead in Fall River they bury you. Here they leave you walk around until your friends notice it. Why did I ever leave Fall River? I was attracted by the glamor of the Great White Way." She waved her red and white umbrella ironically, in salute to the city.

Enders noticed that a hint, a twitch of a smile, played at the corner of Miss Zelinka's mouth. He was glad that she'd heard Wysocki say he was educated, he was going to go a long way.

"If you'd like," he heard his voice boom out suddenly in the direction of Miss Zelinka, "if you'd like, if you're waiting for someone, you can wait in my room. It's not so noisy there."

"No, thank you," Miss Zelinka said, speaking curiously, her lips together, not showing her teeth. Her voice, behind the closed, beautiful lips, was deep and hoarse and moving, and Enders felt it grip at his throat like a cool, firm hand. He turned to Wysocki, determined now that he was not going back to his room.

"I was curious," he said. "Where did Bishop get that chicken he wants to sell me?"

Wysocki looked behind him carefully. "Don't buy those chickens, Enders," he said in a low voice. "I advise you as a good friend. Bishop picks them up on Tenth Avenue, alongside the railroad tracks."

"What're they doing there?" Enders asked.

"The trains bring them in from the farms, from the country," Wysocki said. "The ones that died on the trip for one reason or another, the trainmen throw them off the cars and they're piled up alongside the tracks and Bishop picks out the ones that look as though they died most peaceful and he tries to sell them." Wysocki slid back to the office door, listened guiltily for a moment for Bishop, like a spy in the movies. "I advise you not to buy them. They're not the most nourishing articles of food in the world."

Enders smiled. "Bishop ought to be in Wall Street," he said. "With talent like that."

Miss Zelinka laughed. Feeling twice as tall as he had felt a moment before, Enders noticed that Miss Zelinka was laughing, quietly, and without opening her mouth, but true laughter. He laughed with her and their eyes met in friendly, understanding amusement.

"May I buy you a cup of coffee?" hurled out of his throat, at Miss Zelinka's head, like a hand grenade.

The light of thought, consideration, appeared in the large gray eyes, while Enders waited. Then Miss Zelinka smiled. "All right," she said. She stood up, five feet six inches tall, graceful as a duchess.

"I'll be right back," Enders said, quickly. "Just have to get my coat."

He fled lightly down the hall toward his room.

"That's what keeps me poor," Josephine said. "Girls like that. What a night, what a dirty whore of a night!"

"I'm a dancer," Bertha Zelinka was saying two hours later, her coat off, in Enders' room, as she drank the whisky straight in one of the two water tumblers the room boasted. "Specialty dancing." She put the whisky down, suddenly sank beautifully to the floor in a split. "I'm as supple as a cat."

"I see," Enders said, his eyes furious with admiration for Miss Zelinka, full-breasted, flat-bellied, steel-thighed, supple as a cat, spread magnificently on the dirty carpet. It was more pleasant to look at her body, now that he had seen her eating, mouth opened to reveal the poor, poverty-stricken, ruined teeth jagged and sorrowful in her mouth. "That looks very hard to do."

"My name's been in lights," Miss Zelinka said, from the floor. "Please pass the whisky. From one end of the country to another. I've stopped show after show. I've got an uncanny sense of timing." She stood up, after taking another draught of her whisky, closing her eyes with a kind of harsh rapture as the Four Roses went down past the miserable teeth, down inside the powerful, long white throat. "I'm an actress, too, you know, Mr. Enders."

"I'm an actor," Enders said shyly, feeling the whisky beat in his blood, keeping his eyes fiercely and wonderingly on Miss Zelinka. "That's why I'm in New York. I'm an actor."

"You ought to be a good actor," Miss Zelinka said. "You got the face for it. It's refined." She poured herself another drink, watching the amber liquor pour into her glass with a brooding, intense expression on her face. "I had my name in lights from coast to coast. Don't you believe it?"

"I believe it," Enders said sincerely, noting that half the bottle was already gone.

"That's why I'm here now," she said. She walked beautifully around the small, flaky-walled room, her hands running sorrowfully over the warped bureau, the painted bedstead. "That's why I'm here now." Her voice was faraway and echoing, hoarse with whisky and regret. "I'm very much in demand, you know. I've stopped shows for ten minutes at a time. They wouldn't let me get off the stage. Musicals that cost one hundred and fifty thousand to ring the curtain up. That's why I'm here now," she said mysteriously, and drained her glass. She threw herself on the bed next to Enders, stared moodily through almost closed eyes, at the stained and beaten ceiling. "The Shuberts're putting on a musical. They want me for it. Rehearsals are on Fifty-second Street, so I thought I'd move close by for the time being." She sat up, silently reached for the bottle, poured with the fixed expression, brooding and infatuate, which she reserved for the distillers' product. Enders, too full for words, sitting on the same bed with a woman who looked like Greta Garbo, who had stopped musical shows with specialty dancing from coast to coast, who got drunk with the assured yet ferocious grace of a young society matron, watched her every move, with hope, admiration, growing passion.

"You might ask," Miss Zelinka said, "what is a person like myself doing in a rat-hole like this." She waited, but Enders merely gulped silently at his whisky. She chuckled and patted his hand. "You're a nice boy. Iowa, you said? You come from Iowa?"

"Iowa."

"Corn," Miss Zelinka said. "That's what they grow in Iowa." She nodded, having placed Iowa and Enders firmly in her mind. "I passed through Iowa on my way to Hollywood." Half the whisky in her glass disappeared.

"Have you acted in pictures?" Enders asked, impressed, sitting on the same bed with a woman who had been in Hollywood.

Miss Zelinka laughed moodily. "Hollywood!" She finished her drink. "Don't look for my footprints in front of Grauman's Chinese." She reached fluently for the bottle.

"It seems to me," Enders said seriously, breathing deeply because Miss Zelinka was leaning across him for the moment. "It seems to me you'd do very well. You're beautiful and you've got a wonderful voice."

Miss Zelinka laughed again. "Look at me," she said.

Enders looked at her.

"Do I remind you of anybody?" Miss Zelinka asked.

Enders nodded.

Miss Zelinka drank moodily. "I look like Greta Garbo," she said. "Nobody could deny that. I'm not being vain when I tell you when I photograph you couldn't tell me apart from the Swede." She sipped her whisky, ran it lovingly around in her mouth, swallowed slowly. "A woman who looks like Greta Garbo in Hollywood is like the fifth leg on a race horse. Do you understand what I mean?"

Enders nodded sympathetically.

"It's my private curse," Miss Zelinka said, tears looming in her eyes like mist over the ocean. She jumped up, shaking her head, walked lightly and dramatically around the room. "I have no complaints," she said. "I've done very well. I live in a two-room suite on the twentieth floor of a hotel on Seventy-fifth Street. Overlooking the park. All my trunks and bags are up there. I just took a few things with me, until the rehearsals are over. Seventy-fifth Street, on the East Side, is too far away; when you're rehearsing a musical comedy, you've got to be on tap twenty-four hours a day for the Shuberts. A very luxurious two-room suite in the Hotel Chalmers. It's very exclusive, but it's too far from Fifty-second Street." She poured some more whisky for herself, and Enders noticed that the bottle was almost empty. "Oh, yes," she said, crooning to the glass in her hand, "I've done very well. I've danced all over the country. In the most exclusive nightspots, I was the featured entertainment. I'm very greatly in demand." She sat down, close to him, her body moving gently and rhythmically as she spoke. "Seattle, Chicago, Los Angeles, Detroit." She gulped her whisky and her eyes clouded with a final, deep, vague mist and her voice suddenly got very throaty and hoarse. "Miami, Florida." She sat absolutely still and the cloud dissolved into tears and the tears coursed slowly down her face.

"What's the matter?" Enders asked anxiously. "Did I do something?"

Miss Zelinka threw the empty tumbler against the opposite wall. It broke heavily and sullenly, scattered over the carpet. She threw herself back on the bed, wept. "Miami, Florida," she sobbed. "Miami, Florida . . ."

Enders patted her shoulder consolingly.

"I danced in The Golden Horn in Miami, Florida," she cried. "It was a Turkish night club. Very exclusive."

"Why're you crying, darling?" Enders asked, feeling sorry for her, but elated, too, because he had said "darling."

"Every time I think of Miami, Florida," Miss Zelinka said, "I cry."

"Can I do anything to help?" Enders held her hand softly.

"It was January, 1936." Miss Zelinka's voice throbbed with old, hopeless, broken tragedy, forlorn as the story of a siege of a lost and ruined village. "I was dressed in Turkish garments: a brassiere, and veils around my legs and nothing around the middle. At the end of the dance I had to do a back-bend. I leaned back and touched the floor with my hands, with my hair falling down to the floor. There was a bald man. There was a convention of the Metal-Trades Union in Miami, Florida. He had on a badge. The whole night club was full of them." The tears and the anguish pulled at her face. "I'll remember that bald son of a bitch until the day I die. There was no music at that part of the dance. Drums and tambourines. He leaned over and put an olive in my navel and sprinkled it with salt." Miss Zelinka rolled suddenly over on her face and, clutching the bedspread, her shoulders heaving, burrowed into the grayish cotton. "It was a cartoon. He saw it in a cartoon in a magazine. It's funny in a magazine, but wait until it happens to you! The humiliation," she wept. "Every time I think of the humiliation I want to die. Miami, Florida."

Enders watched the bedspread stain with tears, mascara and rouge. With genuine sympathy, he put his arm around her. "I want to be treated with respect," Miss Zelinka wailed. "I was brought up in a good family, why shouldn't I be treated with respect? That fat, bald man, with the badge from the Metal-Trades Union Convention. He leaned over and put the olive in my navel like an egg in an egg cup and sprinkled salt like he was starting breakfast and everybody laughed and laughed, including the orchestra . . ." Her voice went wailing up the airwell, lost, despairing, full of an ancient and irreparable sorrow.

She sat up and threw her arms around Enders, digging her grief-torn head into his shoulder, clutching him with strong hands, both of them rocking back and forth like Jews praying, on the enameled bed that squeaked and wailed in the little room.

"Hold me tight," she wept, "hold me tight. I haven't got a two-room suite on East Seventy-fifth Street. I got no trunks in the Hotel Chalmers, hold me tight." Her hands dug into him and her tears and rouge and mascara stained his coat. "The Shuberts aren't giving me a job. Why do I lie, why do I always lie?" She lifted her head, kissed his throat fiercely. He shook at the soft, violent pressure, at the wetness of her lips and the tragic and exhilarating trickle of her tears under his chin, knowing that he was going to have this woman, this Bertha Zelinka. Lonely, far from home, on a rainy night, the city was pulling him in, making a place in its wild and ludicrous life for him. As he kissed her, this woman who looked like Greta Garbo, the century's dream of passion and tragedy and beauty, this woman whom he had met in a rat-tenanted lobby off Columbus Circle, among whores thinking of death and a Pole in an orange tie checking in each night's transients, age and sin, at reasonable rates, Enders felt suddenly at home, accounted for. The city had produced for him a great beauty, supple as a cat, full of lies and whisky and ancient shadowy victories, a woman with magnificent proud legs and deep stormy eyes who wept bitterly behind the frail, warped door because once, in 1936, a bald man from a Metal-Trades Union had put an olive in her navel. Enders held Bertha Zelinka's head in his two hands, looked intently at the bony, drunken, beautiful, tear-stained face. Bertha Zelinka peered longingly and sadly at him through half-closed classic lids, her mouth hanging softly open in passion and promise, her poor jagged teeth showing behind the long, heart-breaking lips. He kissed her, feeling deep within him, that in its own way, on this rainy night, the city had put out its hand in greeting, had called, in its own voice, wry and ironic, "Welcome, Citizen."

Gratefully, near tears, hating himself, his hands shaking exultantly, Enders bent to his knees and took the scraped, year-worn shoes, swollen with the streets' rain, from the long and handsome feet of Bertha Zelinka.

1942

# MARY McCARTHY

---

*Mary McCarthy (1912–89) was a central figure in New York intellectual life from the 1940's on. Wickedly acerbic at times, she brought a satiric yet psychologically nuanced approach to the institution of the New York dinner party in her story "The Genial Host." In later years she admitted that the Stalinist lady at the dinner party was modeled on playwright Lillian Hellman, with whom McCarthy was later to engage in a very public quarrel over the veracity of Hellman's memoirs.*

## THE GENIAL HOST

WHEN HE TELEPHONED to ask you to do something he never said baldly, "Can you come to dinner a week from Thursday?" First he let you know who else was going to be there: the Slaters, perhaps, and the Berolzheimers, and John Peterson, the critic. And he could not leave this guest-list to speak for itself, but would annotate it at once with some short character sketches. "Peterson's a queer fellow," he would say. "Of course, he's moody and right now he's too much interested in politics for his own good, but I hope he'll get back soon to his book on Montaigne. That's his real work, and I wish you'd tell him that. You may not like him, of course, but underneath it all John is a marvelous person." He was deferential, ingratiating, concerned for your pleasure, like a waiter with a tray of French pastry in his hand. This one had custard in it and that one was mocha; the chocolate-covered one had whipped cream, and the little one on the side was just a macaroon. With Pflaumen you were always perfectly safe—you never had to order blind.

In a way, it was a kindness he did you, putting it like that. Other acquaintances made the opposite error, calling up to demand, "Are you free Thursday?" before disclosing whether they wanted you to picket a movie house, attend a lecture at the New School, buy tickets for a party for Spain, or go and dance at a new night club. Nevertheless, there was something too explicit about Pflaumen's invitations that made you set down the telephone with a feeling of distaste, made you dress hurriedly, though carefully, for his parties, as if you were going to keep some shameful assignation, made you, stepping out of your door in the new clothes you had bought, look furtively up and down the street before starting for the subway. Pflaumen had taken the risks out of social life, that was the trouble; and you felt that it was wrong to enjoy an evening without having paid for it with some touch of uncertainty, some tiny fear of being bored or out of place. Moreover, behind those bland and humble telephone calls, there was an unpleasant assumption about your character. Plainly Pflaumen must believe that you went out at night not because you liked your friends and wanted to be with them, but because you were anxious to meet new people, celebrities, to enlarge your own rather tacky social circle. No doubt this was at least half true, since with your real friends you seemed to prefer those whose spheres of interest were larger rather than smaller than your own—or at any rate to see more of them, if you could—but in those cases you were able to be sure that you *liked them for themselves.* With Pflaumen, unfortunately, there was never any question of that. Yet every time you accepted one of his invitations you entered into a conspiracy with him to hide the fact that he was a foolish, dull man whom nobody had much use for. And though some of his friends— the rich ones, perhaps—could feel all right about sitting at his table (after all, *they* were doing *him* a favor), you poor ones knew that he had bought your complaisance with his wines and rich food and prominent acquaintances, and you half-hated him before your finger touched his doorbell.

Standing there in the apartment-house corridor, you listened for voices that would mean that other guests had arrived and you would not be alone with him and the unmentionable secret. If you heard nothing, you hesitated, considered hurrying back downstairs and walking round the block till someone else should get there; but perhaps *he* had heard the elevator stop, heard your heels click on the stone floor, and was even now on the other side of the door silently waiting to admit you. You rang, and by the length of time it took him to answer, you knew that he had been in his bedroom after all. He

came to the door in a maroon-colored smoking jacket, evening
trousers, and black patent-leather shoes; he was newly shaved and
scrubbed and powdered, and there was a general odor of Mennen's
about him. His whole stocky, carefully exercised body was full of energy: well-directed arrows of delight and welcome shot at you out of
his black eyes, and his mouth curved downwards in a strenuous,
sickle-shaped smile that gave his face an expression of cruelty.

How ill-suited he was, you thought, to his role of *élégant*! What a
tireless struggle he must wage against his own physical nature!
Looking at him, so black and broad and hairy, you saw that his well-
kept person must appear to him like a settler's plot triumphantly defended against the invading wilderness. No wonder he took such
pride in the fit of his coat, the shine of his nails, the whiteness of his
sharp, jagged teeth. You saw the lines his body ought to have followed; he had the regular merchant's build; though he was not yet
thirty-five, you looked for the crease in the waistcoat, but it was always just absent. Whenever you really noticed Pflaumen, you became aware of an additional person, a comfortable, cigar-smoking,
sentimental family man, a kind of ancestral type on which the man-
about-town had been superimposed, so that his finished personality
came out as a sort of double exposure that was very disconcerting. If
you were in a sympathetic mood, you might think what a pity it was
he had not given in to his real self, had not married some nice girl
and had some children, and reproduced in modern terms that atmosphere of bay rum, whisky, spilled ashes, poker chips, potted
plants, kindness, and solid comfort that must have been his father's
personal climate. How nice he could have been under those circumstances! But if you looked at him hard again, you realized that something else was being held in check, something that did not fit at all
with this picture of easygoing German-Jewish family life—something primitive and hungry and excessively endowed with animal vitality. Though it was true that his figure had a mercantile cast to it,
in other ways he did not look like a German Jew, but like a member
of some early barbarous tribe, a Scythian on a Greek vase. In his
habits he was soft and self-indulgent; yet you felt there was a furnace
of energy burning in him, and you drew back from the blast. It was

this energy that had made it possible for him to discipline his body and his manners into patterns so unnatural to him; and, ironically, it was at the same time this energy that undid him as a society man by making him over-demonstrative, over-polite, over-genial, like a comedian who produces an effect of fatigue in his audience by working too hard at putting his gags across.

He held out his arms to help you with your coat, and what might have been an ordinary service became a tableau of politeness. Your hands shook, missing the buttons, for you felt that the coat was getting too much of the limelight. It would have been kinder to whisk the shabby thing inconspicuously into a closet. If you did not yet know him well, you did not realize that he loved you for that patched fur. It signified that you were the *real thing*, the poet in a garret, and it also opened up for him charming vistas of What He Could Do For You. He led you into his bedroom, where a new novel by one of his friends and a fine edition or two lay open on a table. A lamp with a pale-amber shade (better for the eyes) was burning beside them, and the cushion in the easy chair by the table was slightly mussed. An impression of leisure and the enjoyment of fine things was readily engendered, though you knew that he could not have been back from his office for more than an hour, and that he must have bathed, shaved, dressed, and arranged the final details during that time. Yet he was not a hypocrite, so undoubtedly he had been reading. Five minutes with a book was as good as an hour to him anyway, for he took literature like wine-tasting: you can get all the flavor in the first sip; further indulgence might only blunt your palate. The room was furnished in a half-monastic style; the bed was narrow, with a monkscloth cover. On the walls were pictures by Kunyoshi and Reginald Marsh, some George Grosz water colors and the reproduction of a detail from a mural by Rivera. You sat down behind his desk, a good piece, a little too heavy for the room, in black walnut; it had a great many fancy paper-weights on it, and a large marble cigarette-lighter, gifts, obviously, from clients in the patent law business. He got out the cocktail shaker, and said, "Let's try it before the others come."

He was disappointed, always, if you pronounced it perfect. He wanted to tinker with it a little, add a dash of Cointreau or Curaçao at your suggestion. "You're absolutely right," he would agree at once. "I knew it needed something," and, picking up the shaker, he would hurry out to the bar he had installed in what had once been a linen closet. When he came back the drink would taste exactly the same to you, but Pflaumen's satisfaction in it would be somehow deepened. The process was familiar to you. You had gone through it with other people, at dress rehearsals, at fittings with a tailor or a dressmaker, in a painter's studio, till you had become expert at discovering and pointing out some trifling flaw that in no way invalidated the whole, a prop that was out of place, a coat that wrinkled imperceptibly across the shoulders, sleeves that were a quarter of an inch too short on a dress, a foreground that seemed a little crowded. Once you had made your criticism, everybody would be very happy. It was a form of exorcism: some minor or totally imaginary error is noted and corrected, symbolically, as it were, with the idea that all real and major imperfections have thereby been dealt with—as if by casting out some impudent small devil you had routed Beelzebub himself. Perhaps, also, there was a hope of dispersing responsibility; that cocktail was not Pflaumen's any longer, but yours and his together, as it would never have been if you had merely given it your approval. By arriving early, you had become his hostess, and, all at once, you were sure that Pflaumen had intended this to happen.

Yet this conviction did not disturb you. On the contrary, you felt slightly uplifted, like one of those "good" bums who voluntarily chops half a cord of wood for the lady of the house to square her for the meal she has just put in front of him. Pflaumen rarely gave you a chance to repay his benevolence, so that generally you were uncomfortable with him, dangerously over-stored, explosive, a living battery of undischarged obligations. There were, for example, those letters of introduction, a great pile of them now, lying unopened, gathering dust on your desk. If only you had not drunk too much that one night when you had first known Pflaumen! If you had not let him see that you were frightened because you had no job and almost no money left! Above all, if you had not cried about it! The next morning he had sent you a sheaf of letters of introduction, and you had been touched and a little amused by the lack of judgment behind them. But you had presented them all. You had interviewed a brassière manufacturer in Ozone Park, a crank lawyer downtown who wanted someone to ghostwrite a book on the sunspot theory of economics, an advertising executive who needed some soap slogans, a hotel man, a brilliantine manufacturer. When it was over you were relieved, for somehow you had never felt so out of step, so unwanted, so drably unemployed, as in these offices Pflaumen had sent you to.

But the next week there was a new batch of letters, some of them signed by people you had never heard of, friends of Pflaumen's whom he had got to recommend you for a job; and while you were delivering these, still more letters came in, taking you on errands that grew more and more bizarre. There was a loft in the garment district with AMERICAN RESEARCH printed on the door and inside three large rooms that contained nothing but a filing cabinet and a little man with a cigar—you had never found out what his research consisted of. Then there was a bald man on the seventeenth floor of the St. Moritz hotel who wanted a girl to go round the world with him—he, too, was writing a book, on occultism.

After that, you had presented no more letters, but they kept coming in as relentlessly as bills, and there was Pflaumen's voice on the telephone, patient at first, then hurt and puzzled, but always mysteriously complacent. Had you gone to see the man in the Squibb Building? No? Really, it was impossible to understand you. He had been under the impression that you *wanted* a job. You made explanations at first, halting and shamefaced (after all, you supposed, he was trying to help you). Finally, you had quarreled with him; but your rudeness had only added to your debt, and your air of bravado and Bohemian defiance had quickened his admiration. (Such indifference to the question of survival was impractical, of course, but somehow, he knew, in awfully good taste.) You were for him, you discovered, the perfect object of charity, poor but not bedraggled, independent, stubborn, frivolous, thankless, and proud. He could pity you, deplore you, denounce you, display you, be kind to you, be hurt by you, forgive you. He could, in fact, run through his whole stock of feelings with you. A more grateful beneficiary would have given him no exercise for his masochistic emotions; a more willing one would have left his sadism unsatisfied. He was not going to let you go if he could help it. You stood to him in the relation of Man to God, embraced in an eternal neurotic mystery compounded out of His infinite goodness and your guilt.

When the others came, you all went into the living room, which was done in honey beige. There were pieces of sculpture by Archipenko and Harold Cash, and the head of a beautiful Egyptian queen, Neferteete. Everybody praised the cocktail, and Pflaumen's old friends, of whom there were always a pair, complimented him on a new acquisition—a painting, a vase, a lamp—he had made. All Pflaumen's friends lived on terms of intimacy with his possessions; if someone did not notice a new object, it was as mortifying a slip as a husband's failure to notice his wife's new hat. Indeed, Pflaumen, opening the door of his apartment, often wore that look of owlish mystery that says, "What's new about me?" and the guests, being warned by it, examined the premises sharply till they found the single ornament that was responsible for the host's elation. This acquisitiveness of Pflaumen's was, you thought, just another way of making it easy for his friends to appear to like him. He was giving them something they could honestly admire, and if the objects could be viewed as extensions of Pflaumen's personality, why, then, it followed that his friends admired Pflaumen. It was on such questionable but never questioned syllogisms that his social life was built.

By the time the maid announced dinner and the party moved down to a refectory table set in the foyer, Pflaumen's eyes were damp with happiness. Everything was going well. Voices had risen in lively controversy over the new play, the new strike, the new Moscow trials, the new abstract show at the Modern Museum. Nobody was incoherent; nobody made speeches; nobody lost his temper. Sentences were short, and points in the argument clicked like bright billiard balls. Everyone felt witty. Pflaumen made a great bustle of seating the guests, and finally plumped himself down at the head of the table and beamed at them all as if to say, "Isn't this cozy?"

The steak came in, with an orange and sherry sauce, and everyone exclaimed over it. Pflaumen himself kept casting joyous sheep's eyes up at his maid, commending her for the success of "their" dish. (He had put into circulation a dozen anecdotes designed to prove that this Scotchwoman who worked for him, like the maids of all really smart people, was a Character, full of sweet crotchets, *bons mots*, and rough devotion. Nobody, however, had seen the slightest sign of this, and tonight, as usual, she paid no attention to her employer, but continued to make her rounds with a stony face.) Peas were served, new ones cooked in the French style in their pods, and then the wine was brought in, a Château Latour Rothschild.

This was Pflaumen's apogee. Having tapped on his glass to get the table's attention, he read aloud the Château and the year, and then uncorked the bottle himself, standing up to do it. Somebody at the end of the table, a man with a hearty voice, called, "Look out, there, George Arliss may come out of that bottle!" Pflaumen, pouring a little into his own glass, laughed with the others, but he was not quite pleased—it was the sort of joke he was capable of making himself. "Give us a speech, about the wine," said one of the ladies obligingly. "The way they do at gourmet dinners." "Why," said Pflaumen, still standing at the head of the table with the bottle in his hand, "it's not one of the great Bordeaux. . . ." "I prefer the word 'claret,' " someone else put in, "it's so full of English history." "You mean," retorted Pflaumen, "English history is so full of *it*." He waited for the laugh, which came reluctantly—it was said that Pflaumen had "a pretty wit," but there was something chilling about it; he had never learned how to throw a line away. "Anyway," he went on, with a little laugh, so that no one should think he took all this too seriously, "it's a nice brisk wine, on the astringent side. I thought it would do well with the steak." "Perfect!" exclaimed a lady, though the glasses were still empty. "Of course I think it's silly," continued Pflaumen, starting to go round the table with the bottle, "to be too pedantic about what you drink with what. I'll take a good Burgundy with a broiler and a Rhine wine with a kidney chop any time I can get it." Murmurs of approval greeted this unconventional statement, and Pflaumen passed on down the line, carefully decanting the wine into each glass.

Across the table from you someone refused, and all the rest raised their heads with an identical look of worry. It was the young Russian Jew, the instructor in law at Columbia, who wore a rather quizzical, sardonic expression on a pure Italianate face. His Marxist study of jurisprudence had created a stir. Still, perhaps Fleischer had made a mistake in him. Was it possible that he was not an eccentric but a crank? This act of abstention was a challenge to everyone at the table, an insult to the host. For almost a full minute nobody spoke, but muscles tightened with hostility. In different circumstances the young man might have been lynched.

"You don't *drink?*" said a woman at last in a loud, bewildered voice.

"I drank a cocktail," he admitted. "It went to my head. If I took any more I might make a fool of myself." He twisted his head and looked up at Pflaumen with a disarming boyish grin. "You'll have to give me a course in the art of drinking. That's one subject that was left out of my proletarian education." He pronounced the last words mildly, with a sort of droll self-mockery that deprecated, ever so faintly, his innocence, his poor Russian parents, his studiousness, the Talmudic simplicity of his life. There was a burst of relieved laughter, and after that everyone liked him. Thank God, was the general feeling, he had turned out not to be one of those Marxist prigs!

Once the wine was poured, Pflaumen took very little part in the conversation. He leaned back in his chair with the air of a satisfied impresario, embracing all his guests in a smile of the most intense and proprietary affection. Now and then, this look of commendation would rest particularly on you; whenever this happened, it was as if, in his delight, he had reached over and squeezed you. From time to time, his cup of bliss would appear to run over, and the smile would break into a short high giggle. When the spasm was over, he would take out his handkerchief and carefully wipe his eyes, and the old-fashioned masculinity of this gesture made a strange contrast with the schoolgirlish sound he had just produced. Sitting at his left hand, you looked down at your plate until this display was finished. There was something androgynous about Pflaumen, something not pansy, but psychically hermaphroditic that was always disconcerting you. It was as if the male and female strains in his personality had never blended, but were engaged in some perennial household spat that you were obliged to eavesdrop on. For, when you came to think of it, the Jewish paterfamilias was not the only figure that kept hovering behind your host's well-padded shoulder; there was also a young girl, newly married to a man already coarse and comfortable, a young girl playing house all by herself in a fine establishment full of wedding presents that both astonished and saddened her. Most Jewish men were more feminine than Gentile men of similar social background. You had noticed this and had supposed, vaguely, that it was the mark matriarchy had left on them, but looking at Pflaumen you saw the whole process dramatically. The matriarch had begun by being married off to a husband who was prosperous and settled and older than herself, and her sons she had created in her own image, forlorn little bridegrooms to a middle-aged bride.

In most of the men, the masculine influence had, in the end, overridden or absorbed the feminine, and you saw only vestigial traces of the mother. There might be a tendency to hypochondria, a readiness to take offense, personal vanity, love of comfort, love of being waited on and made much of; and, on the other hand, there would be unusual intuitive powers, sympathy, loyalty, tenderness, domestic graces and kindnesses unknown to the Gentile. But with Pflaumen it was not a question of the survival of a few traits. Two complete personalities had been preserved in him, as in a glacier. Half of him was a successful businessman and half of him was playing house. These dinners of his were like children's tea parties, and in this lay their strength and their weakness. They had the sort of perfection that can only be achieved in miniature. The groaning board was not in Pflaumen's style at all: one exquisite dish, one vegetable, a salad and some cheese were what you got, rarely a soup, never a dessert. You thought of your little electric stove, your cambric tea or hot chocolate and your *petits fours* from the caterer. But more important than the perfection of the appointments was the illusion of a microcosm Pflaumen was able to create, the sense of a little world that was exactly the same as the big world, though it had none of the pain or care.

Each of Pflaumen's guests had been selected, as it were, for his allegorical possibilities, and every dinner was presented as a morality play in which art and science, wealth and poverty, business and literature, sex and scholarship, vice and virtue, Judaism and Christianity, Stalinism and Trotskyism, all the antipodes of life, were personified and yet abstract. Tonight there was John Peterson, who stood for criticism and also for official Communism. There was Jim Berolzheimer, a bright young man in one of the great banking houses, who represented capitalism, and his wife who painted pictures and was going to have a baby, and was therefore both art and motherhood. There was Henry Slater, the publisher, very flirtatious, with a shock of prematurely white hair, who was sex, and his wife, an ash-blond woman with a straight bang, who kept a stable full of horses and had no opinions and was sport. There was a woman psychoanalyst who got herself up in a Medici gown and used a cigarette holder. There was a pretty English girl named Leslie who worked on *Time*. There was the young Jew, Martin Erdman, who did not drink. There was Pflaumen himself, who stood for trade marks and good living, and you, who stood for literature and the Fourth International. After dinner there might be others: a biologist and his wife, a man who was high up in the Newspaper Guild, a matronly young woman who wore her hair in a coronet around her head and was active in the League of Women Shoppers, a Wall Street lawyer, a wine dealer, a statistician.

And here was the striking effect produced by Pflaumen's dinners: you truly felt yourself turning into an abstraction of your beliefs and your circumstances. Contradictions you had known in yourself melted away; challenged by its opposite, your personality hardened into something unequivocal and defiant—your banners were flying. All the guests felt this. If you asserted your Trotskyism, your poverty, your sexual freedom, the expectant mother radiated her pregnancy, the banker basked in his reactionary convictions, and John Peterson forgot about Montaigne and grew pale as an El Greco saint in his defense of Spanish democracy. Everybody, for the moment, knew exactly who he was. Pflaumen had given you all your identity cards, just as a mother will assign personalities to each of her brood of children: Jack is hard-working and steady, Billy is a flash-in-the-pan, never can finish anything he starts. Mary is dreamy, Helen is practical. While it lasted, the feeling was delightful; and at the dinner table everyone was heady with a peculiar, almost lawless excitement, like dancers at a costume ball.

It was only when you caught a glimpse of the author of your happiness, ensconced there, so considerate, so unobtrusive, at the head of his table, that your conviction wavered. To the others, too, he must have been a disturbing factor, for throughout the meal there was a tacit conspiracy to ignore the host, to push him out of the bright circle he had so painstakingly assembled. Once the dinner got under way, nobody accorded him more than a hasty glance. If he dropped a pun or a platitude into the conversation, it was just as if he had dropped a plate: there would be a moment of frozen silence, then the talk would go on as before.

Pflaumen did not appear to mind this; in fact, he seemed to accept it as natural. Here in this apartment, all the rules of ordinary politeness were suspended; and at first you were so caught up in your own gaiety that you hardly noticed this, and it seemed to you, too, perfectly natural that no one should speak to the host. But gradually, as in a dream, you became aware that the laws of the normal world were not operating here, that something was wrong, that nothing was what it seemed to be, that the church bell you were listening to was really the alarm clock. And, just as in a dream, the exhilaration continued for a little, but underneath it ran distrust and terror. You knew that it was not what it pretended to be, this microcosm of your host's, for if it were actually so fine and first-rate, Pflaumen himself would not be in it, even on sufferance. He was the clue in the detective story, the piece of thread, the thumbprint, the bullet in the wainscoting, that stares up at the bright detective and tells him that the well-arranged scene before him is the work, not of Nature, but of Man. You had only to look at him to know that the morality play was just a puppet show, that the other guests did not represent the things they were supposed to, that they could be fitted into this simulacrum of the larger world precisely because they were small, unreal figures, and with growing anxiety you asked yourself, "Why am I in it too?"

The conversation around you began to sound peculiarly flat. "Cultivate your own garden is what I told her," the publisher was saying. "She'll never understand politics." "She'd do better to cultivate her gardener—like Lady Chatterley," put in the English girl. Next to her, John Peterson went on talking through her joke. He was a little tight. "This back-stabbing that goes on here makes me want to vomit," he said. "I can't listen to it after what I've seen in Madrid. I've heard La Pasionara sing. What do these petty political squabbles mean to her? She's got a heart as big as the Spanish earth."

Suddenly you knew that you must cut yourself off from these people, must demonstrate conclusively that you did not belong here. You took a deep breath and leaned across the table toward John Peterson. "God damn you," you said in a very loud voice, such as you had once heard a priest use to denounce sinners from the pulpit, "God damn you, what about Andres Nin?" You felt your body begin to shake with stage fright and the blood rush up into your face and you heard the gasp go around the table, and you were gloriously happy because you had been rude and politically unfashionable, and really carried beyond yourself, an angel warrior with a flaming sword. Surely, there could be no doubt that you had put yourself beyond the pale. But when you looked up you saw that Pflaumen was beaming at you again, his eyes wetter than ever, as proud as if you had just spoken your first word to an audience of aunts.

"Meg is a violent Trotskyist," he said tenderly. "She thinks the rest of us are all GPU agents." The publisher, who had been concentrating on the English girl, looked across the table at you, sizing you up for the first time. "My God," he said, "you're certainly spirited about it." Martin Erdman was watching you, too. He clapped his hands twice in pantomime and gave you a long, ironic smile. You bent your head and blushed, and, though you were excited, your heart sank. You knew that you were not a violent Trotskyist, and Erdman must know it too. It was just that you were temperamentally attracted to unpopular causes: when you were young, it had been the South, the Dauphin, Bonnie Prince Charlie; later it was Debs and now Trotsky that you loved. You admired this romantic trait in yourself and you would confess humorously: "All I have to do is be *for* somebody and he loses." Now it came to you that perhaps this was just another way of showing off, of setting yourself apart from the run of people. Your eyes began to fill with tears of shame; you felt like Peter in the Garden, but yours was, you knew, the greater blasphemy: social pressure had made Peter deny the Master; it had made you affirm him—it was the difference between plain and fancy cowardice.

You held your eyes wide open to keep the tears from falling. The others, staring at you, must certainly think that your brimming eyes testified to the depth of your feeling for the murdered Nin. You tossed your head slightly and the tears began to settle.

"You *are*," you said, "a lot of you, GPU agents. The trouble is you're such idiots you don't even get paid for it."

It was a harsh joke, but it was a joke, and it was your peace offering. There was a cackle of laughter, and then everyone but John Peterson and Erdman was looking at you fondly, as if they were all much older than you were. Peterson cast you a malignant glance from his pale eyes, but he did not say anything. He was not too drunk to know that though the others actually agreed with him about Nin (or else did not care), temporarily, in some way, you had got them on your side. Erdman did not speak either; he nodded his head twice in the same tempo he had clapped his hands in, and kept smiling at you with that strange, mocking, affectionate expression.

You saw how profitable that exchange had been for you: it had earned you an enemy and, you thought, a lover. The first thing made you feel good, and the second saddened you. The next morning the phone would wake you and you would reach out and take it dreamily and it would be Erdman speaking very softly, asking you to have tea with him. You could see how it would all be. You would go to bed with him finally, but it would not last long, because you had both been compromised at this dinner party, and you had both understood this and understood each other. "Have you seen Pflaumen lately?" he would ask from time to time, and you would not be able to meet his eyes when you answered yes or no. He would not pursue the subject (you would never dare discuss Pflaumen together), but both of you would be silently asking the same question: what

weakness, what flimsiness of character, what opportunism or cynicism had put the other into Pflaumen's hands?

On the other hand, you would treat each other gently, with a
special tenderness, as though you were both wounded. For if, in one
way, your love would be full of doubt, in another, it would be over-
full of comprehension, lacking in mystery, like the grave dreary love
between brother and sister. You had recognized him in the scene
about the wine; he had recognized you in the scene about Nin. You
would have liked, both of you, to play a lone hand; but you had not
been strong enough for it. In each case, your war of independence
had been an inglorious *Putsch.* *("Excuse me, Officer, I was only fooling.")*

While the coffee and liqueurs were being served, new people
came in, and the party broke up into smaller units. The publisher
whispered in the English girl's ear; the banker talked Bermuda with
the publisher's wife. John Peterson, glassy-eyed, exhorted the
woman psychoanalyst—"But surely in his later years Freud played
into Hitler's hands." You stood beside Martin Erdman, not talking,
listening to the others, sharing an ironic smile between you. Pflaumen sat on a sofa beside the expectant mother; he was telling her
about a new product he had just had trademarked, while she went
through a pantomime of congratulation. Only she could afford to be
polite, for she had nothing to gain now from social intercourse, and,
being easily fatigued, nothing much to give. She was comfortable
with Pflaumen; he took her hand and she let him hold it; he was one
of her oldest friends.

What had happened to you with Erdman was happening with
others all over the room. Men were taking out address books or repeating phone numbers in low voices. There was a slight shuffle of
impatience; nothing more could be done here; it was time to go and
yet it was much too early.

People got up and shifted around, like people in a railroad station
when the stationmaster has come in to announce that the train will
be forty minutes late. New combinations were formed. The publisher was sitting on the arm of your chair now, asking if you would
like to write an opinion on a manuscript. You agreed, and for you,

too, now the party was over. You had got everything you came for—
a new lover and some work to do. Pflaumen came and sat at your
feet on the floor. "You were wonderful," he said, looking up at you
with that over-energetic expression of delight. You had an unaccountable impulse to kick him exactly where the paunch should have
been. "The Berolzheimers are crazy about you," he went on, ignoring
your angry look, putting it down to "temperament," an inestimable
commodity. "They want me to bring you to dinner next Wednesday."
You raised your eyebrows into circles of surprise; yet you had
known, ever since that scene at the table, that the Berolzheimers
would invite you. They were pleasant and they would have a nice
house with good food, and there would be new people there; it
would be interesting to see the world through a banker's eyes.

"Are you having fun?" asked Pflaumen, drawing his knees up and
hugging them with his arms in a real ecstasy of coziness.

"Yes," you said. "It's a very gay party."

"Erdman is interesting . . ." he began tentatively.

*You don't miss a trick*, you thought, but you answered him impas-
sively. "Is he?" you said. "I can't really tell. I haven't talked much to
him."

Pflaumen looked hurt.

"Of course," he said, "it's none of my business . . ."

"I don't know what you mean," you said, in a stubborn childish
voice.

The warm, twosey smile had died on his lips, but he revived it
with an effort.

"Personally," he went on, "I should have thought Peterson was
more in your line. I asked him specially because I thought he could
do you some good . . ."

He paused. The unresolved sentence hung coaxingly in the air,
begging your denial, your explanation, your attention. But cruelly
you ignored it, and leaned back in your chair, as if to catch the words
of the neighboring conversation. "Did you hear that?" you said finally.
"They are picketing *The Tsar to Lenin*."

Pflaumen glanced up at you, refusing the diversion. "Oh Meg," he
murmured reproachfully, "I thought we were such friends."

"Don't be tiresome!" you exclaimed. "Why don't you get me another highball?" You put your glass in his hand with a decisive gesture.

"All right," he acceded, scrambling to his feet. You thought you had won. At a single sharp word that hungry ego had scuttled back into the shell of function, where friendship and hospitality were identical and every highball was a loving cup. But he had taken only a few steps toward the bar, when he stopped, as if he had forgotten something, and turned back to you with an anxious face. "You're not drinking too much, are you?" he asked, in a true stage whisper. Several people, including Erdman, turned their heads.

At last, you thought, the bill had come in. The dinners, the letters of introduction, the bottle of perfume, the gardenias, the new Soviet film, the play, the ballet, the ice-skating at Rockefeller Plaza had all been invoiced, and a line drawn underneath, and the total computed. How recklessly you had accepted, like a young matron with a charge account ("Take two, madam; the bill will not go out till after the first of the year"). Now, when you looked at it, the total was staggering; it was more than you could pay.

You remembered suddenly all the warning signs. How deep Pflaumen always was in the confidence of his friends, how offended if two of them should meet in his absence! How careful people were to serve the whisky Pflaumen's client made—you recalled how a young husband had hurried out, unshaved, to the liquor store, so that the label on the bottle should be right when Pflaumen arrived for highballs; you remembered another husband pouring wine into a decanter so that Pflaumen should not know that it came from his client's competitor. And how fond Pflaumen was of talking about loyalty! "It's the only thing I expect of my friends," he would say, sententiously. Loyalty, you now perceived, meant that Pflaumen should never be left out of anything. He was like an *x* that you can never drop out of an equation no matter how many times you multiply it or add to it this side of infinity. All at once, you saw how he could be generous and humble and look predatory at the same time; the hawklike mouth was not deceptive, for he was a true bird of prey: he did not demand any of the trifles that serve as coin in the ordinary give-and-take of social intercourse; he wanted something bigger, he wanted part of your life.

For the first time, you understood why it was that this apartment of Pflaumen's affected you so unpleasantly, why you went there almost surreptitiously, not telling anyone, so that your closest friends were hardly aware that you knew Pflaumen. You saw that it was indeed a house of assignation, where business deals, friendships, love affairs were arranged, with Pflaumen, the promoter, taking his inevitable cut. When you had refused to tell Pflaumen about Erdman—though, so far, there was nothing really to tell—you had violated the code. You had tried to cheat him of his rightful share; you had been guilty of disloyalty. And he was going to crack down on you; he had, in fact, already begun.

When he came back from the bar with your glass in his hand, he was smiling, but the down-curved lips were strained and angry. You took the glass and set it down; Erdman in a cheap tweed coat was making his way toward you, ready to say good-bye. You smiled at him faintly, knowing that Pflaumen was watching you, and knowing, too, with a certain vindictive happiness, that of all the things about Erdman, Pflaumen was most envious of that baggy Kollege Kut coat with its raglan collar. You thought of your own poor coat, and you could see the two of them hanging side by side in Pflaumen's closet, like two pairs of shoes outside a hotel room in a naughty French movie, sentinels to a private, serious world that Pflaumen could never—even vicariously—invade.

The two men were shaking hands. "Come again," said Pflaumen, "and I'll get Farwell from the Yale Law School to meet you. And bring your wife," he added, in an emphatic voice. "You ought to meet her, Meg."

"Yes," you said thinly. "I didn't know Mr. Erdman was married."

"He tries to keep it dark," said Pflaumen, suddenly very jovial. He slapped Erdman on the back and began to propel him toward the door.

You went quietly into the bedroom and took your coat out of the closet. By the time Pflaumen returned from the elevator, you were ready to go.

"You're not leaving?" he said, looking alarmed. "If you wait till the others go, I'll drive you."

"Don't bother," you said. "I'm used to the subway."

"But what about the Berolzheimers?" he asked breathlessly, in a sort of panic. Clearly he had not intended that things should go quite so far. "Next Wednesday?"

You had forgotten about the Berolzheimers. Now you hesitated, weighing the invitation. Sooner or later you would break with him, you knew. But not yet, not while you were still so poor, so loverless, so lonely. "All right," you said, "you can pick me up at my place."

The time after the next, you promised yourself, you would surely refuse.

*THE COMPANY SHE KEEPS*, 1942

# ZORA NEALE HURSTON

*Zora Neale Hurston (1891–1960) was one of the major writers of the Harlem Renaissance. Raised in the small town of Eatonville, Florida, she trained in anthropology with Franz Boas and did groundbreaking research in African-American ethnography. Here she applies her talents as a folklorist (including an exceptional ear for dialect), her vivacity and humor as a prose stylist, and her perspective as a woman to an irreverent portrait of male street-corner society.*

## STORY IN HARLEM SLANG

WAIT TILL I light up my coal-pot and I'll tell you about this Zigaboo called Jelly. Well, all right now. He was a sealskin brown and papa-tree-top-tall. Skinny in the hips and solid built for speed. He was born with this rough-dried hair, but when he laid on the grease and pressed it down overnight with his stocking-cap, it looked just like that righteous moss, and had so many waves you got seasick from looking. Solid, man, solid!

His mama named him Marvel, but after a month on Lenox Avenue, he changed all that to Jelly. How come? Well, he put it in the street that when it came to filling that long-felt need, sugar-curing the ladies' feelings, he was in a class by himself and nobody knew his name, so he had to tell 'em. "It must be Jelly, 'cause jam don't shake." Therefore, his name was Jelly. That was what was on his sign. The stuff was there and it was mellow. Whenever he was challenged by a hard-head or a frail eel on the right of his title he would eye-ball the idol-breaker with a slice of ice and put on his ugly-laugh, made up of scorn and pity, and say: "Youse just dumb to the fact, baby. If you don't know what you talking 'bout, you better ask Granny Grunt. I wouldn't mislead you, baby. I don't need to—not with the help I got." Then he would give the pimp's* sign, and percolate on down the Avenue. You can't go behind a fact like that.

So this day he was airing out on the Avenue. It had to be late afternoon, or he would not have been out of bed. All you did by rolling out early was to stir your stomach up. That made you hunt for more dishes to dirty. The longer you slept, the less you had to eat. But you can't collar nods all day. No matter how long you stay in bed, and how quiet you keep, sooner or later that big gut is going to reach over and grab that little one and start to gnaw. That's confidential right from the Bible. You got to get out on the beat and collar yourself a hot.

So Jelly got into his zoot suit with the reet pleats and got out to skivver around and do himself some good. At 132nd Street, he spied one of his colleagues on the opposite sidewalk, standing in front of a café. Jelly figured that if he bull-skated just right, he might confidence Sweet Back out of a thousand on a plate. Maybe a shot of scrap-iron or a reefer. Therefore, Jelly took a quick backward look at his shoe soles to see how his leather was holding out. The way he figured it after the peep was that he had plenty to get across and maybe do a little more cruising besides. So he stanched out into the street and made the crossing.

"Hi there, Sweet Back!" he exploded cheerfully. "Gimme some skin!"

"Lay de skin on me, pal!" Sweet Back grabbed Jelly's outstretched hand and shook hard. "Ain't seen you since the last time, Jelly. What's cookin'?"

"Oh, just like de bear—I ain't nowhere. Like de bear's brother, I ain't no further. Like de bear's daughter—ain't got a quarter."

Right away, he wished he had not been so honest. Sweet Back gave him a top-superior, cut-eye look. Looked at Jelly just like a

---

*In Harlemese, *pimp* has a different meaning than its ordinary definition as a procurer for immoral purposes. The Harlem pimp is a man whose amatory talents are for sale to any woman who will support him, either with a free meal or on a common law basis; in this sense, he is actually a male prostitute.

showman looks at an ape. Just as far above Jelly as fried chicken is over branch water.

"Cold in hand, hunh?" He talked down to Jelly. "A red hot pimp like you *say* you is, ain't got no business in the barrel. Last night when I left you, you was beating up your gums and broadcasting about how hot you was. Just as hot as July-jam, you told me. What you doing cold in hand?"

"Aw, man, can't you take a joke? I was just beating up my gums when I said I was broke. How can I be broke when I got de best woman in Harlem? If I ask her for a dime, she'll give me a ten dollar bill; ask her for drink of likker, and she'll buy me a whiskey still. If I'm lying, I'm flying!"

"Gar, don't hang out dat dirty washing in my back yard! Didn't I see you last night with dat beat chick, scoffing a hot dog? Dat chick you had was beat to de heels. Boy, you ain't no good for what you live."

"If you ain't lying now, you flying. You ain't got de first thin. You ain't got nickel one."

Jelly threw back the long skirt of his coat and rammed his hand down into his pants pocket. "Put your money where your mouth is!" he challenged, as he mock-struggled to haul out a huge roll. "Back your crap with your money. I bet you five dollars!"

Sweet Back made the same gesture of hauling out nonexistent money.

"I been raised in the church. I don't bet, but I'll doubt you. Five rocks!"

"I thought so!" Jelly crowed, and hurriedly pulled his empty hand out of his pocket. "I knowed you'd back up when I drawed my roll on you."

"You ain't drawed no roll on me, Jelly. You ain't drawed nothing but your pocket. You better stop dat boogerbooing. Next time I'm liable to make you do it." There was a splinter of regret in his voice. If Jelly really had had some money, he might have staked him, Sweet Back, to a hot. Good Southern cornbread with a piano on a platter. Oh, well! The right broad would, or might, come along.

"Who boogerbooing?" Jelly snorted. "Jig, I don't have to. Talking about *me* with a beat chick scoffing a hot dog! You must of not seen me, 'cause last night I was riding round in a Yellow Cab, with a yellow gal, drinking yellow likker and spending yellow money. Tell 'em 'bout me, tell 'em!"

"Git out of my face, Jelly! Dat broad I seen you with wasn't no pe-ola. She was one of them coal-scuttle blondes with hair just as close to her head as ninety-nine is to a hundred. She look-ted like she had seventy-five pounds of clear bosom, guts in her feet, and she look-ted like six months in front and nine months behind. Buy you a whiskey still! Dat broad couldn't make the down payment on a pair of sox."

"Sweet Back, you fixing to talk out of place." Jelly stiffened.

"If you trying to jump salty, Jelly, that's your mammy."

"Don't play in de family, Sweet Back. I don't play de dozens. I done told you."

"Who playing de dozens? You trying to get your hips up on your shoulders 'cause I said you was with a beat broad. One of them lam blacks."

"Who? Me? Long as you been knowing me, Sweet Back, you ain't never seen me with nothing but pe-olas. I can get any frail eel I wants to. How come I'm up here in New York? You don't know, do you? Since youse dumb to the fact, I reckon I'll have to make you hep. I had to leave from down south 'cause Miss Anne used to worry me so bad to go with me. Who, me? Man, I don't deal in no coal. Know what I tell 'em? If they's white, they's right! If they's yellow, they's mellow! If they's brown, they can stick around. But if they come black, they better git way back! Tell 'em bout me!"

"Aw, man, you trying to show your grandma how to milk ducks. Best you can do is to confidence some kitchen-mechanic out of a dime or two. Me, I knocks de pad with them cack-broads up on Sugar Hill, and fills 'em full of melody. Man, I'm quick death and easy judgment. Youse just a home-boy, Jelly. Don't try to follow me."

"Me follow *you*! Man, I come on like the Gang Busters, and go off like The March of Time! If dat ain't so, God is gone to Jersey City and you know He wouldn't be messing 'round a place like that.

Know what my woman done? We hauled off and went to church last Sunday, and when they passed 'round the plate for the *penny* collection, I throwed in a dollar. De man looked at me real hard for dat. Dat made my woman mad, so she called him back and throwed in a twenty dollar bill! Told him to take dat and go! Dat's what he got for looking at me 'cause I throwed in a dollar."

"Jelly, de wind may blow and de door may slam; dat what you shooting ain't worth a damn!"

Jelly slammed his hand in his bosom as if to draw a gun. Sweet Back did the same.

"If you wants to fight, Sweet Back, the favor is in me."

"I was deep-thinking then, Jelly. It's a good thing I ain't short-tempered. 'T'aint nothing to you, nohow. You ain't hit me yet."

Both burst into a laugh and changed from fighting to lounging poses.

"Don't get too yaller on me, Jelly. You liable to get hurt some day."

"You over-sports your hand your ownself. Too blamed astorperious. I just don't pay you no mind. Lay de skin on me!"

They broke their handshake hurriedly, because both of them looked up the Avenue and saw the same thing. It was a girl and they both remembered that it was Wednesday afternoon. All of the domestics off for the afternoon with their pay in their pockets. Some of them bound to be hungry for love. That meant a dinner, a shot of scrap-iron, maybe room rent and a reefer or two. Both went into the pose and put on the look.

"Big stars falling!" Jelly said out loud when she was in hearing distance. "It must be just before day!"

"Yeah, man!" Sweet Back agreed. "Must be a recess in Heaven— pretty angel like that out on the ground."

The girl drew abreast of them, reeling and rocking her hips.

"I'd walk clear to Diddy-Wah-Diddy to get a chance to speak to a pretty lil' ground-angel like that," Jelly went on.

"Aw, man, you ain't willing to go very far. Me, I'd go slap to Ginny-Gall, where they eat cow-rump, skin and all."

The girl smiled, so Jelly set his hat and took the plunge.

"Baby," he crooned, "what's on de rail for de lizard?"

The girl halted and braced her hips with her hands. "A Zigaboo down in Georgy, where I come from, asked a woman that one time and the judge told him 'ninety days.'"

"Georgy!" Sweet Back pretended to be elated. "Where 'bouts in Georgy is you from? Delaware?"

"Delaware?" Jelly snorted. "My people! My people! Free schools and dumb jigs! Man, how you going to put Delaware in Georgy? You ought to know dat's in Maryland."

"Oh, don't try to make out youse no northerner, you! Youse from right down in 'Bam your ownself!" The girl turned on Jelly.

"Yeah, I'm *from* there and I aims to stay from there."

"One of them Russians, eh?" the girl retorted. "Rushed up here to get away from a job of work."

That kind of talk was not leading towards the dinner table.

"But baby!" Jelly gasped. "Dat shape you got on you! I bet the Coca Cola Company is paying you good money for the patent!"

The girl smiled with pleasure at this, so Sweet Back jumped in.

"I know youse somebody swell to know. Youse real people. You grins like a regular fellow." He gave her his most killing look and let it simmer in. "These dickty jigs round here tries to smile. S'pose you and me go inside the café here and grab a hot?"

"You got any money?" the girl asked, and stiffened like a ramrod. "Nobody ain't pimping on me. You dig me?"

"Aw, now, baby!"

"I seen you two mullet-heads before. I was uptown when Joe Brown had you all in the go-long last night. Dat cop sure hates a pimp! All he needs to see is the pimps' salute, and he'll out with his night-stick and whip your head to the red. Beat your head just as flat as a dime!" She went off into a great blow of laughter.

"Oh, let's us don't talk about the law. Let's talk about us," Sweet Back persisted. "You going inside with me to holler 'let one come flopping! One come grunting! Snatch one from de rear!'"

"Naw indeed!" the girl laughed harshly. "You skillets is trying to promote a meal on me. But it'll never happen, brother. You barking up the wrong tree. I wouldn't give you air if you was stopped up in a jug. I'm not putting out a thing. I'm just like the cemetery—I'm not putting out, I'm taking in! Dig?"

"I'll tell you like the farmer told the potato—plant you now and dig you later."

The girl made a movement to switch on off. Sweet Back had not dirtied a plate since the day before. He made a weak but desperate gesture.

"Trying to snatch my pocketbook, eh?" she blazed. Instead of running, she grabbed hold of Sweet Back's draping coattail and made a slashing gesture. "How much split you want back here? If your feets don't hurry up and take you 'way from here, you'll *ride* away. I'll spread my lungs all over New York and call the law. Go ahead, Bedbug! Touch me! And I'll holler like a pretty white woman!"

The boys were ready to flee, but she turned suddenly and rocked on off with her ear-rings snapping and her heels popping.

"My people! My people!" Sweet Back sighed.

"I know you feel chewed," Jelly said, in an effort to make it appear that he had had no part in the fiasco.

"Oh, let her go," Sweet Back said magnanimously. "When I see people without the periodical principles they's supposed to have, I just don't fool with 'em. What I want to steal her old pocketbook with all the money I got? I could buy a beat chick like her and give her away. I got money's mammy and Grandma change. One of my women, and not the best one I got neither, is buying me ten shag suits at one time."

He glanced sidewise at Jelly to see if he was convincing. But Jelly's thoughts were far away. He was remembering those full, hot meals he had left back in Alabama to seek wealth and splendor in Harlem without working. He had even forgotten to look cocky and rich.

1942

# RED SMITH

*Red Smith (real name Walter Wellesley, 1905–82) was the dean of American sportswriters. His columns in the New York Herald Tribune and The New York Times were much admired for their seemingly effortless elegance, though Smith once remarked: "There's nothing to writing. All you do is sit down at a typewriter and open a vein." Smith masterfully blended the celebratory and the elegiac: one of the best collections of his work,* To Absent Friends, *consists solely of eulogies— mostly to sports figures, but also to other luminaries of the day, such as New York's colorful mayor Jimmy Walker.*

### AS HE SEEMED TO A HICK

IT SEEMS PRESUMPTUOUS to be writing of Jimmy Walker now, after all that has been written with honest affection by those who knew him longer and more intimately. And yet we hicks out in the Middle West knew the man, too, and perhaps our long-range view of him was as sharply defined and as accurate as the closer slant.

Probably there are many serious-minded New Yorkers who resent the repeated statement that Jimmy was the symbol of his city and his era, feeling that there is a great deal more to the world's greatest city than the things he represented. But the fact is that if Jimmy was a symbol to his townsmen, he was ever so much more than that to us in the hinterlands.

To us he was New York. He was the New York we had come to know, or to think we knew, through the columns of Winchell and O. O. McIntyre. He was the Broadway of George M. Cohan and Texas Guinan, the Polo Grounds of John McGraw, the Madison Square Garden of Tex Rickard and Jimmy Johnston. He was the New York of Babe Ruth and Tammany Hall and Tin Pan Alley.

He was the fiddler who called the turns in a dance which we pictured as never-ending. He was the debonair prophet of gaiety and extravagance and glitter. He was the embodiment of all the qualities which hicks like us resented and admired about New York.

Little things like this made a lasting impression on a visitor to New York in those days:

The crowd was in the Long Island Bowl for the second Sharkey-Stribling fight and the preliminaries were stumbling to a close and there came the rising whine of sirens from outside. A stir and a babble ran through the crowd and heads turned away from the ring and it seemed everyone was standing and craning. Down an aisle swept Jimmy with his retinue, with a hand uplifted in jaunty response to the shouts that greeted him. And that entrance was more exciting than any of the fifteen rounds of brawling that followed.

Afterward, the cab coming back to Manhattan was halted on the bridge by the warning of sirens. A big black limousine hissed by, weaving through the jammed traffic behind its escort. Ahead and below through the darkness the lights of Manhattan glowed. The two hicks in the cab sighed.

"Golly!" one of them breathed. "But they do it big in this town!"

Jimmy hadn't built the bridge, of course, or the towers or turned on the lights, and he hadn't staged the fight or drawn the crowd. And yet, somehow, he seemed to stand for all the things that they did so big in this town.

New York was the perfect background for him. New York set him off. But he was no less a figure of distinction when he crossed the Hudson or the Atlantic.

Al Laney recalls how he took France by storm on his first visit and how his speeches created a schism in the scholarship of the country. Jimmy used the expression "these good-time Charlies," and writers for the French literary journals worked up a fearful sweat trying to translate the term, composing long and ponderous essays defining its hidden meanings.

Jimmy also brought the expression "the cocktail hour" to France. Indeed, he represented that pleasant institution in Parisian eyes. And again the scholars quarreled, practically fighting duels over the comparative merits of the Anglicized spelling and the French *coquetele*.

Mr. Laney remembers, too, how lonesome and homesick Jimmy

was in his later exile in southern France. And how often of an evening, out of loneliness and boredom, he would telephone the *Paris Herald* and just sit there shooting the breeze with any American who happened to answer the phone.

To us out in the country there seemed nothing shocking about the disclosures made or hinted at in the investigation which drove Jimmy out of office and out of the country. So he hadn't been an efficient administrator. Well, whoever said he was? What we felt was a sincere regret in his passing from public life; we'd rather have lost our dearest bootlegger.

Jimmy wasn't supposed to be a statesman. He didn't pretend to be. He was a bandleader, and the most charming one that ever swung a baton. His charm, his urbane graciousness, were his trademarks to the end. To any who had the good fortune to know him, the facts published in his formal obituaries were of small interest. The essential thing about Jimmy was something you hardly ever read on the obituary page, the simple fact that he was the most charming man you ever met.

NEW YORK *HERALD TRIBUNE*, 1946

# DAVID SCHUBERT

*Ever since the city's underground train system was built, watching peo-ple in the subways has been a favorite New York sport. David Schubert (1913–46), the brilliant Brooklyn poet whom William Carlos Williams described as "a nova in the sky" and who died tragically young, brought a rueful, courtly voice to such speculative musings.*

### IT IS STICKY IN THE SUBWAY

How I love this girl who until
This minute, I never knew existed on
The face of this earth.

     I sit opposite
Her, thinking myself as stupid as that
Photograph, maudlin in Mumford, of
Orpheus.

    A kinkled adolescent
Defies the Authorities by
Smoking a butt right next to me. He is
Of Romeos the least attractive who
Has played the role.

     He
Smirks, squints, glues his eyes to her
Tightly entethered teeth, scratches
His moist passion on some scratch paper.

    Her eyes
Accuse Plato of non-en
Tity. Most delightful creature of moment's
      above-ground.

# WELDON KEES

*Weldon Kees (1914–55) was a poet, critic, painter, and musician. His sardonic 1940's "Robinson" poems conjure a world of educated sellouts, conformist admen, and media hacks haunted by their lost inner lives— the Madison Avenue types who would later take center stage in* The Man in the Gray Flannel Suit *and other novels and movies of the 1950's.*

## ASPECTS OF ROBINSON

Robinson at cards at the Algonquin; a thin
Blue light comes down once more outside the blinds.
Gray men in overcoats are ghosts blown past the door.
The taxis streak the avenues with yellow, orange, and red.
This is Grand Central, Mr. Robinson.

Robinson on a roof above the Heights; the boats
Mourn like the lost. Water is slate, far down.
Through sounds of ice cubes dropped in glass, an osteopath,
Dressed for the links, describes an old Intourist tour.
—Here's where old Gibbons jumped from, Robinson.

Robinson walking in the Park, admiring the elephant.
Robinson buying the *Tribune*, Robinson buying the *Times*. Robinson
Saying, "Hello. Yes, this is Robinson. Sunday
At five? I'd love to. Pretty well. And you?"
Robinson alone at Longchamps, staring at the wall.

Robinson afraid, drunk, sobbing. Robinson
In bed with a Mrs. Morse. Robinson at home;
Decisions: Toynbee or luminol? Where the sun
Shines, Robinson in flowered trunks, eyes toward
The breakers. Where the night ends, Robinson in East Side bars.

Robinson in Glen plaid jacket, Scotch-grain shoes,
Black four-in-hand and oxford button-down,
The jeweled and silent watch that winds itself, the brief-
Case, covert topcoat, clothes for spring, all covering
His sad and usual heart, dry as a winter leaf.

RELATING TO ROBINSON

Somewhere in Chelsea, early summer;
And, walking in the twilight toward the docks,
I thought I made out Robinson ahead of me.

From an uncurtained second-story room, a radio
Was playing *There's a Small Hotel*; a kite
Twisted above dark rooftops and slow drifting birds.
We were alone there, he and I,
Inhabiting the empty street.

Under a sign for Natural Bloom Cigars,
While lights clicked softly in the dusk from red to green,
He stopped and gazed into a window
Where a plaster Venus, modeling a truss,
Looked out at Eastbound traffic. (But Robinson,
I knew, was out of town: he summers at a place in Maine,
Sometimes on Fire Island, sometimes the Cape,
Leaves town in June and comes back after Labor Day.)
And yet, I almost called out, "Robinson!"

There was no chance. Just as I passed,
Turning my head to search his face,
His own head turned with mine
And fixed me with dilated, terrifying eyes

That stopped my blood. His voice
Came at me like an echo in the dark.

"I thought I saw the whirlpool opening.
Kicked all night at a bolted door.
You must have followed me from Astor Place.
An empty paper floats down at the last.

*And then a day as huge as yesterday in pairs*
*Unrolled its horror on my face*
*Until it blocked*—" Running in sweat
To reach the docks, I turned back
For a second glance. I had no certainty,
There in the dark, that it was Robinson
Or someone else.
                    The block was bare. The Venus,
Bathed in blue fluorescent light,
Stared toward the river. As I hurried West,
The lights across the bay were coming on.
The boats moved silently and the low whistles blew.

# BERNARD MALAMUD

*Bernard Malamud (1914–86), a grocer's son, came of age in Brooklyn during the Depression and never forgot how economic forces bore down on the small shopkeeper. In austere early stories such as "The Cost of Living" and his novel* The Assistant, *Malamud transformed the obscure struggles of tenants and retailers into a resonant metaphor for human endurance.*

## THE COST OF LIVING

WINTER HAD FLED the city streets but Sam Tomashevsky's face, when he stumbled into the back room of his grocery store, was a blizzard. Sura, who was sitting at the round table eating bread and salted tomato, looked up in fright and the tomato turned a deeper red. She gulped the bite she had bitten and with pudgy fist socked her chest to make it go down. The gesture already was one of mourning for she knew from the wordless sight of him there was trouble.

"My God," Sam croaked.

She screamed, making him shudder, and he fell wearily into a chair. Sura was standing, enraged and frightened.

"Speak, for God's sake."

"Next door," Sam muttered.

"What happened next door?"—upping her voice.

"Comes a store!"

"What kind of a store?" The cry was piercing.

He waved his arms in rage. "A grocery comes next door."

"Oi." She bit her knuckle and sank down moaning. It could not have been worse.

They had, all winter, been haunted by the empty store. An Italian shoemaker had owned it for years and then a streamlined shoe-repair shop had opened up next block where they had three men in red smocks hammering away in the window and everyone stopped to look. Pellegrino's business had slackened off as if someone were

shutting a faucet, and one day he had looked at his workbench and
when everything stopped jumping, it loomed up ugly and empty. All
morning he had sat motionless, but in the afternoon he put down the
hammer he had been clutching and got his jacket and an old darkened Panama hat a customer had never called for when he used to do
hat cleaning and blocking; then he went into the neighborhood, asking among his former customers for work they might want done. He
collected two pairs of shoes, a man's brown and white ones for summertime and a fragile pair of ladies' dancing slippers. At the same
time, Sam found his own soles and heels had been worn paper thin
for being so many hours on his feet—he could feel the cold floor
boards under him as he walked—and that made three pairs all together, which was what Mr. Pellegrino had that week—and another
pair the week after. When the time came for him to pay next month's
rent he sold everything to a junkman and bought candy to peddle
with in the streets; but after a while no one saw the shoemaker any
more, a stocky man with round eyeglasses and a bristling mustache,
wearing a summer hat in wintertime.

When they tore up the counters and other fixtures and moved
them out, when the store was empty except for the sink glowing in
the rear, Sam would occasionally stand there at night, everyone on
the block but him closed, peering into the window exuding darkness. Often, while gazing through the dusty plate glass, which gave
him back the image of a grocer gazing out, he felt as he had when he
was a boy in Kamenets-Podolskiy and going, three of them, to the
river; they would, as they passed, swoop a frightened glance into a
tall wooden house, eerily narrow, topped by a strange double-
steepled roof, where there had once been a ghastly murder and now
the place was haunted. Returning late, at times in early moonlight,
they walked a distance away, speechless, listening to the ravenous silence of the house, room after room fallen into deeper stillness, and
in the midmost a pit of churning quiet from which, if you thought
about it, all evil erupted. And so it seemed in the dark recesses of the
empty store, where so many shoes had been leathered and ham-
mered into life, and so many people had left something of themselves in the coming and going, that even in emptiness the store

contained some memory of their vanished presences, unspoken echoes in declining tiers, and that in a sense was what was so frightening. Afterwards when Sam went by the store, even in daylight he was afraid to look, and quickly walked past, as they had the haunted house when he was a boy.

But whenever he shut his eyes the empty store was stuck in his mind, a long black hole eternally revolving so that while he slept he was not asleep but within revolving: what if it should happen to me? What if after twenty-seven years of eroding toil (he should years ago have got out), what if after all of that, your own store, a place of business . . . after all the years, the years, the multitude of cans he had wiped off and packed away, the milk cases dragged in like rocks from the street before dawn in freeze or heat; insults, petty thievery, doling of credit to the impoverished by the poor; the peeling ceiling, fly-specked shelves, puffed cans, dirt, swollen veins; the back-breaking sixteen-hour day like a heavy hand slapping, upon awaking, the skull, pushing the head to bend the body's bones; the hours; the work, the years, my God, and where is my life now? Who will save me now, and where will I go, where? Often he had thought these thoughts, subdued after months; and the garish FOR RENT sign had yellowed and fallen in the window so how could any one know the place was to let? But they did. Today when he had all but laid the ghost of fear, a streamer in red cracked him across the eyes: National Grocery Will Open Another Of Its Bargain Price Stores On These Premises, and the woe went into him and his heart bled.

At last Sam raised his head and told her, "I will go to the landlord next door."

Sura looked at him through puffy eyelids. "So what will you say?"

"I will talk to him."

Ordinarily she would have said, "Sam, don't be a fool," but she let him go.

Averting his head from the glare of the new red sign in the window, he entered the hall next door. As he labored up the steps the bleak light from the skylight fell on him and grew heavier as he ascended. He went unwillingly, not knowing what he would say to the landlord. Reaching the top floor he paused before the door at the jabbering in Italian of a woman bewailing her fate. Sam already had one foot on the top stair, ready to descend, when he heard the coffee advertisement and realized it had been a radio play. Now the radio was off, the hallway oppressively silent. He listened and at first heard no voices inside so he knocked without allowing himself to think any more. He was a little frightened and lived in suspense until the slow heavy steps of the landlord, who was also the barber across the street, reached the door, and it was—after some impatient fumbling with the lock—opened.

When the barber saw Sam in the hall he was disturbed, and Sam at once knew why he had not been in the store even once in the past two weeks. However, the barber became cordial and invited Sam to step into the kitchen where his wife and a stranger were seated at the table eating from piled-high plates of spaghetti.

"Thanks," said Sam shyly. "I just ate."

The barber came out into the hall, shutting the door behind him. He glanced vaguely down the stairway and then turned to Sam. His movements were unresolved. Since the death of his son in the war he had become absent-minded; and sometimes when he walked one had the impression he was dragging something.

"Is it true?" Sam asked in embarrassment, "What it says downstairs on the sign?"

"Sam," the barber began heavily. He stopped to wipe his mouth with the napkin he held in his hand and said, "Sam, you know this store I had no rent for it for seven months?"

"I know."

"I can't afford. I was waiting for maybe a liquor store or a hardware but I don't have no offers from them. Last month this chain store make me an offer and then I wait five weeks for something else. I had to take it, I couldn't help myself."

Shadows thickened in the growing darkness. In a sense Pellegrino was present, standing with them at the top of the stairs.

"When will they move in?" Sam sighed.

"Not till May."

The grocer was too faint to say anything. They stared at each other, not knowing what to suggest. But the barber forced a laugh and said the chain store wouldn't hurt Sam's business.

"Why not?"

"Because you carry different brands of goods and when the customers want those brands they go to you."

"Why should they go to me if my prices are higher?"

"A chain store brings more customers and they might like things that you got."

Sam felt ashamed. He didn't doubt the barber's sincerity but his stock was meager and he could not imagine chain store customers interested in what he had to sell.

Holding Sam by the arm, the barber told him in confidential tones of a friend who had a meat store next to an A&P Supermarket and was making out very well.

Sam tried hard to believe he would make out well but couldn't.

"So did you sign with them the lease yet?" he asked.

"Friday," said the barber.

"Friday?" Sam had a wild hope. "Maybe," he said, trying to hold it down, "maybe I could find you, before Friday, a new tenant?"

"What kind of a tenant?"

"A tenant," Sam said.

"What kind of store is he interested?"

Sam tried to think. "A shoe store," he said.

"Shoemaker?"

"No, a shoe store where they sell shoes."

The barber pondered it. At last he said if Sam could get a tenant he wouldn't sign the lease with the chain store.

As Sam descended the stairs the light from the top-floor bulb diminished on his shoulders but not the heaviness, for he had no one in mind to take the store.

However, before Friday he thought of two people. One was the red-haired salesman for a wholesale grocery jobber, who had lately been recounting his investments in new stores; but when Sam spoke to him on the phone he said he was only interested in high-income grocery stores, which was no solution to the problem. The other man he hesitated to call, because he didn't like him. That was I.

Kaufman, a former dry goods merchant, with a wart under his left eyebrow. Kaufman had made some fortunate real estate deals and had become quite wealthy. Years ago he and Sam had stores next to one another on Marcy Avenue in Williamsburg. Sam took him for a lout and was not above saying so, for which Sura often ridiculed him, seeing how Kaufman had progressed and where Sam was. Yet they stayed on comparatively good terms, perhaps because the grocer never asked for favors. When Kaufman happened to be around in the Buick, he usually dropped in, which Sam increasingly disliked, for Kaufman gave advice without stint and Sura sandpapered it in when he had left.

Despite qualms he telephoned him. Kaufman was pontifically surprised and said yes he would see what he could do. On Friday morning the barber took the red sign out of the window so as not to prejudice a possible deal. When Kaufman marched in with his cane that forenoon, Sam, who for once, at Sura's request, had dispensed with his apron, explained to him they had thought of the empty store next door as perfect for a shoe store because the neighborhood had none and the rent was reasonable. And since Kaufman was always investing in one project or another they thought he might be interested in this. The barber came over from across the street and unlocked the door. Kaufman clomped into the empty store, appraised the structure of the place, tested the floor, peered through the barred window into the back yard, and squinting, totaled with moving lips how much shelving was necessary and at what cost. Then he asked the barber how much rent and the barber named a modest figure.

Kaufman nodded sagely and said nothing to either of them there, but back in the grocery store he vehemently berated Sam for wasting his time.

"I didn't want to make you ashamed in front of the goy," he said in anger, even his wart red, "but who do you think, if he is in his right mind, will open a shoe store in this stinky neighborhood?"

Before departing, he gave good advice the way a tube bloops toothpaste and ended by saying to Sam, "If a chain store grocery comes in you're finished. Get out of here before the birds pick the meat out of your bones."

Then he drove off in his Buick. Sura was about to begin a commentary but Sam pounded his fist on the table and that ended it.
That evening the barber pasted the red sign back on the window, for
he had signed the lease.

Lying awake nights, Sam knew what was going on inside the
store, though he never went near it. He could see carpenters sawing
the sweet-smelling pine that willingly yielded to the sharp shining
blade and became in tiers the shelves rising to the ceiling. The
painters arrived, a long man and a short one he was positive he
knew, their faces covered with paint drops. They thickly calcimined
the ceiling and painted everything in bright colors, impractical for a
grocery but pleasing to the eye. Electricians appeared with floures-
cent lamps which obliterated the yellow darkness of globed bulbs;
and then the fixture men hauled down from their vans the long
marble-top counters and a gleaming enameled refrigerator containing three windows, for cooking, medium, and best butter; and a case
for frozen foods, creamy white, the latest thing. As he was admiring
it all, he thought he turned to see if anyone was watching him, and
when he had reassured himself and turned again to look through the
window it had been whitened so he could see nothing more. He had
to get up then to smoke a cigarette and was tempted to put on his
pants and go in slippers quietly down the stairs to see if the window
was really soaped. That it might be kept him back so he returned to
bed, and being still unable to sleep, he worked until he had polished,
with a bit of rag, a small hole in the center of the white window, and
enlarged that till he could see everything clearly. The store was assembled now, spic and span, roomy, ready to receive the goods; it
was a pleasure to come in. He whispered to himself this would be
good if it was for me, but then the alarm banged in his ear and he
had to get up and drag in the milk cases. At eight A.M. three enormous trucks rolled down the block and six young men in white duck
jackets jumped off and packed the store in seven hours. All day Sam's
heart beat so hard he sometimes fondled it with his hand as though
trying to calm a wild bird that wanted to fly away.

When the chain store opened in the middle of May, with a horse-
shoe wreath of roses in the window, Sura counted up that night and

proclaimed they were ten dollars short; which wasn't so bad, Sam said, till she reminded him ten times six was sixty. She openly wept, sobbing they must do *something*, driving Sam to a thorough wiping of the shelves with wet cloths she handed him, oiling the floor, and washing, inside and out, the front window, which she redecorated with white tissue paper from the five-and-ten. Then she told him to call the wholesaler, who read off this week's specials; and when they were delivered, Sam packed three cases of cans in a towering pyramid in the window. Only no one seemed to buy. They were fifty dollars short the next week and Sam thought if it stays like this we can exist, and he cut the price of beer, lettering with black crayon on wrapping paper a sign for the window that beer was reduced in price, selling fully five cases more that day, though Sura nagged what was the good of it if they made no profit—lost on paper bags—and the customers who came in for beer went next door for bread and canned goods? Yet Sam still hoped, but the next week they were seventy-two behind, and in two weeks a clean hundred. The chain store, with a manager and two clerks, was busy all day but with Sam there was never, any more, anything resembling a rush. Then he discovered that they carried, next door, every brand he had and many he hadn't, and he felt for the barber a furious anger.

That summer, usually better for his business, was bad, and the fall was worse. The store was so silent it got to be a piercing pleasure when someone opened the door. They sat long hours under the unshaded bulb in the rear, reading and rereading the newspaper and looking up hopefully when anyone passed by in the street, though trying not to look when they could tell he was going next door. Sam now kept open an hour longer, till midnight, although that wearied him greatly, but he was able, during the extra hour, to pick up a dollar or two among the housewives who had run out of milk or needed a last minute loaf of bread for school sandwiches. To cut expenses he put out one of the two lights in the window and a lamp in the store. He had the phone removed, bought his paper bags from peddlers, shaved every second day and, although he would not admit it, ate less. Then in an unexpected burst of optimism he ordered eighteen cases of goods from the jobber and filled the empty sections of his shelves with low-priced items clearly marked, but as Sura said, who saw them if nobody came in? People he had seen every day for ten, fifteen, even twenty years, disappeared as if they had moved or died. Sometimes when he was delivering a small order somewhere, he saw a former customer who either quickly crossed the street, or ducked the other way and walked around the block. The barber, too, avoided him and he avoided the barber. Sam schemed to give short weight on loose items but couldn't bring himself to. He considered canvassing the neighborhood from house to house for orders he would personally deliver but then remembered Mr. Pellegrino and gave up the idea. Sura, who had all their married life, nagged him, now sat silent in the back. When Sam counted the receipts of the first week in December he knew he could no longer hope. The wind blew outside and the store was cold. He offered it for sale but no one would take it.

One morning Sura got up and slowly ripped her cheeks with her fingernails. Sam went across the street for a haircut. He had formerly had his hair cut once a month but now it had grown ten weeks and was thickly pelted at the back of the neck. The barber cut it with his eyes shut. Then Sam called an auctioneer who moved in with two lively assistants and a red auction flag that flapped and furled in the icy breeze as though it were a holiday. The money they got was not a quarter of the sum needed to pay the creditors. Sam and Sura closed the store and moved away. So long as he lived he would not return to the old neighborhood, afraid his store was standing empty, and he dreaded to look through the window.

1949

# ANZIA YEZIERSKA

*Anzia Yezierska (1885–1970) wrote powerful novels and stories (Hungry Hearts, Bread-Givers) about growing up in slums of the Lower East Side, working in sweatshops, and struggling to become an independent writer. In this passage from her autobiography,* Red Ribbon on a White Horse, *Yezierska focuses on the archetypal moment when the ghetto-dweller sees a larger world beckoning and takes her first tentative steps toward it.*

## FROM *RED RIBBON ON A WHITE HORSE*

FROM THE WIDE, sunny windows of my hotel apartment on Fifth Avenue, I could see the Hudson and East Rivers and the skyscrapers of downtown Manhattan. I had been living in my high-towered luxury for three years and still did not feel at home. One Saturday afternoon in June, an overwhelming nostalgia took me back to the East Side. People sprawled about the stoops, leaned out of the windows, the leisure of the Sabbath in their faces.

The rumble of traffic, the feverish jostling and bargain-hunting at the pushcarts were stilled; but from open doorways and windows, radios blared a pandemonium of familiar strains.

On one corner, the water hydrant was turned on to clear the muck from the gutter. Half-naked children in ragged underwear danced and shouted with joy under the shower. In the basement entrance of a tenement sat a white-bearded sage in a black skullcap holding forth to a circle of his neighbors. The sidewalks surged with young folks in their holiday best parading gayly past overflowing garbage cans. They pushed out the walls of their homes to the street on their day of rest.

How often, when I was in Hollywood, had this noisy, crowded ghetto come between me and the parties of "eminent authors." The same dark, irrational compulsion that makes a murderer risk his life to return to the scene of his crime pulled me back to this home that had never been home to me. The very forces that had driven me away drew me back.

The sunset lit up the sky, splashing the drab tenements with gold, bringing memories of Sabbath candles and the smell of *gefüllte* fish. When I had lived on Hester Street, I would stop at the pushcart of Zalmon Shlomoh, the hunchbacked fish peddler, to buy his leftover fish for the Sabbath.

"How goes your luck today?" I used to ask him.

"Except for health and a living, I'm perfectly fine."

He always made the same joke as he wiped his hands on his sweater gleaming with the scales of the fish. His broad, bony cheeks, the deformed curve of his back, and his knotted arthritic hands made him a gnome, a grotesque. But his eyes were alive with the radiance of our secret code. Except for health and a living, we were both perfectly fine.

One day he flashed me a look of bold intimacy. "*Und* how goes it with you? With your red hair, you must be always on fire!"

Startled, I returned his look. All at once the hunchback became a man in my eyes. It had been a long time since I had felt so free with any one. I reached out and touched his arm in responsive gaiety.

"I'm like a sinner in the next world, thrown from one hell into another."

"But you wouldn't be happy except in hell." Zalmon laughed back, exposing the black cavities of his yellow teeth.

That was all I needed to let loose my obsession. "If you want to know what hell is, I'll tell you. Hell is trying to do what you can't do, trying to be what you're not——"

"*Nu?* So what are you trying to be that you're not?" he bantered.

"It wills itself in me to be a writer——"

"A writer?" He gave me a long, sparkling glance. "A young girl like you! For what do you need yet to write?"

"*Oi weh!* I don't know myself." I sighed as he wrapped the fish in a newspaper and there was no longer any reason to linger at the pushcart. "Time is flying. I can't bear to be left out of life an old maid. Tell me, why do I have to write? When will I live?"

In Zalmon Shlomoh's eyes was such a naked look of comprehension that it silenced me. Unmindful of the hurrying crowd, the shrill cries of the hucksters and the housewives pushing past us with their market baskets, we stood looking at each other. We belonged to the shadowy company of those who were withdrawn from their fellows by grief, illness, or the torment of frustration.

Zalmon turned away and scolded with mock impatience. "You ask more questions in a minute than all the wise men can answer in a lifetime."

He shook his head and gave my arm a wicked little pinch. "God sends always to the spinner his flax, to the drinker his wine, and to a *meshugeneh*, a crazy one like you, an answer to your own *meshugass*. If I weren't old enough to be your father, I'd take you away to the end of the earth where we could both go crazy together; but you deserve a young man your own age. Your red hair and white skin cry out for youth."

"I hate young men! They say I have a *dybbuk*, a devil, a book for a heart. They laugh because I want to be a writer."

Always whenever I saw Zalmon Shlomoh I would feel that I too was a cripple. It leaped out of my eyes like the guilt of secret sin, that devouring hunger in me. People ran away from it as from a deformity. Only Zalmon Shlomoh, the hunchback, could feel and see the wild wolves of that hunger and not be frightened away.

I wondered, as I recalled the days when Zalmon was my only friend, whether he was still alive. If I could reach him, would he be glad to see me? Dared I look him up, to find out? But I knew he could never forgive my becoming one of the bloody rich. I never would look him up.

I thought of the time Zalmon had come to see me with a newspaper package under his arm. In the secondhand shop he had picked up, for a dime, an old record of Beethoven's "Moonlight Sonata." Instead of talking, he turned on the record again and again, filling the small room with the melancholy tenderness of all the unspoken love in the world.

One night he had taken me to hear Caruso in *Pagliacci*. The grief of the clown reached up to us in the gallery. That glorious voice cried out the ache of our own unlived lives.

Even while we sat together, cousins in sorrow, I was affronted by Zalmon's fish smells. In his new suit he looked as incongruous as a dog in a praying shawl. His charm was great enough to make me forget the dwarfed deformity of his body, but his fish smells drove me away. I could smell them even now.

They were soaked into me from sweatshop days. Whenever the boss had wanted us to work late without pay, he treated the machine hands to herring and onions. Among themselves the girls grumbled as they bolted the bitter bribe. One night Sara Solomon flared up.

"I got my feller waiting for me on the corner. All I need yet, he should pick himself up another girl——"

"You got to meet your feller?" I said. "*I* got to go to night school. I'm going to be a stenographer——"

"*Nu?* So tell the boss to choke himself with his herring——"

"Sure I will!" I grabbed my shawl and stood up. "I don't care if the shop burns down. We sell him our days, but the nights are ours."

Their faces froze. I felt the boss's hand on my neck.

"Out you go! Out of my shop! I want no fresh-mouthed *Amerikanerins!* Greenhorns! The minute they learn a word English, they get flies in their nose and wanna be ladies. I don't want no ladies here!"

A dark period followed the loss of my job. But I had had enough of the sweatshop. I decided I knew enough typing and stenography to look for work in an office. And then I found myself up against a new barrier—the barrier of being a Jew.

A bank in the Jewish clothing district wanted a beginner. I was among the first to apply. The room was crowded with girls when the door of the inner office opened and the personnel manager stuck his head out. "Are there any Jews here?" he asked, briefly scanning the girls' faces. "If so there's no need to stay. No Jewish girls are wanted for this particular job."

I stood up and walked out quickly. Others followed me. Out in the street I could see nothing but that man's face, hear nothing but that man's voice as he said, "No Jewish girls are wanted."

Again and again I was told "No Jews wanted." But I had to have a job and so I kept on answering ads. I could not give up the hope that somewhere in some office it wasn't a crime to be born a Jew. Late at night, as soon as the morning papers were on the stands, I was there studying the Help Wanted columns.

I answered an ad for a stenographer. It was so early I did not expect to find the office open. I walked past the empty switchboard and reception desk, past a row of darkened cubicles. Then I noticed in the far corner a light. A door was open on an inner office where a man was bent over papers on his desk. I was inside the door before he saw me.

He was a big man, in his middle fifties. A great head strongly modeled; the forehead jutted out, throwing his eyes into deep shadow.

"I came about a job," I said. "Can you tell me where to go?"

He glanced at the clock and then back at me. "I didn't expect any one this early———"

"I wanted to be the first to apply," I said.

"Are you a legal stenographer?"

The lines over his high forehead rushed together like sentinels over his gray eyes. Those eyes, sunk deep in their sockets, had a penetrating intelligence that could see through people. I felt he knew I had come to lie my way into the job.

"The ad calls for an experienced stenographer," he reminded me. "What is your experience?"

"Where shall I get experience if no one gives me a chance to get it?" I burst out. "The last place I applied they wouldn't even try me out when I said I was a Jew. Experience! My God! I'm burning up with experience, but not in offices."

He took off his glasses and stared at me. His brows arched and a slow smile spread over his face. "Well, where did you get your experience?"

"In factories—sewing shirts, making artificial flowers, rolling cigars."

"But what I need is an experienced stenographer———"

"Oh, I'm a stenographer, all right! And a good one! I studied in night school——— "

Suddenly I realized by the quiet look in his eyes that I was shouting the same way that I bargained at the pushcarts. I flushed with embarrassment and lowered my voice. "Just try me out. I'll show you———"

"All right, show me." He handed me a shorthand pad and pencil. As he dictated I became aware of his voice. It was a kind of voice I had never heard before. The charm of courtesy and kindness was in it and the assurance of education. It was like listening to music that quieted fear.

When I handed him what I had typed, I was afraid it wasn't good enough. For such a man even the typing would have to be somehow superior.

He read it and turned to me. "Young lady, you're hired. When can you start?"

My throat was so dry I had to swallow to get the words out. "You want me? I really have the job?"

"Certainly." He laughed, and then, noticing the anxiety in my face. "What's the matter with you? You've shown me you're capable."

Ashamed of my clumsiness, I said, "I've been turned down so much!"

He stood up, stretched his arms, and I saw how tall he was. "Look here," he said casually, "I've been working all night in this office. I'm going for breakfast. Would you like a cup of coffee?"

I gaped at him. Such friendliness from a boss!

"Come on! Let's go!" He opened the door. And suddenly all strangeness between us was gone.

"It's so wonderful to have a job in an office!" I told him. "After what I've been through to be hired—by a person like you—a real American."

His smile showed he liked being appreciated. There were bright pin points of light in his eyes—flecks of sunlight on gray water.

In the restaurant, I spread out the napkin, touched the tablecloth, drank the coffee. Real, I kept telling myself, looking at everything around me but not at him.

"When I put the ad in the *Times* I did not expect to find any one like you," he said. "You are a very unusual person."

He patted my hand. It was a gesture of simple kindness, but it stirred currents in me that had never before been touched. The mountain of hurts I carried on my back from czarist Russia, and the hurts piled up looking for a job in America, dissolved. I had been accepted, recognized as a person. . . . I tasted the bread and wine of equality.

Morrow's office was on the twentieth floor of a Wall Street skyscraper. The sunlight, the air, the view all around New York introduced me to a life outside all my experience. I looked out of the clean windows and saw the grimy, barred windows of Cohen's Shirt Factory. I pitied the people I had left behind in the noisy clatter of the machines.

My desk was just outside Morrow's office. The switchboard and reception desk screened outsiders from us, and we were also removed from the rest of the floor where his assistants worked.

There had always been a chasm between earning my living and living my life. Earning a living had meant drudgery, the chain around my neck—until I worked for John Morrow. Working with him, I was learning and growing every day.

Once, when there was some overtime work, he asked me to dine with him. "My family is out of town and I hate eating alone," he said.

He asked me to take him to an East Side restaurant and we went to Yoneh Shimmel's on Delancey Street.

After dinner we walked through lines of pushcarts to Allen Street, where the basement shops showed brass samovars, old shawls, and trays from Palestine.

"This is like a foreign country!" he said, marveling.

After that staying late for a job was like a holiday, because it meant dining with him when the work was finished.

I had to prove to him that he had made no mistake in choosing an awkward girl from Hester Street instead of the lady-like college secretary he could have had. All I had to offer was the manuscript about the people in the sweatshop. As he was getting ready to go home one afternoon I stuck it into his coat pocket and asked him to read it.

The first thing he said when he came in the following morning was, "I've read it! I've read it! That sweatshop is shocking, terrifying! And you've survived it. You've risen out of it!"

He seemed to be very much moved, and that was all he said. But all that morning I was conscious of his eyes on me. No other man had ever looked at me like that.

Later in the afternoon he came over to me, put the manuscript on my desk. "This is rough now, but alive." His hand touched mine, withdrew instantly. In that brief touch all the unlived in me leaped into life.

I had found some one who saw me, knew me, reassured me that I existed. And writing ceased to have the desperate urgency it used to have. The greatest words ever written were pale and thin beside the new life I was living.

We dined often on the East Side. At first I had been embarrassed about showing him the dirty streets, the haggling and bargaining, and the smells from the alleys of the ghetto where I lived. But what I had thought coarse and commonplace was to him exotic. My Old World was so fresh and new to him it became fresh and new to me.

Sometimes we went to the Yiddish theater. Leaving the theater one night, he stopped to buy baked sweet potatoes from a pushcart peddler, and we ate them as we walked along.

"I thought I'd become a lady working for you," I laughed. "And now you're dragging me down to eating from pushcarts."

He looked into my eyes, and his look burned through me. I was suspended in the concentration of his gaze. "You don't have to become. You suffer from striving. You try to be. But you are, you are already."

There were always pauses in the midst of our work for our private conversations. One afternoon we were talking about a Yiddish play we had seen the evening before. It surprised me how well he understood everything without knowing Yiddish. He said the emotion of the actors was so vivid and the audience so responsive that this interested him more than the play.

"You know, they have something you have too," he said, studying me. "The same intensity. I think it comes from fighting for every inch of ground on which you stand——"

"My fight has been only to keep alive," I protested. "You're a fighter, too, but for others——"

"Oh, my dear." He shook his head. "I've never fought for anything with the spirit that you have. I like the passion with which you live every moment. Everything that has ever happened to you is in your eyes."

The ringing of the telephone interrupted us. I answered it, and then told him that Mrs. Morrow was in the reception room.

He flushed and turned back to his desk. "Ask her to come in," he said.

Mrs. Morrow, a gracious woman in her fifties with an intelligent, attractive face, smiled at me as she entered. It was the first time I had ever seen her, and I felt instantly that she was everything I was not.

The delicate perfume, the slender elegance of her shoes, the softly tailored gray suit, the perfection of her shining gray hair were details of a rich life I had only read about. She had a natural poise and elegance. She was kind with the kindness of one whose position in the world was secure.

Her visit was brief. She had called to drive her husband home. They left the office together.

I went home alone. I was aware for the rest of the evening how far from me he was, how unpossessable. He had withdrawn into a world of culture and beautiful living where I could never enter.

But I consoled myself. I knew him as neither his wife nor children could know him. They had his name, his money, his reputation, but I had something that fed his spirit. He could never share with his family the thoughts he shared with me. Our need for each other burned away the differences between Gentile and Jew, native and immigrant—the barriers of race, class, and education.

In my dreams I felt myself more married to him than his wife, closer to him than his children.

I was twenty-three. I had never loved any one before. On the East Side there was no privacy, couples seized their chance to be together wherever they found it; they embraced in hallways, lay together on roofs. I had passed them all with eyes averted.

My love needed a sanctuary, a solitude of sky and stars. Away from work, away from him, I walked the Brooklyn Bridge night after night, re-creating my every experience with him: the way he looked at me, the words he said, trying to hold close the golden moments of being understood.

1950

# WILLIAM CARLOS WILLIAMS

*William Carlos Williams (1883–1963), the bard of Rutherford, New Jersey, a practicing physician, and a major innovator in modernist poetry, served as an intern in the Hell's Kitchen area of Manhattan, an experience vividly and humorously described in his* Autobiography. *As in Williams' famous story "The Use of Force," the doctor-writer portrays himself as a man pulled between gruff impatience and compassion.*

## HELL'S KITCHEN

HOW I EVER got into the Nursery and Child's Hospital is more than I know. I think I applied and they grabbed me, that's all. I had hardly a week between quitting at the French and beginning there. Doc Richardson was my Senior; there were only two of us. The man I wanted most to work under there was Charles Gilmore Kerley, one of the leading pediatricians of the day. I was extremely happy at my good luck.

This was a very different setup from what I had been experiencing at the French, as different as night and day, a very much looser organization—and no Sisters of Charity. The main building, just completed, was on the corner of Sixty-first Street and Tenth Avenue, a six-story brick structure just across Tenth from the most notorious block in the New York criminal West Side, San Juan Hill or Hell's Kitchen, as you preferred to call it. We didn't go out much after dark unaccompanied, man or woman. There were shootings and near riots and worse practically every week-end. That block, the most heavily populated in the city, was said to be honeycombed with interconnecting tunnels from flat to flat so that a man who had taken it on the lam, once he got inside an entry, was gone from the police forever.

Our children's ward was back of the main building, the maternity section. It was a two-floor brick cube consisting of two small wards, holding eight beds each, right and left, with a similar second floor.

The management of the place, aside from the nursing, was

riddled with corruption. There were a few nurses from various out-lying hospitals who had been sent there for their pediatric and ob-stetric training, but there was no school. Miss Cuthbertson, a large, straightforward Canadian woman, was in charge of the nursing pro-gram. Miss Malzacher, a dark, sweaty-looking creature with furtive, bulging eyes, was in charge of the office, and another mild plump little woman, whose name I have forgotten, was the over-all director in residence, a decorative fiftyish little figure, who kept a wonderful table for Richardson and me, but that was all. She had said, in fact, that that was the only way she could hold any resident physicians in the place: by feeding them well. Our sleeping quarters were noth-ing, worse than nothing, in fact on more than one occasion full of bedbugs. But the food was marvelous and we were interfered with in our work almost not at all. I can still remember those meals with the lady boss herself and Miss Cuthbertson—the four of us. The madam insisted that the Senior in charge carve the roasts, chickens and other meat she served. She felt it was part of her duty to teach us manners. We literally ate it up. Miss Cuthbertson was our pal. It worked out beautifully in that small intimate dining room on the back corridor of the old part of the original building.

There was plenty of work. That's what saved the place, medically speaking. During my time there I delivered three hundred babies and faced every complication that could be thought of. I learned to know and to admire women, of a sort, in that place. They led a tough life and still kept a sort of gentleness and kindness about them that could, I think, beat anything a man might offer under the same cir-cumstances. I never saw one yet, white or black, that didn't give me a break if I treated her half-decently.

Miss Diamond, who wore a gold tooth in the front, was a first-rate Supervisor and head of the delivery room. Miss Becksted, Chief of Pediatric Service, a tough little Englishwoman, was another of my pals. At the beginning it seemed just what I wanted. Miss Diamond was the right woman for her situation. As she once said, "I'm going to run a three-foot streamer around this place below the sixth-floor windows and it's going to read: 'BABIES FRESH EVERY HOUR, ANY COLOR DESIRED, 100% ILLEGITIMATE!' "

She wasn't fooling, either. The women at the Nursery and Child's were the dregs of the city, a fine crew. Once I was called by Miss Diamond to help her separate five of them in a fight. They were lying, all approaching full term, on the stone floor of one of the upper hallways, snarling and spitting like cats. She told me that two or more were pregnant from the same man, and the others had joined in on one side or the other. She'd grab one by the foot and try to pull her out of the pile, but the floor was polished and Diamond was so strong she'd pull the whole sputtering mass in one direction or other. I stood looking at her, somewhat reluctant to join in.

"Grab a leg and pull against me," she yelled. So I did what she wanted but I couldn't hurt the things.

"Pull!" she said. But the women had their hands locked in each other's hair and we got no results.

"All *right*, you bitches," she told them, "I'll get the ether can!" And that she did. She got a towel, soaked it with ether, and waded in among them. They all let go all right and scrambled up without a word. It was the first time I had seen such a thing and told her so.

"Oh, that's nothing. We have it every once in a while around here. All we need is a ringleader and they're at it. I know who it is now, I got my eye on her. It won't happen again."

Miss Diamond—I don't think I ever knew her first name—was a big, sharp-chinned peroxide blond, the gold tooth right in front of her face, young and not at all bad-looking, somewhat of a Mae West type. When she set her jaw and her blue eyes began to snap, the women usually cowered; but she was a good nurse and a fast worker. In the end, the women knew she was for them. They respected her. So did I. She taught me a lot about obstetrics.

When I had come on duty during the first summer with the pediatric work—there had been nothing of that at the French—I was fascinated by it and knew at once that that was my field. We had 'em of all sorts, as you may imagine. We got most of the foundlings from all over the city when Bellevue didn't want them.

I'll never forget that summer. Some charitable-minded woman from the Riverside Drive section, fashionable at that time, offered us her apartment for a convalescent home on one condition, that we were not to put any sick children there, that is, very sick infants who might die on the premises.

It was agreed. She had removed the furniture from her parlor and dining room, covered the mirrors and carpets with proper drapes and runners. On each side we installed cribs and assigned certain nurses and attendants to care for a dozen or more infants who were to be kept there. It was a fine gesture on her part and we lived up to the agreement to the letter.

But something happened, as it usually does under such circumstances, to ruin all our plans. One of the children developed a severe case of infectious gastro-enteritis and before anyone knew it, had died, in three days! Something we were absolutely unprepared for. We couldn't let the lady find it out, but obviously we had to do something with the body. So that I, being on Pediatrics at the hospital, was assigned the job of covering up. I was dispatched by streetcar to the apartment with instructions to bring the dead infant to our morgue in a suitcase, which was provided for me. And I did it, by public conveyance, the suitcase under my knees as I sat there looking about me. I was not happy over it, all sorts of notions going through my head as I thought of what would happen if the rickety container should fly open and the body of the child fall out just at the wrong moment. I tell you I sweated over that job, plenty. When I got back I told them: No more!

In a day or two, the whole group at the residence was affected, we lost 90 per cent of them, but I never went back for another body. They had to close the place up.

It was when I was on duty with the infants and older children in the little building at the back of the Nursery and Child's that I was visited by Viola Baxter, one of Ezra's friends of the Utica days when he was at Hamilton College. She was beautiful and sympathetic, but when she saw what we had under our care, the very scum of the city streets, she was shocked—at our cruelty!

"Cruelty!" I said. "What do you mean? We can't dress them in pretty garments to make a show of them."

"But look at the poor miserable brats! Hear them cry. You're brutal, you're heartless—you're impossible."

"You don't know what you're talking about," I told her. "You ought to have seen this brat when we got him. He was the most bedraggled, neglected, dirty, emaciated piece of garbage—you couldn't possibly imagine what he looked like—sores, rickets, his legs out of shape, and look at him now—he's beautiful!"

"Beautiful? He needs his diaper changed this minute! Where are the nurses? You don't understand these things as a woman does. He smells."

"What do you want me to do?" I asked her. I could have kicked her out of the place. As a matter of fact, that particular infant was our special pride and joy, the most patient little beast I have ever witnessed—and one of the most understanding.

They weren't all like him. Some were enough to drive me half-insane with their screaming. I was, I must confess, to lose my temper one day, at a brat I had broken my heart over trying to recondition him. He'd yell at night, every night and only at night, right under my bedroom window across the alleyway, until one night I went to his crib—I could find nothing the matter with him to make him yell—and slapped a piece of three-inch adhesive over his mouth. He could still breathe through his nose, but I thought better of it after a few minutes and took it off again.

That gave me an idea. One night I got hold of my nurse on duty—she used to wear long drawers—and told her I needed her assistance. We had a somewhat older boy than usual in one of the downstairs isolation rooms who had become particularly troublesome. Nothing we did seemed to make him comfortable. So that evening I primed her. We switched off all the lights, darkened the windows and went into the boy's room.

"Here's a flashlight," I said. "Stand there, right where I put you, and when I say go, you flash that light on the youngster where he lies." Oh, shades of old Krumwiede!

"O.K."

"Ready," I said.

"O.K."

"Go!" and I threw back the covers with one stroke leaving the child naked on the sheet!

About twenty enormous bedbugs darted in all directions from his carcass and disappeared into the corners of the bed. I had solved my problem!

Next day I got permission to buy half a barrel of bar-sulphur, big pieces round as my wrist. I got myself six old enameled basins, put them on bricks in the center of the wards and other rooms of the building, poured half a pint of alcohol into them and, having had the engineer seal up the cracks around the doors and windows, except those about the exit-door—leaving all used sheets, blankets, and clothing in the building—the weather being fine, I had the nurses deliver each child to me, naked, at the one door that remained accessible. There I wrapped each child in a fresh sterile blanket and carried it to a spot outside the building, in the sun, where I laid it on a board along the south wall. It was very amusing to see them lying there. We took pictures.

When this was finished and I had inspected the building to see that everything alive except the bugs was out of it in the fresh air, I set matches to the alcohol in the pans one by one, beginning at the far end of the second floor. The stuff went up like a flash. I had to run for it. Outside I sealed the final door. We all for a while stood outside looking in as the sulphur clouds in the room became denser and denser. I could see the damned stuff in the nearest pan bubbling as it burned.

When we opened the place up later in the day, you never saw such heaps of insects on the floors and in the corners of each bed! We swept them up dead into veritable pyramids.

I had turned out to be such a famous exterminator that I got the nurses' dormitory as my next job—but the heavy fumes trickled out under the main door there, cascaded down the stair and damn near suffocated the private patients in the rooms below.

Once later I did a job on the main business office where an infant, critically ill with diphtheria, had been sitting for two hours while we tried to find a place for it. There I burned a formalin candle. Hours later when I opened the door, one of our famous cats flew out from under Malzacher's desk coughing and spitting. I hope its fleas were impressed.

Then one evening there was a terrific to-do on the avenue: screams and finally a pistol shot followed by the ringing of the out-patient bell. Hell's Kitchen or San Juan Hill was merely living up to its reputation. I thought nothing more of the affair but went about my business as usual until the gossip as to what had happened reached through to me.

The police had brought in a young girl who had been plenty roughed up. We didn't usually care for that sort of case, but under the circumstances the nurses had to straighten her out at least a lit-tle. They discovered that it was not a girl at all, but a boy. He had ap-parently been soliciting trade in doorways and the street entries to the various houses on the block, the usual two-bit stand-up, when one of his customers got wise to him. For the boy or young man had an inflated rubber replica of the female genitalia pulled up and strapped between his legs to make him marketable. It must have gone fine for a while until this guy found himself cheated, got his hands on the thing and then hauled off and clipped the vendor on the jaw. And so the riot began!

A colored gal from the Bahamas at full term went in one of the back wards one day, sat on the toilet and had the child there, keep-ing the water running until it came out under the toilet door onto the tiles until the whole room was flooded. When we broke in, took her off the seat and cut the child's cord, it turned out to be as good as ever. We discharged them both a week later. It was midwinter, and the infant was found next morning wrapped in newspaper under a bench in Prospect Park. Automatically it was sent in to us. One of the girls looked at it and immediately recognized it.

"Why, that's Joe we sent out of here yesterday! Look at him, isn't that Joe?"

Everyone clustered around. Sure enough, it was Joe.

One day I was examining a fifteen-year-old white girl—a cute kid who had been brought into the clinic for diagnosis by her mother who wanted to know what made her belly so big. The kid was not dumb and fought us every step of the way. Finally after threats by the mother and persuasion on my part, we got her dress off, but at that point she flew at us all and in her underwear dashed out the door and up the street like a young doe. That's the last I saw of her.

Another time I was delivering a case when they wheeled in a second. It was neck and neck. I stood between the tables, a glove on both hands and two nurses in attendance, when Miss Diamond brought in a third, dragged in a mattress, covered it with a sterile sheet and told the gal to go to it—on the floor. That was her style.

These were the ward cases. They'd come in around the sixth to the eighth month and work around the floors or just do nothing until they fell into labor, all sorts of women. One I remember was a morphine addict who begged me for a shot of the dope, three grams she wanted. I told her I'd give her a quarter of morphine but that was all. She begged and pleaded for more, but I had no instructions and didn't want to kill her. How did I know what she was up to? I guess I looked easy and they all tried to break me down. I got up to a half with her, then three-quarters of a grain every six to eight hours and kept her there until her time, she saying we were killing her.

We also had a few private rooms. Those women were of a different type. I remember my first twins were on that floor. Then one day I found myself taking the history of a young woman who quietly told me this story!

It was late in June, she had recently finished her year at a local college. The year before she had been seduced by her father's overseer at their farm in the Middle West. Finding herself pregnant, she induced her father to let her go east to college. She visited friends during the Christmas vacation, then at the end of the term, came here with us. It was a simple case. She gave the baby out for adoption and went home for the summer. I grew very fond of the woman.

The hospital backed up on some colored apartments. We would look into them idly sometimes going about our work. There were stray cats everywhere. At night, looking for food, I suppose, they'd climb the dumbwaiters making an awful racket so that someone offered a quarter a tail for any we could do away with. Occasionally we'd corner one in the pharmacy, catch it and give it to the big Swede, and I mean big, who took care of the furnaces. We did it at least until we learned that with his enormous hands he'd avulse the poor beasts' tails, to claim the bounty, then throw the carcass in at the open furnace door—scratch him as the things might.

We often put up our own drugs at night in the pharmacy. One day the new night superintendent of nurses came there for something and before many minutes, I had her in my arms.

She wasn't as young as I, and had a sad story—the place was full of sad stories. Some one of the attending surgeons, a Dr. Tuttle, wanted her to take charge of his convalescent home somewhere in the mountains of Virginia. I never did find out where the girl came from—extremely pretty, unusually well-made, but hardly an intellectual—a futile, dispirited, lonely sort of woman, just the sort that would take the job of night superintendent in such an institution. Miss Cuthbertson seemed to think she was all right, but there certainly was a mystery about her. She seldom smiled. I suppose she had been married, or double-crossed in some way, or maybe her professional credits weren't up to the mark.

It became a bit serious in the pharmacy evenings after that. One day she asked me if I—or perhaps I asked her—if I might visit her in her room, on Twenty-third Street, that old row of houses that used to stand there between Eighth and Ninth Avenues.

"Yes," she said. She had full lips and big baby-doll eyes.

So I went. The room was on the fourth floor, right under the eaves, room for little more than the bed, the dresser and one chair. The poor child seemed really poor and humiliated in such surroundings. She had decorated the place with red candles and a fancy bedspread with roses. I wanted to lie on the bed with her. She shook her head.

"But you asked me to come and here we are."

She demurred. "Just say one word," she told me, "and you can have anything I've got."

So it hung, now, on one word. What word? I wondered, since I'd heard that before. Marriage, obviously. I still remember that little room under the eaves on West Twenty-third Street. It was so neat and futile.

By this time, Richardson had finished his term, the first half-year was ended and I was put in charge. I'd never had anything to do with Malzacher in the office, but we got along all right, so I was wholly unprepared for what was to follow. For at the end of the first month of the year 1909, I was handed the official forms from Albany to report the business of the hospital for that month: patients received, deaths, recoveries, patients discharged and so forth. It was an extensive and explicit sheet which I, as Resident Surgeon, had now to clear and sign.

The hospital, I thus discovered, was in part state-supported, though it had its separate Board of Governors, headed by one of the most distinguished figures in Wall Street banking circles. Each month we received funds from Albany commensurate with the admissions and discharges for that month. Miss Malzacher handed me a slip of paper giving the essential facts, which I was to fill in, in my own handwriting, sign and return the sheets to her to put with the other matters to be sent to the state capital.

"Fine," I said. "But how do you get these figures?"

"From the blue cards, you know," she said.

"Fine again," said I. "Show me the blue cards." The thing was we had blue and salmon cards, one for the out-patient department, which was large, and the others for the kids in the little back ward.

"I can't do that," she said. "This is a business matter, not a medical matter, and we can't release them."

"Is that so?" I said. "Then I can't sign the report."

"Why, no one has ever made such a fuss over so small a matter before. You'll have to sign them."

"Sure, after I see the cards." You see that's what I had been taught by my parents and I had no choice in the matter.

So the report went to Albany without my signature. Then all hell broke out.

They fired the report back at us and Malzacher began all over again on me.

But my back was up and there it was to stay.

After Malzacher, the doctors took their turn. They were some of the leading men in the East, though this was not one of their major appointments: Kerley, Davis, Mabbott and several others— "Maggoty" Mabbott the girls had nicknamed him, because of the way he lingered over a vaginal examination. Kerley was one of the worst, all this at a bad time for me because Kerley had asked me what I intended to do after I had finished at Nursery and Child's. When I told him that I had no plans, he asked me if I would not come into his office for the first year. What an opportunity! A New York specialist. I was practically made, I thought.

Kerley came to me and said, "Look, Williams, why don't you sign that report? This is just a routine matter. It's been going on for years. There's no reason to suspect dishonesty. You know who's at the head of the Board. Sign the damned thing and forget it."

"I'm sorry, Dr. Kerley," I said, "but unless I can verify what I'm signing, I can't put my name to it." He walked off disgusted.

Davis tried to laugh it off without success, and then Mabbott, dear old Maggoty Mabbott, tried his hand at it. Meanwhile our operating funds were being withheld.

"Williams, we all like you in this place. Your work has been excellent, outstanding. You have a brilliant future before you either in pediatrics or obstetrics. I know you're young and a stickler for your principles. But look, we doctors can't go against the business of an institution like this. Our business is to cure patients, not to worry over where the money comes from. You're actually doing everyone an injury by this eccentric conduct. Look, sign those papers and get the silly business over with." He stopped and smiled benignly at me.

I looked at him and said, "Dr. Mabbott, if someone handed you some scribbled figures on a piece of paper and told you to copy them into an official report, figures which you had no way of verifying, could you as a self-respecting person put your name to those figures, and would you do it?" I spoke straight to his face.

He looked hard at me and I could see the color rising. He remained silent only a moment, then he said, "No, I'll be damned if I would," and turned and walked out.

Good old Maggoty Mabbott. But the Board would not release

me. They said that they had arranged for the treasurer of the institution to sign the report and that I was suspended for two weeks for insubordination.

My head seethed, but before I left, Miss Cuthbertson, who had followed the proceedings with mounting excitement, begged me not to quit but to keep on, that she had some information that would be brought forward at the right time and place, please not to quit under attack, not to go back on her. I spent my two weeks at home. Pop had no suggestions other than to say that I was right in doing what I did. At the end of the two weeks, I returned to duty. Everything seemed fine.

But at the end of February, it began again. The previous month's report signed by the treasurer was not satisfactory to Albany. It had to have my signature and the office still refused to let me see and count the cards. Then Miss Cuthbertson played her card—but not officially, only to me where it did no good. She didn't come out publicly with the facts.

One day she had gone, not quite by chance, but knowing someone was in the Board Room, to see why they were so quiet there. Opening the door she discovered Miss M. on the end of the table, the President of the Board facing her, in a position that she, Miss Cuthbertson, would not describe to me. There it was, plain as daylight, the whole reason why the woman was being allowed to get away with her petty graft—that wealthy man.

If I could spill this in the papers, I thought. But Pop advised me against it.

A lawyer?

No. How can we afford to fight it? and with some of the leading specialists of New York too cowardly to back me, afraid of big money and what their stinking little hides might have to take for it. Sick, I had a horrible sore throat, in fact I could hardly talk above a whisper, I resigned. I didn't tell anyone about it, but I wrote a letter to the Board giving them a piece of my mind and started to close up shop.

The girls were marvelous to me. They were coming into my room with hot drinks, putting cold compresses on my throat, all but getting in bed with me to warm me when I had a chill, kissing me good night—but still I wrote the letter, went down and mailed it in the inside box at the door of the office.

Miss Cuthbertson had seen me go and, knowing my mood, rushed up to ask me what I had been up to.

"I've resigned," I said. "I wrote a letter to the Board of Governors telling them what I thought of them and mailed it."

"You fool. Where?"

"In the box at the office."

She ran out my door for it was not a U.S. Mailbox and could be opened with a key. But in a few moments she was back, licked.

"You've done it. That woman was too quick for me. She must have guessed what you were up to. She has taken your letter and has gone out and mailed it at the corner. I asked the officer at the door. He saw her do it. You fool—just when we could have beat them."

I didn't give a damn. I felt better in fact than I had felt in two months, unhappy as I must have been internally. I couldn't work with that gang any longer. My resignation was officially accepted. I packed and said good-bye and went home. My days of internship were over. Not a single doctor of the attending staff had stood by me. To hell with them all, I thought.

*THE AUTOBIOGRAPHY OF WILLIAM*
*CARLOS WILLIAMS*, 1951

# MALCOLM COWLEY

*After World War I, while some members of the "lost generation" of the 1920's found themselves in Paris, a greater number turned up in Greenwich Village. Malcolm Cowley's memoir of the era,* Exile's Return, *cunningly fused his own story with that of his generation. In retrospect, Cowley (1898–1989) managed a detached but tender irony toward some of the more inflated claims of 20's bohemianism.*

## THE LONG FURLOUGH

AFTER COLLEGE and the war, most of us drifted to Manhattan, to the crooked streets south of Fourteenth, where you could rent a furnished hall-bedroom for two or three dollars weekly or the top floor of a rickety house for thirty dollars a month. We came to the Village without any intention of becoming Villagers. We came because living was cheap, because friends of ours had come already (and written us letters full of enchantment), because it seemed that New York was the only city where a young writer could be published. There were some who stayed in Europe after the war and others who carried their college diplomas straight to Paris: they had money. But the rest of us belonged to the proletariat of the arts and we lived in Greenwich Village where everyone else was poor.

"There were," I wrote some years ago, "two schools among us: those who painted the floors black (they were the last of the aesthetes) and those who did not paint the floors. Our college textbooks and the complete works of Jules Laforgue gathered dust on the mantelpiece among a litter of unemptied ashtrays. The streets outside were those of Glenn Coleman's early paintings: low red-brick early nineteenth-century houses, crazy doorways, sidewalks covered with black snow and, in the foreground, an old woman bending under a sack of rags."

The black snow melted: February blustered into March. It was as if the war had never been fought, or had been fought by others. We were about to continue the work begun in high school, of training ourselves as writers, choosing masters to imitate, deciding what we wanted to say and persuading magazines to let us say it. We should have to earn money, think about getting jobs: the war was over. But besides the memories we scarcely mentioned, it had left us with a vast unconcern for the future and an enormous appetite for pleasure. We were like soldiers with a few more days to spend in Blighty: every moment was borrowed from death. It didn't matter that we were penniless: we danced to old squeaky victrola records—*You called me Baby Doll a year ago; Hello, Central, give me No Man's Land*—we had our first love affairs, we stopped in the midst of arguments to laugh at jokes as broad and pointless as the ocean, we were continually drunk with high spirits, transported by the miracle of no longer wearing a uniform. As we walked down Greenwich Avenue we stopped to enjoy the smell of hot bread outside of Cushman's bakery. In the spring morning it seemed that every ash barrel was green-wreathed with spinach.

It was April now, and the long furlough continued. . . . You woke at ten o'clock between soiled sheets in a borrowed apartment; the sun dripped over the edges of the green windowshade. On the dresser was a half-dollar borrowed the night before from the last guest to go downstairs singing: even at wartime prices it was enough to buy breakfast for two—eggs, butter, a loaf of bread, a grapefruit. When the second pot of coffee was emptied a visitor would come, then another; you would borrow fifty-five cents for the cheapest bottle of sherry. Somebody would suggest a ride across the bay to Staten Island. Dinner provided itself, and there was always a program for the evening. On Fridays there were dances in Webster Hall attended by terrible uptown people who came to watch the Villagers at their revels and buy them drinks in return for being insulted; on Saturdays everybody gathered at Luke O'Connor's saloon, the Working Girls' Home; on Sunday nights there were poker games played for imaginary stakes and interrupted from moment to moment by gossip, jokes, plans; everything in those days was an excuse for talking. There were always parties, and if they lasted into the morning they might end in a "community sleep": the mattresses were pulled off the beds and laid side by side on the floor, then double blankets were unfolded and stretched lengthwise across them, so that a dozen people could sleep there in discomfort, provided nobody snored. One night, having fallen asleep, you gave a snore so tremendous that you wakened to its echo and listened to your companions drowsily cursing the snorer, and for good measure cursed him yourself. But always, before going to bed, you borrowed fifty cents for breakfast. Eight hours' foresight was sufficient. Always, after the coffee pot was drained a visitor would come with money enough for a bottle of sherry.

But it couldn't go on forever. Some drizzly morning late in April you woke up to find yourself married (and your wife, perhaps, suffering from a dry cough that threatened consumption). If there had been checks from home, there would be no more of them. Or else it happened after a siege of influenza, which that year had curious effects: it left you weak in body, clear in mind, revolted by humanity and yourself. Tottering from the hospital, you sat in the back room of a saloon and from the whitewood table sour with spilled beer, surveyed your blank prospects. You had been living on borrowed money, on borrowed time, in a borrowed apartment: in three months you had exhausted both your credit and your capacity to beg. There was no army now to clothe and feed you like a kind-hateful parent. No matter where the next meal came from, you would pay for it yourself.

In the following weeks you didn't exactly starve; ways could be found of earning a few dollars. Once a week you went round to the editorial offices of the *Dial*, which was then appearing every two weeks in a format something like that of the *Nation*. One of the editors was a friend of your wife's and he would give you half a dozen bad novels to review in fifty or a hundred words apiece. When the reviews were published you would be paid a dollar for each of them, but that mightn't be for weeks or months, and meanwhile you had to eat. So you would carry the books to a bench in Union Square and page through them hastily, making notes—in two or three hours you would be finished with the whole armful and then you would take them to a secondhand bookstore on Fourth Avenue, where the proprietor paid a flat rate of thirty-five cents for each review copy; you thought it was more than the novels were worth. With exactly $2.10 in your pocket you would buy bread and butter and lamb chops and Bull Durham for cigarettes and order a bag of coal; then at home you would broil the lamb chops over the grate because the landlady had neglected to pay her gas bill, just as you had neglected to pay the rent. You were all good friends and she would be invited to share in the feast. Next morning you would write the reviews, then start on the search for a few dollars more.

You began to feel that one meal a day was all that anyone needed and you wondered why anyone bothered to eat more. Late on a June day you were sitting in Sheridan Square trying to write a poem. "Move along, young fella," said the cop, and the poem was forgotten. Walking southward with the Woolworth Building visible in the distance you imagined a revolution in New York. Revolution was in the air that summer; the general strike had failed in Seattle, but a steel strike was being prepared, and a coal strike, and the railroad men were demanding government ownership—that was all right, but you imagined another kind of revolt, one that would start with a dance through the streets and barrels of cider opened at every corner and beside each barrel a back-country ham fresh from the oven; the juice squirted out of it when you carved the first slice. Then—but only after you had finished the last of the ham and drained a pitcher of cider and stuffed your mouth with apple pie—then you would set about hanging policemen from the lamp posts, or better still from the crossties of the Elevated, and beside each policeman would be hanged a Methodist preacher, and beside each preacher a pansy poet. Editors would be poisoned with printer's ink: they would die horribly, vomiting ink on white paper. You hated editors, pansipoetical poets, police men, preachers, you hated city streets . . . and suddenly the street went black. You hadn't even time to feel faint. The pavement rose and hit you between the eyes.

Nobody came to help, nobody even noticed that you had fallen. You scrambled to your feet, limped into a lunch wagon and spent your last dime for a roll and a cup of coffee. The revolution was postponed (on account of I was hungry, sergeant, honest I was too hungry) and the war was ended (listen, sojer, you're out of that man's army now, you're going back behind the plow, you gotta get rich, you son of a bitch). The war was over now and your long furlough was over. It was time to get a job.

*EXILE'S RETURN*, 1951

# ALFRED KAZIN

*New York has sometimes been compared to a collection of small villages, insular and provincial. As literary critic Alfred Kazin (1915–1998) recalls in his memoir* A Walker in the City, *the psychological distance between his shtetl-like neighborhood of Brownsville, Brooklyn, and the spires of Manhattan could be so great that "going into the city" felt like visiting another country.*

## FROM *A WALKER IN THE CITY*

W HEN I was a child I thought we lived at the end of the world. It was the eternity of the subway ride into the city that first gave me this idea. It took a long time getting to "New York"; it seemed longer getting back. Even the I.R.T. got tired by the time it came to us, and ran up into the open for a breath of air before it got locked into its terminus at New Lots. As the train left the tunnel to rattle along the elevated tracks, I felt I was being jostled on a camel past the last way stations in the desert. Oh that ride from New York! Light came only at Sutter Avenue. First across the many stations of the Gentiles to the East River. Then clear across Brooklyn, almost to the brink of the ocean all our fathers crossed. All those first stations in Brooklyn—Clark, Borough Hall, Hoyt, Nevins, the junction of the East and West Side express lines—told me only that I was on the last leg home, though there was always a stirring of my heart at Hoyt, where the grimy subway platform was suddenly enlivened by Abraham and Straus's windows of ladies' wear. Atlantic Avenue was vaguely exciting, a crossroads, the Long Island railroad; I never saw a soul get in or out at Bergen Street; the Grand Army Plaza, with its great empty caverns smoky with dust and chewing-gum wrappers, meant Prospect Park and that stone path beside a meadow where as a child I ran off from my father one summer twilight just in time to see the lamplighter go up the path lighting from the end of his pole each gas mantle suddenly flaring within its corolla of pleated paper—then, that summer I first strayed off the block for myself, the steps leading up from the boathouse, the long stalks of grass wound between the steps thick with the dust and smell of summer—then, that great summer at sixteen, my discovery in the Brooklyn Museum of Albert Pinkham Ryder's cracked oily fishing boats drifting under the moon. Franklin Avenue was where the Jews began—but all middle-class Jews, *alrightniks*, making out "all right" in the New World, they were still Gentiles to me as they went out into the wide and tree-lined Eastern Parkway. For us the journey went on and on—past Nostrand, past Kingston, past Utica, and only then out into the open at Sutter, overlooking Lincoln Terrace Park, "Tickle-Her" Park, the zoo of our adolescence, through which no girl could pass on a summer evening without its being understood forever after that she was "in"; past the rickety "two-family" private houses built in the fever of Brownsville's last real-estate boom; and then into Brownsville itself—Saratoga, Rockaway, and home. For those who lived still beyond, in East New York, there was Junius, there was Pennsylvania, there was Van Siclen, and so at last into New Lots, where the city goes back to the marsh, and even the subway ends.

Yet it was not just the long pent-up subway ride that led me to think of Brownsville as the margin of the city, the last place, the car barns where they locked up the subway and the trolley cars at night. There were always raw patches of unused city land all around us filled with "monument works" where they cut and stored tombstones, as there were still on our street farmhouses and the remains of old cobbled driveways down which chickens came squealing into our punchball games—but most of it dead land, neither country nor city, with that look of prairie waste I have so often seen on my walks along the fringes of American cities near the freight yards. We were nearer the ocean than the city, but our front on the ocean was Canarsie—in those days the great refuse dump through which I made my first and grimmest walks into the city—a place so celebrated in New York vaudeville houses for its squalor that the very sound of the word was always good for a laugh. CAN-NARR-SIE! They fell into the aisles. But that was the way to the ocean we always took summer evenings—through silent streets of old broken houses whose smoky red Victorian fronts looked as if the paint had clotted like blood and had then been mixed with soot—past infinite weedy lots, the smell of freshly cut boards in the lumber yards, the junk yards, the marshland eating the pavement, the truck farms, the bungalows that had lost a window or a door as they tottered on their poles against the damp and the ocean winds. The place as I have it in my mind still reeks of the fires burning in the refuse dumps. Farms that had once been the outposts of settlers in Revolutionary days had crumbled and sunk like wet sand. Canarsie was where they opened the sluice gates to let the city's muck out into the ocean. But at the end was the roar of the Atlantic and the summer house where we stood outside watching through lattices the sports being served with great pitchers of beer foaming onto the red-checked tablecloths. Summer, my summer! Summer!

We were of the city, but somehow not in it. Whenever I went off on my favorite walk to Highland Park in the "American" district to the north, on the border of Queens, and climbed the hill to the old reservoir from which I could look straight across to the skyscrapers of Manhattan, I saw New York as a foreign city. There, brilliant and unreal, the city had its life, as Brownsville was ours. That the two were joined in me I never knew then—not even on those glorious summer nights of my last weeks in high school when, with what an ache, I would come back into Brownsville along Liberty Avenue, and, as soon as I could see blocks ahead of me the Labor Lyceum, the malted milk and Fatima signs over the candy stores, the old women in their housedresses sitting in front of the tenements like priestesses of an ancient cult, knew I was home.

We were the end of the line. We were the children of the immigrants who had camped at the city's back door, in New York's rawest, remotest, cheapest ghetto, enclosed on one side by the Canarsie flats and on the other by the hallowed middle-class districts that showed the way to New York. "New York" was what we put last on our address, but first in thinking of the others around us. *They* were New York, the Gentiles, America; we were Brownsville—*Brunzvil,* as the old folks said—the dust of the earth to all Jews with money, and notoriously a place that measured all success by our skill in getting away from it. So that when poor Jews left, *even* Negroes, as we said, found it easy to settle on the margins of Brownsville, and with the coming of spring, bands of Gypsies, who would rent empty stores, hang their rugs around them like a desert tent, and bring a dusty and faintly sinister air of carnival into our neighborhood.

They have built a housing project deep down the center of Brownsville, from Rockaway to Stone, cutting clean diagonal forms within the onlooking streets, and leaving at one end only the public school I attended as a boy. As I walked past those indistinguishable red prisms of city houses, I kept remembering what they had pulled down to make this *project*—and despite my pleasure in all this space and light in Brownsville, despite even my envious wonder what our own life would have been if *we* had lived, as soon all of New York's masses will live, just like everybody else, still, I could not quite believe that what I saw before me was real. Brownsville in that model quarter looks like an old crone who has had a plastic operation, and to my amazement I miss her old, sly, and withered face. I miss all those ratty little wooden tenements, born with the smell of damp in them, in which there grew up how many schoolteachers, city accountants, rabbis, cancer specialists, functionaries of the revolution, and strong-arm men for Murder, Inc.; I miss that affected squirt who always wore a paste diamond on his left pinky and one unforgotten day, taught me to say *children* for *kids*; I miss the sinister "Coney Island" dives where before, during, and after the school day we all anxiously gobbled down hot dogs soggy in sauerkraut and mustard, and I slid along the sawdust floor fighting to get back the violin the tough guys always stole from my locker for a joke; I miss the poisonous sweetness I used to breathe in from the caramels melting inside the paper cartons every time I passed the candy wholesaler's on my way back from school; I miss the liturgical refrain *Kosher-Bosher* lettered on the windows of the butcher shops; the ducks at Thanksgiving hanging down the doorways of the chicken store; the clouds of white dust that rose up behind the windows of the mattress factory. Above all I miss the fence to the junk yard where I would wait with my store of little red volumes, THE WORLD'S GREATEST

SELECTED SHORT STORIES, given us gratis by the *Literary Digest*, hoping for a glimpse of a girl named Deborah. At eleven or twelve I was so agonizedly in love with her, not least because she had been named after a prophetess in Israel, that I would stand at the fence for hours, even creep through the junk yard to be near her windows, with those little red books always in my hand. At home I would recite to myself in triumph the great lines from Judges: *Desolate were the open towns in Israel, they were desolate, until that I arose, Deborah. . . .* But near her I was afraid, and always took along volumes of THE WORLD'S GREATEST SELECTED SHORT STORIES as a gift, to ease my way into her house. She had five sisters, and every one of them always seemed to be home whenever I called. They would look up at me standing in their kitchen with the books in my hand, and laugh. "Look, boychik," the eldest once said to me in a kindly way, "you don't have to *buy* your way in here every time with those damned books just to see Deborah! Come on your own!"

There is something uncanny now about seeing the old vistas rear up at each end of that housing project. Despite those fresh diagonal walks, with their trees and children's sandboxes and Negro faces calmly at home with the white, so many of the old tenements have been left undisturbed on every side of the project, the streets beyond are so obviously just as they were when I grew up in them, that it is as if they had been ripped out of their original pattern and then pasted back again behind the unbelievable miniatures of the future.

To make that housing project they have torn away the lumber yard; the wholesale drygoods store where my dressmaker mother bought the first shirts I ever wore that she did not make herself; how many poolrooms; and that to me sinister shed that was so long a garage, but before that, in the days of the silents, a movie house where every week, while peddlers went up and down the aisles hawking ice-cream bricks and orange squeeze, I feasted in my terror and joy on the "episodes." It was there one afternoon, between the damp coldness in the movie house and the covetous cries of the peddlers, that I was first seized by that bitter guilt I always felt in the movies whenever there was still daylight outside. As I saw Monte

Blue being locked into an Iron Maiden, it suddenly came on me that the penalty for my delicious reveries might be just such a death—a death as lonely, as sickeningly remote from all human aid, as the one I saw my hero calmly prepare to face against the yellow shadows of deepest Asia. Though that long-forgotten movie house now comes back on me as a primitive, folksy place—every time the main door was opened to let in peddlers with fresh goods, a hostile mocking wave of daylight fell against the screen, and in the lip-reading silence of the movies I could hear the steady whir and clacking of the machine and the screech of the trolley cars on Rockaway Avenue—I instantly saw in that ominous patch of light the torture box of life-in-death, some reproach calling out the punishment for my sin.

A sin, perhaps, only of my own devising; the sin I recorded against all idle enjoyment, looking on for its own sake alone; but a sin. The daylight was for grimness and labor.

I see that they have also torn out that little clapboard Protestant church that stood so long near the corner of Blake Avenue. It was the only church I ever saw in our neighborhood—the others were the Russian Orthodox meeting-house in East New York, and the Catholic church on East New York Avenue that marked the boundary, as I used to think of it, between us and the Italians stretching down Rockaway and Saratoga to Fulton. That little clapboard church must have been the last of its kind surviving from the days when all that land was owned by Scottish farmers. I remember the hymns that rolled out of the church on Sunday mornings, and how we sniffed as we went by. All those earnest, faded-looking people in their carefully brushed and strangely old-fashioned clothes must have come down there from a long way off. I never saw any of them except on Sunday mornings—the women often surprisingly quite fat, if not so fat as ours, and looking rather timid in their severe dresses and great straw hats with clusters of artificial flowers and wax berries along the brim as they waited for each other on the steps after the service; the men very stiff in their long four-buttoned jackets. They did not belong with us at all; I could never entirely believe that they were really there. One afternoon on my way back from school my curiosity got the better of me despite all my fear of Gentiles, and I stealthily crept in, never having entered a church in my life before, to examine what I was sure would be an exotic and idolatrous horror. It was the plainest thing I had ever seen—not, of course, homey, lived-in, and smelling of sour wine, snuff, and old prayer books, like our little wooden synagogue on Chester Street, but so varnished-clean and empty and austere, like our school auditorium, and so severely reserved above the altar and in the set rows of wooden pews to the service of an enigmatic cult, that the chief impression it made on me, who expected all Christians to be as fantastic as albinos, was that these people were not, apparently, so completely different from us as I had imagined. I was bewildered. What really held me there was the number of things written in English. I had associated God only with a foreign language. Suspended from the ceiling over the altar was a great gold-wood sign on which the black Gothic letters read: I AM THE RESURRECTION AND THE LIFE. I remember standing in the doorway, longing to go all the way up the aisle, then suddenly running away. The distance from that doorway to the altar was the longest gap in space I had ever seen.

1951

# JOSEPH MITCHELL

———

*North Carolina–born Joseph Mitchell (1908–96) became an ardent lover of New York, and celebrated it eloquently. He sought out the city's lesser-known subcultures (Gypsy fortune-tellers, Mohawk construction workers, fishing boat captains, African-American cemetery-keepers in Staten Island) and brought an archaeologist's patience and an unshowy but meticulous prose style to his New Yorker pieces—and in the process set a new literary standard for the urban profile.*

## UP IN THE OLD HOTEL

EVERY NOW AND THEN, seeking to rid my mind of thoughts of death and doom, I get up early and go down to Fulton Fish Market. I usually arrive around five-thirty, and take a walk through the two huge open-fronted market sheds, the Old Market and the New Market, whose fronts rest on South Street and whose backs rest on piles in the East River. At that time, a little while before the trading begins, the stands in the sheds are heaped high and spilling over with forty to sixty kinds of finfish and shellfish from the East Coast, the West Coast, the Gulf Coast, and half a dozen foreign countries. The smoky riverbank dawn, the racket the fishmongers make, the seaweedy smell, and the sight of this plentifulness always give me a feeling of well-being, and sometimes they elate me. I wander among the stands for an hour or so. Then I go into a cheerful market restaurant named Sloppy Louie's and eat a big, inexpensive, invigorating breakfast—a kippered herring and scrambled eggs, or a shad-roe omelet, or split sea scallops and bacon, or some other breakfast specialty of the place.

Sloppy Louie's occupies the ground floor of an old building at 92 South Street, diagonally across the street from the sheds. This building faces the river and looks out on the slip between the Fulton Street fish pier and the old Porto Rico Line dock. It is six floors high, and it has two windows to the floor. Like the majority of the older buildings in the market district, it is made of hand-molded Hudson

River brick, a rosy-pink and relatively narrow kind that used to be turned out in Haverstraw and other kiln towns on the Hudson and sent down to the city in barges. It has an ornamented tin cornice and a slate-covered mansard roof. It is one of those handsome, symmetrical old East River waterfront buildings that have been allowed to dilapidate. The windows of its four upper floors have been boarded over for many years, a rain pipe that runs down the front of it is riddled with rust holes, and there are gaps here and there on its mansard where slates have slipped off. In the afternoons, after two or three, when the trading is over and the stands begin to close, the slimy, overfed gulls that scavenge in the market roost by the hundreds along its cornice, hunched up and gazing downward.

I have been going to Sloppy Louie's for nine or ten years, and the proprietor and I are old friends. His name is Louis Morino, and he is a contemplative and generous and worldly-wise man in his middle sixties. Louie is a North Italian. He was born in Recco, a fishing and bathing-beach village thirteen miles southeast of Genoa, on the Eastern Riviera. Recco is ancient; it dates back to the third century. Families in Genoa and Milan and Turin own villas in and around it, and go there in the summer. Some seasons, a few English and Americans show up. According to a row of colored-postcard views of it Scotch-taped to a mirror on the wall in back of Louie's cash register, it is a village of steep streets and tall, square, whitewashed stone houses. The fronts of the houses are decorated with stenciled designs—madonnas, angels, flowers, fruit, and fish. The fish design is believed to protect against the evil eye and appears most often over doors and windows. Big, lush fig bushes grow in almost every yard. In the center of the village is an open-air market where fishermen and farmers sell their produce off plank-and-sawhorse counters. Louie's father was a fisherman. His name was Giuseppe Morino, and he was called, in Genoese dialect, Beppe du Russu, or Joe the Redhead. "My family was one of the old fishing families in Recco that the priest used to tell us had been fishing along that coast since Roman times," Louis says. "We lived on a street named the Vico Saporito that was paved with broken-up sea shells and wound in and out and led down to the water. My father did a kind of fishing that's called haul-seining over here, and he set lobster traps and jigged for squid and bobbed for octopuses. When the weather was right, he used to row out to an underwater cave he knew about and anchor over it and take a bob consisting of a long line with scraps of raw meat hung from it every foot or so and a stone on the end of it and drop it in the mouth of the cave, and the octopuses would shoot up out of the dark down there and swallow the meat scraps and that would hold them, and then my father would draw the bob up slow and steady and pull the octopuses loose from the meat scraps one by one and toss them in a tub in the boat. He'd bob up enough octopuses in a couple of hours to glut the market in Recco. This cave was full of octopuses; it was choked with them. He had found it, and he had the rights to it. The other fishermen didn't go near it; they called it Beppe du Russu's cave. In addition to fishing, he kept a rickety old bathhouse on the beach for the summer people. It stood on stilts, and I judge it had fifty to sixty rooms. We called it the Bagni Margherita. My mother ran a little buffet in connection with it."

Louie left Recco in 1905, when he was close to eighteen. "I loved my family," he says, "and it tore me in two to leave, but I had five brothers and two sisters, and all my brothers were younger than me, and there were already too many fishermen in Recco, and the bathhouse brought in just so much, and I had a fear kept persisting there might not be enough at home to go around in time to come, so I got passage from Genoa to New York scrubbing pots in the galley of a steamship and went straight from the dock to a chophouse on East 138th Street in the Bronx that was operated by a man named Capurro who came from Recco. Capurro knew my father when they both were boys." Capurro gave Louie a job washing dishes and taught him how to wait on tables. He stayed there two years. For the next twenty-three years, he worked as a waiter in restaurants all over Manhattan and Brooklyn. He has forgotten how many he worked in; he can recall the names of thirteen. Most of them were medium-size restaurants of the Steak-&-Chops, We-Specialize-in-Seafood type. In the winter of 1930, he decided to risk his savings and become his own boss. "At that time," he says, "the stock-market crash had shook everything up and the depression was setting in, and I knew of

several restaurants in midtown that could be bought at a bargain—
lease, furnishings, and good will. All were up-to-date places. Then I
ran into a waiter I used to work with and he told me about this old
run-down restaurant in an old run-down building in the fish market
that was for sale, and I went and saw it, and I took it. The reason I
did, Fulton Fish Market reminds me of Recco. There's a world of
difference between them. At the same time, they're very much alike
—the fish smell, the general gone-to-pot look, the trading that goes
on in the streets, the roofs over the sidewalks, the cats in corners
gnawing on fish heads, the gulls in the gutters, the way everybody's
on to everybody else, the quarreling and the arguing. There's a boss
fishmonger down here, a spry old hardheaded Italian man who's got
a million dollars in the bank and dresses like he's on relief and walks
up and down the fish pier snatching fish out of barrels by their tails
and weighing them in his hands and figuring out in his mind to a
fraction of a fraction how much they're worth and shouting and
singing and enjoying life, and the face on him, the way he conducts
himself, he reminds me so much of my father that sometimes, when
I see him, it puts me in a good humor, and sometimes it breaks my
heart."

Louie is five feet six, and stocky. He has an owl-like face—his
nose is hooked, his eyebrows are tufted, and his eyes are large and
brown and observant. He is white-haired. His complexion is reddish, and his face and the backs of his hands are speckled with freck-
les and liver spots. He wears glasses with flesh-colored frames. He is
bandy-legged, and he carries his left shoulder lower than his right
and walks with a shuffling, hipshot, head-up, old-waiter's walk. He
dresses neatly. He has his suits made by a high-priced tailor in the insurance district, which adjoins the fish-market district. Starting work
in the morning, he always puts on a fresh apron and a fresh brown
linen jacket. He keeps a napkin folded over his left arm even when
he is standing behind the cash register. He is a proud man, and somewhat stiff and formal by nature, but he unbends easily and he has
great curiosity and he knows how to get along with people. During
rush hours, he jokes and laughs with his customers and recommends
his daily specials in extravagant terms and listens to fish-market

gossip and passes it on; afterward, in repose, having a cup of coffee by himself at a table in the rear, he is grave.

Louie is a widower. His wife, Mrs. Victoria Piazza Morino, came from a village named Ruta that is only two and a half miles from Recco, but he first became acquainted with her in Brooklyn. They were married in 1928, and he was deeply devoted to her. She died in 1949. He has two daughters—Jacqueline, who is twenty-two and was recently graduated from the Mills College of Education, a school for nursery, kindergarten, and primary teachers on lower Fifth Avenue, and Lois, who is seventeen and was recently graduated from Fontbonne Hall, a high school on Shore Road in Brooklyn that is operated by the Sisters of St. Joseph. They are smart, bright, slim, vivid, dark-eyed girls. Louie has to be on hand in his restaurant in the early morning, and he usually gets up between four and five, but before leaving home he always squeezes orange juice and puts coffee on the stove for his daughters. Most days, he gets home before they do and cooks dinner.

Louie owns his home, a two-story brick house on a maple-bordered street in the predominantly Norwegian part of the Bay Ridge neighborhood in Brooklyn. There is a saying in Recco that people and fig bushes do best close to salt water; Louie's home is only a few blocks from the Narrows, and fifteen years ago he ordered three tiny fig bushes from a nursery in Virginia and set them out in his back yard, and they have flourished. In the late fall, he wraps an accumulation of worn-out suits and dresses and sweaters and sheets and blankets around their trunks and limbs. "All winter," he says, "when I look out the back window, it looks like I got three mummies stood up out there." At the first sign of spring, he takes the wrappings off. The bushes begin to bear the middle of July and bear abundantly during August. One bush bears small white figs, and the others bear plump black figs that split their skins down one side as they ripen and gape open and show their pink and violet flesh. Louie likes to gather the figs around dusk, when they are still warm from the heat of the day. Sometimes, bending beside a bush, he plunges his face into the leaves and breathes in the musky smell of the ripening figs, a smell that fills his mind with memories of Recco in mid-summer.

Louie doesn't think much of the name of his restaurant. It is an old restaurant with old furnishings that has had a succession of proprietors and a succession of names. Under the proprietor preceding Louie, John Barbagelata, it was named the Fulton Restaurant, and was sometimes called Sloppy John's. When Louie took it over, he changed the name to Louie's Restaurant. One of the fishmongers promptly started calling it Sloppy Louie's, and Louie made a mistake and remonstrated with him. He remonstrated with him on several occasions. As soon as the people in the market caught on to the fact that the name offended Louie, naturally most of them began using it. They got in the habit of using it. Louie brooded about the matter off and on for over three years, and then had a new swinging signboard erected above his door with SLOPPY LOUIE'S RESTAURANT on it in big red letters. He even changed his listing in the telephone book. "I couldn't beat them," he says, "so I joined them."

Sloppy Louie's is small and busy. It can seat eighty, and it crowds up and thins out six or seven times a day. It opens at five in the morning and closes at eight-thirty in the evening. It has a double door in front with a show window on each side. In one window are three sailing-ship models in whiskey bottles, a giant lobster claw with eyes and a mouth painted on it, a bulky oyster shell, and a small skull. Beside the shell is a card on which Louie has neatly written, "Shell of an Oyster dredged from the bottom of Great South Bay. Weighed two and a quarter pounds. Estimated to be fifteen years old. Said to be largest ever dredged in G.S.B." Beside the skull is a similar card, which says, "This is the skull of a Porpoise taken by a dragger off Long Beach, Long Island." In the other window is an old pie cupboard with glass sides. To the left, as you enter, is a combined cigar showcase and cashier's desk, and an iron safe with a cash register on top of it. There are mirrors all around the walls. Four lamps and three electric fans with wooden blades that resemble propellers hang from the stamped tin ceiling. The tables in Louie's are communal, and there are exactly one dozen; six jut out from the wall on one side of the room and six jut out from the wall on the other side, and a broad aisle divides them. They are long tables, and solid and old and plain and built to last. They are made of black walnut; Louie once repaired a leg on one, and said it was like driving a nail in iron. Their tops have been seasoned by drippings and spillings from thousands upon thousands of platters of broiled fish, and their edges have been scratched and scarred by the hatchets and bale hooks that hang from frogs on fishmongers' belts. They are identical in size; some seat six, and some have a chair on the aisle end and seat seven. At the back of the room, hiding the door to the kitchen, is a huge floor mirror on which, each morning, using a piece of moistened chalk, Louie writes the menu for the day. It is sometimes a lengthy menu. A good many dishes are served in Louie's that are rarely served in other restaurants. One day, interspersed among the staple seafood-restaurant dishes, Louie listed cod cheeks, salmon cheeks, cod tongues, sturgeon liver, blue-shark steak, tuna steak, squid stew, and five kinds of roe—shad roe, cod roe, mackerel roe, herring roe, and yellow-pike roe. Cheeks are delectable morsels of flesh that are found in the heads of some species of fish, one on each side, inset in bone and cartilage. The men who dress fish in the fillet houses in the market cut out a few quarts of cheeks whenever they have the time to spare and sell them to Louie. Small shipments of them come down occasionally from the Boston Fish Pier, and the fishmongers, thinking of their own gullets, let Louie buy most of them. The fishmongers use Louie's as a testing kitchen. When anything unusual is shipped to the market, it is taken to Louie's and tried out. In the course of a year, Louie's undoubtedly serves a wider variety of seafood than any other restaurant in the country.

When I go to Sloppy Louie's for breakfast, I always try to get a chair at one of the tables up front, and Louie generally comes out from behind the cash register and tells me what is best to order. Some mornings, if there is a lull in the breakfast rush, he draws himself a cup of coffee and sits down with me. One morning a while back, he sat down, and I asked him how things were going, and he said he couldn't complain, he had about as much business as he could handle. "My breakfast trade still consists almost entirely of fishmongers and fish buyers," he said, "but my lunch trade has undergone a change. The last few years, a good many people in the districts up above the market have taken to walking down here occasionally for lunch—people from the insurance district, the financial district, and the coffee-roasting district. Some days, from noon to three, they outnumber the fishmongers. I hadn't realized myself how great a change had taken place until just the other day I happened to notice the mixed-up nature of a group of people sitting around one table. They were talking back and forth, the way people do in here that never even saw each other before, and passing the ketchup, and I'll tell you who they were. Sitting on one side was an insurance broker from Maiden Lane, and next to him was a fishmonger named Mr. Frank Wilkisson who's a member of a family that's had a stand in the Old Market three generations, and next to him was a young Southerner that you're doing good if you understand half what he says who drives one of those tremendous big refrigerator trucks that they call reefers and hits the market every four or five days with a load of shrimp from little shrimp ports in Florida and Georgia. Sitting on the other side was a lady who holds a responsible position in Continental Casualty up on William Street and comes in here for bouillabaisse, only we call it *ciuppin di pesce* and cook it the way it's cooked fishing-family style back in Recco, and next to her was an old gentleman who works in J. P. Morgan & Company's banking house and you'd think he'd order something expensive like pompano but he always orders cod cheeks and if we're out of that he orders cod roe and if we're out of that he orders broiled cod and God knows we're never out of that, and next to him was one of the bosses in Mooney's coffee-roasting plant at Fulton and Front. And sitting at the aisle end of the table was a man known all over as Cowhide Charlie who goes to slaughterhouses and buys green cowhides and sells them to fishing-boat captains to rig to the undersides of their drag nets to keep them from getting bottom-chafed and rock-cut and he's always bragging that right this very minute his hides are rubbing the bottom of every fishing bank from Nantucket Shoals to the Virginia Capes."

Louie said that some days, particularly Fridays, the place is jammed around one o'clock and latecomers crowd together just inside the door and stand and wait and stare, and he said that this gets on his nerves. He said he had come to the conclusion that he would have to go ahead and put in some tables on the second floor.

"I would've done it long ago," he said, "except I need the second floor for other things. This building doesn't have a cellar. South Street is old filled-in river swamp, and the cellars along here, what few there are, the East River leaks into them every high tide. The second floor is my cellar. I store supplies up there, and I keep my Deepfreeze up there, and the waiters change their clothes up there. I don't know what I'll do without it, only I got to make room someway."

"That ought to be easy," I said. "You've got four empty floors up above."

"You mean those boarded-up floors," Louie said. He hesitated a moment. "Didn't I ever tell you about the upstairs in here?" he asked. "Didn't I ever tell you about those boarded-up floors?"

"No," I said.

"They aren't empty," he said.

"What's in them?" I asked.

"I don't know," he said. "I've heard this and I've heard that, but I don't know. I wish to God I did know. I've wondered about it enough. I've rented this building twenty-two years, and I've never been above the second floor. The reason being, that's as far as the stairs go. After that, you have to get in a queer old elevator and pull yourself up. It's an old-fashioned hand-power elevator, what they used to call a rope-pull. I wouldn't be surprised it's the last of its kind in the city. I don't understand the machinery of it, the balancing weights and the cables and all that, but the way it's operated, there's a big iron wheel up at the top of the shaft and the wheel's got a groove in it, and there's a rope that rides in this groove, and you pull on the part of the rope that hangs down one side of the cage to go up, and you pull on the part that hangs down the other side to go down. Like a dumbwaiter. It used to run from the ground floor to the top, but a long time ago some tenant must've decided he didn't

have any further use for it and wanted it out of the way, so he had
the shaft removed from the ground floor and the second floor. He
had it cut off at the second-floor ceiling. In other words, the way it
is now, the bottom of the shaft is level with the second-floor ceiling—the floor of the elevator cage acts as part of the ceiling. To get
in the elevator, you have to climb a ladder that leads to a trap door
that's cut in the floor of the cage. It's a big, roomy cage, bigger than
the ones nowadays, but it doesn't have a roof on it—just this wooden
floor and some iron-framework sides. I go up the ladder sometimes
and push up the trap door and put my head and shoulders inside the
cage and shine a flashlight up the shaft, but that's as far as I go. Oh,
Jesus, it's dark and dusty in there. The cage is all furry with dust and
there's mold and mildew on the walls of the shaft and the air is dead.

"The first day I came here, I wanted to get right in the elevator
and go up to the upper floors and rummage around up there, see
what I could see, but the man who rented the building ahead of me
was with me, showing me over the place, and he warned me not to.
He didn't trust the elevator. He said you couldn't pay him to get in
it. 'Don't meddle with that thing,' he said. 'It's a rattlesnake. The
rope might break, or that big iron wheel up at the top of the shaft
that's eaten up with rust and hasn't been oiled for a generation might
work loose and drop on your head.' Consequently, I've never even
given the rope a pull. To pull the rope, you got to get inside the cage
and stand up. You can't reach it otherwise. I've been tempted to
many a time. It's a thick hemp rope. It's as thick as a hawser. It might
be rotten, but it certainly looks strong. The way the cage is sitting
now, I figure it'd only take a couple of pulls, a couple of turns of the
wheel, and you'd be far enough up to where you could swing the
cage door open and step out on the third floor. You can't open the
cage door now; you got to draw the cage up just a little. A matter of
inches. I reached into the cage once and tried to poke the door open
with a boat hook I borrowed off one of the fishing boats, but it
wouldn't budge. It's a highly irritating situation to me. I'd just like to
know for certain what's up there. A year goes by sometimes and I
hardly think about it, and then I get to wondering, and it has a tendency to prey on my mind. An old-timer in the market once told me

that many years ago a fishmonger down here got a bug in his head and invented a patented returnable zinc-lined fish box for shipping fish on ice and had hundreds of them built, sunk everything he had in them, and they didn't catch on, and finally he got permission to store them up on the third and fourth floors of this building until he could come to some conclusion what to do with them. This was back before they tinkered with the elevator. Only he never came to any conclusion, and by and by he died. The old-timer said it was his belief the fish boxes are still up there. The man who rented the building ahead of me, he had a different story. He was never above the second floor either, but he told me that one of the men who rented it ahead of him told him it was *his* understanding there was a lot of miscellaneous old hotel junk stored up there—beds and bureaus, pitchers and bowls, chamber pots, mirrors, brass spittoons, odds and ends, old hotel registers that the rats chew on to get paper to line their nests with, God knows what all. That's what he said. I don't know. I've made quite a study of this building for one reason and another, and I've took all kinds of pains tracking things down, but there's a lot about it I still don't know. I do know there was a hotel in here years back. I know that beyond all doubt. It was one of those old steamship hotels that used to face the docks all along South Street."

"Why don't you get a mechanic to inspect the elevator?" I asked. "It might be perfectly safe."

"That would cost money," Louie said. "I'm curious, but I'm not that curious. To tell you the truth, I just don't want to get in that cage by myself. I got a feeling about it, and that's the fact of the matter. It makes me uneasy—all closed in, and all that furry dust. It makes me think of a coffin, the inside of a coffin. Either that or a cave, the mouth of a cave. If I could get somebody to go along with me, somebody to talk to, just so I wouldn't be all alone in there, I'd go; I'd crawl right in. A couple of times, it almost happened I did. The first time was back in 1938. The hurricane we had that fall damaged the roofs on a good many of the old South Street buildings, and the real-estate management company I rented this building from sent a man down here to see if my roof was all right. I asked the man why didn't he take the elevator up to the attic floor, there might be a door

leading out on the roof. I told him I'd go along. He took one look inside the cage and said it would be more trouble than it was worth.
What he did, he went up on the roof of the building next door and
crossed over. Didn't find anything wrong. Six or seven months ago, I
had another disappointment. I was talking with a customer of mine
eats a fish lunch in here Fridays who's a contractor, and it happened
I got on the subject of the upper floors, and he remarked he understood how I felt, my curiosity. He said he seldom passes an old
boarded-up building without he wonders about it, wonders what it's
like in there—all empty and hollow and dark and still, not a sound,
only some rats maybe, racing around in the dark, or maybe some
English sparrows flying around in there in the empty rooms that always get in if there's a crack in one of the boards over a broken win-
dowpane, a crack or a knothole, and sometimes they can't find their
way out and they keep on hopping and flying and hopping and flying
until they starve to death. He said he had been in many such buildings in the course of his work, and had seen some peculiar things.
The next time he came in for lunch, he brought along a couple
of those helmets that they wear around construction work, those
orange-colored helmets, and he said to me, 'Come on, Louie. Put on
one of these, and let's go up and try out that elevator. If the rope
breaks, which I don't think it will—what the hell, a little shaking up
is good for the liver. If the wheel drops, maybe these helmets will
save us.' But he's a big heavy man, and he's not as active as he used
to be. He went up the ladder first, and when he got to the top he
backed right down. He put it on the basis he had a business appointment that afternoon and didn't want to get all dusty and dirty. I kept
the helmets. He wanted them back, but I held on to them. I don't intend to let that elevator stand in my way much longer. One of these
days, I'm going to sit down awhile with a bottle of Strega, and then
I'm going to stick one of those helmets on my head and climb in that
cage and put that damned elevator back in commission. The very
least, I'll pull the rope and see what happens. I do wish I could find
somebody had enough curiosity to go along with me. I've asked my
waiters, and I've tried to interest some of the people in the market,
but they all had the same answer. 'Hell, no,' they said."

Louie suddenly leaned forward. "What about you?" he asked. "Maybe I could persuade you."

I thought it over a few moments, and was about to suggest that we go upstairs at any rate and climb in the cage and look at the elevator, but just then a fishmonger who had finished his breakfast and wanted to pay his check rapped a dictatorial rat-a-tat on the glass top of the cigar showcase with a coin. Louie frowned and clenched his teeth. "I wish they wouldn't do that," he said, getting up. "It goes right through me."

Louie went over and took the man's money and gave him his change. Two waiters were standing at a service table in the rear, filling salt shakers, and Louie gestured to one of them to come up front and take charge of the cash register. Then he got himself another cup of coffee and sat back down and started talking again. "When I bought this restaurant," he said, "I wasn't too enthusiastic about the building. I had it in mind to build up the restaurant and find me a location somewhere else in the market and move, the trade would follow. Instead of which, after a while I got very closely attached to the building. Why I did is one of those matters, it really doesn't make much sense. It's all mixed up with the name of a street in Brooklyn, and it goes back to the last place I worked in before I came here. That was Joe's in Brooklyn, the old Nevins Street Joe's, Nevins just off Flatbush Avenue Extension. I was a waiter there seven years, and it was the best place I ever worked in. Joe's is part of a chain now, the Brass Rail chain. In my time, it was run by a very high-type Italian restaurant man named Joe Sartori, and it was the biggest chophouse in Brooklyn—fifty waiters, a main floor, a balcony, a ladies' dining room, and a Roman Garden. Joe's was a hangout for Brooklyn political bosses and officeholders, and it got a class of trade we called the old Brooklyn family trade, the rich old intermarried families that made their money out of Brooklyn real estate and Brooklyn docks and Brooklyn streetcar lines and Brooklyn gasworks. They had their money sunk way down deep in Brooklyn. I don't know how it is now, they've probably all moved into apartment houses, but in those days a good many of them lived in steep-stoop,

stain-glass mansions sitting up as solid as banks on Brooklyn Heights
and Park Slope and over around Fort Greene Park. They were a big-
eating class of people, and they believed in patronizing the good old
Brooklyn restaurants. You'd see them in Joe's, and you'd see them in
Gage & Tollner's and Lundy's and Tappen's and Villepigue's. There
was a high percentage of rich old independent women among them,
widows and divorced ladies and maiden ladies. They were a class
within a class. They wore clothes that hadn't been the style for years,
and they wore the biggest hats I ever saw, and the ugliest. They all
seemed to know each other since their childhood days, and they all
had some peculiarity, and they all had one foot in the grave, and they
all had big appetites. They had traveled widely, and they were good
judges of food, and they knew how to order a meal. Some were poison, to say the least, and some were just as nice as they could be. On
the whole, I liked them; they broke the monotony. Some always
came to my station; if my tables were full, they'd sit in some leather
chairs Mr. Sartori had up front and wait. One was a widow named
Mrs. Frelinghuysen. She was very old and tiny and delicate, and she
ate like a horse. She ate like she thought any meal might be her last
meal. She was a little lame from rheumatism, and she used a walking
stick that had a snake's head for a knob, a snake's head carved out of
ivory. She had a pleasant voice, a beautiful voice, and she made the
most surprising funny remarks. They were coarse remarks, the humor in them. She made some remarks on occasion that had me wondering did I hear right. Everybody liked her, the way she hung on to
life, and everybody tried to do things for her. I remember Mr.
Sartori one night went out in the rain and got her a cab. 'She's such
a thin little thing,' he said when he came back in. 'There's nothing to
her,' he said, 'but six bones and one gut and a set of teeth and a big
hat with a bird on it.' Her peculiarity was she always brought her
own silver. It was old family silver. She'd have it wrapped up in a
linen napkin in her handbag, and she'd get it out and set her own
place. After she finished eating, I'd take it to the kitchen and wash it,
and she'd stuff it back in her handbag. She'd always start off with one
dozen oysters in winter or one dozen clams in summer, and she'd
gobble them down and go on from there. She could get more out of

a lobster than anybody I ever saw. You'd think she'd got everything she possibly could, and then she'd pull the little legs off that most people don't even bother with, and suck the juice out of them. Sometimes, if it was a slow night and I was just standing around, she'd call me over and talk to me while she ate. She'd talk about people and past times, and she knew a lot; she had kept her eyes open while she was going through life.

"My hours in Joe's were ten in the morning to nine at night. In the afternoons, I'd take a break from three to four-thirty. I saw so much rich food I usually didn't want any lunch, the way old waiters get—just a crust of bread, or some fruit. If it was a nice day, I'd step over to Albee Square and go into an old fancy-fruit store named Ecklebe & Guyer's and pick me out a piece of fruit—an orange or two, or a bunch of grapes, or one of those big red pomegranates that split open when they're ripe the same as figs and their juice is so strong and red it purifies the blood. Then I'd go over to Schermerhorn Street. Schermerhorn was a block and a half west of Joe's. There were some trees along Schermerhorn, and some benches under the trees. Young women would sit along there with their babies, and old men would sit along there the whole day through and read papers and play checkers and discuss matters. And I'd sit there the little time I had and rest my feet and eat my fruit and read the *New York Times*—my purpose reading the *New York Times*, I was trying to improve my English. Schermerhorn Street was a peaceful old backwater street, so nice and quiet, and I liked it. It did me good to sit down there and rest. One afternoon the thought occurred to me, 'Who the hell was Schermerhorn?' So that night it happened Mrs. Frelinghuysen was in, and I asked her who was Schermerhorn that the street's named for. She knew, all right. Oh, Jesus, she more than knew. She saw I was interested, and from then on that was one of the main subjects she talked to me about—Old New York street names and neighborhood names; Old New York this, Old New York that. She knew a great many facts and figures and skeletons in the closet that her mother and her grandmother and her aunts had passed on down to her relating to the old New York Dutch families that they call the Knickerbockers—those that dissipated too much and dissipated all their property away and died out and disappeared, and those that are still around. Holland Dutch, not German Dutch, the way I used to think it meant. The Schermerhorns are one of the oldest of the old Dutch families, according to her, and one of the best. They were big landowners in Dutch days, and they still are, and they go back so deep in Old New York that if you went any deeper you wouldn't find anything but Indians and bones and bears. Mrs. Frelinghuysen was well acquainted with the Schermerhorn family. She had been to Schermerhorn weddings and Schermerhorn funerals. I remember she told about a Schermerhorn girl she went to school with who belonged to the eighth generation, I think it was, in direct descent from old Jacob Schermerhorn who came here from Schermerhorn, Holland, in the sixteen-thirties, and this girl died and was buried in the Schermerhorn plot in Trinity Church cemetery up in Washington Heights, and one day many years later driving down from Connecticut Mrs. Frelinghuysen got to thinking about her and stopped off at the cemetery and looked around in there and located her grave and put some jonquils on it."

At this moment a fishmonger opened the door of the restaurant and put his head in and interrupted Louie. "Hey, Louie," he called out, "has Little Joe been in?"

"Little Joe that's a lumper on the pier," asked Louie, "or Little Joe that works for Chesebro, Robbins?"

"The lumper," said the fishmonger.

"He was in and out an hour ago," said Louie. "He snook in and got a cup of coffee and was out and gone the moment he finished it."

"If you see him," the fishmonger said, "tell him they want him on the pier. A couple of draggers just came in—the *Felicia* from New Bedford and the *Positive* from Gloucester—and the *Ann Elizabeth Kristin* from Stonington is out in the river, on her way in."

Louie nodded, and the fishmonger went away. "To continue about Mrs. Frelinghuysen," Louie said, "she died in 1927. The next year, I got married. The next year was the year the stock market crashed. The next year, I quit Joe's and came over here and bought this restaurant and rented this building. I rented it from a real estate company, the Charles F. Noyes Company, and I paid my rent to them, and I took it for granted they owned it. One afternoon four years later, the early part of 1934, around in March, I was standing at the cash register in here and a long black limousine drove up out front and parked, and a uniform chauffeur got out and came in and said Mrs. Schermerhorn wanted to speak to me, and I looked at him and said, 'What do you mean—Mrs. Schermerhorn?' And he said, 'Mrs. Schermerhorn that owns this building.' So I went out on the sidewalk, and there was a lady sitting in the limousine, her appearance was quite beautiful, and she said she was Mrs. Arthur F. Schermerhorn and her husband had died in September the year before and she was taking a look at some of the buildings the estate owned and the Noyes company was the agent for. So she asked me some questions concerning what shape the building was in, and the like of that. Which I answered to the best of my ability. Then I told her I was certainly surprised for various reasons to hear this was Schermerhorn property. I told her, 'Frankly,' I said, 'I'm amazed to hear it.' I asked her did she know anything about the history of the building, how old it was, and she said she didn't, she hadn't ever even seen it before, it was just one of a number of properties that had come down to her husband from his father. Even her husband, she said, she doubted if he had known much about the building. I had a lot of questions I wanted to ask, and I asked her to get out and come in and have some coffee and take a look around, but I guess she figured the signboard SLOPPY LOUIE'S RESTAURANT meant what it said. She thanked me and said she had to be getting on, and she gave the chauffeur an address, and they drove off and I never saw her again.

"I went back inside and stood there and thought it over, and the effect it had on me, the simple fact my building was an old Schermerhorn building, it may sound foolish, but it pleased me very much. The feeling I had, it connected me with the past. It connected me with Old New York. It connected Sloppy Louie's Restaurant with Old New York. It made the building look much better to me. Instead of just an old run-down building in the fish market, the way it looked to me before, it had a history to it, connections going back, and I liked that. It stirred up my curiosity to know more. A day or so later, I went over and asked the people at the Noyes company would they mind telling me something about the history of the building, but they didn't know anything about it. They had only took over the management of it in 1929, the year before I rented it, and the company that had been the previous agent had gone out of business. They said to go to the City Department of Buildings in the Municipal Building. Which I did, but the man in there, he looked up my building and couldn't find any file on it, and he said it's hard to date a good many old buildings down in my part of town because a fire in the Building Department around 1890 destroyed some cases of papers relating to them—permits and specifications and all that. He advised me to go to the Hall of Records on Chambers Street, where deeds are recorded. I went over there, and they showed me the deed, but it wasn't any help. It described the lot, but all it said about the building, it said 'the building thereon,' and didn't give any date on it. So I gave up. Well, there's a nice old gentleman eats in here sometimes who works for the Title Guarantee & Trust Company, an old Yankee fish-eater, and we were talking one day, and it happened he told me that Title Guarantee has tons and tons of records on New York City property stored away in their vaults that they refer to when they're deciding whether or not the title to a piece of property is clear. 'Do me a favor,' I said, 'and look up the records on 92 South Street—nothing private or financial; just the history—and I'll treat you to the best broiled lobster you ever had. I'll treat you to broiled lobster six Fridays in a row,' I said, 'and I'll broil the lobsters myself.'

"The next time he came in, he said he had took a look in the Title Guarantee vaults for me, and had talked to a title searcher over there who's an expert on South Street property, and he read me off some notes he had made. It seems all this end of South Street used to be under water. The East River flowed over it. Then the city filled it in and divided it into lots. In February, 1804, a merchant by the name of Peter Schermerhorn, a descendant of Jacob Schermerhorn, was given grants to the lot my building now stands on—92 South—and the lot next to it—93 South, a corner lot, the corner of South and Fulton. Schermerhorn put up a four-story brick-and-frame building on each of these lots—stores on the street floors and flats above. In 1872, 1873, or 1874—my friend from Title Guarantee wasn't able to determine the exact year—the heirs and assigns of Peter Schermerhorn ripped these buildings down and put up two six-story brick buildings exactly alike side by side on 92 and 93. Those buildings are this one here and the one next door. The Schermerhorns put them up for hotel purposes, and they were designed so they could be used as one building—there's a party wall between them, and in those days there were sets of doors on each floor leading from one building to the other. This building had that old hand-pull elevator in it from bottom to top, and the other building had a wide staircase in it from bottom to top. The Schermerhorns didn't skimp on materials; they used heart pine for beams and they used hand-molded, air-dried, kiln-burned Hudson River brick. The Schermerhorns leased the buildings to two hotel men named Frederick and Henry Lemmermann, and the first lease on record is 1874. The name of the hotel was the Fulton Ferry Hotel. The hotel saloon occupied the whole bottom floor of the building next door, and the hotel restaurant was right in here, and they had a combined lobby and billiard room that occupied the second floor of both buildings, and they had a reading room in the front half of the third floor of this building and rooms in the rear half, and all the rest of the space in both buildings was single rooms and double rooms and suites. At that time, there were passenger-line steamship docks all along South Street, lines that went to every part of the world, and out-of-town people waiting for passage on the various steamers would stay at the Fulton Ferry Hotel. Also, the Brooklyn Bridge hadn't yet been built, and the Fulton Ferry was the principal ferry to Brooklyn, and the ferryhouse stood directly in front of the hotel. On account of the ferry, Fulton Street was like a funnel; damned near everything headed for Brooklyn went through it. It was full of foot traffic and horse-drawn traffic day and night, and South and Fulton was one of the most ideal saloon corners in the city.

"The Fulton Ferry Hotel lasted forty-five years, but it only had about twenty good years; the rest was downhill. The first bad blow was the bridges over the East River, beginning with the Brooklyn Bridge, that gradually drained off the heavy traffic on the Fulton Ferry that the hotel saloon got most of its trade from. And then, the worst blow of all, the passenger lines began leaving South Street and moving around to bigger, longer docks on the Hudson. Little by little, the Fulton Ferry Hotel got to be one of those waterfront hotels that rummies hole up in, and old men on pensions, and old nuts, and sailors on the beach. Steps going down. Around 1910, somewhere in there, the Lemmermanns gave up the part of the hotel that was in this building, and the Schermerhorn interests boarded up the windows on the four upper floors and bricked up the doors in the party wall connecting the two buildings. And the hotel restaurant, what they did with that, they rented it to a man named MacDonald who turned it into a quick lunch for the people in the fish market. MacDonald ran it awhile. Then a son of his took it over, according to some lease notations in the Title Guarantee records. Then a man named Jimmy Something-or-Other took it over. It was called Jimmy's while he had it. Then two Greek fellows took it over. Then a German fellow and his wife and sister and brother-in-law had it awhile. Then two brothers named Fortunato and Louie Barbagelata took it over. Then John Barbagelata took it over, a nephew of the other Barbagelatas, and eventually I came along and bought the lease and furnishings off of him. After the party wall was bricked up, the Lemmermanns held on to the building next door a few years more, and kept on calling it the Fulton Ferry Hotel, but all it amounted to, it was just a waterfront saloon with rooms for rent up above. They operated it until 1919, when the final blow hit them—prohibition. Those are the bare bones of the matter. If I could get upstairs just once in that damned old elevator and scratch around in those hotel registers up there and whatever to hell else is stored up there, it might be possible I'd find out a whole lot more."

"Look, Louie," I said, "I'll go up in the elevator with you."

"You think you would," Louie said, "but you'd just take a look at it, and then you'd back out."

"I'd like to see inside the cage, at least," I said.

Louie looked at me inquisitively. "You really want to go up there?" he asked.

"Yes," I said.

"The next time you come down here, put on the oldest clothes you got, so the dust don't make any difference," Louie said, "and we'll go up and try out the elevator."

"Oh, no," I said. "Now or never. If I think it over, I'll change my mind."

"It's your own risk," he said.

"Of course," I said.

Louie abruptly stood up. "Let me speak to the waiter at the cash register," he said, "and I'll be with you."

He went over and spoke to the waiter. Then he opened the door of a cupboard in back of the cash register and took out two flashlights and the two construction-work helmets that his customer, the contractor, had brought in. He handed me one of the flashlights and one of the helmets. I put the helmet on and started over to a mirror to see how I looked. "Come on," Louie said, somewhat impatiently. We went up the stairs to the second floor. Along one wall, on this floor, were shelves stacked with restaurant supplies—canned goods and nests of bowls and plates and boxes of soap powder and boxes of paper napkins. Headed up against the wainscoting were half a dozen burlap bags of potatoes. A narrow, round-runged, wooden ladder stood at a slant in a corner up front, and Louie went directly to it. One end of the ladder was fixed to the floor, and the other end was fixed to the ceiling. At the top of the ladder, flush with the ceiling, was the bottom of the elevator cage with the trap door cut in it. The trap door was shut. Louie unbuttoned a shirt button and stuck his flashlight in the front of his shirt, and immediately started up the ladder. At the top, he paused and looked down at me for an instant. His face was set. Then he gave the trap door a shove, and it fell back, and a cloud of black dust burst out. Louie ducked his head and shook it and blew the dust out of his nose. He stood at the top of the ladder for about a minute, waiting for the dust to settle. Then, all of a sudden, he scrambled into the cage. "Oh, God in Heaven," he called out, "the dust in here! It's like somebody emptied a vacuum-cleaner bag in here." I climbed the ladder and entered the cage and closed the trap door. Louie pointed his flashlight up the shaft. "I thought there was only one wheel up there," he said, peering upward. "I see two."

[ 758 ]

The dust had risen to the top of the shaft, and we couldn't see the wheels clearly. There was an iron strut over the top of the cage, and a cable extended from it to one of the wheels. Two thick hemp ropes hung down into the cage from the other wheel. "I'm going to risk it," Louie said. "I'm going to pull the rope. Take both flashlights, and shine one on me and shine the other up the shaft. If I can get the cage up about a foot, it'll be level with the third floor, and we can open the door."

Louie grasped one of the ropes and pulled on it, and dust sprang off it all the way to the top. The wheel screeched as the rope turned it, but the cage didn't move. "The rope feels loose," Louie said. "I don't think it has any grip on the wheel." He pulled again, and nothing happened.

"Maybe you've got the wrong rope," I said.

He disregarded me and pulled again, and the cage shook from side to side. Louie let go of the rope, and looked up the shaft. "That wheel acts all right," he said. He pulled the rope again, and this time the cage rose an inch or two. He pulled five or six times, and the cage rose an inch or two each time. Then we looked down and saw that the floor of the cage was almost even with the third floor. Louie pulled the rope once more. Then he stepped over and pushed on the grilled door of the cage and shook it, trying to swing it open; it rattled, and long, lacy flakes of rust fell off it, but it wouldn't open. I gave Louie the lights of both flashlights, and he examined the door. There were sets of hinges down it in two places. "I see," Louie said. "You're supposed to fold it back in." The hinges were stiff, and he got in a frenzy struggling with the door before he succeeded in folding it back far enough for us to get through. On the landing there was a kind of storm-door-like affair, a three-sided cubbyhole with a plain wooden door in the center side. "I guess they had that there to keep people from falling in the shaft," Louie said. "It'll be just our luck the door's locked on the other side. If it is, I'm not going to monkey around; I'm going to kick it in." He tried the knob, and it turned, and he opened the door, and we walked out and entered the front half of the third floor, the old reading room of the Fulton Ferry Hotel.

It was pitch-dark in the room. We stood still and played the lights of our flashlights across the floor and up and down the walls. Everything we saw was covered with dust. There was a thick, black mat of fleecy dust on the floor—dust and soot and grit and lint and slut's wool. Louie scuffed his shoes in it. "A-a-ah!" he said, and spat. His light fell on a roll-top desk, and he hurried over to it and rolled the top up. I stayed where I was, and continued to look around. The room was rectangular, and it had a stamped-tin ceiling, and tongue-and-groove wainscoting, and plaster walls the color of putty. The plaster had crumbled down to the laths in many places. There was a gas fixture on each wall. High up on one wall was a round hole that had once held a stovepipe. Screwed to the door leading to the rear half of the floor were two framed signs. One said, "THIS READING ROOM WILL BE CLOSED AT 1 A.M. FULTON FERRY HOTEL." The other said, "ALL GAMBLING IN THIS READING ROOM STRICTLY PROHIBITED. BY ORDER OF THE PROPRIETORS. FULTON FERRY HOTEL. F. & H. LEMMERMANN, PROPRIETORS." Some bedsprings and some ugly white knobby iron bedsteads were stacked criss-cross in one corner. The stack was breast-high. Between the boarded-up windows, against the front wall, stood a marble-top table. On it were three seltzer bottles with corroded spouts, a tin water cooler painted to resemble brown marble, a cracked glass bell of the kind used to cover clocks and stuffed birds, and four sugar bowls whose metal flap lids had been eaten away from their hinges by rust. On the floor, beside the table, were an umbrella stand, two brass spittoons, and a wire basket filled to the brim with whiskey bottles of the flask type. I took the bottles out one by one. Dampness had destroyed the labels; pulpy scraps of paper with nothing legible on them were sticking to a few on the bottom. Lined up back to back in the middle of the room were six bureaus with mirrors on their tops. Still curious to see how I looked in the construction-work helmet, I went and peered in one of the mirrors.

Louie, who had been yanking drawers out of the roll-top desk, suddenly said, "God damn it! I thought I'd find those hotel registers in here. There's nothing in here, only rusty paper clips." He went over to the whiskey bottles I had strewn about and examined a few, and then he walked up behind me and looked in the mirror. His face was strained. He had rubbed one cheek with his dusty fingers, and it was streaked with dust. "We're the first faces to look in that mirror in years and years," he said. He held his flashlight with one hand and jerked open the top drawer of the bureau with the other. There were a few hairpins in the drawer, and some buttons, and a comb with several teeth missing, and a needle with a bit of black thread in its eye, and a scattering of worn playing cards; the design on the backs of the cards was a stag at bay. He opened the middle drawer, and it was empty. He opened the bottom drawer, and it was empty. He started in on the next bureau. In the top drawer, he found a square, clear-glass medicine bottle that contained two inches of colorless liquid and half an inch of black sediment. He wrenched the stopper out, and put the bottle to his nose and smelled the liquid. "It's gone dead," he said. "It doesn't smell like anything at all." He poured the liquid on the floor, and handed the bottle to me. Blown in one side of it was "Perry's Pharmacy. Open All Night. Popular Prices. World Building, New York." All at once, while looking at the old bottle, I became conscious of the noises of the market seemingly far below, and I stepped over to one of the boarded-up windows and tried to peep down at South Street through a split in a board, but it wasn't possible. Louie continued to go through the bureau drawers. "Here's something," he said. "Look at this." He handed me a foxed and yellowed photograph of a dark young woman with upswept hair who wore a lace shirtwaist and a long black skirt and sat in a fanciful fan-backed wicker chair. After a while, Louie reached the last drawer in the last bureau, and looked in it and snorted and slammed it shut. "Let's go in the rear part of the floor," he said.

Louie opened the door, and we entered a hall, along which was a row of single rooms. There were six rooms, and on their doors were little oval enameled number plates running from 12 to 17. We looked in Room 12. Two wooden coat hangers were lying on the floor. Room 13 was absolutely empty. Room 14 had evidently last been occupied by someone with a religious turn of mind. There was an old iron bedstead still standing in it, but without springs, and tacked on the wall above the head of the bed was a placard of the kind distributed by some evangelistic religious groups. It said, "The Wages of Sin is Death; but the Gift of God is Eternal Life through Jesus Christ our Lord." Tacked on the wall beside the bed was another religious placard: "Christ is the Head of this House, the Unseen Host at Every Meal, the Silent Listener to Every Conversation." We stared at the placards a few moments, and then Louie turned and started back up the hall.

"Louie," I called, following him, "where are you going?"

"Let's go on back downstairs," he said.

"I thought we were going on up to the floors above," I said. "Let's go up to the fourth floor, at least. We'll take turns pulling the rope."

"There's nothing up here," he said. "I don't want to stay up here another minute. Come on, let's go."

I followed him into the elevator cage. "I'll pull the rope going down," I said.

Louie said nothing, and I glanced at him. He was leaning against the side of the cage, and his shoulders were slumped and his eyes were tired. "I didn't learn much I didn't know before," he said.

"You learned that the wages of sin is death," I said, trying to say something cheerful.

"I knew that before," Louie said. A look of revulsion came on his face. "The wages of sin!" he said. "Sin, death, dust, old empty rooms, old empty whiskey bottles, old empty bureau drawers. Come on, pull the rope faster! Pull it faster! Let's get out of this."

*THE NEW YORKER*, 1952

# WILLIAM  S.  BURROUGHS

*In William S. Burroughs' (1914–97) hard-boiled memoir of heroin ad-
diction,* Junky *(first published as a lurid paperback original by Ace
Books), he describes a ghostly, almost invisible milieu far removed from
the flamboyance of the 60's drug scene. Burroughs' prose here is as discreet and businesslike as the seasoned addicts he describes.*

## FROM  *JUNKY*

ROY CAME BACK from his thirty-day cure on Riker's Island
and introduced me to a peddler who was pushing Mexican
H on 103rd and Broadway. During the early part of the war,
imports of H were virtually cut off and the only junk available was
prescription M. However, lines of communication reformed and
heroin began coming in from Mexico, where there were poppy fields
tended by Chinese. This Mexican H was brown in color since it had
quite a bit of raw opium in it.

103rd and Broadway looks like any Broadway block. A cafeteria, a
movie, stores. In the middle of Broadway is an island with some grass
and benches placed at intervals. 103rd is a subway stop, a crowded
block. This is junk territory. Junk haunts the cafeteria, roams up and
down the block, sometimes half-crossing Broadway to rest on one of
the island benches. A ghost in daylight on a crowded street.

You could always find a few junkies sitting in the cafeteria or
standing around outside with coat collars turned up, spitting on the
sidewalk and looking up and down the street as they waited for the
connection. In summer, they sit on the island benches, huddled like
so many vultures in their dark suits.

The peddler had the face of a withered adolescent. He was fifty-
five but he did not look more than thirty. He was a small, dark man
with a thin Irish face. When he did show up—and like many oldtime
junkies he was completely unpunctual—he would sit at a table in the
cafeteria. You gave him money at the table, and met him around the

corner three minutes later where he would deliver the junk. He never had it on him, but kept it stashed somewhere close by.

This man was known as Irish. At one time he had worked for Dutch Schultz, but big-time racketeers will not keep junkies on the payroll as they are supposed to be unreliable. So Irish was out. Now he peddled from time to time and "worked the hole" (rolling drunks on subways and in cars) when he couldn't make connections to peddle. One night, Irish got nailed in the subway for jostling. He hanged himself in the Tombs.

The job of peddler was a sort of public service that rotated from one member of the group to the other, the average term of office being about three months. All agreed that it was a thankless job. As George the Greek said, "You end up broke and in jail. Everybody calls you cheap if you don't give credit; if you do, they take advantage."

George couldn't turn down a man who came to him sick. People took advantage of his kindness, hitting him for credit and taking their cash to some other pusher. George did three years, and when he got out he refused to do any more pushing.

The hipster-bebop junkies never showed at 103rd Street. The 103rd Street boys were all oldtimers—thin, sallow faces; bitter, twisted mouths; stiff-fingered, stylized gestures. (There is a junk gesture that marks the junky like the limp wrist marks the fag: the hand swings out from the elbow stiff-fingered, palm up.) They were of various nationalities and physical types, but they all looked alike somehow. They all looked like junk. There was Irish, George the Greek, Pantopon Rose, Louie the Bellhop, Eric the Fag, the Beagle, the Sailor, and Joe the Mex. Several of them are dead now, others are doing time.

There are no more junkies at 103rd and Broadway waiting for the connection. The connection has gone somewhere else. But the feel of junk is still there. It hits you at the corner, follows you along the block, then falls away like a discouraged panhandler as you walk on.

Joe the Mex had a thin face with a long, sharp, twitchy nose and a down-curving, toothless mouth. Joe's face was lined and ravaged, but not old. Things had happened to his face, but Joe was not touched. His eyes were bright and young. There was a gentleness about him common to many oldtime junkies. You could spot Joe blocks away. In the anonymous city crowd he stood out sharp and clear, as though you were seeing him through binoculars. He was a liar, and like most liars, he was constantly changing his stories, altering time and personnel from one telling to the next. One time he would tell a story about some friend, next time he would switch the story around to give himself the lead. He would sit in the cafeteria over coffee and pound cake, talking at random about his experiences.

"We know this Chinaman has some stuff stashed, and we try every way to make him tell us where it is. We have him tied to a chair. I light matches"—he made a gesture of lighting a match—"and put them under his feet. He won't say nothing. I feel so sorry for that man. Then my partner hit him in the face with his gun and the blood run all down his face." He put his hands over his face and drew them down to indicate the flow of blood. "When I see that I turn sick at my stomach and I say, 'Let's get out of here and leave the man alone. He ain't going to tell us nothing.'"

Louie was a shoplifter who had lost what nerve he ever had. He wore long, shabby, black overcoats that gave him all the look of a furtive buzzard. Thief and junky stuck out all over him. Louie had a hard time making it. I heard that at one time he had been a stool pigeon, but at the time I knew him he was generally considered right. George the Greek did not like Louie and said he was just a bum. "Don't ever invite him to your home, he'll take advantage. He'll go on the nod in front of your family. He's got no class to him."

George the Greek was the admitted arbiter of this set. He decided who was right and who was wrong. George prided himself on his integrity. "I never beat nobody."

George was a three-time loser. The next time meant life as an habitual criminal. His life narrowed down to the necessity of avoiding any serious involvements. No pushing, no stealing; he worked from time to time on the docks. He was hemmed in on every side and there was no way for him to go but down. When he couldn't get junk—which was about half the time—he drank and took goof balls.

He had two adolescent sons who gave him a lot of trouble. George was half-sick most of the time in this period of scarcity, and no match for these young louts. His face bore the marks of a constant losing fight. The last time I was in New York I couldn't find George. The 103rd Street boys are scattered now and no one I talked to knew what happened to George the Greek.

Fritz the Janitor was a pale thin little man who gave the impression of being crippled. He was on parole after doing five years because he scored for a pigeon. The pigeon was hard up for someone to turn in, and the narcotics agent urgently needed to make an arrest. Between them they built Fritz up to a big-time dope peddler, and smashed a narcotics ring with his arrest. Fritz was glad to attract so much attention and he talked complacently about his "nickel" in Lexington.

The Fag was a brilliantly successful lush-worker. His scores were fabulous. He was the man who gets to a lush first, never the man who arrives on the scene when the lush is lying there with his pockets turned inside out. A sleeping lush—known as a "flop" in the trade—attracts a hierarchy of scavengers. First come the top lush-workers like the Fag, guided by a special radar. They only want cash, good rings, and watches. Then come the punks who will steal anything. They take the hat, shoes, and belt. Finally, brazen, clumsy thieves will try to pull the lush's overcoat or jacket off him.

The Fag was always first on a good lush. One time he scored for a thousand dollars at the 103rd Street Station. Often his scores ran into the hundreds. If the lush woke up, he would simper and feel the man's thigh as though his intentions were sexual. From this angle he got this moniker.

He always dressed well, usually in tweed sport coats and gray flannels. A European charm of manner and a slight Scandinavian accent completed his front. No one could have looked less like a lush-roller. He always worked alone. His luck was good and he was determined to avoid contamination. Sometimes, contact with the lucky can change a man's run of bad luck, but generally it works out the other way. Junkies are an envious lot. 103rd Street envied the Fag his scores. But everyone had to admit he was a right guy, and always good for a small touch.

1953

# BERNARDO VEGA

Bernardo Vega (1885–1965) was a political activist and organizer in the Socialist Party, who came to the city in 1916 as an experienced tabaquero, or cigar factory worker. A gifted writer, he founded the weekly magazine Gráfico in 1927 and contributed frequently to Spanish-language newspapers. His posthumously published memoirs give us a rare detailed picture of the first wave of Puerto Rican immigrants to New York.

FROM *MEMOIRS OF BERNARDO VEGA*
FROM MY HOMETOWN CAYEY TO SAN JUAN, AND HOW I
ARRIVED IN NEW YORK WITHOUT A WATCH

EARLY IN THE MORNING of August 2, 1916, I took leave of Cayey. I got on the bus at the Plaza and sat down, squeezed in between passengers and suitcases. Of my traveling companions I remember nothing. I don't think I opened my mouth the whole way. I just stared at the landscape, sunk in deep sorrow. I was leaving a girlfriend in town . . .

But my readers are very much mistaken if they expect a sentimental love story from me. I don't write to pour my heart out—confessions of love bore me to death, especially my own. So, to make a long story short, the girl's parents, brothers, relatives, and well-wishers declared war on me. That's not exactly why I decided to leave, but that small-town drama of Montagues and Capulets did have an influence. Anyway, I left Cayey that hot summer, heavy of heart, but ready to face a new life.

From an early age I had worked as a cigar-roller in a tobacco factory. I had just turned thirty, and although it was not the first time I had left my hometown, never before had I put the shores of Puerto Rico behind me. I had been to the capital a few times. But now it meant going farther, to a strange and distant world. I hadn't the slightest idea what fate awaited me.

In those days I was taller than most Puerto Ricans. I was white, a peasant from the highlands (a *jíbaro*), and there was that waxen pallor to my face so typical of country folk. I had a round face with high cheekbones, a wide, flat nose, and small blue eyes. As for my lips, well, I'd say they were rather sensual, and I had strong, straight teeth. I had a full head of light chesnut hair, and, in contrast to the roundness of my face, I had square jaws. All in all, I suppose I was rather ugly, though there were women around who thought otherwise.

I did not inspire much sympathy at first sight, I'm sure of that. I have never made friends easily. No doubt my physical appearance has a lot to do with it. I hadn't been living in New York for long before I realized how difficult it was for people to guess where I came from. Time and again I was taken for a Polish Jew, or a Tartar, or even a Japanese . . . God forgive my dear parents for my human countenance, which was after all the only thing they had bequeathed me!

I arrived in San Juan at around ten o'clock in the morning. I ordered the driver to take me to El Comercio, a cheap hotel I knew of on Calle Tetuán. I left my suitcase and went out for a walk in the city.

The sun warmed the pavements of the narrow streets. I longed for the morning chill of my native Toa valley. I decided to go for a ride in a trolley car and say goodbye to an old schoolteacher of mine. To her I owed my first stop. Her name was Elisa Rubio and I have fond memories of her to this day. In her little house in Santurce she told me glowing things about the United States and praised my decision to emigrate. I would have a chance to study there. To this day, after all these years, her exaggerated praise echoes in my mind: "You have talent and ambition. You will get ahead, I am sure. And you'll become famous." Heaven forgive my well-meaning teacher.

On my return to the old section of San Juan, I spent the afternoon taking leave of my comrades. There was Manuel F. Rojas, who had been elected secretary general of the Partido Socialista at the constituent assembly recently held in Cayey, my hometown, which I had attended as a delegate. With him were Santiago Iglesias, Prudencio Rivera Martínez, and Rafael Alonso Torres . . . They all were unhappy about my decision to leave because of the loss it would be for our newly organized workers' movement. But they did

not try hard to dissuade me. As socialists, we dig our trenches everywhere in the world.

I returned to the little hotel tired and sweaty. Before going up to
my room I bought the daily newspapers—*La Correspondencia, El
Tiempo, La Democracia.* In shirtsleeves, I threw myself onto my bed
and plunged into the latest events of the day.

In those days our newspapers were not as big as they are today—
none were over twelve pages. The news, especially about foreign affairs, did not take up much space. But our native writers waxed
eloquent in endless polemics—original commentaries, sharp criticism, and plenty of our local humor. They reflected the life of the
whole society—or rather, of its ruling class—with uneven success,
but in any case they were more truthful than they are today, for sure.

Night fell, and I washed up, dressed, and went back out in the
street. I had a long conversation with Benigno Fernández García, the
son of a prestigious Cayey family. We talked about the European war,
in which the United States was soon to be involved. Then I returned
to my hotel, went to bed, and tried to sleep, but it was impossible.
My mind was full of memories and my heart ached. Until then I had
been acting like a robot, or a man under the influence of drugs. Now,
alone in the darkness of my room, I recalled my mother's tears, the
sad faces of my little brothers . . . I just couldn't get to sleep.

Once again I went back into the streets. It had rained. A pleasant
breeze blew through the city. The bright moon lit up the streets. The
damp pavements glistened. And I took to walking, up one street and
down another, in an intimate chat with the cobblestones of that city
which means so much to Puerto Ricans.

Dawn caught me by surprise, seated on one of the benches in the
Plaza de Armas now and then looking up at the big clock. The cheerful rattle of the first trolley car brought me back to sad reality.
Within a few minutes the bold tropical sun had taken possession of
San Juan, and the streets were crowded with people. Gentlemen in
jackets and hats left home to go to work. But the largest crowds
were made up of people flocking in from the countryside, dealers in
agricultural produce. Cornflakes had not yet replaced corn on the
cob, though things were already headed in that direction.

The hours passed quickly. At around two in the afternoon I boarded the boat, the famous *Coamo* which made so many trips from San Juan to New York and back. I took a quick look at my cabin, and went right back up on deck. I did not want to lose a single breath of those final minutes in my country, perhaps the last ones I would ever have.

Soon the boat pushed off from the dock, turned, and began to move slowly toward El Morro castle at the mouth of the harbor. A nun who worked at the women's home was waving *adiós* from high up on the ramparts; I assumed she meant it for me. As soon as we were on the open sea and the boat started to pitch, the passengers went off to their cabins, most of them already half seasick. Not I. I stayed up on deck, lingering there until the island was lost from sight in the first shadows of nightfall.

The days passed peacefully. Sunrise of the first day and the passengers were already acting as though they belonged to one family. It was not long before we came to know each other's life stories. The topic of conversation, of course, was what lay ahead: life in New York. First savings would be for sending for close relatives. Years later the time would come to return home with pots of money. Everyone's mind was on that farm they'd be buying or the business they'd set up in town . . . All of us were building our own little castles in the sky.

When the fourth day dawned even those who had spent the whole trip cooped up in their cabins showed up on deck. We saw the lights of New York even before the morning mist rose. As the boat entered the harbor the sky was clear and clean. The excitement grew the closer we got to the docks. We recognized the Statue of Liberty in the distance. Countless smaller boats were sailing about in the harbor. In front of us rose the imposing sight of skyscrapers—the same skyline we had admired so often on postcards. Many of the passengers had only heard talk of New York, and stood with their mouths open, spellbound . . . Finally the *Coamo* docked at Hamilton Pier on Staten Island.

First to disembark were the passengers traveling first class— businessmen, well-to-do families, students. In second class, where I

was, there were the emigrants, most of us *tabaqueros*, or cigar workers. We all boarded the ferry that crossed from Staten Island to lower
Manhattan. We sighed as we set foot on solid ground. There, gaping
before us, were the jaws of the iron dragon: the immense New York
metropolis.

All of us new arrivals were well dressed. I mean, we had on our
Sunday best. I myself was wearing a navy blue woolen suit (or *flus,* as
they would say back home), a borsalino hat made of Italian straw,
black shoes with pointy toes, a white vest, and a red tie. I would have
been sporting a shiny wristwatch too, if a traveling companion
hadn't warned me that in New York it was considered effeminate to
wear things like that. So as soon as the city was in sight, and the boat
was entering the harbor, I tossed my watch into the sea . . . And to
think that it wasn't long before those wristwatches came into fashion
and ended up being the rage!

And so I arrived in New York, without a watch.

THE TRIALS AND TRIBULATIONS OF AN
EMIGRANT IN THE IRON TOWER OF BABEL
ON THE EVE OF WORLD WAR I

The Battery, which as I found out later is what they call the tip of
lower Manhattan where our ferry from Staten Island docked, was
also a port of call for all the elevated trains. The Second, Third,
Sixth, and Ninth Avenue lines all met there. I entered the huge station with Ambrosio Fernández, who had come down to meet me at
the dock. The noise of the trains was deafening, and I felt as if I was
drowning in the crowd. Funny, but now that I was on land I started
to feel seasick. People were rushing about every which way, not
seeming to know exactly where they were headed. Now and then
one of them would cast a mocking glance at the funny-looking travelers with their suitcases and other baggage. Finally there I was in a
subway car, crushed by the mobs of passengers, kept afloat only by
the confidence I felt in the presence of my friend.

The train snaked along at breakneck speed. I pretended to take
note of everything, my eyes like the golden deuce in a deck of

Spanish cards. The further along we moved, and as the dingy buildings filed past my view, all the visions I had of the gorgeous splendor
of New York vanished. The skyscrapers seemed like tall gravestones.
I wondered why, if the United States was so rich, as surely it was, did
its biggest city look so grotesque? At that moment I sensed for the
first time that people in New York could not possibly be as happy as
we used to think they were back home in Cayey.

Ambrosio rescued me from my brooding. We were at the 23rd
Street station. We got off and walked down to 22nd Street. We were
on the West Side. At number 228 I took up my first lodgings. It was
a boarding house run by Mrs. Arnao, the place where Ambrosio was
living.

On my first day in New York I didn't go out at all. There was a lot
to talk about, and Ambrosio and I had lengthy conversations. I told
him the latest from Puerto Rico, about our families and friends. He
talked about the city, what life was like, what the chances were of
finding a job . . . To put it mildly, an utterly dismal picture.

Ambrosio himself was out of work, which led me to ask myself,
"Now, if Ambrosio is out of a job, and he's been here a while and
isn't just a cigarworker but a silversmith and watchmaker to boot,
then how am I ever going to find anything?" My mind began to cloud
over with doubts; frightening shadows fell over my immediate future. I dreaded the thought of finding myself out in the streets of
such a big, inhospitable city. I paid the landlady a few weeks' rent in
advance. Then, while continuing my conversation with Ambrosio, I
took the further precautionary measure of sewing the money for my
return to Puerto Rico into the lining of my jacket. I knew I only had
a few months to find work before winter descended on us. If I
didn't, I figured I'd send New York to the devil and haul anchor.

Word was that Mrs. Arnao was married to a Puerto Rican dentist, though I never saw hide nor hair of the alleged tooth-puller
around the house. She was an industrious woman and her rooming
house was furnished in elegant taste. She had a flair for cooking and
could prepare a delectable dinner, down to the peapods. At the time
I arrived her only other boarder was Ambrosio, which led me to suspect that she wasn't doing too well financially.

But in those days you didn't need much to get by in New York. Potatoes were selling for a fraction of a cent a pound; eggs were fifteen cents a dozen; a pound of salt pork was going for twelve cents, and a prime steak for twenty cents. A nickel would buy a lot of vegetables. You could pick up a good suit for $10.00. With a nickel fare you could get anywhere in the city, and change from one line to another without having to pay more.

The next day I went out with Ambrosio to get to know New York. We headed for Fifth Avenue, where we got on a double-decker bus. It was the first time I had ever been on one of those strange contraptions! The tour was terrific. The bus went uptown, crossed over on 110th Street and made its way up Riverside Drive. At 135th Street we took Broadway up to 168th Street, and then St. Nicholas Avenue to 191st. From our comfortable seats on the upper deck we could soak in all the sights—the shiny store windows, then the mansions, and later on the gray panorama of the Hudson River.

In later years I took the same trip many times. But I was never as impressed as I was then, even though on other occasions I was often in better company. Not to say that Ambrosio wasn't good company, don't get me wrong!

At the end of our tour, where we got off the bus, was a little park. We strolled through it, reading the inscriptions commemorating the War of Independence. We couldn't help noticing the young couples kissing right there in public. At first it upset me to witness such an embarrassing scene. But I quickly realized that our presence didn't matter to them, and Ambrosio confirmed my impression. What a difference between our customs back home and the behavior of Puerto Rican men and women in New York!

We returned by the same route, but got off the bus at 110th Street. We walked up Manhattan Avenue to 116th, which is where the León brothers—Antonio, Pepín, and Abelardo—were living. They owned a small cigar factory. They were part of a family from Cayey that had emigrated to New York back in 1904. The members of that family were some of the first Puerto Ricans to settle in the Latin *barrio* of Harlem. In those days the Nadals, Matienzos, Pietris, Escalonas, and Umpierres lived there too; I also knew of a certain

Julio Ortíz. In all, I'd say there were some one hundred and fifty Puerto Ricans living in that part of the city around the turn of the century.

Before our countrymen, there were other Hispanics here. There was a sizable Cuban colony in the last quarter of the nineteenth century, members of the Quesada, Arango, and Mantilla families, as well as Emilia Casanova de Villaverde. They must have been people of some means, since they lived in apartments belonging to Sephardic Jews on 110th Street facing Central Park.

As I was saying, when I took up residence in New York in 1916 the apartment buildings and stores in what came to be known as El Barrio, "our" barrio, or the Barrio Latino, all belonged to Jews. Seventh, St. Nicholas, and Manhattan avenues, and the streets in between, were all inhabited by Jewish people of means, if not great wealth. 110th Street was the professional center of the district. The classy, expensive stores were on Lenox Avenue, while the more modest ones were located east of Fifth Avenue. The ghetto of poor Jews extended along Park Avenue between 110th and 117th and on the streets east of Madison. It was in this lower class Jewish neighborhood that some Puerto Rican and Cuban families, up to about fifty of them, were living at that time. Here, too, was where a good many Puerto Rican cigarworkers, bachelors for the most part, occupied the many furnished rooms in the blocks between Madison and Park.

On Park Avenue was an open-air market where you could buy things at low prices. Early in the morning the vendors would set up their stands on the sidewalk under the elevated train, and in the afternoon they would pack up their goods for the night. The marketplace was dirty and stank to high heaven, and remained that way until the years of Mayor Fiorello La Guardia, who put the market in the condition it is in today.

Many of the Jews who lived there in those days were recent immigrants, which made the whole area seem like a Tower of Babel. There were Sephardic Jews who spoke ancient Spanish or Portuguese; there were those from the Near East and from the Mediterranean, who spoke Italian, French, Provençal, Roumanian, Turkish,

Arabic, or Greek. Many of them, in fact, could get along in five or even six languages. On makeshift shelves and display cases, hanging from walls and wire hangers, all kinds of goods were on display. You could buy everything from the simplest darning needle to a complete trousseau. For a quarter you could get a used pair of shoes and for two or three cents a bag of fruit or vegetables.

At the end of our visit to this neighborhood, Ambrosio and I stopped off for dinner at a restaurant called La Luz. We were attracted by the Spanish name, though the owner was actually a Sephardic Jew. The food was not prepared in the style that was familiar to us, but we did notice that the sauces were of Spanish origin. The customers who frequented the place spoke Castilian Spanish. Their heated discussions centered on the war raging in Europe. From what I could gather, most of them thought that the United States would soon be involved in the conflict, and that the Germans would be defeated in the end.

I was impressed by the restaurant because it was so hard to believe that it was located in the United States. There was something exotic about the atmosphere. The furniture and decor gave it the appearance of a café in Spain or Portugal. Even the people who gathered there, their gestures and speech mannerisms, identified them as from Galicia, Andalusia, Aragon, or some other Iberian region. I began to recognize that New York City was really a modern Babylon, the meeting point for peoples from all over the world.

At this time Harlem was a socialist stronghold. The Socialist Party had set up a large number of clubs in the neighborhood. Young working people would get together not only for political purposes but for cultural and sports activities and all kinds of parties. There were two major community centers organized by the party: the Harlem Terrace on 104th Street (a branch of the Rand School), and the Harlem Educational Center on 106th between Madison and Park. Other cultural societies and a large number of workers' cooperatives also worked out of these centers. Meetings and large indoor activities were held at the Park Palace, an auditorium with a large seating capacity. Outdoor public events were held at the corner of 110th Street and Fifth Avenue. All kinds of political, economic, social, and philosophical issues were discussed there; every night speakers aired their views, with the active participation of the public.

Housing in that growing neighborhood was for the most part owned by people who lived there. In many buildings the owners lived in one apartment and rented out the rest. There was still little or no exploitation of tenants by absentee landlords who had nothing to do with the community. The apartments were spacious and quite comfortable. They were well maintained precisely because the owners themselves lived in the buildings. Clearly, the Jewish people who lived in Harlem back then considered it their neighborhood and felt a sentimental attachment to it. Several generations had grown up there; they had their own schools, synagogues, and theaters . . . But all of this changed rapidly during the war and in the years to follow.

It was late, almost closing time, when we reached the León brothers' little cigar factory. Antonio, the eldest, harbored vivid memories of his little hometown of Cayey, which he had left so many years ago. His younger brothers, Pepín and Abelardo, had emigrated later but felt the same kind of nostalgia. There we were, pining for our distant homeland, when Ambrosio finally brought up the problem at hand: my pressing need for work. "Work, here?" the elder brother exclaimed. "This dump hardly provides for us!" Thus, my dream of rolling cigars in the León brothers' little factory was shattered. My tribulations in the iron Tower of Babel had begun.

PROLETARIANS EXTEND A HAND, BUT HUNGER
PINCHES AND THERE IS NO REMEDY BUT TO
WORK IN A WEAPONS FACTORY

The following day Ambrosio and I began the challenging task of looking for work. We set out for the neighborhood where the bulk of the cigarworkers then lived: the blocks along Third Avenue, between 64th and 106th streets. Spread out over this large area were a lot of Puerto Ricans. There were also a lot in Chelsea, and up on the West Side of Manhattan, which is where the ones with money lived.

After Manhattan, the borough with the largest concentration of Puerto Ricans was Brooklyn, in the Boro Hall area, especially on

Sand, Adams, and Pearl streets, and over near the Navy Yard. Puerto Rican neighborhoods in the Bronx and the outlying parts of Manhattan were still unknown.

Between 15th and 20th streets on the East Side there were the boarding houses that served as residences primarily for Puerto Rican *tabaqueros*. I especially remember the houses owned by Isidro Capdevila and Juan Crusellas. They were where Francisco Ramos, Félix Rodríguez Infanzón, Juan Cruz, Lorenzo Verdeguez, Pedro Juan Alfaro, and Alfonso Baerga were staying.

In 1916 the Puerto Rican colony in New York amounted to about six thousand people, mostly *tabaqueros* and their families. The broader Spanish-speaking population was estimated at 16,000.

There were no notable color differences between the various pockets of Puerto Ricans. Especially in the section between 99th and 106th, there were quite a few black *paisanos*. Some of them, like Arturo Alfonso Schomburg, Agustín Vázquez, and Isidro Manzano, later moved up to the black North American neighborhood. As a rule, people lived in harmony in the Puerto Rican neighborhoods, and racial differences were of no concern.

That day we visited a good many cigar factories. The men on the job were friendly. Many of them even said they would help us out if we needed it. That's how cigarworkers were, the same in Puerto Rico as in Cuba, the same in Tampa as in New York. They had a strong sense of *compañerismo*—we were all brothers. But they couldn't make a place for us at the worktable of any factory.

I spent the days that followed going around the city and visiting places of interest. A "card-carrying" socialist, I made my way down to the editors of the *New York Call*, the Socialist Party paper which back then had a circulation in the hundreds of thousands. I showed a letter of introduction given to me by Santiago Iglesias before I left San Juan, and they welcomed me like a brother. Some of the editorial staff spoke our language and showed great interest in the situation in Puerto Rico. We talked about the conditions of the workers, strikes, and the personality of Iglesias . . . They insisted that I come back that afternoon to talk to Morris Hillquit, the leader of the party.

My conversation with Comrade Hillquit centered around the question of the political sovereignty of Puerto Rico. In his opinion, our country should be constituted as a republic, while maintaining friendly relations with the United States. He told me that was what he advised Santiago Iglesias. "I do not understand," he added, "how that political position could not appear in the program of the Partido Socialista of Puerto Rico."

I left very impressed by my meetings with the North American comrades. A few days later I introduced myself to the Socialist Section of Chelsea. The secretary was an Irishman by the name of Carmichael. He attended to me in a friendly fashion and signed me up as a member, after which he introduced me to a comrade by the name of Henry Gotay. A sailor by trade, Henry was a descendant of Felipe Gotay, that celebrated Puerto Rican who commanded one of the regiments of Narciso López' army in its final and unsuccessful invasion on Cuba. Henry in turn introduced me to Ventura Mijón and Emiliano Ramos, two Puerto Rican *tabaquero* militants. They belonged to an anarchist group led by Pedro Esteves and associated with the newspaper *Cultura Proletaria*, the organ of the Spanish anarchists in New York.

In Henry's judgment, Mijón, Ramos, and Esteves were simply degrading their own intelligence and wasting their time preaching such a utopian cause. Henry was a man of deep socialist convictions. I had lunch that day with him and Carmichael at a Greek place on 27th Street and Eighth Avenue. It was an interesting experience—it was the first time I ever drank whisky. As I was not used to alcoholic beverages, I got very drunk and my two new friends had to carry me home. That was the first time I was dead drunk in New York!

Liquor in those years was dirt cheap. A hearty shot of the best brand went for a dime. All the bars had what was called "free lunch," with an endless assortment of tidbits free for the taking: cheese, ham, smoked fish, eggs, potatoes, onions, olives . . . I must admit I was a frequent client of those taverns in my needier days. I would nurse my ten-cent shot and stuff my face with free goodies. What a shame when a few years later prohibition put an end to those paradises of the poor!

My drunk cost me several days in bed. All I had to do was take a drink of water and the whisky would roll around in my stomach and I'd be drunk all over again. But once I was back on my feet I headed straight for the Socialist Club. I was there often, and Carmichael, Henry, and I became close friends. They helped me straighten out some personal problems and went to great lengths to find me a job. But times were very bad. There simply was no work, and with every passing day I saw my situation grow bleaker and bleaker . . . "As a last resort," my friend said, "when your money runs out and you can't pay your rent, bring your belongings here and sleep in the club. And as for food, don't worry about that either. There'll be some here for you. The party has an emergency fund for cases like this." Those words gave me such a lift!

In the following days I visited Local 90 of the Cigarmakers' Union, which was a local led by the "progressives" in the union. Jacob Ryan held the post of secretary. I showed him my "travel card," establishing me as a member of the Puerto Rico chapter of the International Cigarmakers' Union/A.F.L. I wasn't given much of a welcome; my meeting with the secretary was cold and formal.

I immediately started attending union meetings at the hall up on 84th Street off Second Avenue. There I met many countrymen who had been living in New York since the end of the century. The militancy of those Puerto Rican cigarmakers had been a decisive factor in the election of progressive candidates to leading positions in the local.

Despite all my efforts, after more than a month in New York I was still unemployed. If I didn't find something soon I knew I'd be in serious straits. How much longer could I stretch the little money I had? The bills I had sewn into the lining of my jacket were of course sacred, so I decided to resort to an employment agency and "buy" a job. Yes, sure, I had already been warned of all the traps set to catch the innocent. I knew how mercilessly they would swindle foreigners by "selling" them imaginary jobs. But I had to turn somewhere, and even the slightest hope was better than none. So I showed up, along with my friend Ambrosio, who was also still out of work, at one of those infamous agencies. We paid our $15.00 and set our hopes on the employment due us.

Day in, day out, we would go to the agency and be sent off to some remote "workplace." More often than not it turned out that the street number, and even the street, was completely unknown to anyone. Other times we would track down the address, only to find an abandoned building. We would of course go back to the agency and explain what had happened, but they would only treat us like idiots who couldn't even find our way around town. Finally it began to dawn on us that we were being made fools of.

One day I woke up with that *jíbaro* spirit boiling in my blood. When we got there, the agency was full of innocent new victims. I went straight up to the man in charge and raised holy hell. I yelled at him—partly in English but mostly in Spanish—and demanded my money back immediately. A few Spaniards heard the noise and joined me in a loud chorus, demanding the return of their money too. Two employees of the agency grabbed me by the arms and tried to throw me down the stairs. But the Spaniards jumped to my defense. Finally the boss of the place, afraid of a serious scandal and police involvement, gave all of us our money back.

At the next meeting of the Socialist Club I recounted my experience at the employment agency, and it was decided to make a complaint to the authorities. I later found out that they did in fact conduct an investigation, and that the agency had its license suspended. The fact is, though, that the injustices of those infamous agencies continued, and that Puerto Ricans became their most favored prey.

In those years, and for a long time to come, the Socialist Party, the Cigarmakers' Union, and the Seamen's Union were the only groups that were concerned about defending foreign workers. The other labor unions either showed no interest, or were too weak to do anything, as in the case of the Dressmakers' Union, which later became the powerful International Ladies' Garment Workers' Union. It should also be mentioned that the Fur and Leather Workers' Union showed its solidarity with the struggles of foreign workers.

Socialist influence was strong among the Jews. Many of their organizations worked with the Socialist Party and the labor unions.

Most outstanding of all were the Jewish Workmen's Circle and the liberal-minded newspaper *Forward*.

I began to move in these circles and go to a lot of their activities. Truth is, though, that as far as finding work is concerned none of it did me any good. On top of that, the landlady at our rooming house, Mrs. Arnao, began to ask us every single day whether or not we had found work. Even though we would pay her religiously every week, she started to have an unpleasant look on her face.

At the same time, the warm hospitality we had enjoyed at the boarding house was cooling down. There was not such a variety of food as in our first days there. The rooms weren't cared for as carefully as they had been at the beginning. The hatchet finally fell on a Friday, after dinner. Suddenly Mrs. Arnao informed us that she was thinking of going away on a trip and that we would have to move out.

Figuring that misery makes poor company, Ambrosio and I decided to part ways. We headed off in different directions. Before long word had it that my friend had found work in a gunpowder factory. As for me, I took up lodgings at the house of a certain Rodríguez, a cigar-maker from Bayamón who had a boarding house on East 86th Street. It was actually the first floor of a modern building. The apartment was spacious and comfortable. The roomers in the house were mostly Hungarians and Czechs. The style of life in the neighborhood was strictly European, filled with traces of old Vienna, Berlin, and Prague.

Mr. Rodríguez' wife was an excellent Puerto Rican woman. To her misfortune, however, her husband drank whisky the way a camel drinks water. When he was sober he was mild-mannered and good natured, but when he took to drinking, which was usually the case, he liked to pick fights.

Several Puerto Ricans were also staying in the house, very good people to be sure. Many others of the same caliber came by to visit. Among them I got to know Paco Candelas, J. Amy Sanjurjo, J. Correa, Pablo Ortíz, and Pepe Lleras. It was a pleasant neighborhood: the atmosphere was neat and clean, the people friendly and open-minded. Everyone would express themselves in their own tongue. Most people spoke English, but poorly, and always with a foreign accent.

There were excellent restaurants in the neighborhood. You had your choice—Hungarian, German, Czech, Italian, Montenegran . . . Quite a few of them would imitate the style of cafés in Vienna and Bohemia. The area was full of good-looking women, especially Hungarian. A lot were blonde, though you'd also see dark-haired ones with that distinctive gypsy beauty! I must admit that it was those women, who looked so much like the ones from my home country, that most appealed to the romantic side of me. But what could a man do who was out of work and down to his last pennies?

But I enjoyed the neighborhood anyway. On 86th Street there were five theaters where they not only showed films but put on live shows. I loved the diversity of people. Nearby was the German colony, where the socialists were active in all community affairs. There were many meeting places there, most notably the Labor Temple. Down a little ways was the Czech area, with its center of activity being the Bohemian National Hall (*Narodni Budova*), between First and Second avenues. The followers of Beneš and Masaryk used to meet there before Czechoslovakia became an independent state.

Around the time that I went to live in that part of town a good many Puerto Ricans were beginning to move in too. Many Hispanics, especially Cubans from the time of José Martí, lived on those streets. Right in the heart of that area, in fact, at 235 East 75th Street, is where our illustrious countryman Sotero Figueroa lived for many years.

It certainly was a good thing that I liked the neighborhood, because the truth is that my situation was desperate. Winter was near and I didn't even have adequate clothing. As fall set in I spent my days feeling the lining of my jacket and that precious return fare to Puerto Rico. But I wasn't about to give up until the eleventh hour . . .

One morning my fellow townsman Pepe Lleras invited me to go with him to Kingsland over in New Jersey. My good friend Lleras, who was also unemployed, convinced me that the only place we would be able to find work was in the munitions industry. So off we went to one of those immense plants. When asked in the personnel office if we had any experience, we said yes. I was so set on landing something that I almost went so far as to say I had grown up playing with gunpowder!

That was my first job in the United States. The war in Europe was at its height. The Germans had just suffered a setback at Verdun. In the United States, war material was being produced in enormous quantities. The work in the munitions plant was very hard. Only those hardened by rigorous labor could stand it. It really was too much for the soft hands of *tabaqueros* like ourselves. They would work us for eight hours without a break. Even to do your private business you had to get permission from the lead man of the work crew, and he would only relieve you for a few short minutes. Never before had I experienced, or even witnessed, such brutal working conditions.

Pepe and I would be out of the house at five in the morning. It took us almost two hours to get there. The work day started at seven and we would spend the whole day surrounded by all kinds of grenades and explosives. Most of the workers were Italians of peasant stock, tough as the marble of their country. There were also a lot of Norwegian, Swedish, and Polish workers, most of them as strong as oxen . . . Pepe Lleras and I, though better built than the average Puerto Rican, were beaten to a pulp after two weeks.

On the way home we would collapse onto the seat of the train like two drunks, and when we got home we hardly even felt like eating. Our hands were all beaten and bloody and felt like they were burning. After massaging each other's backs, we would throw ourselves into bed like tired beasts of burden. At the crack of dawn, feeling as though we had hardly slept more than a few minutes, we'd be up and off to another day's labor.

One day—we hadn't been there long—we met up with a stroke of hard luck. We used to get there a few minutes before work began to change into our work clothes. It so happened that one afternoon at the end of the day we couldn't find our street clothes. We complained to the man in charge, but he only responded sneeringly, "What do you think this is, a bank or something? If your clothes are stolen, that's your tough luck."

It sure was our tough luck. The clothes that were stolen were the only good clothes we had, and for me the loss was greater still—for along with my suit jacket went my passage money back to Puerto Rico. It was as though my return ship had gone up in flames.

1955

# FRANK O'HARA

In the 1950's and early 60's, Frank O'Hara (1926–66) developed a type
of diary-poem that replicated the sensation of walking around New
York, noticing both the action on the street and the action inside one's
head: the literary equivalent of Times Square, where avenues converge
and "everything suddenly honks" O'Hara adapted French poetry's col-
lage techniques to colloquial American speech, with doses of the sub-
dialect that Allen Ginsberg called "gay talk"—a mixture of chatty
gossip, camp humor, and cultural sophistication.

### A STEP AWAY FROM THEM

It's my lunch hour, so I go
for a walk among the hum-colored
cabs. First, down the sidewalk
where laborers feed their dirty
glistening torsos sandwiches
and Coca-Cola, with yellow helmets
on. They protect them from falling
bricks, I guess. Then onto the
avenue where skirts are flipping
above heels and blow up over
grates. The sun is hot, but the
cabs stir up the air. I look
at bargains in wristwatches. There
are cats playing in sawdust.
                      On
to Times Square, where the sign
blows smoke over my head, and higher
the waterfall pours lightly. A
Negro stands in a doorway with a
toothpick, languorously agitating.
A blonde chorus girl clicks: he
smiles and rubs his chin. Everything

suddenly honks: it is 12:40 of
a Thursday.
   Neon in daylight is a
great pleasure, as Edwin Denby would
write, as are light bulbs in daylight.
I stop for a cheeseburger at JULIET'S
CORNER. Giulietta Masina, wife of
Federico Fellini, *è bell' attrice.*
And chocolate malted. A lady in
foxes on such a day puts her poodle
in a cab.
   There are several Puerto
Ricans on the avenue today, which
makes it beautiful and warm. First
Bunny died, then John Latouche,
then Jackson Pollock. But is the
earth as full as life was full, of them?
And one has eaten and one walks,
past the magazines with nudes
and the posters for BULLFIGHT and
the Manhattan Storage Warehouse,
which they'll soon tear down. I
used to think they had the Armory
Show there.
   A glass of papaya juice
and back to work. My heart is in my
pocket, it is Poems by Pierre Reverdy.

1 9 5 6

THE DAY LADY DIED

It is 12:20 in New York a Friday
three days after Bastille day, yes
it is 1959 and I go get a shoeshine
because I will get off the 4:19 in Easthampton
at 7:15 and then go straight to dinner
and I don't know the people who will feed me

I walk up the muggy street beginning to sun
and have a hamburger and a malted and buy
an ugly NEW WORLD WRITING to see what the poets
in Ghana are doing these days
                              I go on to the bank
and Miss Stillwagon (first name Linda I once heard)
doesn't even look up my balance for once in her life
and in the GOLDEN GRIFFIN I get a little Verlaine
for Patsy with drawings by Bonnard although I do
think of Hesiod, trans. Richmond Lattimore or
Brendan Behan's new play or *Le Balcon* or *Les Nègres*
of Genet, but I don't, I stick with Verlaine
after practically going to sleep with quandariness

and for Mike I just stroll into the PARK LANE
Liquor Store and ask for a bottle of Strega and
then I go back where I came from to 6th Avenue
and the tobacconist in the Ziegfeld Theatre and
casually ask for a carton of Gauloises and a carton
of Picayunes, and a NEW YORK POST with her face on it

and I am sweating a lot by now and thinking of
leaning on the john door in the 5 SPOT
while she whispered a song along the keyboard
to Mal Waldron and everyone and I stopped breathing

                                                    1959

[ 787 ]

## STEPS

How funny you are today New York
like Ginger Rogers in *Swingtime*
and St. Bridget's steeple leaning a little to the left

here I have just jumped out of a bed full of V-days
(I got tired of D-days) and blue you there still
accepts me foolish and free
all I want is a room up there
and you in it
and even the traffic halt so thick is a way
for people to rub up against each other
and when their surgical appliances lock
they stay together
for the rest of the day (what a day)
I go by to check a slide and I say
that painting's not so blue

where's Lana Turner
she's out eating
and Garbo's backstage at the Met
everyone's taking their coat off
so they can show a rib-cage to the rib-watchers
and the park's full of dancers with their tights and shoes
in little bags
who are often mistaken for worker-outers at the West Side Y
why not
the Pittsburgh Pirates shout because they won
and in a sense we're all winning
we're alive

the apartment was vacated by a gay couple
who moved to the country for fun
they moved a day too soon
even the stabbings are helping the population explosion

though in the wrong country
and all those liars have left the U N
the Seagram Building's no longer rivalled in interest
not that we need liquor (we just like it)

and the little box is out on the sidewalk
next to the delicatessen
so the old man can sit on it and drink beer
and get knocked off it by his wife later in the day
while the sun is still shining

oh god it's wonderful
to get out of bed
and drink too much coffee
and smoke too many cigarettes
and love you so much

1960

# LOREN EISELEY

*Scientist and naturalist Loren Eiseley (1907–77) brought a melancholy sensibility and formidable literary gift to essay-writing. In his auto-biography* All the Strange Hours *(1975), Eiseley demonstrated his capacity for taking the long view, through geological and evolutionary lenses. Here, in an excerpt from his book* The Immense Journey, *he looks at New York City from a similarly elevated perspective.*

## FROM *THE IMMENSE JOURNEY*

NEW YORK IS NOT, on the whole, the best place to enjoy the downright miraculous nature of the planet. There are, I do not doubt, many remarkable stories to be heard there and many strange sights to be seen, but to grasp a marvel fully it must be savored from all aspects. This cannot be done while one is being jostled and hustled along a crowded street. Nevertheless, in any city there are true wildernesses where a man can be alone. It can happen in a hotel room, or on the high roofs at dawn.

One night on the twentieth floor of a midtown hotel I awoke in the dark and grew restless. On an impulse I climbed upon the broad old-fashioned window sill, opened the curtains and peered out. It was the hour just before dawn, the hour when men sigh in their sleep, or, if awake, strive to focus their wavering eyesight upon a world emerging from the shadows. I leaned out sleepily through the open window. I had expected depths, but not the sight I saw.

I found I was looking down from that great height into a series of curious cupolas or lofts that I could just barely make out in the darkness. As I looked, the outlines of these lofts became more distinct because the light was being reflected from the wings of pigeons who, in utter silence, were beginning to float outward upon the city. In and out through the open slits in the cupolas passed the white-winged birds on their mysterious errands. At this hour the city was theirs, and quietly, without the brush of a single wing tip against stone in that high, eerie place, they were taking over the spires of

Manhattan. They were pouring upward in a light that was not yet perceptible to human eyes, while far down in the black darkness of the alleys it was still midnight.

As I crouched half asleep across the sill, I had a moment's illusion that the world had changed in the night, as in some immense snow-fall, and that if I were to leave, it would have to be as these other in-habitants were doing, by the window. I should have to launch out into that great bottomless void with the simple confidence of young birds reared high up there among the familiar chimney pots and in-terposed horrors of the abyss.

I leaned farther out. To and fro went the white wings, to and fro. There were no sounds from any of them. They knew man was asleep and this light for a little while was theirs. Or perhaps I had only dreamed about man in this city of wings—which he could surely never have built. Perhaps I, myself, was one of these birds dreaming unpleasantly a moment of old dangers far below as I teetered on a window ledge.

Around and around went the wings. It needed only a little courage, only a little shove from the window ledge to enter that city of light. The muscles of my hands were already making little pre-monitory lunges. I wanted to enter that city and go away over the roofs in the first dawn. I wanted to enter it so badly that I drew back carefully into the room and opened the hall door. I found my coat on the chair, and it slowly became clear to me that there was a way down through the floors, that I was, after all, only a man.

I dressed then and went back to my own kind, and I have been rather more than usually careful ever since not to look into the city of light. I had seen, just once, man's greatest creation from a strange inverted angle, and it was not really his at all. I will never forget how those wings went round and round, and how, by the merest pressure of the fingers and a feeling for air, one might go away over the roofs. It is a knowledge, however, that is better kept to oneself. I think of it sometimes in such a way that the wings, beginning far down in the black depths of the mind, begin to rise and whirl till all the mind is lit by their spinning, and there is a sense of things passing away, but lightly, as a wing might veer over an obstacle.

1957

# ROBERT MOSES

*No two individuals did more to shape New York City in the twentieth century than Mayor Fiorello H. LaGuardia and Robert Moses (1888–1981), the master planner who worked with "The Little Flower" and who here assesses his career. As Robert Caro showed in his biography of Moses,* The Power Broker, *the man who got bridges, beaches, and parks built also had a destructive side (see also Gay Talese's "Panic in Brooklyn," page 859). Moses was Machiavellian and complex; he was also, it turns out, quite a good writer.*

## FIORELLO H. LAGUARDIA

THERE IS such a thing as moderation even in biography, and it is unnecessary to make the subject either a Galahad or Lohengrin or to exaggerate the warts in the manner of Ghirlandajo and Hogarth. After all, it was not his vulnerable heel that made him Achilles. Every portrait of a great figure by a contemporary must be impressionistic. Few admirers on reflection would wish to see Shelley plain.

A candid photo tells very little. No doubt the fairest method would be to publish in full the impact of a personality on several people. Surely the worst way would be, in the fashion of the big magazine publishers, to put a pack of eager researchers to work on every trace and clue, toss the combined product into a pot, mash it up, and produce a single, smooth, composite result.

We pause in our busy lives to salute Fiorello LaGuardia. He was much more than a colorful personality. We doff our hats to a record of extraordinary accomplishment in almost every field of municipal works, in plan and performance, in health and hospitals, in schools, housing, and recreation, in the arts and sciences, in protection, in personnel. Countless evidences are still about us. Only those who recall the cynicism of the late Twenties and early Thirties and remember how low the City's credit and civic morale had fallen can properly gauge what this man did to lift us up and to attract to New York the lost respect of the nation.

He lifted dispirited civic morale and raised public enterprise and housekeeping to a permanently higher level. There are, no doubt, gaps in this record and chinks in the armor of righteousness. LaGuardia kept promising to raise the subway fare and finance rapid-transit improvements before their cost became prohibitive, but he never got around to it. The issue was always good for one more election, until it was abandoned without the great outcry the politicians feared and prophesied.

Much has been made of LaGuardia's amusing antics, whether calculated or the result of surplus energy—rushing to fires, reading the comics, leading the band, helping Grover Whalen to greet trained seals fresh from swimming the English Channel, jeering at stuffy tycoons knee-deep in soft rugs in Park and Fifth Avenue clubs or at "tinhorns" in the less elegant bistros, crucifying a market inspector for accepting a cheap necktie from a pushcart peddler, acting as a committing magistrate to pillory a welfare inspector who did a favor for somebody on relief, brewing beer at 115th Street and Lenox Avenue to the delight of Harlem, deluging commissioners with letters to the Mayor to which were attached brightly colored slips directing just what was to be done about them, including drafts and copies of replies, which made a gigantic dead-letter office out of City Hall, firing a faithful, if sometimes sappy, secretary for getting tight, driving the gay hurdy-gurdies from the streets, screaming obscenities at Mussolini's Virginio Gayda over the Italian transatlantic radio, denouncing Greyhound bus officials "Grey Mutts," hurrahing for UNRRA, berating offending City Hall reporters, taking away policemen's clubs, directing traffic, laying out airports, acting as impresario of the City Center, cutting salaries of department heads to fit what he considered to be their private means without reference to responsibilities, proposing with impish glee to hang the wet wash in the back of Gracie Mansion where everyone in Carl Schurz Park could see the short and simple flannels of the ruling family, and beating his breast and quoting from *Timothy* that he had fought a good fight and kept the faith.

His moments of omniscience and megalomania were followed by charming public admissions of fallibility. He said that when he made a mistake it was a beaut. When he changed his mind, it was in Macy's window. It may well be asked why a polyglot city of many facets, moods, sympathies, variations, changes, whimsies, generosities, crudities, and enthusiasms should not have a Mayor with a few occasional eccentricities of his own. At any rate that's the way Fiorello LaGuardia figured it as he became more and more adept in the use of blazing, often carefully prepared indiscretions.

True, there were occasional unpredictable thunderstorms, from which he emerged smiling on flora and fauna and drying the eyes of a distracted secretariat, but these became less frequent, no doubt because the doctors threatened tremors and strokes. More and more he used his brains rather than his muscles. The Little Flower was not as much of a Hotspur as he pretended to be. He was bold, but not foolhardy, wore stout buckskin gloves when he grasped the nettle, and rarely got a bloody paw.

The contrast between LaGuardia and Walker was startling. Champagne, caviar, and the Central Park Casino gave way to neat rum, salami, and the Advertising Club, but there were deeper differences. He could speak real Yiddish where Jimmy Walker's vocabulary was limited to *gefilte fish* and *bagels and lox*. He reveled in Italian of the street variety where Jimmy knew only *arrivederci*, *pasta*, and *io compresco tutto*. Jimmy Walker had to make a quick exit to get a big hand. Fiorello LaGuardia had persistence and knowledge and could afford to stick around and make a real impression. One was an entertaining, enormously likable mountebank, the other an accomplished showman.

The Mayor adopted a Lincolnesque approach to Harlem, made broad his phylacteries in East New York, emphasized his ancestral links with and unquestionable respect for the Roman Catholic Church, and attended an occasional Church of England service at the Cathedral of St. John the Divine. If there had been a solid group of Chinese Mohammedans, he would doubtless have discovered strong ties with them. Trojan and Tyrian, he took them all on.

Being Mayor of New York is an exacting job. Any mayor of any great American city—and our Mayor in particular—never has leisure and time for reflection, is always in the limelight, and is subject to the pressure of events, the impact of the unexpected and unguessable, the demand for quick decisions, the dangers of misrepresentation and error. By comparison, the Governor up in Albany is a hermit. It is as hard for a mayor to get into the Hall of Fame as it is for a camel to pass through the eye of a needle.

I shall never forget my first sight of LaGuardia in action on his first day in office. He was sitting at his desk in City Hall flanked by Deputy Comptroller Joseph D. McGoldrick and Bernard Deutsch, president of the Board of Aldermen. All three were small and compact, and they made quite a picture. The Mayor was tossing letters at a pint-sized secretary and shouting, "Say yes, say no, throw it away, tell him to go to hell," etc. The Fusion regime was warming up.

The Mayor in his three terms, and notably in the first, presided over a strange collection of department heads and deputies typical of a fusion administration. Visiting City Hall was like opening a box of animal crackers. You never could tell what kind of beast would come out of the Ark. Adolph Augustus Berle, Jr., was appointed City chamberlain and was a brilliant prime minister without portfolio. When an unfeeling rascal, no doubt a tool of the Beelzebubs of Tammany Hall, vamoosed with a wad of City money, the happy news traveled swiftly to the streets of Gath and Askelon, and there was great rejoicing among the Philistines over Berle's personal liability and hopes that he would never be reimbursed. The prodigies who launched the LaGuardia reform era did not stay long. They moved to larger, greener, and more distant national and global fields. When my friend Adolph Berle was leaving, he said to me, "Bob, it's all very well for you to fuss with street openings. As for me, I'm off to settle the Chinese question."

I cannot speak as one who was in the Mayor's kitchen cabinet with the Gamaliels, the anointed, the pundits and geniuses, the incurable amateurs, the wide-eyed innocents, the second-guessers, the *muchachos* and camp followers of reform. Sometimes I was held in reserve in the pantry, but I was usually in the woodshed. However the Mayor's advisers may be characterized, he was always their boss and never their victim. A new man of the first generation, LaGuardia pretended a mild contempt for old families and professed to believe that nepotism usually accounted for their advancement. Nevertheless, he liked to have representatives of this class on his staff. But a native aristocrat in Fiorello's book was at best a chip of the old munk.

Somehow, even normally intelligent voters still expect a mayor to be all things to all men. If he falls for this demand and faithfully attends all dinners, clambakes, cornerstone layings, communions, bar mitzvahs, weddings, and funerals, he may continue to be popular, but he will certainly not achieve civic immortality. All efforts to shift power and responsibility to a deputy mayor or business manager, on the false assumption that city government is just big business minus the profit motive, and to reduce the mayor to a greeter and symbol, or to lighten his responsibilities by handing them to subordinates with a passion for anonymity—these efforts have failed because in the never-ending clinches and emergencies the people demand leadership, and leadership has its penalties.

LaGuardia was a showoff, but he never confused groundbreakings with openings. He cut red tape and ribbons. He was not content with the dismal succession of announcement, delay, and failure.

The Mayor blandly subscribed to the pet theory of the goo-goos that the deputy mayor should be an executive vice-president, given wide delegated discretion to lift the burden of administrative detail from the top boss, but in practice LaGuardia's deputy was something halfway between a warrant officer loosely attached to a retired admiral and a dignified eunuch at the door of a squirming seraglio.

About a decade after the appearance of Alfred E. Smith on the lower East Side. Fiorello Henry LaGuardia was born in a tenement at 7 Varick Street. He was soon on his way to Arizona and the field where his father was an Army bandmaster.

Smith and LaGuardia had quite a lot in common. First and foremost, they shared the same fierce determination to demonstrate to skeptics and bigots that boys from the sidewalks of Lower Manhattan could run great governments honestly, intelligently, progressively, and to an astonishing degree without degrading politics, and thus wring reluctant admiration from the sticks, the crossroads, the

Southern Tier, and Park Avenue. One had the curious sense in observing Governor Smith that he was living up to a model or example he had established for himself and that the executive was something apart from and superior to the man. It was the same with LaGuardia.

When the Mayor was mad at me, he would say, "The only boss you ever had whom you really respected was Al Smith. You think he was a better executive than I am. What's he got that I don't have?" And I always answered that I admired both of them but thought Smith a better executive partly because he had more loyalty to his men. My wife once charged the Mayor with lack of loyalty. He replied, "I'm loyal to principles, not to men"—a very cute rejoinder but one that still horrifies me, because all genuine loyalties run to individuals.

I cannot forget the impish, almost sadistic quality that led the Mayor to humiliate a department head by calling in a stenographer and shouting at her, "If you were any dumber, I'd make you a commissioner." One of the commissioners talked to me with tears in his eyes about his humiliation at the hands of the Mayor and said he just couldn't stand it but couldn't afford to quit. On the other hand, Bill Carey, the big contractor and part-time sanitation commissioner, was one of the few unterrified department heads. He could always leave the job, and he regarded the Mayor's vaudeville stunts with a mixture of humor, friendly admiration, and amazed incredulity. It was just the best show Bill had ever seen.

Bill Carey's predecessor was an Army colonel whom the Mayor, as a small boy, had known at some western Army reservation where the senior LaGuardia played the cornet and led the band. The colonel's appointment was strictly a matter of sentiment. He didn't last long. One night his boys left open the booms that controlled scow dumping at Pelham Bay Park for the future Orchard Beach. The garbage floated over the entire Sound shorefront of Westchester up to Connecticut. The Westchester health commissioner flew into a rage. I got the Mayor to order the colonel to send several thousand sanitation lads and their equipment to Westchester to clean up the mess.

The Mayor had his ax out for local political leaders. They did not make him, and while he had to use them around elections, he resented it and repudiated even the suggestion of personal obligation. The leaders who were finally lined up in turn resented having to support him. It was up to some of us to appeal periodically to the higher instincts of angry Republican leaders while the Mayor insulted them with public references to clubhouse loafers and bums. Paul Windels, the corporation counsel, and other conservatives would explain blandly that these epithets were LaGuardia terms of endearment.

It must be admitted that in exploiting racial and religious prejudices LaGuardia could run circles around the bosses he despised and derided. When it came to raking ashes of Old World hates, warming ancient grudges, waving the bloody shirt, tuning the ear to ancestral voices, he could easily outdemagogue the demagogues. And for what purpose? To redress old wrongs abroad? To combat foreign levy or malice domestic? To produce peace on the Danube, the Nile, the Jordan? Not on your tintype. Fiorello LaGuardia knew better.

No doubt his own birth and background, his early youth as a bandmaster's son on our western frontier, his experience as an interpreter on the edge of the Balkans, his flying stunts in the south of Europe in World War I, his service in Congress representing a polyglot slum district, UNRRA, the upheavals, the prison camps and furnaces of World War II, the beginnings of the emancipation of colonial people made him sensitive to great issues, but he was too shrewd, too honest, too basically cool, too calculating, too essentially American really to believe in his own occasional lapses into political claptrap. Why, then, did he use the familiar, rabble-rousing technique? He did it to get and stay elected.*

*Like most reformers, the Little Flower occasionally went way off beam on issues of conduct and morals. *The New York Times* reported that in 1942 William N. Conrad, a councilman, "introduced a bill forbidding anyone over 12 years old from appearing solely in a bathing suit or other brief attire on a boardwalk or city street beyond 200 feet of a beach or park. This bill . . . had the backing of . . . religious and civic groups and the opposition of Parks Commissioner Robert Moses, passed. It was signed . . . by Mayor . . . LaGuardia, who suggested that anyone who changed into bathing attire on the front lawn of a private home should be 'fanned' by the police all the way to the station house."

He loved the summer City Halls we rigged up for him, and especially those at the World's Fair in 1939 and 1940 in Flushing Meadow, which gave a fillip to his frequent gestures in the direction of internationalism. LaGuardia always wanted to be a general with one star to begin with, and President Roosevelt agreed to nominate him and assign him to Italy. The Mayor had been a candidate for Secretary of War, but the President had been persuaded not to send in his name. This therefore was a second effort in the military war service direction. So sure was he of the Italian job that he rearranged his pension, ordered his uniform, and canvassed the selection of a temporary successor. He had no thought of retiring as mayor and didn't like the applicable provisions of the City Charter. So with the help of some upstate officials with similar ambitions to eat their cake and have it, an extraordinary bill was passed at Albany under which an elected official could accept a commission in the Army, meanwhile holding on to his local office and picking a temporary successor who would be turfed out as soon as the elected incumbent chose to come home. Any ambitious student interested in the fine art of bill drafting can find this gem.

This strange act superseded all statutory and charter provisions about absence, incapacity, retirement, etc., of the incumbent. The bill was entitled "Absence from Public Office for Military Duty" and was so drawn that its real purpose was unrecognizable—just another bit of patriotic legislation to help win the war. There were plenty of rumors floating around as to the Mayor's departure. They were confirmed when he sent for me and said he had picked me to act in his absence, Judge Thomas D. Thacher having declined this dubious honor. I asked him what about Newbold Morris, who as president of the Council was designated in the Charter to pinch-hit for the Mayor when he was away. He gave no responsive answer.

I told him I wasn't interested in any such shenanigans and didn't believe anyway that he was going to be confirmed by the Senate. Actually Judge Samuel Seabury, Charles C. Burlingham, and other Mammons of civic uprighteousness rushed to Washington and protested to Secretary Stimson, who had already told the President he didn't think the Mayor's fiery, provocative presence in Italy would be helpful and that he could not recommend confirmation. The nomination never went in. The Mayor stayed on at City Hall. I never heard what became of his uniform.

LaGuardia was certainly ill and not himself in his last year in office and in the unfortunate period of random scribbling, pot-boiling, and ill-prepared, raucous radio exhortations that followed. Some way must certainly be found of relieving honest officials—so many of whom come out of office with depleted means and an inadequate pension—from the curse of grabbing undignified employment to provide a backlog for their families.

When the Mayor sent for me late in the summer of 1947, I was shocked at the change in him. He was in bed, so shrunken, so chapfallen yet so spunky, and so obviously on the way out. I felt like crying. It was a battle that not even the most courageous fighter could win.

In retrospect, I shall never forget the Lewisohn Stadium concert in 1944 at which the squatty little Mayor with much fanfare strode onto the stage with the towering General De Gaulle, soul of the French Resistance. They looked at first like Mutt and Jeff. The orchestra struck up the "Marseillaise." Marian Anderson sang. The entire audience joined in.

This is the last letter I received from the Little Flower. I saw him once before he died shortly afterward.

> LA GUARDIA
> 30 Rockefeller Plaza, New York City
> August 18, 1947

Dear Bob:

It was so nice talking to you today. I am so glad you will take my broadcast next Sunday, August 24th. I have 23 minutes which you will find most comfortable in comparison with the 13 minutes time on a 15 minute program.

Two precious building seasons have been lost. I am sure you will be able to tell better than any one else why. Whatever the reason, something must be done. The present situation, now critical, may soon be tragic.

I always felt that lower interest rates would do a great deal but even since that time, there are so many income groups that need housing that every possible kind of development within the rent reach of these groups is helpful.

Morris Novik will be in touch with you regarding detailed arrangements for the broadcast.

Marie will ring up Mary. I do hope to see you real soon.

Sincerely,<br>
Fiorello

1957

# JOHN CHEEVER

*When New York began to feel dangerous, chaotic, and indifferent to the aspirations of middle-class families, the flight to the suburbs began. John Cheever (1912–82), whose stories chronicle the tradeoffs of suburban living, analyzes in this autobiographical essay the process by which he himself began to detach himself from his urban moorings.*

## MOVING OUT

THE WAR was over; so was the shortage of building materials, and from the windows of our apartment near Sutton Place we could see the horizon beginning to change. Everybody was home who was coming back, the girls still had their dewy furlough looks and, after the smoking and carious ruins of Manila, the City of New York with the sky pouring its light onto the rivers looked like a vision of enlightenment. My children were young and my favorite New York was the one they led me through on Sunday afternoons. A girl in high heels can show you Rome, a drinking companion is the best for Dublin, and I enjoyed the New York my children knew. They liked the Central Park lion house at four o'clock on February afternoons, the highest point of the Queensboro Bridge, and a riverside dock in the East Forties, long gone, where I once saw a couple of tarts playing hopscotch with a hotel room key. Oh, it was a long time ago. You could still hear the *Oklahoma!* score during drinking hours, the Mink Decade was just taking hold and the Third Avenue El still rattled the dishes in Bloomingdale's. The East River views were broader then and there was an imposing puissance to those reaches of light and water. We used to ride and play touch football in Central Park and, in October, with the skiing season in mind, I used to climb the ten flights of stairs to our apartment. I used the back stairs, the only stairs, and I was the only one to use them. Most of the kitchen doors stood open and my climb was a breach of privacy, but what could I do? I used to whistle and sometimes sing to warn the tenants of my approach, but in spite of these precautions I once saw a lady wearing nothing but a girdle while she basted a leg of lamb, a cook drinking whiskey out of a bottle, and a housewife sitting on the lap of the sallow-faced delivery boy from the corner butcher's. On Christmas Eve my children and their friends used to sing carols on Sutton Place—mostly to butlers, everyone else having gone to Nassau, which may have been the beginning of the end.

It was a wonderful life and it didn't seem that it would ever end. In the winter there were those days with a smart polish on the air and the buildings, and then there were the first south winds of spring with their exciting and unclean odors of back yards and all the women shoppers walking east at dusk, carrying bunches of apple blossom and lilac that had been trucked up from the Shenandoah Valley the night before. A French-speaking panhandler used to work Beekman Place (*Je le regrette beaucoup, monsieur . . .*), and going out to dinner one night we ran into a bagpiper on the Lexington Avenue subway platform who played a Black Watch march between trains. New York was the place where I had met and married my wife, I had dreamed of its streets during the war, my children had been born here and it was here that I had first experienced the feeling of being free from social and parental strictures. We and our friends seemed to improvise our world and to meet society on the most liberal and spontaneous terms. I don't suppose there was a day, an hour, when the middle class got their marching orders, but toward the end of the 1940's the middle class began to move. It was more of a push than a move and the energy behind the push was the changing economic character of the city. It would all be easier to describe if there had been edicts, proclamations and tables of statistics, but this vast population shift was forced by butcher's bills, tips, increased rental and tuition costs and demolitions. Where are the Wilsons? you might ask. Oh, they've bought a place in Putnam County. And the Renshaws? They've moved to New Jersey. And the Oppers? The Oppers are in White Plains. The ranks were thinning and we watched them go with commiseration and some scorn. They sometimes returned for dinner with mud on their shoes, the women's faces red from weeding the vegetable garden. My God, the suburbs! They encircled the city's boundaries like enemy territory and we thought of them as a loss of privacy, a cesspool of conformity and a life of inde-scribable dreariness in some split-level village where the place name appeared in The New York *Times* only when some bored housewife blew off her head with a shotgun.

That spring, at the closing assembly of my daughter's school, the headmistress took the lectern and announced: "Now school is over and we are *all* going to the country!" We were not going to the coun-try and the exclamation fascinated me because hidden somewhere in her words was a sense, an apprehension of the fact that the rich of the city were getting richer and the friable middle ground where we stood was vanishing. The river views at any rate were vanishing and so were most of the landmarks. Down went a baronial old brewery and up went a de luxe apartment house. Building began on a vacant lot where we used to run the dog and most of the small and pleas-ant houses in the neighborhood, where people who were less than rich could live, were marked for demolition and would be replaced by the glass towers of a new class. I could see the landscape of my children's youth destroyed before my eyes; and don't we impair the richness of our memories with this velocity of reconstruction? The apartment house where we lived changed hands and the new owners prepared to turn the building into a co-operative, but we were given eight months to find another home. Most of the people we knew by then lived either in River House or in downtown tenements where you had to put out pots and pans to catch the leaks when it rained. Girls either came out at the Colony Club or came out, so to speak, on the river embankments, and my sons' friends either played foot-ball for Buckley or practiced snap-knife shots in the shadows of the bridge.

That was the winter when we never had enough money. I looked for another apartment, but it was impossible to find a place for a family of five that suited my wife and my income. We were not poor enough for subsidized housing and not anything like rich enough for the new buildings that were going up around us. The noise of wreck-ing crews seemed aimed directly at our residence in the city. In March one of the obligations that I couldn't—or at least neglected to—meet was the electric bill and our lights were turned off. The children took their baths by candlelight and, while they enjoyed this turn of events, the effect of the dark apartment on my own feelings was somber. We simply didn't have the scratch. I paid the light bill in the morning and went out to Westchester a week later and arranged to rent a little frame house with a sickly shade tree on the lawn.

The farewell parties were numerous and sometimes tearful. The sense was that we were being exiled, like so many thousands before us, by invincible economic pressures and sent out to a barren and provincial life where we would get fat, wear ill-fitting clothes and spend our evenings glued to the television set. What else can you do in the suburbs? On the night before we left we went to Riverview Terrace for dinner where I jumped, in an exuberance of regret, out of a first-story window. I don't think you can do that any more. After the party I walked around the city, beginning my farewells. The customary tinder lights beat up from the streets onto the low clouds overhead. On a sidewalk somewhere in the Eighties I saw a Cuban going through the steps of a rhumba, holding a baby in his arms. A dinner party in the Sixties was breaking up and men and women were standing in a lighted doorway calling good-by and good-night. In the Fifties I saw a scavenger pushing an enormous English perambulator—a carriage for a princess—from ash can to ash can. It was part of the city's imprimatur. It was in the spring and there was a heady, vernal fragrance from Central Park, for in New York the advance of the seasons is not forgotten but intensified. Autumn thunderstorms, leaf fires, the primeval stillness that comes after a heavy snowfall and the randy smells of April all seem magnified by the pavings of the greatest city in the world.

The moving men were due at noon and I took another melancholy walk. I had my shoes shined by a pleasant Italian who always described himself as a dirty-minded man. He blamed it on the smell of shoe polish which he claimed had some venereal persuasions. He had, like many men of his kind, a lively mind and possessed, along with the largest collection of nudist magazines I have ever seen, some exalted memories of Laurence Olivier as Hamlet, or Omletto as he called him. Standing in front of our apartment house was an old lady who not only fed and watered the pigeons that then lived

around the Queensboro Bridge, but whose love of the birds was jealous. A workman had put the crusts of his meal onto the sidewalk for
the birds and she was kicking the crusts into the gutter. "*You* don't
have to feed them," she was telling him. "*You* don't have to worry
about them. *I* take care of them. I spend four dollars a week on grain
and stale bread and in the summer I change their water twice a
day. I don't like strangers to feed them. . . ." The city is raffish and
magnificent and she and the shoeshine man would be advocates of its
raffishness—those millions of lonely but not-discontented men and
women who can be overheard speaking with great intimacy to the
chimpanzee in the zoo, the squirrels in the park and the pigeons
everywhere. That morning the air of New York was full of music.
Bessie Smith was singing *Jazzbo Brown* from a radio in the orange-
drink stand at the corner. Halfway down Sutton Place a blind man
was playing *Make Believe* on a sliding trombone. Beethoven's *Fifth
Symphony*, all threats and revelations, was blowing out of an upstairs
window. Men and women were sunning themselves on Second
Avenue and the vision of urban life seemed to be an amiable one, a
bond of imponderables, a shared risk and at least a gesture toward
the peaceableness of mankind, for who but a peaceable species could
live in such congestion? Fredric March was sitting on a bench in
Central Park. Igor Stravinsky was waiting at the corner for the light
to change. Myrna Loy was coming out of the Plaza and on lower
Sixth Avenue e. e. cummings was buying a bunch of bananas. It was
time to go and I got a cab uptown. "I'm not sleeping," the driver
said. "I'm not sleeping any more. I'm not getting my rest. Spring! It
don't mean nothing to me. My wife, she's left me. She's shacked up
with this fireman, but I told her I'll wait for you, Mildred, I'll wait
for you, it's nothing but bestiality you feel for this fireman and I'm
waiting for you, I'm keeping the home fires burning. . . ." It was the
idiom of the city and one of its many voices, for where else in the
world will strangers bear their intimate secrets to one another with
such urgency and such speed—and I would miss this.

Like so much else in modern life the pathos of our departure was
concealed by a deep cartilege of decorum. When the moving van had
closed its doors and departed, we shook hands with the doorman

and started for the country ourselves, wondering if we would ever return.

As it happened we returned the next week for dinner and continued to drive back into town regularly to see our friends. They shared our prejudices and our anxieties. "Can you bear it?" we would be asked. "Are you all right out there? When do you think you can get back?"

And we found other evacuees in the country who sat on their suburban lawns, planning to go back when the children had finished college; and when the rain fell into the leaves of the rock maples they asked: "Oh, Charlie, do you think it's raining in New York?"

Now on summer nights the smell of the city sometimes drifts northward on the waters of the Hudson River, up to the wooded, inland banks where we live. The odor is like the stales from some enormous laundry, although I expect that an incurable evacuee could detect in it Arpége, stone-cold gin, and might perhaps even imagine that he heard music on the water; but this is not for me. I sometimes go back to walk through the ghostly remains of Sutton Place where the rude, new buildings stand squarely in one another's river views and where the rents would make your head swim, but now my old friends seem insular in their concern about my exile, their apartments seem magnificent but sooty, like the scenery for the national or traveling company of a Broadway hit, and their doormen only remind me of the fact that I don't have to tip a staff of twenty at Christmas and that in my own house I can shout in anger or joy without having someone pound on the radiator for silence. The truth is that I'm crazy about the suburbs and I don't care who knows it. Sometimes my sons and I go fishing for perch in the Hudson, and when the trains for the city come bowling down along the riverbanks I salute the sometimes embarrassed passengers with my beer can, wishing them God-speed and prosperity in the greatest city in the world, but I see them pass without a trace of longing or envy.

ESQUIRE, 1960

# NED ROREM

*Ned Rorem (1923–   ), the composer noted for his art songs, has achieved equal distinction as a candid, worldly, and scathing self-analytic diarist. His willingness to be indiscreet about encounters with the famous is tempered by an alert and rather severe moral intelligence. In this entry from his* New York Diary *(1966), he takes us behind the scenes of the city's gay community in the pre-Stonewall era to describe a largely hidden world of anonymous sex.*

## FROM *THE NEW YORK DIARY*

TURKISH BATH, like the Quaker service, is a place of silent meeting. The silence is shared solely by men, men who come uniquely together not to speak but to act. More even than the army, the bath is by definition a male, if not a masculine, domain. (Though in Paris, whimsically, it's a lady who presents you your *billet d'entrée*, robe and towel.) There are as many varieties of bath as of motel, from the scorpion-ridden hammams of Marrakech, where like Rimbaud in a boxcar you'll be systematically violated by a regiment, to the carpeted saunas of Frisco, where like a corpse in a glossy morgue you'll be a slab of flab on marble with Musak. There is no variety, however, in the purpose served: anonymous carnality. As in a whorehouse, you check interpersonal responsibility at the door; but unlike the whorehouse, here a *ménage* might accidentally meet in mutual infidelity. The ethical value too is like prostitution's: the consolation that no one can prove you are not more fulfilled by a stranger (precisely because there's no responsibility to deflect your fantasies—fantasies which now are real) than by the mate you dearly love, and the realization that Good Sex is not in performing as the other person wants but as you want. You will reconfirm this as you retreat into time through every bath of history.

For decades there has existed in central Manhattan one such establishment, notorious throughout the planet but never written about. Certainly this one seeks no publicity: word of mouth seems sufficient to promote its million-dollar business. Located in the heart of a wholesale floral district, there's small chance that an unsuspecting salesman might happen in for a simple rubdown, the nearest hotel being the Martha Washington—for women only. The customers do constitute as heterogeneous a cross section as you'll ever find. (There are only two uncategorizable phenomena: the care and feeding of so-called creative artists, and the nature of a Turkish bath's clientele.) Minors and majors, beatniks and bartenders, all ages and proclivities of the married and single, the famous and tough, so *many* from Jersey! but curiously few mad queens because it's hard to maintain a style stark naked. To run across your friends is less embarrassing than cumbersome: who wants gossip now?

You enter at any age, in any condition, any time of night or week, pay dearly for a fetid cubicle, and are given a torn gown and a pair of mismated slippers (insufficient against the grime that remains in your toes for days). You penetrate an obscure world, disrobe in private while reading graffiti, emerge rerobed into the public of gray wanderers so often compared to the lost souls of Dante, although this geography is not built of seven circles but of four square stories each capable of housing some eighty mortals. Once, you are told, this was a synagogue; today it's a brothel lit like *Guernica* by one nude bulb. The top floor is a suite of squalid rooms giving onto a corridor from *The Blood of a Poet* with background music of a constant pitty-pat, whips and whispers, slurps and groans. The second floor, more of same, plus massive dormitory. On the ground floor are cubicles, a television room, a monastic refectory. The basement contains fringe benefits: a dryer, a massage room, a large dirty pool, and the famous steam-room wherein *partouzes* are not discouraged.

The personnel, working in shifts, comprises at any given time some ten people, including two masseurs and a uniformed policeman. Each of these appears dull-witted due to years of inhaling the gloomy disinfectant of locker room and hamburger grease.

There are feast and fast days, rough Spanish mornings and sneaky afternoons, even Embryo Night at the Baths. Eternal motion, never action (meaning production): despite a daily ocean of orgasm the ceaseless efforts at cross-breeding could hardly make a mule. Not from want of trying; at any time you may witness couplings of white with black, beauty with horror, aardvark with dinosaur, panda with pachyderm, skinny-old-slate-gray-potbelly-bald with chubby-old-slate-gray-potbelly-bald, heartbreakingly gentle with stimulatingly rugged—but always, paradoxically, like with like. Your pupils widen as a faun mounts that stevedore, or when a mountain descends on Mohammed. Some cluster forever together in a throbbing Medusa's head; others disentangle themselves to squat in foggy corners, immobile as carnivorous orchids, waiting to "go up" on whatever passes. There's one! on his knees, praying with tongue more active than a windmill in a hurricane, neck thrown back like Mata Hari's and smeared with tears nobody notices mingling with steam. All are centered on the spasm that in a fraction switches from sublime to ridiculous, the sickening spasm sought by poets and peasants, and which, like great love, makes the great seem silly. . . . Yet if at those suburban wife-swapping gang-bangs there's risk of pregnancy, these mirthless matings stay sterile—not because the sexes aren't mixed but because the species *are*.

If you don't believe me, says Maldoror, go see for yourself. You won't believe it *of* yourself, the money and months you've passed, a cultured person lurking in shadows governed by groin! Did you *honestly* spend the night? Can you, with your splitting head, manage it down the hall to pee, through shafts of black sunlight and idiot eyes and churning mouths that never say die, and crunched on the floor those tropical roaches you hadn't noticed last evening? Don't slip in the sperm while retching at the fact that it's 8 A.M. and there's still a dull moan and a sound of belts (they've really no sense of proportion). So leave, descend while cackling still rends the ear, reclaim that responsibility checked with your wallet. Hate all those bad people; or, if you will, feel lightened and purged. Allow the sounds to dim—the anticlimatic puffing and shooting and slippery striving, the friendless hasty jerkings that could fertilize a universe in the dirty dark (*quel embarras de richesses!*). Quit the baths to go home and bathe, but make clear to yourself that such uncommitted hilarity doesn't necessarily preclude a throbbing heart. For three times there you found eternal love.

1959-60

# JANE JACOBS

---

*Jane Jacobs' The Death and Life of Great American Cities marked a turning point in thinking about city planning. Jacobs (1916– ), through accessible examples and persuasive prose, advocated learning from the organic, gently self-corrective lessons of neighborhoods such as Greenwich Village, rather than the bulldozing, utopian schemes of urban renewal promoted by Robert Moses and the federal government.*

## FROM *THE DEATH AND LIFE OF GREAT AMERICAN CITIES*

UNDER THE SEEMING DISORDER of the old city, wherever the old city is working successfully, is a marvelous order for maintaining the safety of the streets and the freedom of the city. It is a complex order. Its essence is intricacy of sidewalk use, bringing with it a constant succession of eyes. This order is all composed of movement and change, and although it is life, not art, we may fancifully call it the art form of the city and liken it to the dance—not to a simple-minded precision dance with everyone kicking up at the same time, twirling in unison and bowing off en masse, but to an intricate ballet in which the individual dancers and ensembles all have distinctive parts which miraculously reinforce each other and compose an orderly whole. The ballet of the good city sidewalk never repeats itself from place to place, and in any one place is always replete with new improvisations.

The stretch of Hudson Street where I live is each day the scene of an intricate sidewalk ballet. I make my own first entrance into it a little after eight when I put out the garbage can, surely a prosaic occupation, but I enjoy my part, my little clang, as the droves of junior high school students walk by the center of the stage dropping candy wrappers. (How do they eat so much candy so early in the morning?)

While I sweep up the wrappers I watch the other rituals of morning: Mr. Halpert unlocking the laundry's handcart from its mooring to a cellar door, Joe Cornacchia's son-in-law stacking out the empty crates from the delicatessen, the barber bringing out his sidewalk folding chair, Mr. Goldstein arranging the coils of wire which proclaim the hardware store is open, the wife of the tenement's superintendent depositing her chunky three-year-old with a toy mandolin on the stoop, the vantage point from which he is learning the English his mother cannot speak. Now the primary children, heading for St. Luke's, dribble through to the south; the children for St. Veronica's cross, heading to the west, and the children for P.S. 41, heading toward the east. Two new entrances are being made from the wings: well-dressed and even elegant women and men with brief cases emerge from doorways and side streets. Most of these are heading for the bus and subways, but some hover on the curbs, stopping taxis which have miraculously appeared at the right moment, for the taxis are part of a wider morning ritual: having dropped passengers from midtown in the downtown financial district, they are now bringing downtowners up to midtown. Simultaneously, numbers of women in housedresses have emerged and as they crisscross with one another they pause for quick conversations that sound with either laughter or joint indignation, never, it seems, anything between. It is time for me to hurry to work too, and I exchange my ritual farewell with Mr. Lofaro, the short, thick-bodied, white-aproned fruit man who stands outside his doorway a little up the street, his arms folded, his feet planted, looking solid as earth itself. We nod; we each glance quickly up and down the street, then look back to each other and smile. We have done this many a morning for more than ten years, and we both know what it means: All is well.

The heart-of-the-day ballet I seldom see, because part of the nature of it is that working people who live there, like me, are mostly gone, filling the roles of strangers on other sidewalks. But from days off, I know enough of it to know that it becomes more and more intricate. Longshoremen who are not working that day gather at the White Horse or the Ideal or the International for beer and conversation. The executives and business lunchers from the industries just to the west throng the Dorgene restaurant and the Lion's Head coffee house; meat-market workers and communications scientists fill the bakery lunchroom. Character dancers come on, a strange old man with strings of old shoes over his shoulders, motor-scooter riders with big beards and girl friends who bounce on the back of the scooters and wear their hair long in front of their faces as well as behind, drunks who follow the advice of the Hat Council and are always turned out in hats, but not hats the Council would approve. Mr. Lacey, the locksmith, shuts up his shop for a while and goes to exchange the time of day with Mr. Slube at the cigar store. Mr. Koochagian, the tailor, waters the luxuriant jungle of plants in his window, gives them a critical look from the outside, accepts a compliment on them from two passers-by, fingers the leaves on the plane tree in front of our house with a thoughtful gardener's appraisal, and crosses the street for a bite at the Ideal where he can keep an eye on customers and wigwag across the message that he is coming. The baby carriages come out, and clusters of everyone from toddlers with dolls to teen-agers with homework gather at the stoops.

When I get home after work, the ballet is reaching its crescendo. This is the time of roller skates and stilts and tricycles, and games in the lee of the stoop with bottletops and plastic cowboys; this is the time of bundles and packages, zigzagging from the drug store to the fruit stand and back over to the butcher's; this is the time when teen-agers, all dressed up, are pausing to ask if their slips show or their collars look right; this is the time when beautiful girls get out of MG's; this is the time when the fire engines go through; this is the time when anybody you know around Hudson Street will go by.

As darkness thickens and Mr. Halpert moors the laundry cart to the cellar door again, the ballet goes on under lights, eddying back and forth but intensifying at the bright spotlight pools of Joe's sidewalk pizza dispensary, the bars, the delicatessen, the restaurant and the drug store. The night workers stop now at the delicatessen, to pick up salami and a container of milk. Things have settled down for the evening but the street and its ballet have not come to a stop.

I know the deep night ballet and its seasons best from waking long after midnight to tend a baby and, sitting in the dark, seeing the shadows and hearing the sounds of the sidewalk. Mostly it is a sound like infinitely pattering snatches of party conversation and, about three in the morning, singing, very good singing. Sometimes there is sharpness and anger or sad, sad weeping, or a flurry of search for a string of beads broken. One night a young man came roaring along, bellowing terrible language at two girls whom he had apparently picked up and who were disappointing him. Doors opened, a wary semicircle formed around him, not too close, until the police came. Out came the heads, too, along Hudson Street, offering opinion, "Drunk . . . Crazy . . . A wild kid from the suburbs."*

Deep in the night, I am almost unaware how many people are on the street unless something calls them together, like the bagpipe. Who the piper was and why he favored our street I have no idea. The bagpipe just skirled out in the February night, and as if it were a signal the random, dwindled movements of the sidewalk took on direction. Swiftly, quietly, almost magically a little crowd was there, a crowd that evolved into a circle with a Highland fling inside it. The crowd could be seen on the shadowy sidewalk, the dancers could be seen, but the bagpiper himself was almost invisible because his bravura was all in his music. He was a very little man in a plain brown overcoat. When he finished and vanished, the dancers and watchers applauded, and applause came from the galleries too, half a dozen of the hundred windows on Hudson Street. Then the windows closed, and the little crowd dissolved into the random movements of the night street.

The strangers on Hudson Street, the allies whose eyes help us natives keep the peace of the street, are so many that they always seem to be different people from one day to the next. That does not matter. Whether they are so many always-different people as they seem to be, I do not know. Likely they are. When Jimmy Rogan fell through a plate-glass window (he was separating some scuffling friends) and almost lost his arm, a stranger in an old T shirt emerged from the Ideal bar, swiftly applied an expert tourniquet and, according to the hospital's emergency staff, saved Jimmy's life. Nobody remembered seeing the man before and no one has seen him since. The hospital was called in this way: a woman sitting on the steps next to

*He turned out to be a wild kid from the suburbs. Sometimes, on Hudson Street, we are tempted to believe the suburbs must be a difficult place to bring up children.

the accident ran over to the bus stop, wordlessly snatched the dime from the hand of a stranger who was waiting with his fifteen-cent fare ready, and raced into the Ideal's phone booth. The stranger raced after her to offer the nickel too. Nobody remembered seeing him before, and no one has seen him since. When you see the same stranger three or four times on Hudson Street, you begin to nod. This is almost getting to be an acquaintance, a public acquaintance, of course.

I have made the daily ballet of Hudson Street sound more frenetic than it is, because writing it telescopes it. In real life, it is not that way. In real life, to be sure, something is always going on, the ballet is never at a halt, but the general effect is peaceful and the general tenor even leisurely. People who know well such animated city streets will know how it is. I am afraid people who do not will always have it a little wrong in their heads—like the old prints of rhinoceroses made from travelers' descriptions of rhinoceroses.

On Hudson Street, the same as in the North End of Boston or in any other animated neighborhoods of great cities, we are not innately more competent at keeping the sidewalks safe than are the people who try to live off the hostile truce of Turf in a blind-eyed city. We are the lucky possessors of a city order that makes it relatively simple to keep the peace because there are plenty of eyes on the street. But there is nothing simple about that order itself, or the bewildering number of components that go into it. Most of those components are specialized in one way or another. They unite in their joint effect upon the sidewalk, which is not specialized in the least. That is its strength.

1961

# JAMES MERRILL

That New York is a city that is forever being torn down and built up
again has often been observed, from the mid-nineteenth century onward;
but the emotional consequences of that continuous displacement have
rarely been expressed as affectingly as in this poem by James Merrill
(1926–95). A cosmopolitan, engagingly elegant poet, Merrill was
haunted, as Richard Howard put it, by "the opposition between that
which abides and that which flows."

## AN URBAN CONVALESCENCE

Out for a walk, after a week in bed,
I find them tearing up part of my block
And, chilled through, dazed and lonely, join the dozen
In meek attitudes, watching a huge crane
Fumble luxuriously in the filth of years.
Her jaws dribble rubble. An old man
Laughs and curses in her brain,
Bringing to mind the close of *The White Goddess*.

As usual in New York, everything is torn down
Before you have had time to care for it.
Head bowed, at the shrine of noise, let me try to recall
What building stood here. Was there a building at all?
I have lived on this same street for a decade.

Wait. Yes. Vaguely a presence rises
Some five floors high, of shabby stone
—Or am I confusing it with another one
In another part of town, or of the world?—
And over its lintel into focus vaguely
Misted with blood (my eyes are shut)
A single garland sways, stone fruit, stone leaves,
Which years of grit had etched until it thrust
Roots down, even into the poor soil of my seeing.

When did the garland become part of me?
I ask myself, amused almost,
Then shiver once from head to toe,

Transfixed by a particular cheap engraving of garlands
Bought for a few francs long ago,
All calligraphic tendril and cross-hatched rondure,
Ten years ago, and crumpled up to stanch
Boughs dripping, whose white gestures filled a cab,
And thought of neither then nor since.
Also, to clasp them, the small, red-nailed hand
Of no one I can place. Wait. No. Her name, her features
Lie toppled underneath that year's fashions.
The words she must have spoken, setting her face
To fluttering like a veil, I cannot hear now,
Let alone understand.

So that I am already on the stair,
As it were, of where I lived,
When the whole structure shudders at my tread
And soundlessly collapses, filling
The air with motes of stone.
Onto the still erect building next door
Are pressed levels and hues—
Pocked rose, streaked greens, brown whites.
Who drained the pousse-café?
Wires and pipes, snapped off at the roots, quiver.

Well, that is what life does. I stare
A moment longer, so. And presently
The massive volume of the world
Closes again.

Upon that book I swear
To abide by what it teaches:
Gospels of ugliness and waste,
Of towering voids, of soiled gusts,

Of a shrieking to be faced
Full into, eyes astream with cold—

With cold?
All right then. With self-knowledge.

Indoors at last, the pages of *Time* are apt
To open, and the illustrated mayor of New York,
Given a glimpse of how and where I work,
To note yet one more house that can be scrapped.

Unwillingly I picture
My walls weathering in the general view.
It is not even as though the new
Buildings did very much for architecture.

Suppose they did. The sickness of our time requires
That these as well be blasted in their prime.
You would think the simple fact of having lasted
Threatened our cities like mysterious fires.

There are certain phrases which to use in a poem
Is like rubbing silver with quicksilver. Bright
But facile, the glamour deadens overnight.
For instance, how 'the sickness of our time'

Enhances, then debases, what I feel.
At my desk I swallow in a glass of water
No longer cordial, scarcely wet, a pill
They had told me not to take until much later.

With the result that back into my imagination
The city glides, like cities seen from the air,
Mere smoke and sparkle to the passenger
Having in mind another destination

Which now is not that honey-slow descent
Of the Champs-Elysées, her hand in his,
But the dull need to make some kind of house
Out of the life lived, out of the love spent.

1962

# EDWIN DENBY

---

*The dance critic and poet Edwin Denby (1903–83) possessed a uniquely urban vision: as the title of one of his collections,* Dancers, Buildings and People in the Streets, *indicates, he could articulate the common link between Manhattan's pedestrian flow, the "walk"-based choreography of Merce Cunningham, and the brush strokes of abstract expressionist Willem de Kooning. Here he recounts, from the inside, the early days of what was to become the New York School of painting. Denby was also a fine poet; unlike his friend Frank O'Hara, whose street poems splashed over the page, he pinned down the flux of New York avenues in calm, well-ordered sonnets.*

## THE THIRTIES

PAT PASLOFF asked me to write something for the show about New York painting in the thirties, how it seemed at the time. The part I knew, I saw as a neighbor. I met Willem de Kooning on the fire escape, because a black kitten lost in the rain cried at my fire door, and after the rain it turned out to be his kitten. He was painting on a dark eight-foot-high picture that had sweeps of black across it and a big look. That was early in '36. Soon Rudy Burckhardt and I kept meeting Bill at midnight at the local Stewart's, and having a coffee together. Friends of his often showed up, and when the cafeteria closed we would go to Bill's loft in the next street and talk some more and make coffee. I remember people talking intently and listening intently and then everybody burst out laughing and started off intent on another tack. Seeing the pictures more or less every day, they slowly became beautiful, and then they stayed beautiful. I didn't think of them as painting of the New York School, I thought of them as Bill's pictures.

These early ones are easy to get into now from the later point of view of the New York School. At the time, from the point of view of the School of Paris, they were impenetrable. The resemblances to Picasso and Miro were misleading, because where they led one to expect seduction and climax, one saw instead a vibration. To start from Mondrian might have helped. One could not get into the picture by way of any detail, one had to get into it all at once, so to speak. It often took me several months to be able to.

I remember walking at night in Chelsea with Bill during the depression, and his pointing out to me on the pavement the dispersed compositions—spots and cracks and bits of wrappers and reflections of neon-light—neon-signs were few then—and I remember the scale in the compositions was too big for me to see it. Luckily I could imagine it. At the time Rudy Burckhardt was taking photographs of New York that keep open the moment its transient buildings spread their unknown and unequalled harmonies of scale. I could watch that scale like a magnanimous motion on these undistorted photographs; but in everyday looking about, it kept spreading beyond the field of sight. At the time we all talked a great deal about scale in New York, and about the difference of instinctive scale in signs, painted color, clothes, gestures, everyday expressions between Europe and America. We were happy to be in a city the beauty of which was unknown, uncozy, and not small scale.

While we were talking twenty years ago, I remembered someone saying, "Bill, you haven't said a word for half an hour." "Yes," he answered, his voice rising like a New Yorker's to falsetto with surprise, "I was just noticing that, too." He was likely to join in the talk by vehemently embracing a suggestion or vehemently rejecting it. Right off he imagined what it would be like to act on it and go on acting on it. He didn't, like a wit, imitate the appearance of acting on it; he committed himself full force to what he was imagining. As he went on, characteristic situations in his life or those of friends came back to him as vividly as if they had just happened. He invented others. Objections he accepted, or circumvented, or shouted his opposition to. He kept heading for the image in which a spontaneous action had the force of the general ideas involved. And there he found the energy of contradictory actions. The laugh wasn't ridiculousness, but the fun of being committed to the contrary. He was just as interested in the contrary energy. Self protection bored him.

In the talk then about painting, no doctrine of style was settled at

Bill's. He belligerently brought out the mysterious paradoxes left over. In any style he kept watching the action of the visual paradoxes of painting—the opposition of interchangeable centers, or a volume continued as a space, a value balancing a color. He seemed to consider in them a craft by which the picture seen as an image unpredictably came loose, moved forward and spread. On the other hand, his working idea at the time was to master the plainest problems of painting. I often heard him say that he was beating his brains out about connecting a figure and a background. The basic connection he meant seemed to me a motion from inside them that they interchanged and that continued throughout. He insisted on it during those years stroke by stroke and gained a virtuoso's eye and hand. But he wanted everything in the picture out of equilibrium except spontaneously all of it. That to him was one objective professional standard. That was form the way the standard masterpieces had form—a miraculous force and weight of presence moving from all over the canvas at once.

Later, I saw in some Greek temples contradictory forces operating publicly at full speed. Reading the *Iliad*, the poem at the height of reason presented the irrational and subjective, self-contradictory sweep of action under inspiration. I had missed the point in the talks in 22nd Street. The question Bill was keeping open with an enduring impatience had been that of professional responsibility toward the force of inspiration. That force or scale is there every day here where everybody is. Whose responsibility is it, if not your own? What he said, was "All an artist has left to work with is his self-consciousness."

From such a point of view the Marxist talk of the thirties was one-track. The generous feeling in it was stopped by a rigid perspective, a single center of action, and by jokes with only one side to them. If one overlooked that, what was interesting was the peremptoriness and the paranoia of Marxism as a ferment or method of rhetoric. But artists who looked at painting were used to a brilliance in such a method on the part of the Paris surrealists and to a surrealist humor that the political talk did not have. Politically everybody downtown was anti-fascist, and the talk went on peacefully. Then when friends who had fought in Spain returned, their silence made

an impression so direct that the subject was dropped. Against everybody's intention it had become shameless.

In the presence of New York at the end of the thirties, the paranoia of surrealism looked parlor-sized or arch. But during the war
Bill told me he had been walking uptown one afternoon and at the
corner of 53rd and 7th he had noticed a man across the street who
was making peculiar gestures in front of his face. It was Breton and he
was fighting off a butterfly. A butterfly had attacked the Parisian poet
in the middle of New York. So hospitable nature is to a man of genius.

Talking to Bill and to Rudy for many years, I found I did not see
with a painter's eye. For me the after-image (as Elaine de Kooning
has called it) became one of the ways people behave together, that is,
a moral image. The beauty Bill's depression pictures have kept reminds me of the beauty that instinctive behavior in a complex situation can have—mutual actions one has noticed that do not make one
ashamed of one's self, or others, or of one's surroundings either. I am
assuming that one knows what it is to be ashamed. The joke of art in
this sense is a magnanimity more steady than one notices in everyday
life, and no better justified. Bill's early pictures resemble the later
ones in that the expression of character the picture has seems to me
of the same kind in early and later ones, though the scope of it and
the performance in later ones becomes prodigious.

The general look of painting today strikes me as seductive. It
makes the miles of New York galleries as luxurious to wander
through as a slave market. Room after room, native or imported, the
young prosperity pictures lift their intelligent eyes to the buyer and
tempt him with an independent personality. The honest critics, as
they pass close to a particularly luscious one, give it a tweak in the
soft spots. The picture pinches them in return. At the end of a day's
work, a critic's after-images are black and blue. It takes more character to be serious now.

Twenty years ago Bill's great friend was Gorky. I knew they
talked together about painting more than anyone else. But when
other people were at Bill's, Gorky said so little that he was often forgotten. At one party the talk turned to the condition of the painter
in America, the bitterness and unfairness of his poverty and disre-

gard. People had a great deal to say on the subject, and they said it, but the talk ended in a gloomy silence. In the pause, Gorky's deep voice came from under a table. "Nineteen miserable years have I lived in America." Everybody burst out laughing. There was no whine left. Gorky had not spoken of justice, but of fate, and everybody laughed open-hearted.

At a WPA art occasion, I heard that LaGuardia had made a liberal speech about art and society. After the applause, Gorky who was on the reception committee stepped forward unexpectedly and began, "Your Honor, you know about government, and I know about art." Short LaGuardia looked at tall Gorky, who was earnestly contradicting him in a few sentences. I imagine he saw Gorky's seedy sportclothes and the exhilarating nobility of his point of view and valued them. Maybe he felt like laughing happily the way we did. The last time I saw Gorky, not long after the war, he was sitting with Bill and Elaine in the diner that used to be at Sixth Avenue across from 8th Street, and I went in and joined them for a coffee. I told them I had just read in a paper that when the war was over there were 175 million more people in the world than before it began. He looked at me with those magnificent eyes of his and said quietly, "That is the most terrible thing I have heard." The beauty of Gorky's painting I understood only last year.

I began this train of thought wondering at the cliché about downtown painting in the depression—the accepted idea that everybody had doubts and imitated Picasso and talked politics. None of these features seemed to me remarkable at the time, and they don't now. Downtown everybody loved Picasso then, and why not. But what they painted made no sense as an imitation of him. For myself, something in his steady wide light reminded me then of the light in the streets and lofts we lived in. At that time Tchelitchev was the uptown master, and he had a flickering light. The current painters seem for their part to tend toward a flickering light. The difference that strikes me between downtown then and now is that then everybody drank coffee and nobody had shows. Private life goes on regardless.

1962

## THE CLIMATE

I myself like the climate of New York
I see it in the air up between the street
You use a worn-down cafeteria fork
But the climate you don't use stays fresh and neat.
Even we people who walk about in it
We have to submit to wear too, get muddy,
Air keeps changing but the nose ceases to fit
And sleekness is used up, and the end's shoddy.
Monday, you're down; Tuesday, dying seems a fuss
An adult looks new in the weather's motion
The sky is in the streets with the trucks and us,
Stands awhile, then lifts across land and ocean.
We can take it for granted that here we're home
In our record climate I look pleased or glum.

1948

# AMIRI BARAKA
# (LEROI JONES)

*The New York jazz scene has been one of the city's glories since the days of Ellington at the Cotton Club and Basie at the Famous Door, and it achieved particular splendor in the early 1940's, when Charlie Parker reigned at Minton's. Here, poet and dramatist Amiri Baraka (born LeRoi Jones, 1934–  ), who wrote informed, impassioned jazz criticism for publications like* The Village Voice *in the early 60's, commemorates the era of the bebop revolution.*

## MINTON'S

BY NOW it is almost impossible to find out just what did go on at Minton's during the early 40's. There are so many conflicting stories, many by people who have no way of knowing. But in my adolescence the myth went something like this: "Around 1942, after classical jazz had made its conquests, a small group used to get together every night in a Harlem night club called Minton's Playhouse. It was made up of several young colored boys who, unlike their fellow musicians, no longer felt at home in the atmosphere of 'swing music.' It was becoming urgent to get a little air in a richly decked out palace that was soon going to be a prison. That was the aim of trumpeter Dizzy Gillespie, pianist Thelonius Monk, guitarist Charlie Christian (who died before the group's efforts bore fruit), drummer Kenny Clarke and saxophonist Charlie Parker. Except for Christian, they were poor, unknown and unprepossessing: but Monk stimulated his partners by the boldness of his harmonies, Clarke created a new style of drum playing, and Gillespie and Parker took choruses that seemed crazy to the people who came to listen to them. The bebop style was in the process of being born."

It sounds almost like the beginnings of modern American writing among the emigrés of Paris. But this is the legend which filled most of my adolescence. However, as Thelonius Monk put it, "It's true modern jazz probably began to get popular there, but some of these histories and articles put what happened over the course of ten years into one year. They put people all together in one time in one place. I've seen practically everybody at Minton's, but they were just there playing. They weren't giving lectures."

Minton's opened in 1940 on 118th Street in the Hotel Cecil. Teddy Hill, the band leader, was running the place, and it was only natural that a lot of musicians would fall by whenever they got a chance. Even before the "bop" sessions got under way, musicians who were working up the street at the Apollo would come by after their last show, or even between shows, and sit in with whoever was on the stand. Mondays became the best night for open sessions, because a lot of musicians didn't have to go to their regular gigs. Charlie Christian used to cab it up from midtown, where he was working with Benny Goodman, after his last set and sit on the stand, no matter who was tooting, until four in the morning when the place was supposed to close. (When it did close musicians went further uptown to Monroe's.)

Lester Young, Coleman Hawkins, Ben Webster, Roy Eldridge and a lot of older musicians used to come in the place, too, although, one of the tales about Minton's is that Roy stopped coming in once Gillespie stopped imitating him and started blowing his own thing. Every night was cutting night, but Monday all the axes came out for real because the audiences were just about as hip as the musicians. In fact most of the audience, after a while, were musicians themselves.

There had to be a feeling of freedom and the excitement that goes with individual expression, because all of this began in the midst of the Swing Era, when the arranger, not the soloist was the important man in jazz. There were good soloists in the worst popular swing bands, yet even in the best bands, the arrangement wore the soloists like a Bellevue sport coat. But Minton's was where these young musicians could stand up and blow their brains out all night long, and experimentation led to innovation. A lot of musicians would leave Minton's after one of the Monday sessions claiming Monk, Bird, Dizzy, Klook and the others were purposely "playing weird," just so they could keep the bandstand to themselves.

Bop also carried with it a distinct element of social protest, not only in the sense that it was music that seemed antagonistically non-conformist, but also that the musicians who played it were loudly outspoken about who they thought they were. "If you don't like it, don't listen," was the attitude, which seems to me now as rational as you can get. These musicians seemed no longer to want to be thought of merely as "performers," in the old Cotton Club-yellow hiney sense, but as musicians. And this was an unforgivable change of emphasis for a great many people. Bebopper jokes were as common in the late 40's as were beatnik jokes recently. These Negro musicians were thought of as "weird" and "deep," the bebop glasses and goatees some wore seemed to complete the image.

About four years went by before any of the music that grew up in Minton's (and Monroe's) was heard by a great many people, because of the recording ban in effect at the time. Still the word got out, mouth to ear, that something really wiggy was brewing uptown. In 1944 when Gillespie and Parker started recording and working in some of the 52nd Street clubs, the whole jazz world got turned around, and the non-jazz world as well.

Today, Minton's is still full of sounds, though they are by no means "the new thing" or avant-garde. Usually, the groups that come into Minton's are stand-up replicas of what was highly experimental twenty-five years ago. These are groups that are now more "socially" acceptable, and make up the mainstream of jazz, for the uptown mainstream listener.

The new jazz, for all intents and purposes, is centered downtown on the lower eastside, in lofts, small bohemian-type clubs, although there have been some efforts of late to return the newest expression of the black soul back home.

1962

# GEORGE OPPEN

The seasoned New Yorker sometimes tries to see his city with fresh eyes by looking at it in the guise of a tourist. Here George Oppen (1908–84), a member of the Objectivist group of poets that also included Charles Reznikoff and Louis Zukofsky, brings a craftsman's spare lines and a philosopher's abstraction to his observations in this mode.

### TOURIST EYE

*This activity, beginning in the midst of men . . .*

1
The lights that blaze and promise
Where are so many—What is offered

In the wall and nest of lights?
The land

Lacked center:
We must look to Lever Brothers

Based in a square block.
A thousand lives

Within that glass. What is the final meaning
Of extravagance? Why are the office

Buildings, storehouses of papers,
The centers of extravagance?

2
The solitary are obsessed.
Apartments furnish little solitude. Doors lock

On halls scarred
And painted. One might look everywhere

As tourists do, the halls and stairways
For something bequeathed

From time, some mark
In these most worn places

Where chance moves among the crowd
Unearned and separate

Among the crowd, the living, that other
Marvel among the mineral.

3
Rectangular, rearing
Black windows into daylight: the sound

Of a piano in the deep bulk tying
Generations to a Sunday that holds
As the building holds, only the adamant

Nothing that the child hopes,
Laboring a tune. From any window, the day

Flawless and without exterior
Without alternative. But to the tenant

The future is all chance, all future, and the present
All inanimate, or all herself.

4
The heart pounds
To be among them, the buildings,
The red buildings of Red Hook! In the currents of the harbor
The barn-red ferries on their curving courses
And the tides of Buttermilk Channel
Flow past the Brooklyn Hardware stores

And the homes
The aging homes

Of the workmen. This is a sense of order
And of threat. The essential city,
The necessary city
Among these harbor streets still visible.


5
Down-town
Swarms. Surely the oldest city,


It seems the oldest city in the world. Tho they are new in it.

            But they too can become a fist
Having menace, the power of menace. After the headlines
     of last night

The streets appear unchanged,
Tho they are endangered,

By no means safe, the building tops
Unwarned and unwarnable.

                     1 9 6 2

# JAMES BALDWIN

James Baldwin (1924–87) grew up in a Harlem which, by his account, had become a grimmer and more devastated neighborhood since the Harlem Renaissance. In his novels and essays Baldwin wrote mesmerizingly about his adolescence there—his experience as a boy preacher and subsequent loss of faith, his yearnings to write, his stepfather's death, his struggles over racial anger and sexual orientation—never more vividly than in his apocalyptic book-length essay "The Fire Next Time," excerpted below.

## FROM *THE FIRE NEXT TIME*

I UNDERWENT, during the summer that I became fourteen, a prolonged religious crisis. I use the word "religious" in the common, and arbitrary, sense, meaning that I then discovered God, His saints and angels, and His blazing Hell. And since I had been born in a Christian nation, I accepted this Deity as the only one. I supposed Him to exist only within the walls of a church—in fact, of *our* church—and I also supposed that God and safety were synonymous. The word "safety" brings us to the real meaning of the word "religious" as we use it. Therefore, to state it in another, more accurate way, I became, during my fourteenth year, for the first time in my life, afraid—afraid of the evil within me and afraid of the evil without. What I saw around me that summer in Harlem was what I had always seen; nothing had changed. But now, without any warning, the whores and pimps and racketeers on the Avenue had become a personal menace. It had not before occurred to me that I could become one of them, but now I realized that we had been produced by the same circumstances. Many of my comrades were clearly headed for the Avenue, and my father said that I was headed that way, too. My friends began to drink and smoke, and embarked—at first avid, then groaning—on their sexual careers. Girls, only slightly older than I was, who sang in the choir or taught Sunday school, the children of holy parents, underwent, before my eyes, their incredible metamorphosis, of which the most bewildering aspect was not their budding breasts or their rounding behinds but something deeper and more subtle, in their eyes, their heat, their odor, and the inflection of their voices. Like the strangers on the Avenue, they became, in the twinkling of an eye, unutterably different and fantastically *present*. Owing to the way I had been raised, the abrupt discomfort that all this aroused in me and the fact that I had no idea what my voice or my mind or my body was likely to do next caused me to consider myself one of the most depraved people on earth. Matters were not helped by the fact that these holy girls seemed rather to enjoy my terrified lapses, our grim, guilty, tormented experiments, which were at once as chill and joyless as the Russian steppes and hotter, by far, than all the fires of Hell.

Yet there was something deeper than these changes, and less definable, that frightened me. It was real in both the boys and the girls, but it was, somehow, more vivid in the boys. In the case of the girls, one watched them turning into matrons before they had become women. They began to manifest a curious and really rather terrifying single-mindedness. It is hard to say exactly how this was conveyed: something implacable in the set of the lips, something farseeing (seeing what?) in the eyes, some new and crushing determination in the walk, something peremptory in the voice. They did not tease us, the boys, any more; they reprimanded us sharply, saying, "You better be thinking about your soul!" For the girls also saw the evidence on the Avenue, knew what the price would be, for them, of one misstep, knew that they had to be protected and that we were the only protection there was. They understood that they must act as God's decoys, saving the souls of the boys for Jesus and binding the bodies of the boys in marriage. For this was the beginning of our burning time, and "It is better," said St. Paul—who elsewhere, with a most unusual and stunning exactness, described himself as a "wretched man"—"to marry than to burn." And I began to feel in the boys a curious, wary, bewildered despair, as though they were now settling in for the long, hard winter of life. I did not know then what it was that I was reacting to; I put it to myself that they were letting themselves go. In the same way that the girls were destined to gain as much weight as their mothers, the boys, it was clear, would rise no higher than their fathers. School began to reveal itself, therefore, as a child's game that one could not win, and boys dropped out of school and went to work. My father wanted me to do the same. I refused, even though I no longer had any illusions about what an education could do for me; I had already encountered too many college-graduate handymen. My friends were now "downtown," busy, as they put it, "fighting the man." They began to care less about the way they looked, the way they dressed, the things they did; presently, one found them in twos and threes and fours, in a hallway, sharing a jug of wine or a bottle of whiskey, talking, cursing, fighting, sometimes weeping: lost, and unable to say what it was that oppressed them, except that they knew it was "the man"—the white man. And there seemed to be no way whatever to remove this cloud that stood between them and the sun, between them and love and life and power, between them and whatever it was that they wanted. One did not have to be very bright to realize how little one could do to change one's situation; one did not have to be abnormally sensitive to be worn down to a cutting edge by the incessant and gratuitous humiliation and danger one encountered every working day, all day long. The humiliation did not apply merely to working days, or workers; I was thirteen and was crossing Fifth Avenue on my way to the Forty-second Street library, and the cop in the middle of the street muttered as I passed him, "Why don't you niggers stay uptown where you belong?" When I was ten, and didn't look, certainly, any older, two policemen amused themselves with me by frisking me, making comic (and terrifying) speculations concerning my ancestry and probable sexual prowess, and for good measure, leaving me flat on my back in one of Harlem's empty lots. Just before and then during the Second World War, many of my friends fled into the service, all to be changed there, and rarely for the better, many to be ruined, and many to die. Others fled to other states and cities—that is, to other ghettos. Some went on wine or whiskey or the needle, and are still on it. And others, like me, fled into the church.

For the wages of sin were visible everywhere, in every wine-stained and urine-splashed hallway, in every clanging ambulance bell, in every scar on the faces of the pimps and their whores, in every helpless, newborn baby being brought into this danger, in every knife and pistol fight on the Avenue, and in every disastrous bulletin: a cousin, mother of six, suddenly gone mad, the children parcelled out here and there; an indestructible aunt rewarded for years of hard labor by a slow, agonizing death in a terrible small room; someone's bright son blown into eternity by his own hand; another turned robber and carried off to jail. It was a summer of dreadful speculations and discoveries, of which these were not the worst. Crime became real, for example—for the first time—not as *a* possibility but as *the* possibility. One would never defeat one's circumstances by working and saving one's pennies; one would never, by working, acquire that many pennies, and, besides, the social treatment accorded even the most successful Negroes proved that one needed, in order to be free, something more than a bank account. One needed a handle, a lever, a means of inspiring fear. It was absolutely clear that the police would whip you and take you in as long as they could get away with it, and that everyone else—housewives, taxi-drivers, elevator boys, dishwashers, bartenders, lawyers, judges, doctors, and grocers— would never, by the operation of any generous human feeling, cease to use you as an outlet for his frustrations and hostilities. Neither civilized reason nor Christian love would cause any of those people to treat you as they presumably wanted to be treated; only the fear of your power to retaliate would cause them to do that, or to seem to do it, which was (and is) good enough. There appears to be a vast amount of confusion on this point, but I do not know many Negroes who are eager to be "accepted" by white people, still less to be loved by them; they, the blacks, simply don't wish to be beaten over the head by the whites every instant of our brief passage on this planet. White people in this country will have quite enough to do in learning how to accept and love themselves and each other, and when they have achieved this—which will not be tomorrow and may very well be never—the Negro problem will no longer exist, for it will no longer be needed.

People more advantageously placed than we in Harlem were, and are, will no doubt find the psychology and the view of human nature sketched above dismal and shocking in the extreme. But the Negro's experience of the white world cannot possibly create in him any respect for the standards by which the white world claims to live. His own condition is overwhelming proof that white people do not live by these standards. Negro servants have been smuggling odds and ends out of white homes for generations, and white people have been delighted to have them do it, because it has assuaged a dim guilt and testified to the intrinsic superiority of white people. Even the most doltish and servile Negro could scarcely fail to be impressed by the disparity between his situation and that of the people for whom he worked; Negroes who were neither doltish nor servile did not feel that they were doing anything wrong when they robbed white people. In spite of the Puritan-Yankee equation of virtue with well-being, Negroes had excellent reasons for doubting that money was made or kept by any very striking adherence to the Christian virtues; it certainly did not work that way for black Christians. In any case, white people, who had robbed black people of their liberty and who profited by this theft every hour that they lived, had no moral ground on which to stand. They had the judges, the juries, the shotguns, the law—in a word, power. But it was a criminal power, to be feared but not respected, and to be outwitted in any way whatever. And those virtues preached but not practiced by the white world were merely another means of holding Negroes in subjection.

It turned out, then, that summer, that the moral barriers that I had supposed to exist between me and the dangers of a criminal career were so tenuous as to be nearly nonexistent. I certainly could not discover any principled reason for not becoming a criminal, and it is not my poor, God-fearing parents who are to be indicted for the lack but this society. I was icily determined—more determined, really, than I then knew—never to make my peace with the ghetto but to die and go to Hell before I would let any white man spit on me, before I would accept my "place" in this republic. I did not intend to allow the white people of this country to tell me who I was, and limit me that way, and polish me off that way. And yet, of course, at the same time, I was being spat on and defined and described and limited, and could have been polished off with no effort whatever.

Every Negro boy—in my situation during those years, at least—who reaches this point realizes, at once, profoundly, because he wants to live, that he stands in great peril and must find, with speed, a "thing," a gimmick, to lift him out, to start him on his way. *And it does not matter what the gimmick is.* It was this last realization that terrified me and—since it revealed that the door opened on so many dangers—helped to hurl me into the church. And, by an unforeseeable paradox, it was my career in the church that turned out, precisely, to be my gimmick.

For when I tried to assess my capabilities, I realized that I had almost none. In order to achieve the life I wanted, I had been dealt, it seemed to me, the worst possible hand. I could not become a prizefighter—many of us tried but very few succeeded. I could not sing. I could not dance. I had been well conditioned by the world in which I grew up, so I did not yet dare take the idea of becoming a writer seriously. The only other possibility seemed to involve my becoming one of the sordid people on the Avenue, who were not really as sordid as I then imagined but who frightened me terribly, both because I did not want to live that life and because of what they made me feel. Everything inflamed me, and that was bad enough, but I myself had also become a source of fire and temptation. I had been far too well raised, alas, to suppose that any of the extremely explicit overtures made to me that summer, sometimes by boys and girls but also, more alarmingly, by older men and women, had anything to do with my attractiveness. On the contrary, since the Harlem idea of seduction is, to put it mildly, blunt, whatever these people saw in me merely confirmed my sense of my depravity.

It is certainly sad that the awakening of one's senses should lead to such a merciless judgment of oneself—to say nothing of the time and anguish one spends in the effort to arrive at any other—but it is also inevitable that a literal attempt to mortify the flesh should be made among black people like those with whom I grew up. Negroes in this country—and Negroes do not, strictly or legally speaking, exist in any other—are taught really to despise themselves from the moment their eyes open on the world. This world is white and they are black. White people hold the power, which means that they are superior to blacks (intrinsically, that is: God decreed it so), and the world has innumerable ways of making this difference known and felt and feared. Long before the Negro child perceives this difference, and even longer before he understands it, he has begun to react to it, he has begun to be controlled by it. Every effort made by the child's elders to prepare him for a fate from which they cannot protect him causes him secretly, in terror, to begin to await, without knowing that he is doing so, his mysterious and inexorable punishment. He must be "good" not only in order to please his parents and not only to avoid being punished by them; behind their authority stands another, nameless and impersonal, infinitely harder to please, and bottomlessly cruel. And this filters into the child's consciousness through his parents' tone of voice as he is being exhorted, punished, or loved; in the sudden, uncontrollable note of fear heard in his mother's or his father's voice when he has strayed beyond some particular boundary. He does not know what the boundary is, and he can get no explanation of it, which is frightening enough, but the fear he hears in the voices of his elders is more frightening still. The fear that I heard in my father's voice, for example, when he realized that I really *believed* I could do anything a white boy could do, and had every intention of proving it, was not at all like the fear I heard when one of us was ill or had fallen down the stairs or strayed too far from the house. It was another fear, a fear that the child, in challenging the white world's assumptions, was putting himself in the path of destruction. A child cannot, thank Heaven, know how vast and how merciless is the nature of power, with what unbelievable cruelty people treat each other. He reacts to the fear in his parents' voices because his parents hold up the world for him and he has no protection without them. I defended myself, as I imagined, against the fear my father made me feel by remembering that he was very old-fashioned. Also, I prided myself on the fact that I already knew how to outwit him. To defend oneself against a fear is simply to insure that one will, one day, be conquered by it; fears must be faced. As for one's wits, it is just not true that one can live by them—not, that is, if one wishes really to live. That summer, in any case, all the fears with which I had grown up, and which were now a part of me and controlled my vision of the world, rose up like a wall between the world and me, and drove me into the church.

As I look back, everything I did seems curiously deliberate, though it certainly did not seem deliberate then. For example, I did not join the church of which my father was a member and in which he preached. My best friend in school, who attended a different church, had already "surrendered his life to the Lord," and he was very anxious about my soul's salvation. (I wasn't, but any human attention was better than none.) One Saturday afternoon, he took me to his church. There were no services that day, and the church was empty, except for some women cleaning and some other women praying. My friend took me into the back room to meet his pastor—a woman. There she sat, in her robes, smiling, an extremely proud and handsome woman, with Africa, Europe, and the America of the American Indian blended in her face. She was perhaps forty-five or fifty at this time, and in our world she was a very celebrated woman. My friend was about to introduce me when she looked at me and smiled and said, "Whose little boy are you?" Now this, unbelievably, was precisely the phrase used by pimps and racketeers on the Avenue when they suggested, both humorously and intensely, that I "hang out" with them. Perhaps part of the terror they had caused me to feel came from the fact that I unquestionably wanted to be *somebody's* little boy. I was so frightened, and at the mercy of so many conundrums, that inevitably, that summer, *someone* would have taken me over; one doesn't, in Harlem, long remain standing on any auction block. It was my good luck—perhaps—that I found myself in the church racket instead of some other, and surrendered to a spiritual seduction long before I came to any carnal knowledge. For when the pastor asked me, with that marvellous smile, "Whose little boy are you?" my heart replied at once, "Why, yours."

1 9 6 3

# HARVEY SHAPIRO

*Over the past fifty years Harvey Shapiro (1924–    ) has perfected a tersely sardonic, downbeat poetry, a kind of Jewish blues, cut to the bone, with its own metaphysics based on everyday city life. A* New York Times *editor in his "day job," Shapiro, like the deli countermen imaged below, trims away excess verbiage in his poems.*

## NATIONAL COLD STORAGE COMPANY

The National Cold Storage Company contains
More things than you can dream of.
Hard by the Brooklyn Bridge it stands
In a litter of freight cars,
Tugs to one side; the other, the traffic
Of the Long Island Expressway.
I myself have dropped into it in seven years
Midnight tossings, plans for escape, the shakes.
Add this to the national total—
Grant's tomb, the Civil War, Arlington,
The young President dead.
Above the warehouse and beneath the stars
The poets creep on the harp of the Bridge.
But see,
They fall into the National Cold Storage Company
One by one. The wind off the river is too cold,
Or the times too rough, or the Bridge
Is not a harp at all. Or maybe
A monstrous birth inside the warehouse
Must be fed by everything—ships, poems,
Stars, all the years of our lives.

1963

## 47TH STREET

In the delicatessen
The countermen
Were bantering about the messiah,
Lifting the mounds of corned beef
And tongue. He wouldn't come,
They said, you couldn't
Count on it. Meaning:
They would die in harness.

1988

# GAY TALESE

***

*The functioning working-class neighborhood, once a staple of New York, has become as fragile as it is prized. In this chapter from* The Bridge, *Gay Talese (1932–    ), a leading practitioner of the "new journalism" that emerged in the early 1960's, details one example of how the city government sometimes undermined these old arrangements, with devastating effect on the locals.*

## PANIC IN BROOKLYN

"YOU *sonamabitch!*" the old Italian shoemaker cried, standing in the doorway of the Brooklyn real estate office, glaring at the men who sat behind desks in the rear of the room. "You *sonamabitch,*" he repeated when nobody looked up.

"*Hey,*" snapped one of the men, jumping up from his desk, "who are *you* talking to?"

"You," said the shoemaker, his small disheveled figure leaning against the door unsteadily, as if he'd been drinking, his tiny dark eyes angry and bloodshot. "You take-a my store . . . you no give-a me notting, you . . ."

"Now listen here," said the real estate man, quickly walking to where the shoemaker stood and looking down at him hard, "we will have none of *that* talk around here. In fact I am going to call the cops . . ."

He grabbed the phone nearest him and began to dial. The shoemaker watched for a moment, not seeming to care. Then he shrugged to himself and slowly turned and, without another word, walked out the door and shuffled down the street.

The real estate man, putting down the telephone, watched the shoemaker go. He did not chase him. He wanted nothing further to do with him—neither with him nor with *any* of those boisterous people who had been making so much noise lately, cursing or signing petitions or issuing threats, as if it had been the *real estate men's* idea to build the Verrazano-Narrows Bridge and the big highway leading up to it, the highway that would cut into the Bay Ridge section of Brooklyn where seven thousand people now lived, where eight hundred buildings now stood—including a shoestore—and would level everything in its path into a long, smooth piece of concrete.

No, it was not their idea, it was the idea of Robert Moses and his Triborough Bridge and Tunnel Authority to build the bridge and its adjoining highways—but the real estate men, hired by the Authority, were getting most of the direct blame because it was they, not Moses, who had to face the people and say, "Abandon your homes— we must build a bridge."

Some people, particularly old people, panicked. Many of them pleaded with the Authority's representatives and prayed to God not to destroy these homes where their children had been born, where their husbands had died. Others panicked with anger, saying this was *their* home, *their* castle, and Mr. Moses would have to drag them from it bodily.

Some took the news quietly, waiting without words to be listed among the missing—waiting for the moving van as if it meant death itself. With the money the Authority paid them for their old home, they went to Florida, or to Arizona, or to another home in Brooklyn, any home, not seeming to care very much because now they were old people and new homes were all the same.

The old shoemaker, nearly seventy, returned to Southern Italy, back to his native Cosenza, where he had some farmland he hoped to sell. He had left Cosenza for America when he was twenty-two years old. And now, in 1959, seeing Cosenza again was seeing how little it had changed. There were still goats and donkeys climbing up the narrow roads, and some peasant women carrying clay pots on their heads, and a few men wearing black bands on their sleeves or ribbons in their lapels to show that they were in mourning; and still the same white stone houses speckled against the lush green of the mountainside—houses of many generations.

When he arrived, he was greeted by relatives he had long forgotten, and they welcomed him like a returning hero. But later they began to tell him about their ailments, their poverty, all their problems, and he knew what was coming next. So he quickly began to tell them about *his* problems, sparing few details, recalling how he had fallen behind in the rent of his shoestore in Brooklyn, how the Authority had thrown him out without a dime, and how he now found himself back in Italy where he had started—all because this damned bridge was going to be built, this bridge the Americans were planning to name after an Italian explorer the shoemaker's relatives had never heard of: this Giovanni da Verrazano, who, sailing for the French in 1524, discovered New York Bay. The shoemaker went on and on, gesturing with his hands and making his point, making certain they knew he was no soft touch—and, a day or two later, he went about the business of trying to sell the farmland. . . .

On the Staten Island side, opposition to the bridge was nothing like it was in Brooklyn, where more than twice as many people and buildings were affected by the bridge; in fact, in Staten Island there had long been powerful factions that dreamed of the day when a bridge might be built to link their borough more firmly with the rest of New York City. Staten Island had always been the most isolated, the most ignored of New York's five boroughs; it was separated from Manhattan by five miles of water and a half-hour's ride on the ferry.

While New Yorkers and tourists had always enjoyed riding the Staten Island ferry—"a luxury cruise at a penny a mile"—nobody was ever much interested in getting to the other side. What was there to see? Sixty percent of the island's fifty-four square miles were underdeveloped as of 1958. Most of its 225,000 citizens lived in one-family houses. It was the dullest of New York's boroughs, and when a New York policeman was in the doghouse with headquarters, he was often transferred to Staten Island.

The island first acquired its rural quality when the British controlled it three hundred years ago, encouraging farming rather than manufacturing, and that was the way many Staten Islanders wanted it to remain—quiet and remote. But on the last day of 1958, after years of debate and doubt, plans for the building of the Verrazano-Narrows Bridge finally became definite and the way of those who cherished the traditional life was in decline. But many more Staten

Island residents were overjoyed with the news; they had wanted a change, had grown bored with the provincialism, and now hoped the bridge would trigger a boom—and suddenly they had their wish.

The bridge announcement was followed by a land rush. Real estate values shot up. A small lot that cost $1,200 in 1958 was worth $6,000 in 1959, and larger pieces of property worth $100,000 in the morning often sold for $200,000 that afternoon. Tax-delinquent properties were quickly claimed by the city. Huge foreign syndicates from Brazil, Italy and Switzerland moved in for a quick kill. New construction was planned for almost every part of Staten Island, and despite complaints and suits against contractors for cheaply built homes (one foreman was so ashamed of the shoddy work he was ordered to do that he waited until night to leave the construction site) nothing discouraged the boom or deglamorized the bridge in Staten Island.

The bridge had become, in early 1959, months before any workmen started to put it up, the symbol of hope.

"We are now on our way to surmounting the barrier of isolation," announced the borough president, Albert V. Maniscalco—while other leaders were conceding that the bridge, no matter what it might bring, could not really hurt Staten Island. What was there to hurt? "Nothing has ever been successful in Staten Island in its entire history," said one resident, Robert Regan, husband of opera singer Eileen Farrell. He pointed out that there had been attempts in the past to establish a Staten Island opera company, a semi-professional football team, a dog track, a boxing arena, a symphony orchestra, a midget auto track, a basketball team—and all failed. "The only thing that might save this island," he said, "is a lot of new people."

Over in Brooklyn, however, it was different. They did not need or want new people. They had a flourishing, middle-class, almost all-white community in the Bay Ridge section, and they were satisfied with what they had. Bay Ridge, which is in western Brooklyn along the ridge of Upper New York Bay and Lower New York Bay, commands a superb view of the Narrows, a mile-wide tidal strait that connects the two Bays, and through which pass all the big ships en-

tering or leaving New York. Among its first settlers were thousands
of Scandinavians, most of them Danes, who liked Bay Ridge because
of its nearness to the water and the balmy breeze. And in the late
nineteenth century, Bay Ridge became one of the most exclusive sections of Brooklyn.

It was not that now, in 1959, except possibly along its shorefront
section, which was lined with trees and manicured lawns and with
strong sturdy homes, one of them occupied by Charles Atlas. The
rest of Bay Ridge was almost like any other Brooklyn residential
neighborhood, except that there were few if any Negroes living
among the whites. The whites were mostly Catholic. The big
churches, some with parishes in excess of 12,000, were supported
by the lace-curtain Irish and aspiring Italians, and the politics, usually
Republican, were run by them, too. There were still large numbers
of Swedes and Danes, and also many Syrian shopkeepers, and there
were old Italian immigrants (friends of the shoemaker) who were
hanging on, but it was the younger, second- and third-generation
Italians, together with the Irish, who determined the tone of Bay
Ridge. They lived, those not yet rich enough for the shorefront
homes, in smaller brown brick houses jammed together along tree-
lined streets, and they competed each day for a parking place at the
curb. They shopped along busy sidewalks clustered with tiny neighborhood stores with apartments above, and there were plenty of
small taverns on corners, and there was the Hamilton House for a
good dinner at night—provided they wore a jacket and tie—and
there was a dimly lit sidestreet supper-club on the front barstool of
which sat a curvesome, wrinkled platinum blonde with a cigarette,
but no match.

So Bay Ridge, in 1959, had things in balance; it was no longer
chic, but it was tidy, and most people wanted no change, no new
people, no more traffic. And they certainly wanted no bridge. When
the news came that they would get one, the local politicians were
stunned. Some women began to cry. A number of people refused to
believe it. They had heard this talk before, they said, pointing out
that as far back as 1888 there had been plans for a railroad tunnel
that would link Brooklyn and Staten Island. And in 1923 New York's

Mayor Hylan even broke ground for a combined rail-and-automobile tunnel to Staten Island, and all that happened was that the city lost a half-million dollars and now has a little hole somewhere going nowhere.

And there had been talk about this big bridge across the Narrows for *twenty years*, they said, and each time it turned out to be just talk. In 1950 there was talk that a bridge between Brooklyn and Staten Island was a good thing, but what if the Russians blew it up during a war: would not the United States Navy ships docked in New York harbor be trapped behind the collapsed bridge at the harbor's entrance? And a year later, there was more talk of a tunnel to Staten Island, and then more debate on the bridge, and it went on this way, on and on. So, they said, in 1959, maybe this is *still* all talk, no action, so let's not worry.

What these people failed to realize was that about 1957 the talk changed a little; it became more intense, and Robert Moses was getting more determined, and New York City's Fire Commissioner was so sure in 1957 that the bridge to Staten Island would become a reality that he quickly got in his bid with the City Planning Commission for a big new Staten Island firehouse, asking that he be given $379,500 to build it and $250,000 to equip it. They did not realize that the powerful Brooklyn politician Joseph T. Sharkey saw the bridge as inevitable in 1958, and he had made one last desperate attack, too late, on Robert Moses on the City Council floor, shouting that Moses was getting too much power and was listening only to the engineers, not to the will of the people. And they did not realize, too, that while they were thinking it was still *all talk*, a group of engineers around a drawing board were quietly inking out a large chunk of Brooklyn that would be destroyed for the big approachway to the bridge—and one of the engineers, to his horror, realized that his plan included the demolition of the home of his own mother-in-law. When he told her the news, she screamed and cried and demanded he change the plan. He told her he was helpless to do so; the bridge was inevitable. She died without forgiving him.

The bridge was inevitable—and it was inevitable they would hate it. They saw the coming bridge not as a sign of progress, but as a symbol of destruction, as an enormous sea monster that soon would rise out of the water and destroy eight hundred buildings and force seven thousand Bay Ridge people to move—all sorts of people: housewives, bartenders, a tugboat skipper, doctors, lawyers, a pimp, teetotalers, drunks, secretaries, a retired light-heavyweight fighter, a former Ziegfeld Follies girl, a family of seventeen children (two dogs and a cat), a dentist who had just spent $15,000 installing new chairs, a vegetarian, a bank clerk, an assistant school principal, and two lovers—a divorced man of forty-one and an unhappily married woman who lived across the street. Each afternoon in his apartment they would meet, these lovers, and make love and wonder what next, wonder if she could ever tell her husband and leave her children. And now, suddenly, this bridge was coming between the lovers, would destroy their neighborhood and their quiet afternoons together, and they had no idea, in 1959, what they would do.

What the others did, the angry ones, was join the "Save Bay Ridge" committee which tried to fight Moses until the bulldozers were bashing down their doors. They signed petitions, and made speeches, and screamed, "This bridge—*who needs it?*" News photographers took their photographs and reporters interviewed them, quoting their impassioned pleas, and Robert Moses became furious.

He wrote letters to a newspaper publisher saying that the reporter had distorted the truth, had lied, had emphasized only the bad part, not the good part, of destroying people's homes. Most people in Brooklyn did not, in 1959, understand the good part, and so they held on to their homes with determination. But sooner or later, within the next year or so, they let go. One by one they went, and soon the house lights went out for the last time, and then moving vans rolled in, and then the bulldozers came crashing up and the walls crumbled down, and the roofs caved in and everything was hidden in an avalanche of dust—a sordid scene to be witnessed by the hold-out next door, and soon he, too, would move out, and then another, and another. And that is how it went on each block, in each neighborhood, until, finally, even the most determined hold-out gave in because, when a block is almost completely destroyed, and one is all alone amid the chaos, strange and unfamiliar fears sprout up: the

fear of being alone in a neighborhood that is dying; the fear of a band
of young vagrants who occasionally would roam through the rubble
smashing windows or stealing doors, or picket fences, light fixtures,
or shrubbery, or picking at broken pictures or leftover love letters;
fear of the derelicts who would sleep in the shells of empty apartments or hanging halls; fear of the rats that people said would soon
be crawling up from the shattered sinks or sewers because, it was explained, rats also were being dispossessed in Bay Ridge, Brooklyn.

One of the last hold-outs was a hazel-eyed, very pretty brunette
divorced woman of forty-two named Florence Campbell. She left after the lovers, after the dentist, and after the former Ziegfeld Follies
girl, Bessie Gros Dempsey, who had to pack up her 350 plumed hats
and old scrapbooks; she left after the crazy little man who had been
discovered alone in an empty apartment house because, somehow, he
never heard the bulldozers beneath him and had no idea that a bridge
was being built.

She left after the retired prizefighter, Freddy Fredericksen, who
had only lost twice before, and after Mr. and Mrs. John G. Herbert,
the parents of seventeen children—although Florence Campbell's
leaving was nowhere as complex as the Herberts'. It had taken them
twelve trips to move all their furniture, all the bicycles, sleds, dishes,
dogs to their new house a little more than a mile away—twelve trips
and sixteen hours; and when they had finally gotten everything
there, Mr. Herbert, a Navy Yard worker, discovered that the cat was
missing. So early the next morning he sent two sons back to the old
house, and they discovered the cat beneath the porch. They also discovered an old axe there. And for the next hour they used the axe to
destroy everything they could of the old house; they smashed windows, walls, the floors, they smashed their old bedroom, the kitchen
shelves, and the banister of the porch, where they used to gather on
summer nights, and they smashed without knowing exactly why,
only knowing, as they took turns swinging, that they felt a little wild
and gleeful and sad and mad as they smashed—and then, too tired to
continue, they retrieved the cat from under the smashed porch and
they left their old home for the last time.

In the case of Florence Campbell, it took more than even a murder to make her abandon her home. She had been living, since her divorce, with her young son in a sixty-four-dollar-a-month spacious apartment. It was difficult for her to find anything like it at a rental she could afford. The relocation agent, who had lost patience with her for turning down apartments he considered suitable but she considered too expensive, now forgot about her, and she was on her own to search alone at night after she had returned from her book-keeping job with the Whitehall Club in Manhattan.

Then one morning she started smelling a strange odor in the apartment. She thought perhaps that her son had gone fishing the day before, after school, and had dumped his catch in the dumbwaiter. He denied it, and the next night, when the odor became worse, she telephoned the police. They soon discovered that the elderly man living on the first floor, the only other tenant in the house, had three days before murdered his wife with shotgun bullets and now, dazed and silent, he was sitting next to the corpse, empty whiskey bottles at his feet.

"Lady, do me a favor," the police sergeant said to Florence Campbell. "Get out of this block, will ya?"

She said she would, but she still could not find an apartment during her searchings. She had no relatives she could move in with, no friends within the neighborhood, because they had all moved. When she came home at midnight from apartment hunting, she would find the hall dark—somebody was always stealing the light bulb—or she might stumble over a drunken derelict sleeping on the sidewalk in front of the downstairs door.

A few nights after the sergeant's warning she was awakened from sleep by the sounds of shuffling feet outside her door and the pounding of fists against the wall. Her son, in the adjoining bedroom, jumped up, grabbed a shotgun he kept in his closet, and ran out into the hall. But it was completely dark, the light bulb had been stolen again. He tripped and Florence Campbell screamed.

A strange man raced up the steps to the roof. She called the police. They came quickly but could find no one on the roof. The police sergeant again told her to leave, and she nodded, weeping, that she would. The next day she was too nervous to go to work, and so she went to a nearby bar to get a drink and told the bartender what had happened, and, very excited, he told her he knew of an apartment that was available a block away for sixty-eight dollars a month. She ran to the address, got the apartment—and the landlord could not understand why, after she got it, she began to cry.

*THE BRIDGE*, 1964

# LOUIS AUCHINCLOSS

───────

*Louis Auchincloss (1917–    ) has gracefully, triumphantly, and pretty much exclusively inherited Edith Wharton's mantle as chronicler of New York's beleaguered, ingrown aristocracy. In his nuanced stories and novels, such as* Portrait in Brownstone, *he draws on his professional knowledge of New York law firms and his long study of the city's past. His story "The Landmarker" suggests the complex meaning that historical preservation may have for the patrician class.*

## THE LANDMARKER

CHAUNCEY LEFFERTS had been trained as an "extra man" in a social era when extra men had had still more or less to be men, before the age of the designer, the decorator, the peacock whose cry is as harsh as his plumage is bright. Nobody had minded that Lefferts was drab so long as Lefferts was punctual or that he was dull so long as he was available. Unremarkable of appearance as of opinion, he had been perfectly content to be unnoticed so long as he was present: a slight, round, paunchy gentleman, discreetly dressed, with soft brown hair, all his own and undyed, who never forgot a name or a family relationship and who talked as easily with the men over the brandy as with the ladies in the drawing room.

In his sixties Lefferts began to ask himself the questions that most men would have asked three decades before. Was the New York social game worth the candle? Did the conversation, the food, even the wine justify the effort of getting into a stiff shirt? Now to most people the lateness of such doubts might seem proof of a weak intellect, even of a deranged one, but that would be because they could not comprehend the peculiar combination of Lefferts' sexual inhibition and natural gregariousness, of his fear of competition and his yearning to be identified with those who have competed and won. Only in society can one mingle with beautiful women and successful men and escape unscathed, which was why the opiate had operated so long and so effectively for him. But now, with age, and just when he most needed it, it began to lose its potency, and, catching sight of his black crow's feet and tired eyes in a French mirror, on a grand stairway, he would wonder if the institution of the dinner party, which had once seemed to supply him with the most blessed of veils, did not provide instead a merciless searchlight.

He was sure that the younger people giggled at him, and he hated them for it. He grumbled audibly now when he found himself abandoned at dinner, between two bare backs of partners talking to the men on their other sides, yet, when a lady *was* talking to him, if he was bored, he lapsed into sulky silence. His personal comments became more caustic, his appearances less punctual, his dinner jackets less pressed, his tips to servants less generous, and he was even known on occasion to drink too much. He began to behave, in short, with an independence that was the very opposite of the quality that had made him initially popular. Society will accept any conduct in its inner circles, provided those so conducting themselves have always behaved that way; what it cannot abide is to have its pigeons change their holes. Lefferts' fall was as speedy as social falls always are. He found that he was asked for weekends on Friday night and for dinners on the morning of the party, and soon enough, with the exception of the faithful Bella Hoppin, whose fetish for personal consistency and quasi-royal passion for order fortunately encompassed loyalty to protégés, he was greeted by his old gang with the terrible falsity of the cry: "Chauncey dear! Why do we *never* see you?"

He tried to console himself by saying that society had gone to hell and that he had known, after all, its great days. He tried to consider his years of dining out as a preparation for writing a great novel and played with the idea of becoming a latter-day Proust. He took long walks to recapture the old New York that was dying with him. If he was out-of-date, he was out-of-date like history, out-of-date like the old mansions in which he had dined as a younger man, some of which survived here and there, as boardinghouses or shops, moldering and dowdy, admired only by his faithful self. As time drew on, the façades of these disappearing abodes came to be his sole connection with their former owners, some dead but others merely transplanted and dead now only to him in their distant fashionableness, so that his daily rambles became a sort of social memoir, a retracing in asphalt of his old gay rounds. Living in the past, did people say? Where else *could* he live?

And what a past! He remembered as a young man, before the first war, the exhilaration of riding up Fifth Avenue on the top of an open bus and seeing unfold before him that glorious romp through the Renaissance! He remembered the massive brownstone of the Vanderbilt "twins" at Fifty-first Street, the mellow pink tower of the Gerry château, where the Pierre now stands, and, farther north, the birthday-cake splendor of Senator Clark's and the wide grilled portals of Mrs. Astor that opened to the visitor before he ever touched a bell. And he remembered, too, the long wonderful dinners, to him a peak of civilization, where one arrived happily at eight and departed satisfied at eleven, having spent two of the intervening hours at table over seven courses and five wines.

Oh, people sneered at those parties now, of course. But at least one had known what was expected of one. Today, even at Bella Hoppin's, one never knew how late into the night cocktails might push the battered meal or what ghastly parlor game would be thrust on one afterward. Lefferts lived in a constant secret dread that he would be asked, as a penalty in one of these, to step up on a table and strip before the jeering multitude.

"Well, at least we're *alive*," Bella had once retorted to his protests. "We don't just sit in a row like a herd of dressed-up swine with our noses in the trough. We use our imaginations. I'm afraid you're getting stuffy, Chauncey."

"My idea of heaven," Lefferts muttered, "is a place where one needn't be ashamed to be stuffy."

"Don't turn into a crank, dearie. You haven't the money for that."

Lefferts sighed. It was certainly true that his income, like his invitations, had dropped off. The old grandfather who had limited the modest family trust to railway bonds had ignored the perils of inflation. Had it not been for Bella, who had been his friend since dancing-school days, and a few much younger couples who regarded him beneficently as a social curiosity, rather like a tattered hansom cab parked outside the Plaza, he might have had to dine every night at the Cosmopolitan Club with his maiden sisters who never made even a decent effort to conceal their satisfaction that he should have been dropped at last by Mammon. Poor Lefferts had plenty of opportunity to consider Oscar Wilde's axiom that if to be in society was simply a bore, to be out of it was simply a tragedy.

Happily for him, however, the past did not prove a sterile pursuit. When there were no longer enough houses to visit on his daily walks, he ventured farther afield to seek out other survivals of the great preceding century. In a curious way his need to retreat to it seemed to have a democratizing effect on his attitudes. Anything that shared now in the dignity and grandeur of that greater age—a church, a station, a hotel or a store—shared similarly in his widening affections. He learned the secrets of the rapid transit to be able to visit even the most distant of his new friends, and the same Lefferts who had once walked by the Lady Chapel of St. Patrick's Cathedral and Commodore Farragut's statue in Madison Square without turning his head was now happy to pass a morning traveling underground to the center of Brooklyn for a glimpse of the Gothic gates of Greenwood Cemetery.

It was as if he and the old by-passed city had found each other in a golden twilight. As he stood looking up at Louis Sullivan's terra-cotta angels with their outstretched arms, high on a cornice over Bleecker Street, or wandered amid the chaste Greek porticos of Snug Harbor, or took in the faded grandeur of Colonnade Row in Lafayette Street, he felt a tremendous upsurge of spirit. This was even more intensely the case when the approach to the landmark was through dingy streets, past yawning warehouses, where Lefferts had to piece his way cautiously and self-consciously, peering ahead until at last he saw, shooting up out of the jumbled masonry, like a nymph rising from her bath, the fine thrust of a Florentine campanile. The very mass of the surrounding city, the engulfing, amorphous, indifferent city, like a huge sow smothering her own offspring, gave to his searches some of the excitement of a consecrating act, as though, a monk in a desperate age, he was solacing his soul by lighting little candles in darkest corners. It even charmed him that the landmarks were frequently merely façades, that the interiors were put to vulgar uses, that bales were stored where there had once been counters of silverware, that dull-eyed lodgers, unconscious of the past and hardly aware of the present, moped in what had once been gilded drawing rooms. The very precariousness of surviving beauty, the mask or shell exposed to a world that never looked up, was analogous to his own threadbare elegance. What was he but a sober, four-story brownstone façade, with Gothic arches and an iron grille, such as one might find in Hicks Street over at Brooklyn Heights?

"Have you ever heard of Tinetti's?" he asked Bella Hoppin, one night before dinner, in her splendid yellow-and-gold drawing room that opened up to the arriving guest like an issue of *House and Garden*. Ordinarily he had the tact not to put such a question to his hostess at such a time, but his new obsession made him importunate. "It was the most fashionable department store in the city in 1850. It stood at the corner at Lafayette and Spring streets. A great square iron palazzo with a hundred arched windows, like the Sansovino library in Venice. When your great-grandfather, Mayor Brevoort, opened it, he said that the new world need no longer hang its head before the architecture of the old."

The reference to her ancestor checked the incipient frown on Bella's high brow. "Weren't they divine, those old New Yorkers? Like Hudson River primitives. Whatever put them in your head?"

"Because the Tinetti building is still standing. It's a textile factory, a bit beat up, naturally, but the lines and proportions and the old dignity are still there. I thought it might amuse you to give your St. Andrew's Settlement House ball there. It could be cleaned up in a few days, and we could all go in the costumes of the opening." He watched her closely as he paused. "You would go, of course, as your great-grandmother Brevoort."

Oh, he had her attention now! "Why, Chauncey, what a perfectly divine idea. Do you know I still have some of her dresses? But where would we ever get permission to fix the place up?"

"Right here."

"Here?"

"You own the block, Bella. It's up to you. And so is the fate of Tinetti's, which is scheduled to be torn down, come spring."

Lefferts remembered having read that a hippopotamus is dangerous to man only when he gets between it and the water. The same, he concluded sadly, taking in the sudden opaqueness of Bella's gaze, might be said of the heiress and the sources of her wealth.

"I make it a point never to interfere with my agents," she said in a crisper tone. "They do their job, I mine."

"But, Bella," he protested, "their job is to get you the greatest revenue they can. Yours is a higher responsibility. It is to see that for the sake of a few more dollars that you don't really need———"

"I'm glad you're in a position, Chauncey, to talk of not needing dollars," she interrupted as she moved away to greet a newcomer. "The rest of us find them very useful."

It was not Bella's general reputation that she was a disappointing woman—indeed, if anything, she was deemed to fulfill more richly even than she promised—but to Lefferts this was now her essential quality. He had gone so far, in the bitterness of his recent seventieth birthday, to wonder if his disappointment in Bella was not his disappointment in life. She always appeared so large, so handsome, so full-blown, so fair of breast and straight of carriage, with so noble a brow and nose and such fine luxuriant hair, a Roman mother of heroes, like Cornelia or Volumnia. True, her laugh was a bit too loud, her voice too raucous, her perspiration too quick, but that was even part of the promise. The disappointment was in her ultimate failure to be what she seemed: the perfect mixture of wisdom and worldliness, sentiment and saltiness, horse sense and horsiness, to be instead a Volumnia who blued her hair, a Cornelia who doted on gossip. It never occurred to Bella that "good talk" was anything but a kind of oral album of candid-camera shots of the great, and her world agreed with her. "Isn't Bella wonderful?" they were always saying. Only Lefferts dissented. Bella was not sensitive, but she could sense dissent.

"Chauncey, I'm going to be frank with you," she told him later that night, having beckoned him to her sofa when the gentlemen joined the ladies. "I don't like the way you've been looking. Have you seen a doctor? We're not at an age where we can take chances, you know."

So that was it, he reflected morosely. He was to be "handled." He was to be "fixed." His ears echoed already with the plaudits of the friends: "Bella is really prodigious. She never forgets anyone."

"I have a common or garden variety of arterial trouble," he said dryly. "We can't all have your health. It will kill me in time, but, after all, something must. There are no fountains of eternal youth. Not in New York, anyway. And if there were, somebody'd tear them down."

"I thought you might be looking for one in those rambles you're always taking."

"No, I just go to visit a few old friends. Poor shabby edifices that will probably disappear even before me. And be missed about as much."

"You must stop feeling sorry for yourself," Bella reproached him. "Nothing ages like self-pity."

"I'm not aging. I'm aged."

"Fiddlesticks, seventy isn't old any more. The worse thing you can possibly do is to keep relating yourself to a lot of old tenements waiting for the wrecker. It's turning you into the dullest kind of bore, the one who's always trying to save some shack from a highway or housing development. Mark my words, Chauncey, those people end by losing all discrimination. You'll be wringing your hands over the Third Avenue El."

"As a matter of fact, those Gothic entrances were a great loss!"

"Now, stop! You see? What you need is people. You've got to see more people. It's the only way to stay young."

People! What else had aged him? Surviving to seventy with one's mental faculties intact was like going to a cocktail party while on the wagon. How noisy his contemporaries sounded, how little they listened, how obsessive was their naked concern with their own "pluck" and their trips, their endless jet trips, to Luxor, to Hong Kong, to Tokyo! As though it took pluck to throw their old carcasses into armchairs and be transported from one pleasure to another! No, the only true companions of Lefferts' old age were the shabby, graceful, undemanding façades of his landmarks.

He went down the next morning to visit the doomed, dark, dusty Italian palace, empty now, with broken windows, ready for demolition, but like a marquise in a tumbrel on her way to the guillotine, her neck bared, her head high, her scornful eyes fixed over the heads of the screeching mob. Lefferts tried desperately to imagine the building a century back; he closed his eyes tightly until amid the stars and flashing he had a sense of crinolines and glittering counters. He seemed suddenly to be losing his balance, and he spread his arms out wildly.

He recovered consciousness in a clean, commodious green hospital room with a dazzling view of the Hudson, and he speculated idly that he might be at last in the heaven of old landmarks, until it was borne in upon him with a shock that he was in the Harkness Pavilion. Could his sisters have possibly played so fast and loose with his funds? Nowadays the poor, like himself, did not expect to leave estates; they simply looked to save enough to cover their terminal ailments. But at fifty dollars a day! He reached frantically for the bell just as the door opened, and Bella came in.

"There's not a thing to worry about," she assured him. "Just a slight seizure. It's providential that it happened where it did. My managing agent was in the building when you were brought in, and when he found the card in your wallet he recognized your name and called me. I had you taken right here, and, of course, you're not even to *think* of the bill. In a way, I regard myself as responsible. It was your worry about that old store that brought this on. And you were right about it, too. It *is* a beauty. I went down and looked at it myself this morning. I've given instructions to preserve it. We may even have it done over. It'll be like the Racketty-Packetty House of Frances Hodgson Burnett, do you remember? I used to read it to the girls when they were little. The old dolls' house that was going to be burnt until the little princess spotted it and recognized its true worth and had it refurbished so that it was even grander than Tidy Castle?"

Lefferts spent the next weeks in a kind of euphoria. When Bella took on a job, she did it thoroughly. After he was released from

Harkness she moved him to her apartment where he had a trained nurse and breakfast in bed and was taken out for a short drive in the afternoon in Bella's Bentley. He liked to think that the interest in old buildings that he might have imparted to her would have a softening effect on her, too. It was an odd way to learn humanity, no doubt, but was it not possible, as her interest stretched from interiors to exteriors, from the abodes of the rich to stores and even tenements, that her heart might reach out to *all* who lived under roofs? Or was this merely the loosest kind of sentimentality, the product of what had been—despite all Bella's efforts to conceal it from him—a stroke?

Yes, he was certainly very ill, and, worst of all, the common but deadly disease that had clutched him was at last striking at his memory. He could not remember what he had done the day before, how long he had been at Bella's, when his sisters had last called. He was afraid of seeing in the faces of his nurse and of Bella's discreet, impassive staff just how bad it was, and he smiled vaguely when they asked him questions that troubled him, or affected not to have heard. If only in losing one's memory, one could forget that one had lost it! But the awareness of his growing deficiency stayed with him like a street lamp seen by an insomniac from a darkened house.

He kept reminding himself that Bella had promised to spare Tinetti's, but he could not be sure that he had not imagined it, and he dared not ask her for fear of making her reconsider an act of such uncharacteristic extravagance. It became his fixed idea to visit the old place and see if her offered renovations had been started, but he had not the courage to ask her grand chauffeur to take him so far downtown. One afternoon, however, when the nurse had delivered him to the doorman and returned to the elevator, his chance came. Bella's chauffeur was late.

"Oh, please, tell him I took a cab," Lefferts said eagerly to the hesitant doorman, under orders, no doubt, about Mrs. Hoppin's guest. "Would you be good enough to call me one?"

The cab driver took him down by the East River and turned off at Delancey Street. As he approached the area of Tinetti's down Spring Street under the old dark commercial buildings he felt an excitement that was almost unbearable.

"Please let me out here and wait!" he exclaimed, and getting out of the cab he stumbled along the pavement toward Lafayette Street. He would not look ahead; he would not have the driver witness his shock at what he now realized that he must see. When he had come within visual range of the old store, he closed his eyes, his head still bowed, and uttered a prayer. Then, resolutely, he looked up and opened his eyes.

Of course, it was gone.

On the site was a great pit in the bottom of which a crane was working. The corner was flooded with a new sunlight that made the dull windows of the neighboring buildings blink. Lefferts had an extraordinary and oddly painless sense of inner void, as though a cube in his own mind, comparable to Tinetti's, had been removed by the most competent surgery. But that cube of sensation had nonetheless been the best of him, and he and the departed building were together at the end in his own departing memory. As for the rest of him—well, he would know now what to do with the rest of him.

He was perfectly calm again. He returned to the cab and to Bella's apartment. At tea she asked him, a bit suspiciously, where he had been, and he told her that he had dropped in at the Frick Collection.

"I like to visit the great Holbeins of More and Cromwell once a year. A saint and a sinner, yet they have in common that pale, hard accepting look of Tudor courtiers. They were always willing to gamble, even knowing that they would lose. I sometimes think you're a bit of a Tudor, Bella. But a Tudor queen. *They* always won."

Bella smiled. He would not alienate her now. Obviously she believed that he had forgotten Tinetti's. He would have to be very careful to do nothing to upset that belief. For Bella in the right could be tremendous, but Bella in the wrong might oust him from her apartment. And how he clung to it, that apartment! To be fed and fussed over, to be safe from his censorious siblings, to be able to doze over a drink by a fire while the muted sounds of Bella's social life throbbed from the distant drawing room—it was not to be lost now.

"If you ever have any trouble with Saint Peter, Bella," he continued as he sipped his tea, "just mention what you've done for old

Chauncey Lefferts, and he'll whisk you right past those pearly gates!"

Bella smiled again and even beamed; she loved to be thanked as she loved to be worshipped. Her smile embraced him and reassured him. "Trust me, give yourself up and be cared for," she seemed to be telling him. She was nurse; she was asylum; she was the city itself, with its force and possessiveness. She could be counted on to succor the weak, as she could be counted on to destroy the strong. A Tudor, he repeated to himself, with a pale accepting smile. A terrible Tudor queen.

1964

# MARIO PUZO

———

*Before Mario Puzo (1920–    ) produced his bestseller* The Godfather, *he wrote probably the single best novel about Italian-American life,* The Fortunate Pilgrim. *The book's first chapter conveys, without a shred of sentimentality, the immigrant generation's stubborn existence in New York as urban villagers, close-knit and suspicious of the American ways that would inevitably erode their communal ties.*

### FROM *THE FORTUNATE PILGRIM*

LARRY ANGELUZZI spurred his jet black horse proudly through a canyon formed by two great walls of tenements, and at the foot of each wall, marooned on their separate blue-slate sidewalks, little children stopped their games to watch him with silent admiration. He swung his red lantern in a great arc; sparks flew from the iron hoofs of his horse as they rang on railroad tracks, set flush in the stones of Tenth Avenue, and slowly following horse, rider and lantern came the long freight train, inching its way north from St. John's Park terminal on Hudson Street.

In 1928 the New York Central Railroad used the streets of the city to shuttle trains north and south, sending scouts on horseback to warn traffic. In a few more years this would end, an overhead pass built. But Larry Angeluzzi, not knowing he was the last of the "dummy boys," that he would soon be a tiny scrap of urban history, rode as straight and arrogantly as any western cowboy. His spurs were white, heavy sneakers, his sombrero a peaked cap studded with union buttons. His blue dungarees were fastened at the ankle with shiny, plated bicycle clips.

He cantered through the hot summer night, his desert a city of stone. Women gossiped on wooden boxes, men puffed cigars of the De Nobili while standing on street corners, children risked their lives in dangerous play, leaving their blue-slate islands to climb on the moving freight train. All moved in the smoky yellow light of lamp posts and the naked white-hot bulbs of candy-store windows.

At every intersection a fresh breeze from Twelfth Avenue, concrete bank of the Hudson River, refreshed horse and rider, cooled the hot black engine that gave warning hoots behind them.

At 27th Street the wall on Larry Angeluzzi's right fell away for a whole block. In the cleared space was Chelsea Park packed with dark squatting shapes, kids sitting on the ground to watch the free out-door movies shown by Hudson Guild Settlement House. On the distant giant white screen, Larry Angeluzzi saw a monstrous horse and rider, bathed in false sunlight, thundering down upon him, felt his own horse rise in alarm as its tossing head caught sight of those great ghosts; and then they were past the intersection of 28th Street, and the wall had sprung up again.

Larry was nearly home. There was the pedestrian bridge that spanned Tenth Avenue on 30th Street; when he passed beneath that bridge he would be home, his work done. He set his cap at a jauntier angle, rode straight in the saddle. All the people sitting on the side-walk from 30th to 31st Streets were relatives and friends. Larry made his horse gallop.

He passed swiftly beneath the bridge, waved to the children lean-ing on its rails above his head. He made his horse rear up for the people on the sidewalk on his right, then turned the animal left into the open railroad yards that formed a great spark-filled plain of steel down to the Hudson River.

Behind him the huge black engine chugged white clouds of steam, and as if by magic, the bridge and its children vanished, leav-ing behind them thin beautiful screams of delight rising to the pale, almost invisible stars. The freight train curved into the yards, the bridge reappeared, and scores of damp children hurtled down the stairways to run along the Avenue.

Larry tied his horse to the hitching post by the switchman's shanty and sat on the bench against the shanty wall. On the other side of the Avenue, painted on a flat screen, the familiar world he loved came alive inch by inch.

The brightly lit bakery was near the corner of 30th Street, its fes-tooned lemon-ice stand surrounded by children. The *Panettiere* him-self filled white-ridged paper cups with cherry-red, pale yellow and glittering-white crystals of ice. He scooped generous portions, for he was rich and even went to race tracks to squander his money.

Next to the bakery, toward 31st Street, was the grocery, its window filled with yellow logs of provolone in shiny, waxy skins and prosciutto hams, meaty triangles hanging in gaily colored paper. Then there was the barber shop closed for business but open for card playing, the jealous barber even now alert for any freshly cut heads that did not bear the mark of his scissors. Children covered the pavement, busy as ants, women, almost invisible in black, made little dark mounds before each tenement door. From each mound a buzzing hum of angry gossip rose to the summer, starry sky.

The dwarf-like switchman came from the tracks and said, "No more trains tonight, kid." Larry unhitched his horse, mounted, then made the animal turn and rear up.

As the horse rose in the air, the row of tenements, the western wall of the great city, billowed, tilted toward Larry like some fragile canvas. In the open window of his own home, on the top floor of the tenement directly opposite, Larry saw the dark shape of what must be his little brother Vincent. Larry waved but there was no answering motion until he waved again. In the wall there were only a few scattered panes of yellow light. Everyone was down on the street, everyone was watching him. He struck his horse across the neck and galloped up the cobblestones of Tenth Avenue to the stable on 36th Street.

Earlier that evening, in twilight, when Larry Angeluzzi saddled his horse in St. John's Park, his mother, Lucia Santa Angeluzzi-Corbo, also mother of Octavia and Vincenzo Angeluzzi, widow of Anthony Angeluzzi, now wife of Frank Corbo and mother of his three children, by name Gino, Salvatore and Aileen, prepared to leave her empty flat, escape the choking summer heat, spend her evening with neighbors in quarreling gossip, and most of all, to guard her children playing in the darkness of the city streets.

Lucia Santa was at ease tonight, for summer was the good time—the children never ill with colds or fevers, no worries about warm coats, gloves, boots for the winter snow and extra money for school supplies. Everyone rushed through supper to escape the air-less rooms and move with the tide of life in the streets; there were no evening quarrels. The house was easily kept clean since it was always empty. But, best of all for Lucia Santa, her own evenings were free; the street was a meeting place and summer was a time when neighbors became friends. So now, heavy jet black hair combed into a bun, wearing a clean black dress, she picked up the backless kitchen chair and went down the four flights of stairs to sit on the Avenue.

Each tenement was a village square; each had its group of women, all in black, sitting on stools and boxes and doing more than gossip. They recalled ancient history, argued morals and social law, always taking their precedents from the mountain village in southern Italy they had escaped, fled from many years ago. And with what relish their favorite imaginings! Now: What if their stern fathers were transported by some miracle to face the problems *they* faced every day? Or their mothers of the quick and heavy hands? What shrieks if *they* as daughters had dared as these American children dared? If *they* had presumed.

The women talked of their children as they would of strangers. It was a favorite topic, the corruption of the innocent by the new land. Now: Felicia, who lived around the corner of 31st Street. What type of daughter was she who did not cut short her honeymoon on news of her godmother's illness, the summons issued by her own mother? A real whore. No no, they did not mince words Felicia's mother herself told the story. And a son, poor man, who could not wait another year to marry when his father so commanded? Ahhh, the disrespect. *Figlio disgraziato.* Never could this pass in Italy. The father would kill his arrogant son; yes, kill him. And the daughter? In Italy—Felicia's mother swore in a voice still trembling with passion, though this had all happened three years ago, the godmother recovered, the grandchildren the light of her life—ah, in Italy the mother would pull the whore out of her bridal chamber, drag her to the hospital bed by the hair of her head. Ah, Italia, Italia; how the world changed and for the worse. What madness was it that made them leave such a land? Where fathers commanded and mothers were treated with respect by their children.

Each in turn told a story of insolence and defiance, themselves heroic, long-suffering, the children spitting Lucifers saved by an application of Italian discipline—the razor strop or the *Tackeril*. And at the end of each story each woman recited her requiem. *Mannaggia America!*—Damn America. But in the hot summer night their voices were filled with hope, with a vigor never sounded in their homeland. Here now was money in the bank, children who could read and write, grandchildren who would be professors if all went well. They spoke with guilty loyalty of customs they had themselves trampled into dust.

The truth: These country women from the mountain farms of Italy, whose fathers and grandfathers had died in the same rooms in which they were born, these women loved the clashing steel and stone of the great city, the thunder of trains in the railroad yards across the street, the lights above the Palisades far across the Hudson. As children they had lived in solitude, on land so poor that people scattered themselves singly along the mountain slopes to search out a living.

Audacity had liberated them. They were pioneers, though they never walked an American plain and never felt real soil beneath their feet. They moved in a sadder wilderness, where the language was strange, where their children became members of a different race. It was a price that must be paid.

In all this Lucia Santa was silent. She waited for her friend and ally, Zia Louche. She rested, gathering up her strength for the long hours of happy quarreling that lay ahead. It was still early evening, and they would not return to their homes before midnight. The rooms would not be cool before then. She folded her hands in her lap and turned her face to the gentle breeze that blew from the river below Twelfth Avenue.

A small, round, handsome woman, Lucia Santa stood at the height of her powers in health, mental and physical; courageous and without fear of life and its dangers. But not foolhardy, not reckless. She was strong, experienced, wary and alert, well-equipped for the

great responsibility of bringing a large family to adulthood and freedom. Her only weakness was a lack of that natural cunning and
shrewdness which does so much more for people than virtue.

When she was only seventeen, over twenty years ago, Lucia Santa
had left her home in Italy. She traveled the three thousand miles of
dark ocean to a strange country and a strange people and began a life
with a man she had known only when they had played together as innocent children.

Shaking her head at her own madness, yet with pride, she often
told the story.

There had come a time when her father, with stern pity, told her,
his favorite daughter, that she could not hope for bridal linen. The
farm was too poor. There were debts. Life promised to be even
harder. There it was. There could be found only a husband witless
with love.

In that moment she had lost all respect for her father, for her
home, for her country. A bride without linen was shameful, shameful as a bride rising from an unbloodied nuptial bed; worse, for there
could be no recourse to slyness, no timing of the bridal night near
the period of flood. And even that men had forgiven. But what man
would take a woman with the stigma of hopeless poverty?

Only the poor can understand the shame of poverty, greater than
the shame of the greatest sinner. For the sinner, vanquished by his
own other self, is in one sense the victor. But the poor are truly vanquished: by their world, by their *padrones*, by fortune and by time.
They are beggars always in need of charity. To the poor who have
been poor for centuries, the nobility of honest toil is a legend. Their
virtues lead them to humiliation and shame.

But Lucia Santa was helpless, though her sulky, adolescent rage
endured. Then a letter from America; a boy from the neighboring
farm, her companion when they were both little children, wrote and
asked her to join him in the new land. It was all done correctly
through both fathers. Lucia Santa tried to remember the boy's face.

And so one sunny Italian day Lucia Santa and two other village
maidens were escorted to the town hall and then to the church by
their weeping parents, aunts, and sisters. The three girls went on

board ship, brides by proxy, sailing from Naples to New York, by law Americans.

In a dream Lucia Santa entered a land of stone and steel, bedded that same night with a stranger who was her legal husband, bore that stranger two children, and was pregnant with the third when he carelessly let himself be killed in one of those accidents that were part of the building of the new continent. She accepted all this without self-pity. She lamented, true, but that was not the same thing; she only begged fate for mercy.

So then, a pregnant widow, still young, with no one to turn to, she never succumbed to terror, despair. She had an enormous strength, not unusual in women, to bear adversity. But she was not a stone. Fate did not make her bitter; that was left to friends and neighbors—these very neighbors who so intimately shared the summer night.

Ahh, the young wives, the young mothers, all the other young Italian women in a strange land. What cronies they were. How they ran to each other's apartments, up and down the stairs, into the adjoining tenements. "*Cara* Lucia Santa, taste this special dish"—a platter of new sausage, Easter pie with wheat germ and clotted cheese and a crust glazed with eggs, or plump ravioli for a family saint's day, with a special meat and tomato sauce. What flutters, what compliments and cups of coffee and confidences and promises to be godmother to the yet-to-be-born infant. But after the tragedy, after the initial pity and condolences, the true face of the world showed itself to Lucia Santa.

Greetings were cold, doors were shut, prospective godmothers disappeared. Who wished to be friendly with a young, full-blooded widow? Husbands were weak, there would be calls for assistance. In the tenements life was close; a young woman without a man was dangerous. She could draw off money and goods as the leech draws blood. They were not malicious; they showed only the prudence of the poor, so easy to mock when there is no understanding of the fear which is its root.

One friend stood fast. Zia Louche, an old, childless widow, came to help, stood godmother when the fatherless Vincenzo was born and bought her godson a beautiful gold watch when he was confirmed so that Lucia Santa could hold up her head; for such a magnificent present was a mark of respect and faith. But Zia Louche was the only one, and when mourning time had passed Lucia Santa saw the world with new and wiser eyes.

Time healed the wounds and now they were all friends again. Perhaps—who knows?— the young widow had been too harsh in her judgment, for these same neighbors, true, in their own self-interest, helped her find a second husband who would feed and clothe her children. There was a marriage in church. These same neighbors gave her a glorious wedding-night feast. But Lucia Santa never let the world deceive her again.

And so on this heavy summer night, with her first batch of children grown and safe, her second batch of children no longer infants except for Lena, and with some money in the post office; now, after twenty years of struggle and a fair share of suffering, Lucia Santa Angeluzzi-Corbo stood on that little knoll of prosperity that the poor reach, reach with such effort that they believe the struggle is won and that with ordinary care their lives are safe. She had already lived a lifetime; the story was over.

Enough. Here came Zia Louche, completing the circle. Lucia Santa paid attention, prepared to enter the torrent of gossip. But she saw her daughter Octavia coming from the corner of 30th Street, past the *Panettiere* and his red glass box of pizza and pale tin cans of lemon ice. Then Lucia Santa lost sight of her daughter; for one blinding moment her eyes were filled by the *Panettiere's* wooden tub, brimming with red coppers and gleaming silver fishes of dimes and nickels. She felt a quick, hot surge of passionate anger that she could never possess such treasure and that the ugly baker should find fortune so kind. Then she saw the *Panettiere's* wife—old, mustached, no longer able to bear children—guarding that wooden tub of copper and silver, her wrinkled shell-lidded dragon eyes flashing fire in the summer night.

Lucia Santa felt Octavia sitting beside her on the backless chair;

their hips and thighs touched. This always irritated the mother, but her daughter would be offended if she moved, so she accepted it. Seeing her daughter so oddly handsome, dressed in the American style, she gave the old crone Zia Louche a smile that showed both her pride and a hint of derisive irony. Octavia, dutifully silent and attentive, saw that smile and understood it, yet she was bewildered once again by her mother's nature.

As if her mother could understand that Octavia wanted to be everything these women were not! With the foolish and transparent cleverness of the young, she wore a powder blue suit that hid her bust and squared the roundness of her hips. She wore white gloves, as her high school teacher had done. Her eyebrows were heavy and black, honestly unplucked. Hopelessly she compressed the full red lips to an imaginary sternness, her eyes quietly grave—and all to hide the drowning sensuality that had been the undoing of the women around her. For Octavia reasoned that satisfying the terrible dark need stilled all other needs and she felt a frightened pity for these women enchanted into dreamless slavery by children and the unknown pleasures of a marriage bed.

This would not be *her* fate. She sat with bowed head, listening, Judas-like; pretending to be one of the faithful, she planned treason and escape.

Now with only women around her, Octavia took off her jacket; the white blouse with its tiny red-ribboned tie was more seductive than she could ever know. No disguise could hide the full roundness of her bust. The sensual face, crown of blue-black curls and ringlets, great liquid eyes, all mocked the staidness of her dress. With malice she could not have made herself more provocative than she did in her innocence.

Lucia Santa took the jacket and folded it over her arm, an act of love that was maternal, that meant possession and dominance. But above all an act of reconciliation, for earlier that evening mother and daughter had quarreled.

Octavia wanted to go to night school, study to become a teacher. Lucia Santa refused permission. No; she would become ill working and going to school. "Why? Why?" the mother asked. "You, such a beautiful dressmaker, you earn good money." The mother objected out of superstition. This course was known. Life was unlucky, you followed a new path at your peril. You put yourself at the mercy of fate. Her daughter was too young to understand.

Unexpectedly, shamefacedly, Octavia had said, "I want to be happy," and the older woman became a raging fury, contemptuous—the mother, who had always defended her daughter's toity ways, her reading of books, her tailored suits that were as affected as a lorgnette. The mother had mimicked Octavia in the perfect English of a shallow girl, *"You want to be happy."* And then in Italian, with deadly seriousness, "Thank God you are alive."

In the cool evening air Octavia accepted her mother's act of peace, sat gracefully, hands folded in her lap. Remembering the quarrel, she mused on the mystery of her mother's speaking perfect English when mimicking her children. Out of the corner of her eye Octavia saw Guido, the dark son of the *Panettiere*, wavering through the warm summer night toward the light of her white blouse. In his dark, strong hand he bore a tall paper cup of fruit ice, lemon and or-ange, which he gave her, almost bowing, whispering hurriedly some-thing that sounded like "Don't spoil your shirt," and then hurrying back to the stand to help his father. Octavia smiled, took a few mouthfuls out of politeness, and passed the cup to her mother, who had a passion for ices and sucked on the cup, greedy as a child. The buzz of the old women's voices went on.

Her stepfather turned the corner of 31st Street and entered the Avenue, wheeling the baby carriage before him. Octavia watched him go from 31st Street to 30th and back again. And as her mother's irony bewildered her, this tenderness of the stepfather confused her emotions. For she hated him as someone cruel, villainous, evil. She had seen him give blows to her mother, act the tyrant to his step-children. In the faded memories of Octavia's childhood his courting of her mother followed too swiftly the day of her real father's death.

She wanted to look at the sleeping baby, the little sister she loved passionately, though she was her stepfather's child. But she could not bear speaking to the man, looking into his cold blue eyes and harsh angular face. She knew her stepfather hated her as she hated him and that each feared the other. He had never dared strike her as he some-times struck Vinnie. And she would not have minded his blows to his stepson if he had been paternal in other ways. But he brought pre-sents for Gino and Sal and Aileen and never for Vincent, though Vincent was a child still. She hated him because he never took Vincent for walks or haircuts with his natural children. She feared him because he was strange—the evil mysterious stranger of story books, the blue-eyed Italian with the Mephistophelean face; and yet she knew that really he was an illiterate peasant, a poor, con-temptible immigrant who gave himself airs. One day she had seen him on the subway pretending to read a newspaper. She had rushed to tell her mother, laughing, contemptuous. Her mother had only given her a curious smile and said nothing.

But now one of the black-clad women was telling a story about a villainous young Italian girl (born in America, naturally). Octavia at-tended. "Yes, yes," the woman said. "They were married for a month, they had finished with their honeymoon. Oh, she loved him. She sat on his lap in his mother's home. When they visited she played with his hand. Like this—" two gnarled hands with warty fingers linked themselves lovingly, obscenely, in the storyteller's lap—"and then they went to dance, in the church. The foolishness of those young priests who do not even speak Italian! Her husband won a prize for entering the door. He took the prize and dropped to the earth, dead. His poor heart, he was always sickly. His mother had always warned him, cared for him. But now. The young bride, dancing with another man, is told. Does she rush to the side of her beloved? She shrieks. She cries, 'No, no. I cannot.' She fears death like a child, not a woman. The loved one lies in his own piss, alone, but *she* no longer loves him. She cries out, 'No, I will not look at it.'"

Slyly Zia Louche, her tongue rolling up both meanings, said, "Ah! You may be sure she looked at It when It was alive." A great burst of coarse laughter from all the women filled the Avenue, drawing jeal-ous looks from other circles of women. Octavia was disgusted, angry that even her mother was smiling with delight.

To more serious things. Lucia Santa and Zia Louche stood fast against the rest of the circle on a point of ancient history, the exact details of a scandal twenty years ago across the sea in Italy. It amused Octavia to see her mother defer to Zia Louche, and the old crone valiantly do battle for her mother, each of them treating the other like a duchess. Her mother turning to Zia Louche and asking respectfully, *"E vero, Comare?"* And Zia Louche always answering imperiously, *"Sì, Signora,"* showing no callow familiarity before the others. Octavia knew the relationship behind this, her mother's gratitude for that valuable alliance in the hour of her most terrible misfortune.

But the quarrel was too finely drawn and Octavia became bored. She got up to look at her baby half sister, staring down at the carriage, not greeting her stepfather. She gazed down at the baby girl with an overwhelming tenderness, an emotion she did not even feel for Vincent. Then she walked toward the corner of 31st Street to look for Gino, saw him playing, saw little Sal sitting on the curb. She took Sal back to his mother. Vinnie was missing. Looking up, she saw him far above her, sitting on the window sill of the apartment, dark, motionless, guarding them all.

Frank Corbo, somber, watched his big stepdaughter lean over his baby. Strange with blue eyes, object of amusement (what Italian male wheeled his baby in the summer night?), illiterate, his mind mute, he saw the beauty of the stone city in darkness, felt the hatred of his stepdaughter without returning hatred. The harsh thin face concealed a wordless and consuming anguish. His life was a dream of beauty felt and not understood, of love twisted into cruelty. Countless treasures went by like shadows, the world was locked away. In search of deliverance, he would leave the city tonight and desert his family. In the early morning hours, while it was still dark, he would meet a farm truck and disappear without a word, without quarreling or giving blows. He would work in the brown and green fields of summer, gain peace from love, restore his strength.

He suffered. He suffered as a deaf mute suffers who would sing seeing beauty, who cannot cry out in pain. He felt love and could not give caresses. There were too many people sleeping in the rooms around him, too many beings walked the streets around him. He dreamed terrible dreams. Tapestried on black, his wife and children circled him round, and from their foreheads each drew a dagger. He had cried out.

It was late, late; the children should be in bed, but it was still too hot. Frank Corbo watched his son Gino run crazily in some sort of tagging game incomprehensible to the father, as was the child's American speech, as were the books and newspapers, the colors of the night sky, the beauty of the summer night and all the joys of the world he felt cut off from, all colored with pain. The world was a great mystery. Vast dangers that others could guard their children against would bring him and his loved ones into the dust. They would teach his children to hate him.

But still, the father, never knowing he would be saved, wheeled the carriage back and forth. Not knowing that deep down in his blood, in the tiny mysterious cells of his brain, a new world was forming. Slowly, day by day, pain by pain, beauty by lost beauty, the walls of the world he feared so much were crumbling in the timelessness of his mind, and in a year a new fantastic world would spring up, himself the god and king, his enemies startled and afraid, his loved ones forever lost and yet that loss of love not felt or mourned. A world of such chaotic pain that he would be drowned in ecstasy, mystery and fear banished. He would be free.

But it was like magic, and no hint nor warning could come beforehand. Now, this night, he put his trust in one summer of tilling the earth, as he had done so long ago, a boy in Italy.

The world has a special light for children, and sounds are magical. Gino Corbo moved through the clang of engines, circles of mellow lamp-post lights, heard young girls laughing, and played his game so intently that his head ached. He ran back and forth across 31st Street, trying to capture other children or surround them. But someone always backed against a wall, hand outstretched. Once Gino was trapped, but a taxi cut his opponents off and he ran back to his own sidewalk. He saw his father watching and ran to him shouting, "Gimme a penny for lemon ice." Snatching the coin, he ran along Tenth Avenue and planned a beautiful trick. He tried to run past his mother and her friends. Zia Louche grabbed his arm and pulled him off his feet, her bony fingers a trap of steel.

His dazed, impatient eyes saw a circle of old women's faces, some hairy and mustached. Frantic to be away, afraid the game would end, Gino tried to run. Zia Louche held him like a fly, saying, "Rest—sit with your mother and rest. You'll be sick tomorrow. Feel how your heart is beating." And she put her withered claw upon his chest. He pulled violently. The old crone held him and said with ferocious love, "*Eh, come è faccia brutta.*" He understood she was calling him ugly, and that made him still. He stared at the circle of women. They were laughing, but Gino did not know they laughed with delight at his fierce desire, his blazing eyes.

He spat at Zia Louche, the fake spit of Italian women that shows contempt in a quarrel. It got him free, and he was so quick that his mother hit his face only a glancing blow as he sped away. Around the corner, along 30th Street to Ninth Avenue, up the Avenue to 31st Street, and then through 31st Street to Tenth Avenue he would go; having traveled the four sides of the city block, he would swoop into the game out of the darkness and with one masterly stroke shatter the enemy.

But as he ran full speed toward Ninth Avenue, a line of alien boys formed a wall against him. Gino pumped his legs higher and faster and burst through, shattered them. Clutching hands tore his shirt, the wind rushed against his face. On Ninth Avenue the boys came after him, but when he turned into the darkness at the top of 31st Street they did not dare to follow. Gino stopped running and walked softly along the stoops. He was on the final side of the square and below him, at the foot of the street, near Tenth Avenue, painted into the dim yellow cones of light cast by lamp posts, his friends scurried to and fro like little black rats, still playing. He was in time.

He rested in darkness and then went very softly, slowly, down the street. In a basement room he saw a little girl leaning against a wall half white, half electric blue. She rested her head against her arm upon the wall, hiding her eyes from the cold, artificial light of the room, empty, deserted behind her. Gino knew she was playing hide and seek, not crying, and that if he waited, the deserted room would come magically alive with shrieking girls. But he did not stop, not knowing he would always remember the girl alone, hiding her eyes against a blue and white wall; desolate, never changing, as if by not stopping he left her there forever, enchanted. He went on.

A dim patch of light made him pause. He shivered. Sitting at the window, leaning out of her street-level flat, an old Irish crone rested her head on a furry pillow and watched him move past her down the empty silent street. In that weak yellow light her head was bony with age, her thin, whiskered mouth bloody with the light of a holy red candle. Behind that feral face, faintly visible in the shadows of her room, a vase, a lamp, and a graven image gleamed like old bones. Gino stared at her. The teeth bared in greeting. Gino ran.

Now he could hear the shouts of his friends; he was near the circles of light on Tenth Avenue. He crouched on the steps of a cellar, hidden, powerful, ready to strike. He never thought to be afraid of the dark basement below or of the night. He forgot his mother's anger. He existed only for this moment and the moment he would enter the pool of light and shatter it.

High over Tenth Avenue, Gino Corbo's half brother, Vincenzo Angeluzzi, thirteen years old, brooded to the softened, whispery sound of the summer night that floated up to him. He brooded on his window sill, the long line of rooms behind him dark and empty, the door from the hall to the kitchen securely locked. He was self-exiled.

The dream of summer, freedom, and play had been taken from him. His mother had informed him that in the morning he would start working for the *Panettiere*, and work until school started in the fall. He would carry heavy baskets of bread in the hot sun while other boys swam in the river, played stickball and "Johnny Ride the Pony," and hitched onto the backs of trolley cars to see the city. There would be no sitting in the shade eating lemon ice or reading by the wall of Runkel's factory or playing "Bankers and Brokers" and "Seven-and-a-half" for pennies.

A watcher on the western wall of the city, everything weighed down his soul and spirit, the wasteland of railroad yards, steel tracks, deserted box cars, engines giving off dirty red sparks and low hoots of warning. The Hudson was a black ribbon beneath the cragged Jersey shore.

He dozed on his window sill, and the babel of voices rose like a faint shout. Far down the Avenue he saw the red lantern of a dummy boy leading his freight train from St. John's Park. The children below him played on, and Vincent waited with gloomy satisfaction for their shouts of joy, savoring his bitterness at not sharing their pleasure. And then the children were screaming and scrambling up the steps of the bridge to wait for the damp cloud of steam that would make them invisible.

Vincent was too young to know that he was melancholy by nature, that this distressed his sister Octavia so that she brought him presents and candy. When he was a toddling infant Octavia used to take him into her bed, tell him stories, and sing songs so that he would go to sleep with a remembrance of smiles. But nothing could change his nature.

Below, he could hear Zia Louche quarreling shrilly and his mother's strong voice supporting her. The resentment came that this old crone was his godmother and that the five-dollar gold piece she gave him every birthday must be paid for with a kiss—a kiss he gave only to make his mother happy. He thought his mother beautiful, though she was fat and always dressed in black, and he always obeyed her.

But Zia Louche, ever since he could remember, had made him hate her. Long ago when he played on the kitchen floor between his mother's feet, Zia Louche would study him. The two women would be talking violently, without their public formality, recalling with gusto their misfortunes through the years. There would be a silence. The two women would look at him thoughtfully, sipping coffee. Then Zia Louche would sigh through age-browned teeth and say with hopeless, angry pity to the little boy, "Ah, *miserabile, miserabile.* Your father died before you were born."

That was the climax; the old crone went on to other things, leaving him bewildered and watching his mother's face go pale and her eyes turn red. She would reach down to touch him, but she never spoke.

Down in the street Vincent saw his sister Octavia get up to look at the baby. He hated her, too. She had betrayed him. She had not protested their mother's sending him to work. Then the dummy boy rode under the bridge, and Vincent saw his brother Larry riding like a real cowboy on a black horse.

Even from so far up he could hear a loud clatter of hoofs on cobblestones. The children disappeared and the bridge vanished in a cloud of steam from the engine. With a great shower of sparks, the train slid into the railroad yards.

It was late. The night air had cooled the city. His mother and the other women picked up their stools and crates, called to husbands and children. His stepfather wheeled the baby to the tenement door. It was time to get ready for bed.

Vincent left his window sill and went back through the bedrooms to the kitchen. He unlocked the door to the hallway, opening the house for his family. Then he took the thigh-sized loaf of Italian bread and sliced off three thick, crusty chunks. Over these he poured red wine vinegar, then thick, yellow-green olive oil. He stood back and scattered salt over all three, inspecting them with a satisfied air. The coarse bread was a lovely red dotted with blots of greasy green. Gino and Sal would be delighted with this bedtime snack. They would all eat together. He waited. From the street, through windows still open and coming down the corridor of rooms between, he heard Gino's voice in a loud continuous scream.

That scream froze Lucia Santa with the baby in her arms. Octavia, on the corner of 30th Street, turned toward 31st. Across the Avenue Larry wheeled around on his horse. The father, his temples bursting with fear, started to run and curse. But the child's scream was one of hysterical triumph. Gino had shot out of the darkness and circled his enemies and was screaming, "Burn the city, burn the city, burn the city." So ending the game, he could not stop screaming the magic words or stop running. He aimed himself at his mother's enormous menacing figure with great leaps into the air, remembered his insult to Zia Louche, and swerved away, through the door and up the stairs.

Lucia Santa, with every intention of striking him to the ground, stood overwhelmed by a fierce pride and tenderness at her child's wild joy, the spirit that she must some day break. She let him pass unharmed.

The Neapolitan Italians dissolved from the dark streets and left the city to the clatter of hoofs on cobblestones as Larry Angeluzzi galloped his horse to the stable on 35th Street.

1 9 6 5

# TOM WOLFE

*Even in the most hectic city on the planet there are "down times" when lovers loll around indoors, enjoying their sabbath, taking the morning slowly; such casual epiphanies are the stuff of Tom Wolfe's "A Sunday Kind of Love." Wolfe (1931–   ), the foremost exponent of "new journalism" whose novel* The Bonfire of the Vanities *cast a mordant look on New York City in the 1980's, permits himself more tenderness toward the metropolis in this earlier piece.*

## A SUNDAY KIND OF LOVE

LOVE! Attar of libido in the air! It is 8:45 A.M. Thursday morning in the IRT subway station at 50th Street and Broadway and already two kids are hung up in a kind of herringbone weave of arms and legs, which proves, one has to admit, that love is not *confined* to Sunday in New York. Still, the odds! All the faces come popping in clots out of the Seventh Avenue local, past the King Size Ice Cream machine, and the turnstiles start whacking away as if the world were breaking up on the reefs. Four steps past the turnstiles everybody is already backed up haunch to paunch for the climb up the ramp and the stairs to the surface, a great funnel of flesh, wool, felt, leather, rubber and steaming alumicron, with the blood squeezing through everybody's old sclerotic arteries in hopped-up spurts from too much coffee and the effort of surfacing from the subway at the rush hour. Yet there on the landing are a boy and a girl, both about eighteen, in one of those utter, My Sin, backbreaking embraces.

He envelops her not only with his arms but with his chest, which has the American teen-ager concave shape to it. She has her head cocked at a 90-degree angle and they both have their eyes pressed shut for all they are worth and some incredibly feverish action going with each other's mouths. All round them, ten, scores, it seems like hundreds, of faces and bodies are perspiring, trooping and bellying up the stairs with arteriosclerotic grimaces past a showcase full of such novel items as Joy Buzzers, Squirting Nickels, Finger Rats,

Scary Tarantulas and spoons with realistic dead flies on them, past Fred's barbershop, which is just off the landing and has glossy photographs of young men with the kind of baroque haircuts one can get in there, and up onto 50th Street into a madhouse of traffic and shops with weird lingerie and gray hair-dyeing displays in the windows, signs for free teacup readings and a pool-playing match between the Playboy Bunnies and Downey's Showgirls, and then everybody pounds on toward the Time-Life Building, the Brill Building or NBC.

The boy and the girl just keep on writhing in their embroilment. Her hand is sliding up the back of his neck, which he turns when her fingers wander into the intricate formal gardens of his Chicago Boxcar hairdo at the base of the skull. The turn causes his face to start to mash in the ciliated hull of her beehive hairdo, and so she rolls her head 180 degrees to the other side, using their mouths for the pivot. But aside from good hair grooming, they are oblivious to everything but each other. Everybody gives them a once-over. Disgusting! Amusing! How touching! A few kids pass by and say things like "Swing it, baby." But the great majority in that heaving funnel up the stairs seem to be as much astounded as anything else. The vision of love at rush hour cannot strike anyone exactly as romance. It is a feat, like a fat man crossing the English Channel in a barrel. It is an earnest accomplishment against the tide. It is a piece of slightly gross heroics, after the manner of those knobby, varicose old men who come out from some place in baggy shorts every year and run through the streets of Boston in the Marathon race. And somehow that is the gaffe against love all week long in New York, for everybody, not just two kids writhing under their coiffures in the 50th Street subway station; too hurried, too crowded, too hard, and no time for dalliance. Which explains why the real thing in New York is, as it says in the song, a Sunday kind of love.

There is Saturday, but Saturday is not much better than Monday through Friday. Saturday is the day for errands in New York. More millions of shoppers are pouring in to keep the place jammed up. Everybody is bobbing around, running up to Yorkville to pick up these arty cheeses for this evening, or down to Fourth Avenue to try

to find this Van Vechten book, *Parties*, to complete the set for somebody, or off to the cleaner's, the dentist's, the hairdresser's, or some
guy's who is going to loan you his station wagon to pick up two flush
doors to make tables out of, or over to some place somebody mentioned that is supposed to have fabulous cuts of meat and the butcher
wears a straw hat and arm garters and is colorfully rude.

True, there is Saturday night, and Friday night. They are fine for
dates and good times in New York. But for the dalliance of love, they
are just as stupefying and wound up as the rest of the week. On
Friday and Saturday nights everybody is making some kind of scene.
It may be a cellar cabaret in the Village where five guys from some
place talk "Jamaican" and pound steel drums and the Connecticut
teen-agers wear plaid ponchos and knee-high boots and drink such
things as Passion Climax cocktails, which are made of apple cider
with watermelon balls thrown in. Or it may be some cellar in
the East 50's, a discotheque, where the alabaster kids come on in
sleeveless minksides jackets, tweed evening dresses and cool-it
Modernismus hairdos. But either way, it's a scene, a production, and
soon the evening begins to whirl, like the whole world with the bed-
spins, in a montage of taxis, slithery legs slithering in, slithery legs
slithering out, worsted, piqué, grins, eye teeth, glissandos, buffoon-
dos, tips, par lamps, doormen, lines, magenta ropes, white dickies,
mirrors and bar bottles, pink men and shawl-collared coats, hat-
check girls and neon peach fingernails, taxis, keys, broken lamps and
no coat hangers. . . .

And, then, an unbelievable dawning; Sunday, in New York.

George G., who writes "Z" ads for a department store, keeps saying that all it takes for him is to smell coffee being made at a certain
point in the percolation. It doesn't matter where. It could be the
worst death-ball hamburger dive. All he has to do is smell it, and
suddenly he finds himself swimming, drowning dissolving in his own
reverie of New York's Sunday kind of love.

Anne A.'s apartment was nothing, he keeps saying, and that was
the funny thing. She lived in Chelsea. It was this one room with a
cameo-style carving of a bored Medusa on the facing of the mantelpiece, this one room plus a kitchen, in a brownstone sunk down be-

hind a lot of loft buildings and truck terminals and so forth. Beautiful Chelsea. But on Sunday morning by 10:30 the sun would be hitting cleanly between two rearview buildings and making it through the old no man's land of gas effluvia ducts, restaurant vents, aerials, fire escapes, stairwell doors, clotheslines, chimneys, skylights, vestigial lightning rods, Mansard slopes, and those peculiarly bleak, filthy and misshapen backsides of New York buildings, into Anne's kitchen.

George would be sitting at this rickety little table with an oilcloth over it. How he goes on about it! The place was grimy. You couldn't keep the soot out. The place was beautiful. Anne is at the stove making coffee. The smell of the coffee being made, just the smell . . . already he is turned on. She had on a great terrycloth bathrobe with a sash belt. The way she moved around inside that bathrobe with the sun shining in the window always got him. It was the *at*mosphere of the thing. There she was, moving around in that great fluffy bathrobe with the sun hitting her hair, and they had all the time in the world. There wasn't even one flatulent truck horn out on Eighth Avenue. Nobody was clobbering their way down the stairs in high heels out in the hall at 10 minutes to 9.

Anne would make scrambled eggs, plain scrambled eggs, but it was a feast. It was incredible. She would bring out a couple of these little smoked fish with golden skin and some smoked oysters that always came in a little can with ornate lettering and royal colors and flourishes and some Kissebrot bread and black cherry preserves, and then the coffee. They had about a million cups of coffee apiece, until the warmth seemed to seep through your whole viscera. And then cigarettes. The cigarettes were like some soothing incense. The radiator was always making a hissing sound and then a clunk. The sun was shining in and the fire escapes and effluvia ducts were just silhouettes out there someplace. George would tear off another slice of Kissebrot and pile on some black cherry preserves and drink some more coffee and have another cigarette, and Anne crossed her legs under her terrycloth bathrobe and crossed her arms and drew on her cigarette, and that was the way it went.

"It was the *torpor*, boy," he says. "It was beautiful. Torpor is a beautiful, underrated thing. Torpor is a luxury. Especially in this stupid town. There in that kitchen it was like being in a perfect cocoon of love. Everything was beautiful, a perfect cocoon."

By and by they would get dressed, always in as shiftless a getup as possible. She would put on a big heavy sweater, a raincoat and a pair of faded slacks that gripped her like neopreme rubber. He would put on a pair of corduroy pants, a crew sweater with moth holes and a raincoat. Then they would go out and walk down to 14th Street for the Sunday paper.

All of a sudden it was great out there on the street in New York. All those damnable millions who come careening into Manhattan all week weren't there. The town was empty. To a man and woman shuffling along there, torpid, in the cocoon of love, it was as if all of rotten Gotham had improved overnight. Even the people looked better. There would be one of those old dolls with little flabby arms all hunched up in a coat of pastel oatmeal texture, the kind whose lumpy old legs you keep seeing as she heaves her way up the subway stairs ahead of you and holds everybody up because she is so flabby and decrepit . . . and today, Sunday, on good, clean, empty 14th Street, she just looked like a nice old lady. There was no one around to make her look slow, stupid, unfit, unhip, expendable. That was the thing about Sunday. The weasel millions were absent. And Anne walking along beside him with a thready old pair of slacks gripping her like neopreme rubber looked like possibly the most marvelous vision the world had ever come up with, and the cocoon of love was perfect. It was like having your cake and eating it, too. On the one hand, here it was, boy, the prize: New York. All the buildings, the Gotham spires, were sitting up all over the landscape in silhouette like ikons representing all that was great, glorious and triumphant in New York. And, on the other hand, there were no weasel millions bellying past you and eating crullers on the run with the crumbs flaking off the corners of their mouths as a reminder of how much *Angst* and *Welthustle* you had to put into the town to get any of that out of it for yourself. All there was was the cocoon of love, which was complete. It was like being inside a scenic Easter Egg where you look in and the Gotham spires are just standing there like a little gemlike backdrop.

By and by the two of them would be back in the apartment sprawled out on the floor rustling through the Sunday paper, all that even black ink appliquéd on big fat fronds of paper. Anne would put an E. Power Biggs organ record on the hi-fi, and pretty soon the old trammeler's bass chords would be vibrating through you as if he had clamped a diathermy machine on your solar plexus. So there they would be, sprawled out on the floor, rustling through the Sunday paper, getting bathed and massaged by E. Power Biggs' sonic waves. It was like taking peyote or something. This marvelously high feeling would come over them, as though they were psychedelic, and the most commonplace objects took on this great radiance and significance. It was like old Aldous Huxley in his drug experiments, sitting there hooking down peyote buttons and staring at a clay geranium pot on a table, which gradually became the most fabulous geranium pot in God's world. The way it curved . . . why, it curved 360 d-e-g-r-e-e-s! And the clay . . . why, it was the color of the earth itself! And the top . . . It had a r-i-m on it! George had the same feeling. Anne's apartment . . . it was hung all over the place with the usual New York working girl's modern prints, the Picasso scrawls, the Mondrians curling at the corners . . . somehow nobody ever gets even a mat for a Mondrian print . . . the Toulouse-Lautrecs with that guy with the chin kicking his silhouette leg, the Klees, that Paul Klee is cute . . . why, all of a sudden these were the most beautiful things in the whole hagiology of art . . . the way that guy with the chin k-i-c-k-s t-h-a-t l-e-g, the way that Paul Klee h-i-t-s t-h-a-t b-a-l-l . . . the way that apartment just wrapped around them like a cocoon, with lint under the couch like angel's hair, and the plum cover on the bed lying halfway on the floor in folds like the folds in a Tiepolo cherub's silks, and the bored Medusa on the mantelpiece looking like the most splendidly, gloriously b-o-r-e-d Medusa in the face of time!

"Now, that was love," says George, "and there has never been anything like it. I don't know what happens to it. Unless it's Monday. Monday sort of happens to it in New York."

1965

# JOAN DIDION

*For Joan Didion (1934– ), a native daughter of Sacramento, California, New York City was the right place to be when young: it offered newcomers an anonymity that could absorb the errors of youthful innocence and experimentation. Once one was no longer an ingenue, however, the fun began to wear thin. Didion's chic, enervated partygoers seem like forerunners of the yuppies who would flood Manhattan in the 1980's—and reincarnations of F. Scott Fitzgerald's Jazz Age celebrants.*

## GOODBYE TO ALL THAT

*How many miles to Babylon?*
*Three score miles and ten—*
*Can I get there by candlelight?*
*Yes, and back again—*
*If your feet are nimble and light*
*You can get there by candlelight.*

IT IS EASY to see the beginnings of things, and harder to see the ends. I can remember now, with a clarity that makes the nerves in the back of my neck constrict, when New York began for me, but I cannot lay my finger upon the moment it ended, can never cut through the ambiguities and second starts and broken resolves to the exact place on the page where the heroine is no longer as optimistic as she once was. When I first saw New York I was twenty, and it was summertime, and I got off a DC-7 at the old Idlewild temporary terminal in a new dress which had seemed very smart in Sacramento but seemed less smart already, even in the old Idlewild temporary terminal, and the warm air smelled of mildew and some instinct, programmed by all the movies I had ever seen and all the songs I had ever heard sung and all the stories I had ever read about New York, informed me that it would never be quite the same again. In fact it never was. Some time later there was a song on all the jukeboxes on the upper East Side that went "but where is the schoolgirl who used to be me," and if it was late enough at night I used to wonder that. I know now that almost everyone wonders something like that, sooner or later and no matter what he or she is doing, but one of the mixed blessings of being twenty and twenty-one and even twenty-three is the conviction that nothing like this, all evidence to the contrary notwithstanding, has ever happened to anyone before.

Of course it might have been some other city, had circumstances been different and the time been different and had I been different, might have been Paris or Chicago or even San Francisco, but because I am talking about myself I am talking here about New York. That first night I opened my window on the bus into town and watched for the skyline, but all I could see were the wastes of Queens and the big signs that said MIDTOWN TUNNEL THIS LANE and then a flood of summer rain (even that seemed remarkable and exotic, for I had come out of the West where there was no summer rain), and for the next three days I sat wrapped in blankets in a hotel room air-conditioned to 35° and tried to get over a bad cold and a high fever. It did not occur to me to call a doctor, because I knew none, and although it did occur to me to call the desk and ask that the air conditioner be turned off, I never called, because I did not know how much to tip whoever might come—was anyone ever so young? I am here to tell you that someone was. All I could do during those three days was talk long-distance to the boy I already knew I would never marry in the spring. I would stay in New York, I told him, just six months, and I could see the Brooklyn Bridge from my window. As it turned out the bridge was the Triborough, and I stayed eight years.

In retrospect it seems to me that those days before I knew the names of all the bridges were happier than the ones that came later, but perhaps you will see that as we go along. Part of what I want to tell you is what it is like to be young in New York, how six months can become eight years with the deceptive ease of a film dissolve, for that is how those years appear to me now, in a long sequence of sentimental dissolves and old-fashioned trick shots—the Seagram Building fountains dissolve into snowflakes, I enter a revolving door at twenty and come out a good deal older, and on a different street.

But most particularly I want to explain to you, and in the process perhaps to myself, why I no longer live in New York. It is often said that New York is a city for only the very rich and the very poor. It is less often said that New York is also, at least for those of us who came there from somewhere else, a city for only the very young.

I remember once, one cold bright December evening in New York, suggesting to a friend who complained of having been around too long that he come with me to a party where there would be, I assured him with the bright resourcefulness of twenty-three, "new faces." He laughed literally until he choked, and I had to roll down the taxi window and hit him on the back. "New faces," he said finally, "don't tell me about *new faces*." It seemed that the last time he had gone to a party where he had been promised "new faces," there had been fifteen people in the room, and he had already slept with five of the women and owed money to all but two of the men. I laughed with him, but the first snow had just begun to fall and the big Christmas trees glittered yellow and white as far as I could see up Park Avenue and I had a new dress and it would be a long while before I would come to understand the particular moral of the story.

It would be a long while because, quite simply, I was in love with New York. I do not mean "love" in any colloquial way, I mean that I was in love with the city, the way you love the first person who ever touches you and never love anyone quite that way again. I remember walking across Sixty-second Street one twilight that first spring, or the second spring, they were all alike for a while. I was late to meet someone but I stopped at Lexington Avenue and bought a peach and stood on the corner eating it and knew that I had come out of the West and reached the mirage. I could taste the peach and feel the soft air blowing from a subway grating on my legs and I could smell lilac and garbage and expensive perfume and I knew that it would cost something sooner or later—because I did not belong there, did not come from there—but when you are twenty-two or twenty-three, you figure that later you will have a high emotional balance, and be able to pay whatever it costs. I still believed in possibilities then, still had the sense, so peculiar to New York, that something extraordinary would happen any minute, any day, any month. I was making only $65 or $70 a week then ("Put yourself in Hattie Carnegie's hands," I was advised without the slightest trace of irony by an editor of the magazine for which I worked), so little money that some weeks I had to charge food at Bloomingdale's gourmet shop in order to eat, a fact which went unmentioned in the letters I wrote to California. I never told my father that I needed money because then he would have sent it, and I would never know if I could do it by myself. At that time making a living seemed a game to me, with arbitrary but quite inflexible rules. And except on a certain kind of winter evening—six-thirty in the Seventies, say, already dark and bitter with a wind off the river, when I would be walking very fast toward a bus and would look in the bright windows of brown-stones and see cooks working in clean kitchens and imagine women lighting candles on the floor above and beautiful children being bathed on the floor above that—except on nights like those, I never felt poor; I had the feeling that if I needed money I could always get it. I could write a syndicated column for teenagers under the name "Debbi Lynn" or I could smuggle gold into India or I could become a $100 call girl, and none of it would matter.

Nothing was irrevocable; everything was within reach. Just around every corner lay something curious and interesting, something I had never before seen or done or known about. I could go to a party and meet someone who called himself Mr. Emotional Appeal and ran The Emotional Appeal Institute or Tina Onassis Blandford or a Florida cracker who was then a regular on what he called "the Big C," the Southampton–El Morocco circuit ("I'm well-connected on the Big C, honey," he would tell me over collard greens on his vast borrowed terrace), or the widow of the celery king of the Harlem market or a piano salesman from Bonne Terre, Missouri, or someone who had already made and lost two fortunes in Midland, Texas. I could make promises to myself and to other people and there would be all the time in the world to keep them. I could stay up all night and make mistakes, and none of it would count.

You see I was in a curious position in New York: it never oc-curred to me that I was living a real life there. In my imagination I was always there for just another few months, just until Christmas or

Easter or the first warm day in May. For that reason I was most comfortable in the company of Southerners. They seemed to be in New York as I was, on some indefinitely extended leave from wherever they belonged, disinclined to consider the future, temporary exiles who always knew when the flights left for New Orleans or Memphis or Richmond or, in my case, California. Someone who lives always with a plane schedule in the drawer lives on a slightly different calendar. Christmas, for example, was a difficult season. Other people could take it in stride, going to Stowe or going abroad or going for the day to their mothers' places in Connecticut; those of us who believed that we lived somewhere else would spend it making and canceling airline reservations, waiting for weatherbound flights as if for the last plane out of Lisbon in 1940, and finally comforting one another, those of us who were left, with the oranges and mementos and smoked-oyster stuffings of childhood, gathering close, colonials in a far country.

Which is precisely what we were. I am not sure that it is possible for anyone brought up in the East to appreciate entirely what New York, the idea of New York, means to those of us who came out of the West and the South. To an Eastern child, particularly a child who has always had an uncle on Wall Street and who has spent several hundred Saturdays first at F. A. O. Schwarz and being fitted for shoes at Best's and then waiting under the Biltmore clock and dancing to Lester Lanin, New York is just a city, albeit *the* city, a plausible place for people to live. But to those of us who came from places where no one had heard of Lester Lanin and Grand Central Station was a Saturday radio program, where Wall Street and Fifth Avenue and Madison Avenue were not places at all but abstractions ("Money," and "High Fashion," and "The Hucksters"), New York was no mere city. It was instead an infinitely romantic notion, the mysterious nexus of all love and money and power, the shining and perishable dream itself. To think of "living" there was to reduce the miraculous to the mundane; one does not "live" at Xanadu.

In fact it was difficult in the extreme for me to understand those young women for whom New York was not simply an ephemeral Estoril but a real place, girls who bought toasters and installed new cabinets in their apartments and committed themselves to some reasonable future. I never bought any furniture in New York. For a year or so I lived in other people's apartments; after that I lived in the Nineties in an apartment furnished entirely with things taken from storage by a friend whose wife had moved away. And when I left the apartment in the Nineties (that was when I was leaving everything, when it was all breaking up) I left everything in it, even my winter clothes and the map of Sacramento County I had hung on the bedroom wall to remind me who I was, and I moved into a monastic four-room floor-through on Seventy-fifth Street. "Monastic" is perhaps misleading here, implying some chic severity; until after I was married and my husband moved some furniture in, there was nothing at all in those four rooms except a cheap double mattress and box springs, ordered by telephone the day I decided to move, and two French garden chairs lent me by a friend who imported them. (It strikes me now that the people I knew in New York all had curious and self-defeating sidelines. They imported garden chairs which did not sell very well at Hammacher Schlemmer or they tried to market hair straighteners in Harlem or they ghosted exposés of Murder Incorporated for Sunday supplements. I think that perhaps none of us was very serious, *engagé* only about our most private lives.)

All I ever did to that apartment was hang fifty yards of yellow theatrical silk across the bedroom windows, because I had some idea that the gold light would make me feel better, but I did not bother to weight the curtains correctly and all that summer the long panels of transparent golden silk would blow out the windows and get tangled and drenched in the afternoon thunderstorms. That was the year, my twenty-eighth, when I was discovering that not all of the promises would be kept, that some things are in fact irrevocable and that it had counted after all, every evasion and every procrastination, every mistake, every word, all of it.

That is what it was all about, wasn't it? Promises? Now when New York comes back to me it comes in hallucinatory flashes, so clinically detailed that I sometimes wish that memory would effect the distortion with which it is commonly credited. For a lot of the time I was in New York I used a perfume called *Fleurs de Rocaille*, and then *L'Air du Temps*, and now the slightest trace of either can short-circuit my connections for the rest of the day. Nor can I smell Henri Bendel jasmine soap without falling back into the past, or the particular mixture of spices used for boiling crabs. There were barrels of crab boil in a Czech place in the Eighties where I once shopped. Smells, of course, are notorious memory stimuli, but there are other things which affect me the same way. Blue-and-white striped sheets. Vermouth cassis. Some faded nightgowns which were new in 1959 or 1960, and some chiffon scarves I bought about the same time.

I suppose that a lot of us who have been young in New York have the same scenes on our home screens. I remember sitting in a lot of apartments with a slight headache about five o'clock in the morning. I had a friend who could not sleep, and he knew a few other people who had the same trouble, and we would watch the sky lighten and have a last drink with no ice and then go home in the early morning light, when the streets were clean and wet (had it rained in the night? we never knew) and the few cruising taxis still had their headlights on and the only color was the red and green of traffic signals. The White Rose bars opened very early in the morning; I recall waiting in one of them to watch an astronaut go into space, waiting so long that at the moment it actually happened I had my eyes not on the television screen but on a cockroach on the tile floor. I liked the bleak branches above Washington Square at dawn, and the mono-chromatic flatness of Second Avenue, the fire escapes and the grilled storefronts peculiar and empty in their perspective.

It is relatively hard to fight at six-thirty or seven in the morning without any sleep, which was perhaps one reason we stayed up all night, and it seemed to me a pleasant time of day. The windows were shuttered in that apartment in the Nineties and I could sleep a few hours and then go to work. I could work then on two or three hours' sleep and a container of coffee from Chock Full O' Nuts. I liked going to work, liked the soothing and satisfactory rhythm of getting out a magazine, liked the orderly progression of four-color closings and two-color closings and black-and-white closings and then The Product, no abstraction but something which looked effortlessly glossy and could be picked up on a newsstand and weighed in the hand. I liked all the minutiae of proofs and layouts, liked working late on the nights the magazine went to press, sitting and reading *Variety* and waiting for the copy desk to call. From my office I could look across town to the weather signal on the Mutual of New York Building and the lights that alternately spelled out TIME and LIFE above Rockefeller Plaza; that pleased me obscurely, and so did walking uptown in the mauve eight o'clocks of early summer evenings and looking at things, Lowestoft tureens in Fifty-seventh Street windows, people in evening clothes trying to get taxis, the trees just coming into full leaf, the lambent air, all the sweet promises of money and summer.

Some years passed, but I still did not lose that sense of wonder about New York. I began to cherish the loneliness of it, the sense that at any given time no one need know where I was or what I was doing. I liked walking, from the East River over to the Hudson and back on brisk days, down around the Village on warm days. A friend would leave me the key to her apartment in the West Village when she was out of town, and sometimes I would just move down there, because by that time the telephone was beginning to bother me (the canker, you see, was already in the rose) and not many people had that number. I remember one day when someone who did have the West Village number came to pick me up for lunch there, and we both had hangovers, and I cut my finger opening him a beer and burst into tears, and we walked to a Spanish restaurant and drank Bloody Marys and *gazpacho* until we felt better. I was not then guilt-ridden about spending afternoons that way, because I still had all the afternoons in the world.

And even that late in the game I still liked going to parties, all parties, bad parties, Saturday-afternoon parties given by recently married couples who lived in Stuyvesant Town, West Side parties given by unpublished or failed writers who served cheap red wine and talked about going to Guadalajara, Village parties where all the guests worked for advertising agencies and voted for Reform Democrats, press parties at Sardi's, the worst kinds of parties. You will have perceived by now that I was not one to profit by the experience of others, that it was a very long time indeed before I stopped believing in new faces and began to understand the lesson in that story, which was that it is distinctly possible to stay too long at the Fair.

I could not tell you when I began to understand that. All I know is that it was very bad when I was twenty-eight. Everything that was said to me I seemed to have heard before, and I could no longer listen. I could no longer sit in little bars near Grand Central and listen to someone complaining of his wife's inability to cope with the help while he missed another train to Connecticut. I no longer had any interest in hearing about the advances other people had received from their publishers, about plays which were having second-act trouble in Philadelphia, or about people I would like very much if only I would come out and meet them. I had already met them, always. There were certain parts of the city which I had to avoid. I could not bear upper Madison Avenue on weekday mornings (this was a particularly inconvenient aversion, since I then lived just fifty or sixty feet east of Madison), because I would see women walking Yorkshire terriers and shopping at Gristede's, and some Veblenesque gorge would rise in my throat. I could not go to Times Square in the afternoon, or to the New York Public Library for any reason whatsoever. One day I could not go into a Schrafft's; the next day it would be Bonwit Teller.

I hurt the people I cared about, and insulted those I did not. I cut myself off from the one person who was closer to me than any other. I cried until I was not even aware when I was crying and when I was not, cried in elevators and in taxis and in Chinese laundries, and when I went to the doctor he said only that I seemed to be depressed, and should see a "specialist." He wrote down a psychiatrist's name and address for me, but I did not go.

Instead I got married, which as it turned out was a very good thing to do but badly timed, since I still could not walk on upper Madison Avenue in the mornings and still could not talk to people and still cried in Chinese laundries. I had never before understood what "despair" meant, and I am not sure that I understand now, but I understood that year. Of course I could not work. I could not even get dinner with any degree of certainty, and I would sit in the apartment on Seventy-fifth Street paralyzed until my husband would call from his office and say gently that I did not have to get dinner, that I could meet him at Michael's Pub or at Toots Shor's or at Sardi's East. And then one morning in April (we had been married in January) he called and told me that he wanted to get out of New York for a while, that he would take a six-month leave of absence, that we would go somewhere.

It was three years ago that he told me that, and we have lived in Los Angeles since. Many of the people we knew in New York think this a curious aberration, and in fact tell us so. There is no possible, no adequate answer to that, and so we give certain stock answers, the answers everyone gives. I talk about how difficult it would be for us to "afford" to live in New York right now, about how much "space" we need. All I mean is that I was very young in New York, and that at some point the golden rhythm was broken, and I am not that young any more. The last time I was in New York was in a cold January, and everyone was ill and tired. Many of the people I used to know there had moved to Dallas or had gone on Antabuse or had bought a farm in New Hampshire. We stayed ten days, and then we took an afternoon flight back to Los Angeles, and on the way home from the airport that night I could see the moon on the Pacific and smell jasmine all around and we both knew that there was no longer any point in keeping the apartment we still kept in New York. There were years when I called Los Angeles "the Coast," but they seem a long time ago.

1967

# ISAAC BASHEVIS SINGER

*Preeminent among the refugees from Hitler who so changed New York's (and America's) cultural climate was Isaac Bashevis Singer (1904–91). The Polish-born, Yiddish-language writer was for five decades a familiar sight on Manhattan's Upper West Side. "The Cafeteria," with its characteristic themes of exile, the supernatural, and sexuality, uncannily captures the lives of people still living, years later, under the shadow of the Holocaust.*

## THE CAFETERIA

EVEN THOUGH I have reached the point where a great part of my earnings is given away in taxes, I still have the habit of eating in cafeterias when I am by myself. I like to take a tray with a tin knife, fork, spoon, and paper napkin and to choose at the counter the food I enjoy. Besides, I meet there the *landsleit* from Poland, as well as all kinds of literary beginners and readers who know Yiddish. The moment I sit down at a table, they come over. "Hello, Aaron!" they greet me, and we talk about Yiddish literature, the Holocaust, the state of Israel, and often about acquaintances who were eating rice pudding or stewed prunes the last time I was here and are already in their graves. Since I seldom read a paper, I learn this news only later. Each time, I am startled, but at my age one has to be ready for such tidings. The food sticks in the throat; we look at one another in confusion, and our eyes ask mutely, Whose turn is next? Soon we begin to chew again. I am often reminded of a scene in a film about Africa. A lion attacks a herd of zebras and kills one. The frightened zebras run for a while and then they stop and start to graze again. Do they have a choice?

I cannot spend too long with these Yiddishists, because I am always busy. I am writing a novel, a story, an article. I have to lecture today or tomorrow; my datebook is crowded with all kinds of appointments for weeks and months in advance. It can happen that an hour after I leave the cafeteria I am on a train to Chicago or flying to

California. But meanwhile we converse in the mother language and I hear of intrigues and pettiness about which, from a moral point of view, it would be better not to be informed. Everyone tries in his own way with all his means to grab as many honors and as much money and prestige as he can. None of us learns from all these deaths. Old age does not cleanse us. We don't repent at the gate of hell.

I have been moving around in this neighborhood for over thirty years—as long as I lived in Poland. I know each block, each house. There has been little building here on uptown Broadway in the last decades, and I have the illusion of having put down roots here. I have spoken in most of the synagogues. They know me in some of the stores and in the vegetarian restaurants. Women with whom I have had affairs live on the side streets. Even the pigeons know me; the moment I come out with a bag of feed, they begin to fly toward me from blocks away. It is an area that stretches from Ninety-sixth Street to Seventy-second Street and from Central Park to Riverside Drive. Almost every day on my walk after lunch, I pass the funeral parlor that waits for us and all our ambitions and illusions. Sometimes I imagine that the funeral parlor is also a kind of cafeteria where one gets a quick eulogy or Kaddish on the way to eternity.

The cafeteria people I meet are mostly men: old bachelors like myself, would-be writers, retired teachers, some with dubious doctorate titles, a rabbi without a congregation, a painter of Jewish themes, a few translators—all immigrants from Poland or Russia. I seldom know their names. One of them disappears and I think he is already in the next world; suddenly he reappears and he tells me that he has tried to settle in Tel Aviv or Los Angeles. Again he eats his rice pudding, sweetens his coffee with saccharin. He has a few more wrinkles, but he tells the same stories and makes the same gestures. It may happen that he takes a paper from his pocket and reads me a poem he has written.

It was in the fifties that a woman appeared in the group who looked younger than the rest of us. She must have been in her early thirties; she was short, slim, with a girlish face, brown hair that she wore in a bun, a short nose, and dimples in her cheeks. Her eyes were hazel—actually, of an indefinite color. She dressed in a modest European way. She spoke Polish, Russian, and an idiomatic Yiddish. She always carried Yiddish newspapers and magazines. She had been in a prison camp in Russia and had spent some time in the camps in Germany before she obtained a visa for the United States. The men all hovered around her. They didn't let her pay the check. They gallantly brought her coffee and cheese cake. They listened to her talk and jokes. She had returned from the devastation still gay. She was introduced to me. Her name was Esther. I didn't know if she was unmarried, a widow, a divorcée. She told me she was working in a factory, where she sorted buttons. This fresh young woman did not fit into the group of elderly has-beens. It was also hard to understand why she couldn't find a better job than sorting buttons in New Jersey. But I didn't ask too many questions. She told me that she had read my writing while still in Poland, and later in the camps in Germany after the war. She said to me, "You are my writer."

The moment she uttered those words I imagined I was in love with her. We were sitting alone (the other man at our table had gone to make a telephone call), and I said, "For such words I must kiss you."

"Well, what are you waiting for?"

She gave me both a kiss and a bite.

I said, "You are a ball of fire."

"Yes, fire from Gehenna."

A few days later, she invited me to her home. She lived on a street between Broadway and Riverside Drive with her father, who had no legs and sat in a wheelchair. His legs had been frozen in Siberia. He had tried to run away from one of Stalin's slave camps in the winter of 1944. He looked like a strong man, had a head of thick white hair, a ruddy face, and eyes full of energy. He spoke in a swaggering fashion, with boyish boastfulness and a cheerful laugh. In an hour, he told me his story. He was born in White Russia but he had lived long years in Warsaw, Lodz, and Vilna. In the beginning of the thirties, he became a Communist and soon afterward a functionary in the Party. In 1939 he escaped to Russia with his daughter. His wife and the other children remained in Nazi-occupied Warsaw. In Russia, somebody denounced him as a Trotskyite and he was sent to mine gold in the north. The G.P.U. sent people there to die. Even the strongest could not survive the cold and hunger for more than a year. They were exiled without a sentence. They died together: Zionists, Bundists, members of the Polish Socialist Party, Ukrainian Nationalists, and just refugees, all caught because of the labor shortage. They often died of scurvy or beriberi. Boris Merkin, Esther's father, spoke about this as if it were a big joke. He called the Stalinists outcasts, bandits, sycophants. He assured me that had it not been for the United States Hitler would have overrun all of Russia. He told how prisoners tricked the guards to get an extra piece of bread or a double portion of watery soup, and what methods were used in picking lice.

Esther called out, "Father, enough!"

"What's the matter—am I lying?"

"One can have enough even of *kreplach*."

"Daughter, you did it yourself."

When Esther went to the kitchen to make tea, I learned from her father that she had had a husband in Russia—a Polish Jew who had volunteered in the Red Army and perished in the war. Here in New York she was courted by a refugee, a former smuggler in Germany who had opened a bookbinding factory and become rich. "Persuade her to marry him," Boris Merkin said to me. "It would be good for me, too."

"Maybe she doesn't love him."

"There is no such thing as love. Give me a cigarette. In the camp, people climbed on one another like worms."

## 2.

I had invited Esther to supper, but she called to say she had the grippe and must remain in bed. Then in a few days' time a situation arose that made me leave for Israel. On the way back, I stopped over in London and Paris. I wanted to write to Esther, but I had lost her address. When I returned to New York, I tried to call her, but there was no telephone listing for Boris Merkin or Esther Merkin—father and daughter must have been boarders in somebody else's apartment. Weeks passed and she did not show up in the cafeteria. I asked the group about her; nobody knew where she was. "She has most probably married that bookbinder," I said to myself. One evening, I went to the cafeteria with the premonition that I would find Esther there. I saw a black wall and boarded windows—the cafeteria had burned. The old bachelors were no doubt meeting in another cafeteria, or an Automat. But where? To search is not in my nature. I had plenty of complications without Esther.

The summer passed; it was winter. Late one day, I walked by the cafeteria and again saw lights, a counter, guests. The owners had rebuilt. I entered, took a check, and saw Esther sitting alone at a table reading a Yiddish newspaper. She did not notice me, and I observed her for a while. She wore a man's fur fez and a jacket trimmed with a faded fur collar. She looked pale, as though recuperating from a sickness. Could that grippe have been the start of a serious illness? I went over to her table and asked, "What's new in buttons?"

She started and smiled. Then she called out, "Miracles do happen!"

"Where have you been?"

"Where did you disappear to?" she replied. "I thought you were still abroad."

"Where are our *cafeterianiks?*"

"They now go to the cafeteria on Fifty-seventh Street and Eighth Avenue: They only reopened this place yesterday."

"May I bring you a cup of coffee?"

"I drink too much coffee. All right."

I went to get her coffee and a large egg cookie. While I stood at the counter, I turned my head and looked at her. Esther had taken off her mannish fur hat and smoothed her hair. She folded the newspaper, which meant that she was ready to talk. She got up and tilted the other chair against the table as a sign that the seat was taken. When I sat down, Esther said, "You left without saying goodbye, and there I was about to knock at the pearly gates of heaven."

"What happened?"

"Oh, the grippe became pneumonia. They gave me penicillin, and

I am one of those who cannot take it. I got a rash all over my body. My father, too, is not well."

"What's the matter with your father?"

"High blood pressure. He had a kind of stroke and his mouth became all crooked."

"Oh, I'm sorry. Do you still work with buttons?"

"Yes, with buttons. At least I don't have to use my head, only my hands. I can think my own thoughts."

"What do you think about?"

"What not. The other workers are all Puerto Ricans. They rattle away in Spanish from morning to night."

"Who takes care of your father?"

"Who? Nobody. I come home in the evening to make supper. He has one desire—to marry me off for my own good and, perhaps, for his comfort, but I can't marry a man I don't love."

"What is love?"

"You ask me! You write novels about it. But you're a man—I assume you really don't know what it is. A woman is a piece of merchandise to you. To me a man who talks nonsense or smiles like an idiot is repulsive. I would rather die than live with him. And a man who goes from one woman to another is not for me. I don't want to share with anybody."

"I'm afraid a time is coming when everybody will."

"That is not for me."

"What kind of person was your husband?"

"How did you know I had a husband? My father, I suppose. The minute I leave the room, he prattles. My husband believed in things and was ready to die for them. He was not exactly my type but I respected him and loved him, too. He wanted to die and he died like a hero. What else can I say?"

"And the others?"

"There were no others. Men were after me. The way people behaved in the war—you will never know. They lost all shame. On the bunks near me one time, a mother lay with one man and her daughter with another. People were like beasts—worse than beasts. In the middle of it all, I dreamed about love. Now I have even stopped dreaming. The men who come here are terrible bores. Most of them are half mad, too. One of them tried to read me a forty-page poem. I almost fainted."

"I wouldn't read you anything I'd written."

"I've been told how you behave—no!"

"No is no. Drink your coffee."

"You don't even try to persuade me. Most men around here plague you and you can't get rid of them. In Russia people suffered, but I have never met as many maniacs there as in New York City. The building where I live is a madhouse. My neighbors are lunatics. They accuse each other of all kinds of things. They sing, cry, break dishes. One of them jumped out of the window and killed herself. She was having an affair with a boy twenty years younger. In Russia the problem was to escape the lice; here you're surrounded by insanity."

We drank coffee and shared the egg cookie. Esther put down her cup. "I can't believe that I'm sitting with you at this table. I read all your articles under all your pen names. You tell so much about yourself I have the feeling I've known you for years. Still, you are a riddle to me."

"Men and women can never understand one another."

"No—I cannot understand my own father. Sometimes he is a complete stranger to me. He won't live long."

"Is he so sick?"

"It's everything together. He's lost the will to live. Why live without legs, without friends, without a family? They have all perished. He sits and reads the newspapers all day long. He acts as though he were interested in what's going on in the world. His ideals are gone, but he still hopes for a just revolution. How can a revolution help him? I myself never put my hopes in any movement or party. How can we hope when everything ends in death?"

"Hope in itself is a proof that there is no death."

"Yes, I know you often write about this. For me, death is the only comfort. What do the dead do? They continue to drink coffee and eat egg cookies? They still read newspapers? A life after death would be nothing but a joke."

3.

Some of the *cafeterianiks* came back to the rebuilt cafeteria. New people appeared—all of them Europeans. They launched into long discussions in Yiddish, Polish, Russian, even Hebrew. Some of those who came from Hungary mixed German, Hungarian, Yiddish-German—then all of a sudden they began to speak plain Galician Yiddish. They asked to have their coffee in glasses, and held lumps of sugar between their teeth when they drank. Many of them were my readers. They introduced themselves and reproached me for all kinds of literary errors: I contradicted myself, went too far in descriptions of sex, described Jews in such a way that anti-Semites could use it for propaganda. They told me their experiences in the ghettos, in the Nazi concentration camps, in Russia. They pointed out one another. "Do you see that fellow—in Russia he immediately became a Stalinist. He denounced his own friends. Here in America he has switched to anti-Bolshevism." The one who was spoken about seemed to sense that he was being maligned, because the moment my informant left he took his cup of coffee and his rice pudding, sat down at my table, and said, "Don't believe a word of what you are told. They invent all kinds of lies. What could you do in a country where the rope was always around your neck? You had to adjust yourself if you wanted to live and not die somewhere in Kazakhstan. To get a bowl of soup or a place to stay you had to sell your soul."

There was a table with a group of refugees who ignored me. They were not interested in literature and journalism but strictly in business. In Germany they had been smugglers. They seemed to be doing shady business here, too; they whispered to one another and winked, counted their money, wrote long lists of numbers. Somebody pointed out one of them. "He had a store in Auschwitz."

"What do you mean, a store?"

"God help us. He kept his merchandise in the straw where he slept—a rotten potato, sometimes a piece of soap, a tin spoon, a little fat. Still, he did business. Later, in Germany, he became such a big smuggler they once took forty thousand dollars away from him."

Sometimes months passed between my visits to the cafeteria. A year or two had gone by (perhaps three or four; I lost count), and Esther did not show up. I asked about her a few times. Someone said that she was going to the cafeteria on Forty-second Street; another had heard that she was married. I learned that some of the *cafeteri-aniks* had died. They were beginning to settle down in the United States, had remarried, opened businesses, workshops, even had children again. Then came cancer or a heart attack. The result of the Hitler and Stalin years, it was said.

One day, I entered the cafeteria and saw Esther. She was sitting alone at a table. It was the same Esther. She was even wearing the same fur hat, but a strand of gray hair fell over her forehead. How strange—the fur hat, too, seemed to have grayed. The other *cafeteri-aniks* did not appear to be interested in her any more, or they did not know her. Her face told of the time that had passed. There were shadows under her eyes. Her gaze was no longer so clear. Around her mouth was an expression that could be called bitterness, disenchantment. I greeted her. She smiled, but her smile immediately faded away. I asked, "What happened to you?"

"Oh, I'm still alive."

"May I sit down?"

"Please—certainly."

"May I bring you a cup of coffee?"

"No. Well, if you insist."

I noticed that she was smoking, and also that she was reading not the newspaper to which I contribute but a competition paper. She had gone over to the enemy. I brought her coffee and for myself stewed prunes—a remedy for constipation. I sat down. "Where were you all this time? I have asked for you."

"Really? Thank you."

"What happened?"

"Nothing good." She looked at me. I knew that she saw in me what I saw in her: the slow wilting of the flesh. She said, "You have no hair but you are white."

For a while we were silent. Then I said, "Your father—" and as I said it I knew that her father was not alive.

Esther said, "He has been dead for almost a year."

"Do you still sort buttons?"

"No, I became an operator in a dress shop."

"What happened to you personally, may I ask?"

"Oh nothing—absolutely nothing. You will not believe it, but I was sitting here thinking about you. I have fallen into some kind of trap. I don't know what to call it. I thought perhaps you could advise me. Do you still have the patience to listen to the troubles of little people like me? No, I didn't mean to insult you. I even doubted you would remember me. To make it short, I work but work is growing more difficult for me. I suffer from arthritis. I feel as if my bones would crack. I wake up in the morning and can't sit up. One doctor tells me that it's a disc in my back, others try to cure my nerves. One took X-rays and says that I have a tumor. He wanted me to go to the hospital for a few weeks, but I'm in no hurry for an operation. Suddenly a little lawyer showed up. He is a refugee himself and is connected with the German government. You know they're now giving reparation money. It's true that I escaped to Russia, but I'm a victim of the Nazis just the same. Besides, they don't know my biography so exactly. I could get a pension plus a few thousand dollars, but my dislocated disc is no good for the purpose because I got it later—after the camps. This lawyer says my only chance is to convince them that I am ruined psychically. It's the bitter truth, but how can you prove it? The German doctors, the neurologists, the psychiatrists require proof. Everything has to be according to the textbooks—just so and no different. The lawyer wants me to play insane. Naturally, he gets twenty per cent of the reparation money—maybe more. Why he needs so much money I don't understand. He's already in his seventies, an old bachelor. He tried to make love to me and whatnot. He's half *meshugga* himself. But how can I play insane when actually I *am* insane? The whole thing revolts me and I'm afraid it will really drive me crazy. I hate swindle. But this shyster pursues me. I don't sleep. When the alarm rings in the morning, I wake up as shattered as I used to be in Russia when I had to walk to the forest and saw logs at four in the morning. Naturally, I take sleeping pills—if I didn't, I couldn't sleep at all. That is more or less the situation."

[ 905 ]

"Why don't you get married? You are still a good-looking woman."

"Well, the old question—there is nobody. It's too late. If you knew how I felt, you wouldn't ask such a question."

## 4.

A few weeks passed. Snow had been falling. After the snow came rain, then frost. I stood at my window and looked out at Broadway. The passersby half walked, half slipped. Cars moved slowly. The sky above the roofs shone violet, without a moon, without stars, and even though it was eight o'clock in the evening the light and the emptiness reminded me of dawn. The stores were deserted. For a moment, I had the feeling I was in Warsaw. The telephone rang and I rushed to answer it as I did ten, twenty, thirty years ago—still expecting the good tidings that a telephone call was about to bring me. I said hello, but there was no answer and I was seized by the fear that some evil power was trying to keep back the good news at the last minute. Then I heard a stammering. A woman's voice muttered my name.

"Yes, it is I."

"Excuse me for disturbing you. My name is Esther. We met a few weeks ago in the cafeteria—"

"Esther!" I exclaimed.

"I don't know how I got the courage to phone you. I need to talk to you about something. Naturally, if you have the time and—please forgive my presumption."

"No presumption. Would you like to come to my apartment?"

"If I will not be interrupting. It's difficult to talk in the cafeteria. It's noisy and there are eavesdroppers. What I want to tell you is a secret I wouldn't trust to anyone else."

"Please, come up."

I gave Esther directions. Then I tried to make order in my apartment, but I soon realized this was impossible. Letters, manuscripts lay around on tables and chairs. In the corners books and magazines were piled high. I opened the closets and threw inside whatever was under my hand: jackets, pants, shirts, shoes, slippers. I picked up an envelope and to my amazement saw that it had never been opened. I tore it open and found a check. "What's the matter with me—have I lost my mind?" I said out loud. I tried to read the letter that came with the check, but I had misplaced my glasses; my fountain pen was gone, too. Well—and where were my keys? I heard a bell ring and I didn't know whether it was the door or the telephone. I opened the door and saw Esther. It must have been snowing again, because her hat and the shoulders of her coat were trimmed with white. I asked her in, and my neighbor, the divorcée, who spied on me openly with no shame—and, God knows, with no sense of purpose—opened her door and stared at my guest.

Esther removed her boots and I took her coat and put it on the case of the Encyclopedia Britannica. I shoved a few manuscripts off the sofa so she could sit down. I said, "In my house there is sheer chaos."

"It doesn't matter."

I sat in an armchair strewn with socks and handkerchiefs. For a while we spoke about the weather, about the danger of being out in New York at night—even early in the evening. Then Esther said, "Do you remember the time I spoke to you about my lawyer—that I had to go to a psychiatrist because of the reparation money?"

"Yes, I remember."

"I didn't tell you everything. It was too wild. It still seems unbelievable, even to me. Don't interrupt me, I implore you. I'm not completely healthy—I may even say that I'm sick—but I know the difference between fact and illusion. I haven't slept for nights, and I kept wondering whether I should call you or not. I decided not to—but this evening it occurred to me that if I couldn't trust you with a thing like this, then there is no one I could talk to. I read you and I know that you have a sense of the great mysteries—" Esther said all this stammering and with pauses. For a moment her eyes smiled, and then they became sad and wavering.

I said, "You can tell me everything."

"I am afraid that you'll think me insane."

"I swear I will not."

Esther bit her lower lip. "I want you to know that I saw Hitler," she said.

Even though I was prepared for something unusual, my throat constricted. "When—where?"

"You see, you are frightened already. It happened three years ago—almost four. I saw him here on Broadway."

"On the street?"

"In the cafeteria."

I tried to swallow the lump in my throat. "Most probably someone resembling him," I said finally.

"I knew you would say that. But remember, you've promised to listen. You recall the fire in the cafeteria?"

"Yes, certainly."

"The fire has to do with it. Since you don't believe me anyhow, why draw it out? It happened this way. That night I didn't sleep. Usually when I can't sleep, I get up and make tea, or I try to read a book, but this time some power commanded me to get dressed and go out. I can't explain to you how I dared walk on Broadway at that late hour. It must have been two or three o'clock. I reached the cafeteria, thinking perhaps it stays open all night. I tried to look in, but the large window was covered by a curtain. There was a pale glow inside. I tried the revolving door and it turned. I went in and saw a scene I will not forget to the last day of my life. The tables were shoved together and around them sat men in white robes, like doctors or orderlies, all with swastikas on their sleeves. At the head sat Hitler. I beg you to hear me out—even a deranged person sometimes deserves to be listened to. They all spoke German. They didn't see me. They were busy with the Führer. It grew quiet and he started to talk. That abominable voice—I heard it many times on the radio. I didn't make out exactly what he said. I was too terrified to take it in. Suddenly one of his henchmen looked back at me and jumped up from his chair. How I came out alive I will never know. I ran with all my strength, and I was trembling all over. When I got home, I said to myself, 'Esther, you are not right in the head.' I still don't know how I lived through that night. The next morning, I didn't go straight to work but walked to the cafeteria to see if it was really there. Such an experience makes a person doubt his own senses. When I arrived, I found the place had burned down. When I saw this, I knew it had to do with what I had seen. Those who were there wanted all traces erased. These are the plain facts. I have no reason to fabricate such queer things."

We were both silent. Then I said, "You had a vision."

"What do you mean, a vision?"

"The past is not lost. An image from years ago remained present somewhere in the fourth dimension and it reached you just at that moment."

"As far as I know, Hitler never wore a long white robe."

"Perhaps he did."

"Why did the cafeteria burn down just that night?" Esther asked.

"It could be that the fire evoked the vision."

"There was no fire then. Somehow I foresaw that you would give me this kind of explanation. If this was a vision, my sitting here with you is also a vision."

"It couldn't have been anything else. Even if Hitler is living and is hiding out in the United States, he is not likely to meet his cronies at a cafeteria on Broadway. Besides, the cafeteria belongs to a Jew."

"I saw him as I am seeing you now."

"You had a glimpse back in time."

"Well, let it be so. But since then I have had no rest. I keep thinking about it. If I am destined to lose my mind, this will drive me to it."

The telephone rang and I jumped up with a start. It was a wrong number. I sat down again. "What about the psychiatrist your lawyer sent you to? Tell it to him and you'll get full compensation."

Esther looked at me sidewise and unfriendly. "I know what you mean. I haven't fallen that low yet."

### 5.

I was afraid that Esther would continue to call me. I even planned to change my telephone number. But weeks and months passed and I never heard from her or saw her. I didn't go to the cafeteria. But I often thought about her. How can the brain produce such nightmares? What goes on in that little marrow behind the skull? And what guarantee do I have that the same sort of thing will not happen to me? And how do we know that the human species will not end like this? I have played with the idea that all of humanity suffers from schizophrenia. Along with the atom, the personality of *Homo sapiens* has been splitting. When it comes to technology, the brain still functions, but in everything else degeneration has begun. They are all insane: the Communists, the Fascists, the preachers of democracy, the writers, the painters, the clergy, the atheists. Soon technology, too, will disintegrate. Buildings will collapse, power plants will stop generating electricity. Generals will drop atomic bombs on their own populations. Mad revolutionaries will run in the streets, crying fantastic slogans. I have often thought that it would begin in New York. This metropolis has all the symptoms of a mind gone berserk.

But since insanity has not yet taken over altogether, one has to act as though there were still order—according to Vaihinger's principle of "as if." I continued with my scribbling. I delivered manuscripts to the publisher. I lectured. Four times a year, I sent checks to the federal government, the state. What was left after my expenses I put in the savings bank. A teller entered some numbers in my bankbook and this meant that I was provided for. Somebody printed a few lines in a magazine or newspaper, and this signified that my value as a writer had gone up. I saw with amazement that all my efforts turned into paper. My apartment was one big wastepaper basket. From day to day, all this paper was getting drier and more parched. I woke up at night fearful that it would ignite. There was not an hour when I did not hear the sirens of fire engines.

A year after I had last seen Esther, I was going to Toronto to read a paper about Yiddish in the second half of the nineteenth century. I put a few shirts in my valise as well as papers of all kinds, among them one that made me a citizen of the United States. I had enough paper money in my pocket to pay for a taxi to Grand Central. But the taxis seemed to be taken. Those that were not refused to stop. Didn't the drivers see me? Had I suddenly become one of those who see and are not seen? I decided to take the subway. On my way, I saw Esther. She was not alone but with someone I had known years ago, soon after I arrived in the United States. He was a frequenter of a cafeteria on East Broadway. He used to sit at a table, express opinions, criticize, grumble. He was a small man, with sunken cheeks the color of brick, and bulging eyes. He was angry at the new writers. He belittled the old ones. He rolled his own cigarettes and dropped ashes into the plates from which we ate. Almost two decades had passed since I had last seen him. Suddenly he appears with Esther. He was even holding her arm. I had never seen Esther look so well. She was wearing a new coat, a new hat. She smiled at me and nodded. I wanted to stop her, but my watch showed that it was late. I barely managed to catch the train. In my bedroom, the bed was already made. I undressed and went to sleep.

In the middle of the night, I awoke. My car was being switched, and I almost fell out of bed. I could not sleep any more and I tried to remember the name of the little man I had seen with Esther. But I was unable to. The thing I did remember was that even thirty years ago he had been far from young. He had come to the United States in 1905 after the revolution in Russia. In Europe, he had a reputation as a speaker and public figure. How old must he be now? According to my calculations, he had to be in the late eighties—perhaps even ninety. Is it possible that Esther could be intimate with such an old man? But this evening he had not looked old. The longer I brooded about it in the darkness, the stranger the encounter seemed to me. I even imagined that somewhere in a newspaper I had read that he had died. Do corpses walk around on Broadway? This would mean that Esther, too, was not living. I raised the window shade and sat up and looked out into the night—black, impenetrable, without a moon. A few stars ran along with the train for a while and then they disappeared. A lighted factory emerged; I saw machines but no operators. Then it was swallowed in the darkness and another group of stars began to follow the train. I was turning with the earth on its axis. I was circling with it around the sun and moving in the direction of a constellation whose name I had forgotten. Is there no death? Or is there no life?

I thought about what Esther had told me of seeing Hitler in the cafeteria. It had seemed utter nonsense, but now I began to reappraise the idea. If time and space are nothing more than forms of perception, as Kant argues, and quality, quantity, causality are only categories of thinking, why shouldn't Hitler confer with his Nazis in a cafeteria on Broadway? Esther didn't sound insane. She had seen a piece of reality that the heavenly censorship prohibits as a rule. She had caught a glimpse behind the curtain of the phenomena. I regretted that I had not asked for more details.

In Toronto, I had little time to ponder these matters, but when I returned to New York I went to the cafeteria for some private investigation. I met only one man I knew: a rabbi who had become an agnostic and given up his job. I asked him about Esther. He said, "The pretty little woman who used to come here?"

"Yes."

"I heard that she committed suicide."

"When—how?"

"I don't know. Perhaps we are not speaking about the same person."

No matter how many questions I asked and how much I described Esther, everything remained vague. Some young woman who used to come here had turned on the gas and made an end of herself—that was all the ex-rabbi could tell me.

I decided not to rest until I knew for certain what had happened to Esther and also to that half writer, half politician I remembered from East Broadway. But I grew busier from day to day. The cafeteria closed. The neighborhood changed. Years have passed and I have never seen Esther again. Yes, corpses do walk on Broadway. But why did Esther choose that particular corpse? She could have got a better bargain even in this world.

1 9 6 8

# JIMMY CANNON

---

*The clipped, tough-guy style of tabloid columnists like Walter Winchell, Jimmy Cannon, and Jimmy Breslin is an enduring part of New York's identity and literary record. Cannon (1909–73), a sportswriter for the New York Post whose prose earned praise from his literary mentor Ernest Hemingway, wrote some of his most vivid columns about the city's gritty boxing world.*

## LOU STILLMAN

THE STOOPED old man spoke a private language of insult and a .38 bulged in his hip pocket. The voice was grouchy and harsh. If New York could talk, it would sound like Lou Stillman, who died this week at eighty-two. He ran Stillman's Gym on Eighth Avenue in New York City. Once there was a hockshop on the same block, and winos slept off their afternoon loads in the doorway. Now it is a street of motels and apartment houses.

The great champions worked in the old man's gym and so did the ones with the brains punched soft in their heads. The wreckers tore it down and a lot of the fight racket went with it. It belonged in the great years, going all the way back to Jack Dempsey. It was a bleak loft with dirty windows and you reached it by going up a dark flight of splintered wooden stairs. There were two rings and, in the big days of boxing, fighters stood in line and practiced, two at a time, from morning until dusk. Upstairs, on a balcony, were the heavy bags and the speed bags. The old man realized it was going away from him when he was forced to stay open evenings. TV had ruined the small clubs. There weren't enough places for the kids to fight. They took jobs in the daytime and fought as a sideline.

The fight mob respected Stillman. The gun didn't impress them, because a lot of guys were out of the mobs and killed people for a living. He could shout them down and he rousted all of them and threw them out if he suspected they were locker thieves or were too rough with the towels.

Stillman's was the post office of the fight racket. Promoters from out of town would call the phone booths and there was always a manager around who could fill their cards.

Once I was awakened by a phone call from Rocky Graziano.

"Come on over to Stillman's," he said. "I got a scoop for you."

I dressed rapidly and was gasping for breath after running up the stairs. A guy in a zoot suit under a big hat was waiting for me and steered me back into the dressing room, where Graziano sat on a rubbing table.

"Go," he said to another guy who wore blue working pants and was naked from the waist up.

The guy held a harmonica against his nostrils and blew the breath out of his nose. Slowly, the harmonica wheezed "Swanee River."

"The only man in the world who could play 'Swanee River' with his nose," Graziano said when the concert was over. "He could make a million dollars."

The guy stood there, proud and smiling, and the middleweight champion of the world slapped him on the back and requested an encore. Years afterward there was an underworld outfit called the Gallos, who were getting a big play in the papers. They had challenged the Mafia and I wondered who they were.

"You know them," Graziano said. "Remember the guy in the zoot suit brought you back to hear the jerk play the harmonica with his nose? That was one of the Gallos."

Once I was standing at the lunch counter drinking coffee with Eddie Walker, the fight manager. He turned and there was Chalky Wright, then the featherweight champion of the world. The fighter needed a shave, and his stubble of a beard was white.

"Go down and get a shave," Walker told him. "I told you not to come around here without a shave. They'll pick up your license you look so old. You could be your own father."

There was an afternoon when Tony Kelly, a fight manager, told me he wanted to be described by the name on his birth certificate. He was born Tony Lento. He was standing near the phone when another manager answered it.

"What Tony Kelly you want?" the guy asked. "The Italian one . . . the Irish one . . . the Jewish one?"

He is dead and so are Wright and Walker. And now it's Lou Stillman. The old Garden is a parking lot. Stillman's Gym is an apartment house. The guy who played the harmonica with his nose didn't make the million dollars.

And all around the town the fight mob talked about Lou Stillman and guys laughed. Laughter is a beautiful obituary.

1 9 6 9

# JAMES SCHUYLER

James Schuyler (1923–91) was, along with Frank O'Hara, John Ashbery, Kenneth Koch, and Edwin Denby, a leading light of what became known as the New York School of poetry. Some of Schuyler's New York poems, like "February," have the patient, almost egoless, descriptive purity of classical Chinese verse. Others are unnervingly candid about his mental illnesses, hospitalizations, and unhappy love affairs. A knowledge of New York history underpins his work, as demonstrated in the elegiac poem "Dining Out With Doug and Frank."

## FEBRUARY

A chimney, breathing a little smoke.
The sun, I can't see
making a bit of pink
I can't quite see in the blue.
The pink of five tulips
at five P.M. on the day before March first.
The green of the tulip stems and leaves
like something I can't remember,
finding a jack-in-the-pulpit
a long time ago and far away.
Why it was December then
and the sun was on the sea
by the temples we'd gone to see.
One green wave moved in the violet sea
like the UN building on big evenings,
green and wet
while the sky turns violet.
A few almond trees
had a few flowers, like a few snowflakes
out of the blue looking pink in the light.
A gray hush
in which the boxy trucks roll up Second Avenue

into the sky. They're just
going over the hill.
The green leaves of the tulips on my desk
like grass light on flesh,
and a green-copper steeple
and streaks of cloud beginning to glow.
I can't get over
how it all works in together
like a woman who just came to her window
and stands there filling it
jogging her baby in her arms.
She's so far off. Is it the light
that makes the baby pink?
I can see the little fists
and the rocking-horse motion of her breasts.
It's getting grayer and gold and chilly.
Two dog-size lions face each other
at the corners of a roof.
It's the yellow dust inside the tulips.
It's the shape of a tulip.
It's the water in the drinking glass the tulips are in.
It's a day like any other.

1 9 6 9

## DINING OUT WITH DOUG AND FRANK

For Frank Polach

Not quite yet. First,
around the corner for a visit
to the Bella Landauer Collection
of printed ephemera:
luscious lithos and why did
Fairy Soap vanish and
Crouch and Fitzgerald survive?

Fairy Soap was once a
household word! I've been living
at Broadway and West 74th
for a week and still haven't
ventured on a stroll in
Central Park, two bizarre blocks
away. (Bizarre is for the ex-
town houses, mixing Byzantine
with Gothic and Queen Anne.)
My abstention from the park
is for Billy Nichols who went
bird-watching there and, for
his binoculars, got his
head beat in. Streaming blood,
he made it to an avenue
where no cab would pick him up
until one did and at
Roosevelt Hospital he waited
several hours before any
doctor took him in hand. A
year later he was dead. But
I'll make the park: I carry
more cash than I should and
walk the street at night
without feeling scared unless
someone scary passes.

II

Now it's tomorrow,
as usual. Turned out that
Doug (Douglas Crase, the poet)
had to work (he makes his bread
writing speeches): thirty pages
explaining why Eastman Kodak's
semi-slump (?) is just what
the stockholders ordered. He

looked glum, and declined
a drink. By the by did you know
that John Ashbery's grandfather
was offered an investment-in
when George Eastman founded his
great corporation? He turned it
down. Eastman Kodak will survive.
"Yes" and where would our
John be now? I can't imagine him
any different than he is,
a problem which does not arise,
so I went with Frank (the poet,
he makes his dough as a librarian,
botanical librarian at Rutgers
and as a worker he's a beaver:
up at 5:30, home after 7, but
over striped bass he said he
had begun to see the unwisdom
of his ways and next week will
revert to the seven-hour day
for which he's paid. Good. Time
and energy to write. Poetry
takes it out of you, or you
have to have a surge to bring
to it. Words. So useful and
pleasant) to dine at McFeely's
at West 23rd and Eleventh Avenue
by the West River, which is
the right name for the Hudson
when it bifurcates from
the East River to create
Manhattan "an isle of joy."
Take my word for it, don't
(shall I tell you about my
friend who effectively threw
himself under a train in

the Times Square station?
No. Too tender to touch. In
fact, at the moment I've blocked
out his name. No I haven't:
Peter Kemeny, gifted and tormented
fat man) listen to anyone
else.

### III

Oh. At the Battery all
that water becomes the
North River, which seems
to me to make no sense
at all. I always thought
Castle Garden faced Calais.

### IV

Peconic Bay scallops, the
tiny, the real ones and cooked
in butter, not breaded and
plunged in deep grease. The food
is good and reasonable (for these
days) but the point is McFeely's
itself—the owner's name or
was it always called that? It's
the bar of the old Terminal Hotel
and someone (McFeely?) has had
the wit to restore it to what
it was: all was there, under
layers of paint and abuse, neglect.
You, perhaps, could put a date
on it: I'll vote for 1881
or the 70's. The ceiling is
florid glass, like the cabbage-rose
runners in the grand hotels
at Saratoga: when were they built?

The bar is thick and long and
sinuous, virile. Mirrors: are
the decorations on them cut
or etched? I do remember that
above the men's room door the
word Toilet is etched
on a transom. Beautiful lettering,
but nothing to what lurks
within: the three most
splendid urinals I've ever
seen. Like Roman steles. I
don't know what I was going
to say. Yes. Does the Terminal Hotel
itself still function? (Did you
know that "they" sold all the
old mirror glass out of Gage
and Tollner's? Donald Droll has
a fit every time he eats there.)
"Terminal," I surmise, because
the hotel faced the terminal
of the 23rd Street ferry, a
perfect sunset sail to Hoboken
and the yummies of the Clam
Broth House, which, thank God,
still survives. Not many do:
Gage and Tollner's, the Clam Broth House,
McSorley's and now McFeely's. Was
that the most beautiful of the
ferry houses or am I thinking
of Christopher Street? And there
was another uptown that crossed
to Jersey and back but docking
further downtown: it sailed
on two diagonals. And wasn't
there one at 42nd? It couldn't
matter less, they're gone, all

gone and we are left with just
the Staten Island ferry, all
right in its way but how often
do you want to pass Miss Liberty
and see that awesome spiky postcard
view? The river ferryboats were
squat and low like tugs, old
and wooden and handsome, you
were *in* the water, *in* the shipping:
Millay wrote a poem about
it all. I cannot accept their
death, or any other death. Bill
Aalto, my first lover (five tumultuous
years found Bill chasing me around
the kitchen table—in Wystan Auden's
house in Forio d'Ischia—with
a carving knife. He was serious
and so was I and so I wouldn't go
when he wanted to see me when
he was dying of leukemia. Am I
sorry? Not really. The fear had
gone too deep. The last time I
saw him was in the City Center lobby
and he was jolly—if he just
stared at you and the tears began
it was time to cut and run—
and the cancer had made him lose
a lot of weight and he looked
young and handsome as the night
we picked each other up
in Pop Tunick's long-gone gay bar.
Bill never let me forget that
on the jukebox I kept playing
Lena Horne's "Mad about the Boy."
Why the nagging teasing? It's

a great performance but he
thought it was East Fifties queen
taste. Funny—or, funnily enough—
in dreams, and I dream about him
a lot, he's always the nice guy
I first knew and loved, not
the figure of terror he became.
Oh well. Bill had his hour: he
was a hero, a major in the
Abraham Lincoln Brigade. A dark
Finn who looked not unlike
a butch version of Valentino.
Watch out for Finns. They're
murder when they drink) used
to ride the ferries all the
time, doing the bars along
the waterfront: did you know
Hoboken has—or had—
more bars (Death.
At least twice when
someone I knew and hated
died I felt the joy of vengeance:
I mean I smiled and laughed out
loud: a hateful feeling.
It passes) to the square inch
than any other city? "Trivia,
Goddess . . ." Through dinner
I wanted to talk more than we
did about Frank's poems. All it
came down to was "experiment
more," "try collages," and "write
some skinny poems" but I like
where he's heading now and
Creative Writing has never
been my trip although I understand

the fun of teaching someone
something fun to do although most people
simply have not got the gift
and where's the point? What
puzzles me is what my friends
find to say. Oh, forget it. Reading,
writing, knowing other poets
will do it, if there is
anything doing. The reams
of shit I've read. It would
have been so nice after dinner
to take a ferry boat with Frank
across the Hudson (or West River,
if you prefer). To be on
the water in the dark and
the wonder of electricity—
the real beauty of Manhattan.
Oh well. When they tore down
the Singer Building,
and when I saw the Bogardus Building
rusty and coming unstitched in
a battlefield of rubble I deliberately
withdrew my emotional investments
in loving old New York. Except
you can't. I really like
dining out and last night was
especially fine. A full moon
when we parted hung over
Frank and me. Why is this poem
so long? And full of death?
Frank and Doug are young and
beautiful and have nothing
to do with that. Why is this poem
so long? "Enough is as good
as a feast" and I'm a Herrick fan.
I'd like to take that plunge

into Central Park, only I'm
waiting for Darragh Park to phone.
Oh. Doug and Frank. One is light,
the other dark.
Doug is the tall one.

1980

# ALLEN GINSBERG

The poet Allen Ginsberg (1926–97) lived most of his adult life in the
Lower East Side tenement area he describes here. For Ginsberg, a practicing Buddhist, close observation of the present amounted to a spiritual
discipline. In "Mugging," he draws on Whitman's long lines and his own
deep-breathing practice to come to terms with an all-too-common experience of 1970's New York.

## MUGGING

### I

Tonite I walked out of my red apartment door on East tenth street's
    dusk—

Walked out of my home ten years, walked out in my honking
    neighborhood

Tonite at seven walked out past garbage cans chained to concrete
    anchors

Walked under black painted fire escapes, giant castiron plate
    covering a hole in ground

—Crossed the street, traffic lite red, thirteen bus roaring by liquor
    store,

past corner pharmacy iron grated, past Coca Cola & Mylai posters
    fading scraped on brick

Past Chinese Laundry wood door'd, & broken cement stoop steps
    For Rent hall painted green & purple Puerto Rican style

Along E. 10th's glass splattered pavement, kid blacks & Spanish oiled
    hair adolescents' crowded house fronts—

Ah, tonite I walked out on my block NY City under humid summer
    sky Halloween,

thinking what happened Timothy Leary joining brain police for a
    season?

thinking what's all this Weathermen, secrecy & selfrighteousness
    beyond reason—F.B.I. plots?

Walked past a taxicab controlling the bottle strewn curb—
past young fellows with their umbrella handles & canes leaning
    against a ravaged Buick
—and as I looked at the crowd of kids on the stoop—a boy stepped
    up, put his arm around my neck
tenderly I thought for a moment, squeezed harder, his umbrella
    handle against my skull,
and his friends took my arm, a young brown companion tripped his
    foot 'gainst my ankle—
as I went down shouting Om Ah Hūṃ to gangs of lovers on the
    stoop watching
slowly appreciating, why this is a raid, these strangers mean strange
    business
with what—my pockets, bald head, broken-healed-bone leg, my
    softshoes, my heart—
Have they knives? Om Ah Hūṃ—Have they sharp metal wood to
    shove in eye ear ass? Om Ah Hūṃ
& slowly reclined on the pavement, struggling to keep my woolen
    bag of poetry address calendar & Leary-lawyer notes hung
    from my shoulder
dragged in my neat orlon shirt over the crossbar of a broken metal
    door
dragged slowly onto the fire-soiled floor an abandoned store,
    laundry candy counter 1929—
now a mess of papers & pillows & plastic car seat covers cracked
    cockroach-corpsed ground—
my wallet back pocket passed over the iron foot step guard
and fell out, stole by God Muggers' lost fingers, Strange—
Couldn't tell—snakeskin wallet actually plastic, 70 dollars my bank
    money for a week,
old broken wallet—and dreary plastic contents—Amex card &
    Manf. Hanover Trust Credit too—business card from Mr.
    Spears British Home Minister Drug Squad—my draft card—
    membership ACLU & Naropa Institute Instructor's
    identification
Om Ah Hūṃ I continued chanting Om Ah Hūṃ

Putting my palm on the neck of an 18 year old boy fingering my
    back pocket crying "Where's the money"
"Om Ah Hūm there isn't any"
My card Chief Boo-Hoo Neo American Church New Jersey &
    Lower East Side
Om Ah Hūm—what not forgotten crowded wallet—Mobil Credit,
    Shell? old lovers addresses on cardboard pieces, booksellers
    calling cards—
—"Shut up or we'll murder you"—"Om Ah Hūm take it easy"
Lying on the floor shall I shout more loud?—the metal door closed
    on blackness
one boy felt my broken healed ankle, looking for hundred dollar bills
    behind my stocking weren't even there—a third boy untied my
    Seiko Hong Kong watch rough from right wrist leaving a clasp-
    prick skin tiny bruise
"Shut up and we'll get out of here"—and so they left,
as I rose from the cardboard mattress thinking Om Ah Hūm didn't
    stop em enough,
the tone of voice too loud—my shoulder bag with 10,000 dollars
    full of poetry left on the broken floor—

                                *November 2, 1974*

## II

Went out the door dim eyed, bent down & picked up my glasses
    from step edge I placed them while dragged in the store—
    looked out—
Whole street a bombed-out face, building rows' eyes & teeth
    missing
burned apartments half the long block, gutted cellars, hallways'
    charred beams
hanging over trash plaster mounded entrances, couches &
    bedsprings rusty after sunset
Nobody home, but scattered stoopfuls of scared kids frozen in black
    hair chatted giggling at house doors in black shoes, families
    cooked For Rent some six story houses mid the street's
    wreckage

Nextdoor Bodega, a phone, the police? "I just got mugged" I said
to the man's face under fluorescent grocery light tin ceiling—
puffy, eyes blank & watery, sickness of beer kidney and language
    tongue
thick lips stunned as my own eyes, poor drunken Uncle minding the
    store!
O hopeless city of idiots empty eyed staring afraid, red beam top'd
    car at street curb arrived—
"Hey maybe my wallet's still on the ground got a flashlight?"
Back into the burnt-doored cave, & the policeman's gray flashlight
    broken no eyebeam—
"My partner all he wants is sit in the car never gets out Hey Joe
    bring your flashlight—"
a tiny throwaway beam, dim as a match in the criminal dark
"No I can't see anything here" . . . "Fill out this form"
Neighborhood street crowd behind a car "We didn't see nothing"
Stoop young girls, kids laughing "Listen man last time I messed with
    them see this—"
rolled up his skinny arm shirt, a white knife scar on his brown
    shoulder
"Besides we help you the cops come don't know anybody we all get
    arrested
go to jail I never help no more mind my business everytime"
"Agh!" upstreet think "Gee I don't know anybody here ten years
    lived half block crost Avenue C
and who knows who?"—passing empty apartments, old lady with
    frayed paper bags
sitting in the tin-boarded doorframe of a dead house.

                    *December 10, 1974*

## FOURTH FLOOR, DAWN,
## UP ALL NIGHT WRITING LETTERS

Pigeons shake their wings on the copper church roof
out my window across the street, a bird perched on the cross
surveys the city's blue-gray clouds. Larry Rivers
'll come at 10 A.M. and take my picture. I'm taking
your picture, pigeons. I'm writing you down, Dawn.
I'm immortalizing your exhaust, Avenue A bus.
O Thought, now you'll have to think the same thing forever!

*New York, June 7, 1980, 6:48 A.M.*

# ELIZABETH HARDWICK

*In her memoir-cum-novel* Sleepless Nights, *the distinguished essayist and literary critic Elizabeth Hardwick (1916–    ) memorably describes a Manhattan of the lonely and impoverished, set in a twilit landscape of cheap hotels and jazz clubs. Presiding over this world is the charismatic jazz singer Billie Holiday, whose magical presence is hauntingly evoked here.*

## FROM *SLEEPLESS NIGHTS*

WE LIVED THERE in the center of Manhattan, scorning the ups and downs, somehow believing the very placing of the hotel to be an overwhelming beneficence. No star was to be seen in the heavens, but the sky was always bright with the flicker of distant lights. No tree was to be seen, but as if by a miracle little heaps of twigs and blown leaves gathered in the gutters. To live in the obscuring jungle in the midst of things: close to—what? Within walking distance of all those places one never walked to.

But it was history, wasn't it? The acrimonious twilight fell into the hollows between the gray and red buildings. Inside, the hotel was a sort of underbrush, a swampy footing for the irregular. What a mark the old hotel dwellers leave on your own unsteady heart— their brooding inconsequences, their delusions and disappearances.

These people, and some had been there for years, lived as if in a house recently burglarized, wires cut, their world vandalized, their memory a lament of peculiar losses. It was as if they had robbed themselves, and that gave a certain cheerfulness. Do not imagine that in the reduction to the rented room they received nothing in return. They got a lot, I tell you. They were lifted by insolence above their forgotten loans, their surly arrears, their misspent matrimonies, their many debts which seemed to fall with relief into the wastebaskets where they would be picked up by the night men.

The Automat with its woeful, watery macaroni, its bready meat loaf, the cubicles of drying sandwiches; mud, glue and leather, from these textures you made your choice. The miseries of the deformed diners and their revolting habits; they were necessary, like a sewer, like the Bowery, Klein's, 14th Street. Every great city is a Lourdes where you hope to throw off your crutches but meanwhile must stumble along on them, hobbling under the protection of the shrine.

The Hotel Schuyler was more than a little sleazy and a great deal of sleazy life went on there. Its spotted rugs and walls were a challenge no effort could meet and the rootlessness hardened over everything, like a scab. Repetition—no one ever escapes it, and these poor people who were trying were the most trapped of all.

Midtown—look toward the east, toward many beautiful and bright things for sale. Turn the eyes westward—a nettling thicket of drunks, actors, gamblers, waiters, people who slept all day in their graying underwear and gave off a far from fresh odor when they dressed in their brown suits and brown snap-brim hats for the evening's inchoate activities. At that time these loosely connected persons had about them an air that was sometimes thick and dumb and yet passive; the faces on the streets had not yet frozen into an expression of danger and assault, of malice and fearlessness, the glaze of death in the daylight.

The small, futile shops around us explained how little we know of ourselves and how perplexing are our souvenirs and icons. Watch the strangers in the city, poor people, in a daze, making decisions, exchanging coins and bills for the incurious curiosities, the unexceptional novelties. Sixth Avenue lies buried in the drawers, bureaus, boxes, attics, and cellars of grandchildren. There, blackening, are the dead watches, the long, oval rings for the little finger, the smooth pieces of polished wood shaped into a long-chinned African head, the key rings of the Empire State building. And there were little, blaring shops, narrow as a cell, open most of the night, where were sold old, scratched, worn-thin jazz and race records—Vocalion, Okeh, and Brunswick labels.

And the shifty jazz clubs on 52nd Street, with their large blow-ups of faces, instruments, and names. Little men, chewing on cigars, outside in the cold or the heat, calling out the names of performers, saying: Three Nights Only, or Last New York Appearance.

At the curb, getting out of a taxi, or at the White Rose Bar drinking, there "they" were, the great performers with their worn, brown faces, enigmatic in the early evening, their coughs, their split lips and yellow eyes; their clothes, crisp and bright and hard as the bone-fibered feathers of a bird.

And there she often was— the "bizarre deity," Billie Holiday.

*Real* people: nothing like your mother and father, nothing like those friends from long ago now living in the family house alone, with the silver and the pictures, a few new lamps and a new roof— set up at last, preparing to die.

At night in the cold winter moonlight, around 1943, the city pageantry was of a benign sort. Adolescents were sleeping and the threat was only in the landscape, aesthetic. Dirty slush in the gutters, a lost black overshoe, a pair of white panties, perhaps thrown from a passing car. Murderous dissipation went with the music, inseparable, skin and bone. And always her luminous self-destruction.

She was fat the first time we saw her, large, brilliantly beautiful, fat. She seemed for this moment that never again returned to be almost a matron, someone real and sensible who carried money to the bank, signed papers, had curtains made to match, dresses hung and shoes in pairs, gold and silver, black and white, ready. What a strange, betraying apparition that was, madness, because never was any woman less a wife or mother, less attached; not even a daughter could she easily appear to be. Little called to mind the pitiful sweetness of a young girl. No, she was glittering, somber and solitary, although of course never alone, never. Stately, sinister and determined.

The creamy lips, the oily eyelids, the violent perfume—and in her voice the tropical *l*'s and *r*'s. Her presence, her singing created a large, swelling anxiety. Long red fingernails and the sound of electrified guitars. Here was a woman who had never been a Christian.

To speak as part of the white audience of "knowing" this baroque and puzzling phantom is an immoderation and yet there are many persons who have little splinters of memory that seem to have been *personal.* At times they have remembered an exchange of some sort. And of course the lascivious gardenias, worn like a large, white, beautiful ear, the heavy laugh, marvelous teeth, and the splendid head, archaic, as if washed up from the Aegean. Sometimes she dyed her hair red and the curls lay flat against her skull, like dried blood.

Early in the week the clubs were *dead*, as they spoke of it. And the chill of failure everywhere, always visible in the cold eyes of the owners. These men, always changing, were weary with anxious calculations. They often held their ownership so briefly that one could scarcely believe the ink dry on the license. They started out with the embezzler's hope and moved swiftly to the bankrupt's torpor. The bartenders—thin, watchful, stubbornly crooked, resentful, silent thieves. Wandering soldiers, drunk and worried, musicians, and a few people, couples, looking into each other's eyes, as if they were safe.

My friend and I, peculiar and tense, experienced during the quiet nights a tainted joy. Then, showing our fidelity, it seemed that a sort of *motif* would reveal itself, that under the glaze ancient patterns from a lost world were to be discovered. The mind strains to recover the blank spaces in history and our pale, gray-green eyes looked into her swimming, dark, inconstant pools—and got back nothing.

In her presence on these bedraggled nights, nights when performers all over the world were smiling, dancing, or pretending to be a prince of antiquity, offering their acts to dead rooms, then it was impossible to escape the depths of her disbelief, to refuse the mean, horrible freedom of a savage suspicion of destiny. And yet the heart always drew back from the power of her will and its engagement with disaster. An inclination bred from punishing experiences compelled her to live gregariously and without affections.

Well, it's a life. And some always hung about, as there is always someone in the evening leaning against the monument in the park.

A genuine nihilism; genuine, look twice. Infatuated glances saying, Beautiful black star, can you love me? The answer: No.

Somehow she had retrieved from darkness the miracle of pure style. That was it. Only a fool imagined that it was necessary to love a man, love anyone, love life. Her own people, those around her, feared her. And perhaps even she was often ashamed of the heavy weight of her own spirit, one never tempted to the relief of sentimentality.

In my youth, at home in Kentucky, there was a dance place just outside of town called Joyland Park. In the summer the great bands arrived, Ellington, Louis Armstrong, Chick Webb, sometimes for a Friday and Saturday or merely for one night. When I speak of the great bands it must not be taken to mean that we thought of them as such. No, they were part of the summer nights and the hot dog stands, the fetid swimming pool heavy with chlorine, the screaming roller coaster, the old rain-splintered picnic tables, the broken iron swings. And the bands were also part of Southern drunkenness, couples drinking Coke and whiskey, vomiting, being unfaithful, lovelorn, frantic. The black musicians, with their cumbersome instruments, their tuxedos, were simply there to beat out time for the stumbling, cuddling fox-trotting of the period.

The band buses, parked in the field, the caravans in which they suffered the litter of cigarettes and bottles, the hot, streaking highways, all night, or resting for a few hours in the black quarters: the *via dolorosa* of show business. They arrived at last, nowhere, to audiences large and small, often, with us, depending not upon the musicians but upon the calendar of the park, the other occasions from which the crowd would spill over into the dance hall. Jimmie Lunceford's band? Don't they ever do a slow number?

At our high school dances in the winter, small, cheap local events. We had our curls, red taffeta dresses, satin shoes with their new dye fading in the rain puddles; and most of all we were dressed in our ferocious hope for popularity. This was a hot blanket, an airless tent; gasping, grinning, we stood anxious-eyed, next to the piano, hovering about Fats Waller, who had come from Cincinnati for the occasion. Requests, insolent glances, drunken teen-agers, nodding teacher-chaperones: these we offered to the music, looking upon it, I suppose, as something inevitable, effortlessly pushing up from the common soil.

On 52nd Street: Yeah, I remember your town, she said, without inflection.

And I remember her dog, Mister. She was one of those women who admired large, overwhelming, impressive dogs and who gave to them a care and courteous punctuality denied everything else. Several times we waited in panic for her in the bar of the Hotel Braddock in Harlem. At the Braddock, the porters took plates of meat for the dog to her room. Soon, one of her friends, appearing almost like a child, so easily broken were others by the powerful, energetic horrors of her life, one of those young people would take the great dog to the street. These animals, asleep in her dressing rooms, were like sculptured treasures, fit for the tomb of a queen.

The sheer enormity of her vices. The outrageousness of them. For the grand destruction one must be worthy. Her ruthless talent and the opulent devastation. Onto the heaviest addiction to heroin, she piled up the rocks of her tomb with a prodigiousness of Scotch and brandy. She was never at any hour of the day or night free of these consumptions, never except when she was asleep. And there did not seem to be any pleading need to quit, to modify. With cold anger she spoke of various cures that had been forced upon her and she would say, bearing down heavily, as sure of her rights as if she had been robbed: And I paid for it myself. Out of a term at the Federal Women's Prison in West Virginia she stepped, puffy from a diet of potatoes, onto the stage of Town Hall to pick up some money and start up again the very day of release.

Still, even in her case, authenticity was sometimes pushed aside. A vague stirring in her mind and for just a moment a stereotype burst through and hung there like a balloon over the head of the heroine in a cartoon. The little girl with her mop, clothes on the line, the wife at the stove, a plate or two, candles. An invitation for chili: *my turn.*

J. and I went up to a street in Harlem just as the winter sky was turning black. Darkened windows with thin bands of watchful light above the sills. Inside, the halls were dark and empty, filled only with the scent of dust. We, our faces bleached from the cold, in our thin coats, black gloves, had clinging to us the evangelical diffidence of bell-ringing members of a religious sect. Determination glacial, timid, and yet pedantic. Our frozen alarm and fascination carried us into the void of the dead old tenement. The house was under a police ban, partly boarded up with pieces of tin. A policeman gloomily stood guard near the stoop. When we whispered her name he stared at us with furious incredulity. She was hounded by the police, but for once the occasion was not hers. Somewhere, upstairs, behind another door, there had been a catastrophe.

Her own records played over and over on the turntable; everything else was quiet. All of her living places were temporary in the purest meaning of the term. But she filled even a black hotel room with a stinging, demonic weight. At the moment she was living with a trumpet player who was just becoming known and who soon after faded altogether. He was as thin as a stick, and his lovely, round, light face, with frightened, shiny, round eyes, looked like a sacrifice impaled upon the stalk of his neck. His younger brother came out of the bedroom. He stood before us, wavering between confusing possibilities. Tiny, skinny, perhaps in his twenties, the young man was engrossed in a blur of functions. He was a sort of hectic Hermes, working in Hades, now buying cigarettes, now darting back to the bedroom, now almost inaudible on the phone, ordering or disposing of something in a light, shaking voice.

Lady's a little behind. She's over-scheduled herself. Groans and coughs from the bedroom. In the peach-shaded lights, the wan rosiness of a beaten sofa was visible. A shell, still flushed from the birth of some crustacean, filled with cigarettes. A stocking on the floor. And the record player, on and on, with the bright lift of her songs. Smoke and perfume and somewhere a heart pounding.

One winter she wore a great lynx coat, and in it she moved, menacing and handsome as a Cossack, pacing about in the trap of her vitality. Quarrelsome dreams sometimes rushed through her speech and accounts of wounds she had inflicted with broken glass. And at the White Rose Bar, a thousand cigarettes punctuated her appearances, which, not only in their brilliance but in the fact of their taking place at all, had about them the aspect of magic. Waiting and waiting: that was what the pursuit of her was. One felt like an old carriage horse standing at the entrance, ready for the cold midnight race through the park. She was always behind a closed door—the fate of those addicted to whatever. And then at last she must come forward, emerge in powders and Vaseline, hair twisted with a curling iron, gloves of satin or silk jersey, flowers—the expensive martyrdom of the "entertainer."

At that time not many of her records were in print, and she was seldom heard on the radio because her voice did not accord with popular taste then. The appearances in nightclubs were a necessity. It was a burden to be there night after night, although not a burden to sing, once she had started, in her own way. She knew she could do it, that she had mastered it all, but why not ask the question: Is this all there is? Her work took on, gradually, a destructive cast, as it so often does with the greatly gifted who are doomed to repeat endlessly their own heights of inspiration.

She was late for her mother's funeral. At last she arrived, ferociously appropriate in a black turban. A number of jazz musicians were there. The late morning light fell mercilessly on their unsteady, night faces. In the daytime these people, all except her, had a furtive, suburban aspect, like family men who work the night shift. The marks of a fractured domesticity, signals of a real life that is itself almost a secret existence for the performer, were drifting about the little church, adding to the awkward unreality.

Her mother, Sadie Holiday, was short and sentimental, bewildered to be the bearer of such news to the world. She made efforts to *sneak* into Billie's life, but there was no place and no need for her. She was set up from time to time in small restaurants which she ran without any talent and failed in quickly. She never achieved the aim of her life, the professional dream, which was to be "Billie's dresser." The two women bore no resemblance, neither of face nor of body. The mother seemed to meet each day with the bald hopefulness of a baby and end each evening in a baffled little cry of disappointment. Sadie and Billie Holiday were a violation, a rift in the statistics of life.

The great singer was one of those for whom the word *changeling* was invented. She shared the changeling's spectacular destiny and was acquainted with malevolent forces.

She lived to be forty-four; or should it better be said she died at forty-four. Of "enormous complications." Was it a long or a short life? The "highs" she sought with such concentration of course remained a mystery. I fault Jimmy for all that, someone said once in a taxi, naming her first husband, a fabulous Harlem club owner when she was young.

Once she came to see us in the Hotel Schuyler, accompanied by someone. We sat there in the neat squalor and there was nothing to do and nothing to say and she did not wish to eat. In the anxious gap, I felt the deepest melancholy in her black eyes. She died in misery from the erosions and poisons of her fervent, felonious narcotism. The police were at the hospital bedside, vigilant lest she, in a coma, manage a last chemical inner migration.

Her whole life had taken place in the dark. The spotlight shone down on the black, hushed circle in a café; the moon slowly slid through the clouds. Night—working, smiling, in makeup, in long, silky dresses, singing over and over, again and again. The aim of it all is just to be drifting off to sleep when the first rays of the sun's brightness begin to threaten the theatrical eyelids.

The star, the great person, seen in the night, does not mix in memory with your own shady history. J.—do you remember Lena, running the carpet sweeper at the hotel, she with her *blood*, Portuguese, Indian, and African. Was she one or three disastrously adrift souls? There she is mashing a banana in a small bowl and spreading the mash on a piece of bread. One day she arrives with manic, spendthrift energy and the next, sudden slumps and languors. Sometimes seeing her approaching on the street she walked like an Indian, slow and plain. Another day she arrived as wild and florid and thickly brilliant as a bird.

In the hotel lobby, tired bandsmen, dark glasses, ashen sleeplessness, oppressive overcoats, their wives, blond and tired. Tired creatures of the saxophone, the trumpet, basses; sweating booking agents lying in wait. The "vocalist" carrying a load of long dresses on her arm.

I knew well those in the old furnished rooms up around Columbia. They had about them a left-over, dim, vanquished aspect, depressed spirits living in a conquered territory. The discontent of the people at the Hotel Schuyler was quite different. Most of them were failures, but they lived elated by unreal hopes, ill-considered plans. They drank, they fought, they fornicated. They ran up bills, they lied and fought confusion with mild debaucheries. They were not poverty-stricken, just always a little "behind." Undomestic, restless, unreliable, changeable, disloyal. They were not spinsters, but divorcees, not bachelors but seedy *bons vivants*, deserters from family life, alimony, child-support, from loans long erased from memory. They drank for three days and sobered for three. People with union cards—acrobats, ballroom teams. That act was presented terrible, they would say about the current bill at Radio City Music Hall.

Tell me, is it true that a bad artist suffers as greatly as a good one? There were many performers at the Hotel Schuyler, but they gave no hint of suffering from the failure of their art. Perhaps the art had changed its name and came to their minds as something else—employment.

The sadness of the lost years of practice, the lessons, the exercises, the muscles stretched, the horn-blowing, tap-dancing, the swirling tango, the anguish of the violin. It is too much to think of. Even for these people the horror of mastery had been theirs. They seemed to be from the small towns of large states, such as New Jersey or northern Ohio. Their faces mirrored the bleak urban surface, the jangling provinciality of the old highway suburbs. Old age was unimaginable. When, whither? Perhaps, perhaps lovers would turn into widowers in the nick of time, somebody, somewhere would settle a little property on them. Why not? It was known to happen. Old rakes and "models"—after all, they were not clerks or filling station attendants or grocers. They were only those who wanted a good time, to have fun, to grow blowzy and paunchy in a vivacious, noisy company. The night clerks, rodents with red eyes, gray faces, men who had spent all their lives on the night shift, who greeted the morning as the time to pull down the blinds—how they envied the tenants, the lucky ones we never pass by in life without asking: what do they live on?

1979

# LEWIS MUMFORD

*Lewis Mumford (1895–1990) wrote about cities, in such books as* Sticks and Stones *and* The Brown Decades, *with more historical knowledge and passion than anyone of his generation. His urbanism combined an expertise in architecture, town planning, social policy, and literature. In this passage from his memoir* Sketches from Life, *he retrieves a teenage epiphany on the Brooklyn Bridge.*

## FROM *SKETCHES FROM LIFE*

URING THIS EARLY PERIOD of manhood (1914–1919) I began to experience the waterfront of New York, by repeated rides on ferryboats, in a fashion that has now become impossible. Everywhere the wholesale commitment to bridges and tunnels across and under the rivers and bays, for the sake of speed alone, is depriving us of this primal source of recreation, causing us to go farther in search of enlivening change—and often to fare worse.

But surely the ferryboat was one of the great inventions of the Nineteenth Century: that great turtlelike creature—plodding through waters often iridescent with scum near the ferry slips, doggedly meeting the hazards of time and weather, sometimes serving as a summer excursion boat to Staten Island, sometimes bumping and cracking through the ice floes in the surly black water, so that the salt spray would tingle in one's nostrils.

What endless variations on the simple theme of 'passage' by water! Even the short trips to Jersey City from downtown New York provided a touch of uncertainty and adventure, allowing for the tide, dodging other boats and ships, all with a closeness to the sea and sky and the wide sweep of the city itself that no other form of locomotion could boast.

Ferryboats would have been worthwhile for their value as a source of recreation alone: no, I would go further, they were worth running if only to give sustenance to poets and lovers and lonely young people, from Walt Whitman to Edna St. Vincent Millay, from Alfred Stieglitz and John Sloan to myself. Ferries had uses beyond the ordinary needs for transportation, and their relative slowness was not the least part of their merit—though as to speed, it has often taken far more time to cross by motorcar from Manhattan to Brooklyn or from San Francisco to Oakland during the rush hour, amid poisonous fumes and irritating tensions, than it once did by ferry. Those who put speed above all other values are often cheated even of speed by their dedication to a single mode of mass locomotion.

No poet, hurtling by plane even as far as Cathay, has yet written a poem comparable to 'Crossing Brooklyn Ferry'; no painter has come back with a picture comparable to John Sloan's 'Ferryboat Ride,' which, for me, in its dun colors, recalls one of the moments I liked best on the North River: a lowery sky, a smoke-hung skyline, and the turbid waters of the river. When I read Whitman's poem now, I realize the special historic advantage of belonging to a generation that is "ebbing with the ebb-tide," for I am old enough to have felt every sensation he described, to have seen every sight—except the then-bowered heights of Hoboken—with a sense of identification that even the most active imagination could hardly evoke now.

Those wonderful long ferry rides! Alas for a later generation that cannot guess how they opened the city up, or how the change of pace and place, from swift to slow, from land to water, had a specially stimulating effect upon the mind. But if I loved the ferries, I loved the bridges, too; and one after another I walked over all the bridges that linked Manhattan to Long Island, even that least rewarding one, the Queensboro. But it was the Brooklyn Bridge that I loved best, partly because of its own somber perfection of form, with its spidery lacing of cables contrasting with the great stone piers through which they were suspended: stone masonry that seemed in its harmony of granite pier, classic coping, and ogive arch to crystallize the essence of Roman, Romanesque, and Gothic architecture; while its cables stretched like a bowstring to shoot a steel arrow into our own age.

Since we lived on Brooklyn Heights between 1922 and 1925, I

took every possible occasion to walk back and forth across the Brooklyn Bridge; and I knew it in all weathers and at all times of the day and night: so it is no wonder that when I came to write 'Sticks and Stones' in 1924, I gave perhaps the first critical appreciation of that achievement since Montgomery Schuyler's contemporary essay, published in his 'American Architecture' in 1893.

At that period, as it happened, Hart Crane and I—then personally unknown to each other—were living on Brooklyn Heights, and he, in his poet's way, was engaged in a similar enterprise: indeed, some time later, after I had moved away, he consulted me about biographic materials on the Roeblings, the builders of the Bridge. Thousands of people must have felt the same as we in our different ways had felt, ever since the Bridge was opened; but no one had freshly expressed it until the twenties. Only then did the first formal biography of John Roebling appear, to be followed a decade later by David Steinman's detailed study of the building of the Brooklyn Bridge—a book that by happy chance passed under my favorable editorial eye before my own publishers decided to go ahead with it.

So deeply did the Bridge itself capture my imagination that before I had abandoned my aim of becoming a playwright (as late as 1927), I wrote the first draft of a long play on the theme of the Bridge: a play that I recognized, even while writing it, could be produced only when done over into a motion picture. Fragments of that play still haunt me: not least a love scene, at night, high up on one of the piers of the half-finished structure, with a sense of giddy isolation heightening the passion of the lovers—and the muted whistles and hoots from the river below, in the spreading fog, underscoring with the note of the city itself their private encounter.

That scene no one will of course find in any Roebling biography, but the stuff of it I was soon to encounter, if less exaltedly, in my own life; for many of my written fantasies have turned out to be gropings, forebodings, formative anticipations of unconscious urgings that were soon to take on outward shapes, all the more because of their contrast with the sober, neatly planned, dutiful routine, so close in its more workmanlike qualities to that of an engineer, that characterizes such a large part of my workaday existence.

There was a slightly older contemporary who, as it seemed in 1915, had caught the very beat of the city, a beat that had begun to pulsate with quickening consciousness in all of us. This was Ernest Poole, who in 'The Harbor,' through his choice of scenes, characters, social issues, said something for my generation that no one else had yet said, though he was never—that was perhaps his tragedy!—to say it so well again. Brooklyn Heights and 'The Harbor' took shape almost entirely in Poole's imagination. But he captured the contrast between the depths of Furman Street, on the level of the waterfront, rimmed by a jumble of warehouses and docks, and the top of the stone-walled escarpment, with its seemly rows of brick or serpentine houses which commanded the whole harbor. There on Furman Street in the middle of the afternoon I had already seen an aged, drunken slattern, foul with whiskey and fouler with words—exhibiting the destitution and squalor that the gardens and mansions above both actually and figuratively overlooked.

I hardly dare to look at 'The Harbor' to find out how the printed pages would compare now with the sensations I had in 1915, when I first read the book. Somehow that novel seethed with my own hopeful excitement over the contemporary world of factories and steamships, of employers and labor unions, of political strife and private ambition, giving me much the same reaction I had felt earlier when reading H. G. Wells's 'The New Machiavelli' or his 'Tono-Bungay'—both books that influenced my youth. 'The Harbor' satisfied my appetite for the concrete and the contemporary, which was a very real appetite in those quickening days. The fact that Poole saw the city in much the same way I was beginning to see it gave moral backing and political support to my own efforts.

Not that I needed much backing! We all had a sense that we were on the verge of translation into a new world, a quite magical translation, in which the best hopes of the American Revolution, the French Revolution, and the Industrial Revolution would all be simultaneously fulfilled. The First World War battered and shattered those hopes, but it took years before the messages received through our eyes or felt at our fingers' ends were effectively conveyed to our brains and could be decoded: for long those ominous messages simply did not make sense. Until well into the 1930s we could always see the bright side of the darkest cloud. We did not, while the spirit of our confident years worked in us, guess that the sun upon which we counted might soon be in eclipse.

Yes: I loved the great bridges and walked back and forth over them, year after year. But as often happens with repeated experiences, one memory stands out above all others: a twilight hour in early spring—it was March, I think—when, starting from the Brooklyn end, I faced into the west wind sweeping over the rivers from New Jersey. The ragged, slate-blue cumulus clouds that gathered over the horizon left open patches for the light of the waning sun to shine through, and finally, as I reached the middle of the Brooklyn Bridge, the sunlight spread across the sky, forming a halo around the jagged mountain of skyscrapers, with the darkened loft buildings and warehouses huddling below in the foreground. The towers, topped by the golden pinnacles of the new Woolworth Building, still caught the light even as it began to ebb away. Three-quarters of the way across the Bridge I saw the skyscrapers in the deepening darkness become slowly honeycombed with lights until, before I reached the Manhattan end, these buildings piled up in a dazzling mass against the indigo sky.

Here was my city, immense, overpowering, flooded with energy and light; there below lay the river and the harbor, catching the last flakes of gold on their waters, with the black tugs, free from their barges, plodding dockward, the ferryboats lumbering from pier to pier, the tramp steamers slowly crawling toward the sea, the Statue of Liberty erectly standing, little curls of steam coming out of boat whistles or towered chimneys, while the rumbling elevated trains and trolley cars just below me on the bridge moved in a relentless tide to carry tens of thousands homeward. And there was I, breasting the March wind, drinking in the city and the sky, both vast, yet both contained in me, transmitting through me the great mysterious will that had made them and the promise of the new day that was still to come.

The world, at that moment, opened before me, challenging me, beckoning me, demanding something of me that it would take more than a lifetime to give, but raising all my energies by its own vivid promise to a higher pitch. In that sudden revelation of power and beauty all the confusions of adolescence dropped from me, and I trod the narrow, resilient boards of the footway with a new confidence that came, not from my isolated self alone but from the collective energies I had confronted and risen to.

I cannot hope to bring back the exaltation of that moment: the wonder of it was like the wonder of an orgasm in the body of one's beloved, as if one's whole life had led up to that moment and had swiftly culminated there. And yet I have carried the sense of that occasion, along with two or three other similar moments, equally enveloping and pregnant, through my life: they remain, not as a constant presence, but as a momentary flash reminding me of heights approached and scaled, as a mountain climber might carry with him the memory of some daring ascent, never to be achieved again. Since then I have courted that moment more than once on the Brooklyn Bridge; but the exact conjunction of weather and light and mood and inner readiness has never come back. That experience remains alone: a fleeting glimpse of the utmost possibilities life may hold for man.

1981

# KATE SIMON

As a worldly travel writer, Kate Simon (1912–90) was an epicure of sensual treats and exotic vistas. Yet her most enduring book, Bronx Primitive, a tour de force of memoir writing, re-creates an impoverished and culturally isolated childhood. Her recollections brilliantly blend the viewpoint of the curious and stubborn young girl she was, unwilling to settle for her parents' explanations, and that of the sophisticated writer she would become.

### THE MOVIES AND OTHER SCHOOLS

LIFE ON LAFONTAINE offered several schools. School-school, P.S. 59, was sometimes nice, as when I was chosen to be Prosperity in the class play, blond, plump, dressed in a white pillow case banded with yellow and green crepe paper, for the colors of grasses and grain, and waving something like a sheaf of wheat. The cringing days were usually Fridays, when arithmetic flash cards, too fast, too many, blinded me and I couldn't add or subtract the simplest numbers. (For many years, into adulthood, I carried around a sack of churning entrails on Friday mornings.) The library, which made me my own absolutely special and private person with a card that belonged to no one but me, offered hundreds of books, all mine and no tests on them, a brighter, more generous school than P.S. 59. The brightest, most informative school was the movies. We learned how tennis was played and golf, what a swimming pool was and what to wear if you ever got to drive a car. We learned how tables were set, "How do you do? Pleased to meet you," how primped and starched little girls should be, how neat and straight boys should be, even when they were temporarily ragamuffins. We learned to look up soulfully and make our lips tremble to warn our mothers of a flood of tears, and though they didn't fall for it (they laughed), we kept practicing. We learned how regal mothers were and how stately fathers, and of course we learned about Love, a very foreign country like maybe China or Connecticut. It was smooth and slinky, it shone and rustled. It was petals with Lillian Gish, gay flags with Marion Davies, tiger stripes with Rudolph Valentino, dog's eyes with Charlie Ray. From what I could see, and I searched, there was no Love on the block, nor even its fairy-tale end, Marriage. We had only Being Married, and that included the kids, a big crowded barrel with a family name stamped on it. Of course, there was Being Married in the movies, but except for the terrible cruel people in rags and scowls, it was as silky as Love. Fathers kissed their wives and children when they came home from work and spoke to them quietly and nobly, like kings, and never shouted or hit if the kids came in late or dirty. Mothers in crisp dresses stroked their children's heads tenderly as they presented them with the big ringletted doll and the football Grandma had sent, adding, "Run off and play, darlings." "Darling," "dear," were movie words, and we had few grandmothers, most of them dead or in shadowy conversation pieces reported from At Home, the Old Country. And "Run off and play" was so superbly refined, silken gauze to the rough wool of our hard-working mothers whose rules were to feed their children, see that they were warmly dressed in the wintertime, and run to the druggist on Third Avenue for advice when they were sick. Beyond that it was mostly "Get out of my way." Not all the mothers were so impatient. Miltie's mother helped him with his arithmetic homework; my mother often found us amusing and laughed with and at us a lot. From other apartments, on rainy afternoons: Joey—"What'll I do, Maaa?" His Mother—"*Va te ne! Gherradi!*" (the Italian version of "Get out of here"); Lily—"What'll I do, Maaa?" Mrs. Stavicz—"Scratch your ass on a broken bottle." I sometimes wished my mother would say colorful, tough things like that but I wasn't sure I wouldn't break into tears if she did, which would make her call me a "*pianovi chasto*" (as I remember the Polish phrase), a delicate meringue cake that falls apart easily, which would make me cry more, which would make her more lightly contemptuous, and so on. Despite my occasional wish to see her as one of the big-mouth, storming women, I was willing to settle for her more modest distinction, a lady who won notebooks in her English class at the library and sang many tunes from "Polish operettas" that, with later enlightenment, I realized were *The Student Prince* and *The Merry Widow.*

Being Married had as an important ingredient a nervous father. There must have been other kitchens, not only ours, in which at about seven o'clock, the fathers' coming-home time, children were warned, "Now remember, Papa is coming home soon. He's nervous from working in the factory all day and riding in the crowded El. Sit quiet at the table, don't laugh, don't talk." It was hard not to giggle at the table, when my brother and I, who played with keen concentration a game of mortal enemies at other times, became close conspirators at annoying Them by making faces at each other. The muffled giggles were stopped by a shout of "Respect!" and a long black look, fork poised like a sword in midair while no one breathed. After the silent meal, came the part we disliked most, the after-dinner lecture. There were two. The first was The Hard Life of the Jewish worker, the Jewish father, the deepest funereal sounds unstopped for the cost of electricity (a new and lovely toy but not as pretty as throbbing little mazda lamps) for which he had to pay an immense sum each time we switched it on and off, like the wastrels we were. Did we think butter cost a penny a pound that we slathered it on bread as if it were Coney Island mud pies? Those good expensive shoes he bought us (he was an expert shoe worker, a maker of samples, and tortured us with embarrassment when he displayed his expertise to the salesman, so don't try to fool him), which were old and scuffed and dirty within a week, did we know how much bloody sweat was paid for them? The second lecture was the clever one whose proud, sententious repetitions I listened to with shame for him, wanting to put my head down not to see my handsome father turn into a vaudeville comic whose old monologues strained and fell. This lecture was usually inspired by my brother who, in spite of the "nervous" call, dashed at my father as soon as he heard the key in the lock with "Hello, Pa. Gimme a penny?" That led it off: "You say you want a penny, *only* a penny. I've got dimes and quarters and half-dollars in my pockets, you say, so what's a penny to me? Well, let's see. If you went to the El station and gave the man four cents, he wouldn't let you on the train, you'd need another penny. If Mama gave you two cents for a three-cent ice cream cone, would Mrs. Katz in the candy store give it to you? If Mama had only forty-eight cents for a forty-nine-cent chicken, would the butcher give it to her?" And on and on, a carefully rehearsed long slow aria, with dramatic runs of words and significant questioning pauses. Once or twice I heard my mother mutter as she went out of the room, "That Victrola record again," but her usual policy was to say nothing. She was not afraid of my father, nor particularly in awe of him. (I heard him say frequently how fresh she was, but with a smile, not the way he said it to us.)

In none of my assiduous eavesdropping on the street did I ever hear any mention of unhappy marriage or happy marriage. Married was married. Although a Jewish divorce was a singularly easy matter except for the disgrace it carried, the Jewish women were as firmly imbedded in their marriages as the Catholic. A divorce was as unthinkable as adultery or lipstick. No matter what—beatings, infidelity, drunkenness, verbal abuse, outlandish demands—no woman could run the risk of making her children fatherless. Marriage and children were fate, like being skinny, like skeletal Mr. Roberts, or humpbacked, like the leering watchman at the hat factory. "*Es is mir beschert,*" "It is my fate," was a common sighing phrase, the Amen that closed hymns of woe.

My mother didn't accept her fate as a forever thing. She began to work during our school hours after her English classes had taught her as much as they could, and while I was still young, certainly no more than ten, I began to get her lecture on being a woman. It ended with extraordinary statements, shocking in view of the street mores. "Study. Learn. Go to college. Be a schoolteacher," then a respected, privileged breed, "and don't get married until you have a profession. With a profession you can have men friends and even children, if you want. You're free. But don't get married, at least not until you can support yourself and make a careful choice. Or don't get married at all, better still." This never got into "My mother said" conversations with my friends. I sensed it to be too outrageous. My mother was already tagged "The Princess" because she never went into the street unless fully, carefully dressed: no grease-stained housedress, no bent, melted felt slippers. Rarely, except when she was pregnant with my little sister, did she stop for conversations on the street. She was one of the few in the building who had gone to classes, the only mother who went out alone at night to join her mandolin group. She was sufficiently marked, and though I was proud of her difference, I didn't want to report her as altogether eccentric. In the community fabric, as heavy as the soups we ate and the dark, coarse "soldier's bread" we chomped on, as thick as the cotton on which we practiced our cross-stitch embroidery, was the conviction that girls were to marry as early as possible, the earlier the more triumphant. (Long after we moved from the area, my mother, on a visit to Lafontaine to see appealing, inept little Fannie Herman who had for many years been her charge and mine, met Mrs. Roth, who asked about me. When my mother said I was going to Hunter College, Mrs. Roth, looking both pleased and sympathetic, said, "*My* Helen married a man who makes a nice living, a laundry man. Don't worry, your Katie will find a husband soon." She knew that some of the boys of the block wound up in City College, but a girl in college? From a pretty, polite child, I must have turned into an ugly, bad-tempered shrew whom no one would have. Why else would my marrying years be spent in college?)

I never saw my mother and father kiss or stroke each other as people did in the movies. In company she addressed him, as did most of the Jewish women, by our family name, a mark of respectful distance. They inhabited two separate worlds, he adventuring among anti-Semites to reach a shadowy dungeon called "Factory," where he labored ceaselessly. In the evening he returned to her world for food, bed, children, and fighting. We were accustomed to fighting: the boys and, once in a while, fiery little girls tearing at each other in the street; bigger Italian boys punching and being punched by the Irish gangs that wandered in from Arthur Avenue; females fighting over clotheslines—whose sheets were blocking whose right to the sun—bounced around the courtyard constantly. The Genoese in the houses near 178th Street never spoke to the Sicilians near 179th Street except to complain that somebody's barbaric little southern slob had peed against a northern tree. To my entranced ears and eyes, the Sicilians seemed always to win, hotter, louder, faster with "*Fangu*"—the southern version of "*Fa' in culo*" (up yours)—than the aristocrats who retired before the Sicilians could hit them with "*Mortacci*"—the utterly insupportable insult. My brother and I fought over who grabbed the biggest apple, who hid the skate key, and where he put my baby picture, I lying on a white rug with my bare ass showing, a picture he threatened to pass among his friends and humiliate me beyond recovery. I would have to kill him.

These sorts of fighting were almost literally the spice of daily life, deliciously, lightly menacing, grotesque and entertaining. The fighting between my mother and father was something else entirely, at times so threatening that I still, decades later, cringe in paralyzed stupidity, as if I were being pelted with stones, when I hear a man shouting. The fights often concerned our conduct and my mother's permissiveness. My father had a rich vocabulary which he shaped into theatrical phrases spoken in a voice as black and dangerous as an open sewer. The opening shot was against my brother, who was six or seven when the attacks began. He was becoming a wilderness boy, no sense, no controls, dirty, disobedient, he did badly in school (not true: with a minimum of attention he managed mediocrity). There was no doubt that he would become a bum, then a thief, wind up alone in a prison cell full of rats, given one piece of bread a day and one cup of dirty water. He would come out a gangster and wind up in the electric chair.

When it was my turn, I was disobedient and careless; I didn't do my homework when I should, I didn't practice enough, my head was always in a book, I was always in the street running wild with the Italian and Polish beasts. I didn't take proper care of my brother, I climbed with boys, I ran with boys, I skated with them on far streets. Mr. Kaplan had seen me and told him. And how would this life, this playing with boys, end? I would surely become a street girl, a prostitute, and wind up being shipped to a filthy, diseased brothel crawling with hairy tropical bugs, in Buenos Aires. My mother's response was sharp and short: we acted like other children and played like other children; it was he who was at fault, asking more of us than he should. And enough about prisons and electric chairs and brothels. He went on shouting, entranced by his gorgeous words and visions, until she left the room to wash the dishes or scrub the kitchen floor. We, of course, had heard everything from our bedroom; the oratory was as much for us as for our mother. When the big rats in the windowless cell came to our ears, my brother began to shake with terror beyond crying. I tried to comfort him, as accustomed a role as trying to maim him. I didn't know what a street girl was, and I certainly didn't know what a brothel was, but I wasn't afraid—I was too angry. If our father hated us so, why didn't he go away? I didn't examine consequences, who would feed us and pay the rent. I just wanted him out, out, dead.

Other fights were about money, and that, too, involved us. How dare she, without consulting him, change from a fifty-cent-a-lesson piano teacher to another—and who knows how good *he* was?—who charged a dollar? What about the embroidered tablecloth and the stone bowl with the pigeons that she bought from the Arab peddler, that crook. Did she realize how hard he had to work to pay for our school supplies each fall? And add to that the nickel for candy to eat at the movies every Saturday, and the ten cents each for the movie and the three cents for ice-cream cones on Friday nights. And God only knew how much money she slipped us for the sweet garbage we chewed on, which would certainly rot our teeth, and where would he get the money for dentists? Maybe she thought she was still in her shop in Warsaw, dancing and singing and spilling money like a fool. And on and on it went. These tirades, too, were answered very briefly. Our lives were meager enough. Did he ever think of buying us even the cheapest toy, like the other fathers did, instead of stashing every spare penny in the bank and taking it out only for his relatives? The ignorant Italians he so despised, they had celebrations for their children. Where were our birthday presents?

Long silences followed these fights and we became messengers. "Tell your mother to take my shoes to the shoemaker." "Aw, Pa, I'm doing my homework. Later." "Tell your mother I have no clean shirts." "Aw, Pa, I'm just sitting down to practice. I'll tell her later." We used the operative words "homework" and "practice" mercilessly while he seethed at our delays. My mother heard all these instructions but it was her role neither to notice nor to obey. Those were great days and we exploited our roles fattily, with enormous vengeful pleasure.

One constant set of squabbles that didn't circle around us concerned her relaxed, almost loose judgments of other people. She showed no sympathy when he complained about the nigger sweeper in the factory who talked back to him, when he complained about the Italian who reeked of garlic and almost suffocated him in the train. Most loudly he complained about her availability, spoiling his sleep, letting his supper get cold, neglecting her own children, to run to any Italian idiot who didn't know to take care of her own baby. Let them take care of their own convulsions or get some Wop neighbor to help. It was disgraceful that she sat on Mrs. Santini's porch in open daylight trying to teach her not to feed her infant from her own mouth. If the fat fool wanted to give it germs, let her. If it died, she'd, next year, have another; they bred like rabbits. Why didn't my mother mind her own business, what the hell did these people, these foreign ignoramuses, mean to her? The answer was short and always the same, "*Es is doch a mench*," yet these are human beings, the only religious training we ever had, perhaps quite enough.

There were fights with no messengers, no messages, whispered fights when the door to our bedroom was shut tight and we heard nothing but hissing. The slow unfolding of time and sophistications indicated that these were fights about women, women my father saw some of those evenings when he said he was going to a Workmen's Circle meeting. There was no more "Tell your mother," "Tell your father," and except for the crying of our baby, no more evening sounds. No Caruso, no Rosa Ponselle, no mandolin practice, no lectures. My father busied himself with extra piecework, "skiving" it was called, cutting with breathtaking delicacy leaf and daisy designs into the surface of the sample shoes to be shown to buyers. She, during one such period, crocheted a beaded bag, tiny beads, tiny stitches. We watched, struck dumb by their skill, and because it was no time to open our mouths about anything, anything at all. The silence was dreadful, a creeping, dark thing, a night alley before the murderer appears. The furniture was waiting to be destroyed, the windows to be broken, by a terrible storm. We would all be swept away, my brother and I to a jungle where wild animals would eat us, my parents and the baby, separated, to starve and burn alone in a desert. School now offered the comforts of a church, the street its comforting familiarities, unchanging, predictable. We stayed out as long as we could, dashing up for a speedy supper, and down again. On rainy nights we read a lot, we went to bed early, anything to remove us from our private-faced parents, who made us feel unbearably shy.

One spring evening, invited to jump Double Dutch with a few experts, uncertain that I could leap between two ropes whipping in rapid alternation at precisely the exact moment, and continue to stay between them in small fast hops from side to side, I admitted a need urgent for some time, to go to the toilet. I ran up the stairs to find our door locked, an extraordinary thing. Maybe they had run away. Maybe they had killed each other. Sick with panic, I kept trying the door, it wouldn't give. Then I heard the baby making squirmy, sucking baby noises. No matter what, my mother would never leave the baby, and anyway, maybe they were doing their whispering fighting again. Still uneasy, I knocked on the Hermans' door and asked to use their toilet. When I came out, I asked Fannie Herman if she knew whether my parents were at home. Yes, she said. Her door was wide open and she would have seen or heard them come out, but they hadn't. The Double Dutch on the street was finished when I got down so I joined the race, boys and girls, around the block, running hard, loving my pumping legs and my swinging arms and my open mouth swallowing the breeze. When most of the kids had gone home and it was time for us, too, I couldn't find my brother, who was hiding from me to destroy my power and maybe get me into trouble. I went up alone. The door had been unlocked, and as I walked uneasily through the long hallway of our railroad flat with wary steps, I heard sounds from the kitchen. My mother was sitting on a kitchen chair, her feet in a basin of water. My father was kneeling before her on spread newspaper. Her plump foot rested in his big hand while he cut her toenails, flashing his sharp work knife, dexterous, light, and swift. She was splashing him a little, playing the water with her free foot. They were making jokes, lilting, laughing. Something, another branch in the twisted tree that shaded our lives, was going to keep us safe for a while.

*BRONX PRIMITIVE*, 1983

# EDWARD RIVERA

*The wave of Puerto Rican immigration to New York after World War II took its place with other, earlier waves in altering and enriching the character of the city. For many of these newcomers, as Edward Rivera shows in his lively, piquant memoir* Family Installments, *the adjustment of rural island people to the northern winters and slum conditions of the barrio required considerable resourcefulness. Here he recounts the difficult period when his father, Papi, first came to New York and prepared the way for his family to join him.*

## FROM *FAMILY INSTALLMENTS*

THE BEST WAY to find a position, Santos," Papi used to tell me, "is to stumble into it." That was his way of leading into the story of how he found the gondola job with an Italian construction crew shortly after he and his brother Mito and Mito's wife, Agripina, arrived in New York.

"I didn't have to pay a penny, Santos. Nobody asked me anything about my past. Not until I was hired, anyway. I just walked in off the street."

Wandered in, he meant. Lost. Freezing his testicles. He got off at the wrong stop on the Broadway local. He should have gotten off at 96th Street, taken another local back up to 110th and Lenox, a crosstown bus to Lexington, and walked down to his "home." He lived in a rooming house, a single room occupancy near Saint Misericordia's R.C. Church, his other home.

But he fell asleep that day on the local and got off at 137th Street, a long walk from home. All the money he had on him was some loose change and he didn't want to waste it on another token, so he decided to get back to his SRO on foot. It would do him good, this walk, if it didn't turn him to ice.

Up the cold hill he goes, not sure whether he's heading in the right direction or toward New Jersey, and not caring, he's that lonely. He's also recently unemployed. Burdock Bride Frocks down on Thirty-something and Seventh has relieved him of his duties as an assistant packer for misaddressing one shipment too many. The head packer has been lying on his behalf all along, but now he's had it.

"There's a limit to how many mistakes you're allowed in this life, Geránimo," the headman tells him, making it sound like a moral lapse on Papi's part. And all Papi can plead in self-defense is that he had a "meegraine" at the time he made his fatal error.

"So buy a bottle of Bayer's," the head packer tells him. "On your time."

"In other words, Santos, I am fired. This head packer is polite, and doesn't like to use filthy language like 'fired' and the other things he called me when he was urinated off. I don't argue back. I was expecting for it." Urinated off? Sometimes he liked to coin a euphemism.

The day he got off at the wrong stop, he had been at his brother's and sister-in-law's apartment on Fox Street, East Bronx, taking advantage of their hospitality and their handouts: another free meal (Agripina gets high marks for her cooking, some of the best in the Bronx), guitar music, and singing (solos, duets, and trios). He'd had himself a good time, and returned the favor with his talents. But freeloading has its limits, and he's too polite to push them. Besides, Agripina wouldn't care for his hanging around the apartment too long. Her sense of privacy is strong. He understands. Nobody has to tell him about privacy. So, before he'd like to, he leaves.

He's not looking forward to that SRO on Lexington. It's a lonely place, and it's noisy. His most valuable possession there, aside from his gold-tipped pen and the stationery he uses to write his wife and sons, is a pawnshop radio his brother gave him. He keeps it tuned to *La Voz Hispana*, like someone on hurricane watch. First thing he does when he gets in is turn it on, then the light; then he takes off his secondhand army coat (a Catholic Charities discount), hangs it up on the nail on the door, puts the coffeepot on the hot plate, takes his customary leak in the communal john, and then, with a cup of coffee at his elbow, starts in on his latest letter to Lilia and the boys. His gold-tipped pen was a farewell present from Octavio Cardona, Chuito's godfather, who gave it to him the day he and Mito left the island, and he can't bring himself to pawn it, much as he's tempted to at times.

"My dear Lilia! You have a lucky husband. I fell asleep on the subway train and found a job with some Italians. I push a wheelbarrow. Let me tell you about it, since I have all the time in the world. . . ."

At the top of a cold hill on Amsterdam Avenue, he sees a crew of Italian-looking men working away as if this weren't the coldest day of the year. Some of them are singing in Italian; and at first, in his ignorance, he wonders if maybe they're not a company of professional singers rehearsing for an opera.

He walks up to a couple of them and asks in broken English if they need some help. They take one look at him and laugh—who is this little iceman in the army coat? But he gets the job anyway. Out of compassion, he thinks afterward, since they seem to be all filled up. Maybe they can use some extra comic relief on the job, a butt of jokes during lunch break. For a steady job, he'll put up with whatever ridicule they want to throw at him. "Let them kid me all they want, Santos. For regular work, I'll stand on my head." Maybe he did.

They give him a wheelbarrow and throw in a quick lesson on what to do with it. He fills it with frozen sand on this side of the site and shoves it to that side. A sand-and-rocks man. "The Malánguez Cadillac," some of the men call his wheelbarrow. He calls it his Italian gondola. They get along all right. He keeps his mouth shut, follows orders (everybody's), and keeps to himself. Sometimes the kidding comes close to getting out of hand. How come he doesn't look too much like a Spik? What's he going to do with himself when he grows up? And others of that kind. Some of these questions, and the answers he retaliates with (smiling), he wouldn't repeat in public. It's everybody's way of letting off tension, he thinks. No hard feelings. They were kind enough to give him this job, after all. He opens a savings account and begins putting a few dollars into it every payday. For four plane tickets. Lilia and the boys. And for an apartment, and furnishings.

His Italian colleagues teach him some opera lyrics and explain what they mean. "*Amarilli, mia bella, non credi O del mio cor dolce*

*desio . . ."* *"Sebben, crudele, mi fai languir Sempre fedele ti voglio amar . . ."*
He sometimes hums himself to sleep with these; and years later he
would sing them to himself in our dining room, alternating bel canto
with the le-lo-lais of our old village. A confusion of cultures, mild in
his case.

But there was to be a time limit to this wheelbarrow windfall. It
was seasonal work, and at the end of spring they let him go. Then he
moved on to a laundry, a comedown. They put him to pressing shorts
and folding shirts nine to five. During lunch breaks, he looked
around for something cooler. One of his co-workers told him to try
the Hotel Roosevelt. "They're hiring dishwashers this week." But
when he applied, the man who did the kitchen hiring told him he
didn't meet their qualifications, their height requirements.

"To wash the dishes?" he asked.

Yes, he was told. Besides, it wasn't just his height; it was also his
eyesight.

And since when, he wanted to know, did one need the eyes of a
hawk to wash dishes?

"Since I said so," the man told him. "Listen, Mr. Malan-guéss, I
don't have to defend our hiring policy to anyone who walks in off
the street looking for a job."

"You mispronounced my name," Papi tells him.

"So scram," he's told. He scrams, before the police are called in.

That night he punches the walls of his SRO, damaging private
property as well as his knuckles. His neighbors bang on their own
walls to shut him up. He swabs the back of his right hand with iodine
and spends most of the night blowing on his bleeding knuckles. He
doesn't repeat this outburst. Bad for his handwriting, for one thing.
"That last letter you wrote us," Mami writes back, "was almost illeg-
ible. What's the problem, Gerán?"

"I was in a hurry, Lilia," he answers. "I was on my way to a job interview."

A steam-room colleague put him on to the American Combining
Company, a textile place in Brooklyn. He took the New Lots by
mistake, then switched to the Flatbush when he discovered his
error, and got there at about the time he should have been back in

the laundry. But it ended well; he got the job. The man who did the hiring for the ACC misspelled his name: "Malanga," after a former employee who had gone back to the island after twenty years on this job. Papi didn't correct the misspelling until it made no difference how they spelled his last name.

From his ACC paycheck he had deductions to make: his wife and sons, the savings bank, his father-in-law (installments on a dead mule), and a dentist on Fox Street, who had put a gold crown in his mouth. This was to be a surprise for Lilia, something special.

He was disappointed when we weren't impressed by this gold tooth. Why, Mami asked him once, had he turned his mouth into a gold mine?

It was for her benefit, he told her. "I wanted to look presentable." The sweat of his brow had gone into it. Wasted sweat, it seemed.

He should have asked her first, she said.

"It's my mouth," he told her. He had pushed a gondola for this tooth, and his own wife was ridiculing it. It was the only luxury he had allowed himself during those SRO days. Single Cave Occupancy, he might have called that period of his life.

Even when he had to step outside that room for a trip to the toilet, or for a rapid shower in temperamental water (sometimes lukewarm, usually freezing, and always mixed with rust and other disgusting impurities), he locked his door. Not that the lock was going to keep anyone out. But he didn't want to tempt his neighbors. Besides, Octavio's pen, his brother Mito's radio, his Catholic Charities army coat, were precious possessions, think what anyone would; so were the letters from his wife. He numbered and dated the envelopes, he tied them in a bundle and kept them "locked" inside a shoe box. He reread them often, had memorized some of them, didn't want them stolen by a neighbor.

The place was noisy, a lot of fights broke out on weekends, and it was lonely in there. Always that, the hardest of his problems. Mito and Agripina had just had their first baby, Genoveva, an unattractive name in his opinion. It didn't go with the kid's looks, at any rate. Whatever they called her, this baby picked up his mood. But Agripina was one of those jealous mothers who don't like people handling their babies too much. "Let me have her back, Gerán, before she forgets who her mother is. She needs my breast." He took those remarks as hints: time to go.

His other home, Saint Misericordia's Church, helped some. He went there every morning, including Saturdays, when even the priests looked bored; the altar boys fell asleep on their feet, the parishioners on their knees. He pinched himself to stay awake, considering it sinful to fall asleep during the service. Afterward, he went back to bed. Fire trucks, police sirens, neighbors, bad dreams, woke him up from time to time. He didn't recommend that kind of life, he told me, whispered it to me, as if ashamed of the experience. "Stay away from the SROs."

Eventually, against his better judgment, he made friends with one of the people who lived in that rooming house, a woman in her twenties from Orocovis or Morovis, some place not far from Bautabarro. This young woman, whose name he couldn't recall, he said, worked for Linens of the Week or Month; she washed, starched, pressed, and folded all week. Not exactly a vocation. She had a couple of friends from the island there, but they were all married women with husbands, kids, and other lookouts. So, like him, she was by herself. She had come to join her fiancé, El Prometido, who had disappeared somewhere in the Hunts Point section of the Bronx. Needle in a haystack. She hadn't heard from him going on six months. Something horrible must have happened. Her telegrams and letters were wasted, unacknowledged. So she decided to come and find him herself. She was in love.

After a lot of detective work, including ads in *El Diario* (a waste of money), she found out that El Prometido was living with a divorced woman who had eight or nine kids from previous husbands and lovers. Now she was pregnant by El Prometido. Very fertile, this woman. A cow type. "Which I don't mean as an insult, Santos," Papi said. "Far be it. But—well, I can almost hear her mooing. She was trapped by her own fertility, and whatever else. Those men in her life, for one thing.

"And this El Prometido had the *cojones* to suggest to my friend, La Prometida, that she take up with him by moving to her own apartment on Simpson Street, near that police precinct we've all heard about. The Apache one. That was the same block El Prometido and his pregnant woman were living on. He tried all kinds of tricks to talk La Prometida into going along with this proposal."

He offered to find her a better job in a dress factory and to pay her rent until she got on her own. Some of his friends on Simpson would paint her new apartment. The way El Prometido put this proposal to her, it was as if she had no choice, as if she couldn't wait to jump into it. He's coming on like the head of a numbers syndicate. Big man, a take-charge type. Just leave it to me. Easy Simpson Street. Like a personal friend of Genovese or Costello. When what he is is a big mouth, holes in his pockets, he can use a new pair of heels, but he can't seem to afford them: He's up to his nose in easy payments.

So what does she think of his proposal? "You're going to hell," she tells him. He laughs, she leaves, and ends up in the same rooming house where Papi lives.

"What was her name?" I asked him.

"I can't remember. It's not important." He usually had a good memory for names. "We became very good friends, that's all."

He said he tried talking her into going back to her home village, but she wouldn't. She had been shamed by her fiancé, to go back home would be a disgrace. Maybe she was exaggerating a little, but that was how she felt, and he understood. His own situation was similar, if for different reasons.

What, I asked him, had gone on between the two of them? Nothing, he said, looking embarrassed enough to be holding back the truth. She went to live on the West Side after a while; a lower-rent SRO. He hoped she was married and happy. They'd lost contact. He switched topics quickly, told me about the "tragic" telegram he received one day from "Lilia."

The telegram said she was arriving at La Guardia in two days, Wednesday morning. That made no sense to him. But the name of the sender was Lilia, and he knew only one Lilia. Maybe her father had given her money for plane tickets. Maybe he had died and left her something. Hard to believe, but no less hard than this incredible telegram. Maybe she'd gone insane.

He hardly slept that night, and he was so confused that it didn't occur to him to send back a telegram demanding an explanation. Next day and night, same sleeplessness. He must have smoked a pack of cigarettes in a couple of hours; he went into a bar and grill and got drunk on three beers. Wednesday morning, looking like the original insomniac, he headed for the airport hours before the plane was due to arrive. He took a bus and train, then a cab. The driver took him for someone who didn't know his way around and made him pay for his ignorance, left him close to broke; and Papi was too polite to refuse the thief a tip: two quarters.

He got there a little past sunup and spent close to five hours abusing his stomach and nervous system with cup after cup of black coffee, waiting for the airplane to land and clarify that mysterious telegram. ". . . Starving, but the last thing on my mind was food, if that makes any sense . . . my nerves." The waitresses kept a close eye on him, as if they thought he was going to steal something. They put the salt, pepper, mustard, and ketchup out of his reach; the cream was under the counter, the donuts and turnovers on the other side of it. They had him all wrong.

The plane was late; when it finally arrived, there was no sign of Lilia and the boys, only strangers walking into the arms of waiting loved ones. He was about to break down when this woman with high cheekbones, her face almost a mask from all the makeup, a bony woman, close to breastless, swished up to him as if she had invented sophistication, and introduced herself as Lilia Tapia de Cardona. Her middle name was Pompilia, and he must be Gerán. Doesn't he remember her?

"No," he says, embarrassed. "Almost yes, but no. Forgive me, I had short sleep last night. Fire engines . . ."

She explains that they're second cousins, or maybe only third. "You know how backward they are about keeping birth records in our villages. Some of them have never heard of the twentieth century."

He nods politely. Who is this woman? "Whoever she is, in less than a minute she's talking like an old friend."

"Whatever cousins we are, Gerán," she's going on, "I'm on that side of our family that has a few successful members." And when he asks her what she means by that, she wastes no time telling him about the medical doctor in Mayagüez, the "classical" pianist in Ponce (a poverty-parish organist, he can't help thinking), the schoolteacher in Santurce and the other one in Hato Rey, the parish priest in Caguas, the cement executive in Bayamón. . . . She goes on with this list of family notables he's never heard of; she's sounding more desperate with each name dropped.

"What she wanted, Santos, was a place to stay." So he asks her cautiously, as politely as he can put it, whether she'd mind spending a day or two at his "apartment. My broom closet, I meant. But I didn't want to offend her with language like that."

She wastes about ten seconds pretending to be thinking it over, and while waiting for her guaranteed yes, he sizes up her outfit: a thin purple dress decorated with nondescript tropical flowers, something out of a San Juan bargain store, he can't help thinking; and a pair of white shoes, imperfectly dyed high-heelers, some of the original black showing through the white.

"Very well, Gerán," she tells him nonchalantly, as if doing him a kindness, "maybe for a couple of days until I can find a decent hotel." He tells her she shouldn't have any trouble finding one, and off they go.

"I thought you were my wife and kids," he tells her on the subway back.

"Do I look like her?" She must think he's trying to flatter her.

"I meant that you both have the same name."

"I know," she says.

"You do? May I ask who told you?"

"Octavio's Calpurnia. My cousin. I stayed as her guest before taking the plane."

This Calpurnia must be running her own rooming house. "She must have put this Lilia Pompilia up to the telegram trick. Talk about *maromas*. All kinds of stunts to get something for nothing, Santos."

"Did you sleep in the same bed?" I ask.

"Who, me? What are you getting at?"

"Nothing. One bed, two people. That's always a problem, depending."

"No problem. I slept on the floor."

"I think you're too generous sometimes, Papi. That's one of your——"

"It was good for my back. I was her host, anyway. Where else can I sleep?"

"How long did you have to sleep on the floor?"

"Two weeks."

"Did she leave you a tip?"

"I wouldn't take a tip even if she had anything to tip with. She was almost broke when she arrived."

And he went broke feeding her, taking her to old Mexican movies (he slept through those, he said) and to employment agencies. It turned out she had secretarial skills, so she wasn't all helpless, and she finally found a position (he found it for her) with a Latin American import-export outfit. He got docked for taking off from work so he could escort her around the job agencies. And when he came home from work one day, looking forward to a little companionship, all he found of her was a note pinned to his pillow. It said a friend of hers from work had put her onto a "decent hotel" downtown (no address) and that she had decided to move in right away before someone else took it. She promised to come around as soon as possible, either next day or the day after. "But you know how it is," he told me a long time later. "I never saw her again."

"Did you try to track her down at least?"

"What for? She was on her own now. I have a feeling some man in that import-export place fell in love with her, and that was that."

"And you weren't even angry?"

"For what?"

"For being taken in by this Pompilia Lilia."

"Lilia Pompilia."

"All right."

"No, I wasn't. What for? It happens all the time."

Not angry, he repeated, but frustrated, impatient to get his own family over. "Desperate, Santos." The lonelies hit him hard again, and not for the first time he considered pawning Octavio's gold-tipped pen and Mito's old radio with it; he also thought of giving up his SRO and sleeping in basements for as long as he had to, a small saving. Except that was just another way of committing suicide, a major sin. So he controlled the urge and went to his brother instead. "But only after trying everything else. Mito and Agripina had next to nothing themselves, and I didn't want them to think I was turning them into Household Finance."

Somebody at work put him on to this HFC, and he went to them, the local branch, but they didn't even ask to see his Social Security card; he had no collateral. Same for the two savings banks he approached. "Let me put it to you this way, Mr. Malánguish," one bank manager told him. "It's not what our bank can do for you, but what you can do for our bank, if you see what I'm getting at." No collateral, no loan. The alert guard's eyes followed him to the exit, holding his head up. The revolving door almost brought him back inside, he was that upset.

His favorite confessor at Saint Misericordia's Church, a benevolent old Irishman who had worked his way up to the priesthood ("I spent my boyhood shining shoes, my son. I worked on the docks before I joined the seminary"), suggested he try Catholic Charities, which specialized in emergency cases. "And you look as though you belong in an emergency clinic, Germán. No offense meant." None taken.

Catholic Charities told him they had no money. "We don't dispense cash, Mr. Málangas. Only household items, secondhand necessities. Look around and pick out a few. Take your time." He took as many pawnable items as he could carry: two secondhand shopping bags stuffed with used pots, pans, dinnerware, a pair of shoes without laces, a shadeless lamp shaped like a jug of whiskey with a four-leaf-clover design and some green words in a foreign language, two pairs of pants too big for him, and a couple of shirts he wouldn't be caught in, no matter how desperate. The third pawnshop he approached with these handouts gave him three dollars for both shopping bags and asked him not to come back. He promised not to.

He visited *bodegas* and asked if they could use a part-time delivery man, but they were either all filled up or they had no deliveries. "We're strictly cash-and-carry here, Malánguez," one grocer told him. "Try Don Matos down the block." Don Matos down the block laughed him out of his hole-in-the-wall, and suggested he try shining shoes. Which he considered, but the competition in that field was already fierce; an amateur like him trying to move in on the pros would get swamped, go bankrupt overnight. Same for selling the Sunday *News* Saturday nights. He tried doing that and came back home with five unsold copies. From eight P.M. to two A.M. he had succeeded in selling all of one copy to a heavy drinker in a bar.

And finally, before hitting his brother for an interest-free loan, he discovered empties. There were refundable bottles all over the streets: milk, soda, beer. You didn't even need the entire bottle; from the neck up, an empty bottle was worth two or three cents. Weekends, armed with a potato sack one grocer gave him, he went around collecting discarded empties. He found them in the gutters, in garbage cans, on stoops, in empty lots, and in Central Park. That park was a gold mine of empty beer bottles, each one worth three cents. Grocers and candystore owners began referring to him as "The Empty Bottles Man," "Señor Refundable," "Don Deposits," "Mr. Bottleneck," and other tributes. He couldn't afford to defend himself, a choice between hard cash and swallowing his self-respect. He swallowed the respect, for the time being.

Then the Law, in the form of two mounted policemen, put an end to this scavenging. They caught him coming out of the 106th Street exit with his stuffed sack. This was about two hours past curfew. "Let's see what you got in the sack, Chico," one of them said.

"It is just bottles, officer," he answered, and they said that they'd believe his story as soon as he showed them. So he had to pull every empty out of the sack (some of them were only refundable necks) and upend it to satisfy the officers that there were no jewels or illegal drugs inside: only insects (spiders, a couple of Japanese beetles), but these didn't count as contraband, so they had to let him go. Another nut, they concluded.

"Let's not catch you in the park after curfew." And they

confiscated his flashlight (borrowed from someone at work), a bur-
glar's tool.

As usual whenever the cops stopped someone for any reason,
spectators had gathered around the scene of the frisking ("I felt like
a bum, Santos, which maybe I was just then") and he decided to give
up exchanging bottles for our plane tickets. There had to be a less
humiliating way, and a faster one: Mito again.

Mito had about fifty dollars in the bank (for his children's education, he had said), and something more important: collateral. The
chef at the hotel where he worked—a fancy one on Park Avenue—
and the chef's steward, and a couple of other men with impressive
titles all vouched for Mito's honesty. Good enough for Mito's savings
bank and the local HFC. "We'll pay them back any way we can," he
told Papi, as if there was nothing to worry about, as if this weren't
the first time he had pulled that stunt. As if he weren't peeing in his
own pants.

Papi didn't have too much trouble finding a furnished apartment
for us. He did a lot of asking around and taped hand-lettered signs
on storefronts. Within two weeks he got a response from an old couple who couldn't wait to move back to the island as permanent
guests of their grandchildren and others. Their apartment was furnished and they wanted a hundred dollars in cash, but that was just a
bluff. He had no trouble knocking them down to fifty—a steal, but
he had no choice—thirty cash and twenty in installments. They'd just
have to give him their new address and trust him to come through.
(He did.) They were impatient to leave. "This whole thing has been
a big mistake for us, Gerán," the old man told him. "But you're still
young." He guessed he was; it didn't always feel like it.

And that was what we moved into: fifth floor, five-and-a-half
rooms, a huge hospital one block away to the south, Central Park
less than a block away to the west, the Home and Hospital for the
Sons and Daughters of Israel on one corner, Mr. Cohn and Son's
Farmacia on the other, and, spanning two windows, a fancy fire-
escape for just in case. "Not bad, Lilia, eh?" he told Mami.

She wasn't too sure about that. "Is this what we left Bautabarro for?" she said. "I don't think I want to spend the rest of our lives here, Gerán."

"Don't worry, Lilia, we won't. This is just the beginning." He was hurt. She was disappointed. They'd have to work it out.

It was a strange neighborhood: crowded, littered, smelly, loud. Men, grown, growing, and declining, sat on stoops doing nothing special, just talking or staring into the distance, as if expecting something. They played sidewalk cards and dominoes, using garbage cans as chairs. The table was a piece of rescued plywood resting on two pairs of knees. One wrong move and the whole game would come crashing down. "It's different, all right," Mami concluded.

1983

# JOYCE JOHNSON

*Novelist and nonfiction writer Joyce Johnson (1935–    ) grew up in New York City, and gravitated as a young woman to the Beat crowd of writers and painters. Her indispensable memoir of that period,* Minor Characters, *describes her experiences as Jack Kerouac's companion and as an urban pioneer, nesting in rough tenement lofts and cold-water flats of precisely the sort her parents had striven to escape.*

## FROM *MINOR CHARACTERS*

SCUFFLING WAS WHAT you did in my new neighborhood, soon to be called the East Village. The original poor of the Lower East Side had scuffled without hope, of course, selling their labor for low wages. Their children grew up and fled to Queens or Jersey, leaving room in the tenements for middle-class children loosely defined as "artists," who believed for a while, under the influence of all the new philosophy and rejecting the values of their own parents, that they had no use for money. Nomads without rucksacks, they joyfully camped out among the gloomy Ukrainians, the suspicious Poles, the Italian fruit vendors, the retired Jewish garment workers dying in their fourth-floor walkups. The newcomers to the neighborhood regarded jobs the way jazz musicians regarded gigs— brief engagements. A steady gig (really a contradiction in terms) was valued chiefly as a means of getting unemployment insurance. The great accomplishment was to avoid actual employment for as long as possible and by whatever means. But it was all right for women to go out and earn wages, since they had no important creative endeavors to be distracted from. The women didn't mind, or, if they did, they never said—not until years later.

Meanwhile rents were low, you could eat for next to nothing, toilets were in the hallway, bathtubs were in the kitchen, and you never let the meter man in if you could help it. Con Ed trucks appeared on the streets on Friday mornings to turn delinquent payers off for the weekend, plunging them into penal darkness even if they could have paid up that very afternoon. Yahrzeit candles, or the Puerto Rican kind with rainbow-colored wax, were hoarded for such emergencies. Poems were written about roaches who lived in the stove, the woodwork, the innards of portable radios and shoes, and copulated in the chocolate-smelling gas heat of winter. Wives swapped recipes for chicken-back stew or lentil soup with gizzards; tofu had not yet been discovered in the West.

Bachelor poets, I soon noticed, seemed to live by an aesthetic of grime. Moving into a ruin, a poet would faithfully maintain it as such, filling the air behind the permanently filmed windows with nicotine, and accumulating beer bottles so prodigiously that a monument to Miss Rheingold was created, too sacred for any trashcan.

Another approach to tenement life involved denial of the tenement as a tenement and insistence upon it as "a charming place" once it had been stripped to its core, taken back virtually to its prehistory as a dwelling. Plaster was laboriously scraped off brick that had always been plastered; windowsills and lintels were sanded raw; decades of linoleum were ripped up to reveal floorboards underneath, even parquet, sometimes, perfectly preserved by generations of housewives who, like my mother and Jack's, always put a covering on anything "good."

My mother couldn't understand why I'd returned to the streets my grandparents had struggled so hard to stay out of: "At least we never lived on the Lower East Side. We lived near Bronx Park when it was a beautiful area. At least we never lived in the slums."

I loved the slums, my slums, the sweet slums of Bohemia and beatnikdom, where sunflowers and morning glories would bloom on fire escapes in the summer and old ladies weighed down by breasts leaned on goosedown pillows in windows, self-appointed guardians of the street, and Tompkins Square with its onion-topped church had the greyness of photos of Moscow. Who would not wish to be a scuffler on Second Avenue? I bought seven-cent bagels and ten-cent half-sour pickles and sat up till dawn in Rappaport's, where they gave you a whole basket of rolls free, drinking coffee with a jazz trombonist from St. Louis and a poet just arrived from Chicago.

Thirty years before, Yiddish culture had flowered on Second

Avenue. All that was left were some dairy restaurants. Around the corner from my apartment was a bar called Slugger Anne's—once the Café Royal, the legendary gathering place of Jewish artists and intelligentsia. In his years of exile, Trotsky had published *Novy Mir* in the basement of a house on St. Marks Place, the much-traveled thoroughfare to the West Village. Now you could see W. H. Auden come down his stoop in his bedroom slippers on his way to the A&P, and you could hardly take a walk there without running into someone you'd just met two nights before and might remain friends with for the rest of your life. The East Side was flowering again. If you couldn't live on Gay Street you lived on East Thirteenth, and knew you'd never never go home again to the Upper West Side.

My new apartment was small and had no light. Plants grew pale and died in the air-shaft window. The Pullman kitchen had been painted black by a previous occupant. Since I didn't have much to put in the two rooms, I decorated according to the principle explained to me by a painter in the Cedar, that space between objects created a field of tension around them. Next door to me lived Mike the alcoholic super, who terrified me now and then by pounding on my door at 3 A.M., demanding to come in and "fix the plumbing," while his wife in robe and curlers screamed "Kurva! Kurva!" on the landing. "What's *kurva*?" I asked a sympathetic neighbor, a married ballet dancer whom the super never bothered at all. "I'm not sure," she said, "but I think it's Polish for *whore*." On the other side of me lived a woman in a black wig who was the super's wife's best friend. As I came up the stairs, she'd always open her door to see who was with me, and once I caught her sprinkling perfume on my doorstep—"Because you cook the cabbage all night and you drive me crazy!" she yelled.

I didn't spend a great deal of time at home anyway. To this day I have a triangular scar on my left thumb reminding me of the night I rushed to my apartment after a day of being a temporary typist for an insurance company, determined to rush out again after the boring necessity of making dinner. Two pork chops frozen together threatened to hold me up. I hacked away at them, cut some flesh off my thumb in the process, wrapped a dish towel around the wound, and went out anyway, bleeding all the way crosstown to the Cedar.

Franz Kline asked to examine my thumb, and lectured me. "If I were your father, I'd take you to get stitches."

"Well, I didn't want to miss anything," I told him.

"No. Of course not." Still holding my wrist, he shook his head with a gleam of mischievous understanding in his eyes.

Affluence was spreading among the painters that fall. They'd turn up self-consciously in stiff new brown corduroy suits purchased at Hudson's on the Bowery, on their way to gallery openings all the way uptown. Socialites too would appear at the Cedar, fairy godmothers in extraordinary furs—potential collectors of artists as well as art. Some painters' old ladies were retaliating by picking up the wilder stuff in thrift shops—Spanish combs and beaded dresses from the twenties that ripped under the arms if danced in too energetically. They draped themselves in embroidered piano shawls, put on purple mesh stockings, and called themselves Beat Pre-Raphaelites.

Every Saturday night now there were parties. The word would spread through the Cedar like wildfire that a certain up-and-coming abstract expressionist was inviting over a few close friends, some collectors, and some important gallery people, and shortly the as-tonished host would find himself confronting hordes of crashers who'd trudged up five flights of stairs with six-packs and bottles of Gallo—as well as grass, which was smoked with discreet ceremoni-ousness at these gatherings, in intense little circles of people. Occasionally would-be guests were turned away and fistfights broke out, but most of the time everyone got in. These parties were like giant vibrating rush-hour trains filled with swaying passengers, all being borne along to some further destination—the next love affair, the next party, the next hangover, the next 5 A.M. bowl of wonton soup on Mott Street.

The best place to end up was the Five Spot, which during the summer had materialized like an overnight miracle in a bar on Second Street and the Bowery formerly frequented by bums. The new owners had cleaned it up a little, hauled in a piano, and hung posters on the walls advertising Tenth Street gallery openings. The connection with "the scene" was clear from the beginning. Here for the price of a beer you could hear Coltrane or Thelonius Monk, or an occasional painter/musician like Larry Rivers sitting in and blowing hard and a little self-consciously. Kenneth Rexroth flew in from San Francisco and did a weekend of poetry-and-jazz, staking out his claim on that territory in the East before Jack or Allen or Gregory Corso came back to town and stole his thunder.

But most of all, I remember one night when a middle-aged, sad-faced black woman stood up beside the table where she'd been sitting and sang so beautifully in a cracked, heartbroken voice I was sure I'd heard before. There was silence when she finished, then everyone rose and began clapping. It was the great Lady Day, who had been deprived of her cabaret card by the New York police and was soon to die under arrest in a hospital bed—subject of the famous poem by Frank O'Hara, who also heard Billie Holiday sing that night:

> leaning on the john door in the 5 Spot
> while she whispered a song along the keyboard
> to Mal Waldron and everyone and I stopped breathing

1983

# LIONEL ABEL

*The so-called "New York intellectuals" reached their zenith of cultural eminence in the period from the 1930's through the 50's. Politically engaged, disputatious, and brilliant, often the children of Jewish immigrants, they were for the most part non-academics who supported themselves by writing for magazines and journals on an impressive range of cultural and topical issues. One of the most illustrious of their number, Lionel Abel (1910–   ), in his crankily amusing memoir* The Intellectual Follies, *tells the hilarious and sad tale of the group's demise.*

## FROM *THE INTELLECTUAL FOLLIES*

THERE ARE INTELLECTUALS, any number of them, in New York City today, but is there any one group of them able to speak for the others? I have had reasons for seriously doubting that there is, ever since one evening in 1958.

An evening in the Big Town that was indeed a Big Town evening in its animation and futility! But let me first sketch the political background to it: Boris Pasternak, awarded the Nobel Prize in Stockholm, had been denied permission by the Soviet authorities to go to Sweden and be honored for his work. Moreover, his novel *Dr. Zhivago,* for which he had been given the Nobel award, was denied publication by the Soviet government. Under these circumstances it seemed perfectly proper for politically interested intellectuals in New York City to send the Soviet government a letter of protest. (This our own press would have published, whatever the Russian response.) Surely, I thought, there was no great problem here. One had only to bring together a sampling of the New York City writers who had expressed political views over the years and had in the past been critical of Soviet policies. At least that was how it seemed to me. I consulted Meyer Schapiro on this, and obtained his agreement to suggest to some of the writers of our acquaintance that a meeting be held at which we might discuss the kind of protest which would be appropriate.

Here are some of the writers we invited: Dwight Macdonald, Mary McCarthy (she was then living in New York City), Harold Rosenberg, William Phillips of *Partisan Review* (Philip Rahv was then in Boston), Norman Podhoretz, Paul Goodman, Hannah Arendt, Eric Bentley, Stanley Plastrik of *Dissent* (Irving Howe was in the Midwest). To be sure we did not invite every single writer or scholar whom we knew to be living in New York City. But the ones we did invite were certainly representative; moreover, they were persons who had seen each other with some regularity over the years and had participated, on other occasions, in common actions. These were not the only intellectuals in New York City, but without them, could one say there was an intelligentsia?

We did not invite those intellectuals in the Committee for Cultural Freedom who had taken what I considered to be a cold war position towards the Soviet Union. The position I took, with Schapiro's support, and which I presented at the meeting was this: The Republic of Letters was indeed a reality, if not an actually existing entity. This republic, of which Pasternak was as especially honored member, was not itself a signatory of either the NATO agreements or of the Warsaw Pact. We were making our appeal as citizens of this republic on behalf of a fellow citizen.

Joseph Buttinger had offered us a whole floor of his townhouse on East Eighty-seventh Street, and he had agreed to chair our meeting. Just a word about Mr. Buttinger, who is, by the way, quite well known in left-wing intellectual circles. An Austrian worker with Socialist convictions, he had married a cultivated American woman of great wealth; she was sympathetic to left-wing causes, which the couple often backed. I am told they were very generous to Ortega y Gasset when he was in exile, and I know that Mr. Buttinger has been helpful to *Dissent*. I had visited the Buttingers once before, at their apartment on Central Park West, where they had hosted a party for *Dissent*, and I remember being struck by their library, which was just extraordinary, and also at the availability of the books, which Mr. Buttinger generously offered to lend to anyone at the *Dissent* party.

By 1958, though, the Buttingers had left their apartment for the more grandiose townhouse on Eighty-seventh Street. Mr. Buttinger, needless to say, did not abandon his books. These now occupied the whole ground floor of the new townhouse, and if you wanted to borrow one of them, you had to discuss the matter with a librarian. In fact, if you wanted a book you had to first of all apply for a card, just as in the public libraries. And the date of your borrowing would be duly stamped, the book taken noted, and you could be asked, if need be, not to keep it beyond a certain date. There were many more books on the shelves, as I remember, and every single one of these was less available. Such was the march of progress in the Buttinger household, hardly differing in this respect from the movement of things in the world outside.

To be sure, there were reasons for controlling the coming and going of the Buttinger books. People who are not forced to sign on the dotted line when they borrow a book tend, the Buttingers had found, not to return it, thus depriving others who would also like the pleasure of not signing up for a book, of just this privilege. So what is one to do in such a case? The Buttingers had in fact done the sensible thing. They indexed the books, hired a librarian, gave their prospective book borrowers cards, and quite broke my heart when I arrived that evening in 1958 and saw what had occurred. Mr. Buttinger had of course also limited his own freedom. He could no longer say to a friend who wanted some book: "Take it; it's downstairs." Yes, of course the book was downstairs, or might be there. But wherever it was, it wasn't Buttinger's; it now belonged to his library.

The new order of the Buttinger library gave me my first shock in an evening full of crossed purposes. Here I want to briefly describe the main actors in the drama which was to follow. I shall begin with Paul Goodman who was, I think, the only one we invited who represented a generally dissenting policy with regard to the Pasternak affair. Others raised difficulties about what Schapiro and I proposed, but I think Paul had come *politically* prepared to make trouble for any such proposal. Here is my speculation as to why.

Goodman was at that moment in his career just on the point of becoming famous, but without the knowledge that this was about to happen. Lack of adequate fame, which is to say, a fame extending beyond small circles of admirers, had made him irritable for years, and especially irritable in those small groups where he was well known. I believe he was aware at that time that a consistently anti-Communist, or—what was almost the same—a pro-American government attitude, would prevent any writer from being taken up by the youth. Maybe Paul was even more intuitive than I am suggesting, and, looking into the future, was able to read there that to success-fully combat American military policy in Southeast Asia one would have to make some kind of alliance with the pro-Communists among the young. Let's grant Paul the best of motives. In any case, he had come prepared to sabotage any kind of action on behalf of Pasternak. As he took his seat among us he announced for all to hear that he had not read *Dr. Zhivago* and had no intention of reading it. Then he said: "Pasternak can read me." When the first suggestion was put forward that we draft a letter of protest to the Soviet government, Paul indi-cated that he would sign no such letter. Why not? This was the rea-son he gave: Coming from us, such a protest would be in bad faith, for we had not protested the refusal of a moving picture house in Hicksville, Long Island to show a recent Charlie Chaplin film which made fun of American anti-Communism. "Where were we when this film was denied a showing?" Paul wanted to know. "Where were we?" Mary McCarthy countered, "We were certainly not in Hicksville." She had never been there, had no intention of going there, and just because she hadn't gone to Hicksville did not mean that Pasternak should not be allowed to go to Stockholm. But, as I found on other occasions, a witticism was not going to stop Paul when he felt himself deeply committed. He had two other objections to our projected protests: First of all, we had done nothing for James Joyce during the twenties when *Ulysses* was banned, and secondly, he thought that in banning the publication of certain books, the Soviet leaders showed a respect for literature which American politicians lacked. Miss McCarthy responded: "Then hadn't a certain respect been shown for literature in the banning of *Ulysses*?" And returning to the matter of the Charlie Chaplin film, she added that in her opinion anyone who had respect for Chaplin would not want to live in Hicksville; so why should the film have been shown there? This remark of hers was interpreted by Dwight Macdonald, who was sitting next to me, as an indication that from now on Paul Goodman was fair game, and after that whatever Paul said, Dwight attacked.

In fact, Dwight did have something against Paul, an article in *Dissent* in which Goodman had described Dwight as a man who thought with his typewriter. To complicate matters, Dwight that evening was also involved in a running battle with Harold Rosenberg, who had called him a Philistine in *Dissent* for his views on contemporary art. I think Dwight must have felt that night that Harold was politically allied with Paul and that he would have to do battle with both. But I must say that on this particular evening Rosenberg said little—this was most unusual—and made no really signal contribution to the chaos of our meeting.

In addition to the Macdonald-Goodman conflict, there was Mary McCarthy's feud with me. We had always had friendly relations, and I did admire most of her writings, though not her ventures in dramatic criticism. When she attacked Eugene O'Neill's reputation, remarking that not only was he incapable of writing an entire play, but incapable of composing one single good sentence, I did a piece against her in *The New Leader* in which I indicated that O'Neill was certainly the best of our playwrights and Miss McCarthy was just as certainly not our best dramatic critic. When she swept into the Buttinger living room, Miss McCarthy told me in the roundest terms that she had come, not merely to pay tribute to Pasternak, but also to tell me I should have informed her I was breaking off relations with her *before* I published a piece critical of her views. I replied, as I poured a drink for her from Mr. Buttinger's excellent stock, that I believed in the manners observed in Parliament, where one attacks one's opponent roundly and then exchanges compliments with him or her over drinks. Mary, though, thought this was not a matter of manners, but of morals, and let me know she would do her best to cross me all evening.

As for Hannah Arendt, she was not opposed, of course, to helping Pasternak, but she was doubtful that our intervention would help him. This was a serious consideration, and it is something everyone must think of now who is concerned to help the Russian dissidents. They do insist, and have insisted all along, that American intervention helps them, but of course such intervention has to be properly timed, properly stated, and as we have seen from the fate of Shcharansky, may well be counterproductive. In any case, Miss Arendt urged caution upon us and had nothing more positive to suggest. As for Pasternak, she was doubtful that any statement by us could help him, and quite sure that any but the most perfectly stated protest would actually hurt him, and she gave us the feeling that it was not possible for us to come up with a statement she would feel obliged to sign. At this point practically everyone present helped himself to a drink, and Dwight, by now quite drunk, indicated that he wanted to take the floor. Mr. Buttinger, who was chairing the meeting, denied it to him. I cannot remember what his reason was, but I do remember that at the time I did not think it arbitrary. But Dwight thought it was. "Let's get another chairman," he shouted, as if another could be supplied as easily as an additional drink. He had also forgotten that Mr. Buttinger was not only our chairman, but our host. As I recall, Mr. Buttinger gracefully relinquished his chair, leaving us to our own devices for contriving chaos.

And chaotic it was after he left.

Meyer Schapiro pleaded with us to try and find some measure of real agreement so that we could at the very least express our feeling that Pasternak deserved support. He spoke with the clarity and eloquence which had so often, in past meetings, thrilled most of those in the room. This time, though, his eloquence was unavailing.

Paul once again asserted his unwillingness to sign any statement which implied any approval of the policy of our government, most especially its policy on literary questions. Any attack on Soviet policy, he said, was an endorsement of that of its opposite number. To this I objected that the United States was without any policy on literary matters, at which point William Phillips, who had so far not intervened in the argument, took moderate issue with me and gave support to Paul's position.

I have observed William Phillips's behavior at general meetings and have noticed a certain political line he always seems to follow. During the sixties, at a meeting called by *Commentary* to discuss the civil rights movement in this country, a meeting at which James Baldwin, Nat Glazer, Sidney Hook, and Gunnar Myrdal were the panelists, William Phillips, when he took the floor, announced: "I'm probably the only intellectual here who agrees with Jimmy Baldwin." In fact this was not the case. There were others in the audience who did not agree with what had been said by Sidney Hook, by Gunnar Myrdal, by Nat Glazer, and who did agree with Baldwin's comments. At Buttinger's in 1955, William took what amounted to the same line, though he did not say: "I'm probably the only one here who agrees with Paul." What he said was this: "I'm trying to understand what Paul has said because I would like to agree with him." Now I'm quite sure that this was a correct description of his desire; he did want to agree with Paul. For Paul was clearly the one taking a line that could be interpreted as *left*. But William did not say, "I want to agree with Paul because he is taking a *left* line on this." William has a certain gift for subtlety, and so he put his proposition differently. He said: "I think Paul wants us to respond as writers to the Soviet treatment of Pasternak, rather than as persons committed to a certain political line." According to William, Paul was the one who had talked like a writer, though William did not go so far as to say that he had talked on behalf of literature. What Paul had in fact said was that he did not want to defend Pasternak and that he would not criticize the Soviet government. Somehow, as William saw it, those of us who wanted to defend Pasternak, and who, by the way, unlike Paul, had actually read his novel, were not thinking as *writers* hoping to defend a fellow writer.

It was precisely to rule out this sort of argument that I had suggested at the outset of our meeting that we had come together as citizens of the Republic of Letters, and that it was in the name of this imaginary institution, and not of any actually existing state, that we were determined to protest the Soviets' treatment of Boris Pasternak. What Paul Goodman had done, and what William Phillips supported him in doing, amounted to denying that there was any such thing as a Republic of Letters. There were only states like the

Soviet Union and the United States, hostile to each other, and we could not attack one of these states without giving comfort and support to its opposite number. To cap the confusion, we were now being told by William Phillips that Paul wanted us to think of ourselves as writers in what amounted to nothing less than a round denial that there was any purely literary institution to which we could say we belonged. I replied that Paul was trying to say that we were just United Staters or Soviet Staters, and that the so-called Republic of Letters was just a literary dream.

At this point somebody noticed that our host Mr. Buttinger had left his chair (in fact he had left it in some dudgeon) and suggested that it was only proper to invite him back. Not, however, to resume the function of chairman, Dwight insisted. Somebody said to Dwight, "You won't ask him to leave if he comes back and sits down quietly?" Somebody went to fetch Mr. Buttinger, but when asked to return, he indicated that he had had enough of our drunken shenanigans, and declined.

Just two more details about the meeting. I, too, had helped myself to Mr. Buttinger's bourbon, and no doubt this had been duly noted. When at one point I suggested that we propose to the leading Soviet literary journal that it publish Edmund Wilson's favorable review of *Dr. Zhivago* (which had appeared in the *New Yorker*) and, in return for this concession to American literary opinion, would try to obtain publication in some leading American publication, preferably the *New Yorker*, for any critique of *Dr. Zhivago* by a Russian critic chosen by the Soviet authorities, Miss Arendt airily dismissed my suggestion. She said: "Schnapps's ideas."

When it was finally apparent that no statement would be agreed upon, the meeting broke up. It had been suggested that Harold Rosenberg write a provisional statement which would then be sent to Irving Howe for revision, but as we left the Buttinger drawing room, Eric Bentley, whom I had brought to the meeting, whispered to me, "I'll never sign a political statement edited by Irving Howe." Nor did he. And Harold Rosenberg wrote no statement, and none was presented for Irving Howe to revise. None of those present at that meeting were able to sign a statement on behalf of Pasternak. It was evident that the New York intellectuals could no longer act as a group.

What broke up our meeting? Personal rivalries? Drunkenness? Lack of seriousness? Political differences? All these, of course, played a part. But if I am to single out any one cause that was more than merely contributory to the general disorder, then this cause was none of the ones I have already mentioned, but something quite different; in fact it was fear of a very particular kind which in recent times I have seen dominate many meetings, many movements, much action and inaction. What fear? The fear that what one did or said might be regarded as contrary, and even harmful, to the Left.

One must in no case do anything that might be harmful to the Left. What if the projected action seems a good one? Then one must be all the more careful. One must consider every possible consequence, even the most remote. Many actions that at first sight might seem beneficent, when looked at more closely turn out to involve a possible damage to the Left. What Left? Which Left? Never mind. And do not ask. Indeed there is need not to ask, for the very fact that we don't know what the Left is today means that whatever it be, its situation is precarious. We don't even know what the Left is? Then we must be all the more careful of it. We must do nothing that by any stretch of imagination may be regarded as against whatever it is that remains of this Left, which we can no longer identify. And it was on this fear that Paul Goodman had played when he assailed us for not having done battle for Chaplin's film in Hicksville during the early fifties, or even for Joyce's novel during the twenties, when most of those in the room had been too young to know of Joyce. And it was this fear which William Phillips tried to make us feel when he said that Paul had wanted us to respond to the Pasternak affair like writers. But nobody had been invited to the Buttinger townhouse who could be described as antileftist, and almost everyone there wanted to be thought of as a leftist or as a supporter of the Left. Also, there was not one person in the room who then knew with any degree of clarity just what it was still possible to mean by the term

"Left." I have observed that it is in such moments of political confusion—that is, when we don't know what the Left is—that our fear of being thought against the Left, or anti-Left, is greatest.

But there is reason, I believe, behind this fear of damaging the Left even when one is not sure what the Left stands for or is at any particular moment. For fear of damaging the Left may represent fear of dissolving intellectual unity, the intelligentsia, in fact, which in America in recent times has only been brought together, shaped into some kind of unity, by leftist interests. So for any of my readers who may judge William Phillips's behavior as I described it at the Pasternak meeting as devious or personally motivated, I want to make this clearly contrary judgment: I think William was motivated by a desire to keep the intellectuals together, and this he may have very well believed could only be done by steering clear of any action which could be interpreted as anti-Left. And the fact is that the New York intelligentsia came apart simply because it could not agree that it was in the interest of anything that could be called the Left to protest Pasternak's treatment by the Russians. In Europe, of course, there have been right-wing intelligentsias. I'm thinking of, for instance, *L'Action française*; and even in this country we had for a time at least the grouping of Southern writers led by Donald Davidson and Allen Tate. But this grouping was of only very short duration, and one of its most gifted writers, Robert Penn Warren, threw in his lot finally with more moderate intellectuals in the North. Today of course there are some right-wing writers grouped around the National Review. But generally speaking, whenever there has been any significant coherent activity by intellectuals, involving more than just a few persons, this activity has been leftist in character and motivated by left-wing interests. In a period where it is said that there is a conservative tide sweeping the country, and at a time too, when leftism is in intellectual difficulty and cannot define itself clearly, it is still hard to find any clearly articulated right-wing intelligentsia in this country or in fact in any country in western Europe. If there is going to be an intelligentsia of any sort, it apparently has to be left-wing.

◆  ◆  ◆  ◆  ◆

If any one person was responsible for breaking up that meeting, that person unquestionably was Paul. And his reason for breaking it up was basically that he did not want to make publicly an unfavorable judgment of Soviet literary policy. Yet Paul, however much he may have wanted to get along with leftist youth, was in no sense a Stalinist. And I think he may have felt some regret for his own actions as we left the Buttinger townhouse that night. For as Meyer Schapiro and I were getting into a cab, Paul, who had come up behind us, called to me. What did he want? As I remember, he shook his fist at me, and I interpretated the gesture as hostile, and especially hostile to me. On the other hand, he called out, "Lionel, wait!" But I thought, "Why should we wait? So that he can shake his fist in my face?" And I told the driver to drive off. He did, and we left Paul on the curb calling after us, "But I wanted to come with you!" All the ambiguities and contradictions of the evening were somehow present in that last upsetting scene.

1 9 8 4

# E. L. DOCTOROW

*For native New Yorkers, as well as out-of-towners, the 1939 World's Fair in Flushing Meadows, Queens, constituted a kind of utopian city alongside the real, imperfect one of the prewar 30's. E. L. Doctorow (1931– ) has written eloquently about the city's past in novels such as* Ragtime *and* The Waterworks, *but never more so than in* World's Fair, *a fusion of memoir and fiction that conjures up the mystery and unreality of this miniaturized future world, as seen through the eyes of a Depression-era Bronx kid.*

## FROM *WORLD'S FAIR*

EVEN FROM the elevated station I could see the famous Trylon and Perisphere. They were enormous. They were white in the sun, white spire, white globe, they went together, they belonged together as some sort of partnership in my head. I didn't know what they stood for, it was all very vague in my mind, but to see them, after having seen pictures and posters and buttons of them for so long, made me incredibly happy. I felt like jumping up and down, I felt myself trembling with joy.

I thought of them as friends of mine.

We came down the stairs right into the fairgrounds. Banners flew from the pavilions. The wide streets were painted red, yellow and blue. They were absolutely clean. The buildings were mostly streamlined, with rounded edges, as I supposed buildings of the future should be. We walked on Rainbow Avenue. The day was fine. Thousands of people were here. They smiled and chatted and pointed things out and consulted their guidebooks. We walked along Constitution Mall. Brilliant tulip gardens were in bloom. The Fair had its own buses. It had its own tractor trains, and Norma decided we should have a ride. An orange-and-blue electric-powered tractor pulled a dozen rubber-wheeled cars behind it, and when the driver blew his horn it played the opening measures of "The Sidewalks of New York": "East side, west side, all around the town." Norma wanted us just to look around and get our bearings. We sat on the last car of the train, so that it whipped around a bit at the corners. Of course it was very tame, nothing like the roller coaster we could see in the distance in the amusement area; it had to go slow because it moved among great crowds of strolling people. Everywhere people walked in family groups and stopped to take their pictures in front of exhibit buildings. There were lady guides in grey uniform jackets and hats. The shuffle of feet was like a constant whispering in my ears, or what I imagined a herd of antelope would sound like going in great numbers slowly through high grass. We went around Commerce Circle and through the Plaza of Light and right around the Trylon and Perisphere, which, up close, seemed to fill the sky. The pictures of them hadn't suggested their enormity. They were the only white objects to be seen. They were dazzling. They seemed to be about to take off, they looked lighter than air. A ramp connected them, and I could see a line of people silhouetted against the blue sky. We passed the statue of George Washington. I had my map, which I consulted. But with Norma it wasn't really necessary. She knew everything. "Let's make our plans," she said. She had been so happy to have me with them that she'd arranged to join the fun. "I don't have to go to work yet, so I thought we'd start with a little education. I thought we'd look, for instance, at the interesting foreign pavilions like Iceland or Rumania." My heart sank. Meg said, "Norma, stop your kidding!" and I looked up and saw Norma laughing and realized she was funny for a mother, and she knew what children liked and what they hated. I laughed too.

We rode across the Bridge of Wheels and got out, of course, at the General Motors Building. That was everyone's first stop. We took our places on a long line that went up a ramp and turned a corner and up another, alongside this great streamlined building of rounded corners and windowless walls. It reminded me of the kind of structure I would make by turning over a pail of wet sand at the beach and pounding the bottom of the pail and lifting it off the sand mold. The General Motors exhibit was the most popular in the whole Fair, and so I didn't mind the long wait we had, practically an hour. We inched along Meg held my hand, and Norma just behind us smoked her cigarettes and fanned herself with her hat. We were quiet. In the momentousness everyone was quiet. It was the quiet World of Tomorrow, everyone all dressed up.

Finally we got inside. My stomach tightened and my heart beat as we prepared for the exhibit. We ran and took seats, each of us in a chair with high sides and loudspeakers built into them, they faced the same direction and were on a track. The lights went down. Music played and the chairs lurched and began to move sideways. In front of us a whole world lit up, as if we were flying over it, the most fantastic sight I had ever seen, an entire city of the future, with skyscrapers and fourteen-lane highways, real little cars moving on them at different speeds, the center lanes for the higher speeds, the lanes on the edge for the lower. Cars were regulated by radio control, the drivers didn't even do the driving! This miniature world demonstrated how everything was planned, people lived in these modern streamlined curvilinear buildings, each of them accommodating the population of a small town and holding all the things, schools, food stores, laundries, movies and so on, that they might need, and they wouldn't even have to go outside, just as if 174th Street and all the neighborhood around were packed into one giant building. And we passed bridges and streams, and electrified farms and airports that brought up airliners on elevators from underground hangars. And there were factories with lights and smoke, and lakes and forests and mountains, and it was all real, which is to say, built to scale, the forests had real tiny trees, and the water in the tiny lakes was real, and around it all we went, at different levels, seeing everything in more and more detail, thousands of tiny cars zipping right along on their tracks as if carrying their small beings about their business. And out in the countryside were these tiny houses with people sitting in them and reading the paper and listening to the radio. In the cities of the future, pedestrian bridges connected the buildings and highways were sunken on tracks below them. No one would get run over in this futuristic world. It all made sense, people didn't have to travel except to see the countryside; everything else, their schools, their jobs, were right where they lived. I was very impressed. No matter what I had heard about the Futurama, nothing compared with seeing it for myself: all the small moving parts, all the lights and shadows, the animation, as if I were looking at the largest most complicated toy ever made! In fact this is what I realized and that no one had mentioned to me. It was a toy that any child in the world would want to own. You could play with it forever. The little cars made me think of my toy cars when I was small, the ones I held between my thumb and forefinger, the little coupes and sedans of gunmetal whose wheels spun on axles no thicker than a needle as I drove them along the colored tracks of my plaid carriage blanket. The buildings were models, it was a model world. It was filled with appropriate music, and an announcer was describing all these wonderful things as they went by, these raindrop cars, these air-conditioned cities.

And then the amazing thing was that at the end you saw a particular model street intersection and the show was over, and with your I HAVE SEEN THE FUTURE button in your hand you came out into the sun and you were standing on precisely the corner you had just seen, the future was right where you were standing and what was small had become big, the scale had enlarged and you were no longer looking down at it, but standing in it, on this corner of the future, right here in the World's Fair!

That dazzled me. Perhaps it might only have been the sudden passage from darkness to daylight, but I actually wobbled on my feet. I had the feeling that I too had changed size, and it only lasted a moment but it was quite strange. It alerted me to the sizes of everything at the Fair. Norma took us to the Railroads Building. We sat in an auditorium facing a stage with a scenic diorama of O-gage trains and locomotives rolling through hills and valleys and over rivers and through cities. So we were big again. A model freight train would disappear around a bend just as a model passenger train came over a bridge. An announcer told us they had laid the tracks for this exhibit on seventy thousand tiny railway ties that were fastened with a quarter of a million tiny spikes. And then outside, in the daylight behind the exhibit hall, was a real railroad yard with ancient steam engines on display, "The General," the "Daniel Nason," and the newest most modern locomotive of all, a sleek and monumental monster of dark green whose wheels were taller than a man. So there it was again!

And then at the Consolidated Edison exhibit, again everything was shrunk—it was a diorama of the entire City of New York, showing the life in the city from morning till night. We could see the whole city and across the Hudson River to Jersey, the Statue of Liberty in the harbor. We could see up in Westchester and Connecticut. I looked for my house in the Bronx, but I couldn't see it. Norma thought she saw Claremont Park. But below us were the great stone skyscrapers, the cars and buses in the streets, the subways and elevated trains, all of the working metropolis, all of it sparkling with life, and when afternoon came there was even a thunderstorm, and all the lights of the buildings and streets came up to deal with the darkness.

Everywhere at the World's Fair the world was reduced to tiny size by the cunning and ingenuity of builders and engineers. And then things loomed up that were larger than they ought to have been. The Public Health Building had an exhibit showing the different parts of the body, each of them depicted many times their real size. An enormous ear, and nose, with their canals and valves and cellular bone marrow exposed—big pink plastic organs, bigger than I was. The eye was so big you walked into it! You walked into this eye, saw through its lens, which changed to make you nearsighted or farsighted. We all grew dizzy with that one. And then an enormous man made of Plexiglas, I suppose, with all his giant internal organs visible, but no visible penis, a mistake in representation about which I said nothing to Meg and Norma, thinking it was not polite.

And everywhere outside were stone statues of men and women in various poses, wrestling dogs, or bulls, swimming with dolphins, or standing on one foot, or carrying farm tools. They wore stone dresses or stone pants, or they were naked with stone breasts and backsides. You could see the muscles in their legs or arms, you could see their ribs and spinal columns of stone. They stood or lay about in pools or atop pylons or rose up from shrubbery. Some of them were pressed into the sides of buildings, so only the front halves of them showed, sculptures of concrete pressed in like sand molds. The same kinds of expressionless people were painted on the sides of buildings, enormous murals of them holding beakers of chemicals or blueprints in their hands. They looked like no one I knew, parts of them were immense, other parts were small. They intermingled, so you didn't know which arms belonged to which bodies. I was made light-headed by the looming and shrinking size of things.

We wanted to go everywhere, do everything. "Whoa, whoa, hold your horses," Norma said. We were getting wild. She took us to a dairy counter and we sat down and had egg salad sandwiches on white bread and malted milks, an excellent lunch. We sat at a little metal table under an umbrella and ate and drank while Norma leaned on an elbow and smoked a cigarette and watched us. She had bought a buttermilk for herself. When we had finished, she leaned forward and gently wiped with a paper napkin the malted milk around Meg's mouth, who lifted her chin and closed her eyes while this was done.

Then we were off again. It was late afternoon. We saw a rotating platform on which real cows were milked by electric pumps. The cows stared at us as they turned past. They were like the cows on that farm in Connecticut. That they had to be milked by machines while they were rotated I did not question. I thought this was a new discovery; perhaps it kept the cream from rising. We saw in the General Electric Building hall an artificial lightning generator. This was truly fearsome. Bolts of lightning shot thirty feet through the air. Meg screamed and people around us laughed. You could smell the air burn, the thunder was deafening. This was part of the exhibit showing General Electric Appliances for the home. There was so much to see and do. We watched Coca-Cola being bottled and Philadelphia Cream Cheeses wrapped and we saw France and Spain and Belgium. In the Radio Corporation of America Building, which was shaped like a radio vacuum tube, we saw a demonstration of wireless telegraphy saving a ship at sea, and a new invention, picture radio, or television, in which there were reflected on mirrors tilted over a receiver actual pictures of people talking into microphones at the very moment they were talking from somewhere else in the city, not the World's Fair.

We were tired now and stopped to rest on a bench, and to watch the people walk by. All you had to do was turn around and wherever you were you could see the Trylon and Perisphere.

"OK, kids," Norma said, "now I've got to go to work. I have it all planned out. If you're going to make it through this evening, you've got to rest awhile."

She took us on another tractor train to the section of the Fair where she worked. The Amusement Zone. This was very familiar to me. It looked like the boardwalk at Rockaway, with the same penny arcades and shooting galleries and scales to stand on while the concessionaire guessed your weight. But there were big rides too and showplaces like Gay New Orleans and Forbidden Tibet. Meg tugged my arm. "Look, Edgar!" We were going past what I had thought was only another building. But on the roof was a truly amazing sight, a gigantic red revolving National Cash Register, seven stories high. It showed the day's Fair attendance as if it were ringing up sales. Clouds floated peacefully behind it.

1985

# RALPH ELLISON

---

*Ralph Ellison (1914–94) distilled the contradictions of American race relations in his novel* Invisible Man, *whose protagonist is pulled into a maelstrom of political tensions, divided loyalties, and violence shortly after arriving in New York City. In "New York, 1936"—excerpted from the longer essay "An Extravagance of Laughter"—Ellison writes of his own arrival in the city and his struggle to disentangle New York's often bewildering manners and codes.*

## NEW YORK, 1936

IN 1936, a few weeks after my arrival in New York City, I was lucky enough to be invited by an old hero and newfound friend, Langston Hughes, to be his guest at what would be my introduction to Broadway theater. I was so delighted and grateful for the invitation that I failed to ask my host the title of the play, and it was not until we arrived at the theater that I learned that it would be Jack Kirkland's dramatization of Erskine Caldwell's famous novel *Tobacco Road*. No less successful than in its original form, the play was well on its way to a record-breaking seven-and-a-half-year run, and that alone was enough to increase my expectations. And so much so that I failed to note the irony of circumstance that would have as my introduction to New York theater a play with a southern setting and characters that were based upon a type and class of whites whom I had spent the last three years trying to avoid. Had I been more alert, it might have occurred to me that somehow a group of white Alabama farm folk had learned of my presence in New York, thrown together a theatrical troupe, and flown north to haunt me. But being dazzled by the lights, the theatrical atmosphere, the babble of the playgoing crowd, it didn't. And yet that irony arose precisely from the mixture of motives—practical, educational, and romantic—that had brought me to the North in the first place.

Among these was my desire to enjoy a summer free of the South and its problems while meeting the challenge of being on my own for the first time in a great northern city. Fresh out of Alabama, with my junior year at Tuskegee Institute behind me, I was also in New York seeking funds with which to complete my final year as a music major—a goal at which I was having less success than I had hoped. However, there had been compensations. For between working in the Harlem YMCA cafeteria as a substitute for vacationing waiters and countermen and searching for a more profitable job, I had used my free time exploring the city, making new acquaintances, and enjoying the many forms of social freedom that were unavailable to me in Alabama. The very idea of being in New York was dreamlike, for like many young Negroes of the time, I thought of it as the freest of American cities and considered Harlem as the site and symbol of Afro-American progress and hope. Indeed, I was both young and bookish enough to think of Manhattan as my substitute for Paris and of Harlem as a place of Left Bank excitement.

And yet I soon discovered, much to my chagrin, that while I was physically out of the South, I was restrained—sometimes consciously, sometimes not—by certain internalized thou-shalt-nots that had structured my public conduct in Alabama. It was as though I had come to the Eden of American culture and found myself indecisive as to which of its fruits were free for my picking. Beyond the borders of Harlem's briar patch—which seemed familiar because of my racial and cultural identification with the majority of its people and the lingering spell that had been cast nationwide by the music, dance, and literature of the so-called Harlem Renaissance—I viewed New Yorkers through the overlay of my Alabama experience. Contrasting the whites I encountered with those I had observed in the South, I weighed class against class and compared southern styles with their northern counterparts. I listened to diction and noted dress, and searched for attitudes in inflections, carriage, and manners. And in pursuing this aspect of my extracurricular education, I explored the landscape.

I crossed Manhattan back and forth from river to river and up, down, and around again, from Spuyten Duyvil Creek to the Battery, looking and listening and gadding about; rode streetcar and el, subway and bus; took a hint from Edna Millay and spent an evening riding back and forth on the Staten Island Ferry. From the elevated trains I saw my first penthouses with green trees growing atop tall buildings, caught remote glimpses of homes, businesses, and factories while moving above the teeming streets, and felt a sense of quiet tranquillity despite the bang and clatter. Yes, but the subways were something else again.

In fact, the subways were utterly confusing to my southern-bred idea of good manners, and especially the absence of a certain gallantry that men were expected to extend toward women. Subway cars appeared to be underground arenas where northern social equality took the form of an endless shoving match in which the usual rules of etiquette were turned upside down—or so I concluded after watching a 5:00 footrace in a crowded car.

The contest was between a huge white woman who carried an armful of bundles, and a small Negro man who lugged a large suitcase. At the time I was standing against the track-side door, and when the train stopped at a downtown station I saw the two come charging through the opening doors like racehorses leaving the starting gate at Belmont. And as they spied and dashed for the single empty seat, the outcome appeared up for grabs, but it was the woman, thanks to a bustling, more ruthless stride (and more subway know-how) who won—though but by a hip and a hair. For just as they reached the seat she swung a well-padded hip and knocked the man off stride, thus causing him to lose his balance as she turned, slipped beneath his reeling body, and plopped into the seat. It was a maneuver that produced a startling effect—at least on me.

For as she banged into the seat it caused the man to spin and land smack-dab in her lap—in which massive and heaving center of gravity he froze, stared into her face nose-tip to nose, and then performed a springlike leap to his feet as from a red-hot stove. It was but the briefest conjunction, and then, as he reached down and fumbled for his suitcase, the woman began adjusting her bundles, and with an elegant toss of her head she then looked up into his face with the most ladylike and triumphant of smiles.

I had no idea of what to expect next, but to her sign of good sportswomanship the man let out with an exasperated "Hell, you can have it, I don't want it!" A response that evoked a phrase from an old forgotten ditty to which my startled mind added the unstated line— "Sleeping in the bed with your hand right on it"—and shook me with visions of the train screeching to a stop and a race riot beginning. . . .

But not at all. For while the defeated man pushed his way to another part of the car the crowd of passengers simply looked on and laughed.

Still, for all their noise and tension, it was not the subways that most intrigued me, but the buses. In the South you occupied the back of the bus, and nowhere *but* the back, or so help you God. Being in the North and encouraged by my anonymity, I experimented by riding all *over* New York buses, excluding only the driver's seat—front end, back end, right side, left side, sitting or standing as the route and flow of passengers demanded. *And*, since those were the glorious days of double-deckers, both enclosed and open, I even rode *top*side.

Thus having convinced myself that no questions of racial status would be raised by where I chose to ride, I asked myself whether a seat at the back of the bus wasn't actually more desirable than one at the front. For not only did it provide more legroom, it offered a more inclusive perspective on both the interior and exterior scenes. I found the answer obvious and quite amusing. But now that I was no longer forced by law and compelled by custom to ride at the back, what was more desirable—the possibility of exercising what was routinely accepted in the North as an abstract, highly symbolic (even trivial) form of democratic freedom, or the creature comfort that was to be had by occupying a spot from which more of the passing scene could be observed? And in my own personal terms, what was more important—my individual comfort, or the exercise of the democratic right to be squeezed and jostled by strangers? Such questions were akin to that of whether you lived in a Negro neighborhood because you were forced to do so, or because you preferred living among those of your own background. Having experienced life in mixed neighborhoods as a child, I preferred to live where people spoke my own version of the American language, and where misreading of tone or gesture was less likely to ignite lethal conflict. Segregation laws aside, this was a matter of personal choice, for even though class and cultural differences existed among Negroes, it was far easier to deal with hostilities arising between yourself and your own people than with, say, Jeeter Lester or, more realistically, Lester Maddox.

But my interrogation by the New York scene (for that is what it had become) was not to stop there, for once my mind got rolling on buses, it was difficult to stop and get off. So I became preoccupied with defining the difference between northern and southern buses. Of the two, New York buses were simpler, if only for being earth-bound. They were merely a form of transportation, an inflated version of a taxicab or passenger car that one took to get from one locality to another. And as far as one's destination and motives were concerned they were neutral. But this was far from true of southern buses. For when compared with its New York counterpart, even the most dilapidated of southern buses seemed (from my New York perspective) to be a haunted form of transportation.

A southern bus was a contraption contrived by laying the South's social pyramid on its side, knocking out a few strategic holes, and rendering it vehicular through the addition of engine, windows, and wheels. Thus converted, with the sharp apex of the pyramid blunted and equipped with fare box and steering gear, and its sprawling base curtailed severely and narrowly aligned (and arrayed with jim crow signs), a ride in such a vehicle became, at least for Negroes, as un-predictable as a trip in a spaceship doomed to be caught in the time warp of history—that man-made "fourth dimension," which ever confounds our American grasp of "real," or *actual*, time or duration.

For blacks and whites alike, southern buses were places of hallucination, but especially for Negroes. Because once inside, their journey ended even before the engine fired and the wheels got rolling. Then the engine chugged, the tires scuffed, and the scenery outside flashed and flickered, but they themselves remained, like Zeno's arrow, ever in the same old place. Thus the motorized mobility of the social pyramid did little to advance the Negroes' effort toward equality. Because although they were allowed to enter the section that had been—in its vertical configuration—its top, any semblance of upward mobility ended at the fare box—from whence, once their fares were deposited, they were sent, forthwith, straight to the rear, or horizontalized bottom. And along the way almost *anything* could happen, from push to shove, assaults on hats, heads, or aching corns, to unprovoked tongue-lashings from the driver or from any white passenger, drunk or sober, who took exception to their looks, attitude, or mere existence.

And even as the phantomized bus went lurching and fumbling along its treadmill of a trajectory, the struggle within scuffled and raged in fitful retrograde. Thus, as it moved without moving, those trapped inside played out their roles like figures in dreams—with one group ever forcing the other to the backmost part, and the other ever watching and waiting as they bowed to force and clung to sanity. And indeed the time would come when such bus enscened pantomime would erupt in a sound and fury of action that would engulf the South and change American society.

But of this I had no way of knowing at the time. I only knew that southern bus rides had the power to haunt and confuse my New York passage. Moreover, they were raising the even more troublesome question of to what extent had I failed to grasp a certain degree of freedom that had always existed in my group's state of unfreedom? There was an Afro-American dimension in southern culture, and the lives of many black southerners possessed a certain verve and self-possessed fullness—so to what extent had I overlooked similar opportunities for self-discovery while accepting a definition of possibility laid down by those who would deny me freedom?

Thus, while I enjoyed my summer, such New York-provoked questions made for a certain unease, which I tried to ignore. Nevertheless, they made me aware that whatever its true shape turned out to be, northern freedom could be grasped only by my running the risk of the unknown and by acting in the face of uncertainty. Which meant that I would have to keep moving into racially uncharted areas. Otherwise I would remain physically in Harlem and psychologically in Alabama—neither of which was acceptable. Harlem was "Harlem," a dream place of glamour and excitement—what with its music, its dance, its style. But it was all of this because it was a part of (and apart *from*) the larger city. Harlem, I came to feel, was the shining transcendence of a national negative, and it took its fullest meaning from that which it was not, and without which I would have regarded it as less interesting than, say, Kansas City, Missouri—or South Side Chicago. Harlem, whose ironic inhabitants described it a thousand times a day as being "nowhere," took much of its meaning from the larger metropolis; so I could only achieve the fullest measure of its attractions by experiencing that which it was not.

Prior to stumbling onto *Tobacco Road*, I had already encountered some of the complexity evoked by my probings. As the guest of a white female friend who reported musical events for a magazine, I had occupied a seat in the orchestra section of Carnegie Hall without inciting protest. But shortly thereafter I had been denied admission to a West Side cinema house that featured European movies. Then I had learned that while one midtown restaurant would make you welcome, in another (located in Greenwich Village, Harlem's twin symbol of Manhattan's freedom), the waiters would go through the polite motions of seating you but then fill your food with salt. And to make certain that you got the message, they would enact a rite of exorcism in which the glasses and crockery, now considered hopelessly contaminated by your touch, were enfolded in the tablecloth and smithereened in the fireplace.

Or again, upon arriving at a Central Park West apartment building to deliver a music manuscript for the Tuskegee composer William L. Dawson, you encountered a doorman with a European accent who was so rude that you were tempted to break his nose. Fortunately, you didn't, for after you refused to use the servants' elevator he rang up the tenant into whose hands alone you were instructed to make the delivery, Jacques Gordon of the Gordon String Quartet, who hurried down and invited you up to his apartment. Where, to your surprise and delight, he talked with you without condescension about his recordings, questioned you sympathetically about your musical background, and encouraged you in your ambitions to become a composer. So if you weren't always welcome to break bread in public places, an interest in the arts *could* break down social distance and allow for communication that was uninhibited by questions of race—or so it seemed.

As on a Madison Avenue bus an enthusiastic, bright-eyed little old Jewish lady, fresh from an art exhibition with color catalog in hand, would engage you in conversation and describe knowingly the styles and intentions of French painters of whom you'd never heard.

"Then you must go to galleries," she insisted.

"Stir yourself and go to museums," she demanded.

"This is one of the world's great centers of art, so learn about them! Why are you waiting? Enough already!" she exhorted.

And eventually, God bless her, I did.

But then, on another bus ride, a beautifully groomed and expensively dressed woman would become offended when you retrieved and attempted to return the section of a newspaper that she had dropped when preparing to depart, apparently mistaking what was intended as an act of politeness for a reprimand from a social inferior. So it appeared that in New York one had to choose the time, place, and person even when exercising one's southern good manners.

I had hoped that in New York there would exist generally a type of understanding that obtained in the South between certain individual whites and Negroes. This was a type of southern honor that did little to alter the general system of inequity, but allowed individual whites to make exceptions in exerting the usual gestures of white supremacy. Such individuals refused to use racial epithets and tried, within the limitations of the system, to treat Negroes fairly. This was a saving grace and a balm to the aches and pains of the South's endless racial contention.

Only years later would I learn that during periods of intense social unrest, even sensitive intellectuals who had themselves been victims of discrimination would find it irresistible to use their well-deserved elevation to the upper levels of their professions as platforms from which, in the name of the most abstract—and fashionable—of philosophical ideas, to reduce Negroes to stereotypes that were no less reductive and demeaning than those employed by the most ignorant and bigoted of white southerners.

Fortunately, that knowledge was still in the future, and so, doing unto another as I would have had him do unto me, I dismissed my chance acquaintance as an insecure individual, and not the representative of a group or general attitude. But he did serve as a warning that if I wished to communicate with New Yorkers, I must watch my metaphors, for here one man's cliché was another man's facile opportunity for victimization.

I was learning that exploring New York was a journey without a map, Baedeker, or Henry James, and that how one was received by the natives depended more upon how one presented oneself than upon any ironclad rule of exclusion. Here the portals to many places of interest were guarded by hired help, and if you approached with uncertain mien, you were likely to be turned away by anyone from doormen to waiters to ticket agents. However, if you acted as though you were in fact a New Yorker exercising a routine freedom, chances were that you'd be accepted. Which is to say that in many instances I found that my air and attitude could offset the inescapable fact of my color. For it seemed that in the hustle and bustle of that most theatrical of American cities, one was accepted on the basis of what one *appeared* to be. So, to enjoy the wonders of New York, I assumed a mask which I conceived to be that of a "New Yorker," and decided to leave it to those whites who might object to seek out the questioning Tuskegeean who was hidden behind the mask.

Today, looking back, I suspect that for many observers, my masking was all too transparent. But what remained hidden from them, as from myself, was the possibility that such playacting was also a process of self-transformation—a process through which I was becoming neither an abstract "ex-southwesterner" nor a sophisticated "New Yorker," but an individual variation upon a national type that, after two hundred years of grappling with its racial, religious, and geographical diversity, is still in the process of achieving a full measure of self-consciousness: a product of that democratic hope, uncertainty, and turbulence in the mind and heart which identifies the "American."

*ESQUIRE*, 1986

# OSCAR HIJUELOS

*Oscar Hijuelos (1951–    ) was born in New York City, the child of Cuban immigrants, and grew up in Spanish Harlem, listening to his uncle Pedro tell stories about playing in Xaviar Cugat's orchestra. Hijuelos evokes that Latin music scene in his Pulitzer Prize–winning novel* The Mambo Kings Play Songs of Love, *whose lush, rhythmic prose pays homage to the stylings of salsa.*

FROM *THE MAMBO KINGS PLAY SONGS OF LOVE*

THE MAMBO KING flourished in that ballroom with its friendly crowds, good food, booze, companionship, and music. And when he wasn't out to dance or to play jobs with his orchestra, he was visiting the friends he had made in the Park Palace and other dance halls, fellow Cubans or Puerto Ricans who would invite him over to their apartments to eat dinner, play cards, listen to records, and become a swaying ring of arms in the kitchen, singing and always having fun.

It was at the Park Palace that the Mambo King and his brother found many of their musicians. When he and his brother had first turned up in New York in early 1949, the beginning of the mambo boom, they had gotten jobs through their fat cousin Pablo, with whom they had at first lived, working in a meat-packing plant on 125th Street by day so that they could have enough money to party and set things up at night. They met a lot of people then, a lot of musicians like themselves, good players. There was Pito Pérez, who played the timbales; Benny Domingo on the congas; Ray Alcázar on the piano; Manny Domínguez, who played the guitar and the *cencerro*; Xavier from Puerto Rico, the trombone; Willie Carmen, the flute; Ramón "*El Jamón*" Ortiz, the bass saxophone; José Otero, violin; Rafael Guillón, the rattle gourd; Benny Chacón, accordion; Johnny Bing, saxophone; Johnny Cruz, horn; Francisco Martínez, vibraphone; Johnny Reyes, the *tres* and the eight-stringed *quatro*. And, among them, the brothers themselves: Cesar, who sang, played the trumpet, guitar, accordion, and piano; and Nestor, flute, trumpet, guitar, and vocals.

Like the brothers, many of the musicians were workers by day, and when they played jobs and were on a stage, or went out dancing, they were Stars for a Night. Stars of buying drinks, stars of friendly introductions, stars of female conquest. Some of them were already famous like the Mambo King wanted to be. They met the drummer Mongo Santamaría, who had an act back then called the Black Cuban Diamonds; Pérez Prado,* the emperor of the Mambo; the singer Graciela; the pianist Chico O'Farrill; and that black fellow who liked Cubans so much, Dizzy Gillespie. And they met the great Machito, a dignified and dapper-looking mulatto, who would hang out at the bar of the Park Palace, his diminutive wife by his side, receiving his fans and their gifts of jewelry, which he would calmly tuck into his jacket pocket. Later the jewelry would end up in a teakwood Chinese box that Machito kept in his living room. Visiting with Machito at his apartment in the West Eighties, the brothers would see this box, thick with engraved watches, bracelets, and rings, its lid decorated with Chinese swirls and inlaid with the image of a mother-of-pearl dragon devouring a flower. And Cesar would say, "Don't you worry, brother, that's going to be happening to us one day."

Cesar had a picture from one of those nights, tucked in the soft cloth pocket of his suitcase in the Hotel Splendour: the two brothers decked out in white suits and seated at a round table, the mirrored

---

*Puff of smoke, a swallow of whiskey, the sensation that something was pinching the small of his back, something with razor-like claws, making its way along the mysterious passages of his kidneys and liver . . . *Pérez Prado.* When the Mambo King, ensconced in his room in the Hotel Splendour, thought about Pérez, he recalled the first time he saw the man on a stage, off in another world and bending his body in a hundred shapes, as if he was made of rubber: prowling like a hound, on his haunches like a cat, spreading out like a tree, soaring like a biplane, rushing like a train, vibrating like a tumbling washing machine, rolling like dice, bounding like a kangaroo, bouncing like a spring, skipping like a stone . . . and his face a mask of concentration, conviction, and pure pleasure, a being from another world, his stage another world. Thin Pérez giving the Mambo King some of his jazzier stage moves, the loquacious and cheerful Pérez out by the bar, telling everyone around him, "Fellas, you must come and visit me in Mexico! We'll have the time of our lives, tell you what, my friends. We'll go to the races and the bullfights, we'll eat like princes and drink like the Pope!"

walls and columns behind them reflecting the distant lights, dancers, and the brass of an orchestra. Cesar, a little drunk and pleased to death with himself, a champagne glass in one hand and, in the other, the soft, curvaceous shoulder of an unidentified girl—Paulita? Roxanne? Xiomara?—looking a lot like Rita Hayworth, with her nice breasts pushed up into the top of her dress and a funny smile because Cesar had just leaned over and kissed her, licking her ear with his tongue, and Nestor beside them, a little detached and to the side, staring off, his brows raised slightly in bewilderment.

Those were the days when they'd formed the Mambo Kings. It started with jam sessions that used to drive their landlady, Mrs. Shannon, and their other neighbors, mostly Irish and German people, crazy. Musicians they knew from the dance halls would come over to the apartment with their instruments and set up in the living room, which was often noisy with wacky saxophones, violins, drums, and basses that screeched, floated, banged, and bounced out into the courtyard and street, so that the neighbors slammed down their windows and threatened the Cubans with hammers. The casual jam sessions became regular sessions, certain musicians always showed up, and so one day Cesar simply said, "Let's make a little orchestra, huh?"

His best find, though, was a certain Miguel Montoya, a pianist and good professional who knew the secrets of arranging. He was also Cuban and had been kicking around in different orchestras in New York City since the early 1930s and he was well connected, having played with Antonio Arcana and with Noro Morales. They'd see Montoya over at the Park Palace. Dressed in white from head to toe, he wore large, glittering sapphire rings, and sported an ivory crystal-tipped cane. Rumor had it that although he'd show up in the dance halls with a woman he was effeminate in character. One night they went to Montoya's apartment on Riverside Drive and 155th Street for dinner. Everything in his home was white and fleecy—from the goatskins and plumes that hung on the walls to the statues of Santa Barbara and the Holy Mother that he'd draped in silk, to the furry love seats, sofas, and chairs. In the corner his white baby grand piano, a Steinway, on which he'd placed a thin-necked vase filled with tulips. They dined on delicate slices of veal which Miguel had cooked with lemon, butter, garlic, salt, and olive oil; scalloped potatoes; and a grand salad, which they washed down with one bottle of wine after the other. Later, as the Hudson gleamed silver in the moonlight and New Jersey blinked in the distance, they laughed, turned on the record player, and passed half the night dancing rumbas, mambos, and tangos. Cultivating Miguel through flirtation, Cesar treated him with real affection like a beloved uncle, constantly patting and hugging him. Later in the evening he asked Montoya if he could spare the time to sit in with their orchestra, and that night Montoya gave in and said he would.

They formed a mambo band; that is, a traditional Latin dance band given balls by saxophones and horns. This orchestra consisted of a flute, violin, piano, sax, two trumpets, two drummers, one playing an American kit and the other a battery of congas. Cesar had thought up the Mambo Kings while looking through the advertising pages of the Brooklyn *Herald*, where half the orchestras had names like the Mambo Devils, Romero and the Hot Rumba Orchestra, Mambo Pete and His Caribbean Crooners. There was a certain Eddie Reyes King of the Bronx Mambo, Juan Valentino and His Mad Mambo Rompers, Vic Caruso and His Little Italy Mambonairs, and groups like the Havana Casino Orchestra, the Havana Melody Band, the Havana Dance Orchestra. Those same pages advertising DANCING LESSONS NOW! LEARN THE MAMBO, THE FOX-TROT, THE RUMBA, DANCE YOUR WAY INTO A GIRL'S HEART! Why not Cesar Castillo and the Mambo Kings?

Although Cesar considered himself a singer, he was also quite talented as an instrumentalist and adept at percussion. He was blessed with tremendous energy, a surge of power from too many slaps in the face from his foul-tempered father, Pedro Castillo, and a love of melody because of his mother and the affectionate maid who had helped bring him into the world, Genebria. (Here he listens to a distant trumpeting on a Mambo King recording, "Twilight in Havana," and sighs; it's as if he's a kid again running through the center of Las Piñas at carnival and the porches of the houses are lit with huge lanterns and the balconies garlanded with ribbons and tapers and flowers, and where he runs past so many musicians, musicians everywhere on the street corners, on the church steps, on the porches of the houses, and continuing on toward the plaza, where the big orchestra is set up; that's the trumpet he hears echoing in the arcades of his town as he passes the columns and the shadows of couples hidden behind them and charges down steps past a garden, through the crowds and the dancers, to the bandstand, where that trumpet player, obese in a white suit, head tilted back, blows music up into the sky, and this carries and bounces off the walls of another arcade in Havana, and he's blowing the trumpet now at three in the morning, reeling around in circles and laughing after a night out at the clubs and brothels with friends and his brother, laughing with the notes that whip into the empty dark spaces and bounce back, swirling inside him like youth.)

He and his brother actually preferred the slower ballads and boleros, but they set out with Montoya to build a sound dance band, because that's what the people wanted. It was Montoya who did all the arrangements of pieces like *"Tu Felicidad," "Cachita," "No Te Importe Saber,"* pieces made popular by the likes of René Touzet, Noro Morales, Israel Fajardo. He knew how to read music, which the brothers had never really learned—though they could struggle their way through a chart, they presented their songs with simple chords and with the melodies worked out on instruments or in their heads. This sometimes annoyed the other musicians, but Cesar used to tell them, "What I'm interested in is a man who can really feel the music, instead of someone who can only play the charts." And then he talked about the immortal *conguero* Chano Pozo, who was shot to death in 1948 over a drug deal* and whose ghost was already

---

*From Manuel Flanagan, a trumpet player who knew Chano: "I remember when Chano died. I was down on 52nd when I heard the whole thing. Chano was up on 116th Street at the Caribbean Bar and Grill, looking for this man who'd sold him stuff. That was in the morning. He'd injected it, gotten sick, and then later went out on the street looking for him. He found him in that bar, pulled a knife on him, and demanded his money back. Now, the man wasn't afraid of Chano and Chano wasn't afraid of the man; Chano had already been shot up and stabbed in Havana and had survived it, you know, so that Chano took his knife out and lunged at the man, even though he'd pulled out a gun: Chano kept coming at him because he thought the spirits were protecting him, but these spirits, Yoruba spirits, couldn't stop the bullets from tearing him up and that was that."

turning up in Havana mambos, and of musicians like the great Mongo Santamaría. "Just look at Mongo," Cesar would say to Nestor. "He doesn't read. And did Chano? No, *hombre*, he had the spirit, and that's what we want, too."

They'd rehearse in the living room of their cousin Pablo's apartment, on days when the walls were subject to wild fits of clanking boiler pipes and when the floors rumbled because of the subways, as if in an earthquake. They'd rehearse on days when the boiler had shut down and it was so cold steam oozed out of their cuticles and the musicians would roll their eyes, saying, "Who needs this shit?" But they continued because Cesar Castillo treated them well: they'd show up dead-tired from their day jobs and play their hearts out, knowing that at the end of the rehearsal they would crowd into the little kitchen: Pablo's wife would cook up big platters of steak and pork chops—smuggled out of the meat-packing plant under shirts and long coats—rice and beans, and whatever else they wanted. Having consumed great quantities of food and beer, they'd laugh and head back into the chilly universe feeling as if Cesar Castillo and his brother had really looked out for them.

Hands moving around in circles (after taking a sip of beer, drag of a Chesterfield), he'd explain his ideas about a song: "For this ballad, we should come in quietly like cats. Miguel, first you on the piano, the minor chords and all that business on the high notes, then, Manny, you come in with the bass, but *suavecito, suavecito,* and then, Nestor, you come in with the horn, talatalatalata, then the congas and the other brass. We go through one verse and then we come into the turnaround and I'll sing the verse."

"We'll play," Manny the bassist was saying. "And you sing with that priestly expression on your face."

When they finally had the songs worked out, lyrics and simple chords, the melody lines memorized, he used to take them to his arranger, the elegant Miguel Montoya. Sitting down beside him, he'd whistle the melody or pick it out directly on the piano, so that it could be written down as music. Many a night, passersby on Broadway and Tiemann Place would hear these melodies being worked out by the Mambo King and his brother. People would look up and see their silhouettes in the window, heads arched back. Or sometimes they went up to the rooftop with a few bottles of beer and steak sandwiches on Italian bread, smothered in onions and salt, and set out a blanket, feasted and drank, passing the night improvising songs as if for the red-yellow-blue-and-white-lit buildings of the city.

Jobs were hard to find at first, with so many good dance bands already out there. On his days off, Cesar did a lot of the footwork, going from club to club on Eighth, Ninth, and Tenth Avenues, and to the Bronx and Brooklyn and uptown, Harlem. He was always trying to set up auditions with jaded, tan-suited Puerto Rican gangsters who owned half of the mambo singers in New York. But they did get some jobs: parish dances, grammar-school parties, weddings. Many hours of rehearsal, few dollars of pay. It would help a lot that Cesar Castillo was a white Cuban bolero singer like Desi Arnaz, what they called in those days a Latin-lover type, dark-haired and dark-featured, his skin being what was then called "swarthy." Swarthy to Americans, but light-skinned when compared to many of his friends. Pito, a wiry Cuban from Cienfuegos, was as dark as the mahogany legs of the easy chair in their living room on La Salle. A lot of the fellows who turned up at the apartment with their squealing, guitar-shaped wives and girlfriends were dark, bony-limbed men.

A flier from May 15, 1950:

*The Friendship Club on 79th Street and Broadway presents for your dancing pleasure a double bill of top Mambo Entertainment. Tonight and tomorrow night (Fri. and Sat.) we are proud to present the Glorious Gloria Parker and Her All-Girl Rumba Orchestra! And, sharing this bill, the Fabulous Cesar Castillo and His Mambo Kings of Cuba! Admission $1.04. Doors open at 9 P.M. No zoot suits and no jitterbugs, please.*

They started playing jobs all over the city. The Café Society on 58th Street, the Havana Madrid on Broadway and 51st, the Biltmore Ballroom on Church and Flatbush, the Club 78, the Stardust on Boston Road in the Bronx, the Pan-American Club and the Gayheart Ballroom on Nostrand Avenue, the Hotel Manhattan Towers on 76th Street and at the City Center Casino.

He'd get up on the stage, dancing before the microphone while his musicians took the music forward. The glory of being on a stage with his brother Nestor, playing for crowds of café-society people who jumped, bounced, and wriggled across the dance floor. While Nestor soloed, Cesar's heavy eyelids fluttered like butterfly wings lilting on a rose; for drum solos his hips shook, his arms whipped into the air: he'd take backwards dance steps, gripping his belt with one hand and a crease of trouser with the other, hiking them up, as if to accentuate the valiant masculinity therein: outline of big prick through white silk *pantalones*. Piano taking a ninth chord voicing behind a solo, he'd stare up into the pink and red spotlights, giving the audience a horse's grin. Woman in a strapless dress dancing a slow, grinding rumba, staring at Cesar Castillo. Old woman with hair coiffed upward into a heavenly spiral, staring at Cesar. Teenage girl, Miss Roosevelt High School Class of 1950, thin-legged and thinking about the mystery of boys and love, staring at Cesar Castillo. Old ladies' skin heating up, hips moving like young girls' hips, eyes wide open with admiration and delight.

Audiences everywhere seemed to like them, but if there was one place they "owned," it was the Imperial Ballroom on East 18th Street and Utica Avenue, Brooklyn. Here they were the house band—hired at first because of Miguel Montoya, but kept on because of Cesar and Nestor's popularity. They were constantly playing contests which awarded $25 prizes for the Best Peg Pants, Loudest Shirts, Best-Looking Woman, Best Dancer Holding an Umbrella, Shapeliest Legs, Weirdest Shoes, Most Outrageous Hat, and, on one Saturday night, the Best Baldhead contest, for which a huge crowd turned out. Their greatest moment of glory at the Imperial came on that memorable night when they engaged in a battle in the war between Cuba and Puerto Rico. Under the sterling hip-swinging, pelvis-grinding admiralship of their singer, Cesar Castillo, the orchestra pulled a victory out of, to quote the *Herald's* entertainment column, "the ravages of da-feet."

And, on another night, Cesar met one of his best and lifelong friends, Frankie Pérez. This was in 1950 and the orchestra was playing one of Cesar and Nestor's original compositions, "Twilight in

Havana." Frankie was a hammy dancer, knew every rumba, mambo, and cu-bop* step on earth. He was a *suavecito* who had been a natural wizard on his toes since he was a kid in Havana, and could make any partner look good dancing with him. At that time, he'd make the rounds of the major ballrooms of the city three or four nights a week: the Park Palace, the Palladium, the Savoy, the Imperial. That night he was dressed in a green zoot suit with a pink oversized purple-brimmed hat, cream-colored Cuban-heeled shoes, and green argyle socks. Dancing happily near the stage, he was oblivious to the troubles of the world, when he heard pop, pop coming out of the manager's office. Then the crashing of glass and screaming. Someone shouted, "Get down!" and people scattered across the dance floor and hid behind the mirrored columns and under the tables. Two more pops and the orchestra stopped playing, the musicians ducking behind their music stands and jumping down off the stage and hitting the floor.

Two men came running out of the manager's office onto the dance floor and they spun around firing off shots as they made their way out toward the door. One of them was thin and eagle-beaked and carried a satchel of money. The other man was heavier and seemed to have trouble running, as if he had a lame leg or had been hit by the gunshots fired from the office. They looked as if they were going to make it, but once they got outside they ran into a barrage

---

*"Cu-bop" being the term used to describe the fusion of Afro-Cuban music and hot be-bop Harlem jazz. Its greatest practitioner was the bandleader Machito, who with Maurio Bauza and Chano Pozo hooked up with Dizzy Gillespie and Charlie Parker in the late 1940s. The American jazz players picked up the Cuban rhythms, and the Cubans picked up jazzier rhythms and chord progressions. Machito's orchestra, with Chico O'Farrill as arranger, became famous for dazzling solos played over extended vamps called *montunos*. During these furious breaks, when drummers like Chano Pozo and players like Charlie Parker went nuts, dancers like Frankie Pérez took to the center of the ballroom floor, improvising turns, dips, splits, leaps around the basic mambo steps, in the same way that the musicians improvised during their solos. (Yeah, and there was that other sneaky move he'd picked up from Cesar Castillo. While dancing with a pretty woman he would touch his forehead with his index finger and make a sizzling sound as if he was burning up and then he would fan himself, to cool out from love's mighty heat, sizzle some more, hop around as if on hot coals, fan himself again, and blow a kiss, all the time feeling cu-bop crazy, man.)

of gunfire; some cops had been driving by when they heard the commotion. One of the robbers was hit in the back of the head, the other surrendered. Later, when everyone was huddling by the bar and throwing down drinks, Cesar and Nestor struck up a conversation with Frankie. When they finished with their drinks, they made their way out into the street, where a crowd had gathered. The dead man was still lying face-down in the gutter. He was broad-shouldered and dressed in a pinstriped jacket. Nestor had no stomach for this, but Cesar and Frankie made their way over to the corpse to get a better look. Leaning up against a brick wall, their solemn faces peering out into the world from the shadows, they sadly and confoundedly contemplated the dead man's fate. As he watched, Cesar had one foot lifted behind him, the bottom of his sporty cordovan shoe pressed to the wall, and was lighting a cigarette and listening to all the sirens when a white camera flash went off. Foof. Aside from becoming friends that night, he and Frankie ended up on page 3 of the next morning's *Daily News*, part of the photograph whose caption read: BALLROOM ROBBER DIES IN POOL OF BLOOD.

A spectacular evening among so many spectacular evenings. How the rum flowed then, Jesus, how the bottles of booze multiplied along with the thick latex prophylactics and quivering female thighs like the miracle of fish and bread.

1989

# VIVIAN GORNICK

_____

*Essayist-journalist Vivian Gornick (1935– ) grew up in the Bronx,*
*under the watchful eye of her mother and the other neighborhood*
*women, a process vividly recounted in her memoir* Fierce Attachments.
*Gornick has written bracingly about being a single woman in the New*
*York she continues to love unconditionally yet without illusions. In her*
*long essay "On the Street: Nobody Watches, Everybody Performs," ex-*
*cerpted below, she gives her own twist to the traditional themes of the*
*flaneur: the solace of spectatorship and the loneliness of city life.*

## FROM *APPROACHING EYE LEVEL*

A WRITER who lived at the end of my block died. I'd known this
woman more than twenty years. She admired my work,
shared my politics, liked my face when she saw it coming
toward her, I could see that, but she didn't want to spend time with
me. We'd run into each other on the street, and it was always big
smiles, a wide embrace, kisses on both cheeks, a few minutes of
happy unguarded jabber. Inevitably I'd say, "Let's get together." She'd
nod and say, "Call me." I'd call, and she'd make an excuse to call
back, then she never would. Next time we'd run into each other: big
smile, great hug, kisses on both cheeks, not a word about the unre-
turned call. She was impenetrable: I could not pierce the mask of
smiling politeness. We went on like this for years. Sometimes I'd run
into her in other parts of town. I'd always be startled, she too, New
York is like a country, the neighborhood is your town, you spot
someone from the block or the building in another neighborhood
and the first impulse to the brain is, What are *you* doing here? We'd
each see the thought on the other's face and start to laugh. Then we'd
both give a brief salute and keep walking.

Six months after her death I passed her house one day and felt
stricken. I realized that never again would I look at her retreating
back thinking, Why doesn't she want my friendship? I missed her
then. I missed her terribly. She was gone from the landscape of mar-

ginal encounters. That landscape against which I measure daily the immutable force of all I connect with only on the street, and only when it sees me coming.

At Thirty-eighth Street two men were leaning against a building one afternoon in July. They were both bald, both had cigars in their mouths, and each one had a small dog attached to a leash. In the glare of noise, heat, dust, and confusion, the dogs barked nonstop. Both men looked balefully at their animals. "Yap, yap, stop yapping already," one man said angrily. "Yap, yap, keep on yapping," the other said softly. I burst out laughing. The men looked up at me, and grinned. Satisfaction spread itself across each face. They had performed and I had received. My laughter had given shape to an exchange that would otherwise have evaporated in the chaos. The glare felt less threatening. I realized how often the street achieves composition for me: the flash of experience I extract again and again from the endless stream of event. The street does for me what I cannot do for myself. On the street nobody watches, everyone performs.

Another afternoon that summer I stood at my kitchen sink struggling to make a faulty spray attachment adhere to the inside of the faucet. Finally, I called in the super in my building. He shook his head. The washer inside the spray was too small for the faucet. Maybe the threads had worn down. I should go to the hardware store and find a washer big enough to remedy the situation. I walked down Greenwich Avenue, carrying the faucet and the attachment, trying hard to remember exactly what the super had told me to ask for. I didn't know the language, I wasn't sure I'd get the words right. Suddenly, I felt anxious, terribly anxious. I would not, I knew, be able to get what I needed. The spray would never work again. I walked into Garber's, an old-fashioned hardware store with these tough old Jewish guys behind the counter. One of them—also bald and with a cigar in his mouth—took the faucet and the spray in his hand. He looked at it. Slowly, he began to shake his head. Obviously, there was no hope. "Lady," he said. "It ain't the threads. It definitely ain't the threads." He continued to shake his head. He wanted there to be no hope as long as possible. "And this," he said, holding the gray plastic washer in his open hand, "this is a piece of crap." I stood there in patient despair. He shifted his cigar from one side of his mouth to the other, then moved away from the counter. I saw him puttering about in a drawerful of little cardboard boxes. He removed something from one of them and returned to the counter with the spray magically attached to the faucet. He detached the spray and showed me what he had done. Where there had once been gray plastic there was now gleaming silver. He screwed the spray back on, easy as you please. "Oh," I crowed, "you've done it!" Torn between the triumph of problem-solving and the satisfaction of denial, his mouth twisted up in a grim smile. "Metal," he said philosophically, tapping the perfectly fitted washer in the faucet. "This," he picked up the plastic again, "this is a piece of crap. I'll take two dollars and fifteen cents from you." I thanked him profusely, handed him his money, then clasped my hands together on the counter and said, "It is such a pleasure to have small anxieties easily corrected." He looked at me. "Now," I said, spreading my arms wide, palms up, as though about to introduce a vaudeville act, "you've freed me for large anxieties." He continued to look at me. Then he shifted his cigar again, and spoke. "What you just said. That's a true thing." I walked out of the store happy. That evening I told the story to Laura, a writer. She said, "These are your people." Later in the evening I told it to Leonard, a New Yorker. He said, "He charged you too much."

Street theater can be achieved in a store, on a bus, in your own apartment. The idiom requires enough actors (bit players as well as principals) to complete the action and the rhythm of extended exchange. The city is rich in both. In the city things can be kept moving until they arrive at point. When they do, I come to rest.

I complain to Leonard of having had to spend the evening at a dinner party listening to the tedious husband of an interesting woman I know.

"The nerve," Leonard replies. "He thinks he's a person too."

Marie calls to tell me Em has chosen this moment when her father is dying to tell her that her self-absorption is endemic not circumstantial.

"What bad timing," I commiserate.

"Bad timing!" Marie cries. "It's aggression, pure aggression!" Her voice sounds the way cracked pavement looks.

Lorenzo, a nervous musician I know, tells me he is buying a new apartment.

"Why?" I ask, knowing his old apartment to be a lovely one.

"The bathroom is twenty feet from the bedroom," he confides, then laughs self-consciously. "I know it's only a small detail. But when you live alone it's all details, isn't it?"

I run into Jane on the street. We speak of a woman we both know whose voice is routinely suicidal. Jane tells me the woman called her the other day at seven ayem and she responded with exuberance. "Don't get me wrong," she says, "I wasn't being altruistic. I was trying to pick her up off the ground because it was too early in the morning to bend over so far. I was just protecting my back."

My acquaintanceship—like the city itself—is wide-ranging but unintegrated. The people who are my friends are not the friends of one another. Sometimes—when I am feeling expansive and imagining life in New York all of a piece—these friendships feel like beads on a necklace loosely strung, the beads not touching one another but all lying, nonetheless, lightly and securely against the base of my throat, magically pressing into me the warmth of connection. Then my life seems to mirror an urban essence I prize: the dense and original quality of life on the margin, the risk and excitement of having to put it all together each day anew. The harshness of the city seems alluring. Ah, the pleasures of conflict! The glamour of uncertainty! Hurrah for neurotic friendships and yea to incivility!

At other times—when no one is around and no one is available—I stare out the window, thinking, What a fool you are to glamorize life in the city. Loneliness engulfs me like dry heat. It is New York loneliness, hot with shame, loneliness that tells you you're a fool and a loser. Everyone else is feasting, you alone cannot gain a seat at the banquet. I look down at the street. I see that mine is a workhorse life. As long as I remain in harness I am able to put one foot in front of the other without losing step, but if anything unbalances me I feel again the weight of circumstance hanging from my neck, a millstone beneath which I have taught myself to walk upright.

The day is brilliant: asphalt glimmers, people knife through the crowd, buildings look cut out against a rare blue sky. The sidewalk is mobbed, the sound of traffic deafening. I walk slowly, and people hit against me. Within a mile my pace quickens, my eyes relax, my ears clear out. Here and there, a face, a body, a gesture separates itself from the endlessly advancing crowd, attracts my reviving attention. I begin to hear the city, and feel its presence. Two men in their twenties, thin and well dressed, brush past me, one saying rapidly to the other, "You gotta give her credit. She made herself out of nothing. And I mean nothing." I laugh and lose my rhythm. Excuse me, my fault, beg your pardon. . . . A couple appears in the crowd, dark, attractive, middle-aged. As they come abreast of me the man is saying to the woman, "It's always my problem. It's never your problem." Cars honk, trucks screech, lights change. Sidewalk vendors hawk food, clothing, jewelry. A man standing beside a folding table covered with gold and silver watches speaks quietly into the air. "It's a steal, ladies and gentlemen," he says. "A real steal." Another couple is coming toward me, this time an odd one. The woman is black, a dwarf, around forty years old. The man is Hispanic, a boy, twelve or fourteen. She looks straight ahead as she walks, he dances along beside her. As they pass she says in the voice of a Montessori mother, "It doesn't matter what he thinks. It only matters what you think."

My shoulders straighten, my stride lengthens. The misery in my chest begins to dissolve out. The city is opening itself to me. I feel myself enfolded in the embrace of the crowded street, its heedless expressiveness the only invitation I need to not feel shut out.

There are mornings I awake and, somehow, I have more of myself. I swing my legs over the side of the bed, draw up the blind, and, from my sixteenth-floor window, feel the city spilling itself across my eyes, crowding up into the world, filling in the landscape. Behind it, there in the distance, where it belongs, is the Hudson River and, if I want it, the sky. But I don't want it. What I want is to take this self I now have more of down into those noisy, dirty, dangerous streets and make my way from one end of Manhattan to the other in the midst of that crowd that also may have more of itself. There is no friend, lover, or relative I want to be with as much as I want to swing through the streets being jostled and bumped, catching the eye of the stranger, feeling the stranger's touch. In the street I am grinning like an idiot to myself, walking fast at everyone coming my way. Children stare, men smile, women laugh right into my eyes. The tenderness I encounter in that mood! The impersonal affection of a palm laid against my arm or my back as someone murmurs, "Excuse me," and sidles skillfully past my body: it soothes beyond reasonable explanation. I feel such love then, for the idea of the city as well as the reality. And everyone looks good: handsome, stylish, interesting. Life spills over without stint and without condition. I feel often that I am walking with my head tipped back, my mouth thrown open, a stream of sunlight on water pouring into my throat. When I consider the days on which I find myself looking into one gargoyle face after another—everyone in front of me old, ugly, deformed, and diseased— I have to realize the street gives me back a primitive reflection of whatever load of hope or fear I am carrying about with me that day.

Nothing heals me of a sore and angry heart like a walk through the very city I often feel denying me. To see in the street the fifty different ways people struggle to remain human until the very last minute—the variety and inventiveness of survival technique—is to feel the pressure relieved, the overflow draining off. I join the anxiety. I share the condition. I feel in my nerve endings the common refusal to go under. Never am I less alone than alone in the crowded street. Alone, I imagine myself. Alone, I buy time. Me, and everyone I know. Me, and all the New York friends.

The telephone rings. It's Leonard with a question about an editor he wants to send someone to. I answer his question, and we chat. I hear the bright hard edge in his voice, I hear him struggling against it. I help by talking us into a conversation that interests us both. In ten minutes he's been pulled out of his own black hole. He's laughing now, quite genuinely. Warmed by the effort and the success, I say, "Let's have dinner." "Sure," he responds with only a flicker of hesitation. "Let's see now." He's looking at his book. "God, this is awful!" I can hear the anxiety seeping back into his voice, the panic he feels at being forced to make a date. "How about two weeks from Friday?" "Fine," I say, only a second or two off course myself.

Later in the day the phone rings again. It's Laura. "You won't believe this," she says, and proceeds to entertain us both with the story she's called to tell me. Laura is all solid contact from the moment her voice hears mine. She tells the story, we both laugh, many sentences of psychological wisdom pass between us. "Let's have dinner," I say. "Absolutely," she says. "Let's see now." She too looks at her book. "Omigod, this is ridiculous. I can't do it until early next week. Waitaminnit, waitaminnit." She's enjoying her own self so much during this conversation she doesn't want to let the pleasure evaporate. "There's something here I can change. How about Thursday?"

There are two categories of friendship: those in which people are enlivened by each other and those in which people must be enlivened to be with each other. In the first category one clears the decks to be together. In the second one looks for an empty space in the schedule.

Sometimes I am Laura, sometimes Leonard. Sometimes I am both in the course of a single day. I am eager to remain Laura. She is always responsive to human contact. To be responsive is to feel expressive. I value the expressiveness above all else. Or so I say. But there are moments, even days, when any disinterested observer might justly conclude that I, like Leonard, seem awash in my own melancholy, swamped by the invading instability, suffering a failure of nerve to which I seem devoted.

New York friendship is an education in the struggle between devotion to the melancholy and attraction to the expressive. I had thought it would be different in friendship than it generally is in marriage: attaining to a higher level of equilibrium somehow. But how foolish to have thought that. We are all the formerly married, are we not. Most of us spend our lives fighting an inner battle that is never won, in a war concluded only by death. In each life, however, one element or the other has the edge. The city reels beneath the impact of this dynamic. Why, exactly, it's hard to say.

I put the telephone receiver back in its cradle. I close the apartment door. In thirty seconds I'm on the street. Thank God for the street! Those of us who crave the expressive but can't shake off the melancholy walk the street. The pavements of New York are filled with people escaping the prison sentence of personal history into the promise of an open destiny.

This morning, on Eighth Avenue in Chelsea, I saw a woman I thought I knew, a faculty wife I'd once met somewhere in the South. The woman's face was narrow and fine boned, framed in a waterfall of New York kinky hair, just like Barbara Levinson's. And she was wearing worn leather boots that had once been expensive along with a wool cape three years out of fashion held together by a jade and silver clasp, also just the kind of thing Barbara might have worn. When I got close I saw that it was not Barbara at all. How knowing this face was! It was the face of a woman who had had "expectations," you could see that. The mouth was ravaged, the chin defiant, the lipstick bold, the eyes resigned to intelligent obscurity. The woman looked glamorous to me here on Eighth Avenue at ten in the morning—richly haggard, a jewel in its natural setting—with the street at her back and all that she knew etched clearly in her face. It was a face that could have been made only in the city.

In the South Barbara L. had seemed odd, an embarrassing exotic, and then as she got older just embarrassing. It was the isolation that had done her in, I could see that now. One among the many, she could survive in the South but not flourish. On the way to interesting she had stopped at eccentric. To blossom just "anywhere" one must be either distinguished enough to create one's own environment or humble enough to merge with the one at hand. If one is neither, a critical mass of like-minded spirits is required. It's like the difference between ordinary plants put down in a suburban lawn (one dumb-looking bush here, forlorn flowerbed there) and those in a richly planted garden whose massed profusion makes the same homely bushes and flowers glow with "element." Here on Eighth Avenue what this woman knew made her exciting. Put her down in a southern college town and she'd quickly become forlorn.

That hair. That New York kinky hair. It required more massed profusion than any of us had ever dreamed it would.

On Ninth Avenue, near the bus station, suddenly there is a couple walking beside me, in the gutter, among the cars. They are both black, both thin, and both dressed in rags. The man carries a heavy shopping bag in each hand. The woman walks behind the man, carrying nothing, trembling with fatigue. The man seems beyond speech. He moves stoically ahead. She moves slowly with great hesitation. Her face weeps without sound. She cries out at him, "You no good! You no good at all. You take everything from me. Everything!" The man makes no reply. The woman repeats that he is no good and that he has taken everything from her. "You one no good man," she calls out again. "I gonna call the poh-leece on you. You heah me? I gonna call the poh-leece." To my astonishment she does indeed stop a cop and demand that he attend to her complaint. A crowd begins to gather. The cop hears the woman out. The man with the shopping bags stops walking. I see the effort it costs him to bring his plodding motion to a halt. The cop turns to the man. The man says quietly that he has taken nothing from her, that he is carrying her load as well as his own. The cop nods wearily. He and the man quickly become allies. The cop puts a kindly hand on his arm and one on the woman's arm. He urges them to repair their quarrel and sends them on their way. The woman stands there, helpless, all hope now gone. The man waits, looking patiently at her. He knows he must let her speak. The woman extends her arm, makes a fist of her hand. From the fist she extends her forefinger and shakes it like a thermometer at the man. "I don' want no part of you," she cries out. "You stay away from me! I don' wan' no part of you no more." Slowly, the other fingers of her clenched fist open out. These fingers then begin to curl inward. They open and close in a beckoning motion. "I don' wan' no part of you," she cries. The fingers begin to implore instead of accuse. Swifter and swifter, they beckon. And all the while she keeps on crying, "I don' wan' no part of you."

I stand alone at the edge of the crowd. The woman's voice and gesture thrill me. I am amazed by her eloquence. How well she has put language and movement together to tell her story. I do not feel at one with her. She is alone, I am alone. But there she is, and here I am. She too has New York kinky hair. For the moment that's comradeship enough.

When I was growing up New York was safe, everything was either cheap or free, and, in midtown, no gays, no blacks, no women. Now the city is violent, everything costs the earth, and we are all visible.

1996

# COLSON WHITEHEAD

Colson Whitehead is the author of three novels, The Intuitionist (1999), John Henry Days (2003), and Apex Hides the Hurt (2006), and an urbanist meditation, The Colossus of New York (2003). A native of New York City, born in 1969, and educated at Harvard, he served as the pop culture and television critic for The Village Voice. In 2002 he was awarded a MacArthur grant. In his vivid first novel, The Intuitionist, which was a finalist for the Ernest Hemingway / PEN fiction award, he treated the unnamed metropolis, obviously based on New York, in a Kafkaesque, fable-like manner. On the heels of the World Trade Center attacks in 2001, in The Colossus of New York, he specifically took on the particulars of the city, investigating what quirks and mental habits united its citizens tribally, and what kept the place functioning, in spite of its always bordering on chaos. Whitehead's work is embedded in an exploration of consciousness, which acts as a two-way filter, both detaching the self bemusedly from and reintegrating it with reality. He lives with his family in Brooklyn, New York.

## FROM *THE COLOSSUS OF NEW YORK*

I'M here because I was born here and thus ruined for anywhere else, but I don't know about you. Maybe you're from here, too, and sooner or later it will come out that we used to live a block away from each other and didn't even know it. Or maybe you moved here a couple years ago for a job. Maybe you came here for school. Maybe you saw the brochure. The city has spent a considerable amount of time and money putting the brochure together, what with all the movies, TV shows and songs—the whole If You Can Make It There business. The city also puts a lot of effort into making your hometown look really drab and tiny, just in case you were wondering why it's such a drag to go back sometimes.

No matter how long you have been here, you are a New Yorker the first time you say, That used to be Munsey's, or That used to be the Tic

Toc Lounge. That before the internet cafe plugged itself in, you got your shoes resoled in the mom-and-pop operation that used to be there. You are a New Yorker when what was there before is more real and solid than what is here now.

You start building your private New York the first time you lay eyes on it. Maybe you were in a cab leaving the airport when the sky-line first roused itself into view. All your worldly possessions were in the trunk, and in your hand you held an address on a piece of paper. Look: there's the Empire State Building, over there are the Twin Towers. Somewhere in that fantastic, glorious mess was the address on the piece of paper, your first home here. Maybe your parents dragged you here for a vacation when you were a kid and towed you up and down the gigantic avenues to shop for Christmas gifts. The only skyscrapers visible from your stroller were the legs of adults, but you got to know the ground pretty well and started to wonder why some sidewalks sparkle at certain angles, and others don't. Maybe you came to visit your old buddy, the one who moved here last summer, and there was some mix-up as to where you were supposed to meet. You stepped out of Penn Station into the dizzying hustle of Eighth Avenue and fainted. Freeze it there: that instant is the first brick in your city.

I started building my New York on the uptown No. 1 train. My first city memory is of looking out a subway window as the train erupted from the tunnel on the way to 125th Street and palsied up onto the elevated tracks. It's the early 70's, so everything is filthy. Which means everything is still filthy, because that is my city and I'm sticking to it. I still call it the Pan Am Building, not out of affectation, but because that's what it is. For that new transplant from Des Moines, who is starting her first week of work at a Park Avenue South insurance firm, that titan squatting over Grand Central is the Met Life Building, and for her it always will be. She is wrong, of course—when I look up there, I clearly see the gigantic letters spelling out Pan Am, don't I? And of course I am wrong, in the eyes of the old-timers who maintain the myth that there was a time before Pan Am.

History books and public television documentaries are always trying to tell you all sorts of "facts" about New York. That Canal Street used to be a canal. That Bryant Park used to be a reservoir. It's all hokum. I've been to Canal Street, and the only time I ever saw a river flow through it was during the last water-main explosion. Never listen to what people tell you about old New York, because if you didn't witness it, it is not a part of your New York and might as well be Jersey. Except for that bit about the Dutch buying Manhattan for 24 bucks—there are and always will be braggarts who "got in at the right time."

There are eight million naked cities in this naked city—they dispute and disagree. The New York City you live in is not my New York City; how could it be? This place multiplies when you're not looking. We move over here, we move over there. Over a lifetime, that adds up to a lot of neighborhoods, the motley construction material of your jerry-built metropolis. Your favorite newsstands, restaurants, movie theaters, subway stations and barbershops are replaced by your next neighborhood's favorites. It gets to be quite a sum. Before you know it, you have your own personal skyline.

Go back to your old haunts in your old neighborhoods and what do you find: they remain and have disappeared. The greasy spoon, the deli, the dry cleaner you scouted out when you first arrived and tried to make those new streets yours: they are gone. But look past the windows of the travel agency that replaced your pizza parlor. Beyond the desks and computers and promo posters for tropical adventures, you can still see Neapolitan slices cooling, the pizza cutter lying next to half a pie, the map of Sicily on the wall. It is all still there, I assure you. The man who just paid for a trip to Jamaica sees none of that, sees his romantic getaway, his family vacation, what this little shop on this little street has granted him. The disappeared pizza parlor is still here because you are here, and when the beauty parlor replaces the travel agency, the gentleman will still have his vacation. And that lady will have her manicure.

You swallow hard when you discover that the old coffee shop is now a chain pharmacy, that the place where you first kissed so-and-so is now a discount electronics retailer, that where you bought this very jacket is now rubble behind a blue plywood fence and a future office building. Damage has been done to your city. You say, It happened overnight. But of course it didn't. Your pizza parlor, his shoeshine stand, her hat store: when they were here, we neglected them. For all you know, the place closed down moments after the last time you walked out the door. (Ten months ago? Six years? Fifteen? You can't remember, can you?) And there have been five stores in that spot before the travel agency. Five different neighborhoods coming and going between then and now, other people's other cities. Or fifteen, twenty-five, a hundred neighborhoods. Thousands of people pass that storefront every day, each one haunting the streets of his or her own New York, not one of them seeing the same thing.

We can never make proper goodbyes. It was your last ride in a Checker cab and you had no warning. It was the last time you were going to have Lake Tung Ting shrimp in that kinda shady Chinese restaurant and you had no idea. If you had known, perhaps you would have stepped behind the counter and shaken everyone's hand, pulled out the disposable camera and issued posing instructions. But you had no idea. There are unheralded tipping points, a certain number of times that we will unlock the front door of an apartment. At some point you were closer to the last time than you were to the first time, and you didn't even know it. You didn't know that each time you passed the threshold you were saying goodbye.

I never got a chance to say goodbye to some of my old buildings. Some I lived in, others were part of a skyline I thought would always be there. And they never got a chance to say goodbye to me. I think they would have liked to—I refuse to believe in their indifference. You say you know these streets pretty well? The city knows you better than any living person because it has seen you when you are alone. It saw you steeling yourself for the job interview, slowly walking home after the late date, tripping over nonexistent impediments on the sidewalk. It saw you wince when the single frigid drop fell from the air-conditioner twelve stories up and zapped you. It saw the bewilderment on your face as you stepped out of the stolen matinee, incredulous that there was still daylight after such a long movie. It saw you half-running up the street after you got the keys to your first apartment. The city saw all that. Remembers too.

Consider what all your old apartments would say if they got

together to swap stories. They could piece together the starts and finishes of your relationships, complain about your wardrobe and musical tastes, gossip about who you are after midnight. 7J says, So that's what happened to Lucy—I knew it would never work out. You picked up yoga, you put down yoga, you tried various cures. You tried on selves and got rid of them, and this makes your old rooms wistful: why must things change? 3R goes, Saxophone, you say—I knew him when he played guitar. Cherish your old apartments and pause for a moment when you pass them. Pay tribute, for they are the caretakers of your reinventions.

Our streets are calendars containing who we were and who we will be next. We see ourselves in this city every day when we walk down the sidewalk and catch our reflections in store windows, seek ourselves in this city each time we reminisce about what was there fifteen, ten, forty years ago, because all our old places are proof that we were here. One day the city we built will be gone, and when it goes, we go. When the buildings fall, we topple, too.

Maybe we become New Yorkers the day we realize that New York will go on without us. To put off the inevitable, we try to fix the city in place, remember it as it was, doing to the city what we would never allow to be done to ourselves. The kid on the uptown No. 1 train, the new arrival stepping out of Grand Central, the jerk at the intersection who doesn't know east from west: those people don't exist anymore, ceased to be a couple of apartments ago, and we wouldn't have it any other way. New York City does not hold our former selves against us. Perhaps we can extend the same courtesy.

Our old buildings still stand because we saw them, moved in and out of their long shadows, were lucky enough to know them for a time. They are a part of the city we carry around. It is hard to imagine that something will take their place, but at this very moment the people with the right credentials are considering how to fill the craters. The cement trucks will roll up and spin their bellies, the jackhammers will rattle, and after a while the postcards of the new skyline will be available for purchase. Naturally we will cast a wary eye toward those new kids on the block, but let's be patient and not judge too quickly. We were new here, too, once.

What follows is my city. Making this a guide book, with handy color-coded maps and miniscule fine print you should read very closely so you won't be surprised. It contains your neighborhoods. Or doesn't. We overlap. Or don't. Maybe you've walked these avenues, maybe it's all Jersey to you. I'm not sure what to say. Except that probably we're neighbors. That we walk past each other every day, and never knew it until now.

2003

# VIJAY SESHADRI

_In his two collections_ Wild Kingdom _(1996) and_ The Long
Meadow, _which won the James Laughlin Prize in 2003 for best second
book of poetry, Vijay Seshadri has established himself as one of the most
compelling, singular voices in American poetry today. Seshadri was born
in Bangalore, India, in 1954; his family immigrated to Columbus, Ohio,
when he was five. But Seshadri is suspicious of the conventional immigrant narrative and prefers to be seen as a poet in the classical American
lineage of Walt Whitman, Elizabeth Bishop, and James Schuyler. He
shares with Whitman a hunger to incorporate the flow of humanity into
his poems, to get beyond the narrow, confessional self and take on greater
spiritual, historical, and scientific concerns. His observant imagery, warm
wit, and self-mocking irony co-exist on the page with a larger perspective
edging toward abstraction. The poet, who has lived for many years in
Brooklyn with his family, teaches at Sarah Lawrence College._

## NORTH OF MANHATTAN

You can take the Dyre Avenue bus to where the subway terminates
just inside the Bronx
and be downtown before you realize
how quickly your body has escaped your mind,
stretching down the tracks on a beam
until the band snaps and the body slips free and is gone,
out the crashing doors, through the stiles,
and up the long chutes,
to burn both ways at once down the avenues,
ecstatic in its finitude,
with all the other bodies,
the bundles of molecules
fusing and dispersing on the sidewalks.
Ten to the hundredth power,
bundles of molecules are looking at paintings,

bundles of molecules are eating corn muffins,
crabcakes, shad roe, spring lamb, rice pudding.
Bundles of molecules are talking to each other,
sotto voce or in a commanding voice—
"I agree with you one hundred percent, Dog";
"I looked for you today, but you'd already gone";
"I've left the Amended Restated Sublease Agreement on your desk";
"I'm going home now,
and you think about what you did."
The ear grows accustomed to wider and wider intervals.
The eye senses shapes in the periphery
toward which it dares not turn to look.
One bundle is selling another a playback machine,
a six-square-inch wax-paper reticule
of powdered white rhinoceros horn,
an off-season-discounted ticket to Machu Picchu,
a gas-powered generator
for when the lights go out,
a dime bag of Mexican brown.
It is four o'clock in the afternoon.
The sunlight is stealing inch by inch
down the newly repointed redbrick wall.
She comes into the kitchen wrapped in the quilt
and watches as he fries eggs.
"After what just happened, you want to eat?" she says in disgust.
Will she or will she not, back in the bedroom,
lift the gun from the holster
and put it in her purse? The mind, meanwhile,
is still somewhere around Tremont Avenue,
panting down the tracks, straining
from the past to the vanishing present.
It will never catch up
and touch the moment. It will always be
in this tunnel of its forever,
where aquamarine crusted bulbs feed on a darkness
that looks all around without seeing,

and fungus, earlike, starved for light, sprouts
from walls where drops of rusted water
condense and drip.

Don't say I didn't warn you about this.
Don't say my concern for your welfare
never extended to my sharing the terrible and addictive secrets
that only death can undo.
Because I'm telling you now
that you can also take the same bus north,
crossing over against the traffic spilling out of the mall
and waiting twenty minutes in the kiosk with the Drambuie ad.
There. Isn't that better?
More passengers are getting off than on.
The girl with the skates going home from practice
will soon get off, as will
the old woman whose license to drive has been taken from her.
They will enter houses with little gazebos tucked in their gardens.
And then, for just a while, the mind will disembark from the body,
relaxed on its contoured plastic seat,
and go out to make fresh tracks in the snow
and stand and breathe under the imaginary trees—
the horsehair pine, the ambergris tree,
the tree that the bulbul loves,
the nebula tree  .  .  .

2 0 0 4

# DON DELILLO

---

*Don DeLillo, one of the central figures in contemporary American litera-
ture, was born in the Bronx, New York, in 1936 and has lived for much of
his life in New York City, which he has often used as a backdrop for fiction. His 14 novels, including* Great Jones Street, White Noise, Libra,
Mao II, *and* Underworld, *have influenced a generation of emergent fiction writers. DeLillo has often treated such subjects as terrorism, conspiracy, mass persuasion, the reification of reality through media saturation,
and the numbing impact of future shock on American culture—all of
which seem to anticipate the crisis brought on by September 11, 2001. In
his most recent novel,* Falling Man *(2007), DeLillo begins the book with
a chilling, uncanny description of a man caught in the World Trade Center attack. The* Times Literary Supplement *reviewer, Stephen Abell,
put the matter this way: "It is fitting that the most important writer in
the United States has now provided an enduring account of the most important event in recent American history. One feels that DeLillo —in his
role as cataloguer of the nation's consciousness—is unimprovably
equipped to provide an artistic response to such an occurrence."*

## FROM *FALLING MAN*

IT was not a street anymore but a world, a time and space of
falling ash and near night. He was walking north through rubble
and mud and there were people running past holding towels to
their faces or jackets over their heads. They had handkerchiefs pressed
to their mouths. They had shoes in their hands, a woman with a shoe
in each hand, running past him. They ran and fell, some of them, confused and ungainly, with debris coming down around them, and there
were people taking shelter under cars.

The roar was still in the air, the buckling rumble of the fall. This
was the world now. Smoke and ash came rolling down streets and
turning corners, busting around corners, seismic tides of smoke, with
office paper flashing past, standard sheets with cutting edge, skimming, whipping past, otherworldly things in the morning pall.

He wore a suit and carried a briefcase. There was glass in his hair and face, marbled bolls of blood and light. He walked past a Breakfast Special sign and they went running by, city cops and security guards running, hands pressed down on gun butts to keep the weapons steady.

Things inside were distant and still, where he was supposed to be. It happened everywhere around him, a car half buried in debris, windows smashed and noises coming out, radio voices scratching at the wreckage. He saw people shedding water as they ran, clothes and bodies drenched from sprinkler systems. There were shoes discarded in the street, handbags and laptops, a man seated on the sidewalk coughing up blood. Paper cups went bouncing oddly by.

The world was this as well, figures in windows a thousand feet up, dropping into free space, and the stink of fuel fire, and the steady rip of sirens in the air. The noise lay everywhere they ran, stratified sound collecting around them, and he walked away from it and into it at the same time.

There was something else then, outside all this, not belonging to this, aloft. He watched it coming down. A shirt came down out of the high smoke, a shirt lifted and drifting in the scant light and then falling again, down toward the river.

They ran and then they stopped, some of them, standing there swaying, trying to draw breath out of the burning air, and the fitful cries of disbelief, curses and lost shouts, and the paper massed in the air, contracts, resumés blowing by, intact snatches of business, quick in the wind.

He kept on walking. There were the runners who'd stopped and others veering into sidestreets. Some were walking backwards, looking into the core of it, all those writhing lives back there, and things kept falling, scorched objects trailing lines of fire.

He saw two women sobbing in their reverse march, looking past him, both in running shorts, faces in collapse.

He saw members of the tai chi group from the park nearby, standing with hands extended at roughly chest level, elbows bent, as if all of this, themselves included, might be placed in a state of abeyance.

Someone came out of a diner and tried to hand him a bottle of water. It was a woman wearing a dust mask and a baseball cap and she withdrew the bottle and twisted off the top and then thrust it toward him again. He put down the briefcase to take it, barely aware that he wasn't using his left arm, that he'd had to put down the briefcase before he could take the bottle. Three police vans came veering into the street and sped downtown, sirens sounding. He closed his eyes and drank, feeling the water pass into his body taking dust and soot down with it. She was looking at him. She said something he didn't hear and he handed back the bottle and picked up the brief case. There was an after-taste of blood in the long draft of water.

He started walking again. A supermarket cart stood upright and empty. There was a woman behind it, facing him, with police tape wrapped around her head and face, yellow caution tape that marks the limits of a crime scene. Her eyes were thin white ripples in the bright mask and she gripped the handle of the cart and stood there, looking into the smoke.

In time he heard the sound of the second fall. He crossed Canal Street and began to see things, somehow, differently. Things did not seem charged in the usual ways, the cobbled street, the cast-iron buildings. There was something critically missing from the things around him. They were unfinished, whatever that means. They were unseen, whatever that means, shop windows, loading platforms, paint-sprayed walls. Maybe this is what things look like when there is no one here to see them.

He heard the sound of the second fall, or felt it in the trembling air, the north tower coming down, a soft awe of voices in the distance. That was him coming down, the north tower.

The sky was lighter here and he could breathe more easily. There were others behind him, thousands, filling the middle distance, a mass in near formation, people walking out of the smoke. He kept going until he had to stop. It hit him quickly, the knowledge that he couldn't go any farther.

2 0 0 7

# POSTSCRIPT

IN THE DECADE SINCE THE INITIAL EDITION OF THIS ANTHOLOGY AP-
PEARED (1998–2008), NEW YORK CITY HAS UNDERGONE ONE OF ITS
most eventful and momentous periods. We would do well to consider
briefly, in this expanded second edition, what those challenges and
changes were, and how the literary profession has responded to
them.

First, of course, was the terrorist attack on September 11, 2001,
which leveled the World Trade Center and killed several thousand
people. Such a previously unimaginable act—hijacking commercial
planes and turning them into bombs to bring down two of the tallest
skyscrapers in the world—had a much more visceral and traumatic
impact on New Yorkers than on those who only saw the images on
television. As the city mourned and began picking up the pieces, local
writers shook their heads and wondered how anything they wrote
could possibly reflect intelligently on and not soil with cliché the
enormity of the event. Some said it was a subject, like the Holocaust,
that could not be written about without trivializing; others, that a
number of years would have to elapse before this material could be
transformed into something of literary worth. All these warnings did
not deter distinguished novelists such as Don DeDillo, Lynne Sharon
Schwartz, and Jonathan Safan Foer from making subtle, powerful attempts to describe the impact of that day and its aftermath.

It was remembered also that the city was no stranger to tragedy:
New York carries in its bones the memory of devastating fires and
cholera epidemics, the Civil War draft riots, the General Slocum
tragedy, the 1929 stock market crash, the earlier terrorist attack on
the World Trade Center. Its citizens are ever conscious of the metropolis's vulnerability, from a temporary breakdown of the subway system to a sanitation strike. New York has inspired many apocalyptic,
sci-fi imaginings of its destruction, usually in movies, less so in serious
literature. Writers have tended to focus on the daily life of the city
and to shy away from catastrophe. This stubborn clinging to the everyday, even as it is shot through with a sense of loss (as apotheosized by

the Twin Towers), can be seen in Colson Whitehead's recent meditation *The Colossus of New York*, when he emphasizes the private city
everyone builds in his head: "No matter how long you have been here,
you are a New Yorker the first time you say, That used to be Munsey's,
or That used to be the Tic Toc Lounge. That before the internet cafe
plugged itself in, you got your shoes resoled in the mom-and-pop operation that used to be there. You are a New Yorker when what was
there before is more real and solid than what is there now."

Initially, the September 11th attacks were thought to have dealt
the local economy an incalculably severe blow, running into billions
and billions of dollars, from which it would take decades to recover.
And indeed, many small businesses and restaurants in the downtown
area were forced to shut down permanently. But what is surprising is
how quickly the city's economy recovered its robustness, even its
tourists, and began to show a surplus. As New York's wealth became
increasingly dependent on the interconnected spheres of finance, insurance, legal services, and real estate, its writers have scrambled to
reflect these more abstract, byte-driven modes of livelihood (compared to the more colorful manufacturing and shipping of the city's
past), and to register the enormous emphasis on consumerism—
shopping. The resulting literature has been frequently satiric. As New
York became a demographic magnet for young, college graduate
women, we have witnessed the rise of an urban "chick lit" subgenre,
exemplified by *The Devil Wears Prada*, which updates the earlier, office-
work bestsellers such as Rona Jaffe's *The Best of Everything*.

The continuing high price of New York real estate has made for increasing polarization between the rich and the poor, especially in the
city's center, Manhattan, where the middle class is being priced out of
housing. In consequence, the other boroughs, such as Brooklyn, are
witnessing vast construction, and their classic, low-scale cityscape is
being replaced by a more monolithic high-rise profile. Some authors
have warned that the city's texture, its very character, is being eroded
by a steady stream of luxury condominiums and national chain stores.
In this apocalyptic vision, the destruction of New York will come not
from terrorist attack but from the slow nibbling away of its soul by
greedy, suburbanized blandness. Still, the city's ability to retain its vi-

tality in the midst of this ongoing expansion should not be counted out. We have already seen since 1980 how hundreds of thousands of new immigrants, drawn from around the world, have replaced that part of the older population which fled to warmer climes, and have adapted to and even prospered in the city they found awaiting them. These immigrants have brought their mercantile skills, cultures, and cuisines to neighborhoods such as Flushing, Astoria, Flatbush, and Brighton Beach—and their poetry and prose. Simply restricting ourselves to the diaspora of the Indian subcontinent, we can number Salman Rushdie, Jhumpa Lahiri, Vijay Seshadri, Amitov Gosh, Kiran Desai, and Sukehtu Mehta who have already enriched New York writing. How much richer is that discourse when we factor in the many important Hispanic, African, Chinese, and Russian, and other writers who have recently immigrated to New York.

It is undoubtedly a tall order for today's authors, whether indigenous or transplanted, to assimilate and articulate the enormous changes that are taking place in this city. But if no single writer can be expected to give voice to modern New York as Joyce did Dublin or Dickens, London, we can count on the totality of those novelists, poets, and essayists who are living in and writing about the city to thicken and deepen immeasurably the literary record of this place. It is already happening.

*Phillip Lopate*

# SOURCES & ACKNOWLEDGMENTS

Washington Irving. (from) *A History of New York: Washington Irving: History, Tales, and Sketches* (New York: The Library of America, 1983), pp. 449–55.

James Kirke Paulding. The Stranger at Home; or, a Tour in Broadway: *Washington Irving: History, Tales, and Sketches* (New York: The Library of America, 1983). Text copyright © 1977, 1978 by G.K. Hall & Company.

Frances Trollope. (from) *Domestic Manners of the Americans: Domestic Manners of the Americans* (2 vols. London: Whittaker, Treacher, 1832), Vol. 2, pp. 156–61.

Fanny Kemble. (from) The Journal: Monica Gough (ed.), *Fanny Kemble: The Journal of a Young Actress* (New York: Columbia University Press, 1980). Copyright © 1990 by Columbia University Press. Reprinted by permission.

Philip Hone. (from) The Diary: Allan Nevins (ed.), *The Diary of Philip Hone, 1828–1851* (2 vols. New York: Dodd, Mead & Co., 1927).

Charles Dickens. (from) *American Notes for General Circulation:* Chapter 6, "New York" of *American Notes for General Circulation* (London: Chapman & Hall, 1842).

Henry David Thoreau. Letters from Staten Island: Walter Harding and Carl Bode (eds.), *The Correspondence of Henry David Thoreau* (New York: New York University Press, 1958), excerpts from pp. 98–142.

Nathaniel Parker Willis. (from) Open-Air Musings in the City: *Rural Letters and Other Records of Thought and Leisure, Written in the Intervals of More Hurried Literary Labor* (New York: Baker and Scribners, 1849).

Edgar Allan Poe. (from) Doings of Gotham: Thomas Olive Mabbott (ed.), *Doings of Gotham* (Pottsville, Pa.: Jacob E. Spannuth, 1929).

James Fenimore Cooper. (from) Satanstoe: *Satanstoe, or, The Littlepage Manuscripts: A Tale of the Colony* (Albany: State University of New York Press, 1990), pp. 64–66, 69–70. Text copyright © 1990 by the State University of New York Press. Reprinted by permission of the State University of New York Press. All rights reserved.

Margaret Fuller. Our City Charities: Jeffrey Steele (ed.), *The Essential Margaret Fuller* (New Brunswick: Rutgers University Press, 1992).

George G. Foster. The Eating-Houses: *New York in Slices: By an Experienced Carver* (New York: W.F. Burgess, 1848).

Grant Thorburn. (from) *Life and Writings of Grant Thorburn: Life and Writings of Grant Thorburn, prepared by himself* (New York: E. Walker, 1852), pp. 60–74.

Walt Whitman. Crossing Brooklyn Ferry: *Walt Whitman: Poetry and Prose* (New York: The Library of America, 1982). The Old Bowery: Floyd Stovall (ed.), *The Collected Writings of Walt Whitman: Prose Works 1892, Vol. 2 (New York: New York University Press, 1964).

Herman Melville. Bartleby, the Scrivener: *The Piazza Tales*, by Herman Melville, published by Northwestern University Press/Newberry Library. Copyright

© 1987 by Northwestern University Press and The Newberry Library. Reprinted with permission.

George Templeton Strong. (from) The Diaries: Allan Nevins and Milton Halsey (eds.), *The Diary of George Templeton Strong* (4 vols. New York: Macmillan, 1952). Copyright © 1952 by Macmillan Publishing Company, renewed © 1980 by Milton Halsey Thomas. Reprinted by permission of Simon & Schuster.

Frederick Law Olmsted. Passages in the Life of an Unpractical Man: Charles E. Beveridge and David Schuyler (eds.), *The Papers of Frederick Law Olmsted, Vol. 3: Creating Central Park 1857–1861* (Baltimore: Johns Hopkins University Press, 1983). Copyright © 1983 by the Johns Hopkins University Press. Reprinted by permission.

Ernest Dauvergier de Hauranne. (from) *Eight Months in America:* Ralph H. Bowen (trans. and ed.), *A Frenchman in Lincoln's America* (2 vols. Chicago: The Lakeside Press, 1974), Vol. 1, pp. 384–89.

Fanny Fern. Tyrants of the Shop: Joyce W. Warren (ed.), *Ruth Hall and Other Writings* (New Brunswick: Rutgers University Press, 1986).

Mark Twain. Personals: *Daily Alta California*, June 1, 1867.

James D. McCabe. Impostors: *Lights and Shadows of New York Life; or, the Sights and Sensations of the Great City* (Philadelphia: National Publishing Company, 1872).

Wong Chin Foo. Experience of a Chinese Journalist: *Puck*, April 1885.

José Martí. New York Under the Snow: *The America of José Martí*, trans. Juan de Osís (New York: Noonday Press, 1953). Translation copyright © 1954, renewed copyright © by Farrar, Straus, & Giroux, Inc.

William Dean Howells. (from) *A Hazard of New Fortunes: A Hazard of New Fortunes* (Bloomington and London: Indiana University Press, 1976), pp. 41–52, 58–63. Text copyright © 1976 by Indiana University Press. Reprinted by permission.

Jacob Riis, The Down Town Back-Alleys: *How the Other Half Lives* (New York: Charles Scribner's Sons, 1890).

Stephen Crane. Opium's Varied Dreams; Adventures of a Novelist: *Stephen Crane: Prose and Poetry* (New York: The Library of America, 1984). Text copyright © by The University Press of Virginia. Reprinted by permission.

Abraham Cahan. Drowned Their Sins; Summer Complaint: The Annual Strike: Moses Rischin (ed.): *Grandma Never Lived in America* (Bloomington: Indiana University Press, 1985). Copyright © 1985 by Moses Rischin.

Theodore Dreiser. Whence the Song; A Vanished Seaside Resort: *The Color of a Great City* (New York: Boni and Liveright, 1923). Copyright © The Dreiser Trust. Reprinted by permission of the Dreiser Trust.

George W. Plunkitt and William L. Riordan. Honest Graft and Dishonest Graft; The Curse of Civil Service Reform: *Plunkitt of Tammany Hall: A Series of Very Plain Talks on Very Practical Politics* (New York: McClure, Phillips, 1905).

Maxim Gorky. Boredom: *The Independent*, August 5, 1907.

Henry James. (from) *The American Scene: Henry James: Collected Travel Writings, Great Britain and America* (New York: The Library of America, 1993), pp. 416–28.

O. Henry. The Duel: *Strictly Business* (New York: Doubleday, Page and Company, 1910).

James Weldon Johnson. (from) *The Autobiography of an Ex-Colored Man:* Chapter 6 from *The Autobiography of an Ex-Colored Man* (Boston: Sherman, French & Co., 1912).

James Huneker. The Lungs: *New Cosmopolis* (Charles Scribner's Sons, 1915).

Sara Teasdale. Gramercy Park; In the Metropolitan Museum; Coney Island; Union Square: *Helen of Troy and Other Poems* (New York: G.P Putnam, 1912). Broadway: *Rivers to the Sea* (New York: Macmillan, 1915).

Djuna Barnes. "Come Into the Roof Garden, Maud": *New York Press*, July 14, 1914.

Edna St. Vincent Millay. If I should learn: *Renascence and Other Poems* (New York: Harper and Brothers, 1917). Recuerdo: *A Few Figs from Thistles* (New York: F. Shay, 1921).

Willa Cather. Coming, Aphrodite!: *Willa Cather: Stories, Poems, and Other Writings* (New York: The Library of America, 1992).

Claude McKay. The Tropics in New York; The Harlem Dancer: *Harlem Shadows: The Poems of Claude McKay* (New York: Harcourt, Brace, 1922).

Marianne Moore. New York: *The Complete Poems of Marianne Moore* (New York: The Viking Press, 1967). Copyright © 1935 by Marianne Moore, renewed © 1963 by Marianne Moore and T.S. Eliot. Reprinted by permission of Simon & Schuster.

Paul Rosenfeld. (from) *Port of New York:* "Epilogue" to *Port of New York* (New York: Harcourt, Brace, 1924).

Edmund Wilson. The Finale at the Follies; Thoughts on Leaving New York for New Orleans: *The American Earthquake* (Garden City, N.Y.: Doubleday and Company, 1958). Copyright © 1958 by Edmund Wilson, renewed © 1986 by Helen Miranda Wilson. Reprinted by permission of Farrar, Straus & Giroux, Inc.

Vladimir Mayakovsky. Brooklyn Bridge: Patricia Blake (ed.), *The Bedbug and Selected Poetry*, trans. Max Hayward and George Reavey (Bloomington and London: Indiana University Press, 1975).

Hart Crane. To Brooklyn Bridge: Marc Simon (ed.), *The Poems of Hart Crane* (New York: W.W. Norton, 1984). Copyright © 1933, 1958, 1966 by Liveright Publishing Corporation. Copyright © 1986 by Marc Simon. Reprinted by permission of Liveright Publishing Corporation.

Stephen Graham. Exterior Street: *New York Nights* (New York: George H. Doran, 1927).

Al Smith. (from) *Up to Now: Up to Now* (New York: Viking Press, 1929), pp. 9–13, 14–24.

Helen Keller. I Go Adventuring: *Midstream: My Later Life* (Garden City, N.Y.:

Doubleday, Doran, 1929), pp. 295–300 (excerpt from Chapter 28, "I Go Adventuring"). Copyright © 1929 by Helen Keller and The Crowell Publishing Company. Reprinted by permission of Doubleday, a division of Bantam Doubleday Dell Publishing Group, Inc.

Paul Murand. (from) *New York: New York* (New York: Henry Holt and Company, 1930), pp. 65–74, 174–77, 186–92. Copyright © Flammarion, Paris, 1930. English translation © 1930 Henry Holt, New York, 1930.

Lincoln Steffens. The Police; Roosevelt and Reform: *The Autobiography of Lincoln Steffens* (New York: Harcourt, Brace and Company, 1931). Copyright © 1931, renewed 1959 by Peter Steffens. Reprinted by permission of Harcourt Brace & Company.

Dawn Powell. (from) The Diaries: Tim Page (ed.), *The Diaries of Dawn Powell 1931–1965.* (South Royalton, Vt.: Steerforth Press, 1995). Copyright © 1995 by The Estate of Dawn Powell. Reprinted by permission of Steerforth Press, South Royalton, Vermont.

Louis-Ferdinand Céline. (from) *Journey to the End of the Night: Journey to the End of the Night*, trans. Ralph Mannheim (New York: New Directions, 1983), pp. 166–74. Copyright © 1952 by Ferdinand Céline. Reprinted by permission of New Directions Publishing Corp.

Christopher Morley. West End Avenue: *Internal Revenue* (Garden City, N.Y.: Doubleday, Doran, 1932).

F. Scott Fitzgerald. My Lost City: *The Crack-Up* (New York: New Directions, 1945). Copyright © 1945 by New Directions Publishing Corp. Reprinted by permission of New Directions Publishing Corp.

Edith Wharton. The Background: Chapter One of *A Backward Glance,* in *Edith Wharton: Novellas and Other Writings* (New York: The Library of America, 1990). Copyright © 1933, 1934 Charles Scribner's Sons, renewed © 1961, 1962 by William R. Tyler. Reprinted by permission of Scribner, a division of Simon & Schuster, Inc.

Thomas Wolfe. Only the Dead Know Brooklyn: *From Death to Morning* (New York: Charles Scribner's Sons, 1935). Copyright © 1935 by Charles Scribner's Sons, renewed © 1963 by Paul Gitlin. Reprinted by permission of Scribner, a division of Simon & Schuster, Inc.

Damon Runyon. Sense of Humor: *Money from Home* (New York: Frederick A. Stokes, 1935). © Renewed 1961 by Damon Runyon Jr. and D'Ann McKibben. Reprinted by special arrangement with Sheldon Abend. © 1999 Sheldon Abend, assignee of Damon Runyon's children and grandchildren.

Henry Miller. (from) *Black Spring: Black Spring* (Paris: Obelisk Press, 1936). Copyright © 1936 by Henry Miller. Reprinted by permission of Grove/Atlantic, Inc.

Charles Reznikoff. Millinery District; (from) *Autobiography: New York;* (from) *By the Well of Living and Seeing:* Seamus Cooney, ed., *Poems 1918-1975: The Complete*

*Poems of Charles Reznikoff* (2 vols. Santa Rosa, Ca.: Black Sparrow Press, 1977). Copyright © 1977 by Marie Syrkin Reznikoff. Reprinted by permission of Black Sparrow Press.

A. J. Liebling. Apology for Breathing: *Back Where I Came From*, (New York: Sheridan House, 1938). Copyright © 1938, renewed © 1966 by Jean Stafford Liebling. Reprinted by permission of North Point Press, a division of Farrar, Straus & Giroux, Inc.

Langston Hughes. When the Negro Was In Vogue: *The Big Sea* (New York: Alfred A. Knopf, 1940). Copyright © 1940 by Langston Hughes, renewed © 1968 by Arna Bontemps and George Houston Bass. Reprinted by permission of Hill and Wang, a division of Farrar, Straus & Giroux, Inc.

Elizabeth Bishop. Letter to N.Y.: *The Complete Poems 1927–1979* (New York: Farrar, Straus & Giroux, 1979). Copyright © 1979, 1983 by Alice Helen Methfessel. Reprinted by permission of Farrar, Straus & Giroux, Inc.

John McNulty. Atheist Hit By Truck: *The New Yorker*, April 12, 1941. Copyright © 1941 by John McNulty. All rights reserved. Reprinted by permission. The Television Helps, But Not Very Much: *The New Yorker*, March 18, 1950. Copyright © 1950 by John McNulty. All rights reserved. Reprinted by permission. Both pieces were reprinted in *The World of John McNulty* (Doubleday).

Irwin Shaw. Welcome to the City: *Welcome to the City* (New York: Random House, 1942). Copyright © Irwin Shaw. Reprinted by permission.

Mary McCarthy. The Genial Host: *The Company She Keeps* (New York: Simon and Schuster, 1942). Copyright © The Mary McCarthy Literary Trust. Reprinted by permission.

Zora Neale Hurston. Story in Harlem Slang: *Zora Neale Hurston: Novels and Stories* (New York: The Library of America, 1995).

Red Smith. As He Seemed to a Hick: *To Absent Friends* (New York: Atheneum, 1982). Copyright © 1982 by Atheneum Publishers, Inc. Reprinted by permission of Scribner, a division of Simon & Schuster, Inc.

David Schubert. It Is Sticky in the Subway: *Initial A* (New York: Macmillan and Co, 1961). Copyright David Schubert. By permission of Theodore Weiss.

Weldon Kees. Aspects of Robinson: *Poems: 1947–1954* (San Francisco: A. Wilson and Company, 1954). Copyright © 1975 by the University of Nebraska Press. Reprinted by permission of the University of Nebraska Press; Relating to Robinson: Donald Justice, ed., *The Collected Poems of Weldon Kees* (Lincoln: University of Nebraska Press, 1962). Copyright © 1975 by the University of Nebraska Press.

Bernard Malamud. The Cost of Living: *Idiots First* (New York: Farrar, Straus & Giroux, 1963). Copyright © 1963 by Bernard Malamud, renewed © 1991 by Ann Malamud. Reprinted by permission of Farrar, Straus & Giroux, Inc.

Anzia Yezierska. (from) *Red Ribbon on a White Horse*: *Red Ribbon on a White Horse* (New York: Charles Scribner's Sons, 1950), pp. 101–11. Copyright © 1950 by

Anzia Yezierska, renewed © 1978 by Louise Levitas Henrikson. Reprinted by permission of the Henriksen Family Trust.

William Carlos Williams. Hell's Kitchen: *The Autobiography of William Carlos Williams* (New York: Random House, 1951). The text printed here is an abridged version of Part One, Chapter 17, "Hell's Kitchen." Copyright © 1951 by William Carlos Williams. Reprinted by permission of New Directions Publishing Corp.

Malcolm Cowley. The Long Furlough: *Exile's Return* (New York: Viking Press, 1951), pp. 48–52. Copyright © 1934, 1935, 1941, 1951 by Malcolm Cowley. Reprinted by permission of Viking Penguin, a division of Penguin Putnam Inc.

Alfred Kazin. (from) *A Walker in the City: A Walker in the City* (New York: Harcourt, Brace, 1951), pp. 8–17. Copyright © 1951, renewed © 1979 by Alfred Kazin. Reprinted by permission of Harcourt Brace & Company.

Joseph Mitchell. Up in the Old Hotel: *The Bottom of the Harbor* (Boston: Little, Brown, 1959). Copyright © by Joseph Mitchell.

William S. Burroughs. (from) *Junky: Junky* (New York: Penguin, 1977), pp. 28–32. Copyright © 1977 by William S. Burroughs. Reprinted with the permission of The Wylie Agency, Inc.

Bernardo Vega. (from) *Memoirs of Bernardo Vega:* Chapters 1–3 of Cesar Andreu Iglesias (ed.), *Memoirs of Bernardo Vega*, trans. Juan Flores (Monthly Review Press, 1984) Copyright © 1984 by the Monthly Review Foundation. Reprinted by permission.

Frank O'Hara. A Step Away from Them; The Day Lady Died; Steps: Donald Allen (ed.), *Collected Poems of Frank O'Hara* (New York: Knopf, 1971). Copyright © 1964 by Frank O'Hara. Reprinted by permission of City Lights Books.

Loren Eiseley. (from) *The Immense Journey: The Immense Journey* (New York: Random House, 1957), pp. 195-97. Copyright © 1956 by Loren Eiseley. Reprinted by permission of Random House, Inc.

Robert Moses. Fiorello H. LaGuardia: *Public Works: A Dangerous Trade* (New York: McGraw Hill, 1970). The text printed here has been slightly abridged.

John Cheever. Moving Out: *Esquire*, July 1960. Copyright © 1960 by John Cheever. Reprinted by permission of Donadio & Ashworth, Inc.

Ned Rorem. (from) *The New York Diary: The New York Diary of Ned Rorem* (New York: George Brazillier, 1966), pp. 188–91. Copyright © Ned Rorem. Reprinted by permission of the author.

Jane Jacobs. (from) *The Death and Life of Great American Cities: The Death and Life of Great American Cities* (New York: Random House, 1961), pp. 50–54. Copyright © 1961 by Jane Jacobs. Reprinted by permission of Random House, Inc.

James Merrill. An Urban Convalescence: *Water Street* (New York, Atheneum, 1962). Copyright © 1992 by James Merrill. Reprinted by permission of Alfred A. Knopf, Inc.

Edwin Denby. The Thirties: *Dancers, Buildings, and People in the Street* (New York: Horizon Press, 1965). The Climate: Ron Padgett (ed.), *The Complete Poems of Edwin Denby* (New York: Random House, 1986). Copyright © by Edwin Denby. Reprinted by permission of The Estate of Edwin Denby.

Amiri Baraka (LeRoi Jones). Minton's: *Black Music* (New York: William Morrow, 1967). Copyright © 1967 by LeRoi Jones. Reprinted by permission of William Morrow & Company, Inc.

George Oppen. Tourist Eye: *The Materials* (New York: New Directions, 1962). Copyright © 1975 by George Oppen. Reprinted by permission of New Directions Publishing Corp.

James Baldwin. (from) *The Fire Next Time: James Baldwin: Collected Essays* (New York: The Library of America, 1998), pp. 296–303. Copyright © 1962, 1963 by James Baldwin. Copyright renewed. Published by Vintage Books. Reprinted by arrangement with The James Baldwin Estate.

Harvey Shapiro. National Cold Storage Company; 47th Street: *National Cold Storage Company: New and Selected Poems* (Middletown: Wesleyan University Press, 1988). Copyright © 1988 by Harvey Shapiro and Wesleyan University Press. Reprinted by permission of the University Press of New England.

Gay Talese. Panic in Brooklyn: *The Bridge* (New York: Harper and Row, 1964). Copyright © 1964 by Gay Talese, renewed 1992 by Gay Talese. Reprinted by permission of HarperCollins, Publishers, Inc.

Louis Auchincloss. The Landmarker: *Tales of Manhattan* (Boston: Houghton Mifflin, 1964). Copyright © 1964, 1966, 1967 by Louis Auchincloss. Reprinted by permission of Houghton Mifflin Company. All rights reserved.

Mario Puzo. (from) *The Fortunate Pilgrim:* Chapter One from *The Fortunate Pilgrim* (New York: Atheneum, 1965). Copyright © 1965 by Mario Puzo.

Tom Wolfe. A Sunday Kind of Love: *The Kandy-Kolored Tangerine-Flake Streamline Baby* (New York: Farrar, Straus & Giroux, 1965). Copyright © 1964, renewed © 1993 by Tom Wolfe. Reprinted by permission of Farrar, Straus & Giroux, Inc.

Joan Didion. Goodbye to All That: *Slouching Towards Bethlehem* (New York: Farrar, Straus & Giroux, 1968). Copyright © 1966, 1968, renewed © 1996 by Joan Didion. Reprinted by permission of Farrar, Straus & Giroux, Inc.

Isaac Bashevis Singer. The Cafeteria (trans. by the author and Mirra Ginsburg): *A Friend of Kafka and Other Stories* (New York: Farrar, Straus & Giroux, 1968). Copyright © 1970 by Isaac Bashevis Singer. Reprinted by permission of Farrar, Straus & Giroux, Inc.

Jimmy Cannon. Lou Stillman: *Nobody Asked Me, But . . . The World of Jimmy Cannon* (New York: Holt, Rinehart & Winston, 1978). Copyright © by Jimmy Cannon.

James Schuyler. February; Dining Out with Doug and Frank: *The Collected Poems of James Schuyler* (New York: Farrar, Straus & Giroux, 1993). Copyright © 1993 by The Estate of James Schuyler. Reprinted by permission of Farrar, Straus & Giroux, Inc.

Allen Ginsberg. Mugging: *Mind Breaths: Poems 1972–77* (San Francisco: City Lights Books, 1974); Fourth Floor, Dawn, Up All Night Writing Letters: *Plutonian Ode: Poems 1977–80* (San Francisco: City Lights Books, 1980). Copyright © Allen Ginsberg. Reprinted by permission of HarperCollins, Inc.

Elizabeth Hardwick. (from) *Sleepless Nights: Sleepless Nights* (New York: Random House, 1979), pp. 32–44. Copyright © 1979 by Elizabeth Hardwick. Reprinted by permission of Random House, Inc.

Lewis Mumford. (from) *Sketches from Life: Sketches from Life* (New York: Dial Press, 1982), pp. 125–30. Copyright © 1982 by Lewis Mumford. Reprinted by permission of Doubleday, a division of Bantam Doubleday Dell Publishing Group, Inc.

Kate Simon. The Movies and Other Schools: *Bronx Primitive* (New York: Viking, 1983). Copyright © 1982 by Kate Simon. Reprinted by permission of Viking Penguin, a division of Penguin Putnam Inc.

Edward Rivera. (from) *Family Installments: Family Installments* (New York: William Morrow, 1983), pp. 177–89. Copyright © 1985 by Edwin Rivera. Reprinted by permission of William Morrow & Company, Inc.

Joyce Johnson. (from) *Minor Characters: Minor Characters* (Boston: Houghton Mifflin, 1983), pp. 207–11. Copyright © 1983 by Joyce Johnson. Reprinted by permission of the author.

Lionel Abel. (from) *The Intellectual Follies: The Intellectual Follies: A Memoir of the Literary Venture in New York and Paris* (New York: W.W. Norton and Co., 1984), pp. 242–51, 256–57. Copyright © 1984 by Lionel Abel. Reprinted by permission of W.W. Norton & Company, Inc.

E. L. Doctorow. (from) *World's Fair: World's Fair* (New York: Random House, 1985), pp. 250–56. Copyright © 1985 by E. L. Doctorow. Reprinted by permission of Random House, Inc.

Ralph Ellison. New York, 1936: *Esquire*, July 1986. Copyright © 1986 by Ralph Ellison. Reprinted by permission of Random House, Inc.

Oscar Hijuelos. (from) *The Mambo Kings Play Songs of Love: The Mambo Kings Play Songs of Love* (New York: Farrar, Straus & Giroux, 1989), pp. 21–31. Copyright © 1989 by Oscar Hijuelos. Reprinted by permission of Farrar, Straus & Giroux, Inc.

Vivian Gornick. (from) *Approaching Eye Level: Approaching Eye Level* (Boston: Beacon Press, 1996), pp. 1–14. Copyright © 1996 by Vivian Gornick. Reprinted by permission of Beacon Press, Boston.

Colson Whitehead. (from) *The Colossus of New York: A City in Thirteen Parts* (New York: Doubleday, 2003), pp. 3–11. Copyright © 2003 by Colson Whitehead. Used by permission of Doubleday, a division of Random House, Inc.

Vijay Seshadri. North of Manhattan: *The Long Meadow* (St. Paul, MN: Graywolf Press, 2004), pp. 18–20. Copyright © 2004 by Vijay Seshadri. Reprinted